W9-BZG-780

Statistical Record OF Black America

Statistical Record <u>of</u> Black America

Compiled and Edited by
CARRELL PETERSON HORTON
Fisk University

and

JESSIE CARNEY SMITH
Fisk University

 **Gale Research Inc.** · *DETROIT* · *NEW YORK* · *LONDON*

Carrell Peterson Horton and Jessie Carney Smith, *Editors*
Negather Douglas and Michael Russell, *Production Assistants*

Gale Research Inc. Staff

Mary Beth Trimper, *Production Manager*
Marilyn Jackman, *External Production Assistant*

Arthur Chartow, *Art Director*
Bernadette M. Gornie, *Graphic Designer*

Laura Bryant, *Production Supervisor*
Louise Gagné, *Internal Production Associate*

The paper used in this publication meets the minimum requirements
of American National Standard for Information Sciences—Permanence
Paper for Printed Library Materials, ANSI Z39.48-1984. ∞™

Copyright© 1990
Gale Research Inc.
835 Penobscot Bldg.
Detroit, MI 48226-4094

Library of Congress Catalog Card Number 90-2242X214
ISBN 0-8103-7724-1

Printed in the United States of America

Printed simultaneously in the United Kingdom
by Gale Research International
(An affiliated company of Gale Research Inc.)

TABLE OF CONTENTS

Preface vii
Abbreviations xi

Attitudes, Values, and Behavior 1
Business and Economics 28
Crime, Law Enforcement, and Legal Justice . . 45
Education 98
The Family 260
Government Service 292
Health and Medical Care 294
Housing 369
Income, Spending, and Wealth 379
Labor and Employment 415
Military Affairs 465
Miscellany 473
Politics and Elections 476
Population 515
The Professions 551
Religion 606
Social Services 609
Sports and Leisure 612
Vital Statistics 623

Reference Sources 683
Index 693

PREFACE

This first edition of *Statistical Record of Black America* is designed to fill a need that has long existed and is ever increasing. Its value to librarians and researchers should be apparent, but it is also a volume that contains data of interest to civic and community groups as well as to individuals who are curious about the general and/or specific aspects of conditions and attitudes in the United States.

As the United States continues to become a more highly industrialized and technological society and as its population continues to grow in diversity, the need for information that assists in determining of policy and that facilitates understanding of the nature and quality of life of United States residents grows exponentially. Interest in black Americans and other minorities is particularly acute. And concerning minorities, there is no shortage of information in some areas. The United States government is a prolific publisher of statistics that range in concern from broad issues such as population characteristics to minute details such as the number of children left alone after school, with data presented separately for population subgroups. Government sources are widely used by private organizations—foundations, corporations, and others—to combine data in different ways and rework them to emphasize particular groups and points of interest. Private organizations also collect their own data, and though these data are not always national in coverage, the information provided is equally useful. The problem has been that the majority of separate data sources provide information on a narrow range of subject areas. The broader the interests of researchers and policy-makers whose interests overlap subject areas, the greater the number of sources they must consult. This volume does not eliminate that problem, but it does make the task of researching and understanding black America easier by bringing together in a single source the published information that is most readily accessible and available. It also combines the most recent data available with historical information, providing a perspective on changes that have occurred through the years. Wherever available, comparative information on the total, on the majority and on other minority groups is included to provide a frame of reference.

Scope of This Volume

Tables and figures included have been drawn from both public and private sources. The distinction between such sources is blurred, however, by the fact that information published by a public source may initially have been obtained from a private source (and vice versa), as noted above. The information included for each of the chapters reveals that data are more readily available in some areas than others. Religion, arts and entertainment, and lifestyles are areas for which a paucity of statistical data was unearthed. We invite our readers to suggest additional sources of information that they would like to see included in future editions or that may have been overlooked in the compilation of this work.

A small number of the tables in this volume were compiled by the editors from the original source text or tables, in order to make more explicit the information provided on minorities. The majority, however, are presented with relevant information exactly as presented by the source. Readers are urged, nevertheless, to use this volume as a beginning point, and to consult the sources presented here. Original sources often present data in more detailed form and on a larger number of variables than space in this volume permits; they may also provide additional references to a given topic. The list of sources at the end of this volume is a ready reference to the availability of material.

Interpreting the Data

As readers go through this volume, it will perhaps appear to include multiple items on the same characteristics. In preparation of the volume, the editors noted two characteristics of published data that may contribute to this perception. First, the continuous updating of statistical information leads to the compilation and summarization of data at different data points and by different groups. The specific nature of a trend or the importance of a single data point is clearly related to both when the data were collected and who collected them. Different trend points and single data points are therefore included, along with data on the same characteristics from different sources. Second, the same characteristic is sometimes presented in both tabular and graphic form. Experience suggests that some readers grasp the meaning of data more easily in one form than the other. A pie chart, for example, may be more compelling than a table of numbers.

Items are presented here without comment and without evaluation as to validity and reliability of the information. Sources used do not include the many academic research studies that are conducted and filed initially only in university libraries as theses and dissertations; the majority of such studies have a narrower focus than the information presented in this volume. There are also few items taken from the popular press, since such data may lack the precision and scope deemed essential for this work. Users of *Statistical Record of Black America* should be aware of the additional information that is available through such sources.

Acknowledgements

The editors are grateful to the several private organizations and individuals who recognized the importance of this work and gave permission for their original work to be included. These sources are acknowledged within individual items and are included in the list of sources. Our editorial consultant at Gale Research Incorporated, James E. Person, was instrumental in helping to make the work an enjoyable and stimulating task.

At a more personal level, this volume could not have been completed without the support and assistance of very special individuals whose enthusiasm for this project was almost equal to ours. From the Fisk University family: Henry Ponder, president; George Neely, Jr., and Robert Williams, Fisk University faculty; Dixie Jernigan, Marion Roberts, and Sharon Williams, Fisk University Library staff; and Djuan Hampton, Fisk University student. Others whose help we could not have done without include Vera Stevens Chatman and Eleanor Chippey-Grier, Meharry Medical College, and Philip Neely, Chicago Illinois school system. A very heartfelt thank-you is extended to each of them.

Every effort has been made to trace copyright, but if omissions have been made, please let us know.

Carrell Peterson Horton
Director, Division of Social Science, Fisk University

Jessie Carney Smith
University Librarian, Fisk University

ABBREVIATIONS

ACT	American College Testing
AP	Advanced Placement
EOEI	Equal Opportunity Educational Institutions
HBCU	Historically Black Colleges and Universities
NAACP	National Association for the Advancement of Colored People
NAEP	National Assessment of Educational Progress
NAFEO	National Association for Equality of Opportunity in Higher Education
NRC	National Research Council
PBI	Predominantly Black Institutions
PWI	Predominantly White Institutions
TBI	Traditionally Black Institutions
TWI	Traditionally White Institutions
SAT	Scholastic Aptitude Test
SEF	Southern Education Foundation
SREB	Southern Regional Education Board

Statistical Record OF Black America

ATTITUDES, VALUES, AND BEHAVIOR

★ 1 ★
8th Graders' Attitudes about Classes

Class subject and attitude	Percent who agree with statement					
		Race/ethnicity				
	All 8th graders	White	Black	Hispanic	Asian	American Indian
Mathematics class						
Look forward to	56.6	52.8	69.2	64.2	67.6	63.7
Afraid to ask questions	20.9	19.3	22.0	28.6	23.1	32.5
Useful in my future	88.0	87.4	89.3	89.7	90.4	85.1
English class						
Look forward to	56.9	52.2	72.8	67.5	63.6	66.0
Afraid to ask questions	15.4	14.2	16.7	20.7	17.4	19.6
Useful in my future	84.1	82.9	87.9	88.1	88.0	80.7
Social studies class						
Look forward to	58.5	56.0	67.6	63.3	64.0	60.2
Afraid to ask questions	15.1	13.7	16.5	20.8	19.1	22.2
Useful in my future	59.1	56.9	66.7	63.0	64.7	64.3
Science class						
Look forward to	61.3	59.0	68.3	66.6	67.2	64.3
Afraid to ask questions	14.9	13.5	16.0	20.8	16.2	25.6
Useful in my future	68.7	67.6	71.7	70.4	74.5	67.6

Source: "Eighth Graders' Attitudes about Selected Classes, by Selected Student and School Characteristics: 1988," *Digest of Education Statistics*, 1989, p. 130. Primary source: U.S. Department of Education, National Center for Educational Statistics, "National Education Longitudinal Study of 1988" survey. (This table was prepared June 1989.) *Note:* Data are preliminary.

1

★ 2 ★
8th Graders' Expected Occupations

Expected occupation at age 30	All 8th graders	Race/ethnicity				
		White	Black	Hispanic	Asian	American Indian
Craftsperson or operator	4.2	4.3	3.2	5.3	3.6	6.6
Farmer or farm manager	1.0	1.2	0.1	0.6	0.6	0.3
Housewife/homemaker	2.3	2.5	0.9	2.9	1.1	3.1
Laborer or farm worker	0.6	0.5	0.6	0.8	0.7	0.2
Military, police, or security officer	9.6	9.0	11.4	11.0	7.0	17.0
Professional, business, or managerial	28.6	28.7	29.3	26.0	34.9	23.0
Business owner	6.2	6.3	5.8	5.7	6.4	5.7
Technical	6.2	5.7	8.0	7.3	7.6	6.5
Salesperson, clerical, or office worker	2.8	2.7	2.9	3.8	2.3	2.3
Science or engineering professional	5.9	6.1	4.2	4.8	9.7	6.4
Service worker	4.9	4.9	6.4	3.9	2.3	3.4
Other employment	17.0	17.7	16.3	15.1	13.4	11.9
Don't know	10.5	10.2	10.4	12.5	10.5	13.5

Source: "Expected Occupations of 8th Graders at Age 30, by Selected Student and School Characteristics: 1988," *Digest of Education Statistics*, 1989, p. 130. Primary source: U.S. Department of Education, National Center for Educational Statistics, "National Education Longitudinal Study of 1988" survey. (This table was prepared June 1989.) *Note:* Data are preliminary.

★ 3 ★
Approval of Use of Firearms

By demographic characteristics, United States, 1986. Question: "Do you think people should have the right to shoot someone who breaks into their home, even if they don't know whether the person is armed?" Numbers in percent.

	Yes	No	Don't know/no answer
National	68	24	8
Race, ethnicity			
White	68	24	8
Black	74	21	5
Hispanic	44	50	6
Other	65	13	22

Source: "Attitudes toward Use of a Firearm," *Sourcebook of Criminal Justice Statistics - 1988*, 1989, p. 233. Primary source: Table adapted by SOURCEBOOK staff from table provided by the Media General/Associated Press Poll. Reprinted by permission.

★ 4 ★
Are Handguns OK in Individual Communities?

By demographic characteristics, United States, 1986. Question: "Some communities have passed laws banning the sale and possession of handguns. Would you favor or oppose having such a law in this city/community?" Numbers in percent.

	Favor	Oppose	No opinion
National	47	47	6
Race, ethnicity			
White	45	49	6
Nonwhite	59	35	6
Black	59	34	7
Hispanic	50	41	9

Source: "Attitudes toward Laws Banning the Sale and Possession of Handguns in Own Community," *Sourcebook of Criminal Justice Statistics - 1988*, 1989, p. 239. Primary source: Gallup Jr., George, *The Gallup Report*, Report No. 248 (Princeton, NJ: The Gallup Poll, May 1986), p. 18 and *The Gallup Poll* (Princeton, NJ: The Gallup Poll, May 11, 1986), pp. 2, 3. Table adapted by SOURCEBOOK staff. Reprinted by permission. Published by permission.

★ 5 ★
Attitudes about Current Job: TWI Faculty

Item	Strongly Disagree	Disagree With Reservations	Agree With Reservations	Strongly Agree	n
Salary is Appropriate for Rank and Experience	23.0	18.5	37.7	20.8	443
Compared to Colleagues, Research Rewarded Equitably	14.0	20.8	38.6	26.6	394
Compared to Colleagues, Teaching Rewarded Equitably	13.6	18.1	39.4	28.9	426
Promotion and Tenure Procedures are Equitable	12.8	23.9	43.1	20.3	439
Tenure Status is Appropriate	15.9	11.3	31.4	41.3	433
Student Evaluations Fair and Equitable	8.2	11.2	37.6	43.0	428
Supervisor Evaluations Fair and Equitable	7.0	9.3	40.7	43.0	440

Source: "Black Faculty Attitudes and Perceptions about Salary, Tenure, and Promotion," *Black Faculty in Traditionally White Institutions in Selected Adams States, 1988, p. 77. Primary source:* Black Faculty in Traditionally White Institutions in Selected Adams States: Characteristics, Experiences and Perceptions, Southern Education Foundation, Atlanta, GA 30308, 1988. TWI: Traditionally White Institutions. Published by permission.

★ 6 ★
Attitudes about Racial Climate: TWI Faculty

Item	Strongly Disagree	Disagree With Reservations	Agree With Reservations	Strongly Agree	n
Institution Committed to Improvement in Minority Affairs	21.8	26.6	39.9	11.8	459
Faculty Search Committees Have Sufficient Minority Membership	41.5	33.4	20.1	5.0	443
Department Has Appropriate Minority Faculty Representation	58.3	21.1	13.6	7.0	456
Institution Has Appropriate Minority Faculty Representation	73.4	17.9	7.2	1.5	458
My Ethnic Background Enhances My Opportunity for Advancement	36.6	38.0	20.1	5.1	453

Source: "Black Faculty Attitudes and Perceptions about Racial Climate," *Black Faculty in Traditionally White Institutions in Selected Adams States*, 1988, p. 90. Primary source: *Black Faculty in Traditionally White Institutions in Selected Adams States: Characteristics, Experiences and Perceptions*, Southern Education Foundation, Atlanta, GA 30308. TWI: Traditionally White Institutions. Published by permission.

★7★
Attitudes about Work Environment: TWI Faculty

Item	Strongly Disagree	Disagree with Reservations	Agree with Reservations	Strongly Agree	n
Professional Ambition Achievable at Present Institution	18.4	18.2	35.3	28.1	456
Good Working Relationships Easiliy Developed in Department	9.9	17.7	37.1	35.2	463
Good Working Relationships Easily Developed in Institution	10.2	29.5	45.1	15.2	461
Skills and Experience Could Be Better Utilized	9.1	17.8	34.7	38.4	450
Input in Department Matters Well Received	8.3	15.5	39.6	36.5	457
Have Real Sense of Identification with Department	11.3	17.4	36.2	35.1	459
Have Real Sense of Identification with Institution	13.9	25.7	41.6	18.7	459
Have Had Opportunities to Serve on Important Committees	10.4	13.2	32.1	44.3	461
Difficult to be Appointed to Important Committees	25.2	33.4	25.9	15.9	452
Difficult to be Elected to Important Committees	19.5	29.6	31.6	19.3	446

Source: "Black Faculty Attitudes and Perceptions about Work Environment," *Black Faculty in Traditionally White Institutions (TWI) in Selected Adams States*, 1988, p. 81. Primary source: *Black Faculty in Traditionally White Institutions in Selected Adams States: Characteristics, Experiences and Perceptions*, Southern Education Foundation, Atlanta, GA 30308, 1988. Target state system was isolated for comparisons. Published by permission.

★8★
Attitudes Toward School Busing: Trends

Race	1972	1974	1975	1976	1977	1978	1982	1983	1985	1986	Change, 1986-1972
Black	45	37	53	48	52	48	44	44	43	38	-7
White	87	85	86	87	87	83	84	79	81	75	-12
Difference: black minus white	-42	-48	-33	-39	-35	-35	-40	-35	-38	-37	

Source: "Opposition to School Busing, by Race and Year (in percent)," A Common Destiny: Blacks and American Society, 1989, p. 128. Primary source: Davis, James A., and Tom W. Smith. 1987. General Social Surveys, 1972-1987. *Public Opinion Quarterly*, 43 (Winter): 463-476. *Notes:* The question was as follows: "In general, do you favor or oppose the busing of (Negro/black) and white school children from one district to another?". Published by permission.

★ 9 ★
Attitudes: College Student Interracial Dating

Numbers in percent.

Attitudes Toward Interracial Dating	Total Population	Campus Race	
		Black	White
Equally Acceptable	41.1	41.3	40.9
Not Equally Acceptable	58.9	58.7	59.1
Total	100.0	100.0	100.0
N	(1542)	(860)	(682)

Source: "Attitudes toward Interracial Dating by Student Gender and Campus Race," *Gender and Campus Race Differences in Black Student Academic Performance, Racial Attitudes and College Satisfaction,* 1986, p. 36. Primary source: National Study of Black College Students, 1981 and 1983, University of Michigan, Ann Arbor.

★ 10 ★
Attitudes: Sex Education & Related Topics

Adult characteristics	Percentage of adults who favor the following practices in public schools		
	Teaching sex education	Dispensing birth control information and contraceptives	School clinic referrals to family planning clinics
Total[1]	89	73	80
Race			
White	88	71	81
Black	92	88	75
Hispanic	90	73	73

Source: "Public Attitudes toward Sex Education and Provision of Birth Control Information, Referrals, and Contraceptives in the Public Schools: 1988," *Digest of Educational Statistics,* 1989, p. 131. Primary source: Planned Parenthood Federation of America Inc., Louis Harris and Associates, Inc., *Public Attitudes Toward Teenage Pregnancy, Sex Education and Birth Conrtol,* May 1988. (This table was prepared November 1988.) *Note:* 1. Adults, 18 years old and older.

★ 11 ★
Black College Students' Attitudes toward Fellow Black Students

Numbers in percent.

Attitudes Toward Black Student Unity	Total Population	Campus Race	
		Black	White
A Great Deal	54.1	61.9	44.1
Very Little	45.9	38.1	55.9
Total	100.0	100.0	100.0
N	(1544)	(862)	(682)

Source: "Attitudes toward Black Students by Student Gender and Campus Race," *Gender and Campus Race Differences in Black Student Academic Performance, Racial Attitudes and College Satisfaction,* 1986, p. 37. Primary source: National Study of Black College Students, 1981 and 1983, University of Michigan, Ann Arbor.

★ 12 ★
Black College Students: Relations with White Staff

Numbers in percent.

Relations with White Staff	Total Population	Campus Race	
		Black	White
Excellent	17.0	21.6	12.3
Good	65.6	63.5	67.9
Poor	14.4	12.3	16.5
Very Poor	3.0	2.6	3.4
Total	100.0	100.0	100.0
N	(1378)	(693)	(685)

Source: "Relations with White Staff by Student Gender and Campus Race," *Gender and Campus Race Differences in Black Student Academic Performance, Racial Attitudes and College Satisfaction,* 1986, p. 44. Primary source: National Study of Black College Students, 1981 and 1983, University of Michigan, Ann Arbor. Published by permission.

★ 13 ★
Changes in Attitude Toward Community Crime

By demographic characteristics, United States, 1989. Question: "Is there more crime in your area than there was a year ago, or less?" Numbers in percent.

	More	Less	Same[1]	No opinion
National	47	21	27	5
Race				
White	45	21	29	5
Nonwhite	58	27	14	1
Black	59	28	13	[2]

Source: "Attitudes toward Changes in the Level of Crime in Own Area Compared to a Year Ago," *Sourcebook of Criminal Justice Statistics - 1988,* 1989, p. 201. Primary source: Gallup Jr., George, *The Gallup Report,* Report Nos. 282-283 (Princeton, NJ: The Gallup Poll, March/April 1989), p. 7. Table adapted by SOURCEBOOK staff. Reprinted by permission. *Notes:* 1. Response volunteered. 2. Less than 1 percent. Published by permission.

★ 14 ★
Community Drug Abuse: How Serious is the Problem?

By demographic characteristics, United States, 1986(1). Question: "How important a problem do you think drug abuse is in your community: Is it one of the 2 or 3 worst problems, is it a serious problem but other things are worse, or is it not much of a problem in your community?" Numbers in percent.

	One of two or three worst problems	Serious problem	Not much of a problem	Don't know/ no answer
National	24	35	35	6
Race				
White	23	36	34	6
Black	30	26	41	4

Source: "Attitudes toward the Seriousness of Drug Abuse as a Problem in Respondent's Community," *Sourcebook of Criminal Justice Statistics - 1988*, 1989, p. 260. Primary source: Table adapted by SOURCEBOOK staff from tables provided by The New York Times/CBS News Poll. Copyright 1986 by The New York Times/CBS News Poll. Reprinted by permission. *Notes:* This question was asked of the 87 percent subsample who did not respond "drugs" to the question: "What do you think is the most important problem facing the community you live in?" 1. Percents may not add up to 100 due to rounding.

★ 15 ★
Community Police Performance

By demographic characteristics, United States, 1986. Question: "In general, do you think the police in your community do a good, fair, or poor job against crime?" Numbers in percent.

	Good	Fair	Poor	Don't know/ no answer
National	59	31	8	2
Race, ethnicity				
White	60	30	8	2
Black	39	46	11	4
Hispanic	44	44	6	6
Other	52	44	4	0

Source: "Attitudes toward Community Police Performance," *Sourcebook of Criminal Justice Statistics - 1988*, 1989, p. 207. Primary source: Table adapted by SOURCEBOOK staff from table provided by the Media General/Associated Press Poll. Reprinted by permission.

★ 16 ★
Congruence of College Campus Activities and Student

Numbers in percent.

Campus Activities Represent Interests	Total Population	Campus Race	
		Black	White
Not at all	14.1	10.0	19.4
Very Little	32.2	24.1	42.7
Somewhat	35.9	40.1	30.4
Considerably	17.8	25.7	7.5
Total	100.0	100.0	100.0
N	(1571)	(887)	(684)

Source: "Relation of Campus Activities to Interests by Student Gender and Campus Race," *Gender and Campus Race Differences in Black Student Academic Performance, Racial Attitudes and College Satisfaction*, 1986, p. 40. Primary source: National Study of Black College Students, 1981 and 1983, University of Michigan, Ann Arbor. Published by permission.

★ 17 ★
Drugs and Neighborhood Crime

By demographic characteristics, United States, 1988. Question: "Thinking about the neighborhood where you now live ... is drug-related crime a serious problem, somewhat of a problem, or not a problem at all?" Numbers in percent.

	Serious problem	Somewhat of a problem	Not a problem	No opinion
National	10	34	54	2
Race				
White	10	35	54	2
Nonwhite	17	27	55	1
Black	19	28	52	1

Source: "Attitudes toward Drug-Related Crime in Own Neighborhood," *Sourcebook of Criminal Justice Statistics - 1988*, 1989, p. 261. Primary source: Gallup Jr., George, *The Gallup Report*, Report No. 276 (Princeton, NJ: The Gallup Poll, September 1988), p. 31. Table adapted by SOURCEBOOK staff. Reprinted by permission. Published by permission.

★ 18 ★
Fairness of the Supreme Court

By demographic characteristics, United States, 1987. Question: "Do you think the Supreme Court has been impartial in its decisions or do you think it has tended to favor one group more than another?" Numbers in percent.

	Impartial	Favors one group	No opinion
National	44	37	19
Race, ethnicity			
White	45	36	19
Nonwhite	42	42	16
Black	43	41	16
Hispanic	37	36	27

Source: "Attitudes toward Fairness of the U.S. Supreme Court," *Sourcebook of Criminal Justice Statistics - 1988*, 1989, p. 194. Primary source: Gallup Jr., George, *The Gallup Report*, Report No. 262 (Princeton, NJ: The Gallup Poll, July 1987), p. 27. Table adapted by SOURCEBOOK staff. Reprinted by permission. Published by permission.

★ 19 ★
Feelings of Personal Safety: At Home

By demographic characteristics, United States, 1986. Numbers in percent.

| | First, do you generally feel that your home is secure against crime, or not? | | | Do you lock your doors regularly or not? | | |
	Yes	No	Don't know/ no answer	Yes Yes	No No	Don't know/ no answer
National	72	26	2	88	12	0
Race, ethnicity						
White	75	24	1	86	13	1
Black	57	38	5	95	5	0
Hispanic	81	19	0	94	6	0
Other	70	30	0	83	17	0

Source: "Attitudes toward Personal Safety at Home," *Sourcebook of Criminal Justice Statistics - 1988,* 1989, p. 207. Primary source: Table adapted by SOURCEBOOK staff from table provided by the Media General/Associated Press Poll. Reprinted by permission. *Notes:* For a discussion of public opinion survey sampling procedures, see Appendix 5.

★ 20 ★
Feelings of Personal Safety: In Community

By demographic characteristics, United States, 1986. Numbers in percent.

| | How about the street on which you live? Do you feel it is safe to walk on your street after dark, or not? | | | How about elsewhere in your community? Do you feel it is safe to go walking most places in your community after dark or not? | | |
	Yes	No	Don't know/ no answer	Yes	No	Don't know/ no answer
National	78	20	2	64	35	1
Race, ethnicity						
White	80	18	2	66	33	1
Black	64	36	0	46	53	1
Hispanic	63	31	6	69	31	0
Other	78	22	0	48	48	4

Source: "Attitudes toward Personal Safety in Respondent's Community," *Sourcebook of Criminal Justice Statistics - 1988,* 1989, p. 208. Primary source: Table adapted by SOURCEBOOK staff from table provided by the Media General/Associated Press Poll. Reprinted by permission.

★ 21 ★
Firearms and Home Safety

By demographic characteristics, United States, 1986. Question: "In general, do you think having a gun in the home makes the home a safer place, a more dangerous place or makes no difference at all?" Numbers in percent.

	Safer	More dangerous	No difference	Don't know/no answer
National	28	36	29	7
Race, ethnicity				
White	28	36	29	7
Black	34	31	26	9
Hispanic	25	44	31	0
Other	22	17	44	17

Source: "Attitudes toward Home Safety and Possession of a Firearm," *Sourcebook of Criminal Justice Statistics - 1988*, 1989, p. 233. Primary source: Table adapted by SOURCEBOOK staff from table provided by the Media General/Associated Press Poll. Reprinted by permission.

★ 22 ★
Firearms and Public Policy

By demographic characteristics, United States, 1988. Question: "Would you favor or oppose: a) The registration of all firearms? b) A law requiring that any person who carries a gun outside his home must have a license to do so? c) A national law requiring a 7- day waiting period before a handgun could be purchased, in order to determine whether the prospective buyer has been convicted of a felony or is mentally ill?" Numbers in percent.

	Registration		Licensing		Waiting period	
	Favor	Oppose	Favor	Oppose	Favor	Oppose
National[1]	67	30	84	15	91	8
Race						
White	68	28	83	15	91	7
Nonwhite	59	38	86	11	86	13
Black	59	37	86	13	86	13

Source: "Attitudes toward Public Policies on Firearm Registration," *Sourcebook of Criminal Justice Statistics - 1988*, 1989, p. 242. Primary source: Gallup Jr., George, *The Gallup Report*, Report No. 280 (Princeton, NJ: The Gallup Poll, January 1989), p. 26. Reprinted by permission. *Note:* 1. Responses of "no opinion" were omitted by the Source. Published by permission.

★ 23 ★
High School Seniors' Extra-Curricular Activities: Trends

Student Characteristics	Percent of seniors participating in activities								
	Athletics[1]	Debating, drama, band, chorus[2]	Subject-matter clubs	Vocational education clubs	Newspaper, magazine, or yearbook clubs	Student council, government, political clubs	Hobby clubs	Cheer-leaders, pep clubs, majorettes	Honorary clubs
All 1972 seniors	44.5	32.9	25.8	23.0	20.4	19.6	18.7	17.3	14.8
Race									
White	44.5	32.6	25.0	21.9	20.7	19.2	18.3	17.3	15.7
Black	49.7	40.6	33.1	33.1	21.2	25.5	19.7	20.5	11.6
All 1982 seniors	51.5	34.6	20.6	23.6	18.3	16.3	20.0	13.7	15.6

Continued.

High School Seniors' Extra-Curricular Activities: Trends
[Continued]

Student Characteristics	Athletics[1]	Debating, drama, band, chorus[2]	Subject-matter clubs	Vocational education clubs	Newspaper, magazine, or yearbook clubs	Student council, government, political clubs	Hobby clubs	Cheeer-leaders, pep clubs, majorettes	Honorary clubs
					Percent of seniors participating in activities				
Race									
White	51.1	34.0	19.7	22.2	19.1	15.6	19.1	13.5	16.8
Black	54.5	43.1	23.9	30.0	16.0	19.7	19.5	16.8	12.5

Source: "Participation of High School Seniors in Extracurricular Activities, by Selected Student Characteristics: 1972 and 1982," *Digest of Education Statistics*, 1989, p. 132. Primary source: U.S. Department of Education, National Center for Educational Statistics, "National Longitudinal Study of 1972" and High School and Beyond surveys. (This table was prepared August 1987.) *Notes:* 1. In 1972, includes participation in team athletics, intramurals, letterman's clubs, and sports clubs. In 1982, includes varsity athletic teams and other teams - in or out of school. 2. In 1972, includes debating, drama, band, and chorus. In 1982, includes debating, drama, band, orchestra, chorus, and dance.

★ 24 ★
High School Seniors' Positive Views of Justice System: Trends

By race, United States, 1977-88. NOTE: "Now we'd like you to make some ratings of how good or bad a job you feel each of the following organizations is doing for the country as a whole... How good or bad a job is being done for the country as a whole by...all the courts and the justice system in general?" (Percent responding "good" or "very good").

	Class of 1977 N = 3,144	Class of 1978 N = 3,778	Class of 1979 N = 3,295	Class of 1980 N = 3,299	Class of 1981 N = 3,658	Class of 1982 N = 3,688	Class of 1983 N = 3,382	Class of 1984 N = 3,287	Class of 1985 N = 3,294	Class of 1986 N = 3,159	Class of 1987 N = 3,357	Class of 1988 N = 3,378
Total	26.7	24.9	24.4	24.2	26.9	25.7	25.7	28.7	28.7	34.4	33.7	31.6
Race												
White	26.8	24.1	23.9	24.4	27.3	25.7	26.3	29.0	28.8	34.7	33.8	34.0
Black	24.5	28.3	24.5	22.1	25.7	28.0	23.5	26.4	28.9	35.4	30.9	21.6

Source: "High School Seniors Reporting Positive Attitudes towards the Performance of the Courts and the Justice System in General." *Sourcebook of Criminal Justice Statistics — 1988*, 1989, p. 252. Primary source: Lloyd D. Johnston, Jerald G. Bachman, and Patrick M. O'Malley, *Monitoring the Future 1977*, p. 126; *1979*, p. 127; *1981*, p. 128; *1983*, p. 127; *1985*, p. 127 (Ann Arbor, MI: Institute for Social Research, University of Michigan); Jerald G. Bachman, Lloyd D. Johnston, and Patrick M. O'Malley, *Monitoring the Future 1978*, p. 125; *1980*, p. 128; *1982*, p. 127; *1984*, p. 127; *1986*, p. 130 (Ann Arbor, MI: Institute for Social Research, University of Michigan); and data provided by the Monitoring the Future Project, Survey Research Center, Lloyd D. Johnston and Jerald G. Bachman, Principal Investigators. Table adapted by SOURCEBOOK staff. Reprinted by permission. *Notes:* Response categories were "very poor," "fair," "very good," and "no opinion." Readers interested in responses to this question for 1975 and 1976 should consult previous editions of SOURCEBOOK.

★ 25 ★
High School Seniors' Positive Views of Police: Trends

By race, United States, 1977-88. NOTE: Question: "Now we'd like you to make some ratings of how good or bad a job you feel each of the following organizations is doing for the country as a whole... How good or bad a job is being done for the country as a whole by... the police and other law enforcement agencies?" (Percent responding "good" or "very good").

	Class of 1977 N= 3,144	Class of 1978 N= 3,778	Class of 1979 N= 3,295	Class of 1980 N= 3,299	Class of 1981 N= 3,658	Class of 1982 N= 3,688	Class of 1983 N= 3,382	Class of 1984 N= 3,287	Class of 1985 N= 3,294	Class of 1986 N= 3,159	Class of 1987 N= 3,357	Class of 1988 N= 3,378
Total	36.2	37.0	37.6	37.2	35.0	37.2	37.4	36.9	37.3	40.5	39.5	37.4
Race												
White	37.7	39.3	39.5	39.7	36.9	38.6	38.7	37.6	38.9	42.4	41.9	40.5
Black	27.8	24.2	28.9	23.1	24.7	30.3	29.8	31.7	29.4	30.3	24.8	22.6

Source: "High School Seniors Reporting Positive Attitudes towards the Performance of the Police and Other Law Enforcement Agencies." *Sourcebook of Criminal Justice Statistics — 1988*, 1989, p. 250. Primary source: Lloyd D. Johnston, Jerald G. Bachman, and Patrick M. O'Malley, *Monitoring the Future 1977*, p. 126; *1979*, p. 127; *1981*, p. 128; *1983*, p. 128; *1985*, p. 128 (Ann Arbor, MI: Institute for Social Research, University of Michigan); Jerald G. Bachman, Lloyd D. Johnston, and Patrick M. O'Malley, *Monitoring the Future 1978*, p. 128; *1980*, p. 128; *1982*, p. 128; *1984*, p. 128; *1986*, p. 131 (Ann Arbor, MI: Institute for Social Research, University of Michigan); and data provided by the Monitoring the Future Project, Survey Research Center, Lloyd D. Johnston and Jerald G. Bachman, Principal Investigators. Table adapted by SOURCEBOOK staff. Reprinted by permission. *Notes:* Response categories were "very poor," "poor," "fair," "good" "very good" and "no opinion." Readers interested in responses to this question for 1975 and 1976 should consult previous editions of SOURCEBOOK.

★ 26 ★
High School Seniors' Positive Views of Supreme Court: Trends

By race, United States, 1977-88 Question: "Now we'd like you to make some ratings of how good or bad a job you feel each of the following organizations is doing for the country as a whole ... How good or bad a job is being done for the country as a whole by ... the U.S. Supreme Court?" Percent responding "good" or "very good".

	Class of 1977 N= 3,144	Class of 1978 N= 3,778	Class of 1979 N= 3,295	Class of 1980 N= 3,299	Class of 1981 N= 3,658	Class of 1982 N= 3,688	Class of 1983 N= 3,382	Class of 1984 N= 3,287	Class of 1985 N= 3,294	Class of 1986 N= 3,159	Class of 1987 N= 3,357	Class of 1988 N= 3,378
Total	37.0	34.9	32.3	30.0	37.2	37.5	36.4	43.1	42.1	46.3	45.7	42.1
Race												
White	37.8	35.2	33.0	29.9	37.8	38.8	37.8	45.2	43.8	48.1	47.9	45.0
Black	31.0	34.5	31.2	30.6	35.6	37.9	30.8	35.5	37.8	42.3	38.5	32.0

Source: "High School Seniors Reporting Positive Attitudes toward the Performance of the U.S. Supreme Court," *Sourcebook of Criminal Justice Statistics - 1988*, 1989, p. 251. Primary source: Lloyd D. Johnston, Jerald G. Bachman, and Patrick M. O'Malley, *Monitoring the Future 1977*, p. 126; *1979*, p. 127; *1981*, p. 128; *1983*, p. 127; *1985*, p. 127. (Ann Arbor, MI: Institute for Social Research, University of Michigan); Jerald G. Bachman, Lloyd D. Johnston, and Patrick M. O'Malley, *Monitoring the Future 1978*, p. 125; *1980*, p. 128; *1982*, p. 127; *1984*, p. 127; *1986*, p. 130 (Ann Arbor, MI: Institute for Social Research, University of Michigan); and data provided by the Monitoring the Future Project, Survey Research Center, Lloyd D. Johnston and Jerald G. Bachman, Principal Investigators. Table adapted by SOURCEBOOK staff. Reprinted by permission. *Notes:* Response categories were "very poor," "poor," "fair," "good," "very good," and "no opinion." Readers interested in responses to this question for 1975 and 1976 should consult previous editions of the SOURCEBOOK.

★ 27 ★
High School Seniors' Views on Crime and Violence: Trends

By race, United States, 1977-88. Question: "Of all the problems facing the nation today, how often do you worry about ... crime and violence?" (Percent responding "often" or "sometimes").

	Class of 1977 N= 3,117	Class of 1978 N= 3,770	Class of 1979 N= 3,308	Class of 1980 N= 3,286	Class of 1981 N= 3,656	Class of 1982 N= 3,616	Class of 1983 N= 3,339	Class of 1984 N= 3,294	Class of 1985 N= 3,286	Class of 1986 N= 3,073	Class of 1987 N= 3,370	Class of 1988 N= 3,326
Total	87.2	86.6	84.6	81.2	87.8	86.3	85.4	83.9	82.3	79.4	81.9	83.9
Race												
White	86.8	86.2	83.8	80.7	87.3	85.1	84.5	83.3	80.9	78.4	80.8	82.8
Black	91.5	88.8	89.1	83.3	91.0	91.2	91.6	90.4	88.9	81.9	94.2	88.2

Source: "High School Seniors' Reporting that They Worry about Crime and Violence," *Sourcebook of Criminal Justice Statistics - 1988*, 1989, p. 246. Primary source: Lloyd D. Johnston, Jerald G. Bachman, and Patrick M. O'Malley, *Monitoring the Future 1977*, pp. 170, 171; *1979*, pp. 171, 172; *1981*, pp. 172, 173; *1983*, pp. 174, 175; *1985*, p. 174 (Ann Arbor, MI: Institute for Social Research, University of Michigan); Jerald G. Bachman, Lloyd D. Johnston, and Patrick M. O'Malley, *Monitoring the Future 1978*, pp. 170, 171; *1980*, pp. 172, 173; *1982*, p. 174; *1984*, p. 174; *1986*, p. 176 (Ann Arbor, MI: Institute for Social Research, University of Michigan); and data provided by the Monitoring Project, Survey Research Center, Lloyd D. Johnston and Jerald G. Bachman, Principal Investigators. Table adapted by SOURCEBOOK staff. Reprinted by permission. Percentages and Table Ns are based on weighted cases. *Notes:* Data are given for those who identify themselves as White or Caucasian and those who identify themselves as Black or Afro-American because these are the two largest racial/ethnic subgroups in the population. Data are not given for the other 3 percent of the sample in any given year (Source, 1982, p. 9). "College plans" distinguishes those seniors who expect to graduate from a 4- year college from those who expect to receive some college training or none. The four drug use categories are based on an index of seriousness of involvement. The term "pills" may contain people who indicate that they use any of a number of drugs including some that usually are not taken in pill form. "Few pills" refers to respondents indicating the use of one or more of a number of illicit drugs but who had not used any one class of them on three or more occasions. "More pills" refers to respondents indicating such use on three or more occassions. Respondents reporting heroin use were included in a separate category that is not presented here due to the small number of respondents indicating such use. (Source, 1982, pp. 8,9,14.) Response categories were "never," "seldom," "sometimes," and "often." Readers interested in responses to this question for 1975 and 1976 should consult previous editions of SOURCEBOOK.

★ 28 ★
High School Seniors' Views on Justice System: Trends

By race, United States, 1977-88. Question: "Now we'd like to ask you to make some ratings of how honest and moral the people are who run the following organizations. To what extent are there problems of dishonesty and immorality in the leadership of ... all the courts and the justice system in general?" (Percent responding "considerable" or "great").

	Class of 1977 N= 3,197	Class of 1978 N= 3,785	Class of 1979 N= 3,348	Class of 1980 N= 3,327	Class of 1981 N= 3,655	Class of 1982 N= 3,678	Class of 1983 N= 3,435	Class of 1984 N= 3,322	Class of 1985 N= 3,327	Class of 1986 N= 3,179	Class of 1987 N= 3,361	Class of 1988 N= 3,350
Total	25.4	23.9	24.1	24.5	22.2	22.8	21.7	23.3	22.8	22.8	22.9	23.1
Race												
White	24.9	23.2	23.7	24.0	21.8	22.1	20.6	22.1	22.1	22.5	21.4	22.5
Black	26.5	26.4	26.4	29.4	29.2	25.6	28.3	29.2	26.8	28.9	32.1	24.1

Source: "High School Seniors' Beliefs that Problems of Dishonesty and Immorality Exist in the Leadership of the Courts and the Justice System in General," *Sourcebook of Criminal Justice Statistics - 1988*, 1989, p. 248. Primary source: Lloyd D. Johnston, Jerald G. Bachman, and Patrick M. O'Malley, *Monitoring the Future 1977*, p. 106; *1979*, p. 107; *1981*, p. 107; *1983*, p. 107; *1985*, p. 106 (Ann Arbor, MI: Institute for Social Research, University of Michigan); Jerald G. Bachman, Lloyd D.Johnston, and Patrick O'Malley M., *Monitoring the Future 1978*, p. 106; *1980*, p. 107; *1982*, p. 107; *1984*, p. 106; *1986*, p. 109, 177 (Ann Arbor, MI: Institute for Social Research, University of Michigan); and data provided by the Monitoring Project, Survey Research Center, Lloyd D. Johnston and Jerald G. Bachman, Principal Investigators. Table adapted by SOURCEBOOK staff. Reprinted by permission. *Notes:* Response categories were "not at all," "slight," "moderate," "considerable," "great," and "no opinion." Readers interested in responses to this question for 1975 and 1976 should consult previous editions of SOURCEBOOK.

★ 29 ★
High School Seniors' Views on Police: Trends

By race, United States, 1977-88. Question: "Now we'd like to ask you to make some ratings of how honest and moral the people are who run the following organizations. To what extent are there problems of dishonesty and immorality in the leadership of ... the police and other law enforcement agencies?" (Percent responding "considerable" or "great").

	Class of 1977 N= 3,197	Class of 1978 N= 3,785	Class of 1979 N= 3,348	Class of 1980 N= 3,327	Class of 1981 N= 3,655	Class of 1982 N= 3,678	Class of 1983 N= 3,435	Class of 1984 N= 3,322	Class of 1985 N= 3,327	Class of 1986 N= 3,179	Class of 1987 N= 3,361	Class of 1988 N= 3,350
Total	32.5	32.8	32.5	31.5	29.9	30.6	30.3	29.3	27.2	28.4	27.8	30.3
Race												
White	31.4	31.6	32.2	30.4	28.4	29.6	28.7	28.7	26.7	27.1	26.5	28.2
Black	38.0	36.4	35.1	37.9	40.1	33.6	39.0	32.4	29.7	32.6	37.3	37.7

Source: "High School Seniors' Beliefs that Problems of Dishonesty and Immorality Exist in the Leadership of the Police and Other Law Enforcement Agencies," *Sourcebook of Criminal Justice Statistics - 1988*, 1989, p. 246. Primary source: Lloyd D. Johnston, Jerald G. Bachman, and Patrick M. O'Malley, *Monitoring the Future 1977*, p. 107; *1979*, p. 108; *1981*, p. 108; *1983*, p. 108; *1985*, p. 107 (Ann Arbor, MI: Institute for Social Research, University of Michigan); Jerald G. Bachman, Lloyd D. Johnston, and Patrick O'Malley M., *Monitoring the Future 1978*, p. 107; *1980*, p. 108; *1982*, p. 108; *1984*, p. 107; *1986*, p. 110 (Ann Arbor, MI: Institute for Social Research, University of Michigan); and data provided by the Monitoring Project, Survey Research Center, Lloyd D. Johnston and Jerald G. Bachman, Principal Investigators. Table adapted by SOURCEBOOK staff. Reprinted by permission. Percentages and Table Ns are based on weighted cases. *Notes:* Response categories were "not at all," "slight," "moderate," "considerable," "great," and "no opinion." Readers interested in responses to this question for 1975 and 1976 should consult previous editions of SOURCEBOOK.

★ 30 ★
High School Seniors' Views on Supreme Court: Trends

By race, United States, 1977-88. Question: "Now we'd like to ask you to make some ratings of how honest and moral the people are who run the following organizations. To what extent are there problems of dishonesty and immorality in the leadership of ... the U.S. Supreme Court?" (Percent responding "considerable" or "great").

	Class of 1977 N= 3,197	Class of 1978 N= 3,785	Class of 1979 N= 3,348	Class of 1980 N= 3,327	Class of 1981 N= 3,655	Class of 1982 N= 3,678	Class of 1983 N= 3,435	Class of 1984 N= 3,322	Class of 1985 N= 3,327	Class of 1986 N= 3,179	Class of 1987 N= 3,361	Class of 1988 N= 3,350
Total	23.0	22.1	24.3	22.8	20.0	20.7	19.1	22.7	22.5	23.2	23.1	21.9
Race												
White	22.3	21.0	23.3	21.8	18.9	19.9	17.0	21.1	21.6	22.5	21.7	21.1
Black	27.9	27.4	32.0	30.7	27.7	23.9	28.3	29.0	27.6	29.7	31.0	25.7

Source: "High School Seniors' Beliefs that Problems of Dishonesty and Immorality Exist in the Leadership of the U.S. Supreme Court," *Sourcebook of Criminal Justice Statistics - 1988*, 1989, p. 247. Primary source: Lloyd D. Johnston, Jerald G. Bachman, and Patrick M. O'Malley, *Monitoring the Future 1977*, p. 106; *1979*, p. 107; *1981*, p. 107; *1983*, p. 107; *1985*, p. 106 (Ann Arbor, MI: Institute for Social Research, University of Michigan); Jerald G. Bachman, Lloyd D. Johnston, and Patrick O'Malley M., *Monitoring the Future 1978*, p. 106; *1980*, p. 107; *1982*, p. 107; *1984*, p. 106; *1986*, p. 109, 177 (Ann Arbor, MI: Institute for Social Research, University of Michigan); and data provided by the Monitoring Project, Survey Research Center, Lloyd D. Johnston and Jerald G. Bachman, Principal Investigators. Table adapted by SOURCEBOOK staff. Reprinted by permission. *Notes:* Response categories were "not at all," "slight," "moderate," "considerable," "great," and "no opinion." Readers interested in responses to this question for 1975 and 1976 should consult previous editions of SOURCEBOOK.

★ 31 ★
How do 8th Graders Feel About School?

Statements about school climate	Percent who strongly agree or agree with statement					
		Race/ethnicity				
	All 8th graders	White	Black	Hispanic	Asian	American Indian
Students get along well with teachers	67.1	68.1	60.5	66.4	73.0	65.2
There is real school spirit	68.6	69.8	65.0	64.9	66.7	67.4
Rules for behavior are strict	68.5	68.5	68.7	68.4	67.3	65.4
Discipline is fair	69.1	69.7	65.0	70.7	72.5	63.5
Other students often disrupt classs	77.9	77.3	80.5	79.1	76.1	79.0
Teaching is good	80.2	80.0	80.0	81.3	83.4	76.7
Teachers are interested in students	75.2	74.7	76.6	76.8	78.6	68.5
Teachers praise my effort when I work hard	63.3	60.3	72.1	70.7	70.8	63.3
I often feel "put down" by my teachers	21.8	21.7	21.5	22.6	17.1	30.5
Teachers listen to what I have to say	68.4	67.1	73.2	70.6	74.9	62.1
Disruptions by other students interfere with my learning	39.6	35.7	54.9	44.9	45.1	55.2
Misbehaving students often get away with it	52.8	51.9	53.4	55.7	55.3	59.0

Source: "Eighth Graders' Attitudes about School Climate, by Student and School Characteristics: 1988," *Education Statistics*, 1989, p. 133. Primary source: U.S. Department of Education, National Center for Educational Statistics, "National Education Longitudinal Study of 1988" survey. (This table was prepared June 1989.) *Note:* Data are preliminary.

★ 32 ★
Important Community Problems

By sex and race, United States, 1986(1). Question: "What do you think is the most important problem facing the community you live in?".

	National	Sex		Race	
		Male	Female	White	Black
War	0	0	0	0	0
Taxes	3	4	3	4	1
Unemployment	17	18	16	16	17
Economy, inflation	6	6	5	6	1
Politicians inept	2	2	1	2	2
Nuclear sites	0	0	0	0	0
Environment, pollution	3	3	3	3	0
Road maintenance	1	1	2	1	0
Development	2	3	2	3	0
Population, traffic	2	3	1	2	0
Mass transit	0	0	0	0	0
Welfare	1	1	0	1	0

Continued.

Important Community Problems
[Continued]

	National	Sex		Race	
		Male	Female	White	Black
Health, AIDS[2]	0	0	1	0	1
Farmers	2	2	2	3	0
Social Security, elderly	0	0	0	0	0
Poor	1	0	2	1	1
Crime	8	7	8	7	10
Oil	1	2	1	1	0
Homeless	1	0	1	1	2
Minorities, race relations	1	1	0	1	0
Education	3	2	3	3	0
Housing	2	3	2	2	7
Immigrants	1	1	0	1	0
Gangs	1	1	1	0	6
Labor	0	0	0	0	0
Youth	0	0	0	0	0
Morality, values	1	1	2	1	3
Indifference, nobody cares	1	1	1	1	0
Drugs	13	12	14	12	18
Alcohol	1	0	1	1	0
Other	1	1	2	1	2
Don't know/no answer	24	24	25	24	29

Source: "Attitudes toward the Most Important Problem Facing Respondent's Community," Sourcebook of Criminal Justice Statistics — 1988, 1989, p. 183. Primary source: Table adopted by SOURCEBOOK staff from tables provided by The New York Times/CBS News Poll. Copyright 1986 by the New York Times/CBS News Poll. Reprinted by permission. Notes: 1. Percents may not add to 100 due to rounding. Some 0 entries may be less than one-half of 1 percent. 2. Acquired immunodeficiency syndrome.

★ 33 ★
Important National Problems - Part I

By demographic characteristics, United States, 1988(1). Question: "What do you think is the most important problem facing this country today?"

	Economic problems								
	Economic problems (total)	Federal budget deficit	Economy (general)	Unemploy-ment	Trade deficit/ trade relations	High cost of living/ inflation	Other specific economic problems	Drugs/ drug abuse	Poverty/ hunger/ homeless
	Numbers in percent								
National	45	12		12	9	3	2	7	11	7
Race									
White	46	14		13	8	3	2	6	11	7
Black	41	5	6	1	6	3	3	8	17	10

Source: "Attitudes toward the Most Important Problem Facing the Country," Sourcebook of Criminal Justice Statistics - 1988, 1989, pp. 184-185. Primary source: Gallup, Jr., George. The Gallup Report, Report No. 277 (Princeton, NJ: The Gallup Poll, October, 1988), pp. 6,7. Table adapted by SOURCEBOOK staff. Reprinted by permission. Notes: 1. Totals add up to more than 100 percent due to multiple responses. 2. Less than 1 percent. Published by permission.

★ 34 ★
Important National Problems - Part II

By demographic characteristics, United States, 1988(1). Question: "What do you think is the most important problem facing this country today?"

	Fear of war/ nuclear war problems	International problems/ foreign affairs	Quality of education	Crime	Moral/ religious decline in society	Other non-economic problems	None/ no opinion
			Numbers in percent				
National	5	4	2	2	1	11	12
Race							
White	5	4	2	2	1	11	11
Black	4	3	2	1	1	5	18

Source: "Attitudes toward the Most Important Problem Facing the Country," *Sourcebook of Criminal Justice Statistics - 1988*, 1989, pp. 184-185. Primary source: Gallup, Jr., George. *The Gallup Report*, Report No. 277 (Princeton, NJ: The Gallup Poll, October, 1988), pp. 6,7. Table adapted by SOURCEBOOK staff. Reprinted by permission. *Notes:* 1. Totals add up to more than 100 percent due to multiple responses. 2. Less than 1 percent. Published by permission.

★ 35 ★
Index to Satisfaction with College

Consider Leaving	Total Population	Campus Race	
		Black	White
Yes	36.7	39.7	33
No	63.3	60.3	67
Total	100.0	100.0	100.0
N	(1560)	(869)	(691)

Source: "Whether Considered Leaving College by Student Gender and Campus Race," *Gender and Campus Race Differences in Black Student Academic Performance, Racial Attitudes and College Satisfaction*, 1986, p. 41. Primary source: National Study of Black College Students, 1981 and 1983, University of Michigan, Ann Arbor. Published by permission.

★ 36 ★
Is the Death Penalty Imposed Fairly?

By demographic characteristics, United States, 1986. Question: "Some people say the death penalty is not carried out fairly from case to case. Others say it is. Do you think the death penalty is carried out fairly from case to case, or not?" Numbers in percent.

	Carried out fairly	Not carried out fairly	Don't know/no answer
National	32	50	18
Race, ethnicity			
White	33	49	18
Black	21	59	20
Hispanic	25	62	13
Other	57	26	17

Source: "Attitudes toward Fairness in the Imposition of the Death Penalty," *Sourcebook of Criminal Justice Statistics - 1988*, 1989, p. 231. Primary source: Table adapted by SOURCEBOOK staff from table provided by the Media General/Associated Press Poll. Reprinted by permission.

★ 37 ★
Local Teenage Drug Abuse

By demographic characteristics, United States, 1986. Question: "How serious a problem do you think drug abuse is among teenagers in the community where you live — a very serious problem, a somewhat serious problem, or not much of a problem?"

	Very serious	Somewhat serious	Not much of a problem	Don't know/ no answer
National[1]	29	42	23	6
Race				
White	27	45	22	6
Black	39	23	32	7

Source: "Attitudes toward the Severity of Teenage Drug Abuse in Respondent's Community," *Sourcebook of Criminal Justice Statistics - 1988,* 1989, p. 261. Primary source: Table adapted by SOURCEBOOK staff from tables provided by The New York Times/CBS News Poll. Copyright 1986 by The New York Times/CBS News Poll. Reprinted by permission. *Note:* 1. Percents may not add to 100 due to rounding.

★ 38 ★
Murder and the Death Penalty

By demographic characteristics, United States, 1986. Question: "In general, do you feel the death penalty should be allowed in all murder cases, only in certain murder cases, or should there be no death penalty at all?" Numbers in percent.

	All murder cases	In certain murder cases	No death penalty	Don't know/no answer
National	29	56	11	4
Race, ethnicity				
White	30	58	9	3
Black	20	38	33	9
Hispanic	19	50	31	0
Other	39	48	13	0

Source: "Attitudes toward the Death Penalty for Murder," *Sourcebook of Criminal Justice Statistics - 1988,* 1989, p. 230. Primary source: Table adapted by SOURCEBOOK staff provided by the Media General/Associated Press Poll. Reprinted by permission.

★ 39 ★
Parents' and Teachers' Beliefs About Education

Selected activities and programs	Percent of parents, by race			
	All parents	White parents	Black parents	Hispanic parents
Having the school notify the parents immediately about any problems involving their child	88	88	89	88
Having parents limit television until all homework is finished	79	77	86	83
Having parents spend much more time with their children in support of school and teachers	70	69	73	69
Distributing a newsletter to keep parents informed about what's happening in school	68	66	71	80
Establishing a homework hotline which students can call for advice on how to deal with homework assignments	64	62	70	72
Having the school give more guidance to teachers about how to involve				

Continued.

Parents' and Teachers' Beliefs About Education
[Continued]

Selected activities and programs	Percent of parents, by race			
	All parents	White parents	Black parents	Hispanic parents
parents better in the future	60	57	72	61
Getting teachers and parents to meet together and talk about school policies	58	56	71	62
Providing counseling and support services to children with emotional, mental, social, or family problems	80	79	85	84
Developing school programs to involve parents with students who have special needs	73	72	76	72
Developing school programs to involve members of the community with students who have special needs	62	60	73	62
Developing educational programs designed for students who are frequently absent from school	54	53	57	61
Beginning the education process earlier by enrolling students in pre-school education programs	49	43	73	55
Developing different approaches to education outside the traditional school	40	39	49	40
Providing optional day-care programs with an educational component after the regular school hours	39	33	64	50

Source: "Beliefs Held by the Parents and Teachers of Public School Students about what Activities and Programs would 'Help a Lot' to Improve Education: 1987," *Digest of Education Statistics*, 1989, p. 28. Primary Source: Metropolitan Life/Louis Harris Associates, Inc., *The American Teacher*, 1987. (This table was prepared September 1987.).

★ 40 ★
Penalties for Murder - Death or Life Imprisonment?

By demographic characteristics, United States, 1986. Question: "What do you think should be the penalty for murder — the death penalty or life imprisonment with absolutely no possibility of parole?"

	Death penalty	Life imprisonment	Neither[1]	No opinion
	Numbers in percent			
National	55	35	4	6
Race, ethnicity				
White	57	33	3	7
Nonwhite	38	52	4	6
Black	38	52	4	6
Hispanic	44	42	4	10

Source: "Attitudes toward the Death Penalty Versus Life Imprisonment with No Possibility of Parole as Penalties for Murder," *Sourcebook of Criminal Justice Statistics - 1988*, 1989, p. 229. Primary source: Gallup Jr., George, *The Gallup Report*, Report Nos. 244/245 (Princeton, NJ: The Gallup Poll, January/February 1986), p. 13. Table adapted by SOURCEBOOK staff. Reprinted by permission. *Note:* 1. Responses volunteered. Published by permission.

★ 41 ★
Problems Teenagers Have

By demographic characteristics, United States, 1987. Question: "What do you feel is the biggest problem facing people your age?" Numbers in percent.

	Drug abuse	Alcohol abuse	Teenage pregnancy	Peer pressures	AIDS[2]	Problems with parents	Maturity, independence	Unemployment	Teenage suicide	Other	No opinion
National[1]	54	12	11	10	5	2	2	2	2	9	8
Race											
White	54	14	9	10	5	2	2	2	2	8	9
Black	55	2	25	12	6	4	3	[3]	[3]	8	4

Source: "Teenager Attitudes toward Problems Facing Young People," *Sourcebook of Criminal Justice Statistics - 1988*, 1989, p. 187. Primary source: Gallup Jr., George, *The Gallup Report*, Report No. 265 (Princeton, NJ: The Gallup Poll, October 1987), p. 43. Table adapted by SOURCEBOOK staff. Reprinted by permission. *Notes:* 1. Totals exceed 100 percent due to multiple responses. 2. Acquired immunodeficiency syndrome. 3. Less than 1 percent. . Published by permission.

★ 42 ★
Punishment for Drug Dealers

By demographic characteristics, United States, 1986(1). Question: "What do you think should happen to people who are convicted of *selling* cocaine or crack for the first time? Should they be fined and put on probation, OR should they get 30 days in jail, OR a year in jail, OR more than a year in jail?" Numbers in percent.

	Fine and probation	30 days in jail	1 year in jail	More than 1 year in jail	Life imprisonment[2]	Death[2]	Don't know/ no answer
National	12	16	22	42	0	1	6
Race							
White	12	15	23	42	0	1	5
Black	18	28	13	28	0	0	12

Source: "Attitudes toward the Punishment of First-Time Convicted Cocaine or Crack Sellers," *Sourcebook of Criminal Justice Statistics - 1988*, 1989, p. 272. Primary source: Table adapted by SOURCEBOOK staff from tables provided by The New York Times/CBS News Poll. Copyright 1986 by The New York Times/CBS News Poll. Reprinted by permission. *Notes:* "Crack" is a highly potent and addictive form of cocaine. 1. Percents may not add to 100 due to rounding. Some 0 entries may be less than one-half of 1 percent. 2. Response volunteered.

★ 43 ★
Should Abortion Be Legal?

By demographic characteristics, United States, 1988. Question: "Do you think abortions should be legal under any circumstances, legal only under certain circumstances, or illegal in all circumstances?" Number in percent.

	Always legal	Legal under certain circumstances	Always illegal	No opinion
National	24	57	17	2
Race				
White	25	57	15	3
Nonwhite	15	55	28	2
Black	14	56	28	2

Source: "Attitudes Toward Abortion," *Sourcebook of Criminal Justice Statistics - 1988*, 1989, p. 214. Primary source: Gallup Jr., George, *The Gallup Report*, Report No. 281 (Princeton, NJ: The Gallup Poll, February 1989), p. 17. Reprinted by permission. Published by permission.

★ 44 ★
Should Gun Sales be Regulated?

By demographic characteristics, United States, 1989(1). Numbers in percent.

	Do you favor or oppose federal laws which control the sale of guns, such as making all persons register all gun purchases, no matter where the purchases are made?			Do you favor or oppose a federal law requiring that all handguns people own be registered by federal authorities?		
	Favor	Oppose	Not sure	Favor	Oppose	Not sure
National	79	18	3	78	20	2
Race, ethnicity						
White	79	19	3	78	20	2
Black	83	12	4	79	16	5
Hispanic	74	24	2	71	27	2

Source: "Attitudes toward Federal Laws Regulating the Sale and Registration of All Guns," *Sourcebook of Criminal Justice Statistics - 1988*, 1989, p. 235. Primary source: Table adapted by SOURCEBOOK staff from table provided by Louis Harris & Associates, Inc. Reprinted by permission. *Note:* 1. Percent may not add to 100 due to rounding. Published by permission.

★ 45 ★
Should the Legal "Drinking Age" be 21?

By demographic characteristics, United States, 1986. Question: "Would you favor or oppose a national law that would raise the legal drinking age in all States to 21?" Numbers in percent.

	Favor	Oppose	No opinion
National	80	17	3
Race			
White	81	17	2
Nonwhite	79	18	3
Black	80	17	4

Source: "Attitudes toward a National Law Raising the Drinking Age to 21," *Sourcebook of Criminal Justice Statistics - 1988*, 1989, p. 273. Primary source: Gallup Jr., George, *The Gallup Report*, Report No. 265 (Princeton, NJ: The Gallup Report, October 1987), p. 15. Reprinted by permission. Published by permission.

★ 46 ★
Standards of Ethics/Honesty of Lawyers

By demographic characteristics, United States, 1988. Question: "How would you rate the honesty and ethical standards of people in these different fields — very high, high, average, low, or very low: Lawyers?" Numbers in percent.

	Very high	High	Average	Low	Very low	No opinion
National	3	15	45	23	10	4
Race						
White	2	14	45	25	11	3
Nonwhite	5	21	48	16	5	5
Black	6	21	51	13	6	3

Source: "Respondents' Ratings of the Honesty and Ethical Stanadrds of Lawyers," *Sourcebook of Criminal Justice Statistics - 1988*, 1989, p. 196. Primary source: Gallup Jr., George, *The Gallup Report*, Report No. 279 (Princeton, NJ: The Gallup Poll, December 1988), p. 18. Table adapted by SOURCEBOOK staff. Reprinted by permission. Published by permission.

★ 47 ★
Standards of Ethics/Honesty of Policepersons

By demographic characteristics, United States, 1988. Question: "How would you rate the honesty and ethical standards of people in these different fields — very high, high, average, low, or very low: Policemen?" Numbers in percent.

	Very high	High	Average	Low	Very low	No opinion
National	10	37	39	8	3	3
Race						
White	11	38	39	7	3	2
Nonwhite	3	30	46	11	4	6
Black	4	29	47	10	3	7

Source: "Respondents' Ratings of the Honesty and Ethical Stanadrds of Policemen," *Sourcebook of Criminal Justice Statistics - 1988*, 1989, p. 196. Primary source: Gallup Jr., George, *The Gallup Report*, Report No. 279 (Princeton, NJ: The Gallup Poll, December 1988), p. 10. Table adapted by SOURCEBOOK staff. Reprinted by permission. Published by permission.

★ 48 ★
Striving for Success on Black/White College Campuses

Numbers in percent.

Occupational Success Striving	Total Population	Campus Race	
		Black	White
Well Enough	5.8	7.1	4.1
As Well As Most	3.9	4.2	3.5
Better Than Most	9.4	7.9	11.4
Much Better Than Most	23.7	19.3	29.5
Among Top in Profession	57.1	61.4	51.5
Total	100.0	100.0	100.0
N	(1507)	(856)	(651)

Source: "Occupation Eminence Striving by Student Gender and Campus Race," *Gender and Campus Race Differences in Black Student Academic Performance, Racial Attitudes and College Satisfaction*, 1986, p. 56 Primary source: National Study of Black College Students, 1981 and 1983, University of Michigan, Ann Arbor. Published by permission.

★ 49 ★
Student Self-Concept on Black/White College Campuses

Self-Concept	Total Population	Campus Race	
		Black	White
Below Average	.4	.1	.7
Average	20.2	24.8	14.3
Above Average	52.3	49.0	56.4
High	27.2	26.1	28.5
Total	100.0	100.0	100.0
N	(1550)	(866)	(684)

Source: "Self-Concept by Student Gender and Campus Race," *Gender and Campus Race Differences in Black Student Academic Performance, Racial Attitudes and College Satisfaction*, 1986, p. 54. Primary source: National Study of Black College Students, 1981 and 1983, University of Michigan, Ann Arbor. Published by permission.

★ 50 ★
Supreme Court Ratings

By demographic characteristics, United States, 1987 Question: "In general, what kind of rating would you give the U.S. Supreme Court — excellent, good, fair, or poor?" Numbers in percent.

	Excellent	Good	Fair	Poor	No opinion
National	10	40	35	7	8
Race, ethnicity					
White	10	41	34	7	8
Nonwhite	8	34	44	8	6
Black	9	33	45	9	4
Hispanic	7	37	33	11	12

Source: "Respondents' Ratings of the U.S. Supreme Court," *Sourcebook of Criminal Justice Statistics - 1988*, 1989, p. 194. Primary source: Gallup Jr., George, *The Gallup Report*, Report No. 262 (Princeton, NJ: The Gallup Poll, July 1987), p. 26. Table adapted by SOURCEBOOK staff. Reprinted by permission. Published by permission.

★ 51 ★
Testing Prisoners for AIDS

By demographic characteristic, United States, 1987. Question: "In your opinion which of the following group of people, if any should be tested for AIDS?: Inmates of federal prisons." Numbers in percent.

	Should	Should Not	No opinion
National	88	10	2
Race			
White	88	10	2
Nonwhite	90	9	1
Black	89	10	1

Source: "Attitudes toward Testing Federal Prison Inmates for AIDS," *Sourcebook of Criminal Justice Statistics - 1988*, 1989, p. 280. Primary source: Gallup Jr., George, *The Gallup Report*, Report No. 261 (Princeton, NJ: The Gallup Poll, June 1987), p. 4. Reprinted by permission. AIDS - Acquired Immunodeficiency Syndrome. Published by permission.

★ 52 ★
The 1989 College Freshman: Why Go to College?

Reasons	All Institutions	Predominantly Black Colleges	Predominantly Black Colleges	
			Public	Private
Parents wanted me to go	34.4	53.4	54.4	51.6
Could not find a job	7.0	11.6	11.5	11.8
Wanted to get away from home	15.0	26.7	26.9	26.3
Get a better job	75.9	81.6	81.4	81.8
Gain general education	62.5	77.0	76.6	77.9
Improve reading and study skills	40.5	65.3	66.1	64.1
Nothing better to do	2.4	4.6	3.9	5.7
Become a more cultured person	35.6	55.6	53.1	60.0
Make more money	72.2	84.0	84.2	83.7
Learn more about things	72.4	79.2	78.4	80.5
Prepare for graduate school	51.5	73.3	70.6	78.0

Source: "Reasons Noted as Very Important in Deciding to Go to College," *The American Freshman: National Norms for Fall 1989*, p. 44. Primary source: Cooperative Institutional Research Program, American Council on Education, University of California, Los Angeles, 1989. Figures for predominantly Black colleges includes all ethnic groups. Published by permission.

★ 53 ★
The Death Penalty for Murder

By demographic characteristics, United States, 1986. Numbers in percent.

	Do you favor or oppose the death penalty for murder?			Suppose new evidence showed that the death penalty does not act as a deterrent to murder, that it does not lower the murder rate. Would you favor or oppose the death penalty?[1]			Suppose new evidence showed that the death penalty acts as a deterrent to murder, that it lowers the murder rate. Would you favor or oppose the death penalty?[2]		
	Favor	Oppose	No opinion	Favor	Oppose	No opinion	Would now favor	Would now oppose	No opinion
National	70	22	8	73	19	8	18	71	11
Race, ethnicity									
White	73	19	8	3	19	8	19	69	12
Nonwhite	50	41	9	70	22	8	16	76	8
Black	47	43	10	68	24	8	14	77	9
Hispanic	60	30	10	57	35	8	17	60	23

Source: "Attitudes toward the Death Penalty for Murder," *Sourcebook of Criminal Justice Statistics - 1988*, 1989, p. 228. Primary source: Gallup Jr., George, *The Gallup Report*, Report Nos. 244/245 (Princeton, NJ: The Gallup Poll, January/February 1986), pp. 12, 15. Reprinted by permission. *Notes:* 1. This question was asked of the 70 percent subsample who reported that they favor the death penalty. 2. This question was asked of the 22 percent subsample who reported that they oppose the death penalty. Published by permission.

★ 54 ★
When is Abortion Approved?

By demographic characteristics, United States, 1988. Question: "Please tell me whether you think abortions should or should not be legal under each of the following circumstances:"(1) Numbers in percent.

	If a woman's life is endangered?		If the woman may suffer severe physical health damage?		If there is any chance the baby will be born deformed?		If the pregnancy is the result of rape or incest?		If the family cannot afford to have the child?	
	Approve	Disapprove	Approve	Disapprove	Approve	Disapprove	Approve	Disapprove	Approve	Disapprove
National	94	2	84	11	60	29	85	11	19	75
Race										
White	94	2	85	11	58	30	85	11	18	76
Nonwhite	91	6	82	11	69	26	84	14	23	72
Black	92	7	84	9	68	27	84	13	22	71

Source: "Attitudes toward the Circumstances of Abortion," *Sourcebook of Criminal Justice Statistics - 1988*, 1989, p. 215. Primary source: Gallup Jr., George, *The Gallup Report*, Report No. 281 (Princeton, NJ: The Gallup Poll, February 1989), p. 18. Reprinted by permission. *Notes:* This question was asked of the 57 percent subsample responding "legal under certain circumstances" to a question presented earlier. 1. Responses of "no opinion" were omitted by the Source. Published by permission.

★ 55 ★
When is the Death Penalty Justifiable?

By demographic characteristics, United States, 1988. Question: "Do you favor or oppose the death penalty for people convicted of:" Numbers in percent.

	Murder?		Rape?		Hijacking an airplane?		Attempting to assassinate the President?		Spying for a foreign nation during peace-time?		Drug dealers not convicted of murder?	
	Favor	Oppose	Favor	Oppose	Favor	Oppose	Favor	Oppose	Favor	Oppose	Favor	Oppose
National	79	16	51	42	49	45	63	33	42	50	38	55
Race												
White	82	14	53	41	51	43	66	31	43	49	39	54
Nonwhite	61	28	45	46	41	53	44	49	38	51	33	61
Black	57	31	40	50	40	55	42	52	38	51	28	67

Source: "Attitudes toward the Death Penalty for Persons Convicted of Murder and Other Offenses," *Sourcebook of Criminal Justice Statistics - 1988*, 1989, p. 223. Primary source: Gallup Jr., George, *The Gallup Report*, Report No. 280 (Princeton, NJ: The Gallup Poll, January 1989), p. 28, 29. Table adapted by SOURCEBOOK staff. Reprinted by permission. *Note:* Responses of "no opinion" were omitted by the Source. Published by permission.

★ 56 ★
Young Adult Political Participation: Trends

Political participation	Total	Race/ethnicity			
		White, non-Hispanic	Black, non-Hispanic	Hispanic	Asian
1979[1]					
Tried to persuade someone to vote for or against a candidate	34.3	35.6	26.9	28.7	35.3
Gave money or bought tickets to help a candidate	20.6	19.8	27.7	23.1	19.3
Attended a social-political gathering [2]	21.3	20.3	30.0	24.2	20.4
Voted in a local, State, or national election[3]	68.4	70.2	63.4	53.7	59.0
1986[4]					
Tried to persuade someone to vote for or against a candidate	25.0	25.2	26.8	23.2	24.5
Gave money or bought tickets to help a candidate	13.7	12.5	19.6	17.1	11.1
Attended a social-political gathering [2]	15.7	15.0	21.9	15.5	16.0
Registered to vote	72.3	71.8	77.8	70.3	71.8
Voted in a local, State, or national election[5]	60.7	61.4	62.5	52.8	56.8

Continued.

Young Adult Political Participation: Trends
[Continued]

Political participation	Total	Race/ethnicity			
		White, non-Hispanic	Black, non-Hispanic	Hispanic	Asian
Voted in the 1984 presidential election	59.0	60.0	60.0	51.8	54.1

Source: "Political Participation of Young Adults, by Sex, Race/Ethnicity, and Socioeconomic Status: 1979 and 1986," *Digest of Educational Statistics*, 1989, p. 377. Primary source: U.S. Department of Education, National Center for Educational Statistics, "High School and Beyond, Third Follow-up, 1986" and "National Longitudinal Study, Fourth Follow-up, 1980" surveys. (This table was prepared September 1987.) *Notes:* Because of the different time frames of the political participation inquiries, care should be used when interpreting this data. 1. Sample survey in 1979-80 based on people who were high school seniors during the 1971-72 school year. Survey participants were asked about their political activities over a 3- year period, 1976 to 1979. 2. Includes attendance at political meetings, rallies, barbecues, fish fries, or similar events in connection with an election. 3. Survey participants were asked whether or not they voted in any local, State, or national election November 1976 and October 1979. 4. Sample survey in 1986 based on people who were high schol seniors in spring 1980. Survey participants were asked about their political activities over a 2- year period, 1984 to 1986. 5. Survey participants were asked whether or not they voted in any local, State, or national election between March 1974 and February 1986.

BUSINESS AND ECONOMICS

★ 57 ★
Automobile Dealerships

Numbers in percent.

Manufacturer	Percent
Ford	48.8
General Motors	21.3
Chrysler	16.7
General Motors/Foreign	5.2
General Motors/Ford	2.3
Ford/Toyota	2.1
General/Jeep	1.5
Honda	0.8
Chrysler/Foreign	0.8
Acura	0.5

Source: "B.E. Dealerships by Manufacturer." *Black Enterprise* 20 (June 1990), p. 102. Primary source: *Black Enterprise* 20 (June 1990).

★ 58 ★
Black Banks

Ranked by total assets as of Dec. 31, 1988.

Rank, Bank, Location, and Chief Executive	Year Started	Staff	Assets[1]	Deposits[1]	Loans[1]
1. Seaway National Bank of Chicago, Chicago, IL **Walter E. Grady**	1965	142	149.942	126.920	45.322
2. Citizens Trust Bank, Atlanta, GA **I. Owen Funderburg**	1921	138	121.289	110.938	46.076
3. Freedom National Bank of New York, New York, NY **George A. Russell, Jr.**	1964	111	119.498	97.228	52.660
4. Independence Bank of Chicago, Chicago, IL **Alvin J. Boutte**	1964	101	117.299	101.994	48.790
5. Industrial Bank of Washington, Washington, DC **B. Doyle Mitchell**	1934	98	110.159	100.919	58.378
6. First Texas Bank, Dallas, TX **William E. Stahnke**	1975	60	96.323	86.304	54.626
7. Mechanics and Farmers Bank, Durham, NC **Julia W. Taylor**	1908	96	85.982	75.952	46.542
8. First Independence National Bank of Detroit, Detroit, MI **Lester W. Robinson**	1970	92	84.776	78.092	25.830
9. City National Bank of New Jersey, Newark, NJ **Milton Plummer**	1973	40	70.413	65.430	16.757
10. Consolidated Bank and Trust Co., Richmond, VA	1903	69	60.117	54.483	35.187

Continued.

Black Banks
[Continued]

Rank, Bank, Location, and Chief Executive	Year Started	Staff	Assets[1]	Deposits[1]	Loans[1]
Vernard W. Henley					
11. Highland Community Bank, Chicago, IL	1970	60	58.058	51.586	14.392
George R. Brokemond					
12. Tri-State Bank of Memphis, Memphis, TN	1946	55	56.967	49.775	24.300
Jesse H. Turner					
13. Boston Bank of Commerce, Boston, MA	1982	45	55.253	51.292	44.205
Ronald A. Homer					
14. Liberty Bank and Trust Co., New Orleans, LA	1972	62	48.338	45.209	25.241
Alden J. McDonald, Jr.					
15. The Douglass Bank, Kansas City, KS	1983	34	43.234	36.144	21.293
Donald D. Ford					
16. First National Bank Association, Cleveland, OH	1974	46	40.705	38.834	25.591
Arthur Humphrey					
17. Citizens Savings Bank and Trust Co., Nashville, TN	1904	28	35.754	3.932	19.852
Rick Davidson					
18. The Harbor Bank of Maryland, Baltimore, MD	1982	27	32.067	28.814	21.980
Joseph Haskins, Jr.					
19. Community Bank of Lawndale, Chicago, IL	1977	44	27.790	25.385	11.535
Joyce K. Wade					
20. Peoples National Bank of Commerce, Miami, FL	1982	19	24.000	22.000	8.000
Arthur J. Hill					

Source: "Banks," *Black Enterprise*, June 1989, pp. 251-252. Primary source: Prepared by BE Research. Reviewed by Mitchell/Titus & Co. *Note:* 1. In millions of dollars, to nearest thousand.

★ 59 ★
Black Insurance Companies Ranked by Assets

Ranked by total assets as of Dec. 31, 1988.

Rank, Company, Location, and Chief Executive	Year Started	Staff	Assets[1]	Insurance in force[1]	Premium Income[1]	Net Investment Income[1]
1. North Carolina Mutual Life Insurance Company, Durham, NC	1989	837	217.413	8982.418	69.622	14.718
W.J. Kennedy, III						
2. Atlanta Life Insurance, Atlanta, GA	1905	975	133.863	2064.798	22.089	8.139
Jesse Hill, Jr.						
3. Golden State Mutual Life Insuarnce Company, Los Angeles, CA	1925	410	116.818	4824.863	16.065	9.393
Ivan J. Houston						
4. Universal Life Insurance Company, Memphis, TN	1923	773	65.563	680.457	21.468	4.683
A. Maceo Walker, Sr.						
5. Supreme Life Insurance Company of America, Chicago, IL	1921	46	55.179	2332.495	16.942	2.258
John H. Johnson						
6. Chicago Metropolitan Mutual Assurance Company, Chicago, IL	1927	188	53.738	2551.740	20.590	2.665
Anderson M. Schweich						
7. Booker T. Washington Insurance Company, Birmingham, AL	1932	197	35.515	760.449	10.071	2.283
Louis J. Willie						
8. Mammoth Life and Accident Insurance Company, Louisville, KY	1915	213	29.050	302.505	3.746	2.065
Edwin Chestnut, Sr.						
9. The Pilgrim Health and Life Insurance Company, Augusta, GA	1898	171	15.832	154.044	3.448	1.038
Solomon W. Walker, II						
10. Protective Industrial Insurance Co. of Alabama Inc., Birmingham, AL	1923	123	13.145	70.746	3.386	.838
Paul E. Harris						
11. United Mutual Life Insurance Company, New York, NY	1933	15	12.418	1388.257	12.669	.907

Continued.

Black Insurance Companies Ranked by Assets
[Continued]

Rank, Company, Location, and Chief Executive	Year Started	Staff	Assets[1]	Insurance in force[1]	Premium Income[1]	Net Investment Income[1]
Edward J. Babb						
12. Winnfield Life Insurance Company, Natchitoches, LA	1936	27	8.960	57.800	1.936	.336
Ben D. Johnson						
13. Golden Circle Life Insurance Company, Brownsville, TN	1958	70	7.693	20.591	1.543	.539
William D. Rawls, Sr.						
14. American Woodmen's Life Insurance Company, Denver, CO	1966	27	5.337	327.411	1.035	.170
Lillie Anne Owens						
15. Central Life Insurance of Florida, Tampa, FL	1922	86	4.885	53.000	1.906	.271
Joseph B. Williams						
16. Williams-Progressive Life & Accident Insurance Company, Opelousas, LA	1947	55	4.691	36.554	1.265	.380
Borel C. Dauphin						
17. Wright Mutual Insuarcne Company, Detroit, MI	1942	44	4.418	33.104	.874	.232
Wardell C. Croft						
18. Gertrude Geddes Willis Life Insurance Company, New Orleans, LA	1941	49	3.831	36.250	1.204	.282
Joseph O. Misshore, Jr.						
19. Reliable Life Insurance Company, Monroe, LA	1940	80	3.446	24.108	1.156	.171
Joseph H. Miller, Jr.						
20. Benevolent Life Insurance Company Inc., Shreveport, LA	1934	82	2.749	16.085	.695	.190
Granville L. Smith						

Source: "Insurance," *Black Enterprise*, June 1989, pp. 290-291. *Note:* 1. In millions of dollars, to nearest thousand.

★ 60 ★
Black Thrifts

Ranked by total assets as of Dec. 31,1988.

Rank, Company, Location, and Chief Executive	Year Started	Staff	Assets[1]	Deposits[1]	Loans[1]
1. Independence Federal Savings Bank, Washington, DC	1968	70	264.637	171.670	228.150
William B. Fitzgerald					
2. Carver Federal Savings Bank, New York, NY	1948	80	167.386	149.854	129.393
Richard T. Greene					
3. Family Savings & Loan Association, Los Angeles, CA	1948	66	153.000	138.000	126.000
Robert Bowdoin					
4. Founders Savings & Loan Association, Los Angeles, CA	1974	77	132.600	159.577	109.185
Wayne Bradshaw					
5. Illinois Service/Federal S&L Association of Chicago, Chicago, IL	1934	37	105.219	101.571	76.276
Thelma J. Smith					
6. Broadway Federal Savings & Loan Association, Los Angeles, CA	1946	55	96.898	88.739	77.725
Elbert T. Hudson					
7. Time Savings & Loan Association, San Francisco, CA	1975	41	65.000	56.000	140.000
Mark Seidenberg					
8. Citizens Federal Savings Bank, Birmingham, AL	1957	37	62.181	55.450	42.753
Bunny Stokes, Jr.					
9. United Federal Savings & Loan Association, New Orleans, LA	1964	35	58.273	45.199	40.002
Beverly N. Staes					
10. First Federal S&L Association of Scotlandville, Baton Rouge, LA	1956	21	41.111	43.210	31.299
Henry J. Stamper					
11. Sentry Federal Savings Bank, Norfolk, VA	1913	64	40.319	34.937	32.210
Kenneth Clark					
12. Mutual Federal S&L Association of Atlanta, Atlanta, GA	1925	18	37.621	33.601	24.234

Continued.

Black Thrifts
[Continued]

Rank, Company, Location, and Chief Executive	Year Started	Staff	Assets[1]	Deposits[1]	Loans[1]
Fletcher Coombs 13. Advance Federal Savings & Loan Association, Baltimore, MD	1957	31	35.618	30.371	25.602
Winfred O. Bryson Jr. 14. Berean Savings Association, Philadelphia, PA	1888	19	33.770	30.390	21.220
I. Maximilian Martin 15. Tuskegee Federal Savings & Loan Association, Tuskegee, AL	1894	19	32.886	28.744	27.506
Richard R. Harvey 16. Mutual Savings & Loan Association, Durham, NC	1921	12	25.348	21.292	20.099
Ferdinand V. Allison Jr. 17. People's Savings and Loan Association, F.A., Hampton, VA	1889	9	25.329	24.033	18.003
John E. Coles 18. Home Federal Savings Bank, Detroit, MI	1947	15	23.503	20.319	16.852
Wilburn R. Phillips 19. American Federal Savings & Loan Association, Greensboro, NC	1959	17	22.000	17.000	18.000
Bernard J. Battle 20. Connecticut Savings and Loan Association, Hartford, CT **John A. Hogan**	1968	11	19.684	13.504	17.701

Source: "Savings & Loans," *Black Enterprise*, June 1989, pp. 271-72. Prepared by BE Research. Reviewed by Mitchell/Titus & Co. *Note:* 1. In millions of dollars, to nearest thousand.

★ 61 ★
Businesses as Growth Leaders

Company and location	1989 Sales[1]	1988 Sales[1]	Percent Increase
Wesley Industries Inc., Flint, MI[2]	36.500	8.500	329.41
Jerry Watkins Cadillac-GMC Truck, Inc., Winston-Salem, NC	107.916	32.143	235.74
V-Tech Inc., Pomona, CA	15.000	7.418	102.21
Advanced Consumer Marketing Corp., Burlingame, CA	47.800	26.895	77.73
Wise Construction Co., Inc., Dayton, OH	8.900	5.701	56.11
Shoals Ford Inc., Muscle Shoals, AL	24.715	15.988	54.58
Texcom Inc., Lanham, MD	15.392	10.000	53.92
Baranco Lincoln-Mercury Inc., Duluth, GA	50.424	32.981	52.89
C.H. James & Co., Charleston, WV	10.101	6.607	52.88
Alan Young Buick-GMC Truck Inc., Fort Worth, TX	23.925	15.655	52.83

Source: "B.E. 100s Top Ten Growth Leaders," *Black Enterprise* 20 (June 1990), p. 104. Primary source: *Black Enterprise* 20 (June 1990), p. 104. *Notes:* 1. In millions of dollars, to nearest thousand. As of Dec. 31, 1989. 2. Formerly Flint Coatings, Inc.

★ 62 ★
Characteristics of Black-Owned Banks

	1988	1989	Percent Change
Number of Banks	35	37	5.7
Number of Employees	1,641	1,803	9.9
Assets[1]	1,680.005	1,880.131	11.9
Deposits[1]	1,497.743	1,681.527	12.3
Loans[1]	761.191	834.402	9.6

Source: "Black-Owned Banks," *Black Enterprise* 20, June 1990, p. 174. Primary source: *Black Enterprise*, June 1989. Reviewed by Mitchell/Titus & Co. *Note:* 1. In millions of dollars, to nearest thousand.

★ 63 ★
Employment Leaders, 1989

Company	Location		Number of Employees	1989 Sales[1]	Employee to Sales Ratio[2]
TLC Beatrice International Holdings, Inc.	New York	NY	6,000	1,514,000	1:252
Johnson Publishing Co., Inc.	Chicago	IL	2,370	241,327	1:102
Keys Group Company	Detroit	MI	2,300	18,600	1:8
The Gourmet Companies	Atlanta	GA	1,367	27,150	1:20
Trans Jones, Inc./Jones Transfer Company	Monroe	MI	1,264	78,555	1:62
Philadelphia Coca-Cola Bottling Co., Inc.	Philadelphia	PA	985	240,000	1:244
The Maxima Corporation	Rockville	MD	918	58,383	1:64
Centennial One, Inc.	Lanham	MD	800	8,300	1:10
J.J.S. Services Inc.	Peabody	MA	800	8,625	1:11
Kass Management Services, Inc.	Oakland	CA	775	13,065	1:17

Source: "Top Ten Employment Leaders," *Black Enterprise* 20, June 1990, p. 108. Primary source: Prepared by BE Research. Reviewed by Mitchell/Titus Co. *Notes:* 1. In millions of dollars, to nearest thousand. 2. In thousands of dollars. As of Dec. 31, 1989.

★ 64 ★
Geographical Location of Businesses

State	Number of businesses
Alabama	2
Arkansas	3
California	23
Connecticut	2
Florida	3
Georgia	9
Illinois	17
Indiana	4
Iowa	2
Kentucky	3
Louisiana	3

Continued.

Geographical Location of Businesses
[Continued]

State	Number of businesses
Maryland	7
Massachusetts	3
Michigan	22
Minnesota	1
Mississippi	1
Missouri	5
Nebraska	2
New Jersey	5
New York	19
North Carolina	5
Ohio	13
Oklahoma	2
Oregon	2
Pennsylvania	4
South Carolina	1
Tennessee	3
Texas	11
Virginia	8
Washington	4
Washington, DC	1
West Virginia	2
Wisconsin	3

Source: "BE 100 Companies by State, 1990," *Black Enterprise* 20, June 1990, p. 106. Primary source: Prepared by BE Research. Reviewed by Mitchell/Titus & Co.

★ 65 ★
Growth of Insurance Companies

Black-Owned Insurance Companies	1988	1989	Percent Change
Number of Companies	31	30	-3.2
Number of Employees	5,088	4,711	-7.4
Assets[1]	806.217	802.954	-.4
Insurance in Force[1]	24,795.140	23,451.234	-5.4
Premium Income[1]	215.324	215.206	-.1
New Investment Income[1]	52.217	52.244	.1

Source: "Black-Owned Insurance Companies, 1987, 1988," *Black Enterprise* 20, June 1990, p. 206. Primary source: Prepared by BE Research. Reviewed by Mitchell/Titus & Co. *Note:* 1. In millions of dollars to nearest thousand.

★ 66 ★
Growth of Savings and Loan Associations

Characteristic	1988	1989	Percent Change
Number of Savings & Loan Associations	33	24	-27.3
Number of Employees	850	636	-25.2
Savings Capital/ Deposits[1]	1,394.678	1,140.000	-18.3
Assets[1]	1,579.307	1,325.721	-16.1
Loans[1]	1,319.043	1,049.261	-20.5

Source: "Savings and Loan Associations," *Black Enterprise*, June 1990, p. 194. Primary source: Prepared by BE Research. Reviewed by Mitchell/Titus & Co. *Note:* 1. In millions of dollars to nearest thousand.

★ 67 ★
Income of Black Industries

Characteristics	Blk Rcpt	Wht Rcpt	B/W	Rcpt Gap	Blk Firm	Wht Firm	B/W	Firm Gap
Total	13.83	8,411.19	.012	1,155.92	301.43	14,315	.151	1,689.38
Construction	1.17	398.65	.021	54.27	23.06	1,551	.107	192.64
Manufacturing	1.16	2,804.56	.003	388.87	4.17	531	.056	69.68
Transportation and Public Utilities	.94	747.75	.009	103.06	24.40	585	.300	56.96
Wholesale Trade	1.01	1,308.24	.006	180.93	3.65	1,135	.022	59.76
Retail Trade	4.85	1,319.54	.026	178.66	84.05	2,949	.025	326.07
Finance, Insurance, and Real Estate	.88	1,209.60	.005	167.53	14.83	2,150	.050	284.18
Selected Services	3.82	622.87	.044	82.80	147.26	5,374	.197	600.11

Source: "Total Receipts (in Billions of 1987$) and Number of Firms (1,000's) in 1982, by Industry," *The State of Black America, 1990*, January 1990, p. 43. Primary source: U.S. Department of Commerce, Bureau of the Census, *Surveys of Minority-Owned Businesses: Black*, 1972, 1977, 1982.

★ 68 ★
Industries

Represents standard metropolitan statistical areas (SMSAs) established by the Office of Management and Budget, as of January 1, 1982.

	Number of firms	Receipts (millions)
SMSA and Industry Group		
Black-Owned		
Los Angeles-Long Beach, CA	23,520	775
New York, NY-NJ	20,242	725
Washington, DC-MD-VA	18,805	556
Chicago, IL	13,660	934
Houston, TX	12,206	328
San Francisco-Oakland, CA	9,388	390
Detroit, MI	8,731	369
Philadelphia, PA-NJ	8,581	354
Dallas-Fort Worth, TX	7,825	210
Atlanta, GA	7,077	336
Hispanic-Owned		
Los Angeles-Long Beach, CA	29,982	1,717
Miami, FL	24,898	2,236
New York, NY-NJ	12,292	882
San Antonio, TX	10,341	555
Houston, TX	9,276	441
San Francisco-Oakland, CA	7,649	418
El Paso, TX	5,994	402
McAllen-Pharr-Edinburg, TX	5,766	322
Anaheim-Santa Ana-Garden Grove, CA	5,317	306
Riverside-San Bernardino-Ontario, CA	5,218	272
Industry		
Black-Owned		
Automotive dealers and service stations (55)	3,448	1,307
Miscellaneous retail(59)	53,981	993
Food stores (54)	9,187	883
Eating and drinking places (58)	11,629	675
Health services (80)	17,195	595
Special trade contractors 17)	18,399	578
Personal services (72)	40,394	561
Wholesale trade - nondurable goods (51)	2,441	550
Trucking and warehousing (42)	13,029	530
Wholesale trade - durable goods (50)	1,210	309
Hispanic-Owned		
Automotive dealers and service stations (55)	3,746	1,309
Wholesale trade - nondurable goods (51)	2,279	1,286
Food stores (54)	7,692	1,095
Eating and drinking places (58)	10,791	1,076
Special trade contractors (17)	22,017	1,042
Health services (80)	8,401	579

Continued.

Industries
[Continued]

	Number of firms	Receipts (millions)
Wholesale trade - durable goods (50)	1,343	531
Trucking and warehousing (42)	9,201	419
Personal services (72)	22,382	410
Auto repair, services, and garages (75)	6,873	363

Source: "Women-Owned and Minority-Owned Firms - Number and Receipts for Ten Largest SMSAs and Industries by Type of Ownership: 1982," *Statistical Abstract,* 1989, p. 528. Primary source: U.S. Bureau of the Census, *1982 Survey of Minority-Owned Business Enterprises,* Series MB82-1, MB82-2, MB82-3.

★ 69 ★
Leading Black Businesses

Industry	Percent
Telecommunications	1.35
Transportation	1.60
Auto Dealers	37.07
Security/Maintenance	0.60
Manufacturing	5.67
Construction	4.94
Health & Beauty Aids	2.53
Food/Beverage	30.48
Computer/Office Supplies	5.43
Entertainment	2.20
Media	6.40
Commodities	0.88
Petroleum Sales	0.16
Miscellaneous	0.70

Source: "1990 Black Enterprise 100s Companies by Industry," *Black Enterprise,* June 1990, p. 100. In millions of dollars to the nearest thousand. Prepared by BE Research. Reviewed by Mitchell/Titus & Co.

★ 70 ★
Leading Black Companies

	1988	1990	Difference	Percent Change
Total Sales[1]	4,461.274	4,288.354	(172.900)	-3.8
Total Staff	37,048	33,196	(3,852)	-10.4
1989 Automobile Dealers (Auto 100)				
Total Sales[1]	2,330.310	2,526.140	195.830	8.4
Total Staff	6,455	6,369	(86)	-1.3
The 1989 Black Enterprise 100s				

Continued.

Leading Black Companies
[Continued]

	1988	1990	Difference	Percent Change
Total Sales[1]	6,791.584	6,814.494	22.910	0.3
Total Staff	43,503	39,565	(3,938)	-9.0

Source: "1990 B.E. Industrial/Service 100; 1990 Top 100 Automobile Dealers; 1990 Black Enterprise 100s," *Black Enterprise*, June 1990, p. 100. Prepared by BE Research. Reviewed by Mitchell/Titus & Co. *Notes:* 1. In millions of dollars to the nearest thousand. .

★ 71 ★
Minority Thrifts

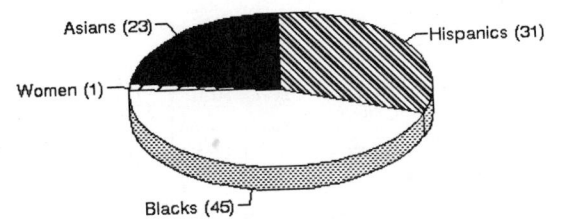
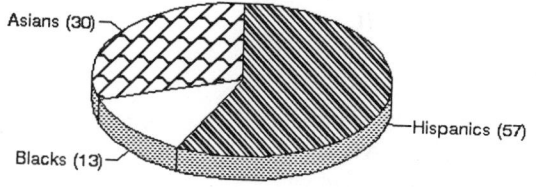

Numbers in percent.

Minority characteristic	Institution	Assets
Blacks	45	13
Hispanics	31	57
Asians	23	30
Women	1	Less than 1/10 of 1%

Source: "Asset Distribution Among Minority Thrifts." *Black Enterprise* 20 (June 1990), p. 226. Primary source: Irons, Edward D. *The S&L Industry: An Industry In Transition,* 1990 *Notes:* Minority S&Ls comprise only 2% of the thrift industry by number and control only .1% of the industry's assets. As of the end of 1989, there were 71 minority S&Ls (those controlled by Blacks, Hispanics, Asians, or Women) with a total of $11.5 billion in assets. The charts above illustrate the distribution of the thrifts and their assets among minority groups. The left chart shows control, the chart on the right shows shows assets. Women owned less than one-tenth of 1% of the assets and hence are not shown in that graphic.

★ 72 ★
Thirty Largest Insurance Companies

Ranked by total assets as of Dec. 31, 1989.

Company and Location	Rank	Year Started	Staff	Assets[1]	Insurance in Force[1]	Premium Income[1]	Net Invest- ment Income[1]
North Carolina Mutual Life Insurance Co., Durham, NC	1	1898	728	215.709	7966.545	58.358	13.670
Atlanta Life Insurance Co., Atlanta, GA	2	1905	975	134.379	2093.059	22.070	8.933
Golden State Mutual Life Insurance Co., Los Angeles, CA	3	1925	347	113.959	4635.562	31.108	9.294
Universal Life Insurance Co., Memphis, TN	4	1923	770	66.442	672.077	21.027	4.818
Supreme Life Insurance Co. of America, Chicago, IL	5	1921	214	54.191	2143.602	15.743	2.212
Chicago Metropolitan Mutual Assurance Co., Chicago, IL	6	1927	164	54.185	2603.303	17.525	2.488
Booker T. Washington Insurance Co., Birmingham, AL	7	1932	210	36.795	754.340	10.213	2.316
Mammoth Life and Accident Insurance Co., Louisville, KY	8	1915	183	29.035	273.072	3.527	2.173
The Pilgrim Health and Life Insurance Co., Augusta, GA	9	1898	143	16.414	166.648	3.558	.968
Protective Industrial Insurance Co. of Alabama, Inc., Birmingham, AL	10	1923	124	13.832	67.298	3.265	.880
United Mutual Life Insurance Co., New York, NY	11	1933	13	12.378	1487.655	14.619	.967
Winnfield Life Insurance Co., Natchitoches, LA	12	1936	25	8.220	59.510	1.823	.345
Golden Circle Life Insurance Co., Brownsville, TN	13	1958	70	8.175	20.011	1.516	.557
American Woodsmen's Life Insurance Co., Denver, CO	14	1966	23	5.054	257.639	1.294	.098
Williams-Progressive Life & Accident Insurance Co., Opelousas, LA	15	1947	60	4.968	36.233	1.266	.439
Wright Mutual Insurance Co., Detroit, MI	16	1942	40	4.535	32.524	.926	.305
Getrude Geddes Willis Life Insurance Co., New Orleans, LA	17	1941	49	4.017	33.640	1.140	.301
Reliable Life Insurance Co., Monroe, LA	18	1940	70	3.769	25.179	1.185	.162
Central Life Insurance Co. of Florida, Tampa, FL	19	1922	80	3.537	42.427	1.518	.312
Benevolent Life Insurance Co., Inc., Shreveport, LA	20	1934	75	2.878	17.530	.671	.182
Majestic Life Insurance Co., Inc., New Orleans, LA	21	1947	24	2.444	11.930	.393	.145
National Service Industrial Life Insurance Co., New Orleans, LA	22	1940	36	2.070	11.625	.590	.135
Valley Life Insurance Group, Phoenix, AZ	23	1958	11	1.957	4.800	.350	.097
Lighthouse Life Insurance Co., Shreveport, LA	24	1949	75	1.044	12.379	.581	.089

Continued.

Thirty Largest Insurance Companies
[Continued]

Company and Location	Rank	Year Started	Staff	Assets[1]	Insurance in Force[1]	Premium Income[1]	Net Investment Income[1]
Rhodes Life Insurance Co. of Louisiana, New Orleans, LA	25	1927	18	.888	5.040	.302	.050
Rhodes Mutual Life Insurance Co. of Alabama, Mobile, AL	26	1949	17	.749	3.388	.216	.024
American Trust Life Insurance Co., Birmingham, AL	27	1932	17	.510	2.001	.035	.058
Unity Life Insurance Co., Jackson, MS	28	1978	21	.325	3.367	.120	.193
Peoples Assured Family Life Insurance Co., Jackson, MS	29	1985	110	.290	5.090	.127	.019
Peoples Progressive Burial Insurance Co., Rayville, LA	30	1936	19	.205	3.760	.140	.014

Source: "Insurance," *Black Enterprise*, 20 (June 1990), pp. 210-211. Primary source: *Black Enterprise*, 20 (June 1990), pp. 210-211. *Note:* 1. In millions of dollars, to nearest thousand.

★ 73 ★
Thrift Companies

Eight of the 33 thrifts ranked on last year's BLACK ENTERPRISE S&L LIST were taken over by the Federal Deposit Insurance Corporation (FDIC) since last year. In order to return to the list, the S&Ls must be sold to a black institution or investor.

Company	1989 Rank	City	State	Year Started
Founders Savings and Loan Association	4	Los Angeles	CA	1974
First Federal S&L Association of Scotlandville	10	Baton Rouge	LA	1956
People's Saving and Loan Association, F.A.	17	Hampton	VA	1889
Standard Savings Association	22	Houston	TX	1958
Community Federal S&L Association of Tampa	27	Tampa	FL	1967
State Mutual Federal Savings & Loan Assoc.	28	Jackson	MS	1955
Community Federal Savings & Loan Assoc.	29	Newport News	VA	1957
Equity Federal Savings & Loan Assoc.	33	Denver	CO	1954

Source: "Black Thrifts in Receivership." *Black Enterprise* 20 (June 1990), p. 196. Primary source: *Black Enterprise* 20 (June 1990).

★ 74 ★
Top Twenty Industrial/Service Companies

As of Dec. 31, 1989.

Company, Location and Chief Executive	Rank This year	Rank Last year	Year Started	Staff	Type of Business	1989 Sales[1]
TLC Beatrice International Holdings Inc., New York, NY/Reginald F. Lewis	1	1	1983	6,000	Processing & distribution food prod.	1,514.000
Johnson Publishing Co., Inc.					Publishing; broadcasting;	

Continued.

Top Twenty Industrial/Service Companies
[Continued]

Company, Location and Chief Executive	Rank		Year Started	Staff	Type of Business	1989 Sales[1]
	This year	Last year				
Chicago, IL John H. Johnson	2	2	1942	2,370	cosmetics; hair care	241.327
Philadelphia Coca-Cola Bottling Co., Inc., Philadelphia, PA/ J. Bruce Llewellyn	3	3	1985	985	Soft-drink bottling	240.000
H.J. Russell & Co. Atlanta, GA Herman J. Russell	4	4	1958	668	Construction; communica- tions; food & beverages	132.876
The Gordy Co., Los Angeles, CA/ Berry Gordy	5	5	1958	70	Entertainment	100.000
Soft Sheen Products Inc., Chicago, IL Edward G. Gardner	6	6	1964	565	Hair-care pro- ducts manu- facturing	87.200
Trans Jones Inc./Jones Transfer Co., Monroe, MI/Gary L. White	7	7	1986	1,264	Transportation services	78.555
The Bing Group[2] Detroit, MI David Bing	8	10	1980	170	Steel proces- sing & dis- tribution	73.883
The Maxima Corp. Rockville, MD Joshua I. Smith	9	9	1978	918	Systems engi- neering & comp. mgt.	58.383
Dick Griffey Productions, Hollywood, CA/Dick Griffey	10	11	1975	86	Entertainment	50.162
Network Solutions Inc., Herndon, VA/Emmit J. McHenry	11	-	1979	480	Systems integration	48.800
Integrated Systems Analysts Inc. Arlington, VA C. Michael Gooden	12	14	1980	640	Engineering & technical supp. serv.	48.710
Advanced Consumer Marketing Corp. Burlingame, CA Harry W. Brooks, Jr.	13	25	1984	427	Systems intergra- tion; mail order prod.	47.800
Community Foods Inc., Baltimore, MD/Oscar A. Smith, Jr.	14	12	1970	450	Retail foods	47.200
Yancy Minerals, Woodbridge, CT/ Woodbridge, CT					Industrial metals,	

Continued.

Top Twenty Industrial/Service Companies
[Continued]

Company, Location and Chief Executive	Rank This year	Rank Last year	Year Started	Staff	Type of Business	1989 Sales[1]
Earl J. Yancy	15	-	1977	8	minerals and coal distrib.	45.000
Crescent Distributing Co. Inc., Harahan, LA/Stanley S. Scott	16	12	1988	165	Beer distrib.	45.000
The Thacker Organization, Decatur, GA/Floyd G. Thacker	17	20	1970	98	Construction & engineering	42.100
Granite Broadcasting Corp., New York, NY/W. Don Cornwell	18	-	1988	350	TV broadcasting	38.611
Essence Communications Inc. New York, NY Edward Lewis	19	16	1969	85	Publishing; TV production; direct-mail catalog sales	38.037
Systems Management America Corp. Norfolk, VA Herman E. Valentine	20	8	1970	390	Computer systems integration	38.000

Source: "B.E. 100s: Industrial/Service Companies," *Black Enterprise* 20 (June 1990), p. 113. Primary source: *Black Enterprise* 20 (June 1990), p. 113. Condensed by the editors from a list of 100. *Notes:* 1. In millions of dollars, to the nearest thousand. 2. Formerly Bing Steel Inc.

★ 75 ★
Twenty Leading Black Banks

Ranked by total assets as of Dec. 31, 1989.

Bank, Location, and Chief Executive	Rank	Year Started	Employment	Assets[1]	Deposits[1]	Loans[1]
Seaway National Bank of Chicago, Chicago, IL/Walter E. Grady	1	1965	142	163.840	139.150	45.405
Citizens Trust Bank, Atlanta, GA/ I. Owen Funderburg	2	1921	157	126.486	116.557	51.520
Industrial Bank of Washington, Washington, DC/B. Doyle Mitchell	3	1934	97	121.982	110.653	60.044
Freedom National Bank of New York, New York, NY/George A. Russell, Jr.	4	1964	126	120.648	101.794	53.945
Independence Bank of Chicago, Chicago, IL/Alvin J. Boutte	5	1964	106	117.990	102.544	44.240
Drexel National Bank, Chicago, IL/ Alvin J. Boutte	6	1989	86	108.919	100.298	36.896
First Independence National Bank of Detroit, Detroit, MI/Gerald E. Harrington	7	1970	96	100.607	89.741	33.898
First Texas Bank, Dallas, TX/ William E. Stahnke	8	1975	67	95.550	85.357	54.866

Continued.

Twenty Leading Black Banks
[Continued]

Bank, Location, and Chief Executive	Rank	Year Started	Employ-ment	Assets[1]	Deposits[1]	Loans[1]
Mechanics and Farmers Bank, Durham, NC/Julia W. Taylor	9	1908	96	92.108	81.354	51.388
Highland Community Bank, Chicago, IL/George R. Brokemond	10	1970	70	74.041	66.838	12.987
Boston Bank of Commerce, Boston, MA/ Ronald A. Homer	11	1982	50	67.721	63.442	57.230
Consolidated Bank and Trust Co., Richmond, VA/Vernard W. Henley	12	1903	72	61.995	55.698	39.390
Tri-State Bank of Memphis, Memphis, TN/ Jesse H. Turner, Jr.	13	1946	67	59.301	52.374	22.836
Liberty Bank and Trust Co., New Orleans, LA/Alden J. McDonald, Jr.	14	1972	60	51.160	48.116	25.671
City National Bank of New Jersey, Newark, NJ/Louis Prezeau	15	1973	44	50.622	47.053	15.027
The Douglass Bank, Kansas City, KS/ Donald D. Ford	16	1983	34	39.006	36.399	16.565
Citizens Savings Bank and Trust Co., Nashville, TN/Rick Davidson	17	1904	32	38.432	35.586	17.421
The Harbor Bank of Maryland, Baltimore, MD/Joseph Haskins, Jr.	18	1982	28	37.514	33.674	23.191
First Bank National Association, Warrensville Hts., OH/Arthur Humphrey	19	1974	30	32.956	32.698	22.840
Community Bank of Lawndale, Chicago, IL/ Joyce K. Wade	20	1977	42	31.316	28.637	12.354

Source: "Banks," *Black Enterprise*, 20 (June 1990), p. 179. Primary source: *Black Enterprise*, 20 (June 1990), p. 179. Condensed by the editors from a list of 100. *Note:* 1. In millions of dollars.

★ 76 ★
Twenty Leading Savings and Loan Companies

Ranked by total assets as of Dec. 31, 1989.

Company, Location, and Chief Executive	Rank	Year Started	Staff	Assets[1]	Deposits[1]	Loans[1]
Independence Federal Savings Bank, Washington, DC/William B. Fitzgerald	1	1968	80	254.269	191.968	214.404
Carver Federal Savings Bank, New York, NY/Richard T. Greene	2	1948	95	238.016	206.118	190.449
Family Savings and Loan Association, Los Angeles, CA/Wayne-Kent Bradshaw	3	1948	68	138.002	119.727	117.578
Illinois Service/Federal S&L Associa- tion of Chicago, Chicago, IL/Thelma J. Smith	4	1934	37	104.102	98.694	74.697
Broadway Federal Savings & Loan Asso- ciation, Los Angeles, CA/Elbert T. Hudson	5	1946	55	95.162	87.993	81.023
Citizens Federal Savings Bank, Bir- mingham, AL/Bunny Stokes, Jr.	6	1957	31	68.883	62.479	46.588
Time Savings & Loan Association, San Francisco, CA/Michael Perri, Jr.	7	1975	43	61.579	56.225	45.200
United Federal Savings & Loan Association, New Orleans, LA/						

Continued.

Twenty Leading Savings and Loan Companies
[Continued]

Company, Location, and Chief Executive	Rank	Year Started	Staff	Assets[1]	Deposits[1]	Loans[1]
Beverly N. Staes	8	1964	22	53.566	43.358	38.304
Mutual Federal S&L Association of Atlanta, Atlanta, GA/Fletcher Coombs	9	1925	17	36.946	33.205	24.877
Advance Federal Savings & Loan Association, Baltimore, MD/Winfred O. Bryson, Jr.	10	1957	34	36.378	29.816	26.837
Berean Savings Bank, PASA, Philadelphia, PA/I. Maximilian Martin	11	1888	18	33.943	29.914	26.290
Tuskegee Federal Savings & Loan Association, Tuskegee, AL/Richard R. Harvey	12	1894	19	33.849	29.051	28.333
Mutual Savings & Loan Association, Durham, NC/Ferdinand V. Allison, Jr.	13	1921	15	27.015	22.727	22.823
Home Federal Savings Bank, Detroit, MI/ Wilburn R. Phillips	14	1947	15	22.122	20.645	16.631
American Federal Savings & Loan Association, Greensboro, NC/Bernard J. Battle	15	1959	13	19.871	17.897	16.399
Connecticut Savings & Loan Association, Hartford, CT/John A. Hogan	16	1968	10	18.258	13.766	16.764
Enterprise Savings & Loan Association, Long Beach, CA/Cornell R. Kirkland	17	1963	13	16.276	15.450	12.110
Dwelling House Savings & Loan Association, Pittsburgh, PA/Robert R. Lavelle	18	1957	7	13.145	11.443	8.609
Columbia Savings & Loan Association, Milwaukee, WI/Thalia B. Winfield	19	1924	9	11.961	10.692	9.768
New Age Federal Savings & Loan Association, St. Louis, MO/David Harper	20	1915	7	9.837	9.86	8.416

Source: "Savings & Loans," *Black Enterprise* 20 (June 1990), p. 201. Primary source: *Black Enterprise* 20 (June 1990), p. 201. *Note:* 1. In millions of dollars, to nearest thousand. Published by permission.

★ 77 ★
Twenty Top Automobile Dealers

Company, Location, and Chief Executive	Rank This year	Rank Last year	Year Started	Staff	Type of Dealership	1989 Sales[1]
Shack-Woods & Associates, Long Beach, CA/William E. Shack, Jr. and Timothy L. Woods	1	1	1977	400	Ford	138.000
Jerry Watkins Cadillac-GMC Truck Inc., Winston-Salem, NC/Jerry D. Watkins	2	15	1983	70	GM	107.916
S&J Enterprises, Charlotte, NC/Sam Johnson	3	11	1973	216	Ford	97.882
Dick Gidron Cadillac & Ford Inc., Bronx, NY/Richard D. Gidron	4	3	1972	283	GM-Ford	57.500
Mel Farr Automotive Group, Oak Park, MI/Mel Farr	5	17	1975	160	Ford-Toyota	52.100
Baranco Lincoln-Mercury, Inc., Duluth, GA/Gregory T. Baranco	6	14	1987	55	Ford	50.424
Gulf Freeway Dodge Inc., Houston, TX/Richard L. Prophet, Jr.	7	6	1985	85	Chrysler	50.127
Mort Hall Ford, Inc., Houston, TX/ Donald Wolfe	8	-	1988	200	Ford	47.000

Continued.

Twenty Top Automobile Dealers
[Continued]

Company, Location, and Chief Executive	Rank		Year Started	Staff	Type of Dealer-ship	1989 Sales[1]
	This year	Last year				
Al Bennett Inc., Flint, MI/Al Bennett	9	2	1979	147	Ford	46.492
Baranco Pontiac-GMC Truck-Subaru Inc., Decatur, GA/Gregory T. Baranco	10	4	1978	99	GM-Foreign	45.096
Southside Ford Truck Sales Inc., Chicago, IL/Carl Statham	11	9	1984	89	Ford	43.394
Al Johnson Cadillac-Saab Inc., Tinley Park, IL/Albert W. Johnson, Sr.	12	27	1967	103	GM-Foreign	37.260
Metrolina Dodge Inc., Charlotte, NC/ Reginald T. Hubbard	13	28	1986	58	Chrysler	36.427
Bob Ross Buick-Mercedes GMC Inc./ Centerville, OH/Robert P. Ross	14	8	1974	105	GM-Foreign	35.666
Pavillion Lincoln-Mercury Inc., Austin, TX/James M. Chargois	15	-	1988	80	Ford	35.040
Northwestern Dodge, Ferndale, MI/ Jesse J. Jones, Jr.	16	30	1980	68	Chrysler	34.900
Pochelon Lincoln-Mercury Inc., Saginaw, MI/James W. Woodruff	17	-	1988	36	Ford	34.424
Leader Motors Inc., St. Louis, MO/ Jesse Morrow	18	12	1983	78	Ford	32.260
North Seattle Chrysler-Plymouth Inc., Seattle, WA/William E. McIntosh, Jr.	19	13	1985	64	Chrysler	30.000
Chino Hills Ford Inc., Chino, CA/ Timothy L. Woods	20	18	1982	68	Ford	29.705

Source: "B.E. 100s: Auto Dealers," *Black Enterprise* 20 (June 1990), p. 125. Primary source: *Black Enterprise* 20 (June 1990), p. 125. Condensed by the editors from a list of 100. *Notes:* 1. In millions of dollars, to the nearest thousand. As of Dec. 31, 1989.

CRIME, LAW ENFORCEMENT, AND LEGAL JUSTICE

★ 78 ★
Age and Personal Victimization - Part I

Age and race of victim	Total population	Crimes of violence									
		Total	Com-pleted	At-tempted	Rape	Robbery			Assault		
						Total	With injury	Without injury	Total	Aggra-vated	Simple
White											
12 to 15 years	10,686,480	51.7	23.3	28.5	1.0[1]	6.2	1.8	4.4	44.5	10.4	34.1
16 to 19 years	12,082,870	66.4	24.7	41.7	1.9	7.8	2.4	5.4	56.7	18.7	38.0
20 to 24 years	15,958,400	65.1	21.0	44.1	1.2	9.6	4.1	5.5	54.3	17.3	36.9
25 to 34 years	36,312,460	31.7	11.7	19.9	0.9	6.2	2.1	4.1	24.6	8.1	16.5
35 to 49 years	40,344,880	18.5	5.4	13.1	0.1[1]	2.8	1.2	1.6	15.6	5.5	10.2
50 to 64 years	28,925,810	7.9	2.7	5.2	0.0[1]	1.9	0.8	1.2	5.9	2.2	3.7
65 years and older	25,604,390	4.6	2.3	2.3	0.1[1]	1.6	0.9	0.7	2.9	1.3	1.7
Black											
12 to 15 years	2,081,050	78.2	34.4	43.8	3.0[1]	13.3	3.7[1]	9.6	61.9	23.5	38.3
16 to 19 years	2,207,900	77.3	20.6	56.8	3.3[1]	15.8	3.8[1]	11.9	58.2	38.9	19.3
20 to 24 years	2,570,380	53.0	21.6	31.4	3.4[1]	12.5	4.7[1]	7.8	37.1	11.0	26.1
25 to 34 years	5,273,990	49.7	23.6	26.1	3.0[1]	19.0	4.7	14.3	27.6	12.5	15.2
35 to 49 years	4,988,680	18.6	6.4	12.3	0.4[1]	7.2	2.8[1]	4.3	11.1	6.8	4.2
50 to 64 years	3,239,450	12.8	9.2	3.6[1]	0.0[1]	7.8	2.8[1]	5.0	5.1	2.1[1]	3.0[1]
65 years and older	2,364,230	14.3	4.7[1]	9.6	0.0[1]	4.9[1]	4.2[1]	0.7[1]	9.4	1.5[1]	7.9

Source: "Estimated Rate (per 1,000 Population in Each Age Group) of Personal Victimization," *Sourcebook of Criminal Justice Statistics - 1988*, 1989, p. 299. Primary source: U.S. Department of Justice, Bureau of Justice Statistics, *Criminal Victimization in the United States, 1987*, National Crime Survey Report NCJ-115-524 (Washington, DC: U.S. Department of Justice, 1989), Table 9. *Notes:* Subcategories may not sum to total because of rounding. 1. Estimate is based on about 10 or fewer sample cases.

★ 79 ★
Age and Personal Victimization - Part II

	Crimes of theft				
	Total	Com-pleted	At-tempted	Personal larceny	
				With contact	Without contact
White					
12 to 15 years	111.2	108.0	3.2	2.1	109.1
16 to 19 years	124.5	120.0	4.5	3.2	121.3
20 to 24 years	113.2	105.1	8.2	3.7	109.5
25 to 34 years	80.2	74.3	5.9	2.2	78.1
35 to 49 years	64.9	60.7	4.2	2.1	62.9

Continued.

Age and Personal Victimization - Part II
[Continued]

		Crimes of theft			
	Total	Com-pleted	At-tempted	Personal larceny	
				With contact	Without contact
50 to 64 years	37.4	34.6	2.8	1.6	35.8
65 years and older	18.7	17.4	1.3	2.2	16.4
Black					
12 to 15 years	98.1	93.9	4.2[1]	6.6[1]	91.5
16 to 19 years	98.6	87.0	11.6	5.5[1]	93.1
20 to 24 years	87.1	78.4	8.7	9.5	77.5
25 to 34 years	67.4	63.9	3.6	1.0[1]	66.4
35 to 49 years	54.0	49.9	4.1	2.5[1]	51.5
50 to 64 years	36.3	34.2	2.1[1]	3.8[1]	32.5
65 years and older	17.9	17.9	0.0[1]	7.5	10.4

Source: "Estimated Rate (per 1,000 Population in Each Age Group) of Personal Victimization," *Sourcebook of Criminal Justice Statistics - 1988*, 1989, p. 299. Primary source: U.S. Department of Justice, Bureau of Justice Statistics, *Criminal Victimization in the United States, 1987*, National Crime Survey Report NCJ-115524 (Washington, DC: U.S. Department of Justice, 1989), Table 9. *Notes:* Subcategories may not sum to total because of rounding. 1. Estimate is based on about 10 or fewer sample cases.

★ 80 ★
Arrests

1975-1981 data represent agencies reporting 6 to 12 months; thereafter, data represent those agencies reporting 12 months. See also *Historical Statistics, Colonial Times to 1970*, series H 999-1011.

Item	Unit	1975	1980	1981	1982	1983	1984	1985	1986	1987
Persons arrested[1]	1,000	7,671	9,684	10,264	10,000	10,248	8,891	10,239	10,336	10,750
White	1,000	5,539	7,146	7,482	7,070	7,291	6,529	7,338	7,371	7,387
Black	1,000	1,935	2,375	2,619	2,777	2,796	2,216	2,721	2,789	3,168
Other	1,000	197	163	163	153	161	146	181	176	196

Source: "Persons Arrested by Race: 1975 to 1987," *Statistical Abstract*, 1989, p. 173. Primary source: U.S. Federal Bureau of Investigation, *Crime in the United States*, annual. *Notes:* 1. Represents each person arrested rather than number of charges filed against each. Through 1981, includes persons for whom age was not known, not shown separately in breakdown by age.

★ 81 ★
Cases Litigated by the NAACP: Trends

Category of Case	Years			
	1940-1959	1960-1969	1970-1983	Total
All cases[1]	198	569	840	1,607
School desegregation	67	203	248	518
Employment discrimi- nation	8	43	265	316
Prisons	3	12	72	87
Public accommodations	16	52	4	72
Housing and real estate	15	20	34	69
Demonstration rights	1	53	8	62

Continued.

Cases Litigated by the NAACP: Trends
[Continued]

Category of Case	Years 1940-1959	1960-1969	1970-1983	Total
Voting rights	10	21	28	59
Habeas corpus	5	23	22	50
Jury proceedings	7	21	16	44
Capital punishment	4	15	23	42
Social services	1	19	12	32
Police brutality	3	10	15	28

Source: "Federal and State Litigation by NAACP Legal Defense Fund, by Category of Case, 1940-1983," *A Common Destiny: Blacks And American Society*, 1989, p. 185. Primary source: Unpublished data from the National Association for the Advancement of Colored People (NAACP). *Note:* 1. Totals include cases not covered below.

★ 82 ★
Child Neglect and Abuse

In percent, except as indicated. Total number of children reported is generally a duplicate count in that a child may be reported and therefore enumerated more than once each year. Because of differences in enumeration methods, a relatively small number of States (5 to 10) can provide only unduplicated reports, whereas most states provide only duplicated counts.

Item	1976	1977	1978	1979	1980	1981	1982	1983	1984	1985
Characteristics of child involved:										
Race:										
White	61.1	67.7	67.1	65.7	69.4	67.8	64.9	67.5	67.0	NA
Black	19.8	19.1	21.1	22.2	18.8	21.7	21.7	19.7	20.8	NA
Hispanic	11.1	6.8	8.0	9.2	9.7	8.6	10.9	9.9	9.6	NA
Other	8.0	6.3	3.8	2.9	2.0	1.9	2.4	2.9	2.6	NA
Characteristics of caretaker:										
Race:										
White	65.3	71.5	70.4	72.1	72.7	73.0	70.8	73.1	74.5	NA
Black	17.0	15.9	17.2	17.5	16.6	18.6	19.1	17.5	17.5	NA
Hispanic	10.0	6.4	9.6	4.9	5.1	4.7	6.1	6.8	5.5	NA
Other	7.7	6.2	2.8	5.5	5.6	3.7	4.0	2.6	2.5	NA
Characteristics of perpetrator:										
Race:										
White	65.1	71.2	71.2	71.2	72.0	71.1	69.0	69.5	69.9	NA
Black	17.7	16.5	18.4	19.1	17.6	19.7	19.7	18.7	19.1	NA
Hispanic	9.5	6.3	7.4	7.2	8.3	7.5	9.2	9.8	9.3	NA
Other	7.7	6.0	3.0	2.5	2.1	1.7	2.1	2.0	1.9	NA

Source: "Child Maltreatment Cases Reported — Summary: 1976 to 1985," *Statistical Abstract*, 1989, p. 172. Primary source: American Humane Association, Denver, CO, *National Study on Child Neglect and Abuse Reporting*, annual. *Note:* NA - Not available.

★ 83 ★
Crime and Victim-Neighborhood Characteristics: Trends

Racial Makeup of Neighborhood (% black)	1973 Victim		1977 Victim		1981 Victim	
	Black	White	Black	White	Black	White
0	4.8	49.8	6.1	50.5	10	50.3
1-10	11.8	36.5	15.3	36.4	15.5	36.9
11+	83.4	13.7	78.3	13.1	74.5	12.8
Total (%)	100.0	100.0	100.0	100.0	100.0	100.0
Less than or equal to 45	44.8		51.8		54.5	
46 to 89	34.3		32.5		28.6	
Greater than or equal to 90	20.9		15.7		16.9	
Total (%)	100.0		100.0		100.0	

Source: "Criminal Incidents by Racial Makeup of Neighborhood and Race of Victim, 1973-1981," *A Common Destiny: Blacks And American Society*, 1989, p. 471. Primary source: Myers, Samuel L. and William J. Sabol. 1987. *Crime and the Black Community: Issues in the Understanding of Race and Crime in America*. Paper prepared for the Committee on the Status of Black Americans, National Research Council, Washington, DC. *Note:* Total percent does not always equal 100 because of rounding. Published by permission.

★ 84 ★
Crime Victims

Rates per 1,000 persons, 12 years old and over. Includes attempted crimes. Data based on National Crime Survey; see text, section 5, and Appendix III. Totals exclude personal larceny.

Year and Crime	Total[1]	White	Black	Hispanic[2]	Male			Female		
					White	Black	Hispanic[2]	White	Black	Hispanic[2]
1973	33	32	42	36	43	53	53	21	32	22
1975	33	32	43	40	42	53	50	21	34	30
1976	33	31	44	35	42	55	55	21	36	23
1977	34	33	42	40	45	57	50	22	29	32
1978	34	33	41	37	45	54	54	22	30	23
1979	35	34	42	41	44	53	55	24	32	29
1980	33	32	41	40	43	53	54	22	31	27
1981	35	33	50	39	44	61	53	23	40	26
1982	34	33	44	40	42	57	49	25	33	32
1983	31	30	41	38	39	50	48	21	33	29
1984	31	30	41	35	38	51	45	22	33	26
1985	30	29	38	30	38	47	33	21	31	27
1986	28	28	33	27	35	39	39	21	29	15

Source: "Victimization Rates for Crimes Against Persons: 1973 to 1986," *Statistical Abstract*, 1989, p. 171. Primary source: U.S. Law Enforcement Assistance Administration; thereafter, U.S. Bureau of Justice Statistics, *Criminal Victimization in the United States*, annual. *Notes:* 1. Includes races not shown separately. 2. Hispanic persons may be of any race.

★ 85 ★
Crime Victims' Educational Level - Part I

Rate per 1,000 population age 12 and over.

Level of educational attainment and race	Crimes of violence	Completed violent crimes	Attempted violent crimes	Rape	Robbery		
					Total	With Injury	Without injury
Elementary school							
All races (30,182,470)[1]	30.4	14.1	16.3	.6	5.3	1.9	3.4
White (24,633,350)	28.0	12.7	15.2	.4[3]	4.3	1.6	2.7
Black (4,622,210)	43.0	21.7	21.4	1.3	11.1	3.7	7.4
0-4 years[2]							
All races (4,090,940)[1]	16.5	6.5	10.0	0[3]	6.4	3.3[3]	3.2[3]
White (2,990,450)	19.0	6.8	12.2	0[3]	5.8	3.0[3]	2.8[3]
Black (878,680)	12.0[3]	7.1[3]	4.9[3]	0[3]	10.1[3]	5.1[3]	5.1[3]
5-7 years							
All races (14,475,850)[1]	38.1	17.4	20.7	.7[3]	5.8	2.0	3.8
White (11,678,120)	35.0	15.7	19.2	.3[3]	4.7	1.8	3.0
Black (2,324,360)	51.1	25.9	25.2	2.7[3]	11.6	3.3[3]	8.3
8 years							
All races (11,615,680)[1]	25.8	12.7	13.1	.6[3]	4.2	1.2[3]	3.0
White (9,964,780)	22.5	11.0	11.5	.7[3]	3.4	1.0[3]	2.4
Black (1,419,170)	48.9	23.7	25.2	0[3]	10.8[3]	3.3[3]	7.5[3]
High school							
All races (99,586,320)[1]	30.2	11.8	18.5	.9	5.8	2.1	3.7
White (85,336,960)	28.8	11.0	17.8	.7	4.8	1.8	2.9
Black (12,270,570)	40.6	16.6	24.0	1.6	12.9	4.1	8.8
1-3 years							
All races (29,815,030)[1]	42.7	15.9	26.8	1.4	7.5	3.0	4.4
White (24,436,570)	42.1	15.8	26.3	1.3	6.5	2.6	3.8
Black (4,750,660)	47.8	17.7	30.1	1.4[3]	13.6	5.6	8.0
4 years							
All races (69,412,550)[1]	24.9	10.0	14.9	.6	5.1	1.7	3.3
White (60,900,390)	23.5	9.1	14.4	.4	4.1	1.5	2.6
Black (7,519,910)	36.1	16.0	20.1	1.7[3]	12.5	3.2	9.4
College							
All races (66,412,550)[1]	25.5	7.1	18.5	.6	4.2	1.5	2.8
White (58,748,430)	24.9	6.7	18.1	.4	3.8	1.3	2.5
Black (5,506,300)	34.2	10.3	23.9	2.6[3]	9.8	3.4	6.4
1-3 years							
All races (33,610,070)[1]	33.3	10.3	23.0	.7	5.7	2.1	3.5
White (29,332,710)	32.6	9.8	22.8	.4[3]	5.2	2.0	3.2
Black (3,408,740)	40.9	13.4	27.4	2.9[3]	11.0	3.5[3]	7.5
4 or more years							
All races (32,802,480)[1]	17.6	3.8	13.8	.5[3]	2.8	.8	2.0
White (29,415,720)	17.2	3.7	13.5	.3[3]	2.4	.7	1.8
Black (2,097,570)	23.3	5.1[3]	18.2	2.2[3]	7.9	3.2[3]	4.7[3]

Source: "Victimization Rates for Persons age 12 and Over, by level of Educational Attainment and Race of Victims and Type of Crime," *Criminal Victimization in the United States - 1987,* June 1989, pp. 28-29. Primary source: *Criminal Victimization in the United States, 1987.* U.S. Department of Justice, Washington, D.C., NCJ-115-524, June, 1989. *Notes:* 1. Includes data on "other" races, not shown separately. 2. Includes persons who never attended or who attended kindergarten only. 3. Estimate is based on about 10 or fewer sample cases. NOTE: Detail may not add to total shown because of rounding. Numbers in parentheses refer to population in the group; excludes data on persons age 12 and over whose level of education was not ascertained.

★ 86 ★
Crime Victims' Educational Level - Part II

Rate per 1,000 population age 12 and over.

| | Assault | | | Crimes of theft | Completed theft | Attempted theft | Personal larceny | |
	Total	Aggravated	Simple				With contact	Without contac
Elementary school								
All races (30,182,470)[1]	24.6	7.6	17.0	53.1	51.0	2.1	3.1	50.1
White (24,633,350)	23.2	6.6	16.6	54.0	52.0	2.0	2.2	51.8
Black (4,622,210)	30.6	10.7	19.9	49.0	46.6	2.4[3]	7.7	41.3
0-4 years[2]								
All races (4,090,940)[1]	10.0	5.1	5.0	26.3	21.4	4.9	3.1[3]	23.3
White (2,990,450)	13.2	6.4	6.8	23.6	19.7	4.0[3]	1.9[3]	21.8
Black (878,680)	1.9[3]	1.9[3]	0[3]	34.3	27.1	7.2[3]	7.9[3]	26.4
5-7 years								
All races (14,475,850)[1]	31.6	9.5	22.1	64.8	62.9	1.9	3.1	61.7
White (11,678,120)	29.9	8.8	21.1	66.8	64.9	1.9	2.2	64.6
Black (2,324,360)	36.8	10.3	26.5	56.1	53.9	2.1[3]	7.9	48.1
8 years								
All races (11,615,680)[1]	21.0	6.2	14.8	48.1	46.7	1.4[3]	3.1	45.0
White (9,964,780)	18.4	4.2	14.2	48.2	46.6	1.6[3]	2.4	45.8
Black (1,419,170)	38.1	16.8	21.3	46.7	46.7	0[3]	7.2[3]	39.4
High school								
All races (99,586,320)[1]	23.6	8.6	15.0	61.2	57.5	3.7	2.3	58.9
White (85,336,960)	23.4	7.8	15.6	60.8	57.3	3.6	1.9	58.9
Black (12,270,570)	26.1	14.3	11.8	63.5	58.5	5.0	4.6	58.9
1-3 years								
All races (29,815,030)[1]	33.8	11.9	21.9	69.3	65.9	3.4	2.6	66.7
White (24,436,570)	34.3	10.6	23.7	70.9	67.8	3.1	2.2	68.8
Black (4,750,660)	32.8	19.6	13.2	60.6	55.9	4.7	5.1	55.5
4 years								
All races (69,412,550)[1]	19.2	7.1	12.1	57.7	53.8	3.9	2.1	55.5
White (60,900,390)	19.0	6.7	12.3	56.8	53.1	3.7	1.8	55.0
Black (7,519,910)	21.9	11.0	10.9	65.4	60.2	5.2	4.3	61.1
College								
All races (66,412,550)[1]	20.7	6.7	13.9	84.1	78.1	6.0	2.8	81.3
White (58,748,430)	20.7	6.6	14.1	85.3	79.1	6.2	2.9	82.5
Black (5,506,300)	21.7	7.7	14.0	75.9	70.6	5.3	.9[3]	75.1
1-3 years								
All races (33,610,070)[1]	20.9	9.4	17.5	86.3	80.2	6.1	2.4	83.9
White (29,332,710)	26.9	9.3	17.5	88.5	82.1	6.4	2.6	85.8
Black (3,408,740)	27.0	9.5	17.5	73.1	68.6	4.4[3]	.9[3]	72.2
4 or more years								
All races (32,802,480)[1]	14.3	4.0	10.3	81.8	75.9	5.9	3.2	78.6
White (29,415,720)	14.5	4.0	10.5	82.2	76.2	6.0	3.1	79.1
Black (2,097,570)	13.2	4.8[3]	8.4	80.6	73.8	6.8[3]	.8[3]	79.7

Source: "Victimization Rates for Persons age 12 and Over, by level of Educational Attainment and Race of Victims and Type of Crime," *Criminal Victimization in the United States - 1987,* June 1989, pp. 28-29. Primary source: *Criminal Victimization in the United States, 1987.* U.S. Department of Justice, Washington, D.C., NCJ-115-524, June, 1989. *Notes:* 1. Includes data on "other" races, not shown separately. 2. Includes persons who never attended or who attended kindergarten only. 3. Estimate is based on about 10 or fewer sample cases. NOTE: Detail may not add to total shown because of rounding. Numbers in parentheses refer to population in the group; excludes data on persons age 12 and over whose level of education was not ascertained.

★ 87 ★
Crime Victims' Reports to Police

Type of crime	All victimizations		Involving strangers		Involving nonstrangers	
	White	Black	White	Black	White	Black
Crimes of violence	47.9	52.8	50.0	53.7	45.1	51.5
Completed	55.1	67.5	57.9	72.5	51.8	60.9
Attempted	43.9	42.5	46.0	40.6	40.9	45.1
Rape	56.2	54.1	52.6	60.6	59.4	38.7[1]
Robbery	56.4	57.7	56.1	57.0	57.2	60.6
Completed	64.5	72.0	67.4	74.4	55.1	63.1
With injury	73.6	80.7	75.1	75.2	69.2	100.0[1]
From seroius assault	74.9	90.4	78.0	88.3	63.7[1]	100.0[1]
From minor assault	72.5	72.4	72.3	62.8[1]	73.0	100.0[1]
Without injury	56.8	68.5	61.1	74.1	42.6	47.8[1]
Attempted	42.0	23.2	38.2	20.1[1]	62.6	48.7[1]
With injury	72.7	36.3[1]	67.2	31.8[1]	89.3[1]	48.7[1]
From serious assault	76.8	33.9[1]	78.2	17.3[1]	70.0[1]	100.0[1]
From minor assault	67.9	37.3[1]	50.5[1]	38.8[1]	100.0[1]	33.5[1]
Without injury	32.4	28.4[1]	30.4	14.1[1]	46.0[1]	0[1]
Assault	46.1	50.5	48.2	50.2	43.7	50.7
Aggravated	61.8	52.0	63.3	52.7	59.4	51.2
Completed with injury	63.1	61.1	60.4	83.0	65.7	47.9
Attempted with weapon	61.2	48.4	64.3	45.7	55.0	53.6
Simple	38.6	49.1	39.2	46.7	38.0	50.4
Completed with injury	44.4	64.2	45.0	58.1[1]	44.0	66.4
Attempted with weapon	36.1	43.3	37.3	43.5	34.9	43.2
Crimes of theft	27.8	26.9	...	...	...	...
Completed	28.0	27.8	...	...	...	...
Attempted	24.1	15.3[1]	...	...	...	...
Personal larceny with contact	35.5	31.2	36.6	28.1	0[1]	69.0[1]
Purse snatching	46.8	45.8[1]	46.8	41.4[1]	0[1]	100.0[1]
Completed	61.5	72.3[1]	61.5	68.5[1]	0[1]	100.0[1]
Attempted	21.1[1]	0[1]	21.1[1]	0[1]	0[1]	0[1]
Pocket picking	29.0	23.9[1]	30.4	21.6[1]	0[1]	53.1[1]
Personal larceny without contact	27.5	26.6	...	...	...	...
Completed	27.7	27.3	...	...	...	...
Less than $50	11.0	10.8	...	...	...	...
$50 or more	42.0	40.3	...	...	...	...
Amount not available	29.5	29.4	...	...	...	...
Attempted	24.3	17.3[1]	...	...	...	...

Source: "Percent of Victimizations Reported to the Police, by Type of Crime, Victim-Offender Relationship, and Race of Victims," *Criminal Victimization in the United States - 1987*, June 1989, p. 82. Primary source: *Criminal Victimization in the United States, 1987*. U.S. Department of Justice, Washington, DC, NCJ-115-524, June, 1989. *Notes:* ... Not available. The distinction between stranger and nonstranger is not made for the noncontact larcenies because victims rarely see the offender. 1. Estimate is based on about 10 or fewer sample cases.

★ 88 ★
Crime Victims' Self-Protective Measures

Characteristic	Crimes of violence	Completed violent crimes	Attempted violent crimes	Rape	Robbery			Assault		
					Total	With Injury	Without Injury	Total	Aggra-vated	Simple
Race										
White	69.9	68.3	70.8	88.6	64.8	67.0	63.5	70.5	70.2	70.6
Black	63.7	58.2	67.6	71.5	50.5	70.1	41.1	69.2	68.6	69.7

Source: "Percent of Victimizations in which Victims Took Self-Protective Measures, by Characteristics of Victims and Type of Crime," *Criminal Victimization in the United States - 1987*, June 1989, p. 65. Primary source: *Criminal Victimization in the United States, 1987*. U.S. Department of Justice, Washington, DC, NCJ-115-524, June, 1989.

★ 89 ★
Crime Victims: Residence

Rate per 1,000 households.

Area and Race	Household crimes	Completed household crimes	Attempted household crimes	Burglary	Household larcency	Motor vehicle theft
All areas						
White	163.6	139.0	24.7	57.0	91.4	15.2
Black	232.0	189.7	42.3	94.4	116.2	21.4
Metropolitan areas						
Central cities						
White	216.8	181.8	35.1	68.8	125.6	22.4
Black	254.3	205.6	48.6	105.5	125.8	22.9
Outside central cities						
White	151.0	128.6	22.4	52.9	82.1	16.0
Black	210.6	171.6	39.0	73.0	106.8	30.7
Nonmetropolitan areas						
White	130.8	112.8	18.0	51.7	72.2	7.0
Black	181.8	157.6	24.2	84.0	94.4	3.5[1]

Source: "Victimization Rates, by Type of Locality of Residence, Race of Head of Household, and Type of Crime," *Criminal Victimization in the United States - 1987*, June, 1989, p. 42. Primary source: *Criminal Victimization in the United States, 1987*. U.S. Department of Justice, Washington, DC, NCJ-115-524, June, 1989. *Notes:* Numbers in parentheses refer to households in the group. 1. Estimate is based on about 10 or fewer sample cases.

★ 90 ★
Crime Victims: Sex/Race/Age

Rate per 1,000 population in each age group.

Race, sex, and age	Crimes of violence	Crimes of theft
White		
Male		
12-15 (5,467,390)	65.7	114.0
16-19 (6,109,030)	89.4	125.3
20-24 (7,882,380)	82.1	125.1
25-34 (18,265,560)	37.3	85.2
35-49 (19,962,380)	22.9	65.2

Continued.

Crime Victims: Sex/Race/Age
[Continued]

Race, sex, and age	Crimes of violence	Crimes of theft
50-64 (13,803,010	9.7	38.0
65 and over (10,618,990)	4.5	18.1
Female		
12-15 (5,219,090)	37.1	108.2
16-19 (5,973,830)	42.9	123.7
20-24 (8,076,010)	48.5	101.7
25-34 (18,046,900)	25.9	75.2
35-49 (20,382,500)	14.2	64.6
50-64 (15,122,800)	6.1	36.9
65 and over (14,985,400)	4.6	19.1
Black		
Male		
12-15 (1,053,880)	90.8	88.3
16-19 (1,086,640)	101.0	119.2
20-24 (1,181,860)	49.2	104.5
25-34 (2,423,580)	62.5	82.0
35-49 (2,250,140)	21.1	51.5
50-64 (1,414,730)	22.9[1]	37.8
65 and over (971,300)	15.4[1]	19.9
Female		
12-15 (1,027,170)	65.2	108.1
16-19 (1,121,260)	54.4	78.6
20-24 (1,388,520)	56.3	72.3
25-34 (2,850,410)	38.8	55.0
35-49 (2,738,540)	16.6[1]	56.0
50-64 (1,824,730)	5.0[1]	35.1
65 and over (1,392,930)	13.6	16.5

Source: "Victimization Rates for Persons Age 12 and Over, by Race, Sex and Age of Victims and Type of Crime," *Criminal Victimization in the United States - 1987*, June 1989, p. 22. Primary source: *Criminal Victimization in the United States, 1987.* U.S. Department of Justice, Washington, DC, NCJ-115-524, June, 1989. *Notes:* Numbers in parentheses refer to population in the group. 1. Estimate is based on about 10 or fewer sample cases.

★ 91 ★
Crimes

Rates per 100,000 resident population in specified group. Beginning 1970, excludes deaths to nonresidents of U.S. Beginning 1980, deaths classified according to the ninth revision of the *International Classification of Diseases*; for earlier years, classified according to revision in use at the time; see text, section 2. See also *Historical Statistics, Colonial Times to 1970*, series H 971-978.

Year	Homicide Victims					Homicide Rate[2]				
	Total[1]	White		Black		Total[1]	White		Black	
		Male	Female	Male	Female		Male	Female	Male	Female
1960	8,464	2,832	1,154	3,345	1,013	4.7	3.6	1.4	36.7	10.4
1970	16,848	5,865	1,938	7,265	1,569	8.3	6.8	2.1	67.6	13.3
1975	21,310	8,222	2,751	8,092	1,929	9.9	9.0	2.9	69.0	14.9
1980	24,278	10,381	3,177	8,385	1,898	10.7	10.9	3.2	66.6	13.5
1981	23,646	9,941	3,125	8,312	1,825	10.3	10.4	3.1	64.8	12.7
1982	22,358	9,260	3,179	7,730	1,743	9.6	9.6	3.1	59.1	12.0

Continued.

Crimes
[Continued]

Year	Homicide Victims					Homicide Rate[2]				
	Total[1]	White		Black		Total[1]	White		Black	
		Male	Female	Male	Female		Male	Female	Male	Female
1983	20,191	8,355	2,880	6,822	1,672	8.6	8.6	2.8	51.4	11.3
1984	19,796	8,171	2,956	6,563	1,677	8.4	8.3	2.9	48.7	11.2
1985	19,893	8,122	3,041	6,616	1,666	8.3	8.2	2.9	48.4	11.0
1986	21,731	8,567	3,123	7,634	1,861	9.0	8.6	3.0	55.0	12.1

Source: "Homicide Victims, by Race and Sex: 1960 to 1986," *Statistical Abstract,* 1989, p. 168. Primary source: U.S. National Center for Health Statistics, *Vital Statistics of the United States,* annual. *Notes:* 1. Includes races not shown separately. 2. Rate based on enumerated population figures as of April 1 for 1960, 1970, and 1980, July 1 estimates for other years.

★ 92 ★
Criminal Victimization by Strangers

Sex and race	Crimes of violence	Completed violent crimes	Attempted violent crimes	Rape	Robbery			Assault		
					Total	With injury	Without injury	Total	Aggravated	Simple
Both sexes										
White	57.0	53.3	59.1	46.8	79.2	75.3	81.5	52.9	61.0	49.1
Black	56.8	56.9	56.8	70.3	81.6	76.3	84.2	44.7	57.9	33.4
Male										
White	66.1	64.0	67.2	55.4[1]	85.1	82.3	86.6	62.5	67.2	59.8
Black	59.9	59.5	60.2	0[1]	77.9	71.9	80.9	51.9	62.6	39.4
Female										
White	42.3	37.9	45.0	45.7	69.4	65.5	72.2	36.6	46.2	33.3
Black	52.8	54.4	51.3	70.3	87.1	83.3	88.7	34.2	47.1	27.3

Source: "Percent of Victimizations Involving Strangers, by Sex and Race of Victims and Type of Crime," *Criminal Victimization in the United States - 1987,* June 1989, p. 44. Primary source: *Criminal Victimization in the United States, 1987.* U.S. Department of Justice, Washington, DC, NCJ-115-524, June, 1989. *Note:* 1. Estimate is based on about 10 or fewer sample cases.

★ 93 ★
Current Offense of Confined Youth

By age and race, United States, year end 1987(1). Percents are estimated.

Age and current offense	Total	Race	
		White	Black
Less than 18 years old			
Total	100.0	100.0	100.0
Violent offenses	39.3	32.9	47.0
Murder[2]	1.8	2.0	1.4
Negligent manslaughter	0.6	0.6	0.7
Kidnaping	0.3	0.2	0.4
Rape	2.4	1.8	3.3
Other sexual assault	3.5	4.3	2.8
Robbery	13.1	10.8	15.9
Assault	16.3	11.9	21.4
Other violent	1.2	1.2	1.2

Continued.

Current Offense of Confined Youth
[Continued]

Age and current offense	Total	Race	
		White	Black
Property offenses	45.6	51.1	38.6
Burglary	23.8	27.2	19.4
Larceny/theft	7.3	8.0	6.3
Motor vehicle theft	7.8	8.2	7.1
Arson	1.8	2.1	1.5
Fraud	1.1	1.7	0.5
Stolen property	1.4	1.1	1.7
Other property	2.5	2.7	2.1
Drug offenses	5.6	4.2	7.4
Possession	2.9	2.7	3.5
Trafficking	2.5	1.3	3.8
Other drug	0.2	0.3	0.1
Public-order offenses	7.2	8.8	5.4
Weapons	1.9	1.6	2.2
Other public-order	5.3	7.2	3.2
Juvenile status offenses[3]	2.2	7.2	3.2
Other offenses	0.2	0.3	0.0
18 years and older			
Total	100.0	100.0	100.0
Violent offenses	52.3	48.2	56.0
Murder[2]	7.1	8.1	5.6
Negligent manslaughter	2.2	2.5	1.8
Kidnaping	1.4	2.0	0.4
Rape	5.1	4.4	5.8
Other sexual assault	1.6	2.5	0.4
Robbery	18.0	14.0	22.6
Assault	16.6	14.5	18.9
Other violent	0.3	0.2	0.5
Property offenses	29.0	34.2	22.6
Burglary	17.1	21.4	11.5
Larceny/theft	3.5	4.5	2.6
Motor vehicle theft	3.3	3.3	3.7
Arson	1.0	0.9	0.8
Fraud	1.4	1.6	0.9
Stolen property	2.3	2.2	2.7
Other property	0.4	0.3	0.2
Drug offenses	11.3	8.8	14.9
Possession	5.6	5.2	6.1
Trafficking	5.4	3.7	8.1
Other drug	0.3	0.0	0.7
Public-order offenses	6.8	8.4	5.5
Weapons	2.5	2.2	3.0

Continued.

Current Offense of Confined Youth
[Continued]

Age and current offense	Total	Race	
		White	Black
Other public-order	4.3	6.1	2.4
Juvenile status offenses[3]	0.3	0.0	0.8
Other offenses	0.3	0.4	0.2

Source: "Current Offense of Youth in Long-Term, State-Operated Juvenile Institutions," *Sourcebook of Criminal Justice Institutions — 1988,* 1989, p. 599. Primary source: U.S. Department of Justice, Bureau of Justice Statistics, *Survey of Youth in Custody,* 1987, Special Report NCJ-113365 (Washington, DC: U.S. Department of Justice, September 1988), p. 3, Table 3. *Notes:* 1. Percents may not add to 100 due to rounding. 2. Includes nonnegligent manslaughter. 3. Includes noncriminal juvenile offenses, such as truancy, running away, and incorrigible behavior.

★ 94 ★
Death Row Inmates

	Number	Percent
Total	2210	100.0
Race of Defendant:		
Black	877	39.68
White	1141	51.63
Hispanic	134	6.06
Native American	36	1.63
Asian	13	.59
Unknown at this issue	9	.41

Source: "Death Row, U.S.A," NAACP Legal Defense and Educational Fund, Inc., July, 1989. Primary source: NAACP Legal Defense and Educational Fund, Inc. Published by permission.

★ 95 ★
Drug Use in Prison

By race, and frequency of use, United States, 1986.

	Estimated percent of all inmates who:				
		Used drugs			
	Never used drugs	Anytime in the past	Regularly in the past	In the month before the offense	
				At all	Daily
Any drug[1]	20.4	79.6	63.4	52.3	42.6
Race					
White	20.0	80.1	65.0	53.9	44.8
Black	20.8	79.2	62.0	50.9	40.7
Other	19.8	80.1	62.8	49.8	38.8
Major drug[2]	47.6	52.4	35.8	24.7	18.6
Race					
White	43.2	56.8	38.9	26.5	19.3

Continued.

Drug Use in Prison
[Continued]

	Estimated percent of all inmates who:				
		Used drugs			
	Never used drugs	Anytime in the past	Regularly in the past	In the month before the offense	
				At all	Daily
Black	52.5	47.6	32.7	23.0	17.9
Other	44.1	55.9	35.1	24.0	17.5

Source: "Drug Use History of State Prison Inmates," *Sourcebook of Criminal Justice Statistics - 1988*, 1989, p. 624. Primary source: U.S. Department of Justice, Bureau of Justice Statistics, *Profile of State Prison Inmates, 1986*, Special Report NCJ-109926 (Washington, DC: U.S. Department of Justice, January 1988), p. 6, Table 12. *Notes:* These data are based on the 1986 Survey of State Prison Inmates conducted by the U.S. Bureau of the Census for the Bureau of Justice Statistics. The sample design employed a stratified two-stage selection procedure with the probability of selection proportional to the size of the correctional facility. In 1986, 13,711 inmates in 275 facilities were interviewed regarding their background, employment, criminal history, and drug and alcohol use. 1. Includes major drugs (cocaine, heroin, PCP, LSD, and methadone) and marijuana or hashish, amphetamines, barbituates, methaqualone, and all other drugs. 2. Includes cocaine, heroin, PCP, LSD, and methadone.

★ 96 ★
Economic Losses of Crime Victims

Race and type of crime	Total	No monetary value	Less than $50	$50-$99	$100-$249	$250-$499	$500 or more	Not known and not available
All races[1]								
All personal crimes (14,238,550)	100.0	.9	39.4	14.0	16.3	7.7	8.5	13.3
Crimes of violence (1,343,610)[2]	100.0	4.0	21.8	7.8	9.3	8.2	9.6	39.4
Completed (989,300)	100.0	2.0	23.3	9.8	10.5	9.6	10.9	33.8
Attempted (354,310)	100.0	9.4	17.6	2.3[3]	5.6	4.1[3]	5.8	55.2
Robbery (714,910)	100.0	1.0[3]	26.3	13.0	12.0	13.7	15.1	18.9
Completed (678,150)	100.0	0[3]	27.1	13.7	12.7	13.8	15.3	17.4
With Injury (275,650)	100.0	0[3]	23.8	11.7	17.2	11.1	16.5	19.7
Without Injury (402,490)	100.0	0[3]	29.4	15.0	9.6	15.6	14.5	15.8
Attempted (36,770)	100.0	19.4[3]	12.0[3]	0[3]	0[3]	11.5[3]	10.9[3]	46.1[3]
With Injury (13,230)	100.0[3]	54.0[3]	0[3]	0[3]	0[3]	0[3]	0[3]	46.0[3]
Without Injury (23,530)	100.0	0[3]	18.8[3]	0[3]	0[3]	17.9[3]	17.1[3]	46.2[3]
Assault (596,490)	100.0	7.4	14.9	2.1[3]	6.1	1.7[3]	3.4[3]	64.4
Aggravated (255,840)	100.0	7.3	12.2	2.3[3]	8.2	3.1[3]	2.1[3]	64.7
Simple (340,650)	100.0	7.5	16.9	1.9[3]	4.5[3]	.6[3]	4.4[3]	64.2
Crimes of theft (12,894,940)	100.0	.6	41.2	14.7	17.1	7.6	8.4	10.5
Completed (12,509,770)	100.0	.3	42.1	14.9	17.2	7.7	8.5	9.3
Attempted (385,170)	100.0	9.1	11.3	6.2	12.2	6.3	4.9	49.9
Personal larceny with contact (454,090)	100.0	0[3]	43.7	15.4	24.2	6.3	5.0	5.3
Personal larceny without contact (12,440,860)	100.0	.6	41.1	14.6	16.8	7.7	8.5	10.7
All household crimes (14,309,860)	100.0	1.9	28.9	12.3	13.9	8.1	19.7	15.2
Completed (12,839,440)	100.0	.8	30.0	13.0	14.8	8.5	21.5	11.4
Attempted (1,470,430)	100.0	12.2	19.4	6.4	6.0	4.4	3.4	48.3
Burglary (4,776,120)	100.0	3.8	16.3	8.1	12.3	8.5	27.1	23.9

Continued.

Economic Losses of Crime Victims
[Continued]

Race and type of crime	Total	No monetary value	Less than $50	$50-$99	$100-$249	$250-$499	$500 or more	Not known and not available
Completed (3,852,780)	100.0	1.2	14.9	9.2	14.2	10.4	33.3	16.9
Forcible entry (1,856,150)	100.0	1.9	7.9	3.8	7.8	8.8	44.7	25.1
Unlawful entry without force (1,996,630)	100.0	.5³	21.4	14.2	20.1	11.8	22.6	9.3
Attempted forcible entry (923,340)	100.0	15.0	21.9	3.4	4.1	.6³	1.5³	53.4
Household larceny (8,222,950)	100.0	1.0	40.5	16.1	16.4	8.0	7.6	10.5
Completed (8,017,840)	100.0	7.7	40.9	16.3	16.6	8.2	7.6	9.7
Attempted (205,110)	100.0	12.3	25.9	8.7	5.5³	2.6³	5.3³	39.7
Motor vehicle theft (1,310,800)	100.0	1.2	2.4	3.7	4.3	6.7	68.5	13.2
Completed (968,820)	100.0	.2³	.2³	.4³	1.7	3.5	90.1	3.8
Attempted (341,980)	100.0	4.2³	8.5	13.1	11.5	15.7	7.3	39
White								
All personal crimes (12,258,140)	100.0	.9	39.8	13.9	16.6	7.7	8.3	12.8
Crimes of violence (1,039,830)²	100.0	4.0	21.8	7.3	9.4	7.0	8.0	42.5
Completed (732,720)	100.0	2.0³	23.4	9.5	10.6	8.2	9.6	36.7
Attempted (307,110)	100.0	8.8	18.2	1.9³	6.5	4.1³	4.2³	56.4
Robbery (511,790)	100.0	1.4³	27.6	12.8	11.6	12.2	13.7	20.7
Completed (476,940)	100.0	0³	29.1	13.7	12.5	12.2	13.8	18.6
With injury (217,750)	100.0	0³	26.9	10.4	16.3	11.2	15.1	20.0
Without injury (259,190)	100.0	0³	30.9	16.5	9.2	13.1	12.8	17.5
Attempted (34,840)	100.0	20.5³	7.2³	0³	0³	12.1³	11.5³	48.7
With injury (13,230)	100.0³	54.0³	0³	0³	0³	0³	0³	46.0³
Without injury (21,610)	100.0	0³	11.6³	0³	0³	19.5³	18.6³	50.3³
Assault (511,040)	100.0	6.4	15.4	20.0³	7.1	2.0³	2.5³	64.6
Aggravated (226,170)	100.0	5.9³	13.0	2.7³	9.3	3.5³	2.4	63.1
Simple (284,870)	100.0	6.7	17.3	1.5³	5.3³	.7³	2.6³	65.8
Crimes of theft (11,218,310)	100.0	.6	41.4	14.5	17.2	7.8	8.4	10.0
Completed (10,875,510)	100.0	.3	42.4	14.8	17.4	7.8	8.5	8.8
Attempted (342,790)	100.0	9.2	10.4	6.6	11.3	7.1	5.5	49.9
Personal larceny with contact (344,600)	100.0	0³	43.1	13.5	26.9	6.0	5.2	5.3
Personal larceny without contact (10,873,710)	100.0	.6	41.4	14.6	16.9	7.9	8.5	10.2
White								
All household crimes (11,821,320)	100.0	1.9	30.2	12.0	13.9	8.0	19.6	14.4
Completed (10,678,380)	100.0	.8	31.1	12.7	14.6	8.5	21.4	10.8
Attempted (1,142,940)	100.0	11.9	21.6	5.2	6.9	3.9	3.2	47.3
Burglary (3,847,350)	100.0	3.8	17.2	8.0	12.5	8.7	27.3	22.5
Completed (3,125,520)	100.0	1.3	15.4	9.1	14.2	10.6	33.3	15.9
Forcible entry (1,420,670)	100.0	2.4	7.8	3.4	8.2	8.9	45.4	43.9
Unlawful entry without force (1,704,850)	100.0	.4³	21.8	13.9	19.2	12.1	23.3	9.3
Attempted forcible entry (721,830)	100.0	14.6	24.7	3.2	5.0	.5³	1.2³	50.8
Household larceny (6,908,190)	100.0	1.0	41.7	15.6	16.1	7.9	7.5	10.2
Completed (6,742,160)	100.0	.7	42.1	15.9	16.3	8.0	7.5	9.4
Attempted (166,030)	100.0	12.5	25.9	14.3³	5.7³	3.2³	5.4³	43.0
Motor vehicle theft (1,065,780)	100.0	1.0³	2.5	3.2	4.5	6.1	70.6	12.0
Completed (810,690)	100.0	.2³	.2³	.5³	1.9³	3.6	90.4	3.2
Attempted (255,090)	100.0	3.7³	9.8	11.6	12.9	14.2	7.6	40.1
Black								

Continued.

Economic Losses of Crime Victims
[Continued]

Race and type of crime	Total	No monetary value	Less than $50	$50-$99	$100-$249	$250 $499	$500 or more	Not known and not available
All personal crimes (1,642,490)	100.0	.8[3]	35.9	14.6	14.9	8.0	8.8	16.9
Crimes of violence (277,830)[2]	100.0	3.5[3]	21.0	9.0	9.6	13.4	14.3	29.2
Completed (238,930)	100.0	2.3[3]	21.6	10.5	11.2	14.7	13.5	26.3
Attempted (38,900)	100.0	11.3[3]	17.1[3]	0[3]	0[3]	5.2[3]	19.4[3]	47.0
Robbery (191,130)	100.0	0[3]	22.6	13.1	14.0	18.4	16.8	15.2
Completed (189,210)	100.0	0[3]	21.8	13.2	14.1	18.6	17.0	15.3
With injury (53,620)	100.0	0[3]	13.0[3]	13.7[3]	21.9[3]	11.4[3]	19.7[3]	20.3[3]
Without injury (135,590)	100.0	0[3]	25.3	13.0	11.0[3]	21.4	16.0	13.4
Attempted (1,920)	100.0[3]	0[3]	100.0[3]	0[3]	0[3]	0[3]	0[3]	0[3]
With injury (0)	100.0[3]	0[3]	0[3]	0[3]	0[3]	0[3]	0[3]	0[3]
Without injury (1,920)	100.0[3]	0[3]	100.0[3]	0[3]	0[3]	0[3]	0[3]	0[3]
Assault (77,140)	100.0	12.7[3]	13.1[3]	0[3]	0[3]	0[3]	9.8[3]	64.4
Aggravated (27,760)	100.0	19.1[3]	6.1[3]	0[3]	0[3]	0[3]	0[3]	74.8
Simple (49,380)	100.0	9.2[3]	17.0[3]	0[3]	0[3]	0[3]	15.3[3]	58.5
Crimes of theft (1,364,660)	100.0	.3[3]	39.0	15.7	16.0	7.0	7.7	14.4
Completed (1,327,650)	100.0	.2[3]	39.6	16.1	15.8	7.1	7.9	13.3
Attempted (37,000)	100.0	5.0[3]	15.9[3]	4.3[3]	22.0[3]	0[3]	0[3]	52.9
Personal larceny with contact (86,130)	100.0	0[3]	46.7	20.5	17.4[3]	7.3[3]	5.9[3]	2.1[3]
Personal larceny without contact (1,278,530)	100.0	.3[3]	38.4	15.4	15.9	6.9	7.8	15.2
All household crimes (2,182,060)	100.0	2.1	22.5	13.6	13.7	8.2	19.8	20.1
Completed (1,901,530)	100.0	.6[3]	24.1	14.2	15.3	8.7	22.9	15.1
Attempted (280,530)	100.0	12.1	11.7	9.4	3.0[3]	4.8[3]	4.5[3]	54.4
Burglary (825,580)	100.0	3.8	12.1	8.3	11.2	7.6	25.4	31.6
Completed (637,280)	100.0	.5[3]	11.9	9.4	14.2	9.5	32.1	22.4
Forcible entry (381,670)	100.0	.5[3]	8.8	4.6	6.0	8.8	40.6	30.8
Unlawful entry without force (255,600)	100.0	.7[3]	16.5	16.7	26.5	10.5	19.3	9.8
Attempted forcible entry (188,310)	100.0	14.9	12.9	4.4[3]	1.1[3]	1.2[3]	2.8[3]	62.7
Household larceny (1,158,410)	100.0	1.1[3]	33.5	19.0	17.0	8.6	8.3	12.5
Completed (1,126,910)	100.0	.7[3]	34.0	18.6	17.5	8.8	8.4	11.9
Attempted (31,500)	100.0	14.4[3]	13.9[3]	33.8[3]	0[3]	0[3]	5.7[3]	32.2[3]
Motor vehicle theft (198,070)	100.0	.8[3]	2.0[3]	3.8[3]	4.2[3]	8.3	63.8	17.1
Completed (137,350)	100.0	0[3]	0[3]	0[3]	1.3[3]	3.7[3]	88.0	7.1[3]
Attempted (60,720)	100.0	2.5[3]	6.6[3]	12.5[3]	10.7[3]	18.7[3]	9.1[3]	39.9

Source: "Percent Distribution of Victimizations Resulting in Economic Loss, by Race of Victims, Type of Crime, and Value of Loss," *Criminal Victimization in the United States - 1987,* June 1989, p. 75. Primary source: *Criminal Victimization in the United States, 1987.* U.S. Department of Justice, Washington, DC, NCJ-115-524, June, 1989. *Notes:* Detail may not add to total shown because of rounding. Number of victimizations shown in parentheses. 1. Includes data on "other" races, not shown separately. 2. Includes data on rape, not shown separately. 3. Estimate is based on about 10 or fewer sample cases.

★ 97 ★
Educational Attainment of Arrestees

City	Black[1]	White[1]	Hispanic[1]
Males			
San Antonio	55	50	81
Kansas City	58	70	[2]
St. Louis	64	70	[2]
Philadelphia	55	54	69
Dallas	56	69	86
Cleveland	55	52	[2]
New Orleans	60	34	[2]
New York	55	36	65
Indianapolis	60	68	[2]
Miami	46	57	68
Chicago	56	50	65
Detroit	62	47	[2]
Portland	46	54	71
Birmingham	49	57	[2]
Los Angeles	34	38	72
Houston	52	34	75
Omaha	36	54	[2]
Phoenix	36	37	74
San Diego	34	37	61
Ft. Lauderdale	45	28	[2]
Females			
San Antonio	[2]	42	74
Kansas City	51	[2]	[2]
St. Louis	52	38	[2]
Philadelphia	56	42	[2]
Dallas	46	49	[2]
New Orleans	48	44	[2]
New York	57	54	64
Indianapolis	36	64	[2]
Chicago	48	[2]	[2]
Detroit	54	67	[2]
Portland	51	65	[2]
Birmingham	52	55	[2]
Los Angeles	29	42	72
Phoenix	47	50	74
San Diego	31	46	71

Source: "Percentage of Arrestees who Completed Less Than 12 Grades of School," *National Institute of Justice/Research in Action*, December 1989, p. 7. Primary source: National Institute of Justice/Drug Use Forecasting Program, Washington, DC, 1988. *Notes:* 1. Data based on voluntary self-reports, 1988. Sample sizes for males are: Black-5622, White-2936, Hispanic-1794. Sample sizes for females are: Black-1533, White-1169, Hispanic-438. 2. Less than 20 cases. Published by permission.

★ 98 ★
Executed Defendants and their Victims

	Number	Percent
Race of Defendants Executed		
Total	121	---
White	65	53.72
Black	49	40.50
Hispanic	7	5.79
Race of Victims		
Total[1]	122	---
White	100	82.79
Black	15	12.30
Hispanic	4	3.38
Asian	1	.82
Victim/Defendant Racial Combinations		
White Victim and		
... White Defendant	65	53.28
... Black Defendant	33	27.05
... Hispanic Defendant	4	3.28
Black Victim and		
...Black Defendant	14	11.48
Hispanic Victim and		
...Hispanic Defendant	3	2.46
...Black Defendant	1	.82
Asian Victim and		
...Black Defendant	1	.82

Source: "Execution Update," NAACP Legal Defense and Educational Fund, Inc., January 18, 1990. Primary source: NAACP Legal Defense and Educational Fund, Inc. Published by permission. Total includes the years 1977-1990. *Note:* 1. One defendant killed a white and a black victim.

★ 99 ★
Execution of Female Prisoners: Trends

By race, and jurisdiction, United States, 1930-87.

Year	Offense	
	Murder	Other
1930-87	31	2
1984	1	0
1962	1	0
1957	1	0
1955	1	0
1954	2	0
1953	1	2
1951	1	0
1947	2	0
1946	1	0
1945	1	0
1944	3	0
1943	3	0

Continued.

Execution of Female Prisoners: Trends
[Continued]

Year	Offense	
	Murder	Other
1942	1	0
1941	1	0
1938	2	0
1937	1	0
1936	1	0
1935	3	0
1934	1	0
1931	1	0
1930	2	0

Source: "Female Prisoners Executed Under Civil Authority," *Sourcebook of Criminal Justice Statistics - 1988*, 1989, p. 673. Primary source: U.S. Department of Justice, Bureau of Justice Statistics, *Capital Punishment 1984*, NCJ-99562, Table 4; *1986*, Bulletin NCJ-106483, p. 9, Appendix table 2; *1987*, Bulletin NCJ-111939, p. 2. (Washington, DC: U.S. Department of Justice). Table adapted by SOURCEBOOK staff. The death penalty was not legal in all States for the total period covered in the Table. *Note:* No females were executed in the years that are not listed.

★ 100 ★
Executions of Prisoners: Trends

Year	Total	Murder	Rape	Other Offenses[1]	Total	Murder	Rape	Other Offenses[1]	Total	Murder	Rape	Other Offenses[1]
1930-87	3,952	3,427	455	70	1,808	1,721	48	39	2,102	1,666	405	31
1987	25	25			13	13			12	12		
1986	18	18			11	11			7	7		
1985	18	18			11	11			7	7		
1984	21	21			13	13			8	8		
1983	5	5			4	4			1	1		
1982	2	2			1	1			1	1		
1981	1	1			1	1						
1980												
1939	160	145	12	3	80	79		1	77	63	12	2
1938	190	154	25	11	96	89	1	6	92	63	24	5
1937	147	133	13	1	69	67	2		74	62	11	1
1936	195	181	10	4	92	86	2	4	101	93	8	
1935	199	184	13	2	119	115	2	2	77	66	11	
1934	168	154	14		65	64	1		192	89	13	
1933	160	151	7	2	77	75	1	1	81	74	6	1
1932	140	128	10	2	62	62			75	63	10	2
1931	153	137	15	1	77	76	1		72	57	14	1
1930	155	147	6	2	90	90			65	57	6	2

Source: "Prisoners Executed Under Civil Authority," *Sourcebook of Criminal Justice Statistics - 1988*, 1989, p. 672. Primary source: U.S. Department of Justice, Bureau of Justice Statistics, *Correctional Populations in the United States, 1987*, NCJ-118762 (Washington, DC: U.S. Department of Justice, 1989), Table 7.26. Table adapted by SOURCEBOOK staff. *Notes:* 1. Includes 25 executed for armed robbery, 20 for kidnaping, 11 for burglary, 6 for sabotage, 6 for aggravated assault, and 2 for espionage.

★ 101 ★
Facilities Housing Juvenile Offenders

By demographic characteristics and adjudication status, on Feb. 2, 1987.

	Total		Public facilities		Private facilities	
	Number	Percent	Number	Percent	Number	Percent
Total	91,646	100	53,503	58	38,143	42
Race/ethnicity						
White, nonhispanic	47,577	52	23,375	44	24,202	63
Black, nonhispanic	31,080	34	20,898	39	10,182	27
Hispanic[1]	10,699	12	7,887	15	2,812	7
Other[2]	2,290	2	1,343	3	947	2

Source: "Juveniles Held in Public and Private Facilities," *Sourcebook of Criminal Justice Institutions - 1988*, 1989, p. 595. Primary source: Table provided to SOURCEBOOK staff by the U.S. Department of Justice, Office of Juvenile Justice and Delinquency Prevention. *Notes:* "Detained" juveniles refer to those awaiting adjudication, disposition, or placement. "Committed" juveniles have been adjudicated and placed, and "Voluntarily admitted" refers to juveniles admitted but not adjudicated. 1. Of Hispanic origin, either black or white. 2. American Indians, Alaskan natives, Asians and Pacific Islanders.

★ 102 ★
Failure to Report Criminal Victimization - Part I

Race and type of crime	Total	Object recovered, offender unsuccessful	Not important enough	Private or personal matter	Reported to someone else	Not aware crime occurred until later	Unable to recover property because no ID number	Lack of proof
White								
All personal crimes (12,792,020)	100.0	26.1	2.8	7.5	16.3	5.2	6.7	10.8
Crimes of violence (2,722,260)	100.0	19.1	4.6	24.5	10.4	.3[1]	.6	7.4
Rape (54,810)	100.0	4.0[1]	0[1]	18.8[1]	2.9[1]	3.7[1]	0[1]	0[1]
Robbery (388,380)	100.0	18.2	.5[1]	14.2	6.6	.6[1]	4.0[1]	14.5
Assault (2,279,070)	100.0	19.7	5.4	26.4	11.2	.2[1]	.1[1]	6.3
Crimes of theft (10,069,760)	100.0	28.0	2.3	3.0	17.9	6.5	8.4	11.7
Personal larceny with contact (293,810)	100.0	19.0	4.1[1]	5.5	17.0	5.2[1]	4.7[1]	15.1
Personal larceny without contact (9,775,950)	100.0	28.3	2.3	2.9	17.9	6.6	8.5	11.6
Black								
All personal crimes (1,757,570)	100.0	18.3	3.4	8.0	16.0	3.3	6.9	11.5
Crimes of violence (516,190)	100.0	9.5	6.9	19.8	17.2	.3[1]	1.3[1]	10.4
Rape (23,090)	100.0	0[1]	0[1]	6.0[1]	6.0[1]	0[1]	0[1]	0[1]
Robbery (128,030)	100.0	3.6[1]	0[1]	24.3	0[1]	1.3[1]	5.1[1]	25.6
Assault (365,070)	100.0	12.1	9.7	19.1	9.8	0[1]	0[1]	5.7
Crimes of theft (1,241,380)	100.0	22.0	1.9	3.1	19.7	4.6	9.3	12.0
Personal larceny with contact (71,050)	100.0	24.8	0[1]	0[1]	6.1[1]	8.7[1]	18.3[1]	13.2[1]
Personal larceny without contact (1,170,340)	100.0	21.9	2.0	3.3	20.5	4.3	8.7	11.9

Source: "Percent Distribution of Reasons for Not Reporting Victimizations to the Police, by Race of Victims and Type of Crime," *Criminal Victimizations in the United States - 1987*, June 1989, pp. 90-91. Primary source: *Criminal Victimizations in the United States, 1987*. U.S. Department of Justice, Washington, DC, NCJ-115-524, June, 1989. *Notes:* Detail may not add to total shown because of rounding. Number of reasons shown in parentheses. Some respondents may have cited more than one reason for not reporting victimizations to police. 1. Estimate is based on about 10 or fewer sample cases.

★ 103 ★
Failure to Report Criminal Victimization - Part II

Race and type of crime	Police not want to be bothered	Police would be inefficient, ineffective, insensitive	Fear of reprisal	Too incon- venient or time consuming	Other and not given
White					
All personal crimes (12,792,020)	6.4	2.2	1.3	3.6	11.0
Crimes of violence (2,722,260)	6.5	3.1	4.9	4.1	14.5
Rape (54,810)	0[1]	15.9[1]	18.0[1]	0[1]	36.6
Robbery (388,380)	9.2	4.7	5.2	4.3	18.1
Assault (2,279,070)	6.2	2.5	4.5	4.2	13.3
Crimes of theft (10,069,760)	6.4	2.0	0.3	3.4	10.0
Personal larceny with contact (293,810)	6.6	5.2[1]	2.1[1]	4.8	10.7
Personal larceny without contact (9,775,950)	6.4	1.9	0.2	3.4	10.0
Black					
All personal crimes (1,757,570)	9.6	3.7	1.9	3.9	13.4
Crimes of violence (516,190)	6.3	7.2	6.2	3.3	21.7
Rape (23,090)	11.6[1]	8.0[1]	27.4[1]	0[1]	41.0[1]
Robbery (128,030)	7.1[1]	7.6[1]	9.0[1]	0[1]	16.4
Assault (365,070)	5.7	7.1	3.8[1]	4.7	22.3
Crimes of theft (1,241,380)	11.0	2.2	0.2[1]	4.2	9.9
Personal larceny with contact (71,050)	9.8[1]	4.5[1]	3.2[1]	2.4[1]	8.9[1]
Personal larceny without contact (1,170,340)	11.1	2.0	0[1]	4.3	10.0

Source: "Percent Distribution of Reasons for Not Reporting Victimizations to the Police, by Race of Victims and Type of Crime," *Criminal Victimizations in the United States - 1987,* June 1989, pp. 90-91. Primary source: *Criminal Victimizations in the United States, 1987.* U.S. Department of Justice, Washington, DC, NCJ-115-524, June, 1989. *Notes:* Detail may not add to total shown because of rounding. Number of reasons shown in parentheses. Some respondents may have cited more than one reason for not reporting victimizations to police. 1. Estimate is based on about 10 or fewer sample cases.

★ 104 ★
Family Income of Burglary Victims

Rate per 1,000 households.

Race and income	Completed burglary			Attempted forcible entry
	All burglaries	Forcible entry	Unlawful entry without force	
White				
Less than $7,500 (10,219,800)	80.6	21.4	40.5	18.6
$7,500-$9,999 (4,005,600)	55.8	20.0	25.1	10.8
$10,000-$14,999 (9,641,800)	65.8	23.7	25.6	16.4
$15,000-$24,999 (15,515,800)	54.3	17.3	25.0	11.9
$25,000-$29,999 (6,610,400)	52.8	21.9	19.0	11.9
$30,000-$49,999 (16,178,100)	48.2	18.4	18.7	11.2
$50,000 or more (8,777,800)	52.1	16.3	25.0	10.7
Black				
Less than $7,500 (3,094,400)	105.8	39.8	28.0	38.0
$7,500-$9,999 (720,300)	158.4	56.1	62.8	39.5
$10,000-$14,999 (1,464,400)	104.4	47.1	32.7	24.6

Continued.

Family Income of Burglary Victims
[Continued]

	Completed burglary			
Race and income	All burglaries	Forcible entry	Unlawful entry without force	Attempted forcible entry
$15,000-$24,999 (1,733,500)	83.2	35.4	25.8	22.0
$25,000-$29,999 (565,500)	85.0	33.1	22.8[1]	29.1
$30,000-$49,999 (1,088,000)	70.7	37.2	11.6[1]	21.9
$50,000 or more (373,500)	28.9[1]	0[1]	24.7[1]	4.2[1]

Source: "Victimization Rates, by Race of Head of Household, Annual Family Income, and Type of Burglary," *Criminal Victimization in the United States - 1987*, June 1989, p. 38. Primary source:Criminal Victimization in the United States, 1987. U.S. Department of Justice, Washington, DC, NCJ-115-524, June 1989. *Notes:* Detail may not add to total shown because of rounding. Numbers in parentheses refer to households in the group; excludes data on families whose income level was not ascertained. 1. Estimate is based on about 10 or fewer sample cases.

★ 105 ★
Family Income of Crime Victims - Part I

Rate per 1,000 population age 12 and over.

Race and income	Crimes of violence	Completed violent crimes	Attempted violent crimes	Rape	Robbery		
					Total	With injury	Without injury
White							
Less than $7,500 (16,350,700)	53.1	22.3	30.8	1.96	9.5	4.0	5.5
$7,500-$9,999 (7,129,200)	42.1	16.9	25.3	.3[1]	8.5	3.9	4.7
$10,000-$14,999 (18,722,500)	32.0	11.1	20.9	.3[1]	4.4	1.0	3.4
$15,000-$24,999 (32,887,700)	25.1	7.8	17.4	.4[1]	3.4	1.4	2.0
$25,000-$29,999 (14,977,600)	26.8	10.4	16.4	.4[1]	4.0	1.1	2.8
$30,000-$49,999 (39,738,100)	20.4	6.7	13.6	.3[1]	3.5	1.4	2.1
$50,000 or more (22,722,900)	20.5	6.0	14.5	.5[1]	2.7	.4[1]	2.3
Black							
Less than $7,500 (5,637,100)	57.8	25.0	32.8	3.9	18.5	4.4	14.1
$7,500-$9,999 (1,635,300)	33.4	18.2	15.2	0[1]	6.0[1]	3.5[1]	2.5[1]
$10,000-$14,999 (3,253,500)	51.0	22.5	28.5	.6[1]	14.2	5.9	8.3
$15,000-$24,999 (4,065,600)	24.6	9.1	15.5	1.7[1]	6.0	2.6[1]	3.4[1]
$25,000-$29,999 (1,415,700)	28.2	8.0[1]	20.2	3.2[1]	6.7[1]	2.8[1]	4.0[1]
$30,000-$49,999 (2,972,300)	23.1	11.1	12.0	.9[1]	4.9[1]	.7[1]	4.2[1]
$50,000 or more (1,123,500)	23.6	7.7[1]	15.9	0[1]	4.5[1]	2.5[1]	2.0[1]

Source: "Victimization Rates for Persons 12 and Over, by Race and Annual Family Income of Victims and Type of Crime," *Criminal Victimization in the United States - 1987*, June 1989, pp. 26-27. Primary source: Criminal Victimization in the United States, 1987. U.S. Department of Justice, Washington, DC, NCJ-115-524, June 1989. *Notes:* Detail may not add to total shown because of rounding. Numbers in parentheses refer to population in the group; excludes data on persons whose income level was not ascertained. 1. Estimate is based on about 10 or fewer sample cases.

★ 106 ★
Family Income of Crime Victims - Part II

Rate per 1,000 population age 12 and over.

		Assault		Crimes of theft	Com-pleted theft	At-tempted theft	Personal larceny	
	Total	Aggravated	Simple				With contact	Without contact
White								
Less than $7,500 (16,350,700)	41.8	13.6	28.2	75.8	72.4	3.3	4.2	71.5
$7,500-$9,999 (7,129,200)	33.3	10.1	23.2	60.9	56.8	4.0	4.9	56.0
$10,000-$14,999 (18,722,500)	27.3	8.8	18.5	56.5	53.1	3.4	1.7	54.9
$15,000-$24,999 (32,887,700)	21.4	7.1	14.3	65.7	61.1	4.6	1.7	64.0
$25,000-$29,999 (14,977,600)	22.4	8.3	14.1	70.5	65.4	4.5	2.0	68.5
$30,000-$49,999 (39,738,100)	16.6	4.5	12.1	69.1	65.9	3.7	2.2	66.9
$50,000 or more (22,722,900)	17.3	5.6	11.7	84.5	78.7	5.8	1.8	82.7
Black								
Less than $7,500 (5,637,100)	35.5	15.9	19.6	54.5	50.3	4.2	5.9	48.6
$7,500-$9,999 (1,635,300)	27.4	15.2	12.2	76.2	69.3	6.9[1]	14.7	61.5
$10,000-$14,999 (3,253,500)	36.1	16.7	19.4	82.7	70.9	11.8	3.7[1]	79.0
$15,000-$24,999 (4,065,600)	16.9	9.1	7.8	60.1	57.7	2.4[1]	3.6[1]	56.5
$25,000-$29,999 (1,415,700)	18.3	7.4[1]	10.9[1]	55.0	55.0	0[1]	0[1]	55.0
$30,000-$49,999 (2,972,300)	17.3	8.7	8.6	63.4	59.3	4.1[1]	1.2[1]	62.2
$50,000 or more (1,123,500)	19.1	0[1]	19.1	67.9	64.7	3.2[1]	0[1]	67.9

Source: "Victimization Rates for Persons 12 and Over, by Race and Annual Family Income of Victims and Type of Crime," *Criminal Victimization in the United States - 1987*, June 1989, pp. 26-27. Primary source: Criminal Victimization in the United States, 1987. U.S. Department of Justice, Washington, DC, NCJ-115-524, June 1989. *Notes:* Detail may not add to total shown because of rounding. Numbers in parentheses refer to population in the group; excludes data on persons whose income level was not ascertained. 1. Estimate is based on about 10 or fewer sample cases.

★ 107 ★
Family Income of Larceny Victims

Rate per 1,000 households.

	All household larcenies[1]	Completed larceny		Attempted larceny
		Less than $50	$50 or more	
White				
Less than $7,500 (10,219,800)	97.0	45.6	38.8	9.0
$7,500-$9,999 (4,005,600)	78.4	32.4	31.4	7.1
$10,000-$14,999 (9,641,800)	86.8	39.6	38.3	4.7
$15,000-$24,999 (15,515,800)	96.8	38.0	47.9	5.9
$25,000-$29,999 (6,610,400)	99.3	41.0	43.4	11.0
$30,000-$49,999 (16,178,100)	94.8	39.5	43.1	6.5
$50,000 or more (8,777,800)	95.3	35.1	47.6	7.0
Black				
Less than $7,500 (3,094,400)	108.3	44.3	50.8	3.5[2]
$7,500-$9,999 (720,300)	153.2	45.7	88.1	10.9[2]
$10,000-$14,999 (1,464,400)	111.0	41.5	61.3	5.0[2]
$15,000-$24,999 (1,733,500)	108.3	37.4	61.9	6.8[2]
$25,000-$29,999 (565,500)	38.5	28.[2]	86.3	14.1[2]

Continued.

Family Income of Larceny Victims
[Continued]

	All household larcenies[1]	Completed larceny		Attempted larceny
		Less than $50	$50 or more	
$30,000-$49,999 (1,088,000)	127.9	37.5	69.3	7.3[2]
$50,000 or more (373,500)	106.7	27.1[2]	79.6	0[2]

Source: "Victimization Rates, by Race of Head of Household, Annual Family Income, and Type of Larceny," *Criminal Victimization in the United States - 1987*, June 1989, p. 38. Primary source: Criminal Victimization in the United States, 1987. U.S. Department of Justice, Washington, DC, NCJ-115-524, June 1989. *Notes:* Detail may not add to total shown because of rounding. Numbers in parentheses refer to households in the group; excludes data on families whose income level was not ascertained. 1. Includes data, not shown separately, on larcenies for which the value of loss was not ascertained. 2. Estimate is based on about 10 or fewer sample cases.

★ 108 ★
Family Income of Theft Victims

Rate per 1,000 households.

Race and income	All vehicle thefts	Completed thefts	Attempted thefts
White			
Less than $7,500 (10,219,800)	12.7	8.8	3.9
$7,500-$9,999 (4,005,600)	13.8	7.2	6.5
$10,000-$14,999 (9,641,800)	11.6	7.3	4.3
$15,000-$24,999 (15,515,800)	16.2	11.8	4.4
$25,000-$29,999 (6,610,400)	15.7	9.4	6.2
$30,000-$49,999 (16,178,100)	16.6	9.7	6.9
$50,000 or more (8,777,800)	19.7	14.8	4.9
Black			
Less than $7,500 (3,094,400)	10.2	8.6	1.6[1]
$7,500-$9,999 (720,300)	28.0	24.3	3.7[1]
$10,000-$14,999 (1,464,400)	17.4	13.2	4.2[1]
$15,000-$24,999 (1,733,500)	19.3	11.1	8.2[1]
$25,000-$29,999 (565,500)	21.2[1]	18.4[1]	2.8[1]
$30,000-$49,999 (1,088,000)	37.6	16.4	21.2
$50,000 or more (373,500)	65.3	31.7[1]	31.8[1]

Source: "Victimization Rates, by Race of Head of Household, Annual Family Income, and Type of Theft," *Criminal Victimization in the United States - 1987*, June 1989, p. 39. Primary source: Criminal Victimization in the United States, 1987. U.S. Department of Justice, Washington, DC, NCJ-115-524, June 1989. *Notes:* Detail may not add to total shown because of rounding. Numbers in parentheses refer to households in the group; excludes data on families whose income level was not ascertained. 1. Estimate is based on about 10 or fewer sample cases.

★ 109 ★
Federal Defendants: Detention Rate

By selected demographic characteristics, United States, 1983 and 1985.

| | Percent of defendants held until trial | | | |
| | Total | | Pretrial only[1] | |
Defendant characteristics	1983	1985	1983	1985
Race				
White	23.7	30.0	1.8	18.5
Black	23.2	26.4	1.7	19.1
Other	30.2	30.1	1.2	22.9

Source: "Detention Rate of Federal Defendants Held Until Trial," *Sourcebook of Criminal Justice Statistics - 1988*, 1989, p. 545. Primary source: U.S. Department of Justice, Bureau of Justice Statistics, *Pretrial Release and Detention: The Bail Reform Act of 1984*, Special Report NCJ-109929 (Washington, DC: U.S. Department of Justice, February 1988), p. 4, Table 8. Includes only cases reaching final disposition within 12 months after initiation. *Notes:* 1. Includes defendants held until trial without the option of release on bail.

★ 110 ★
Federal Drug and Non-Drug Crimes

By type of offense and demographic characteristics, 1986.

| | Estimated percent of persons arrested | | |
| | Race | | |
Offense	White	Black	Other
All offenses	71	25	4
Drug offenses	79	19	2
Distribution/manufacture	81	18	2
Importation	81	15	4
Possession	60	39	1
General trafficking/miscellaneous	83		
Non-drug offenses	67	28	4
Violent	52	32	16
General property	57	39	4
Fraudulent property	63	35	2
Regulatory	81	15	4
Public-order	81	16	3

Source: "Persons Arrested for Federal Drug and Non-Drug Offenses," *Sourcebook of Criminal Justice Statistics - 1988*, 1989, p. 519. Primary source: U.S. Department of Justice, Bureau of Justice Statistics, *Drug Law Violators, 1980-86*, Special Report NCJ-111763 (Washington, DC: U.S. Department of Justice, June 1988), p. 2, Table 1. *Notes:* These data are from the Bureau of Justice Statistics' Federal Justice Statistics data base maintained by Abt Associates, Inc. Sources of information include the Executive Office for U.S. Attorneys, the Administrative Office of the U.S. Courts, and the U.S. Parole Commission. The data in this table describe 31,660 defendants interviewed by the Pretrial Services Agency in calendar year 1986. Twenty-six percent of the interviews did not record race or ethnicity; 30 percent did not record educational level. There were 21,188 drug suspects arrested by the Drug Enforcement Administration and the Federal Bureau of Investigation in the 12 months preceding September 30, 1986.

★ 111 ★
Hospitalization of Crime Victims

Characteristic and type of crime	Total	Emergency room care	Inpatient care				
			Total	Less than 1 day	1-3 days	4 days or more	Not available
Race							
White							
Crimes of violence(332,640)[1]	100.0	56.6	43.5	24.3	7.8	11.4	0[2]
Robbery (81,430)	100.0	61.1	38.8	14.2[2]	7.9[2]	16.7[2]	0[2]
Assault (227,680)	100.0	53.0	47.0	29.6	7.6	9.8	0[2]
Black							
Crimes of violence(69,490)[1]	100.0	38.3	61.7	17.5[2]	27.6	13.2[2]	3.5[2]
Robbery (23,530)	100.0	33.5[2]	66.5[2]	26.4[2]	19.5[2]	20.6[2]	0[2]
Assault (37,280)	100.0	44.3	55.7	4.0[2]	39.1[2]	6.1[2]	6.4[2]

Source: "Percent Distribution of Victimization in which Injured Victims Received Hospital Care, by Selected Characteristics of Victims, Type of Crime, and Type of Hospital Care," *Criminal Victimization in the United States - 1987*, June 1989, p. 71. Primary source: *Criminal Victimizations in the United States, 1987*. U.S. Department of Justice, Washington, DC, NCJ-115-524, June, 1989. *Notes:* Detail may not add to total shown because of rounding. Number of victimizations shown in parentheses. 1. Includes data on rape, not shown separately. 2. Estimate is based on about 10 or fewer sample cases.

★ 112 ★
Household Crime Victims

Rates per 1,000 households. Includes attempted offenses. Data based on National Crime Survey, see text, section 5, and Appendix III.

Year and Household Characteristic	Total	Burglary			Larceny			Motor Vehicle Theft		
		Total[1]	White	Black	Total[1]	White	Black	Total[1]	White	Black
1973	218	92	87	133	107	108	104	19	18	24
1975	237	92	87	129	125	127	115	19	19	27
1976	229	89	84	131	124	126	112	17	16	21
1977	229	89	84	122	123	124	116	17	16	21
1978	223	86	83	115	120	120	121	18	17	21
1979	235	84	80	114	134	133	133	18	17	22
1980	227	84	81	115	127	125	134	17	16	25
1981	226	88	83	134	121	119	142	17	16	24
1982	208	78	73	117	114	111	132	16	15	25
1983	190	70	67	98	105	103	119	15	13	25
1984	179	64	61	92	99	97	115	15	14	26
1985	174	63	60	83	97	95	120	14	13	22
1986: All households	170	61	58	92	94	92	102	15	14	24
Homeowner	138	48	45	78	78	77	93	13	12	23
Renter	226	86	82	103	121	124	109	19	18	24
Households with income of--										
Under $7,500	201	91	87	102	99	109	70	11	11	10
$7,500-$9,999	179	56	52	81	111	110	118	12	11	14
$20.000-$14,999	170	65	59	107	90	86	116	15	13	30
$15,000-$24,999	166	55	52	73	97	93	127	14	12	31
$25,000-$29,999	168	55	50	133	97	95	126	16	14	41

Continued.

Household Crime Victims
[Continued]

Year and Household Characteristic	Total	Burglary			Larceny			Motor Vehicle Theft		
		Total[1]	White	Black	Total[1]	White	Black	Total[1]	White	Black
$30,000-$49,999	166	54	52	83	93	91	140	19	17	45
$50,000 and over	164	61	59	135	84	83	127	18	17	41

Source: "Victimization Rates for Crimes against Households: 1973 to 1986," *Statistical Abstracts*, 1989, p. 171. Primary source: Through 1975, U.S. Law Enforcement Assistance Administration; thereafter, U.S. Bureau of Justice Statistics, *Criminal Victimization in the United States*, annual. *Note:* 1. Includes other races not shown separately.

★ 113 ★
Household Head and Type of Victimization

Rate per 1,000 households.

Type of crime	All races (91,763,950)	White (79,543,810)	Black (10,229,530)	Other (1,990,600)
Household crimes	171.4	163.6	232.0	169.3
Completed	144.5	139.0	189.7	135.5
Attempted	26.8	24.7	42.3	33.9
Burglary	61.3	57.0	94.4	62.6
Completed	46.6	44.0	66.1	50.3
Forcible entry	21.4	18.9	39.3	28.8
Unlawful entry without force	25.2	25.1	26.8	21.5
Attempted forcible entry	14.7	13.0	28.3	12.3
Household larceny	94.0	91.4	116.2	82.2
Completed	87.4	84.8	110.2	74.7
Less than $50	37.7	37.7	40.1	26.5
$50 or more	44.5	42.3	61.5	44.7
Amount not available	5.2	4.8	8.5	3.6[1]
Attempted	6.6	6.7	6.0	7.5[1]
Motor vehicle theft	16.1	15.2	21.4	24.5
Completed	10.6	10.2	13.4	10.4
Attempted	5.6	5.0	8.0	14.1

Source: "Victimization Rates, by Type of Crime and Race of Head of Household," *Criminal Victimization in the United States - 1987*, June, 1989, p. 35. Primary source: *Criminal Victimization in the United States, 1987*. U.S. Department of Justice, Washington, DC, NCJ-115-524, June, 1989. *Notes:* Detail may not add to total shown because of rounding. Numbers in parentheses refer to households in the group. 1. Estimate is based on 10 or fewer sample cases.

★ 114 ★
Household Ownership of Crime Victims

Rate per 1,000 households.

Type of crime	Owned or being bought			Rented		
	All races[1] (58,715,510)	White (53,266,170)	Black (4,498,240)	All races[1] (33,048,430)	White (26,277,640)	Black (5,731,300)
Household crimes	140.8	135.9	196.1	225.8	219.9	260.1
Completed	121.1	117.5	164.0	186.2	182.5	209.9
Attempted	19.7	18.4	32.2	39.6	37.4	50.2
Burglary	47.8	46.2	66.5	85.3	78.8	116.3
Completed	38.0	37.2	48.7	61.8	57.9	79.8

Continued.

Household Ownership of Crime Victims
[Continued]

	Owned or being bought			Rented		
Type of crime	All races[1] (58,715,510)	White (53,266,170)	Black (4,498,240)	All races[1] (33,048,430)	White (26,277,640)	Black (5,731,300)
Forcible entry	17.7	16.7	28.1	28.0	23.4	48.1
Unlawful entry without force	20.4	20.4	20.7	33.8	34.4	31.7
Attempted forcible entry	9.7	9.1	17.8	23.5	20.9	36.5
Household larceny	80.3	77.9	106.7	118.4	118.8	123.6
Completed	74.7	72.4	101.7	109.9	109.9	116.8
Less than $50	33.9	33.6	39.0	44.5	45.9	41.0
$50 or more	36.2	34.4	54.0	59.2	58.3	67.5
Amount not available	4.7	4.4	8.8	6.1	5.7	8.3
Attempted	5.5	5.6	5.0	8.5	8.9	6.8
Motor vehicle theft	12.7	11.7	22.9	22.1	22.4	20.3
Completed	8.4	7.9	13.5	14.5	14.8	13.3
Attempted	4.4	3.8	9.3	7.7	7.6	6.9

Source: "Victimization Rates, by Types of Crime, form of Tenure, and Race of Head of Household," *Criminal Victimization in the United States - 1987*, June 1989, p. 40. Primary source: *Criminal Victimization in the United States, 1987*. U.S. Department of Justice, Washington, DC, NCJ-115-524, June, 1989. *Notes:* Detail may not add to total shown because of rounding. Numbers in parentheses refer to households in the group. 1. Includes data on "other" races, not shown separately.

★ 115 ★
Household Victims of Crimes

A household is considered "touched by crime" if during the year it experienced a burglary, auto theft or household theft or if a household member was raped, robbed, or assaulted, or a victim of personal theft, no matter where the crime occurred. Data based on the National Crime Survey.

	1987 Percent Touched		
Type of Crime	Total[1]	White	Black
Total[2]	24.4	23.9	27.8
Violent crime	4.6	4.4	5.8
Rape	.1	.1	.2
Robbery	1.0	.8	2.2
Assault	3.7	3.7	3.8
Theft	17.1	17.2	16.8
Personal	11.0	11.2	9.6
Household	7.9	7.7	9.4
Burglary	5.2	4.8	7.9
Motor vehicle theft	1.5	1.4	2.3

Source: "Households Touched by Crime, and by Characteristic, 1987," *Statistical Abstract*, 1989, p. 171. Primary source: U.S. Bureau of Justice Statistics, *Households Touched by Crime*, annual. *Notes:* 1. Includes other races not shown separately. 2. Types of crime will not add to "total" since each household may report as many crime categories as experienced.

★ 116 ★
Households Victimized by Crime

By type of victimization and race of head of household, United States, 1987(1).

	Race of head of household		
	White	Black	Other
Any crime	23.9	27.8	25.0
Violent crime	4.4	5.8	5.3
Rape	0.1	0.2	0.1
Robbery	0.8	2.2	1.2
Assault	3.7	3.8	4.0
Aggravated	1.3	1.7	2.0
Simple	2.6	2.4	2.5
Total theft	17.2	16.8	16.4
Personal	11.2	9.6	11.3
Household	7.7	9.4	7.4
Burglary	4.8	7.9	6.0
Motor vehicle theft	1.4	2.3	2.0
Serious violent crime[2]	2.2	3.8	3.3
Crimes of high concern[3]	7.0	10.4	8.8

Source: "Percent of 'Households Touched by Crime' During the Last 12 Months," *Sourcebook of Criminal Justice Statistics — 1988,* 1989, p. 321. Primary source: U.S. Department of Justice, Bureau of Justice Statistics, *Households Touched by Crime, 1987,* Bulletin NCJ-111240 (Washington, DC: U.S. Department of Justice, May 1988), p. 3. Tables 3 and 4. Table adopted by SOURCEBOOK staff. *Notes:* See Notes, tables 3.1 and 3.49. The entries for white "households touched by crime" are computed as a percent of the total number of white households and the entries for black "households touched by crime" are computed as a percent of the total number of other households. "Other" households refer to those headed by an individual whose racial identification is other than white or black. For survey methodology and definitions of terms, see Appendix 6. 1. Detail does not add to total because of overlap in households touched by different crimes. 2. Rape, robbery, aggravated assault. 3. Rape, robbery, assault by stranger, or burglary.

★ 117 ★
Jail Inmates: 1984-1987

By sex and race, United States, 1984-87 (estimated).

	Percent of jail inmates on June 30			
	1984	1985	1986	1987
Race[2]				
White	59	59	58	57
Male	55	55	54	53
Female	4	4	4	4
Black	40	40	41	42
Male	37	37	37	38
Female	3	3	3	4
Other[3]	1	1	1	1
Male	1	1	1	1
Female	4	4	4	4

Source: "Jail Inmates on June 30," *Sourcebook of Criminal Justice Statistics — 1988,* 1989, p. 606. Primary source: U.S. Department of Justice, Bureau of Justice Statistics, *Jail Inmates, 1985,* NCJ-105586 (Washington, DC: USGPO, 1987, p. 6, Table 3: and U.S. Department of Justice, Bureau of Justice, Statistics, *Jail Inmates 1987,* Bulletin NCJ-114319 (Washington, DC: U.S. Department of Justice, December 1988), p. 2, Table 3. Table adopted by SOURCEBOOK staff. *Notes:* 1. Percents may not add to total because of rounding. 2. Sex was reported for all inmates for all 4 years. Race and ethnicity were reported for 88 percent of the inmates in 1984, 80 percent in 1985, 97 percent in 1986, and 93 percent in 1987. 3. Native Americans, Aleuts, Asians, and Pacific Islanders. 4. Less than 0.5 percent.

★ 118 ★
Jurisdiction Over Prisoners Sentenced to Die

By race or ethnicity and jurisdiction, on Mar. 1, 1989.

		Race or ethnicity					
Jurisdiction	Total	White	Black	Hispanic	Native American	Asian	Unknown
United States	2,186	1,132	871	131	35	13	4
Federal civil	0	X	X	X	X	X	X
U.S. Military	5	1	3	0	0	0	1
Alabama	94	44[1,2,3]	49[2,4]	0	0	1	0
Arizona	84	60[3]	8	14[2]	2[3]	0	0
Arkansas	30	20	8	1	1	0	0
California	241	105[3]	93	32	6	5	0
Colorado	3	2	0	1	0	0	0
Connecticut	1	1	0	0	0	0	0
Delaware	7	2	55[2,4]	0	0	0	0
Florida	290	169[1,5,6]	88	19	2	1	0
Georgia	107	58[3,4,7]	48	0	0	0	1
Idaho	15	14	0	1	0	0	0
Illinois	120	41	73	6	0	0	0
Indiana	50	28[4]	21[2,5,8]	1	0	0	0
Kentucky	30	22[4]	8	0	0	0	0
Louisiana	39	17	22	0	0	0	0
Maryland	18	5[2]	13	0	0	0	0
Mississippi	46	18	27	1	0	0	0
Missouri	71	42[2,8]	28[2,3]	0	1	0	0
Montana	7	4	1	0	1	0	0
Nebraska	13	9	3	0	1	0	0
Nevada	47	31	11	5	0	0	0
New Hampshire	0	X	X	X	X	X	X
New Jersey	25	11	13	1	0	0	0
New Mexico	2	1	0	0	1	0	0
North Carolina	82	37[8,4]	39	1	5	0	0
Ohio	88	36	47	2	2	0	1
Oklahoma	98	68[8,4,6]	19	1	9[3]	1	0
Oregon	15	10	2	2	1	0	0
Pennsylvania	115	45	64	4	0	1	1
South Carolina	42	23	19	0	0	0	0
South Dakota	0	X	X	X	X	X	X
Tennessee	70	47[4]	22[3,4,9]	0	1	0	0
Texas	287	137[1,6]	106	39[2]	2	3	0
Utah	6	3	3	0	0	0	0
Vermont	0	X	X	X	X	X	X
Virginia	40	18	22	0	0	0	0

Continued.

Jurisdiction Over Prisoners Sentenced to Die
[Continued]

Jurisdiction	Total	Race or ethnicity					
		White	Black	Hispanic	Native American	Asian	Unknown
Washington	7	5	1	0	0	1	0
Wyoming	2	2	0	0	0	0	0

Source: "Prisoners Under Sentence of Death," *Sourcebook of Criminal Justice Statistics — 1988*, 1989, p. 663. Primary source: Table constructed by SOURCEBOOK staff from data provided by the NAACP Legal Defense and Educational Fund, Inc. *Notes:* The NAACP Legal Defense and Educational Fund, Inc. periodically collects data on persons on death row. As of Mar. 1, 1989, 37 jurisdictions, the Federal Government, and the United States military had capital punishment laws, and 34 jurisdictions and the United States military had at least 1 prisoner under sentence of death. Between Jan. 1, 1973 and Mar. 1, 1989, an estimated 558 death sentences have been vacated as unconstitutional and an estimated 932 convictions or sentences have been reversed or vacated on other grounds. 1. Includes three females. 2. Includes one person who was a juvenile at the time of the offense. 3. Includes one person sentenced to death in the State but serving another sentence in another State. 4. Includes one female. 5. Includes two persons sentenced to death in the State but serving other sentences in other States. 6. Includes two persons who were juveniles at the time of offense. 7. Includes three persons who were juveniles at the time of the offense. 8. Includes two females. 9. Includes four persons who were juveniles at the time of the offense. Published by permission.

★ 119 ★
Killers of Law Enforcement Officers

By demographic characteristics, United States, 1978-87 (aggregate) and 1987.

Characteristics of persons identified	1978 to 1987		1987	
	Number	Percent	Number	Percent
Total	1,145	100	85	100
Race, ethnicity				
White	632	55	55	65
Black	487	42	30	35
Other	26	2	0	0

Source: "Persons Identified in the Killing of Law Enforcement Officers," *Sourcebook of Criminal Justice Statistics - 1988*, 1989, p. 466. Primary source: U.S. Department of Justice, Federal Bureau of Investigation, *Law Enforcement Officers Killed and Assaulted, 1987*, FBI Uniform Crime Reports (Washington, DC: USGPO, 1988), p. 21. Table constructed by SOURCEBOOK staff. Data includes Federal, State, and local officers killed in the U.S., its territories, Puerto Rico, and abroad.

★ 120 ★
Law Enforcement Officers Slain

By selected characteristics of officers, United States, 1978-87(1).

Characteristics of officers killed	1978 (N=93)	1979 (N=106)	1980 (N=104)	1981 (N=91)	1982 (N=92)	1983 (N=80)	1984 (N=72)	1985 (N=78)	1986 (N=66)	1987 (N=73)
Race										
White	91	88	86	85	84	84	85	88	89	90
Black	9	9	13	14	15	13	14	10	11	10
Other	0	3	0	1	1	4	1	1	0	0

Source: "Percent Distribution of Law Enforcement Officers Killed," *Sourcebook of Criminal Justice Statistics — 1988*, 1989, p. 465. Primary source: U.S. Department of Justice, Federal Bureau of Investigation, *Law Enforcement Officers Killed, 1978*, p. 22; *1979*, p. 22; *1980*, p. 23; *1981*, p. 18; FBI Uniform Crime Reports (Washington, DC: USGPO); *Law Enforcement Officers Killed and Assaulted, 1982*, FBI Uniform Crime Reports (Washington, DC: U.S. Department of Justice, 1983), p. 20; *1984*, p. 20; FBI Uniform Crime Reports (Washington, DC: USGPO); *Law Enforcement Officers Killed and Assaulted, 1985*, FBI Uniform Crime Reports (Washington, DC: U.S. Department of Justice, 1986), p. 21; and *Law Enforcement Officers Killed and Assaulted, 1986*, p. 22; *1987*, p. 20. FBI Uniform Crime Reports (Washington, DC: USGPO). Table constructed by SOURCEBOOK staff. Data include Federal, State, and local officers killed in the U.S., its territories, Puerto Rico, and abroad. *Note:* 1. Because of rounding, percents may not add to 100.

★ 121 ★
Locality of Residence and Victimization Rates - Part I

Rate per 1,000 population age 12 and over.

Race and income	Crimes of violence	Completed violent crimes	Attempted violent crimes	Rape	Robbery		
					Total	With injury	Without injury
All areas							
White male (82,108,740)	35.0	12.0	23.0	.1[1]	5.7	2.0	3.7
White female (87,806,540)	20.1	7.7	12.3	.9	3.2	1.3	1.9
Black male (10,382,130)	49.1	17.5	31.6	0[1]	15.2	5.1	10.1
Black female (12,343,560)	31.6	15.2	16.4	3.3	8.9	2.7	6.2
Metropolitan areas							
Central cities							
White male (20,767,760)	48.6	18.3	30.3	.2[1]	11.2	4.6	6.6
White female (23,570,370)	30.5	11.8	18.7	1.6	6.1	2.6	3.6
Black male (5,795,690)	59.4	22.1	37.3	0[1]	19.9	5.6	14.3
Black female (7,192,700)	37.8	20.2	17.7	3.6	12.5	3.9	8.6
Metropolitan areas							
Outside central cities							
White male (37,628,320)	30.5	10.1	20.5	.2[1]	4.8	1.3	3.5
White female (39,149,960)	15.4	5.8	9.5	.6	2.3	.9	1.3
Black male (2,598,990)	34.9	11.9	23.0	0[1]	11.2	7.2	4.1[1]
Black female (2,904,720)	21.1	6.4	14.7	4.0[1]	4.2[1]	.7[1]	3.5[1]
Nonmetropolitan areas							
White male (23,712,670)	30.2	9.5	20.6	0[1]	2.3	.9	1.4
White female (25,086,210)	17.6	6.9	10.7	.8	2.0	.8	1.1
Black male (1,987,450)	37.7	11.6	26.1	0[1]	6.8[1]	1.1[1]	5.7[1]
Black female (2,246,130)	25.2	10.9	14.3	1.2[1]	3.5[1]	1.2[1]	2.3[1]

Source: "Victimization Rates for Persons age 12 and Over, by Type of Locality of Residence, Race and Sex of Victims, and Type of Crime, *Criminal Victimization in the United States - 1987,* June 1989, pp. 32-33. Primary source: *Criminal Victimization in the United States, 1987.* U.S. Department of Justice, Washington, DC, NCJ-115-524, June, 1989. *Notes:* Detail may not add to total shown because of rounding. Numbers in parentheses refer to population in the group. 1. Estimate is based on about 10 or fewer sample cases.

★ 122 ★
Locality of Residence and Victimization Rates - Part II

Rate per 1,000 population age 12 and over.

	Assault			Crimes of theft	Completed theft	Attempted theft	Personal larceny	
	Total	Aggravated	Simple				With contact	Without contac
All areas								
White male (82,108,740)	29.2	10.5	18.7	72.5	67.7	4.7	1.9	70.6
White female (87,806,540)	15.9	4.1	11.8	64.3	60.5	3.8	2.7	61.6
Black male (10,382,130)	33.9	18.3	15.6	70.6	64.1	6.6	4.4	66.2
Black female (12,343,560)	19.5	6.8	12.7	56.4	53.7	2.8	4.2	52.2
Metropolitan areas								
Central cities								
White male (20,767,760)	37.3	15.8	21.4	89.4	82.0	7.4	3.9	85.5
White female (23,570,370)	22.8	6.2	16.6	79.8	74.0	5.8	6.6	73.2
Black male (5,795,690)	39.5	22.7	16.9	79.4	69.9	9.5	6.0	73.3
Black female (7,192,700)	21.8	8.5	13.3	56.6	53.2	3.4	6.1	50.5
Metropolitan areas								
Outside central cities								
White male (37,628,320)	25.6	8.4	7.2	74.5	69.6	4.9	1.6	72.9
White female (39,149,960)	12.5	3.0	9.5	65.7	61.6	4.0	1.6	64.1
Black male (2,598,990)	23.7	11.2	12.4	70.2	70.2	0[1]	1.2[1]	69.0
Black female (2,904,720)	12.9	2.1[1]	10.8	68.3	65.6	2.7[1]	2.8[1]	65.5

Continued.

Locality of Residence and Victimization Rates - Part II
[Continued]

		Assault		Crimes of theft	Completed theft	Attempted theft	Personal larceny	
	Total	Aggravated	Simple				With contact	Without contac
Nonmetropolitan areas								
White male (23,712,670)	27.9	9.4	18.6	54.5	52.4	2.2	.6[1]	54.0
White female (25,086,210)	14.9	3.9	11.0	47.5	46.1	1.4	.6[1]	46.9
Black male (1,987,450)	30.9	14.7	16.2	45.7	39.0	6.7[1]	3.9[1]	41.8
Black female (2,246,130)	20.5	7.4	13.2	40.6	39.8	.8[1]	0[1]	40.6

Source: "Victimization Rates for Persons age and Over, by Type of Locality of Residence, Race and Sex of Victims, and Type of Crime, *Criminal Victimization in the United States - 1987*, June 1989, pp. 32-33. Primary source: *Criminal Victimization in the United States, 1987*. U.S. Department of Justice, Washington, DC, NCJ-115-524, June, 1989. *Notes:* 1. Estimate is based on about 10 or fewer sample cases. NOTE: Detail may not add to total shown because of rounding. Numbers in parentheses refer to population in the group.

★ 123 ★
Multiple-Offender Crimes: Victim and Offender Race

Type of crime and race of victim	Total	Perceived race of offenders				
		All white	All black	All other	Mixed races	Not known and not available
Crimes of violence[1]						
White (1,094,190)	100.0	56.9	23.9	6.1	10.4	2.8
Black (241,830)	100.0	5.1[2]	82.6	.9[2]	11.4	0[2]
Robbery						
White (337,870)	100.0	35.7	43.7	6.5	11.6	2.4[2]
Black (101,890)	100.0	2.8[2]	85.6	0[2]	11.6[2]	0[2]
Assault						
White (746,510)	100.0	67.2	13.9	6.0	9.9	3.0
Black (139,940)	100.0	6.8[2]	80.5	1.6[2]	11.2[2]	0[2]

Source: "Percent Distribution of Multiple-Offender Victimizations, by Type of Crime, Race of Victims, and Perceived Race of Offenders," *Criminal Victimization in the United States - 1987*, June 1989, p. 53. Primary source: *Criminal Victimization in the United States, 1987*. U.S. Department of Justice, Washington, DC, NCJ-115-524, June, 1989. *Notes:* Detail may not add to total shown because of rounding. Number of victimizations shown in parentheses. 1. Includes data on rape, not shown separately. 2. Estimate is based on about 10 or fewer sample cases.

★ 124 ★
Outcomes of Parole

By method of parole release, and race, 33 States, 1984(1).

Method of parole release	Percent of persons discharged from parole	
	Sex	
	Male	Female
All parole releases	100.0	100.0
Successful completion	75.0	84.1
Absconded	1.4	1.1
Return to jail or prison[2]	21.7	13.6
Other	1.9	1.2
Number of releases	55,343	3,904

Source: "Releases from Parole," *Sourcebook of Criminal Justice Statistics - 1988*, 1989, p. 653. Primary source: U.S. Department of Justice, Bureau of Justice Statistics, *Time Served in Prison and on Parole 1984*, Special Report NCJ-108554 (Washington, DC: U.S. Department of Justice, January 1988), p. 6, Table 10. Data include approxiamtely three-fourths of total State prison releases during 1984. *Notes:* Data based on persons who had received sentences of more than a year and include those on supervised release even if not technically termed "parole." 1. Percents may not add to 100 due to rounding. 2. Includes those returned to jail or prison with a new sentence, technical parole violators, and those returned pending parole revocation.

★ 125 ★
People in Prisons: Trends

Year	White	Black	Percent Black
1939	47,971	17,324	26
1949	38,155	15,640	29
1960	108,920	67,781	38
1974	97,700	89,700	48
1979	161,642	145,383	47
1985	260,847	227,137	46

Source: "Prison Population, by Race, 1939-1985," *A Common Destiny: Blacks And American Society*, 1989, p. 461. Primary source: Hawkins, Darnell F. 1987. Paper prepared for the Committee on the Status of Black Americans, National Research Council, Washington, DC. *Notes:* Data for 1939 are for all court-received prisoners or flows during each year. Data for 1949 are for male felony prisoners received from courts during each year, including federal and state courts but excluding data from Georgia, Michigan, and Mississippi. Data for 1960 include all nonwhites and are the year-end felony population. Data for 1974-1985 are for the year-end stock population. Published by permission.

★ 126 ★
Physical Injury of Crime Victims

Characteristic	Robbery and assault	Robbery	Assault
Race			
White	31.3	37.8	30.1
Black	29.4	32.1	28.2

Source: "Percent of Victimizations in which Victims Sustained Physical Injury, by Selected Characteristics of Victims and Type of Crime," *Criminal Victimization in the United States - 1987,* June 1989, p. 67. Primary source: *Criminal Victimization in the United States, 1987.* U.S. Department of Justice, Washington, DC, NCJ-115-524, June, 1989.

★ 127 ★
Police Agency Employees

By size of population served, United States, 1987.

Population served	Total	Percent of sworn employees who are [1]							
		White		Black		Hispanic		Other	
		Male	Female	Male	Female	Male	Female	Male	Female
All sizes	100.0	79.9	5.5	7.7	1.6	4.1	0.4	0.7	0.1
1,000,000 or more	100.0	69.5	6.0	12.2	3.5	7.1	1.1	0.6	0.1
500,000 to 999,999	100.0	69.8	5.1	14.9	3.8	4.9	0.4	1.0	0.1
250,000 to 499,999	100.0	71.7	6.1	11.2	2.4	7.0	0.5	1.0	0.1
100,000 to 249,999	100.0	78.7	5.7	8.7	1.5	3.9	0.3	1.1	0.1
50,000 to 99,999	100.0	84.0	4.8	5.5	0.7	4.1	0.2	0.7	0.0
25,000 to 49,999	100.0	87.5	5.1	4.2	0.5	1.8	0.1	0.8	0.0
10,000 to 24,999	100.0	87.8	4.8	3.5	0.3	2.8	0.3	0.5	0.0
2,500 to 9,999	100.0	87.2	6.1	3.5	0.5	2.1	0.1	0.5	0.1
Under 2,500	100.0	88.3	5.7	4.2	0.3	1.0	0.1	0.3	0.0

Source: "Estimated Percent Distribution of Characteristics of Sworn Employees in Local Police Agencies," *Sourcebook of Criminal Justice Statistics — 1988,* 1989, p. 79. Primary source: U.S. Department of Justice, Bureau of Justice Statistics, *Profile of State and Local Law Enforcement Agencies, 1987,* Bulletin NCJ-113949 (Washington, DC: U.S. Department of Justice, March 1989), p. 3, Table 7. *Notes:* Both full-time and part-time employees. Breakdown of blacks and whites does not include Hispanics. "Other" includes American Indians, Alaska Natives, Asians, and Pacific Islanders. 1. Percents may not add to 100 due to rounding.

★ 128 ★
Police Knowledge of Murders/Manslaughters

By race of victim, United States, 1964-87.

Year	Race of victim			Total[1]	Total number of murders and nonnegligent manslaughters
	White	Black	All others (including race unknown)		
1964	45	54	1	100	7,990
1965	45	54	1	100	8,773
1966	45	54	1	100	9,552
1967	45	54	1	100	11,114
1968	45	54	1	100	12,503

Continued.

Police Knowledge of Murders/Manslaughters
[Continued]

Year	Race of victim			Total[1]	Total number of murders and nonnegligent manslaughters
	White	Black	All others (including race unknown)		
1969	44	55	2	100	13,575
1970	44	55	1	100	13,649
1971	44	55	2	100	16,183
1972	45	53	2	100	15,832
1973	47	52	1	100	17,123
1974	48	50	2	100	18,632
1975	51	47	2	100	18,642
1976	51	47	2	100	16,605
1977	52	45	2	100	18,033
1978	54	44	2	100	18,714
1979	54	43	2	100	20,591
1980	53	42	4	100	21,860
1981	54	44	2	100	20,053
1982	55	42	2	100	19,485
1983	55	42	3	100	18,673
1984	56	41	3	100	16,689
1985	56	42	3	100	17,545
1986	53	44	3	100	19,257
1987	52	45	3	100	17,859

Source: "Percent Distribution of Murders and Nonnegligent Manslaughters Known to Police," *Sourcebook of Criminal Justice Statistics — 1988*, 1989, p. 452. Primary source: U.S. Department of Justice, Federal Bureau of Investigation, *Crime in the United States, 1964*, p. 104, Table 17; *1965*, p. 106, Table 17; *1966*, p. 107, Table 21; *1967*, p. 112, Table 21; *1968*, p. 108, Table 21; *1969*, p. 106, Table 22; *1970*, p. 118, Table 22; *1971*, p. 114, Table 21; *1972*, p. 12; *1978*, p. 9; *1979*, p. 10; *1980*, p. 11; *1981*, p. 10; *1982*, p. 8; *1983*, p. 8; *1984*, p. 8; *1985*, p. 9; *1986*, p. 9; (Washington DC: USGPO). Table constructed by SOURCEBOOK staff. Table presents yearly data based on number of agencies reporting, which may vary annually. *Note:* 1. Because of rounding, percents may not add to total.

★ 129 ★
Policepersons in Big Cities

1983 and 1988.

City	Total number of officers		Black Officers				Black representation			Affirmative action plan
	1983	1988	1983		1988		1983	1988	Percent change	
			Number	Percent	Number	Percent				
New York, NY	23,408	27,312	2,395	10.2	2,992	10.9	0.40	0.43	7.5	Yes
Chicago, IL	12,472	12,362	2,508	20.1	2,805	22.0	0.51	0.55	7.8	Yes
Los Angeles, CA	6,928	7,305	657	9.4	873	11.9	0.55	0.70	27.2	Yes
Philadelphia, PA	7,265	6,519	1,201	16.5	1,300	19.9	0.44	0.53	20.4	Yes
Houston, TX	3,629	4,323	355	9.7	595	13.7	0.35	0.50	42.8	Yes
Detroit, MI	4,032	4,944	1,238	30.7	2,806	56.7	0.49	0.90	83.6	Yes[1]
Dallas, TX	2,053	2,381	169	8.2	324	13.6	0.28	0.46	64.2	Yes[1]
San Diego, CA	1,363	1,704	76	5.5	114	6.6	0.62	0.74	19.3	[3]
Phoenix, AZ	1,660	1,888	48	2.8	69	3.6	0.58	0.75	29.3	[3]
Baltimore, MD	3,056	2,992	537	17.5	701	23.4	0.32	0.43	34.3	[3]
San Antonio, TX[2]	1,164	[3]	54	4.6	[3]	[3]	[3]	[3]	[3]	[3]

Continued.

Policepersons in Big Cities
[Continued]

City	Total number of officers		Black Officers				Black representation			Affirmative action plan
			1983		1988				Percent	
	1983	1988	Number	Percent	Number	Percent	1983	1988	change	
Indianapolis, IN	936	989	123	13.1	139	14.0	0.60	0.64	6.6	Yes
San Francisco, CA	1,957	1,846	159	8.1	158	8.5	0.64	0.67	4.6	Yes
Memphis, TN	1,216	1,264	268	22.0	371	29.3	0.46	0.62	34.7	Yes[1]
Washington, DC	3,851	3,855	1,931	50.1	1,596	41.4	0.71	0.59	-16.9	[3]
Milwaukee, WI	1,438	1,974	168	11.6	225	11.3	0.50	0.49	-2.0	Yes
San Jose, CA	915	1,009	20	2.1	35	3.4	0.46	0.74	60.8	Yes
Cleveland, OH	2,091	[3]	238	11.3	[3]	[3]	[3]	[3]	[3]	[3]
Columbus, OH	1,197	1,370	133	11.1	195	14.2	0.50	0.64	28.0	Yes
Boston, MA	1,871	1,943	248	13.2	336	17.2	0.59	0.77	30.5	Yes

Source: "Number of Police Officers and Number of Black Police Officers in the 50 Largest Cities," *Sourcebook of Criminal Justice Statistics — 1988*, 1989, p. 89. Primary source: Samuel Walker, "Employment of Black and Hispanic Police Officers," *Review of Applied Urban Research* XI (October 1983), p. 3; and Samuel Walker, "Employment of Black and Hispanic Police Officers, 1983- 1988: A follow-up Study," Center for Applied Urban Research (Omaha: University of Nebraska at Omaha, 1989). Table adapted by SOURCEBOOK staff. *Notes:* Data for 1983 were obtained through a questionnaire mailed to the office of the chief of police and the office of the municipal director of personnel (or equivalent position) in the 50 largest cities in the United States. The data for 1988 are the result of a 5- year follow-up to the 1983 study. For both surveys, 47 cities returned completed questionnaires. Cities are listed in rank order of size based on the 1980 Census of the population. The index of Black representation is calculated by dividing the percent of Black police officers in a department by the percent of Blacks in the local population. An index approaching 1.0 indicates that a city is closer to achieving a representation of Black police officers equal to their proportion in the local population. The Black population of a city is derived from the 1980 census of the population. A "yes" in the table indicates the presence of an affirmative action plan for Blacks operating at some point during 1983-88. 1. Voluntary plan. All others are court-ordered. 2. Data for 1983 are based on 1980-81 information from the Police Executive Research Forum, *Survey of Police Operational and Administration Practices 1981* (Washington, DC: Police Executive Research Forum, 1981). 3. Not available.

★ 130 ★
Prisoner Characteristics

Based on a sample survey of about 13,711 inmates in 1986 and 11,397 inmates in 1979; subject to sampling variability.

Characteristic	Number		Percent of Prisoner Inmates	
	1979	1986	1979	1986
Total	274,564	447,185	100.0	100.0
White	136,295	223,648	49.6	49.7
Black	131,329	221,021	47.8	46.9
Other races	6,939	15,412	2.6	3.4

Source: "State Prison Inmates — Selected Characteristics: 1979 and 1986," *Statistical Abstract*, 1989, p. 198. Primary source: U.S. Bureau of Justice Statistics, *Profile of State Prison Inmates, 1986*, January 1988.

★ 131 ★
Prisoner Characteristics

Excludes Federal and State prisons or other corectional institutions; institutions exclusively for juveniles; State-operated jails in Connecticut, Delaware, Hawaii, Rhode Island, and Vermont; and other facilities which retain persons for less than 48 hours. As of June 30. For the years 1982 and 1984-1986 data based on sample survey and subject to sampling variability; 1978 and 1983, based on the National Jail Census.

Characteristic	1978	1982	1983	1984	1985	1986
Total inmates[1]	158,394	209,582	223,552	234,500[1]	256,615[1]	274,444[1]
White	89,418	[3]	130,118	138,355	151,403	159,178
Black	65,104	[3]	87,508	93,800	102,646	112,522
Hispanic[2]	16,349	[3]	31,297	30,485	35,926	38,422

Source: "Jail Inmates, by Race and Detention Status: 1978 to 1986," *Statistical Abstract*, 1989, p. 183. Primary source: U.S. Bureau of Justice Statistics, *Profile of Jail Inmates, 1976*, and *Jail Inmates*, annual. *Notes:* 1. Includes juveniles not shown separately by sex. 2. Hispanic persons may be of any race. 3. Not available.

★ 132 ★
Prisoner Characteristics

Based on a sample survey of about 13,711 inmates. Violent/nonviolent refers to the current or past criminal offense for which the inmate is or was incarcerated; subject to sampling variability.

	Criminal History of Prison Inmates								
		First-timers			Recidivists[1]				
Characteristic	Total	Total	Non-violent	Violent	Total	Non-violent	Prior violent only	Current violent only	Current and prior violent
Prison inmates, total	447,185	82,791	23,808	58,983	364,393	129,465	49,827	98,946	86,155
Percent distribution:									
White	49.7	54.2	63.2	50.7	48.6	56.9	44.9	47.1	40.2
Black	46.9	42.0	33.3	45.6	48.0	40.5	51.6	48.9	56.2
Other races	3.4	3.6	3.5	3.7	3.4	2.6	3.5	4.0	3.6

Source: "State Prison Inmates, by Criminal History and Selected Characteristics of the Inmate: 1986," *Statistical Abstract*, 1989, p. 184. Primary source: U.S. Bureau of Justice Statistics, *Profiles of State Prison Inmates, 1986*, January 1988. *Notes:* 1. An individual who has been previously sentenced to probation or incarceration as a juvenile or adult.

★ 133 ★
Prisoners and Probationers in California

Conviction crime type and sample type	Weighted number of offenders	Defendant's race (Percent)		
		Black	Latino	White
Assault				
Prisoners	460	39	32	29
Probationers	684	27	32	41
Robbery				
Prisoners	1870	43	25	32
Probationers	753	36	32	33
Burglary				
Prisoners	1877	33	31	37

Continued.

Prisoners and Probationers in California
[Continued]

Conviction crime type and sample type	Weighted number of offenders	Defendant's race (Percent)		
		Black	Latino	White
Probationers	3644	26	32	41
Theft				
Prisoners	969	39	17	44
Probationers	3044	32	22	46
Forgery				
Prisoners	169	35	15	49
Probationers	369	31	15	55
Drugs				
Prisoners	419	23	58	20
Probationers	1079	23	33	44

Source: "Number of Prisoners and Probationers, and the Percentage in Each Racial Group by Crime Type," *Science*, 16 February, 1990, p. 813. Primary source: Klein, S., Petersilia, J., and Turner, S. "Race and Imprisonment Decisions in California," *Science*. *Notes:* The sum of the percentages within a row may not equal 100 because of rounding off.

★ 134 ★
Average Prison Term in California

Offenders	Prison term (months) for					
	Assault	Robbery	Burglary	Theft	Forgery	Drugs
All	48	58	32	26	27	36
Blacks	49	57	33	26	29	35
Latinos	47	58	31	26	26	37
Whites	48	59	33	26	26	35

Source: "Average Prison Term Imposed, by Race and Crime Type," *Science*, 16 February, 1990, p. 815. Primary source: Klein, S., Petersilia, J., and Turner, S. "Race and Imprisonment Decsions in California," *Science*.

★ 135 ★
Prisoners Arrested Again After 1983 Release

By number of prior adult arrests and selected characteristics.

	Number of released prisoners	Total all released prisoners	Percent of prisoners who were rearrested within 3 years whose number of adult arrests prior to release was:				
			One prior arrest	2 to 3 prior arrests	4 to 6 prior arrests	7 to 10 prior arrests	11 or more prior arrests
Race/ethnicity[1]							
White, non-Hispanic	46,205	56.1	31.1	46.3	54.8	63.0	73.2
Black, non-Hispanic	47,854	67.1	45.1	56.2	64.1	71.6	81.4
Hispanic	13,079	68.4	40.9	53.3	69.6	67.8	84.5

Source: "Estimated Rearrest Rates of State Prisoners Released in 11 States in 1983," *Sourcebook of Criminal Justice Statistics - 1988*, 1989, p. 660. Primary source: U.S. Department of Justice, Bureau of Justice Statistics, *Recidivism of Prisoners Released in 1983*, Special Report NCJ-116261 (Washington, DC: U.S. Department of Justice, April 1989), p. 8, Tables 13-15. Table adapted by SOURCEBOOK staff. Information collected only on felonies and serious misdemeanors that occurred within 3 years of release. *Notes:* 1. Too few cases of other racial or ethnic groups existed to provide reliable estimates.

★ 136 ★
Prisoners Released in 1983: Recidivism Rates

By selected characteristics(1).

Prisoner Characteristics	Percent of all released prisoners	Percent of released prisoners		
		Rearrested within 3 years	Reconvicted within 3 years[2]	Reincarcerated within 3 years[2]
All released prisoners[3]	100	62.9	46.8	41.4
Race				
White	54.1	58.7	44.2	38.0
Black	45.1	67.1	49.9	45.3
Other	0.8	58.7	50.6	45.3

Source: "Estimated Recidivism Rates of State Prisoners Released in 11 States," *Sourcebook of Criminal Justice Statistics — 1988,* 1989, p. 658. Primary source: U.S. Department of Justice, Bureau of Justice Statistics, *Recidivism of Prisoners Released in 1983,* Special Report NCJ-116261 (Washington, DC: U.S. Department of Justice, April 1989), p. 5, Table 7. *Notes:* These data are derived from a sample of 16,355 prison releases, representing 108,580 persons released from prison in 11 States during 1983. The sample was obtained from records submitted by States participating in the National Corrections Reporting Program (NCRP). Criminal history data for the sample of released prisoners were obtained from the criminal identification bureaus in the 11 participating States and from the Federal Bureau of Investigation. Information was collected only on felonies and serious misdemeanors occurring within 3 years of a prisoner's release. Demographic characteristics of prisoners were collected from the departments of correction in each State, as part of the NCRP conducted annually by the Bureau of Justice Statistics. (Source, p. 2.) The 11 States are California, Florida, Illinois, Michigan, Minnesota, New Jersey, New York, North Carolina, Ohio, Oregon, and Texas. These States accounted for more than 57 percent of all State prisoners released in the nation during 1983. (Source, p. 1.) 1. Subcategories may not add to totals because of the exclusion of missing data. 2. Because of the underreporting of court and custody data in Ohio, the percents reconvicted and reincarcerated exclude data from Ohio. 3. Data on sex were reported for 100 percent of releases, data on race for 99.6 percent, Hispanic origin for 99.9 percent, age at time of release 96.8 percent, and education for 46.6 percent.

★ 137 ★
Prisoners Sentenced to Die

By demographic characteristics, prior felony conviction history, and legal status, United States, on Dec. 31, 1987.

Characteristic	Number and Percent
Total number	1,984
Percent	
Race	
White	57.4
Black	41.4
Other[1]	1.3

Source: "Prisoners Under Sentence of Death," *Sourcebook of Criminal Justice Statistics - 1988,* 1989, p. 665. Primary source: U.S. Department of Justice, Bureau of Justice Statistics, *Capital Punishment 1987,* Bulletin NCJ-111939 (Washington, DC: U.S. Department of Justice, July 1988), p. 7, Table 5, p. 8. Table adapted by SOURCEBOOK staff. *Notes:* Thirty-seven States had death penalty statutes in effect on Dec. 31, 1987. At year end 1987, ethnicity data were not reported for 216 prisoners, education data were not reported for 210 prisoners, marital status was not reported for 99 prisoners, prior felony conviction history was not reported for 122 prisoners, and legal status was not reported for 290 prisoners. 1. Consists of 16 American Indians and 9 Asians present at the end of 1987.

★ 138 ★
Prisoners' Criminal Histories

By selected characteristics, United States, 1986 (estimated).

		First-timers		Recidivists[1]			
	Total	Nonviolent	Violent	Non-violent	Prior violent only	Current violent only	Current and prior violent
Number of prison inmates	447,185[2]	23,808	58,983	129,465	49,827	98,946	86,155
Percent of all inmates	100.0	5.3	13.2	29.0	11.1	22.1	19.3
Race							
White	49.7	63.2	50.7	56.9	44.9	47.1	40.2
Black	46.9	33.3	45.6	40.5	51.6	48.9	56.2
Other	3.4	3.5	3.7	2.6	3.5	4.0	3.6

Source: "Criminal Histories of State Prison Inmates," *Sourcebook of Criminal Justice Statistics - 1988,* 1989, p. 621. Primary source: U.S. Department of Justice, Bureau of Justice Statistics, *Profile of State Prison Inmates 1986,* Special Report NCJ-109926 (Washington, DC: U.S. Department of Justice, January 1988), p. 4, Table 5. *Notes:* Criminal history information was based on the self-reports of inmates. The median is the point above which and below which 50 percent of all the ages fall. 1. Defined as having previously been sentenced to probation or incarceration as a juvenile or adult. 2. This number differs from that in table 6.38 because criminal history information was not available for an estimated 3,231 inmates.

★ 139 ★
Prisoners' Educational Attainment

	Percent of prison inmates by educational level						
	No. of inmates	0-6 years	7-8	9-11	GED	H.S. graduate	Some college or more
All prisoners	448,694	6.7	14.2	40.8	43.0	27.5	6.6
Race							
White	222,823	7.7	15.7	33.6	4.4	30.6	8.0
Black	210,223	5.3	12.3	48.8	4.2	24.4	5.0
Other	15,312	8.9	16.3	37.1	5.7	24.5	7.5

Source: "Educational Attainment of State Prison Inmates, 1986," *Black Issues in Higher Education,* September 28, 1989, p. 7. Primary source: *Bureau of Justice Statistics,* date not specified.

★ 140 ★
Prisoners, Capital Punishment

Prisoners reported under sentence of death by civil authorities. The term "under sentence of death" begins when the court pronounces the first sentence of death for a capital offense. As a result of a major procedural change, beginning 1977, all data except executions are not strictly comparable to corresponding data for earlier years. See source for explanation.

Status	1975	1977	1978	1979	1980	1981	1982	1983	1984	1985	1986	1987
Under sentence of death, Jan 1	244	420	423	483	595	697	865	1,072	1,216	1,420	1,575	1,800
Received death sentence[1]	322	159	210	173	203	250	287	263	296	281	297	299
White	145	82	123	104	125	131	166	156	173	165	164	190
Black	174	75	85	67	77	115	117	105	119	114	123	106
Under sentence of death, Dec. 31 [1]	488	423	483	595	697	864	1,073	1,214	1,420	1,575	1,781	1,984
White	218	229	281	354	425	499	615	694	809	896	1,006	1,138
Black	262	192	198	238	268	357	446	508	595	664	750	821

Source: Movement of Prisoners under Sentence of Death: 1975 to 1987," *Statistical Abstract,* 1989, p. 187. Primary source: Through 1978, U.S. Law Enforcement Assistance Administration; thereafter, U.S. Bureau of Justice Statistics, *Capital Punishment,* annual. *Note:* 1. Includes races other than White and Black.

★ 141 ★
Prisoners, Capital Punishment

As of December 31. Excludes prisoners under sentence of death who remained within local correctional systems pending exhaustion of appellate process or who had not been committed to prison.

Race	1980	1984	1985	1986	1987
Total	714	1,405	1,575[1]	1,781	1,984
White	427	804	896	1,006	1,138
Black and other	287	601	679	775	846

Source: "Prisoners under Sentence of Death: 1980 to 1987," *Statistical Abstract*, 1989, p. 186. Primary source: U.S. Bureau of Justice Statistics, *Capital Punishment*, annual. *Notes:* 1. Revisions to the total number of prisoners were not carried to the characteristics except for race.

★ 142 ★
Prisoners, Capital Punishment

Excludes executions by military authorities. The Army (including the Air Force) carried out 160 (148 between 1942 and 1950, 3 each in 1954, 1955, and 1957, and 1 each in 1958, 1959, and 1961). Of the total, 106 were executed for murder (including 21 involving rape), 53 for rape, and 1 for desertion. The Navy carried out no executions during the period. See also *Historical Statistics, Colonial Times to 1970*, series H 1155 - 1167.

Year or Period	Total[1]	White	Black	Executed for Murder			Executed for Rape			Other Offenses[2]		
				Total[1]	White	Black	Total[1]	White	Black	Total[1]	White	Black
All years	3,909	1,784	2,083	3,384	1,697	1,647	455	48	405	70	39	31
1930-1939	1,667	827	816	1,514	803	687	125	10	115	28	14	14
1940-1949	1,284	490	781	1,064	458	595	200	19	179	20	13	7
1950-1959	717	336	376	601	316	280	102	13	89	14	7	7
1960-1964	181	90	91	145	79	66	28	6	22	8	5	3
1965-1967	10	8	2	10	8	2	3	3	3	3	3	3
1968-1976	3	3	3	3	3	3	3	3	3	3	3	3
1977-1980	3	3	3	3	3	3	3	3	3	3	3	3
1981	1	1	3	1	1	3	3	3	3	3	3	3
1982	2	1	1	2	1	1	3	3	3	3	3	3
1983	5	4	1	5	4	1	3	3	3	3	3	3
1984	21	13	8	21	13	8	3	3	3	3	3	3
1985	18	11	7	18	11	7	3	3	3	3	3	3
1986	18	11	7	18	11	7	3	3	3	3	3	3
1987	25	13	12	25	13	12	3	3	3	3	3	3

Source: "Prisoners Executed under Civil Authority: 1930 to 1987," *Statistical Abstract*, 1989, p. 187. Primary source: Through 1978, U.S. Law Enforcement Assistance Administration; thereafter, U.S. Bureau of Justice Statistics, *Correctional Projections in the United States*, annual. *Notes:* 1. Includes races other than White or Black. 2. Armed robbery, 20 kidnapping, 11 burglary, 8 espionage (6 in 1942 and 2 in 1953), and 6 aggravated assault. 3. Represents zero.

★ 143 ★
Prisoners: Sentence Length and Time Served

By type of conviction offense and race, 33 States, 1984.

Most serious offense	Percent of first releases with a prior felony incarceration		
	Total[1]	Race	
		White	Black
All offenses	25.6	21.9	31.0
Violent offenses	17.3	14.7	20.7
Murder	12.4	10.6	14.3
Manslaughter	12.9	9.7	17.6
Kidnapping	13.1	12.9	14.3
Rape	13.1	12.2	13.8
Other sexual assault	11.7	10.7	14.4
Robbery	18.7	16.7	20.7
Assault	20.6	16.7	26.2
Other violent	26.6	21.4	37.1
Property offenses	30.9	25.6	38.3
Burglary	27.3	22.9	34.2
Larceny/theft	37.3	31.0	44.4
Motor vehicle theft	25.8	20.0	33.3
Arson	19.9	19.9	19.7
Fraud	33.2	28.8	40.3
Stolen property	39.1	30.8	47.3
Other Property	22.2	19.4	25.2
Drug offenses	22.0	18.4	28.4
Possession	30.1	26.8	35.1
Trafficking	20.7	17.1	27.6
Other drug	14.9	12.6	19.1
Public-order offenses	38.1	36.4	41.3
Weapons	31.4	27.0	37.0
Other public-order	40.0	38.5	43.2
Other offenses	11.2	9.6	14.4
Number of releases	51,191	28,628	21,489

Source: "Average Sentence Length and Time Served in Jail or Prison for State Prison Releases," *Sourcebook of Criminal Justice Statistics-1988,* 1989, p. 642 Primary source: U.S. Department of Justice, Bureau of Justice Statistics, *Time Served in Prison and on Parole 1984,* Special Report NCJ-108544 (Washington, DC: U.S. Department of Justice, January 1988), p. 5, Table 7. Data include approximately three-fourths of total State prison releases during 1984. *Notes:* Data on prior felony incarceration were reported for 56 percent of the first releases in 1984 with sentences of more than a year. 1. "Total" category includes information on persons of "other races" as well as those whose race and sex was not known.

★ 144 ★
Rate of Motor Vehicle Thefts

Characteristic	Based on households			Based on vehicles owned		
	Number of households	Number of thefts	Rate per 1,000	Number of vehicles owned	Number of thefts	Rate per 1,000
Race of head of household						
All races	91,763,950	1,478,750	16.1	165,528,650	1,575,760	9.5
White	79,543,810	1,210,840	15.2	149,881,430	1,304,220	8.7
Black	10,229,530	219,120	21.4	12,393,100	222,750	18.0
Other	1,990,600	48,790	24.5	3,254,120	48,790	15.0

Source: "Victimization Rates on the Basis of Thefts per 1,000 Households and of Thefts per 1,000 Vehicles Owned, by Selected Household Characteristics," *Criminal Victimization in the United States - 1987*, June, 1989, p. 36. Primary source: *Criminal Victimization in the United States, 1987*. U.S. Department of Justice, Washington, DC, NCJ-115-524, June, 1989. *Notes:* The number of thefts based on vehicles owned is equal to or higher than the corresponding figure based on households because the former includes all completed or attempted vehicle thefts, regardless of the final classification of the event; personal crimes of contact and burglary occurring in conjunction with motor vehicle thefts take precedence in determining the final classification based on the number of households.

★ 145 ★
Recidivism Rates of Young Adults

By selected demographic characteristics, United States.

	Number paroled	Percent of parolees		
		Rearrested within 6 years	Reconvicted within 6 years	Reincarcerated within 6 years
All parolees	11,347	69	53	49
Race and ethnic origin				
White non-Hispanic	6,540	64	49	45
Black non-Hispanic	4,206	76	60	56
Hispanic	374	71	50	44
Other	143	75	65	63

Source: Recidivism Rates of Young Adults Paroled in 22 States in 1978," *Sourcebook of Criminal Justice Statistics — 1988*, 1989, p. 657. Primary source: U.S. Department of Justice, Bureau of Justice Statistics, *Recidivism of Young Parolees*, Special Report NCJ-104916 (Washington, DC: U..S. Department of Justice, May 1987), p. 3, Table 2. *Notes:* These findings are based on a sample of 3,995 parolees, representing 11,347 persons between the ages of 17 and 22, who were paroled from prisons in 22 States in 1978. These States accounted for 50 percent of all State prisoners paroled in the Nation during that year. (Source, p. 1.) The 22 States are: Alabama, Delaware, Florida, Georgia, Illinois, Kansas, Kentucky, Maine, Michigan, Nebraska, Nevada, New Hampshire, New Mexico, North Carolina, North Dakota, Ohio, Pennsylvania, South Dakota, Texas, Utah, Virginia, and Wyoming. Subcategories may not add to total because of exclusion of missing data.

★ 146 ★
Robbery/Theft Loss & Proportion Recovered

Race and type of crime	Total	None recovered[3]	Some recovered				All recovered	Not available
			Total	Less than half	Half or more	Proportion unknown[4]		
All races[1]								
All personal crimes (13,199,780)[2]	100.0	73.5	5.9	1.1	1.2	3.5	3.6	17.0
Robbery (678,150)	100.0	59.8	13.8	3.5	2.1[5]	8.2	6.2	20.3
Crimes of theft (12,509,770)	100.0	74.2	5.5	1.0	1.2	3.3	3.4	16.9
Personal larceny with contact (445,660)	100.0	67.3	12.6	2.9[5]	.8[5]	8.9	6.4	13.7
Personal larceny without contact (12,064,110)	100.0	74.5	5.2	.9	1.2	3.0	3.3	17.0
All household crimes (12,532,820)	100.0	70.3	7.9	1.2	1.7	5.1	5.5	16.2
Burglary (3,546,160)	100.0	62.6	6.4	1.5	1.4	3.5	4.0	27.0
Household larceny (8,017,840)	100.0	80.8	3.5	.8	.8	1.9	4.2	11.5
Motor vehicle theft (968,820)	100.0	12.0	50.1	3.0	10.1	37.0	22.1	15.6
White								
All personal crimes (11,359,400)[2]	100.0	72.9	6.0	1.2	1.2	3.5	3.7	17.5
Robbery (476,940)	100.0	55.4	15.2	4.6	2.6[5]	8.0	7.7	21.7
Crimes of theft (10,875,510)	100.0	73.6	5.6	1.1	1.2	3.3	3.5	17.3
Personal larceny with contact (336,180)	100.0	63.8	15.1	2.7[5]	1.0[5]	11.4	7.4	13.7
Personal larceny without contact (10,539,340)	100.0	73.9	5.3	1.0	1.2	3.1	3.4	17.4
All household crimes (10,430,310)	100.0	69.2	8.2	1.2	1.8	5.2	5.8	16.8
Burglary (2,877,450)	100.0	59.8	6.8	1.6	1.5	3.6	4.2	29.3
Household larceny (6,742,160)	100.0	80.1	3.8	.8	.9	2.2	4.5	11.5
Motor vehicle theft (810,690)	100.0	12.1	49.3	2.8	10.3	36.2	22.1	16.3
Black								
All personal crimes (1,521,790)[2]	100.0	77.1	6.3	.6[5]	1.5	4.2	2.7	14.0
Robbery (189,210)	100.0	69.6	11.0	.9[5]	.9[5]	9.2	2.8[5]	16.6
Crimes of theft (1,327,650)	100.0	78.4	5.5	.6[5]	1.6	3.3	2.5	13.6
Personal larceny with contact (86,130)	100.0	81.1	6.1[5]	4.2[5]	0[5]	1.9[5]	0[5]	12.8[5]
Personal larceny without contact (1,241,530)	100.0	78.2	5.4	.4[5]	1.7	3.4	2.7	13.7
All household crimes (1,842,980)	100.0	76.2	7.0	1.0	1.4	4.7	4.0	12.7
Burglary (578,730)	100.0	75.6	4.4	.6[5]	.9[5]	2.9	3.4	16.7
Household larceny (1,126,910)	100.0	84.5	2.1	.7[5]	.7[5]	.7[5]	2.4	11.1
Motor vehicle theft (137,350)	100.0	10.9[5]	59.0	4.8[5]	9.3[5]	44.9	20.2	9.9[5]

Source: "Percent Distribution of Victimizations Resulting in Theft Loss, by Race of Victims, Type of Crime, and Value of Loss," *Criminal Victimization in the United States - 1987*, June 1989, p. 76. Primary source: *Criminal Victimization in the United States, 1987*. U.S. Department of Justice, Washington, DC, NCJ-115-524, June 1989. *Notes:* Detail may not add to total shown because of rounding. Number of victimizations shown in parentheses. 1. Includes data on "other" races, not shown separately. 2. Includes data on rape, not shown separately, but excludes data on assault, which by definition does not involve theft. 3. Includes items that were taken that had no value. 4. Includes items that were recovered that had no value. 5. Estimate is absed on about 10 or fewer sample cases.

★ 147 ★
Same-Race Homicide Victims/Assailants

	Percentage
Race of victim	
White	85.0
Black	95.0
Other	62.0

Source: "Percentage of Homicide Victims Killed by Assailants of the Same Race, U.S. 1976-1989," *Black Issues in Higher Education*, December 7, 1989, p. 13. Primary source: "High Risk Racial and Ethnic Groups - Blacks, Hispanics, 1970-1983," *Centers for Disease Control*, 1986. *Notes:* Graph excludes 41,270 Homicides (26.3%) for which the race of either assailant or victim was unknown.

★ 148 ★
Sheriffs' Agency Employees

By size of population served, United States, 1987.

Population served	Total[1]	Percent of sworn employees who are:							
		White		Black		Hispanic		Other	
		Male	Female	Male	Female	Male	Female	Male	Female
All sizes	100.0	76.5	10.1	6.4	1.9	3.8	0.5	0.7	0.1
1,000,000 or more	100.0	70.9	9.5	6.6	2.4	8.0	1.0	1.5	0.1
500,000 to 999,999	100.0	74.0	8.7	7.9	2.4	4.8	1.2	0.9	0.1
250,000 to 499,999	100.0	75.8	7.3	6.5	2.4	3.9	0.5	0.6	0.0
100,000 to 249,999	100.0	77.2	9.9	7.3	2.2	2.6	0.3	0.5	0.1
50,000 to 99,999	100.0	80.5	9.7	5.7	1.1	2.3	0.3	0.2	0.1
25,000 to 49,999	100.0	80.4	10.8	6.4	1.7	0.4	0.0	0.3	0.0
10,000 to 24,999	100.0	77.8	10.7	5.3	1.0	3.7	0.4	1.2	0.0
Under 10,000	100.0	80.3	14.8	1.7	0.2	2.6	0.0	0.2	0.2

Source: "Estimated Percent Distribution of Characteristics of Sworn Employees in Sheriffs' Agencies," *Sourcebook of Criminal Justice Statistics — 1988,* 1989, p. 82. Primary source: U.S. Department of Justice, Bureau of Justice Statistics, *Profile of State and Local Law Enforcement Agencies, 1987,* Bulletin NCJ-113949 (Washington, DC: U.S. Department of Justice, March 1989), p. 6, Table 18. *Note:* 1. Percents may not add to 100 due to rounding.

★ 149 ★
Single-Offender Crimes: Victim and Offender Race

Type of crime and race of victim	Perceived race of offender				
	Total	White	Black	Other	Not known and not available
Crimes of violence	(4,093,360)	(2,785,140)	(1,047,830)	(201,500)	(58,890)
White	84.4	97.3	50.0	85.7	80.6
Black	15.6	2.7	50.0	14.3	19.4[1]
Completed	(1,419,260)	(948,650)	(390,440)	(61,940)	(18,230)
White	83.1	98.2	44.9	95.8	77.0[1]
Black	16.9	1.8	55.1	4.2[1]	23.0[1]
Attempted	(2,674,090)	(1,836,490)	(657,390)	(139,570)	(40,650)
White	85.1	96.9	53.1	81.2	82.2
Black	14.9	3.1	46.9	18.8	17.8[1]
Rape	(121,610)	(68,230)	(40,020)	(13,360)	(0)
White	66.9	93.5	29.2[1]	44.1[1]	0[1]
Black	33.1	6.5[1]	70.8	55.9[1]	0[1]
Robbery	(554,170)	(224,550)	(285,700)	(32,250)	(11,660)
White	71.6	94.3	52.6	85.3	60.1[1]
Black	28.4	5.7[1]	47.4	14.7[1]	39.9[1]
Completed	(343,590)	(134,370)	(186,370)	(16,160)	(6,690)
White	70.2	93.6	52.1	83.8[1]	71.6[1]
Black	29.8	6.4[1]	47.9	16.2[1]	28.4[1]
With Injury	(139,560)	(62,510)	(70,550)	(3,770)	(2,730)
White	73.5	94.2	52.7	100.0[1]	100.0[1]
Black	26.5	5.8[1]	47.3	0[1]	0[1]
Without Injury	(204,030)	(71,870)	(115,810)	(12,390)	(3,950)
White	68.0	93.1	51.8	78.9[1]	51.9[1]
Black	32.0	6.9[1]	48.2	21.1[1]	48.1[1]
Attempted	(210,580)	(90,180)	(99,340)	(16,090)	(4,970)
White	73.8	95.4	53.6	86.8[1]	44.7[1]

Continued.

Single-Offender Crimes: Victim and Offender Race
[Continued]

Type of crime and race of victim	Perceived race of offender				
	Total	White	Black	Other	Not known and not available
Black	26.2	4.6[1]	46.4	13.2[1]	55.3[1]
With Injury	(62,330)	(33,240)	(27,180)	(1,900)	(0)
White	62.2	87.6	28.6[1]	100.0[1]	0[1]
Black	37.8	12.4[1]	71.4	0[1]	0[1]
Without Injury	(148,250)	(56,940)	(72,140)	(14,180)	(4,970)
White	78.7	100.0	63.0	85.0[1]	44.7[1]
Black	21.3	0[1]	37.0	15.0[1]	55.3[1]
Assault	(3,417,590)	(2,492,360)	(722,110)	(155,890)	(47,220)
White	87.1	97.7	50.2	89.3	85.6
Black	12.9	2.3	49.8	10.7	14.4[1]
Aggravated	(1,065,650)	(705,680)	(282,950)	(62,610)	(14,410)
White	82.3	97.5	44.3	87.1	66.5[1]
Black	17.7	2.5	55.7	12.9[1]	33.5[1]
Simple	(2,351,940)	(1,786,680)	(439,150)	(93,280)	(32,810)
White	89.3	97.8	53.9	90.9	94.1
Black	10.7	2.2	46.1	9.1[1]	5.9[1]

Source: "Percent Distribution of Single-Offender Victimizations, based on Perceived Race of Offender, by Type of Crime and Race of Victims," *Criminal Victimization in the United States - 1987*, June 1989, p. 50. Primary source: *Criminal Victimization in the United States - 1987*. U.S. Department of Justice, Washington, DC, NCJ-115-524, June, 1989. *Notes:* Number of victimizations shown in parentheses. 1. Estimate is based on about 10 or fewer sample cases.

★ 150 ★
State Police Employees

United States, 1987.

	Percent of sworn employees[1]		
	Total	Male	Female
Total	100.0	95.8	4.2
White	88.7	85.1	3.6
Black	6.5	6.1	0.4
Hispanic	3.8	3.7	0.2
Other	0.9	0.8	[2]

Source: "Estimated Percent Distribution of Characteristics of Sworn Employees in State Police Agencies," *Sourcebook of Criminal Justice Statistics - 1988*, 1989, p. 83. Primary source: U.S. Department of Justice, Washington, DC, Bureau of Justice Statistics, *Profile of State and Local Law Enforcement Agencies, 1987*, Bulletin NCJ-113949 (Washington, DC: U.S. Department of Justice, Washington, DC, March 1989), p. 7, Table 27. *Notes:* 1. Percents may not add to 100 due to rounding. 2. Less than .05 percent.

★ 151 ★
Type of Crime and Arrests

By offense charged, age group, and race, United States, 1987. 10,545 agencies; 1987 estimated population 201,675,000.

	Total Arrests					Percent[1]				
Offense charged	Total	White	Black	American Indian or Alaskan Native	Asian or Pacific Islander	Total	White	Black	American Indian or Alaskan Native	Asian or Pacific Islander
Total	10,750,309	7,386,639	3,168,129	116,916	78,625	100.0	68.7	29.5	1.1	0.7
Violent crime [2]	471,690	241,510	223,337	3,827	3,016	100.0	51.2	47.3	0.8	0.6
Property crime [3]	1,790,289	1,174,887	579,633	17,834	17,935	100.0	65.6	32.4	1.0	1.0
Total Crime Index[4]	2,261,979	1,416,397	802,970	21,661	20,951	100.0	62.6	35.5	1.0	0.9

Source: "Arrest," Sourcebook of Criminal Justice Statistics — 1988, 1989 p. 494- 496. U.S. Department of Justice, Federal Bureau of Investigation, *Crime in the United States, 1987* (Washington, DC:USGPO, 1988), pp. 182-184. *Notes:* Estimates by the U.S. Bureau of the Census indicate that on July 1, 1987, whites comprised 84.6 percent, blacks 12.2 percent, and other racial categories 3.2 percent of the total U.S. resident population (U.S. Department of Commerce, Bureau of the Census, *United States Population Estimates by Age, Sex, and Race: 1980 to 1987, Population Estimates and Projections*, Series P-25, No. 1022 (Washington, DC: USGPO, 1988), p. 22). 1. Because of rounding, percents may not add to total. 2. Violent crimes are offenses of murder, forcible rape, robbery, and aggravated assault. 3. Property crimes are offenses of burglary, larceny-theft, motor vehicle theft, and arson. 4. Includes arson.

★ 152 ★
Types of Crime and Victimization Rates

By type of victimization and race of victim, United States, 1987(1).

Type of victimization	White N=169,915,280	Black N=22,725,690	Other N=5,128,510
Crimes of violence	27.3	39.6	24.6
Completed	9.8	16.3	10.5
Attempted	17.5	23.3	14.1
Rape	0.5	1.8	1.9[2]
Robbery	4.4	11.8	3.0[2]
Completed	2.8	8.3	2.3[2]
With Injury	1.3	2.4	0.8[2]
From serious assault	0.6	1.1	0.8[2]
From minor assault	0.7	1.3	0.0[2]
Without injury	1.5	6.0	1.5[2]
Attempted	1.6	3.4	0.6[2]
With injury	0.4	1.4	0.0[2]
From serious assault	0.2	0.4[2]	0.0[2]
From minor assault	0.2	1.0	0.0[2]
Without injury	1.2	2.0	0.6[2]
Assault	22.3	26.1	19.7
Aggravated	7.2	12.0	8.9
Completed with injury	2.3	3.5	3.1[2]
Attempted with weapon	4.9	8.6	5.8
Simple	15.1	14.0	10.9
Completed with injury	4.4	3.9	3.7
Attempted without weapon	10.7	10.1	7.2
Crimes of theft	68.2	62.9	62.4
Completed	64.0	58.4	59.8
Attempted	4.2	4.5	2.7[2]
Personal larceny with contact	2.3	4.3	4.6
Purse snatching	0.8	1.4	2.3[2]
Pocket picking	1.5	2.9	2.3[2]
Personal larceny without contact	66.0	58.6	57.9

Continued.

Types of Crime and Victimization Rates
[Continued]

Type of victimization	White N=169,915,280	Black N=22,725,690	Other N=5,128,510
Completed	62.0	54.6	55.2
Less than $50	27.6	22.1	25.9
$50 or more	31.8	27.4	27.2
Amount not available	2.7	5.2	2.1[2]
Attempted	3.9	4.0	2.7[2]

Source: "Estimated Rate (per 1,000 Population age 12 and Over) of Personal Victimization," *Sourcebook of Criminal Justice Statistics - 1988,* 1989, p. 298. Primary source: U.S. Department of Justice, Bureau of Justice Statistics, *Criminal Victimization in the United States, 1987,* National Crime Survey Report NCJ-115524 (Washington,DC: U.S. Department of Justice, 1989), Table 6. Data include 96% of all eligible housing units. Vital Statistics *Notes:* The racial category "other" includes minority groups such as Asians, Pacific Islanders, Native Americans, etc. 1. Subcategories may not sum to total because of rounding. 2. Estimate is based on about 10 or fewer sample cases.

★ 153 ★
Value of Robbery/Theft Losses

Race and type of crime	Total	No monetary value	Less than $10	$10-$49	$50-$99	$100-$249	$250-$999	$1,000 or more	Not known and not available
All races[1]									
Robbery (678,150)	100.0	0[3]	8.4	21.8	14.6	14.3	23.5	9.4	8.1
Crimes of theft (12,509,770)[2]	100.0	.3	11.7	32.1	15.8	18.8	13.2	3.3	4.8
White									
Robbery (476,940)	100.0	0[3]	9.3	22.8	14.5	13.8	20.9	9.1	9.5
Crimes of theft (10,875,510)[2]	100.0	.3	11.9	32.2	15.6	19.0	13.4	3.4	4.3
Black									
Robbery (189,210)	100.0	0[3]	6.8[3]	18.7	14.3	16.2	30.4	8.6	5.0[3]
Crimes of theft (1,327,650)[2]	100.0	.2[3]	10.4	30.2	17.4	17.0	12.8	3.0	9.1

Source: "Percent Distribution of Victimizations Resulting in Theft Loss, by Race of Victims, Type of Crime, and Value of Loss," *Criminal Victimization in the United States - 1987,* June 1989, p. 76. Primary source: *Criminal Victimization in the United States, 1987.* U.S. Department of Justice, Washington, DC, NCJ-115-524, June, 1989. *Notes:* Detail may not add to total shown because of rounding. Number of victimizations shown in parentheses. 1. Includes data on "other" races, not shown separately. 2. Includes both personal larceny with contact and personal larceny without contact. 3. Estimate is based on about 10 or fewer sample cases.

★ 154 ★
Vehicles Registered and Vehicles Stolen

By household characteristics, United States, 1973-85 (aggregate).

Characteristic	Motor vehicle theft victimization rate per:		Number of vehicles per household
	1,000 households	1,000 registered motor vehicles	
Total	18.6	11.3	1.7
Race of head of household			
White	17.7	10.3	1.7
Black	26.1	24.2	1.1
Other	19.0	12.6	1.5

Source: "Estimated Rate of Motor Vehicle Theft Victimization," *Sourcebook of Criminal Justice Statistics - 1988*, 1989, p. 307. Primary source: *Motor Vehicle Theft*. Bureau of Justice Statistics, U.S. Department of Justice, Washington, DC, NCJ-109978, March, 1988, p. 6. *Notes:* These data are based on all motor vehicle thefts reported in the National Crime Survey (NCS) conducted for the Bureau of Justice Statistics by the U.S. Bureau of the Census. Estimates presented here are higher than other NCS data because: (1) motor vehicle thefts occurring during other, more serious crimes, are included, and (2) series crimes — three or more incidents about which the victim is unable to provide separate detail — are counted as three incidents each. Approximately 7.7 percent of motor vehicle thefts reported in these tables involved a rape, robbery, or burglary and 3.6 percent constituted serious crimes. Motor vehicle thefts were weighted to represent both households and incidents, since for crimes defined as a household crimes, the household as a whole is considered the victim, with one household per theft.

★ 155 ★
Victim/Offender Race and Police Knowledge of Crime

By race of victim and offender, United States, 1987.

Characteristics of victim	Total victims/ offenders	Characteristics of offender						
		Race				Sex		
		White	Black	Other	Unknown	Male	Female	Unknown
Race								
White	5,268	4,605	571	52	40	4,659	569	40
Black	4,719	285	4,410	9	15	3,875	829	15
Other	195	52	25	115	3	168	24	3
Unknown	46	15	10	1	20	23	3	20

Source: "Murders and Nonnegligent Manslaughters Known to Police," *Sourcebook of Criminal Justice Statistics — 1988*, 1989, p. 453. Primary source: U.S. Department of Justice, Federal Bureau of Investigation, *Crime in the United States, 1987* (Washington, DC: USGPO, 1988), p. 9. *Notes:* These data pertain only to the 10,228 murders and nonnegligent manslaughters in which there was a single offender and a single victim.

★ 156 ★
Victimization by Strangers & Victims' Income

Race and annual family income	Crimes of violence	Completed violent crimes	Attempted violent crimes	Rape	Robbery			Assault		
					Total	With injury	Without injury	Total	Aggravated	Simple
All races[1]										
Less than $7,500	48.3	46.4	49.8	45.0	70.9	66.4	73.2	41.9	44.8	40.3
$7,500-$9,999	56.4	48.2	62.6	100.0[2]	74.3	69.5	78.6	51.7	58.9	47.7
$10,000-$14,999	56.1	50.4	59.4	100.0[2]	82.6	71.1	87.6	50.2	64.1	42.9
$15,000-$24,999	56.0	55.6	56.1	59.8[2]	87.2	86.2	87.9	50.3	55.9	47.4
$25,000-$29,999	63.6	59.7	65.9	38.4[2]	90.4	77.6	95.9	59.4	73.7	51.0
$30,000-$49,999	59.5	57.8	60.3	48.7[2]	80.5	77.4	82.3	55.2	71.9	48.3
$50,000 or more	65.1	58.9	67.7	61.6[2]	76.9	84.8[2]	74.6	63.3	73.1	58.9
White										
Less than $7,500	46.8	43.9	48.9	19.0[2]	69.9	65.7	73.0	42.8	43.6	42.4
$7,500-$9,999	60.8	55.4	64.3	100.0[2]	79.6	84.0	76.0	55.7	68.1	50.3
$10,000-$14,999	56.0	48.4	60.0	100.0[2]	75.1	51.4[2]	82.3	52.5	63.7	47.0
$15,000-$24,999	56.9	56.8	57.0	57.6[2]	91.9	88.6	94.2	51.4	55.9	49.2
$25,000-$29,999	63.2	58.0	66.6	65.3[2]	88.8	72.4[2]	95.3	58.7	72.5	50.4
$30,000-$49,999	58.4	56.6	59.4	36.2[2]	78.2	76.6	79.3	54.6	69.2	49.2
$50,000 or more	64.9	60.6	66.7	61.6[2]	77.9	100.0[2]	73.6	63.0	71.9	58.7
Black										
Less than $7,500	52.1	51.0	52.9	76.2	70.3	65.7	71.7	39.9	47.8	33.6
$7,500-$9,999	38.1	28.5[2]	49.6[2]	0[2]	41.5[2]	0[2]	100.0[2]	37.3	46.1[2]	26.4[2]
$10,000-$14,999	57.3	59.6	55.4	100.0[2]	96.2	91.0	100.0	41.2	63.8	21.9[2]
$15,000-$24,999	50.2	49.9	50.3	68.8[2]	64.0[2]	75.6[2]	55.1[2]	43.4	47.9	38.0[2]
$25,000-$29,999	73.1	84.4[2]	68.7	0[2]	100.0[2]	100.0[2]	100.0[2]	76.2	83.2[2]	71.5[2]
$30,000-$49,999	65.8	67.7	64.1	100.0[2]	100.0[2]	100.0[2]	100.0[2]	54.4	86.1	22.3[2]
$50,000 or more	74.0	58.2[2]	81.6[2]	0[2]	100.0[2]	100.0[2]	100.0[2]	68.0[2]	0[2]	68.0[2]

Source: "Percent of Victimizations Involving Strangers, by Race and Annual Family Income of Victims and Type of Crime," *Criminal Victimization in the United States - 1987*, June 1989, p. 46. Primary source: *Criminal Victimization in the United States - 1987*. U.S. Department of Justice, Washington, DC, NCJ-115-524, June, 1989. *Notes:* Excludes data on persons whose family income level was not ascertained. 1. Includes data on "other" races, not shown separately. 2. Estimate is based on about 10 or fewer sample cases.

★ 157 ★
Victims and Offenders in Multiple-Offender Crimes

By type of victimization, race of victim, and perceived races of offenders, United States, 1987(1).

Type of victimization and race of victim	Number of victimi-zations	Perceived races of multiple offenders					
		Total	All white	All black	All other	Mixed races	Not known and not available
Crimes of violence[2]							
White	1,494,190	100.0	56.9	23.9	6.1	10.4	2.8
Black	241,830	100.0	5.1[3]	82.6	0.9[3]	11.4	0.0[3]
Robbery							
White	337,870	100.0	35.7	43.7	66.5	11.6	2.4[3]
Black	101,890	100.0	2.8[3]	85.6	0.0[3]	11.6[3]	0.0[3]
Assault							
White	746,510	100.0	67.2	13.9	6.0	9.9	3.0
Black	139,940	100.0	6.8[3]	80.5	1.6[3]	11.2[3]	0.0[3]

Source: "Estimated Percent Distribution of Multiple-Offender Victimizations," *Sourcebook of Criminal Justice Statistics - 1988*, 1989, p. 312. U.S. Department of Justice, Bureau of Justice Statistics, *Criminal Victimization in the United States - 1987*, National Crime Survey Report NCJ-115524 (Washington, DC: U.S. Department of Justice, 1989), Table 50. *Notes:* 1. Subcategories may not sum to total because of rounding. 2. Includes data on rape, not shown separately. 3. Estimate is based on about 10 or fewer sample cases.

★ 158 ★
Victims of Juveniles' Violent Offenses

By type of current offense, United States, year end 1987(1). Percents are estimated.

Victim characteristics	Type of violent offense					
	All violent	Homicide[2]	Sexual assault[3]	Robbery	Assault	Other violent
Race						
White	61.6	57.3	62.2	68.3	54.6	69.1
Black	24.8	31.9	31.4	13.9	33.9	11.8
Other	9.7	9.4	5.1	13.0	8.1	8.3
Mixed[4]	3.9	1.4	1.3	4.7	3.4	10.8

Source: "Characteristics of Victims of Juveniles Held for Violent Offenses in Long-Term, State-Operated Juvenile Institutions," *Sourcebook of Criminal Justice Statistics — 1988*, 1989, p. 323. Primary source: U.S. Department of Justice, Bureau of Justice Statistics, *Survey of Youth in Custody, 1987*, Special Report NCJ-113365 (Washington, DC: U.S. Department of Justice, September 1988), p. 2. *Notes:* This information was obtained from a survey of juveniles and young adults in custody conducted by the U.S. Bureau of the Census for the Bureau of Justice Statistics. This survey was based on personal interviews with a nationally representative sample of 2,621 juveniles and young adults. Interviews were conducted in 50 institutions in 26 States, representing 1 in 4 long-term, State-operated institutions. Data presented are estimates of characteristics of the 18,226 juveniles and 6,798 young adults represented by the sample. Participation in the survey was voluntary and the response rate was 89 percent. The sample design was a stratified sample based on the size of the correctional facility. Facilities that were long-term and State-operated with institutional environments were included in the sampling frame. The majority of these institutions described themselves as training schools. Excluded from the survey were institutions that were locally operated, State facilities not designed for secure custody and all short-term or privately-operated facilities and institutions. Primarily as a result of the inclusion of California's Youth Authority facilities, more than a quarter of the sample was made up of young adults who are age 18 and older (up to 25 years of age). This older population is referred to as young adults, while those less than the age of 18 will be referred to as juveniles. All residents regardless of age are referred to as youth. (Source, pp. 1, 9.) 1. Percents may not add to 100 due to rounding. 2. Includes murder and all forms of manslaughter. 3. Includes rape and other sexual assaults. 4. For cases with multiple victims.

★ 159 ★
Victims of State Prisoners' Violent Offenses

By current offense and victim characteristics, United States, 1986 (estimated).

Victim characteristics	Current offense								
	Total[1]	Murder[2]	Negligent man-slaughter	Kid-napping	Rape	Other sexual assault	Robbery	Assault	Other violent
Race									
White	64.6	62.9	48.0	74.3	69.4	77.5	66.7	55.6	70.8
Black	27.5	32.7	47.4	18.5	26.0	17.5	20.7	37.2	26.8
Other	3.3	2.9	3.3	2.4	3.0	4.1	3.7	2.6	2.0
Mixed[3]	4.7	1.4	1.3	4.8	1.7	0.9	8.8	4.6	0.3

Source: "Characteristics of Victims of State Prison Inmates Incarcerated for Violent Crimes," *Sourcebook of Criminal Justice Statistics - 1988*, 1989, p. 322. Primary source: U.S. Department of Justice, Bureau of Justice Statistics, *Profile of State Prison Inmates 1986*, Special Report NCJ-109926 (Washington, DC: Department of Justice, January 1988), p. 7. *Notes:* These data were collected by the U.S. Bureau of the Census for the Bureau of Justice Statistics through the Survey of Inmates of State Correctional Facilities. This survey employs a stratified probability sampling design with the probabilities proportional to the size of correctional facility. In 1986, 13,711 interviews were conducted at 275 prisons from a sample of approximately 15,000 inmates. The estimated prison population for 1986 was 450,416. 1. Percents may not add to 100 due to rounding. 2. Includes nonnegligent manslaughter. 3. Cases involving multiple victims.

★ 160 ★
Who Populates the State Prisons?

United States, 1979 and 1986 (estimated).

	Percent of prison inmates	
	1979	1986
Race		
White	49.6	49.7
Black	47.8	46.9
Other	2.6	3.4

Source: "Characteristics of State Prison Inmates," *Sourcebook of Criminal Justice Statistics - 1988*, 1989, p. 620. Primary source: U.S. Department of Justice, Bureau of Justice Statistics, *Profile of State Prison Inmates 1986*, Special Report NCJ-109926 (Washington, DC: U.S. Department of Justice, January 1988), p. 3, Tables 1 and 2. Table adapted by SOURCEBOOK staff. *Notes:* These data were collected by the U.S. Bureau of the Census for the Bureau of Justice Statistics through the Survey of Inmates of State Correctional Facilities. This survey, conducted in 1979 and 1986, employs a stratified probability sampling design with the probabilities proportional to the size of the correctional facility. In 1979, 11,397 interviews were conducted at 215 prisons with a selected sample of about 12,000 inmates. In 1986, 13,7121 interviews were conducted at 275 prisons from a sample of approximately 15,000 inmates. In 1979, the State prison population was an estimated 274,563. In 1986, the estimated prison population was 450,416. For each characteristic other than ethnicity and income, data were available for at least 99 percent of the inmates. Ethnicity data were available for 95 percent of the inmates in both 1979 and 1986. Income data were available for 50 percent of the inmates in 1979 and 89 percent of the inmates in 1986.

★ 161 ★
Work-Time Lost due to Criminal Victimization

Race and type of crime	Total	Less than 1 day	1-5 days	6-10 days	11 days or more	Not known and not available
White						
All personal crimes (895,980)	100.0	39.5	42.3	4.0	9.0	5.2
Crimes of violence (442,850)	100.0	20.0	50.0	6.3	14.9	8.8
Crimes of theft (453,130)	100.0	58.5	34.9	1.7[1]	3.3[1]	1.7[1]
All household crimes (719,850)	100.0	45.1	45.4	1.8[1]	1.4[1]	4.3
Burglary (278,560)	100.0	44.9	45.7	1.2[1]	2.3[1]	4.0[1]
Household larceny (208,520)	100.0	57.3	33.0	0[1]	1.9[1]	5.1[1]
Motor vehicle theft (232,770)	100.0	34.3	56.0	4.0[1]	0[1]	3.9[1]
Black						
All personal crimes (140,610)	100.0	28.5	47.8	1.5[1]	18.6	3.7[1]
Crimes of violence (84,850)	100.0	12.9[1]	47.7	2.5[1]	30.7	6.1[1]
Crimes of theft (55,760)	100.0	52.1	47.9	0[1]	0[1]	0[1]
All household crimes (117,260)	100.0	38.9	47.4	2.8[1]	7.1[1]	3.8[1]
Burglary (52,080)	100.0	24.5[1]	60.0	0[1]	10.1[1]	5.4[1]

Continued.

Work-Time Lost due to Criminal Victimization
[Continued]

Race and type of crime	Total	Less than 1 day	1-5 days	6-10 days	11 days or more	Not known and not available
Household larceny (26,060)	100.0	63.0	37.0[1]	0[1]	0[1]	0[1]
Motor vehicle theft (39,110)	100.0	42.0	37.7[1]	8.5[1]	7.7[1]	4.1[1]

Source: "Percent Distribution of Victimizations Resulting in Loss of Time from Work, by Race of Victims, Type of Crime and Number of Days Lost," *Criminal Victimization in the United States - 1987*, June 1989, p. 79. Primary source: *Criminal Victimization in the United States, 1987*. U.S. Department of Justice, Washington, DC, NCJ-115-524, June, 1989. *Notes:* Detail may not add to total shown because of rounding. Number of victimizations shown in parentheses. 1. Estimate is based on about 10 or fewer sample cases.

★ 162 ★
Young People in Long-Term Institutions

By demographic characteristics, United States, year end 1987(1).

Characteristics	Estimated percent of youth			
	Total	11 to 14 years old	15 to 17 years old	18 years and older
Estimated number of youth	25,024	3,096	15,130	6,798
Race				
White	53.1	46.4	53.8	54.6
Black	41.1	46.7	40.3	40.5
Other[2]	5.7	6.9	5.9	4.8

Source: "Youth in Long-Term, State-Operated Juvenile Institutions," *Sourcebook of Criminal Justice Statistics — 1988*, 1989, p. 598. Primary source: U.S. Department of Justice, Bureau of Justice Statistics, *Survey of Youth in Custody, 1987*, Special Report NCJ-113365 (Washington, DC: U.S. Department of Justice, September 1988), p. 2. *Notes:* This information was obtained from a survey of juveniles and young adults in custody conducted by the U.S. Bureau of the Census for the Bureau of Justice Statistics. This survey was based on personal interviews with a nationally representative sample of 2,621 juveniles and young adults. Interviews were conducted in 50 institutions in 26 States, representing 1 in 4 long-term, State-operated institutions. Data presented are estimates of characteristics of the 18,226 juveniles and 6,798 young adults represented by the sample. Participation in the survey was voluntary and the response rate was 89 percent. The sample design was a stratified sample based on the size of the correctional facility. Facilities that were long-term and State-operated with institutional environments were included in the sampling frame. The majority of these institutions described themselves as training schools. Excluded from the survey were institutions that were locally operated, State facilities not designed for secure custody and all short-term or privately-operated facilities and institutions. Primarily as a result of the inclusion of California's Youth Authority facilities, more than a quarter of the sample was made up of young adults who are age 18 and older (up to 25 years of age). This older population is referred to as young adults, while those less than the age of 18 will be referred to as juveniles. All residents regardless of age are referred to as youth. (Source, pp. 1, 9.) 1. Percents may not add to 100 due to rounding. 2. Includes American Indians, Alaskan natives, Asians, and Pacific Islanders.

EDUCATION

★ 163 ★
1980 High School Grad in 4-year Colleges

Race/ethnicity	Fall 1980 Full-time	Fall 1980 Part-time	Fall 1981 Full-time	Fall 1981 Part-time	Fall 1982 Full-time	Fall 1982 Part-time	Fall 1983 Full-time	Fall 1983 Part-time	Fall 1984 Full-time	Fall 1984 Part-time	Fall 1985 Full-time	Fall 1985 Part-time
Total	30.3	1.5	28.9	1.6	26.3	3.4	27.9	2.7	13.8	4.3	7.9	4.2
Race/ethnicity												
White, non-Hispanic	31.8	1.5	30.6	1.6	28.0	3.5	29.8	2.7	14.7	4.4	8.3	4.2
Black, non-Hispanic	28.2	1.1	26.1	1.3	21.2	3.2	21.3	2.1	9.1	3.0	5.6	3.2
Hispanic	16.7	1.3	14.2	1.5	13.9	2.0	15.5	2.8	9.1	4.7	6.2	4.3
American Indian	14.5	1.3	14.4	1.8	13.2	2.7	15.7	2.3	9.8	1.0	6.6	1.0
Asian	44.6	4.0	43.1	4.0	42.6	6.6	46.4	4.7	34.0	8.5	18.3	8.3

Source: "Percent of the High School Class of 1980 Enrolled in 4- Year Colleges, by Attendance Status, Sex, Race/Ethnicity, Socioeconomic Status, and Ability Level: Fall 1980 to Fall 1985," *Digest of Educational Statistics,* 1989, p. 275. Primary source: U.S. Department of Education, National Center for Education Statistics, High School and Beyond survey. (This table was prepared October 1988.).

★ 164 ★
1980 High School Seniors: Educational Attainment

Race/ethnicity and October 1980 post-secondary education attendance status	Highest educational attainment of 1980 high school seniors in 1986						
	Total	No high school diploma[1]	High school diploma	License[2]	Associate degree	Bachelor's degree	Graduate/professional degree
All students							
Part-time 2-year public college	100.0	0.7	66.4	17.7	8.8	6.5	[3]
Part-time 4-year public college	100.0	2.7	57.1	15.4	1.6	22.6	0.6
Full-time 2-year public college	100.0	[3]	49.5	11.7	20.7	17.6	0.5
Full-time 4-year public college	100.0	[3]	41.7	7.6	4.5	44.9	1.3
Full-time 4-year private college	100.0	[3]	31.1	8.8	5.1	51.9	3.0
Not a student	100.0	1.8	78.2	12.8	3.6	3.5	0.2
White							
Part-time 2-year public college	100.0	0.8	67.7	17.9	6.9	6.7	[3]
Part-time 4-year public college	100.0	3.4	54.8	14.5	0.3	27.0	[3]
Full-time 2-year public college	100.0	[3]	48.6	10.8	20.7	19.3	0.7
Full-time 4-year public college	100.0	[3]	39.0	6.8	4.8	48.0	1.5
Full-time 4-year private college	100.0	[3]	28.1	7.9	5.1	55.7	3.3
Not a student	100.0	1.6	78.5	12.7	3.5	3.5	0.2
Black							
Part-time 2-year public college	100.0	[3]	65.8	22.1	9.8	2.3	[3]

Continued.

1980 High School Seniors: Educational Attainment
[Continued]

Race/ethnicity and October 1980 post-secondary education attendance status	Highest educational attainment of 1980 high school seniors in 1986						
	Total	No high school diploma[1]	High school diploma	License[2]	Asso-ciate degree	Bache-lor's degree	Graduate/ profes-sional degree
Part-time 4-year public college	100.0	[3]	58.5	25.1	6.0	8.5	1.8
Full-time 2-year public college	100.0	[3]	52.8	19.2	18.9	9.1	[3]
Full-time 4-year public college	100.0	[3]	59.4	11.2	3.4	25.6	0.5
Full-time 4-year private college	100.0	[3]	50.5	15.0	5.5	28.5	0.6
Not a student	100.0	2.2	78.1	13.3	3.6	2.8	[3]
Hispanic							
Part-time 2-year public college	100.0	[3]	57.4	14.9	23.4	4.4	[3]
Part-time 4-year public college	[4]	[4]	[4]	[4]	[4]	[4]	[4]
Full-time 2-year public college	100.0	[3]	53.9	14.9	22.7	8.5	[3]
Full-time 4-year public college	100.0	[3]	51.1	18.4	4.1	25.6	0.9
Full-time 4-year private college	100.0	[3]	46.8	19.4	6.1	26.8	1.0
Not a student	100.0	3.1	83.2	10.3	2.4	0.9	[3]

Source: "Highest Level of Education Attained by 1980 High School Seniors, by Race/Ethnicity and October 1980 Postsecondary Attendance Status: Spring 1986," *Digest of Educational Statistics*, 1989, p. 278. Primary source: U.S. Department of Education, National Center for Educational Statistics, High School and Beyond survey. (This table was prepared September 1987.) *Notes:* Because of rounding, percents may not add to 100.0 1. Seniors who dropped out of high school after spring 1980 survey and had not completed high school by 1986. 2. Includes persons who earned a certificate for completing a program of study. 3. Less than .05 percent. 4. Fewer than 30 cases available for analysis. Estimates are suppressed because they are unreliable.

★ 165 ★
1986 Doctorate Degrees

Fields	All Ethnic Groups	White	Black	Black As a % Total
Engineering	1,379	1,224	14	1.0
Physical Sciences	3,003	2,714	25	.8
Life Sciences	4,342	3,958	64	1.5
Social Sciences	4,548	4,080	163	3.6
Humanities	2,728	2,496	70	2.7
Professional & Other	1,289	1,246	63	4.5
Education	5,595	4,820	421	7.5

Source: "Doctorates Earned by Blacks and Whites in 1986," *Black Faculty in Traditionally White Institutions in Selected Adams States*, 1988, p. 35. Summary Report 1986: Doctorate Recipients from United States Universities. National Academy Press, Washington, D.C., 1987.

★ 166 ★
1989 Doctorate Recipients and 10-Year Change

Race	1989	10-Year change (%)
White	20,668	-5.6
Black	811	-23.2
Hispanic	569	+23.2
Asian	624	+45.8
American Indian	93	+14.8
Race unknown	387	---
All U.S. citizens	23,172	-9.0

Source: "Doctorate Recipients: U.S. Citizens by Ethnic Group," *The Chronicle of Higher Education*, April 25, 1990, p. A-1. Primary source: National Research Council.

★ 167 ★
Academic Competition on College Campuses

Numbers in percent.

Level of Academic Competition on Campus	Total Population	Campus Race	
		Black	White
None	2.4	8.9	.9
Very Little	9.7	27.1	6.1
Some	41.6	51.0	31.9
Considerable Amount	46.3	13.0	61.1
Total	100.0	100.0	100.0
N	(1574)	(853)	(689)

Source: "Academic Competition by Student Gender and Campus Race," *Gender and Campus Race Differences in Black Student Academic Performance, Racial Attitudes and College Satisfaction*, 1986, p. 51. Primary source: National Study of Black College Students, 1981 and 1983, University of Michigan, Ann Arbor. *Notes:* Total N does not seem to be correct in Table, but no other information provides a clue as to nature of error. Published by permission.

★ 168 ★
Academic, Vocational, and Continuing Education

Numbers in thousands.

	Type of postsecondary education					
	Academic[1]		Vocational[2]		Continuing[3]	
Race	Number	Percent	Number	Percent	Number	Percent
Total	9,243	100.0	3,787	100.0	5,177	100.0
White	7,933	85.8	3,199	84.5	4,731	91.4
Black	918	9.9	449	11.9	255	4.9
Other races	392	4.2	138	3.6	190	3.7

Source: "Participants in Postsecondary Academic, Vocational, and Continuing Education, by Sex, Race, Age Group, and Labor Force Status: October 1982," *Digest of Educational Statistics*, 1989, p. 318. Primary source: U.S. Department of Education, National Center for Education Statistics, *Participants in Postsecondary Education: October 1982*. (This table was prepared May 1986.) *Notes:* Data based on a sample survey of the civilian noninstitutional population. Because of rounding, details may not add up to totals. 1. Academic students pursued coursework, either full-or part-time, for the purpose of obtaining an undergraduate, graduate, or postsecondary degree. 2. Vocational students took coursework, either full-or part-time, in an occupational or technical field for the purpose of obtaining a vocational credential, such as a vocational certificate, occupational license, or other vocational degree or diploma. 3. Continuing education students were postsecondary education participants not otherwise classified as academic or vocational students who were taking college credit courses but not seeking a degree or who were taking noncredit courses for job improvement, personal developement, or social/recreational purposes (excluding adult basic education courses to improve basic skills in reading, writing, or arithmetic).

★ 169 ★
Acceptances and Yields in 4-Year Institutions, 1985.

Institutional Type and Group	Number of Institutions	Average Number of Applications	Average Number of Acceptances	Acceptance Rate	Number of Institutions	Average Number of Acceptances	Average Number of Freshmen	Yield Rate
Four-Year Public								
Total	328	3,958	2,844	72	331	2,847	1,567	55
American Indians	151	23	18	76	148	16	10	64
Asians	157	218	144	66	159	135	68	51
Blacks	181	396	257	65	184	254	149	59
Hispanics	163	178	123	69	165	119	73	61
Whites	183	3,413	2,462	72	186	2,443	1,348	55
Others	107	287	175	61	105	163	57	35
Four-Year Private								
Total	688	1,042	864	62	692	859	388	45
American Indians	174	8	5	63	165	3	2	66
Asians	286	88	43	48	289	36	16	45
Blacks	354	98	60	61	357	57	28	49
Hispanics	273	54	32	59	279	26	13	48
Whites	381	1,243	752	60	387	738	335	45
Others	122	102	47	46	117	32	14	45

Source: "Acceptance and Yield Rates in Four-Year Institutions," *Demographics, Standards, and Equity*, 1986, p. 40. Primary source: *Demographics, Standards, and Equity: Challenges in College Admissions*. American Association of Collegiate Registars & Admission Officers, American College Testing Program, College Board, Educational Testing Service, National Association of College Admission Counselors, November 1986. *Notes:* 1. Number reporting both applications and acceptances. 2. Number reporting both acceptances and enrolled freshmen.

★ 170 ★
Acceptances in 4-Year Institutions: Trends

	Four-Year Public		Four-Year Private	
	N	%	N	%
Total				
Less	133	36	253	34
Same	73	20	172	23
More	165	44	318	43
	371	100	743	100
Blacks				
Less	85	27	135	22
Same	101	32	262	44
More	128	41	304	34
	314	100	701	100
Hispanics				
Less	40	14	69	12
Same	143	48	338	60
More	112	38	160	28
	295	100	567	100
Asians				
Less	32	11	53	9
Same	140	48	309	55
More	118	41	201	36
	290	100	563	100
American Indians				
Less	48	174	61	11
Same	177	62	422	77
More	61	21	63	12
	286	100	546	100
Whites				
Less	95	30	159	26
Same	68	22	177	29
More	149	48	266	44

Source: "Self-Reported Trends in Acceptances by Four-Year Institutions, 1980- 1985," *Demographics, Standards, and Equity*, 1986, p. 45. Primary source: *Demographics, Standards, and Equity: Challenges in College Admissions*. American Association of Collegiate Registars & Admission Officers, American College Testing Program, College Board, Educational Testing Service, National Association of College Admission Counselors, November 1986.

★ 171 ★
Achievement in Mathematics: Trends

Ethnicity	1973	1978	1982	1986
9-year-olds				
Total	219.1	218.6	219.0	221.7
White	224.9	224.1	224.0	226.9
Black	190.0	192.4	194.9	201.6
Hispanic	202.1	202.9	204.0	205.4
13-year-olds				
Total	266.0	264.1	268.6	269.0
White	273.7	271.6	274.4	273.6
Black	227.7	229.6	240.4	249.2
Hispanic	238.8	238.0	252.4	254.3
17-year-olds				
Total	304.4	300.4	298.5	302.0
White	310.1	305.9	303.7	307.5
Black	269.8	268.4	271.8	278.6
Hispanic	277.2	276.3	276.7	283.1

Source: "Achievement Scores in Mathematics, by Age, Gender, and Ethnicity: 1973- 86," *Science and Engineering Indicators - 1989*, 1989, p. 190. Primary source: National Assessment of Educational Progress, *The Mathematics Report Card: Are We Measuring Up?*, Report No. 17- M-01 (Princeton: Educational Testing Service, 1988).

★ 172 ★
Achievement in Science: Trends

Ethnicity	1970	1973	1977	1982	1986
9-year-olds					
Total	224.9	220.3	219.9	220.9	224.3
White	235.9	231.1	229.6	229.1	231.9
Black	178.7	176.5	174.9	187.1	196.2
Hispanic	[1]	[1]	191.9	189.0	199.4
13-year-olds					
Total	254.9	249.5	247.4	250.2	251.4
White	263.4	258.6	256.1	257.3	259.2
Black	214.9	205.3	208.1	217.2	221.6
Hispanic	[1]	[1]	213.4	225.5	226.1
17-year-olds					
Total	804.8	295.8	289.6	283.3	288.5
White	311.8	303.9	297.7	293.2	297.5

Continued.

Achievement in Science: Trends
[Continued]

Ethnicity	1970	1973	1977	1982	1986
Black	257.8	250.4	240.3	234.8	252.8
Hispanic	[1]	[1]	262.3	248.7	259.3

Source: "Achievement Scores in Science, by Age, Gender, and Ethnicity: 1970-86," *Science and Engineering Indicators - 1989*, 1989, p. 186. Primary source: National Assessment of Educational Progress, *The Science Report Card: Elements of Risk and Recovery*, Report No. 17- S-01 (Princeton: Educational Testing Service, 1988). *Note:* 1. Not available.

★ 173 ★
Achievement: 8th Grade Students

Achievement test and score quartile	Distribution of eighth graders' achievement by score quartile[1]				
	White	Black	Hispanic	Asian	American Indian
History	100.0	100.0	100.0	100.0	100.0
Lower quartile	19.6	41.9	40.4	21.7	43.1
Lower middle quartile	23.0	31.9	26.2	19.9	31.0
Upper middle quartile	28.2	17.4	20.1	26.4	18.4
Upper quartile	29.2	8.8	13.3	32.1	7.4
Mathematics	100.0	100.0	100.0	100.0	100.0
Lower quartile	18.3	49.0	39.2	18.8	46.3
Lower middle quartile	24.1	28.7	30.1	19.7	29.1
Upper middle quartile	27.0	15.1	19.9	22.3	16.3
Upper quartile	30.6	7.2	10.8	39.2	8.3
Reading	100.0	100.0	100.0	100.0	100.0
Lower quartile	19.9	45.0	38.2	23.5	44.9
Lower middle quartile	23.5	29.4	30.5	22.6	30.0
Upper middle quartile	26.2	16.6	20.1	24.6	18.5
Upper quartile	30.4	9.0	11.2	29.3	6.6
Science	100.0	100.0	100.0	100.0	100.0
Lower quartile	19.2	47.7	37.8	22.0	46.9
Lower middle quartile	22.4	30.1	30.7	23.0	27.4
Upper middle quartile	28.8	15.9	20.6	24.6	17.4
Upper quartile	29.6	6.3	10.9	30.3	8.3

Source: "Eighth Graders' Achievement on American History, Mathematics, Reading, and Science Tests: 1988," *Digest of Educational Statistics*, 1989, p. 118. Primary source: U.S. Department of Education, National Center for Educational Statistics, "National Education Longitudinal Study of 1988" survey. (This table was prepared June 1989). *Notes:* Because of rounding, details may not add to totals. Data are preliminary. 1. Twenty-five percent of all students fall into each one of the quartile groups.

★ 174 ★
ACT Scores: Trends

Reference Group	Year	# Students	English	Math	Social Sciences	Natural Sciences	Composite
Afro-American/Black							
National	1985	58,988	13.5	10.1	11.4	15.1	12.6
National	1986	58,793	14.0	10.4	11.7	15.5	13.0
National	1987	61,763	14.4	11.0	12.1	15.7	13.4
National	1988	69.509	14.5	11.3	12.2	15.9	13.6
National	1989	74,227	14.4	11.6	12.0	15.7	13.6
American Indian/Alaskan Native							
National	1985	6,858	13.9	11.8	12.7	17.3	14.1
National	1986	6,712	14.4	12.1	13.0	17.7	14.4
National	1987	7,358	14.6	12.5	13.2	17.8	14.6
National	1988	8,096	14.7	12.8	13.3	18.1	14.9
National	1989	9,115	14.6	12.8	13.0	17.9	14.7
Caucasian							
National	1985	593,785	18.9	18.1	18.3	22.1	19.5
National	1986	579,989	19.2	18.2	18.6	22.2	19.7
National	1987	610,759	19.1	18.0	18.3	22.2	19.6
National	1988	650,999	19.2	18.0	18.3	22.3	19.6
National	1989	661,010	19.2	17.9	18.1	22.1	19.4
Mexican American/Chicano							
National	1985	11,081	15.0	12.8	13.3	17.3	14.7
National	1986	16,023	15.6	13.2	13.7	17.8	15.2
National	1987	17,448	15.6	13.7	13.9	17.9	15.4
National	1988	19,717	15.9	14.0	14.1	18.2	15.7
National	1989	22,685	15.6	14.1	13.7	17.8	15.4
Asian American/Pacific Islander							
National	1985	11,081	17.4	20.6	17.0	21.5	19.2
National	1986	11,968	18.0	20.8	17.4	21.9	19.6
National	1987	13,885	18.2	20.9	17.7	22.0	19.8
National	1988	15,854	18.4	21.0	17.7	22.1	19.9
National	1989	17,751	18.5	21.2	17.9	21.9	20.0
Puerto Rican/Cuban/Other Hispanic							
National	1985	6,762	15.9	14.8	14.8	18.6	16.2
National	1986	6,856	16.4	15.1	15.2	18.9	16.5
National	1987	7,564	16.7	15.5	15.5	19.3	16.9
National	1988	8,622	16.9	15.8	15.8	19.3	17.1
National	1989	9,880	16.8	15.9	15.5	19.2	17.0

Source: "Average ACT Scores by Racial-Ethnic Groups," *Black Issues in Higher Education, September 28, 1989, p. 12. Primary source: National ACT Assessment Results 1989.*

★ 175 ★
Adult Education

For the year ending in May 1984. Persons 17 years of age and over on the date of the survey. Adult education participants are involved in part-time organized educational activities such as college courses, employee training, continuing education and private instruction. Based on Current Population Survey.

Characteristic	Number adults in population (1,000)	Participants in Adult Education					
		Total		Full-time Students[1]		Not full-time Students[1,2]	
		Number (1,000)	Percent	Number (1,000)	Percent	Number (1,000)	Percent
Racial/ethnic group:							
White, non-Hispanic	139,777	20,429	14.6	939	7	19,491	13.9
Black, non-Hispanic	18,628	1,506	8.1	88	5	1,418	7.6
Hispanic	9,706	796	8.2	63	6	733	7.6
Other	4,472	571	12.8	28	6	543	12.1

Source: "Participants in Adult Education, by Selected Characteristics: 1984," *Statistical Abstracts*, 1989, p. 161. Primary source: U.S. Department of Education, National Center for Education Statistics, "Survey of Adult Education, Current Population Survey, May 1984," unpublished data. *Notes:* 1. In high school or college degree programs on the date of the survey. 2. Includes part-time undergraduate students and college students who indicated that they were also adult education participants.

★ 176 ★
Age, Education, and Poverty Status

Numbers in thousands. Persons as of March 1989.

Years of school completed and age	Total			White			Black			Hispanic origin[1]		
	Total	Below poverty level		Total	Below poverty level		Total	Below poverty level		Total	Below poverty level	
		Number	Percent		Number	Percent		Number	Percent		Number	Percent
All Persons												
Persons 18 years and over	179,783	19,294	10.7	154,032	13,282	8.6	19,984	5,063	25.3	13,061	2,726	28.9
Less than 4 years of high school	41,308	9,689	23.5	33,139	6,468	19.5	6,812	2,743	40.3	6,313	1,933	30.6
High school graduate but no college	70,340	6,476	9.2	61,031	4,464	7.3	7,662	1,755	22.9	3,879	555	14.6
College 1 year or more	68,135	3,129	4.6	59,862	2,349	3.9	5,511	564	10.2	2,869	238	8.3
Persons 18 to 24 years	25,628	3,998	15.6	21,128	2,633	12.5	3,589	1,151	32.1	2,624	652	24.8
Less than 4 years of high school	5,667	1,680	29.6	4,456	1,099	24.7	1,013	505	49.8	1,185	416	35.1
High school graduate but no college	11,004	1,566	14.2	9,021	965	10.7	1,674	523	31.2	972	192	19.8
College 1 year or more	8,957	752	8.4	7,651	569	7.4	903	123	13.6	466	43	9.2
Persons 25 to 44 years	79,112	7,766	9.8	66,958	5,238	7.8	9,288	2,083	22.4	6,637	1,349	20.3
Less than 4 years of high school	10,605	3,090	29.1	8,356	2,102	25.2	1,784	796	44.6	2,763	894	32.3
High school graduate but no college	31,266	3,055	9.8	26,401	2,009	7.6	4,081	922	22.6	2,066	283	13.7
College 1 year or more	37,242	1,621	4.4	32,201	1,126	3.5	3,424	365	10.6	1,808	172	9.5
Persons 45 to 64 years	46,021	4,047	8.8	39,944	2,816	7.0	4,670	1,045	22.4	2,796	500	17.9
Less than 4 years of high school	11,940	2,390	20.0	9,377	1,522	16.2	2,177	739	33.9	1,638	423	25.8
High school graduate but no college	18,435	1,167	6.3	16,530	888	5.4	1,521	242	15.9	666	64	9.6
College 1 year or more	15,645	490	3.1	14,037	405	2.9	972	64	6.6	491	13	2.6
Persons 65 years and over	29,022	3,482	12.0	26,001	2,595	10.0	2,436	785	32.2	1,005	225	22.4
Less than 4 years of high school	13,096	2,528	19.3	10,951	1,744	15.9	1,838	704	38.3	726	200	27.5
High school graduate but no college	9,635	688	7.1	9,078	603	6.6	386	68	17.6	175	15	8.5
College 1 year or more	6,291	266	4.2	5,972	248	4.2	212	13	6.0	103	10	10.1

Source: "Years of School Completed of Persons 18 Years and Over, by Type of Family, Related Children Under 18, Work Experience, Race and Hispanic Origin, and Poverty Status in 1988," *Money Income and Poverty Status in the United States: 1988*, 1989, pp. 79-81. Primary source: U.S. Bureau of the Census, Current Population Reports, Series P-60, No. 166. *Notes:* 1. Persons of Hispanic origin may be of any race. 2. Base less than 75,000. 3. Represents zero or rounds to zero.

★ 177 ★
Anticipated College Major and SAT Score

	Mean Composite SAT				
	Whites	Blacks	Chicanos	Puerto Ricans	American Indians
Arts and humanities	930	732	845	831	808
Education	884	632	751	738	755
Social sciences	1,029	735	866	796	839
Business	950	695	807	814	798
Allied health fields	958	710	846	800	868
Biological sciences	1,066	807	921	897	855
Engineering	1,109	848	1,018	918	969
Physical sciences and mathematics	1,142	845	1,016	915	979

Source: "SAT Test Scores of High School Seniors by Racial or Ethnic Group and Anticipated Major in College," *Equality and Excellence: The Educational Status of Black Americans*, 1985, p. 21. Primary source: Astin, Alexander W. *Minorities in American Higher Education*, San Francisco: Jossey-Bass, 1982, p. 70. Published by permission.

★ 178 ★
Anticipated Graduate Field and GRE Score

Expected Graduate Field	Total	White	Black	Mexican American	Puerto Rican	American Indian	Asian American
Total	1,015	1,039	733	847	801	925	1,054
Arts	979	992	773	820	739	882	997
Other humanities	1,049	1,064	774	851	784	969	1,026
Education	900	929	661	751	718	808	924
Behavioral sciences	1,030	1,055	765	902	804	933	1,054
Health fields	995	1,015	774	882	798	903	1,032
Biological sciences	1,093	1,110	822	1,013	798	1,001	1,102
Engineering	1,184	1,202	964	1,063	965	1,111	1,126
Mathematics	1,182	1,208	834	1,044	923	1,129	1,104
Physical sciences	1,162	1,170	884	985	885	1,140	1,163

Source: "1980-81 Combined Verbal and Quantitative Graduate Record Examination Scores by Expected Graduate Fields and Race and Ethnicity," *Equality and Excellence: The Educational Status of Black Americans*, 1985, p. 21. Primary source: Goodison, Marlene B., *A Summary of Data Collected from Graduate Record Examinations Test-Takers During 1980-81*. Princeton: Educational Testing Service, May 1982, pp. 74-77 and 79-80. Published by permission.

★ 179 ★
Applications in 4-Year Institutions: Trends

	Four-Year Public		Four-Year Private	
	N	%	N	%
Total				
Less	137	37	254	34
Same	62	16	132	18
More	175	47	359	48
	374	100	745	100

Continued.

Applications in 4-Year Institutions: Trends
[Continued]

	Four-Year Public		Four-Year Private	
	N	%	N	%
Blacks				
Less	90	29	134	22
Same	96	30	253	42
More	128	41	215	36
	314	100	602	100
Hispanics				
Less	40	14	76	13
Same	147	50	329	58
More	109	37	163	29
	296	101	568	100
Asians				
Less	36	12	54	10
Same	134	46	300	53
More	123	42	210	37
	293	100	564	100
American Indians				
Less	53	18	64	12
Same	167	58	415	76
More	67	23	70	13
	287	99	549	101
Whites				
Less	97	31	156	26
Same	57	18	155	26
More	158	51	292	48
	312	100	603	100

Source: "Self-Reported Trends in Applications in Four-Year Institutions, 1980- 1985," *Demographics, Standards, and Equity*, 1986, p. 43. Primary source: *Demographics, Standards, and Equity: Challenges in College Admissions*. American Association of Collegiate Registars & Admission Officers, American College Testing Program, College Board, Educational Testing Service, National Association of College Admission Counselors, November 1986.

★ 180 ★
Average SAT Scores: Trends

	1979	1980	1981	1982	1983	1984	1985	1986[1]	1987	1988	1989	10 year Change
SAT Verbal												
American Indian	386	390	391	388	388	390	392	NA	393	393	384	-2
Asian American	396	396	397	398	395	398	404	NA	405	408	409	+13
Black	330	330	332	341	339	342	346	NA	351	353	351	+21
Mexican American	370	372	373	377	375	376	382	NA	379	382	381	+11
Puerto Rican	345	350	353	360	358	358	368	NA	360	355	360	+15

Continued.

Average SAT Scores: Trends
[Continued]

	1979	1980	1981	1982	1983	1984	1985	1986[1]	1987	1988	1989	10 year Change
Other Hispanic	NA	NA	NA	NA	NA	NA	NA	NA	387	387	389	NA
White	444	442	442	444	443	445	449	NA	447	445	446	+2
Other	393	394	388	392	386	388	391	NA	405	410	414	+21
All Students	427	424	424	426	425	426	431	431	430	428	427	0
SAT Mathematical												
American Indian	421	426	425	424	425	427	428	NA	432	435	428	+7
Asian American	511	509	513	513	514	519	518	NA	521	522	525	+14
Black	358	360	362	366	369	373	376	NA	377	384	386	+28
Mexican American	410	413	415	416	417	420	426	NA	424	428	430	+20
Puerto Rican	388	394	398	403	403	405	409	NA	400	402	406	+18
Other Hispanic	NA	NA	NA	NA	NA	NA	NA	NA	432	433	436	NA
White	483	482	483	483	484	487	490	NA	489	490	491	+8
Other	447	449	447	449	446	450	448	NA	455	460	467	+20
All Students	467	466	466	467	468	471	475	475	476	476	476	+9

Source: "SAT Averages by Ethnic Group, 1979-85, 1987-89," *Black Issues in Higher Education*, September 28, 1989, p. 13. Primary source: The College Board, 1989. *Notes:* 1. SAT scores by ethnic group are not available for 1986 due to changes in the Student Descriptive Questionnaire (SDQ) that students complete when they register for the tests. The SDQ question on ethnic background was changed to include the "Other Hispanic" category for 1987.

★ 181 ★
Average/Overall Acceptance at 4-Year Colleges, 1985

	Four-Year Public			Four-Year Private		
Group	Number of Institutions	Average Acceptance Rate	Overall Acceptance Rate	Number of Institutions	Average Acceptance Rate	Overall Acceptance Rate
Total	328	76%	72%	689	76%	62%
American Indian	166	74%	76%	304	72%	63%
Asian	167	75%	66%	338	76%	48%
Black	182	70%	65%	372	71%	61%
Hispanic	171	74%	69%	331	74%	59%

Source: "Acceptance Rates in Four-Year Institutions Computed by Two Methods, by Racial/Ethnic Group," *Demographics, Stands, and Equity*, 1986, p. 13. Primary source: *Demographics, Stands, and Equity: Challenges in College Admissions*. American Association of Collegiate Registrars & Admission Officers, American College Testing Program, College Board, Educational Testing Service, National Association of College Admission Counselors, November, 1986. *Notes:* Two methods were used to compute acceptance rates. Average Acceptance Rate: The acceptance rate was computed first for each institution separately, then these acceptance rates were averaged across institutions. Overall Acceptance Rate: The total number of acceptances reported for all institutions was divided by the total number of applications reported for all institutions.

★ 182 ★
Baccalaureate Enrollment & Graduates in AACSB Business Schools

| | Baccalaureate | | | |
| | Enrollment | | Graduates | |
Characteristic	Number	Percent	Number	Percent
Total number reported	601,639	---	128,798	---
No. of schools responding	310	---	288	---
No. of schools responding				
w/demographic breakdowns	265	---	283	---
Ethnic/racial status				
(U.S. citizens only)				
White	398,543	54.0	87,205	85.2
Black	37,710	7.7	5,270	5.2
Hispanic	23,723	4.8	4,542	4.4
Asian American	16,528	3.4	3,073	3.0
Native American	2,099	0.4	267	0.3
Other, No Response, or				
Non-Reporting	12,065	2.5	1,957	1.9
Total	490,668	100.0	102,314	100.0

Source: "Business School Matriculation Rate," *Black Issues in Higher Education*, March 29, 1990, p. 6. Primary source: American Assembly of Collegiate Schools of Business (AACSB) - 1986, 1987, 1988 Surveys of Student Demographics and Doctoral Production; 1986, 1987, 1988 School Fact Forum. *Notes:* Totals for various categories will not add up to total enrollment because not all schools could provide breakdowns in all categories.

★ 183 ★
Baccalaureate Origins of Recent Ph.D.s

Ranked on number of Ph.D.s(1).

Race and institution	Number
Asian-Americans	
University of California-Berkeley	104
University of Hawaii-Manoa	102
University of California-Los Angeles	63
Massachusetts Institute of	
Technology	45
University of California-Davis	31
Stanford University	30
University of Illinois-Urbana	29
Cornell University	27
University of Washington	27
University of Michigan	26
Blacks	
Howard University[2]	81
Tuskegee University[2]	50
Morgan State University[2]	41
Spelman College[2]	41
Hampton University[2]	38
Jackson State University[2]	36
Southern University[2]	34
Wayne State University	30
North Carolina Central University[2]	30

Continued.

Baccalaureate Origins of Recent Ph.D.s
[Continued]

Race and institution	Number
University of the District of Columbia[2]	29
Hispanics	
University of Puerto Rico-Rio Piedras	232
University of Puerto Rico-Mayaguez	62
University of Texas-El Paso	34
University of Texas-Austin	31
University of California-Berkeley	30
University of California-Los Angeles	30
University of New Mexico	27
University of Miami	25
California State University-Los Angeles	24
University of Florida	22
Whites	
University of California-Berkeley	783
University of Michigan	716
University of Illinois-Urbana	667
Pennsylvania State University	652
Cornell University	647
University of Wisconsin-Milwaukee	609
Michigan State University	530
University of California-Los Angeles	528
Ohio State University	500
University of Minnesota-Minneapolis	495

Source: "Ph.D.s by Race/Ethnicity: Institutions Feeding Ph.D. Pipeline 1986- 1988," *Black Issues in Higher Education,* June 7, 1990, p. 9. Primary source: National Research Council, Doctorate Records Projects. *Notes:* 1. Because of the small numbers of doctorates awarded to American Indians, baccalaureate institutions for this group are not included. 2. Predominantly Black Institution.

★ 184 ★
Bachelor's Degree Areas: Trends

Discipline/Division	1975-1976		1978-1979		1980-1981		1982-1983		1984-1985	
	Degrees Awarded	% of Total	Degrees Awarded	% of Total	Degrees Awarded	% of Total	Degrees Awarded	% of Total	Degrees Awarded	% of Total
Total	59,122	6.4	60,130	6.6	60,533	6.5	57,129	5.8	54,964	5.5
Architecture and environmental design	259	2.8	316	3.4	300	3.2	334	3.4	324	3.5
Biological sciences	2,326	4.3	2,487	8.6	2,266	5.2	2,073	5.1	1,972	5.0
Business and management	9,489	6.7	11,430	6.6	13,388	6.7	13,777	6.0	14,172	6.0
Computer and information sciences	323	5.8	505	5.8	784	5.2	1,274	5.2	2,087	5.3
Education	14,209	9.2	11,509	9.1	9,494	8.8	6,826	6.8	5,221	5.8

Continued.

Bachelor's Degree Areas: Trends
[Continued]

Discipline/Division	1975-1976		1978-1979		1980-1981		1982-1983		1984-1985	
	Degrees Awarded	% of Total	Degrees Awarded	% of Total	Degrees Awarded	% of Total	Degrees Awarded	% of Total	Degrees Awarded	% of Total
Engineering	1,370	3.0	1,756	2.9	2,432	3.3	2,848	3.2	3,013	3.1
Health professions	2,741	5.1	3,380	5.4	3,603	5.7	3,774	5.8	3,704	5.6
Law	27	5.2	53	7.9	22	2.8	40	3.6	83	7.1
Mathematics	799	5.1	652	5.6	582	5.3	629	5.0	757	5.0
Physical sciences	647	3.0	691	3.0	886	3.8	839	3.6	803	3.4

Source: "Bachelor's Degrees Awarded to Black Students by Selected Discipline Division, 1976, 1979, 1981, 1983, 1985," *NAFEO INROADS*, April/May 1988, p. 3. Primary source: Office for Civil Rights (OCR), ED (Washington, 1976, 1979, 1981, 1983, and 1985. Unpublished data.) *Notes:* Figures for U.S. Outlying Areas are not included for 1976, 1979, and 1981. Percent of total column refers to percent of total degrees awarded to all U.S. students. Published by permission.

★ 185 ★
Bachelor's Degree-Granting TBIs

Name of College	Number of Degrees granted to Respondents
Florida A&M University	29
Howard University	14
North Carolina Central University	14
Tuskegee College	13
A&T University	10
Fisk University	9
Alabama State	9
Bennett College	7
Hampton University	7
Fort Valley State College	7
South Carolina State College	7
Morehouse College	6
Stillman College	6
Talladega College	6
Tennessee State University	6
Spelman College	5
Virginia State College	5
Winston Salem State University	5

Source: "Selected TBIs Granting Bachelor's Degrees to Black Respondents," *Black Faculty in Traditionally White Institutions in Selected Adams States*, 1988, p. 30 Primary source: *Black Faculty in Traditionally White Institutions in Selected Adams States: Characteristics, Experiences and Perceptions*, Southern Education Foundation, Inc., Atlanta, GA 30308, 1988 Adams States: Alabama, Florida, Georgis, Kentucky, Maryland, North Carolina, South Carolina, Tennessee, Virginia. Published by permission.

★ 186 ★
Bachelor's Degrees in Education and in Business/Management

Location	1977	1985
United States:		
Education	12,943	5,491
Business and Management	10,001	14,194
SREB States		
Education	8,085	3,614
Business and Management	5,541	7,597

Source: "Bachelor's Degrees Awarded to Black Students," *Regional Spotlight*, April 1989, p. 3. Published by permission, unspecified source. *Note:* SREB: Southern Regional Education Board.

★ 187 ★
Bachelor's Degrees in Education: Trends

Year	Total	Group	
		Black	White
1975-76	156,538	14,229	135,514
1978-79	127,633	11,538	108,984
1980-81	110,715	9,517	93,750
1982-83	100,171	6,826	81,663
1984-85	90,511	5,221	74,918

Source: "Bachelor's Degrees Conferred to [sic] Blacks and Whites in Education by All U.S. Institutions," *NAFEO INROADS*, February/March 1988, p. 7. Primary source: *OCR Unpublished Data on Degrees Awarded by Major Field, Race/Ethnicity, and Sex*; National Advisory Committee Staff Analysis, 1975- 76, 1977-78, NAFEO Research Institute Staff Analysis, 1980-81, 1982-83, 1984-85. Published by permission.

★ 188 ★
Black College Students: High School Grade-Point Average

High School Grade Point Average	Total Population	Campus Race	
		Black	White
Below 2.5	10.0	15.0	4.1
2.5-2.99	22.4	27.8	15.9
3.0-3.5	35.7	39.2	31.5
Above 3.5	31.9	17.9	48.5
Total	100.0	100.0	100.0
N	(1376)	(747)	(629)

Source: "High School Grade Point Average by Student Gender and Campus Race," *Gender and Campus Race Differences in Black Student Academic Performance, Racial Attitudes and College Satisfaction*, 1986, p. 48. Primary source: National Study of Black College Students, 1981 and 1983, University of Michigan, Ann Arbor. Published by permission.

★ 189 ★
Black College Students: Sex & Type of Instruction

Numbers in thousands.

Control and Sex	1976	1978	1980	1982	1984	1986
Total -						
number	1,033	1,054	1,107	1,101	1,076	1,081
%	9.4	9.4	9.2	8.9	8.8	8.6
Public -						
number	831	840	876	873	844	855
%	7.6	7.5	7.2	7.0	6.9	6.8
Private -						
number	202	215	231	228	232	226
%	1.8	1.9	1.9	1.8	1.9	1.8
Sex						
Male -						
number	470	453	464	458	437	436
%	4.3	4.0	3.8	3.7	3.6	3.5
Female -						
number	563	601	643	644	639	645
%	5.1	5.4	5.3	5.2	5.2	5.2

Source: "Black Enrollment and Percent Distribution in Institutions of Higher Education by Control and Sex, Fall 1976-1986," *NAFEO INROADS*, February/March-April/May, 1989, p. 12. Primary source: *Survey Report: Trends in Minority Enrollment in Higher Education, Fall 1976- Fall 1986*, U.S. Department of Education, Office of Educational Research and Improvement, April 1988. Published by permission.

★ 190 ★
Black Enrollment at HBCUs

Control and Sex	Number						Percent Distribution					
	1986		1987		1988		1986		1987		1988	
	Male	Female	Male	Female	Male	Female	Male	Female	Male	Female	Male	Female
All HBCUs	73,495	103,115	74,447	107,573	77,741	115,107	41.6	58.4	41.0	59.0	40.3	59.7
Four Year	70,434	98,211	71,584	102,754	74,220	108,938	41.8	58.2	41.0	59.0	40.5	59.5
Two Year	3,061	4,904	2,863	4,819	3,521	6,169	38.4	61.6	37.3	62.7	36.3	63.7
Public HBCUs	50,592	70,338	51,177	73,572	53,206	78,861	41.8	58.2	41.0	59.0	40.3	59.7
Four Year	48,305	66,430	49,074	69,740	50,604	73,955	42.1	57.9	41.3	58.7	40.6	59.4
Two Year	2,287	3,908	2,103	3,832	2,602	4,906	36.9	63.1	35.4	64.6	34.7	65.3
Private HBCUs	22,903	32,777	32,270	34,001	24,535	36,246	41.5	58.9	40.6	59.4	40.4	59.6
Four Year	22,129	31,781	22,510	33,014	23,616	34,983	41.0	59.0	40.5	59.5	40.3	59.7
Two Year	774	996	760	987	919	1,263	43.7	56.3	43.5	56.5	42.1	57.9
Grand Total												
All Races	92,643	120,471	92,307	125,363	95,851	134,907	43.1	56.5	42.4	57.6	41.5	58.5

Source: "Black Enrollment at HBCUs by Control, Level, and Sex, Fall 1986-1988, *NAFEO INROADS*, February/March-April/May, 1989, p. 13. Primary source: NAFEO Annual Fall Enrollment Survey: 1986, 1987, and 1988. *Note:* Number of Institutions: 1986 and 1987 (N=104), 1988 (N=106).

★ 191 ★
Black Faculty in Higher Education

				Percent Distribution		
Control	All Insti- tutions	HBCUs/EOEIs	Non-HBCUs	All Institutions	HBCUs/EOEIs	Non-HBCUs
All Institutions - Total	19,571	7,020	12,551	100.0	35.9	64.1
Male	10,541	3,784	6,757	100.0	35.9	64.1
Female	9,030	3,236	5,794	100.0	35.9	64.1
Public Institutions - Total	13,636	4,118	9,518	100.0	30.2	69.8
Male	7,094	2,118	4,976	100.0	30.0	70.1
Female	6,542	2,000	4,542	100.0	30.6	69.4
Private Institutions - Total	5,935	2,902	3,033	100.0	48.9	51.1
Male	3,447	1,666	1,781	100.0	48.3	51.7
Female	2,488	1,236	1,252	100.0	49.7	50.3

Source: "Number and Percent of Full-Time Black Faculty in HBCUs/EOEIs and All Institutions of Higher Education by Control and Sex, 1983, *NAFEO INROADS*, February/March - April/May, 1989, p. 14. Primary source: NAFEO Research Institute Staff Analysis of EEO-6 Survey Data from the Equal Employment Opportunity Commission, 1983. *Notes:* HBCU: Historically Black Colleges and Universities EOEI: Equal Opportunity Employment Institutions NAFEO: National Association for Equal Opportunity in Higher Education. Published by permission.

★ 192 ★
Black/White Campuses and Academic Performance

Numbers in percent.

College Grade Point Average	Total Population	Campus Race	
		Black	White
Below 2.5	31.7	28.0	36.4
2.6 to 2.99	38.6	38.1	39.2
3.0 to 3.49	23.7	26.1	20.7
Above 3.5	6.0	7.8	3.7
Total	100.0	100.0	100.0
N	(149.7)	(844)	(653)

Source: "Academic Performance by Student Gender and Campus Race," *Gender and Campus Race Differences in Black Student Academic Performance, Racial Attitudes and College Satisfaction,*" 1986, p. 33. Primary source: National Study of Black College Students, 1981 and 1983, University of Michigan, Ann Arbor. Published by permission.

★ 193 ★
Black/White Enrollment in Historically Black Colleges and Universities.

State/Institutions	Date Estab.	Control/ Level[3]	Total Students	Black		White	
				Total	Percent	Total	Percent
ALABAMA							
Alabama A&M University[2]	1875	PU-4+G	4,045	3,039	75.1	238	5.9
Alabama State University	1874	PU-4+G	3,540	3,451	97.5	24	0.7
S.D. Bishop State Jr. College	1936	PU-2	1,664	1,338	80.4	306	18.4
Concordia College	1922	PR-2	410	401	97.8	0	0
Lawson State Community College[1]	1949	PU-2	1,522	1,509	99.1	13	0.8
Miles College[1]	1905	PR-4	456	443	97.1	1	0.2
Oakwood College	1896	PR-4	1,000	888	88.8	0	0
Selma University	1878	PR-2	206	206	100	0	0

Continued.

Black/White Enrollment in Historically Black Colleges and Universities.
[Continued]

State/Institutions	Date Estab.	Control/ Level[3]	Total Students	Black		White	
				Total	Percent	Total	Percent
Stillman College	1876	PR-4	793	764	96.3	2	0.3
Talladega College[1]	1867	PR-4	442	437	98.9	1	0.2
Tuskegee University[2]	1888	PR-4+GP	3,070	2,718	88.5	103	3.4
ARKANSAS							
Arkansas Baptist College	1884	PR-4	233	225	96.6	8	3.4
Philander Smith College	1877	PR-4	572	489	85.5	4	0.7
Shorter College	1886	PR-2	120	99	82.5	13	10.8
University of Arkansas[2]	1873	PU-4	2,900	2,321	80	567	19.6
DELAWARE							
Delaware State College[2]	1891	PU-4	2,327	1,253	53.8	1,000	43
DISTRICT OF COLUMBIA							
Howard University	1867	PR-4+GP	11,053	8,805	79.7	171	1.5
University of the District of Columbia[2]	1851	PU-4+G	11,098	9,897	89.2	556	5
FLORIDA							
Bethune-Cookman College	1904	PR-4	1,815	1,711	94.3	16	0.9
Edward Waters College[1]	1866	PR-4	712	667	93.7	10	1.4
Florida A&M University[2]	1887	PU-4+G	5,377	4,429	82.4	678	12.6
Florida Memorial College	1879	PR-4	2,172	1,797	82.7	5	0.2
GEORGIA							
Albany State College	1903	PU-4+G	1,754	1,463	83.4	282	16.1
Atlanta University	1865	PR-G	1,072	833	77.7	12	1.1
Clark College	1869	PR-4	1,883	1,850	98.2	0	0
Fort Valley State College[2]	1895	PU-4+G	1,811	1,656	91.4	118	6.5
Morehouse College	1967	PR-4	2,121	2,066	97.4	0	0
Morehouse School of Medicine	1981	PR-GP	132	101	76.5	16	12.1
Morris Brown College[1]	1881	PR-4	1,086	1,065	98.1	0	0
Paine College	1882	PR-4	789	724	91.8	44	5.6
Savannah State College	1890	PU-4+G	1,694	1,330	78.5	303	17.9
Spelman College[1]	1881	PR-4	1,586	1,550	97.7	0	0
KENTUCKY							
Kentucky State University[2]	1886	PU-4+G	2,205	895	40.6	1,266	57.4
Simmons University Bible College	1873	PR-4	99	99	100	0	0
LOUISIANA							
Dillard University	1869	PR-4	1,275	1,266	99.3	1	0.1
Grambling State University	1901	PU-4+G	5,224	4,984	95.4	71	1.4
Southern University (Baton Rouge)[2]	1880	PR-GP	9,110	8,000	87.8	375	4.1
Southern University (New Orleans)	1956	PU-4+G	3,302	2,868	86.9	251	7.6
Southern University (Shreveport)	1964	PU-2	756	725	95.9	31	4.1
Xavier University	1925	PR-4+G	1,992	1,800	90.4	143	7.2
MARYLAND							

Continued.

Black/White Enrollment in Historically Black Colleges and Universities.
[Continued]

State/Institutions	Date Estab.	Control/ Level[3]	Total Students	Black		White	
				Total	Percent	Total	Percent
Bowie State College	1865	PU-4+G	2,902	1,668	57.5	942	32.5
Coppin State College	1900	PU-4+G	2,315	2,000	86.4	80	3.5
Morgan State University	1867	PU-4+G	3,702	3,130	84.5	170	4.6
University of Maryland Eastern Shore[2]	1886	PU-4+G	1,259	920	73.1	257	20.4
MISSISSIPPI							
Alcorn State University[2]	1871	PU-4+G	2,319	2,245	96.8	103	4.4
Coahoma Jr. College	1949	PU-2	1,362	1,339	98.3	23	1.7
Jackson State University	1877	PU-4+G	6,319	5,858	92.7	150	2.4
Mary Holmes College	1892	PR-2	345	336	97.4	1	0.3
Mississippi Valley State University[1]	1950	PU-4+G	2,344	2,330	99.4	7	0.3
Natchez Jr. College	1885	PR-2	107	107	100	0	0
Prentiss Institute Jr. College	1907	PR-2	124	124	100	0	0
Rust College	1866	PR-4	915	893	97.6	4	0.4
Tougaloo College	1869	PR-4	902	890	98.7	12	1.3
Utica Jr. College[1]	1903	PU-2	640	632	98.8	5	0.8
MISSOURI							
Harris-Stowe State College	1857	PU-4	1,374	983	71.5	344	25
Lincoln University[2]	1866	PU-4+G	2,486	772	31.1	1600	64.6
NORTH CAROLINA							
Barber-Scotia College	1867	PR-4	383	382	99.7	1	0.3
Bennett College[1]	1873	PR-4	576	574	99.7	2	0.3
Elizabeth City State University	1891	PU-4	1,615	1,321	81.8	283	17.5
Fayetteville State University	1877	PU-4+G	2,921	2,173	74.4	679	23.2
Johnson C. Smith University	1867	PR-4	1,130	1,105	97.8	0	0
Livingstone College	1879	PR-4	733	712	97.1	4	0.5
|North Carolina A&T	1891	PU-4+G	5,966	4,978	83.4	705	11.8
State University[2]	1910	PU-4+G	4,988	4,113	82.5	804	16.1
North Carolina Central University	1867	PR-4	1,636	1,636	100	0	0
Saint Augustine's College	1865	PR-4	1,742	1,373	78.8	17	1
Shaw University[1]	1892	PU-4	2,570	2,187	85.1	388	15.1
Winston-Salem State University							
OHIO							
Central State University	1856	PU-4	2,670	2,358	88.3	230	8.6
Wilberforce University	1856	PR-4	797	794	99.6	2	0.3
OKLAHOMA							
Langston University[2]	1897	PU-4	2,030	968	47.7	841	41.4
PENNSYLVANIA							
Cheyney University	1837	PU-4+G	1,507	1,437	95.4	0	0
Lincoln University[1]	1854	PU-4	1,245	1,111	89.2	98	7.9
SOUTH CAROLINA							
Allen University	1870	PR-4	233	219	94	14	6

Continued.

Black/White Enrollment in Historically Black Colleges and Universities.
[Continued]

State/Institutions	Date Estab.	Control/ Level[3]	Total Students	Black		White	
				Total	Percent	Total	Percent
Benedict College	1870	PR-4	1,510	1,453	96.2	16	1.1
Claflin College	1869	PR-4	757	747	98.7	3	0.4
Clinton Jr. College[1]	1894	PR-2	95	95	100	0	0
Denmark Technical College	1948	PU-2	689	652	94.6	32	4.6
Morris College	1908	PR-4	675	674	99.9	1	0.1
South Carolina State College[2]	1896	PU-4+G	3,869	3,570	92.3	261	6.7
Voorhees College	1897	PR-4	576	571	99.1	0	0
TENNESSEE							
Fisk University	1866	PR-4+G	538	509	94.6	1	0.2
Knoxville College	1875	PR-4	436	393	90.1	30	6.9
Lane College	1882	PR-4	531	529	99.6	2	0.4
LeMoyne-Owen College[1]	1862	PR-4	844	827	98	0	0
Meharry Medical College	1876	PR-GP	678	534	78.8	39	5.8
Morristown College	1881	PR-2	178	176	98.9	2	1.1
Tennessee State University[2]	1912	PU-4+G	6,737	4,263	63.3	2,141	31.8
TEXAS							
Bishop College	1881	PR-4	946	608	64.3	0	0
Huston-Tillotson College	1876	PR-4	520	327	62.9	5	1
Jarvis Christian College[1]	1912	PR-4	533	531	99.6	1	0.2
Paul Quinn College	1872	PR-4	464	444	95.7	11	2.4
Prarie View A&M University[2]	1876	PU-4	4,499	3,658	81.3	399	8.9
Southwestern Christian College	1949	PR-2	251	226	90	2	0.8
Texas College	1894	PR-4	478	356	74.5	1	0.2
Texas Southern University	1947	PU-4+G	7,246	5,320	73.4	181	2.5
Wiley College[1]	1873	PR-4	537	503	93.7	1	0.2
VIRGIN ISLANDS							
University of the Virgin Islands	1962	PU-4+G	2,495	1,911	76.6	222	8.9
VIRGINIA							
Hampton University	1868	PR-4+G	4,482	4,186	93.4	228	5.1
Norfolk State University	1935	PU-4+G	7,458	6,324	84.8	864	11.6
Saint Paul's College	1888	PR-4	736	711	96.6	16	2.2
The Virginia College	1888	PR-4	40	40	100	0	0
Virginia State University[2]	1882	PU-4+G	3,583	3,070	85.7	42.5	11.9
Virginia Union University	1865	PR-4+G	1,108	1,091	98.5	8	0.7
WEST VIRGINIA							
West Virginia State College	1891	PU-4	4,029	517	12.8	3,464	86

Source: "Percent of Black and White Students Enrolled in Historically Black Colleges and Universities, Fall 1986, NAFEO Membership (n = 104), *NAFEO INROADS*, February/March 1987, pp. 5-7. Primary source: NAFEO Annual Fall Enrollment Survey (1986) of Undergraduate, Graduate and Professional Students. University of Arkansas in table refers to University of Arkansas - Pine Bluff. *Notes:* Other historically black colleges not included in the analysis are: Bluefield State College, Bluefield, WV (founded in 1895 and presently a predominantly white institution), and Interdenominational Theological Center, Atlanta, GA (founded in 1958 and currently a viable institution). 1. 1986 racial/ethnic data are not available for 15 of the 104 historically black colleges and universities. Racial/ethnic data for these 15 institutions were imputed from the 1984 Office of Civil Rights *Racial, Ethnic and Sex Enrollment Data for Institutions of Higher Education* (Unpublished data). Analysis does not include unclassified students. 2. The 1890 Land Grant Institutions. 3. Legend: PU-4 Public 4 Year; PU-4+G Public 4 Year + Graduate; PU-2 Public 2 Year; PR-4 Private 4 Year; PR-4+G Private 4 Year + Graduate; PR-2 Private 2 Year; PR-4+GP Private 4 Year + Graduate Professional; PR-G Private Graduate Only.

★ 194 ★
Changes in Performance in Mathematics

Selected Characteristics of Participants	Age 9			Age 13			Age 17		
	Mean % Correct		Mean	Mean % Correct		Mean	Mean % Correct		Mean
	1977-78	1981-82	Change	1977-78	1981-82	Change	1977-78	1981-82	Change
All participants	55.4	56.4	1.0	56.6	60.5	3.9	60.4	60.2	-0.2
Race:									
Black	43.1	45.2	2.1	41.7	48.2	6.5	43.7	45.0	1.3
White	58.1	58.8	0.7	59.9	63.1	3.2	63.2	63.1	-0.1
Hispanic	46.6	47.7	1.1	45.4	51.9	6.5	48.5	49.4	0.9

Source: "National Assessment of Educational Progress in Mathematics for 9-, 13-, and 17- Year-Olds by Selected Characteristics of Participants: United States, 1977-78 and 1981-82," *Equality and Excellence: The Educational Status of Black Americans*, 1985, p. 27. Primary source: Derived from data available in the files of the National Assessment of Educational Progress, July 1983. Published by permission.

★ 195 ★
Characteristics of Doctorate Recipients: Trends

Race/Ethnicity	1982	1983	1984	1985	1986
Men					
American Indian					
U.S.	44	50	53	39	58
Permanent Visas[1]	-	1	-	-	-
Temporary Visas[1]	-	-	-	-	1
Asian					
U.S.	281	312	338	329	347
Permanent Visas	444	431	389	437	412
Temporary Visas	1,567	1,731	1,982	2,137	2,252
Black					
U.S.	483	412	427	379	321
Permanent Visas	81	73	81	117	106
Temporary Visas	340	339	382	354	275
Hispanic					
U.S.	344	288	313	300	299
Permanent Visas	52	45	47	50	71
Temporary Visas	247	288	252	294	288
White					
U.S.	13,984	13,599	13,155	12,778	12,257
Permanent Visas	309	381	350	367	409
Temporary Visas	1,242	1,287	1,223	1,272	1,214
Women					
American Indian					
U.S.	33	30	20	56	41
Permanent Visas[1]	-	-	-	-	-
Temporary Visas[1]	-	-	-	-	-
Asian					
U.S.	171	180	174	187	180
Permanent Visas	108	120	118	116	111
Temporary Visas	262	275	313	389	387
Black					
U.S.	564	509	526	533	499

Continued.

Characteristics of Doctorate Recipients: Trends
[Continued]

Race/Ethnicity	1982	1983	1984	1985	1986
Permanent Visas	15	10	21	14	20
Temporary Visas	33	244	37	41	38
Hispanic					
U.S.	191	250	222	261	268
Permanent Visas	27	24	24	23	36
Temporary Visas	47	54	48	67	83
White					
U.S.	7,689	8,074	8,168	7,926	8,281
Permanent Visas	154	163	163	167	183
Temporary Visas	216	252	267	295	290

Source: "Doctorate Recipients by Sex, Race and Citizenship," *Black Issues in Higher Education,* March 30, 1989, p. 20. Primary source: Summary Report 1986, Doctorate Recipients from United States Universities, National Research Council. *Notes:* 1. In most cases, non-U.S. American Indians are citizens of Canada or Latin American coutries.

★ 196 ★
Children: Computer Competence

Student Groups	Grade 3	Grade 7	Grade 11
All Students	33.7	41.2	46.2
Race/Hispanic			
White	34.9	43.1	47.6
Black	29.4	35.6	39.9
Hispanic	29.8	36.1	40.2

Source: "National Assessment of Educational Progress Overall Computer Competence Scores (mean percent correct), by Grade, Sex, and Race/Hispanic Origin, 1985-86," *U.S. Children and their Families,* 1989, p. 153. Primary source: The National Assessment of Educational Progress, *Computer Competence: The First National Assessment,* Educational Testing Service, April 1988. *Notes:* National Assessment test results are based on national probability samples of students at the specified grade levels. Computer competence was assessed by a written test covering three general categories: knowledge of computer technology, computer applications, and computer programming. Scores represent the average percent correct answers achieved by students in each of the three grade levels. Different tests were used for each age, so comparisons across age groups are inappropriate.

★ 197 ★
Closed Predominantly Black Institutions

Institution	City	State
Butler Junior College	Tyler	TX
Daniel Payne College	Birmingham	AL
Durham College	Durham,	NC
Friendship College	Rock Hill	SC
J.P. Campbell College	Jackson	MS
Kittrell College	Kittrell	NC
Mary Allen Junior College	Crockett	TX
Mississippi Industrial College	Holly Spring	MS
Okolona College	Okolona	MS
Saints Junior College	Lexington	MS

Continued.

Closed Predominantly Black Institutions
[Continued]

Institution	City	State
Shaw College of Detroit	Detroit	MI
Storer College	Harper Ferry	WV
T.J. Harris Junior College	Meridan	MS
Piney Woods County Life School	Piney Woods	MS
(Now offering a nursery through 12th grade program).		

Source: "Historically and Predominantly Black Colleges Now Closed, *NAFEO INROADS*, February/March 1987, p. 14. Source: NAFEO Archives. Published by permission.

★ 198 ★
College Acceptance Rates and Institution Selectivity, 1985

Selectivity/Group	Four-Year Public			Four-Year Private		
	Number of Institutions	Average Acceptance Rate	Overall Acceptance Rate	Number of Institutions	Average Acceptance Rate	Overall Acceptance Rate
Most Selective Institutions						
Total	28	42%	38%	69	42%	34%
American Indian	13	55%	42%	38	44%	41%
Asian	14	49%	47%	44	47%	30%
Black	14	45%	40%	44	53%	45%
Hispanic	14	46%	50%	43	49%	40%
More Selective Institutions						
Total	151	68%	68%	276	72%	68%
American Indian	85	68%	68%	108	72%	64%
Asian	85	71%	67%	126	76%	69%
Black	94	61%	60%	142	64%	60%
Hispanic	86	69%	65%	125	69%	63%
Less Selective Institutions						
Total	105	88%	87%	274	85%	84%
American Indian	46	84%	85%	119	77%	72%
Asian	45	82%	81%	128	84%	82%
Black	51	81%	80%	141	78%	67%
Hispanic	48	82%	85%	127	85%	82%
Least Selective Institutions						
Total	44	98%	97%	67	94%	93%
American Indian	22	94%	93%	37	97%	97%
Asian	23	97%	98%	38	93%	88%
Black	23	95%	96%	42	91%	96%
Hispanic	23	94%	97%	34	97%	92%

Source: "Acceptance Rates in Four-Year Institutions Computed by Two Methods, by Racial/Ethnic Group and Selectivity," *Demographics, Stands, and Equity*, 1986, p. 14. Primary source: *Demographics, Stands, and Equity: Challenges in College Admissions.* American Association of Collegiate Registrars & Admission Officers, American College Testing Program, College Board, Educational Testing Service, National Association of College Admission Counselors, November, 1986. *Notes:* Two methods were used to compute acceptance rates. Average Acceptance Rate: The acceptance rate was computed first for each institution separately, then these acceptance rates were averaged across institutions. Overall Acceptance Rate: The total number of acceptances reported for all institutions was divided by the total number of applications reported for all institutions.

★ 199 ★
College Completion Rates: Trends

Student characteristics	1972 high school seniors											
	1- to 2-year degree, by year of attainment[1]						Bachelor's degree, by year of attainment					
	June 1976	June 1978	June 1980	June 1982	June 1984	June 1986	June 1976	June 1978	June 1980	June 1982	June 1984	June 1986
Total	6.39	7.87	9.35	11.76	14.22	16.59	14.33	23.71	25.14	26.42	27.08	27.68
Race/ethnicity												
White	6.94	8.52	9.91	12.11	14.72	16.99	15.61	25.46	26.98	28.05	28.76	29.39
Black	2.14	3.48	4.89	9.36	11.09	14.61	7.75	13.49	14.69	18.29	18.66	19.18
Hispanic	3.29	4.01	6.59	9.07	10.99	13.69	3.09	9.13	9.70	10.44	10.81	10.88
Asian	8.02	8.02	12.77	21.00	25.49	27.66	5.76	5.76	5.76	10.72	15.29	18.52
American Indian	4.11	5.51	11.36	20.06	23.46	26.23	29.19	48.48	53.23	54.93	54.93	56.06

Source: "Cumulative Percent of 1972, 1980, and 1982 High School Graduates Completing College, by Level of Degree and Selected Student Characteristics: 1976 to 1986," *Digest of Educational Statistics,* 1989, p. 279. Primary source: U.S. Department of Education, National Center for Educational Statistics, High School and Beyond and National Longitudinal Study surveys, unpublished tabulations. (This table was prepared November 1988.) *Notes:* 1. Includes licenses, awards, and associate degree programs of 1 to 2 years duration. 2. Ability level as measured by a test battery administered as part of the High School and Beyond survey.

★ 200 ★
College Default Rates

Name of College	Percent
Alabama State University[1]	52.9
Alcorn State University[1]	19.2
Apex Technical School (N.Y.)	45.7
Arkansas Baptist College	60.0
Arizona State University	16.2
Bowie State University[1]	33.8
Chicago State University	4.8
Cuyahoga Community College	33.8
Fisk University[1]	11.8
Florida A&M University[1]	15.8
Nevada Gaming School	59.9
Oklahoma City Community College	62.7
Princeton University	1.5
San Antonio Trade School	65.1
Southern University[1]	24.2
Southwest Texas Jr. College	19.8
Spelman College[1]	28.2
Stanford University	2.3
University of Virginia	2.5
Voorhees College[1]	57.3
Virginia Western Comm. College	3.9

Source: "A Sampling of College Default Rates, "*Black Issues in Higher Education,* June 22, 1989, p. 11. Primary source: U.S. Education Department. *Note:* 1. Predominantly black or Equal Opportunity Educational Institutions.

★ 201 ★
College Endowments at UNCF Institutions: Trends

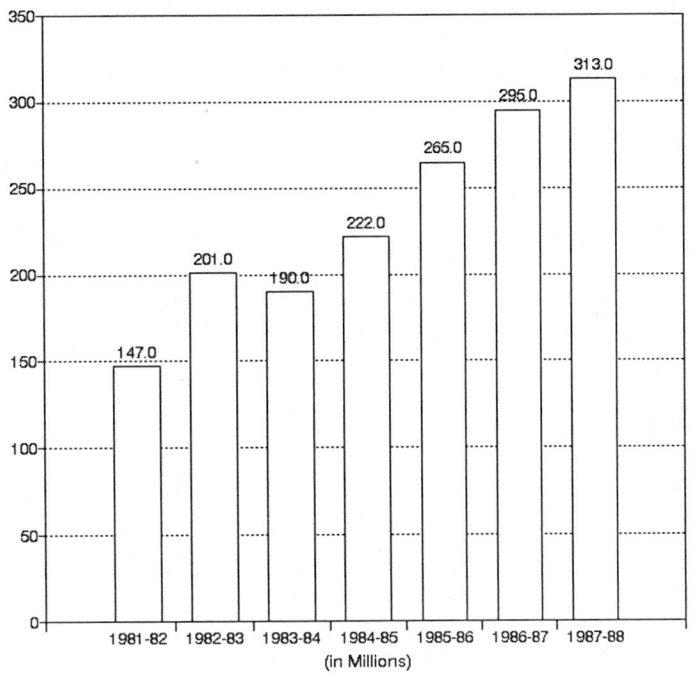

(in Millions)

In millions.

Year	Dollar amount
1981-82	147
1982-83	201
1983-84	190
1984-85	222
1985-86	265
1986-87	295
1987-88	313

Source: "Total Endowment, UNCF Member Institutions," *UNCF 1989 Statistical Report,* p. 17. Primary source: United Negro College Fund (UNCF), Inc., UNCF 1989 Statistical Report (undated), New York, NY.

★ 202 ★
College Enrollment in Relation to Population - Part I

	1972	1973	1974	1975	1976	1977	1978	1979
White male								
Population[1]	5,973	6,1296	6,373	6,545	6,651	6,730	6,783	6,827
Enrollment[1]	2,304	2,194	2,210	2,417	2,317	2,396	2,278	2,250
Percent	38.6	35.8	34.7	36.9	34.8	35.6	33.5	33.0
White female								
Population[1]	6,481	6,573	6,784	6,903	6,991	7,051	7,073	7,072
Enrollment[1]	2,024	1,952	2,039	2,238	2,368	2,282	2,251	2,327
Percent	31.2	29.7	30.1	32.4	33.9	32.4	31.8	32.9
Black male								
Population[1]	825	854	865	941	957	946	951	956

Continued.

College Enrollment in Relation to Population - Part I
[Continued]

	1972	1973	1974	1975	1976	1977	1978	1979
Enrollment[1]	193	189	202	218	234	205	220	220
Percent	23.4	22.1	23.4	23.2	24.5	21.7	23.1	23.0
Black female								
Population[1]	980	998	1,031	1,085	1,110	1,130	1,132	1,137
Enrollment[1]	204	168	222	280	320	326	288	283
Percent	20.8	16.8	21.5	25.8	28.8	28.8	25.4	24.9
Hispanic male								
Population[1]	372	355	428	416	458	462	439	486
Enrollment[1]	83	76	99	105	108	99	83	110
Percent	22.3	21.4	23.1	25.2	23.6	21.4	18.9	22.6
Hispanic female								
Population[1]	419	382	466	484	507	519	521	525
Enrollment[1]	68	77	107	114	119	120	94	110
Percent	16.2	20.2	23.0	23.6	23.5	23.1	18.0	21.0

Source: "U.S. Population and College Enrollment of 18- to 21- Year-Olds, by Selected Race and Gender: 1970-88," *Science and Engineering Indicators — 1989*, 1989, p. 212. Primary source: U.S. Bureau of the Census, *Current Population Reports*, Series P-20 (Washington, DC: U.S. Bureau of the Census), various issues; and unpublished tabulations. *Note:* 1. In thousands.

★ 203 ★
College Enrollment in Relation to Population - Part II

	1980	1981	1982	1983	1984	1985	1986	1987	1988
White male									
Population[1]	6,793	6,820	6,626	6,501	6,289	6,069	5,850	5,757	5,765
Enrollment[1]	2,346	2,363	2,377	2,346	2,367	2,313	2,216	2,416	2,308
Percent	34.5	34.6	35.9	36.1	37.6	38.1	37.9	42.0	40.0
White female									
Population[1]	7,033	7,051	6,895	6,689	6,461	6,280	6,065	5,951	5,955
Enrollment[1]	2,363	2,514	2,519	2,412	2,380	2,483	2,295	2,401	2,601
Percent	33.6	35.7	36.5	36.1	36.8	39.5	37.8	40.3	43.7
Black male									
Population[1]	967	1,032	1,058	1,059	1,040	1,017	985	964	962
Enrollment[1]	199	225	216	205	241	261	227	278	198
Percent	20.6	21.8	20.4	19.4	23.2	25.7	23.0	28.8	20.6
Black female									
Population[1]	1,148	1,193	1,194	1,177	1,167	1,132	1,107	1,085	1,079
Enrollment[1]	309	312	300	295	298	272	318	326	356
Percent	26.9	26.2	25.1	25.1	25.5	24.0	28.7	30.0	33.0
Hispanic male									
Population[1]	589	611	559	577	508	551	716	710	762
Enrollment[1]	120	125	99	102	105	97	151	176	151
Percent	20.4	20.5	17.7	17.7	20.7	17.6	21.1	24.8	19.8
Hispanic female									
Population[1]	578	642	561	610	579	594	658	662	719

Continued.

College Enrollment in Relation to Population - Part II
[Continued]

	1980	1981	1982	1983	1984	1985	1986	1987	1988
Enrollment[1]	110	127	148	157	164	157	155	132	164
Percent	19.0	19.8	26.4	25.7	28.3	26.4	23.6	19.9	22.8

Source: "U.S. Population and College Enrollment of 18- to 21- Year-Olds, by Selected Race and Gender: 1970-88," *Science and Engineering Indicators — 1989*, 1989, p. 212. Primary source: U.S. Bureau of the Census, *Current Population Reports*, Series P-20 (Washington, DC: U.S. Bureau of the Census), various issues; and unpublished tabulations. *Note:* 1. In thousands.

★ 204 ★
College Enrollment in Relation to Population

Racial/Ethnic Group and Year	Numbers in Thousands			Percent		
	Popula-tion	High School Graduates	College Enrollment	High School Graduates as % of Population	College Enroll-ment as % of Population	College Enrollment as % of High School Graduates
White						
1970	19,6085	15,960	5,305	81.4	27.1	33.2
1975	22,703	18,883	6,116	83.2	26.9	32.4
1980	23,975	19,787	6,334	82.5	26.4	32.0
Black						
1970	2,692	1,602	416	59.5	15.5	26.0
1975	3,213	2,081	665	64.8	20.7	32.0
1980	3,555	2,479	688	69.7	19.4	27.8
Hispanic						
1970	---	---	---	---	---	---
1975	1,446	832	295	57.5	20.4	35.4
1980	1,962	1,054	315	53.7	16.1	29.9

Source: "Population, High School Graduates, and College Enrollment of 18- to 24- Year-Olds, by Racial/Ethnic Group: 1970, 1975, and 1980," *Equality and Excellence: The Educational Status of Black Americans*, 1985, p. 12. Primary source: U.S. Department of Commerce, *Current Population Report*, "School Enrollment — Social and Economic Characteristics of Students," Series P-20, Nos. 222, 303, 362. Published by permission.

★ 205 ★
College Enrollment Rates: Trends - Part I

Numbers in thousands.

Year	High school graduates			
	Total	White[2]	Black[2,3]	Hispanic[3]
1970	2,757	2,461	[4]	[4]
1971	2,872	2,596	[4]	[4]
1972	2,961	2,614	[4]	[4]
1973	3,059	2,707	[4]	[4]
1974	3,101	2,736	[4]	[4]
1975	3,186	2,825	[4]	[4]
1976	2,987	2,640	320	152
1977	3,140	2,768	335	156

Continued.

College Enrollment Rates: Trends - Part I
[Continued]

| Year | High school graduates | | | |
	Total	White[2]	Black[2,3]	Hispanic[3]
1978	3,161	2,750	352	133
1979	3,160	2,776	324	154
1980	3,089	2,682	361	129
1981	3,053	2,626	359	146
1982	3,100	2,644	384	174
1983	2,964	2,496	392	138
1984	3,012	2,514	438	185
1985	2,666	2,241	333	141
1986	2,786	2,307	386	169
1987	2,647	2,207	337	176

Source: "College Enrollment Rates of High School Graduates, by Race/Ethnicity: 1960 to 1987," Digest of Education Statistics, 1989, p. 369. Primary source: American College Testing Program, unpublished tabulations, 1987, derived from statistics collected by the U.S. Department of Labor; and U.S. Department of Labor, unpublished tabulations. (This table was prepared December 1988.) *Notes:* Data based on sample surveys of the civilian population. High school graduate data in this table differ from figures appearing in other tables because of varying survey procedures and coverage. 1. Enrollment in college as of October of each year for individuals age 16 to 24 who graduated from high school during the preceding 12 months. 2. Includes persons of Hispanic origin. 3. Due to the small sample size, data are subject to relatively large amounts of sampling error. 4. Data not available.

★ 206 ★
College Enrollment Rates: Trends - Part II

Numbers in thousands.

| Year | Enrolled in college[1] | | | | | | | |
| | Total | | White[2] | | Black[2,3] | | Hispanic[3] | |
	Number	Percent	Number	Percent	Number	Percent	Number	Percent
1970	1,427	51.8	1,280	52.0	4	4	4	4
1971	1,535	53.4	1,402	54.0	4	4	4	4
1972	1,457	49.2	1,292	49.4	4	4	4	4
1973	1,425	46.6	1,302	48.1	4	4	4	4
1974	1,474	47.5	1,288	47.1	4	4	4	4
1975	1,615	50.7	1,446	51.2	4	4	4	4
1976	1,458	48.8	1,291	48.9	134	41.9	80	52.6
1977	1,590	50.6	1,403	50.7	166	49.6	80	51.3
1978	1,584	50.1	1,378	50.1	161	45.7	57	42.9
1979	1,559	49.3	1,376	49.6	147	45.4	69	44.8
1980	1,524	49.3	1,339	49.9	151	41.8	68	52.7
1981	1,646	53.9	1,434	54.6	154	42.9	76	52.1
1982	1,568	50.6	1,376	52.0	140	36.5	75	43.1
1983	1,562	52.7	1,372	55.0	151	38.5	75	54.3
1984	1,662	55.2	1,455	57.9	176	40.2	82	44.3
1985	1,539	57.7	1,332	59.4	141	42.3	72	51.1

Continued.

College Enrollment Rates: Trends - Part II
[Continued]

| Year | Enrolled in college[1] | | | | | | | |
| | Total | | White[2] | | Black[2,3] | | Hispanic[3] | |
	Number	Percent	Number	Percent	Number	Percent	Number	Percent
1986	1,499	53.8	1,292	56.0	141	36.5	75	44.4
1987	1,503	56.8	1,249	56.6	175	51.9	59	33.5

Source: "College Enrollment Rates of High School Graduates, by Race/Ethnicity: 1960 to 1987," *Demographics, Stands, and Equity,* 1989, p. 369. Primary source: American College Testing Program, unpublished tabulations, 1987, derived from statistics collected by the U.S. Department of Labor; and U.S. Department of Labor, unpublished tabulations. (This table was prepared December 1988.) *Notes:* Data based on sample surveys of the civilian population. High school graduate data in this table differ from figures appearing in other tables because of varying survey procedures and coverage. 1. Enrollment in college as of October of each year for individuals age 16 to 24 who graduated from high school during the preceding 12 months. 2. Includes persons of Hispanic origin. 3. Due to the small sample size, data are subject to relatively large amounts of sampling error. 4. Data not available.

★ 207 ★
College Faculty Initial Ranks: Black TWI Faculty

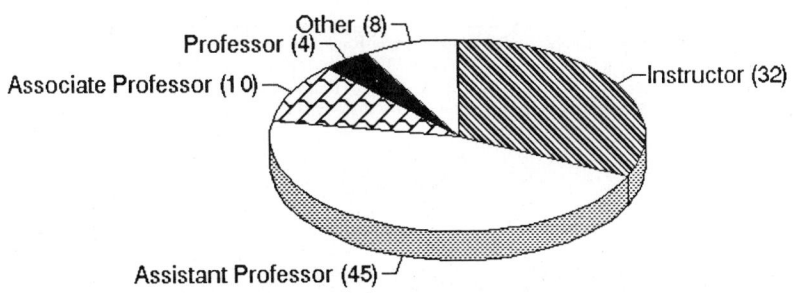

Position	Percent
Instructor	32
Assistant Professor	45
Associate Professor	10
Professor	4
Other	8

Source: "Proportion of Black Faculty at Each Rank at Initial Hire," *Black Faculty in Traditionally White Institutions in Selected Adams States,* 1988, p. 108. Primary source: *Black Faculty in Traditionally White Institutions in Selected Adams States: Characteristics, Experiences and Perceptions,* Southern Education Foundation, Atlanta, GA 30308, 1988. TWI: Traditionally White Institutions. Published by permission.

★ 208 ★
College Faculty Present Ranks: Black TWI Faculty

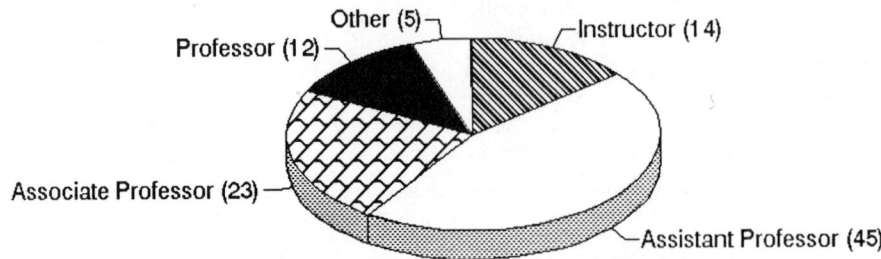

Position	Percent
Instructor	14
Assistant Professor	45
Associate Professor	23
Professor	12
Other	5

Source: "Proportion of Black Faculty at Each Rank, Present Rank," *Black Faculty in Traditionally White Institutions in Selected Adams States,* 1988, p. 109. Primary source: *Black Faculty in Traditionally White Institutions in Selected Adams States: Characteristics, Experiences and Perceptions,* Southern Education Foundation, Atlanta, GA 30308, 1988. TWI: Traditionally White Institutions.

★ 209 ★
College Faculty Salaries: TWI Faculty

Length of Service	Blacks	Whites
Up to 5 years	25,450	27,550
5 to 10 years	25,900	25,350
10 to 15 years	28,400	26,500
15 or more years	29,600	31,600

Source: "Salary by Length of Service: Target State," *Black Faculty in Traditionally White Institutions in Selected Adams States,* 1988, p. 98. Primary source: *Black Faculty in Traditionally White Institutions in Selected Adam States: Characteristics, Experiences and Perceptions,* Southern Education Foundation, Atlanta, GA 30308, 1988. TWI: Traditionally White Institutions Target state system was isolated for comparisons.

★ 210 ★
College Faculty Tenure Status: TWI Faculty

Years Tenured	Black	White
0	67.0	83.3
1	5.2	1.1
2	4.1	1.1
3	4.1	1.1
4	3.1	0
5	7.2	2.2
6	1.0	1.1

Continued.

College Faculty Tenure Status: TWI Faculty
[Continued]

Years Tenured	Black	White
7	1.0	0
8	1.0	0
9	6.2	10.0

Source: "Tenure Status by Race," *Black Faculty in Traditionally White Institutions in Selected Adams States,* 1988, p. 92. Primary source: *Black Faculty in Traditionally White Institutions in Selected Adams States: Characteristics, Experiences and Perceptions,* Southern Education Foundation, Atlanta, GA 30308, 1988. TWI: Traditionally White Institutions.

★ 211 ★
College Faculty Years of Service at TWIs

Number of Years	n = 468	Percent Total Respondents	Female As a %	Male As a %
0	54	11.5	46.3	53.7
1	34	7.3	47.1	52.9
2	38	8.1	55.3	44.7
3	31	6.6	54.8	45.2
4	28	6.0	42.9	57.1
5	25	5.3	56.0	44.0
6	25	5.3	44.0	56.0
7	15	3.2	53.3	46.7
8	26	5.6	42.9	57.1
9	15	3.2	42.3	57.7
10	27	5.8	51.9	48.1
11	12	2.6	50.0	50.0
12	18	3.8	61.1	38.9
13	24	5.1	41.7	58.3
14	23	4.9	56.5	43.5
15	19	4.1	52.6	47.4
16	14	3.0	57.1	42.9
17	14	3.0	7.1	92.9
18	10	2.1	50.0	50.0
19	2	.4	50.0	50.0
20	6	1.3	16.7	83.3
Over 20	7	1.5	13.0	87.8

Source: "Years of Service at TWIs," *Black Faculty in Traditionally White Institutions in Selected Adams States,* 1988, p. 45. Primary Source: *Black Faculty in Traditionally White Institutions in Selected Adams States: Characteristics, Experiences and Perceptions,* Southern Education Foundation, Inc., Atlanta,GA 30308, 1988. TWI: Traditionally White Institutions. Published by permission.

★ 212 ★
College Faculty: UNCF Institutions

UNCF Institutions	1987-88				1988-89			
	Percent Faculty with Doctorate	No. Black	No. Non-Black	Total	Percent Faculty with Doctorate	No. Black	No. Non-Black	Total
Atlanta University	72	60	21	81	93	57	33	90
Barber-Scotia College	45	23	8	31	41	25	9	34
Benedict College	35	69	39	108	31	71	38	109
Bennett College	55	27	15	42	60	29	16	45
Bethune-Cookman College	44	70	67	137	43	63	65	128
Claflin College	48	28	21	50	56	28	22	50
Clark College	46	84	25	109	47	104	22	126
Dillard University	48	75	26	101	45	76	24	100
Edward Waters College	33	35	14	49	28	36	14	50
Fisk University	49	44	28	72	48	38	29	67
Florida Mem. College	70	83	54	137	69	52	33	85
Huston-Tillotson College	42	19	14	33	43	21	14	35
Inter. Denom. Center	73	21	5	26	73	23	3	26
Jarvis Christian College	43	26	14	40	39	31	15	46
Johnson C. Smith University	45	44	31	75	48	43	36	79
Knoxville College	36	20	22	42	28	27	29	56
Lane College	26	23	12	35	29	25	19	44
Lemoyne-Owen College	47	29	18	47	44	39	15	54
Livingstone College	49	39	16	55	32	37	16	53
Miles College	40	31	12	43	43	27	12	39
Morehouse College	65	66	34	100	65	83	27	110
Morris College	43	28	16	44	49	25	20	45
Morris Brown College	57	56	7	63	53	70	9	79
Oakwood College	40	72	15	87	45	73	16	89
Paine College	26	34	35	69	35	39	32	71
Paul Quinn College	43	21	19	40	42	23	20	43
Philander Smith College	35	23	8	31	31	23	13	36
Rust College	43	36	11	47	42	38	12	50
St. Augustine's College	50	59	15	74	52	55	18	73
St. Paul's University	49	34	11	45	57	23	10	33
Shaw University	52	33	27	60	55	35	23	58
Spelman College	64	94	37	131	66	103	31	134
Stillman College	40	25	27	52	44	25	30	55
Talladega College	52	20	22	42	63	21	20	41
Texas College	52	19	10	29	46	17	11	28
Tougaloo College	57	32	31	63	51	53	0	53
Tuskegee University	54	171	107	278	62	188	109	297
Virginia Union University	39	58	22	80	40	57	32	89
Voorhees College	26	27	15	42	30	25	18	43
Wilberforce University	23	26	22	48	26	27	26	53
Wiley College	37	29	1	30	40	31	4	35
Xavier University	63	46	84	130	61	53	100	153

Continued.

College Faculty: UNCF Institutions
[Continued]

UNCF Institutions	1987-88				1988-89			
	Percent Faculty with Doctorate	No. Black	No. Non-Black	Total	Percent Faculty with Doctorate	No. Black	No. Non-Black	Total
Total		1,860	1,038	2,898		1,939	1,045	2,984
Percent	46.5	64.1	35.8		49.4	65.0	35.0	

Source: "Faculty by Race and Degrees, UNCF Institutions, 1987-88 and 1988-89," *UNCF 1989 Statistical Report*, p. 37. Primary source: United Negro College Fund (UNCF), Inc., UNCF 1989 Statistical Report (undated), New York, NY.

★ 213 ★
College Majors on Black/White Campuses

Numbers in percent.

College Major	Total Population	Campus Race	
		Black	White
Natural/Life Science	8.9	8.1	9.8
Entrepreneurial Professions	50.8	57.2	42.9
Human Service Professions	12.0	14.8	8.4
Social Sciences	19.6	16.3	23.8
Humanities	5.6	2.9	9.1
Undecided	3.0	.7	6.0
Total	100.0	100.0	100.0
N	(1544)	(863)	(681)

Source: "College Major by Student Gender and Campus Race," *Gender and Campus Race Differences in Black Student Academic Performance, Racial Attitudes and College Satisfaction*, 1986, p. 50. Primary source: National Study of Black College Students, 1981 and 1983, University of Michigan, Ann Arbor. Published by permission.

★ 214 ★
College Participation Rates: Trends

Figures in thousands.

Years	Women			Men		
	Total Population	H.S. Grad[1]	Enrolled in College	Total Population	H.S. Grad[1]	Enrolled in College
Black						
1982	1,786	1,171	331	2,086	1,572	436
1983	1,807	1,202	31	2,058	1,539	411
1984	1,811	1,272	367	2,052	1,613	419
1985	1,720	1,244	345	1,996	1,565	389
1986	1,699	1,225	340	1,966	1,576	461
White						
1982	11,874	9,611	3,308	12,332	10,333	3,285
1983	11,787	9,411	3,335	12,112	10,233	3,129

Continued.

College Participation Rates: Trends
[Continued]

	Women			Men		
Years	Total Population	H.S. Grad[1]	Enrolled in College	Total Population	H.S. Grad[1]	Enrolled in College
1984	11,521	9,348	3,406	11,826	10,026	3,120
1985	11,108	9,077	3,254	11,524	9,840	3,247
1986	10,803	8,771	3,127	11,205	9,509	3,112
Hispanic						
1982	944	519	141	1,056	634	196
1983	968	476	152	1,057	634	198
1984	956	549	154	1,061	661	207
1985	1,132	659	168	1,091	734	205
1986	1,338	772	224	1,175	737	220

Source: "College Participation Rates for 18- to-24 Year-Old High School Graduates, by Race/ Ethnicity and Sex, 1982 to 1986," *Black Issues in Higher Education*, March 30, 1989, p. 17. Primary source: Seventh Annual Status Report: Minorities In Higher Education, American Council on Education Office of Minority Concerns. *Notes:* 1. The number of high school graduates was calculated by adding the number in this age group as of October of that year and the number of high school graduates not enrolled in college; these figures include individuals who enrolled in college without receiving a high school diploma or GED. Therefore these high school completion figures will be slightly higher than figures that do not include this relatively small population.

★ 215 ★
College Professors' Faculty Ranks

	FACULTY							
	Black				White			
	Male		Female		Male		Female	
Rank	All Insts.	HBCUs	All Insts.	HBCUs	All Insts.	HBCUs	All Insts.	HBCUs
Professors	19.3	23.7	9.2	11.9	34.0	29.8	11.3	25.0
Associate Professors	23.3	23.8	16.9	17.7	25.6	28.4	19.7	18.7
Assistant Professors	28.1	30.9	32.4	38.8	21.0	27.7	30.7	31.7
Instructors	22.0	17.9	31.5	26.6	13.6	11.5	27.3	21.7
Lecturers	2.9	1.9	3.6	2.2	1.5	1.3	3.3	1.9
No Rank	4.4	1.8	6.5	2.8	4.4	1.3	7.7	1.0
Total Percent	100.0	100.0	100.0	100.0	100.0	100.0	100.0	100.0

Source: NAFEO INROADS, February/March - April/May, 1989, p. 14. Primary source: NAFEO Research Institute Staff Analysis of EEO-6 Survey Data from the Equal Employment Commission, 1983. Published by permission.

★ 216 ★
College Students and Computers

As of October. Based on Current Population Survey.

	Total students (1,000)	Place of Use of Computer							
		Number (1,000)				Percent			
		Total[1]	School	Home	Work	Total[1]	School	Home	Work
Total enrolled	12,305	5,461	3,677	1,224	2,261	44.4	29.9	9.9	18.4
White	10,522	4,767	3,151	1,108	2,002	45.3	29.9	10.5	19.0
Black	1,274	468	342	68	177	36.7	26.8	5.3	13.9
Other	509	226	184	48	82	44.4	36.1	9.4	16.7
Hispanic[2]	563	231	171	27	97	41.0	30.4	4.8	17.2
Non-Hispanic	11,742	5,230	3,506	1,197	2,164	44.5	29.9	10.2	18.4

Source: "Computer Use by College Students — Selected Characteristics by Place of Use: 1984," *Statistical Abstract*, 1989, p. 151. Primary source: U.S. Bureau of the Census, *Current Population Reports*, series P-23, No. 155. *Notes:* 1. Total who use computers at home, school, or work. Excludes duplication. 2. Persons of Hispanic origin may be of any race.

★ 217 ★
College Withdrawal and Graduation Rates

Student Characteristic	Total Withdrawal Rate[1]								Graduation Rate for 2-Year College Students	
	4-Year College Students				2-Year College Students					
	Aided		Not Aided		Aided		Not Aided		Aided	Not Aided
Race:										
White	20.9	(15.6)	29.0	(22.5)	34.0	(25.5)	49.1	(42.4)	25.5	12.2
Black	24.4	(18.4)	46.2	(37.5)	43.5	(33.5)	67.1	(58.0)	11.0	4.1

Source: "Total Withdrawal Rate for Two-Year and Four-Year College Students and Graduation Rates for Two-Year College Students by Financial Aid Status, Academic Ability, Race, Educational Aspirations, and SES: 1974," *Equality and Excellence: The Educational Status of Black Americans*, 1985, p. 15. Primary source: National Center for Education Statistics, *Students and Schools*, 1979, Table 3,14. *Notes:* 1. Includes those who withdrew for academic and nonacademic reasons. Figures in parentheses are nonacademic withdrawal rates; subtracting these figures from the ones preceding them will give academic withdrawal rates for that subgroup. Published by permission.

★ 218 ★
College-Bound Seniors - SAT Scores: Trends

For school year ending in year shown.

Type of Test and Characteristic	Unit	1967	1970	1975	1980	1981	1982	1983	1984	1985	1986	1987
Test Scores[1]												
Participants												
Total	1,000	[2]	[2]	996	992	994	989	963	965	977	1,001	1,080
White	Percent	[2]	[2]	86.0	82.1	81.9	81.7	81.1	80.3	81.0	[2]	72.9
Black	Percent	[2]	[2]	7.9	9.1	9.0	8.9	8.8	9.1	7.5	[2]	8.1

Source: "Scholastic Aptitude Test (SAT) Scores and Characteristics of College Bound Seniors: 1967 to 1987, *Statistical Abstract*, 1989, p. 144. Primary source: College Entrance Examination Board, New York, NY, *National College-Bound Senior*, annual. (Copyright). *Notes:* 1. Minimum score, 200; maximum score, 800. 2. Not available.

★ 219 ★
College-Bound Seniors: Science/Math Achievement

Scores on the mathematics portion of the aptitude test, ranging from 200 to 800.

Achievement and SAT-M tests	Total	White	Black	Asian	Native American	Mexican American	Puerto Rican	Latin American
Chemistry	577	578	514	588	542	522	521	556
SAT-M	641	643	561	654	604	594	574	609
Biology	553	556	489	554	516	497	519	539
SAT-M	594	596	513	613	551	531	546	566
Physics	599	600	528	607	557	535	535	568
SAT-M	662	667	583	667	617	624	604	622
Mathematics Level I	549	552	491	575	519	495	504	515
SAT-M (1)	570	577	598	582	537	496	512	525
Mathematics Level II	664	664	597	681	630	604	619	640
SAT-M	655	659	576	658	623	590	603	621

Source: "Achievement Test Scores in Science and Mathematics for College-Bound Seniors, by Gender and Racial/Ethnic Group: 1988," *Women and Minorities in Science and Engineering,* January 1990, p. 126. Primary source: Admissions Testing Program of the College Entrance Examination Board, 1988 PROFILES OF SAT AND ACHIEVEMENT TEST TAKERS, (Princeton, N.J.: Educational Testing Service, 1988). Published by permission.

★ 220 ★
College-Bound Seniors: Science/Math Advanced Placement Scores

Advanced placement test	Total	White	Black	Asian	Native American	Mexican American	Puerto Rican	Latin American
Biology	3.05	3.04	2.17	3.39	2.61	2.31	2.72	2.67
Chemistry	2.94	2.94	1.99	3.14	2.64	2.42	2.69	2.38
Physics B	2.85	2.85	1.97	2.99	2.12	2.10	3.06	2.58
Physics C-Mechanics	3.29	3.31	2.34	3.36	3.00	1.98	2.89	2.73
Physics C-Electricity and Magnetism	3.29	3.28	2.69	3.34	3.00	2.06	2.50	3.36
Mathematics/Calculus AB	3.10	3.11	2.16	3.34	2.74	2.67	2.47	2.77
Mathematics/Calculus BC	3.53	3.50	2.98	3.67	2.64	2.59	3.21	3.18
Computer Science AB	2.56	2.64	1.81	2.47	2.12	2.13	1.57	2.04
Computer Science A	2.87	2.94	1.95	2.88	2.75	2.45	1.75	2.34

Source: "Advanced Placement Test Scores in Science and Mathematics for College-Bound Seniors, by Gender and Racial/Ethnic Group: 1988," *Women and Minorites in Science and Engineering,* January 1990, p. 127. Primary source: Advanced Placement Program of the College Entrance Examination Board, 1988 ADVANCED PLACEMENT PROGRAM, NATIONAL SUMMARY REPORTS, (Princeton, N.J.: Educational Testing Service, 1988). *Notes:* Score range is from 1 to 5: (a) 1 = no recommendation for college credit; (b) 2 = possibly qualified; (c) 3 = qualified; (d) 4 = well qualified; and (e) 5 = extremely well qualified. Published by permission.

★ 221 ★
Completing, Transferring, or Withdrawing from College

Characteristics	4-Year College			2-Year College		
	Persister	Transfer	Completer/Withdrawer[2]	Persister	Transfer	Completer/Withdrawer[2]
All students[1]	75	15[3]	10	59	16[4]	26
Racial/ethnic group:						
Hispanic	66	17	17	65	11	24
Black	71	14	15	61	15	24
White	75	15	9	57	16	27
Asian American	86	12	2	70	21	9
American Indian	81	11	9	61	21	18

Source: "Percentage of Two-and Four-Year College Entrants who had Persisted, Transferred, Completed Short-Term Programs, or Wtihdrawn, by Selected Student Characteristics: February 1982," *Equality and Excellence: The Educational Status of Black Americans,* 1985, p. 16. Primary source: National Center for Education Statistics, High School and Beyond data base, *Two Years After High School: A Capsule Description of 1980 Seniors, p. 9. Notes:* 1. Percentages are based on those individuals who entered college before June 1981. 2. Students who had completed short-term programs(i.e., completers) and students who had left school without completing programs (i.e., withdrawers) were not differentiated in this table because the information needed for so doing was not available in the HS&B first follow-up survey. 3. Includes 10 percent 4- to-4 year college transfers and 5 percent 4- to-2 year college transfers. 4. Includes 8 percent 2- to-2 year college transfers and 8 percent 2- to-4 year college transfers. . Published by permission.

★ 222 ★
Courses Taken by College-Bound High School Seniors

Coursework	Percent							
	Total	White	Black	Asian	Native American	Mexican American	Puerto Rican	Latin American
Natural science								
Biology	97	97	96	95	97	96	96	96
Chemistry	78	80	70	86	70	71	73	76
Physics	42	43	31	63	30	32	41	42
Honors course	20	21	12	29	11	18	12	19
Social Science								
Anthropology	3	3	2	3	3	2	3	3
Economics	46	45	49	50	46	69	35	53
Psychology	29	31	20	22	28	21	22	26
Sociology	17	18	13	11	17	10	16	14
Honors course	19	20	13	26	11	17	12	19
Mathematics								
Algebra	97	97	96	96	96	98	95	96
Geometry	93	94	85	95	89	92	88	92
Trigonometry	55	57	43	73	43	43	50	54
Precalculus	28	29	16	45	18	21	24	25
Calculus	18	18	9	36	9	12	10	16
Honors course	22	23	13	34	12	20	15	20

Source: "Percentage of College-Bound Seniors who Took Natual Science, Social Science, or Mathematics Coursework in High School, by Gender and Racial/Ethnic Group: 1988," *Women and Minorities in Science and Engineering,* January 1990, p. 124. Primary source: Admissions Testing Program of the College Entrance Examination Board, COLLEGE-BOUND SENIORS, 1988 PROFILE OF SAT AND ACHIEVEMENT TEST TAKERS, (Princeton, N.J.: Educational Testing Service, 1988). Published by permission.

★ 223 ★
Current TWI Faculty: Service at TBIs

Number of Years	n = 462	% Total Respondents	Female As a %	Male As a %
0	330	71.4	46.7	53.3
1	27	5.8	48.1	51.9
2	15	3.2	66.7	33.3
3	11	2.4	36.4	63.6
4	9	1.9	77.8	22.2
5	10	2.2	40.0	60.0
6	7	1.5	57.1	42.9
7	6	1.3	16.7	83.3
8	9	1.9	44.4	55.6
9	5	1.1	60.0	40.0
10	10	2.2	40.0	60.0
11	3	.6	33.3	66.7
12	2	.4	0	100.0
13	4	.9	75.0	25.0
14	2	.4	50.0	50.0
15	0	0	0	0
16	0	0	0	0
17	3	.6	100.0	0
18	1	.2	100.0	0
19	1	.2	0	100.0
20	0	0	0	0
Over 20	7	1.5	86.6	13.3

Source: "Years of Service at TBIs," *Black Faculty at Traditionally White Institutions in Selected Adams States*, 1988, p. 46. Primary source: *Black Faculty in Traditionally White Institutions in Selected Adams States: Characteristics, Experiences and Perceptions*, Southern Education Foundation, Atlanta, GA 30308, 1988. TWI: Traditionally White Institutions. TBI: Traditionally Black Institutions.

★ 224 ★
Degrees Awarded

Characteristic	All Fields				1987							Social Sciences	
	1975	1980	1985	1986	All fields[1]	Engineering	Physical sciences[2]	Mathematics	Computer sciences	Psychology	Biological sciences[3]	Economics	Other social sciences[4]
White[5]	86.7	84.6	86.2	86.6	86.2	76.2	87.8	80.6	83.3	89.5	87.9	83.4	84.8
Asian[5]	3.6	4.2	4.3	4.3	4.8	17.1	6.0	10.4	9.5	1.7	5.3	8.7	4.7
Blacks and others[5]	4.9	6.3	7.2	7.0	6.8	3.4	3.4	5.5	3.2	7.4	4.3	5.6	7.6

Source: "Doctorates Conferred, by Recipients' Characteristics, 1975 to 1987, and by Selected Science and Engineering Fields, 1987," *Statistical Abstract*, 1989, p. 584. Primary source: U.S. National Science Foundation, Division of Science Resources Studies, *Survey of Earned Doctorates. Notes:* 1. Includes other fields, not shown separately. 2. Astronomy, physics, chemistry, and earth sciences. 3. Biochemistry, botany, microbiology, physiology, zoology, and related fields. 4. Anthropology, sociology, political science, and international relations. 5. Data on race limited to U.S. citizens and non-U.S. citizens with permanent government visas.

★ 225 ★
Degrees Awarded at UNCF Institutions

Field of Study	Number	Percent of Total
Afro-American Studies	4	<1
Agriculture	25	<1
Architecture	27	<1
Art	28	<1
Biological Science	314	5
Business:		
Accounting	350	6
Business Administartion	630	11
Banking & Finance	106	2
Management	289	5
Marketing	131	2
Office Administration	39	<1
Other	98	2
Total Business	1,643	29
Communications:		
General Communications	50	<1
Journalism	24	<1
Radio/TV/Film	89	2
Speech/Drama	14	<1
Other	77	1
Total Communications	254	4
Computer Science	337	6
Criminal Justice	169	3
Education:		
Business Education	15	<1
Child Development	65	1
Educational Administration	12	<1
Special Education	19	<1
Elementary Education	148	2
Physical Education	97	2
Social Education	7	<1
Other	203	4
Total Education	466	10
Engineering:		
Electrical Engineering	69	1
Mechanical Engineering	24	<1
Other	9	<1
Total Engineering	101	2
English	176	3
Foreign Languages	8	<1
Health Professions:		
Medical Technician	16	<1
Nursing	64	1
Nutrition	17	<1
Veterinary Medicine	54	<1
Other	189	3

Continued.

Degrees Awarded at UNCF Institutions
[Continued]

Field of Study	Number	Percent of Total
Total Health Professions	340	6
Home Economics	17	<1
Library Science	28	<1
Mathematics	185	3
Music	48	<1
Physical Sciences:		
Chemistry	130	2
Physics	48	<1
Other	37	<1
Total Physical Science	215	4
Psychology	259	4
Religion/Philosophy	149	3
Social Sciences:		
General Social Science	3	<1
Economics	80	1
History	49	<1
Political Science	192	3
Social Work	137	2
Sociology	221	4
Urban Studies	11	<1
Other	52	<1
Total Social Sciences	745	13
Other Majors	86	2
GRAND TOTAL	5,727	100

Source: "Degrees Awarded at UNCF Institutions by Subject Area, 1987-88, *UNCF 1989 Statistical Report*, p. 9. Primary source: United Negro College Fund, Inc., UNCF 1989 Statistical Report, (undated), New York, NY. UNCF: United Negro College Fund.

★ 226 ★
Disability Status of Postsecondary Students

Selected student characteristics	Disabled students[1]	Nondisabled students
Race/ethnicity	100.0	100.0
White, non-Hispanic	78.5	78.2
Black, non-Hispanic	8.0	9.0
Hispanic	7.5	6.5
Asian American	4.1	5.5
American Indian	1.9	.8

Source: "Students Enrolled in Postsecondary Institutions, by Disability Status and Selected Student Characteristics: Fall 1986," *Digest of Educational Statistics*, 1989, p. 196. Primary source: U.S. Department of Education, National Center for Education Statistics, "The 1987 National Postsecondary Student Aid Study." (This table was prepared March 1989.) *Notes:* 1. Disabled students are those who reported that they had one or more of the following conditions: a specific learning disability, a visual handicap, hard of hearing, deafness, a speech disability, an orthopedic handicap, or a health impairment.

★ 227 ★
Doctoral Major of TWI Faculty

Major	Number	Percent
Education	93	20.1
Nursing	24	5.1
Psychology	24	5.1
English	19	4.0
Social Work	18	3.8
Business	16	3.4
Music	13	2.7
Law	12	2.5
History	12	2.5
Biology	12	2.5
Math	11	2.3
Social Science	9	1.9
Sociology	8	1.7
Political Science	8	1.7
Agriculture	7	1.5
Engineering	6	1.3
Chemistry	4	.8
Architecture	3	.6
Physical Education	2	.4
Zoology	1	.2
Foreign Language	1	.2
Physics	0	0
Computer Science	0	0

Source: "Selected Majors of Respondents - Doctoral Degree," *Black Faculty in Traditionally White Institutions in Selected Adams States*, 1988, p. 34. Primary source: *Black Faculty in Traditionally White Institutions in Selected Adams States: Characteristics, Experiences and Perceptions*, Southern Education Foundation, Atlanta, GA 30308, 1988. TWI: Traditionally White Institutions.

★ 228 ★
Doctorate Recipients: Trends

Year and sex of student	Total	White non-Hispanic	Black non-Hispanic	Hispanic	Asian or Pacific Islander	American Indian/ Alaskan Native	Non-resident alien
1976-77							
Total[2]	33,126	26,851	1.253	522	658	95	3,747
Men	25,036	20,032	766	383	540	67	3,248
Women	8,090	6,819	487	139	118	28	499
1978-79							
Total[3]	32,675	26,138	1,268	439	811	104	3,915
Men	23,488	18,433	734	294	646	69	3,312
Women	9,187	7,705	534	145	165	35	639
1980-81							
Total[4]	32,839	25,908	1,265	456	877	130	4,203
Men	22,595	17,310	694	277	655	95	3,564
Women	10,244	8,598	571	179	222	35	639
1984-85							
Total[5]	32,307	23,934	1,154	677	1,106	119	5,317
Men	21,296	15,017	561	431	802	64	4,421
Women	11,011	8,917	593	246	304	55	896
1986-87							
Total[6]	34,033	24,435	1,060	750	1,097	104	6,587
Men	22,059	14,813	488	439	795	58	5,466
Women	11,974	9,622	572	311	302	46	1,121

Source: "Doctor's Degrees Conferred by Institutions of Higher Education, by Racial/Ethnic Group and Sex of Student: 1976-77 to 1986-87," *Digest of Educational Statistics*, 1989, p. 248. Primary source: U.S. Department of Education, National Center for Educational Statistics, "Degrees and Other Formal Awards Conferred" surveys, and Integrated Postsecondary Education Data System (IPEDS), "Completions" survey. (This table was prepared June 1989.) *Notes:* 1. Includes Ph.D., Ed.D., and comparable degrees at the doctoral level. Excludes first-professional degrees. 2. Excludes 106 men whose racial/ethnic group was not available. 3. Excludes 53 men and 2 women whose racial/ethnic group was not available. 4. Excludes 116 men and 3 women whose racial/ethnic group was not available. 5. Excludes 404 men and 232 women whose racial/ethnic group was not available. 6. Excludes 40 men and 47 women whose racial/ethnic group was not available. Data are preliminary.

★ 229 ★
Doctorates in Education: Trends

Item	1977-78	1978-79	1979-80	1980-81	1981-82	1982-83	1983-84	1984-85	1985-86	1986-87
Number of doctorates	7,190	7,370	7,576	7,489	7,226	7,147	6,780	6,717	6,602	6,447
Racial/ethnic group (percent) [1]										
American Indian	0.8	0.9	0.7	0.6	0.4	0.6	0.5	0.6	0.4	0.6
Asian	2.8	2.9	3.2	3.4	3.9	4.2	4.2	4.2	3.8	4.1
Black	9.5	9.0	9.2	9.3	9.9	8.8	9.3	9.1	8.3	7.3
Mexican-American	[2]	[2]	0.7	1.1	1.1	1.1	1.1	0.8	1.3	1.1
Puerto Rican	[2]	[2]	0.3	0.5	0.6	0.7	0.5	1.1	0.4	0.8
Other Hispanic	[2]	[2]	1.4	1.1	1.3	1.5	1.2	1.6	1.8	1.3

Continued.

Doctorates in Education: Trends
[Continued]

Item	1977-78	1978-79	1979-80	1980-81	1981-82	1982-83	1983-84	1984-85	1985-86	1986-87
White	77.3	76.4	77.7	77.3	77.3	78.5	78.2	76.5	76.3	76.7
Other and unknown	7.1	7.9	6.8	6.8	5.4	4.7	5.0	6.0	7.7	8.0

Source: "Statistical Profile of Persons Receiving Doctor's Degrees in Education: 1977-78 to 1986-87," *Digest of Education Statistics*, 1989, p. 270. Primary source: National Academy of Sciences, National Research Council, Office of Scientific and Engineering Personnel, Doctorate Records File. (This table was prepared March 1989). *Notes:* The National Research Council's classification of degrees by field differs somewhat from that in most publications of the National Center for Education Statistics (NCES). The number of degrees also differs slightly from that reported in the NCES "Degrees and Other Formal Awards Conferred" survey. Because of rounding, percents may not add to 100.0. 1. Longitudinal comparisons by race/ethnicity should be done with extreme care, due to periodic changes in the survey. 2. Hispanic subcategories were not collected until 1980. Published by permission.

★ 230 ★
Educational Aspirations on Black/White College Campuses

Numbers in percent.

Educational Aspirations	Total Population	Campus Race	
		Black	White
B.A. Degree	31.5	31.2	31.8
M.A. Degree	38.5	43.6	31.7
J.D. or M.D. Degree	16.7	7.8	28.7
Ph.D. Degree	13.3	17.4	7.8
Total	100.0	100.0	100.0
N	(1495)	(860)	(638)

Source: "Educational Aspirations by Student Gender and Campus Race," *Gender and Campus Race Differences in Black Student Academic Performance, Racial Attitudes and College Satisfaction*, 1986, p. 61. Primary source: National Study of Black College Students, 1981 and 1983, University of Michigan, Ann Arbor. *Note:* Total N does not match "Campus Race" total. Published by permission.

★ 231 ★
Educational Attainment after High School

Socioeconomic status in 1980 and race/ethnicity	Highest educational attainment of 1980 high school in 1986						
	Total	No high school diploma[2]	High school diploma	License[3]	Associate degree	Bachelor's degree	Graduate/ professional degree
Lower 25 percent							
White, non-Hispanic	100.0	0.9	75.1	12.2	5.0	6.6	0.3
Black, non-Hispanic	100.0	1.4	73.0	12.7	5.1	7.7	0.1
Hispanic	100.0	1.6	73.9	11.8	7.8	4.9	[4]
Asian	100.0	[4]	53.4	17.3	15.7	12.0	1.6
Middle 50 percent							
White, non-Hispanic	100.0	0.3	62.0	13.0	8.0	16.3	0.4
Black, non-Hispanic	100.0	0.3	67.5	14.7	6.5	10.7	0.3
Hispanic	100.0	1.0	67.0	14.7	6.5	10.7	0.2
Asian	100.0	[4]	51.1	11.7	11.1	26.1	[4]
Upper 25 percent							
White, non-Hispanic	100.0	[4]	44.9	8.6	6.2	38.2	2.2
Black, non-Hispanic	100.0	[4]	56.3	12.4	5.4	25.5	0.4

Continued.

Educational Attainment after High School
[Continued]

Socioeconomic status in 1980 and race/ethnicity	Highest educational attainment of 1980 high school in 1986						
	Total	No high school diploma[2]	High school diploma	License[3]	Associate degree	Bachelor's degree	Graduate/ professional degree
Hispanic	100.0	0.3	60.0	11.4	9.6	18.0	0.7
Asian	100.0	[4]	42.9	6.5	4.8	40.0	5.9

Source: "Highest Level of Education Attained by 1980 High School Seniors, by Socioeconomic Status and Race/Ethnicity: Spring 1986," *Digest of Educational Statistics*, 1989, p. 278. Primary source: U.S. Department of Education, National Center for Educational Statistics, High School and Beyond survey. (This table was prepared September 1987.) *Notes:* Because of rounding, percents may not add to 100.0. 1. Socioeconomic status was measured by a composite score on parental education, family income, father's occupation, and household characteristics in 1980. 2. Seniors who dropped out of high school after spring 1980 survey and had not completed high school by 1986. 3. Includes persons who earned a certificate for completing a program of study. 4. Less than .05 percent.

★ 232 ★
Educational Attainment at Age 18 and Over

In thousands.

Age and race	Total Population[1]	Elementary level		High school		College		
		Less than 8 years	8 years	1 to 3 years	4 years	1 to 3 years	4 years	5 years or more
Total[1]								
18 and over	177,677	10,876	8,403	22,464	70,194	32,932	19,622	13,188
18 and 19 years old	7,221	88	132	2,610	3,453	935	3	---
20 to 24 years old	18,840	446	312	2,041	7,801	6,213	1,749	277
25 years old and over	151,616	10,341	7,959	17,813	58,940	25,784	17,870	12,911
25 to 29 years old	21,523	502	330	2,205	9,093	4,514	3,483	1,397
30 to 34 years old	21,446	635	288	1,877	8,796	4,554	3,345	1,951
35 to 39 years old	18,854	697	285	1,523	7,162	4,164	2,772	2,251
40 to 49 years old	28,604	1,203	735	2,854	11,345	5,261	3,636	3,571
50 to 59 years old	21,870	1,673	1,285	3,080	8,943	3,047	2,049	1,793
60 to 69 years old	20,595	2,212	1,888	3,309	8,039	2,475	1,499	1,174
70 years old and over	18,724	3,417	3,148	2,967	5,562	1,769	1,086	773
White[2]								
18 and over	152,644	8,299	7,262	18,119	61,090	28,640	17,402	11,833
18 and 19 years old	5,927	72	95	2,036	2,905	817	3	---
20 to 24 years old	15,625	389	245	1,563	6,390	5,224	1,557	259
25 years old and over	131,092	7,839	6,923	14,520	51,795	22,599	15,842	11,574
25 to 29 years old	18,070	437	269	1,710	7,637	3,764	3,031	1,222
30 to 34 years old	18,078	531	236	1,431	7,415	3,857	2,922	1,686
35 to 39 years old	16,059	582	228	1,142	6,073	3,598	2,421	2,016
40 to 49 years old	24,683	942	595	2,240	9,857	4,624	3,197	3,228
50 to 59 years old	19,001	1,247	1,091	2,465	8,055	2,730	1,824	1,589
60 to 69 years old	18,308	1,550	1,617	2,830	7,465	2,350	1,413	1,085
70 years old and over	16,894	2,552	2,887	2,702	5,294	1,678	1,034	747

Continued.

Educational Attainment at Age 18 and Over
[Continued]

| Age and race | Total Population[1] | Elementary level | | High school | | College | | |
		Less than 8 years	8 years	1 to 3 years	4 years	1 to 3 years	4 years	5 years or more
Black[2]								
18 and over	19,549	2,067	961	3,877	7,541	3,173	1,227	702
18 and 19 years old	1,043	15	30	486	432	79	---	---
20 to 24 years old	2,576	49	61	424	1,195	712	125	9
25 years old and over	15,930	2,003	870	2,966	5,914	2,382	1,102	693
25 to 29 years old	2,701	26	48	444	1,279	573	254	78
30 to 34 years old	2,571	76	37	397	1,167	532	248	113
35 to 39 years old	2,122	71	38	336	931	432	196	119
40 to 49 years old	2,913	174	119	557	1,216	455	201	190
50 to 59 years old	2,250	345	165	561	706	234	120	118
60 to 69 years old	1,861	575	227	442	421	95	49	52
70 years old and over	1,512	736	236	229	194	61	34	23
Hispanic origin[3]								
18 and over	12,605	3,067	803	2,108	3,854	1,696	702	373
18 and 19 years old	690	45	33	304	260	48	---	---
20 to 24 years old	1,975	247	88	389	780	390	68	12
25 years old and over	9,940	2,775	682	1.415	2,813	1,258	634	361
25 to 29 years old	2,044	327	90	353	701	342	165	65
30 to 34 years old	1,741	359	74	243	538	305	150	70
35 to 39 years old	1,553	372	71	217	495	229	97	73
40 to 49 years old	1,857	519	124	262	553	215	106	79
50 to 59 years old	1,322	498	132	180	297	96	70	50
60 to 69 years old	852	376	98	118	156	55	31	17
70 years old and over	571	324	93	42	74	16	15	8

Source: "Years of School Completed by Persons Age 18 and Over, by Age, Sex, and Race/Ethnicity: 1988," *Digest of Education Statistics,* 189, p. 16. Primary Source: U.S. Department of Commerce, Bureau of the Census, Current Population Survey, unpublished data. (This table was prepared December 1988.) *Notes:* Data are based on sample surveys of the noninstitutional population. Although cells with fewer than 75,000 people are subject to relatively wide sampling variation, they are included in the table to permit various types of aggregations. Because of rounding, details may not add to totals. 1. Civilian noninstitutional population. 2. Includes persons of Hispanic origin. 3. Persons of Hispanic origin may be of any race.

★ 233 ★
Educational Attainment of 1980 High School Graduates

| Student and school chrarcterisitcs | Highest educational attainment of 1980 high school seniors in 1986 | | | | | | |
	Total	No high school diploma[1]	High school diploma	License[2]	Associate degree	Bachelor's degree	Graduate/pro-fessional degree
Total	100.0	0.9	61.8	11.9	6.5	18.2	0.7
Race/ethnicity							
White, non-Hispanic	100.0	0.8	60.0	11.5	6.6	20.2	0.9
Black, non-Hispanic	100.0	1.2	69.4	13.9	5.3	9.9	0.2
Hispanic	100.0	1.7	70.2	13.8	7.3	6.8	0.1

Continued.

Educational Attainment of 1980 High School Graduates
[Continued]

Student and school chrarcterisitcs		Highest educational attainment of 1980 high school seniors in 1986					
	Total	No high school diploma[1]	High school diploma	License[2]	Associate degree	Bachelor's degree	Graduate/pro-fessional degree
Asian	100.0	[3]	49.6	12.6	8.7	27.3	1.7
American Indian	100.0	[3]	61.3	18.6	9.3	10.8	[3]

Source: "Highest Level of Education Attained by 1980 High School Seniors, by Selected Student and School Characterisitcs: Spring 1986," *Digest of Educational Statistics*, 1989, p. 277. Primary source: U.S. Department of Education, National Center for Education Statistics, High School and Beyond survey. (This table was prepared September 1987.) *Notes:* Beacuse of rounding, percents may not add to 100.0. 1. Seniors who dropped out of high school after spring 1980 survey had not completed high school by 1986. 2. Persons who earned a certificate for completing a program of study. Less than .05 percent.

★ 234 ★
Elementary and Secondary School Students

	Population Total 1987	Public Elementary and Secondary Education			
		Public K-12 Students 1987	Percent Minority		Change in High School Grads 1985-1990
			1980	1987	
United States	243,308	40,200	26.8	30.0	-2.4
SREB States	82,797	14,406	32.2	35.0	3.1
Alabama	4,086	731	33.6	38.0	-1.6
Arkansas	2,386	437	23.5	25.0	2.2
Florida	11,962	1,664	32.2	35.0	15.9
Georgia	6,244	1,159	34.3	39.0	-1.9
Kentucky	3,733	643	9.1	11.0	0.9
Louisiana	4,504	795	43.5	43.0	-5.8
Maryland	4,532	680	33.5	40.0	-10.1
Mississippi	2,643	506	51.6	56.0	0.7
North Carolina	6,422	1,085	31.8	32.0	-2.9
Oklahoma	3,295	599	20.8	21.0	1.2
South Carolina	3,402	615	43.5	45.0	3.8
Tennessee	4,848	819	24.5	23.0	7.0
Texas	16,937	3,351	46.1	49.0	9.8
Virginia	5,883	979	27.5	27.0	1.9
West Virginia	1,902	344	4.3	4.0	-2.5

Source: "Population, Education, and Economy," *NAFEO INROADS*, December-January 1990, p. 4. Primary source: Southern Regional Education Board (SREB) Fact Book on Higher Education, 1988. Published by permission.

★ 235 ★
Elementary/Secondary Students and Computer Use

As of October. Based on Current Population Survey.

	Total students (1,000)	Place of Use of Computer							
		Number (1,000)				Percent			
Item		Total[1]	School	Home	Both	Total[1]	School	Home	Both
Total enrolled	44,221	15,248	12,335	5,425	2,512	34.5	27.9	12.3	5.7
White	35,860	13,483	10,850	4,939	2,306	37.6	30.3	13.8	6.4
Black	6,760	1,252	1,046	346	140	18.5	15.5	5.1	2.1
Other	1,601	513	439	140	66	32.0	27.4	8.7	4.1
Hispanic[2]	3,653	714	636	127	49	19.5	17.4	3.5	1.3
Non-Hispanic	40,568	14,534	11,699	5,298	2,463	35.8	28.8	13.1	6.1

Source: "Computer Use by Students, Grades K-12 — Selected Characteristics by Place of Use: 1984," *Statistical Abstract*, p. 141. Primary source: U.S. bureau of the Census, *Current Population Reports*, series P-23, No. 155 and unpublished data. *Notes:* 1. Total who use computers at home or at school. Excludes duplication. 2. Persons of Hispanic origin may be of any race.

★ 236 ★
Engineering Enrollment

	Women		Blacks		Hispanics[1]		American Indians		Asian/ Pacific	
	1987	1988	1987	1988	1987	1988	1987	1988	1987	1988
Full Time Undergraduates:										
First Year	15,004	15,837	6,145	7,075	4,465	4,872	354	433	7,074	7,510
Second Year	11,820	11,465	3,777	3,911	3,424	3,221	215	209	6,015	6,174
Third Year	11,775	11,356	3,298	3,357	3,396	3,315	228	212	6,984	7,101
Fourth Year	15,640	15,011	3,892	3,697	4,456	4,228	325	302	9,441	9,227
Fifth Year	1,232	1,103	188	187	1,390	1,391	14	8	616	340
Total Full Time Undergraduates	55,471	54,772	17,300	18,227	17,131	17,027	1,136	1,164	30,130	30,352
Part Time Undergraduates	4,810	5,616	1,842	2,178	1,122	1,673	109	120	2,665	3,699
Full Time Graduate Students										
M.S. or Prof. Engrg.	5,546	5,813	626	651	878	752	66	70	2,818	2,875
Doctorate	2,533	2,960	165	215	254	310	25	31	1,497	1,789
Total Full Time graduates	8,079	8,773	791	866	1,132	1,062	91	101	4,315	4,664
Part Time Graduate Students	5,836	6,545	888	899	700	697	56	70	3,590	3,645

Source: "Women, Minorities, and Foreign Nationals Enrolled in Engineering, 1987- 1988." *Engineering Manpower Bulletin* 95, May 1989, p. 3. American Association of Engineering Societies. *Notes:* 1. Includes 4,150 full-time undergraduates, 118 part-time undergraduates, 113 full-time graduate students, and two part-time graduate students at the University of Puerto Rico in 1987, and 3,889 full-time undergraduates, 99 part-time undergraduates, 102 full-time graduate students, and one part-time graduate student at the same institution in 1988.

★ 237 ★
Enrollment

As of October, except as noted. Covers civilian noninstitutional population 14 to 24 years old.

Item and Year	All Persons			Male			Female		
	Total[1]	White	Black	Total[1]	White	Black	Total[1]	White	Black
College enrollment (1,000): 1960[2]	2,279	2,138	141[3]	1,365	1,297	68[3]	914	841	73[3]
1970	6,065	5,535	437	3,461	3,213	202	2,604	2,322	236
1980	7,475	6,546	718	3,700	3,303	292	3,778	3,243	426
1985	7,799	6,729	755	3,880	3,374	355	3,917	3,357	400
1986	7,613	6,426	820	3,739	3,206	350	3,874	3,221	471
Percent of high school students enrolled:									
1960[2]	23.8	24.3	18.7[3]	30.4	31.1	21.1[3]	18.0	18.1	16.9[3]
1970	33.3	33.9	26.7	41.8	42.9	29.5	26.3	26.3	24.7
1980	32.3	32.5	28.3	33.8	34.3	27.0	30.9	30.9	29.2
1985	34.3	35.0	26.5	36.0	36.6	28.2	32.8	33.6	25.1
1986	34.4	34.6	28.8	35.7	36.1	28.2	33.3	33.3	29.4
Percent of high school graduates enrolled in college or completed 1 or more years of college: 1960[2]	40.4	41.0	32.5[3]	46.1	47.1	33.5[3]	35.3	35.6	31.8[3]
1970	52.3	53.4	40.0	59.2	60.8	41.2	46.5	47.1	39.0
1980	51.1	51.4	46.2	51.4	51.8	44.4	51.0	51.0	47.5
1985	54.3	55.3	43.8	54.6	55.5	43.5	54.0	55.2	43.9
1986	54.8	55.3	47.4	54.2	55.0	43.7	55.3	55.6	50.2

Source: "College Enrollment and Percent of High School Graduates Enrolled in, or Completed One or More Years of College, by Sex and Race: 1960 to 1986," *Statistical Abstract*, 1989, p. 147. Primary source: U.S. Bureau of the Census: *U.S. Census of Population: 1960*, vol. I; *Characteristics of the Population*, part 1; *Current Population Reports*, Series P-20, No. 429. *Notes:* 1. Includes other races, not shown separately. 2. As of April. 3. Black and other races.

★ 238 ★
Enrollment

In thousands. As of October. Covers civilian noninstitutional population, 14 years old and over. Degree credit enrollment only.

Sex and Race	1972	1975	1978	1979	1980	1981[1]	1981[2]	1982	1983	1984	1985	1986
Total	9,095	10,880	11,140	11,380	11,387	11,814	12,127	12,309	12,320	12,304	12,524	12,402
White	8,147	9,547	9,662	9,956	9,926	10,166	10,352	10,550	10,566	10,521	10,782	10,497
Male	4,723	5,263	4,913	4,823	4,804	4,900	5,011	5,078	5,162	5,111	5,101	4,987
Female	3,427	4,285	4,748	5,132	5,123	5,265	5,342	5,474	5,404	5,410	5,680	5,510
Black and other races	949	1,333	1,479	1,424	1,461	1,648	1,775	1,758	1,754	1,784	1,742	1,905
Male	496	648	668	657	626	735	814	821	848	878	805	861
Female	450	684	811	768	834	913	961	936	906	906	938	1,044

Source: "College Enrollment, by Sex, Age, and Race: 1972 to 1986," *Statistical Abstract*, 1989, p. 147. Primary source: U.S. Bureau of the Census, *Current Population Reports*, series P-20, No. 429 and earlier reports; and unpublished data. *Notes:* 1. Population controls based on 1970 census; see text, sections 1 and 4. 2. Population controls based on 1980 census; see text, sections 1 and 4.

★ 239 ★
Enrollment

As of October. Civilian noninstitutional population. Includes public and nonpublic nursery school and kindergarten programs. Excludes 5 year olds enrolled in elementary school. The method of identifying Hispanic children was changed in 1980 from allocation based on status of mother to status reported for each child. The number of Hispanic children using the new method is larger. Based on Current Population Survey.

Item	1972	1975	1979	1980	1981	1982	1983	1984	1985	1986
Number of children (1,000)										
White	3,542	4,105	3,786	3,994	4,038	4,165	4,430	4,411	4,757	4,851
Black	619	731	750	725	725	769	758	845	919	892
Hispanic[2]	3	3	289	370	399	368	406	380	496	593
3 years old	535	683	746	857	891	928	1,005	1,004	1,035	1,041
4 years old	1,121	1,418	1,393	1,423	1,442	1,496	1,619	1,603	1,765	1,772
5 years old	2,575	2,852	2,525	2,598	2,604	2,681	2,762	2,872	3,065	3,157
Enrollment Rate										
Total enrolled	41.6	48.6	51.1	52.5	51.2	51.7	52.5	51.6	54.6	55.0
White										
Black	43.0	48.1	53.3	51.8	50.0	52.0	48.8	51.3	55.8	54.1
Hispanic[2]	3	3	40.3	43.3	40.2	41.2	42.7	41.6	43.3	47.8
3 years old	15.5	21.5	24.6	27.3	27.3	27.4	28.1	27.8	28.8	28.9
4 years old	33.5	40.5	45.4	46.3	44.9	45.7	47.4	41.8	49.1	49.0
5 years old	76.1	81.3	83.5	84.7	82.1	83.4	84.6	83.9	86.5	86.7

Source: "Preprimary School Enrollment - Summary: 1972 to 1986," *Statistical Abstract*, 1989, p. 129. Primary source: U.S. Bureau of the Census, *Current Population Reports*, series P-20, No. 318; and unpublished data. *Notes:* 1. Includes races not shown separately. 2. Persons of Hispanic origin may be of any race. 3. Not available.

★ 240 ★
Enrollment

As of October. Civilian noninstitutional population. Includes public and nonpublic nursery school and kindergarten programs. Excludes 5 year olds enrolled in elementary school.

			Percent Enrolled in								
			Nursery school				Kindergarten			Percet not	
	All children		Total		Full-day		Total		Full-day	enrolled	
Race and Labor Force Status	1972	1986	1972	1986	1972	1986	1972	1986	1986	1972	1986
White											
Children 3 to 5 years old	8,560	8,785	12.5	24.3	3.1	7.5	28.8	30.9	10.5	58.6	44.8
Living with mother	8,409	8,520	12.6	24.5	3.1	7.5	28.9	30.7	10.3	58.5	44.8
Mother in labor force	2,623	4,733	15.9	27.1	7.2	11.6	28.7	31.8	11.8	55.4	41.0
Employed	2,419	4,383	16.5	28.1	7.7	12.3	28.7	31.8	11.8	54.8	40.1
Full-time	1,499	2,732	15.8	28.5	11.1	16.1	27.7	31.0	12.9	56.5	40.4
Part-time	920	1,651	17.7	27.3	2.0	5.2	30.3	33.0	10.0	52.0	39.7
Unemployed	205	350	8.9	15.5	1.0	2.9	28.6	32.3	12.3	62.5	52.2
Mother not in labor force	5,785	3,787	11.1	21.1	1.2	2.4	29.0	29.3	8.3	59.9	49.6
Black											
Children 3 to 5 years old	1,442	1,649	12.8	19.1	9.5	12.6	30.1	35.0	21.8	57.0	45.9
Living with mother	1,414	1,560	12.8	19.4	9.4	12.9	30.2	34.7	21.7	56.7	45.9
Mother in labor force	639	846	15.0	25.1	12.7	19.6	29.5	33.4	23.1	55.5	41.5
Employed	537	715	15.1	26.0	13.4	21.2	30.9	33.3	23.7	54.0	40.7

Continued.

Enrollment
[Continued]

			Percent Enrolled in								
			Nursery school				Kindergarten			Percet not	
	All children		Total		Full-day		Total		Full-day	enrolled	
Race and Labor Force Status	1972	1986	1972	1986	1972	1986	1972	1986	1986	1972	1986
Full-time	407	575	15.0	26.9	13.0	22.9	28.7	35.2	26.1	56.3	37.9
Part-time	130	140	15.5	22.4	14.6	14.2	37.7	25.6	14.1	46.8	52.0
Unemployed	103	130	14.5	19.9	8.7	11.2	22.5	34.0	20.0	63.0	46.1
Mother not in labor force	774	715	11.0	12.7	6.7	4.9	30.8	36.3	19.9	58.1	51.0

Source: "Preprimary School Enrollment, by Level of Enrollment and Labor Force Status of Mother: 1972 and 1986," *Statistical Abstract*, 1989, p. 129. *Current Population Reports*, Series P-20, No. 318, U.S. Bureau of the Census and unpublished data.

★ 241 ★
Enrollment Characteristics

As of October. For the civilian noninstitutional population. Based on the Current Population Survey.

					Percent Distribution							
					High school graduates							
	Total persons (1,000)		Enrolled in high school		Total		In college		Not in college		Not high school graduates	
Characteristic	1975	1986	1975	1986	1975	1986	1975	1986	1975	1986	1975	1986
Total[1]	15,693	14,453	5.7	7.0	78.0	79.4	33.5	36.6	44.5	42.8	16.3	13.6
White	13,448	11,915	4.7	6.1	80.6	80.8	34.6	37.9	46.0	42.9	14.7	13.1
Black	1,997	2,092	12.5	11.5	60.4	72.0	24.9	26.1	35.6	45.9	27.0	16.5
Hispanic[2]	899	1,374	12.0	9.6	57.2	58.9	24.4	22.2	32.8	36.8	30.8	31.2
Male[1]	7,584	7,068	7.4	8.9	76.6	76.3	35.4	36.4	41.3	40.2	15.9	14.7
White	6,545	5,850	6.2	7.4	79.7	78.2	36.9	37.9	42.8	40.3	14.1	14.4
Black	911	985	15.9	16.5	55.0	66.4	23.9	23.0	31.1	43.4	29.0	17.2
Hispanic[2]	416	716	17.3	9.1	54.6	56.4	25.2	21.1	29.3	35.3	27.9	34.4
Female[1]	8,109	7,385	4.2	5.3	79.2	82.3	31.8	36.9	47.4	45.4	16.6	12.5
White	6,903	6,065	3.2	4.7	81.4	83.3	32.4	37.8	49.0	45.4	15.3	12.0
Black	1,085	1,107	9.7	7.0	65.0	77.0	25.8	28.7	39.2	48.2	25.4	16.0
Hispanic[2]	484	658	7.6	10.2	59.3	62.2	23.6	23.6	35.7	38.6	33.1	27.8

Source: "Enrollment Status of Persons 18 to 21 Years Old, by Race, Hispanic Origin, and Sex: 1975 and 1986," *Statistical Abstract*, 1989, p. 146. Primary source: *Current Population Reports*, Series P-20, Nos. 303 and 429. U.S. Bureau of the Census. *Notes:* 1. Includes other races not shown separately. 2. Persons of Hispanic origin may be of any race.

★ 242 ★
Enrollment in 2- and 4-Year Higher Education Institutions: Trends

Type of institution and race/ethnicity of student	Numbers, in thousands				Percentage distribution of total enrollment			
	1980	1982	1984[1]	1986[1]	1980	1982	1984	1986
All institutions	12,087	12,388	12,235	12,489	100.0	100.0	100.0	100.0
White, non-Hispanic	9,833	9,997	9,815	9,911	81.4	80.7	80.2	79.4
Total minority	1,949	2,059	2,085	2,235	16.1	16.6	17.0	17.9
Black, non-Hispanic	1,107	1,101	1,076	1,080	9.2	8.9	8.8	8.7
Hispanic	472	519	535	617	3.9	4.2	4.4	4.9
Asian or Pacific Islander	286	351	390	448	2.4	2.8	3.2	3.6
American Indian/Alaskan Native	84	88	84	90	0.7	0.7	0.7	0.7

Continued.

Enrollment in 2- and 4-Year Higher Education Institutions: Trends
[Continued]

Type of institution and race/ethnicity of student	Numbers, in thousands				Percentage distribution of total enrollment			
	1980	1982	1984[1]	1986[1]	1980	1982	1984	1986
Nonresident alien	305	331	335	344	2.5	2.7	2.7	2.8
4-year institutions	7,565	7,648	7,708	7,818	62.6	61.7	63.0	62.6
White, non-Hispanic	6,275	6,306	6,301	6,333	51.9	50.9	51.5	50.7
Total minority	1,050	1,073	1,124	1,194	8.7	8.7	9.2	9.6
Black, non-Hispanic	634	612	617	615	5.2	4.9	5.0	4.9
Hispanic	217	229	246	278	1.8	1.8	2.0	2.2
Asian or Pacific Islander	162	193	223	262	1.3	1.6	1.8	2.1
American Indian/Alaskan Native	37	39	38	39	0.3	0.3	0.3	0.3
Nonresident alien	241	270	282	291	2.0	2.2	2.3	2.3
2-year institutions	4,521	4,740	4,527	4,671	37.4	38.3	37.0	37.4
White, non-Hispanic	3,558	3,692	3,514	3,575	29.4	29.8	28.7	28.6
Total minority	899	987	961	1,040	7.4	8.0	7.9	8.3
Black, non-Hispanic	472	489	459	466	3.9	3.9	3.7	3.7
Hispanic	255	291	289	338	2.1	2.3	2.4	2.7
Asian or Pacific Islander	124	158	167	186	1.0	1.3	1.4	1.5
American Indian/Alaskan Native	47	49	46	51	0.4	0.4	0.4	0.4
Nonresident alien	64	61	53	53	0.5	0.5	0.4	0.4

Source: "Total Enrollment in Institutions of Higher Education, by Type of Institution and Race/Ethnicity of Student: Fall 1976 to Fall 1986," *Digest of Education Statistics,* 1989, p. 193. Primary source: U.S. Department of Education, National Center for Educational Statistics, "Fall Enrollment in Colleges and Universities"; and Integrated Postsecondary Education Data System (IPEDS), "Fall Enrollment, 1986" survey and unpublished tabulations. (This table was prepared February 1989.) *Notes:* Because of underreporting and nonreporting of racial/ethnic data, figures are slightly lower than corresponding data in other tables. Because of rounding, details may not add to totals. 1. Data have been revised from previously published figures.

★ 243 ★
Enrollment in Gifted/Talented Programs in 5 School Districts

	American Indian	Asian	Hispanic	Black	Minority	White	Total
Name: New York City Public Schools							
Number of Schools: 1,000							
Enrollment:							
Number	470	37,071	286,870	361,555	685,966	245,227	931,193
Percent	0.1	4.0	30.8	38.8	73.7	26.3	100.0
Gifted/Talented:							
Number	247	5,008	10,906	18,285	34,446	26,378	60,824
Percent	0.4	8.2	17.9	30.1	56.6	43.4	100.0
Name: Los Angeles Unified School Districts							
Number of Schools: 685							
Enrollment:							
Number	2,379	38,761	243,070	125,441	409,651	128,387	538,038
Percent	0.4	7.2	45.2	23.3	76.1	23.9	100.0
Gifted/Talented:							
Number	117	4,024	5,382	3,772	13,295	11,943	25,238
Percent	0.5	15.9	21.3	14.9	52.7	47.3	100.0
Name: Chicago City School District							
Number of Schools: 617							
Enrollment:							
Number	657	9,546	82,669	269,132	362,004	83,265	445,269
Percent	0.1	2.1	18.6	60.4	81.3	18.7	100.0
Gifted/Talented:							

Continued.

Enrollment in Gifted/Talented Programs in 5 School Districts
[Continued]

	American Indian	Asian	Hispanic	Black	Minority	White	Total
Number	16	213	1,051	5,108	6,388	2,624	9,012
Percent	0.2	2.4	11.7	56.7	70.9	29.1	100.0
Name: Detroit City School Districts							
Number of Schools: 292							
Enrollment:							
Number	347	751	3,583	182,452	187,133	25,944	213,077
Percent	0.2	0.4	1.7	85.6	87.8	12.2	100.0
Gifted/Talented:							
Number	2	12	20	1,296	1,330	290	1,620
Percent	0.1	0.7	1.2	80.0	82.1	17.9	100.0
Name: Philadelphia Public Schools							
Number of Schools: 271							
Enrollment:							
Number	117	3,319	15,964	140,336	159,736	64,416	224,152
Percent	0.1	1.5	7.1	62.6	71.3	28.7	100.0
Gifted/Talented:							
Number	1	71	74	1,548	1,694	3,254	4,948
Percent	0.0	1.4	1.5	31.3	34.2	65.8	100.0

Source: "Racial/Ethnic Enrollment in Gifted and Talented Programs — 25 Largest School Districts, 1980," *Equality and Excellence: The Educational Status of Black Americans*, 1985, pp. 31-33. Primary source: Office of Civil Rights, U.S. Department of Education. Data supplied upon request. Published by permission.

★ 244 ★
Enrollment in Grades K-12

	Public K-12 Enrollment			
	Thousands 1987	Percent Change 1977-1987	Percent Minority	
			1980	1987
United States	40,200	-8.1	26.8	30.0
SREB States	14,406	0.6	32.2	35.0
SREB States as a Percent of U.S.	35.8			
Alabama	731	-4.1	33.6	38.0
Arkansas	437	-4.7	23.5	25.0
Florida	1,664	8.3	32.2	35.0
Georgia	1,159	6.4	34.3	39.0
Kentucky	643	-7.8	9.1	11.0
Louisiana	795	-5.2	43.5	43.0
Maryland	680	-18.7	33.5	40.0
Mississippi	506	0.7	51.6	56.0
North Carolina	1,085	-8.2	31.8	32.0
Oklahoma	599	0.7	20.8	21.0

Continued.

Enrollment in Grades K-12
[Continued]

| | Public K-12 Enrollment | | | |
| | Thousands 1987 | Percent Change 1977-1987 | Percent Minority | |
			1980	1987
South Carolina	615	-0.9	43.5	45.0
Tennessee	819	-6.7	24.5	23.0
Texas	3,351	17.9	46.1	49.0
Virginia	979	-9.5	27.5	27.0
West Virginia	344	-14.2	4.3	4.0

Source: "Elementary and Secondary School Enrollment," *NAFEO INROADS*, December-January 1990, p. 5. Primary source: *Digest of Education Statistics, 1979 and 1987*; "Key Statistics for Public Elementary and Secondary Education: Early Estimates, School Year 1987-88," National Center for Education Statistics. "State Education Statistics, 1972 and 1982, 1982 and 1987," U.S. Department of Education. *Notes:* The graduation rates represent the number of students who graduate in a given year compared to the 9th-grade enrollment four years earlier. The "SREB States" high school graduation rate is the median of the rates in the SREB states. Published by permission.

★ 245 ★
Enrollment in Independent Schools: Trends

Number of students and percent of total.

	1971/72	Percent	1976/77	Percent	1979/80	Percent	1986/87	Percent
Number of Schools Reporting	730				673		815	
Total Enrollment	259,540		268,914		262,907		324,025	
African American	9,627	3.7	11,711	4.4	11,883	4.5	15,096	4.7
Hispanic American	1,610	0.6	3,333	1.2	5,297	2.0	5,709	1.8
Asian American	1,581	0.6	3,572	1.3	5,717	2.2	15,193	4.7
Native American	159	0.1	208	0.1	324	0.1	347	0.1
Totals	12,977	5.0	18,824	7.0	23,221	8.8	36,345	11.2

Source: "Minority Enrollments in Independent Schools," *Black Issues in Higher Education*, June 15, 1987, p. 9. Primary source: National Association of Independent Schools. Independent schools include over 1,000 member institutions.

★ 246 ★
Enrollment in Newer Predominantly Black Institutions

State/Institutions	Date Estab.	Control/ Level[1]	Total Students	Percent Black
ALABAMA				
Alabama Christian College	1942	PR-4	1,602	52.4
Booker T. Washington Business	1939	PR-2	308	100.0
Southern Junior College of Business	1969	PR-2	1,783	58.7
Trenholm State Technical College	1965	PU-2	700	75.0
ARKANSAS				
American College	1955	PR-2	1,889	70.6
Capital City Junior College	1927	PR-2	567	58.0

Continued.

Enrollment in Newer Predominantly Black Institutions
[Continued]

State/Institutions	Date Estab.	Control/Level[1]	Total Students	Percent Black
CALIFORNIA				
Los Angeles Southwest College	1967	PU-2	3,552	94.7
West Los Angeles College	1968	PU-2	4,922	56.7
Pattern College	1945	PR-4	109	51.4
GEORGIA				
Draughons Junior College (The Loop)	1899	PU-2	696	60.3
ILLINOIS				
City College Chicago (The Loop)	1962	PU-2	6,149	65.7
City College Chicago (Malcolm X)	1911	PU-2	2,756	86.8
City College (Olive/Harvey)	1957	PU-2	2,984	92.8
East/West University	1978	PR-2	396	88.4
Illinois Technical College	1950	PR-2	326	66.3
State Community College at East St. Louis	1969	PU-2	1,372	97.2
INDIANA				
Clark College	1843	PU-4	528	56.3
Martin Center College	1977	PR-4	140	92.1
KANSAS				
Donnelly College	1949	PR-2	766	63.2
KENTUCKY				
Watterson College	1963	PR-2	2,950	71.2
MARYLAND				
Community College of Baltimore	1947	PU-2	75.6	78.0
MICHIGAN				
Marygrove College	1910	PR-4	964	76.1
NEW JERSEY				
Essex County College	1966	PU-2	5,806	62.4
NEW YORK				
College for Human Services	1964	PR-4	287	76.0
College of New Rochelle	1898	PR-4	3,834	61.3
Interboro Institute	1888	PR-2	854	78.1
Long Island University/Brooklyn Campus	1926	PR-4	2,859	52.0
Taylor Business Institute	1963	PR-2	1,372	58.1
NORTH CAROLINA				
Edgecombe Technical College	1967	PU-2	723	51.5
Rutledge College of Greensboro	1973	PR-2	276	79.7
Rutledge College of Raleigh	1901	PR-2	246	89.8
Rutledge College of Winston-Salem	1962	PR-2	325	77.2

Continued.

Enrollment in Newer Predominantly Black Institutions
[Continued]

State/Institutions	Date Estab.	Control/ Level[1]	Total Students	Percent Black
OHIO				
Dyke College	1848	PR-4	1,242	59.9
PENNSYLVANIA				
Berean Institute	1899	PR-2	172	88.4
Community College of Philadelphia	1965	PU-2	14,965	52.4
Lyons Technical Institute	1968	PR-2	98	51.0
McCarrie Schools of Health Science	1917	PR-2	251	50.6
Tracy Warner School	1956	PR-2	94	57.4
SOUTH CAROLINA				
Columbia Junior College of Business	1935	PR-2	515	75.6
Nielsen Electronic Institute	1965	PR-2	291	67.0
Rutledge College of Columbia	1911	PR-2	504	85.1
Rutledge College of Greenville	1910	PR-2	332	56.9
Rutledge College of Spartanburg	1910	PR-2	383	50.1
Williamsburh Technical College	1969	PU-2	248	60.1
TENNESSEE				
American Baptist Theological Seminary	1924	PR-4	121	87.6
Draughons Junior College	1890	PR-2	743	78.2
Shelby St. Community College	1969	PU-2	4,093	60.9

Source: "Percent of Black Students Enrolled in Newer Predominantly Black Colleges, Fall 1984, Non-NAFEO Membership (N = 47)," *NAFEO INROADS,* February/March 1987, pp. 10-11. Primary source: The 1984 Civil Rights Racial, Ethnic and Sex Enrollment Survey for Higher Education (unpublished data). Analysis does not include unclassified students. Data only include only reporting institutions. *Notes:* NAFEO - National Association for Equal Opportunity in Higher Education. 1. Legend: PU-4 Public 4 Year; PU-2 Public 2 Year; PR-4 Private 4 Year; PR-2 Private 2 Year. Published by permission.

★ 247 ★
Enrollment in Private/Public Higher Education Institutions

Control of institution and race/ethnicity of student	Number, in thousands				Percent distribution			
	1980	1982	1984[1]	1986[1]	1980	1982	1984	1986
All institutions	12,087	12,388	12,235	12,489	100.0	100.0	100.0	100.0
White, non-Hispanic	9,833	9,997	9,815	9,911	81.4	80.7	80.2	79.4
Black, non-Hispanic	1,107	1,101	1,076	1,080	9.2	8.9	8.8	8.7
Hispanic	472	519	535	617	3.9	4.2	4.4	4.9
Asian or Pacific Islander	286	351	390	448	2.4	2.8	3.2	3.6
American Indian/Alaskan Native	84	88	84	90	0.7	0.7	0.7	0.7
Nonresident alien	305	331	335	344	2.5	2.7	2.7	2.8
Public institutions	9,456	9,695	9,458	9,714	100.0	100.0	100.0	100.0
White, non-Hispanic	7,656	7,785	7,543	7,654	81.0	80.3	79.8	78.8
Black, non-Hispanic	876	873	844	854	9.3	9.0	8.9	8.8
Hispanic	406	446	456	532	4.3	4.6	4.8	5.5

Continued.

153

Enrollment in Private/Public Higher Education Institutions
[Continued]

Control of institution and race/ethnicity of student	Number, in thousands				Percent distribution			
	1980	1982	1984[1]	1986[1]	1980	1982	1984	1986
Asian or Pacific Islander	240	296	323	371	2.5	3.0	3.4	3.8
American Indian/Alaskan Native	74	77	72	79	0.8	0.8	0.8	0.8
Nonresident alien	204	219	219	225	2.2	2.3	2.3	2.3
Private institutions	2,630	2,293	2,777	2,775	100.0	100.0	100.0	100.0
White, non-Hispanic	2,177	2,212	2,272	2,257	82.8	82.2	81.8	81.3
Black, non-Hispanic	231	228	232	226	8.8	8.5	8.3	8.2
Hispanic	66	74	79	84	2.5	2.7	2.8	3.0
Asian or Pacific Islander	47	55	67	77	1.8	2.1	2.4	2.8
American Indian/Alaskan Native	10	10	11	11	0.4	0.4	0.4	0.4
Nonresident alien	101	113	116	119	3.8	4.2	4.2	4.3
Men, total	5,868	5,999	5,859	5,880	100.0	100.0	100.0	100.0
White, non-Hispanic	4,773	4,830	4,690	4,644	81.3	80.5	80.0	79.0
Black, non-Hispanic	464	458	437	436	7.9	7.6	7.5	7.4
Hispanic	232	252	254	290	3.9	4.2	4.3	4.9
Asian or Pacific Islander	151	189	210	239	2.6	3.2	3.6	4.1
American Indian/Alaskan Native	38	40	38	40	0.6	0.7	0.6	0.7
Nonresident alien	211	230	231	232	3.6	3.8	3.9	3.9
Women, total	6,219	6,389	6,376	6,609	100.0	100.0	100.0	100.0
White, non-Hispanic	5,060	5,167	5,125	5,267	81.4	80.9	80.4	79.7
Black, non-Hispanic	643	644	639	645	10.3	10.1	10.0	9.8
Hispanic	240	267	281	327	3.9	4.2	4.4	4.9
Asian or Pacific Islander	135	162	180	209	2.2	2.5	2.8	3.2
American Indian/Alaskan Native	46	48	46	51	0.7	0.7	0.7	0.8
Nonresident alien	94	101	104	111	1.5	1.6	1.6	1.7

Source: "Total Enrollment in Institutions of Higher Education, by Control of Institution, Sex of Student and Race/Ethnicity: Fall 1976 to Fall 1986," Digest of Education Statistics, 1989, p. 192. Primary source: U.S. Department of Education, National Center for Educational Statistics, "Fall Enrollment in Colleges and Universities"; and Integrated Postsecondary Education Data System (IPEDS), "Fall Enrollment, 1986" survey. (This table was prepared February 1989.) *Notes:* Because of underreporting and nonreporting of racial/ethnic data, figures are slightly lower than corresponding data in other tables. Because of rounding, details may not add to totals. 1. Data have been revised from previously published figures.

★ 248 ★
Enrollment of Males

Year	White	Black[1]	Differ-ence[2]	Ratio[3]
1850	56.2	1.8	54.4	.32
1860	59.6	1.9	57.7	.32
1870	54.4	9.9	44.5	.182
1880	62.0	33.8	28.2	.545
1890	57.9	32.9	25.0	.568
1900	53.6	31.1	22.5	.580
1910	61.3	44.8	16.5	.731
1920	65.7	53.5	12.2	.814
1930	71.2	60.3	10.9	.847

Continued.

Enrollment of Males
[Continued]

Year	White	Black[1]	Differ-ence[2]	Ratio[3]
1940	75.6	68.4	7.2	.905
1950	79.3	74.8	4.5	.943
1960	84.8	81.5	3.3	.961
1970	88.3	85.3	3.0	.966

Source: "Enrollment Per 100 Males of School Age by Race," *The Economic Progress of Black Men in America*, p. 56. Primary source: U.S. Bureau of the Census, *Historical Statistics of the United States, Colonial Times to 1970*, table H-433-441. *Notes:* The ages included in the enrolled and school-age populations differ as follows: 1850-1880: Enrollment includes all persons enrolled regardless of age; the school-age population is 5-19 years. 1890 and 1940-1970: Enrollment and population include persons 5-19 years old. 1900-1930: Enrollment and population include persons 5-20 years old. 1. Includes other nonwhite races. 2. White rate minus black rate. 3. Black rate divided by white rate.

★ 249 ★
Equal Opportunity Educational Institutions: Date Established

Date Established	Number	Control		Level			
		Public	Private	4-Year	2-Year	4-Year + Graduate	Graduate and Professional
1979-1987							
1964-1978	7	5	2	2	4		1
1949-1963							
1924-1948	3	2	1		3		
1909-1923	1	1			1		
1894-1908							
1879-1893							
1864-1878	1	1				1	
1849-1863							
1834-1848							
Total	12	9	3	2	8	1	1
Percent	100	75	25	17	67	8	8

Source: "A Summary: Other NAFEO Equal Opportunity Educational Colleges and Universities by Control, Level and Date Established - NAFEO Membership (N=12)," *NAFEO INROADS*, February/March 1987, p. 9. Published by permission.

★ 250 ★
Faculty Ranks of Male/Female College Faculty

Rank	Females		Males	
	Number	Percent	Number	Percent
Instructors & Assistant Professors (Lower)	179	49.5	182	50.4
Associate and Full Professors (Upper)	23	35.4	42	64.6

Source: "Gender Representation in Lower and Upper Faculty Ranks," *Black Faculty in Traditionally White Institutions in Selected Adams States*, p. 29. Primary source: *Black Faculty in Traditionally White Institutions in Selected Adams States: Characteristics, Experiences and Perceptions*, Southern Education Foundation, Inc. Atlanta, GA 30308, 1988 Adams States: Alabama, Florida, Georgia, Kentucky, Maryland, North Carolina, South Carolina, Tennessee, Virginia. Published by permission.

★ 251 ★
Faculty/Student Relationships

Relationship with White Faculty	Total Population	Campus Race	
		Black	White
Very Poor	1.9	2.0	1.7
Poor	11.6	8.5	15.2
Good	65.4	63.4	67.7
Excellent	21.2	26.2	15.3
Total	100.0	100.0	100.0
N	(1494)	(803)	(691)

Source: "Faculty Relationships by Student Gender and Campus Race," *Gender and Campus Race Differences in Black Student Academic Performance, Racial Attitudes and College Satisfaction,* 1986, p. 53. Primary source: National Study of Black College Students, 1981 and 1983, University of Michigan, Ann Arbor. Published by permission.

★ 252 ★
Federal R&D Support to Historically Black Colleges/Universities - Part I

Dollars in thousands.

Institutions (Ranked by Amount Received)	Total	UDSA	COM	DOD	ED	DOE	EPA	HHS	INT	NASA	NSF	OTHER
1. Howard University	6,719	97	0	248	439	125	53	3,210	0	1,190	1,357	0
2. NC A&T State University	4,234	2,121	0	840	147	274	0	132	0	353	367	0
3. Meharry Medical College	3,865	0	0	140	0	74	0	2,811	0	0	840	0
4. Alabama A & M University	3,863	1,419	0	0	0	104	0	0	0	1,053	1,287	0
5. Tuskegee University	3,323	1,326	0	565	0	150	0	896	0	386	0	0
6. Tennessee State University	2,751	1,591	0	0	0	0	0	842	0	315	0	0
7. Prairie View A&M University	2,526	2,155	0	0	0	157	0	0	0	214	0	0
8. Jackson State University	2,314	18	0	203	0	1,364	0	175	0	315	239	0
9. Morehouse School of Medicine	2,211	0	0	0	0	0	0	2,211	0	0	0	0
10. Florida A&M University	2,194	1,060	0	50	0	0	0	997	0	87	0	0
11. Atlanta University	2,142	17	0	740	0	473	0	688	0	144	80	0
12. Kentucky State University	1,789	1,682	0	0	107	0	0	0	0	0	0	0
13. Hampton University	1,686	0	0	152	0	50	0	30	0	1,376	755	0
14. Virginia State University	1,625	1,385	0	0	0	94	0	0	0	146	0	0
15. Fort Valley State College	1,594	1,471	0	0	0	50	0	35	0	0	38	0
16. Texas Southern University	1,554	0	0	0	0	106	0	926	0	229	293	0
17. Lincoln University (MO)	1,552	1,552	0	0	0	0	0	0	0	0	0	0
18. Southern U & A&M College	1,543	1,069	0	0	0	0	0	75	0	306	93	0
19. Alcorn State University	1,378	1,378	0	0	0	0	0	0	0	0	0	0
20. Univ of Ark Pine Bluff	1,215	1,155	0	0	0	0	0	60	0	0	0	0
21. South Carolina St. College	1,154	1,154	0	0	0	0	0	0	0	0	0	0
22. Langston University	1,114	1,065	0	0	0	12	0	0	37	0	0	0
23. U of the Virgin Islands	1,091	906	0	0	0	0	0	0	105	0	80	0
24. Xavier University (LA)	998	0	0	0	0	0	0	998	0	0	0	0
25. Clark College	817	0	0	0	0	97	0	0	0	0	720	0
26. U of MD Eastern Shore	810	772	0	0	0	0	0	0	26	0	12	0
27. University of DC	633	477	0	45	0	0	0	0	105	0	6	0
28. Miss Valley State University	606	606	0	0	0	0	0	0	0	0	0	.0
29. Fisk University	574	12	0	0	0	33	11	0	0	518	0	0
30. North Carolina Central University	545	10	0	82	0	30	70	0	0	0	352	0
31. Delaware State College	481	481	0	0	0	0	0	0	0	0	0	0
32. Morgan State University	469	0	0	0	0	0	0	0	0	356	0	113
33. Morehouse College	428	0	0	30	0	0	330	0	60	0	2	6
34. Albany State College	380	0	0	0	0	0	0	0	0	0	380	0
35. Grambling State University	378	0	0	0	0	159	0	124	0	0	10	85
36. Norfolk State University	315	0	0	0	0	0	0	0	0	211	104	0
37. Spelman College	294	0	0	80	0	0	0	0	0	154	60	0
38. Lincoln University (PA)	272	0	0	113	0	0	88	0	0	0	71	0
39. Selma University	183	0	0	0	0	183	0	0	0	0	0	0

Continued.

Federal R&D Support to Historically Black Colleges/Universities - Part I
[Continued]

Institutions (Ranked by Amount Received)	Total	UDSA	COM	DOD	ED	DOE	EPA	HHS	INT	NASA	NSF	OTHER
40. Bowie State College	171	0	0	0	0	0	0	0	0	171	0	0
41. Tougaloo College	156	0	0	0	0	0	0	144	0	0	12	0
42. Central State University	135	0	0	0	0	10	0	0	0	125	0	0
43. Winston-Salem State University	127	0	0	0	0	0	0	127	0	0	0	0
44. Savannah State College	90	0	23	0	0	67	0	0	0	0	0	0
45. Alabama State University	90	0	0	0	0	51	0	0	0	0	39	0
46. Claflin College	76	0	0	0	0	76	0	0	0	0	0	0
47. Rust College	76	17	0	0	0	0	0	59	0	0	0	0
48. Bishop College	67	0	0	0	0	0	0	67	0	0	0	0
49. Voorhees College	62	0	0	0	0	62	0	0	0	0	0	0
50. Paine College	43	0	0	0	0	0	0	43	0	0	0	0
Total 1st 50 Institutions	62,713	24,996	23	3,288	693	3,801	552	14,650	333	7,652	6,521	204

Source: "Federal Obligations for Research and Development to Historically Black Colleges, Fiscal Year 1988," *Black Issues in Higher Education*, December 21, 1989, pp. 30-31. Primary source: National Science Foundation, SRS. *Notes:* Includes DOT, AID, HUD, Labor and NRC ranked in descending order of total amount received, by agency. Published by permission.

★ 253 ★
Federal R&D Support to Historically Black Colleges/Universities - Part II

Dollars in thousands.

Institutions (Ranked by Amount Received)	Total	ENG	PHY SCI	MATH/ COMP SCI	ENV SCI	LIFE SCI	PSY	SOC SCI	OTHER SCI, NEC
1. Howard University	6,719	1,063	1,042	307	345	3,449	53	22	418
2. NC A&T State University	4,234	1,424	150	100	0	1,521	0	698	341
3. Meharry Medical College	3,865	0	0	0	0	2,890	0	0	975
4. Alabama A & M University	3,863	236	1,518	0	0	1,754	0	251	104
5. Tuskegee University	3,323	614	143	0	350	1,244	0	181	791
6. Tennessee State University	2,751	164	453	0	0	712	0	774	648
7. Prairie View A&M University	2,526	114	324	0	0	1,648	0	433	7
8. Jackson State University	2,314	71	166	1,770	0	227	0	80	0
9. Morehouse School of Medicine	2,211	0	0	0	0	1,230	72	0	909
10. Florida A&M University	2,194	0	146	130	0	880	0	41	997
11. Atlanta University	2,142	74	640	529	0	47	0	25	827
12. Kentucky State University	1,789	0	0	0	0	1,139	0	543	107
13. Hampton University	1,686	380	783	103	320	0	0	30	70
14. Virginia State University	1,625	94	146	0	0	947	0	435	0
15. Fort Valley State College	1,594	67	12	0	0	1,206	0	259	50
16. Texas Southern University	1,554	106	343	57	0	233	0	0	815
17. Lincoln University (MO)	1,552	0	0	0	0	1,505	0	47	0
18. Southern U & A&M College	1,543	0	31	368	0	961	0	183	0
19. Alcorn State University	1,378	0	47	0	0	813	0	518	0
20. Univ of Ark Pine Bluff	1,215	0	49	0	0	939	0	227	0
21. South Carolina St. College	1,154	0	0	0	0	357	0	797	0
22. Langston University	1,114	0	0	0	37	1,065	0	0	12
23. U of the Virgin Islands	1,091	83	0	0	185	751	0	72	0
24. Xavier University (LA)	998	0	0	0	0	0	0	0	998
25. Clark College	817	97	0	0	0	720	0	0	0
26. U of MD Eastern Shore	810	0	242	0	0	374	0	194	0
27. University of DC	633	0	111	51	105	302	0	64	0
28. Miss Valley State University	606	0	0	0	0	606	0	0	0

Continued.

Federal R&D Support to Historically Black Colleges/Universities - Part II
[Continued]

Institutions (Ranked by Amount Received)	Total	ENG	PHY SCI	MATH/ COMP SCI	ENV SCI	LIFE SCI	PSY	SOC SCI	OTHER SCI, NEC
29. Fisk University	574	11	322	196	12	0	0	0	33
30. North Carolina Central University	545	0	112	82	353	10	0	70	0
31. Delaware State College	481	0	0	0	0	437	0	44	0
32. Morgan State University	469	0	380	0	0	0	0	69	20
33. Morehouse College	428	60	0	0	94	266	0	6	2
34. Albany State College	380	0	273	0	107	0	0	0	0
35. Grambling State University	378	159	0	0	0	10	0	209	0
36. Norfolk State University	315	0	145	66	0	0	0	0	104
37. Spelman College	294	54	0	150	0	90	0	0	0
38. Lincoln University (PA)	272	0	84	0	0	188	0	0	0
39. Selma University	183	0	0	0	0	0	0	0	153
40. Bowie State College	171	75	0	96	0	0	0	0	0
41. Tougaloo College	156	0	0	12	0	144	0	0	0
42. Central State University	135	125	0	0	0	0	0	0	10
43. Winston-Salem State University	127	0	0	0	0	61	66	0	0
44. Savannah State College	90	0	0	0	0	23	0	0	67
45. Alabama State University	90	51	0	39	0	0	0	0	0
46. Claflin College	76	0	0	0	0	0	0	0	74
47. Rust College	76	0	0	0	0	76	0	0	0
48. Bishop College	67	0	0	0	0	67	0	0	0
49. Voorhees College	62	0	0	0	0	0	0	62	
50. Paine College	43	0	0	0	0	43	0	0	
Total 1st 50 Institutions	62,713	5,122	7,662	3,974	1,908	28,955	191	6,275	8,626

Source: "Federal Obligations for Research and Development to Historically Black Colleges, Fiscal Year 1988," *Black Issues in Higher Education*, December 21, 1989, pp. 30-31 Primary source: National Science Foundation, SRS. *Notes:* Includes DOT, AID, HUD, Labor and NRC ranked in descending order of total mount received, by agency.

★ 254 ★
Fields of Associate Degrees

Major field of study and sex of student	Total	White non-Hispanic	Black non-Hispanic	Hispanic	Asian or or Pacific Islander	American Indian/ Alaskan Native	Non-resident alien
All fields, total[1]	436,308	361,819	35,466	19,345	11,794	3,196	4,688
Agriculture and natural resources, total	5,458	5,149	62	125	27	51	44
Architecture and environmental design, total	1,665	1,448	56	73	54	4	30
Area and ethnic studies, total	14	3	3	2	0	6	0
Business and management, total	115,231	93,990	11,699	4,694	2,853	811	1,184
Communications, total	3,541	2,972	329	124	41	22	53
Computer and information sciences, total	9,101	7,110	954	415	404	47	171
Education, total	7,333	5,942	639	414	130	134	74
Engineering, total	4,539	3,400	261	337	387	28	126
Engineering technologies, total	57,973	47,936	4,019	2,445	2,592	332	649
Foreign languages, total	421	353	14	22	13	11	8
Health professions, total	62,547	53,876	4,878	2,046	1,028	403	316

Continued.

Fields of Associate Degrees
[Continued]

Major field of study and sex of student	Total	White non-Hispanic	Black non-Hispanic	Hispanic	Asian or or Pacific Islander	American Indian/ Alaskan Native	Non-resident alien
Home economics, total	9,328	7,618	969	396	207	54	84
Law, total	2,498	2,179	170	94	40	11	4
Letters, total	508	390	35	29	33	6	15
Liberal/general studies, total	108,097	89,365	7,885	5,838	2,718	813	1,478
Library and archival science, total	117	104	5	4	3	0	1
Life sciences, total	892	617	105	54	62	18	36
Mathematics, total	666	499	39	40	72	4	12
Military sciences, total	50	39	9	1	0	1	0
Multi/interdisciplinary studies, total	9,794	8,800	399	239	273	33	50
Parks and recreation, total	551	478	38	21	8	0	6
Philosophy and religion, total	100	90	4	3	1	2	0
Physical sciences, total	2,061	1,767	104	78	67	6	39
Protective services, total	11,910	9,739	1,132	788	134	81	36
Psychology, total	1,014	825	77	67	20	17	8
Public affairs, total	3,560	2,774	459	141	69	63	54
Social sciences, total	2,584	1,853	304	256	95	52	24
Theology, total	594	527	34	18	3	1	11
Visual and performing arts, total	14,161	11,976	784	581	460	185	175

Source: "Associate Degrees Conferred by Institutions of Higher Education, by Racial/Ethnic Group, Major Field of Study, and Sex of Student: 1986-87," Digest of Education Statistics, 1989, pp. 240-241. Primary source: U.S. Department of Education, National Center for Educational Statistics, Integrated Postsecondary Education Data System (IPEDS), "Completions" survey. (This table was prepared June 1989.) *Notes:* 1. This tabulation excludes 683 men and 146 women whose racial/ethnic group could not be imputed. Because of imputation methods, fields of study totals by race/ethnicity may differ slightly from field of study by sex. Data are preliminary.

★ 255 ★
Fields of Bachelor's Degrees: Trends

Field of study	1977	1979	1981	1985
	White, non-Hispanic			
Total degrees	805,186	799,617	807,319	826,106
Humanities and social/behavioral sciences	271,490	249,100	238,522	224,152
Humanities	130,327	120,305	118,286	113,084
Social and behavioral sciences	141,163	128,795	120,236	111,068
Natural and computer sciences and engineering	127,177	132,701	141,380	172,388
Natural sciences	80,313	73,523	67,967	64,629
Computer sciences and engineering	46,864	59,178	73,413	107,759
Technical/professional[1]	406,519	417,816	427,417	429,566
Education	125,148	108,949	93,724	77,531
Business and other technical/professional[1]	281,371	308,867	333,693	352,035
	Black, non-Hispanic			
Total degrees	58,515	60,130	60,673	57,473
Humanities and social/behavioral sciences	20,107	19,266	18,045	15,272
Humanities	6,567	7,014	6,608	6,505
Social and behavioral sciences	13,540	12,252	11,437	8,767

Continued.

Fields of Bachelor's Degrees: Trends
[Continued]

Field of study	1977	1979	1981	1985
Natural and computer sciences and engineering	5,514	6,091	6,994	8,942
Natural sciences	3,785	3,830	3,759	3,640
Computer sciences and engineering	1,729	2,261	3,235	5,302
Technical/professional[1]	32,894	34,773	35,634	33,259
Education	12,992	11,509	9,494	5,456
Business and other technical/professional[1]	19,972	23,264	26,140	27,803
Hispanic				
Total degrees	18,663	20,029	21,832	25,874
Humanities and social/behavioral sciences	7,764	7,594	7,754	8,049
Humanities	3,537	3,469	3,561	3,872
Social and behavioral sciences	4,227	4,125	4,193	4,177
Natural and computer sciences and engineering	2,514	2,914	3,469	4,983
Natural sciences	1,534	1,642	1,734	1,915
Computer sciences and engineering	980	1,272	1,735	3,068
Technical/professional[1]	8,385	9,521	10,609	12,842
Education	3,050	3,029	2,847	2,533
Business and other technical/professional[1]	5,353	6,492	7,762	10,309
American Indian/Alaskan Native				
Total degrees	3,319	3,404	3,593	4,246
Humanities and social/behavioral sciences	1,143	1,144	1,211	1,260
Humanities	504	470	541	612
Social and behavioral sciences	639	674	670	648
Natural and computer sciences and engineering	399	425	436	770
Natural sciences	250	252	220	318
Computer sciences and engineering	149	173	216	452
Technical/professional[1]	1,777	1,835	1,946	2,216
Education	707	645	569	483
Business and other technical/professional[1]	1,070	1,190	1,377	1,733
Asian or Pacific Islander				
Total degrees	13,745	15,336	18,794	25,395
Humanities and social/behavioral sciences	4,442	4,400	4,807	5,618
Humanities	1,993	2,032	2,323	2,754
Social and behavioral sciences	2,449	2,368	2,484	2,864
Natural and computer sciences and engineering	3,358	4,303	6,211	10,650
Natural sciences	1,996	2,204	2,476	3,593
Computer sciences and engineering	1,362	2,099	3,735	7,057
Technical/professional[1]	5,945	6,633	7,776	9,127
Education	894	785	723	770
Business and other technical/professional[1]	5,051	5,848	7,053	8,357

Source: "Number of Bachelor's Degrees Conferred, by Field and Race and Ethnicity: Selected Academic Years Ending 1977-1985," *1989 Education Indicators*, pp. 241-243. U.S. Department of Education, Office for Civil Rights, Survey of Earned Degrees Conferred by Institutions of Higher Education by Race, Ethnicity, and Sex, academic years ending 1977 and 1979; National Center for Education Statistics, Degrees and Other Formal Awards Conferred surveys, academic years ending 1981 and 1985. *Notes:* Distributions for 1977 through 1981 exclude degrees not reported by race and ethnicity. Distributions for 1985 include degrees for which missing race and ethnicity could be imputed. The number of degrees reported for 1977 and 1979 excludes degrees conferred by U.S. Service Schools (0.4 percent or less of degrees). 1. In contrast to previous editions of *The Condition of Education*, computer sciences and engineering are not included in the technical/professional category.

★ 256 ★
Fields of Doctoral Degrees: Trend

Field of study	1977	1979	1981	1985
	White, non-Hispanic			
Total degrees	26,836	26,128	25,908	23,934
Humanities and social/behavioral sciences	10,042	9,633	9,050	8,067
Humanities	4,481	4,575	3,948	3,554
Social and behavioral sciences	5,561	5,058	5,102	4,513
Natural and computer sciences and engineering	7,800	7,494	7,665	7,055
Natural sciences	6,087	5,926	6,129	5,528
Computer sciences and engineering	1,713	1,568	1,536	1,527
Technical/professional[1]	8,994	9,001	9,193	8,812
Education	6,616	6,333	6,391	5,615
Business and other technical/professional[1]	2,378	2,668	2,802	3,197
	Black, non-Hispanic			
Total degrees	1,253	1,267	1,265	1,154
Humanities and social/behavioral sciences	357	395	361	342
Humanities	135	152	145	117
Social and behavioral sciences	222	243	216	225
Natural and computer sciences and engineering	131	136	130	138
Natural sciences	107	108	105	95
Computer sciences and engineering	24	28	25	43
Technical/professional[1]	765	736	774	674
Education	685	625	614	521
Business and other technical/professional[1]	80	111	160	153
	Hispanic			
Total degrees	522	439	456	677
Humanities and social/behavioral sciences	205	195	185	231
Humanities	88	92	68	100
Social and behavioral sciences	117	103	117	131
Natural and computer sciences and engineering	111	80	92	223
Natural sciences	86	57	69	132
Computer sciences and engineering	25	23	23	91
Technical/professional[1]	206	164	179	223
Education	164	136	140	163
Business and other technical/professional[1]	42	28	39	60
	American Indian/Alaskan Native			
Total degrees	95	104	130	119
Humanities and social/behavioral sciences	27	37	36	27
Humanities	11	10	14	12
Social and behavioral sciences	16	27	22	15
Natural and computer sciences and engineering	27	16	20	24
Natural sciences	24	14	14	16
Computer sciences and engineering	3	2	6	8
Technical/professional[1]	41	51	74	68
Education	32	43	57	51
Business and other technical/professional[1]	9	8	17	17

Continued.

Fields of Doctoral Degrees: Trend
[Continued]

Field of study	1977	1979	1981	1985
	Asian or Pacific Islander			
Total degrees	658	811	877	1,106
Humanities and social/behavioral sciences	146	165	184	230
Humanities	48	77	79	112
Social and behavioral sciences	98	88	105	118
Natural and computer sciences and engineering	354	468	482	621
Natural sciences	221	277	277	344
Computer sciences and engineering	133	191	205	277
Technical/professional[1]	158	178	211	255
Education	77	97	105	84
Business and other technical/professional[1]	81	81	106	171

Source: "Number of Doctor's Degrees Conferred, by Field and Race and Ethnicity: Selected Academic Years Ending 1977-1985," *1989 Education Indicators*, pp. 247-249. U.S. Department of Education, Office for Civil Rights, Survey of Earned Degrees Conferred by Institutions of Higher Education by Race, Ethnicity, and Sex, academic years ending 1977 and 1979; National Center for Education Statistics, Degrees and Other Formal Awards Conferred surveys, academic years ending 1981 and 1985. *Notes:* Distributions for 1977 through 1981 exclude degrees not reported by race and ethnicity. Distributions for 1985 include degrees for which missing race and ethnicity could be imputed. The number of degrees reported for 1977 and 1979 excludes degrees conferred by U.S. Service Schools (0.4 percent or less of degrees). 1. In contrast to previous editions of *the condition of Education*, computer sciences and engineering are not included in the technical/professional category.

★ 257 ★
Fields of Recent Doctorate Recipients

Maror field of study and sex of student	Total	White non-Hispanic	Black non-Hispanic	Hispanic	Asian or Pacific Islander	American Indian/ Alaskan Native	Non-resident alien
All fields, total[1]	34,033	24,435	1,060	750	1,097	104	6,587
Agriculture and natural resources, total	1,048	650	18	15	32	2	331
Architecture and environmental design, total	92	45	7	0	1	0	39
Area and ethnic studies, total	132	99	7	2	1	1	22
Business and management, total	1,094	688	296	10	50	2	315
Communications, total	280	209	17	11	1	0	42
Computer and information sciences, total	374	219	2	6	20	1	126
Education, total	6,909	5,495	468	207	104	49	586
Engineering, total	3,807	1,672	29	68	258	3	1,777
Engineering technologies, total	11	5	1	0	0	0	5
Foreign languages, total	441	300	16	42	4	0	79
Health professions, total	1,213	932	33	17	40	3	188
Home economics, total	297	225	23	6	6	0	37
Law, total	120	71	3	19	0	0	27
Letters, total	1,181	950	28	26	21	6	150
Liberal/general studies, total	29	22	2	1	0	0	4
Library and archival science, total	57	43	1	0	2	1	10
Life sciences, total	3,417	2,624	53	59	149	5	527
Mathematics, total	723	349	9	9	367	1	318
Military sciences, total	0	0	0	0	0	0	0
Multi/interdisciplinary studies, total	276	215	2	8	4	1	46

Continued.

Fields of Recent Doctorate Recipients
[Continued]

Maror field of study and sex of student	Total	White non-Hispanic	Black non-Hispanic	Hispanic	Asian or Pacific Islander	American Indian/ Alaskan Native	Non-resident alien
Parks and recreation, total	33	28	2	0	0	0	3
Philosophy and religion, total	420	346	7	5	9	0	53
Physical sciences, total	3,671	2,441	26	60	166	3	975
Protective services, total	19	15	0	0	3	0	1
Psychology, total	3,056	2,725	97	71	51	16	96
Public affairs, total	397	292	34	18	6	2	45
Social sciences, total	2,915	2,051	95	68	77	4	620
Theology, total	1,230	1,040	39	11	37	2	101
Visual and performing arts, total	791	684	12	11	18	2	64

Source: "Doctor's Degrees Conferred by Institutions of Higher Education, by Racial/Ethnic Group, Major Field of Study, and Sex of Student: 1986-87," Digest of Education Statistics, 1989, pp. 249-250. Primary source: U.S. Department of Education, National Center for Educational Statistics, Integrated Postsecondary Education Data System (IPEDS), "Completions" survey. (This table was prepared June 1989.) *Notes:* 1. This tabulation excludes 40 men and 47 women whose racial/ ethnic group could not be imputed. Because of imputation methods, fields of study totals by race/ethnicity may differ slightly from field of study by sex. Data are preliminary.

★ 258 ★
Financial Aid Categories at UNCF Institutions

Type of Aid	No. of Students	Percentage of all UNCF Students	Total Award	Percent of Total	Average Grant/Loan
Pell Grant	25,450	55	41,591	24	1,634
SEOG	15,410	33	13,447	8	870
College Work Study	16,734	36	16,932	10	1,012
GSL's (Stafford Loans)	22,236	48	53,061	31	2,386
NDSL's (Perkins Loans)	4,349	9	4,832	3	1,111
State Scholarships	15,049	33	15,553	9	1,033
Institutional Scholarships	11,279	24	17,636	10	1,564
Veteran Benefits	238	<1	342	<1	1,437
ROTC	158	<1	642	<1	3,949
Other	5,264	11	8,318	5	1,580
Total			172,336		

Source: "Financial Aid by Category, 1987-88," *UNCF 1989 Statistical Report*, p. 11. Primary source: United Negro College Fund, Inc., UNCF 1989 Statistical Report, (undated), New York, NY. UNCF: United Negro College Fund.

★ 259 ★
Financial Aid to Undergraduates

Selected student characteristics	Enrollment of under-graduates[1] in thousands	Any Aid			Grants			Loans			Work Study		
		Total[2]	Federal	Non-Federal	Total	Federal	Non-Federal	Total	Federal	Non-Federal	Total	Federal	Non-Federal
					Percent of all undergraduates receiving aid								
All undergraduates	11,213	45.5	34.9	28.8	37.6	24.6	27.2	24.4	23.3	1.6	6.1	4.7	1.8
Race/ethnicity													
White, non-Hispanic	8,724	43.3	32.0	28.4	35.1	20.9	26.8	23.6	22.6	1.6	5.6	4.1	1.8
Black, non-Hispanic	1,043	63.8	55.7	33.2	56.6	47.0	31.2	35.0	32.7	2.6	9.8	8.6	1.7
Hispanic	763	47.8	40.9	27.2	41.1	33.2	25.9	24.0	23.4	1.0	5.8	4.5	1.3
Asian American	572	40.5	33.3	28.5	36.2	27.0	27.7	18.4	18.1	1.0	7.6	6.2	1.6
American Indian	112	48.9	40.3	28.7	41.2	35.0	26.1	19.7	18.5	1.1	6.8	5.3	2.1
					Average 1986-87 award for full-time, full-year undergraduates enrolled in fall 1986 (in dollars)								
All full-time, full-year undergraduates	5,621	3,813	2,973	2,113	2,630	1,598	2,033	2,456	2,425	1,723	1,077	1,002	1,105
Race/ethnicity													
White, non-Hispanic	4,454	3,716	2,970	2,043	2,525	1,554	1,953	2,484	2,441	1,879	1,044	983	1,029
Black, non-Hispanic	492	4,126	3,132	2,308	2,827	1,785	2,248	2,257	2,299	1,141	1,170	1,003	1,632
Hispanic	333	3,817	2,741	2,161	2,728	1,518	2,129	2,439	2,420	4	1,186	1,163	1,214
Asian American	299	4,374	2,903	2,546	3,280	1,640	2,474	2,478	2,464	4	1,206	1,082	1,443
American Indian	44	4,201	3,020	2,413	3,299	1,859	2,556	2,762	2,762	4	4	4	4
					Average 1986-87 award for other undergraduates enrolled in fall 1986 (in dollars)								
All other undergraduates[3]	5,592	2,199	2,203	1,145	1,458	1,223	1,079	2,121	2,121	1,197	913	856	949
Race/ethnicity													
White, non-Hispanic	4,270	2,061	2,123	1,137	1,373	1,163	1,059	2,137	2,114	1,277	906	840	916
Black, non-Hispanic	551	2,410	2,295	1,026	1,574	1,333	963	2,007	2,084	4	1,001	916	4
Hispanic	429	2,499	2,454	1,142	1,546	1,233	1,132	2,257	2,271	4	4	4	4
Asian American	273	2,842	2,488	1,520	1,972	1,452	1,473	2,138	2,072	4	4	4	4
American Indian	68	2,126	1,893	4	1,834	1,236	4	4	4	4	4	4	4

Source: "Percent of Undergraduates Enrolled in Fall 1986 and Average Amount Awarded per Student, by Type and Source of Aid and Selected Student Characteristics," *Digest of Education Statistics*, 1989, pp. 284-285. U.S. Department of Education, National Center for Education Statistics, *Undergraduate Financing of Postsecondary Education: A Report of the 1987 National Postsecondary Student Aid Study*. (This table was prepared February 1989). *Notes:* Because of rounding and/or the fact that some students receive aid from multiple sources, details may not add to totals. 1. Numbers of undergraduates may not equal figures reported in other tables, since these data are based on a sample survey. 2. Includes students who reported they were awarded aid, but did nto specify the source or type of aid. 3. Enrollment data include persons whose attendance status was not reported. 4. Data not available.

★ 260 ★
Freshman Admissions at UNCF Institutions: Trends

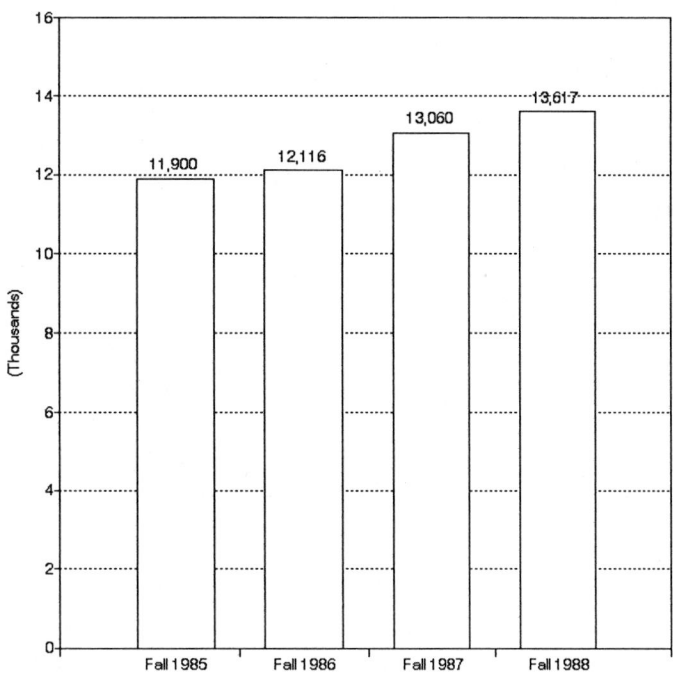

In thousands.

Year	Number
Fall 1985	11,900
Fall 1986	12,116
Fall 1987	13,060
Fall 1988	13,617

Source: "Admissions, New Freshmen — 1985 ... 1988," *UNCF 1989 Statistical Report*, p. 5. Primary source: United Negro College Fund (UNCF), Inc., UNCF 1989 Statistical Report (undated), New York, NY.

★ 261 ★
Freshman Enrollment in 2-Year Institutions: Trends

	Two-Year Public		Two-Year Private	
	N	%	N	%
Total				
Less	164	31	45	28
Same	186	35	53	34
More	180	34	60	38
	530	100	158	100
Blacks				
Less	149	27	25	15
Same	251	45	90	54
More	161	29	53	32
	561	101	168	101

Continued.

Freshman Enrollment in 2-Year Institutions: Trends
[Continued]

	Two-Year Public		Two-Year Private	
	N	%	N	%
Hispanics				
Less	92	17	22	14
Same	304	57	100	63
More	138	26	36	23
	534	100	158	100
Asians				
Less	78	15	19	13
Same	314	59	108	72
More	141	26	23	15
	533	100	150	100
American Indians				
Less	82	16	17	12
Same	347	66	115	78
More	98	19	15	10
	527	101	147	100
Whites				
Less	150	27	39	23
Same	230	41	79	47
More	179	32	51	30
	559	100	169	100

Source: "Self-Reported Trends in Freshman Enrollment in Two-Year Institutions, 1980-1985," *Demographics, Standards, and Equity,* 1986, p. 42. Primary source: *Demographics, Standards, and Equity: Challenges in College Admissions.* American Association of Collegiate Registars & Admission Officers, American College Testing Program, College Board, Educational Testing Service, National Association of College Admission Counselors, November 1986.

★ 262 ★
Freshman Major/Career Preferences: Trends

	Percent of Entering Freshmen Students by Year									
	1977		1979		1981		1983		1985	
Major or College Preference	All	HBCU	All	HBCU	All	HBCU	All	HBCU	All	HBCU
Major:										
Accounting	6.4	7.3	6.2	6.4	5.8	6.0	6.3	7.5	6.5	7.1
Elementary Education	2.6	3.9	2.2	3.2	2.6	1.9	2.4	1.9	3.2	2.9
Electrical or Electronic Engineering	3.2	2.4	3.2	3.7	3.6	2.5	4.3	2.9	3.9	3.3
Mechanical Engineering	1.8	1.2	2.0	.7	2.4	1.0	2.2	1.1	2.1	1.4
Nursing	4.4	4.2	3.6	3.4	3.8	6.2	4.4	2.3	3.3	6.1
Computer Science	1.0	.9	1.8	2.5	3.8	6.0	4.5	8.2	2.3	7.9

Continued.

Freshman Major/Career Preferences: Trends
[Continued]

Major or College Preference	Percent of Entering Freshmen Students by Year									
	1977		1979		1981		1983		1985	
	All	HBCU	All	HBCU	All	HBCU	All	HBCU	All	HBCU
Career Preferences:										
Lawyer	4.4	4.8	3.4	4.2	3.9	4.4	3.9	5.7	3.9	6.4
Physician	3.2	4.1	2.9	3.7	3.4	4.2	3.9	4.4	3.8	5.0

Source: "Trends in Preferences for College Majors and Careers for Freshmen at All Institutions and at HBCUs," *NAFEO INROADS*, April/May, 1988, p. 3. Primary source: *The American College Freshman: National Norms for Fall, 1977, 1979, 1981, 1983, and 1985*, UCLA/ACE Cooperative Institutional Research Project. *Note:* The data represent weighted national norms. Published by permission.

★ 263 ★
Freshmen Enrollment in 4-Year Institutions: Trends

	Four-Year Public		Four-Year Private	
	N	%	N	%
Total				
Less	153	40	294	39
Same	71	19	176	23
More	155	41	288	38
	379	100	758	100
Blacks				
Less	94	28	155	24
Same	96	29	263	41
More	141	43	218	34
	331	100	636	99
Hispanics				
Less	46	15	85	14
Same	155	50	344	58
More	112	36	167	28
	313	101	596	100
Asians				
Less	40	13	60	10
Same	142	46	320	54
More	125	41	215	36
	307	100	595	100
American Indians				
Less	50	16	72	12
Same	187	62	432	75
More	66	22	71	12
	303	100	575	100
Whites				
Less	115	35	202	32
Same	71	22	187	30
More	144	44	242	38

Continued.

Freshmen Enrollment in 4-Year Institutions: Trends
[Continued]

	Four-Year Public		Four-Year Private	
	N	%	N	%
	330	101	631	100

Source: "Self-Reported Trends in Freshmen Enrolled in Four-Year Institutions, 1980-1985," *Demographics, Stands, and Equity*, 1986, p. 41. Primary source: *Demographics, Stands, and Equity: Challenges in College Admissions*. American Association of Collegiate Registars & Admission Officers, American College Testing Program, College Board, Educational Testing Service, National Association of College Admission Counselors, November 1986.

★ 264 ★
Freshmen Racial/Ethnic Diversity in 4-Year Institutions, 1985

Institutional Type and Group	Applications	Acceptances	Enrolled Freshmen
Four-Year Public			
American Indians	0.5	0.4	0.6
Asians	4.3	4.0	3.8
Blacks	8.8	8.3	8.7
Hispanics	3.8	3.6	3.8
Whites	78.6	80.3	81.0
Others	4.1	3.3	2.1
	100.1	99.9	100.0
Four-Year Private			
American Indians	0.3	0.3	0.4
Asians	4.5	3.6	3.5
Blacks	6.2	6.4	8.2
Hispanics	2.7	2.6	2.8
Whites	84.1	85.3	83.1
Others	2.2	1.7	1.9
	100.0	99.9	99.9

Source: "Subgroup Representation Among Applications, Acceptances, and Enrolled Freshmen Reported for Four-Year Institutions," *Demographics, Stands, and Equity*, 1986, p. 40. Primary source: *Demographics, Stands, and Equity: Challenges in College Admissions*. American Association of Collegiate Registars & Admission Officers, American College Testing Program, College Board, Educational Testing Service, National Association of College Admission Counselors, November 1986. *Notes:* Since different numbers of institutions reported applications, acceptances, and enrolled freshmen, precise comparisons across stages of the enrollment process are not possible.

★ 265 ★
From High School through Graduate/Professional School

	Percentage
Graduate from High School	
Anglos	83
Blacks	72
Chicanos	55
Puerto Ricans	55
American Indians	55
Enter College	
Anglos	238
Blacks	29
Chicanos	22
Puerto Ricans	25
American Indians	17
Complete College	
Anglos	23
Blacks	12
Chicanos	7
Puerto Ricans	7
American Indians	6
Enter Graduate or Professional College	
Anglos	14
Blacks	8
Chicanos	4
Puerto Ricans	4
American Indians	4
Complete Graduate or Professional School	
Anglos	9
Blacks	4
Chicanos	2
Puerto Ricans	2
American Indians	2

Source: "The Educational Pipeline in the United States," *Equality and Excellence: The Educational Status of Black Americans,* 1985, p. 13. Primary source: Astin, Alexander, *Minorities in American Higher Education* (San Francisco: Jossey-Bass, 1982). Published by permission.

★ 266 ★
Full- and Part-Time Postsecondary Students

	Full-Time	Part-Time
	Numbers in percent	
White	79.0	80.0
Black	9.0	8.0
Hispanic	4.0	6.0
Asian/Pacific Islander	3.7	3.5
Nonresident Alien	3.7	1.7
American Indian/Alaskan Native	0.6	0.8

Continued.

Full- and Part-Time Postsecondary Students
[Continued]

	Full-Time	Part-Time
	Numbers in hundred thousands	
White	5,609,470	4,304,713
Black	636,344	444,555
American Indian	46,106	44,027
Hispanic	305,336	318,255
Asian/Pacific Islander	260,721	187,591
Nonresident alien	258,526	85,244

Source: "Percentage of Full-time vs. Part-time Students by Race, Ethnicity," *Black Issues in Higher Education*, March 1, 1990, p. 7. Primary source: U.S. Department of Education, Center for Education Statistics, Integrated Postsecondary Education Data System, "Fall Enrollment, 1986." *Note:* 1. Percentages rounded.

★ 267 ★
Full-Time Higher Education Faculty: Characteristics

Academic rank and sex	Total	White non-Hispanic	Black non-Hispanic	Hispanic	Asian or Pacific Islander	American Indian/ Alaskan Native
			Race/ethnicity			
Men and women, all ranks	464,072	417,036	19,227	7,704	18,370	1,735
Professors	129,269	119,868	2,859	1,455	4,788	299
Associate professors	111,092	100,630	4,201	1,727	4,130	404
Assistant professors	111,308	97,496	5,895	1,968	5,469	480
Instructors	75,411	66,799	4,572	1,798	1,806	436
Lecturers	9,766	8,477	631	251	360	47
Other faculty	27,226	23,766	1,069	505	1,817	69
Men, all ranks	336,009	303,953	10,456	5,360	14,846	1,394
Professors	114,258	106,335	2,058	1,206	4,395	264
Associate professors	85,156	77,483	2,595	1,280	3,451	347
Assistant professors	71,463	62,582	2,923	1,316	4,240	402
Instructors	43,251	38,592	2,107	1,141	1,105	306
Lecturers	5,098	4,436	304	117	212	29
Other faculty	16,783	14,525	469	300	1,443	46
Women, all ranks	128,063	113,083	8,771	2,344	3,524	341
Professors	15,011	13,533	801	249	393	35
Associate professors	25,936	23,147	1,606	447	679	57
Assistant professors	39,845	34,914	2,972	652	1,229	78
Instructors	32,160	28,207	2,465	657	701	130
Lecturers	4,668	4,041	327	134	148	18
Other faculty	10,443	9,241	600	205	374	23

Source: "Full-Time Instructional Faculty in Institutions of Higher Education, by Race/Ethnicity, Academic Rank, and Sex: Fall 1985," *Digest of Education Statistics*, 1989, p. 212. Primary source: U.S. Equal Opportunity Commission, Higher Education Staff Information Report File, 1985, unpublished data. (This table was prepared June 1989.) *Notes:* Data exclude faculty employed by system offices. Totals may differ from figures reported on other tables because of varying survey methodologies.

★ 268 ★
HBCU Degrees Conferred: Trends

Degrees	1976	1978	1980	1983[1]	1985	% Change 1976-85
Blacks						
First Professional	537	601	622	747	692	28.0
Doctorate[2]	50	54	69	87	105	110.0
Masters	4,548	3,939	3,185	2,956	2,553	-43.9
Bachelors	21,971	21,616	19,528	17,694	16,758	-23.7
Associate	1,662	1,700	1,855	1,730	1,698	2.2
Total	28,768	27,910	25,259	23,214	21,806	-24.2
Whites						
First Professional	145	111	159	116	165	13.8
Doctorate[2]	2	5	10	7	22	1000.0
Masters	989	850	832	774	799	-19.2
Bachelors	980	1,113	1,517	1,344	1,427	45.6
Associate	90	168	344	292	318	253.3
Total	2,206	2,347	2,862	2,533	2,731	23.8

Source: "Degrees Conferred to [sic] Blacks and Whites by HBCUs, Selected Years 1976, 1979, 1981, 1983, and 1985," *NAFEO INROADS*, February/March-April/May, 1989, p. 13. Primary source: *Data on Earned Degrees Conferred from Institutions of Higher Education, by Race/Ethnicity, and Sex, Academic Year 1975-76, 1976-77, 1978-79*, National Advisory Committee Staff Analysis ED/OCR; *Data on Earned Degrees Conferred from Institutions of Higher Education by Race/Ethnicity, and Sex, Academic Year 1980-81, 1982-83, and 1984-85*, NAFEO Research Institute Staff Analysis ED/OCR. *Notes:* 1. All persons did not indicate race in OCR data for 1983; therefore, numbers may be greater. 2. In 1976, four HBCUs conferred the doctorate and by 1985 the number had increased to eight. Published by permission.

★ 269 ★
HBCU Education Degrees Awarded: Trends

Year	Total Degrees	Institution	
		HBCUs	Non-HBCUs
1965-66	118,339	7,065	111,334
1966-67	120,874	6,773	114,101
1967-68	135,848	6,914	128,934
1968-69	153,248	7,558	145,690
1969-70	166,423	8,197	158,226
1970-71	177,638	8,430	169,208
1975-76	156,538	7,420	149,118
1978-79	127,633	5,740	121,893
1980-81	110,715	3,691	107,024
1982-83	100,171	3,600	96,571
1984-85	90,511	2,747	87,764
Number and Percent Change			
1966-71	59,239	1,365	57,874
	(50.0)	(19.3)	(52.0)

Continued.

HBCU Education Degrees Awarded: Trends
[Continued]

| Year | Total Degrees | Institution | |
		HBCUs	Non-HBCUs
1971-76	-21,100	-1,010	-20,090
	(-11.9)	(-12.0)	(-11.9)
1976-81	-45,823	-3,729	-42,094
	(-29.3)	(-50.3)	(-28.2)
1981-85	-20,204	-944	-19,260
	(-18.3)	(-25.6)	(-18.0)
1966-85	-27,888	-4,318	-23,570
	(-23.6)	(-61.1)	(-21.2)

Source: "Number and Percent Change of Bachelor's Degrees Awarded in Education by Historically Black Colleges and Universities (HBCUs) and All U.S. Institutions, 1965-66 to 1984-85," *NAFEO INROADS,* February/March 1988, p. 19. *Degrees Granted and Enrollment Trends in Historically Black Colleges: And Eight Year Study,* Institute for Services to Education, 1974. National Advisory Committee Staff Analysis, OCR Unpublished Data on Degrees Awarded by Major Field Race/Ethnicity, and Sex - 1975-76, 1976-77, 1978-79. NAFEO Research Institute Staff Analysis of OCR Unpublished Data on Degrees Awarded by Major Field, Race/Ethnicity, and Sex - 1980-81, 1982-83, 1984-85. Published by permission.

★ 270 ★
HBCU Regional Accreditation

| Institution | Number | Regional Accrediting Body | | | | | Total |
		EH	M	NH	SC	WJ	
Two-Year:							
Public	12	1	0	4	7	1	13
Private	11	0	0	2	4	0	6
Four-Year:							
Public	41	0	10	7	24	0	41
Private	48	0	2	3	40	0	45
Grad/Professional	4	0	0	0	3	0	3
Total	116	1	12	16	78	1	108

Source: "A Summary Profile: Regional Accreditation, Historically Black Colleges and Universities (HBCUs) (N = 116)," *NAFEO INROADS,* April/May 1987, p. 8. Primary source: Center for Statistics, *Education Directory, Colleges and Universities, 1985-86;* NAFEO Survey. *Notes:* NAFEO has no Member Institutions in the region covered by the Northwest Association of Schools and Colleges (NW). NAFEO: National Association for Equality of Opportunity in Higher Education. Legend: EH: New England Association of Schools and Colleges, Commission on Institutions of HI ED. M: Middle States Association of Colleges and Schools, Commission on HI ED. NH: North Central Association of Colleges and Schools, Commission on Institutions of HI ED. SC: Southern Association of Colleges and Schools, Commission on Colleges. WJ: Western Association of Schools and Colleges, Accrediting Commission for Community and Junior Colleges.   Published by permission.

★ 271 ★
HBCU Specialized Accreditation

	Two-year:		Four-year:		Grad/	
	Public	Private	Public	Private	Professional	Total
Specialized Accrediting Body						
Number	12	11	41	48	4	116
ADNUR -National League for Nursing	3	0	6	0	0	9
ADVET - American Veterinary Med. Assoc.: Assoc. Degree in Anim. Tech.	1	0	1	0	0	2
APCP - AMA: Assistant to Prim. Care Phy.[1]	1	0	0	1	0	2
ARCH - Natl. Arch. Accred. Bd.: Arch.	0	0	2	3	0	5
ART - Natl. Assoc. of Sch. of Art and Design	0	0	3	1	0	4
BUS - Natl. Assem. O Collegi. Sch. of Bus.	0	0	2	2	1	5
CCR - Natl. Shorthand Rep. Assoc.	1	0	0	0	0	1
CHE - Coun. on Ed. for Pub. Health	0	0	0	1	0	1
CHEM - Amer. Chem. Soc.: Chem.	0	0	3	1	0	4
CT - Amer. Corr. Thera. Assoc: Correc. Thera.	0	0	1	0	0	1
DA - Amer. Dent. Assoc.: Dent. Asst.[1]	2	0	0	0	0	2
DE - Coun. of Deaf Ed.	0	0	1	0	0	1
DENT - Amer. Dent. Assoc.: Dent.[1]	0	0	0	1	1	2
DH - Amer. Dent Assoc.: Dent. Hyg.[1]	1	0	0	1	1	3
DIET - Amer. Dent. Assoc. (UG)[1]	1	0	2	2	0	5
DLT - Amer. Dent. Assoc. Com. on Accred.: Dent. Lab. Tech.	1	0	0	0	0	1
EMT - AMA: Emerg. Med. Ser.	0	0	1	0	0	1
END - Accred. Bd. for Eng. and Tech.: Eng.	0	0	5	2	0	7
ENGT - Accred. Bd. for Eng. Tech.: Eng. Tech.	0	0	6	0	0	6
FS - Amer. Diet. Assoc.: Food Sc. and Nutr.	0	0	1	0	0	1
FUSER - Amer. Bd. of Funeral Ser. Ed.	0	0	1	0	0	1
HE - Amer. Home Ec. Assoc.	0	0	2	0	0	2
HSA - Accred. Com. on Ed. for Health Ser. Adm.	0	0	0	1	0	1
IPSY - APA: Pre-Doc. Intern.	0	0	0	1	0	1
IT - Natl. Assoc. of Ind. Tech.	0	0	1	0	0	1
JOUR - Accred. Coun. on Ed. in Journ. and Mass Comm.	0	0	2	0	0	2
LAW - ABA: Law[1]	0	0	3	1	0	4
LIB - Amer Lib. Assoc.	0	0	1	2	1	4
MAC - AMA: Med. Asst. Ed.[1]	1	0	0	0	0	1
MED - Liaison Com. on Med. Ed.	0	0	0	1	2	3
MIDWF - Amer. Coll. of Nurs.-Midwives	0	0	0	0	1	1
MLTAD - AMA: Med Lab Tech (A.A. Degree)	1	0	0	0	0	1
MR - Amer. Med. Rec. Assoc.: Med. Rec. Adm.	0	0	1	0	0	1
MRA - AMA: Med. Rec. Adm. Ed.	0	0	2	0	0	2
MRT - AMA: Med. Rec. Tech. Ed.	1	0	0	0	0	1
MT - AMA: Med. Tech.	0	0	2	3	1	6
MUS - Natl. Assoc. of Sch. of Mus.[1]	0	0	14	6	0	20
NMT - AMA Nuc. Med. Tech.[1]	0	0	1	0	0	1
NUR - NLN: Bacc. Deg. or Higher	0	0	15	4	0	19
OD - AMA: Occ. Therapy	1	0	0	0	0	1
OT - Amer. Occ. Ther. Assoc.: Occ. Ther. Asst.	0	0	1	2	0	3
OTA - Coun. on Ed. for Pub. Health: Sch. of Pub. Health	1	0	0	0	0	1
PHAR - Amer. Coun. on Phar. Ed.	0	0	2	2	0	4
PTA - Amer. Phy. Therapy Assoc.: Phy. Therapist	0	0	2	1	0	3
PTAA - Amer. Phy. Therapy Assoc.: Phy. Therapy	1	0	0	0	0	1
RAD - AMA: Radiography	1	0	1	2	0	4
RC - Coun. on Rehab. Ed.: Rehab. Couns.	0	0	1	0	0	1
RCE - Coun. on Rehab. Ed.: Rehab. Couns. Ed.	0	0	1	0	0	1
REC - Coun. on Accred. of Natl. Rec. and Parks Assoc.	0	0	1	0	0	1
RSTH - AMA: Respir. Ther.	2	0	2	0	0	4
RSTHT - AMA: Respir. Ther. Tech.	2	0	0	0	0	2
RTT - AMA: Rad. Ther. Tech.	0	0	1	1	0	2
SP - Amer. Speech Lang. Hear. Assoc.: Speech-Lang. Path.[1]	0	0	2	2	0	4
SURGA - AMA: Surg. Assist.[1]	1	0	0	0	0	1
SW - Coun. on Soc. Wk. Ed.	0	0	20	7	1	28
TE - Natl. Assoc. for Indus. Tech.: Tech. Ed.	0	0	1	0	0	1
TED - Natl. Coun. for Accred. of Teach. Ed.[1]	0	0	33	3	1	37
THEA	0	0	1	0	0	1

Continued.

HBCU Specialized Accreditation
[Continued]

	Two-year:		Four-year:		Grad/	
	Public	Private	Public	Private	Professional	Total
THEOL - Assoc. of Theo. Sch. in the USA and Canada	0	0	0	2	0	2
VET - Amer. Vet. Med. Assoc.	0	0	0	1	0	1
31C - Indicates that Inst. qualified for listing via the three-Inst cert. procedure.	0	3	0	1	0	4

Source: "A Summary Profile: Specialized Accreditation, Historically Black Colleges and Universities (HBCUs) (N = 116)," *NAFEO INROADS*, April/May 1987, p. 10. Primary source: Center for Statistics, *Education Directory of Colleges and Universities*, 1985-86; and NAFEO Survey. *Note:* 1. Did not provide 1985-86 updated certification.

★ 272 ★
HBCU Transfer Institutions

Responding Institutions = 32.

HBCU State	1983			1984			1985		
	4-yr	2-yr	Tot	4-yr	2-yr	Tot	4-yr	2-yr	Tot
Alabama	139	195	334	169	183	352	192	179	371
Arkansas	131	32	163	139	41	180	141	35	176
Florida	25	115	140	44	94	138	83	111	194
Georgia	201	79	280	158	97	255	221	111	332
Louisiana	110	22	132	116	23	139	96	48	144
Mississippi	36	59	95	46	40	86	41	62	103
N. Carolina	230	418	648	261	359	620	368	348	716
Ohio	14	20	34	14	18	32	25	16	41
S. Carolina	33	63	96	41	60	101	28	63	91
Tennessee	69	38	107	42	32	74	23	37	60
Texas	81	74	155	43	33	76	80	59	139
Virginia	6	14	20	12	15	27	3	16	19
Total	1072	1129	2204	1085	995	2080	1301	1085	2386
Percent	49	51	100	52	48	100	55	45	100

Source: "HBCU Transfer Students by State and Level, Fall, 1983-1985," *NAFEO INROADS*, June/July 1987, p. 6. Primary source: Patel, Narenda H. *Students Transfers from White to Black Colleges*. NAFEO Research Institute, 1988.

★ 273 ★
HBCU Transfer Students: Characteristics

Responding Institutions(1) = 32.

HBCU State	1983				1984				1985			
	4-yr		2-yr		4-yr		2-yr		4-yr		2-yr	
	Wht	Blk	Wht	Blk	Wht	Blk	Wht	Blk	Wht	Blk	Wht	Blk
Alabama	82	57	102	93	91	78	115	68	116	76	98	81
Arkansas	109	22	17	15	129	10	4	37	118	23	15	20
Florida	19	6	33	82	24	20	84	10	32	51	99	12
Georgia	134	67	54	25	57	101	46	51	99	122	92	19
Louisiana	70	40	16	6	86	30	15	8	58	38	32	16
Mississippi	15	21	42	17	10	36	27	13	14	27	38	24
N. Carolina	131	99	368	50	151	110	270	89	263	105	328	20

Continued.

HBCU Transfer Students: Characteristics
[Continued]

HBCU State	1983				1984				1985			
	4-yr		2-yr		4-yr		2-yr		4-yr		2-yr	
	Wht	Blk	Wht	Blk	Wht	Blk	Wht	Blk	Wht	Blk	Wht	Blk
Ohio	14	0	20	0	14	0	16	2	20	5	16	0
S. Carolina	11	22	57	6	9	32	55	5	13	15	62	1
Tennessee	56	13	20	18	27	15	20	12	13	10	23	14
Texas	58	23	68	6	24	19	30	3	60	20	41	18
Virginia	1	5	14	0	6	6	14	1	2	1	16	0
Total	700	375	811	318	628	457	696	299	808	493	860	225

Source: "HBCU Transfer Students by Institutional Type, State and Level, Fall, 1983-1985," *NAFEO INROADS*, June/July 1987, p. 5. Patel, Narenda H. "Student Transfers from White to Black Colleges," NAFEO Research Institute, 1988. *Notes:* 1. Institutional Type: Wht - Predominately White; Blk - Predominately Black. Published by permission.

★ 274 ★
HBCU Transfers: Where They Come From

HBCU State	Level		Institution[1]			Average Enrollment
	4-yr	2-yr	Wht	Blk	Tot	
Alabama	166	186	201	151	352	5918
Arkansas	137	36	131	42	173	3118
Florida	51	106	97	60	157	3560
Georgia	193	96	161	128	289	5167
Louisiana	107	31	92	46	138	3197
Mississippi	41	54	49	46	95	1584
N. Carolina	286	375	503	158	661	11303
Ohio	18	18	33	3	36	865
S. Carolina	34	62	69	27	96	2715
Tennessee	44	36	53	27	80	1797
Texas	68	55	94	29	123	2006
Virginia	7	15	18	6	24	705
Total	1152	1070	1501	723	2224	(5%)41935
Percent	52	48	68	32	100	

Source: "Three-Year Average of HBCU Transfer Students by State, Institutional Type, and Level, Fall, 1983-1985 (Responding Institutions = 32)," *NAFEO INROADS*, June/July, 1987, p. 7. Primary source: Patel, Narenda H. *Student Transfers from White to Black Colleges*, NAFEO Research Institute, 1988 *Notes:* HBCU: Historically Black Colleges and Universities Institutional Type: Wht - Predominately White Institutions Blk - Predominately Black Institutions . Published by permission.

★ 275 ★
HBCU/EOEI Changes in Enrollment

Control/Level Total	Number of Institutions	Black				White				Total			
		Year		Difference		Year		Difference		Year		Difference	
		1986	1987	Number	%	1986	1987	Number	%	1986	1987	Number	%
HBCUs & EOEIs[1,2]	116	210,084	213,938	3,904	1.9	44,233	43,397	-836	-1.9	271,812	275,053	3,241	1.2
HBCUs	104	176,596	182,019	5,423	3.1	22,651	23,225	574	2.5	213,093	217,367	4,274	2.0
EOEIs	12	33,488	31,919	-1,569	-4.7	21,582	20,172	-1,410	-6.5	58,719	57,686	-1,033	-1.8
HBCUs													
Public (Total)	45	120,916	124,974	3,833	3.2	21,677	21,939	262	1.2	151,468	154,682	3,214	2.1
Four Year	(39)	114,721	118,814	4,093	3.6	21,367	21,538	171	0.8	144,835	148,306	3,471	2.4
Two Year	(6)	6,195	5,935	-260	-4.2	310	401	91	29.4	6,633	6,376	-257	-3.9
Private (Total)	59	55,680	57,270	1,590	2.9	974	1,286	312	33	61,625	62,685	1,060	1.8
Graduate/Professional Only	(3)	1,468	1,472	4	0.3	67	62	-5	-7.5	1,882	1,883	1	-0.1
Four Year	(47)	52,442	54,052	1,610	3.1	889	1,212	323	36	57,907	58,995	1,088	1.9
Two Year	(9)	1,770	1,746	-24	-1.4	18	12	-6	-33.3	1,836	1,807	-29	-1.6
EOEIs													
Public (Total)	9	31,820	30,306	-1,514	-4.8	21,580	20,168	-1,412	-6.5	57,048	56,068	980	1.7
Four Year	(2)	9,004	8,261	-743	-8.3	951	877	-74	-7.8	10,306	9,591	-715	-6.9
Two Year	(7)	22,816	22,045	-771	-3.4	20,629	19,291	-1,338	-6.5	46,742	46,477	-265	-0.6
Private (Total)	3	1,668	1,613	-55	-3.3	2	4	2	100	1,671	1,618	-53	-3.2
Graduate/Professional Only	(1)	950	950	-	-	0	0	-	-	950	950	-	-
Four Year	(1)	380	402	22	5.8	2	2	-	-	383	405	22	5.7
Two Year	(1)	338	261	-77	-23	0	2	2	-	338	263	-75	-22.2

Source: "Change in Enrollment at HBCUs and EOEIs from Fall 1986-87," *NAFEO INROADS*, February/March 1988, p. 24. Primary source: NAFEO Annual Fall 1987 Enrollment Survey of Undergraduate, Graduate, and Professional Students. *Notes:* Fall 1987 racial/ethnic data were not available for twelve institutions. Data for these institutions were imputed from NAFEO's Fall 1986 Annual Enrollment Survey. 1. HBCUs - Historically Black Colleges and Universities (N=104) 2. EOEIs - NAFEO's Other Equal Opportunity Educational Institutions (N=12) . Published by permission.

★ 276 ★
High School Courses Taken

Numbers in thousands.

Courses taken	Total[1]	Race	
		White	Black
Persons over 18 who have attended 12 years of school or more	129,856	114,366	12,180
Number of persons completing courses			
Algebra	102,696	90,689	9,272
Trigonometry or geometry	71,429	63,582	5,662
Chemistry or physics	62,352	54,268	5,922
English, 3 years or more	121,383	107,092	11,486
Foreign language, 2 years or more	56,855	50,493	4,456
Industrial arts, shop, or home economics, 2 years or more	73,883	63,758	8,230
Business courses, 2 years or more	54,297	47,865	5,190
Percentage of persons completing courses			
Algebra	79.1	79.3	76.1
Trigonometry or geometry	55.0	55.6	46.5
Chemistry or physics	48.0	47.5	48.6
English, 3 years or more	93.5	93.6	94.3

Continued.

High School Courses Taken
[Continued]

Courses taken	Total[1]	Race	
		White	Black
Foreign language, 2 years or more	43.8	44.2	36.6
Industrial arts, shop, or home economics, 2 years or more	56.9	55.7	67.6
Business courses, 2 years or more	41.8	41.9	42.6

Source: "High School Courses Taken by Persons Age 16 and Over, by Sex, Race, and Age: Spring 1984," *Digest of Educational Statistics,* 1989, p. 129. Primary source: U.S. Department of Commerce, Bureau of the Census, *Current Population Reports,* Series P-70, No. 11, "Educational Background and Economic Status: Spring 1984." (This table was prepared October 1987.) *Notes:* Data based on sample surveys of the civilian noninstitutional population. 1. Includes only persons completing 12 years of school or more.

★ 277 ★
High School Credits in Science & Mathematics: Trends

Race/ethnicity	Science		Mathematics		Computer science	
	1982	1987	1982	1987	1982	1987
White	2.27	2.68	2.59	2.97	0.12	0.43
Black	1.99	2.41	2.44	2.92	0.10	0.36
Hispanic	1.79	2.39	2.22	2.82	0.07	0.35
Asian/Pacific Islander	2.56	3.23	3.11	3.79	0.19	0.56
Other	2.02	2.57	2.21	3.01	0.05	0.31
Race not reported	[1]	2.55	[1]	3.03	[1]	0.48

Source: "Mean Number of Credits Earned by High School Graduates in Science and Mathematics, by Race/Ethnicity: 1982 and 1987," *Science and Engineering Indicators - 1989,* 1989, p. 201. Primary source: Westat, Inc., *Tabulations for the Nation At Risk Update Study as Part of the 1987 High School Transcript Study* (Washington, DC: U.S. Department of Education, National Center for Education Statistics, 1988). *Note:* 1. Not available.

★ 278 ★
High School Dropouts' Work Status: Trends

Numbers in thousands.

Year and race	Civilian noninstitutional population		Civilian labor force[1]				
				Labor force participation rate		Unemployed	
	Number	Percent	Number		Employed	Number	Unemployment rate
1979-80 high school dropouts in October 1980[2]	739	100.0	471	63.7	322	149	31.6
White[3]	580	78.5	392	67.6	286	106	27.0
Black[3]	146	19.8	73	50.0	33	40	[4]
Hispanic origin[5]	91	12.3	60	65.9	43	17	[4]
1983-84 high school dropouts							

Continued.

High School Dropouts' Work Status: Trends
[Continued]

Year and race	Civilian noninstitutional population		Civilian labor force[1]				
	Number	Percent	Number	Labor force participation rate	Employed	Unemployed	
						Number	Unemployment rate
in October 1984[6]	601	100.0	387	64.4	257	129	33.3
White[3]	483	80.4	321	66.5	229	92	28.7
Black[3]	109	18.1	61	56.0	25	36	[4]
Hispanic origin[5]	91	15.1	47	51.6	32	15	[4]
1984-85 high school dropouts in October 1985[7]	612	100.0	413	67.5	266	147	35.6
White[3]	458	74.1	330	72.1	214	116	35.2
Black[3]	132	21.6	69	52.3	39	30	[4]
Hispanic origin[5]	106	17.3	73	68.9	40	33	[4]
1985-86 high school dropouts in October 1986[8]	562	100.0	359	63.9	259	100	27.9
White[3]	449	79.9	289	64.4	213	76	26.3
Black[3]	90	16.0	50	55.6	29	21	[4]
Hispanic origin[5]	127	22.6	77	60.6	58	19	24.7
1986-87 high school dropouts in October 1987[9]	502	100.0	333	66.4	207	126	37.8
White[3]	373	74.3	257	68.9	172	85	33.0
Black[3]	115	22.9	69	60.1	30	39	[4]
Hispanic origin[5]	57	11.4	37	[4]	22	15	[4]

Source: "Labor Force Status of 1979-80 to 1986-87 High School Dropouts 18 to 24 Years Old, by Sex and Race/Ethnicity: October 1980 to October 1987," *Digest of Educational Statistics*, 1989, p. 371. Primary source: U.S. Department of Labor, Bureau of Labor Statistics, *Students, Graduates, and Dropouts, October 1980-82*; and *Employment of School-Age Youth, Graduates, and Dropouts*, various years, and "Nearly Half of College Freshmen Also Hold a Job or Are Looking for One," June 1987. (This table was prepared December 1988.) *Notes:* Data based on sample surveys of the civilian noninstitutional population. Percents are only shown when the base is 75,000 or greater. Even though the standard errors are large, smaller estimates are shown to permit users to combine categories in various ways. Because of rounding, details may not add to totals. 1. The labor force includes all employed persons plus those seeking employment. The labor force participation rate is the percentage of persons either employed or seeking employment. 2. Includes persons who dropped out of school between October 1979 and October 1980. 3. Includes persons of Hispanic origin. 4. Data not shown where base is less than 75,000. 5. Persons of Hispanic origin may be of any race. 6. Includes persons who dropped out of school between October 1983 and October 1984. 7. Includes persons who dropped out of school between October 1984 and October 1985. 8. Includes persons who dropped out of school between October 1985 and October 1986. 9. Includes persons who dropped out of school between October 1986 and October 1987. 10. Data not available.

★ 279 ★
High School Dropouts: Trends

Year, race/ethnicity, and sex	Total, 14 to 34 years	14 and 15 years	16 and 17 years	18 and 19 years	20 and 21 years	22 to 24 years	25 to 29 years	30 to 34 years
October 1980								
All races	13.0	1.7	8.8	15.7	15.9	15.2	13.9	14.6
Male	13.2	1.3	8.9	16.9	17.8	16.4	13.8	14.0
Female	12.8	2.2	8.8	14.7	14.3	14.0	14.0	15.2
White[1]	12.1	1.7	9.2	14.9	14.5	13.9	12.7	13.4
Male	12.4	1.2	9.3	16.1	15.6	15.4	12.7	13.1

Continued.

High School Dropouts: Trends
[Continued]

Year, race/ethnicity, and sex	Total, 14 to 34 years	14 and 15 years	16 and 17 years	18 and 19 years	20 and 21 years	22 to 24 years	25 to 29 years	30 to 34 years
Female	11.8	2.1	9.2	13.8	13.4	12.6	12.7	13.6
Black[1]	18.8	2.0	6.9	21.2	24.8	24.0	22.6	23.5
Male	19.0	1.5	7.2	22.7	31.3	24.9	22.1	21.9
Female	18.7	2.5	6.6	19.8	19.6	23.3	22.9	24.8
Hispanic origin[2]	35.2	5.7	16.5	39.0	41.6	40.6	40.9	45.4
Male	35.6	3.3	18.1	43.1	41.4	42.9	40.1	43.9
Female	34.9	7.9	15.0	34.6	41.9	38.6	41.7	47.0
October 1986								
All races	11.9	2.4	6.1	12.3	14.8	14.3	13.9	12.6
Male	12.4	2.4	6.5	13.1	16.3	15.3	14.3	13.0
Female	11.4	2.5	5.7	11.5	13.4	13.4	13.5	12.1
White[1]	11.3	2.2	6.5	11.9	14.3	14.3	13.3	11.3
Male	12.1	2.2	6.9	12.8	15.9	15.0	14.2	11.9
Female	10.6	2.2	6.0	11.0	12.9	13.0	12.4	10.7
Black[1]	15.5	3.4	4.7	14.9	18.1	17.3	18.2	20.8
Male	15.5	3.0	4.7	14.6	19.8	19.4	16.7	21.7
Female	15.5	3.8	4.7	15.2	16.7	15.6	19.4	20.1
Hispanic origin[2]	32.2	3.7	14.5	26.8	34.9	38.2	38.5	40.5
Male	33.9	3.7	14.4	29.1	38.7	40.8	40.3	39.8
Female	30.4	3.7	14.7	24.1	30.9	35.1	36.7	41.1

Source: "Percentage of High School Dropouts among Persons 14 to 34 Years Old, by Age, Race/Ethnicity, and Sex: October 1970, 1975, 1980, and 1986," *Digest of Education Statistics*, 1989, p. 106. Primary source: U.S. Department of Commerce, Bureau of the Census, Current Population Reports, Series P-20, Nos. 222, 303, 392, 409, and 429; and unpublished data. (This table was prepared October 1987.) *Notes:* Dropouts are persons who are not enrolled in school and who are not high school graduates. People who have received GED credentials are counted as graduates. Data based on sample surveys of the civilian noninstitutional population. 1. Includes persons of Hispanic origin. 2. Persons of Hispanic origin may be of any race.

★ 280 ★
High School Graduates & the "New Basics"

Racial/ethnic category of students	1982	1987	Percent change 1982 to 1987
All students	13.4	28.6	15.2[1]
White	14.9	29.7	14.8[1]
Black	10.1	24.3	14.2[1]
Hispanic	6.3	17.9	11.6[1]
Asian	21.0	48.3	27.3[1]
Other	5.9	28.9	23.0[1]

Source: "Percent of High School Graduates Earning Recommended Credits in "New Basics", by Racial/Ethnic Category: 1982 and 1987," *1989 Education Indicators*, p. 159. U.S. Department of Education, National Center for Education Statistics, 1987 High School Transcript Study, unpublished tabulations. *Notes:* In this table "new basics" includes 4 years of English and 3 years each of social studies, mathematics, and science. 1. Difference between 1982 and 1987 graduates is significant at the p < 0.05 level.

★ 281 ★
High School Graduates: Academic Course Credits

Students	Year of graduation and course combinations taken[1]	Race/ethnicity			
		White	Black	Hispanic	Asian
1982 graduates					
4 ENG, 3 SS, 3 SCI, 3 MATH, .5 COMP, & 2 FL[2]	1.9	2.2	0.7	0.5	6.0
4 ENG, 3 SS, 3 SCI, 3 MATH, & .5 COMP[3]	2.7	3.1	1.0	0.9	7.1
4 ENG, 3 SS, 3 SCI, 3 MATH, & 2 FL	8.8	10.1	5.2	3.5	17.0
4 ENG, 3 SS, 3 SCI, & 3 MATH	13.4	14.9	10.1	6.3	21.0
4 ENG, 3 SS, 2 SCI, & 2 MATH	29.2	30.2	28.1	23.5	34.5
1987 graduates					
4 ENG, 3 SS, 3 SCI, 3 MATH, .5 COMP, & 2 FL[2]	12.0	12.7	8.3	5.5	24.3
4 ENG, 3 SS, 3 SCI, 3 MATH, & .5 COMP[3]	16.3	17.2	11.7	8.6	28.1
4 ENG, 3 SS, 3 SCI, 3 MATH, & 2 FL	20.9	21.8	16.1	11.8	41.9
4 ENG, 3 SS, 3 SCI, & 3 MATH	28.6	29.7	24.3	17.9	48.3
4 ENG, 3 SS, 2 SCI, & 2 MATH	54.6	53.5	57.2	55.1	71.8
	Increase from 1982 to 1987, in percentage points				
Difference from 1982 to 1987					
4 ENG, 3 SS, 3 SCI, 3 MATH, .5 COMP, & 2 FL[2]	10.2	10.5	7.6	5.0	18.2
4 ENG, 3 SS, 3 SCI, 3 MATH, & .5 COMP[3]	13.6	14.1	10.7	7.7	21.0
4 ENG, 3 SS, 3 SCI, 3 MATH, & 2 FL	12.1	11.7	10.9	8.4	24.9
4 ENG, 3 SS, 3 SCI, & 3 MATH	15.2	14.8	14.2	11.6	27.2
4 ENG, 3 SS, 2 SCI, & 2 MATH	25.4	23.4	29.1	31.6	37.3

Source: "Percentage of High School Graduates Earning Minimum Credits in Selected Combinations of Academic Courses: 1982 and 1987," *Digest of Educational Statistics,* 1989, p. 128. Primary source: U.S. Department of Education, National Center for Educational Statistics, "1987 High School Transcript Study," unpublished tabulations. (This table was prepared December 1988.) *Notes:* Calculations based on unrounded figures. 1. ENG = English; SS = Social Studies; SCI = Science; COMP = Computer Science; and FL = Foreign Language. 2. The National Commission on Excellence in Education recommended that all college-bound high school students follow these courses as a minimum. 3. The National Commission on Excellence in Education recommended that all high school students follow these courses as a minimum.

★ 282 ★
High School Graduates: Credits in Subject Fields

Characteristic	Total	English	History/ social studies	Math	Computer science	Science	Foreign language	Vocational education[1]	Arts	Physical education	Other[2]
1982 graduates											
All students	21.2	3.80	3.10	2.54	0.11	2.19	1.05	3.98	1.39	1.93	1.14
Race											
White	21.4	3.78	3.15	2.59	0.12	2.27	1.13	3.89	1.45	1.89	1.12
Black	20.5	3.90	2.97	2.44	0.10	1.99	0.73	4.15	1.18	1.98	1.07
Hispanic	20.8	3.79	2.94	2.22	0.07	1.79	0.78	4.55	1.27	2.13	1.25
Asian	22.0	3.94	3.04	3.11	0.19	2.56	1.81	2.56	1.22	2.21	1.34
1987 graduates											
All students	23.0	4.03	3.33	2.97	0.43	2.59	1.46	3.65	1.43	1.97	1.14
Race											
White	23.1	3.99	3.30	2.98	0.45	2.64	1.50	3.69	1.48	1.94	1.11
Black	22.5	4.14	3.31	2.90	0.35	2.39	1.12	4.01	1.20	2.01	1.11
Hispanic	22.9	4.23	3.23	2.77	0.36	2.33	1.27	3.57	1.35	2.40	1.37
Asian	24.5	4.31	3.64	3.72	0.57	3.17	2.17	2.08	1.12	2.57	1.14

Source: "Average Number of Carnegie Units Earned by High School Graduates in Various Subject Fields, by Student Characteristic: 1982 and 1987," *Digest of Educational Statistics*, 1989, p. 126. Primary source: U.S. Department of Education, National Center for Educational Statistics, "1987 High School Transcript Study." (This table was prepared December 1988.) *Notes:* The Carnegie unit is a standard of measurement that represents one credit for the completion of a 1- year course. 1. Includes non-occupational vocational education, vocational general introduction, agriculture, business, marketing, health, occupational home economics, trade and industry, and technical courses. 2. Includes personal and social courses, religion and theology, and all other courses not included in the other subject fields.

★ 283 ★
High School Graduates: Vocational Education Course Credits

Characteristic	Total	Non-occupational vocational education	Vocational general introduction	Agriculture	Business	Marketing	Health	Occupational home economics	Trade and industry	Technical
1982 graduates										
All students	3.98	1.84	0.37	0.17	0.78	0.08	0.04	0.09	0.60	0.01
Race										
White	3.89	1.78	0.36	0.18	0.80	0.08	0.03	0.09	0.55	0.02
Black	4.15	1.96	0.41	0.06	0.74	0.10	0.10	0.10	0.67	0.01
Hispanic	4.55	2.17	0.43	0.18	0.73	0.07	0.05	0.10	0.81	0.01
Asian	2.56	1.37	0.18	0.05	0.45	0.03	0.03	0.03	0.41	0.01
1987 graduates										
All students	3.65	1.64	0.34	0.17	0.68	0.10	0.05	0.10	0.56	0.01
Race										
White	3.69	1.66	0.33	0.20	0.69	0.10	0.04	0.09	0.57	0.01

Continued.

High School Graduates: Vocational Education Course Credits
[Continued]

Characteristic	Total	Non-occupational vocational education	Vocational general introduction	Agriculture	Business	Marketing	Health	Occupational home economics	Trade and industry	Technical
Black	4.01	1.83	0.44	0.09	0.74	0.11	0.09	0.19	0.50	0.02
Hispanic	3.57	1.64	0.30	0.06	0.70	0.11	0.05	0.09	0.62	0.00
Asian	2.08	1.01	0.20	0.01	0.44	0.08	0.03	0.05	0.25	0.01

Source: "Average Number of Carnegie Units Earned by High School Graduates in Vocational Education Courses, by Student Characteristic: 1982 and 1987," *Digest of Educational Statistics,* 1989, p. 127. Primary source: U.S. Department of Education, National Center for Educational Statistics, "1987 High School Transcript Study." (This table was prepared December 1988.) *Notes:* The Carnegie unit is a standard of measurement that represents one credit for the completion of a 1- year course.

★ 284 ★
High School Juniors' History & Literature Proficiency

Selected characteristics	Average scores[1]	
	History	Literature
Total	285.0	285.0
Race/ethnicity		
White	290.8	289.9
Black	263.1	267.5
Hispanic	262.5	264.8

Source: "Average Proficiency on the U.S. History and Literature Scales of High School Juniors, by Selected Characteristics: 1986," *1989 Education Indicators,* p. 150. Primary source: National Assessment of Educational Progress, *Literature and U.S. History: The Instructional Experience and Factual Knowledge of High School Juniors,* 1987. *Note:* 1. The history and literature scales range from 0 to 500.

★ 285 ★
Higher Education Enrollment at Ages 14-34 - Part I

Characteristic	Numbers in thousands									
	1965	1970	1975	1976	1977	1978	1979	1980	1981[2]	1982
All students[1]	5,675	7,413	9,697	9,950	10,217	9,838	9,978	10,180	10,734	10,919
White										
Total	5,317	6,759	8,514	8,644	8,812	8,514	8,709	8,875	9,162	9,328
Men	3,326	4,066	4,771	4,658	4,717	4,508	4,400	4,438	4,620	4,650
Women	1,991	2,693	3,743	3,986	4,495	4,006	4,309	4,437	4,543	4,679
Black										
Total	274	522	948	1,062	1,103	1,022	1,002	1,007	1,133	1,127
Men	126	253	442	489	490	452	434	437	505	42
Women	148	269	506	573	614	569	568	570	628	645
Hispanic origin[3]										
Total	4	4	411	427	418	377	440	443	510	493
Men	4	4	219	223	223	196	226	222	258	216

Continued.

Higher Education Enrollment at Ages 14-34 - Part I
[Continued]

Characteristic	Numbers in thousands									
	1965	1970	1975	1976	1977	1978	1979	1980	1981[2]	1982
Women	4	4	192	204	194	181	214	221	252	278

Percentage Distribution

All students[1]	100.0	100.0	100.0	100.0	100.0	100.0	100.0	100.0	100.0	100.0
White										
Total	93.7	91.2	87.8	86.9	86.2	86.5	87.3	87.2	85.4	85.4
Men	58.6	54.8	49.2	46.8	46.2	45.8	44.1	43.6	43.0	42.6
Women	35.1	36.3	38.6	40.1	40.1	40.7	43.2	43.6	42.3	42.9
Black										
Total	4.8	7.0	9.8	10.7	10.8	10.4	10.0	9.9	10.6	10.3
Men	2.2	3.4	4.6	4.9	4.8	4.6	4.3	4.3	4.7	4.4
Women	2.6	3.6	5.2	5.8	6.0	5.8	5.7	5.6	5.9	5.9
Hispanic origin[3]										
Total	4	4	4.2	4.3	4.1	3.8	4.4	4.4	4.8	4.5
Men	4	4	2.3	2.2	2.2	2.0	2.3	2.2	2.4	2.0
Women	4	4	2.0	2.1	1.9	1.8	2.1	2.2	2.3	2.5

Source: "Enrollment of Persons 14 to 34 in Institutions of Higer Education, by Race/Ethnicity, Sex, and Year of College: October 1965 to October 1987," *Digest of Education Statistics,* 1989, p. 197. U.S. Department of Commerce, Bureau of the Census, *Current Population Reports,* Series P-20, No. 409; and unpublished data. (This table was prepared March 1989). *Notes:* Data are based upon sample surveys of the civilian noninstitutional population. Because of rounding, details may not add to totals. 1. Totals differ from those shown in other tables. This table presents data collected in sample surveys of households rather than surveys of institutions. Excludes persons age 35 and over. 2. Data for 1981 and later years are controlled to 1980 census base. 3. Persons of Hispanic origin may be of any race. 4. Data not available.

★ 286 ★
Higher Education Enrollment at Ages 14-34 - Part II

Characteristic	Numbers in thousands				
	1983	1984	1985	1986	1987
All students[1]	10,825	10,859	10,863	10,605	10,918
White					
Total	9,242	9,269	9,334	8,943	9,146
Men	4,718	4,709	4,633	4,485	4,563
Women	4,524	4,559	4,701	4,459	4,583
Black					
Total	1,102	1,138	1,049	1,138	1,196
Men	497	544	458	488	525
Women	605	594	591	649	671
Hispanic origin[3]					
Total	523	524	579	677	667
Men	253	532	280	331	369
Women	270	2921	299	346	298

Percentage Distribution

All students[1]	100.0	100.0	100.0	100.0	100.0
White					
Total	85.4	85.4	85.9	84.3	93.8
Men	43.6	43.4	42.6	42.3	41.8

Continued.

Higher Education Enrollment at Ages 14-34 - Part II
[Continued]

Characteristic	Numbers in thousands				
	1983	1984	1985	1986	1987
Women	41.8	42.0	43.3	42.0	42.0
Black					
Total	10.2	10.5	9.7	10.7	11.0
Men	4.6	5.0	4.2	4.6	4.8
Women	5.6	5.5	5.4	6.1	6.1
Hispanic origin[3]					
Total	4.8	4.8	5.3	6.4	6.1
Men	2.3	2.1	2.6	3.1	3.4
Women	2.5	2.7	2.8	3.3	2.7

Source: "Enrollment of Persons 14 to 34 in Institutions of Higer Education, by Race/Ethnicity, Sex, and Year of College: October 1965 to October 1987," *Digest of Education Statistics*, 1989, p. 197. Primary source: U.S. Department of Commerce, Bureau of the Census, *Current Population Reports*, Series P-20, No. 409; and unpublished data. (This table was prepared March 1989). *Notes:* Data are based upon sample surveys of the civilian noninstitutional population. Because of rounding, details may not add to totals. 1. Totals differ from those shown in other tables. This table presents data collected in sample surveys of households rather than surveys of institutions. Excludes persons age 35 and over. 2. Data for 1981 and later years are controlled to 1980 census base. 3. Persons of Hispanic origin may be of any race. 4. Data not available.

★ 287 ★
Higher Education Enrollment by State of Institution

State or other area	Total	White non-Hispanic	Minority enrollment, by race/ethnicity						Non-resident alien
			Total	Per-cent minor-ity[2]	Black non-Hispanic	Hispanic	Asian Pacific Islander	American Indian/ Alaskan Native	
United States[1]	12,489,142	9,910,765	2,234,680	18.4	1,080,326	616,521	447,736	90,097	343,697
Alabama	181,443	137,301	40,072	22.6	37,687	828	1,181	376	4,070
Alaska	27,482	22,654	3,985	15.0	976	442	577	1,990	843
Arizona	226,593	181,555	39,008	17.7	6,166	20,943	4,276	7,623	6,030
Arkansas	79,182	65,807	11,709	15.1	10,520	323	540	326	1,666
California	1,727,605	1,141,929	524,625	31.5	116,909	194,514	192,643	20,559	61,051
Colorado	177,387	151,937	20,571	11.9	4,283	10,685	4,087	1,516	4,879
Connecticut	158,278	140,091	14,460	9.4	7,584	3,730	2,744	402	3,727
Delaware	33,893	28,726	4,538	13.6	3,703	362	417	56	629
District of Columbia	77,651	41,533	27,348	39.7	22,886	1,878	2,262	322	8,770
Florida	477,211	362,347	100,176	21.7	44,301	47,434	7,219	1,222	14,688
Georgia	195,122	150,952	38,842	20.5	34,303	1,806	2,427	306	5,328
Hawaii	51,697	15,370	34,305	69.1	938	673	32,532	162	2,022
Idaho	45,260	42,534	1,922	4.3	260	713	575	374	804
Illinois	686,895	519,851	153,815	22.8	91,800	35,720	24,148	2,147	13,229
Indiana	250,178	223,687	20,296	8.3	13,570	3,210	2,868	648	6,195
Iowa	155,369	142,680	6,508	4.4	3,164	1,198	1,756	390	6,181
Kansas	143,203	126,518	12,389	8.9	6,475	2,424	1,811	1,679	4,296
Kentucky	144,551	132,584	10,339	7.2	8,803	341	872	323	1,628
Louisana	171,338	119,316	45,477	27.6	39,326	3,210	2,468	473	6,545
Maine	46,231	44,284	1,749	3.8	540	188	688	333	198
Maryland	233,492	179,928	48,015	21.1	35,217	3,637	8,510	651	5,549
Massachusetts	417,548	361,942	38,609	9.6	16,788	9,807	10,884	1,130	16,997
Michigan	520,423	444,505	63,946	12.6	46,891	6,677	7,147	3,231	11,972
Minnesota	226,557	212,298	9,404	4.2	2,969	1,279	3,682	1,474	4,855
Mississippi	101,104	69,240	30,088	30.3	28,785	631	427	245	1,776
Missouri	246,185	216,229	24,976	10.4	18,499	2,361	3,447	669	4,980
Montana	35,238	32,203	2,372	6.9	146	190	151	1,885	663
Nebraska	100,401	93,090	5,355	5.4	2,744	1,098	833	680	1,956

Continued.

Higher Education Enrollment by State of Institution
[Continued]

State or other area	Total	White non-Hispanic	Total	Percent minority[2]	Black non-Hispanic	Hispanic	Asian Pacific Islander	American Indian/ Alaskan Native	Non-resident alien
			Minority enrollment, by race/ethnicity						
Nevada	46,796	40,428	5,725	12.4	1,861	1,917	1,251	696	643
New Hampshire	53,880	51,525	1,662	3.1	667	465	382	148	693
New Jersey	295,313	230,426	54,913	19.2	27,026	17,292	9,735	860	9,974
New Mexico	80,270	50,343	28,396	36.1	1,888	20,604	970	4,934	1,531
New York	997,793	747,300	217,961	22.6	110,057	67,100	36,010	4,794	32,532
North Carolina	332,979	253,074	65,099	20.5	57,371	1,957	3,313	2,458	4,806
North Dakota	37,309	34,354	2,005	5.5	241	125	171	1,468	950
Ohio	520,486	459,186	48,869	9.6	37,687	4,206	5,699	1,277	12,431
Oklahoma	170,840	141,066	23,114	14.1	10,546	2,189	2,711	7,668	6,660
Oregon	144,798	128,742	10,848	7.8	1,836	2,102	5,565	1,345	5,208
Pennsylvania	454,923	483,822	50,126	9.4	35,103	5,515	8,658	850	11,975
Rhode Island	69,569	63,825	4,436	6.5	2,014	1,055	1,164	203	1,308
South Carolina	134,115	103,800	28,074	21.3	25,924	965	978	207	2,241
South Dakota	30,935	28,322	1,952	6.4	190	96	92	1,574	661
Tennessee	197,068	162,535	30,213	15.7	27,506	983	1,383	341	4,320
Texas	776,020	543,904	208,282	27.7	66,662	118,333	20,688	2,599	23,834
Utah	106,218	96,144	5,381	5.3	728	1,731	1,773	1,149	4,693
Vermont	32,459	31,160	760	2.4	298	167	241	54	539
Virginia	308,318	250,004	53,261	17.6	41,545	3,278	7,793	645	5,053
Washington	242,443	211,111	26,503	11.2	5,899	4,289	12,773	3,542	4,829
West Virginia	76,781	71,890	3,777	5.0	2,865	281	535	96	1,114
Wisconsin	283,653	260,294	18,036	6.5	9,334	3,149	3,913	1,640	5,323
Wyoming	24,357	22,717	1,188	5.0	243	545	123	277	452
U.S. Service Schools	53,302	43,702	9,200	17.4	6,602	1,875	643	80	400
Outlying areas	165,620	676	163,622	99.6	1,959	156,537	5,101	25	1,322
American Samoa	759	0	622	100.0	0	0	607	15	137
Guam	4,477	378	3,281	89.7	38	74	3,162	7	818
Northern Marianas	514	29	433	93.7	0	0	433	0	52
Puerto Rico	156,580	46	156,460	100.0	10	156,371	79	0	74
Trust Territory of the Pacific	795	1	794	99.9	0	0	794	0	0
Virgin Islands	2,495	222	2,032	90.2	1,911	92	26	3	241

Source: "Total Enrollment in Institutions of Higher Education, by Race/Ethnicity of Student and by State: Fall 1986," *Digest of Education Statistics,* 1989, p. 195. Primary Source: U.S. Department of Education, National Center for Education Statistics, Integrated Postsecondary Education Data System (IPEDS), "Fall Enrollment, 1986" survey. (This table was prepared February 1989). *Notes:* Because of adjustments to underreported and nonreported racial/ethnic data, figures are slightly different from corresponding data in other tables. 1. Revised from previously published data. 2. Percent minority based on U.S. citizen enrollment (total enrollment less enrollment of nonresident aliens).

★ 288 ★
Higher Education Enrollment: Percent Change

	Fall 1986	Percent Change 1976 to 1986	
		Total	Black
United States	121,682,407	14.0	3.1
SREB States	3,576,335	26.5	10.8
Alabama	181,443	16.2	14.2
Arkansas	79,182	17.8	3.3
Florida	483,964	40.0	11.0
Georgia	195,123	15.0	11.1
Kentucky	144,562	12.2	-8.1

Continued.

Higher Education Enrollment: Percent Change
[Continued]

	Fall 1986	Percent Change 1976 to 1986	
		Total	Black
Louisiana	171,344	11.0	9.2
Maryland	233,492	11.6	-4.7
Mississippi	101,104	3.5	-1.9
North Carolina	322,979	30.0	21.0
Oklahoma	170,840	17.7	11.0
South Carolina	134,115	10.3	2.0
Tennessee	197,069	8.5	4.1
Texas	776,019	24.9	9.0
Virginia	308,318	26.2	15.9
West Virginia	76,781	-4.2	-17.6

Source: "Headcount Enrollment in Institutions of Higher Education," *NAFEO INROADS,* December-January 1990, p. 6. Primary source: Southern Regional Education Board (SREB) Fact Book on Higher Education, 1988. Published by permission.

★ 289 ★
Higher Education Enrollment: Trends

Percentage increase in enrollment in independent colleges and universities. Figured from enrollment in all 50 states, Washington and U.S. territories.

Characteristic	Percent
All minorities	
1982-1986	3.3
1986-1988	5.3
Black	
1982-1986	-5.4
1986-1988	7.1

Source: "Increasing Black Enrollment," *The New York Times,* March 30, 1990, p. A10. Primary source: National Association of Independent Colleges and Universities.

★ 290 ★
Higher Education Institutions: Trends

Type of Institution	All Institutions	NAFEO Membership			Other than NAFEO's HBCUs /EOEIs
		HBCUs	EOEIs	Total	
All Institutions	3,406	104	12	116	3,290
Public	1,533	45	9	54	1,479
Private	1,873	59	3	62	1,811
Four-year Institutions	2,070	89	4	93	1,977
Public	573	39	2	41	532
Private	1,497	50	2	52	1,445

Continued.

Higher Education Institutions: Trends
[Continued]

Type of Institution	All Institutions	NAFEO Membership			Other than NAFEO's HBCUs /EOEIs
		HBCUs	EOEIs	Total	
Two-year Institutions	1,336	15	8	23	1,313
Public	960	6	7	13	947
Private	376	9	1	10	366

Source: "Total Number of U.S. Institutions of Higher Education by Level and Control of Institution, 1987," *NAFEO INROADS,* February/March-April/May, 1989, p. 11. Primary source: NAFEO Research Staff Analysis of the Historically Black Colleges and Universities (HBCUs) and NAFEO's Other Equal Opportunity Educational Institutions (EOEIs); *Education Directory, Colleges and Universities,* 1987- 88, National Center for Education Statistics. *Notes:* One of the thirty-nine (39) NAFEO four-year public institutions is located in the Virgin Islands. All of the other institutions are located in the U.S. and the District of Columbia. Four-year institutions include four-year schools and above (plus universities and other four year schools). Two-year institutions include two-year schools and above (but less than four (4) years). Published by permission.

★ 291 ★
Highest Degree Earned at 18 and Over

Numbers in thousands.

Sex, race, and age	Total	Not high school graduate	High school graduate only	Some college, no degree	Voca-tional	Asso-ciate degree	Bache-lor's degree	Master's degree	Profes-sional degree	Doctor's degree
Total population, 18 and over	170,232	44,324	60,358	30,301	3,105	5,768	18,069	5,795	1,744	768
Men	80,834	20,448	26,407	15,444	1,023	2,804	9,581	3,110	1,432	585
Women	89,398	23,876	33,951	14,857	2,082	2,964	8,488	2,685	312	183
White, total	147,147	35,855	53,129	26,255	2,769	5,108	16,339	5,353	1,634	705
Men	70,276	16,606	23,270	13,444	919	2,498	8,703	2,923	1,355	558
Women	76,871	19,249	29,859	12,811	1,850	2,610	7,636	2,430	279	147
Black, total	18,475	7,133	6,043	3,229	254	482	963	286	53	32
Men	8,274	3,263	2,589	1,589	70	197	416	101	35	14
Women	10,201	3,870	3,454	1,640	184	285	547	185	18	18
Percent distribution, by highest degree earned										
Total population, 18 and over	100.0	26.0	35.5	17.8	1.8	3.4	10.6	3.4	1.0	0.5
Men	100.0	25.3	32.7	19.1	1.3	3.5	11.9	3.8	1.8	0.7
Women	100.0	26.7	38.0	16.6	2.3	3.3	9.5	3.0	0.3	0.2
White, total	100.0	24.4	36.1	17.8	1.9	3.5	11.1	3.6	1.1	0.5
Men	100.0	23.6	33.1	19.1	1.3	3.6	12.4	4.2	1.9	0.8
Women	100.0	25.0	38.8	16.7	2.4	3.4	9.9	3.2	0.4	0.2
Black. total	100.0	38.6	32.7	17.5	1.4	2.6	5.2	1.5	0.3	0.2
Men	100.0	39.4	31.3	19.2	0.8	2.4	5.0	1.2	0.4	0.2
Women	100.0	37.9	33.9	16.1	1.8	2.8	5.4	1.8	0.2	0.2

Source: "Highest Educational Level and Degree Earned by Persons Age 18 and Over, by Sex, Race, and Age: Spring 1984," Digest of Education Statistics, 1989, p. 18. Primary source: U.S. Department of Commerce, Bureau of the Census, *Current Population Reports,* Series P-70, No. 11, "Educational Background and Economic Status: Spring 1984." (This table was prepared October 1987.) *Notes:* Data based on sample surveys of the civilian noninstitutional population. Because of rounding, details may not add to totals.

★ 292 ★
Historically Black Colleges and Universities: Date Established

| Date established | Number | Control | | Level | | | | |
		Public	Private	4-Year	2-Year	4-Year + Graduate	Grad. and Professional	Graduate Only
1979-1987	1		1				1	
1964-1978	1	1			1			
1949-1963	6	5	1		3	3		
1924-1948	5	4	1		2	3		
1909-1923	4	2	2	1	1	2		
1894-1908	16	8	8	7	3	6		
1879-1893	25	10	15	14	4	5	2	
1864-1878	39	10	29	24	1	11	2	1
1849-1863	6	4	2	5		1		
1834-1848	1	1				1		
Total	104	145	59	51	15	32	5	1
Percent	100	43	57	49	14	31	5	1

Source: "A Summary: Historically Black Colleges and Universities by Control, Level and Date Established - NAFEO Membership (N = 104)," *NAFEO INROADS*, February/March 1987, p. 8. Published by permission.

★ 293 ★
Historically Black Public Colleges: Support

Campus	"Gap" (mil.dol.)	Total Voluntary Support (dol.)	Corp. Support (dol.)	Corp. Percent of Total Voluntary Support
University of Arkansas -Pine Bluff	10.9	132,650	58,994	45
Delaware State College	6.6	169,597	73,215	43
Kentucky State University	7.8	654,511	304,273	46
Bowie State University	7.3	255,116	136,778	54
Coppin State College	5.9	253,387	27,245	11
Alcorn State University	5.9	169,717	51,730	30
Elizabeth City State University	8.1	281,632	17,347	6
Fayetteville State University	11.3	105,241	40,575	39
Cheyney University	2.2	72,940	9,280	13
North Carolina A&T State University	22.3	1.4 mil.	828,846	59
Winston-Salem State University	6.2	296,757	106,129	36

Continued.

Historically Black Public Colleges: Support
[Continued]

Campus	"Gap" (mil.dol.)	Total Voluntary Support (dol.)	Corp. Support (dol.)	Corp. Percent of Total Voluntary Support
Prairie View A&M University	13.7	937,499	405,689	43

Source: "1987-88 Breakdown of Support for Some Historically Black Public Colleges," *Black Issues in Higher Education*, March 29, 1990, p. 12. Primary source: Council for Aid to Education (CAFE).

★ 294 ★
Institutional Origins of HBCU Transfer Students

HBCU States	1983			1984			1985		
	Wht	Blk	Tot	Wht	Blk	Tot	Wht	Blk	Tot
Alabama	184	150	334	206	146	352	214	157	371
Arkansas	126	37	163	133	47	180	133	43	176
Florida	52	88	140	108	30	138	131	63	194
Georgia	188	92	280	103	152	255	191	141	332
Louisiana	86	46	132	101	38	139	90	54	144
Mississippi	57	38	95	37	49	86	52	51	103
N. Carolina	499	149	648	421	199	620	591	125	716
Ohio	34	0	34	30	2	32	36	5	41
S. Carolina	68	28	96	64	37	101	75	16	91
Tennessee	76	31	107	47	27	74	36	24	60
Texas	126	29	155	54	22	76	101	38	139
Virginia	15	5	20	20	7	27	18	1	29
Total	1511	693	2204	1324	756	2080	1668	718	2386
Percent	69	31	100	64	36	100	70	30	100

Source: "HBCU Transfer Students by Institutional Type and State, Fall, 1983-1985 (Responding Institutions=32)," *NAFEO INROADS*, June/July, 1987, p.7. Primary source: Patel, Narenda H. *Student Transfers from White to Black Colleges.* NAFEO Research Institute, 1988. *Notes:* NAFEO: National Association for Equal Opportunity in Higher Education. Institutional Type: Wht - Predominately White Institutions Blk - Predominately Black Institutions. Published by permission.

★ 295 ★
K-12 Enrollment and Teachers: SREB States

	Minority enrollment as % of K-12 Enrollment[1]		Percent of Minority Teachers[2]	
	1985	1987	1986	1987
Alabama	36	38	26	25
Arkansas	26	25	14	[3]
Florida	32	35	20	20
Georgia	37	39	[3]	[3]
Kentucky	11	11	[3]	4

Continued.

K-12 Enrollment and Teachers: SREB States
[Continued]

	Minority enrollment as % of K-12 Enrollment[1]		Percent of Minority Teachers[2]	
	1985	1987	1986	1987
Louisiana	44	43	33	32
Maryland	42	40	23	23
Mississippi	51	56	[3]	35
North Carolina	34	32	23	19
Oklahoma	24	21	7	7
South Carolina	41	45	23	22
Tennessee	22	23	[3]	[3]
Texas	43	49	23	[3]
Virginia	28	27	19	19
West Virginia	5	4	[3]	[3]

Source: "Minority Enrollment and Teachers, SREB States," *Regional Spotlight*, April 1989, p. 1. Primary source: U.S. Department of Education; State Departments of Education. Published by permission. *Notes:* SREB: Southern Regional Education Board 1. U.S. Department of Education, calendar years 2. Information from the State Departments of Education, school years. 3. Not available. Published by permission.

★ 296 ★
Key Area Expenditures at UNCF Institutions: Trends

Characteristic	1984-85	1985-86	1986-87	1987-88
Instruction	25	23	24	23
Institutional Support	18	19	20	19
Scholarships and Fellowships	9	12	11	15

Source: "Percent of Funds Expended in Three Areas — 1984-85 through 1986-87," *UNCF 1989 Statistical Report*, p. 16. Primary source: United Negro College Fund, Inc., UNCF 1989 Statistical Report, (undated), New York, NY. UNCF: United Negro College Fund.

★ 297 ★
Leading B.A. Sources of Doctorates

	Output	
Institution	n/N	Type[1]
Howard University/DC	31	II, Private
Morgan State University/MD	23	III, Public
Tennessee State University	20	III, Public
Hampton University/VA	19	III, Private
Tuskegee University/AL	18	III, Private
Fisk University/TN	17	IV, Private
North Carolina Central Univ.	14	III, Public
North Carolina Ag & Tech	13	III, Public
Jackson State University/MS	12	III, Public
Spelman College/GA	12	IV, Private

Continued.

Leading B.A. Sources of Doctorates
[Continued]

Institution	Output	
	n/N	Type[1]
	Productivity	
Fisk University/TN	17/275	IV, Private
Bennett College/NC	4/72	IV, Private
Spelman College/GA	12/219	IV, Private
Morehouse College/GA	10/183	IV, Private
Tougaloo College/MS	7/162	IV, Private
Lincoln University/PA	7/172	IV, Public
Hampton University/VA	19/484	III, Private
Wiley College/TX	3/79	IV, Private
Tuskegee University/AL	18/482	III, Private
Clark College/GA	6/172	III, Private

Source: "Leading B.A. Sources of 1984 Black Doctorate Recipients," *NAFEO INROADS*, December 1986/ January 1987, p. 2. Primary source: National Research Council, *Summary Report 1984 Doctorate Recipients From United States Universities, 1986. Notes:* All institutions listed are Historically Black Colleges and Universities. 1. Type Legend: I=Type I - Research Institutions; II=Type II - Other Doctorate-Granting Universities; III=Type III - Comprehensive Colleges and Universities; IV=Type IV - Liberal Arts Colleges; V=Type V - Specialized Institutions.

★ 298 ★
Level of Education

For persons 25 years and over. As of March. Persons of Hispanic origin may be of any race. Data for other States are not available. Based on Current Population Survey and subject to sampling error. See text, section 1, and Appendix III.

Item	Total persons (1,000)	Percent Completing	
		High school	College
California:			
Total	16,781	78.9	23.5
White	14,220	78.4	23.3
Black	1,093	80.0	13.4
Hispanic origin	3,021	49.1	5.6
Florida:			
Total	7,727	77.1	19.7
White	6,712	79.8	21.1
Black	956	59.4	9.1
Hispanic origin	774	61.2	16.4
Georgia:			
Total	3,788	71.2	19.1
White	2,750	74.9	23.2
Black	1,012	60.9	7.3
Hispanic origin	40	[1]	[1]
Illinois:			
Total	7,124	76.4	20.2
White	6,060	77.7	20.7
Black	912	66.2	10.9
Hispanic origin	314	48.4	11.5
Indiana:			
Total	3,376	76.0	13.3

Continued.

Level of Education
[Continued]

Item	Total persons (1,000)	Percent Completing	
		High school	College
White	3,100	76.5	13.4
Black	253	69.2	11.9
Hispanic origin	21	[1]	[1]
Massachusetts:			
Total	3,699	80.4	26.5
White	3,513	80.7	26.5
Black	132	77.3	21.2
Hispanic origin	80	52.5	11.3
Michigan:			
Total	5,505	75.5	16.5
White	4,809	76.7	16.8
Black	589	64.5	9.7
Hispanic origin	66	[1]	[1]
Missouri:			
Total	3,102	78.1	17.9
White	2,827	79.1	18.1
Black	242	59.9	7.4
Hispanic origin	18	[1]	[1]
New Jersey:			
Total	4,884	76.9	23.3
White	4,231	78.1	24.2
Black	521	63.3	6.7
Hispanic origin	385	57.7	12.2
New York:			
Total	11,255	75.0	23.2
White	9,460	76.4	23.8
Black	1,347	64.1	13.1
Hispanic origin	1,141	51.4	8.5
North Carolina:			
Total	3,955	67.8	16.6
White	3,179	78.6	18.6
Black	717	55.8	8.2
Hispanic origin	17	[1]	[1]
Ohio:			
Total	6,687	75.6	15.0
White	6,057	76.6	15.3
Black	577	64.1	7.5
Hispanic origin	48	[1]	[1]
Pennsylvania:			
Total	7,805	75.5	17.2
White	7,137	76.5	17.6
Black	602	65.0	10.6
Hispanic origin	72	[1]	[1]
Texas:			
Total	9,816	72.0	19.8
White	8,577	72.0	20.4
Black	1,060	68.7	11.1
Hispanic origin	2,065	43.1	7.5
Virginia:			

Continued.

Level of Education
[Continued]

Item	Total persons (1,000)	Percent Completing	
		High school	College
Total	3,605	72.3	23.5
White	2,857	75.4	25.9
Black	667	56.7	10.9
Hispanic origin	50	[1]	[1]

Source: "Years of School Completed, by Sex, Race, and Hispanic Origin - 15 Largest States, 1987," *Statistical Abstract*, 1989, p. 132. Primary source: U.S. Bureau of the Census, *Current Population Reports*, Series P-20, No. 428. *Notes:* 1. Base figure too small to meet standards for reliability of derived figure.

★ 299 ★
Level of Education

Persons 25 years and over. As of April 1970 and 1980, and March 1975 and 1987.

Race and Hispanic Origin	1970	1975	1980	1987				
				Total	25-34 yr.	35-44 yr.	45-64 yr.	65 yr. and over
Less than 5 years of school								
All races[1]	5.5	4.2	3.6	2.4	.9	1.1	2.6	6.1
White	4.5	3.3	2.6	2.0	.9	1.1	2.1	4.6
Black	14.6	12.3	8.2	5.0	.6	.8	5.9	19.6
Hispanic[2]	19.5	18.5	15.5	11.9	5.6	8.9	17.0	31.2
Mexican	28.5	24.6	20.1	15.4	7.7	12.1	21.7	42.4
Puerto Rican	20.5	17.4	14.1	10.3	2.2	5.6	22.5	29.2
Cuban	8.2	7.3	7.3	6.1	1.2	1.6	8.6	12.2
Other[3]	8.8	7.6	8.3	5.7	2.3	4.8	7.0	17.5
4 years of high school or more								
All races[1]	52.3	62.5	66.5	75.6	86.5	85.9	72.8	51.2
White	54.5	64.6	68.8	77.0	87.2	87.1	75.1	53.7
Black	31.4	42.5	51.2	63.4	81.7	76.2	52.4	24.7
Hispanic[2]	32.1	37.9	44.0	50.9	60.3	57.4	41.9	20.8
Mexican	24.2	31.0	37.6	44.8	54.0	51.2	33.9	15.4
Puerto Rican	23.4	28.7	40.1	53.8	68.4	58.8	36.1	19.4
Cuban	43.9	51.7	55.3	61.6	83.1	68.1	56.5	35.9
Other[3]	44.9	58.0	57.4	61.5	68.8	69.2	56.8	25.6

Source: "Percent of Population with Less than 5 Years of School and with 4 Years of High School or More, by Age, Race, and Hispanic Origin: 1970 to 1987," *Statistical Abstract*, 1989, p. 133. Primary source: *Census of Population*: 1970, vol. I and II; 1980, vol. I, chapter C, U.S. Bureau of the Census. *Current Population Reports*, Series P-20, No. 416. *Notes:* 1. Includes races not shown separately. 2. Hispanic persons may be of any race. 3. Includes Central or South America and other Hispanic origin.

★ 300 ★
Level of Education

For persons 25 years and over. As of March. Persons of Hispanic origin may be of any race. Data for other States are not available.

Item	Total persons (1,000)	Percent Completing	
		High school	College
California:			
Total	16,781	78.9	23.5
Male	8,151	79.0	27.0
Female	8,630	78.7	20.2
White	14,220	78.4	23.3
Black	1,093	80.0	13.4
Hispanic origin	3,021	49.1	5.6
Florida:			
Total	7,727	77.1	19.7
Male	3,634	77.2	24.4
Female	4,093	77.1	15.5
White	6,712	79.8	21.1
Black	957	59.4	9.1
Hispanic origin	774	61.2	16.4
Georgia:			
Total	3,788	71.2	19.1
Male	1,745	72.6	22.8
Female	2,043	70.0	16.0
White	2,750	74.9	23.2
Black	1,012	60.9	7.3
Hispanic origin	40	[1]	[1]
Illinois:			
Total	7,124	76.4	20.2
Male	3,283	78.2	23.7
Female	3,841	74.8	17.3
White	6,060	77.7	20.7
Black	912	66.2	10.9
Hispanic origin	314	48.4	11.5
Indiana:			
Total	3,376	76.0	13.3
Male	1,600	74.8	15.5
Female	1,777	77.0	11.3
White	3,100	76.5	13.4
Black	253	69.2	11.9
Hispanic origin	21	[1]	[1]
Massachusetts:			
Total	3,699	80.4	26.5
Male	1,705	81.3	31.9
Female	1,994	79.7	21.9
White	3,513	80.7	26.5

Continued.

194

Level of Education
[Continued]

Item	Total persons (1,000)	Percent Completing	
		High school	College
Black	132	77.3	21.2
Hispanic origin	80	52.5	11.3
Michigan:			
Total	5,505	75.5	16.5
Male	2,587	74.0	20.5
Female	2,918	76.8	13.0
White	4,809	76.7	16.8
Black	589	64.5	9.7
Hispanic origin	66	[1]	[1]
Missouri:			
Total	3,102	78.1	17.9
Male	1,466	78.5	22.0
Female	1,636	77.8	14.2
White	2,827	79.7	18.1
Black	242	59.9	7.4
Hispanic origin	18	[1]	[1]
New Jersey:			
Total	4,884	76.9	23.3
Male	2,269	78.4	28.5
Female	2,616	75.5	18.7
White	4,231	78.1	24.2
Black	521	63.3	6.7
Hispanic origin	385	57.7	12.2
New York:			
Total	11,255	75.0	23.2
Male	5,186	76.2	27.1
Female	6,069	73.9	20.0
White	9,460	76.4	23.8
Black	1,347	64.1	13.1
Hispanic origin	1,141	51.4	8.5
North Carolina:			
Total	3,955	67.8	16.6
Male	1,835	67.1	19.5
Female	2,120	68.3	14.1
White	3,179	70.6	18.6
Black	717	55.8	8.2
Hispanic origin	17	[1]	[1]
Ohio:			
Total	6,687	75.6	15.0
Male	3,134	75.6	17.5
Female	3,553	75.6	12.8
White	6,057	76.6	15.3

Continued.

Level of Education
[Continued]

| Item | Total persons (1,000) | Percent Completing | |
		High school	College
Black	577	64.1	7.5
Hispanic origin	48	[1]	[1]
Pennsylvania:			
Total	7,805	75.5	17.2
Male	3,656	75.4	21.1
Female	4,149	75.6	13.9
White	7,137	76.5	17.6
Black	602	65.0	10.6
Hispanic origin	72	[1]	[1]
Texas:			
Total	9,816	72.0	19.8
Male	4,862	71.7	23.0
Female	4,954	72.2	16.7
White	8,577	72.0	20.4
Black	1,060	68.7	11.1
Hispanic origin	2,065	43.1	7.5
Virginia:			
Total	3,605	72.3	23.5
Male	1,757	71.9	30.1
Female	1,848	72.6	17.3
White	2,857	75.4	25.9
Black	667	56.7	10.9
Hispanic origin	50	[1]	[1]

Source: Based on "Current Population Survey", section 1 and Appendix III, *Statistical Abstract*, 1989, p. 132. Primary source: *Current Population Reports*, Series P-20, No. 428. U.S. Bureau of the Census. *Notes:* 1. Base figure too small to meet standards for reliability of derived figure.

★ 301 ★
Level of Education

| Age and year | Percent not high school graduates | | Percent with 4 years of high school or more | | Median school years completed |
	Total	With less than 5 years of school	Total	College, 4 years or more	
			All persons		
25 years and over:					
1940	75.5	13.7	24.5	4.6	8.6
1950	65.7	11.1	34.3	6.2	9.3
1960	58.9	8.3	41.1	7.7	10.6
1970	47.7	5.5	52.3	10.7	12.1

Continued.

Level of Education
[Continued]

| Age and year | Percent not high school graduates | | Percent with 4 years of high school or more | | Median school years completed |
	Total	With less than 5 years of school	Total	College, 4 years or more	
1980	33.5	3.6	66.5	16.2	12.5
1985	26.1	2.7	73.9	19.4	12.6
1986	25.3	2.7	74.7	19.4	12.6
1987	24.4	2.4	75.6	19.9	12.7
25-29 years:					
1940	61.9	5.9	38.1	5.9	10.3
1950	49.5	4.7	52.8	7.7	12.0
1960	39.3	2.8	60.7	11.1	12.3
1970	26.2	1.7	73.8	16.3	12.6
1980	15.5	1.1	84.5	22.1	12.9
1985	13.9	.7	86.1	22.2	12.9
1986	13.9	.9	86.1	22.4	12.9
1987	14.0	.9	86.0	22.0	12.8

Black persons

Age and year	Total	With less than 5	Total	College, 4 years or more	Median
25 years and over:					
1940	92.7	42.0	7.3	1.3	5.7
1950	87.1	32.9	12.9	2.1	6.8
1960	79.9	23.8	20.1	3.1	8.0
1970	68.6	14.6	31.4	4.4	9.8
1980	48.8	8.2	51.2	8.4	12.0
1985	40.2	6.2	59.8	11.1	12.3
1986	37.7	5.4	62.3	10.9	12.3
1987	36.6	5.0	63.4	10.7	12.4
25-29 years:					
1940	88.4	27.7	11.6	1.6	7.0
1950	80.4	16.8	22.2	2.7	8.6
1960	62.3	7.0	37.7	48.9	9.9
1970	44.6	3.2	55.4	6.0	12.1
1980	24.8	1.1	75.2	11.4	12.6
1985	19.4	.4	80.6	11.5	12.7
1986	16.7	.5	83.4	11.8	12.7
1987	16.7	.4	83.3	11.4	12.7

Source: "Current Population Survey, 1985," *Statistical Abstract*, 1989, p. 130. Primary source: *U.S. Census of Population, 1940, 1950, 1960, 1970, and 1980*, vol. 1; *Current Population Reports*, Series P-20, No. 415, U.S. Bureau of the Census.

★ 302 ★
Level of Education

Persons 25 years old and over. Hispanic persons may be of any race.

Year, Race, Hispanic Origin, and Sex	Population	Percent of Population Completing							Median school years completed
		Elementary school			High school		College		
		0-4 years	5-7 years	8 years	1-3 years	4 years	1-3 years	4 years or more	
1970, total persons[1]	109,899	5.5	10.0	12.8	19.4	31.1	10.6	10.7	12.1
White	98,246	4.5	9.1	13.0	18.8	32.2	11.1	11.3	12.1
Male	46,527	4.8	9.7	13.3	19.2	28.5	11.1	14.4	12.1
Female	51,718	4.1	8.6	12.8	19.4	35.5	11.1	8.4	12.1
Black	10,375	14.6	18.7	10.5	24.8	21.2	5.9	4.4	9.8
Male	4,714	17.7	19.1	10.2	22.9	20.0	6.0	4.2	9.4
Female	5,661	12.0	18.3	10.8	26.4	22.2	5.8	4.6	10.1
Hispanic	3,946	19.5	18.6	11.5	18.2	21.1	6.5	4.5	9.1
Male	1,897	19.1	18.0	11.3	18.1	19.9	7.6	5.9	9.3
Female	2,050	19.9	19.2	11.6	18.3	22.3	5.4	3.2	8.9
1980, total persons[1]	132,836	3.6	6.7	8.0	15.3	34.6	15.7	16.2	12.5
White	114,290	2.6	5.8	8.2	14.6	35.7	16.0	17.1	12.5
Male	53,941	2.8	6.0	8.0	13.6	31.8	16.4	21.3	12.5
Female	60,349	2.5	5.6	8.4	15.5	39.1	15.6	13.3	12.6
Black	13,195	8.2	11.7	7.1	21.8	29.3	13.5	8.4	12.0
Male	5,895	10.0	12.0	6.7	20.5	28.3	14.0	8.4	12.0
Female	7,300	6.7	11.6	7.3	22.9	30.0	13.2	8.3	12.0
Hispanic	6,739	15.5	16.6	8.1	15.8	24.4	12.0	7.6	10.8
Male	3,247	15.2	16.2	7.7	15.5	22.6	13.4	9.4	11.1
Female	3,493	15.8	17.1	8.4	16.1	26.0	10.6	6.0	10.6
1987, total persons[1]	149,144	2.4	4.5	5.8	11.7	38.7	71.1	19.9	12.7
White	129,170	2.0	4.1	5.9	11.0	39.2	17.2	20.5	12.7
Male	61,678	2.1	4.2	5.8	10.6	35.6	17.2	24.5	12.8
Female	67,492	2.0	4.0	6.0	11.4	42.6	17.3	16.9	12.6
Black	15,580	5.0	8.0	5.3	18.2	37.1	15.7	10.7	12.4
Male	6,919	5.9	8.6	5.2	17.2	36.5	15.5	11.0	12.4
Female	8,661	4.3	7.6	5.4	19.0	37.5	15.8	10.4	12.4
Hispanic	9,449	11.9	15.2	8.1	13.9	29.0	13.3	8.6	12.0
Male	4,614	11.8	14.8	7.4	14.2	28.0	14.2	9.7	12.1
Female	4,835	12.0	15.6	8.8	13.6	30.0	12.5	7.5	12.0

Source: "Historical Statistics, Colonial Times to 1970, Series H 602-617," *Statistical Abstract*, 1989, p. 131. Primary source: *U.S. Census of Population: 1970*, vols. I and II; *1980*, vol I, chapter C; and *Current Population Reports*, Series P-20, No. 428, U.S. Bureau of the Census. *Note:* 1. Includes other races, not shown separately.

★ 303 ★
Level of Education

Persons 25 years old and over. As of March, 1987.

Sex, Age, Race, and Hispanic Origin	Population	Percent of Population Completing							Median school years completed
		Elementary school			High school		College		
		0-4 years	5-7 years	8 years	1-3 years	4 years	1-3 years	4 years or more	
Total persons	149,144	2.4	4.5	5.8	11.7	38.7	17.1	19.9	12.7
Male	70,677	2.5	4.6	5.7	11.2	35.4	17.1	23.6	12.7
Female	78,467	2.4	4.4	5.8	12.1	41.6	17.1	16.5	12.6
25-29 years old	21,636	.9	1.6	1.7	9.9	42.4	21.5	22.0	12.8
30-34 years old	20,999	1.0	1.8	1.3	8.8	39.8	21.4	25.8	12.9
35-44 years old	33,632	1.1	2.3	2.2	8.4	39.1	20.3	26.5	12.9
45-54 years old	23,018	2.0	3.7	4.4	12.3	42.1	16.0	19.5	12.7
55-64 years old	21,883	3.2	6.0	8.0	15.0	39.8	13.1	14.9	12.4
65 years and over	27,975	6.1	10.9	15.8	16.0	30.8	10.5	9.9	12.0
Black	15,580	5.0	8.0	5.3	18.2	37.1	15.7	10.7	12.4
15-29 years old	2,683	.4	.7	1.0	14.5	47.4	24.6	11.4	12.7
30-34 years old	2,513	.6	1.4	2.2	15.8	45.9	20.6	13.3	12.7
35-44 years old	3,552	.8	3.4	2.6	17.1	43.7	18.5	14.0	12.6
45-54 years old	2,437	3.5	6.6	4.9	23.8	37.5	12.6	11.1	12.3
55-64 years old	2,063	8.7	16.4	10.9	22.0	25.3	10.1	6.6	10.9
65 years and over	2,331	19.6	24.8	13.5	17.4	15.5	3.9	5.3	8.4
Hispanic origin[1]	9,449	11.9	15.2	8.1	13.9	29.0	13.3	8.6	12.0
25-29 years old	1,936	4.8	12.0	5.9	17.5	33.1	18.0	8.7	12.3
30-34 years old	1,677	6.5	13.8	4.5	14.4	33.2	16.6	11.0	12.3
35-44 years old	2,437	8.9	13.7	7.0	12.9	32.6	5.2	9.6	12.2
45-54 years old	1,451	13.6	16.3	9.5	14.1	27.6	10.1	8.8	11.3
55-64 years old	1,042	21.8	18.0	13.1	11.8	21.8	7.7	5.9	8.8
65 years and over	906	31.2	23.5	14.6	9.7	13.4	3.9	3.7	7.4

Source: "Years of School Completed, by Sex, Age, Race, and Hispanic Origin: 1987," *Statistical Abstract*, 1989, p. 131. Primary source: U.S. Bureau of the Census, unpublished data. *Note:* 1. Hispanic persons may be of any race.

★ 304 ★
Level of Education

Characteristic	1940	1950	1960	1970	1980
White					
25-34	9.95	10.87	11.55	12.48	13.40
35-44	9.02	10.06	11.05	11.85	12.96
45-54	8.11	9.13	10.05	11.24	12.14
55-64	7.61	8.18	8.96	10.16	11.41
Black					
25-34	6.12	7.77	9.17	10.74	12.25
35-44	5.49	6.61	8.05	9.65	11.50
45-54	4.98	5.66	6.69	8.34	10.12
55-64	4.43	4.88	5.67	6.85	8.60
Differential (white minus black)					
25-34	3.83	3.10	2.38	1.74	1.15
35-44	3.53	3.45	3.00	2.20	1.45

Continued.

Level of Education
[Continued]

Characteristic	1940	1950	1960	1970	1980
45-54	3.13	3.47	3.36	2.90	2.03
55-64	3.18	3.30	3.29	3.32	2.81

Source: "Mean Years of School Completed by Race and Age (Male Civilian Population)," *The Economic Progress of Black Men in America*, p. 56. Primary source: Census of Population, 1940-1980; Public Use Sample.

★ 305 ★
Level of Higher Education Degrees Conferred

Race and ethnicity and degree level	Men		Women	
	1977	1985	1977	1985
Bachelor's degrees				
White, non-Hispanic	435,659	405,085	369,527	421,021
Black, non-hispanic	25,026	23,018	33,489	34,455
Hispanic	10,238	12,402	8,425	13,472
Asian or Pacific Islander	7,590	13,554	6,155	11,841
American Indian/Alaskan Native	1,797	1,998	1,552	2,248
Master's degrees				
White, non-Hispanic	138,303	106,059	126,844	117,569
Black, non-hispanic	7,769	5,200	13,255	8,739
Hispanic	3,266	3,059	2,803	3,805
Asian or Pacific Islander	3,116	4,842	1,999	2,940
American Indian/Alaskan Native	521	583	446	673
Doctor's degrees				
White, non-Hispanic	20,017	15,017	6,819	8,917
Black, non-hispanic	766	561	487	593
Hispanic	383	431	139	246
Asian or Pacific Islander	540	802	118	304
American Indian/Alaskan Native	67	64	28	55
First-professional degrees				
White, non-Hispanic	47,777	42,630	10,645	20,589
Black, non-hispanic	1,761	1,623	776	1,406
Hispanic	893	1,239	183	645
Asian or Pacific Islander	776	1,152	245	664
American Indian/Alaskan Native	159	176	37	72

Source: "Number of Degrees Conferred, by Race and Ethnicity, Degree Level, and Gender: Academic Years Ending 1977-1985," *1989 Education Indicators*, p. 231. Primary source: U.S. Department of Education, National Center for Education Statistics, *Digest of Education Statistics*, various years (based on the HEGIS survey Degrees and Other Formal Awards Conferred). *Notes:* Data for nonresident aliens are not shown. Data for 1977 exclude degrees conferred by U.S. Service Schools (0.4 percent or less of degrees conferred).

★ 306 ★
Level of Higher Education Enrollment: Trends

Characteristic	1978	1980	1982	1984	1986	1988	10-year change (%)
American Indian							
All	78,000	84,000	88,000	84,000	90,000	93,000	+19.2
Undergraduate	72,000	79,000	82,000	78,000	83,000	86,000	+19.4
Graduate	4,000	4,000	5,000	5,000	5,000	6,000	+50.0
Professional	1,000	1,000	1,000	1,000	1,000	1,000	0.0
Asian							
All	235,000	286,000	351,000	390,000	448,000	497,000	+111.5
Undergraduate	206,000	253,000	313,000	343,000	393,000	437,000	+112.1
Graduate	24,000	28,000	30,000	37,000	43,000	46,000	+91.7
Professional	5,000	6,000	8,000	9,000	11,000	14,000	+180.0
Black							
All	1,054,000	1,107,000	1,101,000	1,076,000	1,082,000	1,130,000	+7.2
Undergraduate	975,000	1,028,000	1,028,000	995,000	996,000	1,039,000	+6.6
Graduate	68,000	66,000	61,000	67,000	72,000	76,000	+11.8
Professional	11,000	13,000	13,000	13,000	14,000	14,000	+27.3
Hispanic							
All	417,000	472,000	519,000	535,000	618,000	680,000	+63.1
Undergraduate	388,000	438,000	485,000	495,000	563,000	631,000	+62.6
Graduate	24,000	27,000	27,000	32,000	46,000	39,000	+62.5
Professional	5,000	7,000	7,000	8,000	9,000	9,000	+80.0
White							
All	9,194,000	9,833,000	9,997,000	9,815,000	9,921,000	10,283,000	+11.8
Undergraduate	7,946,000	8,556,000	8,749,000	8,484,000	8,558,000	8,907,000	+12.1
Graduate	1,019,000	1,030,000	1,002,000	1,087,000	1,133,000	1,153,000	+13.2
Professional	229,000	248,000	246,000	243,000	231,000	223,000	-2.6
Foreign							
All	253,000	305,000	331,000	335,000	345,000	361,000	+42.7
Undergraduate	169,000	208,000	220,000	216,000	205,000	205,000	+21.3
Graduate	80,000	94,000	108,000	115,000	136,000	151,000	+88.8
Professional	3,000	3,000	3,000	3,000	4,000	5,000	+66.7
All							
All	11,231,000	12,087,000	12,388,000	12,235,000	12,504,000	13,043,000	+16.1
Undergraduate	9,757,000	10,560,000	10,875,000	10,610,000	10,798,000	11,304,000	+15.9
Graduate	1,219,000	1,250,000	1,235,000	1,344,000	1,435,000	1,472,000	+20.8
Professional	255,000	277,000	278,000	278,000	270,000	267,000	+4.7

Source: "Enrollment Trends by Race, 1978-88," *The Chronicle of Higher Education*, April 11, 1990, p. A36. Primary source: U.S. Department of Education. *Note:* Because of rounding, detail may not add to totals.

★ 307 ★
Level of Higher Education Study: Trends

Level of study and race/ethnicity of student	Number, in thousands						Percent distribution, by level of study					
	1976	1978	1980	1982	1984[1]	1986[1]	1976	1978	1980	1982	1984	1986
Undergraduate, total	9,520	9,757	10,560	10,875	10,610	10,787	100.0	100.0	100.0	100.0	100.0	100.0
White, non-Hispanic	7,827	7,946	8,556	8,749	8,484	8,550	82.2	81.4	81.0	80.5	80.0	79.3
Total minority	1,550	1,642	1,797	1,907	1,911	2,033	16.3	16.8	17.0	17.5	18.0	18.8
Black, non-Hispanic	950	975	1,028	1,028	995	995	10.0	10.0	9.7	9.4	9.4	9.2
Hispanic	357	388	438	485	495	562	3.7	4.0	4.1	4.5	4.7	5.2
Asian or Pacific Islander	173	206	253	313	343	393	1.8	2.1	2.4	2.9	3.2	3.6
American Indian/Alaskan Native	70	72	79	82	78	83	0.7	0.7	0.7	0.8	0.7	0.8
Nonresident alien	142	169	208	220	216	204	1.5	1.7	2.0	2.0	2.0	1.9
Graduate, total	1,222	1,219	1,249	1,233	1,344	1,432	100.0	100.0	100.0	100.0	100.0	100.0
White, non-Hispanic	1,030	1,019	1,030	1,002	1,087	1,130	84.2	83.6	82.4	81.2	80.9	78.9
Total minority	119	120	125	123	141	166	9.8	9.8	10.0	10.0	10.5	11.6
Black, non-Hispanic	72	68	66	61	67	72	5.9	5.6	5.3	4.9	5.0	5.0
Hispanic	22	24	27	27	32	46	1.8	1.9	2.2	2.2	2.4	3.2
Asian or Pacific Islander	21	24	28	30	37	43	1.7	2.0	2.2	2.5	2.8	3.0
American Indian/Alaskan Native	4	4	4	5	5	5	0.4	0.4	0.4	0.4	0.4	0.4
Nonresident alien	73	80	94	108	115	136	6.0	6.6	7.5	8.8	8.6	9.5
First-professional, total	244	255	277	278	278	270	100.0	100.0	100.0	100.0	100.0	100.0
White, non-Hispanic	220	229	248	246	243	230	90.1	90.2	89.5	88.5	87.4	85.3
Total minority	21	22	26	29	32	36	8.6	8.7	9.5	10.4	11.4	13.2
Black, non-Hispanic	11	11	13	13	13	14	4.6	4.3	4.6	4.7	4.8	5.2
Hispanic	5	5	7	7	8	9	1.9	2.0	2.4	2.5	2.9	3.4
Asian or Pacific Islander	4	5	6	8	9	11	1.7	2.0	2.2	2.9	3.4	4.2
American Indian/Alaskan Native	1	1	1	1	1	1	0.5	0.4	0.3	0.4	0.4	0.4
Nonresident alien	3	3	3	3	3	4	1.3	1.2	1.0	1.1	1.2	1.5

Source: "Total Enrollment in Institutions of Higher Education, by Level of Study and Race/Ethnicity of Student: Fall 1976 to Fall 1986," *Digest of Educational Statistics,* 1989, p. 194. Primary source: U.S. Department of Education, National Center for Educational Statistics, "Fall Enrollment in Colleges and Universities," and Integrated Postsecondary Education Data System (IPEDS), "Fall Enrollment, 1986" survey and unpublished tabulations. (This table was prepared February 1989.) *Notes:* Because of underreporting and nonreporting of racial/ethnic data, figures are slightly lower than corresponding data in other tables. Because of rounding, details may not add to totals. 1. Data revised from previously published figures.

★ 308 ★
Library Resources at Selected Colleges

Institutions	FTE sts/fac	Current volumes	Volumes needed	Cost to Acquire		Aggregate Budget
				@ $30	@ $40	
Atlanta Univ. Center	9,000/-	670,000	319,870	$9,596,100-	12,794,800	$390,440
Benedict College	1,457/86	31,000	30,455	913,455-	1,218,200	
Bennett College	575/ -	[1]	[1]	[1]	[1]	[1]
Bethune-Cookman Collg.	1,626/-	106,000	148,000	4,440,000-	5,920,000	78,800
Dillard University	1,108/-	127,000	127,000	3,810,000-	5,080,000	58,400
Fisk University	746/64	186,000	18,650	559,500-	746,000	5,200
Hampton Institute	4,063/221	306,000	63,155	1,894,650-	2,526,200	88,000
Johnson C. Smith Univ.	1,346/74	94,000	27,590	827,700-	1,103,600	64,600
Paine College	752/50	74,000	16,280	488,400-	651,200	38,000
St. Augustine's Collg.	1,596/81	114,691	31,935	958,050-	1,277,400	135,000
Stillman College	661/48	77,000	14,715	441,450-	588,600	46,000
Talladega College	643/58	78,000	15,445	463,350-	617,800	[1]
Tougaloo College	651/66	91,000	10,325	309,750-	413,000	6,000
Tuskegee University	3,400/-	242,000	268,000	8,040,000-	10,720,000	183,000

Continued.

Library Resources at Selected Colleges
[Continued]

Institutions	FTE sts/fac	Current volumes	Volumes needed	Cost to Acquire		Aggregate Budget
				@ $30	@ $40	
Virginia Union	1,100/-	140,000	85,000	2,550,000-	3,400,000	43,000
Xavier University	1,687/119	100,000	26,495	794,850-	1,059,800	43,000

Source: "Survey of Librarians at Selected Private HBCUs, January 1986," *Black Issues in Higher Education*, February 15, 1990, p. 17. Primary source: Southern Education Foundation. HBCU: Historically Black Colleges and Universities. *Note:* 1. Not available.

★ 309 ★
Literacy and Reading Skills

Young adult characteristics	Prose literacy scale, % with score of-				[C4|D[2]] ocument litera cy, % with[3] score of-				Quantitative literacy, % with score of-[4]				
	200 or more	250 or more	300 or more	350 or more	200 or more	250 or more	300 or more	350 or more	200 or more	250 or more	300 or more	350 or more	
Total	96.1	82.7	56.4	21.1	95.5	83.8	57.2	20.2	96.4	84.7	56.0	22.5	
Race/ethnicity													
White, non-Hispanic	98.1	89.7	63.0	24.3	98.2	89.5	64.1	24.9	98.1	89.4	62.9	24.8	
Black, non-Hispanic	86.3	57.2	21.3	3.5	84.4	56.5	20.1	2.2	87.8	58.0	21.4	3.3	
Hispanic	93.5	73.6	40.9	13.5	92.0	69.8	35.9	9.4	92.8	72.5	35.2	9.2	

Source: "Literacy Skills and Reading Scores of Young Adults, by Race/Ethnicity and Level of Education: 1985," *Digest of Educational Statistics*, 1989, p. 376. Primary source: U.S. Department of Education, National Center for Educational Statistics, *Young Adult Literacy and Schooling*. (This table was prepared May 1989.) *Notes:* 1. Includes persons 21 to 25 years old. Excludes persons not living in households and those who were unable to speak English. 2. Prose comprehension test measures the knowledge and skills needed to gain understanding and use information from tests such as editorials, news stories, and poems. A score of 200 indicates an ability to write a simple description of the type of job one would like to have. A score of 300 indicates an ability to locate information in a news article or an almanac. A score of 350 indicates an ability to synthesize the main argument from a lengthy newspaper editorial. 3. Document literacy test measures the knowledge and skills required to locate and use information from documents such as indexes, tables, paycheck stubs, and order forms. A score of 200 indicates ability to match money-saving coupons to a shopping list of several items. A score of 300 indicates an ability to follow directions to travel from one location to another using a map. A score of 350 indicates an ability to use a bus schedule to select the appropriate bus for given departures and arrivals. 4. Quantitative literacy test measures the knowledge and skills needed to apply the arithmetic operations of addition, subtraction, multiplication, and division, either alone or sequentially. A score of 200 indicates an ability to total two entries on a bank deposit slip. A score of 300 indicates an ability to enter deposits and checks and balance a checkbook. A score of 350 indicates an ability to determine the amount of a tip in a restaurant using a given percentage.

★ 310 ★
Literacy in Young Adults

Scores	Percent Performing at or above Indicated Score					
	Prose		Documents		Quantitative	
	White	Black	White	Black	White	Black
150	100.0	97.7	99.9	98.6	99.8	98.3
200	98.0	86.2	97.9	82.3	98.0	87.4
250	88.0	57.5	89.9	55.5	89.4	60.4
300	63.2	23.7	65.4	19.8	63.3	22.0
350	24.9	3.1	24.3	2.5	27.2	2.4
375	10.8	0.7	10.5	0.9	11.5	0.8

Source: "Results of Three Literacy Tasks by Adults Aged 21-25, by Race, 1985," *A Common Destiny: Blacks And American Society*, 1989, p. 353. Primary source: Kirsch, Irvin S., and Ann Jungeblut. 1986. *Literacy Profiles of America's Young Adults*. Princeton, NJ: Educational Testing Service. *Notes:* Each scale ranges from a minimum of 0 to a maximum of 500, with a standard deviation of approximately 50. Published by permission.

★ 311 ★
Male Illiteracy Rates: Trends

| | Cohort | | Percentage illiterate | | |
Birth year	Year reached age 10	Year reached age 40	Blacks	Whites	Difference
1840	1850	1880	74.8	8.0	66.8
1850	1860	1890	60.6	7.7	52.9
1860	1870	1900	43.0	6.3	36.7
1870	1880	1910	27.7	5.5	22.2
1880	1890	1920	22.0	5.3	16.7
1890	1900	1930	17.3	3.4	13.9
1900	1910	1940	14.1	2.0	12.1
1910	1920	1950	7.5	1.2	6.3
1920	1930	1960	6.1	0.7	5.4
1930	1940	1970	3.4	0.5	2.9
1940	1950	1980	1.7	0.4	1.3
1950	1960	1990	0.8	0.3	0.5
1960	1970	2000	0.4	0.3	0.1

Source: "Male Illiteracy Rate by Cohort and Race," *The Economic Progress of Black Men in America*, 1986, p. 66. Primary source: Smith, J.P. "Race and Human Capital," American Economic Review 4 (1984): 685-98.

★ 312 ★
Master's Degrees: Number and Field

Major field of study and sex of student	Total	White non-Hispanic	Black non-Hispanic	Hispanic	Asian or Pacific Islander	American Indian/ Alaskan Native	Non-resident Alien
All fields, total[1]	289,341	228,870	13,867	7,044	8,558	1,104	29,898
Agriculture and natural resources, total	3,521	2,536	79	44	58	6	798
Architecture and environmental design, total	3,164	2,250	77	93	92	8	644
Area and ethnic studies, total	853	585	39	53	38	5	133
Business and management, total	67,504	53,582	2,810	1,437	2,304	170	7,201
Communications, total	3,892	3,072	225	70	79	12	434
Computer and information sciences, total	8,041	5,053	222	132	834	23	2,217
Education, total	75,473	64,492	5,250	2,232	724	376	2,399
Engineering, total	22,046	13,343	419	521	1,715	39	6,009
Engineering technologies, total	612	405	30	8	42	25	102
Foreign languages, total	1,745	1,179	29	162	36	4	335
Health professions, total	18,421	15,724	856	378	489	62	912
Home economics, total	2,069	1,731	90	25	49	17	157
Law, total	1,944	1,100	44	50	78	4	668
Letters, total	6,125	5,149	141	89	130	20	596
Liberal/general studies, total	1,129	1,038	19	10	12	8	42
Library and archival science, total	3,814	3,318	146	48	93	9	200
Life sciences, total	4,950	3,944	175	86	198	11	536
Mathematics, total	3,319	2,113	76	55	193	3	879
Military sciences, total	119	101	8	5	0	0	5
Multi/interdisciplinary studies, total	3,035	2,585	114	55	66	31	184

Continued.

Master's Degrees: Number and Field
[Continued]

Major field of study and sex of student	Total	White non-Hispanic	Black non-Hispanic	Hispanic	Asian or Pacific Islander	American Indian/ Alaskan Native	Non-resident Alien
Parks and recreation, total	475	414	25	3	14	1	18
Philosophy and religion, total	1,109	894	41	29	29	3	113
Physical sciences, total	5,630	4,062	84	116	241	9	1,118
Protective services, total	1,019	808	140	15	10	8	38
Psychology, total	8,124	7,093	398	243	120	37	233
Public affairs, total	17,029	13,645	1,553	610	313	135	773
Social sciences, total	10,395	7,441	416	245	250	23	2,020
Theology, total	4,841	4,1085	121	88	112	8	404
Visual and performing arts, total	8,503	7,105	240	142	239	47	730

Source: "Master's Degrees Conferred by Institutions of Higher Education, by Racial/Ethnic Group, Major Field of Study, and Sex of Student: 1986-87," Digest of Education Statistics, 1989, pp. 246-247. Primary source: U.S. Department of Education, National Center for Educational Statistics, Integrated Postsecondary Education Data System (IPEDS), "Completions" survey. (This table was prepared June 1989.) *Notes:* 1. This tabulation excludes 99 men and 117 women whose racial/ethnic group could not be imputed. Because of imputation methods, fields of study totals by race/ethnicity may differ slightly from field of study by sex. Data are preliminary.

★ 313 ★
Math and First- or Second-Generation College Students

Racial and Ethnic Group	Percent Quantitative Majors	
	First Generation College Freshmen	Second Generation College Freshmen
White	17.2	21.8
Black	12.0	19.5
American Indian	12.9	19.0
Chicano	15.2	20.8
Puerto Rican	12.1	22.0
Asian American	41.2	40.2
All	16.7	21.9

Source: "Percent of First and Second Generation 1981 College Freshmen Choosing Quantitative College Majors by Race and Ethnicity," *Equality and Excellence: The Educational Status of Black Americans*, 1985, p. 22. Primary source: Berryman, Sue E., *Who Will Do Science?* The Rockefeller Foundation, 1983.

★ 314 ★
Mathematics Proficiency: Trends

Year, age, and race/ethnicity	Simple arith-metic facts	Begin-ning skills and under-standing	Basic opera-tions and beginning problem solving	Moder-ately complex proce-dures and reasoning	Multi-step problem and algebra
1977-78					
9-year-olds	96.5	70.3	19.4	0.8	[1]
White	98.3	76.0	22.5	0.9	[1]
Black	87.8	42.5	4.3	[1]	[1]
Hispanic	93.5	54.3	10.8	0.5	[1]
13-year-olds	[2]	94.5	64.9	17.9	0.9
White	[2]	97.5	72.5	21.4	1.1
Black	[2]	79.5	28.9	2.1	[1]
Hispanic	[2]	85.9	35.6	3.4	0.1
17-year-olds	[2]	99.8	92.1	51.4	7.4
White	[2]	100.0	95.8	57.3	8.6
Black	[2]	98.7	70.0	18.0	0.4
Hispanic	[2]	99.3	77.4	22.1	1.1
1981-82					
9-year-olds	97.2	71.5	18.7	0.6	[1]
White	98.6	76.9	21.5	0.7	[1]
Black	90.4	46.7	4.5	[1]	[1]
Hispanic	95.0	55.0	9.2	[1]	[1]
13-year-olds	[2]	97.6	71.6	17.8	0.5
White	[2]	99.1	78.5	20.9	0.6
Black	[2]	98.0	38.1	3.3	[1]
Hispanic	[2]	96.1	54.2	6.2	0.2
17-year-olds	[2]	99.9	92.9	48.3	5.4
White	[2]	100.0	96.3	54.5	6.3
Black	[2]	99.6	75.3	17.3	0.6
Hispanic	[2]	99.9	81.3	20.6	0.5
1985-86					
9-year-olds	97.8	73.9	20.8	0.6	[1]
White	98.9	79.2	24.5	0.7	[1]
Black	93.0	53.3	5.4	[1]	[1]
Hispanic	96.4	58.7	8.0	[1]	[1]
13-year-olds	[2]	98.5	73.1	15.9	0.4
White	[2]	99.2	78.7	18.6	0.5
Black	[2]	95.5	49.4	4.0	0.1
Hispanic	[2]	96.1	55.2	5.4	0.3
17-year-olds	[2]	99.9	96.0	51.1	6.4
White	[2]	99.9	98.3	58.0	7.6

Continued.

Mathematics Proficiency: Trends
[Continued]

Year, age, and race/ethnicity	Simple arith-metic facts	Begin-ning skills and under-standing	Basic opera-tions and beginning problem solving	Moder-ately complex proce-dures and reasoning	Multi-step problem and algebra
Black	2	100.0	86.0	21.7	0.3
Hispanic	2	98.9	90.8	26.8	1.2

Source: "Percentage of Students At or Above Five Mathematics Proficiency Levels, by Race/Ethnicity and Age: 1977-78, 1981-82, and 1985-86," *Digest of Education Statistics*, 1989, p. 115. Primary source: U.S. Department of Education, National Center for Education Statistics, National Assessment of Educational Progress. *The Mathematics Report Card*, prepared by Educational Testing Service. (This table was prepared, January 1989.) *Notes:* 1. Virtually no students were able to perform at this level 2. Virtually all students were able to perform at this level.

★ 315 ★
Newer Predominately Black Institutions

Date Established	Number	Control		Level	
		Public	Private	4-Year	2-Year
1979-Present					
1964-1978	16	9	7	2	14
1949-1963	9	2	7	-	9
1924-1948	8	1	7	4	4
1909-1923	6	1	5	1	5
1894-1908	4	-	4	1	3
1879-1893	2	-	2	-	2
Prior to 1879	2	1	1	2	-
Total	47	14	33	10	37
Percent	100	30	70	21	79

Source: "A Summary: Newer Predominately Black Institutions (PBIs) by Control, Level, and Date Established, Fall 1984, Non-NAFEO Membership (N=47)," *NAFEO INROADS*, February/March, 1987, p. 12. Primary source: 1984 Civil Rights *Racial, Ethnic and Sex Enrollment Survey for Higher Education*. NAFEO - National Association for Equal Opportunity in Higher Education *Notes:* Analysis does not include unclassified students. Data include only reporting institutions. Published by permission.

★ 316 ★
Occupational Aspirations on Black/White College Campuses

Numbers in percent.

Prestige Rating of Occupational Goal (100 point scale)	Total Population	Campus Race	
		Black	White
Below 60 points	13.8	12.5	15.5
61-69 points	34.6	35.7	33.1
70-84	33.6	40.2	25.0
Above 85 points	18.0	11.6	26.4

Continued.

Occupational Aspirations on Black/White College Campuses
[Continued]

Prestige Rating of Occupational Goal (100 point scale)	Total Population	Campus Race	
		Black	White
Total	100.0	100.0	100.0
N	(1499)	(848)	(651)

Source: "Occupational Aspirations by Student Gender and Campus Race," *Gender and Campus Race Differences in Black Student Academic Performance, Racial Attitudes and College Satisfaction*, 1986, p. 59. Primary source: National Study of Black College Students, 1981 and 1983, University of Michigan, Ann Arbor. Published by permission.

★ 317 ★
Ph.D. Recipients: Trends

Year	PhD Recipients
1982	1,047
1983	921
1984	953
1985	912
1986	820

Source: "American Blacks Receiving Ph.Ds," *Black Issues in Higher Education*, March 30, 1989, p. 21. Primary source: National Research Council.

★ 318 ★
Physical Science Doctorates: Trends

Item	1977-1978	1978-1979	1979-1980	1980-1981	1981-1982	1982-1983	1983-1984	1984-1985	1985-1986	1986-1987
Number of doctorates	3,234	3,321	3,151	3,208	3,348	3,438	3,459	3,531	3,679	3,837
Racial/ethnic group (percent)[1]										
American Indian	0.5	0.4	0.2	[2]	0.1	0.2	0.2	0.1	0.2	0.2
Asian	13.8	13.7	14.7	15.1	15.5	15.8	17.8	17.8	19.8	20.3
Black	1.8	1.7	1.2	1.7	1.6	1.4	1.8	1.5	1.4	1.2
Mexican-American	[3]	[3]	0.4	0.3	0.2	0.2	0.3	0.5	0.3	0.3
Puerto Rican	[3]	[3]	0.1	0.3	0.2	0.2	0.3	0.2	0.3	0.7
Other Hispanic	[3]	[3]	1.7	1.7	1.8	2.1	2.6	2.2	2.4	2.2
White	73.0	73.2	73.1	73.0	74.8	73.6	71.3	70.3	65.7	64.7
Other and unknown	8.6	8.6	8.6	7.7	5.8	6.3	5.8	7.6	9.9	10.4

Source: "Statistical Profile of Persons Receiving Doctor's Degrees in the Physical Sciences: 1977-78 to 1986-87," *Digest of Educational Statistics*, 1989, p. 272. Primary source: National Academy of Sciences, National Research Council, Office of Scientific and Engineering Personnel, Doctorate Records File. (This table was prepared March 1989.) *Notes:* The National Research Council's classification of degrees by field differs somewhat from that in most publications of the National Center for Educational Statistics (NCES). The number of degrees also differs somewhat from that reported in the NCES "Degrees and Other Formal Awards Conferred" survey. Because of rounding, percents may not add to 100.0 1. Longitudinal comparisons by race/ethnicity should be done with extreme care, due to periodic changes in the survey. 2. Less than 0.05 percent. 3. Hispanic subcategories were not collected until 1980. Published by permission.

★ 319 ★
Postsecondary Degree Holders: Number and Field

Numbers in thousands.

Field of study	Total	Race	
		White	Black
Total population, 18 and over	170,232	147,147	18,475
Number of persons with bachelor's or higher degree	26,381	24,036	1,334
Percent of population	15.5	16.3	7.2
Agriculture and forestry	427	419	[1]
Biology	620	556	21
Business and management	4,462	4,058	238
Economics	462	403	23
Education	5,297	4,890	347
Engineering	2,176	1,952	72
English and journalism	1,029	975	35
Home economics	366	330	23
Law	928	860	45
Liberal arts and humanities	2,371	2,215	73
Mathematics and statistics	541	488	33
Medicine and dentistry	872	776	32
Nursing, pharmacy, and health technologies	1,151	997	57
Physical and earth sciences	741	669	17
Police science and law enforcement	154	140	14
Psychology	749	707	27
Religion and theology	467	445	18
Social sciences	1,764	1,560	156
Vocational and technical studies	157	138	15
Other fields	1,647	1,458	88
	Percentage distribution of degree holders, by field		
Total	100.0	100.0	100.0
Agriculture and forestry	1.6	1.7	[1]
Biology	2.4	2.3	1.6
Business and management	16.9	16.9	17.8
Economics	1.8	1.7	1.7
Education	20.1	20.3	26.0
Engineering	8.2	8.1	5.4
English and journalism	3.9	4.1	2.6
Home economics	1.4	1.4	1.7
Law	3.5	3.6	3.4
Liberal arts and humanities	9.0	9.2	5.5
Mathematics and statistics	2.1	2.0	2.5
Medicine and dentistry	3.3	3.2	2.4
Nursing, pharmacy, and health technologies	4.4	4.1	4.3
Physical and earth sciences	2.8	2.8	1.6
Police science and law enforcement	0.6	0.6	1.0
Psychology	2.8	2.9	2.0
Religion and theology	1.8	1.9	1.3
Social sciences	6.7	6.5	11.7

Continued.

Postsecondary Degree Holders: Number and Field
[Continued]

Field of study	Total	Race	
		White	Black
Vocational and technical studies	0.6	0.6	1.1
Other fields	6.2	6.1	6.6

Source: "Number of Persons age 18 and Over Who Hold a Bachelor's or Higher Degree, by Field of Study, Sex, Race, and Age: Spring 1984," *Digest of Education Statistics,* 1989, p. 17. Primary source: U.S. Department of Commerce, Bureau of the Census, *Current Population Reports,* Series P-70, No. 11, "Educational Background and Economic Status: Spring 1984." (This table was prepared October 1987.) *Notes:* Note — Data are based on sample surveys of the civilian noninstitutional population. Because of rounding, details may not add to totals. 1. Data not available or not applicable.

★ 320 ★
Postsecondary Enrollment of 1980 High School Grads: Trends

Race/ethnicity	Fall 1980		Fall 1981		Fall 1982		Fall 1983		Fall 1984		Fall 1985	
	Full-time	Part-time	Full-time	Part-time	Full-time	Part-time	Full-time	Part-time	Full-time	Part-time	Full-time	Part-time
Total	46.1	5.8	43.1	6.6	34.1	9.9	33.3	6.8	17.1	7.5	10.4	7.6
Race/ethnicity												
White, non-Hispanic	47.7	5.8	44.6	6.6	35.5	10.2	34.7	6.7	18.0	7.6	10.5	7.6
Black, non-Hispanic	42.0	4.1	39.8	4.8	29.8	8.1	28.3	6.0	12.7	5.4	8.9	6.2
Hispanic	34.9	7.8	30.5	9.4	23.6	10.6	22.9	8.0	11.6	8.0	10.0	8.3
American Indian	34.2	5.3	35.0	6.9	21.0	11.9	22.4	8.2	14.8	2.1	10.5	2.6
Asian	67.4	12.0	64.6	12.8	57.7	15.8	53.8	10.9	37.2	13.6	20.8	16.8

Source: "Percent of the High School Class of 1980 Enrolled in Postsecondary Education, by Attendance Status, Sex, Race/Ethnicity, Socioeconomic Status, and Ability Level: Fall 1980 to Fall 1985," *Digest of Education Statistics,* 1989, p. 275. Primary source: U.S. Department of Education, National Center for Education Statistics, High School and Beyond survey. (This table was prepared October 1988).

★ 321 ★
Private School Teachers

Teacher characteristics	All private schools	Level of school				Religious affiliation of school		
		Elementary	Secondary	Combined	Other	Catholic[2]	Other religiously affiliated[2]	Not religiously affiliated
Number of teachers, in thousands[1]	404	190	83	96	35	185	127	92
Race/ethnicity (percent)								
Total	100.0	100.0	100.0	100.0	100.0	100.0	100.0	100.0
White	92.2	91.1	95.0	92.6	91.1	93.5	91.9	90.2
Black	3.8	4.8	1.4	3.3	5.0	2.5	4.0	5.9
Hispanic	2.9	2.9	2.9	3.3	2.4	3.4	2.9	2.2
Other	1.1	1.3	0.7	0.8	1.5	0.7	1.1	1.8

Source: "Characteristics of Private School Teachers, by Level and Affiliation of School: 1985-86," *Digest of Educational Statistics,* 1989, p. 65. Primary source: U.S. Department of Education, National Center for Education Statistics, "1985-86 Private School Survey." (This table was prepared October 1986.) *Notes:* Data based on a sample survey and may not be strictly comparable with data reported elsewhere. Elementary schools have no grade higher than 8. Secondary schools have no grade lower than 7. Combined schools have any other grade spans. Other schools includes special education, alternative, and vocational schools. Includes only schools which offer first grade or above. Data in other tables reflect full-time-equivalent teachers. Because of rounding, details may not add to totals. 1. Tabulation includes full-time and part-time students. 2. Includes schools with a religious orientation or religious affiliation.

★ 322 ★
Private Schools

For school year ending in year shown. Based on survey and subject to sampling error; for details see source.

Item	Total	Level of School				Religious Affiliation		
		Elementary	Secondary	Combined	Other	Catholic	Other	None
Race:								
White non-Hispanic	92.2	91.1	95.0	92.6	91.1	93.5	91.9	90.2
Black non-Hispanic	3.8	4.8	1.4	3.3	5.0	2.5	4.0	5.9
Hispanic	2.9	2.9	2.9	3.3	2.4	3.4	2.9	2.2

Source: "Characteristics of Private Elementary and Secondary Schools and Teachers, by Level and Affiliation of School: 1986," *Statistical Abstract*, 1989, p. 143. Primary source: U.S. Dept. of Education, National Center for Education Statistics, *Digest of Education Statistics*, 1987.

★ 323 ★
Public Elementary and Secondary Schools

	Non-South All	South		Ratio of Southern Black to:	
		Black	White	Southern White	Non-South
Days of attendance[1]					
1920	146.8	86.0	112.8	.76	.59
1935	156.8	111.0	134.0	.83	.71
1940	156.0	127.9	143.4	.89	.82
1951	158.3	149.6	153.2	.98	.94
1953	160.9	151.2	156.7	.96	.94
Student-teacher ratio[2]					
1920	25.0	38.6	26.4	1.46	1.54
1935	32.3	44.8	33.5	1.34	1.39
1940	23.9	30.5	25.3	1.21	1.28
1951	25.3	27.7	27.6	1.00	1.09
1953	25.4	27.7	27.6	1.00	1.09
Teacher salary per school day[3]					
1920	7.82	3.10	5.60	.55	.40
1935	8.60	2.94	5.35	.55	.34
1940	10.10	4.07	6.42	.63	.40
1951	20.47	13.22	16.70	.79	.65
1953	22.25	15.83	17.59	.90	.71

Source: "Measures of School Resources in Public Elementary and Secondary Schools by Race," *The Economic Progress of Black Men in America*, p. 64. Primary source: These data were obtained primarily from various issues of the Biennial Survey of Education, supplemented by other sources cited in the bibliography. *Notes:* 1. Average days of attendance per enrolled student in public schools. 2. Ratio of student enrollment to number of public school teachers weighted by the attendance rate. The attendance rate is the proportion of total school term days attended by the average student. 3. Average annual teacher's salary per day of school term.

★ 324 ★
Public School Enrollment

State	Percent of enrollment, by race or ethnicity					American Indian/ Alaskan Native
	Total	White[1]	Black[1]	Hispanic	Asian or Pacific Islander	
United States	100.0	70.4	16.1	9.9	2.8	0.9
Alabama	100.0	62.0	37.0	0.1	0.4	0.5
Alaska	100.0	65.7	4.3	1.7	3.3	25.1
Arizona	100.0	62.2	4.0	26.4	1.3	6.1
Arkansas	100.0	74.7	24.2	0.4	0.6	0.2
California	100.0	53.7	9.0	27.5	9.1	0.7
Colorado	100.0	78.7	4.5	13.7	2.0	1.0
Connecticut	100.0	77.2	12.1	8.9	1.5	0.2
Delaware	100.0	68.3	27.7	2.5	1.4	0.2
District of Columbia	100.0	4.0	91.1	3.9	0.9	0.1
Florida	100.0	65.4	23.7	9.5	1.2	0.2
Georgia	100.0	60.7	37.9	0.6	0.8	[2]
Hawaii	100.0	23.5	2.3	2.2	71.7	0.3
Idaho	100.0	82.6	0.3	4.9	0.8	1.3
Illinois	100.0	69.8	18.7	9.2	2.3	0.1
Indiana	100.0	88.7	9.0	1.7	0.5	0.1
Iowa	100.0	94.6	3.0	0.9	1.2	0.3
Kansas	100.0	85.6	7.6	4.4	1.9	0.6
Kentucky	100.0	89.2	10.2	0.1	0.5	0.0
Louisiana	100.0	56.5	41.3	0.8	1.1	0.3
Maine	100.0	98.3	0.5	0.2	0.8	0.2
Maryland	100.0	59.7	35.3	1.7	3.1	0.2
Massachusetts	100.0	83.7	7.4	6.0	2.8	0.1
Michigan	100.0	76.4	19.8	1.8	1.2	0.8
Minnesota	100.0	93.9	2.1	0.9	1.7	1.5
Mississippi	100.0	43.9	55.5	0.1	0.4	0.1
Missouri	100.0	83.4	14.9	0.7	0.8	0.2
Montana	100.0	92.7	0.3	0.9	0.5	5.5
Nebraska	100.0	91.4	4.4	2.4	0.8	1.0
Nevada	100.0	77.4	9.6	7.5	3.2	2.3
New Hampshire	100.0	98.0	0.7	0.5	0.8	0.1
New Jersey	100.0	69.1	17.4	10.7	2.7	0.1
New Mexico	100.0	43.1	2.3	45.1	0.8	8.7
New York	100.0	68.4	16.5	12.3	2.7	0.2
North Carolina	100.0	68.4	28.9	0.4	0.6	1.7
North Dakota	100.0	92.4	0.6	1.1	0.8	5.0
Ohio	100.0	83.1	15.0	1.0	0.7	0.1
Oklahoma	100.0	79.0	7.8	1.6	1.0	10.6
Oregon	100.0	89.8	2.2	3.9	2.4	1.7
Pennsylvania	100.0	84.4	12.6	1.8	1.2	0.1
Rhode Island	100.0	87.9	5.6	3.7	2.4	0.3
South Carolina	100.0	54.6	44.5	0.2	0.6	0.1
South Dakota	100.0	90.6	0.5	0.6	0.7	7.6
Tennessee	100.0	76.5	22.6	0.2	0.6	[2]
Texas	100.0	51.0	14.4	32.5	2.0	0.2
Utah	100.0	93.7	0.4	3.0	1.5	1.5

Continued.

Public School Enrollment
[Continued]

State	Percent of enrollment, by race or ethnicity					American Indian/ Alaskan Native
	Total	White[1]	Black[1]	Hispanic	Asian or Pacific Islander	
Vermont	100.0	98.4	0.3	0.2	0.6	0.6
Virginia	100.0	72.6	23.7	1.0	2.6	0.1
Washington	100.0	84.5	4.2	3.8	5.1	2.3
West Virginia	100.0	95.9	3.7	0.1	0.3	0.0
Wisconsin	100.0	86.6	8.9	1.9	1.7	1.0.
Wyoming	100.0	90.7	0.9	5.9	0.6	1.9

Source: "Enrollment in Public Elementary and Secondary Schools, by Race or Ethnicity and State: Fall 1986," *Digest of Education Statistics*, 1989, p. 56. Primary source: U.S. Department of Education, Office for Civil Rights, *1986 State Summaries of Elementary and Secondary School Civil Rights Survey*. (This table was prepared July 1989.) *Notes:* The above tabulation was derived from a sample survey of public school districts from the 1986 Elementary and Secondary School Civil Rights Survey. State estimates may differ from other data sources because of variations in survey methodology. Because of rounding, details may not add up to totals. 1. Excludes persons of Hispanic origin. 2. Less than 0.05 percent.

★ 325 ★
Quantitative GRE Scores

Score	Percent of Group Below Score									
	American Indian	Black/ Afro- American	Mexican American	Oriental or or Asian	Puerto Rican	Other Hispanic/ Latin American	White	Other	No Response	Total
800[1]	99.5	100.0	100.0	98.3	100.0	99.7	99.2	99.3	98.8	99.3
750	98.4	99.8	99.3	92.6	99.7	98.7	96.1	95.7	94.9	96.3
700	94.4	99.4	97.9	81.5	98.4	95.7	90.0	88.2	87.7	90.6
650	90.7	98.5	94.6	68.4	95.6	90.0	81.7	80.4	78.5	82.7
600	83.0	96.6	89.1	53.8	91.2	81.4	70.1	68.4	66.2	71.9
550	72.0	93.1	81.4	38.5	84.5	71.5	56.0	54.1	52.5	58.6
500	59.8	87.3	70.8	26.5	74.0	58.4	40.7	39.1	39.6	44.2
450	46.2	78.4	58.4	15.7	58.7	45.2	26.1	25.5	26.5	30.1
400	32.9	64.8	43.8	8.9	43.9	31.3	14.4	15.3	16.4	18.4
350	19.6	49.4	31.1	5.2	29.7	18.7	7.2	8.5	9.8	10.5
300	10.4	30.4	15.5	1.8	16.5	9.7	2.7	3.8	4.6	4.8
250	4.2	13.8	6.0	0.4	7.5	3.5	0.7	1.2	1.8	1.7
200	0.0	0.0	0.0	0.0	0.0	0.0	0.0	0.0	0.0	0.0
N	1,096	11,133	2,150	2,940	1,282	1,437	148,513	30,339	6,567	178,457

Source: "Distributions of GRE Aptitude Test Quantitative Scores by Ethnic Group (U.S. Citizens Only)," *Equality and Excellence: The Educational Status of Black Americans*, 1985, p. 22. Primary source: Goodison, Marlene B. *A Summary of Data Collected from Graduate Record Examinations Test-Takers During 1980-81*. Princeton: Educational Testing Service, 1982. *Note:* 1. Theoretical maximum score is 900. Published by permission.

★ 326 ★
Reading Proficiency: Trends

Year, age, and race/ethnicity	Rudiment.[1]	Basic[2]	Interm.[3]	Adept[4]	Advanced[5]
1974-75					
9-year-olds	93.3	61.7	14.0	0.7	[6]
White	95.9	68.4	16.6	0.8	[6]
Black	81.5	32.0	1.9	0.0	[6]
Hispanic	82.3	33.5	3.2	0.0	[6]
13-year-olds	99.6	92.8	57.5	9.7	[6]
White	100.0	96.2	64.3	11.5	[6]
Black	98.0	75.3	23.9	1.5	[6]
Hispanic	98.2	81.4	29.8	1.3	[6]
17-year-olds	[7]	97.5	82.0	36.1	3.5
White	[7]	99.1	87.5	40.6	4.0
Black	[7]	86.0	45.0	7.1	0.0
Hispanic	[7]	92.4	56.5	12.9	0.5
1979-80					
9-year-olds	94.4	65.1	17.0	0.8	[6]
White	96.8	71.7	20.3	1.0	[6]
Black	85.3	39.4	3.9	0.0	[6]
Hispanic	84.3	37.6	4.4	0.0	[6]
13-year-olds	99.8	94.3	59.3	10.9	[6]
White	99.9	96.7	66.0	13.1	[6]
Black	99.4	84.1	29.6	1.4	[6]
Hispanic	99.4	85.2	33.7	2.7	[6]
17-year-olds	[7]	97.9	82.8	34.8	3.1
White	[7]	99.3	88.9	39.9	3.6
Black	[7]	88.8	45.8	6.1	0.0
Hispanic	[7]	96.5	63.2	12.7	0.4
1983-84					
9-year-olds	93.9	64.2	18.1	1.0	[6]
White	96.4	71.1	22.0	1.2	[6]
Black	83.6	39.3	4.5	0.1	[6]
Hispanic	88.2	43.8	4.7	0.0	[6]
13-year-olds	99.8	94.5	60.3	11.3	[6]
White	99.9	96.5	66.9	13.6	[6]
Black	99.4	87.1	35.3	2.3	[6]
Hispanic	100.0	88.3	39.4	1.7	[6]
17-year-olds	[7]	98.6	83.6	39.2	4.9
White	[7]	99.2	88.9	45.1	5.8

Continued.

Reading Proficiency: Trends
[Continued]

Year, age, and race/ethnicity	Rudiment.[1]	Basic[2]	Interm.[3]	Adept[4]	Advanced[5]
Black	[7]	96.5	65.8	15.5	0.8
Hispanic	[7]	96.8	69.1	19.9	1.5

Source: "Percentage of Students At or Above Selected Reading Proficiency Levels, by Race/Ethnicity, and Age: 1970-71 to 1983-84," Digest of Education Statistics, 1989, p. 110. Primary source: U.S. Department of Education, National Institute of Education, National Assessment of Educational Progress, *The Reading Report Card.* (This table was prepared May 1986.) *Notes:* 1. Able to follow brief written directions and select phrases to describe pictures. 2. Able to understand combined ideas and make references based on short uncomplicated passages about specific or sequentially related information. 3. Able to search for specific information, interrelate ideas, and make generalizations about literature, science, and social studies materials. 4. Able to find, understand, summarize, and explain relatively complicated literary and informational material. 5. Able to understand the links between ideas even when those links are not explicitly stated and to make appropriate generalizations even when the texts lack clear introductions or explanations. 6. Virtually no students were able to read at this level. 7. Virtually all students were able to read material at this level.

★ 327 ★
Recent Bachelor's Degree Recipients

Major field of study and sex of student	Total	White non-Hispanic	Black non-Hispanic	Hispanic	Asian or or Pacific Islander	American Indian/ Alaskan Native	Non-resident alien
All fields, total[1]	991,260	841,820	56,555	26,990	32,618	3,971	29,306
Agriculture and natural resources, total	14,991	13,657	299	231	283	58	463
Architecture and environmental design, total	8,950	7,271	277	338	365	26	673
Area and ethnic studies, total	3,307	2,649	201	146	214	29	68
Business and management, total	241,100	205,118	14,686	6,397	6,002	783	8,114
Communications, total	45,393	39,493	3,228	1,011	919	132	610
Computer and information sciences, total	39,590	30,251	2,928	1,077	2,546	116	2,672
Education, total	87,083	78,216	4,253	2,223	1,092	452	847
Engineering, total	73,839	57,563	2,356	2,007	5,695	214	6,004
Engineering technologies, total	19,258	15,725	1,145	546	802	75	965
Foreign languages, total	10,197	8,421	321	808	341	24	282
Health professions, total	63,213	55,410	3,822	1,332	1,577	274	798
Home economics, total	14,940	13,072	879	232	423	119	215
Law, total	1,177	1,074	52	25	22	2	2
Letters, total	37,132	33,499	1,589	736	780	99	429
Liberal/general studies, total	21,366	18,066	1,620	893	356	133	298
Library and archival science, total	140	122	9	3	0	0	6
Life sciences, total	38,120	31,279	1,932	1,259	2,620	147	883
Mathematics, total	16,444	13,556	846	269	1,050	53	607
Military sciences, total	384	360	1	13	1	1	8
Multi/interdisciplinary studies, total	16,399	13,754	1,074	527	625	101	318
Parks and recreation, total	4,106	3,735	186	60	71	19	35
Philosophy and religion, total	5,984	5,324	233	142	163	11	111
Physical sciences, total	20,071	17,159	844	423	919	74	653
Protective services, total	12,930	10,177	1,930	534	140	53	96
Psychology, total	42,835	37,014	2,535	1,401	1,188	186	511
Public affairs, total	14,178	11,289	1,822	542	197	127	201
Social sciences, total	96,172	81,659	5,942	2,883	2,942	464	2,282
Theology, total	5,728	5,236	177	81	92	15	127

Continued.

Recent Bachelor's Degree Recipients
[Continued]

Major field of study and sex of student	Total	White non-Hispanic	Black non-Hispanic	Hispanic	Asian or or Pacific Islander	American Indian/ Alaskan Native	Non-resident alien
Visual and performing arts, total	36,233	31,671	1,368	851	1,194	184	965

Source: "Bachelor's Degrees Conferred by Institutions of Higher Education, by Racial/Ethnic Group, Major Field of Study, and Sex of Student: 1986-87," *Digest of Education Statistics, 1989*, pp. 243-244. Primary source: U.S. Department of Education, National Center for Educational Statistics, Integrated Postsecondary Education Data System (IPEDS), "Completions" survey. (This table was prepared June 1989.) *Notes:* 1. This tabulation excludes 74 men and 5 women whose racial/ethnic group could not be imputed. Because of imputation methods, fields of study totals by race/ethnicity may differ slightly from field of study by sex. Data are preliminary.

★ 328 ★
Recent Recipients of Doctorates

Item	All fields	Education	Engineering	Humanities	Life sciences	Mathematics	Physical sciences	Business and management	Social sciences	Other professional fields[2]
Doctor's degrees conferred (number)[1]	32,278[3]	6,447	3,716	3,504	5,742	740	3,837	980	5,718	1,083
Racial/ethnic group (percent)										
American Indian	0.4	0.6	0.2	0.3	0.3	[4]	0.2[4]	[5]	0.4	0.4[6]
Asian	12.7	4.1	34.6	4.8	11.8	[4]	20.3[4]	[5]	7.5	12.9[6]
Black	3.8	7.3	1.5	3.4	3.0	[4]	1.2[4]	[5]	4.0	4.9[6]
Mexican-American	0.6	1.1	0.4	0.5	0.4	[4]	0.3[4]	[5]	0.8	0.4[6]
Puerto Rican	0.6	0.8	0.1	0.9	0.5	[4]	0.7[4]	[5]	0.4	0.5[6]
Other Hispanic	2.1	1.3	2.2	2.7	2.6	[4]	2.2[4]	[5]	2.3	0.9[6]
White	70.0	76.7	49.2	77.3	72.4	[4]	64.7[4]	[5]	73.9	69.1[6]
Other and unknown	9.9	8.0	11.9	10.0	9.1	[4]	10.4[4]	[5]	10.8	10.8[6]

Source: "Statistical Profile of Persons Receiving Doctor's Degrees, by Field of Study: 1986-87," *Digest of Educational Statistics*, 1989, p. 269. Primary source: National Academy of Sciences, National Research Council, Office of Scientific and Engineering Personnel, *Summary Report, 1987: Doctorate Recipients From United States Universities*. (This table was prepared March 1988.) *Notes:* The above classification of degrees by field differs somewhat from that in most publications of the National Center for Educational Statistics (NCES). The major differences are that history is included under social sciences. The number of degrees also differs slightly from that reported in the NCES "Degrees and Other Formal Awards Conferred" survey. The above tabulation excludes some non-research doctorate degrees such as doctor's degrees in theology. Because of rounding, percents may not add to 100.0. 1. Includes Ph.D., Ed.D., and comparable degrees at the doctoral level. Excludes first-professional degrees, such as M.D., D.D.S., and D.V.M. 2. Includes communications. 3. Includes 540 degrees in computer sciences and 61 degrees in other or unspecified fields not shown separately. 4. Within the racial/ethnic category, mathematics and computer sciences are included under physical sciences. 5. Business administration is included under other professional fields. 6. Includes business administration, communications, other professional fields, and other and unspecified. Published by permission.

★ 329 ★
Regional Changes in Schoolchildren's Reading Performance

	Performance			Change		
Age Group, Race, and Region	1971	1975	1980	1971 to 1975	1975 to 1980	1971 to 1980
Average Percent Correct						
9-years-olds	64.0	65.3	67.9	1.3[1]	2.6[1]	3.9[1]
White	66.4	67.0	69.3	.6	2.3[1]	2.8[1]
Northeast	67.8	69.0	71.6	1.2	2.6[1]	3.7[1]
Southeast	63.9	65.3	69.2	1.4	3.9[1]	5.3[1]
Central	68.0	69.1	70.3	1.1	1.2	2.3[1]

Continued.

Regional Changes in Schoolchildren's Reading Performance
[Continued]

	Performance			Change		
				1971 to	1975 to	1971 to
Age Group, Race, and Region	1971	1975	1980	1975	1980	1980
West	64.8	66.6	68.8	1.8	2.2[1]	4.0[1]
Black	49.7	54.5	59.6	4.8[1]	5.1[1]	9.9[1]
Northeast	54.1	56.4	62.0	2.2	5.6[1]	7.8[1]
Southeast	45.4	53.1	58.1	7.6[1]	5.0[1]	12.7[1]
Central	51.0	56.8	60.6	5.8[1]	3.8[1]	9.7[1]
West	51.7	52.6	57.2	.9	4.6	5.5
13-year-olds:	60.0	59.9	60.8	-.1	.9	.8
White	62.6	61.9	62.6	-.7	.7	[2]
Northeast	64.3	63.1	63.6	-1.2	.5	-.7
Southeast	59.9	60.4	61.6	.6	1.1	1.7
Central	64.4	64.3	64.8	.0	.5	.4
West	61.1	62.1	63.2	1.0	1.1	2.2[1]
Black	45.4	46.4	49.6	1.0	3.2[1]	4.2[1]
Northeast	48.8	48.5	53.2	-.3	4.7[1]	4.4
Southeast	41.5	45.5	45.5	4.0[1]	-.1	3.9
Central	47.7	48.6	52.4	.9	3.7	4.7
West	48.1	42.6	50.5	-5.6[1]	-7.9[1]	2.4
17-year-olds:	68.9	69.0	68.2	[2]	-.8	-.7
White	71.2	71.2	70.6	[2]	-.6	-.7
Northeast	72.7	72.6	70.8	-.1	-1.8	-1.9
Southeast	68.3	70.2	70.2	2.0	.0	2.0
Central	72.6	72.9	71.6	.3	-1.3	-1.0
West	69.9	70.6	71.6	.6	1.0	1.7
Black	51.7	52.1	52.2	.5	.1	.5
Northeast	56.1	54.1	56.1	-1.9	1.9	0
Southeast	47.7	50.7	49.8	3.0	-.9	2.1
Central	53.8	54.9	54.2	1.1	-.7	.4
West	51.8	49.4	50.8	-2.4	1.4	-1.0

Source: "Average Reading Performance of 9-, 13-, and 17- Year-Old Students by Race and Region: 1970-71, 1974-75, and 1979-80," *Equality and Excellence: The Educational Status of Black Americans,* 1985, p. 24. Primary source: National Assessment of Educational Progress, *Three National Assessments of Reading: Changes in Performance, 1970-80,* April 1981. *Notes:* 1. Indicates statistically significant change in performance between assessments. 2. Less than 0.05 percent. Published by permission.

★ 330 ★
Regional Educational Attainment

Numbers in thousands .

Educational attainment and region	Black			White		
	Both sexes	Male	Female	Both sexes	Male	Female
United States						
Total, 25 years old and over	15,929	7,067	8,863	131,092	62,679	68,414
Percent	100.0	100.0	100.0	100.0	100.0	100.0
Elementary: Total	18.0	18.9	17.3	11.3	11.4	11.2
0 to 4 years	4.8	5.7	4.2	2.0	2.1	1.9
5 to 7 years	7.7	8.4	7.2	3.9	4.1	3.8
8 years	5.5	4.8	6.0	5.3	5.1	5.4
High School: Total	55.7	54.4	56.8	50.6	46.9	54.0
1 to 3 years	18.6	17.5	19.5	11.1	10.9	11.2
4 years	37.1	37.0	37.3	39.5	36.0	42.8
College: Total	26.2	26.6	25.9	38.2	41.8	34.8
1 to 3 years	15.0	15.4	14.6	17.2	16.9	17.6
4 or more years	11.3	11.2	11.3	20.9	24.9	17.3
4 years of high school or more	63.3	63.6	63.1	77.7	77.7	77.6
South						
Total, 25 years old and over	8,736	3,857	4,879	42,071	19,971	22,100
Percent	100.0	100.0	100.0	100.0	100.0	100.0
Elementary: Total	21.6	22.6	20.8	13.7	14.3	13.1
0 to 4 years	6.1	7.3	5.1	2.9	3.3	2.6
5 to 7 years	9.7	10.5	9.1	5.6	5.9	5.4
8 years	5.8	4.8	6.6	5.2	5.2	5.1
High School: Total	55.1	54.1	55.9	49.2	44.9	53.1
1 to 3 years	18.9	17.7	19.9	12.5	11.9	13.0
4 years	36.2	36.5	36.0	36.7	33.0	40.0
College: Total	23.3	23.3	23.2	37.1	40.8	33.8
1 to 3 years	12.6	13.8	11.7	16.9	16.5	17.1
4 or more years	10.6	9.5	11.6	20.3	24.3	16.6
4 years of high school or more	59.5	59.8	59.3	73.8	73.8	73.8
North and West						
Total, 25 years old and over	7,194	3,210	3,984	89,022	42,708	46,314
Percent	100.0	100.0	100.0	100.0	100.0	100.0
Elementary: Total	13.7	14.5	13.0	10.1	10.0	10.2
0 to 4 years	3.3	3.7	3.0	1.6	1.6	1.6
5 to 7 years	5.3	6.0	4.8	3.1	3.3	3.0
8 years	5.0	4.8	5.2	5.3	5.1	5.6
High School: Total	56.5	54.8	57.9	51.2	47.8	54.4
1 to 3 years	18.3	17.3	19.1	10.4	10.4	10.4
4 years	38.2	37.5	38.8	40.8	37.3	44.1
College: Total	29.8	30.7	29.1	38.6	42.2	35.3
1 to 3 years	17.8	17.4	18.1	17.4	17.0	17.8
4 or more years	12.0	13.3	11.0	21.2	25.2	17.6
4 years of high school or more	68.0	68.2	67.9	79.5	79.6	79.4

Source: "Educational Attainment of Persons 25 Years Old and Over, by Sex, Region, and Race: March 1988," *The Black Population in the United States: March 1988, pp. 25-27.* Primary source: Current Population Reports, Series P-20, No. 442, *The Black Population in the United States: March 1988.*

★ 331 ★
Regional Educational Attainment: Trends

Number in thousands.

Educational attainment	1988		1985		1980	
	Black	White	Black	White	Black	White
United States						
Total, 25 years old and over	15,929	131,092	14,820	124,905	12,927	114,763
Percent completed--						
Less than 5 years of school	4.8	2.0	6.2	2.2	9.2	2.6
4 years of high school or more	63.3	77.7	59.8	75.5	51.2	70.5
4 years of college or more	11.3	20.9	11.1	20.0	7.9	17.8
South						
Total, 25 years old and over	8,736	42,071	7,828	40,137	6,655	36,029
Percent completed--						
Less than 5 years of school	6.1	2.9	8.6	3.2	13.2	4.0
4 years of high school or more	59.5	73.8	55.4	71.6	44.7	67.0
4 years of college or more	10.6	20.3	10.4	18.7	7.5	17.0
North and West						
Total, 25 years old and over	7,194	89,022	6,991	84,768	6,272	78,734
Percent completed--						
Less than 5 years of school	3.3	1.6	3.5	1.7	4.9	2.0
4 years of high school or more	68.0	79.5	64.6	77.4	58.1	72.2
4 years of college or more	12.0	21.2	11.8	20.6	8.4	18.2

Source: "Selected Summary Measures of the Educational Attainment of Persons 25 Years Old and Over, by Region, Age, and Race: March 1988, 1985, and 1980," *The Black Population in the United States: March 1988*, p. 7. Primary source: Current Population Reports, Series P-20, No. 442, *The Black Population in the United States: March 1989*.

★ 332 ★
Regional High School Graduation Rates: Trends

	1980	1988
United States	75.4	80.5
South	73.4	79.4
North and West	77.4	81.8

Source: "High School Graduation Rates for Blacks 25-34 Years Old, by Region: 1980 and 1988," *The Black Population in the United States: March 1988*, p. 6. Primary source: Current Population Reports, Series P-20, No. 442, *The Black Population in the United States*: March 1988.

★ 333 ★
Regional Source of UNCF Students

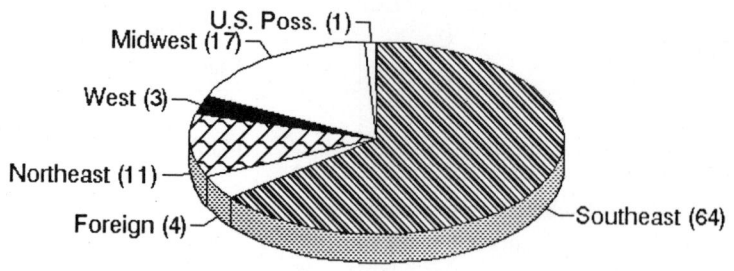

Region	Percent
Southeast	64.0
Midwest	17.0
Northeast	11.0
Foreign	4.0
West	3.0
U.S. Poss.	1.0

Source: "Enrollment by Region, UNCF Member Institutions, Fall 1988," *UNCF 1989 Statistical Report*, p. 4. Primary source: United Negro College Fund (UNCF), Inc., UNCF 1989 Statistical Report (undated), New York, NY.

★ 334 ★
Relative 2-Year Gains in College Enrollment

Race	1988 college enroll- ment	2-year gains (%)
White	10,283,000	3.6
Black	1,130,000	4.4
Hispanic	680,000	10.0
Asian	497,000	10.9
American Indian	93,000	3.3
Foreign	361,000	4.6
Total	13,043,000	4.3

Source: "1988 College Enrollment and 2- Year Gains," *The Chronicle of Higher Education*, April 11, 1990, p. A1. Primary source: U.S. Department of Education. .

★ 335 ★
Relative Change in Higher Education Degrees Conferred

Race and ethnicity	Total	Men	Women
Bachelor's degrees			
Total[1]	6.5	-2.6	17.2
White, non-Hispanic	2.6	-7.0	13.9
Black, non-Hispanic	-1.8	-8.0	2.9
Hispanic	38.6	21.1	59.9
Asian or Pacific Islander	84.8	78.6	92.4
American Indian/Alaskan Native	27.9	11.2	47.7
Master's degrees			
Total[1]	-9.7	-14.5	-4.4
White, non-Hispanic	-15.7	-23.3	-7.3
Black, non-Hispanic	-33.7	-33.1	-34.1
Hispanic	13.1	-6.3	35.7
Asian or Pacific Islander	52.1	55.4	47.1
American Indian/Alaskan Native	29.9	11.9	50.9
Doctor's degrees			
Total[1]	-0.9	-13.7	39.0
White, non-Hispanic	-10.8	-25.0	30.8
Black, non-Hispanic	-7.9	-26.8	21.8
Hispanic	29.7	12.5	77.0
Asian or Pacific Islander	68.1	48.5	157.6
American Indian/Alaskan Native	25.3	-4.5	96.4
First-professional degrees			
Total[1]	16.6	-3.7	105.3
White, non-Hispanic	8.2	-10.8	93.4
Black, non-Hispanic	9.4	-7.8	81.2
Hispanic	75.1	38.7	252.5
Asian or Pacific Islander	77.9	48.5	171.0
American Indian/Alaskan Native	26.5	10.7	94.6

Source: "Percent Change in Number of Degrees Conferred, Between Academic Years Ending 1977 and 1985, by Race and Ethnicity, Degree Level, and Gender," *1989 Education Indicators,* p. 230. Primary source: U.S. Department of Education, National Center for Education Statistics, Digest of Education Statistics, various years (based on the HEGIS survey Degrees and Other Formal Awards Conferred). *Notes:* Data for 1977 exclude degrees conferred by U.S. Service schools (0.4 percent or less of degrees conferred). 1. Includes degrees conferred to nonresident aliens and to those of unknown race/ethnicity.

★ 336 ★
Relative Distribution of Doctoral Degree Fields: Trends

Field of study	1977	1979	1981	1985
White, non-Hispanic				
Total percent	100.0	100.0	100.0	100.0
Humanities and social/behavioral sciences	37.4	36.9	34.9	33.7
Humanities	16.7	17.5	15.2	14.8
Social and behavioral sciences	20.7	19.4	19.7	18.9
Natural and computer sciences and engineering	29.1	28.7	29.6	29.5
Natural sciences	22.7	22.7	23.7	23.1
Computer sciences and engineering	6.4	6.0	5.9	6.4
Technical/professional[1]	33.5	34.4	35.5	36.8
Education	24.7	24.2	24.7	23.5
Business and other technical/professional[1]	8.9	10.2	10.8	13.4
Black, non-Hispanic				
Total percent	100.0	100.0	100.0	100.0
Humanities and social/behavioral sciences	28.5	31.2	28.5	29.6
Humanities	10.8	12.0	11.5	10.1
Social and behavioral sciences	17.7	19.2	17.1	19.5
Natural and computer sciences and engineering	10.5	10.7	10.3	12.0
Natural sciences	8.5	8.5	8.3	8.2
Computer sciences and engineering	1.9	2.2	2.0	3.7
Technical/professional[1]	61.1	58.1	61.2	58.4
Education	54.7	49.3	48.5	45.1
Business and other technical/professional[1]	6.4	8.8	12.6	13.3
Hispanic				
Total percent	100.0	100.0	100.0	100.0
Humanities and social/behavioral sciences	39.3	44.4	40.6	34.1
Humanities	16.9	21.0	14.9	14.8
Social and behavioral sciences	22.4	23.5	25.7	19.4
Natural and computer sciences and engineering	21.3	18.2	20.2	32.9
Natural sciences	16.5	13.0	15.1	19.5
Computer sciences and engineering	4.8	5.2	5.0	13.4
Technical/professional[1]	39.5	37.4	39.3	32.9
Education	31.4	31.0	30.7	24.1
Business and other technical/professional[1]	8.0	6.4	8.6	8.9
American Indian/Alaskan Native				
Total Percent	100.0	100.0	100.0	100.0
Humanities and social/behavioral sciences	28.4	35.6	27.7	22.7
Humanities	11.6	9.6	10.8	10.1
Social and behavioral sciences	16.8	26.0	16.9	12.6
Natural and computer sciences and engineering	28.4	15.4	15.4	20.2
Natural sciences	25.3	13.5	10.8	13.4
Computer sciences and engineering	3.2	1.9	4.6	6.7
Technical/professional[1]	43.2	49.0	56.9	57.1
Education	33.7	41.3	43.8	42.9
Business and other technical/professional[1]	9.5	7.7	13.1	14.3

Continued.

Relative Distribution of Doctoral Degree Fields: Trends
[Continued]

Field of study	1977	1979	1981	1985
	Asian or Pacific Islander			
Total percent	100.0	100.0	100.0	100.0
Humanities and social/behavioral sciences	22.2	20.3	21.0	20.8
Humanities	7.3	9.5	9.0	10.1
Social and behavioral sciences	14.9	10.9	12.0	10.7
Natural and computer sciences and engineering	53.8	57.7	55.0	56.1
Natural sciences	33.6	34.2	31.6	31.1
Computer sciences and engineering	20.2	23.6	23.4	25.0
Technical/professional[1]	24.0	21.9	24.1	23.1
Education	11.7	12.0	12.0	7.6
Business and other technical/professional[1]	12.3	10.0	12.1	15.5

Source: "Percentage Distribution of Doctor's Degrees, by Field and Race and Ethnicity: Selected Academic Years Ending 1977-1985," *1989 Education Indicators*, pp. 238-240 U.S. Department of Education, Office for Civil Rights, Survey of Earned Degrees Conferred by Institutions of Higher Education by Race, Ethnicity and Sex, academic years ending 1977 and 1979; National Center for Education Statistics, Degrees and Other Formal Awards Conferred surveys, academic years ending 1981 and 1985. *Notes:* Distributions for 1977 through 1981 exclude degrees not reported by race and ethnicity. Distributions for 1985 include degrees for which missing race and ethnicity could be imputed. The number of degrees reported for 1977 and 1979 excludes degrees conferred by U.S. Service Schools (0.4 percent or less of degrees). Detail may not add to totals due to rounding. 1. In contrast to previous editions of *The Condition of Education*, computer sciences and engineering are not included in the technical/professional category.

★ 337 ★
Relative Distribution of Master's Degree Fields: Trends

Field of study	1977	1979	1981	1985
	White, non-Hispanic			
Total percent	100.0	100.0	100.0	100.0
Humanities and social/behavioral sciences	17.6	17.0	16.7	15.9
Humanities	10.2	10.1	10.0	9.4
Social and behavioral sciences	7.4	6.9	6.7	6.5
Natural and computer sciences and engineering	10.1	10.0	10.0	12.1
Natural sciences	5.1	5.1	4.6	4.5
Computer sciences and engineering	5.0	4.9	5.4	7.6
Technical/professional[1]	72.3	73.1	73.3	72.0
Education	40.4	37.7	34.3	28.3
Business and other technical/professional[1]	31.9	35.3	39.0	43.7
	Black, non-Hispanic			
Total percent	100.0	100.0	100.0	100.0
Humanities and social/behavioral sciences	12.1	10.9	11.1	11.0
Humanities	5.0	4.6	5.0	4.9
Social and behavioral sciences	7.0	6.3	6.1	6.1
Natural and computer sciences and engineering	3.5	3.5	3.9	6.0
Natural sciences	2.1	1.9	2.0	2.1
Computer sciences and engineering	1.4	1.6	1.9	3.9
Technical/professional[1]	84.4	85.5	84.9	83.0
Education	60.4	55.8	50.5	41.7

Continued.

Relative Distribution of Master's Degree Fields: Trends
[Continued]

Field of study	1977	1979	1981	1985
Business and other technical/professional[1]	24.1	29.7	34.5	41.3
Hispanic				
Total percent	100.0	100.0	100.0	100.0
Humanities and social/behavioral sciences	22.5	18.4	16.5	17.4
Humanities	11.8	10.7	9.4	9.5
Social and behavioral sciences	10.7	7.7	7.1	7.9
Natural and computer sciences and engineering	7.6	6.6	7.8	10.2
Natural sciences	2.8	2.6	2.5	3.9
Computer sciences and engineering	4.8	4.0	5.2	6.3
Technical/professional[1]	69.9	75.0	75.7	72.4
Education	43.9	46.1	43.8	36.7
Business and other technical/professional[1]	25.9	28.9	31.9	35.7
American Indian/Alaskan Native				
Total percent	100.0	100.0	100.0	100.0
Humanities and social/behavioral sciences	13.7	14.5	15.0	14.2
Humanities	7.2	8.0	7.6	7.8
Social and behavioral sciences	6.4	6.5	7.4	6.4
Natural and computer sciences and engineering	7.7	9.3	7.4	10.8
Natural sciences	5.0	5.3	3.2	3.7
Computer sciences and engineering	2.7	4.0	4.2	7.2
Technical/professional[1]	78.7	76.2	77.7	75.0
Education	50.1	45.1	43.8	37.3
Business and other technical/professional[1]	28.6	31.0	33.8	37.7
Asian or Pacific Islander				
Total percent	100.0	100.0	100.0	100.0
Humanities and social/behavioral sciences	17.2	13.4	12.0	12.9
Humanities	10.0	7.5	7.1	7.1
Social and behavioral sciences	7.2	5.8	4.9	5.9
Natural and computer sciences and engineering	24.1	26.7	27.9	35.3
Natural sciences	7.7	8.5	6.3	7.1
Computer sciences and engineering	16.4	18.2	21.6	28.1
Technical/professional[1]	58.7	59.9	60.1	51.8
Education	19.4	17.2	15.5	10.3
Business and other technical/professional[1]	39.3	42.7	44.6	41.5

Source: "Percentage of Master Degrees, by Field and Race and Ethnicity: Selected Academic Years Ending 1977-1985," *1989 Education Indicators*, pp. 235-237. U.S. Department of Education, Office for Civil Rights, Survey of Earned Degrees Conferred by Institutions of Higher Education by Race, Ethnicity, and Sex, academic years ending 1977 and 1979; National Center for Education Statistics, Degrees and Other Formal Awards Conferred surveys, academic years ending 1981 and 1985. *Notes:* Distributions for 1977 through 1981 exclude degrees not reported by race and ethnicity. Distributions for 1985 include degrees for which missing race and ethnicity could be imputed. The number of degrees reported for 1977 and 1979 excludes degrees conferred by U.S. Service Schools (0.4 percent or less of degrees). Detail may not add to totals due to rounding. 1. In contrast to previous editions of *The Condition of Education*, computer sciences and engineering are not included in the technical/professional category.

★ 338 ★
Remediation and Enrichment in English and Math

Student Characteristic	Remedial		Advanced or Honors	
	English	Mathematics	English	Mathematics
	Percent			
All sophomores	34.1	34.2	22.9	24.2
Race/ethnicity:				
White[1]	34.6	33.5	22.7	24.4
Black[1]	32.5	37.0[2]	22.3	21.8[2]
Hispanic	35.5	39.1[2]	19.6[2]	19.9[2]
American Indian	44.2	45.4[2]	18.1	17.3
Asian/Pacific Islanders	27.7	24.6[2]	36.4[2]	39.7[2]
All seniors	30.8	30.0	26.9	23.0
Race/ethnicity:				
White[1]	30.8	29.3	27.0	23.4
Black[1]	31.3	34.3[2]	25.7	20.3[2]
Hispanic	33.1	37.5[2]	23.0[2]	18.0[2]
American Indian	39.7	41.9[2]	25.7	18.7
Asian/Pacific Islanders	30.5	22.4[2]	34.3	41.9[2]

Source: "Remedial and Advanced Courses in English and Mathematics Taken by High School Sophomores and Seniors, by Race/Ethnicity, Sex, and Socioeconomic Status — 1980," *Equality and Excellence: The Educational Status of Black Americans*, 1985, p. 39. Primary source: U.S. Department of Education, National Center for Education Statistics, unpublished tabulation from the High School and Beyond Survey. *Notes:* 1. Non-Hispanic. 2. Represents significant difference from the white population at the . Published by permission.

★ 339 ★
Salary/Length of Service Comparisons: TWI Faculty

Characteristic	Frequency of Higher Level of Characteristic		
	Black Faculty Higher[1]	White Faculty Higher[1]	No Difference
Present Rank	5	9	6
Beginning Rank	10	7	4
Initial Salary	11	7	3
Years Experience	12	6	4

Source: "Comparison of Characteristics of Blacks and Whites Within Same Salary and Length of Service Level," *Black Faculty in Traditionally White Institutions*, 1988, p.99. Primary source: *Black Faculty in Traditionally White Instiutions in Selected Adams States: Characteristics, Experiences and Perceptions*, Southern Education on Foundation, Atlanta, GA 30308, 1988. TWI: Traditionally White Institutions. *Note:* 1. Based on mean levels.

★ 340 ★
SAT Component Averages: Trends

Racial/ethnic background	1975-1976	1976-1977	1977-1978	1978-1979	1979-1980	1980-1981	1981-1982	1982-1983	1983-1984	1984-1985	1986-1987	1987-1988
SAT-Verbal												
All students	431	429	429	427	424	424	426	425	426	431	430	428
White	451	448	446	444	442	442	444	443	445	449	447	445
Black	332	330	332	330	330	332	341	339	342	346	351	353
Mexican-American	371	370	370	370	372	373	377	375	376	382	379	382
Puerto Rican	364	355	349	345	350	353	360	358	358	368	360	355
Asian-American	414	405	401	396	396	397	398	395	398	404	405	408
American Indian	388	390	387	386	390	391	388	388	390	392	393	393
Other	410	402	399	393	394	388	392	386	388	391	405	410
SAT-Mathematics												
All students	472	470	468	467	466	466	467	468	471	475	476	476
White	493	489	485	483	482	483	483	484	487	490	489	490
Black	354	357	354	358	360	362	366	369	373	376	377	384
Mexican-American	410	408	402	410	413	415	416	417	420	426	424	428
Puerto Rican	401	397	388	388	394	398	403	403	405	409	400	402
Asian-American	518	514	510	511	509	513	513	514	519	518	521	522
American Indian	420	421	419	421	426	425	424	425	427	428	432	435
Other	458	457	450	447	449	447	449	446	450	448	455	460

Source: "Scholastic Aptitude Test Score Averages, by Race/Ethnicity: 1975-76 to 1987-88," *Digest of Education Statistics*, 1989, p. 120. Primary source: College Entrance Examination Board, *National Report on College Bound Seniors*, 1988. (Copyright 1988 by the College Entrance Examination Board. All rights reserved). (This table was prepared October 1988). *Notes:* Possible scores on each part of the SAT range from 200 to 800. No race/ethnic group data are available prior to 1975-76. No data are available for 1985-86 due to changes in the Student Descriptive Questionnaire completed when students registered for the test. Published by permission.

★ 341 ★
SAT Component Percentile Ranks

Component and Score	Total	White	Black	Asian	Native American	Mexican American	Puerto Rican	Latin American
Verbal								
700-800	1	1	0	1	0	0	0	0
650-699	2	3	0	3	1	1	0	1
600-649	4	5	1	5	2	2	1	3
500-599	20	23	7	17	11	11	8	13
400-499	33	36	22	26	33	29	23	27
Mathematics								
700-800	4	4	0	10	1	1	1	1
650-699	5	6	1	10	2	2	2	3
600-649	8	9	2	12	4	4	3	5
500-599	25	28	11	26	20	19	14	19
400-499	29	30	25	24	33	33	28	29

Source: "Percentile Rankings on the Scholastic Aptitude Test, by Gender and Racial/Ethnic Group: 1988," *Women and Minorities in Science and Engineering*, January 1990, p. 126. Primary source: Admissions Testing Program of the College Entrance Examination Board, 1988 PROFILES OF SAT AND ACHIEVEMENT TEST TAKERS, (Princeton, N.J.: Educational Testing Service, 1988). Published by permission.

★ 342 ★
SAT Math Score and Intended College Major

Area of Study	Total	White	Black	Asian	Native American	Mexican American	Puerto Rican	Latin American
					Percent			
Total	100.0	100.0	100.0	100.0	100.0	100.0	100.0	100.0
Science and engineering	32.1	31.3	33.7	38.5	27.9	34.4	33.8	35.5
Biological science	3.5	3.5	2.3	4.7	3.2	3.0	3.4	3.4
Agriculture	1.3	1.5	0.4	0.4	1.7	0.9	0.9	0.7
Computer science	3.3	2.6	7.5	4.8	3.2	3.9	5.4	4.4
Mathematics	0.7	0.7	0.4	0.8	0.6	0.5	0.3	0.4
Physical science	1.4	1.6	0.6	1.5	1.0	1.0	0.9	1.0
Social science	11.8	12.0	12.0	8.0	10.3	13.1	11.3	13.4
Engineering	10.2	9.4	10.5	18.4	8.0	12.0	11.7	12.3
Non-science & Engineering[1]	67.9	68.7	66.3	61.5	72.1	65.6	66.2	64.5
Business	23.1	22.7	26.5	22.7	25.3	22.2	22.9	23.3
Education	6.7	7.5	4.1	2.6	7.9	5.9	4.2	4.0
					SAT Mathematics score[2]			
Total	---	---	---	---	---	---	---	---
Science and engineering	---	---	---	---	---	---	---	---
Biological science	514	522	418	567	462	459	426	461
Agriculture	447	451	365	474	427	405	408	422
Computer science	470	509	371	513	433	425	389	414
Mathematics	596	608	479	605	535	528	535	534
Physical science	568	575	448	611	496	503	436	519
Social science	482	496	389	525	442	429	405	440
Engineering	547	566	443	570	501	491	452	486
Non-science & Engineering[1]	---	---	---	---	---	---	---	---
Business	462	476	376	492	431	420	395	423
Education	442	450	354	465	407	397	380	398

Source: "Intended Undergraduate Majors and Corresponding SAT Mathematics Scores of College-Bound Seniors, by Field, Gender, and Racial/Ethnic Group: 1988," *Women and Minorities in Science and Engineering,* January 1990, p. 128. Primary source: Admissions Testing Program of the College Entrance Examination Board, *1988 Profiles of SAT and Achievement Test Takers,* (Princeton, N.J.: Educational Testing Service, 1988). *Notes:* 1. Detail will not add to total because "other" and "undecided" are not included. 2. Mathematics score on the aptitude portion of the SAT. Published by permission.

★ 343 ★
School Attendance Patterns: 8th Graders

Attendance pattern	Percent of 8th graders					
		Race/ethnicity				
	All 8th graders	White	Black	Hispanic	Asian	American Indian
Number of days missed over the past 4 weeks						
None	45.2	44.6	50.0	41.8	57.9	32.6
1 or 2 days	33.7	35.1	27.8	31.9	28.5	35.1
3 or 4 days	13.3	13.0	13.8	16.1	7.3	21.0
5 or more days	7.7	7.2	8.4	10.2	6.2	11.2
Number of times late over the past 4 weeks						
None	63.1	66.3	53.8	52.4	66.2	52.9
1 or 2 days	25.2	24.2	28.6	28.1	23.5	28.9
3 or more days	11.7	9.5	17.6	19.5	10.3	18.2
Cut classes						
Never or almost never	91.1	92.0	91.0	85.6	91.7	87.3
At least sometimes	8.9	8.0	9.0	14.4	8.3	12.7

Source: "Eighth Graders' Attendance Patterns, by Student and School Characteristics: 1988," *Digest of Education Statistics*, 1989, p. 133. Primary source: U.S. Department of Education, National Center for Educational Statistics, "National Education Longitudinal Study of 1988" survey. (This table was prepared June 1989.) *Note:* Data are preliminary.

★ 344 ★
School Children's Mathematics Performance

Characteristic	9-Year-Olds			13-Year-Olds			17-Year-Olds		
	1973	1978	Change	1973	1978	Change	1973	1978	Change
	Mean Percent Correct								
National average	38.1	36.8	-1.3	52.6	50.6	-2.0	51.7	48.1	-3.6
Race:									
White	41.1	39.1	-2.0	56.6	54.2	-2.4	54.5	51.0	-3.5
Black	23.4	26.3	2.9	31.8	32.4	0.6	33.5	30.9	-2.6

Source: "Mean Mathematics Performance of 9-, 13-, and 17- Year-Olds, by Race, Type of Community, and Parental Education: 1973 and 1978," *Equality and Excellence: The Educational Status of Black Americans*, 1985, p. 27. Primary source: National Assessment of Educational Progress, *Mathematical Technical Report: Summary Volume*, April 1980. Published by permission.

★ 345 ★
School Children's Reading Achievement

Age Group and Characteristic	Lowest Achievement Group			Highest Achievement Group		
	1971	1975	1980	1971	1975	1980
	Percent (Average = 25.0)					
9-year-olds:	25.0	25.0	25.0	25.0	25.0	25.0
Racial/ethnic group:						
White	19.6	21.1	21.6	28.3	27.7	27.4
Black	56.4	48.8	45.4	5.8	8.4	10.4
13-year-olds:	25.0	25.0	25.0	25.0	25.0	25.0
Racial/ethnic group:						
White	19.4	20.3	20.9	28.4	27.8	28.0
Black	56.1	56.2	49.8	6.0	5.9	6.7
17-year-olds:	25.0	25.0	25.0	25.0	25.0	25.0
Racial/ethnic group:						
White	19.9	20.1	19.7	27.6	27.7	28.2
Black	62.7	61.7	61.8	5.7	4.9	3.9

Source: "Distribution of 9-, 13-, and 17- Year-Olds Within the Lowes and Highest Reading Achievement Groups, by Region, Sex, and Racial/Ethnic Group: 1970- 71, 1974-75, and 1979-80," *Equality and Excellence: The Educational Status of Black Americans*, 1985, p. 25. Primary source: National Assessment of Educational Progress, *Three National Assessments of Reading: Changes in Performance, 1970-80*, April 1981. Published by permission.

★ 346 ★
School Dropouts

As of October.

Age and Race	Number of Dropouts (1,000)								Percent of Population			
	1970	1975	1980	1982	1983	1984	1985	1986	1970	1980	1985	1986
Total dropouts[1,2]	4,670	4,974	5,212	5,160	5,025	4,784	4,456	4,318	12.2	12.0	10.6	10.5
16-17 years	617	715	709	556	494	485	505	455	8.0	8.8	7.0	6.1
18-21 years	2,138	2,557	2,578	2,646	2,419	2,297	2,095	1,961	16.4	15.8	14.1	13.6
22-24 years	1,770	1,553	1,798	1,854	1,991	1,845	1,724	1,726	18.7	15.2	14.1	14.3
White[2]	3,577	3,861	4,169	4,080	3,950	3,831	3,583	3,497	10.8	11.3	10.3	10.3
16-17 years	485	594	619	478	424	421	424	394	7.3	9.2	7.1	6.5
18-21 years	1,618	1,980	2,032	2,056	1,897	1,852	1,678	1,566	14.3	14.7	13.6	13.1
22-24 years	1,356	1,169	1,416	1,467	1,531	1,429	1,372	1,408	16.3	14.0	13.3	13.9
Black[2]	1,047	1,024	934	937	918	789	748	707	22.2	16.0	12.6	12.0
16-17 years	125	116	80	66	62	55	70	52	12.8	6.9	6.5	4.7
18-21 years	500	540	486	519	436	373	376	345	30.5	23.0	17.5	16.5
22-24 years	397	337	346	332	396	339	279	272	37.8	24.0	17.8	17.3

Source: "High School Dropouts 14 to 24 Years Old, by Age and Race: 1970 to 1986," *Statistical Abstract*, 1989, p. 145. Primary source: U.S. Bureau of the Census, *Current Population Reports*, series P-20, No. 409 and earlier reports; and unpublished data. *Notes:* 1. Includes other race groups not shown separately. 2. Includes persons 14-15 years, not shown separately.

★ 347 ★
School Enrollment at Ages 3-34

Sex and age	All races	White	Black	Hispanic Origin[2]
Both sexes[1]				
Total, 3 to 34 years	48.6	47.7	51.7	45.3
3 and 4 years	38.3	38.2	36.8	28.3
5 and 6 years	95.1	94.8	95.8	92.5
7 to 9 years	99.6	99.6	99.7	99.0
10 to 13 years	99.5	99.4	99.8	99.3
14 and 15 years	98.6	98.5	98.3	97.5
16 and 17 years	91.7	91.8	91.5	86.4
18 and 19 years	55.6	55.3	53.2	41.2
20 and 21 years	38.7	39.6	28.7	28.3
22 to 24 years	17.5	17.3	15.0	12.6
25 to 29 years	9.0	8.7	9.3	8.1
30 to 34 years	5.8	5.7	6.0	4.4
Male				
Total, 3 to 34 years	49.8	48.8	54.0	45.2
3 and 4 years	40.0	39.8	39.0	27.7
5 and 6 years	95.7	95.2	97.4	93.6
7 to 9 years	99.7	99.7	100.0	99.4
10 to 13 years	99.7	99.7	99.8	100.0
14 and 15 years	98.7	98.8	98.1	99.4
16 and 17 years	92.3	92.5	91.8	91.0
18 and 19 years	57.9	57.3	58.7	44.4
20 and 21 years	41.2	42.1	30.3	30.1
22 to 24 years	18.7	18.4	15.5	10.6
25 to 29 years	9.1	8.6	8.4	8.3
30 to 34 years	5.0	5.0	3.4	3.7
Female				
Total, 3 to 34 years	47.4	46.7	49.6	45.4
3 and 4 years	36.5	36.4	34.4	28.9
5 and 6 years	94.5	94.4	94.1	91.2
7 to 9 years	99.5	99.5	99.3	98.7
10 to 13 years	99.2	99.1	99.7	98.6
14 and 15 years	98.4	98.3	98.6	95.2
16 and 17 years	91.1	91.0	91.2	81.8
18 and 19 years	53.4	53.3	48.2	38.6
20 and 21 years	36.4	37.3	27.4	25.6
22 to 24 years	16.4	16.2	14.6	14.7

Continued.

School Enrollment at Ages 3-34
[Continued]

Sex and age	All races	White	Black	Hispanic Origin[2]
25 to 29 years	9.0	8.7	10.0	7.9
30 to 34 years	6.7	6.4	8.1	5.1

Source: "Percent of the Population 3 to 34 Years Old Enrolled in School, by Race/Ethnicity, Sex, and Age: October, 1987," *Digest of Education Statistics*, 1989, p. 14. Primary source: U.S. Department of Commerce, Bureau of the Census, Current Population Survey, unpublished data. (This table was prepared March 1989.) *Notes:* Data based on a sample survey of the civilian noninstitutional population. 1. Includes enrollment in any type of graded public, parochial, or other private school in regular school systems. Includes nursery schools, kindergartens, elementary schools, high schools, colleges, universities, and professional schools. Attendance may be on either a full-time or part-time basis and during the day or night. Enrollments in "special" schools, such as trade schools, business colleges, or correspondence schools, are not included. 2. Persons of Hispanic origin may be of any race.

★ 348 ★
School Enrollment, Characteristics of

As of October. Covers civilian noninstitutional population enrolled in nursery school and above. Based on Current Population Survey, section 1. See *Historical Statistics, Colonial Times to 1970*, Series H-442-476 for enrollment 5-34 years old.

Age and race	Enrollment (1,000)				Rate			
	1970	1980	1985	1986	1970	1980	1985	1986
White: Total 3 to 34 years old	51,719	47,673	47,542	47,267	56.2	48.9	47.8	47.4
3 and 4 years old	1,181	1,844	2,250	2,296	19.9	36.3	38.6	39.1
5 and 6 years old	5,899	4,781	5,437	5,524	90.3	95.8	96.4	95.3
7 to 13 years old	24,564	19,585	18,464	18,579	99.2	99.2	99.3	99.2
14 and 15 years old	6,761	6,038	6,007	5,677	98.2	98.3	98.1	97.8
16 and 17 years old	6,008	5,937	5,449	5,587	90.6	88.6	91.6	92.0
18 and 19 years old	2,924	3,199	3,105	3,192	48.7	46.3	52.4	54.8
20 and 21 years old	1,750	2,206	2,318	2,042	33.1	31.9	36.1	33.5
22 to 24 years old	1,305	1,669	1,744	1,759	15.7	16.4	17.0	17.4
25 to 29 years old	910	1,473	1,635	1,589	7.7	9.2	9.2	8.8
30 to 34 years old	416	942	1,043	1,021	4.2	6.3	6.2	5.9
35 years and over	[2]	1,104	1,533	1,644	[2]	1.3	1.7	1.8
Black: 3 to 34 years old	7,829	8,251	8,444	8,556	57.4	53.9	50.9	51.1
3 and 4 years old	250	371	469	411	22.7	38.2	42.7	38.2
5 and 6 years old	999	904	1,030	1,100	84.9	95.4	95.7	95.2
7 to 13 years old	3,998	3,598	3,549	3,564	99.3	99.4	99.1	99.4
14 and 15 years old	1,025	1,088	1,106	1,079	97.6	97.9	97.9	96.6
16 and 17 years old	837	1,047	994	1,015	85.7	98.6	91.7	93.2
18 and 19 years old	352	494	472	518	40.1	45.7	44.1	49.4
20 and 21 years old	174	242	298	268	22.8	23.4	27.7	25.7
22 to 24 years old	84	196	215	261	8.0	13.6	13.7	16.6
25 to 29 years old	68	187	192	197	4.8	8.8	7.4	7.5
30 to 34 years old	41	124	119	143	3.4	6.8	5.1	5.9
35 years and over[1]	[2]	186	233	265	[2]	1.8	1.9	2.0

Source: "School Enrollment, by Age and Race: 1970 to 1986," *Statistical Abstract*, 1989, p. 128. Primary source: *Current Population Reports*, Series P-20, No. 429; and unpublished data. *Notes:* 1. Black and other races. 2. Not available.

★ 349 ★
School for 3-to 5-Year-Olds: Trends

	1977	1980	1984	1985	1986
3 and 4 Year Olds					
Total Enrolled	32	37	36	39	39
White	31	36	36	39	39
Black	35	38	38	43	38
Hispanic	20	29	24	27	29
5 Year Olds					
Total Enrolled	82	85	84	87	87
White	83	86	85	88	88
Black	80	80	80	82	83
Hispanic	79	78	78	79	83

Source: "Proportion of 3, 4, and 5 Year Olds Enrolled in Pre-Primary School by Race/Hispanic Origin and Age, 1977-1986," *U.S. Children and their Families*, 1989, p. 137. Primary source: Calculations by Child Trends, Inc., from unpublished data from the Current Population Survey provided by the Education and Social Stratification Branch of the Bureau of the Census, 1988. *Notes:* Preprimary enrollment refers to pre-kindergarten and kindergarten enrollment in regular public schools and enrollment in independently operated public and private nursery schools and kindergartens. Published by permission.

★ 350 ★
Science Doctorates: Trends

Race/Ethnic Background and Sex	1978	1988
Total	11,825	11,069
Total Men	9,063	7,133
Total Women	2,762	3,936
White non-Hispanic	10,410	10,432
Total Men	8,001	6,473
Total Women	2,409	3,559
Total Minorities	639	827
Total Men	437	495
Total Women	202	332
Black non-Hispanic	269	212
Total Men	166	112
Total Women	103	100
Hispanic	141	276
Total Men	101	159
Total Women	40	117
Asian/Pacific Islander	212	300
Total Men	154	199
Total Women	58	101
Native American	19	39
Total Men	16	25
Total Women	3	14
Other and unknown	776	210

Continued.

Science Doctorates: Trends
[Continued]

Race/Ethnic Background and Sex	1978	1988
Total Men	625	165
Total Women	151	45

Source: "Source Doctorates Awarded to U.S. Citizens, Sex and Racial/Ethnic Background: 1978 and 1988," *Black Issues in Higher Education*, December 21, 1989, p. 7. Primary source: National Science Foundation, SRS. *Note:* Excludes foreign students, whether on temporary or permanent visas.

★ 351 ★
Science Proficiency: Trends

Year, age, and race/ethnicity	Know everyday science facts	Understand simple scientific principles	Apply basic scientific information	Analyze scientific procedures and data	Integrate specialized scientific information
1976-77					
9-year olds	93.6	67.9	26.2	3.5	[1]
White	97.8	76.5	31.3	4.3	[1]
Black	83.1	42.1	3.8	0.5	[1]
Hispanic	73.1	27.7	8.5	0.1	[1]
13-year olds	[2]	85.9	49.2	10.9	0.7
White	[2]	91.9	56.7	13.1	0.9
Black	[2]	63.1	19.1	2.3	0.2
Hispanic	[2]	57.1	15.1	1.2	[1]
17-year olds	[2]	97.2	81.8	41.7	8.5
White	[2]	99.2	88.4	47.4	9.9
Black	[2]	92.7	61.7	19.1	2.0
Hispanic	[2]	84.5	40.9	8.3	0.6
1981-82					
9-year olds	95.0	70.4	24.8	2.2	[1]
White	98.1	78.0	30.1	2.7	[1]
Black	84.6	41.8	3.8	[1]	[1]
Hispanic	81.2	38.7	4.4	0.4	[1]
13-year olds	[2]	89.6	51.5	9.4	0.4
White	[2]	94.5	58.7	11.2	0.4
Black	[2]	74.5	25.8	2.4	[1]
Hispanic	[2]	66.8	18.6	0.8	[1]
17-year olds	[2]	95.8	76.8	37.5	7.2
White	[2]	98.7	85.0	44.0	8.8
Black	[2]	86.1	46.6	12.5	1.4
Hispanic	[2]	81.0	36.5	6.7	0.1
1985-86					
9-year olds	96.3	71.4	27.6	3.4	[1]
White	98.5	78.4	32.6	4.3	[1]
Black	89.6	49.1	8.8	0.2	[1]
Hispanic	87.5	45.1	10.7	0.4	[1]

Continued.

Science Proficiency: Trends
[Continued]

Year, age, and race/ethnicity	Know everyday science facts	Understand simple scientific principles	Apply basic scientific information	Analyze scientific procedures and data	Integrate specialized scientific information
13-year olds	[2]	91.8	53.4	9.4	0.2
White	[2]	96.4	61.9	11.8	0.3
Black	[2]	76.1	27.6	1.6	[1]
Hispanic	[2]	74.3	20.2	0.9	[1]
17-year olds	[2]	96.7	80.8	41.4	7.5
White	[2]	98.6	87.6	48.8	9.0
Black	[2]	92.9	61.6	15.5	0.5
Hispanic	[2]	89.8	52.9	12.3	1.0

Source: "Percentage of Students At or Above Five Science Proficiency Levels, by Race/Ethnicity and Age: 1976-77, 1981-82, and 1985-86," *Digest of Educational Statistics*, 1989, p. 117. Primary source: U.S. Department of Education, National Center for Educational Statistics, *The Science Report Card, 1988*, prepared by Educational Testing Service (This table was prepared January 1989). *Notes:* 1. Virtually no students were able to perform at this level. 2. Virtually all students were able to perform at this level.

★ 352 ★
Secondary School Principals: Trends

Percentage discount.

Item	1965	1977	1987
Race			
Total	100	100	100
White	[1]	96	94
Black	[1]	3	4
Other	[1]	1	3

Source: "Selected Characteristics of Secondary School Principals: 1965, 1977, and 1987," *Digest of Educational Statistics*, 1989, p. 88. Primary source: National Association of Secondary School Principals, *High School Leaders and Their Schools*, Vol. I, 1988. (This table was prepared November 1988.) *Note:* 1. Data not available. Published by permission.

★ 353 ★
Senior College/University Faculty: Adams States

State	Number of Teaching Faculty[1,2]	Reported Black Teaching[1] Faculty	Blacks As a %
Alabama	6,176	88	1.4
Florida	6,252	226	3.6
Georgia	6,080	195	3.2
Kentucky	4,562	93	2.0
Maryland	3,203	70	2.2
North Carolina	6,710	186	2.8
South Carolina	4,834	97	2.0
Tennessee	5,453	156	2.9

Continued.

Senior College/University Faculty: Adams States
[Continued]

State	Number of Teaching Faculty[1,2]	Reported Black Teaching[1] Faculty	Blacks As a %
Virginia	8,825	157	1.8
TOTALS	52,095	1,268	2.4[3]

Source: "Reported Black Teaching Faculty in Targeted Adams States (Senior Colleges and Universities)," *Black Faculty in Traditionally White Institutions in Selected Adams States*, 1988, p. 20. Primary source: *Black Faculty in Traditionally White Institutions in Selected Adams States: Characteristics, Experiences and Perceptions*, Southern Education Foundation, Inc. Atlanta, GA 30308, 1988 *Notes:* 1. Source: Chief Academic Officers and System Officers. 2. Source: *American Universities and Colleges* 13 ed., American Council on Education, New York: Walter de Gruyter, 1987. 3. This figure drops to about 1.8 percent when administrators and librarians with faculty rank are screened out. Published by permission.

★ 354 ★
Sex of Bachelor's Degree Recipients: Trends

Year and sex of student	Total	White non-Hispanic	Black non-Hispanic	Hispanic	Asian or or Pacific Islander	American Indian/ Alaskan Native	Non-resident alien
Number of degrees conferred							
1980-81							
Total[1]	934,800	807,319	60,673	21,832	18,794	3,593	22,589
Men	469,625	406,173	24,511	10,810	10,107	1,700	16,324
Women	465,175	401,146	36,162	11,022	8,687	1,893	6,265
1984-85							
Total[2]	968,311	826,106	57,473	25,874	25,395	4,246	29,217
Men	476,148	405,085	23,018	12,402	13,554	1,998	20,091
Women	492,163	421,021	34,455	13,472	11,841	2,248	9,126
1986-87							
Total[3]	991,260	841,820	56,555	26,990	32,618	3,971	29,306
Men	480,780	406,751	22,499	12,864	17,249	1,819	19,598
Women	510,480	435,069	34,056	14,126	15,369	2,152	9,708
Percentage distribution of degrees conferred							
1980-81							
Total[1]	100.0	86.4	6.5	2.3	2.0	0.4	2.4
Men	100.0	86.5	5.2	2.3	2.0	0.4	2.4
Women	100.0	86.2	7.8	2.4	1.9	0.4	1.3
1984-85							
Total[2]	100.0	85.3	5.9	2.7	2.6	0.4	3.0
Men	100.0	85.1	4.8	2.6	2.8	0.4	4.2

Continued.

Sex of Bachelor's Degree Recipients: Trends
[Continued]

Year and sex of student	Total	White non-Hispanic	Black non-Hispanic	Hispanic	Asian or or Pacific Islander	American Indian/ Alaskan Native	Non-resident alien
Women	100.0	85.5	7.0	2.7	2.4	0.5	1.9
1986-87							
Total[3]	100.0	84.9	5.7	2.7	3.3	0.4	3.0
Men	100.0	84.6	4.7	2.7	3.6	0.4	4.1
Women	100.0	85.2	6.7	2.8	3.0	0.4	1.9

Source: "Bachelor's Degrees Conferred by Institutions of Higher Education, by Racial/Ethnic Group and Sex of Student: 1976-77 to 1986-87," Digest of Education Statistics, 1989, p. 242. Primary source: U.S. Department of Education, National Center for Educational Statistics, "Degrees and Other Formal Awards Conferred" surveys, and Integrated Postsecondary Education Data System (IPEDS), "Completions" survey. (This table was prepared June 1989.) *Notes:* 1. Excludes 258 men and 82 women whose racial/ethnic group was not available. 2. Excludes 6,380 men and 4,786 women whose racial/ethnic group was not available. 3. Excludes 74 men and 5 women whose racial/ethnic group was not available. Data are preliminary.

★ 355 ★
Sex of Master's Degree Recipients: Trends

Year and sex of student	Total	White non-Hispanic	Black non-Hispanic	Hispanic	Asian or Pacific Islander	American Indian/ Alaskan Native	Non-resident alien
1976-77							
Total[1]	316,602	266,061	21,037	6,071	5,122	967	17,344
Men	167,396	139,210	7,781	3,268	3,123	521	13,493
Women	149,206	126,851	13,256	2,803	1,999	446	3,851
1978-79							
Total[2]	300,255	249,360	19,418	5,555	5,496	999	19,427
Men	152,637	124,058	7,070	2,786	3,325	495	14,903
Women	147,618	125,302	12,348	2,769	2,171	504	4,524
1980-81							
Total[3]	294,183	241,216	17,133	6,461	6,282	1,034	22,057
Men	145,666	115,562	6,156	3,085	3,773	501	16,587
Women	148,517	125,654	10,975	3,376	2,509	533	5,470
1984-85							
Total[4]	280,421	223,628	13,939	6,864	7,782	1,256	26,952
Men	139,417	106,059	5,200	3,059	4,842	583	19,674
Women	141,004	117,569	8,739	3,805	2,940	673	7,278
1986-87							
Total[5]	289,341	228,870	13,867	7,044	8,558	1,104	29,898

Continued.

Sex of Master's Degree Recipients: Trends
[Continued]

Year and sex of student	Total	White non-Hispanic	Black non-Hispanic	Hispanic	Asian or Pacific Islander	American Indian/ Alaskan Native	Non-resident alien
Men	141,264	105,573	5,151	3,330	5,238	517	21,455
Women	148,077	123,297	8,716	3,714	3,320	587	8,443

Source: "Master's Degrees Conferred by Institutions of Higher Education, by Racial/Ethnic Group and Sex of Student: 1976-77 to 1986-87," *Digest of Education Statistics*, 1989, p. 245. Primary source: U.S. Department of Education, National Center for Educational Statistics, "Degrees and Other Formal Awards Conferred" surveys, and Integrated Postsecondary Education Data System (IPEDS), "Completions" survey. (This table was prepared June 1989.) *Notes:* 1. Excludes 387 men and 175 women whose racial/ethnic group was not available. 2. Excludes 733 men and 91 women whose racial/ethnic group was not available. 3. Excludes 1,377 men and 179 women whose racial/ethnic group was not available. 4. Excludes 3,973 men and 1,857 women whose racial/ethnic was not available. 5. Excludes 99 men and 117 women whose racial/ethnic group was not available. Data are preliminary.

★ 356 ★
Social Science Doctorates: Trends

Item	1977-1978	1978-1979	1979-1980	1980-1981	1981-1982	1982-1983	1983-1984	1984-1985	1985-1986	1986-1987
Number of doctorates	6,453	6,379	6,253	6,505	6,250	6,055	5,895	5,720	5,841	5,718
Racial/ethnic group (percent)[1]										
American Indian	0.4	0.6	0.3	0.2	0.3	0.2	0.2	0.3	0.3	0.4
Asian	4.2	5.1	5.4	4.8	5.9	5.8	6.5	7.0	6.6	7.5
Black	4.2	4.6	4.4	4.5	5.0	4.3	4.8	4.8	4.3	4.0
Mexican-American	[2]	[2]	0.4	0.8	0.8	0.8	0.8	0.8	0.8	0.8
Puerto Rican	[2]	[2]	0.3	0.2	0.5	0.3	0.5	0.4	0.5	0.4
Other Hispanic	[2]	[2]	1.8	1.6	1.5	1.9	1.9	1.8	2.4	2.3
White	78.5	77.9	79.5	80.2	78.2	79.7	77.6	76.4	75.6	73.9
Other and unknown	10.0	9.3	7.9	7.6	7.9	6.9	7.6	8.4	9.5	10.8

Source: "Statistical Profile of Persons Receiving Doctor's Degrees in the Social Sciences: 1977-78 to 1986-87," *Digest of Educational Statistics*, 1989, p. 273. Primary source: National Academy of Sciences, National Research Council, Office of Scientific and Engineering Personnel, Doctorate Records File. (This table was prepared March 1989.) *Notes:* The National Research Council's classification of degrees by field differs somewhat from that in most publications of the National Center for Educational Statistics (NCES). The major differences are that history is included under humanities rather social sciences and that psychology is included under social sciences. The number of degrees also differs somewhat from that reported in the NCES "Degrees and Other Formal Awards Conferred" survey. Because of rounding, percents may not add to 100.0 1. Longitudinal comparisons by race/ethnicity should be done with extreme care, due to periodic changes in the survey. 2. Hispanic subcategories were not collected until 1980.

★ 357 ★
Sources of Bachelor's Degrees in Education

Year	No. of Institutes Awarding Degrees	Total Degrees	Race/Ethnicity				
			Black	Total Minority	White	N-R Alien	Balance
1975-76							
Total	1,184	156,538	14,229	20,254	135,514	770	0
HBCUs	80	7,420	7,059	7,074	298	48	0
Non-HBCUs	1,104	149,118	7,170	13,180	135,216	722	0
1978-79							
Total	1,182	127,633	11,538	17,778	108,984	871	0
HBCUs	80	5,740	5,468	5,480	227	33	0
Non-HBCUs	1,102	121,893	6,070	12,298	108,767	838	0
1980-81							
Total	1,183	110,715	9,517	16,045	93,750	920	0
HBCUs	82	3,691	3,353	3,375	271	45	0
Non-HBCUs	1,101	107,024	6,164	12,670	93,479	875	0
1982-83							
Total	1,206	100,171	6,826	11,490	81,663	1,110	5,908
HBCUs	81	3,600	3,248	3,271	271	130	-72
Non-HBCUs	1,125	96,571	3,578	8,221	81,392	980	5,836
1984-85							
Total	1,206	90,511	5,221	9,383	74,918	968	5,232
HBCUs	80	2,747	2,190	2,216	242	134	155
Non-HBCUs	1,126	87,764	3,031	7,167	74,676	834	5,077

Source: "Number of Bachelor's Degrees Awarded in Education by Historically Black Colleges and Universities (HBCUs) and All U.S. Institutions by Race/Ethnicity: 1976, 1979, 1983, and 1985," *NAFEO INROADS*, February/March 1987, p. 20. Primary source: National Advisory Committee Staff Analysis, OCR Unpublished Data on Degrees Awarded by Major Field, Race/Ethnicity, and Sex - 1975-76, 1976-77. NAFEO Research Institute Staff Analysis of OCR Unpublished Data on Degrees Awarded by Major Field, Race/Ethnicity, and Sex - 1980-81, 1982-83, and 1984-85. *Notes:* Positive numbers indicate that racial distributions were not indicated. Negative numbers indicate that the racial distributions exceeded the total. Published by permission.

★ 358 ★
Southern Applicants Who Pass Teacher Examinations: Trends

State	Year	Whites	Blacks
AL	81-82	86	43
AR	80-82	88	33
FL	80-86	88	45
GA	78-83	87	34
LA	78-86	78	15
MS	1982	97-100	54-70
NC	85-86	92	42

Continued.

Southern Applicants Who Pass Teacher Examinations: Trends
[Continued]

State	Year	Whites	Blacks
TX	84-85	73	23
VA	1986	99	83

Source: "Percentage of Whites and Blacks Passing Teacher Examinations, Southern States, Selected Years," *Legislative Bulletin*, Summer 1987, p. 1. Primary source: G. Pritchy Smith, "Unresolved Issues and New Developments in Teacher Competency Testing," 8 *Urban Educator* (Fall, 1986), 1-16; North Carolina figures from State Department of Public Education. Florida figures from "Minority Teachers For Florida's Classroom," by the Florida Education Standards Commission. Mississippi scores broken out according to whether the college attended was predominantly white or black. For the coming school year, 627 Georgia teachers may be denied certificates as a result of recertification tests. Of these 420 or 67 percent are black. Published by permission.

★ 359 ★
Student Exposure to Computers

Numbers in percent.

Type of Exposure	Grade 3	Grade 7	Grade 11
Has Used a Computer			
Total	75	89	87
Race/Ethnicity			
White	78	92	89
Black	65	81	81
Hispanic	69	83	80
Currently Studying Computers[1]			
Total	48	40	21
Race/Ethnicity			
White	49	41	20
Black	42	35	21
Hispanic	48	38	19
Has a Computer at Home			
Total	29	33	30
Race/Ethnicity			
White	30	36	32
Black	25	26	22
Hispanic	25	21	21

Source: "Proportion of Students Exposed to Computers, by Type of Exposure, Grade, Sex, and Race/Hispanic Origin, 1985-86," *U.S. Children and their Families*, 1989, p. 155. Primary source: The National Assessment of Educational Progress, *Computer Competence: The First National Assessment*, Educational Testing Service, April 1988, Tables 3.1, 3.3, 3.8, and Figures 4.5 and 4.8, April 1988. *Notes:* 1. The lower proportion for 11th graders may be explained in part by the timing of courses: most high school computer courses are taken before the eleventh grade. Published by permission.

★ 360 ★
Student Loan Default Rates: 1988

Institution	Default Rate (%)	Dollars in Default
Professional Career Centers, Houston	49.0	7,602,935
Chicago Truck Driving School	45.8	847,811
Florida College of Business	45.0	579,515
Long Beach Community College	42.1	1,595,222
Southwest Virginia Community College	27.9	112,126
Morris Brown College[1]	25.7	430,760
Johnson C. Smith University[1]	22.7	305,599
Fisk University[1]	20.1	192,316
California State University, Los Angeles	17.1	562,750
Florida A&M University[1]	13.5	325,129
NW Alabama Community College	10.8	25,095
Howard University[1]	10.3	1,621,321
Temple University	7.9	1,439,320
New York University	3.6	1,708,071
Morehouse College School of Medicine[1]	3.3	35,800
Yale University	1.4	377,825

Source: "Random Profile of Loan Default Rates — 1988," *Black Issues in Higher Education*, May 10, 1990, p. 3. Primary source: Department of Education. *Note:* 1. Predominantly Black Institution.

★ 361 ★
Teacher Competency as Judged by Examinations

State	All	Whites	Asians	Blacks	Hispanics	Native Americans
Alabama	81	86		43		
Arizona						
January 6, 1983	66	73	50	24	42	22
July 9, 1983	59	70	25	41	36	19
California	68	76	50	26	38	67
Florida						
June 1982	85	92	67	37	57	90
February 1983	84	90	63	35	51	100
Georgia	78	87		34		
Louisiana	77	78		15		
Mississippi		97[1]		54[1]		
		100[2]		70[2]		
Oklahoma	78	79	82	45	71	70
Texas	54	62	47	10	19	47
Virginia (trial testing)						
Communication skills		97		56		
General knowledge		99		69		

Continued.

Teacher Competency as Judged by Examinations
[Continued]

State	All	Whites	Asians	Blacks	Hispanics	Native Americans
Professional knowledge		99		83		

Source: "Pass Rates on Teacher Competency Tests in 10 States, 1982," *A Common Destiny: Blacks And American Society*, 1989, p. 364. Primary source: Data from American Association of Colleges of Teacher Education. *Notes:* 1. Pass rates at predominantly white public institutions. 2. Pass rates at predominantly black public institutions. Published by permission.

★ 362 ★
Teaching Field Changes: Faculty at TWIs

	Initial Teaching Field		Female	Male	Present Teaching Field		Female	Male
	n	% Total	n	n	n	% of Total	n	n
Nursing	30	6.3	29	1	31	6.6	30	1
Social Work	22	4.6	17	5	22	4.7	17	5
Developmental Studies	10	2.1	6	4	12	2.5	9	3
English	20	4.2	14	6	25	5.3	18	7
Sociology	7	1.5	5	2	7	1.5	5	2
Education	51	10.8	21	630	84	18	38	46
Mathematics	5	1.1	0	5	5	1	0	1
Computer Science	2	.4	1	1	4	.8	1	3
Engineering	3	.6	---	---	5	1	1	4
Biology	2	.4	0	2	10	2	2	8
Law	5	1.1	1	4	5	1	1	4
Business	15	3.2	5	10	17	4.9	5	12
Medicine	14	2.9	5	9	18	4	8	10
Political Science	8	1.7	0	8	9	1.9	1	8
Physics	1	.2	0	1	3	.6	1	2
Chemistry	2	.4	1	1	2	.4	1	1
Dentistry	4	.8	2	2	4	.8	1	3
Foreign Language	4	.8	1	3	4	.8	1	3
Geography	1	.2	0	1	1	.2	0	1
History	10	2.1	6	4	12	2.5	6	6
Music	13	2.7	2	11	13	2.8	2	11
Psychology	19	4.0	7	12	19	4.0	8	11

Source: "Blacks in Selected Teaching Fields," *Black Faculty in Traditionally White Institutions in Selected Adams States*, 1988, p. 37. Primary source: *Black Faculty in Traditionally White Institutions in Selected Adams States: Characteristics, Experiences and Perceptions*, Southern Education Foundation, Atlanta, GA 30308. TWI: Traditionally White Institutions.

★ 363 ★
Test Scores

For academic year ending in year shown. Except as indicated, test scores and characteristics of college-bound students. Through 1985, data based on 10 percent sample; thereafter, based on all ACT tested seniors.

Type of Test and Characteristic	Unit	1970	1975	1979	1980	1981	1982	1983	1984	1985	1986	1987
Participants[1]												
Total	1,000	788	714	780	822	836	805	835	849	739	730	777
Male	Percent	52	46	45	45	45	45	46	46	46	46	46
White	Percent	[2]	77	84	83	83	83	82	82	82	82	81
Black	Percent	4	7	8	8	8	8	9	9	8	8	8

Source: "American College Testing (ACT) Program Scores and Characteristics of College-Bound Students: 1970 to 1987," *Statistical Abstract*, 1989, p. 144. Primary source: The American College Testing Program, Iowa City, IA, *High School Profile Report*, annual. *Notes:* 1. Beginning 1985, data are for seniors who graduated in year shown and had taken the ACT in their junior or senior years. 2. Not available.

★ 364 ★
The 1989 College Freshman: Degree Aspirations

Characteristic	All Institutions	Predominantly Black Colleges	Predominantly Black Colleges	
			Public	Private
Highest Degree Planned Anywhere				
None	1.1	1.5	1.8	1.0
Vocational certificate	0.9	0.3	0.3	0.3
Associate (A.A. or equivalent)	4.5	0.7	0.8	0.5
Bachelor's (B.A., B.S.)	32.3	22.1	26.5	14.9
Master's (M.A., M.S.)	37.0	39.7	42.0	36.1
Ph.D. or Ed.D.	11.7	18.5	15.3	23.7
M.D., D.O., D.D.S., D.V.M.	5.7	7.2	4.0	12.3
LL.B. or J.D. (law)	4.9	6.5	5.4	8.3
B.D. or M.Div. (divinity)	0.3	1.0	1.1	0.8
Other	1.6	2.4	2.7	2.0
Highest Degree Planned at Freshman College				
None	3.7	2.3	3.1	1.2
Vocational certificate	1.3	0.5	0.6	0.4
Associate (A.A. or equivalent)	18.1	3.4	4.5	1.7
Bachelor's (B.A., B.S.)	58.2	66.2	62.3	72.0
Master's (M.A., M.S.)	13.2	19.0	21.2	15.8
Ph.D. or Ed.D.	1.9	3.3	3.0	3.7
M.D., D.O., D.D.S., D.V.M.	1.1	1.0	0.6	1.5
LL.B. or J.D. (law)	0.9	1.5	1.6	1.3
B.D. or M.Div. (divinity)	0.2	0.6	0.6	0.7
Other	1.4	2.2	2.5	1.6

Source: "Highest Degree Planned Anywhere and at Freshman College," *The American Freshman: National Norms for Fall 1989*, p. 48. Primary source: Cooperative Institutional Research Program, American Council on Education, University of California, Los Angeles, 1989. Figures for predominantly Black colleges include all ethnic groups.

★ 365 ★
The 1989 College Freshman: Financial Assistance

Sources	All Institutions	Predominantly Black Colleges	Predominantly Black Colleges	
			Public	Private
Received Any Aid From				
Parents or family	78.8	73.6	70.6	79.0
Spouse	1.1	1.6	1.6	1.6
Savings from summer work	54.3	34.2	33.3	36.0
Other savings	28.6	19.4	18.2	21.7
Part-time job on campus	19.8	21.0	16.1	29.9
Other part-time job while at college	24.3	17.9	16.6	20.3
Full-time job while at college	2.0	4.3	4.2	4.5
Pell Grant	21.6	39.0	36.5	43.6
Supplemental Education Opportunity Grant	6.0	11.7	8.5	17.4
State scholarship or grant	15.0	14.1	12.9	16.1
College Work-Study Grant	10.1	15.2	9.2	26.0
Other college grant	20.3	17.8	13.5	25.6
Other private grant	9.2	8.2	6.3	11.6
Other government aid (ROTC, BIA, GI, etc.)	2.5	4.1	4.0	4.1
Federal Guaranteed Student Loan	22.7	30.3	26.2	37.7
National Direct Student Loan	2.4	4.6	4.1	5.5
Other college loan	7.7	8.1	7.1	10.0
Other loan	6.3	7.6	7.3	8.2
Other	3.1	2.5	2.0	3.5

Source: "Sources for Educational Expenses (Aid received from)," *The American Freshman: National Norms for Fall 1989*, p. 55. Primary source: Cooperative Institutional Research Program, American Council on Education, University of California, Los Angeles, 1989. Figures for predominantly Black colleges includes all ethnic groups. Published by permission.

★ 366 ★
The 1989 College Freshman: Probable Majors

Probable Major Field of Study	All institutions	Predominantly Black Colleges	Predominantly Black Colleges	
			Public	Private
Arts and Humanities				
Art, fine and applied	2.1	0.7	0.8	0.7
English (language and literature)	1.3	1.0	1.0	1.0
History	0.8	0.4	0.4	0.4
Journalism	1.4	1.4	1.1	1.9
Language or literature	0.5	0.1	0.1	0.2
Music	0.9	0.6	0.5	0.7
Philosophy	0.2	0.0	0.0	0.1
Speech	0.1	0.1	0.1	0.2
Theater or drama	0.6	0.3	0.1	0.5
Theology or religion	0.1	0.0	0.0	0.0
Other arts and humanities	0.7	0.4	0.4	0.3

Continued.

The 1989 College Freshman: Probable Majors
[Continued]

Probable Major Field of Study	All institutions	Predominant-ly Black Colleges	Predominantly Black Colleges	
			Public	Private
Biological Sciences				
General Biology	1.8	2.7	1.4	4.8
Biochemistry or biophysics	0.4	0.4	0.2	0.6
Botany	0.0	0.0	0.0	0.0
Marine (life) science	0.5	0.0	0.0	0.1
Microbiology or bacteriology	0.2	0.2	0.1	0.2
Zoology	0.3	0.4	0.5	0.2
Other biological sciences	0.5	0.5	0.5	0.4
Business				
Accounting	6.1	9.2	10.6	6.7
Business Administration	6.5	9.6	11.5	6.2
Finance	1.9	1.8	2.0	1.5
Marketing	3.0	3.7	4.2	3.0
Management	4.5	5.7	6.7	3.9
Secretarial studies	0.9	0.2	0.3	0.1
Other business	1.6	1.6	2.0	0.8
Education				
Business education	0.3	0.7	1.0	0.2
Elementary education	4.6	2.9	3.1	2.5
Music or art education	0.4	0.3	0.4	0.2
Physical education or recreation	1.1	0.9	1.3	0.3
Secondary education	1.8	1.1	1.4	0.7
Special education	0.6	0.4	0.6	0.1
Other education	0.4	0.3	0.3	0.2
Engineering				
Aeronautical/astronautical engineering	1.5	1.0	0.3	2.3
Civil engineering	1.1	0.8	0.8	0.7
Chemical engineering	0.7	0.8	0.3	1.6
Electrical engineering	3.0	3.3	3.1	3.5
Industrial engineering	0.3	0.2	0.1	0.4
Mechanical engineering	2.0	1.4	1.2	1.8
Other engineering	1.6	1.0	0.9	1.1
Physical Sciences				
Astronomy	0.1	0.1	0.0	0.1
Atmospheric science	0.1	0.0	0.0	0.0
Chemistry	0.6	0.6	0.2	1.2
Earth science	0.1	0.0	0.0	0.0
Marine science	0.2	0.0	0.0	0.0
Mathematics	0.6	0.2	0.0	0.6
Physics	0.4	0.2	0.2	0.2
Statistics	0.0	0.0	0.1	0.0
Other physical sciences	0.1	0.2	0.2	0.1
Professional				
Architecture or urban planning	1.3	0.5	0.3	0.8
Home economics	0.2	0.3	0.4	0.0
Health technology (med, dent, lab)	0.9	0.9	0.9	0.9
Library or archival science	0.0	0.0	0.0	0.0
Nursing	2.8	2.4	2.3	2.6

Continued.

The 1989 College Freshman: Probable Majors
[Continued]

Probable Major Field of Study	All institutions	Predominant-ly Black Colleges	Predominantly Black Colleges	
			Public	Private
Pharmacy	0.9	1.2	0.4	2.7
Predent, premed, prevet	3.0	3.4	1.4	6.8
Therapy (occup, phys, speech)	2.3	0.8	0.5	1.1
Other professional	1.3	0.8	0.7	1.1
Social Sciences				
Anthropology	0.2	0.0	0.0	0.0
Economics	0.4	0.3	0.1	0.6
Ethnic studies	0.0	0.0	0.0	0.0
Geography	0.0	0.0	0.0	0.0
Political science	3.1	3.7	2.9	5.2
Psychology	4.2	5.5	5.4	5.8
Social work	1.0	1.5	1.9	0.8
Sociology	0.4	1.3	1.4	1.1
Women's studies	0.0	0.0	0.0	0.0
Other social sciences	0.3	0.2	0.2	0.3
Technical				
Building trades	0.4	0.0	0.0	0.0
Data processing	1.0	2.2	2.6	1.4
Drafting or design	0.5	0.5	0.7	0.2
Electronics	0.4	0.3	0.4	0.1
Mechanics	0.5	0.0	0.0	0.0
Other technical	0.5	0.1	0.1	0.1
Other Fields				
Agriculture	0.8	1.0	1.4	0.3
Communications	2.7	4.6	4.3	5.1
Computer science	1.6	4.5	4.7	4.1
Forestry	0.4	0.1	0.2	0.1
Law enforcement	1.5	1.6	1.8	1.3
Military science	0.1	0.2	0.2	0.1
Other fields	1.7	1.3	1.5	1.1
Undecided	6.9	3.2	3.0	3.7

Source: "Probable Major Field of Study," *The American Freshman: National Norms for Fall 1989*, pp. 50-51. Primary source: Cooperative Institutional Research Program, American Council on Education, University of California, Los Angeles, 1989. Figures for Predominately Black colleges include all ethnic groups.

★ 367 ★
The American Freshman: Racial Background

Racial Background	All Institutions	Predominantly Black Colleges	Predominantly Black Colleges	
			Public	Private
White/Caucasian	84.3	1.5	2.0	0.7
Black/Negro/Afro-American	9.2	97.4	96.6	99.0
American Indian	0.9	1.3	1.0	1.7
Asian American/Oriental	2.9	0.2	0.2	0.2
Mexican American/Chicano	1.4	0.2	0.2	0.1
Puerto Rican-American	0.8	0.3	0.3	0.3
Other	2.1	1.3	1.3	1.3

Source: "Racial Background," *The American Freshman: National Norms for Fall 1989,* p. 43. Primary source: Cooperative Institutional Research Program, American Council on Education, University of California, Los Angeles, 1989. *Notes:* Percentages will sum to more than 100 if any students check more than one category. Published by permission.

★ 368 ★
Time Taken to Attain Doctoral Degrees

RTD = Registered time-to-degree. TTD = Total time-to degree (number of years elapsed between earning the baccalaureate and the doctorate).

	Field of Doctorate							
	All Fields	Phys. Sci.[1]	Engi-neering	Life Sci.	Social Sci.	Human-ities	Educ-ation	Prof/Other
RTD Years[1]								
All Ph.D.s	6.9	6.1	5.9	6.5	7.4	8.5	8.1	7.3
Men	6.7	6.2	5.9	6.5	7.3	8.3	8.2	7.3
Women	7.4	6.0	5.8	6.7	7.5	8.7	8.0	7.4
U.S. Citizens	7.2	6.1	5.9	6.6	7.5	8.7	8.3	7.6
Permt. Res.	7.0	6.6	6.2	6.7	8.0	7.5	7.6	7.8
Temp. Res	6.2	6.1	5.8	6.2	6.8	7.2	6.2	6.4
U.S. Citizens[2]								
Asians	7.0	6.4	6.1	6.9	7.8	8.5	8.4	8.5
Blacks	8.1	6.5	6.1	6.6	8.1	9.0	8.6	7.8
Hispanics	7.4	6.4	5.8	6.4	7.8	9.4	8.3	7.5
Whites	7.2	6.1	5.8	6.6	7.4	8.7	8.3	7.5
TTD Years[2]								
All Ph.D.s	10.5	7.4	8.1	8.9	10.5	12.2	16.9	13.0
Men	9.7	7.5	8.2	8.6	10.3	11.9	16.5	12.6
Women	12.3	7.3	7.0	9.3	10.9	12.6	17.2	14.0
U.S. Citizens	11.0	7.1	7.5	8.6	10.5	12.5	17.3	14.0
Permt. Res.	10.0	8.6	8.9	10.0	11.2	10.9	12.9	11.6
Temp. Res	9.3	8.5	8.4	9.7	9.9	10.8	12.9	10.5
U.S. Citizens[2]								
Asians	9.9	7.9	8.7	8.3	10.5	12.6	19.7	15.0
Blacks	14.9	7.8	8.3	10.4	11.0	14.3	17.9	16.0

Continued.

Time Taken to Attain Doctoral Degrees
[Continued]

	Field of Doctorate							
	All Fields	Phys. Sci.[1]	Engi- neering	Life Sci.	Social Sci.	Human- ities	Educ- ation	Prof/ Other
Hispanics	10.9	7.1	7.7	7.7	10.0	13.0	16.2	15.0
Whites	10.9	7.0	7.4	8.6	10.5	12.4	17.3	13.8

Source: "Median Years to Degree for Doctorate Recipients, by Demographic Group and Broad Field, 1988," *Black Issues in Higher Education,* February 1, 1990, p. 9. Primary source: Summary Report 1988: Doctorate Recipients from United States Universities, National Research Council. *Notes:* 1. Includes mathematics and computer sciences. 2. American Indians are not shown because their numerical distribution among fields was too small for averages to be meaningful.

★ 369 ★
Total Enrollment at UNCF Institutions: Trends

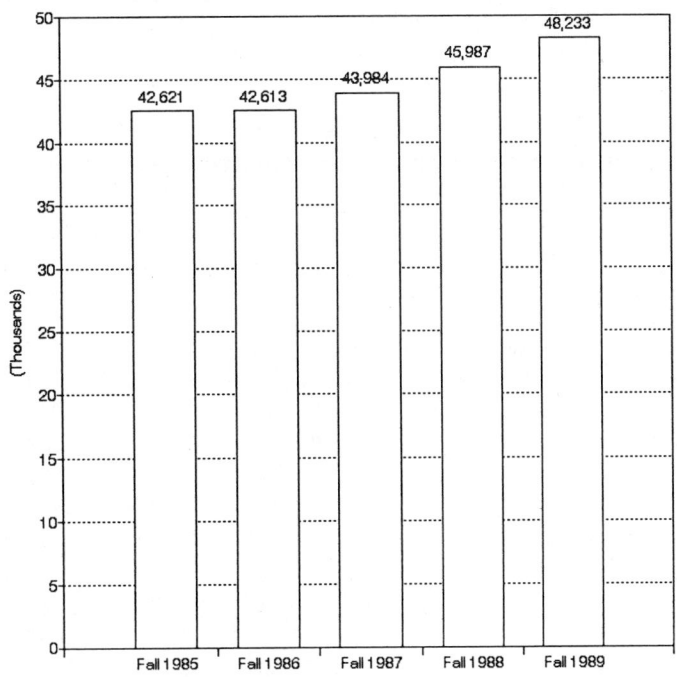

In thousands.

Year	Number
Fall 1985	42,621
Fall 1986	42,613
Fall 1987	43,984
Fall 1988	45,987
Fall 1989	48,233

Source: "Fall Enrollment, UNCF Member Institutions," *UNCF 1989 Statistical Report,* p. 1. Primary source: United Negro College Fund (UNCF), Inc., UNCF 1989 Statistical Report (undated), New York, NY.

★ 370 ★
Total HBCU Transfer Students

Responding Institutions(1) = 32.

Level	1983			1984			1985		
	Wht	Blk	Tot	Wht	Blk	Tot	Wht	Blk	Tot
Two-Year									
Number	811	318	1129	696	299	995	860	221	1085
Percent	72	28	100	70	30	100	79	21	100
Four-Year									
Number	700	375	1075	628	457	1085	808	493	1301
Percent	65	35	100	58	42	100	62	38	100
Total	1511	693	2204	1324	756	2080	1668	718	2386
Percent	69	31	100	64	36	100	70	30	100

Source: "Total Number and Percent of Transfer Students to HBCUs by Institutional Type and Level, Fall, 1983-1985," *NAFEO INROADS*, June/July 1987, p. 6. Primary source: Patel, Narenda H. *Student Transfers from White to Black Colleges*. NAFEO Research Institute, 1988. *Notes:* 1. Institutional Type: Wht - Predominately White Institutions; Blk - Predominately Black Institutions. Published by permission.

★ 371 ★
Traditionally Black Higher Education Institutions: Characteristics

Item	Total	Public		Private	
		4-year	2-year	4-year	2-year
Number of institutions, fall 1987[1]	99	38	5	49	7
Financial statistics, 1985-86, in thousands of dollars					
Current-fund revenues	1,966,778	1,098,481	29,529	827,517	11,251
Tuition and fees	364,622	150,588	2,917	208,037	3,081
Federal Government[2]	403,162	134,818	4,743	261,114	2,487
State governments[2]	575,813	546,340	16,830	12,643	0
Local governments[2]	74,322	71,863	1,438	1,021	0
Private gifts, grants, and contracts	93,950	9,304	771	80,787	3,088
Endowment income	22,630	1,391	40	20,890	309
Sales and services	386,087	156,341	1,732	226,296	1,719
Other sources	46,191	27,837	1,057	16,729	569
Current-fund expenditures	1,954,606	1,078,351	27,851	839,074	9,330
Educational and general expenditures	1,569,158	921,003	26,553	613,560	8,042
Auxiliary enterprises	235,211	157,348	1,298	75,278	1,288
Hospitals	150,237	[3]	[3]	150,237	[3]
Endowments, market value	438,773	20,187	1,149	416,766	670
Buildings, replacement value	4,186,359	2,636,038	57,391	1,468,530	24,400

Source: "Selected Statistics on Traditionally Black Institutions of Higher Education: 1985-86, 1986-87, and Fall 1987," Digest of Education Statistics, 1989, p. 211. Primary source: U.S. Department of Education, National Center for Educational Statistics, "Fall Enrollment in Institutions of Higher Education" and "Financial Statistics of Institutions of Higher Education, Fiscal Year 1986" surveys, and Integrated Postsecondary Education Data System (IPEDS), "Fall Enrollment" and "Completions" surveys. (This table was prepared April 1989.) *Notes:* 1. Includes institutions, mainly in the southern and border States, which were established prior to 1954 for the education of black students during legal segregation. 2. Includes appropriations, grants, and contracts. 3. Data not reported or not applicable.

★ 372 ★
TWI Faculty's Doctoral Institution

Name of Institution	Number of Ph.Ds Granted to Respondents
University of Georgia	11
Florida State University	11
Indiana State University	11
University of Florida	10
Ohio State University	9
University of North Carolina at Chapel Hill	8
University of Michigan	7
North Carolina State University	7
Howard University[1]	7
University of Alabama	5
University of Pittsburgh	5
Michigan State University	5
Atlanta University[1]	4
Columbia University	4

Source: "Selected Colleges/Universities Granting the Doctoral Degree to Respondent Population," *Black Faculty in Traditionally White Institutions in Selected Adams States*, 1988, p. 31. Primary source: *Black Faculty in Traditionally White Institutions in Selected Adams States: Characteristics, Experiences and Perceptions*, Southern Education Foundation, Atlanta, GA 30308, 1988. *Note:* 1. Historically Black College/University.

★ 373 ★
TWI Faculty: Avenues to Position

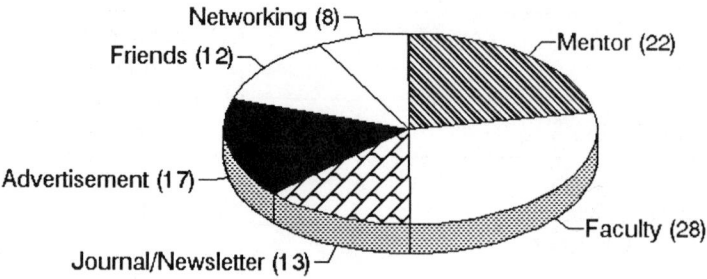

Numbers in percent.

Locating Factor	0 to 5 Years Ago	5 to 10 Years Ago	10 to 15 Years Ago	15 or More Years Ago
Mentor	22	20	28	25
Faculty at Institution	28	30	35	41
Journal/Newsletter	13	10	11	0
Advertisement	17	13	8	7
Friends	12	18	11	23
Networking	8	8	6	5

Source: "Recruiting Factors Used by Black Faculty in Locating Position," *Black Faculty in Traditionally White Institutions in Selected Adams States*, 1988, p. 66. Primary source: *Black Faculty in Traditionally White Institutions in Selected Adams States: Characteristics, Experiences and Perceptions*, Southern Education Foundation, Atlanta, GA 30308, 1988. TWI: Traditionally White Institutions.

★ 374 ★
TWI Faculty: Salary Changes

Salary	Initial		Present	
	Black	White	Black	White
Less than 15,000	32.3	31.8	1.0	0
15,000 < 20,000	22.9	31.8	2.0	3.3
20,000 < 25,000	24.0	13.6	28.6	18.5
25,000 < 30,000	10.4	11.4	34.7	30.4
30,000 < 35,000	4.2	6.8	13.3	26.1
35,000 < 40,000	3.1	1.1	12.2	15.2
40,000 < 45,000	1.0	1.1	2.0	3.3
45,000 < 50,000	0	1.1	2.0	1.1
50,000 < 55,000	1.0	1.1	3.1	0
55,000 < 60,000	0	0	1.0	1.1
75,000 < 80,000	0	0	0	1.1

Source: "Initial Salary and Present Salary: Target State," *Black Faculty in Traditionally White Institutions (TWI) in Selected Adams States*, 1988, p. 100. Primary source: *Black Faculty in Traditionally White Institutions (TWI) in Selected Adams States: Characteristics, Experiences and Perceptions*, Southern Education Foundation, Atlanta, GA 30308, 1988. Target state system was isolated for comparisons.

★ 375 ★
U.S. Degrees Conferred: Types and Trends

Degrees	Year					% Change
	1976	1978	1980	1983	1985	1976-85
First Professional	2,694	2,836	2,929	2,743	2,937	9.0
Doctorate	1,213	1,217	1,265	1,129	1,065	-12.2
Masters	20,351	19,397	17,152	15,099	13,097	-35.6
Bachelors	59,187	60,185	60,589	57,129	54,964	-7.1
Associate	40,958	54,762	46,077	51,346	47,221	15.3
Total	124,403	129,447	128,012	127,446	119,284	-4.1

Source: "Degrees Conferred to [sic] Blacks and Whites by All U.S. Institutions, Selected Years 1976, 1979, 1981, 1983, and 1985," *NAFEO INROADS*, February/March-April/May, 1989, p. 13. Primary source: *Data on Earned Degrees Conferred from Institutions of Higher Education, by Race/Ethnicity, and Sex, Academic Year 1975-76, 1976-77, 1978-79*, National Advisory Committee Staff Analysis ED/OCR; *Data on Earned Degrees Conferred from Institutions of Higher Education by Race/Ethnicity, and Sex, Academic Year 1980-81, 1982-83, and 1984-85*, NAFEO Research Institute Staff Analysis ED/OCR. *Notes:* All persons did not indicate race in OCR data for 1983; therefore, numbers may be greater. Published by permission.

★ 376 ★
UNCF Faculty with Doctorates: Trends

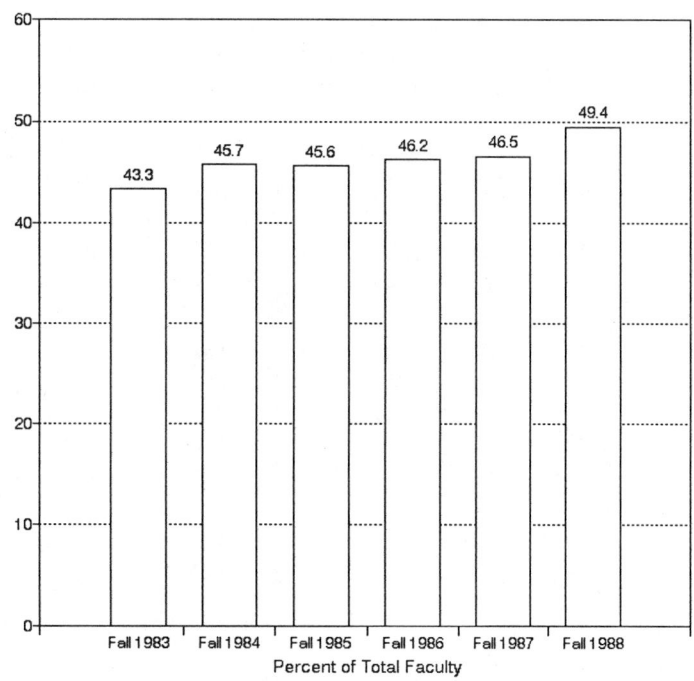

Percent of total faculty.

Year	Percent
Fall 1983	43.3
Fall 1984	45.7
Fall 1985	45.6
Fall 1986	46.2
Fall 1987	46.5

Continued.

251

UNCF Faculty with Doctorates: Trends
[Continued]

Year	Percent
Fall 1988	49.4

Source: "Faculty, Percent with Doctorates," *UNCF 1989 Statistical Report*, p. 6. Primary source: United Negro College Fund (UNCF), Inc., UNCF 1989 Statistical Report (undated), New York, NY.

★ 377 ★
Undergraduate Major and GRE Scores

Undergraduate major and year	Total	White	Black	Asian	Native American	Mexican American	Puerto Rican	Latin American
					Verbal			
All majors								
1979	488	511	363	480	459	419	389	465
1987	487	516	386	476	471	440	389	469
				Students who majored in science or engineering				
Physical sciences								
1979	519	541	391	495	482	509	418	509
1987	505	546	422	516	521	490	391	496
Mathematical sciences								
1979	505	537	364	476	494	420	375	468
1987	483	537	371	441	500	472	414	468
Biological sciences								
1979	492	521	358	494	447	407	398	473
1987	504	527	404	511	479	471	380	494
Behavioral sciences								
1979	507	528	386	503	483	446	399	481
1987	507	528	401	504	487	458	401	482
Social sciences								
1979	454	484	343	453	451	409	363	465
1987	458	488	358	460	447	421	361	446
Engineering								
1979	468	527	403	459	478	434	390	476
1987	466	532	436	451	487	460	401	477
					Quantitative			
All majors								
1979	514	525	358	566	457	422	418	468
1987	539	541	390	604	473	456	443	495
				Students who majored in science or engineering				
Physical sciences								
1979	630	639	462	658	581	600	532	592
1987	639	645	499	672	602	584	517	615
Mathematical sciences								
1979	665	682	486	660	671	595	550	626
1987	657	673	472	658	652	613	573	603

Continued.

Undergraduate Major and GRE Scores
[Continued]

Undergraduate major and year	Total	White	Black	Asian	Native American	Mexican American	Puerto Rican	Latin American
Biological sciences								
1979	555	569	381	596	479	448	450	509
1987	570	581	428	612	521	517	456	542
Behavioral sciences								
1979	500	514	366	528	457	427	387	460
1987	513	522	382	547	459	446	403	479
Social sciences								
1979	474	496	337	494	443	413	378	429
1987	479	495	346	517	439	405	378	436
Engineering								
1979	654	675	521	675	570	595	583	624
1987	673	688	579	682	636	626	601	634
Analytical								
All majors								
1979	503	529	352	510	457	412	385	460
1987	528	554	404	537	487	459	421	493
Students who majored in science or engineering								
Physical sciences								
1979	557	581	406	546	523	516	433	524
1987	572	608	468	583	574	529	437	542
Mathematical sciences								
1979	567	602	401	549	553	467	412	530
1987	588	639	435	553	615	546	491	546
Biological sciences								
1979	521	553	359	537	456	421	401	484
1987	557	582	432	564	510	504	426	528
Behavioral sciences								
1979	511	535	371	510	468	435	382	473
1987	530	551	409	531	490	469	418	500
Social sciences								
1979	471	506	333	464	455	404	362	448
1987	494	526	379	484	457	431	383	458
Engineering								
1979	526	587	437	533	505	487	439	520
1987	563	626	502	554	563	539	491	542

Source: "Graduate Record Examination Scores by Undergraduate Major, Gender, and Racial/Ethnic Group: 1979 and 1987," *Women and Minorities in Science and Engineering,* January 1990, pp. 131-132. Graduate Record Examination Board, *A Summary of Data Collected from Graduate Record Examination Test-Takers During 1978-79, Data Summary Report No. 4; Report No. 12* (Princeton, NJ: Educational Testing Service). *Note:* Score range is 200 to 800 for each component. Published by permission.

★ 378 ★
What Programs Do High Schoolers Take?

Characteristic	Total	Academic	General	Vocational								Sample Size
				Total Vocational	Agriculture	Office Occupations	Distributions	Health	Occupational Home Economics	Technical	Trade and Industry	
							Percentage Distribution					
Total[1]	100.0	38.73	6.9	24.5	2.7	9.8	2.1	1.1	1.3	2.1	5.4	27,775
Racial/ethnic group:												
White												
non-Hispanic	100.0	39.8	37.1	23.1	2.5	9.4	2.0	1.0	.9	2.0	5.3	19,618
Black												
non-Hispanic	100.0	33.0	35.2	31.8	3.7	11.9	3.0	1.6	3.6	1.8	6.2	3,695
Hispanic	100.0	26.9	41.6	31.5	4.4	10.5	2.2	1.4	2.3	2.8	7.9	3,107
American Indian/Alaskan Native	100.0	24.4	45.5	30.1	4.7	9.2	1.3	1.4	.7	1.3	11.5	211
Asian or Pacific Islander	100.0	52.4	29.0	18.5	1.8	8.2	1.6	1.2	1.3	3.0	1.5	362

Source: "Curricular Programs of 1980 High School Seniors, by Sex, Racial/Ethnic Group, Ability, and Socioeconomic Status: Spring 1980," *Equality and Excellence: The Educational Status of Black Americans*, 1985, p. 34. Primary source: U.S. Department of Education, National Center for Education Statistics, High School and Beyond Study, unpublished tabulations, August 1982. *Notes:* 1. Curricular programs can be generally defined as follows: academic - those preparing students for college; vocational - those preparing students for employment immediately following high school graduation; general - those with students considering themselves to be in neither academic nor vocational programs. Published by permission.

★ 379 ★
Where Are Recent High School Graduates?

Numbers in thousands.

Item	Civilian noninstitutional population			Civilian labor force[1]				
	Number	Percent	Percent of high school graduates	Number	Labor force participation rate	Employed	Unemployed	
							Number	Unemployment rate
1986 high school graduates[2]								
Total	2,786	100.0	100.0	1,764	63.3	1,462	302	17.1
White[3]	2,307	82.8	82.8	1,512	65.5	1,288	224	14.8
Black[3]	386	13.9	13.9	208	53.9	136	72	34.6
Hispanic origin[4]	169	6.1	6.1	109	64.5	91	18	16.5
Enrolled in college, October 1986	1,499	100.0	53.8	717	47.8	623	94	13.1
White[3]	1,292	86.2	46.4	651	50.4	569	82	12.6
Black[3]	141	9.4	5.1	41	29.1	33	8	5
Hispanic origin[4]	75	5.0	2.7	33	44.0	30	3	5
Not enrolled in college, October 1986	1,287	100.0	46.2	1,047	81.4	839	208	19.9
White[3]	1,015	78.9	36.4	861	84.8	719	142	16.5
Black[3]	245	19.0	8.8	167	68.2	103	64	38.3
Hispanic origin[4]	94	7.3	3.4	76	80.9	61	15	19.7
1987 high school graduates[6]								
Total	2,647	100.0	100.0	1,657	62.6	1,400	257	15.5
White[3]	2,207	83.4	83.4	1,405	63.7	1,226	179	12.8
Black[3]	337	12.7	12.7	198	58.6	132	66	33.4
Hispanic								

Continued.

Where Are Recent High School Graduates?

[Continued]

	Civilian noninstitutional population			Civilian labor force[1]				
Item	Number	Percent	Percent of high school graduates	Number	Labor force partici-pation rate	Employed	Unemployed	
							Number	Unemploy-ment rate
origin[4]	176	6.6	6.6	102	58.0	84	18	17.7
Enrolled in college,								
October 1987	1,503	100.0	56.8	698	46.5	612	86	12.3
White[3]	1,249	83.1	47.2	584	46.8	528	57	9.7
Black[3]	175	11.6	6.6	79	45.0	56	23	29.4
Hispanic origin[4]	59	3.9	2.2	21	5	21	---	5
Not enrolled in college,								
October 1987	1,144	100.0	43.2	959	83.8	788	171	17.8
White[3]	959	83.8	36.2	821	85.6	698	123	15.0
Black[3]	162	14.2	6.1	119	73.4	76	43	36.1
Hispanic origin[4]	117	10.2	4.4	81	69.5	63	18	22.2

Source: "College Enrollment and Labor Force Status of 1986 and 1987 High School Graduates 16 to 24 Years Old, by Sex and Race/Ethnicity: October 1986 and October 1987," *Digest of Educational Statistics,* 1989, p. 368. Primary source: U.S. Department of Labor, Bureau of Labor Statistics, *Employment of School-Age Youth, High School Graduates, and Dropouts, October 1987,* October 1988. (This table was prepared December 1988.) *Notes:* Data based on sample surveys of the civilian noninstitutional population. Percents are only shown when the base is 75,000 or greater. Even though the standard errors are large, smaller estimates are shown to permit users to combine categories in various ways. Because of rounding, details may not add up to totals. 1. The labor force includes all employed persons plus those seeking employment. The labor force participation rate is the percentage of persons either employed or seeking employment. 2. Includes persons who graduated from high school between October 1985 and October 1986. 3. Includes persons of Hispanic origin. 4. Persons of Hispanic origin may be of any race. 5. Data not shown where base is less than 75,000. 6. Includes persons who graduated from high school October 1986 and October 1987.

★ 380 ★
Who Takes Advanced Placement Tests?

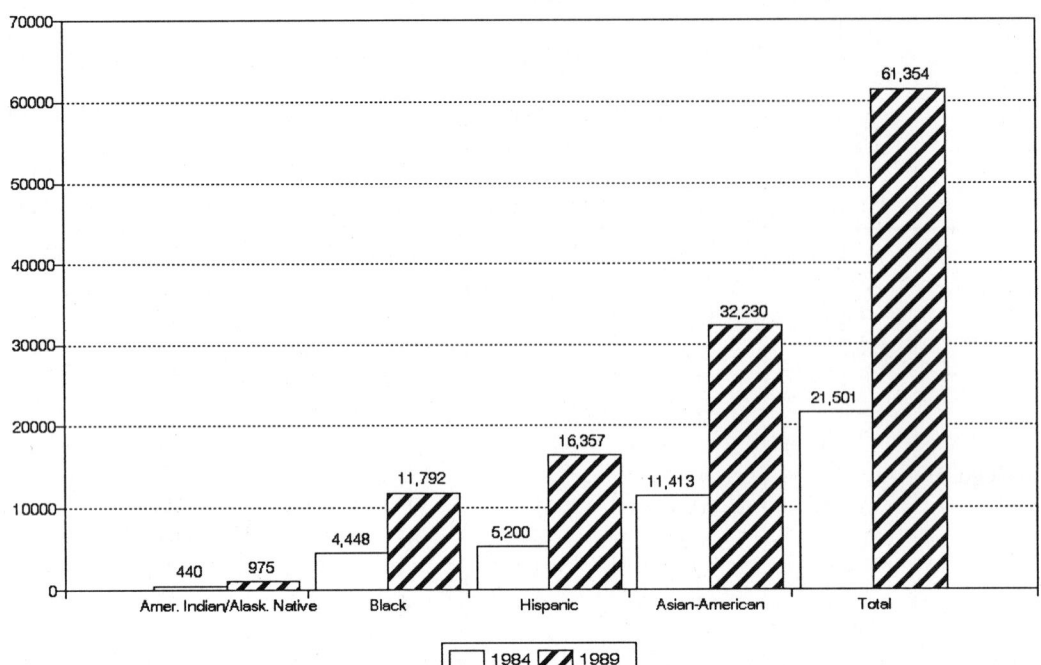

Characteristic	1984	1989
American Indian/ Alaskan Native	440	975
Black	4,448	11,972
Hispanic	5,200	16,357
Asian American	11,413	32,230
Total	21,501	61,354

Source: "Five-Year Growth in U.S. Minority Students Participating in Advanced Placement," *The College Board Review*, Winter 1989-90, p. 20. Primary source: The College Board. Published by permission.

★ 381 ★
Writing Proficiency: Trends

Age, writing task, and year	All Students[1]	Race/ethnicity		
		White	Black	Hispanic
Age 9				
Informative writing				
1979	53.4	58.4	33.5	29.1
1984	55.7	59.7	36.0	51.9
Persuasive writing				
1979	63.7	68.0	44.1	45.4
1984	58.2	62.6	40.1	50.9
Imaginative writing				
1974	36.7	41.3	17.3	22.4

Continued.

Writing Proficiency: Trends
[Continued]

Age, writing task, and year	All Students[1]	Race/ethnicity		
		White	Black	Hispanic
1979	41.4	43.6	29.9	36.6
1984	54.6	57.3	44.8	46.2
Age 13				
Informative writing				
1979	74.4	77.3	60.6	65.3
1984	81.4	84.9	64.4	78.8
Persuasive writing				
1979	27.8	30.1	18.2	18.6
1984	34.1	37.0	26.2	19.9
Imaginative writing				
1974	69.0	70.8	57.1	67.0
1979	60.7	62.3	53.1	58.3
1984	66.7	65.3	75.3	65.7
Age 17[2]				
Informative writing				
1979	87.1	89.4	72.8	78.1
1984	89.0	91.3	79.5	86.1
Persuasive writing				
1979	60.6	62.7	52.5	46.3
1984	63.8	67.2	55.7	52.9
Imaginative writing				
1974	76.4	77.6	70.3	67.8
1979	71.3	72.5	64.7	55.2
1984	75.1	76.4	68.4	76.2

Source: "Percentage of Students Writing at a Minimal Level or Better, by Sex and Race/Ethnicity, by Age: 1974, 1979, 1984," *Digest of Education Statistics*, 1989, p. 113. Primary source: U.S. Department of Education, Office of Educational Research and improvement, National Assessment of Educational Progress, *Writing: Trends Across the Decade, 1974-1984.* (This table was prepared June 1987.) *Notes:* Information writing is used to share knowledge and convey messages, instructions, and ideas. Persuasive writing attempts to bring about some action or change. Imaginative writing provides a special way of sharing our experiences and understanding the world. Five levels of proficiency were defined for each task: non-rateable, unsatisfactory, minimal, adequate, and elaborated. Non-rateable responses included those that were blank, off-task, and unreadable. Unsatisfactory responses were those that failed to reflect a basic understanding of the purpose of the writing. Minimal responses recognized the elements needed to complete the task, but were not managed well enough to ensure that the intended purpose of the writing was achieved. Adequate responses included the features critical to accomplishing the purpose of the writing and were likely to have the intended effect. Elaborated responses went beyond the merely adequate, reflecting a higher level of coherence and elaboration. 1. Standards for minimal performance level differ by grade level. 2. All participants of this age group were in school.

★ 382 ★
Years of Math Taken related to Achievement in Math

	Mathematics Test I Scores[1] Numbers of Years of Mathematics Taken					Mathematics Test II Scores[1] Number of Years of Mathematics Taken				
Characteristic	None	Less than 1 Year	Less than 2 Years	Less than 3 Years	3 Years or More	None	Less than 1 Year	Less than 2 Years	Less than 3 Years	3 Years or More
	Mean Test Score									
Racial/ethnic group:										
White	45.66	48.07	52.39	57.54	58.87	45.04	47.41	51.09	56.52	58.60
Hispanic	41.92	42.06	44.44	49.92	50.27	45.04	44.53	46.32	50.22	51.69
Black	40.51	41.13	42.62	46.80	48.88	42.71	43.60	45.50	47.49	49.90
American Indian or Alaskan Native	41.13	45.96	45.68	51.97	53.30	41.57	45.08	46.77	50.71	50.06
Asian or Pacific Islander	51.27	47.27	51.58	58.30	60.16	44.94	46.05	52.46	59.82	62.41

Source: "Mean Mathematics Test Scores of High School Seniors, by Number of Years of Mathematics Taken, Racial/Ethnic Group, Sex, and Socioeconomic Status: 1980," *Equality and Excellence: The Educational Status of Black Americans*, 1985, p. 37. Primary source: U.S. Department of Education, National Center for Education Statistics, 1980 High School and Beyond Study, unpublished tabulations. *Notes:* Scores are standardized to a mean of 50 points and a standard deviation of 10 points. 1. Mathematics test I was designed to measure basic competence in quantitative skills, while mathematics test II measured the skills at a higher level. Because each set of test scores is standardized, comparisons can only be made within each test. Published by permission.

★ 383 ★
Young Adult College Enrollment: Trends

Numbers in thousands.

Year	Total	Black Americans	Percent
1975	6935	665	9.6
1980	7226	688	9.5
1981	7575	750	9.9
1982	7678	767	10.0
1983	7477	741	9.9
1984	7591	786	10.4

Source: "Number and Percent of Black Americans 18-24 Years Old Enrolled in College, 1975-1984," *NAFEO INROADS*, October/November 1987, p. 3. Primary source: U.S. Bureau of the Census, *U.S. Statistical Abstracts*, 1981, 1982-83, 1984, 1985, 1986.

★ 384 ★
Young Adult Educational Attainment: Trends

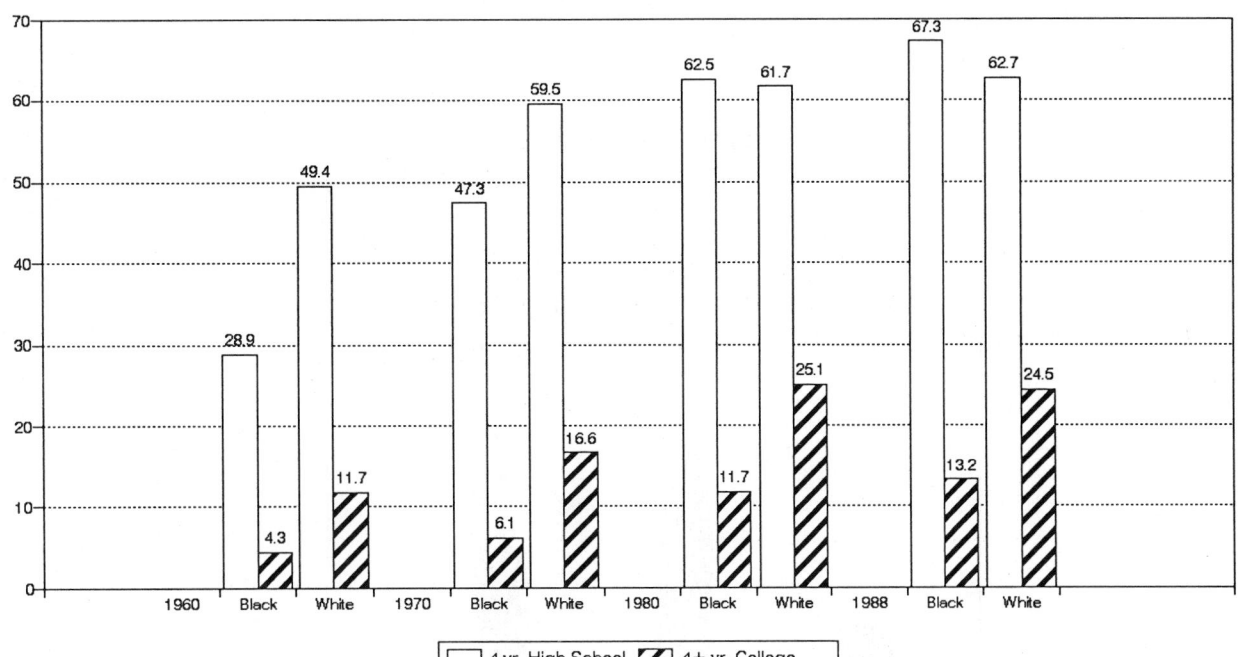

Numbers in percent.

Characteristic	1960		1970		1980		1988	
	Black	White	Black	White	Black	White	Black	White
Four or more years of college	28.9	49.4	47.3	59.5	62.5	61.7	67.3	62.7
Four years of high school or college, 1-3 years	4.3	11.7	6.1	16.6	11.7	25.1	13.2	24.5
High school graduate	33.2	61.1	53.4	76.1	74.2	86.8	80.5	87.2

Source: "Educational Attainment of Persons 25 to 34 Years Old, by Race: 1960 to 1988 (Percent)," *Population Profile of the United States, 1989*, p. 37. Primary source: *Population Profile of the United States 1989*, Special Studies, Bureau of the Census.

THE FAMILY

★ 385 ★
Basic Skills Levels of Young Parents

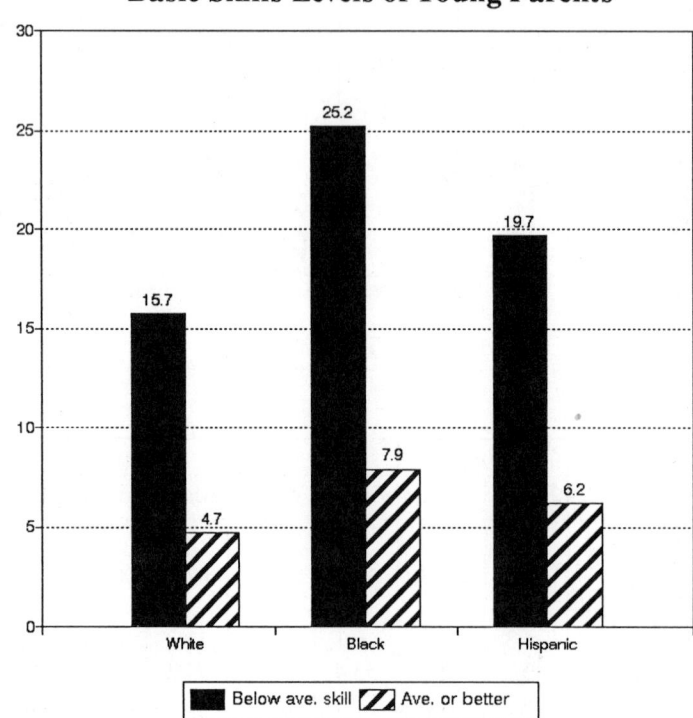

Characteristics	Below average skills	Average or better skills
White	15.7	4.7
Black	25.2	7.9
Hispanic	19.7	6.2

Source: "Parenthood by Basic Skills Levels, 16-19 Year-Old Men and Women, 1981", *The Urban League Review*, Summer 1988/ Winter 1988-89, p. 57. Primary source: Unpublished analyses of the National Longitudinal Survey, courtesy of Andrew Sum, Northeastern University. Extracted from: *The Urban League Review*, Summer 1988/ Winter 1988-89. Published by permission.

★ 386 ★
Breadwinners in Married-Couple Families

In 1987 dollars.

	Husband and wife earners		Husband only earner	
	Black	White	Black	White
1979	33,290	39,650	19,080	29,980
1987	35,280	41,600	18,810	30,000

Source: "Median income of Married-Couple Families, by Earner Status: 1979 and 1987," *The Black Population in the United States: March 1988,* p. 13. Primary source: Current Population Reports, Series P-20, No. 442.

★ 387 ★
Characteristics of Mothers Who Work

Number values in millions.

Characteristic	Mother Worked Full-Time, Full-Year		Mother Worked Part-Time or Part-Year		Mother Did Not Work For Pay During Year	
	Number	Percent	Number	Percent	Number	Percent
All Children Living With their Mothers	18.1	30	21.5	36	19.8	33
Race and Family Type						
White children	14.5	30	18.5	38	15.5	32
- in two-parent families	11.4	28	16.0	40	12.9	32
- in mother-only families	3.0	37	2.5	31	2.6	32
Black children	2.9	33	2.5	29	3.3	39
- in two-parent families	1.6	44	1.1	29	1.0	27
- in mother-only families	1.2	25	1.4	28	2.4	48

Source: "Number and Proportion of Children Whose Mothers Worked Full-Time Full-Year, Part-Time or Part-Year, or Did Not Work for Pay At All During Calendar Year 1987, by Age of Child, Race and Family Type, and Poverty Status," *U.S. Children and their Families,* 1989, p. 87. Primary source: Child Trends, Inc., calculated from U.S. Bureau of the Census, Current Population Reports, Series P-20, No. 163, Table 24 (unpublished corrected version). Data from March 1988 Current Population Survey. Published by permission.

★ 388 ★
Child Abuse

Race/Hispanic Origin	Percent Distribution
White[1]	67
Black[1]	18
Hispanic	11
Other	4

Source: "Characteristics of Maltreated Children, 1986," *U.S. Children and their Families*, 1989, p. 191. Primary source: American Association for Protecting Children, *Highlights of Official Child Neglect and Abuse Reporting, 1984* (Denver, Colorado: The American Humane Association, 1986); American Association for Protecting Children, *Highlights of Official Aggregate Child Neglect and Abuse Reporting, 1987* (Denver, Colorado: The American Humane Association, 1989); Select Committee on Children, Youth, and Families, *Abused Children in America: Victims of Official Neglect*, 1987. *Notes:* Except for five states, reported totals include duplicate reports; i.e., a particular child may be reported more than once in a given year. 1. Non-Hispanic.

★ 389 ★
Child Support in Father-Absent Families: Trends

Characteristic	Percent Who Received Any Child Support[1]				Percent Awarded Child Support Payments			
	1978	1981	1983	1985	1978	1981	1983	1985
All women with minor children from an absent father	35	35	35	37	59	59	58	61
Race and Hispanic Origin								
White	43	42	42	43	71	69	67	71
Black	14	16	16	20	29	34	34	36
Hispanic origin	24	24	20	24	44	44	41	42

Source: "Award and Receipt of Child Support by Women With Minor Children From an Absent Father, 1978-1985," *U.S. Children and Their Families*, 1989, p. 119. Primary source: Calculated from U.S. Bureau of the Census, Current Population Reports, Series P-23, No. 112, 1981, Tables B, 1; No. 140, 1985, Tables B, 1; No. 141, 1985, Tables C, 1; No. 152, 1987, Tables E, 1. *Notes:* 1. Percentages shown are based on all women with children from an absent father, not just those with child support awards.

★ 390 ★
Children in Families

As of March. Excludes persons under 18 years old who maintained house-holds or family groups. It is likely that most of the sizeable increase in children living with never married mothers is the result of new and more definitive coding procedures introduced by the Census Bureau in 1982. Based on Current Population Survey.

Race, Hispanic Origin, and Year	Number (1,000)	Both parents	Percent Living With--						Father only	Neither parent
			Mother only							
			Total	Divorced	Married, spouse absent	Single[1]	Widowed			
All Races[2]										
1970	69,162	85.2	10.8	3.3	4.7	.8	2.0		1.1	2.9
1980	63,427	76.7	18.0	7.5	5.7	2.8	2.0		1.7	3.6
1985	62,475	73.9	20.9	8.5	5.4	5.6	1.5		2.5	2.7
1986	62,763	73.9	21.0	8.5	5.3	5.7	1.4		2.5	2.6
1987	62,932	73.1	21.3	8.5	5.2	6.3	1.3		2.6	2.9
White										
1970	58,790	89.5	7.8	3.1	2.8	.2	1.7		.9	1.8

Continued.

Children in Families
[Continued]

Race, Hispanic Origin, and Year	Number (1,000)	Both parents	Percent Living With--					Father only	Neither parent
			Mother only						
			Total	Divorced	Married, spouse absent	Single[1]	Widowed		
1980	52,242	82.7	13.5	7.0	3.9	1.0	1.7	1.6	2.2
1985	50,836	80.0	15.6	8.1	4.1	2.1	1.3	2.4	2.0
1986	50,931	79.9	15.7	8.2	4.1	2.3	1.2	2.5	1.9
1987	51,112	79.1	16.1	8.4	4.0	2.7	1.1	2.6	2.2
Black									
1970	9,422	58.5	29.5	4.6	16.3	4.4	4.2	2.3	9.7
1980	9,375	42.2	43.9	10.9	16.2	12.8	4.0	1.9	11.9
1985	9,479	39.5	51.0	11.3	12.4	24.8	2.5	2.9	6.6
1986	9,532	40.6	50.6	11.1	12.0	24.9	2.6	2.4	6.3
1987	9,612	40.1	50.4	9.6	12.0	26.3	2.6	2.5	7.0
Hispanic[3]									
1970	4,006[4]	77.7	[5]	[5]	[5]	[5]	[5]	[5]	[5]
1980	5,459	75.4	19.6	5.9	8.2	4.0	1.5	1.5	3.5
1985	6,057	67.9	26.6	7.3	11.1	6.5	1.7	2.2	3.3
1986	6,430	66.5	27.7	8.6	10.7	7.0	1.4	2.7	3.1
1987	6,647	65.5	27.7	8.0	9.3	8.8	1.6	2.8	4.0

Source: "Children Under 18 Years Old, by Presence of Parents: 1970 to 1987," *Statistical Abstract,* 1989, p. 52. Primary source: U.S. Bureau of the Census, *Current Population Reports,* series P-20, No. 423 and earlier reports. *Notes:* 1. Never married. 2. Includes other races not shown separately. 3. Hispanic persons may be of any race. 4. All persons under 18 years old. 5. Not available.

★ 391 ★
Children Left Alone After School

	Number parents responding	How often the child is left alone after school - Percent of parents responding		
		Never	1 or 2 days a week	Almost every day
Total parents	2,011	58	17	24
Race				
White	1,573	59	17	23
Black	211	51	17	31
Hispanic	150	62	15	21

Source: "Characteristics of Children, by How Often They are Left Alone After School, According to Parents: 1987," *1989 Education Indicators,* pp. 205- 206. Primary source: *The Metropolitan Life Survey of The American Teacher 1987: Strengthening Links Between Home and School.*.

★ 392 ★
Children Living Away from Parents: Trends

Living Away from Parents	1982	1985	1987	1988
Number, in thousands	2,035	1,789	1,974	2,039
Percent				
All Children Under 18	3.2	2.9	3.1	3.2
Race/Hispanic Origin				
White	2.2	2.1	2.4	2.4
Black	8.4	6.7	7.2	7.4
Hispanic	4.5	3.6	4.3	3.8

Source: "Number and Percent of Children Under 18 Living Away From Their Parents, by Age, Sex, and Race: 1982-1988," *U.S. Children and their Families*, 1989, p. 67. Primary source: U.S. Bureau of the Census, Current Population Reports, Series P-20, Nos. 380, 410, 423, and 433; *Marital Status and Living Arrangements, March 1982, 1985, 1987,* and *1988,* Tables 2 and 3. *Notes:* Children who live away from their parents include all persons under 18 who do not live with one or both parents (a parent can be either a natural or an adoptive parent) and all persons under 18 who have formed families or unrelated subfamilies of their own. Examples include those living with relatives other than their parents, those living in foster homes, those who have established households of their own, those living in dorms and other group quarters, and those living in households with unrelated roommates. Those who are married or have children are included unless they form a subfamily that is related to the householder, in which case the householder will usually be a parent of the individual.

★ 393 ★
Distribution of Income

Families as of March of the following year. Beginning with 1980, based on householder concept and restricted to primary families. Based on Current Population Survey; 14. See *Historical Statistics, Colonial Times to 1970,* series G 1-8, G 16-23, G 190-192, and G 197-199.

Race and Hispanic Origin of Householder and Year	Number of families (1,000)	Percent Distribution Of Families, By Income Level								Median Income ($)
		Under $5,000	$5,000-$9,900	$10,000-$14,999	$15,000-$19,999	$20,000-$24,999	$25,000-$34,999	$35,000-$49,999	$50,000 and over	
All families										
1970	52,227	3.5	7.6	9.1	9.9	11.3	22.0	21.2	15.4	28,880
1975	56,245	2.9	8.1	10.0	10.2	10.4	20.9	21.0	16.4	28,970
1980	60,309	3.7	8.2	9.8	10.2	10.2	20.0	20.5	17.5	28,996
1983	62,015	4.8	8.4	10.3	10.1	10.2	19.0	19.2	17.9	28,147
1984	62,706	4.5	8.3	9.7	10.0	9.7	18.4	19.7	19.6	28,923
1985	63,558	4.4	8.0	9.7	9.9	9.9	18.3	19.2	20.6	29,302
1986	64,491	4.5	7.5	9.2	9.6	9.5	17.7	19.8	22.2	30,534
1987	65,133	4.4	7.3	9.1	9.5	9.2	17.5	20.2	22.9	30,853
White										
1970	46,535	2.9	6.7	8.5	9.5	11.3	22.6	22.2	16.4	29,960
1975	49,873	2.3	6.9	9.5	10.0	10.3	21.5	21.9	17.6	30,129
1980	52,710	2.7	6.9	9.2	10.0	10.3	20.6	21.5	18.7	30,211
1983	53,890	3.7	7.1	9.9	10.1	10.4	19.5	20.2	19.2	29,474
1984	54,400	3.4	7.0	9.2	9.9	9.8	19.0	20.7	21.0	30,294
1985	54,991	3.5	6.9	9.1	9.6	10.0	18.8	20.1	22.1	30,799
1986	55,676	3.3	6.5	8.6	9.4	9.5	18.2	20.8	23.7	31,935
1987	56,044	3.2	6.1	8.6	9.3	9.1	18.1	21.2	24.4	32,274
Black										
1970	4,928	9.0	16.7	14.6	14.3	12.0	15.6	12.0	5.7	18,378
1975	5,586	7.4	19.0	15.2	12.2	11.7	16.1	12.5	6.1	18,538
1980	6,317	10.7	18.5	15.1	12.0	9.3	15.6	12.0	6.9	17,481
1983	6,681	13.5	19.2	14.1	11.1	9.4	15.1	10.9	6.9	16,610
1984	6,778	13.3	18.4	14.2	11.6	9.4	14.3	10.9	8.0	16,884
1985	6,921	12.4	16.8	14.1	12.4	8.8	15.0	12.2	8.3	17,734
1986	7,096	13.4	15.9	13.5	10.6	9.7	14.5	13.0	9.5	18,247

Continued.

Distribution of Income
[Continued]

Race and Hispanic Origin of Householder and Year	Number of families (1,000)	Percent Distribution Of Families, By Income Level								Median Income ($)
		Under $5,000	$5,000-$9,900	$10,000-$14,999	$15,000-$19,999	$20,000-$24,999	$25,000-$34,999	$35,000-$49,999	$50,000 and over	
1987	7,177	13.5	16.5	12.5	11.8	10.0	13.6	12.8	9.5	18,098
Hispanic										
1970	2,499	5.8	14.9	15.8	13.0	12.2	19.8	12.8	5.8	20,168
1975	3,235	6.5	14.1	15.5	13.5	11.4	17.3	14.1	7.5	20,297
1980	3,788	8.3	16.0	14.1	13.6	11.4	16.3	12.3	7.9	19,313
1983	3,939	8.6	14.5	13.9	12.7	9.9	17.5	14.1	9.0	20,606
1984	4,206	7.4	16.0	14.8	11.7	11.1	16.6	13.0	9.6	20,102
1985	4,403	8.2	14.3	14.8	11.8	10.6	16.1	13.3	11.0	20,726
1986	4,588	8.6	14.4	14.7	11.7	10.2	15.7	14.1	10.9	20,306
1987										

Source: "Money Income of Families — Percent Distribution by Income Level in Constant (1987) Dollars, by Race and Hispanic Origin of Householder: 1970 to 1987," *Statistical Abstract*, 1989, p. 455. Primary source: Current Population Reports, U.S. Bureau of the Census, series P-60, No. 161, and unpublished data. *Note:* Hispanic persons may be of any race.

★ 394 ★
Distribution of Income

Families as of March 1988. See headnote, table 720. For definitions, see text section 1. For definition of median, see Guide to Tabular Presentation. See *Historical Statistics, Colonial Times to 1970*, series G1-8 for U.S. data on total, White, Black and other races.

Race of Householder, Region, and Education	Number of families (1,000)	Percent Distribution of Families, by Income Level--								Median income (dol.)
		Under $5,000	$5,000-$9,999	$10,000-$14,999	$15,000-$24,999	$25,000-$34,999	$35,000-$49,999	$50,000-$74,999	$75,000 and over	
All families[1]	65,133	4.4	7.3	9.0	18.7	17.5	20.2	15.1	7.8	30,853
White, total	56,044	3.2	6.1	8.5	18.4	18.1	21.2	16.1	8.4	32,274
Northeast	11,855	2.9	5.6	6.9	16.5	17.7	21.9	17.7	10.8	35,262
Midwest	14,240	2.9	6.0	8.1	18.7	19.4	22.0	16.2	6.6	32,149
South	18,559	3.8	6.9	9.5	19.2	17.5	20.8	14.7	7.5	30,729
West	11,389	2.9	5.7	9.2	18.7	17.7	20.0	16.4	9.4	32,521
Householder completed--[2]										
Elementary school:										
Less than 8 years	3,259	7.7	21.1	20.3	23.9	13.1	8.7	4.1	1.1	15,264
8 years	2,798	5.8	13.0	18.5	29.6	16.6	10.5	4.4	1.5	18,718
High school:										
1-3 years	6,036	5.0	10.3	13.4	26.1	19.1	15.5	8.2	2.5	22,653
4 years	20,020	2.7	5.0	8.2	20.5	21.7	23.6	14.1	4.1	30,958
College:										
1-3 years	9,184	1.9	3.2	5.6	15.1	19.4	26.9	20.2	7.9	37,324
4 years or more	12,398	.7	1.0	2.3	8.2	12.3	24.0	28.2	23.3	50,908
Black, total	7,177	13.5	16.4	12.5	21.8	13.6	12.8	7.0	2.5	18,098
Northeast	1,189	12.6	14.4	10.2	21.6	12.7	16.0	8.6	3.8	20,678
Midwest	1,389	15.1	18.6	11.7	18.8	14.0	12.9	6.1	2.7	16,755
South	3,972	14.3	16.6	13.4	21.9	13.5	11.6	7.0	1.7	17,302
West	627	6.2	14.5	12.3	27.6	14.7	14.4	5.6	4.8	20,627
Householder completed--[2]										
Elementary school:										
Less than 8 years	821	11.2	28.2	20.2	20.6	11.6	5.4	2.3	.5	12,149
8 years	382	15.2	23.6	17.8	22.0	7.6	7.9	5.5	.5	13,210
High school:										
1-3 years	1,306	18.1	23.6	15.5	19.4	10.4	8.8	3.6	.5	12,166
4 years	2,467	13.2	13.4	11.4	22.7	16.0	14.9	7.1	1.4	20,263
College:										

Continued.

265

Distribution of Income
[Continued]

Race of Householder, Region, and Education	Number of families (1,000)	Percent Distribution of Families, by Income Level--								Median income (dol.)
		Under $5,000	$5,000-$9,999	$10,000-$14,999	$15,000-$24,999	$25,000-$34,999	$35,000-$49,999	$50,000-$74,999	$75,000 and over	
1-3 years	1,006	5.5	9.0	8.2	27.1	16.2	19.3	11.2	3.5	25,115
4 years or more	692	1.9	3.3	3.9	22.2	15.3	21.5	17.9	14.0	36,568

Source: "Money Income of Families — Percent Distribution by Income Level, by Race and Hispanic Origin of Householder, and Selected Characteristics: 1987," *Statistical Abstract,* 1989, p. 447. Primary source: U.S. Bureau of the Census, *Current Population Reports,* series P-60, No. 161, and unpublished data. *Notes:* 1. Includes other races not shown separately. 2. Restricted to families with householder 25 years old and over.

★ 395 ★
Extended Families: Parents, Children, & Other Adults

Numbers in percent.

Characteristic	Grandparent, Older Sibling, or Other Adult Relative	Unmarried Partner, Housekeeper or Other Non-Relative	Parent(s) Only
All children who live with one or both parents			
Children under 18	18	4	79
Type of family:			
Married-couple	15	1	85
Mother only	27	12	62
Father only	26	30	49
Children under 6	12	5	83
Type of family:			
Married-couple	7	1	93
Mother only	31	15	55
Father only	23	50	34
Black children who live with one or both parents			
Children under 18	26	6	69
Type of family:			
Married-couple	17	1	83
Mother only	33	8	60
Father only	24	37	45
Children under 6	27	8	67
Type of family:			
Married-couple	8	1	92
Mother only	40	10	52
Father only	24	54	30
Hispanic children who live with one or both parents			
Children under 18	24	5	72
Type of family:			
Married-couple	21	2	78
Mother only	30	9	62
Father only	26	42	36
Children under 6	19	6	75

Continued.

Extended Families: Parents, Children, & Other Adults
[Continued]

Characteristic	Grandparent, Older Sibling, or Other Adult Relative	Unmarried Partner, Housekeeper or Other Non-Relative	Parent(s) Only
Type of family:			
Married-couple	14	2	84
Mother only	31	11	60
Father only	27	57	22

Source: "Proportion of Children Living With One or Both Parents Who Have Other Adult Relatives or Non-Relatives in the Household as Well, by Family Type, Age of Child, and Race/Hispanic Origin, 1988," *U.S. Children and their Families*, 1989, p. 65. Primary source: U.S. Bureau of the Census, Current Population Reports, Series P-20, No. 433, *Marital Status and Living Arrangements: March 1988*, Table 9.

★ 396 ★
Families & Poverty Status, & Other Characteristics

	Total			White			Black			Hispanic origin[1]		
		Below poverty level			Below poverty level			Below poverty level			Below poverty level	
Years of school completed and age	Total	Number	Percent	Total	Number	Percent	Total	Number	Percent	Total	Number	Percent
All Families												
Householder, all ages	65,837	6,876	10.4	56,492	4,471	7.9	7,409	2,090	28.2	4,823	1,141	23.7
Less than 4 years of high school	15,318	3,436	22.4	12,286	2,213	18.0	2,583	1,053	40.8	2,417	818	33.8
High school graduate but no college	24,543	2,466	10.0	21,261	1,593	7.5	2,792	788	28.2	1,325	233	17.6
College 1 year or more	25,975	974	3.7	22,945	665	2.9	2,034	249	12.2	1,081	90	8.3
Householder under 25 years	3,006	892	29.7	2,378	551	23.2	547	326	59.6	428	163	38.2
Less than 4 years of high school	791	410	51.5	621	273	43.9	158	129	81.9	222	115	51.7
High school graduate but no college	1,482	402	27.1	1,151	227	19.7	294	172	58.3	138	44	31.7 [2]
College 1 year or more	727	80	11.0	606	51	8.5	95	25	26.4	68	5	[2]
Householder 25 to 44 years	31,399	3,773	12.0	26,377	2,426	9.2	3,984	1,161	29.1	2,692	681	25.3
Less than 4 years of high school	4,379	1,544	35.3	3,400	1,023	30.1	794	432	54.5	1,142	441	38.6
High school graduate but no college	12,215	1,575	12.9	10,254	991	9.7	1,729	530	30.7	848	169	19.9
College 1 year or more	14,805	654	4.4	12,723	411	3.2	1,461	198	13.6	702	71	10.1
Householder 45 to 64 years	20,805	1,510	7.3	18,172	1,033	5.7	2,013	394	19.6	1,322	232	17.5
Less than 4 years of high school	5,338	953	17.8	4,215	604	14.3	978	298	30.4	777	205	26.3
High school graduate but no college	7,559	367	4.9	6,760	274	4.1	634	74	11.6	279	20	7.3
College 1 year or more	7,908	190	2.4	7,197	155	2.1	401	23	5.7	266	7	2.7
Householder 65 years and over	10,626	701	6.6	9,565	461	4.8	866	209	24.2	381	65	17.1
Less than 4 years of high school	4,805	259	11.0	4,051	313	7.7	653	194	29.6	276	57	20.8
High school graduate but no college	3,286	122	3.7	3,096	101	3.3	135	13	9.7	60	1	[2]
College 1 year or more	2,535	50	2.0	2,419	47	2.0	78	3	3.3	45	7	[2]

Source: "Selected Characteristics of Families, by Type of Family, Related Children Under 18, Number of Workers, Race and Hispanic Origin of Householder, and Poverty Status in 1988," *Money Income and Poverty Status in the United States:1988*, 1989, pp. 82-85. Notes: 1. Persons of Hispanic origin may be of any race. 2. Base less than 75,000.

★ 397 ★
Families in Poverty: Trends

Characteristic	1959	1970	1975	1980	1985	1986	1987
All Families with Children <18							
All Races	20.3	11.6	13.3	14.7	16.7	16.3	16.2
Whites	15.8	8.5	10.3	11.2	13.3	13.0	12.4
Blacks	[1]	34.9	33.9	35.5	36.0	35.4	37.3
Hispanics	[1]	[1]	29.1	27.2	32.1	30.8	32.1

Continued.

Families in Poverty: Trends
[Continued]

Characteristic	1959	1970	1975	1980	1985	1986	1987
Married-Couple Families							
with Children <18							
All Races	[1]	[1]	7.2	7.7	8.9	8.0	7.8
Whites	[1]	[1]	6.3	6.8	8.2	7.5	7.0
Blacks	[1]	[1]	16.5	15.5	12.9	11.5	13.6
Hispanics	[1]	[1]	[1]	[1]	[1]	[1]	[1]
Female-Headed Families							
with Children <18							
All Races	59.9	43.8	44.0	42.9	45.4	46.0	46.1
Whites	51.7	[1]	37.3	35.9	38.7	39.8	38.7
Blacks	[1]	[1]	57.5	56.0	58.9	58.0	59.5
Hispanics	[1]	[1]	[1]	[1]	64.0	59.5	60.7
All Families							
with Children <6							
All Races	[1]	[1]	16.1	18.4	20.6	19.6	19.8
Whites	[1]	[1]	12.8	14.0	16.7	15.7	15.2
Blacks	[1]	[1]	36.6	41.7	42.0	41.2	43.1
Married-Couple Families							
with Children <6							
All Races	[1]	[1]	9.0	9.8	11.1	9.8	9.9
Whites	[1]	[1]	8.0	8.7	10.4	9.3	8.7
Blacks	[1]	[1]	17.7	18.2	14.6	13.0	18.2
Female-Headed Families							
with Children <6							
All Races	[1]	[1]	57.3	60.6	61.3	60.6	60.5
Whites	[1]	[1]	54.1	55.1	55.4	55.0	54.8
Blacks	[1]	[1]	62.8	67.4	70.4	68.9	68.0

Source: "Families in Poverty by Race/Hispanic Origin and Family Type, 1959- 1987," *U.S. Children and their Families,* 1989, p. 113. Primary source: U.S. Bureau of the Census, Current Population Reports, Series P-60, No. 106, Table 20; No. 133, Table 19; No. 147, Table 19; No. 158, Table 15; No. 160, Table 15; No. 163, February 1989, Tables 3 and 15. *Notes:* Related children include biological, step-, and adopted children of the householder, and any other children related to the householder by blood, marriage, or adoption. Hispanic data for children under 6 are not available. 1. Not available.

★ 398 ★
Families in Poverty: Trends by Region

Numbers in thousands. Families as of March 1988.

Characteristic	1987 Black	1987 White	1982 Black	1982 White	1979 Black	1979 White
United States						
Type of Family						
All families	2,149	4,592	2,158	5,118	1,666	3,515
Percent below poverty level	29.9	8.2	33.0	9.6	27.6	6.8
Married-couple	454	2,440	543	3,104	437	2,058
Percent below poverty level	12.3	5.2	15.6	6.9	13.0	7.4
Female householder, no husband present	1,593	1,930	1,535	1,813	1,195	1,328
Percent below poverty level	51.8	26.7	56.2	27.9	49.2	22.3
All other families	102	223	79	201	34	130

Continued.

Families in Poverty: Trends by Region
[Continued]

Characteristic	1987 Black	1987 White	1982 Black	1982 White	1979 Black	1979 White
Percent below poverty level	24.3	10.3	25.6	12.2	13.3	9.1
Householder 65 years and older	215	511	239	632	205	587
Percent below poverty level	23.7	5.4	29.4	7.3	25.9	7.4
South						
Type of Family						
All families	1,237	1,636	1,177	1,850	922	1,297
Percent below poverty level	31.1	8.8	34.2	10.6	30.0	8.0
Female householder, no husband present	864	601	778	557	616	338
Percent below poverty level	52.6	26.1	56.4	28.0	52.8	20.2
All other families	373	1,034	399	1,294	306	960
Percent below poverty level	16.0	6.4	19.3	8.4	16.1	6.6
Householder 65 years and older	151	235	177	337	151	290
Percent below poverty level	27.9	7.4	36.3	11.4	3104	11.2
North and West						
Type of Family						
All families	913	2,957	981	3,268	745	2.218
Percent below poverty level	28.5	7.9	31.8	9.1	25.1	6.3
Female householder, no husband present	729	1,328	757	1,256	580	990
Percent below poverty level	50.9	26.9	56.0	27.8	46.0	23.1
All other families	183	1,628	114	2,012	166	1,228
Percent below poverty level	10.4	5.0	12.9	6.4	9.7	4.0
Householder 65 years and older	64	276	62	296	54	298
Percent below poverty level	17.6	4.4	19.1	5.2	17.5	5.6

Source: "Selected Characteristics of Families Below the Poverty Level: 1987, 1982, and 1979," *The Black Population in the United States: March 1988*, p. 16. Primary source: Current Population Reports, Series p-20, No. 442, *The Black Population in the United States: March 1988.*

★ 399 ★
Families with Children

In thousands, except as indicated. As of March. Excludes members of Armed Forces except those living off post or with their families on post. Based on Current Population Survey.

Percent Distribution	1987 All races[1] Total[2]	Married couple	Female house- holder[3]	White Total[2]	Married couple	Black Total[2]	Married couple	Hispanic[4] Total[2]	Married couple
Total	100.0	100.0	100.0	100.0	100.0	100.0	100.0	100.0	100.0
Size of family:									
2 persons	40.8	38.4	46.9	42.2	39.6	32.9	28.3	25.3	20.7
3 persons	23.9	22.7	29.8	23.6	22.6	26.4	24.3	22.8	20.7
4 persons	21.1	23.3	13.5	21.2	23.3	20.2	23.6	25.0	27.6
5 persons	9.1	10.2	5.3	8.8	9.9	10.8	12.7	14.9	17.3
6 persons	3.2	3.5	2.4	2.9	3.2	5.1	6.2	6.7	7.9
7 or more persons	1.8	1.8	2.0	1.4	1.5	4.7	4.9	5.3	5.9
Own children under age 18:									
None	50.5	52.2	39.7	52.0	53.1	41.0	45.9	35.1	34.8
1	21.3	19.5	29.5	20.7	19.2	25.1	22.0	22.3	21.6

Continued.

Families with Children
[Continued]

Percent Distribution	1987							
	All races[1]			White		Black		Hispanic[4]	
	Total[2]	Married couple	Female house-holder[3]	Total[2]	Married couple	Total[2]	Married couple	Total[2]	Married couple
2	18.5	18.6	19.8	18.3	18.5	19.5	18.6	23.2	23.7
3	6.9	7.0	7.3	6.6	6.8	8.8	8.5	12.9	13.4
4 or more	2.8	2.7	3.6	2.4	2.5	5.6	5.0	6.5	6.6
Own children under age 6:									
None	77.2	76.8	76.9	77.7	77.0	74.3	75.3	64.2	62.2
1	15.6	15.6	16.9	15.2	15.3	18.1	17.7	22.7	23.6
2 or more	7.2	7.6	6.2	7.1	7.6	7.6	7.0	13.1	14.2

Source: "Families, by Size and Presence of Children: 1980 to 1987," *Statistical Abstract*, 1989, p. 50. Primary source: U.S. Bureau of the Census, *Current Population Reports*, Series P-20, No. 424 and earlier reports. *Notes:* 1. Includes other races, not shown separately. 2. Includes other types of families, not shown separately. 3. No spouse present. 4. Hispanic persons may be of any race.

★ 400 ★
Families with Children: Income

Race	Total Children[1]	Children With Both Parents	Children With Mom Only	Mother Only	
				Divorced/ Spouse Absent	Never Married
All Races					
Number of Children	61,271	45,942	13,521	8,381	4,302
<$10,000	18.1	6.2	57.6	48.4	79.2
$10,000-19,999	17.0	14.6	24.0	27.8	15.3
$20,000-29,999	16.7	18.4	11.0	14.3	3.5
$30,000-49,999	28.6	35.5	6.1	7.8	1.8
$50,000 and over	19.6	25.4	1.3	1.7	.2
Mean Income	33,394	40,067	11,989	13,934	7,054
White					
Number of Children	49,911	40,287	8,160	6,137	1,482
<$10,000	13.5	5.7	50.4	45.5	75.6
$10,000-19,999	16.0	13.7	26.1	28.2	17.6
$20,000-29,999	17.6	18.3	14.0	15.9	4.0
$30,000-49,999	31.1	36.2	7.6	8.6	2.2
$50,000 and over	21.8	26.2	1.9	1.9	.5
Mean Income	35,953	40,833	13,754	14,658	7,829
Black					
Number of Children	8,986	3,739	4,959	1,981	2,736
<$10,000	43.9	9.4	70.0	57.3	81.2
$10,000-19,999	21.7	22.8	20.3	26.2	14.2
$20,000-29,999	12.6	21.5	6.0	10.2	3.1
$30,000-49,999	15.3	31.2	3.4	5.4	1.5
$50,000 and over	6.5	15.1	.3	.8	.0
Mean Income	18,500	31,423	8,929	11,617	6,596
Hispanic					
Number of Children	6,544	4,497	1,845	1,135	600

Continued.

Families with Children: Income
[Continued]

Race	Total Children[1]	Children With Both Parents	Children With Mom Only	Mother Only Divorced/ Spouse Absent	Mother Only Never Married
<$10,000	30.7	14.7	68.9	65.3	79.7
$10,000-19,999	27.1	29.4	22.1	25.2	13.8
$20,000-29,999	16.7	21.0	5.6	6.0	3.3
$30,000-49,999	17.6	23.8	2.8	3.0	2.7
$50,000 and over	8.0	11.1	.7	.4	.3
Mean Income	21,921	27,159	9,507	9,976	7,540

Source: "Distribution of Family Income of Children by Family Type and Race/Hispanic Origin, 1987," *U.S. Children and their Families,* 1989, p. 105. Primary source: Calculations by Child Trends, Inc., from data in Current Population Survey, *Marital Status and Living Arrangements: March 1988,* Series P-20, No. 433, Table 9. *Notes:* 1. Refers to all children living with one or both parents, under 18 years. Published by permission.

★ 401 ★
Families, Characteristics of

Except as noted, as of March and based on Current Population Survey. See also *Historical Statistics, Colonial Times to 1970,* series A353-358.

Race, Hispanic Origin, and Year	Number of families	Percent Distribution by Number of Own Children Under 18 Years Old						Average size of family
		All families	None	1	2	3	4 or more	
All Families[1]								
1970	51,586	100.0	44.1	18.2	17.4	10.6	9.8	3.58
1975	55,712	100.0	46.0	19.7	18.0	9.3	6.9	3.42
1980	59,550	100.0	47.9	20.9	19.3	7.8	4.1	3.29
1985	62,706	100.0	50.4	20.9	18.6	7.2	3.0	3.23
1987	64,491	100.0	50.5	21.3	18.5	6.9	2.8	3.19
White Families								
1970	46,261	100.0	44.8	18.2	17.7	10.5	8.8	3.52
1975	49,451	100.0	47.2	19.4	18.0	9.2	6.2	3.36
1980	52,243	100.0	49.3	20.5	19.1	7.5	3.6	3.23
1985	54,400	100.0	51.8	20.5	18.3	6.8	2.6	3.16
1987	55,676	100.0	52.0	20.7	18.3	6.6	2.4	3.13
Black Families								
1970	4,887	100.0	38.9	17.6	14.8	10.1	18.5	4.13
1975	5,498	100.0	36.8	22.0	17.0	10.6	13.6	3.90
1980	6,184	100.0	38.2	23.4	20.0	10.2	8.2	3.67
1985	6,778	100.0	42.6	23.3	19.6	9.0	5.5	3.60
1987	7,096	100.0	41.0	25.1	19.5	8.8	5.6	3.52
Hispanic Families[2]								
1970	2,004	100.0	29.8	19.5	19.4	13.3	18.1	[3]
1975	2,447	100.0	29.4	23.1	19.7	13.4	14.5	[3]
1980	3,029	100.0	31.2	22.4	23.0	13.4	9.9	3.90
1985	3,939	100.0	33.9	22.9	22.0	12.2	8.9	3.88

Continued.

Families, Characteristics of
[Continued]

Race, Hispanic Origin, and Year	Number of families	Percent Distribution by Number of Own Children Under 18 Years Old						Average size of family
		All families	None	1	2	3	4 or more	
1987	4,403	100.0	35.1	22.3	23.2	12.9	6.5	3.83

Source: "Families, by Number of Own Children Under 18 Years Old: 1970 to 1987," *Statistical Abstract,* 1989, p. 51. Primary source: U.S. Bureau of the Census: *U.S. Census of Population, 1970; Current Population Reports,* Series P-20, No. 424 and earlier reports. *Notes:* 1. Includes other races, not shown separately. 2. Hispanic persons may be of any race. 1970 data as of April. Based on Census of Population. 3. Not available.

★ 402 ★
Families, Characteristics of

As of March.

Presence of Parents and Marital Status	1987					
	Number (1,000)			Percent distribution		
	Total[1]	White	Black	Total[1]	White	Black
Total with children under 18	34,242	28,180	4,963	100.0	100.0	100.0
Two-parent family groups	25,005	22,076	2,058	73.0	78.3	41.5
One-parent family groups	9,236	6,104	2,904	27.0	21.7	58.5
Maintained by mother	8,128	5,190	2,747	23.7	18.4	55.3
Never married	2,575	1,015	1,512	7.5	3.6	30.5
Spouse absent	1,734	1,116	563	5.1	4.0	11.3
Separated	1,512	970	499	4.4	3.4	10.1
Divorced	3,309	2,708	535	9.7	9.6	10.8
Widowed	511	353	139	1.5	1.3	2.8
Maintained by father	1,107	914	157	3.2	3.2	3.2
Never married	209	148	55	.6	.5	1.1
Spouse absent	252	209	29	.7	.7	.6
Divorced	576	497	65	1.7	1.8	1.3
Widowed	69	58	7	.2	.2	.1

Source: "Family Groups with Children Under 18, by Race and Type: 1970 to 1987," *Statistical Abstract,* 1989, p. 50. Primary source: Based on Current Population Survey. *Note:* 1. Includes other races, not shown separately.

★ 403 ★
Families: Poverty Status & Other Characteristics

Numbers in thousands. Families as of March 1989.

Characteristic	Total			White			Black			Hispanic origin[1]		
		Below poverty level			Below poverty level			Below poverty level			Below poverty level	
	Total	No.	% of total	Total	No.	% of total	Total	No.	% of total	Total	No.	% of total
All Families												
Educational Attainment of Householder												
Total, 25 years or older	62,831	5,984	9.5	54,114	3,920	7.2	6,863	1,764	25.7	4,396	978	22.2
No years of school completed	268	110	41.2	165	59	35.9	42	15	[4]	129	50	39.0
Elementary: Less than 8 years	3,841	962	25.0	2,978	662	22.2	746	262	35.1	1,073	343	31.9
8 years	3,106	491	15.8	2,696	348	12.9	322	112	34.9	305	91	30.0
High school: 1 to 3 years	7,308	1,462	20.0	5,827	871	14.9	1,315	535	40.7	690	219	31.7
4 years	23,061	2,064	8.9	20,110	1,366	6.8	2,498	617	24.7	1,187	190	16.0
College: 1 year or more	25,248	894	3.5	22,339	613	2.7	1,940	224	11.5	1,013	85	8.4
Percent a high school graduate	76.9	49.4	[3]	78.4	50.5	[3]	64.7	47.6	[3]	50.1	28.1	[3]
Number of Workers[2]												
Total	65,066	6,844	10.5	55,875	4,445	8.0	7,276	2,084	28.6	4,759	1,137	23.9

Continued.

Families: Poverty Status & Other Characteristics
[Continued]

Characteristic	Total	Total Below poverty level No.	Total Below poverty level % of total	White Total	White Below poverty level No.	White Below poverty level % of total	Black Total	Black Below poverty level No.	Black Below poverty level % of total	Hispanic origin[1] Total	Hispanic origin[1] Below poverty level No.	Hispanic origin[1] Below poverty level % of total
No workers	9,444	2,814	29.8	7,823	1,672	21.4	1,366	993	72.7	624	429	68.8
One worker	17,872	2,802	15.7	14,831	1,869	12.6	2,542	840	33.0	1,538	472	30.5
Two workers	28,571	1,028	3.6	25,201	767	3.0	2,562	212	8.3	1,847	183	9.9
Three worker or more	9,180	200	2.2	8,020	137	1.7	807	39	4.9	741	52	7.1
Employment Status of Householder												
Employed	46,764	2,592	5.5	40,860	1,898	4.6	4,517	598	13.2	3,453	516	15.0
Unemployed	1,965	675	34.4	1,449	381	26.3	435	259	59.4	186	82	43.9
Not in labor force	16,338	3,576	21.9	13,566	2,165	16.0	2,325	1,228	52.8	1,120	538	48.1
In Armed Forces	770	32	4.1	617	26	4.2	133	6	4.1	64	4	4

Source: "Selected Characteristics of Families, by Type of Family, Race, and Hispanic Origin of Householder, and Poverty Status in 1988," *Money Income and Poverty Status in the United States: 1988,* 1989, pp. 68-75. Primary source: U.S. Bureau of the Census, Current Population Reports, Series P-60, No. 166. *Notes:* 1. Persons of Hispanic origin may be of any race. 2. Restricted to families with civilian householder. 3. Not applicable. Base less than 75,000.

★ 404 ★
Families: Types and Characteristics

Numbers in thousands.

Characteristics	Black Total	Black Married couple families	Black Other families Female house-holder, no husband present	Black Other families Male house-holder, no wife present	White Total	White Married couple families	White Other families Female house-holder, no husband present	White Other families Male house-holder, no wife present
Total, all families	7,177	3,682	3,074	421	56,044	46,644	7,235	2,165
Size of Family								
Mean number of persons	3.49	3.63	3.41	2.89	3.12	3.19	2.79	2.63
Age of Householder								
Percent	100.0	100.0	100.0	100.0	100.0	100.0	100.0	100.0
15 to 34 years	34.6	29.2	41.4	33.7	26.6	25.7	30.5	33.4
35 to 44 years	24.6	25.1	24.3	21.9	24.2	23.8	26.8	23.9
45 to 54 years	16.6	17.6	15.1	17.8	17.0	17.4	15.0	15.5
55 years and over	24.2	28.1	19.2	26.6	32.3	33.2	27.7	27.2
Related Children Under 18 Years								
Percent	100.0	100.0	100.0	100.0	100.0	100.0	100.0	100.0
No related children	32.2	40.0	20.7	48.0	50.2	52.0	37.7	53.9
With related children	67.8	60.0	79.2	51.8	49.8	48.0	62.3	46.1
Mean number of related children	1.32	1.15	1.59	0.85	0.90	0.89	1.06	0.70
Own Children Under 18 Years								
Percent	100.0	100.0	100.0	100.0	100.0	100.0	100.0	100.0
No own children	41.5	45.2	34.3	62.0	52.5	53.5	43.8	60.6
With own children	58.5	54.8	65.7	38.0	47.5	46.5	56.2	39.4
Mean number per family with own children	1.85	1.86	1.87	1.57	1.80	1.84	1.67	1.50
Own Children Under 6 Years								
Percent	100.0	100.0	100.0	100.0	100.0	100.0	100.0	100.0
No own children	73.8	73.6	72.6	84.3	78.1	77.5	79.5	87.3
With own children	26.2	26.4	27.4	15.7	21.9	22.5	20.5	12.7

Continued.

Families: Types and Characteristics
[Continued]

Characteristics	Black				White			
			Other families				Other families	
	Total	Married couple families	Female householder, no husband present	Male householder, no wife present	Total	Married couple families	Female householder, no husband present	Male householder, no wife present
Mean number per family with own children	1.28	1.26	1.28		1.35	1.36	1.29	1.31

Source: "Characteristics of Families, by Type and Race of Householder: March 1988, *The Black Population in the United States: March 1988,* p. 24. Primary source: Current Population Reports, Series P-20, No. 442. *The Black Population in the United States: March 1988.*

★ 405 ★
Families: Who is Unemployed

Characteristics	African American	White
Total in Families		
No employed person	40.9	27.3
At least one employed person	59.1	72.
At least one full-time employed person	49.8	63.5
Husbands		
No employed person	35.6	37.6
At least one employed person	64.4	62.4
At least one full-time employed person	52.5	47.6
Wives		
No employed person	22.2	15.6
At least one employed person	77.8	84.4
At least one full-time employed person	67.8	77.9
Female Heads		
No employed person	88.1	80.0
At least one employed person	11.9	20.0
At least one full-time employed person	6.5	12.6

Source: "Percentage Comparison of African American and White Unemployed by Family Relationship and Presence of Other Employed Family Members, 1988," *The State of Black American 1990,* January 1990, p. 219. Primary source: Bureau of Labor Statistics, *Employment and Earnings,* January 1989, Table 50, p. 215. Extracted from: *The State of Black America,* January 1990. Published by permission.

★ 406 ★
Family Income

Minus sign (-) indicates decrease.

Year	Median Income in Current Dollars				Median Income in Constant (1987) Dollars				Annual Percent Change of Median Income of All Families	
	All families[1]	White	Black	Hispanic[2]	All families[1]	White	Black	Hispanic[2]	Current dollars	Constant dollars
1960	5,620	5,835	3,230[3]	[5]	21,567	22,393	12,396	[5]	4.9[4]	2.9[4]
1965	6,957	7,251	3,993[3]	[5]	25,059	26,119	14,383	[5]	4.4	3.1
1970	9,867	10,236	6,279	[5]	28,880	29,960	18,378	[5]	7.2	2.9
1971	10,285	10,672	6,440	[5]	28,862	29,949	18,072	[5]	4.2	-.1
1972	11,116	11,549	6,864	8,183	30,199	31,375	18,647	22,231	8.1	4.6
1973	12,051	12,595	7,269	8,715	30,820	32,211	18,590	22,289	8.4	2.1
1974	12,902	13,408	8,006	9,540	29,735	30,901	18,451	21,986	7.1	-3.5
1975	13,719	14,268	8,779	9,551	28,970	30,129	18,538	20,168	6.3	-2.6
1976	14,958	15,537	9,242	10,259	29,863	31,019	18,451	20,482	9.0	3.1
1977	16,009	16,740	9,563	11,421	30,025	31,396	17,935	21,420	7.0	.5
1978	17,640	18,368	10,879	12,566	30,730	31,998	18,952	21,891	10.2	2.3
1979	19,587	20,439	11,574	14,169	30,669	32,003	18,122	22,185	11.0	-.2
1980	21,023	21,904	12,674	14,716	28,996	30,211	17,481	20,297	7.3	-5.5
1981	22,388	23,517	13,266	16,401	27,977	29,388	16,578	20,495	6.5	-3.5
1982	23,433	24,603	13,598	16,227	27,591	28,969	16,011	19,106	4.7	-1.4
1983	24,674	25,837	14,561	16,930	28,147	29,474	16,610	19,313	5.3	2.0
1984	26,433	27,686	15,432	18,833	28,923	30,294	16,884	20,606	7.1	2.8
1985	27,735	29,152	16,786	19,027	29,302	30,799	17,734	20,102	4.9	1.3
1986	29,458	30,809	17,604	19,995	30,534	31,935	18,247	20,726	6.2	4.2
1987	30,853	32,274	18,098	20,306	30,853	32,274	18,098	20,306	4.7	1.0

Source: "Money Income of Families — Median Family Income in Current and Constant (1987) Dollars, by Race and Hispanic Origin of Householder: 1960 to 1987," *Statistical Abstract*, 1989, p. 445. Primary source: Current Population Reports, U.S. Bureau of the Census, series P-60, No. 161, and unpublished data. *Notes:* 1. Includes other races not shown separately. 2. Hispanic persons may be of any race. 3. For 1960 and 1965, Black and other races. 4. Change from 1955. 5. Not available.

★ 407 ★
Family Income Ranges: Trends

Income	1988		1987		1986		1978		1970		1980	
	Blk	Wht	Blk	Wht	Blk	Wht	Blk	Wht	Blk	Wht	Blk	Wht
Under $5,000	11.9	3.0	12.6	3.0	12.5	3.1	8.1	2.4	8.4	2.3	10.1	2.6
Less Than $10,000	27.3	8.5	28.5	8.7	28.0	9.1	25.6	8.5	24.6	8.0	27.4	9.0
$10,000 - 34,999	46.7	43.2	46.9	43.3	47.5	44.2	51.2	47.7	56.3	45.4	51.9	48.0
More Than $35,000	25.9	48.4	24.6	47.8	24.4	46.7	23.3	43.8	19.2	46.6	20.7	43.0
More Than $50,000	12.6	27.4	10.8	26.8	10.8	25.8	10.0	21.1	6.1	23.2	8.0	21.0

Source: "Percentage of Black Families Receiving Incomes in Selected Ranges," *The State of Black American 1990*, January 1990, p. 29. Primary source: U.S. Department of Commerce, Bureau of the Census, *Money Income and Poverty Status in 1988*, Table 7-7. Extracted from: *The State of Black America*, January 1990. Published by permission. *Note:* Totals may not equal to 100.0 due to rounding.

★ 408 ★
Family Income Related to Unemployment

Characteristics	No Unemploy- ment	African- American Some Unemploy- ment	Percent Unemploy- ment
Total	24,883	13,553	-45.5
Husbands	30,759	16,757	-45.5
Wives	32,635	2,894	-36.0
Female heads	15,971	5,204	-67.4
		White	
Total	33,465	21,175	-36.7
Husbands	37,092	21,175	-41.5
Wives	37,587	26,998	-28.2
Female heads	20,679	8,567	-58.6

Source: "Comparison of African American and White Family Income by Occurrence of Unemployment, 1985," *The State of Black America 1990*, January 1990, p. 216. Primary source: Bureau of Labor Statistics, *Linking Employment Problems to Economic Status*, August 1987, Table 4, p. 11. Extracted from: *The State of Black America*, January 1990. Published by permission.

★ 409 ★
Family Median Income: Trends

Year	Median Family Income		B/W	B/W	Aggregate[1] Gap (bil.)
	Black	White			
1988	19,329	33,915	57.0	14,586	111
1987	19,168	33,725	56.8	14,557	107
1986	19,001	33,255	57.1	14,254	104
1985	18,455	32,051	57.6	13,596	99
1982	16,670	30,161	55.3	13,491	91
1980	18,196	31,447	57.9	13,251	83
1978	19,739	33,327	59.2	13,588	80
1970	19,144	31,209	61.3	12,065	61

Source: "Median Family Income, Selected Years (1988$)," *The State of Black America 1990*, January 1990, p. 28. Primary source: U.S. Department of Commerce, Bureau of the Census, *Money Income and Poverty Status in 1988*, Table 7. Calculations of aggregates and gaps done by author. Extracted from: *The State of Black America*, January 1990. Published by permission. *Notes:* 1. Equals (Mean White Family Income - Mean Black Family Income) x Number of Black Families.

★ 410 ★
Family Social Class: Trends

Characteristic	1969		1983		1986	
	Families	%	Families	%	Families	%
Upper Class	143,000	3	267,000	4	624,000	9
Middle Class	1,100,000	25	1,500,000	25	1,910,000	27
Working Class (Non Poor)	2,100,000	44	2,400,000	36	2,420,000	34
Working Class (Poor)	688,000	14	963,000	14	---	---
Under Class (Nonworking Poor)	716,000	14	1,500,00	23	2,142,000	30

Source: "Social Class of African-American Families, 1969-1986," *Black Issues in Higher Education*, February 1, 1990, p. 27. Primary source: U.S. Bureau of Census.

★ 411 ★
Family Structure and Social Class

Numbers in percent.

Class	Married Couple	Single-Parent	Working-Wife
Upper Class	96	4	50
Middle Class	83	17	78
Working Class (Nonpoor)	60	40	45
Working Class (Poor)	33	67	33
Under Class (Nonworking Poor)	25	75	25

Source: "African-American Social Class and Family Structure," *Black Issues in Higher Education*, February 1, 1990, p. 27. Primary source: U.S. Bureau of the Census..

★ 412 ★
Family Structure: Trends

Families with children:	1960	1970	1975	1980	1985	1990[1]
Two Parents	78	64	54	48	40	37
Mother only	20	33	44	49	57	60
Father only	2	3	3	3	3	3

Source: "African-American Family Structure, 1960-1990 (in percentages)," *The State of Black America 1990*, January 1990, p. 91. Primary source: U.S. Bureau of the Census, *Household and Family Characteristics*, March 1985 (Current Population Reports, Population Characteristics, Series P-20, No. 411), p. 9. Extracted from: *The State of Black America*, January 1990. Published by permission. *Note:* 1. 1990 estimated by author.

★ 413 ★
Family Total Money Income: Characteristics

Numbers in thousands.

	Black						White					
		Married-couple families			Female house-holder, no husband present	Male house-holder, no wife present		Married-couple families			Female house-holder, no husband present	Male house-holder, no wife present
	All families	Total[1]	Husband only earner	Husband and wife earners			All families	Total[1]	Husband only earner	Husband and wife earners		
United States												
Total	7,177	3,682	520	2,226	3,074	421	56,044	46,644	8,538	26,630	7,235	2,165
Median income (dollars)	18,098	27,182	18,812	35,276	9,710	17,455	32,274	35,295	30,002	41,596	17,018	26,230
Standard error (dollars)	390	701	1,227	663	300	1,242	147	163	311	212	300	562
Mean income (dollars)	23,252	31,426	20,482	39,103	13,744	21,183	38,203	41,118	36,687	47,295	21,529	31,112
Standard error (dollars)	345	521	838	691	333	1,338	175	196	482	259	302	806
South												
Total	3,972	2,101	283	1,326	1,642	229	18,559	15,656	2,871	8,997	2,302	601
Median income (dollars)	17,302	25,293	17,210	32,644	9,431	15,002	30,729	33,390	27,992	39,951	16,395	23,058
Standard error (dollars)	447	755	1,312	766	414	1,609	263	370	561	364	576	1,518
Mean income (dollars)	22,135	29,528	18,812	36,215	13,112	18,999	36,336	39,038	34,954	45,090	20,107	28,115
Standard error (dollars)	411	628	1,000	817	435	1,556	294	329	830	430	486	1,257
North and West												
Total	3,204	1,581	237	900	1,432	192	37,485	30,988	5,667	17,633	4,933	1,564
Median income (dollars)	19,124	30,138	20,942	38,794	10,001	19,129	33,129	36,086	30,846	42,531	17,282	26,887
Standard error (dollars)	516	836	935	915	462	1,212	206	193	311	266	353	549
Mean income (dollars)	24,637	33,949	22,474	43,361	14,469	23,794	39,127	42,168	37,565	48,419	22,193	32,264
Standard error (dollars)	481	774	1,225	1,044	451	2,002	208	234	567	310	364	958

Source: "Total Money Income in 1987 of Families, by Type, Earner Status, Region, and Race: March 1988," *The Black Population in the United States: March 1988*, p. 30. Primary source: Current Population Reports, Series P-20, No. 442, *The Black Population in the United States: March 1988. Notes:* 1. Includes other combinations of earners such as wife only, and wife and children, not shown separately.

★ 414 ★
Family Type and Employment Profile

Characteristics	African American	White
All Families		
No employed person	40.7	25.0
At least one employed person	59.3	75.0
At least one full-time employed person	50.1	65.7
Married-Couple Families		
No employed person	18.5	18.3
At least one employed person	81.5	81.7
At least one full-time employed person	71.7	72.6
Female-Headed Families		
No employed person	57.7	48.7
At least one employed person	42.3	51.3
At least one full-time employed person	33.3	41.2

Source: "Percentage Comparison of African American and White Families Affected by Unemployment by Presence of Other Employed Members, 1988, *The State of Black America 1990*, January 1990, p. 218. Primary source: Bureau of Labor Statistics, *Employment and Earnings*, January 1989, Table 49, p. 214. Extracted from: *The State of Black America*, January 1990. Published by permission.

★ 415 ★
Family Types: Trends

Race of householder	Number (thou.)					Percent				
	1960	1970	1975	1980	1981	1960	1970	1975	1980	1981
Families, total	45,111	51,586[1]	55,712[1]	59,550[1]	60,309[1]	---	---	---	---	---
White	40,869	46,261	49,451	52,243	52,710	100.0	100.0	100.0	100.0	100.0
Married couple	36,212	41,049	42,969	44,751	44,860	88.7	88.7	86.9	85.7	85.1
Male householder[2]	1,100	1,048	1,270	1,441	1,584	2.6	2.3	2.6	2.8	3.0
Female householder[2]	3,557	4,165	5,212	6,052	6,266	8.7	9.0	10.5	11.6	11.9
Black	4,242[3]	4,887	5,498	6,184	6,317	100.0[3]	100.0	100.0	100.0	100.0
Married couple	3,117[3]	3,323	3,346	3,433	3,392	73.6[3]	68.0	60.9	55.5	53.7
Male householder[2]	175[3]	182	212	256	291	4.0[3]	3.7	3.9	4.1	4.6
Female householder[2]	950[3]	1,382	1,940	2,495	2,634	22.4[3]	28.3	35.3	40.3	41.7

Source: "Families, by Race of Householder: 1960-1981," *Running the Gauntlet: Black Men in America*, August 1984 (Table 1, no page given). Primary source: U.S. Bureau of the Census, Current Population Reports, Series P-20, No. 371 and unpublished data. *Historical Statistics, Colonial Times to 1970*, Series A 292-295 and A 320-334. Extracted from: McGhee, James D., *Running the Gauntlet: Black Men in America*, National Urban League, Inc., Washington, DC, August 1984. Published by permission. *Notes:* 1. Includes other races, not shown separately. 2. No spouse present. 3. Black and other races.

★ 416 ★
Father-Absent Minor Children: Trends

Characteristic	Number in U.S. Population (in millions)			
	1978	1981	1983	1985
All women with minor children from an absent father	7.1	8.4	8.7	8.8
Race and Hispanic Origin				
White	5.1	6.0	6.2	6.3
Black	1.9	2.3	2.3	2.3
Hispanic origin	.5	.6	.8	.8

Source: "Women with Minor Children From an Absent Father, 1978-1985, *U.S. Children and their Families*, 1989, p. 120. Primary source: U.S. Bureau of the Census, Current Population Reports, Series P-23, No. 112, 1981, Tables B, 1; No. 140, 1985, Tables B, 1; No. 141, 1985, Tables C, 1; No. 152, 1987, Tables E, 1.

★ 417 ★
Household Presence of Parents: Trends

Characteristic	1960	1970	1980	1985	1987	1988
All children under 18						
Two Parents	87.7	85.2	76.7	73.9	73.1	72.7
Mother only	8.0	10.8	18.0	20.9	21.3	21.4
Father only	1.1	1.1	1.7	2.5	2.6	2.9
Neither parent	3.2	2.9	3.6	2.7	2.8	3.0
White children						
Two parents	90.9	89.5	82.7	80.0	79.1	78.9
Mother only	6.1	7.8	13.5	15.6	16.1	16.0
Father only	1.0	.9	1.6	2.4	2.6	2.9
Neither parent	1.9	1.8	2.2	2.0	2.1	2.2

Continued.

Household Presence of Parents: Trends
[Continued]

Characteristic	1960	1970	1980	1985	1987	1988
Black children						
Two parents	67.0	58.5	42.2	39.5	40.1	38.1
Mother only	19.9	29.5	43.9	51.0	50.4	51.
Father only	2.0	2.3	1.9	2.9	2.5	3.0
Neither parent	11.1	9.7	12.0	6.6	6.8	7.4
Hispanic children						
Two parents	1	77.7	75.4	67.9	65.5	66.3
Mother only	1	1	19.6	26.6	27.7	27.2
Father only	1	1	1.5	2.2	2.8	3.0
Neither parent	1	1	3.5	3.3	3.7	3.6

Source: "Percent Distribution of U.S. Children by Presence of Parents in Household," *U.S. Children and their Families*, 1989, p. 53. Primary source: U.S. Bureau of the Census, *Statistical Abstract of the United States, 1988*, Table 69; Current Population Reports, Series P-20, Nos. 410, 418, 423, 433, *Marital Status and Living Arrangements: March 1985, March 1986, March 1987, March 1988*, Table 4 in each report and Table E in 1986 report. *Notes:* Children living with two parents include those living with a parent and stepparent and those living with adoptive parents. Children living with neither parent include those living with relatives other than their parents, with non-relatives, or in group quarters. The small number of persons under 18 maintaining their own households are not included. 1. Not available.

★ 418 ★
Households, Characteristics of

As of March. 1970 covers persons 14 years old and over; beginning 1980, covers persons 15 years old and over. Based on Current Population Survey.

Characteristic	Unit	White					Black				
		1970	1980	1985	1986	1987	1970	1980	1985	1986	1987
Female family house holder	1,000	4,185	6,052	6,941	7,111	7,227	1,349	2,495	2,964	2,874	2,967
Percent of all families	Percent	9.1	11.6	12.8	12.9	13.0	28.3	40.3	43.7	41.5	41.8
Median age	Years	50.4	43.7	42.7	42.4	42.1	41.3	37.4	38.0	37.9	37.5
Marital status:											
Single (never married)	Percent	9.2	10.6	11.9	12.8	13.8	16.2	27.3	33.4	35.4	37.3
Married, spouse absent	Percent	18.5	16.9	16.0	15.8	16.0	39.7	28.6	21.1	21.2	20.7
Separated	Percent	11.4	13.9	13.8	13.5	13.8	33.8	26.8	19.3	19.7	18.6
Other	Percent	7.2	3.0	2.1	2.3	2.2	5.9	1.8	1.7	1.5	2.1
Widowed	Percent	47.0	32.7	28.3	28.6	27.8	29.9	22.2	21.2	18.4	18.0
Divorced	Percent	25.3	39.8	43.8	42.8	42.4	14.2	21.9	24.5	25.1	24.0
Presence of children under 18:											
No own children	Percent	52.0	41.2	43.5	43.2	42.7	33.5	28.1	34.5	32.7	31.8
With own children	Percent	48.0	58.8	56.5	56.8	57.3	66.6	71.9	65.5	67.3	68.3
1 child	Percent	18.8	28.1	28.9	29.3	29.6	19.1	26.3	27.5	25.0	29.2
2 children	Percent	15.0	19.9	18.6	19.2	19.1	14.4	23.2	21.6	22.8	22.1
3 children	Percent	7.8	7.4	6.4	5.9	6.3	12.5	11.1	10.1	11.7	10.0
4 or more children	Percent	6.4	3.4	2.6	2.4	2.3	20.6	11.3	6.3	7.8	6.9
Children per family	Number	1.00	1.03	.96	.95	.96	1.83	1.51	1.29	1.34	1.28

Source: "Female Family Householders with No Spouse Present — Characteristics, by Race: 1970 to 1987," *Statistical Abstracts*, 1989, p. 52. Primary source: U.S. Bureau of the Census, *Current Population Reports*, series P-20, No 424 and earlier reports.

★ 419 ★
Income Characteristics

Families as of March 1988. Based on Current Population Survey.

	Number (1,000)				Median Family Income (dollars)			
Characteristic	All families	White	Black	Hispanic[1]	All families	White	Black	Hispanic[1]
All families	65,133	56,044	7,177	4,588	30,853	32,274	18,098	20,306
Region:								
Northeast	13,382	11,855	1,189	916	33,938	35,262	20,678	16,750
Midwest	15,905	14,240	1,389	306	30,991	32,149	16,755	21,985
South	22,846	18,559	3,972	1,477	28,250	30,729	17,302	18,798
West	13,000	11,389	627	1,889	32,026	32,521	20,627	22,142
Type of family:								
Married-couple families	51,809	46,644	3,682	3,204	34,700	35,295	27,182	24,677
Wife in paid labor force	29,112	25,800	2,424	1,655	40,422	41,023	33,333	31,354
Wife not in paid labor force	22,698	20,844	1,258	1,549	26,652	27,394	16,822	17,967
Male householder, no wife present	2,715	2,165	421	312	24,804	26,230	17,455	19,411
Female householder, no husband present	10,608	7,235	3,074	1,072	14,620	17,018	9,710	9,805
Number of earners:[2]								
Total	64,228	55,324	7,030	4,514	30,951	32,372	17,990	20,264
No earners	9,440	7,803	1,396	648	12,849	14,924	5,528	6,262
One earner	18,009	15,064	2,396	1,458	23,192	25,369	13,774	15,148
Two earners	27,748	24,559	2,442	1,791	36,990	37,731	29,922	27,201
Three earners	6,329	5,545	569	419	46,961	47,860	37,458	34,183
Four or more earners	2,703	2,353	227	199	59,445	60,221	49,929	49,004

Source: "Money Income of Families — Median Family Income by Race and Hispanic Origin: 1987," *Statistical Abstract,* 1989, p. 446. Primary source: U.S. Bureau of the Census, *Current Population Reports,* series P-60, No. 161. *Notes:* 1. Hispanic persons may be of any race. 2. Excludes families with members who are in the Armed Forces.

★ 420 ★
Income Level

Families as of March of following year. Based on Current Population Survey. See *Historical Statistics, Colonial Times to 1970,* series G 31-138.

		1987			
			Race		
	All families, 1980	All families	White	Black and other	
Item				Total	Black
Number (1,000)	60,309	65,133	56,044	9,089	7,177
Income at Selected Positions (dol.)					
Upper limit of each fifth:					
Lowest	10,286	14,450	16,057	7,514	6,800
Second	17,390	25,100	27,000	15,500	13,801
Third	24,630	36,600	38,200	25,500	22,590
Fourth	34,534	52,910	54,280	41,338	36,652
Top 5 percent	54,060	86,300	88,472	69,901	62,000

Continued.

Income Level
[Continued]

Item	All families, 1980	1987			
				Race	
		All families	White	Black and other	
				Total	Black
Lowest fifth	5.1	4.6	5.1	3.2	3.3
Second fifth	11.6	10.8	11.2	8.5	8.7
Third fifth	17.5	16.9	17.0	15.3	15.5
Fourth fifth	24.3	24.1	23.8	24.8	25.1
Highest fifth	41.6	43.7	42.9	48.3	47.4
Top 5 percent	15.3	16.9	16.7	18.4	17.4

Source: "Money Income of Families — Income at Selected Positions and Percent of Aggregate Income Received by Each Fifth and Top 5 Percent of Families: 1980-1987, *Statistical Abstract,* 1989, p. 446. Primary source: U.S. Bureau of the Census, *Current Population Reports,* series P-60, No. 132 and 161.

★ 421 ★
Mothers On Their Own

Age of Youngest Child	Total	White	Black
1 year or under	45	44	47
2 years	53	59	43
3 years	59	61	57
4 years	61	66	57
5 years	64	66	59
Under 6 Years, total	54	57	51
6-17 Years, total	76	78	70
Total with Children Under 18	67	70	62

Source: "Women Maintaining Families On Their Own," *U.S. Children and their Families,* 1989, p. 81. Primary source: Unpublished data from the Bureau of Labor Statistics, 1989.

★ 422 ★
Mothers Who Work

Age, youngest child	Total	White	Black
1 year or younger	52	51	72
2 years	62	60	76
3 years	59	58	76
4 years	61	61	70
5 years	64	64	63
Under 6 years, total	57	56	73

Continued.

Mothers Who Work
[Continued]

Age, youngest child	Total	White	Black
6-17 years, total	73	72	79
Total with Children under 18[1]	65	64	76

Source: "Percentage of Mothers of Children Under 18 Who Were in the Labor Force, March 1988," *U.S. Children and their Families,* 1989, p. 81. Primary source: Unpublished data from the Bureau of Labor Statistics, 1989. *Note:* 1. Married mothers with husbands present.

★ 423 ★
Poverty

In thousands, except percent. Families as of March 1988.

Characteristic		Number Below Poverty Level			
		All races[1]	White	Black	Hispanic[2]
Total	n	7,059	4,592	2,149	1,183
	%	10.8	8.2	29.9	25.8
Age of householder					
15-24 years old	n	863	558	285	157
	%	29.5	23.8	56.7	37.8
25-34 years old	n	2,317	1,429	782	415
	%	15.4	11.4	39.4	28.9
25-44 years old	n	1,595	1,081	431	304
	%	10.1	8.0	24.4	25.5
45-54 years old	n	774	478	247	140
	%	7.0	5.0	20.8	19.6
55-64 years old	n	759	535	190	97
	%	7.8	6.2	22.9	19.0
65 years old and over	n	751	511	215	70
	%	7.2	5.4	23.7	21.6
Northeast	n	1,220	859	312	320
	%	9.1	7.2	26.3	34.9
Midwest	n	1,620	1,090	467	82
	%	10.2	7.7	33.6	26.7
South	n	2,925	1,636	1,237	398
	%	12.8	8.8	31.1	27.0
West	n	1,293	1,007	133	383
	%	9.9	8.8	21.3	30.3
Size of Family:					
2 persons	n	2,346	1,645	609	234
	%	8.7	6.9	25.4	20.0
3 persons	n	1,622	1,040	518	268
	%	10.5	7.9	28.4	24.0
4 persons	n	1,414	906	457	255
	%	10.3	7.7	29.5	22.7
5 persons	n	864	538	280	212
	%	14.8	11.1	37.4	33.9
6 persons	n	453	273	137	114
	%	22.0	17.1	40.3	35.8
7 persons	n	360	191	148	101
	%	29.5	23.5	46.6	42.3

Continued.

Poverty
[Continued]

Characteristic		Number Below Poverty Level			
		All races[1]	White	Black	Hispanic[2]
Mean size	n	3.54	3.44	3.70	4.10
	%	5	5	5	5
Mean number of children per family with children	n	2.25	2.19	2.36	2.61
	%	5	5	5	5
Education of householder:[3]					
Elementary:					
Less than 8 years	n	1,207	827	299	476
	%	28.3	25.4	36.4	40.9
8 years	n	552	403	133	89
	%	17.1	14.4	34.9	31.3
High school:					
1 to 3 years	n	1,406	810	556	203
	%	18.8	13.4	42.6	30.6
4 years	n	2,132	1,377	685	187
	%	9.3	6.9	27.8	16.3
College: 1 year or more	n	899	617	191	72
	%	3.7	2.9	11.2	7.8
Work experience of householder in 1987:[4]					
Total	n	7,022	4,567	2,137	1,178
	%	10.9	8.2	30.4	26.1
Worked	n	3,311	2,349	840	563
	%	6.7	5.4	17.5	16.2
50 to 52 weeks	n	1,334	1,012	286	269
	%	3.4	2.9	8.2	10.2
1 to 49 weeks	n	1,977	1,337	555	295
	%	19.9	16.2	41.3	34.4
Did not work	n	3,712	2,219	1,297	615
	%	25.3	18.4	58.2	59.0

Source: "Families Below Poverty Level — Selected Characteristics, by Race and Hispanic Origin: 1987," *Statistical Abstract*, 1989, p. 455. Primary source: *Current Population Reports*, Series P-60, No. 161. U.S. Bureau of the Census. *Notes:* 1. Includes other races not shown separately. 2. Hispanic persons may be of any race. 3. Householder 25 years and over. 4. Restricted to families with civilian workers. 5. Not applicable.

★ 424 ★
Poverty

Persons as of March of following year.

Characteristics	Number Below Poverty Level (1,000)					Percent Below Poverty Level				
	1970	1979[1]	1985	1986	1987	1970	1979[1]	1985	1986	1987
Persons, 65 yr. and over[2]	4,793	3,682	3,456	3,477	3,491	24.6	15.2	12.6	12.4	12.2
White	4,011	2,911	2,698	2,689	2,597	22.6	13.3	11.0	10.7	10.1
Black	735	740	717	722	808	47.7	36.3	31.5	31.0	33.9
Hispanic[3]	4	154	219	204	247	4	26.8	23.9	22.5	27.4

Source: "Persons 65 Years Old and Over Below Poverty Level, by Selected Characteristics: 1970 to 1987," *Statistical Abstract*, 1989, p. 454. Primary Source: U.S. Bureau of the Census, *Current Population Reports*, series P-60, No. 161, and unpublished data *Notes:* 1. Population controls based on 1980 census; see text, section 14. 2. Beginning 1979, includes members of unrelated subfamilies not shown separately. For earlier years, unrelated subfamily members are included in the "infamilies" category. 3. Hispanic persons may of any race. 4. Not available.

★ 425 ★
Poverty

Persons as of March of the following year.

Year	Number Below Poverty Level				Percent Below Poverty Level			
	All races[1]	White	Black	Hispanic[2]	All races[1]	White	Black	Hispanic[2]
1959	39.5	28.5	9.9	[5]	22.4	18.1	55.1	[5]
1960	39.9	28.3	[5]	[5]	22.2	17.8	[5]	[5]
1966	28.5	20.8	8.9	[5]	14.7	12.2	41.8	[5]
1969	24.1	16.7	7.1	[5]	12.1	9.5	32.2	[5]
1970	25.4	17.5	7.5	[5]	12.6	9.9	33.5	[5]
1975	25.9	17.8	7.5	3.0	12.3	9.7	31.3	26.9
1976	25.5	16.7	7.6	2.8	11.8	9.1	31.1	24.7
1977	24.7	16.4	7.7	2.7	11.6	8.9	31.3	22.4
1978	24.5	16.3	7.6	2.6	11.4	8.7	30.6	21.6
1979[3]	25.3	16.8	7.8	2.9	11.6	8.9	30.9	21.6
1979[4]	26.1	17.2	8.1	2.9	11.7	9.0	31.0	21.8
1980	29.3	19.7	8.6	3.5	13.0	10.2	32.5	25.7
1981	31.8	21.6	9.2	3.7	14.0	11.1	34.2	26.5
1982	34.4	23.5	9.7	4.3	15.0	12.0	35.6	29.9
1983	35.3	24.0	9.9	4.6	15.2	12.1	35.7	28.0
1984	33.7	23.0	9.5	4.8	14.4	11.5	33.8	28.4
1985	33.1	22.9	8.9	5.2	14.0	11.4	31.3	29.0
1986	32.4	22.2	9.0	5.1	13.6	11.0	31.1	27.3
1987	32.5	21.4	9.7	5.5	13.5	10.5	33.1	28.2

Source: "Persons Below Poverty Level and Below 125 Percent of Poverty Level: 1959 to 1987," *Statistical Abstract*, 1989, p. 452. Primary source: *Current Population Reports*, series P-60, No. 161. U.S. Bureau of the Census. *Notes:* 1. Includes other races not shown separately. 2. Hispanic persons may be of any race. 3. Population controls based on 1970 Census; see text, section 14. 4. Population controls based on 1980 Census; see text, sections 1 and 14. 5. Not available.

★ 426 ★
Poverty

Persons as of March of following year.

Race of Householder and Family Status	Below Poverty Level					Below 125 Percent of Poverty Level				
	1979[1]	1984	1985	1986	1987	1979[1]	1984	1985	1986	1987
Number (mil.)										
All persons[2]	26.1	33.7	33.1	32.4	32.5	36.6	45.3	44.2	43.5	43.5
White	17.2	23.0	22.9	22.2	21.4	25.2	32.1	31.5	30.7	30.0
In families	12.5	17.3	17.1	16.4	15.8	18.4	24.2	23.7	22.6	22.0
Householder	3.6	4.9	5.0	4.8	4.6	5.3	7.0	7.0	6.7	6.5
Related children under 18 years	5.9	8.1	7.8	7.7	7.6	8.2	10.7	10.3	10.0	9.9
Other family members	3.0	4.3	4.3	3.9	3.7	4.8	6.6	6.4	5.9	5.7
Unrelated individuals	4.5	5.2	5.3	5.2	5.1	6.5	7.3	7.3	7.4	7.4
Black	8.1	9.5	8.9	9.0	9.7	10.3	11.6	11.1	11.2	11.8
In families	6.8	8.1	7.5	7.4	8.0	8.8	9.9	9.3	9.2	9.7
Householder	1.7	2.1	2.0	2.0	2.1	2.2	2.6	2.5	2.5	2.6
Related children under 18 years	3.7	4.3	4.1	4.0	4.3	4.7	5.1	4.8	4.8	5.0
Other family members	1.3	1.7	1.5	1.4	1.5	1.9	2.3	2.1	1.9	2.0
Unrelated individuals	1.2	1.3	1.3	1.4	1.5	1.4	1.6	1.6	1.8	1.9

Continued.

Poverty
[Continued]

Race of Householder and Family Status	Below Poverty Level					Below 125 Percent of Poverty Level				
	1979[1]	1984	1985	1986	1987	1979[1]	1984	1985	1986	1987
Percent of Population										
All persons[2]	11.7	14.4	14.0	13.6	13.5	16.4	19.4	18.7	18.2	18.1
White	9.0	11.5	11.4	11.0	10.5	13.1	16.1	15.7	15.2	14.7
In families	7.4	10.1	9.9	9.4	9.1	10.9	14.1	13.7	13.0	12.6
Householder	6.9	9.1	9.1	8.6	8.2	10.2	12.8	12.7	12.0	11.5
Related children under 18 years	11.4	16.1	15.6	15.3	15.0	15.9	21.3	20.5	20.0	19.6
Other family members	4.7	6.4	6.4	5.7	5.4	7.5	9.8	9.5	8.6	8.3
Unrelated individuals	19.7	19.9	19.6	19.2	18.2	28.6	27.9	27.0	27.3	26.3
Black	31.0	33.8	31.3	31.1	33.1	39.9	41.4	38.8	38.7	40.2
In families	30.0	33.2	30.5	29.7	31.8	39.0	40.7	37.9	37.1	38.6
Householder	27.8	30.9	28.7	28.0	29.9	36.2	38.2	35.8	35.0	36.4
Related children under 18 years	40.8	46.2	43.1	42.7	45.1	51.1	54.1	51.0	50.8	52.8
Other family member	18.2	20.5	17.7	16.5	18.1	26.1	27.7	24.8	23.3	24.2
Unrelated indiviuals	37.3	35.8	34.7	38.5	38.3	45.4	44.6	42.7	47.3	47.2

Source: "Persons Below Poverty Level and Below 125 Percent of Poverty Level, by Race of Householder and Family Status, 1979 to 1987," *Statistical Abstract*, 1989, p. 453. Primary Source: U.S. Bureau of the Census, *Current Population Reports*, series P-60, No. 161, and unpublished data. *Notes:* 1. Population controls based on 1980 census; see text section 14. 2. Includes races and members of unrelated subfamilies not shown separately.

★ 427 ★
Poverty

Persons as of March of the following year. Covers only related children in families under 18 years old. Based on Current Population Survey.

Year and Region	Number Below Poverty Level (1,000)				Percent Below Poverty Level			
	All races[1]	White	Black	Hispanic[2]	All races[1]	White	Black	Hispanic[2]
1970	10,235	6,138	3,922	[3]	14.9	10.5	41.5	[3]
1971	10,344	6,341	3,836	[3]	15.1	10.9	40.7	[3]
1972	10,082	5,462	4,025	[3]	14.9	10.1	42.7	[3]
1973	9,453	5,462	3,822	1,364	14.2	9.7	40.6	27.8
1974	9,967	6,079	3,713	1,414	15.1	11.0	39.6	28.6
1975	10,882	6,748	3,884	1,619	16.8	12.5	41.4	33.1
1976	10,081	6,034	3,758	1,424	15.8	11.3	40.4	30.1
1977	10,028	5,943	3,850	1,402	16.0	11.4	41.6	28.0
1978	9,722	5,674	3,781	1,354	15.7	11.0	41.2	27.2
1979	9,993	5,909	3,745	1,505	16.0	11.4	40.8	27.7
1980	11,114	6,817	3,906	1,718	17.9	13.4	42.1	33.0
1981	12,068	7,429	4,170	1,874	19.5	14.7	44.9	35.4
1982	13,139	8,282	4,388	2,117	21.3	16.5	47.3	38.9
1983	13,427	8,534	4,273	2,251	21.8	17.0	46.2	37.7
1984	12,929	8,086	4,320	2,317	21.0	16.1	46.2	38.7
1985	12,483	7,838	4,057	2,512	20.1	15.6	43.1	39.6
1986	12,257	7,714	4,039	2,413	19.8	15.3	42.7	37.1
1987	12,435	7,550	4,297	2,631	20.0	15.0	45.1	39.3
Northeast	1,986	1,342	571	600	16.9	13.5	39.4	52.9
Midwest	2,874	1,821	942	184	18.4	13.6	51.5	35.3

Continued.

Poverty
[Continued]

Year and Region	Number Below Poverty Level (1,000)				Percent Below Poverty Level			
	All races[1]	White	Black	Hispanic[2]	All races[1]	White	Black	Hispanic[2]
South	5,052	2,465	2,511	893	23.4	15.7	45.9	43.7
West	2,522	1,922	273	953	18.9	16.9	35.4	31.9

Source: "Children Below the Poverty Level, by Race and Hispanic Origin: 1970 to 1987," *Statistical Abstract*, 1989, p. 454. Primary source: U.S. Bureau of the Census, *Current Population Reports*, series P-60, No. 161, and earlier reports. *Notes:* 1. Includes persons of other races, not shown separately. 2. Hispanic persons may be of any race. 3. Not available.

★ 428 ★
Poverty

Families as of March of the following year.

Year	Number Below Provery Level (1000)				Percent Below Poverty Level				Below 125 Percent of Poverty Level	
	All races[1]	White	Black	Hispanic[2]	All races[1]	White	Black	Hispanic[2]	Number (1,000)	Percent
1960	8,243	6,115	[3]	[3]	18.1	14.9	[3]	[3]	11,525	25.4
1970	5,260	3,708	1,481	[3]	10.1	8.0	29.5	[3]	7,516	14.4
1980	6,217	4,195	1,826	751	10.3	8.0	28.9	23.2	8,764	14.5
1981	6,851	4,670	1,972	792	11.2	8.8	30.8	24.0	9,568	15.7
1982	7,512	5,118	2,158	916	12.2	9.6	33.0	27.2	10,279	16.7
1983	7,681	5,254	2,161	985	12.4	9.7	32.3	26.0	10,410	16.8
1984	7,277	4,925	2,094	991	11.6	9.1	30.9	25.2	9,901	15.8
1985	7,223	4,983	1,983	1,074	11.4	9.1	28.7	25.5	9,753	15.3
1986	7,023	4,811	1,987	1,085	10.9	8.6	28.0	24.7	9,476	14.7
1987	7,059	4,592	2,149	1,183	10.8	8.2	29.9	25.8	9,458	14.5

Source: "Families Below Poverty Level and Below 125 Percent of Poverty Level: 1959 to 1987," *Statistical Abstract*, 1989, p. 455. Primary source: U.S. Bureau of the Census, *Current Population Reports*, Series P-60, No. 161. *Notes:* 1. Includes other races not shown separately. 2. Hispanic persons may be of any race. 3. Not available.

★ 429 ★
Poverty in Families with Unemployed Members

Workers Unemployed	African American	White
Total below poverty level	36.9	18.2
Husband unemployed	24.3	18.8
Wife unemployed	17.5	9.1
Female head unemployed	76.6	49.1

Source: "Incidence of Poverty among African American and White Families with Unemployment [sic] Worker," *The State of Black America 1990*, January 1990, p. 217. Primary source: Bureau of Labor Statistics, *Linking Employment Problems to Economic Status*, August 1987, Table 3, p. 10. Extracted from: *The State of Black America*, January 1990. Published by permission.

★ 430 ★
Poverty/Non-Poverty and Basic Skills Levels of Young Mothers

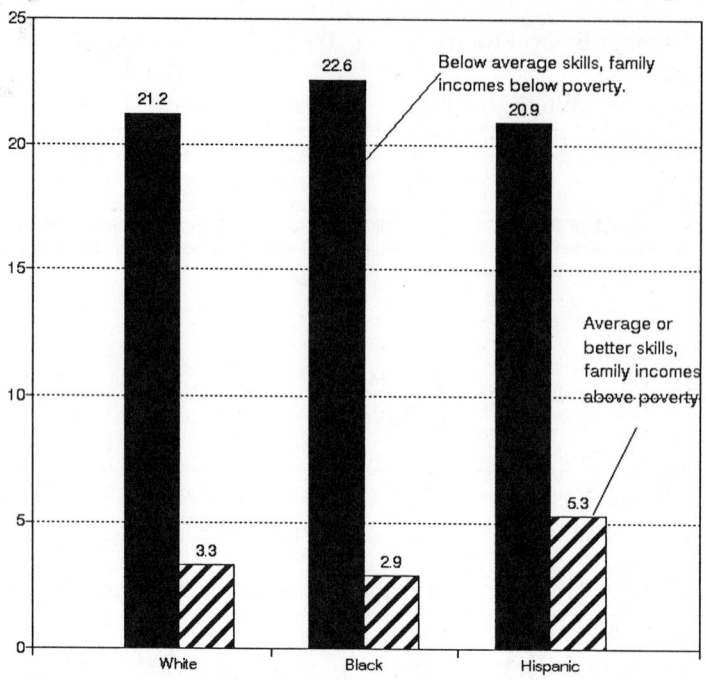

Characteristic	White	Black	Hispanic
Below average skills, family incomes below poverty	21.2	22.6	20.9
Average or better skills, family incomes above poverty	3.3	2.9	5.3

Source: "Parenthood by Poverty and Basic Skills Levels, 16-19 Year-Old Women, 1981," *The Urban League Review*, Summer 1988/ Winter 1988-89, p. 58. Primary source: Unpublished analyses of the National Longitudinal Survey, courtesy of Andrew Sum, Northeastern University. Extracted from: *The Urban League Review*, Summer 1988/ Winter 1988-89. Published by permission.

★ 431 ★
Regional Characteristics of Families: Trends

Numbers in thousands.

Characteristic	1988		1985		1980	
	Black	White	Black	White	Black	White
United States						
Type of Family						
All families	7,177	56,044	6,778	54,400	6,184	52,243
Percent	100.0	100.0	100.0	100.0	100.0	100.0
Married-couple families	51.3	83.2	51.2	83.9	55.5	85.7
Female householder, no husband present	42.8	12.9	43.7	12.8	40.3	11.6
Male householder, no wife present	5.9	3.9	5.1	3.3	4.1	2.8
South						
Type of Family						
All families	3,972	18,559	3,561	17,953	3,202	16,773

Continued.

Regional Characteristics of Families: Trends
[Continued]

Characteristic	1988 Black	1988 White	1985 Black	1985 White	1980 Black	1980 White
Percent	100.0	100.0	100.0	100.0	100.0	100.0
Married-couple families	52.9	84.4	55.2	85.1	57.9	87.2
Female householder, no husband present	41.3	12.4	39.8	11.9	38.2	10.4
Male householder, no wife present	5.8	3.2	5.0	3.1	3.9	2.5
North and West						
Type of Family						
All families	3,204	37,485	3,217	36,447	2,983	35,470
Percent	100.0	100.0	100.0	100.0	100.0	100.0
Married-couple families	49.3	82.7	46.8	83.3	53.0	85.0
Female householder, no husband present	44.7	13.2	48.1	13.2	42.6	12.2
Male householder, no wife present	6.0	4.2	5.1	3.5	4.4	2.9

Source: "Selected Characteristics of Families, by Region and Race: March 1988, 1985, and 1980," *The Black Population in the United States: March 1988*, p. 8. Primary source: Current Population Reports, Series P-20, No. 442, *The Black Population in the United States: March 1988*.

★ 432 ★
Regional Median Family Income: Trends

Year	NORTHEAST Black	NORTHEAST White	NORTHEAST Blk/Wht	MIDWEST Black	MIDWEST White	MIDWEST Blk/Wht	SOUTH Black	SOUTH White	SOUTH Blk/Wht	WEST Black	WEST White	WEST Blk/Wht
1988	$24,495	37,588	65.2	17,469	34,246	51.0	17,545	31,475	55.7	25,840	33,478	77.2
1987	21,534	36,722	58.6	17,449	33,480	52.1	18,081	32,001	56.3	21,481	33,867	63.3
1986	22,533	35,982	62.7	18,732	32,921	56.9	17,518	31,433	55.7	23,898	33,856	70.6
1982	17,891	31,347	57.1	15,025	30,240	49.7	15,840	28,037	56.5	20,046	30,660	65.4
1980							16,696	29,620	56.4	24,601	32,469	75.8
1978	20,946	33,670	62.2	24,572	34,170	71.9	17,679	30,770	57.5	19,405	33,838	57.4
1970	23,685	33,329	71.1	23,514	32,015	73.4	15,922	28,152	56.6	24,377	31,632	77.1

Source: "Median Family Income by Regions," *The State of Black America 1990*, January 1990, p. 32. Primary source: David Swinton, "The Economic Status of Blacks" in Janet Dewart (ed.), *The State of Black America 1988* (New York: National Urban League, 1989), Table 5, page 135. U.S. Department of Commerce, Bureau of the Census, *Money Income and Poverty Status in 1988*, pages 32-35, Table 6. Extracted from: *The State of Black America*, January 1990. Published by permission.

★ 433 ★
Where Do Children Live?

Characteristic	Number (millions) 1976	Number (millions) 1988	Percent Distribution 1976	Percent Distribution 1988
All related children under 18	64.8	62.3	100.0	100.0
Living in metro areas	43.1	47.7	66.5	76.6
Inside central cities	17.4	19.0	26.9	30.4
Outside central cities	25.6	28.7	39.6	46.1
Living outside metro areas	21.6	14.6	33.5	23.4
Living in poverty areas	13.5	11.1	20.9	18.9
Poor children in areas	5.0	5.8	46.1	46.8[1]
White children	54.1	50.4	100.0	100.0

Continued.

Where Do Children Live?
[Continued]

Characteristic	Number (millions)		Percent Distribution	
	1976	1988	1976	1988
Living in metro areas	35.2	37.9	65.0	75.3
Inside central cities	11.6	12.6	21.5	25.0
Outside central cities	23.5	25.3	43.5	50.3
Living outside metro areas	19.0	12.5	35.0	24.7
Living in poverty areas	8.2	6.2	12.7	12.3
Poor children in areas	2.2	2.5	32.7	32.6[1]
Black children	9.4	9.5	100.0	100.0
Living in metro areas	6.9	7.8	73.9	81.5
Inside central cities	5.3	5.4	56.9	56.3
Outside central cities	1.6	2.4	17.0	25.2
Living outside metro areas	2.4	1.8	26.1	18.5
Living in poverty areas	5.1	5.0	54.0	52.7
Poor children in areas	2.7	3.1	70.7	71.1[1]
Hispanic children	4.9	6.7	100.0	100.0
Living in metro areas	4.0	6.1	80.8	91.6
Inside central cities	2.3	3.6	46.8	53.9
Outside central cities	1.7	2.5	34.0	37.8
Living outside metro areas	.9	.6	19.2	8.4
Living in poverty areas	1.7	2.7	33.9	40.6
Poor children in areas	.8	1.5	51.3	57.5[1]

Source: "Distribution of Child Population in Central Cities, Suburbs, and Non-Metropolitan Areas, and in Poverty Areas, 1976 and 1988," *U.S. Children and their Families*, 1989, p. 23. Primary source: Child Trends, calculated from U.S. Bureau of the Census, Current Population Reports, Series P-60, Tables 9 and 42, and No. 163, Tables 4 and 12, and unpublished data. *Notes:* Shifts in metro residence are partly due to changes in definition of metropolitan statistical areas. The changes in definition have increased the area and population of metropolitan areas. Determination of poverty status is based on family income in previous year (i.e., 1975 and 1987). 1. Percentage of poor children in ethnic group who live in poverty areas. Published by permission.

★ 434 ★
Who Adopts Children?

Data based on household interviews of the civilian noninstitutionalized population. The survey design, general qualifications, and information on the reliability of the estimates are given in the technical notes.

Characteristic	Year of adoption		
	All years[1]	1970-79	1980-87
	Number in thousands		
All children[2]	1,081	404	315
	Percent distribution		
Total	100.0	100.0	100.0
Race of adoptive mother			
White	93.2	96.0	87.0
Black	4.5	3.6	9.0
Other	2.3	0.4	4.1
Race of adoptive mother and child[3]			
Same race	92.4	---	---

Continued.

Who Adopts Children?
[Continued]

Characteristic	Year of adoption		
	All years[1]	1970-79	1980-87
White	85.4	---	---
Black	5.9	---	---
Other	1.1	---	---
Different race	7.6	---	---
White mother, black child	1.2	---	---
White mother, child of race other than black	4.8	---	---
Mother of other race, white child	1.6	---	---
All other	0.0	---	---

Source: Number of Unrelated Children Ever Adopted by Women 20-54 Years of Age and Percent Distribution by Selected Characteristics According to Year of Adoption: National Health Interview Survey, 1987," *Advance Data*, January 5, 1990, p. 5. Primary source: National Center for Health Statistics. *Notes:* 1. Includes adopted children for whom date of adoption not ascertained and children adopted before 1970. 2. Includes adopted children for whom information on specific characteristics is not ascertained; percent distributions based on known cases. 3. Based on adoptive children known to be living in household with adoptive mother at time of survey.

GOVERNMENT SERVICE

★ 435 ★
Labor Force

As of June 30. Excludes school systems and educational institutions. Based on reports from State governments (44 in 1973, 48 in 1975 and 1976, 47 in 1977, 45 in 1978, 48 in 1979, 42 in 1980, 49 in 1981, 47 in 1983, 50 in 1984 through 1986) and a sample of county, municipal, township, and special district jurisdictions employing 15 or more nonelected, nonappointed full-time employees.

| Year and Occupation | Employment (1,000) | | | | | Median Annual Salary ($1,000) | | | |
| | | | Minority | | | | | Minority | |
	Total	White[1]	Total[2]	Black[1]	Hispanic[3]	White[1]	Total[2]	Black[1]	Hispanic[3]
1973	3,809	3,115	693	523	125	8.8	7.5	7.4	7.4
1975	3,899	3,102	797	602	147	10.2	8.8	8.6	8.9
1976	4,369	3,490	880	664	165	10.7	9.2	9.1	9.4
1977	4,415	3,480	935	705	175	11.3	9.7	9.5	9.9
1978	4,447	3,481	966	723	181	12.0	10.4	10.1	10.7
1979	4,576	3,568	1,008	751	192	12.8	10.9	10.6	11.4
1980	3,987	3,146	842	619	163	13.8	11.8	11.5	12.3
1981	4,665	3,591	1,074	780	205	16.1	13.5	13.3	14.7
1983	4,492	3,423	1,069	768	219	18.5	15.9	15.6	17.3
1984	4,580	3,458	1,121	799	233	19.6	17.4	16.5	18.4
1985	4,742	1,952	1,179	835	248	20.6	18.4	17.5	19.2
1986, total	4,779	3,549	1,230	865	259	21.5	19.6	18.7	20.2
Officials/administrators	260	226	34	23	7	34.3	33.0	32.4	33.0
Professionals	1,005	812	194	119	36	27.1	25.6	24.8	27.0
Technicians	459	360	99	65	22	21.7	20.7	19.1	21.5
Protective service	736	586	150	105	37	24.3	24.1	22.5	26.2
Paraprofessionals	364	228	136	113	18	16.2	16.8	15.9	17.1
Office/Clerical	868	626	242	165	56	15.9	16.7	16.6	16.9
Skilled craft	401	312	98	57	25	21.7	21.3	20.6	22.4
Service/maintenance	686	400	286	219	57	17.3	16.7	16.5	17.9

Source: "State and Local Government — Full-Time Employment and Salary, by Sex and Race/Ethnic Group: 1973 to 1986," *Statistical Abstract,* 1989, p. 294. Primary source: U.S. Equal Employment Opportunity Commission, *State and Local Government Information Report,* annual. *Notes:* 1. Nonhispanic. 2. Includes other minority groups, now shown separately. 3. Hispanic may be of any race.

★ 436 ★
Labor Force

As of Sept. 30. Covers total employment for only Executive Branch agencies participating in OPM's central personnel data file. Excludes foreign nationals abroad and U.S. Postal Service.

	1982					1986, est.				
	Total employees (1,000)	Race/Hispanic origin				Total employees (1,000)	Race/Hispanic origin			
Pay System		Total[1] (1,000)	Percent of total	Black, non-Hispanic (1,000)	Hispanic (1,000)		Total[1] (1,000)	Percent of total	Black, non-Hispanic (1,000)	Hispanic (1,000)
All pay systems, total[2]	2,008.6	484.0	24.1	311.1	90.0	2,084.0	541.8	26.0	339.8	105.2
General schedule and equivalent[3]	1,508.3	336.2	22.3	222.0	59.0	1,592.7	392.6	24.6	253.6	72.4
GS 1-4 ($9,339- $16,723)	303.6	101.9	33.6	71.0	16.1	282.8	108.6	38.4	75.7	17.9
GS 5-8 ($14,390-$25,662)	464.9	126.5	27.2	90.2	20.2	491.3	148.1	30.1	102.8	25.0
GS 9-12 ($21,804-$41,105)	530.0	87.6	16.5	50.1	18.7	590.0	111.3	18.9	62.6	24.5
GS 13-15 ($37,599-$67,940)	209.8	20.1	9.6	10.7	4.0	228.6	24.6	10.8	12.5	5.0
Executive, total	7.8	.6	7.2	.3	.1	8.9	.6	6.6	.4	.1
Wage systems	414.0	134.6	32.5	83.5	28.0	409.2	135.2	33.0	80.9	29.7
Other pay systems[4]	69.3	10.1	14.6	3.7	2.3	69.0	11.8	17.1	3.8	2.7

Source: "Federal Government Employment, by Race and Hispanic Origin, and by Pay System: 1982 and 1986," *Statistical Abstract*, 1989, p. 321. Primary source: U.S. Office of Personnel Management, *1986 Affirmative Employment Statistics*; biennial, and unpublished data. *Notes:* 1. Includes American Indians, Alaska Natives, Asians, and Pacific Islanders, not shown separately. 2. Due to the inclusion of unspecified employee records, the pay system listed do not add to the total. 3. Pay rates as of January 1986 for general schedule. Each grade (except Executive) includes several salary steps. Range is from lowest to highest step of grades shown. 4. Includes white-collar employment in other than General Schedule and Equivalent or Executive pay plans.

HEALTH AND MEDICAL CARE

★ 437 ★
"Bed Days" - Home from School/Work, Trends

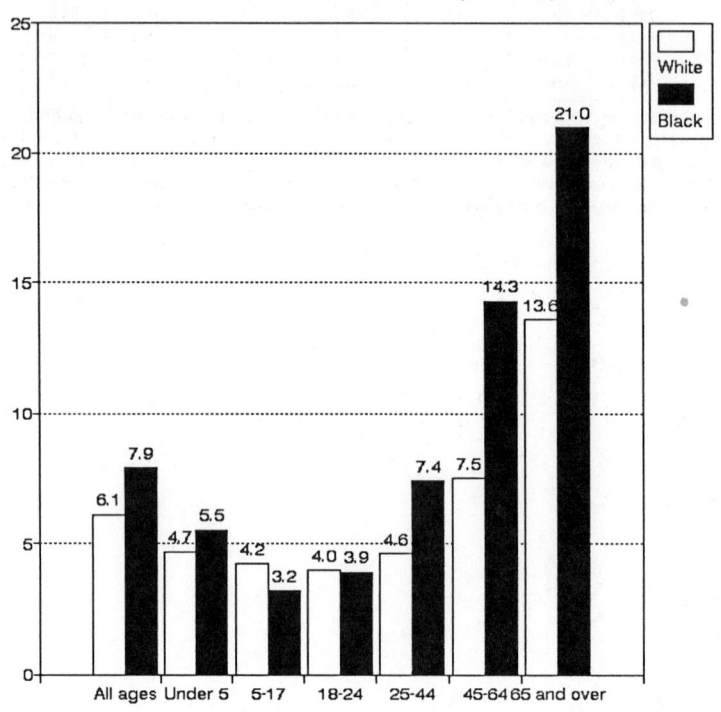

Days per person per year.

Characteristic	White	Black
All family incomes[1]		
All ages	6.1	7.9
Under 5 years	4.7	5.5
5-17 years	4.2	3.2
18-24 years	4.0	3.9
25-44 years	4.5	7.4
45-64 years	7.5	14.3
65 years and over	13.6	21.0
Less than $20,000		
All ages	9.0	9.8
Under 5 years	5.4	5.8
5-17 years	4.8	3.5
18-24 years	5.0	4.8
25-44 years	6.9	10.5

Continued.

294

"Bed Days" - Home from School/Work, Trends
[Continued]

Characteristic	White	Black
45-64 years	14.3	19.9
65 years and over	14.8	20.8
$20,000 or more		
All ages	4.5	4.8
Under 5 years	4.4	5.5
5-17 years	4.0	2.7
18-24 years	3.4	2.2
25-44 years	3.6	5.0
45-64 years	5.0	7.4
65 years and over	11.1	12.7

Source: "Average Annual Number of Bed Days per Person by Race, Age, and Family Income: United States, 1985-87," *Health of Black and White Americans, 1985- 87*, 1990, p. 13. Primary source: National Health Interview Survey, U.S. Department of Health and Human Services, Public Health Service, Centers for Disease Control, Division of Health Statistics, Hyattsville, MD, January 1990. *Note:* 1. Includes unknown family income.

★ 438 ★
Acute Conditions - Rate and Related Factors: Trends

Family income and type of acute condition	White				Black			
	All ages	Under 18 years	18-44 years	45 years and over	All ages	Under 18 years	18-44 years	45 years and over
Number per 100 persons per year								
All family incomes[1]								
All acute conditions	185.7	293.2	176.2	111.9	137.4	178.9	127.2	96.6
Infective and parasitic diseases	23.6	48.6	20.5	7.6	15.6	30.5	9.1	5.9
Respiratory conditions	91.7	144.6	88.3	53.6	62.7	85.8	54.3	44.8
Digestive system conditions	6.2	8.8	5.5	4.9	8.8	9.6	8.8	7.6
Injuries	28.3	34.2	30.9	20.0	20.9	21.6	24.2	14.2
Other selected acute conditions	26.0	46.5	22.3	14.4	18.4	22.6	19.0	11.5
All other acute conditions	10.0	10.4	8.6	11.4	11.0	8.9	11.8	12.7
Family income less than $20,000								
All acute conditions	192.4	280.6	206.9	120.1	147.2	183.2	141.8	99.9
Infective and parasitic diseases	20.5	41.0	20.1	7.6	16.6	31.7	9.2	4.7
Respiratory conditions	94.7	146.3	101.3	54.3	65.7	85.4	59.7	44.8
Digestive system conditions	6.1	6.7	6.6	5.1	10.4	9.9	11.7	9.1
Injuries	31.5	30.0	41.4	22.1	21.8	21.5	26.8	14.2
Other selected acute conditions	27.5	45.2	26.2	17.4	20.9	24.4	22.1	13.9

Continued.

Acute Conditions - Rate and Related Factors: Trends
[Continued]

Family income and type of acute condition	White				Black			
	All ages	Under 18 years	18-44 years	45 years and over	All ages	Under 18 years	18-44 years	45 years and over
All other acute conditions	12.2	11.6	11.3	13.6	11.7	10.3	12.3	13.1
Family income $20,000 or more								
All acute conditions	190.0	305.2	168.8	108.4	127.7	176.1	112.9	89.1
Infective and parasitic diseases	26.9	54.5	21.3	8.2	15.8	31.8	8.8	8.4
Respiratory conditions	93.6	145.7	85.9	53.3	61.0	83.1	51.7	49.7
Digestive system conditions	6.3	10.1	5.0	4.6	6.2	10.5	5.2	2.0
Injuries	28.3	36.7	28.1	20.1	18.8	24.1	18.3	11.8
Other selected acute conditions	26.1	48.1	21.1	12.1	14.9	19.8	16.0	4.6
All other acute conditions	8.8	10.1	7.3	10.1	11.0	6.8	13.0	12.6

Source: "Average Annual Number of Acute Conditions per 100 Persons per Year by Race, Age, Family Income, and Type of Condition: United States, 1985-87," *Health of Black and White Americans, 1985-87,* 1990, p. 9. Primary source: National Health Interview Survey, U.S. Department of Health and Human Services, Public Health Service, Centers for Disease Control, Division of Health. *Notes:* 1. Includes unknown family income. this category.

★ 439 ★
Acute Conditions - Rate and Type: Trends

Covers civilian noninstitutional population. Estimates includes only acute conditions which were medically attended or caused at least one day of restricted activity. Based on National Health Interview Survey.

Year and Characteristic	Number of Conditions (mil.)					Rate per 100 Population				
	Infective and parasitic	Respiratory		Digestive system	Injuries	Infective and parasitic	Respiratory		Digestive system	Injuries
		Upper	Other				Upper	Other		
1986, total[1]	54.4	85.2	143.6	15.0	64.3	23.0	36.1	60.8	6.3	27.2
White	50.1	72.4	130.0	12.0	56.9	25.0	36.2	65.0	6.0	28.4
Black	3.6	9.0	10.1	2.1	5.9	12.7	31.6	35.3	7.5	20.5

Source: "Acute Conditions by Type, 1970 to 1986, and by Selected Characteristics, 1986," *Statistical Abstract,* 1989, p. 114. U.S. National Center for Health Statistics, *Vital and Health Statistics,* series 10, and unpublished data. *Note:* 1. Includes other races and unknown income, not shown separately.

★ 440 ★
Acute Conditions and Family Income

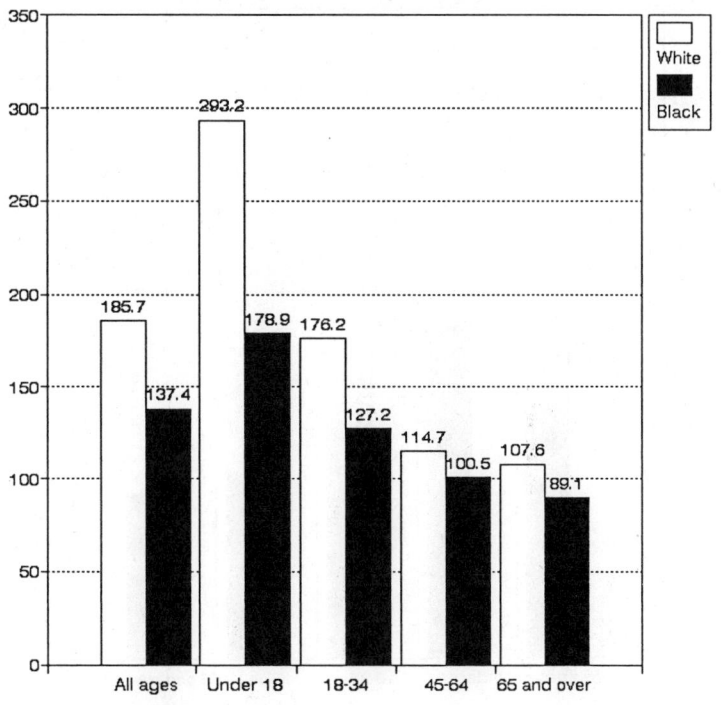

Number per 100 persons per year.

Characteristic	White	Black
All family incomes[1]		
All ages	185.7	137.4
Under 18 years	293.2	178.9
18-44 years	176.2	127.2
45-64 years	114.7	100.5
65 years and over	107.6	89.1
Less than $20,000		
All ages	192.4	147.2
Under 18 years	280.6	183.2
18-44 years	206.9	141.8
45-64 years	134.6	104.4
65 years and over	109.6	94.1
$20,000 or more		
All ages	190.0	127.7
Under 18 years	305.2	176.1
18-44 years	168.8	112.9
45-64 years	108.8	93.0
65 years and over	107.4	65.0

Source: "Average Annual Number of Acute Conditions per 100 Persons by Race, Age, and Family Income: United States, 1985-87," *Health of Black and White Americans, 1985-87*, 1990, p. 7. Primary source: National Health Interview Survey, U.S. Department of Health and Human Services, Public Health Service, Centers for Disease Control, Division of Health Statistics, Hyattsville, MD, January 1990. *Note:* 1. Includes unknown health status.

★ 441 ★
Acute Conditions and Health Self-Assessment: Trends

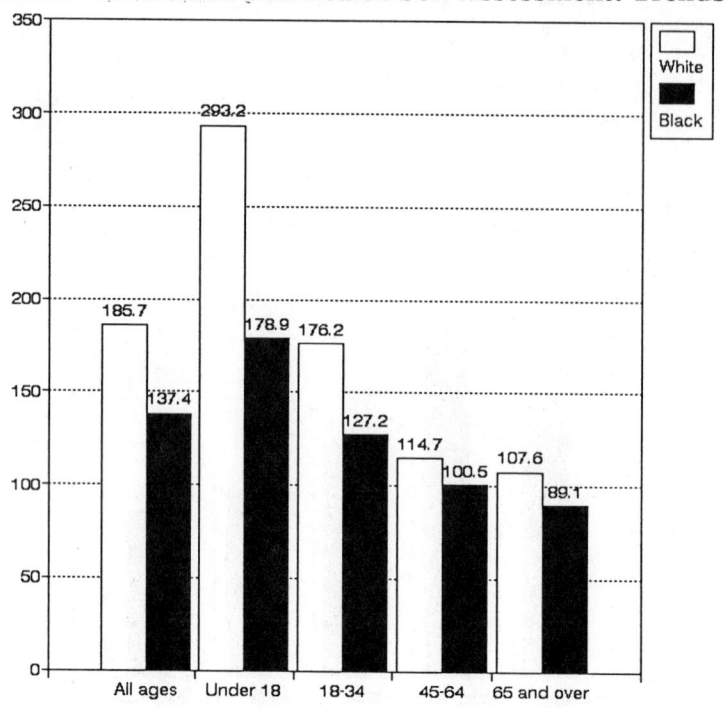

Number per 100 persons per year.

Characteristic	White	Black
All health statuses[1]		
All ages	185.7	137.4
Under 18 years	293.2	178.9
18-44 years	176.2	127.2
45-64 years	114.7	100.5
65 years and over	107.6	89.1
Fair or poor health[2]		
All ages	210.1	180.6
Under 18 years	505.1	322.2
18-44 years	291.9	237.4
45-64 years	171.1	130.4
65 years and over	153.2	117.0
Good to excellent health[2]		
All ages	183.0	129.9
Under 18 years	288.7	172.2
18-44 years	170.1	113.7
45-64 years	103.5	85.9
65 years and over	89.5	66.0

Source: "Average Annual Number of Acute Conditions per 100 Persons by Race, Age, and Respondent-Assessed Health Status: United States, 1985-87," *Health of Black and White Americans, 1985-87,* 1990, p. 8. Primary source: National Health Interview Survey, U.S. Department of Health and Human Services, Public Health Service, Centers for Disease Control, Division of Health Statistics, Hyattsville, MD, January 1990. *Notes:* 1. Includes unknown health status. 2. As assessed by self or responsible family member.

★ 442 ★
Adults at Risk for Cardiovascular Disease

SE - Standard error.

Race - sex group	Risk factor groups[1,2]											
	None				One				Two or more			
	1971-1975		1976-1980		1971-1975		1976-1980		1971-1975		1976-1980	
	Percent	SE	Percent	SE	Percent	SE	Percent	SE	Percent	SE	Percent	SE
White males	39.0	1.3	42.5	1.1	46.2	1.3	44.5	1.1	14.8	0.8	13.0	0.6
White females	45.4	1.1	47.0	0.9	41.9	1.0	42.9	0.8	12.7	0.7	10.1	0.5
Black males	23.4	3.2	29.3	2.0	44.3	3.9	50.9	2.3	32.3	4.1	19.8	2.1
Black females	28.0	2.4	41.4	2.3	49.2	2.5	43.7	2.0	22.8	1.8	14.9	1.2

Source: "Age-Adjusted Percent Distribution Among Groups with Zero, One, and Two or More Risk Factors for Cardiovascular Disease for Persons Aged 25-74 Years, by Race and Sex: First National Health and Nutrition Examination Survey, 1971-74, and Second National Health and Nutrition Examination Survey, 1976-80 (Rowland and Fulwood, 1984)," *Nutrition Monitoring in the United States*, September 1989, p. 119. Primary source: Rowland, M.L., and R. Fulwood. 1984. Coronary Heart Disease Risk Factor Trends in Blacks Between the First and Second National Health and Nutrition Examination Surveys, United States, 1971-1980. *Am. J.* 108: 771-779. *Notes:* 1. Age-adjusted by direct method to the total U.S., population estimated at the midpoint of the 1976-80 NHANES II. 2. Risk factors included the following: systolic blood pressure of at least 160mm mercury and/or diastolic blood pressure of at least 95 mm mercury, serum cholesterol level of at least 6.70 mmol/L (260 mg/dl), or smoker. .

★ 443 ★
Adults with Diabetes

Age group/survey/ ethnic group or race	Prevalence (percent)	Approximate 95 percent confidence interval
20-44 years		
HHANES		
Mexican American	3.8	2.0-5.5
Cuban	2.4	0.0-5.0
Puerto Rican	4.1	2.8-5.3
NHANES II		
Non-Hispanic white	1.6	1.1-2.2
Non-Hispanic black	3.3	0.0-5.7
45-74 years		
HHANES		
Mexican American	23.9	20.8-27.1
Cuban	15.8	10.5-21.1
Puerto Rican	26.1	22.2-30.1
NHANES II		
Non-Hispanic white	12.0	10.7-13.2
Non-Hispanic black	19.3	15.1-23.6

Source: "Total Prevalence of Diabetes (Sum of Previously Diagnosed Diabetes and Undiagnosed Diabetes), by Age Group, Survey, and Ethnic Group or Race: Hispanic Health and Nutrition Examination Survey, 1982-84, and Second National Health and Nutrition Examination Survey, 1976-80," *Nutrition Monitoring in the United States*, September 1989, p. 81. Primary source: Flegal, K.M., Ezzati, T.M., Harris, M.I. et al. 1988. *Prevalence of Diabetes in Mexican Americans, Cubans, and Puerto Ricans from the Hispanic Health and Nutrition Examination Survey, 1982-84.* (Preliminary draft).

★ 444 ★
Age and Rate of Inpatient Psychiatric Services

Race, Hispanic origin, and age	Inpatient psychiatric services			
	State and county mental hospitals	Private psychiatric hospitals	Non-Federal general hospitals	VA medical centers
Total, all races[1]	163.6	62.6	295.3	70.4
Under 18	26.1	26.3	75.7	[3]
18-24	264.6	79.6	396.9	38.2
25-44	282.9	89.1	42.8	129.9
45-64	175.7	71.0	316.9	135.0
65 and over	78.0	54.1	230.4	25.2
White	136.8	63.4	284.9	64.9
Under 18	23.7	28.1	75.8	[3]
18-24	214.5	79.3	357.9	31.7
25-44	225.3	87.0	454.5	108.6
45-64	156.5	73.2	316.2	135.6
65 and over	70.8	55.1	232.8	25.7
Black	364.2	62.9	386.6	118.2
Under 18	35.2	17.0	73.7	-
18-24	598.5	89.2	641.7	85.2
25-44	753.0	118.2	753.9	312.0
45-64	354.3	60.0	349.6	143.2
65 and over	162.2	46.0	199.5	21.3
All other races	142.0	29.6	221.7	33.4
Under 18	49.9	23.3	85.2	-
18-24	231.9	34.9	457.9	[3]
25-44	196.3	37.2	277.5	65.0
45-64	185.8	20.4	179.5	61.3
65 and over	[3]	35.7	[3]	[3]
Hispanic origin[2]	146.0	34.4	227.0	44.1
Under 18	20.4	18.5	20.9	-
18-24	215.8	41.8	362.4	16.1
25-44	296.6	45.4	446.2	114.2
45-64	135.6	46.3	208.8	63.7
65 and over	86.0	40.5	226.6	[3]

Source: "Rate per 100,000 Civilian Population of Admissions to Selected Inpatient Psychiatric Services, by Race, Hispanic Origin, and Sex: United States, 1980," *Mental Health United States*, 1987, p. 78. Primary source: 1980 Patient Sample Surveys, Division of Biometry and Applied Sciences, National Institute of Mental Health. *Notes:* 1. Civilian population estimates used as denominators for rate computations for total all races, whites, and blacks are from the U.S. Bureau of the Census, *Current Population Reports*, Series P-25, No. 929, table 3, p. 19. Population estimates used as denominators for rate computations for American Indians or Alaskan Natives, Asian or Pacific Islanders, and Hispanics are derived from the *1980 Census of Population, General Population Characteristics*, PC80-1- B1, table 43, pp. 32-36, and adjusted to the civilian population estimates. 2. Persons of Hispanics origin may be from any racial group. 3. Based on five or fewer sample cases; rate not shown because it does not meet standards of reliability.

★ 445 ★
Age-Adjusted Cancer Mortality Rates: U.S.

Primary Site	Whites[1]	Blacks	Japanese	Chinese	Filipinos	Native Hawaiians	Native Americans
All sites	163.6	208.5	104.2	131.5	69.7	200.5	87.4
Bladder	3.9	3.8	1.8	1.7	1.5	1.6	1.0
Breast, Female	26.6	26.3	9.9	13.0	8.0	33.0	8.2
Ages <40	1.6	2.5	1.1	0.8	0.9	1.2	1.1
Ages 40+	70.2	68.1	25.2	34.6	20.6	88.7	20.6
Cervix Uteri	3.2	8.8	2.7	2.9	1.6	4.2	5.8
Colon & Rectum	21.6	22.3	17.2	19.3	8.1	15.0	8.6
Colon	18.1	18.8	13.6	15.5	5.8	11.4	6.8
Rectum	3.5	3.5	3.6	3.8	2.3	3.6	1.8
Corpus Uteri	3.9	6.6	3.9	4.3	2.0	3.0	1.8
Esophagus	2.6	9.2	1.9	3.3	1.9	6.5	2.1
Larynx	1.3	2.5	0.2	0.7	0.4	1.4	0.9
Lung, Male	69.3	91.4	32.7	48.2	20.0	88.0	28.0
Lung, Female	20.2	20.1	8.6	21.2	6.8	31.5	8.6
Multiple Myeloma	2.4	5.0	1.2	1.2	1.2	2.8	1.9
Ovary	8.1	6.4	4.3	4.2	2.8	7.0	3.3
Pancreas	8.4	11.0	7.0	7.4	3.3	10.9	4.5
Prostate	21.0	43.9	8.8	7.5	8.2	11.6	15.5
Stomach	5.3	10.0	17.5	7.8	3.3	25.3	6.2

Source: "Average Annual Age-adjusted Cancer Mortality Rates per 100,000 by Primary Site and Racial/Ethnic Group, Total United States, 1978-81," *Cancer Among Blacks and Other Minorities,* (undated), p. 10. Primary source: National Center for Health Statistics.
Notes: 1. The National Center for Health Statistics from which these data are derived does not code ethnicity for Hispanics.

★ 446 ★
Age-Adjusted Cancer Rates: SEER Program

Primary Site	Whites	Blacks	Hispanics[1]	Japanese	Chinese	Filipinos	Native Hawaiians	Native Americans
All sites	335.0	372.5	246.2	247.8	252.9	222.4	357.9	164.2
Bladder	15.4	8.6	8.2	7.7	7.7	5.1	8.2	1.1
Breast, Female	86.5	71.9	54.1	53.1	54.0	43.4	111.1	28.5
Ages <40	8.2	10.7	7.9	8.6	7.4	7.1	7.1	4.0
Ages 40+	221.1	179.3	134.9	146.5	141.0	117.0	300.0	71.4
Cervix Uteri	8.8	20.2	17.7	7.6	11.2	8.8	14.1	22.6
Colon & Rectum	49.6	48.9	25.2	50.4	40.8	30.1	32.7	9.9
Colon	34.6	37.9	15.8	34.0	27.7	17.7	18.4	8.0
Rectum	15.0	11.7	9.4	16.4	13.1	12.4	14.3	1.9
Corpus Uteri	25.1	13.4	11.1	18.6	17.6	11.7	27.1	2.6
Esophagus	3.0	11.5	1.6	2.4	3.4	3.6	6.4	2.4
Larynx	4.6	6.6	2.6	2.6	1.9	1.8	5.2	0.9
Lung, Male	81.0	119.0	34.3	45.1	62.6	38.1	100.9	14.6
Lung, Female	28.2	30.5	13.0	14.1	31.2	18.4	38.6	3.1
Multiple Myeloma	3.4	7.9	2.5	1.2	1.6	4.1	5.5	2.8
Ovary	13.6	9.5	10.4	8.7	9.1	9.4	13.5	3.2
Pancreas	8.9	13.6	10.8	7.4	9.3	6.7	10.0	6.0

Continued.

Age-Adjusted Cancer Rates: SEER Program
[Continued]

Primary Site	Whites	Blacks	Hispanics[1]	Japanese	Chinese	Filipinos	Native Hawaiians	Native Americans
Prostate	75.1	120.3	76.5	44.2	26.1	48.9	57.9	45.4
Stomach	8.0	13.8	15.7	27.9	9.0	7.0	32.4	19.3

Source: "Average Annual Age-adjusted Cancer Incidence Rates per 100,000 by Primary Site and Racial/Ethnic Group, SEER Program, 1978-1981," *Cancer Among Blacks and Other Minorities*, (undated), p. 9. Primary source: Surveillance, Epidemiology and End Results (SEER) Program of the National Cancer Institute. SEER program covers 11 population-based U.S. areas. *Note:* 1. Cancer incidence data for Hispanics come from New Mexico only.

★ 447 ★
AIDS in Children and Young Adults

Age Group	Total	White	Black	Hispanic	Asian	American Indian
Under 5 Years Old						
Males	640	118	357	160	3	1
Females	592	109	346	132	1	2
5-12 Years Old						
Males	169	95	45	26	3	0
Females	88	22	43	21	2	0
Pediatric Total	1,489	344	791	339	9	3
13-19 Years Old						
Males	294	150	82	54	5	2
Females	65	14	39	11	1	0
20-24 Years Old						
Males	3,468	1,858	997	576	22	8
Females	538	148	251	133	2	0
Adult/Adolescent Total	89,501	51,643	23,537	13,472	531	104
Total AIDS cases	90,990	51,987	24,328	13,811	540	107

Source: "Total U.S. AIDS Cases Reported through March 1989, by Age Group, Sex, and Race/Hispanic Origin," *U.S. Children and their Families*, 1989, p. 197. Primary source: Center for Disease Control, *HIV/AIDS Surveillance Report*, April 1989: 1-16, Tables 4 and 6. *Note:* Whites and blacks are those who are non-Hispanic.

★ 448 ★
Amniocentesis Among Older Expectant Mothers

Year	Percent of women 35 years and over who had amniocentesis		
	All races	White	Black
1980	29.0	30.0	16.7

Source: Health United States 1989, March 1990, p. 35. Primary source: National Center for Health Statistics, Division of Vital Statistics.

★ 449 ★
Average Days of Hospitalization: Trends

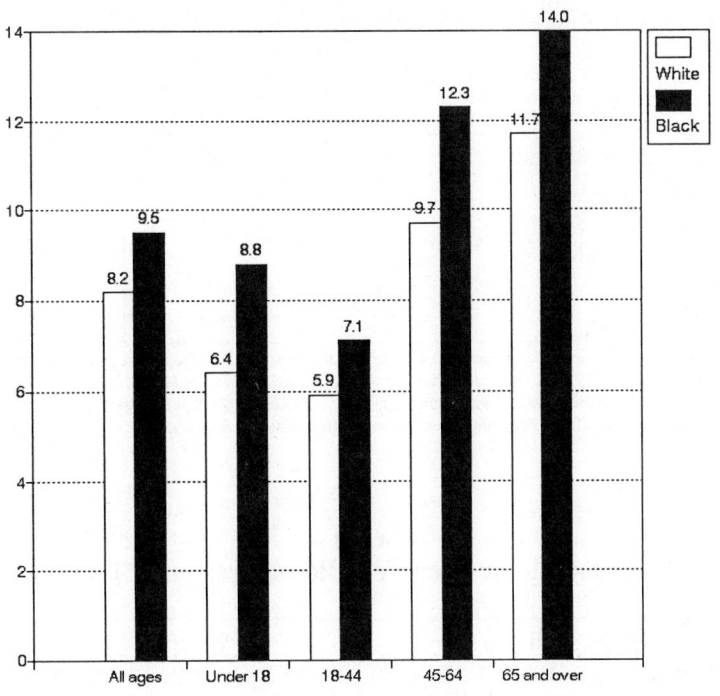

Days per person.

Characteristic	White	Black
All family incomes[1]		
All ages	8.2	9.5
Under 18 years	6.4	8.8
18-44 years	5.9	7.1
45-64 years	9.7	12.3
65 years and over	11.7	14.0
Less than $20,000		
All ages	9.5	10.0
Under 18 years	6.5	9.4
18-44 years	6.6	7.4
45-64 years	11.7	13.5
65 years and over	12.1	13.5
$20,000 or more		
All ages	6.9	7.7
Under 18 years	6.2	7.4
18-44 years	5.4	6.2
45-64 years	8.4	10.6
65 years and over	10.5	13.7

Source: "Average Annual Number of Days Hospitalized per Person Hospitalized during the Year Preceding Interview by Race, Age, and Family Income: United States, 1985-87," *Health of Black and White Americans, 1985-87,* 1990, p. 21. Primary source: National Health Interview Survey, U.S. Department of Health and Human Services, Public Health Service, Centers for Disease Control, Division of Health Statistics, Hyattsville, MD, January 1990. *Note:* 1. Includes unknown family income.

★ 450 ★
Black-White Differences in Cancer Survival: SEER Program

Primary Site	5-Year Relative Survival		Difference
	Blacks	Whites	
All Sites Combined	38	50	12
Corpus Uteri	57	88	31
Bladder	50	74	24
Breast-Female	63	75	12
Rectum	37	49	12
Prostate	59	69	10

Source: "Five-Year Relative Survival for Selected Cancer Sites: Black and White Differences, SEER Program, 1973-81 (percent)," *Cancer Among Blacks and Other Minorities*, (undated), p. 13. Primary source: Surveillance, Epidemiology, and End Results (SEER) Program of the National Cancer Institute. SEER Program covers 11 population-based U.S. areas.

★ 451 ★
Borderline or Elevated Blood Pressure: Trends

Sex, race, and age	All races			White			Black		
	1960-62	1971-74	1976-80	1960-62	1971-74	1976-80	1960-62	1971-74	1976-80
	Percent of population								
Age adjusted, 25-74 years	41.0	42.1	41.3	39.6	40.8	40.1	53.8	55.1	51.3
25-34 years	15.6	19.6	20.8	14.7	18.8	20.7	22.4	28.2	22.4
35-44 years	29.8	32.2	33.0	28.1	29.6	30.8	43.5	54.5	47.9
45-54 years	44.4	46.9	47.1	42.4	45.8	45.9	60.6	57.4	58.9
55-64 years	62.3	59.4	56.7	60.9	58.4	55.2	78.8	71.8	70.5
65-74 years	73.8	70.3	63.1	73.1	69.3	61.9	85.2	80.0	71.7
Male	43.7	46.1	46.6	42.8	45.4	45.9	53.6	55.9	52.8
Age adjusted, 25-74 years	23.3	27.5	31.2	22.3	27.2	31.5	31.9	33.6	31.5
25-34 years	37.4	38.1	39.5	37.0	36.0	37.6	44.2	60.5	53.8
35-44 years	47.2	52.8	52.1	46.0	53.0	52.0	56.3	53.3	50.9
45-54 years	59.3	59.3	58.6	58.3	58.9	57.6	74.8	67.5	71.7
55-64 years	65.9	65.4	62.0	65.0	64.0	60.6	76.8[1]	79.3	68.7
65-74 years	38.4	38.4	36.2	36.5	36.4	34.6	54.7	54.6	50.1
Female									
Age adjusted, 25-74 years	8.6	12.3	11.0	7.6	10.8	10.4	16.1	24.2	15.1
25-34 years	22.7	26.7	27.0	19.8	23.6	24.6	43.0	49.9	43.4
35-44 years	41.8	41.5	42.3	39.1	39.1	40.1	64.8	61.0	65.8
45-54 years	65.0	59.9	55.0	63.3	57.9	53.1	82.8	75.3	69.4
55-64 years	80.3	74.1	63.9	79.8	73.4	63.0	92.1[1]	80.6	74.0
65-74 years									

Source: "Borderline of Definite Elevated Blood Pressure for Persons 25-74 Years of Age, according to Race, Sex, and Age: United States, 1960-62, 1971-74, and 1976-80," *Health United States - 1988*, March 1989, p. 99. Primary source: Division of Health Examination Statistics, National Center for Health Statistics. Notes: Borderline or definite elevated blood pressure is defined as either systolic pressure of at least 140 mmHg of diastolic pressure of at least 90 mmHg or both based on a single measurement. 1. Based on fewer than 45 persons.

★ 452 ★
Cancer Incidence and Mortality: Black to White Ratio

Primary Site	Incidence Rates	Mortality Rates
All Sites Combined	1.11	1.27
Bladder	0.56	0.97
Breast, Female	0.84	0.99
Cervix Uteri	2.30	2.75
Colon & Rectum	1.00	1.03
Colon	1.10	1.04
Rectum	0.78	1.00
Corpus Uteri	0.53	1.69
Esophagus	3.89	3.47
Larynx	1.43	1.92
Lung		
Male	1.47	1.32
Female	1.08	1.00
Multiple Myeolma	2.30	2.08
Ovary	0.70	0.79
Pancreas	1.43	1.31
Prostate	1.60	2.09
Stomach	1.72	1.89

Source: "Ratio of Black to White Age-Adjusted (1970 U.S. Standard) Cancer Incidence and Mortality Rates by Primary Site, SEER Program, 1978-81, *Cancer Among Blacks and Other Minorities,* (undated), p. 12. Primary source: Surveillance, Epidemiology, and End Results (SEER) Program of the National Cancer Institute, and National Center for Health Statistics. SEER Program covers 11 population-based U.S. areas.

★ 453 ★
Cancer Survival Rates

Site	Percent
Japanese	51
Anglo	50
Hispanic	47
Filipino	45
Chinese	44
Hawaiian	44
Black	38
Native American	34

Source: "Five-Year Cancer Survival Rates by Racial/Ethnic Group: 1973-81 (percent), All Sites Combined," *Cancer Among Blacks and Other Minorities,* (undated), p. 130. Primary source: Surveillance, Epidemiology, and End Results (SEER) Program of the National Cancer Institute. SEER Program covers 11 population-based U.S. areas.

★ 454 ★
Cancer Survival Rates: SEER Program

Primary Site	Anglos[3]	Blacks	Hispanics	Japanese	Chinese	Filipinos	Native Hawaiians	Native Americans
All sites	50	38	47	51	44	45	44	34
Bladder	74	50	70	72	74[1]	49[1]	48[2]	37[2]
Breast, Female	75	63	72	85	78	72	76	53[1]
Cervix Uteri	68	63	69	72	72[1]	72[1]	73	67[1]
Colon & Rectum	51	44	46	59	50	41	51[1]	37[1]
Colon	52	46	48	61	53	38	59[1]	44[1]
Rectum	49	37	44	55	44	45	42[1]	24[1]
Corpus Uteri	88	57	86	86	87	78[1]	80[1]	66[2]
Esophagus	5	3	--	--	11[1]	--	--	--
Larynx	67	59	60[1]	75[1]	67[2]	57[2]	79[2]	--
Lung & Bronchus	12	11	11	14	15	12	16	5
Male	11	10	9	13	15	12	13	2
Female	16	14	15	17	15	11	24	--
Multiple Myeloma	24	27	21	30[1]	24[1]	29[1]	26[1]	--
Ovary	37	39	41	41	42[1]	52[1]	36[1]	43[1]
Pancreas	3	3	2	3	3	2	--	--
Prostate	69	59	71	76	76[1]	73	85[1]	47[1]
Stomach	14	15	16	28	16	16	14	9

Source: "Five-Year Relative Survival Rates by Primary Site and Racial/Ethnic Group, SEER Program, 1973-81 (percent)," *Cancer Among Blacks and Other Minorities,* (undated), p. 11. Primary source: Surveillance, Epidemiology, and End Results (SEER) Program of the National Cancer Institute. SEER Program covers 11 population-based U.S. areas. *Notes:* 1. Standard error between 5 & 10%. 2. Standard error 10%. 3. Caucasians not of Hispanic origin or surname.

★ 455 ★
Cancer Survival Rates: Trends

Data are based on the Surveillance, Epidemiology, and End Results Program's population-based registries in Atlanta, Detroit, Seattle-Puget Sound, San Francisco-Oakland, Connecticut, Iowa, New Mexico, Utah, and Hawaii. .

Site	All races			White			Black		
	1974-76	1977-79	1980-85	1974-76	1977-79	1980-85	1974-76	1977-79	1980-85
	Percent of patients								
Male									
All sites	40.5	42.5	41.6	43.8	31.8	45.6	31.0	31.8	32.7
Prostate gland	66.4	70.3	67.4	71.3	61.9	73.4	57.6	61.9	62.8
Lung and bronchus	10.9	11.6	10.9	11.9	8.8	11.7	10.8	8.8	10.4
Colon	49.2	51.1	49.6	51.4	45.2	55.0	43.4	45.2	46.9
Rectum	47.2	48.5	47.5	49.6	38.5	51.4	34.2	38.5	35.9
Urinary bladder	73.4	75.9	74.3	76.3	61.2	78.7	53.5	61.2	59.6
Oral cavity and pharynx	51.8	50.3	54.0	52.6	30.6	52.9	30.8	30.6	25.5
Stomach	13.6	15.0	12.8	14.2	14.3	14.2	15.6	14.3	18.1
Esophagus	3.6	4.56	4.3	5.3	2.3	7.4	2.2	2.3	4.7
Leukemia	32.4	34.4	32.9	35.1	29.9	34.5	31.1	29.9	25.2
Non-Hodgkin's lymphoma	46.8	45.0	47.5	45.6	41.1	49.5	43.5	41.1	38.7
Pancreas	3.0	2.1	3.2	2.0	2.8	2.7	1.1	2.8	3.6

Continued.

Cancer Survival Rates: Trends
[Continued]

Site	All races			White			Black		
	1974-76	1977-79	1980-85	1974-76	1977-79	1980-85	1974-76	1977-79	1980-85
Female									
All sites	56.3	55.4	55.2	57.1	56.2	56.1	46.5	45.7	44.3
Breast	74.0	74.0	75.4	74.6	74.7	76.3	62.6	62.2	63.5
Colon	50.2	53.2	54.8	50.4	53.3	55.3	46.4	49.0	48.6
Rectum	49.1	50.4	53.9	49.4	51.0	54.6	48.2	37.9	42.9
Lung and bronchus	15.4	16.7	15.2	15.6	16.8	15.7	12.9	16.6	14.7
Corpus uteri	88.1	85.1	81.9	89.0	86.5	83.4	62.2	57.1	52.0
Ovary	36.4	37.7	38.6	36.1	32.7	38.4	40.8	39.1	38.3
Cervic uteri	68.2	67.3	66.0	69.0	68.4	66.9	63.0	61.4	59.3
Pancreas	2.4	2.4	3.1	2.3	2.2	2.6	3.4	4.6	6.2
Non-Hodgkin's lymphoma	47.0	50.0	52.1	47.1	49.9	52.4	52.7	58.4	50.9
Melanoma of skin	84.0	84.9	86.5	84.1	85.3	86.6	-	-	77.6[2]

Source: "Five-Year Relative Cancer Survival Rates for Selected Sites, according to Race: 1974-76, 1977-78, and 1980-85," *Health United States - 1988*, March 1989, p. 92. National Cancer Institute, National Institutes of Health, *1988 Annual Cancer Statistics Review, Including a Report on the Status of Cancer Control*, NIH Pub. No. 89-2789. U.S. Department of Health and Human Services, Public Health Service, Bethesda, Md., 1989; National Cancer Institute, Division of Cancer Prevention and Control: Unpublished data. *Notes:* Rates are based on follow up of patients through 1986. The rate is the ratio of the observed survival rate for the patient group to the expected survival rate for persons in the general population similar to the patient group with respect to age, sex, race, and calendar year of observation. It estimates the chance of surviving the effects of cancer. 1. Standard error is greater than 10 percentage points.

★ 456 ★
Cancer: Distribution of Histologic Type

Number of Cases and Histologic Type		Whites	Blacks
Total number of cancer cases		522,065	46,800
Cases microscopically confirmed	n	491,263	43,898
	%	94.1	93.8
Numbers in percent			
Adenocarcinoma[1]		39.2	39.1
Squamous cell carcinoma		11.3	19.3
Carcinoma[1]		5.3	6.6
Duct carcinoma		5.0	4.0
Non-Hodgkin's Lymphoma		4.8	3.0
Leukemia		4.3	3.8
Papillary adenocarcinoma		3.8	3.2
All Others		26.3	21.0
		100.0	100.0

Source: "Percent Distribution of Cases by Histologic Type of Cancer for Blacks and Whites, SEER Program: 1978-81, All Sites Combined," *Cancer Among Blacks and Other Minorities*, (undated), p. 215. Primary Source: Surveillance, Epidemiology, and End Results (SEER) Program of the National Cancer Institute. SEER Program covers 11 population-based U.S. areas. *Note:* 1. NOS = Not otherwise specified.

★ 457 ★
Children's Health Insurance Coverage

Characteristic	Some form of health insurance			Medicaid		
	All	Poor		All	Poor	
	====	====		====	====	
Children 0-17 years	80%	68%		13%	51%	
	Poor	Near-Poor	Non-Poor	Poor	Near-Poor	Non-Poor
	====	====	====	====	====	====
Age Group						
0-5 years	70	68	87	53	14	3
6-17 years	66	67	86	49	12	2
Race/Hispanic Origin						
White	69	70	89	46	14	2
Black	77	62	76	67	20	8
Hispanic	60	65	75	50	10	5
Other	72	64	83	55	7	2

Source: Health Insurance and Medicaid Coverage of Children, by Age Group, Poverty Status, Family Type, Employment of Parents, and Race/Hispanic Origin, 1985, *U.S. Children and their Parents*, 1989, p. 213. Primary source: Child Trends, Inc., special tabulations prepared from the March 1986 Current Population Survey. *Notes:* White, black, and other are those who not Hispanic. Some form of insurance includes Medicaid. Medicaid "coverage" includes all persons enrolled in the Medicaid program at any time during 1984; the persons did not necessarily receive medical care paid for by Medicaid. The **near-poor** are those whose family incomes put them between 1 and 1.5 times the government-established poverty line. Published by permission.

★ 458 ★
Children's Health Ratings

Parent Rating of Child's Health	Percent Distributions					
	Preschool Children (under 5 years) Race, 1987			School-Aged Children (5-17 years) Race, 1987		
	Total	Whites	Blacks	Total	Whites	Blacks
Excellent	54	56	46	53	56	40
Very Good	27	28	25	27	27	26
Good	16	14	25	17	15	31
Fair or Poor	3	2	5	2	2	4

Source: "Health Ratings for Preschool and School-Aged Children, by Race and Poverty Status in 1987, and by Year, 1983-87," *U.S. Children and their Families*, 1989, p. 207. Primary source: National Center for Health Statistics, "Current Estimates From the National Health Interview Survey: United States, 1983;" 1985; and 1987; *Vital and Health Statistics*, Series 10, Nos. 154, 160, and 166, September 1988, Table 70 in each.

★ 459 ★
Children's Physician Visits: Trends

	Number of Physician Visits per Child per Year		Percent with No Physician Visit in Two Years or More	
	1985	1987	1985	1987
All children under 18	4.2	4.2	8.9	8.3
Race				
White	4.5	4.6	8.6	7.9
Black	3.0	3.0	11.0	10.1

Source: "Number of Physician Visits Per Year by Children and Percent of Children with No Visits by Age, Race, and Income, 1985 and 1987," *U.S. Children and their Families*, 1989, p. 211. Primary source: National Center for Health Statistics, "Current Estimates from the National Health Interview Survey, United States, 1987," *Vital and Health Statistics*, Series 10, Nos. 160, 166, September 1988, Tables 71 and 72 in each report. *Notes:* Physician visits as measured in the National Health Interview Survey include contacts with physicians by telephone.

★ 460 ★
Children: Activity Limitations

	In thousands		Percent	
	Total With Activity Limitation	Limitation in Major Activity	Total With Activity Limitation	Limitation in Major Activity
Characteristic				
All children under 18	3,164	2,222	5.0	3.5
Race				
White	2,563	1,764	5.0	3.4
Black	540	403	5.6	4.1

Source: "Children With Activity Limitations by Sex, Race, and Family Income, 1987," *U.S. Children and their Families*, 1989, p. 205. Primary source: National Center for Health Statistics, "Current Estimates From the National Health Interview Survey: United States," 1983, 1985, 1987, *Vital and Health Statistics*, Series 10, Nos. 154, 160, and 166, September 1988, Tables 67 and 68 in each report.

★ 461 ★
Choice of Health Occupations: Trends

Enrollment and health occupation	Number of students All races, both sexes		Percent of students					
			Black		Other minority		Women	
	1976-77[1]	1986-87[2]	1976-77[1]	1986-87[2]	1976-77[1]	1986-87[2]	1976-77[1]	1986-87[2]
Medicine								
Allopathic	57,765	66,125	6.1	5.9	5.6	13.1	24.7	33.4
Osteopathic	3,671	6,640	1.9	1.8	2.3	7.0	12.9	27.9
Podiatry	2,295	2,832	3.2	7.6	2.7	7.4	6.8	23.7
Dentistry[3]	20,790	18,403	4.6	5.6	5.5	14.4	11.2	27.1
Optometry	4,033	4,562	2.2	2.4	5.2	12.9	13.4	33.2
Pharmacy[4]	23,465	25,643	4.0	6.7	4.9	11.0	36.8	58.6
Veterinary medicine	6,571	8,887	-	2.3	-	3.9	27.3	53.0
Registered nurses[5]	239,486	193,712	5.8	6.4	2.7	3.7	93.7	95.6

Continued.

Choice of Health Occupations: Trends
[Continued]

Enrollment and health occupation	Number of students All races, both sexes		Percent of students					
			Black		Other minority		Women	
	1976-77[1]	1986-87[2]	1976-77[1]	1986-87[2]	1976-77[1]	1986-87[2]	1976-77[1]	1986-87[2]
First-year enrollment								
Medicine:								
Allopathic	15,613	16,819	6.7	7.0	6.3	15.0	24.7	35.0
Osteopathic	1,088	1,724	2.4	1.5	3.0	8.0	16.5	27.3
Podiatry	650	815	3.8	9.6	3.2	10.3	-	-
Dentistry[3]	5,869	4,494	4.9	6.4	6.1	17.0	13.5	30.1
Optometry	1,111	1,251	-	-	-	-	15.5	39.0
Pharmacy	8,208	6,584	4.5	6.0	4.9	10.4	33.2	54.5
Veterinary medicine	1,866	2,273	-	-	-	-	33.7	58.5
Registered nurses[5]	110,950	100,791	7.2	9.3	3.9	5.3	95.3	93.4

Source: "Total and First-Year Enrollment of Minorities and Women in Schools for Selected Health Occupations: United States, Academic Years 1976-77 and 1986-87," *Health United States - 1988*, March 1989, p. 137. Primary source:Bureau of Health Professions: *Minorities and Women in the Health Fields*, 1978. DHEW Pub. No. (HRA) 79-22. Health Resources Administration. Washington. U.S. Government Printing Office, Oct. 1978; *Minorities and Women in the Health Fields, 1984 Edition*. DHHS Pub. No. (HRSA) HRS-DV 84- 5. Health Resources and Services Administration. Washington. U.S. Government Printing Office, Sept. 1984; *Minorities and Women in the Health Fields,1987 Edition*. DHHS Pub. No. (HRSA) HRS-P-DV 87-1. Rockville, Md., Sept. 1987; and *Sixth Report to the President and Congress on the Status of Health Personnel in the United States*. Health Resources and Services Administration. DHHS Pub. No. HRS-P-OD-88-1, Rockville, Md., 1988; American Association of Colleges of Osteopathic Medicine: *Annual Statistical Report*, 1987. Rockville, Md., 1987; National League for Nursing: *Nursing Student Census*, 1987. New York, 1988. *Notes:* 1. Data for registered nurses are for 1977-78. 2. Data for total enrollment for optometry and registered nurses and for first-year enrollment for optometry, pharmacy, and registered nurses are for 1985-86. 3. Excludes Puerto Rican schools. 4. Prior to 1986-87, pharmacy enrollments are for students in the final 3 years of pharmacy education. Beginning in 1986-87, data for all pharmacy students are shown. 5. Percent distribution based only on schools reporting minority data.

★ 462 ★
Chronic Conditions and Activity Limitation: Trends

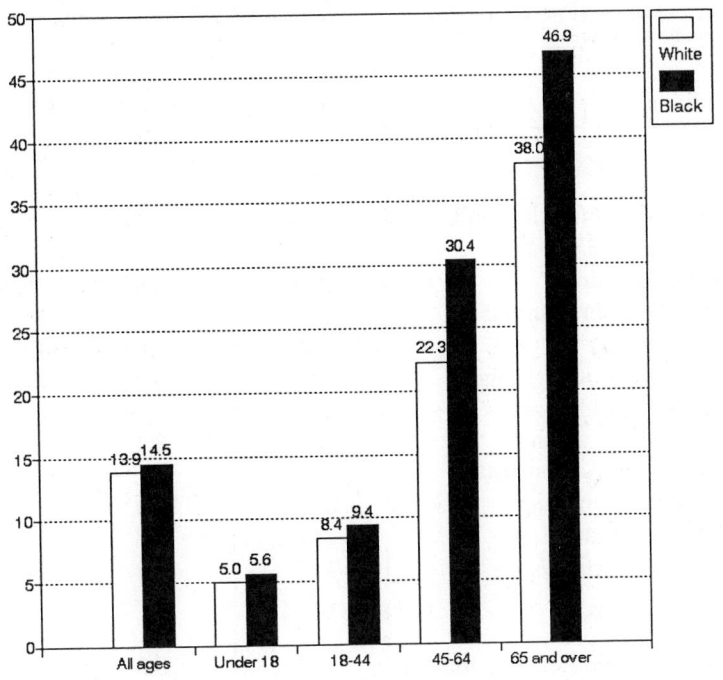

Percent.

Characteristic	White	Black
All family incomes[1]		
All ages	13.9	14.5
Under 18 years	5.0	5.6
18-44 years	8.4	9.4
45-64 years	22.3	30.4
65 years and over	38.0	46.9
Less than $20,000		
All ages	21.4	18.3
Under 18 years	6.5	6.6
18-44 years	12.1	12.6
45-64 years	39.1	42.3
65 years and over	42.3	49.2
$20,000 or more		
All ages	9.7	7.3
Under 18 years	4.5	3.8
18-44 years	6.9	5.4
45-64 years	15.9	14.9
65 years and over	31.3	30.9

Source: "Average Annual Percent of Persons with Limitation of Activity due to Chronic Conditions by Race, Age, and Family Income: United States, 1985- 87," *Health of Black and White Americans, 1985-87*, 1990, p. 12. Primary source: National Health Interview Survey, U.S. Department of Health and Human Services, Public Health Service, Centers for Disease Control, Division of Health Statistics, Hyattsville, MD, January 1990. *Note:* 1. Includes unknown family income.

★ 463 ★
Chronic Conditions that Limit Activity: Trends

Covers civilian noninstitutional population. Conditions classified according to ninth revision of International Classification of Diseases. Based on National Health Interview Survey.

Condition	Total[1]	Race White	Race Black
1980			
Persons with limitation (mil.)	31.4	27.1	3.9
Percent limited by-			
Heart conditions	16.4	16.6	15.2
Arthritis and rheumatism	17.5	17.4	18.3
Hypertension[2]	9.9	8.6	19.2
Impairment of back/spine	9.2	9.4	7.7
Impairment of lower extremities and hips	8.0	8.1	7.2
Percent of all persons with-			
No activity limitation	85.6	85.6	84.9
Activity limitation	14.4	14.4	15.1
In major activity	10.9	10.8	12.2
1985			
Persons with limitation (mil.)	32.7	28.0	4.1
Percent limited by-			
Heart conditions	17.4	17.5	16.9
Arthritis and rheumatism	18.9	18.9	20.3
Hypertension[2]	10.5	9.0	21.3
Impairment of back/spine	9.2	9.4	7.0
Impairment of lower extremities and hips	8.9	9.0	8.1
Percent of all persons with-			
No activity limitation	86.0	85.9	85.5
Activity limitation	14.0	14.1	14.5
In major activity	9.5	9.4	11.1

Source: "Persons with Activity Limitation by Selected Chronic Conditions: 1980 and 1985," *Statistical Abstract*, 1989, p. 115. Primary source: U.S. National Center for Health Statistics, *Vital and Health Statistics*, series 10, and unpublished data. *Notes:* 1. Includes other races, not shown separately. 2. Covers all cases of hypertension, regardless of other conditions.

★ 464 ★
Cigarette Smokers 18 and Over: Trends

Data based on household interviews of a sample of the civilian noninstitutionalized population.

Sex, race, and education	1965	1974	1983	1987
	Percent of persons 18 years of age and over			
All persons				
18 years and over, age adjusted	42.3	37.2	32.2	28.7
18 years and over, crude	42.4	37.1	32.1	28.8
All males				
18 years and over, age adjusted	51.6	42.9	34.7	31.0

Continued.

Cigarette Smokers 18 and Over: Trends
[Continued]

Sex, race, and education	1965	1974	1983	1987
18 years and over, crude	51.9	43.1	35.1	31.2
18-24 years	54.1	42.1	32.9	28.2
25-34 years	60.7	50.5	38.8	34.8
35-44 years	58.2	51.0	41.0	36.6
45-64 years	51.9	42.6	35.9	33.5
65 years and over	28.5	24.8	22.0	17.2
White:				
18 years and over, age adjusted	50.8	41.7	34.1	30.4
18-24 years	53.0	40.8	32.5	29.2
25-34 years	60.1	49.5	38.6	33.8
35-44 years	57.3	50.1	40.8	36.2
45-64 years	51.3	41.2	35.0	32.4
65 years and over	27.7	24.3	20.6	16.0
Black:				
18 years and over, age adjusted	59.2	54.0	41.3	39.0
18-24 years	62.8	54.9	34.2	24.9
25-34 years	68.4	58.5	39.9	44.9
35-44 years	67.3	61.5	45.5	44.0
45-64 years	57.9	57.8	44.8	44.3
65 years and over	36.4	29.7	38.9	30.3
All females				
18 years and over, age adjusted	34.0	32.5	29.9	26.7
18 years and over, crude	33.9	32.1	29.5	26.5
18-24 years	38.1	34.1	35.5	26.1
25-34 years	43.7	38.8	32.6	31.8
35-44 years	43.7	39.8	33.8	29.6
45-64 years	32.0	33.4	31.0	28.6
65 years and over	9.6	12.0	13.1	13.7
White:				
18 years and over, age adjusted	34.3	32.3	30.1	27.2
18-24 years	38.4	34.0	36.5	27.8
25-34 years	43.4	38.6	32.2	31.9
35-44 years	43.9	39.3	34.8	29.2
45-64 years	32.7	33.0	30.6	29.0
65 years and over	9.8	12.3	13.2	13.9
Black:				
18 years and over, age adjusted	32.1	35.9	31.8	27.2
18-24 years	37.1	35.6	32.0	20.4
25-34 years	47.8	42.2	38.0	35.8
35-44 years	42.8	46.4	32.7	35.3
45-64 years	25.7	38.9	36.3	28.4
65 years and over	7.1	8.9	13.1	11.7

Source: "Current Cigarette Smoking by Persons 18 Years of Age and Over, according to Sex, Race, and Education: United States, Selected Years 1974- 87," *Health United States 1989*, March 1990, p. 165. Primary source: Division of Health Interview Statistics, National Center for Health Statistics: Data from the National Health Interview Survey; Data computed by the Division of Epidemiology and Health Promotion from data compiled by the Division of Health Interview Statistics. *Notes:* A current smoker is a person who has smoked at least 100 cigarettes and who now smokes; includes occasional smokers. Excludes unknown smoking status.

★ 465 ★
Cigarette Smokers 25 and Over: Trends

Data based on household interviews of a sample of the civilian noninstitutionalized population.

Sex, race, and education	1974	1979	1983	1985	1987
	Percent of persons 25 years of age and over, age adjusted				
All persons[1]	37.1	33.3	31.7	30.2	29.1
Less than 12 years	43.8	41.1	40.8	41.0	40.6
12 years	36.4	33.7	33.6	32.1	31.8
13-15 years	35.8	33.2	30.3	29.7	27.2
16 or more years	27.5	22.8	20.7	18.6	16.7
All males[1]	43.0	37.6	35.1	32.9	31.5
Less than 12 years	52.4	48.1	47.2	46.0	45.7
12 years	42.6	39.1	37.4	35.6	35.2
13-15 years	41.6	36.5	33.0	33.0	28.4
16 or more years	28.6	23.1	21.8	19.7	17.3
White males[1]	41.9	36.9	34.5	31.1	30.6
Less than 12 years	51.6	48.0	47.9	45.2	45.3
12 years	42.2	38.6	37.1	34.8	34.6
13-15 years	41.1	36.4	32.6	32.3	28.0
16 or more years	28.1	22.8	21.1	19.2	17.4
Black males[1]	53.8	44.9	42.8	45.2	41.9
Less than 12 years	58.3	50.1	46.0	51.1	49.4
12 years	51.2[2]	48.4	47.2	41.9	43.6
13-15 years	45.7[2]	39.3	44.7	42.3	32.4
16 or more years	41.8[2]	37.9[2]	31.3[2]	30.0[2]	20.9
All females[1]	32.2	29.6	28.8	27.8	26.9
Less than 12 years	36.8	35.0	35.3	36.7	36.1
12 years	32.5	29.9	30.9	29.6	29.2
13-15 years	30.2	30.0	27.5	26.7	26.0
16 or more years	26.1	22.5	19.2	17.4	16.1
White females[1]	31.9	29.8	28.8	27.6	27.0
Less than 12 years	37.0	36.1	35.5	37.1	37.0
12 years	32.1	29.9	30.9	29.4	29.4
13-15 years	30.5	30.6	28.0	27.1	26.2
16 or more years	35.8	21.9	18.9	16.8	16.4
Black females[1]	35.9	30.6	31.8	32.1	28.6
Less than 12 years	36.4	31.9	36.9	39.2	39.0
12 years	41.9	33.0	35.2	32.3	28.1
13-15 years	33.2	28.8[2]	26.5	23.7	27.2
16 or more years	35.2[2]	43.4[2]	38.7[2]	27.5	19.5

Source: "Age-Adjusted Prevalence of Current Cigarette Smoking by Persons 25 Years of Age and Over, according to Sex, Race, and Education: United States, Selected Years 1974-87," *Health United States 1989*, March 1990, p. 166. Primary source: Data compiled by the Division of Epidemiology and Health Promotion, National Center for Health Statistics from data compiled by the Division of Health Interview Statistics. *Notes:* A current smoker is a person who has smoked at least 100 cigarettes and who now smokes; includes occasional smokers. Excludes unknown smoking status. 1. Includes unknown education. 2. For age groups where percent smoking was 0 or 100 the age-adjustment procedure was modified to substitute the percent from the next lower education group. These age-adjusted percents should be considered unreliable because of small sample size.

★ 466 ★
Cumulative Risk and Incidence of AIDS in the 80s

Category	White		Black		Hispanic		Other	
	Number	Percent	Number	Percent	Number	Percent	Number	Percent
Adults, total[2]	380.8	1.0	1,068.1	2.8[1]	1,036.3	2.7[1]	141.0	0.4[1]
Adult men	188.9	1.0	578.2	3.1[1]	564.4	3.0[1]	74.4	0.4[1]
Adult women	12.2	1.0	161.1	13.2[1]	104.6	8.6[1]	11.1	0.9
Homosexual men	298.6	1.0	413.8	1.4[1]	513.9	1.7[1]	94.7	0.3[1]
Bisexual men	46.8	1.0	177.7	3.8[1]	126.3	2.7[1]	24.9	0.5[1]
Heterosexual IV								
drug users	10.1	1.0	201.2	19.9[1]	195.1	19.3[1]	4.2	0.3[1]
Hemophiliacs	2.6	1.0	1.4	0.6[1]	2.7	1.0	1.7	0.7
Transfusion								
recipients	5.1	1.0	7.5	1.5	6.5	1.3	5.0	1.0
Pediatric, total[3]	3.8	1.0	46.3	12.1[1]	26.1	6.8[1]	3.2	0.8
Mother, IV drug user	0.8	1.0	21.8	26.4[1]	13.9	16.9[1]	1.3	1.6
Mother's partner, IV								
drug user	0.2	1.0	5.5	25.8[1]	6.2	29.2[1]	0.0	0.0
Transfusion-								
associated	1.1	1.0	2.7	2.3[1]	2.1	1.9	0.0	0.0
Hemophiliacs	0.6	1.0	0.7	1.0	1.3	2.0	0.6	1.0

Source: "Cumulative Incidence of AIDS and Relative Risk, by Race and Ethnic Groups, Age, and Transmission Category, 1981-1987," *A Common Destiny: Blacks And American Society*, 1989, p. 420. Primary source: Curran, J.W., H.W. Jaffe, A.M. Hardy, W.M. Morgan, R.M. Selik, and T.J. Dondero. 1988. Epidemiology of HIV Infection and AIDS in the United States. *Science* 239 (4840): 610-616. *Notes:* Cumulative incidence is given per 1 million population. Relative risk is given in parentheses. Relative risk is the ratio of the cumulative incidence in each race or ethnic group to the incidence in whites. 1. Relative risk significantly different from 1.0 (P<0.05). 2. For all men, homosexual men, and bisexual men, the denomiator consisted of all men >15 years; for all women, the denominator was all women >15 years; for other adult categories, the denominators included all men and women >15 years. 3. For pediatric categories, the denominators consisted of all children <15 years. Published by permission.

★ 467 ★
Current and Former Smokers: Trends

Sex, race, and age	Current smoker[1]				Former smoker			
	1965	1976	1983	1987	1965	1976	1983	1987
	Percent of persons							
Male								
20 years and over, age adjusted	52.1	41.6	35.4	31.5	20.3	29.6	31.1	31.4
20 years and over, crude	52.4	41.9	35.7	31.7	20.5	28.9	29.5	30.1
20-24 years	59.2	45.9	36.9	31.1	9.0	12.2	9.1	7.8
25-34 years	60.7	48.5	38.8	34.8	14.7	18.3	19.8	17.4
35-44 years	58.2	47.6	41.0	36.6	20.6	27.3	27.5	28.1
45-64 years	51.9	41.3	35.9	33.5	24.1	37.1	40.1	40.1
65 years and over	28.5	23.0	22.0	17.2	28.1	44.4	48.1	53.4
White:								
20 years and over, age adjusted	51.3	41.0	34.7	30.7	21.2	30.7	32.0	32.6
20-44 years	58.5	46.8	38.8	34.3	16.9	20.5	20.5	20.4
20-24 years	58.1	45.3	36.1	31.6	9.6	13.3	9.7	8.3
25-34 years	60.1	47.7	38.6	33.8	15.5	18.9	20.5	18.1
35-44 years	57.3	46.8	40.8	36.2	21.5	28.9	27.8	29.3
45 years and over	44.4	35.0	30.1	26.3	26.1	40.5	44.1	46.6
45-64 years	51.3	40.6	35.0	32.4	25.1	38.1	41.2	41.6

Continued.

Current and Former Smokers: Trends
[Continued]

Sex, race, and age	Current smoker[1]				Former smoker			
	1965	1976	1983	1987	1965	1976	1983	1987
65 years and over	27.7	22.8	20.6	16.0	28.7	45.6	49.9	55.1
Black:								
20 years and over, age adjusted	59.6	50.1	42.6	40.3	12.6	20.2	23.2	22.2
20-44 years	67.7	57.4	41.8	41.3	8.3	10.2	15.4	12.9
45 years and over	52.3	42.3	42.9	39.5	17.0	30.0	30.6	32.0
Female								
20 years and over, age adjusted	34.2	32.5	29.9	27.0	8.2	13.9	16.4	18.0
20 years and over, crude	34.1	32.0	29.4	26.8	8.2	13.8	16.2	17.9
20-24 years	41.9	34.2	37.5	28.1	7.3	10.4	10.8	10.5
25-34 years	43.7	37.5	32.6	31.8	9.9	12.9	13.8	15.6
35-44 years	43.7	38.2	33.8	29.6	9.6	15.8	17.1	19.4
45-64 years	32.0	34.8	31.0	28.6	8.6	15.9	18.6	20.7
65 years and over	9.6	12.8	13.1	13.7	4.5	11.7	18.7	19.8
White:								
20 years and over, age adjusted	34.5	32.4	29.8	27.3	8.5	14.6	17.2	18.9
20-44 years	43.3	36.8	34.3	30.5	9.6	14.2	15.2	17.2
20-24 years	41.9	34.4	37.5	29.4	8.0	11.4	11.6	11.5
25-34 years	43.4	37.1	32.2	31.9	10.3	13.7	15.1	16.9
35-44 years	43.9	38.1	34.8	29.2	9.9	17.0	18.0	20.6
45 years and over	25.1	26.7	23.6	22.7	7.4	14.6	19.2	20.9
45-64 years	32.7	34.7	30.6	29.0	8.8	16.4	19.0	21.4
65 years and over	9.8	13.2	13.2	14.0	4.5	11.5	19.5	20.2
Black:								
20 years and over, age adjusted	32.7	34.7	32.5	27.9	5.9	10.2	10.7	13.2
20-44 years	45.0	40.1	36.2	32.7	5.9	8.1	7.7	8.9
45 years and over	20.6	28.3	28.1	22.7	6.0	12.4	13.4	17.4

Source: "Cigarette Smoking by Persons 20 Years of Age and Over, according to Sex, Race, and Age: United States, 1965, 1976, 1983, and 1987," *Health United States - 1988*, March 1989, p. 96. Primary source: National Health Interview Survey, National Center for Health Statistics. *Notes:* Excludes unknown smoking status. 1. A current smoker is a person who has smoked at least 100 cigarettes and who now smokes; includes occasional smokers.

★ 468 ★
Days in Short-Stay Hospitals: Trends

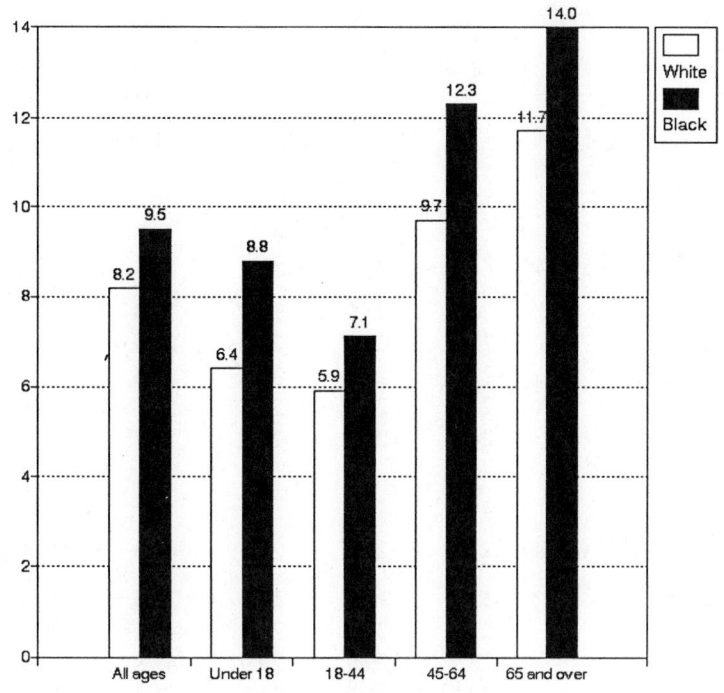

Days per person.

Characteristic	White	Black
All health statuses[1]		
All ages	8.2	9.5
Under 18 years	6.4	8.8
18-44 years	5.9	7.1
45-64 years	9.7	12.3
65 years and over	11.7	14.0
Fair or poor health[2]		
All ages	13.3	14.7
Under 18 years	12.8	19.1
18-44 years	11.4	12.0
45-64 years	13.7	15.1
65 years and over	14.0	15.9
Good to excellent health[2]		
All ages	6.3	6.4
Under 18 years	5.7	6.4
18-44 years	5.0	5.7
45-64 years	6.9	7.8
65 years and over	9.5	9.8

Source: "Average Annual Number of Days in Short-Stay Hospitals per Person Hospitalized during the Year Preceding by Race, Age, and Respondent-Assessed Health Status: United States, 1985-87," *Health of Black and White Americans, 1985-87*, 1990, p. 14. Primary source: National Health Interview Survey, U.S. Department of Health and Human Services, Public Health Service, Centers for Disease Control, Division of Health Statistics, Hyattsville, MD, January 1990. *Notes:* 1. Includes unknown health status. 2. As assessed by self or responsible family member.

★ 469 ★
Demographic Characteristics of Overweight Adults: Trends

Sex and age	White			Black		
	1960-62	1971-74	1976-80	1960-62	1971-74	1976-80
	Percent of population[1]					
Male						
Age adjusted, 25-74 years	25.1	26.0	26.7	24.1	27.6	30.9
25-34 years	21.4	23.6	20.9	34.3	26.1	17.5
35-44 years	22.4	28.9	28.2	28.6	39.3	40.9
45-54 years	29.3	28.2	30.5	18.5	22.4	41.4
55-64 years	28.5	24.9	28.6	20.1	25.6	26.0
65-74 years	24.8	23.1	25.8	11.7[2]	21.6	26.4
Female						
Age adjusted, 25-74 years	27.3	27.4	27.5	47.3	47.8	49.5
25-34 years	13.9	15.9	17.9	29.6	31.5	33.5
35-44 years	21.2	24.5	24.8	46.1	49.9	40.8
45-54 years	28.5	29.9	29.9	47.8	53.5	61.2
55-64 years	40.5	36.6	34.8	71.4	58.7	59.4
65-74 years	43.2	37.0	36.5	47.8[2]	49.2	60.8

Source: "Overweight Persons Aged 25-74 Years, by Race, Sex, and Age: National Health Examination Survey, 1960-62; First National Health and Nutrition Examination Survey, 1971-74; and Second National Health and Nutrition Examination Survey, 1976-80 (NCHS, 1988)," *Nutrition Monitoring in the United States*, September 1989, p. 109. Primary source: National Center for Health Statistics. 1988. *Health, United States, 1987.* DHHS Pub. No. (PHS) 88-1232. Public Health Service. Washington: U.S. Government Printing Office. *Notes:* 1. Overweight is defined for men as body mass index greater than or equal to 27.8 kilograms/square meter, and for women as body mass index greater than or equal to 27.3 kilograms/square meter. These cutoff points were used because they represent the sex-specific 85th percentiles for persons aged 20-29 years in the second National Health and Nutrition Examination Survey. Excludes pregnant women. 2. Based on fewer than 45 persons.

★ 470 ★
Dependency & Other Characteristics of Nursing Home Discharges

Discharge status, characteristics, and duration of stay	All dis-charges	Depen-dent in mobil-ity[1]	Depen-dent in conti-nence[2]	Partial index of dependency in activities of daily living			
				Not depen-dent in mobility or con-tinence	Depen-dent in mobility only	Depen-dent in con-tinence only	Depen-dent in mobility and conti-nence
	Number						
All discharges[3]	1,223,500	736,900	662,900	379,000	181,600	107,600	555,300
Race:							
White	1,135,900	679,300	611,700	354,600	169,600	102,000	509,700
Black	82,000	54,000	48,200	22,400	11,400	5,600	42,600
Other	5,600	4	4	4	4	5	4

Continued.

Dependency & Other Characteristics of Nursing Home Discharges
[Continued]

Discharge status, characteristics, and duration of stay	All dis-charges	Depen-dent in mobil-ity[1]	Depen-dent in conti-nence[2]	Partial index of dependency in activities of daily living			
				Not depen-dent in mobility or con-tinence	Depen-dent in mobility only	Depen-dent in con-tinence only	Depen-dent in mobility and conti-nence
Live discharges	877,000	437,300	383,300	346,900	146,800	92,700	290,500
Race:							
White	811,200	399,600	349,800	323,900	137,400	87,700	262,200
Black	61,200	35,200	31,300	21,000	9,000	5,100	26,200
Other	[4]	[4]	[4]	[4]	[4]	[5]	[4]
Dead discharges	344,200	299,100	279,400	30,200	34,500	14,900	264,600
Race:							
White	322,500	279,200	261,600	28,900	31,900	14,300	247,300
Black	20,700	18,800	17,000	[4]	[4]	[4]	16,400
Other	[4]	[4]	[4]	[5]	[4]	[5]	[4]

Source: "Number of Nursing Home Discharges, by Dependencies in Mobility and Continence, Partial Index of Dependency, Discharge Status, Selected Characteristics, and Duration of Stay, and Median Age and Average Duration of Stay, by Dependencies in Mobility and Continence and Partial Index of Dependency: United States, 1984-85," *Discharges from Nursing Homes: 1985 National Nursing Home Survey*, March 1990, pp. 35-38. Primary source: *Vital and Health Statistics*, Series 13, No. 103. *Notes:* Figures may not add to totals because of rounding. 1. Refers to discharge who was chairfast or bedfast. 2. Refers to discharge who had trouble controlling bowel or bladder, or both, or who had an ostomy. 3. Includes small number of discharges with unknown discharge status. 4. Figure does not meet standard of reliability or precision. 5. Quantity zero.

★ 471 ★
Disability Days and Employment Industry

Data based on household interviews of the civilian noninstitutionalized population.

Race and industry of longest employment	Estimated popu-lation (thou.)	Days per person per year	
		Restric-ted-activity days	Bed-disa-bility days
White			
All persons	140,022	21.0	7.0
Agriculture	4,251	26.3	7.2
Forestry and fisheries	203	28.6	6.8[1]
Mining	1,240	25.9	7.5
Construction	6,969	20.2	6.4
Manufacturing	31,980	22.3	6.9
Transportation and public utilities	8,000	23.6	7.2
Wholesale and retail trade	28,243	18.1	6.6
Finance, insurance, and real estate	6,939	16.5	5.7
Services and miscellaneous	33,851	19.6	6.8
Public administration	7,050	21.3	6.3

Continued.

Disability Days and Employment Industry
[Continued]

Race and industry of longest employment	Estimated population (thou.)	Days per person per year	
		Restricted-activity days	Bed-disability days
Ever worked, industry unknown	6,376	23.0	9.7
Never worked	4,921	31.4	11.3
Black			
All persons	16,842	30.0	12.8
Agriculture	509	43.7	15.3
Forestry and fisheries	9[1]	48.8[1]	48.8[1]
Mining	61	24.8[1]	22.0[1]
Construction	665	35.0	10.2
Manufacturing	3,370	29.1	14.5
Transportation and public utilities	908	29.1	11.2
Wholesale and retail trade	2,159	25.1	11.7
Finance, insurance, and real estate	586	23.9	7.9[1]
Services and miscellaneous	5,428	32.6	13.7
Public administration	1,314	22.7	10.2
Ever worked, industry unknown	877	34.2	14.1
Never worked	957	28.9	10.3

Source: "Number of Persons 17 Years of Age and Over and Number of Days of Disability Per Person Per Year, by Race and Industry of Longest Employment: United States, 1980," Health Characteristics by Occupation and Industry of Longest Employment, June 1989, p. 47. Primary source: *Vital and Health Statistics*, Series 10, Data from the National Health Survey, No. 168. *Note:* 1. Figure does not meet standard of reliability or precision.

★ 472 ★
Disability Days and Occupational Category

Data based on household interviews of the civilian noninstitutionalized population.

Race and occupation of longest employment	Estimated population (thou.)	Restricted-activity days	Bed-disability days
	Days per person per year		
All persons	160,149	21.8	7.6
White-collar workers	72,895	17.1	6.0
Blue-collar workers	48,058	24.5	8.1
Farm workers	4,177	27.8	7.9
Service workers	21,120	27.6	10.2
Ever worked, occupation unknown	7,752	23.7	10.1

Continued.

Disability Days and Occupational Category
[Continued]

Race and occupation of longest employment	Esti-mated population (thou.)	Restric-ted-activity days	Bed-dis-ability days
Never worked	6,146	30.4	10.8
White			
All persons	140,022	21.0	7.0
White-collar workers	66,815	17.1	5.9
Blue-collar workers	41,604	23.8	7.2
Farm workers	3,592	26.1	6.9
Service workers	16,523	24.5	8.5
Ever worked, occupation unknown	6,566	22.9	9.8
Never worked	4,921	31.4	11.3
Black			
All persons	16,842	30.0	12.8
White-collar workers	4,702	18.9	7.4
Blue-collar workers	5,608	30.4	13.8
Farm workers	472	44.3	16.5
Service workers	4,159	39.7	17.5
Ever worked, occupation unknown	944	33.8	13.5
Never worked	957	28.9	10.3

Source: "Number and Percent Distribution of Persons 17 Years of Age and Over by Limitation of Activity Due to Chronic Conditions, According to Race and Occupation of Longest Employment: United States, 1980," *Health Characteristics by Occupation and Industry of Longest Employment,* June 1989, p. 42. Primary source: *Vital and Health Statistics*, Series 10, Data from the National Health Survey, No. 168.

★ 473 ★
Disability Days: Trends

Item	Total Days of Disability (millions)						Days per person					
	1970	1980	1983	1984	1985	1986	1970	1980	1983	1984	1985	1986
Restricted-activity days[1]	2,913	4,165	3,318	3,427	3,453	3,597	14.6	19.1	14.5	14.8	14.8	15.2
White[2]	2,526	3,518	2,813	2,905	2,899	3,048	14.4	18.7	14.3	14.7	14.5	15.2
Black[2]	365	580	452	461	489	473	16.2	22.7	16.6	16.6	17.4	16.6
Hispanic[3]	[4]	[4]	[4]	229	228	226	[4]	[4]	[4]	12.9	13.2	12.5

Source: "Days of Disability, by Type and Selected Characteristics: 1970 to 1986," *Statistical Abstract*, 1989, p. 110. Primary source: U.S. National Center for Health Statistics, *Vital and Health Statistics*, series 10; and unpublished data. *Notes:* 1. A day when a person cuts down on his usual activities for the whole day because of illness or injury. Includes bed-disability, work-loss, and school-loss days. Total includes other races and unknown income, not shown separately. 2. Beginning 1980 race was determined by asking the household respondent to report his race. In earlier years the racial classification of respondents was determined by interviewer observation. 3. Hispanic persons may be of any race 4. Not available.

★ 474 ★
Discharges from Nursing Homes

Discharge status and characteristic	All stays	Less than 1 month	1 month to less than 3 months	3 months to less than 6 months	6 months to less than 12 months	1 year to less than 3 years	3 years to less than 5 years	5 years or more	Ave. duration stay	Median duration of stay
All discharges[1]	1,223,500	379,000	252,200	136,700	137,400	185,200	63,200	69,800	401	82
Race:										
White	1,135,900	352,900	234,400	124,900	126,300	172,000	59,600	65,700	406	82
Black	82,000	23,900	16,200	11,800	10,800	12,200	2	2	333	101
Other	5,600	2	2	3	2	2	2	2	472	44
Live discharges	877,000	283,100	202,400	106,700	98,200	121,900	33,500	31,300	307	70
Race:										
White	811,200	263,600	187,700	96,500	90,400	113,000	31,300	28,700	308	68
Black	61,200	17,600	13,100	10,100	7,500	8,200	2	2	305	87
Other	2	2	2	3	2	2	3	3	2	2
Dead discharges	344,200	95,700	49,200	30,000	38,300	63,100	29,600	38,300	640	163
Race:										
White	322,500	89,100	46,100	28,300	35,100	58,800	28,300	36,800	650	165
Black	20,700	6,400	2	2	2	2	2	2	413	113
Other	2	2	3	3	3	2	2	2	2	2

Source: "Number of Nursing Home Discharges by Duration of Stay, Discharge Status, and Selected Characteristics, and Average and Median Durations of Stay, by Discharge Status and Selected Characteristics: United States, 1984-85," *Discharges from Nursing Homes: 1985 National Nursing Home Survey*, March 1990, pp. 29-31. Primary source: *Vital and Health Statistics*, Series 13, No. 103. *Notes:* Figures may not add to totals because of rounding. 1. Includes small number of discharges with unknown discharge status. 2. Figure does not meet standard of reliability or precision. 3. Quantity zero.

★ 475 ★
Discharges from Short-Stay Hospitals: Trends

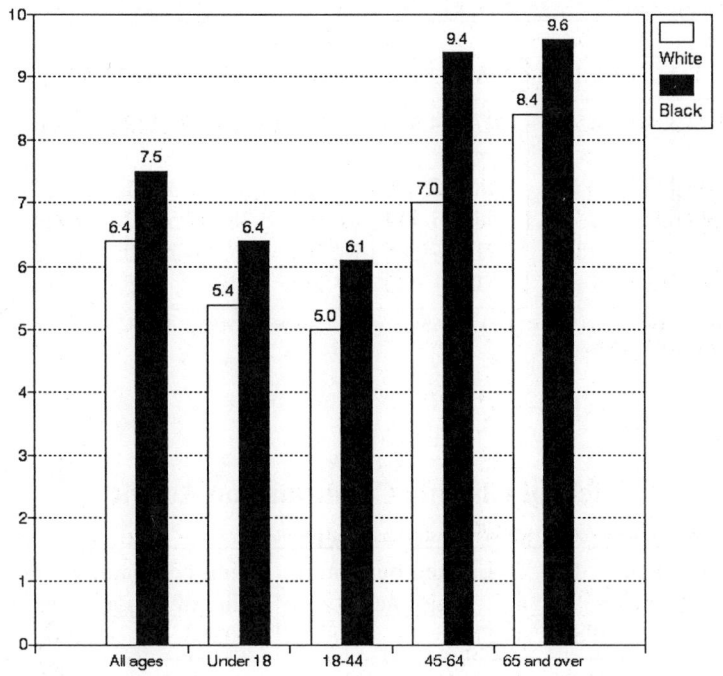

Days per discharge.

Characteristic	White	Black
All health statuses[1]		
All ages	6.4	7.5
Under 18 years	5.4	6.4
18-44 years	5.0	6.1
45-64 years	7.0	9.4
65 years and over	8.4	9.6
Fair or poor health[2]		
All ages	8.5	9.9
Under 18 years	9.6	9.4
18-44 years	7.6	8.6
45-64 years	8.3	10.6
65 years and over	8.9	10.3
Good to excellent health[2]		
All ages	5.3	5.6
Under 18 years	4.7	5.4
18-44 years	4.4	5.1
45-64 years	5.8	6.7
65 years and over	7.6	8.0

Source: "Average Annual Length of Stay per Short-Stay Hospital Discharges by Race, Age, and Respondent-Assessed Health Status: United States, 1985-87," *Health of Black and White Americans, 1985-87,* 1990, p. 20. Primary source: National Health Interview Survey, U.S. Department of Health and Human Services, Public Health Service, Centers for Disease Control, Division of Health Statistics, Hyattsville, MD, January 1990. *Notes:* 1. Includes unknown family income. 2. As assessed by self or responsible family member.

★ 476 ★
Diseases

Provisional. For cases reported in the year shown.

| Characteristic | Number | | | | | | | | Percent Distribution | |
	Total	1981-82	1983	1984	1985	1986	1987	1988[1]	1981-82	1988[1]
Total	73,394	858	2,073	4,448	8,232	13,169	21,118	23,496	100.0	100.0
Race/ethnic group										
White, non-Hispanic	43,423	482	1,181	2,696	5,012	7,889	13,001	13,162	56.3	56.0
Black, non-Hispanic	19,692	253	563	1,114	2,090	3,381	5,362	6,929	29.6	29.5
Hispanic	9,616	119	311	605	1,071	1,780	2,540	3,190	13.9	13.6
Other	663	4	18	33	59	119	215	215	.2	.9

Source: AIDS Cases Reported, by Patient Characteristic: 1981 to 1988, *Statistical Abstract*, 1989, p. 113. U.S. Centers for Disease Control, Atlanta, GA, unpublished data. *Note:* 1. January 1 until late September.

★ 477 ★
Effect of Chronic Conditions on Activity

Data based on household interviews of a sample of the civilian noninstitutionalized population.

| Characteristic | Total with limitation of activity | | Limited but not in major activity | | Limited in amount or kind of major activity | | Unable to carry on major activity | |
	1983	1987	1983	1987	1983	1987	1983	1987
Total[1,2]	13.8	12.9	4.1	4.0	6.0	5.2	3.6	3.7
Race[1]								
White	13.4	12.7	4.2	4.1	5.9	5.2	3.3	3.4
Black	17.5	16.0	3.8	3.5	7.5	6.2	6.2	6.2

Source: "Limitation of Activity Caused by Chronic Conditions, according to Selected Characteristics: United States, 1983 and 1987," *Health United States - 1988*, March 1989, p. 93. Primary source: National Health Interview Survey, National Center for Health Statistics. *Notes:* 1. Age adjusted. 2. Includes all other races not shown separately.

★ 478 ★
Elevated Blood Pressure at Ages 25-74: Trends

Data based on physical examinations of a sample of the civilian noninstitutionalized population.

| Sex and age | All races | | | White | | | Black | | |
	1960-1962	1971-1974	1976-1980	1960-1962	1971-1974	1976-1980	1960-1962	1971-1974	1976-1980
	Percent of population								
Both sexes									
Age adjusted, 25-74 years	20.9	21.7	20.1	19.2	20.1	19.2	36.8	36.6	27.7
25-34 years	5.3	6.7	7.7	4.2	6.0	7.6	14.0	12.9	9.2
35-44 years	13.3	15.5	13.9	11.4	13.5	12.5	28.7	31.9	24.3
45-54 years	21.4	24.3	25.3	19.2	22.2	24.2	39.5	43.7	36.6
55-64 years	31.8	33.2	28.1	30.1	31.6	26.9	50.1	52.1	39.5
65-74 years	48.7	40.9	34.5	46.9	39.5	34.0	71.9	55.7	36.6
Male									
Age adjusted, 25-74 years	20.7	22.9	23.0	19.0	21.7	22.3	36.3	35.8	29.7

Continued.

Elevated Blood Pressure at Ages 25-74: Trends
[Continued]

Sex and age	All races 1960-1962	All races 1971-1974	All races 1976-1980	White 1960-1962	White 1971-1974	White 1976-1980	Black 1960-1962	Black 1971-1974	Black 1976-1980
25-34 years	7.8	8.9	12.2	6.1	8.3	12.2	21.8	16.1	13.4
35-44 years	16.2	19.1	16.9	14.9	17.2	15.2	28.1	36.8	33.2
45-54 years	21.4	26.8	28.5	19.6	25.8	28.6	34.6	37.0	29.3
55-64 years	29.3	32.5	31.1	27.5	31.2	29.7	49.7	49.5	45.7
65-74 years	40.5	36.4	33.3	38.6	35.1	32.7	63.3[1]	50.3	32.1
Female									
Age adjusted, 25-74 years	21.0	20.4	17.4	19.2	18.5	16.3	37.7	37.4	26.2
25-34 years	3.1	4.6	3.6	2.3	3.8	3.2	8.8	10.7	5.8
35-44 years	10.6	12.1	11.1	8.2	9.9	9.9	29.2	28.2	17.4
45-54 years	21.5	21.9	22.4	18.8	18.8	20.1	44.3	49.4	42.9
55-64 years	34.1	33.9	25.3	32.5	32.0	24.4	50.5	54.2	34.2
65-74 years	55.4	44.4	35.5	53.8	42.9	35.0	79.0[1]	59.8	40.0

Source: "Definite Elevated Blood Pressure for Persons 25-74 Years According to Race, Sex, and Age: United States, 1960-62, 1971-74, and 1976-80," *Health United States - 1988*, March 1989, p. 100. Primary source: Division of Health Examination Statistics, National Center for Health Statistics: unpublished data. *Notes:* Definite elevated blood pressure is defined as either systolic pressure of at least 160 mmHg or diastolic pressure of at least 95 mmHg or both based on a single measurement. 1. Based on fewer than 45 persons.

★ 479 ★
Employment Industry and Acute Conditions

Data based on households interviews of the civilian noninstitutionalized population.

Race and occupation of longest employment	Estima-ted population (thou.)	All acute conditions Incidence per 100 persons per year	All acute conditions Percent medically attended	Acute respiratory conditions Incidence per 100 persons per year	Acute respiratory conditions Percent medically attended
White					
All persons	140,022	185.1	52.0	97.9	34.8
Agriculture	4,251	143.4	45.2	81.8	33.2
Forestry and fisheries	203	242.9[1]	54.2[1]	159.1[1]	61.0[1]
Mining	1,240	168.8	53.0	83.5	29.9[1]
Construction	6,969	162.7	51.6	90.7	33.1
Manufacturing	31,980	162.3	53.4	84.8	35.7
Transportation and public utilities	8,000	168.4	46.9	98.5	27.6
Wholesale and retail trade	28,243	193.7	54.6	97.4	39.7
Finance, insurance, and real estate	6,939	190.4	47.5	103.5	30.8
Services and miscellaneous	33,851	219.9	51.9	115.7	34.2
Public administration	7,050	193.7	43.7	106.1	27.7
Ever worked, industry unknown	6,376	173.0	58.9	91.7	38.4

Continued.

Employment Industry and Acute Conditions
[Continued]

Race and occupation of longest employment	Estimated population (thou.)	All acute conditions			Acute respiratory conditions	
		Incidence per 100 persons per year	Percent medically attended		Incidence per 100 persons per year	Percent medically attended
Never worked	4,921	135.9	51.6		75.1	35.4
Black						
All persons	16,842	178.8	58.2		77.9	43.5
Agriculture	509	110.8[1]	69.9[1]		25.1[1]	53.1[1]
Forestry and fisheries	9[1]	[2]	[2]		[2]	[2]
Mining	61	600.0[1]	36.6[1]		380.3[1]	[2]
Construction	665	123.8	39.4[1]		39.1[1]	[2]
Manufacturing	3,370	145.7	68.6		61.6	56.0
Transportation and public utilities	908	155.3	64.8		80.8	51.9[1]
Wholesale and retail trade	2,159	203.2	56.5		83.0	33.4[1]
Finance, insurance, and real estate	586	186.2	48.9[1]		106.5	38.9[1]
Services and miscellaneous	5,428	191.0	58.0		83.1	46.4
Public administration	1,314	199.0	46.8		95.1	38.4[1]
Ever worked, industry unknown	877	206.3	68.9		84.8	48.8[1]
Never worked	957	185.0	50.6		80.3	41.9[1]

Source: "Number and Percent Distribution of Persons 17 Years of Age and Over, Incidence of Acute Conditions and Acute Respiratory Conditions per 100 Persons per Year, and Percent Medically Attended, by Race and Industry of Longest Employment: United States, 1980," *Health Characteristics by Occupation and Industry of Longest Employment*, June 1989, p. 58. Primary source: *Vital and Health Statistics*, Series 10, Data from the National Health Survey, No. 168. *Notes:* Excluded from these statistics are all conditions that involved neither restricted activity nor medical attention. 1. Figure does not meet standard of reliability or precision. 2. Quantity zero.

★ 480 ★
Employment Industry and Professional Care

Data based on household interviews of the civilian noninstitutionalized population.

Race and industry of longest employment	Estimated population (thousands)	Short-stay hospitals			Physician visits		Dental visits	
		Percent with episode in year	Discharges per 100 persons per year	Length of stay per discharge in days	Percent with visit in year	Visits per person per year	Percent with visit in year	Visits per person per year
White								
All persons	140,022	12.2	16.6	7.7	74.3	4.9	51.8	1.7
Agriculture	4,251	12.2	18.3	8.4	67.9	3.8	40.3	1.2
Forestry and fisheries	203	14.8[1]	22.7[1]	5.6[1]	75.9	3.3[1]	46.8	0.7[1]
Mining	1,240	15.3	21.3	12.3	70.6	5.5	41.9	1.1
Construction	6,969	10.8	15.1	9.1	64.4	3.6	44.5	1.5
Manufacturing	31,980	12.5	16.7	7.4	73.0	4.7	46.9	1.7
Transportation and public utilities	8,000	11.4	15.9	9.6	74.8	5.3	50.5	1.8
Wholesale and retail trade	28,243	12.3	17.0	7.2	75.0	5.0	52.4	1.7

Continued.

Employment Industry and Professional Care
[Continued]

Race and industry of longest employment	Estimated population (thousands)	Short-stay hospitals			Physician visits		Dental visits	
		Percent with episode in year	Discharges per 100 persons per year	Length of stay per discharge in days	Percent with visit in year	Visits per person per year	Percent with visit in year	Visits per person per year
Finance, insurance, and real estate	6,939	10.3	13.0	5.6	77.5	4.9	63.9	2.3
Services and miscellaneous	33,851	12.6	16.2	7.0	77.5	5.4	58.7	1.9
Public administration	7,050	12.3	18.2	10.2	77.4	4.9	57.0	1.9
Ever worked, industry unknown	6,376	9.9	14.6	9.0	68.4	4.1	46.6	1.6
Never worked	4,921	16.1	22.4	7.6	74.3	4.9	39.0	1.4
Black								
All persons	16,842	13.3	18.4	10.1	75.5	5.2	34.2	1.1
Agriculture	509	10.6	20.2	14.9	69.2	5.2	18.3	1.2[1]
Forestry and fisheries	9[1]	22.2[1]	[1,2]	[1,2]	66.7[1]	6.3[1]	22.2[1]	[1,2]
Mining	61	19.7[1]	27.9[1]	4.8[1]	78.7	6.3[1]	27.9[1]	1.0[1]
Construction	665	11.4	18.9	9.9	69.2	4.3	24.2	1.0[1]
Manufacturing	3,370	15.1	21.9	10.1	75.5	5.4	34.1	1.1
Transportation and public utilities	908	14.8	23.1	7.0	74.7	4.8	35.4	1.7
Wholesale and retail trade	2,159	11.9	15.2	10.8	72.6	5.0	36.7	1.1
Finance, insurance, and real estate	586	14.0	16.2	7.0[1]	80.5	4.4	43.0	0.5[1]
Services and miscellaneous	5,428	12.9	16.6	10.4	80.3	5.6	35.7	1.1
Public administration	1,314	14.2	19.3	8.9	75.8	5.4	38.3	0.9
Ever worked, industry unknown	877	10.9	15.7	13.1	63.2	3.9	31.2	2.1
Never worked	957	14.6	20.1	10.1	70.6	4.4	27.1	0.5[1]

Source: "Number of Persons 17 Years of Age and Over and Average Rate of Utilization of Medical and Dental Services, by Race and Industry of Longest Employment: United States, 1980," *Health Characteristics by Occupation and Industry of Longest Employment*, June 1989, p. 71. Primary source: *Vital and Health Statistics*, Series 10, Data from the National Health Survey, No. 168. *Notes:* 1. Figure does not meet standard of reliability or precision. 2. Quantity zero.

★ 481 ★
Energy, Fats, and Cholesterol Intake of Adults: Trends

Dietary component, sex and race	1971-1974	1976-1980	Change in mean
Energy (kilocalories)			
White			
Male	2,483	2,481	-2
Female	1,558	1,541	-17
Black			
Male	2,233	2,227	-6
Female	1,410	1,439	+29
Total fat (percent)			
White			
Male	36.9	36.8	-0.1
Female	36.1	36.0	-0.1
Black			
Male	36.2	36.2	0

Continued.

Energy, Fats, and Cholesterol Intake of Adults: Trends
[Continued]

Dietary component, sex and race	1971-1974	1976-1980	Change in mean
Female	35.5	35.8	+0.3
Saturated fat (percent)			
White			
Male	13.6	13.3	-0.3
Female	13.0	12.5	-.05
Black			
Male	12.7	12.8	-0.1
Female	12.4	12.3	-0.1
Linoleic acid (percent)			
White			
Male	3.9	5.1	+1.2
Female	4.0	5.4	+1.4
Black			
Male	3.7	4.9	+1.2
Female	4.0	5.3	+1.3
Cholesterol (milligrams)			
White			
Male	483	436	-47
Female	310	272	-38
Black			
Male	535	476	-59
Female	313	295	-18

Source: "Trends in Age-Adjusted Mean Intakes of Energy, Fats, and Cholesterol for Persons Aged 20-74 Years, by Sex and Age: First National Health and Nutrition Examination Survey, 1971-74, and Second National Health and Nutrition Examination Survey, 1976-80 (Sempos et al., 1987)," *Nutrition Monitoring in the United States*, September 1989, p. 116. Primary source: Sempos, C., Cooper, R., Kovar, M.G., and McMillen, M. 1988. Divergence of the Recent Trends in Coronary Mortality for the Four Major Race-Sex Groups in the United States. *Am. J. Public Health.* 78: 1422-1427. *Notes:* Dietary component is age-adjusted by the direct method to the U.S. population at the midpoint of the NHANES II.

★ 482 ★
Excess Weight at Ages 25-74: Trends

Data based on physical examinations of a sample of the civilian noninstitutionalized population.

Sex and age	All races			White			Black		
	1960-1962	1971-1974	1976-1986	1960-1962	1971-1974	1976-1980	1960-1962	1971-1974	1976-1980
	Percent of population								
Both sexes									
Age adjusted, 25-74 years	27.4	27.9	28.4	26.4	26.8	27.2	35.9	38.8	41.1
25-34 years	18.9	20.5	20.2	17.6	19.7	19.4	31.6	29.1	26.3
35-44 years	23.8	28.4	27.9	21.8	26.6	26.4	38.0	45.3	40.8
45-54 years	29.6	30.0	31.7	28.8	29.1	30.2	33.2	39.4	52.1
55-64 years	35.7	32.0	32.8	34.8	31.0	31.9	45.5	43.9	44.2
65-74 years	34.6	31.5	32.7	35.0	31.0	31.9	31.5	37.3	46.0

Continued.

Excess Weight at Ages 25-74: Trends
[Continued]

Sex and age	All races			White			Black		
	1960-1962	1971-1974	1976-1986	1960-1962	1971-1974	1976-1980	1960-1962	1971-1974	1976-1980
Male									
Age adjusted, 25-74 years	24.8	26.0	26.7	25.1	26.0	26.7	24.1	27.6	30.9
25-34 years	22.0	23.6	20.4	21.4	23.6	20.9	34.3	26.1	17.5
35-44 years	23.2	29.4	28.9	22.4	28.9	28.2	28.6	39.3	40.9
45-54 years	28.1	27.6	31.0	29.3	28.2	30.5	18.5	22.4	41.4
55-64 years	27.2	24.8	28.1	28.5	24.9	28.6	20.1	25.6	26.0
65-74 years	23.8	23.0	25.2	24.8	23.1	25.8	11.7[1]	21.6	26.4
Female									
Age adjusted, 25-74 years	29.6	29.4	29.8	27.3	27.4	27.5	47.3	47.8	49.5
25-34 years	15.9	17.6	20.0	13.9	15.9	17.9	29.6	31.5	33.5
35-44 years	24.4	27.3	27.0	21.2	24.5	24.8	46.1	49.9	40.8
45-54 years	30.9	32.3	32.5	28.5	29.9	29.9	47.8	53.5	61.2
55-64 years	43.6	38.5	37.0	40.5	36.6	34.8	71.4	58.7	59.4
65-74 years	43.3	38.0	38.5	43.2	37.0	36.5	47.8[1]	49.2	60.8

Source: "Overweight Persons 25-74 Years of Age, according to Race, Sex, and Age: United States, 1960-62, 1971-74, and 1976-80," *Health United States - 1988*, March 1989, p. 102. Primary source: Division of Health Examination Statistics, National Center for Health Statistics. *Notes:* Overweight is defined for men as body mass index greater than or equal to 27.8 kilograms/square meter, and for women as body mass index greater than or equal to 27.3 kilograms/square meter. These cut points were used because they represent the sex-specific 85th percentiles for persons 20-29 years of age in the 1976-80 National Health and Nutrition Examination Survey. Excludes pregnant women. 1. Based on fewer than 45 persons.

★ 483 ★
Frequency and Recency of Dental Care: Trends

Data based on household interviews of a sample of the civilian noninstitutionalized population.

Characteristic	Dental visits Number per person			Interval since last dental visit[1] Percent of Population								
				Less than 1 year			2 years or more			Never visited dentist		
	1964	1981	1986	1964	1981	1986	1964	1981	1986	1964	1981	1986
Total[2,3]	1.6	1.7	2.0	42.7	50.4	56.3	28.7	25.1	25.0	15.5	11.0	10.4
Race[2]												
White	1.7	1.8	2.1	45.3	52.6	58.4	27.8	24.0	23.6	13.8	10.4	9.9
Black[4]	0.8	1.1	1.3	22.3	36.3	42.6	37.6	33.9	35.6	28.0	14.4	12.7

Source: "Dental Visits and Interval since Last Visit, according to Selected Patient Characteristics: United States, 1964, 1981, and 1986," *Health United States - 1988*, March 1989, p. 110. Primary source: National Health Interview Survey, National Center for Health Statistics. *Notes:* 1. Percent not shown for an interval of 1 year - less than 2 years. 2. Age adjusted. 3. Includes all other races not shown separately. 4. 1984 data are for all other races.

★ 484 ★
Geographic Distribution of Cancer Cases: SEER Program

Area	Total for all racial/ ethnic groups[2]	Anglos[3]	Blacks	Hispanics	Japanese	Chinese	Filipinos	Native Hawaiians	Native Americans
Total number of cases	297,751	252,095	23,952	6,158	3,682	2,299	1,815	1,331	872
Percent residing in:									
All areas[1]	100.0	100.0	100.0	100.0	100.0	100.0	100.0	100.0	100.0
San Francisco-Oakland	16.8	15.7	20.4	33.5	9.2	64.1	36.1	2.4	3.8
Connecticut	16.9	18.8	8.6	5.4	0.2	1.0	0.1	0.1	1.4
Detroit	19.4	18.3	45.9	1.4	0.4	1.4	1.7	0.1	1.5
Hawaii	3.4	1.4	0.2	---	82.9	28.6	55.8	97.0	---
Iowa	15.1	17.6	1.8	1.6	0.2	0.2	0.2	---	1.7
New Mexico	4.4	3.8	0.8	51.3	0.1	0.2	---	---	42.4
Seattle	12.7	13.7	3.2	1.6	5.6	3.8	6.6	0.4	12.6
Utah	4.3	4.8	0.2	4.8	1.3	0.2	0.2	---	3.2
Atlanta	3.1	5.6	16.6	0.6	0.1	0.3	0.1	0.1	0.4
Arizona Indians	0.1	---	---	---	---	---	---	---	32.7

Source: "Percent Distribution of Cancer Cases by Geographic Area, for Eight Racial/Ethnic Groups, SEER Program, 1978-81," *Cancer Among Blacks and Other Minorities,* (undated), p. 27. Primary source: Surveillance, Epidemiology, and End Results (SEER) Program of the National Cancer Institute. SEER Program covers 11 population-based U.S. areas. *Notes:* 1. Puerto Rico and New Jersey are not included. 2. Total includes 5,367 cases of unknown and other racial/ethnic background. 3. Caucasians not of Hispanic origin or surname.

★ 485 ★
Health Examinations

In percent, except as indicated. For women 18 years of age and older. Based on National Health Interview Survey.

Characteristic	Number of women (1,000)	Breast self-examination		Had a breast exam[2]	Had a PAP smear[2]
		Knew how to do	Did[1]		
RACE					
White	77,657	87.9	36.2	49.5	44.7
Black	10,333	83.6	46.4	57.0	52.9
Hispanic Origin					
Hispanic	5,390	75.4	35.7	49.5	47.1
Non-Hispanic	84,430	87.7	37.3	50.4	45.6

Source: "Women who knew how to do breast self-examination aand women who had a breast examination or PAP smear-selected characteristics: 1985," *Statistical Abstract,* 1989, p. 117. U.S. National Center for Health Statistics, *Vital and Health Statistics,* series 10, No. 163 *Notes:* 1. At least 12 times a year. 2. In the past year 3. Includes persons with unknown characteristics and other races not shown separately.

★ 486 ★
Health Insurance Coverage

Data represents monthly averages for fourth quarter 1985. Government health insurance includes Medicare, Medicaid, and military plans. Based on Survey of Income and Program Participation.

	Number (mil)						Percent				
		Covered by private or government health insurance				Not covered by health insur-ance		Covered by private or government health insurance			Not covered by health insur-ance
			Private insurance		Covered by Medicaid					Covered by Medicaid	
Characteristic	Total	Total[1]	Total	Related to Employment[2]			Total	Total[1]	Private		
Total persons[3]	235.5	204.2	180.1	147.1	17.2	31.3	100.0	86.7	76.5	7.3	13.3
Male	114.2	97.5	87.5	73.2	6.4	16.7	100.0	85.4	76.6	5.6	14.6
Female	121.4	106.8	92.6	73.8	10.8	14.6	100.0	88.0	76.3	8.9	12.0
White	200.1	175.2	159.3	129.9	10.1	24.8	100.0	87.6	79.6	5.0	12.4
Black	28.5	23.0	15.9	13.2	6.2	5.5	100.0	80.7	55.7	21.6	19.3
Hispanic origin[4]	14.2	10.4	7.8	7.0	2.3	3.8	100.0	73.0	55.2	15.98	27.0

Source: "Health Insurance Coverage Status, by Selected Characteristics: 1985," *Statistical Abstract*, 1989, p. 96. Primary source: U.S. Bureau of the Census, *Current Population Reports*, series P-70, No. 8 and unpublished data. *Notes:* 1. Includes other Government Insurance, not shown separately. 2. Related to current or prior employment of self or other family members. 3. Includes other races, not shown separately. 4. Hispanic persons may be of any race.

★ 487 ★
Health Insurance Coverage at 65 and Over: Trends

Data based on household interviews of a sample of the civilian noninstitutionalized population.

| Characteristic | Medicare and private insurance | | | Medicare and Medicaid[1] | | | Medicare[2] | | |
	1980	1982	1986	1980	1982	1986	1980	1982	1986
Total[3,4]	64.4	65.5	71.6	8.1	6.1	5.8	22.7	23.1	17.9
Race[3]									
White	68.3	68.9	75.4	6.6	4.8	4.5	21.0	21.6	16.1
Black	26.5	33.0	34.2	23.3	18.2	19.7	40.6	38.5	34.9

Source: "Health Care Coverage for Persons 65 Years of Age and Over, according to Type of Coverage and Selected Characteristics: United States, 1980, 1982, and 1986," *Health United States - 1988*, March 1989, p. 172. Primary source: National Health Interview Survey, National Center for Health Statistics. *Notes:* Persons with Medicare, private insurance, and Medicaid appear in both columns. Denominators include persons with unknown health insurance (0.8 percent in 1986). In 1986, 5.0 percent of all persons 65 years of age and over had no Medicare but only 0.6 percent were without health insurance. 1. Includes persons receiving Aid to Families with Dependent Children or Supplemental Security Income or those with current Medicaid cards. 2. Includes persons not covered by private insurance or Medicaid. 3. Age adjusted. 4. Includes all other races not shown separately.

★ 488 ★
Health Insurance Coverage at Under 65: Trends

Data based on household interviews of a sample of the civilian noninstitutionalized population.

Characteristic	Private insurance			Medicaid[1]			Not covered[2]		
	1980	1982	1986	1980	1982	1986	1980	1982	1986
Total[3,4]	78.8	77.3	75.9	5.9	5.6	5.9	12.5	14.7	15.3
Race[3]									
White	81.9	80.4	79.1	3.9	3.6	4.0	11.4	13.5	14.0
Black	60.1	59.6	57.0	17.9	17.2	17.4	19.0	21.2	22.6

Source: "Health Care Coverage for Persons Under 65 Years of Age, according to Type of Coverage and Selected Characteristics: United States, 1980, 1982, and 1986," *Health United States - 1988*, March 1989, p. 171. Primary source: National Health Interview Survey, National Center for Health Statistics. *Notes:* Denominators include persons with unknown health insurance (1.7 percent in 1986). Percents do not add up to 100 because the percent with other types of health insurance (e.g., Medicare, military) and unknown health insurance are not shown, and because persons with both private and Medicaid insurance appear in both columns. 1. Includes persons receiving Aid to Families with Dependent Children or Supplemental Security Income or those with current Medicaid cards. 2. Includes persons not covered by private insurance, Medicaid, Medicare, and military plans. 3. Age adjusted. 4. Includes all other races not shown separately.

★ 489 ★
Health Insurance Coverage for Those Under Age 65

Race	Percent
Blacks	22.6
Whites	14.0

Source: "Percent Under Age 65 with No Health Insurance Coverage," *The State of Black America 1990*, January 1990, p. 125. Primary source: National Center for Health Statistics (NCHS), 1986. Extracted from: *The State of Black America*, January 1990. Published by permission.

★ 490 ★
Health Insurance Coverage of Unemployed Workers

Characteristic	Coverage During Spell[1]		
	All Months	Some Months	No Months
African American			
All workers	33.0	12.9	54.1
Covered before unemployment	70.1	17.2	12.6
In own name	62.3	21.6	16.2
Not covered before	2.7	9.4	87.8
White			
All workers	56.6	9.5	33.9
Covered before unemployment	80.9	10.5	8.6

Continued.

Health Insurance Coverage of Unemployed Workers
[Continued]

Characteristic	Coverage During Spell[1]		
	All Months	Some Months	No Months
In own name	72.0	15.4	12.6
Not covered before	5.5	7.3	87.2

Source: "Percentage Comparison of Health Insurance Coverage Among African American and White Unemployed," *The State of Black America 1990*, January 1990, p. 221. Primary source: U.S. Bureau of the Census, *Current Population Reports*, "Spells of Job Search and Layoff...and Their Outcomes," July 1989, Table F, p. 8. Extracted from: *The State of Black America*, January 1990. Published by permission. *Note:* 1. Spells beginning and ending between 1984 and 1986.

★ 491 ★
Health Practices

In percent, For persons 18 years of age and over. Based on National Health Interview Survey.

Characteristics	Sleeps 6 hours or less	Never eats break-fast	Snacks every day	Less physically active than contem-poraries	Had 5 or more drinks on any one day[1]	Current smoker	30 percent or more above desirable weight[2]
All persons[3]	22.0	24.3	39.0	16.4	37.5	30.1	13.0
RACE							
White	21.3	24.5	39.4	16.7	38.3	29.6	12.4
All other	26.6	23.2	36.3	14.3	29.9	33.1	16.4
Black	27.8	23.6	37.2	13.9	29.3	34.9	18.7
Other	21.4	21.5	32.6	16.5	33.3	24.8	6.7

Source: Statistical Abstract, 1989, p. 118. U.S. National Center for Health Statistics, *Health Promotion and Disease Prevention, United States 1985*, series 10, No. 163 and unpublished data. *Notes:* 1. Percent of drinkers who had 5 or more drinks on any one day in the past year. 2. Based on 1960 Metropolitan Life Insurance Company standards. Data are self-reported. 3. Excludes persons whose health practices are unknown.

★ 492 ★
Health Problems

Covers civilian noninstitutional population 18 years old and over. Annual average. Based on subsamples of households in the National Health Interview Survey.

Sex and Race	Number (1,000)				Rate per 1,000 Population			
	Total	Under 45 years	45-64 years	65 years and over	Total	Under 45 years	45-64 years	65 years and over
Total persons with known diabetes[1]	6,585	1,029	2,848	2,707	27.9	6.3	63.7	98.3
White	5,478	890	2,326	2,262	27.4	6.5	59.7	91.4
Black	1,007	139	472	396	35.3	6.4[2]	105.1	172.3

Source: "Persons with Known Cases of Diabetes, by Selected Characteristics: 1986," *Statistical Abstract*, 1989, p. 116. Primary source: U.S. National Center for Health Statistics, unpublished data *Notes:* 1. Includes other races not shown separately. 2. Figure does not meet standards of reliability or precision.

★ 493 ★
Health Self-Assessments and Income: Trends

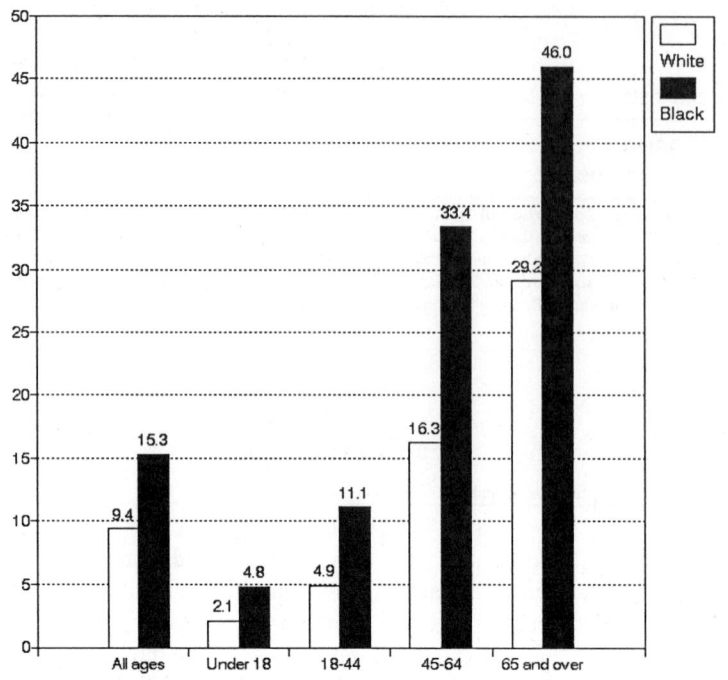

Percent.

Characteristic	White	Black
All family incomes[1]		
All ages	9.4	15.3
Under 18 years	2.1	4.8
18-44 years	4.9	11.1
45-64 years	16.3	33.4
65 years and over	29.2	46.0
Less than $20,000		
All ages	16.6	19.0
Under 18 years	3.7	6.0
18-44 years	8.5	14.8
45-64 years	32.9	44.2
65 years and over	34.2	48.3
$20,000 or more		
All ages	5.1	7.6
Under 18 years	1.4	2.2
18-44 years	3.1	6.2
45-64 years	9.7	18.3
65 years and over	20.7	25.7

Source: "Average Annual Percent of Persons Assessed by Respondents to be in Fair or Poor Health by Race, Age, and Family Income: United States, 1985-87," *Health of Black and White Americans, 1985-87*, 1990, p. 14. Primary source: National Health Interview Survey, U.S. Department of Health and Human Services, Public Health Service, Centers for Disease Control, Division of Health Statistics, Hyattsville, MD, January 1990. *Note:* 1. Includes unknown family income.

★ 494 ★
Health Self-Assessments: Trends

Data are based on household interviews of a sample of the civilian noninstitutionalized population.

Characteristic	Total	Excellent 1983	Excellent 1987	Very good 1983	Very good 1987	Good 1983	Good 1987	Fair or Poor 1983	Fair or Poor 1987
				Percent distribution					
Total[1,2]	100.0	40.7	40.3	25.4	27.8	23.2	22.4	10.7	9.5
Race[1]									
White	100.0	42.6	42.1	25.8	28.2	22.1	21.1	9.6	8.5
Black	100.0	28.5	29.5	21.8	24.4	30.0	29.4	19.7	16.7

Source: "Self-Assessment of Health, according to Selected Characteristics: United States, 1983 and 1987, *Health United States - 1988*, March 1989, p.95. Division of Health Interview Statistics, National Center for Health Statistics: Data from the National Health Interview Survey. *Notes:* 1. Age adjusted. 2. Includes all other races not shown separately and unknown family income.

★ 495 ★
Health-Related Limitations of Activity and Employment Industry

Data based on household interviews of the civilian noninstitutionalized population.

Race and occupation of longest employment	Estimated population (thou.)	Percent	No limita-tion of activity	Limitation of activity Total	Limitation of activity Limited but not in major activity[1]	Limitation of activity Limited in major activity[1]
White						
All persons	140,022	100.0	82.0	18.0	4.2	13.8
Agriculture	4,251	100.0	71.4	28.6	4.1	24.4
Forestry and fisheries	203	100.0	81.8	18.7	3.0[2]	15.8[2]
Mining	1,240	100.0	71.7	28.3	4.2	24.1
Construction	6,969	100.0	80.9	19.1	3.9	15.2
Manufacturing	31,980	100.0	80.8	19.2	4.3	14.9
Transportation and public utilities	8,000	100.0	81.5	18.5	4.1	14.4
Wholesale and retail trade	28,243	100.0	84.6	15.4	3.6	11.7
Finance, insurance, and real estate	6,939	100.0	88.2	11.8	4.2	7.7
Services and miscellaneous	33,851	100.0	84.0	16.0	4.5	11.5
Public administration	7,050	100.0	80.7	19.3	4.6	14.6
Ever worked, industry unknown	6,376	100.0	80.4	19.6	4.3	15.4
Never worked	4,921	100.0	70.1	29.9	5.0	24.8
Black						
All persons	16,842	100.0	79.1	20.9	3.6	17.3
Agriculture	509	100.0	57.4	42.6	6.7[2]	36.1
Forestry and fisheries	9[2]	100.0	77.8[2]	22.2[2]	22.2[2]	[3]
Mining	61	100.0	78.7[2]	19.7[2]	[3]	19.7[2]
Construction	665	100.0	75.0	24.8	2.6[2]	22.3
Manufacturing	3,370	100.0	81.1	18.9	3.2	15.7

Continued.

Health-Related Limitations of Activity and Employment Industry
[Continued]

Race and occupation of longest employment	Estimated population (thou.)	Percent	No limita-tion of activity	Limitation of activity		
				Total	Limited but not in major activity[1]	Limited in major activity[1]
Transportation and public utilities	908	100.0	80.3	19.7	2.3[2]	17.4
Wholesale and retail trade	2,159	100.0	82.1	17.9	3.5	14.4
Finance, insurance, and real estate	586	100.0	91.0	8.9	1.5[2]	7.3
Services and miscellaneous	5,428	100.0	76.7	23.3	3.9	19.4
Public administration	1,314	100.0	83.2	26.9	3.9	13.0
Ever worked, industry unknown	877	100.0	79.2	20.8	3.2[2]	17.6
Never worked	957	100.0	78.3	21.7	5.2	16.5

Source: "Number and Percent Distribution of Persons 17 Years of Age and Over by Limitation of Activity Due to Chronic Conditions, According to Race and Occupation of Longest Employment: United States, 1980," *Health Characteristics by Occupation and Industry of Longest Employment*, June 1989, p. 37. Primary source: *Vital and Health Statistics*, Series 10, Data from the National Health Survey, No. 168. *Notes:* 1. Major activity refers to ability to work, keep house, or engage in school activities. 2. Figure does not meet standard of reliability or precision. 3. Quantity zero.

★ 496 ★

Health-Related Limitations of Activity and Occupational Category

Data based on household interviews of the civilian noninstitutionalized population.

Race and occupation of longest employment	Estimated population (thou.)	Percent	No limita-tion of activity	Limitation of activity		
				Total	Limited but not in major activity[1]	Limited in major activity[1]
Percent distribution						
All persons	160,149	100.0	81.8	18.2	4.1	14.1
White-collar workers	72,895	100.0	85.8	14.2	4.3	10.0
Blue-collar workers	48,058	100.0	79.2	20.8	3.8	16.9
Farm workers	4,177	100.0	68.5	31.5	4.2	27.3
Service workers	21,120	100.0	79.9	20.1	4.0	16.1
Ever worked, occupation unknown	7,752	100.0	80.0	20.0	4.1	15.9
Never worked	6,146	100.0	72.0	28.0	5.1	22.9
White						
All persons	140,022	100.0	82.0	18.0	4.2	13.8
White-collar workers	66,815	100.0	85.4	14.6	4.4	10.2
Blue-collar workers	41,604	100.0	79.3	20.7	4.0	16.7
Farm workers	3,592	100.0	69.5	30.5	3.9	26.6
Service workers	16,523	100.0	82.0	18.0	3.9	14.2
Ever worked, occupation unknown	6,566	100.0	79.9	20.1	4.2	15.9

Continued.

Health-Related Limitations of Activity and Occupational Category
[Continued]

Race and occupation of longest employment	Estimated population (thou.)	Percent	No limita- tion of activity	Limitation of activity		
				Total	Limited but not in major activity[1]	Limited in major activity[1]
Never worked	4,921	100.0	70.1	29.9	5.0	24.8
Black						
All persons	16,842	100.0	79.1	20.9	3.6	17.3
White-collar workers	4,702	100.0	89.3	10.7	2.8	7.9
Blue-collar workers	5,608	100.0	78.0	22.0	3.0	19.1
Farm workers	472	100.0	58.7	41.1	6.1	35.2
Service workers	4,159	100.0	71.6	28.4	4.8	23.6
Ever worked, occupation unknown	944	100.0	78.3	21.7	3.5	18.1
Never worked	957	100.0	78.3	21.7	5.2	16.5

Source: "Number and Percent Distribution of Persons 17 Years of Age and Over by Limitation of Activity Due to Chronic Conditions, According to Race and Occupation of Longest Employment: United States, 1980," *Health Characteristics by Occupation and Industry of Longest Employment*, June 1989, pp. 31-32. Primary source: *Vital and Health Statistics*, Series 10, Data from the National Health Survey, No. 168. *Notes:* 1. Major activity refers to ability to work, keep house, or engage in school activities.

★ 497 ★
Hospital Discharges and Income: Trends

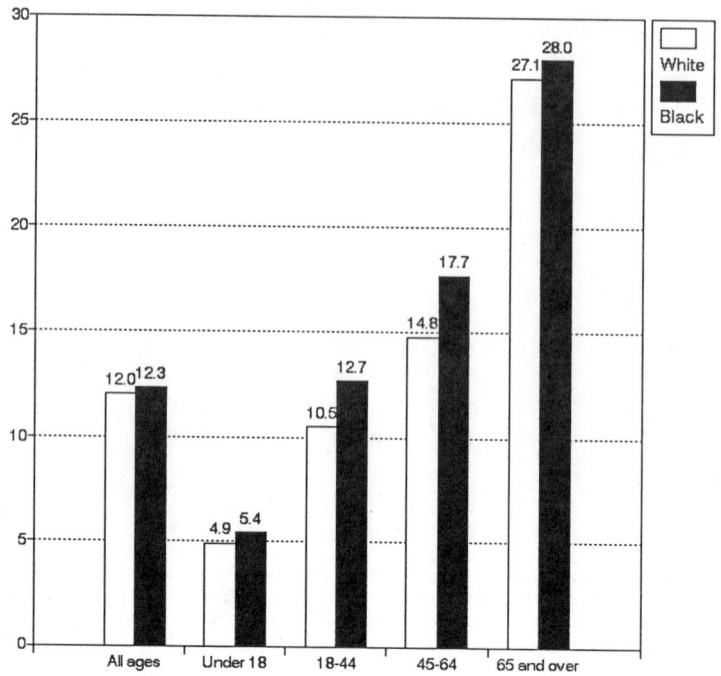

Number per 100 persons per year.

Characteristic	White	Black
All family incomes[1]		
All ages	12.0	12.3
Under 18 years	4.9	5.4
18-44 years	10.5	12.7
45-64 years	14.8	17.7
65 years and over	27.1	28.0
Less than $20,000		
All ages	16.1	14.0
Under 18 years	6.2	5.8
18-44 years	13.1	15.4
45-64 years	21.7	22.7
65 years and over	28.3	26.4
$20,000 or more		
All ages	9.8	8.7
Under 18 years	4.5	4.0
18-44 years	9.6	10.1
45-64 years	12.5	11.1
65 years and over	25.0	21.1

Source: "Average Annual Number of Short-Stay Hospital Discharges per 100 Persons by Race, Age, and Family Income: United States, 1985-87," *Health of Black and White Americans, 1985-87*, 1990, p. 18. Primary source: National Health Interview Survey, U.S. Department of Health and Human Services, Public Health Service, Centers for Disease Control, Division of Health Statistics, Hyattsville, MD, January 1990. *Note:* 1. Includes unknown family income.

★ 498 ★
Hospitalized AIDS Patients in Selected Cities

Numbers in parentheses represent percent of acute care hospitals.

City and race	1985	1987	Percent Change
New York and Newark (23%)			
Caucasian	12	12	-1
Black	51	54	3
Hispanic	32	33	0
Other	5	2	-3
% of City's AIDS Patients	63	53	
San Francisco (36%)			
Caucasian	55	70	15
Black	18	9	-9
Hispanic	18	15	-3
Other	9	6	-3
% of City's AIDS Patients	46	36	
Los Angeles (17%)			
Caucasian	83	60	-23
Black	6	16	10
Hispanic	9	17	8
Other	3	7	4
% of City's AIDS Patients	35	20	
Houston (10%)			
Caucasian	69	58	-11
Black	20	30	10
Hispanic	11	11	0
Other	0	1	1
% of City's AIDS Patients	36	37	
Washington, DC (60%)			
Caucasian	58	54	-4
Black	35	40	5
Hispanic	4	4	0
Other	3	3	-1
% of City's AIDS Patients	63	41	
Chicago (6%)			
Caucasian	42	52	10
Black	46	30	16
Hispanic	12	11	0
Other	0	6	6
% of City's AIDS Patients	32	27	

Source: "Comparison of Study Group with Total City Hospitals and AIDS Caseloads, 1985 and 1987" and "Characteristics of AIDS Patients in New York and Newark, San Francisco, Los Angeles, Houston, Washington, DC, and Chicago," *New Perspectives on HIV-Related Illnesses: Progress in Health Services Research*, September 1989, pp. 59-66. *Notes:* Primary source: Adapted by the editors from Scitovsky, A.A., "Past Lessons and Future Directions: The Economics of Health Services Delivery for HIV-Related Illnesses," *New Perspectives on HIV-Related Illnesses.*

★ 499 ★
How do Children Contract AIDS?

Type of Exposure	Total	White	Black	Hispanic	Asian	American Indian
Mother with/at-risk for AIDS/HIV infection	1,168	174	710	275	3	3
--IV drug use	609	76	363	167	1	2
--Sex with IV drug user	229	37	116	75	0	0
--Born in Pattern II Country	132	2	128	1	0	0
--Unspecified	127	29	73	22	2	1
--Other	71	30	30	10	0	0
Transfusion	181	99	41	38	3	0
Hemophilia/Coagulation Dis.	87	61	10	13	3	0
Undetermined	53	10	30	13	0	0
Total	1,489	344	791	339	9	3

Source: "Total Pediatric AIDS Cases, by Type of Exposure and Race/Hispanic Origin," *U.S. Children and their Families,* 1989, p. 197. Primary source: Centers for Disease Control, *HIV/AIDS Surveillance Report,* April 1989: 1-16, Tables 4 and 6. *Notes:* Whites and blacks are those who are non-Hispanic. Pattern II countries are areas of Africa and some Caribbean countries where most of the reported cases occur in heterosexuals. Other types of exposure include mothers who had AIDS due to: sex with a bisexual male, person with hemophilia, person born in pattern II country, or transfusion recipient with HIV infection; or receipt of transfusion of infected blood or tissue. Unspecified cases are those where the original transmission was not specified.

★ 500 ★
Hypertensive Adults

Ethnic Group or Race	Male	Female
Mexican American	23.9	20.3
Cuban	20.7	14.4
Puerto Rican	21.4	19.2
Non-Hispanic white	33.8	25.1
Non-Hispanic black	41.6	43.8

Source: "Age-Adjusted Prevalence of Hypertension in Persons Aged 20-74 Years, by Ethnic Group or Race: Hispanic Health and Nutrition Examination Survey, 1982-84, and Second National Health and Nutrition Examination Survey, 1976- 80," *Nutrition Monitoring in the United States,* September 1989, p. 69. Primary source: U.S. Department of Health and Human Services and U.S. Department of Agriculture.

★ 501 ★
Incidence of AIDS

Data are based on reporting by State health departments.

Sex and race/ethnicity	Number, by year of report								All years[1,2] Percent distribution	12 mos. ending Nov. 30, 1988 Cases per 100,000 population[1]
	All years[1,2]	1982	1983	1984	1985	1986	1987	1988[2]		
Total[3]	77,883	664	2,073	4,449	8,233	13,174	21,123	27,975		12.6
Male										
All males, 13 years and over[3]	70,239	603	1,898	4,122	7,581	12,025	19,136	24,688	100.0	28.56
White, not Hispanic	43,696	345	1,141	2,610	4,846	7,577	12,377	14,680	62.2	21.42
Black, not Hispanic	16,950	173	475	945	1,722	2,757	4,316	6,521	24.1	67.65

Continued.

Incidence of AIDS
[Continued]

Sex and race/ethnicity	All years[1,2]	Number, by year of report							All years[1,2] Percent distribution	12 mos. ending Nov. 30, 1988 Cases per 100,000 population[1]
		1982	1983	1984	1985	1986	1987	1988[2]		
Hispanic	8,944	83	268	536	961	1,584	2,242	3,246	12.7	52.34
Female										
All females, 13 years and over[3]	6,423	48	141	277	523	963	1,668	2,797	100.0	3.0
White, not Hispanic	1,856	9	34	79	141	271	545	776	28.9	1.07
Black, not Hispanic	3,467	32	66	141	283	520	883	1,540	54.0	14.06
Hispanic	1,034	7	37	57	94	160	228	449	16.1	7.03
Children										
All children, under 13 years[3]	1,221	13	34	50	129	186	319	490	100.0	1.17
White, not Hispanic	294	5	6	10	25	42	81	125	24.1	0.43
Black, not Hispanic	675	5	22	29	86	106	162	265	55.3	4.08
Hispanic	242	3	6	11	18	37	73	94	19.8	2.19

Source: "Acquired Immunodeficiency Syndrome (AIDS) Cases, according to Age, Sex, and Race/Ethnicity: United States, 1982-1988," *Health United States - 1988*, March 1989, p. 82. Center for Disease Control, Center for Infectious Diseases, AIDS Program *Notes:* The AIDS case definition was changed in September 1987 to allow for the presumptive diagnosis of AIDS-associated diseases and conditions and to expand the spectrum of human immunodeficiency virus-associated diseases reportable as AIDS. Excludes residents of U.S. territories. 1. Includes cases prior to 1982. 2. Data are as of November 30, 1988, and reflects reporting delays. 3. Includes all other races not shown separately.

★ 502 ★
Incidence of High Cholesterol: Trends

Data based on physical examinations of a sample of the civilian noninstitutionalized population.

Sex and age	All races			White			Black		
	1960-1962	1971-1974	1976-1980	1960-1962	1971-1974	1976-1980	1960-1962	1971-1974	1976-1980
Percent of population									
Both sexes									
Age adjusted, 25-74 years	26.9	23.2	21.9	27.6	23.2	21.9	22.1	23.7	22.8
25-34 years	20.4	19.9	18.7	20.9	19.8	18.5	19.0	20.6	19.7
35-44 years	21.2	17.5	16.8	22.0	17.3	16.6	14.5	18.2	18.8
45-54 years	26.4	24.2	22.0	26.8	24.4	21.8	25.5	24.1	25.5
55-64 years	36.0	27.9	29.0	37.8	28.0	29.3	20.9	29.3	27.5
65-74 years	37.3	31.3	27.2	37.4	31.5	27.7	38.0	31.1	24.0
Male									
Age adjusted, 25-74 years	24.1	22.1	20.1	25.1	22.0	20.1	17.1	22.7	23.4
25-34 years	23.6	22.7	19.2	24.7	22.8	18.7	16.3	22.3	24.8
35-44 years	26.3	22.6	20.5	27.7	22.2	20.1	13.4	23.7	24.5
45-54 years	25.3	24.1	20.1	26.1	24.6	20.8	21.1	20.4	25.3
55-64 years	22.8	19.5	22.0	23.9	19.3	22.4	13.7	23.0	22.1
65-74 years	20.8	19.9	18.1	20.7	19.5	18.4	22.9[1]	25.8	16.6
Female									
Age adjusted, 25-74 years	29.3	24.0	23.3	29.7	23.9	23.4	26.8	24.6	22.3
25-34 years	17.5	17.2	18.2	17.3	16.9	18.4	20.8	19.4	15.6

Continued.

Incidence of High Cholesterol: Trends
[Continued]

Sex and age	All races			White			Black		
	1960-1962	1971-1974	1976-1980	1960-1962	1971-1974	1976-1980	1960-1962	1971-1974	1976-1980
35-44 years	16.5	12.9	13.4	16.7	12.7	13.3	15.5	14.1	14.3
45-54 years	27.4	24.3	22.9	27.5	24.1	22.7	29.9	27.2	25.8
55-64 years	48.5	35.5	35.3	50.6	35.8	35.6	29.1[1]	34.4	32.0
65-74 years	50.8	40.0	34.3	51.2	40.6	34.8	50.1[1]	35.1	29.5

Source: "High-Risk Serum Cholesterol Levels for Persons 25-74 Years of Age, according to Race, Sex, and Age: United States, 1960-62, 1971-74, and 1976-80," *Health United States - 1988*, March 1989, p. 101. Primary source: Division of Health Examination Statistics, National Center for Health Statistics: unpublished data. *Notes:* High-risk serum cholesterol levels are defined by age-specific cut points of the cholesterol distribution: 20-29 years of age, greater than 220 milligrams/deciliter; 30-39 years of age, greater than 240 milligrams/deciliter; and 40 years of age and over, greater than 260 milligrams/deciliter. Risk levels defined by NIH Consensus Development conference statement on lowering blood cholesterol, December 10, 1984. 1. Based on fewer than 45 persons.

★ 503 ★
Iron Deficiency in 1-4-Year-Old Children

Race	Age (years)	n	Percent	Standard error of the percent
All races	1-2	542	9.4	1.4
	3-4	989	3.9	0.7
White	1-2	434	8.4	1.5
	3-4	803	3.2	0.6
Black	1-2	89	10.9	3.0
	3-4	157	8.5	0.9

Source: "Prevalence of Iron Deficiency Determined by the MCV Model in Children Aged 1-4 Years, by Age, Race, and Poverty Status: Second National Health and Nutrition Examination Survey, 1976-80 (LSRO, 1984)," *Nutrition Monitoring in the United States*, September 1989, p. 150. Primary source: Life Sciences Research Office, S.M. Pilch and F.R. Senti, eds. 1984. *Assessment of the Iron Nutritional Status of the U.S. Population Based on Data Collected in the Second National Health and Nutrition Examination Survey, 1976-80*. Bethesda, MD: Federation of American Societies for Experimental Biology. MCV - Mean corpuscular value.

★ 504 ★
Iron Deficiency in Pregnant Women

Race or ethnic group	Total		First trimester		Second trimester		Third trimester	
	n[1]	Percent low	n	Percent low	n	Percent low	n	Percent low
Total	77,771	14.7	15,261	5.6	36,367	9.9	26,143	26.8
White	43,908	9.4	10,575	3.2	19,885	5.8	13,448	19.4
Black	25,702	24.2	3,609	12.2	12,584	16.8	9,509	38.6
Hispanic	7,130	13.6	902	7.5	3,450	7.9	2,778	22.8
Native American	263	9.1	48	0	111	4.5	104	18.2

Continued.

Iron Deficiency in Pregnant Women
[Continued]

Race or ethnic group	Total		First trimester		Second trimester		Third trimester	
	n[1]	Percent low	n	Percent low	n	Percent low	n	Percent low
Asian	592	15.2	99	9.1	265	12.1	228	21.5

Source: "Prevalence of Low Hematocrit at Initial Visit, Race or Ethnic and Trimester of Pregnancy: CDC Pregnancy Nutrition Surveillance System, 1987," *Nutrion Monitoring in the United States,* September 1989, p. 87. Primary source: Centers for Disease Control. *Notes:* 1. n is the number of persons in the sample; for n < 100, interpret data with caution.

★ 505 ★
Length of Psychiatric Hospital Stay

Race, Hispanic origin, and selected primary diagnoses	Inpatient psychiatric services			
	State and county mental hospitals	Private psychiatric hospitals	Non-Federal general hospitals	VA medical centers
Total, all races	23	19	11	22
Alcohol- and drug-related	12	20	6	20
Organic disorders	71	17	14	33
Affective disorders	22	20	14	26
Schizophrenia	42	18	14	24
White	23	19	12	23
Alcohol- and drug-related	12	20	6	21
Organic disorders	80	17	14	32
Affective disorders	25	20	14	26
Schizophrenia	48	19	14	25
Black	22	18	11	19
Alcohol- and drug-related	12	19	9	15
Organic disorders	27	17	15	52
Affective disorders	16	20	14	28
Schizophrenia	32	16	13	21
American Indian or Alaskan Native	17	10	14	15
Alcohol- and drug-related	12	2	8	18
Organic disorders	3	2	2	2
Affective disorders	6	10	14	2
Schizophrenia	20	2	17	6
Asian or Pacific Islander	35	13	12	18
Alcohol- and drug-related	16	2	2	2
Organic disorders	3	-	2	-
Affective disorders	3	18	10	2
Schizophrenia	52	13	15	2
Hispanic origin[1]	24	15	12	19
Alcohol- and drug-related	13	10	6	18
Organic disorders	19	38	14	-

Continued.

Length of Psychiatric Hospital Stay
[Continued]

Race, Hispanic origin, and selected primary diagnoses	Inpatient psychiatric services			
	State and county mental hospitals	Private psychiatric hospitals	Non-Federal general hospitals	VA medical centers
Affective disorders	14	14	10	17
Schizophrenia	54	17	14	20

Source: "Median Days of Inpatient Stay for Admissions (Excluding Deaths) to Selected Inpatient Psychiatric Services, by Race, Hispanic Origin, and Selected Primary Diagnoses: United States, 1980," *Mental Health United States,* 1987, p. 80. Primary source: 1980 Patient Sample Surveys. Division of Biometry and Applied Sciences, National Institute of Mental Health. *Notes:* 1. Persons of Hispanic origin may be from any racial group. 2. Based on five or fewer sample cases; median days of stay not shown because it does not meet standards of reliability. 3. Since over one-half of the admissions in this group were not discharged during the survey period, median days of stay could not be determined.

★ 506 ★
Length of Stay/Discharge from Short-Stay Hospitals: Trends

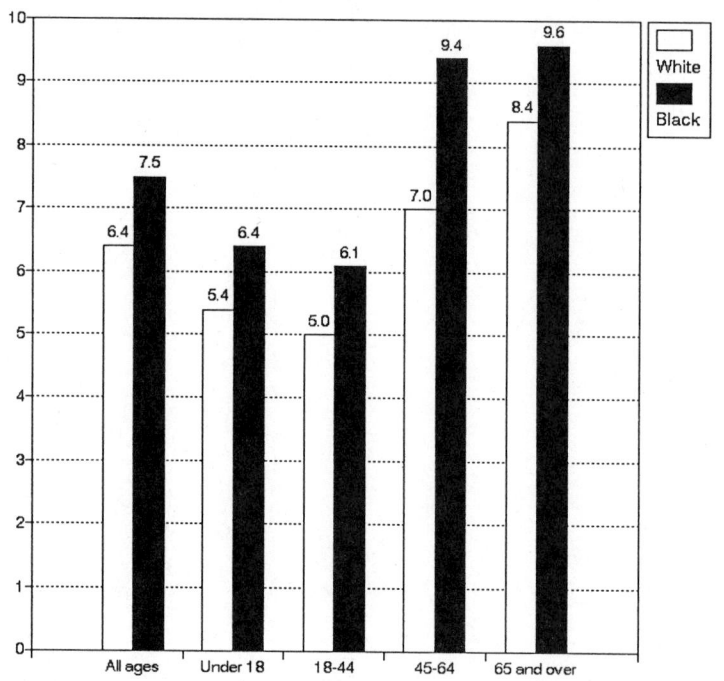

Days per discharge.

Characteristic	White	Black
All family incomes[1]		
All ages	6.4	7.5
Under 18 years	5.4	6.4
18-44 years	5.0	6.1
45-64 years	7.0	9.4
65 years and over	8.4	9.6
Less than $20,000		
All ages	7.1	7.9
Under 18 years	5.1	7.1
18-44 years	5.4	6.1

Continued.

Length of Stay/Discharge from Short-Stay Hospitals: Trends
[Continued]

Characteristic	White	Black
45-64 years	7.8	10.5
65 years and over	8.6	9.4
$20,000 or more		
All ages	5.6	6.6
Under 18 years	5.5	5.4
18-44 years	4.6	5.5
45-64 years	6.2	8.6
65 years and over	7.6	11.0

Source: "Average Annual Length of Stay per Short-Stay Hospital Discharge by Race, Age, and Family Income: United States, 1985-87," *Health of Black and White Americans, 1985-87,* 1990, p. 19. Primary source: National Health Interview Survey, U.S. Department of Health and Human Services, Public Health Service, Centers for Disease Control, Division of Health Statistics, Hyattsville, MD, January 1990. *Note:* 1. Includes unknown family income.

★ 507 ★
Medical Care: Needed but Not Received

Numbers in percent.

Indicator	White	Black	p<
Not receiving health care for economic reasons	5.0	9.1	.01
Individuals with a chronic or serious illness not having ann ambulatory visit in last year	16.6	25.1	.01
People with hypertension without an annual blood-pressure check	19.0	30.0	.01
No dental visit in a year	36.1	50.3	.01

Source: "Indicators of Inequities in Medical Care by Race," *The State of Black America 1990,* January 1990, p. 123. Primary source: *Journal of the American Medical Association,* 261:279, Table 4, January 13, 1989. Extracted from: *The State of Black America,* January 1990. Published by permission.

★ 508 ★
Mineral and Vitamin Deficiencies

Race and age	Serum copper[1,2]		Age	Serum zinc[3]		Serum vitamin C[3]		Serum vitamin A[3-5]	
	Male	Female		Male	Female	Male	Female	Male	Female
White									
3-5 yr	[6]	0.2	3-5yr	3.1	3.8	0.1	[6]	2.8	6.1
6-11 yr	0.6	0.1	6-11yr	1.9	1.2	0.4	[6]	2.0	1.6
12-14 yr	0.8	0.8	12-17yr	1.0	0.8	1.6	1.7		
15-17 yr	1.6	0.3							

Continued.

345

Mineral and Vitamin Deficiencies
[Continued]

Race and age	Serum copper[1,2]		Age	Serum zinc[3]		Serum vitamin C[3]		Serum vitamin A[3-5]	
	Male	Female		Male	Female	Male	Female	Male	Female
18-24 yr	1.9	0.5	18-24yr	0.2	3.6	2.1	1.9		
25-44 yr	0.9	0.4	25-54yr	1.0	3.0	5.4	2.9		
45-64 yr	0.9	0.2							
65-74 yr	0.4	0.1	55-74yr	1.9	2.4	6.5	1.8		
Black									
3-5 yr	6	6	3-5yr	2.7	1.0	6	6	5.9	3.0
6-11 yr	6	1.4	6-11yr	3.0	3.9	6	1.0	2.9	1.6
12-14 yr	6	6	12-17yr	1.3	3.2	1.4	0.6		
15-17 yr	1.3	6							
18-24 yr	6	1.1	18-24yr	2.1	5.9	3.0	2.5		
25-44 yr	6	6	25-54yr	1.4	5.5	9.6	4.7		
45-64 yr	6	6							
65-74 yr	6	6	55-74yr	3.3	3.8	16.2	5.3		

Source: "Percent of Population Below Standard Values for Serum Copper, Zinc, Vitamin C, and Vitamin A, by Race, Age, and Sex: Second National Health and Nutrition Examination Survey, 1976-80 *Notes:* 1. National Center for Health Statistics, R. Fulwood, C.L. Johnson, J.D. Bryner, E.W. Gunter, C.W. McGrath: Hematological and nutritional biochemistry reference data for persons 6 months - 74 years of age: United States, 1976-80. *Vital and Health Statistics*, Series 11 - No. 232. DHHS Pub. No. (PHS) 83-1682. Public Health Service. Washington. U.S. Government Printing Office, Dec. 1982. 2. Cutoff value of <70 mugrams/deciliter from Sauberlich, H.E. Current laboratory tests for assessing nutritional status. *Surv. Synth. Path. Res.* 2:120-133, 1983. 3. U.S. Department of Health and Human Services and U.S. Department of Agriculture: *Nutrition Monitoring in the United States - A Report from the Joint Nutrition Monitoring Evaluation Committee.* DHHS Publication No. (PHS) 86-1255. Public Health Service. Washington. U.S. Government Printing Office, July 1986, pp. 102, 140, 180, 309, 311, 315. Cutoff values used: Zinc: <70 mugrams/deciliter - a.m., fasting; <65 mugrams/deciliter - a.m., nonfasting; 60 mugrams/deciliter - p.m. Vitamin C: <0.25 mugrams/deciliter. Vitamin A: <0.20 mugrams/deciliter. 4. Vitamin A status was assessed only in children 3-11 years of age. 5. Pilch, S.M., editor: Assessment of the vitamin A nutritional status of the U.S. population based on data collected in the National Health and Nutrition Examination Surveys. Prepared for the Center for Food Safety and Applied Nutrition, Food and Drug Administration, under Contract No. FDA 223-84-2059 by the Life Sciences Research Office, Federation of American Societies for Experimental Biology, Bethesda, MD, 1985, p. 31. 6. Insufficient sample size for analysis.

★ 509 ★
Most Prevalent Chronic Conditions: Trends

Number per 1,000 persons per year.

Condition	Percent	
	White	Black
Respiratory		
Chronic sinusitis	146.7	106.7
Hay fever or allergic rhinitis without asthma	95.4	59.8
Asthma	39.6	42.2
Chronic bronchitis	53.5	35.3
Skin and musculoskeletal		
Arthritis	134.4	122.6
Dermatitis	40.0	29.3
Trouble with corns or calluses	19.0	29.7
Circulatory		
Hypertension	120.0	145.7
Hemorrhoids	45.9	30.7
Ischemic heart disease	32.8	10.0
Varicose veins of lower extremities	32.7	17.2

Continued.

Most Prevalent Chronic Conditions: Trends
[Continued]

Condition	Percent	
	White	Black
Digestive		
Frequent indigestion	25.3	17.2
Impairments		
Bilnd, both eyes	2.1	1.8
Other visual impairments	34.2	26.4
Deaf, both ears	7.5	2.4
Other hearing impairments	88.2	45.8
Orthopedic impairments of upper body	47.4	37.8
Orthopedic impairments of lower extremities (excluding flat feet or club foot)	38.0	27.8
Tinnitus	28.7	15.4
Other		
Diabetes	26.5	36.0
Migraine headache	37.5	28.0
Other headache (excluding tension headache)	35.9	35.1

Source: "Average Annual Number of the Most Prevalent Reported Chronic Conditions per 1,000 Persons by Race: United States, 1985-87," *Health of Black and White Americans, 1985-87,* 1990, p. 11. Primary source: National Health Interview Survey, U.S. Department of Health and Human Services, Public Health Service, Centers for Disease Control, Division of Health Statistics, Hyattsville, MD, January 1990.

★ 510 ★
Nursing Homes

Based on the National Nursing Home Survey and subject to sampling variation, see source.

Characteristic	Discharges				Median Duration of Stay (days)	
	Total (1,000)		Percent distribution			
	1976	1985	1976	1985	1976	1985
All discharges[1]	1,117.5	1,223.5	100.0	100.0	75	82
Age at discharge:						
Under 65 years old	136.2	129.4	12.1	10.6	56	69
65 years old and over	981.3	1,094.1	87.8	89.4	78	84
65-74 years old	203.6	182.9	18.2	15.0	52	57
75-84 years old	445.8	452.2	39.9	37.0	67	65
85-94 years old	300.6	389.8	26.9	31.8	123	145
95 years old and over	31.1	69.2	2.8	5.7	379	239
Male	407.7	455.5	36.5	37.2	60	66
Female	709.8	768.0	63.5	62.8	88	93
White	[3]	1,135.9	[3]	92.8	[3]	82
Black	[3]	82.0	[3]	6.7	[3]	101
Other	[3]	5.6	[3]	.5	[3]	44
Hispanic[2]	[3]	35.5	[3]	2.9	[3]	113
Non-Hispanic	[3]	1,130.7	[3]	92.4	[3]	83

Continued.

Nursing Homes
[Continued]

| Characteristic | Discharges | | | | Median Duration of Stay (days) | |
| | Total (1,000) | | Percent distribution | | | |
	1976	1985	1976	1985	1976	1985
Unknown	3	57.4	3	4.7	3	71

Source: "Nursing Home Discharges, by Selected Characteristics: 1976 and 1985," *Statistical Abstract*, 1989, p. 108. Primary source: U.S. National Center for Health Statistics, *Discharge From Nursing Homes: Preliminary Data From the 1985 National Nursing Home Survey*, Advance Data. No. 142, September 1987. *Notes:* 1. Total includes small number of unknown by discharge status. 2. Persons of Hispanic origin may be of any race. 3. Not available.

★ 511 ★
Occupational Category and Acute Conditions

Data based on household interviews of the civilian noninstitutionalized population.

| Race and occupation of longest employment | Estimated population (thou.) | All acute conditions | | Acute respiratory conditions | |
		Incidence per 100 persons per year	Percent medically attended	Incidence per 100 persons per year	Percent medically attended
White					
All persons	140,022	185.1	52.0	97.9	34.8
White-collar workers	66,815	197.1	49.5	106.5	32.9
Blue-collar workers	41,604	162.5	54.4	82.1	34.6
Farm workers	3,592	135.4	50.6	76.6	39.0
Service workers	16,523	223.6	55.2	115.7	41.3
Ever worked, occupation unknown	6,566	172.1	56.6	93.7	37.0
Never worked	4,921	135.9	51.6	75.1	35.4
Black					
All persons	16,842	178.8	58.2	77.9	43.5
White-collar workers	4,702	216.0	57.3	93.8	48.0
Blue-collar workers	5,608	149.2	61.3	63.5	40.3
Farm workers	472	119.5[1]	69.9[1]	27.1[1]	53.1[1]
Service workers	4,159	185.8	53.7	87.9	37.7
Ever worked, occupation unknown	944	162.2	74.7	63.1[1]	65.3[1]
Never worked	957	185.0	50.6	80.3	41.9[1]

Source: "Number and Percent Distribution of Persons 17 Years of Age and Over, Incidence of Acute Conditions and Acute Respiratory Conditions per 100 Persons per Year, and Percent Medically Attended, by Race and Occupation of Longest Employment: United States, 1980," *Health Characteristics by Occupation and Industry of Longest Employment*, June 1989, pp. 52-53. Primary source: *Vital and Health Statistics*, Series 10, Data from the National Health Survey, No. 168. *Notes:* Excluded from these statistics are all conditions that involved neither restricted activity nor medical attention. 1. Figure does not meet standard of reliability or precision.

★ 512 ★
Occupational Category and Professional Care

Data based on households interviews of the civilian noninstitutionalized population.

Race and occupation of longest employment	Estima-ted population (thou.)	Short-stay hospitals			Physician visits		Dental visits	
		Percent with episode in year	Dischar-ges per 100 persons per year	Length of stay per discharge in days	Percent with visit in year	Visits per person per year	Percent with visit in year	Visits per person per year
All races[1]								
All persons	160,149	12.3	16.7	8.0	74.3	4.9	49.8	1.7
White-collar workers	72,895	11.4	14.8	6.9	77.0	5.1	60.2	2.1
Blue-collar workers	48,058	12.7	17.6	8.8	70.5	4.5	39.9	1.3
Farm workers	4,177	12.5	18.6	9.2	67.2	4.1	34.6	0.9
Service workers	21,120	14.2	19.4	7.8	77.0	5.5	44.6	1.4
Ever worked, occupation unknown	7,752	10.6	15.5	11.6	68.6	4.2	45.4	1.6
Never worked	6,146	15.6	21.5	8.0	73.2	4.8	37.1	1.2
White								
All persons	140,022	12.2	16.6	7.7	74.3	4.9	51.8	1.7
White-collar workers	66,815	11.3	15.0	6.9	76.9	5.2	61.5	2.1
Blue-collar workers	41,604	12.7	17.5	8.5	70.5	4.4	41.1	1.3
Farm workers	3,592	12.4	18.2	8.3	66.7	4.0	37.6	1.0
Service workers	16,523	14.2	19.5	7.2	76.8	5.4	48.1	1.5
Ever worked, occupation unknown	6,566	10.4	15.2	11.1	69.1	4.2	47.3	1.5
Never worked	4,921	16.1	22.4	7.6	74.3	4.9	39.0	1.4
Black								
All persons	16,842	13.3	18.4	10.1	75.5	5.2	34.2	1.1
White-collar workers	4,702	12.6	14.4	6.8	80.9	4.9	44.3	1.2
Blue-collar workers	5,608	13.0	19.8	11.1	71.8	5.1	31.5	1.0
Farm workers	472	13.3	22.9	14.9	70.1	5.4	15.5	0.5[2]
Service workers	4,159	14.4	19.7	9.8	78.6	5.9	30.8	1.0
Ever worked, occupation unknown	944	12.3	20.6	14.7	64.4	4.6	31.8	2.0
Never worked	957	14.6	20.1	10.1	70.6	4.4	27.1	0.5[2]

Source: "Number of Persons 17 Years of Age and Over and Average Rate of Utilization of Medical and Dental Services, by Race and Occupation of Longest Employment: United States, 1980," *Health Characteristics by Occupation and Industry of Longest Employment*, June 1989, pp. 52-53. Primary source: *Vital and Health Statistics*, Series 10, Data from the National Health Survey, No. 168. *Notes:* 1. Includes all other races not shown as separate categories. 2. Figure does not meet standard of reliability or precision.

★ 513 ★
Overweight and Severely Overweight Adults

Ethnic group or race	Percent overweight		Percent severely overweight	
	Male	Female	Male	Female
Mexican American	30.9	41.6	10.8	16.9
Cuban	27.6	31.6	10.7	6.6
Puerto Rican	25.6	40.2	8.0	15.7
Non-Hispanic white	24.2	23.9	7.7	9.4
Non-Hispanic black	26.0	44.4	10.0	19.8

Source: "Age-Adjusted Percent of Overweight and Severely Overweight Persons Aged 20-74 Years, by Sex and Ethnic Group or Race: Hispanic Health and Nutrition Examination Survey, 1982-84, and Second National Health and Nutrition Examination Survey, 1976-80," *Nutrition Monitoring in the United States*, September 1989, p. 49. Primary source: U.S. Department of Health and Human Services and U.S. Department of Agriculture.

★ 514 ★
Paying for Nursing Home Care When Admitted

Discharge status and characteristic	Primary source of payment for admission month						
	Dis-charges	All sources	Own income or family support	Medi-care	Medi-caid, skilled	Medi-caid, inter-mediate	All other sources
	Percent distribution						
All discharges[1]	1,223,500	100.0	41.9	17.6	15.5	19.6	5.4
Race:							
White	1,135,900	100.0	43.9	18.0	14.6	18.4	5.2
Black	82,000	100.0	16.3	14.1	26.2	35.3	8.0
Other	5,600	100.0	[2]	[3]	[2]	[2]	[2]
Live discharges	877,000	100.0	40.1	17.8	15.6	20.5	5.9
Race:							
White	811,200	100.0	42.1	18.4	14.6	19.2	5.6
Black	61,200	100.0	14.6	11.3	27.0	37.8	9.4
Other	[2]	[2]	[2]	[3]	[2]	[2]	[2]
Dead discharges	344,200	100.0	46.6	17.2	15.0	17.2	4.0
Race:							
White	322,500	100.0	48.3	16.9	14.5	16.3	4.0
Black	20,700	100.0	[2]	[2]	23.7	28.3	[2]
Other	[2]	[2]	[2]	[3]	[2]	[2]	[3]

Source: "Number of Nursing Home Discharges by Discharge Status and Selected Characteristics, and Percent Distribution of Nursing Home Discharges by Primary Sources of Payment for Admission Month, According to Discharge Status and Selected Characteristics: United States, 1984-85," *Discharges from Nursing Homes: 1985 National Nursing Home Survey*, March 1990, pp. 47- 50. Primary source: *Vital and Health Statistics*, Series 13, No. 103. *Notes:* Figures may not add to totals because of rounding. 1. Includes small number of discharges with unknown discharge status. 2. Figure does not meet standard of reliability or precision. 3. Quantity zero.

★ 515 ★
Paying for Nursing Home Care When Discharged

Discharge status and characteristic	Number Dis- charges	Percent distribution Primary source of payment for discharge month					
		All sources	Own income or family support	Medi- care	Medi- caid, skilled	Medi- caid, inter- mediate	All other sources
All discharges[1]	1,223,500	100.0	41.8	12.1	18.9	21.3	6.0
Race:							
White	1,135,900	100.0	43.7	12.5	17.9	20.1	5.8
Black	82,000	100.0	16.8	7.3	31.5	36.9	7.4
Other	5,600	100.0	[2]	[3]	[2]	[2]	[2]
Live discharges	877,000	100.0	41.4	11.9	18.0	21.9	6.8
Race:							
White	811,200	100.0	43.5	12.4	17.0	20.6	6.6
Black	61,200	100.0	15.7	[2]	30.4	39.7	8.9
Other	[2]	[2]	[2]	[3]	[2]	[2]	[2]
Dead discharges	344,200	100.0	42.8	12.7	21.1	19.7	3.7
Race:							
White	322,500	100.0	44.3	12.7	20.3	19.0	3.7
Black	20,700	100.0	[2]	[2]	34.7	28.9	[2]
Other	[2]	[2]	[2]	[3]	[2]	[2]	[3]

Source: "Number of Nursing Home Discharges by Discharge Status and Selected Characteristics, and Percent Distribution of Nursing Home Discharges by Primary Sources of Payment for Discharge Month, According to Discharge Status and Selected Characteristics: United States, 1984-85," *Discharges from Nursing Homes: 1985 National Nursing Home Survey,* March 1990, pp. 51-54. Primary source: *Vital and Health Statistics,* Series 13, No. 103. *Notes:* Figures may not add to totals because of rounding. 1. Includes small number of discharges with unknown discharge status. 2. Figure does not meet standard of reliability or precision. 3. Quantity zero.

★ 516 ★
Personal and Nursing Home Care: Trends

Data based on a sample of nursing homes.

Age and race	Residents				Residents per 1,000 population[1]			
	1963	1973-74[2]	1977[3]	1985	1963	1973-74[2]	1977[3]	1985
Age								
All ages	445,600	961,500	1,126,000	1,318,300	25.4	44.7	47.1	46.2
65-74 years	89,600	163,100	211,400	212,100	7.9	12.3	14.4	12.5
75-84 years	207,200	384,900	464,700	509,000	39.6	57.7	64.0	57.7
85 years and over	148,700	413,600	449,900	597,300	148.4	257.3	225.9	220.3
Race[4]								
White	431,700	920,600	1,059,900	1,227,400	26.6	46.9	48.9	47.7
65-74 years	84,400	150,100	187,500	187,800	8.1	12.5	14.2	12.3
75-84 years	202,000	369,700	443,200	473,600	41.7	60.3	67.0	59.1
85 years and over	145,400	400,800	429,100	566,000	157.7	270.8	234.2	228.7
Black	13,800	37,700	60,800	82,000	10.3	22.0	30.7	35.0
65-74 years	5,200	12,200	22,000	22,500	5.9	11.1	17.6	15.4

Continued.

Personal and Nursing Home Care: Trends
[Continued]

Age and race	Residents				Residents per 1,000 population[1]			
	1963	1973-74[2]	1977[3]	1985	1963	1973-74[2]	1977[3]	1985
75-84 years	5,300	13,400	19,700	30,600	13.8	26.7	33.4	45.3
85 years and over	3,300	12,100	19,100	29,000	41.8	105.7	133.6	141.5

Source: "Nursing Home and Personal Care Home Residents 65 Years of Age and Over and Rate per 1,000 Population, according to Sex and Race: United States, 1963, 1973-74, 1977, and 1985," *Health United States - 1988*, March 1989, p. 123. Primary source: Wunderlich, G.S. "Characteristics of residents in institutions for the aged and chronically ill, United States, April-June 1963," National Center for Health Statistics. *Vital and Health Statistics*: Series 12, No. 2, DHEW Pub. No. 1000, Public Health Service; Series 13, No. 27, DHEW Pub. No. 77-1778, Health Resources Administration; Series 13, No. 51, DHHS Pub. No. 81-1712, Public Health Service; Series 13, No. 97, U.S. Bureau of the Census. Zappolo, A. "Characteristics, social contacts, and activities of nursing home residents, United States," 1973-74 National Nursing Home Survey, U.S. Government Printing Office, Washington, DC., September 1965. Hing, E. "Characteristics of nursing home residents, health status, and care received: National Nursing Home Survey, United States, May-December 1977," U.S. Government Printing Office, Washington, DC, May 1977. Hing, E., Sekscenski, E., and Strahan, G. "The National Nursing Home Survey: 1985 summary for the United States," U.S. Government Printing Office, Washington, DC, April 1981. "Preliminary estimates of the population of the United States by age, sex, and race: 1970-1981," *Current Population Reports*, Series P-25, No. 917, U.S. Bureau of the Census, U.S. Government Printing Office, Washington, DC, July 1982. *Notes:* 1. Residents per 1,000 population for 1973-74 and 1977 will differ from those presented in the sources because the rates have been recomputed using revised census estimates for these years. 2. Excludes residents in personal care or domiciliary care homes. 3. Includes residents in domiciliary care homes. 4. For data years 1973-74 and 1977, all Hispanics were included in the white category. For 1963, black includes all other races.

★ 517 ★
Physician Contacts: Trends

Data based on household interviews of a sample of the civilian noninstitutionalized population.

Characteristic	Number per person Physician contacts		Place of Contact Percent distribution										
			Total	Doctor's office		Hospital outpatient department[1]		Telephone		Home		Other[2]	
	1983	1987		1983	1987	1983	1987	1983	1987	1983	1987	1983	1987
Total[3,4]	5.1	5.4	100.0	56.1	57.1	14.9	14.1	15.5	13.4	1.5	2.1	12.0	13.4
Race[3]													
White	5.2	5.5	100.0	57.6	58.6	13.4	12.8	16.3	14.1	1.5	2.0	11.1	12.5
Black	4.9	5.1	100.0	44.3	47.2	26.8	23.5	9.7	7.8	1.1	3.1	18.2	18.3

Source: "Physician Contacts, according to Place of Contact and Selected Patient Characteristics: United States, 1983 and 1987," *Health United States - 1988*, March 1989, p. 106. Primary source: National Health Interview Survey, Division of Health Interview Statistics, National Center for Health Statistics. *Notes:* In previous editions of *Health, United States*, physician contacts were labeled physician visits. 1. Includes hospital outpatient clinic, emergency room, and other hospital contacts. 2. Includes clinics or other places outside a hospital. 3. Age adjusted. 4. Includes all other races not shown separately.

★ 518 ★
Prenatal Care and Live Births: Trends

Numbers in percent.

	1970	1975	1980	1985	1986	1987
Prenatal care began:						
First trimester						
All races and origins	68	72	76	76	76	76
White	72	76	79	79	79	79
Black	44	56	63	62	62	61
All Hispanic women	[1]	[1]	60	61	60	61
Cuban			83	83	82	83
Mexican			60	60	59	60
Puerto Rican			58	58	57	57

Continued.

Prenatal Care and Live Births: Trends
[Continued]

	1970	1975	1980	1985	1986	1987
Non-Hispanic women			77	77	77	77
Third trimester or						
no prenatal care						
All races and origins	8	6	5	6	6	6
White	6	5	4	5	5	5
Black	17	10	9	10	11	11
All Hispanic women	1	1	12	12	13	13
Cuban			4	4	4	4
Mexican			12	13	13	13
Puerto Rican			16	16	17	17
Non-Hispanic women			5	5	6	6

Source: "Percentage of Live Births by Trimester Prenatal Care Began, Race, and Hispanic Origin, 1970-1987," *U.S. Children and their Families*, 1989, p. 163. Primary source: National Center for Health Statistics, *Health, United States, 1982*, Table 24; *Vital Statistics of the United States*, 1985, Vol. 1 - Natality, Table 1-84. *Monthly Vital Statistics Report*, Vol. 31, No. 8, Supplement, November 1982, Tables 13, 20; Vol. 35, No. 4, Supplement, July 1986, Table 25; Vol. 36, No. 4, Supplement, July 1987, Table 25; Vol. 37, No. 3, Supplement, June 1989, Tables 27 and 30. Birth figures for Hispanic women in 1985-87 are based on data for 23 states and the District of Columbia which report Hispanic origin of the mother on the birth certificate. These states accounted for 90 percent of the Hispanic population in 1980. Hispanic data for 1980 from: *Monthly Vital Statistics Report*, Vol. 32, No. 6, Supplement, September 1983, Table 13 (based on 22 states). *Notes:* Non-Hispanic women are white, black, and other women not of Hispanic origin, in the same 23 states that report data on origin. 1. Not applicable.

★ 519 ★
Prenatal Care in the First Trimester: Trends

Year	Percent with no prenatal care during the first trimester			
	White	Black	American Indian	Hispanic
1978	21.8	39.8	43.7	43.0
1979	20.9	38.4	41.3	39.5
1980	20.7	37.3	41.3	39.8
1981	20.6	37.6	40.7	39.4
1982	20.7	38.5	39.5	39.0
1983	20.6	38.5	40.3	39.0
1984	20.4	37.8	40.0	38.5
1985	20.6	38.2	39.7	38.8
1986	20.8	38.4	39.3	39.7
1987	20.6	38.9	39.8	39.0
1990	10.0	10.0	10.0	10.0

Source: Health United States 1989, March 1990, p. 35. Primary source: Data from the National Center for Health Statistics, Division of Vital Statistics.

★ 520 ★
Psychiatric Diagnosis and Type of Inpatient Service Facility

Race, Hispanic origin, and primary diagnosis	Inpatient psychiatric services			
	State and county mental hospitals	Private psychiatric hospitals	Non-Federal general hospitals	VA medical centers
Total, all races	369,049	141,209	666,300	158,931
Alcohol-related disorders	21.7	9.3	7.6	34.5
Drug-related disorders	4.8	2.9	2.9	5.1
Organic disorders	4.2	3.5	3.3	2.5
Affective disorders	13.4	42.9	31.1	14.4
Schizophrenia	38.0	21.2	25.2	29.9
Personality disorders	5.7	4.8	4.6	4.7
All other	12.3	15.4	25.2	8.9
White	265,442	123,051	552,679	125,966
Alcohol-related disorders	23.8	9.4	7.8	36.7
Drug-related disorders	5.3	2.8	2.8	3.5
Organic disorders	4.2	3.4	3.1	2.6
Affective disorders	15.6	44.5	33.9	16.4
Schizophrenia	31.5	19.2	22.7	26.4
Personality disorders	6.5	5.1	4.7	4.8
All other	13.1	15.5	25.0	9.6
Black	96,299	16,633	102,212	31,245
Alcohol-related disorders	15.5	8.8	6.4	25.1
Drug-related disorders	3.1	3.7	3.3	11.2
Organic disorders	4.2	4.7	4.1	2.1
Affective disorders	7.7	30.8	16.8	6.4
Schizophrenia	56.3	35.7	38.0	44.5
Personality disorders	3.5	2.4	4.6	4.5
All other	9.8	14.0	26.8	6.2
All other races	7,308	1,525	1,409	1,720
Alcohol-related disorders	27.2	[2]	8.0	45.2
Drug-related disorders	7.3	[2]	[2]	[2]
Organic disorders	3.6	[2]	6.5	[2]
Affective disorders	10.1	39.1	23.9	15.1
Schizophrenia	32.4	27.2	31.3	21.0
Personality disorders	4.1	[2]	[2]	[2]
All other	15.4	24.6	21.9	9.1
Hispanic origin[1]	21,231	4,998	33,017	6,410
Alcohol-related disorders	18.4	4.3	6.0	21.7
Drug-related disorders	7.5	[2]	[2]	10.2
Organic disorders	2.7	[2]	2.5	-
Affective disorders	15.2	40.4	27.4	20.8
Schizophrenia	43.9	27.2	36.7	26.6
Personality disorders	7.2	3.2	2.0	9.0
All other	5.1	22.6	24.2	11.5

Source: "Percent Distribution of Admissions to Selected Inpatient Psychiatric Services, by Race, Hispanic Origin, and Primary Diagnosis: United States, 1980," *Mental Health United States,* 1987, p. 79. Primary source: 1980 Patient Sample Surveys, Division of Biometry and Applied Sciences, National Institute of Mental Health. *Notes:* Percentages may not add up to 100 percent because of rounding. 1. Persons of Hispanic origin may be from any racial group. 2. Five or fewer sample cases; estimate not shown because it does not meet standards of reliability.

★ 521 ★
Rate of Inpatient Psychiatric Admissions

Race and Hispanic origin	Inpatient psychiatric services				
	Total	State and county mental hospitals	Private psychiatric hospitals	Non-Federal general hospitals	VA medical centers
Number					
Total, all races	1,335,489	369,049	141,209	666,300	158,931
White	1,067,138	265,442	123,051	552,679	125,966
Black	246,389	96,299	16,633	102,212	31,245
American Indian or Alaskan Native	12,150	4,547	611	5,515	1,477
Asian or Pacific Islander	9,812	2,761	914	5,894	243
Hispanic origin	65,656	21,232	4,998	33,017	6,410
Percent distribution					
Total, all races	100.0	100.0	100.0	100.0	100.0
White	79.9	71.9	87.1	82.9	79.3
Black	18.4	26.1	11.8	15.3	19.7
American Indian or Alaskan Native	0.9	1.2	0.4	0.8	0.9
Asian or Pacific Islander	0.7	0.7	0.6	0.9	0.2
Hispanic origin	4.9	5.8	3.5	5.0	4.0
Rate per 100,000 civilian population					
Total, all races	592.0	163.6	62.6	295.3	70.4
White	550.0	136.8	63.4	284.9	64.9
Black	931.8	364.2	62.9	386.6	118.2
American Indian or Alaskan Native	818.7	306.4	41.2	371.6	99.5
Asian or Pacific Islander	268.1	75.4	25.0	161.0	6.6
Hispanic origin	451.4	146.0	34.4	227.0	44.1

Source: "Number, Percent Distribution, and Rate per 100,000 Civilian Population of Admissions to Selected Inpatient Psychiatric Services, by Race and Hispanic Origin: United States, 1980," *Mental Health United States,* 1987, p. 76. Primary source: 1980 Patient Sample Surveys, Survey and Reports Branch, Division of Biometry and Applied Sciences, National Institute of Mental Health. *Notes:* Percentages may not add to 100 percent because of rounding. Civilian population estimates used as denominators for rate computations for total all races, whites, and blacks are from the U.S. Bureau of the Census, *Current Population Reports,* Series P-25, No. 929, table 3, p. 19. Population estimates used as denominators for rate computations for American Indians or Alaskan Natives, Asian or Pacific Islanders, and Hispanics are derived from the *1980 Census of Population, General Population Characteristics,* PC80-1- B1, table 43, pp. 32-36, and adjusted to the civilian population estimates. Persons of Hispanic origin may be from any racial group.

★ 522 ★
Inpatient Psychiatric Admissions

	Percent
White	80.0
American Indian or Alaskan Native	1.0
Asian or Pacific Islander	1.0
Black	18.0

Source: "Percent Distribution of Admissions to Selected Inpatient Psychiatric Services, by Race and Hispanic Origin: United States, 1980," *Mental Health United States*, 1987, p. 66. Primary source: 1980 Patient Sample Surveys, Survey and Reports Branch, Division of Biometry and Applied Sciences, National Institute of Mental Health. *Notes:* Includes the inpatient psychiatric services of State and county mental hospitals, private psychiatric hospitals, non-Federal general hospitals, and Veterans Administration medical centers.

★ 523 ★
Rate of Inpatient Psychiatric Services

Race, Hispanic origin, and sex	Inpatient psychiatric services			
	State and county mental hospitals	Private psychiatric hospitals	Non-Federal general hospitals	VA medical centers
Total, all races[1]	163.6	62.6	295.3	70.4
Male	219.8	61.9	276.4	141.9
Female	111.1	63.3	313.1	3.7
White	136.8	63.4	284.9	64.9
Male	182.2	61.7	265.0	130.1
Female	94.1	65.0	303.6	3.6
Black	364.2	62.9	386.6	118.2
Male	512.7	70.4	369.4	247.1
Female	233.5	56.3	401.6	4.7
American Indian or Alaskan Native	306.4	41.2	371.6	99.5
Male	381.1	46.0	450.8	192.9
Female	234.1	36.5	295.0	[3]
Asian or Pacific Islander	75.4	25.0	161.0	6.6
Male	104.2	15.7	159.1	11.8
Female	48.8	33.6	162.8	[3]
Hispanic origin[2]	146.0	34.4	227.0	44.1
Male	206.3	35.2	234.3	87.1
Female	86.8	33.6	219.9	1.9

Source: "Rate per 100,000 Civilian Population of Admissions to Selected Inpatient Psychiatric Services, by Race, Hispanic Origin, and Sex: United States, 1980," *Mental Health United States*, 1987, p. 77. Primary source: 1980 Patient Sample Surveys, Division of Biometry and Applied Sciences, National Institute of Mental Health. *Notes:* 1. Civilian population estimates used as denominators for rate computations for total all races, whites, and blacks are from the U.S. Bureau of the Census, *Current Population Reports*, Series P-25, No. 929, table 3, p. 19. Population estimates used as denominators for rate computations for American Indians or Alaskan Natives, Asian or Pacific Islanders, and Hispanics are derived from the *1980 Census of Population, General Population Characteristics*, PC80-1- B1, table 43, pp. 32-36, and adjusted to the civilian population estimates. 2. Persons of Hispanics origin may be from any racial group. 3. Based on five or fewer sample cases; rate not shown because it does not meet standards of reliability.

★ 524 ★
Rate of Physician Contacts: Trends

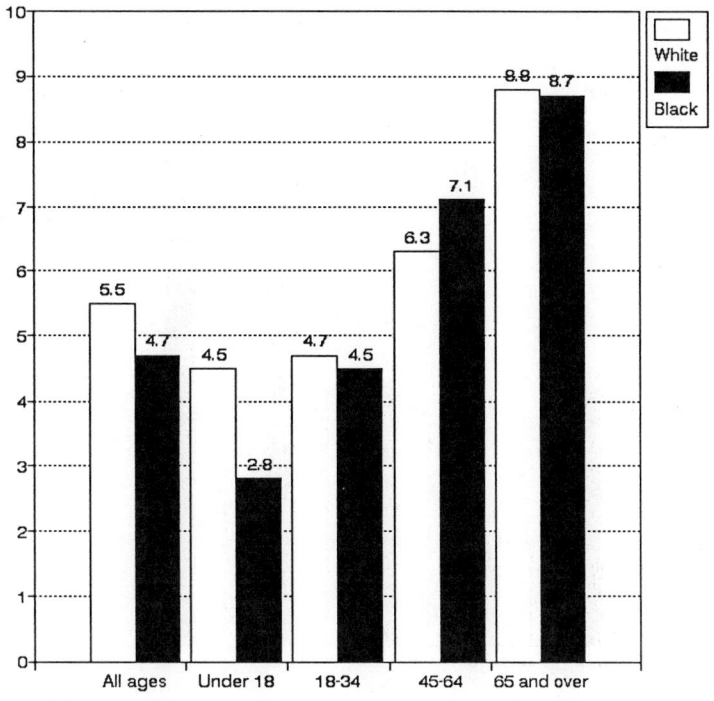

Contacts per person per year.

Characteristic	White	Black
All family incomes[1]		
All ages	5.5	4.7
Under 18 years	4.5	2.8
18-44 years	4.7	4.5
45-64 years	6.3	7.1
65 years and over	8.8	8.7
Less than $20,000		
All ages	6.3	5.1
Under 18 years	4.2	2.9
18-44 years	5.2	5.2
45-64 years	8.3	8.0
65 years and over	9.0	9.1
$20,000 or more		
All ages	5.2	4.4
Under 18 years	4.9	3.0
18-44 years	4.7	4.4
45-64 years	5.8	6.3
65 years and over	8.9	8.1

Source: "Average Annual Number of Physician Contacts per Person by Race, Age, and Family Income: United States, 1985-87," *Health of Black and White Americans, 1985-87*, 1990, p. 16. Primary source: National Health Interview Survey, U.S. Department of Health and Human Services, Public Health Service, Centers for Disease Control, Division of Health Statistics, Hyattsville, MD, January 1990. *Note:* 1. Includes unknown family income.

★ 525 ★
Rate of Short-Stay Hospital Discharges: Trends

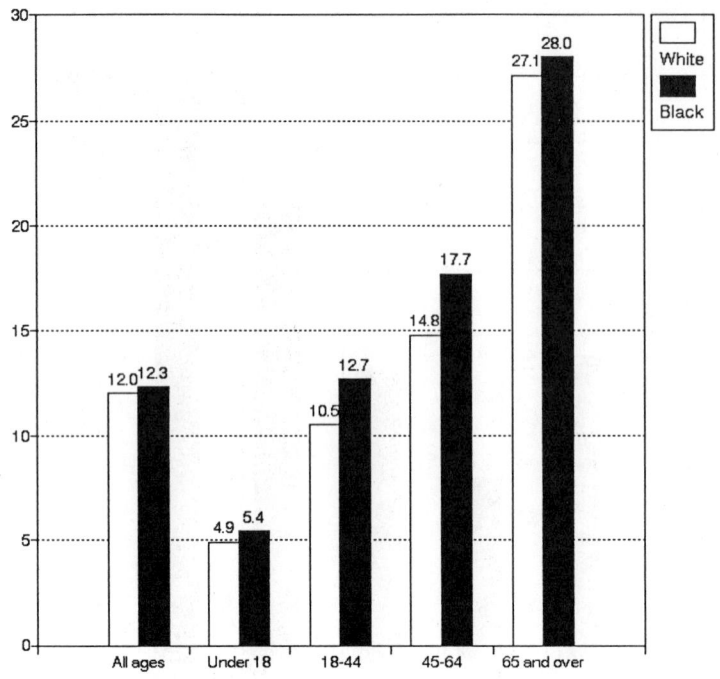

Number per 100 persons per year.

Characteristic	White	Black
All health statuses[1]		
All ages	12.0	12.3
Under 18 years	4.9	5.4
18-44 years	10.5	12.7
45-64 years	14.8	17.7
65 years and over	27.1	28.0
Fair or poor health[2]		
All ages	44.5	36.7
Under 18 years	29.9	28.1
18-44 years	37.9	32.9
45-64 years	44.0	37.4
65 years and over	51.0	44.5
Good to excellent health[2]		
All ages	8.6	7.8
Under 18 years	4.4	4.2
18-44 years	9.1	10.1
45-64 years	9.0	7.8
65 years and over	17.2	13.7

Source: "Average Annual Number of Short-Stay Hospital Discharges per 100 Persons by Race, Age, and Respondent-Assessed Health Status: United States, 1985- 87," *Health of Black and White Americans, 1985-87*, 1990, p. 19. Primary source: National Health Interview Survey, U.S. Department of Health and Human Services, Public Health Service, Centers for Disease Control, Division of Health Statistics, Hyattsville, MD, January 1990. *Notes:* 1. Includes unknown family income. 2. As assessed by self or responsible family member.

★ 526 ★
Recency of Physician Contacts: Trends

Data are based on household interviews of a sample of the civilian noninstitutionalized population.

Characteristic	Total	Less than 1 year			1 year--less than 2 years			2 years or more[1]		
		1964	1982	1987	1964	1982	1987	1964	1982	1987
Percent distribution										
Total[2,3]	100.0	66.9	75.8	76.6	14.0	11.0	10.6	19.1	13.2	12.8
Race[2]										
White	100.0	68.1	76.1	77.1	13.8	10.8	10.4	18.1	13.1	12.6
Black[4]	100.0	58.3	74.9	75.1	15.1	12.4	11.8	26.6	12.7	13.1

Source: "Interval since Last Physician Contact, according to Selected Patient Characteristics: United States, 1964, 1982, and 1987," *Health United States - 1988,* March 1989, p. 107. Primary source: Division of Health Statistics, National Health Interview Survey, National Center for Health Statistics: Data from the National Health Survey. *Notes:* In previous editions of *Health, United States,* physician contacts were labeled physician visits. 1. Includes persons who never visited a physician. 2. Age adjusted. 3. Includes all other races not shown separately. 4. 1964 data include all other races.

★ 527 ★
Restricted-Activity Days: Trends

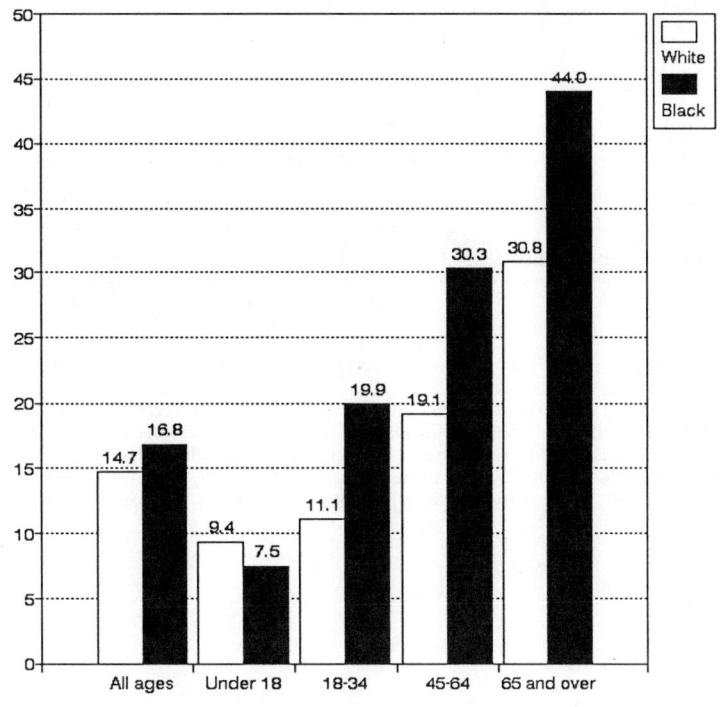

Days per person per year.

Characteristic	White	Black
All family incomes[1]		
All ages	14.7	16.8
Under 18 years	9.4	7.5
18-44 years	11.1	13.9
45-64 years	19.1	30.3

Continued.

Restricted-Activity Days: Trends
[Continued]

Characteristic	White	Black
65 years and over	30.8	44.0
Less than $20,000		
All ages	20.8	20.1
Under 18 years	10.2	8.2
18-44 years	14.8	16.9
45-64 years	32.9	40.7
65 years and over	34.8	47.3
$20,000 or more		
All ages	11.4	11.4
Under 18 years	9.4	6.5
18-44 years	9.7	11.5
45-64 years	13.9	18.6
65 years and over	24.6	21.8

Source: "Average Annual Number of Restricted-Activity Days per Person, by Race, Age, and Family Income: United States, 1985-87," *Health of Black and White Americans, 1985-87*, 1990, p. 12. Primary source: National Health Interview Survey, U.S. Department of Health and Human Services, Public Health Service, Centers for Disease Control, Division of Health Statistics, Hyattsville, MD, January 1990. *Note:* 1. Includes unknown family income.

★ 528 ★
Self-Assessment of Health

Respondent-assessed health status	Percent distribution		Number in thousands	
	White	Black	White	Black
All persons[1]	100.0	100.0	200,554	28,563
Fair or poor	9.4	15.3	18,823	4,358
Good to excellent	90.6	84.7	180,767	24,037

Source: "Average Annual Percent Distribution and Number of Black and White Persons by Age, Family Income, and Respondent-Assessed Health Status: United States, 1985-87," *Health of Black and White Americans, 1985-87*, 1990, p. 5. Primary source: National Health Interview Survey, U.S. Department of Health and Human Services, Public Health Service, Centers for Disease Control, Division of Health Statistics, Hyattsville, MD, January 1990. *Notes:* 1. Percent distribution for assessed health status excludes unknowns. Frequencies include the unknowns for these characteristics.

★ 529 ★
Short-Term Hospital Stay: Trends

Data based on household interviews of a sample of the civilian noninstitutionalized population.

| | Number per 1,000 population | | | | | | Number of days | | |
| | Discharges | | | Days of care | | | Average length of stay | | |
Characteristic	1964	1981	1987	1964	1981	1987	1964	1981	1987
Total[1,2]	109.1	121.7	96.5	970.9	952.1	649.7	8.9	7.8	6.7
Race[1]									
White	112.4	120.0	94.8	961.4	912.5	621.5	8.6	7.6	6.6
Black[3]	84.0	137.7	117.4	1,062.9	1,302.4	942.8	12.7	9.5	8.0

Source: "Discharges, Days of Care, and Average Length of Stay in Short-Stay Hospitals, According to Selected Characteristics: United States, 1964, 1981, and 1987," *Health United States - 1988*, March 1989, p. 111. Primary source: Data from the National Health Interview Survey: Division of Health Interview Statistics, National Center for Health Statistics. *Notes:* Excludes deliveries. 1. Age adjusted. 2. Includes all other races not shown separately. 3. 1964 data include all other races.

★ 530 ★
Signs of Morbidity Among the Elderly

| Selected Morbidity Indicator | White | | | | Black | | | |
| | All Ages | | 65 and Over | | All Ages | | 65 and Over | |
	Male	Female	Male	Female	Male	Female	Male	Female
Limitation in major activity due to chronic condition (%)	11.2	10.5	42.5	34.2	12.7	12.2	56.5	46.5
Restricted activity (days per year)	16.6	20.6	34.1	41.4	19.0	20.5	54.3	58.7
Bed disability (days per year)	5.5	7.6	11.4	13.9	8.0	10.7	24.8	21.5
Time (days) lost from work	4.6	5.1	3.5	4.9	7.1	8.3	3.5	6.5

Source: "Selected Morbidity Indicators for Elderly People, by Race, 1978-1980," *A Common Destiny: Blacks And American Society*, 1989, p. 429. Primary source: Data from National Center for Health Statistics (1984). Published by permission.

★ 531 ★
Smoking and Low Birth Weight

| Race or ethnic group | Total | | Smokers | | Nonsmokers | |
	n[1]	Percent low	n	Percent low	n	Percent low
Total	69,346	6.7	20,393	9.3	48,953	5.6
White	37,207	5.6	15,335	8.3	21,872	3.7
Black	24,290	9.0	4,328	13.8	19,962	8.0
Hispanic	7,024	4.5	645	5.6	6,379	4.4
Native American	267	7.1	57	7.0	210	7.1
Asian	558	5.4	28	0.0	530	5.7

Source: "Prevalence of Low Birth Weight (<2500 Grams), by Race or Ethnic Group and Smoking Status: CDC Pregnancy Nutrition Surveillance System, 1987," *Nutrition Monitoring in the United States*, September 1989, p. 84. Primary source: Centers for Disease Control. *Notes:* 1. n is the number of persons in the sample; for n<100, interpret data with caution.

★ 532 ★
Source of Hospital Payments

Covers non-Federal short stay hospitals. Discharges excludes newborn infants. Based on the National Hospital Discharge Survey.

| Characteristic | Total dis-charged (1,000) | Private insurance | Principal Source of Expected Payment-Percent Distribution | | | | | | | |
| | | | Government | | | | | Self-pay | No charge | Other[1] |
			Medicare	Medicaid	Worker Compensation	Other			
Race									
White	25,363	44.8	36.7	6.8	1.9	2.0	5.9	.5	1.5
Black	4,015	33.0	22.3	25.5	1.7	2.8	11.0	1.7	2.0
All other	4,877	45.7	26.5	11.2	1.9	3.2	7.7	1.0	2.7

Source: "Patients Discharged from Hospitals — Principal Source of Payment, by Selected Characteristic: 1986," *Statistical Abstract*, 1989, p. 106. U.S. National Center for Health Statistics, *Advance Data from Vital and Health Statistics*, No. 145, and unpublished data. *Notes:* Includes all other nonprofit sources of payment such as church, welfare, or United Way.

★ 533 ★
Teenage Alcohol Use

By demographic characteristics, United States, 1985 and 1987. Question: "Do you, yourself, drink alcoholic beverages, or not?" Numbers in percent.

| | 1985 | | 1987[1] | |
	Yes	No	Yes	No
National	39	61	22	78
Race				
White	43	57	24	76
Black	21	79	8	92

Source: "Reported Alcohol Use Among Teenagers," *Sourcebook of Criminal Justice Statistics - 1988*, 1989, p. 379. Primary source: Gallup Jr., George, *The Gallup Report*, Report No. 242, p. 50; Report No. 265, p. 41 (Princeton, NJ: The Gallup Poll). Table adapted by SOURCEBOOK staff. Reprinted by permission. *Note:* 1. Data for 1987 do not include 18 year olds. Published by permission.

★ 534 ★
Transmission of AIDS Cases: Trends

Data are based on reporting by State health departments.

| Race/ethnicity and transmission category | Number, by year of report | | | | | | | | Percent distribution | | | |
	All years[1,2]	1982	1983	1984	1985	1986	1987	1988[2]	All years[1,2]	1984	1986	1988[2]
Total[3]	76,662	651	2,039	4,399	8,104	12,988	20,804	27,485	100.0	100.0	100.0	100.0
Male homosexual/bisexual	48,198	394	1,267	2,869	5,443	8,541	13,501	16,033	62.9	65.2	65.8	58.3
Intravenous drug use	14,542	121	368	773	1,392	2,222	3,502	6,142	19.0	17.6	17.1	22.4
Male homosexual/bisexual and intravenous drug use	5,421	56	199	408	589	972	1,505	1,680	7.1	9.3	7.5	6.1
Hemophilia/coagulation disorder	744	7	12	35	74	125	218	273	1.0	0.8	1.0	1.0
Born in Caribbean/African countries	1,226	45	84	10	143	217	266	356	1.6	2.5	1.7	1.3
Heterosexual[4]	2,123	7	23	57	129	333	594	979	2.8	1.3	2.6	3.6
Sexual contact with intravenous drug user	1,505	6	15	43	97	224	398	721	2.0	1.0	1.7	2.6
Transfusion	1,937	6	26	53	165	300	621	766	2.5	1.2	2.3	2.8
Undetermined[5]	2,471	15	60	94	169	278	597	1,256	3.2	2.1	2.1	4.6
Race/ethnicity												
White, not Hispanic	45,552	354	1,175	2,689	4,987	7,848	12,922	15,456	100.0	100.0	100.0	100.0
Male homosexual/bisexual	35,451	279	929	2,162	4,083	6,253	10,033	11,603	77.8	80.4	79.7	75.1

Continued.

Transmission of AIDS Cases: Trends
[Continued]

Race/ethnicity and transmission category	Number, by year of report								Percent distribution			
	All years[1,2]	1982	1983	1984	1985	1986	1987	1988[2]	All years[1,2]	1984	1986	1988[2]
Intravenous drug use	3,041	31	71	145	251	406	816	1,317	6.7	5.4	5.2	8.5
Male homosexual/bisexual and												
intravenous drug use	3,388	25	124	265	376	646	971	974	7.4	9.9	8.2	6.3
Hemphilia/coagulation disorder	631	7	11	25	63	113	187	225	1.4	0.9	1.4	1.5
Born in Caribbean/African countries	5	-	-	1	1	1	1	1	0.0	0.0	0.0	0.0
Heterosexual[4]	647	1	2	16	31	93	196	308	1.4	0.6	1.2	2.0
Sexual contact with intravenous												
drug user	349	1	-	9	16	39	99	185	0.8	0.3	0.5	1.2
Transfusion	1,446	5	21	40	127	232	469	552	3.2	1.5	3.0	3.6
Undetermined[5]	943	6	17	35	55	104	249	476	2.1	1.3	1.3	3.1
Black, not Hispanic	20,417	205	541	1,086	2,005	3,277	5,199	8,061	100.0	100.0	100.0	100.0
Male homosexual/bisexual	7,616	77	192	399	794	1,321	2,083	2,727	37.3	36.7	40.3	33.8
Intravenous drug use	7,796	55	108	404	747	1,191	1,853	3,355	38.2	37.2	36.3	41.6
Male/homosexual/bisexual and												
intravenous drug use	1,416	17	44	94	142	228	380	507	6.9	8.7	7.0	6.3
Hemophilia/coagulation disorder	50	-	-	5	4	5	12	24	0.2	0.5	0.2	0.3
Born in Caribbean/African countries	1,210	44	83	109	142	214	262	351	5.9	100.0	6.5	4.4
Heterosexual[4]	1,038	4	11	23	73	160	293	474	5.1	2.1	4.9	5.9
Sexual contact with intravenous												
drug user	799	4	6	18	59	116	223	373	3.9	1.7	3.5	4.6
Transfusion	313	-	2	10	27	44	92	138	1.5	0.9	1.3	1.7
Undetermined	978	8	29	42	76	114	224	485	4.8	3.9	3.5	6.0
Hispanic	9,978	90	305	593	1,055	1,744	2,470	3,695	100.0	100.0	100.0	100.0
Male homosexual/bisexual	4,643	37	137	286	526	882	1,235	1,523	46.5	48.2	50.6	41.2
Intravenous drug use	3,639	34	113	222	386	613	822	1,443	36.5	37.4	35.2	39.1
Male homosexual/bisexual and												
intravenous drug use	589	14	29	47	69	95	140	194	5.9	7.9	5.5	5.3
Hemophilia/coagulation disorder	49	-	1	4	7	5	12	20	0.5	0.7	0.3	0.5
Born in Caribbean/African countries	8	1	1	-	-	1	3	2	0.1	-	0.1	0.1
Heterosexual[4]	419	2	10	18	25	77	102	184	4.2	3.0	4.4	5.0
Sexual contact with intravenous												
drug user	349	1	9	16	22	69	75	156	3.5	2.7	4.0	4.2
Transfusion	132	1	2	2	7	19	42	59	1.3	0.3	1.1	1.6
Undetermined[5]	499	1	12	14	35	52	114	270	5.0	2.4	3.0	7.3

Source: "Acquired Immunideficiency Syndrome (AIDS) Cases, according to Race/Ethnicity, Sex, and Transmission Category for Persons 13 Years of Age and Over: United States, 1982-88," *Health United States - 1988*, March 1989, pp.84-85. Primary source:Centers for Disease Control, Center for Infectious Diseases, AIDS Program. *Notes:* The AIDS case definition was changed in September 1987 to allow for the presumptive diagnosis of AIDS-associated diseases and conditions and to expand the spectrum of human immunodeficiency virus-associated diseases reportable as AIDS. Excludes residents of U.S. territories. 1. Includes cases prior to 1982. 2. Data are as of November 30, 1988 and reflect reporting delays. 3. Includes all other races not shown separately. 4. Includes persons who have had heterosexual contact with a person with human immunodeficiency virus (HIV) infection or at risk of HIV infection. 5. Includes persons for whom risk information is incomplete (because of death, refusal to be interviewed, or loss to followup), persons still under investigation, men reported only to have had heterosexual contact with prostitutes, and interviewed persons for whom no specific risk is identified.

★ 535 ★
Treatment of Hypertensive Adults: Trends

Hypertension Prevalence	All People[1]	White Men	White Women	Black Men	Black Women
In the population					
1960-1962	20.3	16.3	20.4	31.8	39.8
1974-1976	22.1	21.4	19.6	37.1	35.5
1976-1980	22.0	21.2	20.0	28.3	39.8
Hypertension never diagnosed[2]					
1960-1962	51.1	57.6	43.9	70.5	35.1
1974-1976	36.4	42.3	29.7	41.0	28.9
1976-1980	26.6	40.6	25.2	35.7	14.5
On medication					
1960-1962	31.3	22.4	38.2	18.5	48.1
1974-1976	34.2	25.9	48.5	24.0	36.4
1976-1980	56.2	38.3	58.6	40.9	60.6
On medication and controlled[3]					
1960-1962	16.0	11.8	21.9	5.0	20.2
1974-1976	19.6	15.1	28.1	12.7	22.3
1976-1980	36.1	20.9	40.3	16.1	30.9

Source: "Prevalence Rates of Hypertension for Persons Aged 25-74 (in percent) by Treatment History, Race, and Sex, 1960-1980," *A Common Destiny: Blacks And American Society,* 1989, p. 423. Primary source: Data from the U.S. Department of Health and Human Services. *Notes:* Hypertension is defined as elevated blood pressure, that is, a systolic measurement of at least 160 mm Hg or a diastolic measurement of at least 95 mm Hg, or as taking antihypertensive medication. Populations are age adjusted by the direct method to the population at the midpoint of the 1976-1980 National Health and Nutrition Examination Survey. 1. Includes all other races not shown separately. 2. Reported that was never told by physician that he or she had high blood pressure or hypertension. 3. Subset of "on medication" group; those taking antihypertensive medication whose blood pressure was not elevated at the time of the examination. Published by permission.

★ 536 ★
Vietnam Veterans and Inpatient Psychiatric Services

Race		Inpatient psychiatric services			
	Total	State and county mental hospitals	Private psychiatric hospitals	Non-Federal general hospitals	VA medical centers
		Number			
Total, Vietnam era veterans	118,705	18,459	5,675	27,979	66,592
Race:					
White	88,788	13,336	4,879	23,539	47,034
Black	28,229	4,824	782	3,881	18,742
Other	1,688	299	[2]	[2]	816
		Percent distribution			
Total, Vietnam era veterans	100.0	100.0	100.0	100.0	100.0
Race:					

Continued.

Vietnam Veterans and Inpatient Psychiatric Services
[Continued]

Race		Inpatient psychiatric services			
	Total	State and county mental hospitals	Private psychiatric hospitals	Non-Federal general hospitals	VA medical centers
White	74.8	72.2	86.0	84.1	70.6
Black	23.8	26.1	13.8	13.9	28.1
Other	1.4	1.6	[2]	[2]	1.2
Rate per 100,000 Vietnam era veterans in civilian population[1]					
Total, Vietnam era veterans	477.0	229.7	70.6	348.1	828.6
Race:					
White	1,271.5	191.0	69.9	337.1	673.5
Black	3,860.6	659.7	106.9	530.8	2,563.2
Other	591.2	104.7	[2]	[2]	285.8

Source: "Number, Percent Distribution, and Rate per 100,000 Vietnam Era Veterans in the Civilian Population for Vietnam Era Veterans Admitted to Selected Inpatient Psychiatric Services, by Age, Sex, and Race: United States, 1980," *Mental Health United States*, 1987, p. 90. Primary source: 1980 Patient Sample Surveys, Division of Biometry and Applied Sciences, National Institute of Mental Health. *Notes:* Percentages may not add to 100 percent because of rounding. 1. Population estimates used as denominators in rate computations for total age, and sex are from *Veterans in the United States, a Statistical Portrait from the 1980 Census*, Office of Information Management and Statistics, Veterans Administration, October, 1984. Population estimates used as denominators in rate computations for race are from the Office of Information Management and Statistics and have been inflated to sum to the total number of Vietnam era veterans in the U.S. civilian population, 1980. 2. Five or fewer sample cases; estimate not shown because it does not meet standards of reliability.

★ 537 ★
Visits to Physicians and Dentists: Trends

Based on National Health Interview Survey.

Type of Visit and Year	Total Visits Race		Visits Per Person Race	
	White	Black	White	Black
Physicians: 1970	832	87	4.8	3.9
1975	929	116	5.1	4.7
1980	903	115	4.8	4.5
1983	1,018	126	5.2	4.6
1985	1,074	132	5.4	4.7
1986	1,110	131	5.5	4.6
Dentists: 1970	283	17	1.6	.8
1975	313	23	1.7	1.0
1980	333	26	1.8	1.0
1983	382	31	1.9	1.1
1986	416	37	2.1	1.4

Source: "Physician and Dental Visits by Patient Characteristics: 1970 to 1986," *Statistical Abstract*, 1989, p. 99. Primary source: U.S. National Center for Health Statistics, *Vital and Health Statistics*, series 10, and unpublished data.

★ 538 ★
Who Does Not Have Health Insurance?

Characteristic	Population uninsured (mill.)	Proportion of group without insurance (percent)
Race and ethnicity		
White	10.5	11.1
African-American	2.6	21.7
Hispanic	3.5	28.8

Source: "Characteristics of Groups Without Health Insurance. 1987," *Setting National Priorities*, 1990, p. 257. Primary source: Moyer, M. Eugene, "A Revised Look at the Number of Uninsured Americans," *Health Affairs*, Summer 1989, pp. 102-10. Published by permission.

★ 539 ★
Who Goes to Physicians? - Trends

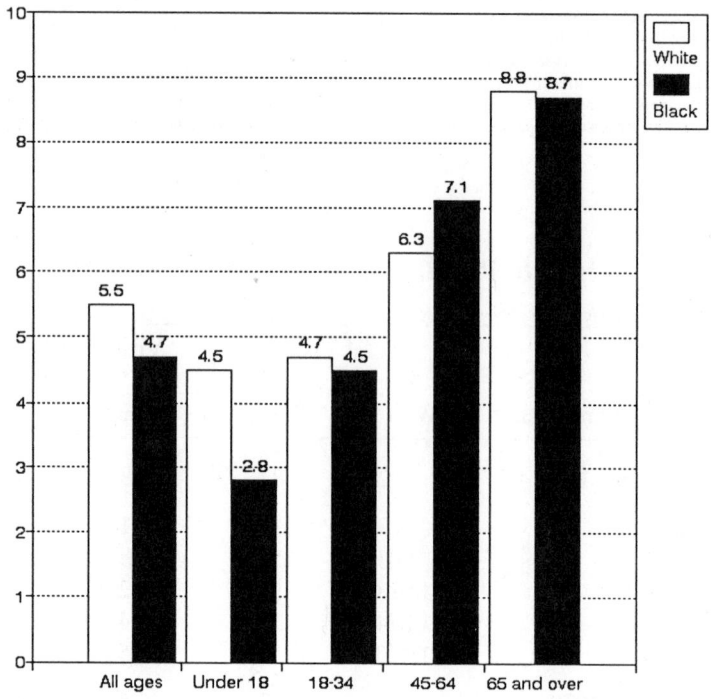

Contacts per person per year.

Characteristic	White	Black
All health statuses[1]		
All ages	5.5	4.7
Under 18 years	4.5	2.8
18-44 years	4.7	4.5
45-64 years	6.3	7.1
65 years and over	8.8	8.7
Fair or poor health[2]		
All ages	14.9	11.8
Under 18 years	15.5	6.5

Continued.

Who Goes to Physicians? - Trends
[Continued]

Characteristic	White	Black
18-44 years	15.6	11.2
45-64 years	15.1	13.0
65 years and over	14.4	13.0
Good to excellent health[2]		
All ages	4.5	3.4
Under 18 years	4.3	2.7
18-44 years	4.2	3.7
45-64 years	4.6	4.2
65 years and over	6.5	5.0

Source: "Average Annual Number of Physician Contacts per Person by Race, Age, and Respondent-Assessed Health Status: United States, 1985-87," *Health of Black and White Americans, 1985-87*, 1990, p. 17. Primary source: National Health Interview Survey, U.S. Department of Health and Human Services, Public Health Service, Centers for Disease Control, Division of Health Statistics, Hyattsville, MD, January 1990. *Notes:* 1. Includes unknown health status. 2. As assessed by self or responsible family member.

★ 540 ★
Who Uses Heroin?

By age group and other demographic characteristics, United States, 1985. Percent reporting ever used.

	Total all ages	Age Group			
		12 to 17 years	18 to 25 years	26 to 34 years	35 years and older
Total (N = 8,038)	1.0	[1]	1.2	2.6	0.5
Race/ethnicity					
White	1.0	[1]	1.1	2.8	[1]
Black	1.4	[1]	1.5	1.6	1.6
Hispanic	0.8	[1]	1.4	2.1	[1]

Source: "Estimated Prevalence of Heroin Use," *Sourcebook of Criminal Justice Statistics — 1988*, 1989, p. 371. Primary source: U.S. Department of Health and Human Services, National Institute on Drug Abuse, *National Household Survey on Drug Abuse: Main Findings 1985* (Washington, DC: USGPO, 1988), p. 63. Table adapted by SOURCEBOOK staff. *Note:* 1. Less than 0.5 percent.

★ 541 ★
Work-Days Lost and Income

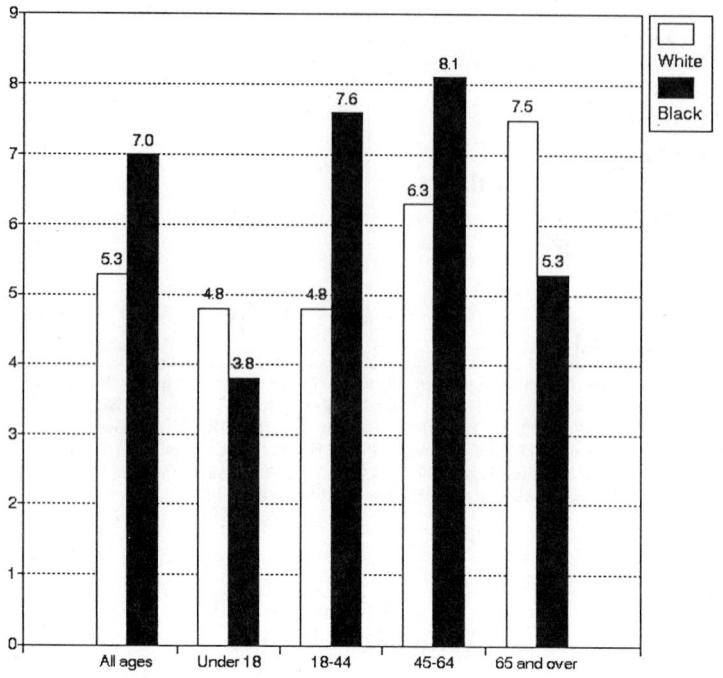

Days per person per year.

Characteristic	White	Black
All family incomes[1]		
All ages	5.3	7.0
Under 18 years	4.8	3.8
18-44 years	4.8	7.6
45-64 years	6.3	8.1
65 years and over	7.5	5.3
Less than $20,000		
All ages	6.4	7.7
Under 18 years	5.2	3.2
18-44 years	5.8	9.6
45-64 years	9.0	7.6
65 years and over	7.6	5.8
$20,000 or more		
All ages	4.9	7.3
Under 18 years	4.8	5.0
18-44 years	4.5	7.0
45-64 years	5.8	9.4
65 years and over	7.5	3.8

Source: "Average Annual Number of Work-Loss Days per Currently Employed Person by Race, Age, and Family Income: United States, 1985-87," *Health of Black and White Americans, 1985-87,* 1990, p. 14. Primary source: National Health Interview Survey, U.S. Department of Health and Human Services, Public Health Service, Centers for Disease Control, Division of Health Statistics, Hyattsville, MD, January 1990. *Note:* 1. Includes unknown family income.

HOUSING

★ 542 ★
Construction and Housing

Covers only units performing repairs, improvements, or alterations in the 2 years prior to the survey. Based on the American Housing Survey.

Characteristic	Number (1,000)			Percent of Total Owner Occupied Units		
	Total owner occupied units	Household characteristics		Total owner occupied units	Household characteristics	
		Black	Hispanic[1]		Black	Hispanic[1]
Total units	56,145	4,310	2,012	100.0	100.0	100.0
Roof replaced	9,161	800	418	16.3	18.6	20.8
Work mostly done by others	6,463	616	246	11.5	14.3	12.2
Costing more than $500	5,863	447	237	10.4	10.4	11.8
Additions built	3,502	233	141	6.2	5.4	7.0
Work mostly done by others	1,524	130	60	2.7	3.0	3.0
Costing more than $500	2,623	169	85	4.7	3.9	4.2
Kitchen remodeled or added	4,631	314	184	8.2	7.3	9.1
Work mostly done by others	2,114	199	76	3.8	4.6	3.8
Costing more than $500	2,959	179	96	5.3	4.2	4.8
Bathroom remodeled or added	5,534	369	239	9.9	8.6	11.9
Work mostly done by others	2,106	200	89	3.8	4.6	4.4
Costing more than $500	2,741	159	106	4.9	3.7	5.3
Siding replaced or added	3,293	238	109	5.9	5.5	5.4
Work mostly done by others	1,942	166	68	3.5	3.9	3.4
Costing more than $500	1,836	137	52	3.3	3.2	2.6
Storm doors/windows installed	8,820	696	187	15.7	16.1	9.3
Work mostly done by others	4,476	477	87	8.0	11.1	4.3
Costing more than $500	3,006	230	68	5.4	5.3	3.4
Major equipment replaced or added	5,063	292	140	9.0	6.8	7.0
Work mostly done by others	3,777	222	110	6.7	5.2	5.5
Costing more than $500	3,625	174	99	6.5	4.0	4.9
Insulation added	6,959	350	256	12.4	8.1	12.7
Work mostly done by others	2,965	201	157	5.3	4.7	7.8
Costing more than $500	1,696	69	65	3.0	1.6	3.2

Source: "Owner Occupied Housing Units — Home Improvements and Repairs, by Selected Characteristics of the Householder: 1985," *Statistical Abstract*, 1989, p. 710. Primary source: U.S. Bureau of the Census, *Current Housing Reports*, series H-150-85, American Housing Survey. *Note:* 1. Persons of Hispanic origin may be of any race.

369

★ 543 ★
Construction and Housing

In thousands of units. Based on the American Housing Survey.

Characteristic	Total occupied units	Black Owner	Black Renter	Hispanic Origin[1] Owner	Hispanic Origin[1] Renter
Total units	88,425	4,310	5,593	2,012	3,066
Amenities:					
Porch, deck, balcony or patio	64,120	3,202	2,968	1,503	1,339
Usable fireplace	25,353	894	342	568	201
Separate dining room	34,164	2,041	1,275	828	592
With 2 or more living rooms or recreation rooms	28,228	1,515	405	648	174
Garage or carport with home	48,727	2,128	814	1,375	843
Cars available:					
None	13,931	755	2,622	223	1,175
1 car	42,270	1,910	2,320	905	1,387
2 cars	24,978	1,226	594	680	419
3 or more cars	7,247	419	57	204	86
Trucks or vans available:					
None	62,831	3,357	5,243	1,195	2,648
1	21,804	876	334	707	395
2 or more	3,791	78	16	110	22
Internal deficiencies:					
Holes in floors	1,483	143	406	40	165
Open cracks or holes	5,572	422	1,114	120	165
Broken plaster or peeling paint (interior of unit)	4,992	311	907	103	442
No electrical wiring	17	[3]	7	[3]	[3]
Exposed wiring	2,009	128	325	51	13
Rooms without outlet	2,502	158	397	48	174
Water leakage[2]	29,110	1,718	2,454	551	1,072

Source: "Occupied Housing Units — Housing Indicators, by Selected Characteristics of the Householder: 1985," *Statistical Abstract*, 1989, p. 710. Primary source: U.S. Bureau of the Census, *Current Housing Reports*, series H-150-85, American Housing Survey. *Notes:* 1. Persons of Hispanic origin may be of any race. 2. During the 12 months prior to the survey. 3. Represents zero.

★ 544 ★
Construction and Housing

Based on the American Housing Survey.

Characteristic	Number (1,000) Total owner occupied units (1,000)	Number (1,000) Household characteristics Black	Number (1,000) Household characteristics Hispanic[1]	Percent of Total Owner Occupied Units Total owner occupied units (1,000)	Percent of Total Owner Occupied Units Household characteristics Black	Percent of Total Owner Occupied Units Household characteristics Hispanic[1]
Total units	56,145	4,310	2,012	100.0	100.0	100.0
Mortgages currently on property:						
None, owned free and clear	23,950	1,742	686	42.7	40.4	34.1
Mortgaged	32,195	2,568	1,326	57.3	59.6	65.9
Two mortgages or more	3,283	261	162	5.8	6.1	8.1
Units with mortgages	32,195	2,568	1,326	100.0	100.0	100.0
Type of primary mortgage:						
FHA	4,586	768	288	14.2	29.9	21.7
VA	3,187	357	129	9.9	13.9	9.7

Continued.

Construction and Housing
[Continued]

Characteristic	Number (1,000)			Percent of Total Owner Occupied Units		
	Total owner occupied units (1,000)	Household characteristics		Total owner occupied units (1,000)	Household characteristics	
		Black	Hispanic[1]		Black	Hispanic[1]
Farmers Home Administration	599	110	20	1.9	4.3	1.5
Other types	22,570	1,177	827	70.1	45.8	62.4
Not reported[2]	1,253	155	61	3.9	6.0	4.6
Payment plan of primary mortgage:						
Fixed payment, self amortizing	25,383	2,088	1,105	78.8	81.3	83.3
Adjustable rate mortgage	2,191	97	65	6.8	3.8	4.9
Graduated payment mortgage	585	27	27	1.8	1.1	2.0
Other[2]	4,036	357	131	12.5	13.9	9.9
Term of primary mortgage:						
Less than 18 years	4,913	283	204	15.3	11.0	15.4
18-22 years	3,978	294	141	12.4	11.4	10.6
23-27 years	4,103	183	123	12.7	7.1	9.3
28 years or more	14,403	1,393	689	44.7	54.2	52.0
Other (incl. variable)	4,798	416	169	14.9	16.2	12.7
Current interest rate:						
Less than 6 percent	1,880	99	57	5.8	3.9	4.3
6.0-7.9 percent	3,377	229	113	10.5	8.9	8.5
8.0-9.9 percent	5,697	332	216	17.7	12.9	16.3
10.0-11.9 percent	4,547	296	155	14.1	11.5	11.7
12.0-13.9 percent	4,327	234	208	13.4	9.1	15.7
14.0 percent or more	1,155	111	69	3.6	4.3	5.2
Other[2]	11,212	1,264	508	34.8	49.2	38.3
Median rate (percent)	9.3	9.4	9.8	[3]	[3]	[3]

Source: "Owner Occupied Housing Units - Mortgage Characteristics, by Selected Characteristics of the Householder: 1985," *Statistical Abstract*, 1989, p. 708. Primary source: U.S. Bureau of the Census, *Current Housing Reports*, Series H-150-85, American Housing Survey. *Notes:* 1. Hispanic persons may be of any race. 2. Includes units that did not know or did not report. 3. Not applicable.

★ 545 ★
Construction and Housing

In thousands of units. Housing costs include real estate taxes, property insurance, utilities, fuel, water, garbage collection, and mortgage.

	Total occupied units	Black		Hispanic Origin[1]	
		Owner	Renter	Owner	Renter
Total units[2]	88,425	4,310	5,593	2,012	3,066
Monthly housing costs:					
Less than $300	32,838	1,938	2,465	726	1,020
$300-$399	13,905	502	1,319	225	807
$400-$499	10,969	397	840	200	523
$500-$599	7,411	347	386	138	305
$600-$699	4,874	211	165	128	133
$700-$799	3,381	152	79	93	60
$800-$999	3,804	195	45	160	28
$1,000 or more	4,709	158	38	165	54

Continued.

Construction and Housing
[Continued]

	Total occupied units	Black		Hispanic Origin[1]	
		Owner	Renter	Owner	Renter
Median amount (dol.)	357	302	314	385	349
Monthly housing costs as percent of income:					
Less than 5 percent	2,105	91	20	64	17
5-9 percent	9,978	557	93	285	77
10-14 percent	12,741	629	469	306	202
15-19 percent	12,741	584	615	220	396
20-24 percent	10,890	476	653	240	369
25-29 percent	8,458	342	667	191	340
30-34 percent	5,733	301	438	126	238
35-39 percent	3,773	172	310	97	211
40 percent or more	14,362	701	1,885	294	991
Median amount (percent)	21	21	31	21	30
Median monthly costs (dol.)					
Electricity	57	63	44	61	40
Piped gas	49	66	40	39	25[3]
Fuel oil	64	64	64	74	62

Source: "American Housing Survey," *Statistical Abstract*, 1989, p. 708. Primary source: *Current Housing Reports*, Series H-150-85. U.S. Bureau of the Census. *Notes:* 1. Persons of Hispanic origin may be of any race. 2. Includes units with mortgage payments not reported and no cash rent not shown separately. 3. Less than $25.

★ 546 ★
Housing and Black Householders

Numbers in percent.

Characteristic	Black House- holds	All House- holds
Ownership rate	44	64
Buildings w/5 or more units	25	16
Married couples	36	57
Female householders (2+ persons)	31	13
Housing costs as percent of income	27	21
Public or subsidized housing	16	5
No savings or invest- ments	52	24
Income below poverty level	34	12
No cars, trucks, or vans	32	12

Source: "Selected Characteristics of Black Households," *Housing in America 1985/86*, p. 60. Primary source: U.S. Bureau of the Census, Current Housing Report, Series H-121, No. 19. *Housing in America 1985/86.* U.S. Government Printing Office, Washington, DC, 1989.

★ 547 ★
Living Arrangements of Children

Numbers in thousands.

| Marital status | 1988 | 1980 | 1970 | 1960 | Percent distribution | | | |
					1988	1980	1970	1960
Total children	15,329	12,466	8,199	5,829	100.0	100.0	100.0	100.0
White children	9,624	7,901	5,110	3,932	100.0	100.0	100.0	100.0
Marital status of parent:								
Divorced	4,829	4,106	1,997	1,118	50.2	52.0	39.1	28.4
Married, spouse absent	2,401	2,243	1,822	1,615	24.9	28.4	35.7	41.1
Separated	2,047	1,817	1,111	779	21.3	23.0	21.7	19.8
Other	287	426	711	836	3.0	5.4	13.9	21.3
Widowed	659	1,000	1,160	1,139	6.8	12.7	22.7	29.0
Never married	1,734	552	131	61	18.0	7.0	2.6	1.6
Black children[1]	5,247	4,297	2,995	1,897	100.0	100.0	100.0	100.0
Marital status of parent:								
Divorced	897	1,078	438	225	17.1	25.1	14.6	11.9
Married, spouse absent	1,253	1,573	1,651	1,085	23.9	36.6	55.1	57.2
Separated	1,100	1,463	1,343	829	21.0	34.0	44.8	43.7
Other	132	110	308	256	2.5	2.6	10.3	13.5
Widowed	254	411	482	405	4.8	9.6	16.1	21.3
Never married	2,843	1,235	423	182	54.2	28.7	14.1	9.6
Hispanic children[2]	2,048	1,152	[3]	[3]	100.0	100.0	[3]	[3]
Marital status of parent:								
Divorced	615	353	[3]	[3]	30.0	30.6	[3]	[3]
Married, spouse absent	643	468	[3]	[3]	31.3	40.6	[3]	[3]
Separated	531	400	[3]	[3]	25.9	34.7	[3]	[3]
Other	105	68	[3]	[3]	5.1	5.9	[3]	[3]
Widowed	118	103	[3]	[3]	5.8	8.9	[3]	[3]
Never married	672	228	[3]	[3]	32.8	19.8	[3]	[3]

Source: "Children Under 18 Years Living With One Parent, by Marital Status of Parent and Race of Child: 1988, 1980, 1970, and 1960," *Marital Status and Living Arrangements: March 1988*, p. 62. Primary source: U.S. Bureau of the Census, Current Population Reports, Series P-20, No. 44. *Marital Status and Living Arrangements: March 1988. Notes:* 1. Non-White in 1960. 2. Persons of Hispanic origin may be of any race. 3. Not available.

★ 548 ★
Living Arrangements of Children

Excludes persons under 18 years old who were maintaining households or family groups. Numbers in thousands.

| Living arrangement | 1988 | 1980 | 1970 | 1960 | Percent distribution | | | |
					1988	1980	1970	1960
White								
Children under 18 years	51,030	52,242	58,790	55,077	100.0	100.0	100.0	100.0
Living with-								
Two parents	40,287	43,200	52,624	50,082	78.9	82.7	89.5	90.9
One parent	9,624	7,901	5,109	3,932	18.9	15.1	8.7	7.1
Mother only	8,160	7,059	4,581	3,381	16.0	13.5	7.8	6.1
Father only	1,464	842	528	551	2.9	1.6	0.9	1.0
Other relatives	818	887	696	774	1.6	1.7	1.2	1.4
Nonrelatives only	301	254	362	288	0.6	0.5	0.6	0.5
Black[1]								
Children under 18 years	9,699	9,375	9,422	8,650	100.0	100.0	100.0	100.0

Continued.

Living Arrangements of Children
[Continued]

Living arrangement	1988	1980	1970	1960	Percent distribution			
					1988	1980	1970	1960
Living with-								
Two parents	3,739	3,956	5,508	5,795	38.6	42.2	58.5	67.0
One parent	5,247	4,297	2,996	1,897	54.1	45.8	31.8	21.9
Mother only	4,959	4,117	2,783	1,723	51.1	43.9	29.5	19.9
Father only	288	180	213	173	3.0	1.9	2.3	2.0
Other relatives	620	999	820	827	6.4	7.7	8.7	9.6
Nonrelatives only	94	123	97	132	1.0	1.3	1.0	1.5
Hispanic[2]								
Children under 18 years	6,786	5,459	4,006[3]	[4]	100.0	100.0	100.0	[4]
Living with-								
Two parents	4,497	4,116	3,111	[4]	66.3	75.4	77.7	[4]
One parent	2,047	1,152	[4]	[4]	30.2	21.1	[4]	[4]
Mother only	1,845	1,069	[4]	[4]	27.2	19.6	[4]	[4]
Father only	202	83	[4]	[4]	3.0	1.5	[4]	[4]
Other relatives	180	183	[4]	[4]	2.7	3.4	[4]	[4]
Nonrelatives only	62	8	[4]	[4]	0.9	0.1	[4]	[4]

Source: "Living Arrangements of Children Under 18 Years Living, by Race and Hispanic Origin: 1988, 1980, 1970, and 1960," *Marital Status and Living Arrangements: March 1988*, p. 61. Primary source: U.S. Bureau of the Census, Current Population Reports, Series P-20, No. 44. *Marital Status and Living Arrangements: March 1988. Notes:* 1. Non-White in 1960. 2. Persons of Hispanic origin may be of any race. 3. Persons under 18 years. 4. Not applicable.

★ 549 ★
Occupied Housing Units: Trends

In thousands, except as indicated. As of April 1, except 1985, as of fall. Prior to 1960, excludes Alaska and Hawaii. Statistics on the number of occupied units are essentially comparable although identified by various terms — the term "family" applies to figures for 1920 and 1930; "occupied dwelling unit," 1940 and 1950; and "occupied housing unit," 1960 to 1985. For 1920, includes the small numbers of quasifamilies; for 1930, represents private families only. See also *Historical Statistics, Colonial Times to 1970*, series N 238-245.

Race of householder and tenure	1920	1930	1940	1950	1960	1970	1980	1985
All Races								
Occupied units, total	24,352	29,905	34,855	42,826	53,024	63,445	80,390	88,425
Owner occupied	11,114	14,280	15,196	23,560	32,797	39,886	51,795	56,145
Percent of occupied	45.6	47.8	43.6	55.0	61.9	62.9	64.4	63.5
Renter occupied	13,238	15,624	19,659	19,266	20,227	23,560	28,595	32,280
White								
Occupied units, total	21,826	26,983	31,561	39,044	47,880	56,606	68,810	76,266
Owner occupied	10,511	13,544	14,418	22,241	30,823	37,005	46,671	50,938
Percent of occupied	48.2	50.2	45.7	57.0	64.4	65.4	67.8	66.8
Renter occupied	11,315	13,439	17,143	16,508	17,057	19,601	22,139	25,328
Black and Other								
Occupied units, total	2,526	2,922	3,293	3,783	5,144	6,839	11,580	12,160
Owner occupied	603	737	778	1,319	1,974	2,881	5,124	5,208

Continued.

Occupied Housing Units: Trends
[Continued]

Race of householder and tenure	1920	1930	1940	1950	1960	1970	1980	1985
Percent of occupied	23.9	25.2	23.6	34.9	38.4	42.1	44.2	42.8
Renter occupied	1,923	2,185	2,516	2,464	3,170	3,959	6,456	6,952

Source: Occupied Housing Units - Tenure, by Race of Householder: 1920 to 1985," *Statistical Abstract*, 1989, p. 706. Primary source: U.S. Bureau of the Census, *Census of Housing: 1960*, vol. 1; *1970*, vol. 1; *1980 Census of Housing*, vol. 1, chapter A (HC80-1- A); and *Current Housing Reports*, series h-150-85, American Housing Survey: 1985.

★ 550 ★
Occupied Housing, Characteristics of

In thousands of units, except as indicated. Based on the American Housing Survey; see Appendix III.

Characteristic	Tenure		Black		Hispanic Origin[1]	
	Owner	Renter	Owner	Renter	Owner	Renter
Total units	56,145	32,280	4,310	5,593	2,012	3,066
Units in structure:						
Single family detached	46,703	8,373	3,427	1,249	1,660	729
Single family attached	2,211	1,890	359	400	70	160
2-4 units	1,996	8,221	171	1,554	110	763
5-9 units	344	4,029	8	780	14	392
10-19 units	261	3,500	31	597	9	325
20-49 units	287	2,627	16	390	14	397
50 or more units	438	2,792	57	577	17	256
Mobile home or trailer	3,906	848	240	45	117	44
Stories in structure:						
One story	26,188	9,255	2,439	1,557	1,491	1,093
2 stories	16,561	10,112	796	1,725	302	860
3 stories	11,741	7,466	865	1,167	170	388
4-6 stories	1,295	3,530	156	677	34	503
7 or more stories	360	1,917	54	467	15	223
Year structure built:						
1939 or earlier	12,029	9,022	1,139	1,733	295	969
1940 to 1949	5,001	2,919	586	656	238	413
1950 to 1959	9,419	3,376	648	621	391	395
1960 to 1969	10,035	4,915	734	813	327	375
1970 to 1979	14,128	9,254	915	1,471	559	706
1980 or later	5,534	2,796	287	297	200	208
Median year	1962	1962	1957	1957	1962	1954
Percent of total occupied units--						
Lacking some or all plumbing facilities	.4	1.3	1.2	3.0	.4	1.0
With public water system or private company	81.1	93.0	88.2	96.3	94.6	97.2
With public sewer	68.7	88.7	78.7	96.3	94.6	97.2
With air conditioning	37.0	26.9	25.7	20.2	32.7	17.9

Source: "Occupied Housing Units — Tenure, by Selected Characteristics of the Unit Householder: 1985," *Statistical Abstract*, 1989, p. 707. Primary source: U.S. Bureau of the Census, *Current Housing Reports*, series H-150-85, American Housing Survey. *Note:* 1. Persons of Hispanic origin may be of any race.

★ 551 ★
Residential Segregation

	Black-White Segregation in 16 Areas[1]	Segregation in Three Metropolitan Areas[2]	
		Black-White	Asian-White
Family income in 1979			
Under $5,000	76	77	66
$5,000-$7,499	76	77	71
$7,500-$9,999	76	78	69
$10,000-$14,999	75	76	59
$15,000-$19,999	75	78	58
$20,000-$24,999	76	77	57
$25,000-$34,999	76	78	53
$35,000-$49,999	76	78	53
$50,000 or more	79	79	56
Educational attainment of persons aged 25 and over			
Less than 9 years	76	77	57
High school, 1-3 years	77	79	56
High school, 4 years	76	44	50
College, 1-3 years	74	74	48
College, 4 years or more	71	69	47

Source: "Indices of Segregation by Income and Educational Level, 1980, " A Common Destiny: Blacks and American Society, 1989, p. 145. Primary source: 1980 decennial census. *Notes:* 1. These residential segregation scores are average values for 16 metropolitan areas (Atlanta, Baltimore, Chicago, Cleveland, Dallas, Detroit, Houston, Los Angeles, Miami, New Orleans, New York, Newark, Philadelphia, St. Louis, San Francisco, and Washington, D.C.) computed from census tract data. The index shown for an income of $20,000-$24,999, 76, compared the residential distribution of black families in this income category to that of white families in the identical category. 2. These segregation scores are average values for those three metropolitan areas that contained at least one-quarter million blacks and one-quarter million Asians: Los Angeles, New York, and San Francisco-Oakland.

★ 552 ★
Residential Segregation

Metropolitan Area	Population in 1980 (in thousands)		Indices of Black-White Residential Segregation[1]			Interracial Contact Measures[2]			
	Total	Black	1980	1970	1960	% Black for Whites	% White for Blacks	% White for Whites	% Black for Blacks
New York	9,120	1,941	78	74	74	9	28	84	64
Chicago	7,140	1,428	88	91	91	4	15	90	84
Los Angeles	7,748	944	79	89	89	6	30	79	61
Detroit	4,353	890	88	89	87	5	20	93	80
Philadelphia	4,717	884	78	78	77	7	28	92	70
Washington, D.C.	3,061	853	71	81	78	12	30	84	69
Baltimore	2,174	557	75	81	87	9	26	89	73
Houston	2,905	529	74	78	81	8	31	85	66
Atlanta	2,030	499	78	82	77	9	26	90	73
Dallas	2,975	419	78	87	81	5	30	90	67
Newark	1,966	418	80	79	73	8	27	89	70
St. Louis	2,356	408	83	87	86	5	24	94	75

Continued.

Residential Segregation
[Continued]

Metropolitan Area	Population in 1980 (in thousands)		Indices of Black-White Residential Segregation[1]			Interracial Contact Measures[2]			
	Total	Black	1980	1970	1960	% Black for Whites	% White for Blacks	% White for Whites	% Black for Blacks
San Francisco	3,251	391	71	77	79	7	42	81	51
New Orleans	1,187	387	73	74	65	14	27	85	72
Memphis	913	364	71	79	73	16	24	83	76
Cleveland	1,899	346	88	90	90	4	18	94	81
Miami	1,626	280	79	86	90	7	30	89	68
Birmingham	847	240	75	68	64	10	26	89	74
Norfolk	807	224	63	77	77	14	36	83	63
Pittsburgh	2,264	176	73	75	74	4	44	96	55
Richmond	632	221	66	77	75	13	34	86	66
Cincinnati	1,401	174	79	82	83	5	36	94	59
Kansas City	1,327	173	79	87	83	5	30	96	69
Nassau-Suffolk	2,606	162	77	---	---	3	49	95	49
Greensboro	827	160	69	75	67	9	37	90	63
Boston	2,763	160	77	79	81	3	40	95	55
Jacksonville	737	158	68	82	78	10	35	89	65
Indianapolis	1,167	152	80	84	79	5	33	94	67
Milwaukee	1,397	151	84	90	90	4	29	95	70
Average	2,617	472	77	81	80	8	31	89	68

Source: "Measures of Residential Segregation for Metropolitan Areas with the Largest Black Population in 1980," *A Common Destiny: Blacks in American Society*, 1989, pp. 78-79. Primary source: 1960, 1970, and 1980 Decennial Censuses. Published by permission. *Notes:* 1. These are indices of dissimilarity comparing the distributions of the white and black populations across census tracts. If individuals were randomly distributed, the index would approach its minimum value of zero. In a situation of total separation, the index would equal 100. The 1970 and 1980 indices compare blacks and whites; the 1960 indices compare whites and nonwhites. 2. These measures of potential interracial contact for 1980 show the percentage of blacks in the census tract of the typical white, the percentage of whites for blacks, the percentage of whites for whites, and the percentage of blacks for blacks. These measures are calculated from data for census tracts. No adjustments have been made for changes over time in the boundaries of metropolitan areas.

★ 553 ★
Value and Rent

In thousands of units, except as indicated.

	Total units	Black	Hispanic[1]
	Owner Occupied Units		
Specified owner occupied	44,875	3,668	1,695
Less than $20,000	2,506	622	136
$20,000-$29,999	2,492	432	89
$30,000-$39,999	4,282	602	146
$40,000-$49,999	5,279	511	198
$50,000-$59,999	4,686	338	156
$60,000-$69,999	5,048	318	177
$70,000-$79,999	4,014	227	150
$80,000-$89,999	5,977	309	264
$100,000-$119,999	3,046	115	140
$120,000-$149,999	2,881	103	130
$150,000-$199,999	2,319	58	57
$200,000-$299,999	1,621	24	34
$300,000 and over	723	8	18
Median value (dol.)	66,300	43,500	66,900

Continued.

Value and Rent
[Continued]

	Total units	Black	Hispanic[1]
	Renter Occupied Units		
Specified renter occupied	31,806	5,549	3,050
Less than $200	4,369	1,360	422
$200-$249	2,634	499	247
$250-$299	3,233	594	348
$300-$349	3,717	724	457
$350-$399	3,658	595	347
$400-$449	3,246	528	322
$450-$499	2,382	312	201
$500-$599	3,133	383	305
$600-$699	1,694	165	133
$700-$799	832	79	60
$800-$999	673	45	28
$1,000 and over	482	38	54
No cash rent	1,753	226	123
Median amount(dol.)	365	314	339

Source: "American Housing Survey," *Statistical Abstract*, 1989, p. 707. Primary source: *Current Housing Reports*, Series H-150-85. U.S. Bureau of the Census. *Note:* 1. Persons of Hispanic origin may be of any race.

INCOME, SPENDING, AND WEALTH

★ 554 ★
1987 & 1988 Income Summary Measures

Households, families, and persons as of March 1989.

Characteristic	1988		1987 median income (in 1988 dols.)	Percent change in real income
	Number (000)	Median income		
Families				
All families	65,837	32,191	32,251	-0.2
Race and Hispanic Origin of Householder				
White	56,492	33,915	33,725	0.6
Black	7,409	19,329	19,168	0.8
Hispanic[1]	4,823	21,769	21,140	3.0
Type of Family				
All races:				
Married-couple families	52,100	36,389	36,322	0.2
Female householder, no husband present	10,890	15,346	15,290	0.4
White:				
Married-couple families	46,877	36,840	36,900	-0.2
Female householder, no husband present	7,342	17,672	17,717	-0.3
Black:				
Married-couple families	3,722	30,385	28,441	6.8[2]
Female householder, no husband present	3,223	10,657	10,251	4.0
Hispanic origin[1]				
Married-couple families	3,398	25,667	25,394	1.1
Female householder, no husband present	1,112	10,687	10,101	5.8
Per Capita Income				
All races	...	13,123	12,904	1.7[2]
White	...	13,896	13,687	1.5[2]
Black	...	8,271	7,961	3.9[2]
Hispanic origin[1]	...	7,956	7,970	-0.2

Source: "Comparison of Income Summary Measures Between 1988 and 1987, by Selected Characteristics," *Money Income and Poverty Status in the United States: 1988*, 1989, p. 3. Primary source: U.S. Bureau of the Census, Current Population Reports, Series P-60, No. 166. *Notes:* 1. Persons of Hispanic origin may be of any race 2. Represents statistically significant percent change.

★ 555 ★
Age of Workers and Poverty Status

In thousands.

Age and sex	Total	White	Black	Hispanic origin	Below poverty level				At or above the poverty level			
					Total	White	Black	Hispanic origin	Total	White	Black	Hispanic origin
Total 16 years and over	113,489	98,296	11,836	8,053	6,400	4,647	1,567	986	107,089	93,649	10,269	7,068
16 to 19 years	4,769	4,229	426	349	494	375	108	65	4,275	3,854	317	284
20 to 24 years	13,013	11,210	1,480	1,337	1,175	893	261	169	11,837	10,317	1,219	1,169
25 to 34 years	34,021	29,075	3,934	2,786	2,069	1,449	561	343	31,952	27,626	3,373	2,442
35 to 44 years	28,131	24,327	2,874	1,890	1,397	1,025	327	229	26,734	23,301	2,548	1,661
45 to 54 years	18,501	16,006	1,850	1,013	697	490	181	114	17,804	15,516	1,669	899
55 to 64 years	11,800	10,554	989	594	459	345	92	64	11,341	10,209	896	529
65 years and over	3,254	2,896	283	84	109	71	37	2	3,146	2,825	246	82
Men, 16 years and over	63,368	55,561	5,917	4,963	3,346	2,608	622	656	60,022	52,953	5,295	4,306
16 to 19 years	2,383	2,148	176	207	224	169	46	37	2,159	1,979	130	170
20 to 24 years	6,898	5,952	780	822	626	477	142	105	6,272	5,475	639	718
25 to 34 years	19,226	16,636	2,005	1,777	1,119	875	203	252	18,107	15,761	1,802	1,525
35 to 44 years	15,643	13,742	1,387	1,134	706	570	107	141	14,936	13,172	1,279	993
45 to 54 years	10,391	9,121	911	614	362	275	72	80	10,029	8,847	839	534
55 to 64 years	6,917	6,262	493	352	254	203	38	40	6,663	6,059	454	312
65 years and over	1,910	1,700	165	56	53	39	14	1	1,856	1,660	152	55
Women, 16 years and over	50,121	42,734	5,918	3,091	3,054	2,039	945	329	47,067	40,696	4,973	2,761
16 to 19 years	2,386	2,081	249	142	270	205	62	28	2,115	1,875	187	114
20 to 24 years	6,114	5,258	700	515	549	416	119	64	5,565	4,842	581	451
25 to 34 years	14,795	12,439	1,929	1,009	950	574	358	91	13,845	11,865	1,571	918
35 to 44 years	12,489	10,585	1,488	756	691	455	219	88	11,798	10,129	1,268	668
45 to 54 years	8,111	6,885	939	399	335	215	109	34	7,776	6,669	830	365
55 to 64 years	4,883	4,292	496	241	204	142	54	24	4,678	4,150	442	217
65 years and over	1,345	1,196	118	28	55	31	23	1	1,289	1,165	94	27

Source: "Poverty Status of Persons in the Labor Force 27 Weeks or More by Age, Sex, Race, and Hispanic Origin: 1987," *A Profile of the Working Poor*, December 1989, p. 19 Primary source: U.S. Department of Labor, Bureau of Labor Statistics. *Notes:* Detail for race and Hispanic-origin groups will not sum to total because data for the "other races" group are not presented and Hispanics are included in both the white and black population groups.

★ 556 ★
Differences in Aggregate Income Share - Part I

Households, families, and unrelated individuals as of March 1989.

Race and Hispanic origin of householder	Number	Income at selected positions (dollars)				
		Upper limit of each fifth				Top 5 percent
		Lowest	Second	Third	Fourth	
Households						
All races	92,830	11,382	21,500	33,506	50,593	85,640
White	79,734	12,559	23,017	35,022	52,071	87,700
Black	10,561	5,941	12,000	21,196	36,069	61,650
Hispanic origin[1]	5,910	8,216	15,800	25,020	38,856	66,150
Families						
All races	65,837	15,102	26,182	38,500	55,906	92,001
White	56,492	16,814	28,000	40,000	57,350	93,900
Black	7,409	7,148	14,400	24,425	40,300	65,927
Hispanic origin[1]	4,823	9,798	17,000	26,848	40,720	66,900
Unrelated individuals						
All races	34,340	5,840	10,450	17,148	27,208	47,163
White	29,315	6,252	11,100	18,000	28,228	48,800
Black	4,095	4,248	6,480	12,000	20,150	35,000

Continued.

Differences in Aggregate Income Share - Part I
[Continued]

Race and Hispanic origin of householder	Number	Income at selected positions (dollars)				
		Upper limit of each fifth				Top 5 percent
		Lowest	Second	Third	Fourth	
Hispanic origin[1]	1,864	4,200	7,768	12,100	20,006	36,600

Source: "Share of Aggregate Income in 1988 of Households, Families, and Unrelated Individuals, by Race and Hispanic Origin of Householder," *Money Income and Poverty Status in the United States: 1988*, 1989, p. 31. Primary source: U.S. Bureau of the Census, Current Population Reports, Series P-60, No. 166. *Note:* 1. Persons of Hispanic origin may be of any race.

★ 557 ★
Differences in Aggregate Income Share - Part II

Households, families, and unrelated individuals as of March 1989.

Race and Hispanic origin of householder	Percent distribution of aggregate income						Mean income (dol.)	Gini ratio
	Lowest fifth	Second fifth	Third fifth	Fourth fifth	Highest fifth	Top 5 percent		
Households								
All races	3.8	9.6	16.0	24.2	46.3	18.3	34,017	.426
White	4.1	10.0	16.2	24.1	45.6	18.0	35,468	.416
Black	3.3	7.7	14.6	24.7	49.7	18.7	22,477	.468
Hispanic origin[1]	3.7	9.3	15.6	24.2	47.2	19.0	25,993	.437
Families								
All races	4.6	10.7	16.7	24.0	44.0	17.2	38,608	.395
White	5.1	11.1	16.8	23.7	43.3	17.0	40,312	.382
Black	3.3	8.5	15.2	25.1	47.9	17.7	25,316	.450
Hispanic origin[1]	3.9	9.8	15.9	24.2	46.1	18.4	27,326	.424
Unrelated individuals								
All races	3.7	8.7	15.0	23.8	48.8	20.3	18,242	.454
White	3.9	9.0	15.1	23.7	48.3	20.0	19,003	.446
Black	3.2	8.2	13.7	25.1	49.8	19.0	12,611	.470
Hispanic origin[1]	2.5	8.7	14.8	24.2	49.8	20.0	13,145	.472

Source: "Share of Aggregate Income in 1988 of Households, Families, and Unrelated Individuals, by Race and Hispanic Origin of Householder," *Money Income and Poverty Status in the United States: 1988*, 1989, p. 31. Primary source: U.S. Bureau of the Census, Current Population Reports, Series P-60, No. 166. *Note:* 1. Persons of Hispanic origin may be of any race.

★ 558 ★
Earnings

	1940-1950	1950-1960	1960-1970	1970-1980
Ages 25-34				
Whites	3.5	3.9	2.9	-0.2
Blacks	6.5	3.4	4.5	0.6
Ages 35-44				
Whites	2.2	3.9	3.0	1.0
Blacks	5.7	3.6	4.0	2.0
Ages 45-54				
Whites	1.9	3.4	3.3	1.3
Blacks	5.4	3.2	4.4	2.5

Continued.

Earnings
[Continued]

	1940-1950	1950-1960	1960-1970	1970-1980
55-64				
Whites	1.9	3.6	2.8	1.6
Blacks	5.0	3.3	4.1	2.6
Total				
Whites	2.5	3.8	3.0	0.6
Blacks	5.9	3.4	4.2	1.7

Source: "Real Earnings Growth: Average Annual Percentage Rates of Change for Men by Race and Age," *The Economic Progress of Black Men in America*, p. 11. Census Population, 1940-1980; Public Use Sample *Notes:* Tabulations based on annual wage and salary earnings of male wage and salary workers with any earnings during the year. The self-employed and unpaid family workers are excluded.

★ 559 ★
Earnings and Educational Attainment: Trends

	Median earnings: 4 years of high school	Earning ratios[1]	
		1-3 years college to 4 years high school	4 or more years college to 4 years high school
White			
1978	$11,825	1.07	1.20
1979	12,351	1.09	1.24
1980	13,357	1.13	1.24
1981	14,563	1.09	1.24
1982	15,308	1.10	1.33
1983	15,754	1.14	1.32
1984	16,356	1.15	1.32
1985	17,597	1.14	1.30
1986	17,708	1.18	1.43
1987	18,238	1.16	1.41
1988	18,869	1.12	1.41
Black			
1978	$9,330	1.12	1.38
1979	10,410	1.15	1.27
1980	10,950	1.14	1.35
1981	12,001	1.08	1.29
1982	13,106	1.06	1.27
1983	13,083	1.12	1.34
1984	13,229	1.19	1.38
1985	13,337	1.14	1.50
1986	14,276	1.09	1.46

Continued.

Earnings and Educational Attainment: Trends
[Continued]

	Median earnings: 4 years of high school	Earning ratios[1]	
		1-3 years college to 4 years high school	4 or more years college to 4 years high school
1987	14,357	1.12	1.49
1988	14,699	1.21	1.45

Source: "Median Earnings and Earnings Ratio of Year-Round, Full-Time Workers 25-34 Years Old, by Educational Attainment and by Race and Gender: 1978- 1988," *1989 Education Indicators,* p. 264. Primary source: U.S. Department of Commerce, Bureau of the Census, Current Population Survey, March of various years; and unpublished tabulations. *Notes:* 1. The earnings ratio is the earnings of those completing 1-3 or 4 or more years of college divided by the earnings of those completing only 4 years of high school.

★ 560 ★
Earnings, Characteristics of

	25-34 years of age			45-54 years of age		
	Annual earnings	Weekly earnings	Hourly earnings	Annual earnings	Weekly earnings	Hourly earnings
Non-South						
8-11 yrs.	20.0	12.7	5.4	15.2	12.6	6.9
High school	19.3	14.5	9.0	18.9	15.8	10.7
College	11.7	8.6	3.5	28.5	26.1	20.4
All levels	20.3	15.1	8.6	27.8	24.9	19.9
South						
8-11 yrs.	22.7	19.6	13.2	30.8	27.7	21.3
High school	23.9	20.5	13.6	30.1	27.9	23.5
College	19.0	16.5	9.8	37.3	33.2	28.7
All levels	26.7	22.9	16.2	39.4	36.6	31.2
All regions						
8-11 yrs.	22.8	18.4	12.9	23.7	20.9	15.4
High school	23.1	19.5	14.1	24.2	21.5	19.1
College	15.4	13.0	7.8	33.1	29.9	23.2
All levels	24.7	20.6	14.8	34.6	31.8	31.3

Source: "Black-White Earnings Gap in 1980 by Region, Age, and Education," *The Economic Progress of Black Men in America,* p. 114. *Notes:* The earnings gap is measured as 100 percent minus the black-white earnings ratio.

★ 561 ★
Educational Attainment and Workers' Poverty Status

Educational attainment	Poverty rates			
	Men		Women	
	White	Black	White	Black
Total	4.7	10.5	4.8	16.0
Fewer than 4 years of high school	11.7	17.4	11.8	28.7
4 years of high school only	4.4	9.6	5.0	17.8
1 to 3 years of college	3.0	7.4	3.4	8.6
4 years of college or more	1.6	3.5	1.3	3.2

Source: "Poverty Rates of Workers in the Labor Force 27 Weeks or More by Educational Attainment, Sex, and Race, 1987," *A Profile of the Working Poor,* December 1989, p. 14. Primary source: U.S. Department of Labor, Bureau of Labor Statistics. *Notes:* Poverty rates are the percent of persons in the labor force 27 weeks or more who are poor.

★ 562 ★
Families in Poverty: Characteristics and Trends

Numbers in thousands. Families as of March of the following year.

Year and characteristic	All families			Married couple families			Male householder, no wife present			Female householder, no husband present		
	Total	Below poverty		Total	Below poverty		Total	Below poverty		Total	Below poverty	
		No.	%		No.	%		No.	%		No.	%
All Races												
With Children Under 18 Years												
1988	34,251	5,373	15.7	25,598	1,847	7.2	1,292	232	18.0	7,361	3,294	44.7
1987	33,991	5,465	16.1	25,462	1,963	7.7	1,316	221	16.8	7,213	3,281	45.5
1986	33,801	5,516	16.3	25,571	2,050	8.0	1,136	202	17.8	7,094	3,264	46.0
1985	33,536	5,586	16.7	25,496	2,258	8.9	1,147	197	17.1	6,892	3,131	45.4
White												
With Children Under 18 Years												
1988	27,995	3,321	11.9	22,433	1,434	6.4	1,012	147	14.5	4,550	1,740	38.2
1987	27,926	3,433	12.3	22,334	1,538	6.9	1,047	154	14.7	4,545	1,742	38.3
1986	27,929	3,637	13.0	22,466	1,692	7.5	911	132	14.5	4,552	1,812	39.8
1985	27,795	3,695	13.3	22,399	1,827	8.2	926	138	14.9	4,470	1,730	38.7
Black												
With Children Under 18 Years												
1988	5,010	1,803	36.0	2,181	272	12.5	246	77	31.4	2,583	1,454	56.3
1987	4,880	1,788	36.6	2,205	290	13.2	222	61	27.5	2,453	1,437	58.6
1986	4,806	1,699	35.4	2,236	257	11.5	185	58	31.5	2,386	1,384	58.0
1985	4,636	1,670	36.0	2,185	281	12.9	182	53	29.0	2,269	1,336	58.9
Hispanic Origin[1]												
With Children Under 18 Years												
1988	3,325	988	29.7	2,339	445	19.0	125	33	26.1	861	510	59.2
1987	3,201	1,022	31.9	2,197	460	20.9	139	35	25.2	865	527	60.9
1986	3,080	949	30.8	NA	NA	NA	NA	NA	822	489	59.5	
1985	2,973	955	32.1	NA	NA	NA	NA	NA	NA	771	493	

Source: "Poverty Status of Families, by Type of Family, Presence of Related Children, Race, and Hispanic Origin: 1959 to 1988," *Money Income and Poverty Status in the United States: 1988,* 1989, pp. 62-65. Primary source: U.S. Bureau of the Census, Current Population Reports, Series P-60, No. 166. *Notes:* Prior to 1979 unrelated subfamilies were included in all families. Beginning in 1979 unrelated subfamilies are excluded from all families. 1. Persons of Hispanic origin may be of any race.

★ 563 ★
Full-time Worker Income By Sex and Race

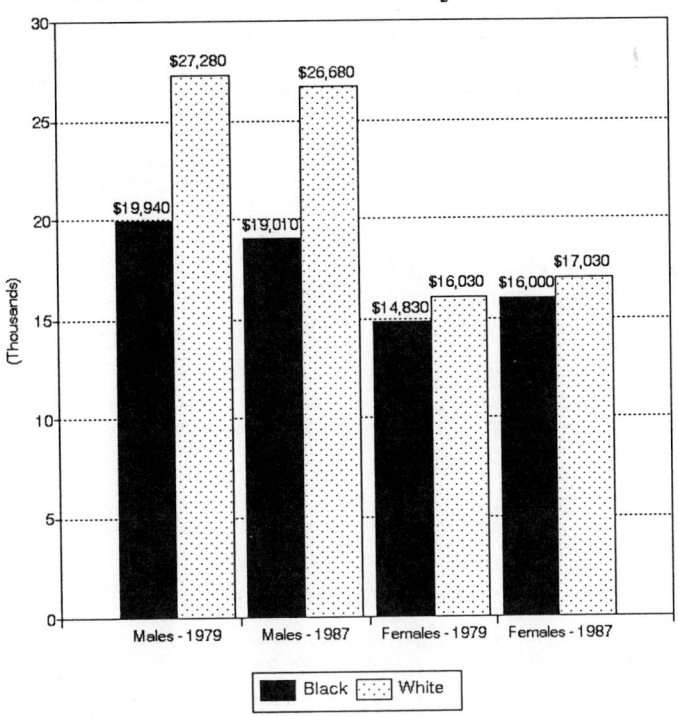

Race and gender	1979	1987
Males		
Black	19,940	19,010
White	27,280	26,680
Females		
Black	14,830	16,000
White	16,030	17,030
Ratio: Black to White		
Males	0.73	0.71
Females	0.93	0.94

Source: "Median Earnings of Year-Round, Full-Time Workers, by Sex and Race: 1979 and 1987:
The Black Population in The United States: March 1988, p. 15. Primary source: Current Population
Reports, Series P-20, No. 442, *The Black Population in the United States: March 1988.*

★ 564 ★
Full-Time Worker Median Income

In 1987 dollars.

Income	1979	1987
Earnings		
Female	14,830	16,000
Male	19,940	19,010
Ratio Female to Male	0.74	0.84

Source: "Median Earnings of Year-Round, Full-Time, Black Workers, by Sex: 1979 and 1987," *The
Black Population in the United States: March 1988,* p. 14. Primary source: Current Population
Reports, Series P-20, No. 442, *The Black Population in the United States: March 1988..*

★ 565 ★
Household Income

Households as of March 1987.

Characteristic	Mean Household Income		Income per Household Member		Taxes as a percent of income
	Before taxes	After taxes	Before taxes	After taxes	
All households	30,759	23,633	11,552	8,894	23.0
Race and Hispanic origin:					
White	32,040	24,570	12,239	9,385	23.3
Black	20,232	16,398	6,952	5,635	18.9
Hispanic[1]	23,173	18,817	6,767	5,495	18.8

Source: Money Income of Households — Mean Income and Income per Household Member Before and After Taxes, by Selected Characteristics: 1986," *Statistical Abstract*, 1989, p. 444. Primary source: U.S. Bureau of the Census, *Current Population Reports*, series P-23, No. 157, and unpublished data. *Note:* 1. Hispanic persons may be of any race.

★ 566 ★
Household Income

Households as of March 1983 and income figures are for the preceding year, expressed in 1984 dollars. Discretionary income is the amount of money which would permit a household to maintain a living standard comfortably higher (30% or more) than the average for similar households. For methodology, see source.

Characteristic	All Households		Households with Discretionary Income					
			Households		Average income		Spendable discretionary income	
	Number (1,000)	Aggregate income after taxes (bil.)	Number (1,000)	Percent of all house-hold	Before taxes (dol.)	After taxes (dol.)	Aggregate income (bil.)	Average income (dol.)
Total	83,918	1,707.3	26,409	31.5	46,764	34,562	277.9	10,525
Race and Hispanic origin of householder:								
White	73,182	1,544.0	24,697	33.7	46,935	34,667	263.3	10,661
Black	10,736	163.3	1,712	16.0	44,301	33,049	14.6	8,555
Hispanic[1]	4,085	67.2	660	16.1	46,172	34,879	6.0	9,119

Source: "Households with Discretionary Income — Selected Income Measures in Constant (1984) Dollars: 1982," *Statistical Abstract*, 1989, p. 444. Primary source: U.S. Bureau of the Census and the Conference Board, *A Marketer's Guide to Discretionary Income*, 1985. *Note:* 1. Hispanic persons may be of any race.

★ 567 ★
Household Income

Households of March of follwing year. Based on Current Population Survey. Minus sign (-) indicates decrease.

Year	Median Income in Current Dollars (dol.)				Median Income in Constant (1987) Dollars (dol.)			
	All house-holds[1]	White	Black	Hispanic[2]	All house-holds[1]	White	Black	Hispanic[2]
1970	8,734	9,097	5,537	[3]	25,563	26,626	16,206	[3]
1971	9,028	9,443	5,578	[3]	25,335	26,499	15,654	[3]
1972	9,697	10,173	5,938	7,677	26,344	27,637	16,132	20,856
1973	10,512	11,017	6,485	8,144	26,884	28,175	16,586	20,828
1974	11,197	11,710	6,964	8,906	25,806	26,987	16,050	20,526
1975	11,800	12,340	7,408	8,865	24,917	26,058	15,643	18,720

Continued.

Household Income
[Continued]

Year	Median Income in Current Dollars (dol.)				Median Income in Constant (1987) Dollars (dol.)			
	All house-holds[1]	White	Black	Hispanic[2]	All house-holds[1]	White	Black	Hispanic[2]
1976	12,686	13,289	7,902	9,569	25,328	26,531	15,776	19,104
1977	13,572	14,272	8,422	10,647	25,454	26,767	15,795	19,968
1978	15,064	15,660	9,411	11,803	26,242	27,281	16,395	20,562
1979	16,461	17,259	10,133	13,042	25,775	27,024	15,866	20,421
1980	17,710	18,684	10,764	13,651	24,426	25,770	14,846	18,826
1981	19,074	20,153	11,309	15,300	23,835	25,184	14,132	19,119
1982	20,171	21,117	11,968	15,178	23,750	24,865	14,092	17,871
1983	21,018	22,035	12,473	15,794	23,976	25,136	14,229	18,017
1984	22,415	23,647	13,471	16,992	24,526	25,874	14,740	18,592
1985	23,618	24,908	14,819	17,465	24,952	26,315	15,656	18,451
1986	24,897	26,175	15,080	18,352	25,807	27,131	15,631	19,023
1987	25,986	27,427	15,475	19,305	25,986	27,427	15,475	19,305

Source: "Money Income of Household — Median Income in Current and Constant (1987) Dollars, by Race and Hispanic Origin of Householder: 1970 to 1987," *Statistical Abstract,* 1989, p. 440. Primary source: Source of tables 711 and 712: U.S. Bureau of the Census, *Current Population Reports,* series P-60, No. 161, and unpublished data. *Notes:* 1. Includes other races not shown separately. 2. Hispanic persons may be of any race. 3. Not available.

★ 568 ★
Household Income

Households as of March of following year. Based on Current Population Survey; see text, sections 1 and 14, and Appendix III. Hispanic persons may be of any race.

Race of Householder and Year	Number of households (1,000)	Percent Distribution, by Income Level								Median income (dol.)
		Under $5,000	$5,000 -$9,999	$10,000 -$14,999	$15,000 -$19,999	$20,000 -$24,999	$25,000 -$34,999	$35,000 -$49,999	$50,000 and over	
White										
1970	57,575	7.0	9.9	9.3	12.3	8.1	25.8	13.9	13.6	26,626
1975	64,392	5.6	11.4	10.6	10.4	9.9	21.6	15.9	14.6	26,058
1980	71,872	6.7	10.7	10.8	10.5	10.1	18.1	18.0	15.1	25,770
1982	73,182	6.9	11.3	11.1	10.8	10.4	17.6	16.8	15.1	24,865
1983	74,170	6.6	10.9	11.3	10.7	10.3	17.3	17.0	15.9	25,136
1984	75,328	6.0	11.1	10.8	10.5	9.9	17.4	17.1	17.1	25,874
1985	76,576	6.0	11.1	10.6	10.3	9.9	17.3	17.0	17.9	26,315
1986	77,284	5.9	10.6	10.3	10.0	9.5	16.9	17.6	19.3	27,131
1987	78,469	5.4	10.7	10.3	10.0	9.2	16.7	18.1	19.7	27,427
Black										
1970	6,180	14.8	17.8	14.1	15.1	8.7	17.5	7.4	4.7	16,206
1975	7,489	13.5	21.0	14.0	11.6	10.6	15.6	8.9	4.9	15,643
1980	8,847	16.8	19.4	14.6	11.4	9.3	13.2	9.8	5.5	14,846
1982	8,916	18.4	19.2	15.0	11.0	9.0	13.3	9.8	4.2	14,092
1983	9,243	18.5	19.5	14.3	11.6	8.6	12.3	9.6	5.6	14,229
1984	9,480	17.0	19.3	14.7	11.5	9.0	12.7	9.3	6.6	14,740
1985	9,797	16.6	18.2	13.7	12.0	8.8	13.2	10.3	7.0	15,656
1986	9,922	18.0	17.3	13.3	10.8	9.2	13.0	10.8	7.6	16,631

Continued.

387

Household Income
[Continued]

Race of Householder and Year	Number of households (1,000)	Percent Distribution, by Income Level								Median income (dol.)
		Under $5,000	$5,000 -$9,999	$10,000 -$14,999	$15,000 -$19,999	$20,000 -$24,999	$25,000 -$34,999	$35,000 -$49,999	$50,000 and over	
1987	10,186	17.9	17.7	13.3	11.0	9.7	12.2	10.8	7.5	15,475

Source: Money Income of Households — Percent Distribution by Income Level in Constant (1987) Dollars, by Race of Householder: 1970 to 1987," *Statistical Abstract,* 1989, p. 440. Primary source: U.S. Bureau of the Census, *Current Population Reports,* series P-60, No. 161, and unpublished data.

★ 569 ★
Household Income

Households as of March 1988.

Characteristics	Total households (1,000)	Percent Distribution of Households by Income Level (in dollars)								Median income (dollars)
		Under 5,000	5,000- 9,999	10,000- 14,999	15,000- 24,999	25,000- 34,999	35,000- 49,999	50,000- 74,999	75,000 and over	
Total[1]	91,066	6.9	11.5	10.6	19.2	16.1	17.2	12.2	6.3	25,986
White	78,469	5.4	10.7	10.2	19.2	16.7	18.1	13.0	6.7	27,427
Black	10,186	17.9	17.7	13.3	20.7	12.2	10.8	5.5	2.0	15,475
Hispanic[2]	5,698	10.4	15.5	14.2	21.7	14.9	13.4	7.0	2.9	19,305

Source: "Money Income of Households — Percent Distribution By Money Income Level: 1987," *Statistical Abstract,* 1989, p. 441. Primary source: U.S. Bureau of the Census, *Current Population Reports,* series P-60, No. 161. *Notes:* 1. Includes other races not shown separately. 2. Hispanic persons may be of any race.

★ 570 ★
Household Income

In dollars, except percent. Households as of March of following year. Estimates of after-tax income were derived from tax simulation procedures based on a "statistical" combination of data from the Internal Revenue Service, summaries of State individual income tax regulations, data on the characteristics of persons paying FICA payroll taxes from the Social Security Administration, property tax information from the Annual Housing Survey, and the March Current Population Survey microdata file.

Characteristics	After-Tax Household Income						Average Annual Percent Change				
	1980	1982	1983	1984	1985	1986	1980- 1982	1982- 1983	1983- 1984	1984- 1985	1985- 1986
Race and Hispanic origin:											
White	22,424	22,293	23,011	23,614	23,936	24,570	-.3	3.2	2.6	1.4	2.6
Black	15,236	14,723	15,113	15,622	16,094	16,398	-.7	2.6	3.4	3.0	1.9
Hispanic[1]	18,030	17,371	17,660	18,324	18,265	18,817	-1.8	1.7	3.8	-.3	3.0

Source: "Money Income of Households — Mean After-Tax Household Income in Constant (1986) Dollars, by Selected Characteristics: 1980 to 1986," *Statistical Abstract,* 1989, p. 443 U.S. Bureau of the Census, *Current Population Reports,* series P-23, No. 157, and unpublished data. *Note:* 1. Hispanic persons may be of any race.

★ 571 ★
Household Income Level

Household as of March 1988.

Item	All households	Family Households					Nonfamily Households				
		Total	Married couple	Male house-holder, wife absent	Female house-holder, husband absent	Total	Single-Person household				Multiple-person household
							Total	Male house-holder	Female house-holder	
Median income (dol.):											
All households	25,986	31,135	34,786	26,157	15,419	14,685	12,544	16,703	10,576	30,573
White	27,427	32,556	35,355	27,574	17,961	15,522	13,281	17,901	11,029	31,889
Black	15,475	18,561	27,238	18,758	10,017	5,529	7,981	10,383	6,730	19,504
Hispanic[1]	19,305	20,852	25,081	22,030	10,627	12,138	9,883	11,739	7,834	23,500

Source: "Household Type, by Median Income and Income Level: 1987," *Statistical Abstract,* 1989, p. 442. Primary source: U.S. Bureau of the Census, *Current Population Reports,* series P-60, No. 161. *Note:* 1. Hispanic persons may be of any race.

★ 572 ★
Household Worth

In dollars. Balances of assets and liabilities held at the end of months August-November 1984. Data exclude group quarters. Based on the Survey of Income and Program Participation.

Characteristic	Net worth	Interest earning deposits[1]	Other interest-earning assets[2]	Regular checking accounts[3]	Equity in--					IRA and KEOGH accounts
					Own home	Rental property	Other real estate	Motor vehicles	Own business or profession	
Race of householder:										
White	39,135	3,457	9,826	457	41,999	34,516	15,488	4,293	7,113	4,922
Black	3,397	739	5	318	24,077	27,291	10,423	2,691	2,054	2,450
Hispanic[4]	4,913	1,178	5	359	38,867	23,772	10,689	2,091	6,580	3,257

Source: "Household Net Worth — Median Value of Holdings: 1984," *Statistical Abstract,* 1989, p. 459. Primary source: U.S. Bureau of the Census, *Current Population Reports,* series P-70, No. 7. *Notes:* 1. At financial institutions. Includes passbook savings accounts, money market deposit accounts, certificates of deposit, and interest-earning checking accounts. 2. Includes money market funds, U.S. Government securities, municipal and corporate bonds, and other interest-earning assets. 3. Excludes interest-earning checking. 4. Hispanic persons may be of any race. 5. Base figure too small to meet statistical standards for reliability of derived figure.

★ 573 ★
Household Worth

Characteristic	Number of house-holds (1,000)	Percent Distribution of Households by Net Worth								Median (dol.)
		Zero or negative	$1 to $4,999	$5,000 to $9,999	$10,000 to $24,999	$25,000 to $49,999	$50,000 to $99,999	$100,000 to $249,999	$250,000 and over	
Total	86,790	11.0	15.3	6.4	12.4	14.5	19.3	15.3	5.9	32,667
Race of householder:										
White	75,343	8.4	14.0	6.3	12.2	15.0	20.7	16.9	6.5	39,135
Black	9,509	30.5	23.9	6.8	14.0	11.7	9.3	3.3	.6	3,397
Hispanic[1]	4,162	23.9	26.3	7.6	11.4	9.5	13.1	5.1	3.1	4,913

Source: "Household Net Worth — Percent Distribution by Selected Characteristics: 1984," *Statistical Abstract*, 1989, p. 459. Primary source: U.S. Bureau of the Census, *Current Population Reports*, series P-70, No. 7. *Note:* 1. Hispanic persons may be of any race.

★ 574 ★
Households Types and Total Money Income: Trends

Numbers in thousands. Households as of March 1989.

Total money income	Total	Family households				Nonfamily households				
		Total	Type of family			Total	Sex of householder			
			Married-couple families	Male householder, no wife present	Female householder, no husband present		Male		Female	
							Total	Living alone	Total	Living alone
All Races										
Total	92,830	65,837	52,100	2,847	10,890	26,994	11,874	9,193	15,120	13,515
Median income (dollars)	27,225	32,491	36,436	28,642	16,051	16,148	20,999	18,284	12,877	11,622
Standard error (dollars)	132	180	180	730	274	176	295	350	228	175
Mean income (dollars)	34,017	38,913	42,875	34,291	21,167	22,077	26,992	23,404	18,218	16,017
Standard error (dollars)	151	188	216	971	278	205	361	358	221	199
Income per household member (dollars)	12,976	12,176	13,265	11,359	6,900	18,077	20,312	23,404	16,026	16,017
Standard error (dollars)	73	81	91	394	113	224	373	532	273	296
Gini ratio	.425	.391	.362	.388	.450	.458	.438	.438	.454	.438
Standard error	.0038	.0045	.0050	.0231	.0111	.0075	.0111	.0127	.0101	.0107
White										
Total	79,734	56,492	46,877	2,274	7,342	23,242	10,013	7,716	13,229	11,798
Median income (dollars)	28,781	34,222	36,883	30,689	18,685	16,932	22,196	19,584	13,548	12,115
Standard error (dollars)	168	205	186	797	394	189	312	357	236	177
Mean income (dollars)	35,468	40,603	43,471	36,430	23,582	22,987	28,359	24,703	18,922	16,601
Standard error (dollars)	166	207	230	1,167	358	225	399	406	243	220
Income per household member (dollars)	13,751	12,933	13,650	12,394	8,095	18,881	21,421	24,703	16,643	16,601
Standard error (dollars)	84	93	95	46	158	251	422	610	302	329
Gini ratio	.415	.378	.359	.384	.430	.452	.4296	.429	.449	.432
Standard error	.0041	.0049	.0053	.0262	.0135	.0081	.0120	.0139	.0109	.0115
Black										
Total	10,561	7,409	3,722	464	3,223	3,152	1,508	1,218	1,644	1,515
Median income (dollars)	16,407	19,823	30,424	19,501	10,995	9,826	13,010	10,859	7,489	7,107
Standard error (dollars)	339	445	748	1,177	366	411	771	842	372	246
Mean income (dollars)	22,477	25,689	34,758	23,560	15,524	14,926	17,765	15,185	12,321	11,267
Standard error (dollars)	325	414	639	1,231	419	424	718	644	454	402
Income per household member (dollars)	7,978	7,351	9,699	7,159	4,538	12,173	13,188	15,185	11,048	11,267
Standard error (dollars)	137	151	229	524	143	500	773	1,082	647	701
Gini ratio	.466	.443	.365	.374	.467	.470	.458	.450	.463	.451
Standard error	.0116	.0135	.0184	.0514	.0216	.0223	.0316	.0341	.0311	.0309
Hispanic Origin[1]										
Total	5,910	4,823	3,398	314	1,112	1,087	623	465	464	399
Median income (dollars)	20,359	22,157	25,769	23,656	11,321	12,889	15,153	12,654	9,508	7,495

Continued.

Households Types and Total Money Income: Trends
[Continued]

Total money income	Total	Family households					Nonfamily households				
		Total	Type of family			Total	Sex of householder				
			Married-couple families	Male householder, no wife present	Female householder, no husband present		Male		Female		
							Total	Living alone	Total	Living alone	
Standard error (dollars)	459	547	555	2,099	662	895	1,321	1,079	1,258	872	
Mean income (dollars)	25,993	27,819	31,361	27,880	16,982	17,890	19,520	16,096	17,703	12,998	
Standard error (dollars)	505	581	735	1,777	844	840	1,128	1,047	1,241	1,020	
Income per household member (dollars)	7,703	7,275	7,924	7,806	4,869	12,967	12,717	16,096	13,405	12,998	
Standard error (dollars)	182	191	240	686	282	876	1,076	1,831	1,554	1,663	
Gini ratio	.434	.419	.386	.366	.487	.463	.436	.419	.492	.466	
Standard error	.0162	.0179	.0214	.0651	.0386	.0386	.0494	.0541	.0631	.0644	

Source: "Type of Household — Households, by Total Money Income in 1988, Race, and Hispanic Origin of Householder," *Money Income and Poverty Status in the United States: 1988*, 1989, pp. 25-26. Primary source: U.S. Bureau of the Census, Current Population Reports, Series P-60, No. 166. Gini: Gross income/net income *Note:* 1. Persons of Hispanic origin may be of any race.

★ 575 ★
Income and Education

	Black	White
Master's	$1,996	$2,287
Bachelor's	$1,388	$1,881
Associate	$1,158	$1,367
Vocational	$860	$1,248
Some College	$862	$1,213
High School Only	$765	$1,080
Not High School Grad	$513	$734

Source: "Average Monthly Income and Educational Attainment, by Race, 1984," *NAFEO INROADS*, October/November, 1987, p. 8. Primary source: U.S. Bureau of the Census, 1984. Published by permission.

★ 576 ★
Income and Family Type

In 1987 dollars.

Race	1979	1987
Married couple		
Black	26,300	27,180
White	34,050	35,300
Female householder, no husband present		
Black	10,750	9,710
White	17,890	17,020

Source: "Median Family Income, by Type of Family and Race of Householder: 1979 and 1987," *The Black Population in the United States: March 1988*, p. 13. Primary source: Current Population Reports, Series P-20, No. 442, *The Black Population in the United States: March 1988*.

★ 577 ★
Income and Household Characteristics

Households as of March 1989.

Characteristic	Percent distribution				Median income (dollars)			
	All races	White	Black	Hispanic origin[1]	All races	White	Black	Hispanic origin[1]
Total								
All households	92,830	79,734	10,561	5,910	27,225	28,781	16,407	20,359
Percent	100.0	100.0	100.0	100.0	27,225	28,781	16,407	20,359
Family households[2]	70.9	70.9	70.2	81.6	32,491	34,222	19,823	22,157
Nonfamily households	29.1	29.1	29.8	18.4	16,148	16,932	9,826	12,889
Householder Year-Round, Full-Time Worker								
All households	49,938	43,756	4,768	3,156	37,678	38,764	27,552	28,828
Percent	53.8	54.9	45.2	53.4	37,678	38,764	27,552	28,828
Family households[2]	41.5	42.4	33.1	45.4	41,283	42,090	31,499	30,199
Nonfamily households	12.3	12.4	12.0	8.0	27,272	28,278	20,773	22,201

Source: "Educational Attainment of Householder — Percent Distribution and Median Income in 1988 of Households, by Type of Household, Age, Work Experience, Race, and Hispanic Origin of Householder," Money Income and Poverty Status in the United States: 1988, 1989, pp. 27-30. Primary source: U.S. Bureau of the Census, Current Population Reports, Series P-60, No. 166. *Notes:* 1. Persons of Hispanic origin may be of any race. 2. Includes male householder, no wife present, not shown separately.

★ 578 ★
Income at Selected Distribution Points: Trends

Figures in dollars; ratios in percent.

Characteristic	1988			1980			1970		
	Black	White	Blk/ Wht	Black	White	Blk/ Wht	Black	White	Blk/ Wht
Upper Limit of									
Lowest Fifth	7,148	16,814	42.5	8,511	16,238	.52	9,054	16,756	.54
Second	14,400	28,000	51.4	15,219	26,478	.57	15,983	26,588	.60
Third	24,425	40,000	61,1	25,023	36,584	.68	24,069	35,619	.68
Fourth	40,300	57,350	70.3	38,477	50,825	.76	35,646	48,532	.73
Lower Limit of Top 5%	65,927	93,900	70.2	62,311	79,252	.79	56,428	75,927	.74

Source: "Income at Selected Positions of the Income Distribution, 1970, 1980, 1988 by Race (Constant 1988 Dollars)," *The State of Black America 1990*, January 1990, p. 31. Primary source: Swinton, David, "The Economic Status of the Black Population," Table 3, page 93, in *The State of Black America 1983* (New York: National Urban League); U.S. Department of Commerce, Bureau of the Census, *Money Income and Poverty Status in 1988*, Table 5.

★ 579 ★
Income Characteristics and Comparisons: Trends

Figures in dollars; ratios in percent.

Year	Aggregate Black Income (bil)	Per Capita Income			Parity Gap	
		Black	White	B/W	Per Capita	Aggregate (bil)
1988	242	8,271	13,896	0.595	5,625	165
1987	234	7,961	13,687	0.582	5.726	168
1986	226	7,779	13,332	0.583	5,553	161
1982	179	6,571	11,679	0.563	5,108	139
1978	183	7,319	12,333	0.593	5,014	126

Continued.

Income Characteristics and Comparisons: Trends
[Continued]

Year	Aggregate Black Income (bil)	Per Capita Income			Parity Gap	
		Black	White	B/W	Per Capita	Aggregate (bil)
1970	137	5,699	10,226	0.557	4,527	105

Source: "Per Capita Income, Aggregate Income, and Income Gaps, Selected Years (1988$)," The State of Black America 1990, January 1990, p. 27. Primary source: U.S. Department of Commerce, Bureau of the Census, *Money Income and Poverty Status in 1988*, Table 16. Calculations of aggregates and gaps done by author.

★ 580 ★
Income Deficit of Families in Poverty

Numbers in thousands. Families as of March 1989.

Size of income deficit	Total			White			Black			Hispanic origin[1]		
	Total	Married-couple families	Families with female householder, no husband present	Total	Married-couple families	Families with female householder, no husband present	Total	Married-couple families	Families with female householder, no husband present	Total	Married-couple families	Families with female householder, no husband present
Total	7,133	2,907	3,884	4,636	2,301	2,097	2,170	424	1,659	1,167	553	566
Less than $250	240	146	76	182	122	45	48	16	32	33	296	1
$250 to $499	198	104	84	146	81	56	48	22	26	23	11	11
$500 to $999	414	241	150	298	198	77	92	33	59	58	30	21
$1,000 to $1,499	435	222	186	285	154	117	120	55	54	55	27	27
$1,500 to $1,999	490	279	195	362	222	129	101	43	54	69	46	23
$2,000 to $2,999	825	358	442	550	287	244	236	40	190	127	66	57
$3,000 to $3,999	771	298	419	496	437	427	239	46	178	115	48	58
$4,000 to $4,999	698	261	390	464	207	223	211	40	160	122	71	44
$5,000 to $5,999	695	200	456	477	184	263	204	9	186	111	40	66
$6,000 to $6,999	573	184	378	361	136	220	187	27	153	111	46	60
$7,000 to $7,999	514	187	302	329	155	162	163	21	130	109	49	57
$8,000 and over	1,278	426	806	685	318	335	521	71	435	235	88	142
						In dollars						
Median income deficit	4,276	3,342	4,999	3,997	3,365	4,694	4,949	3,075	5,407	4,859	4,251	5,640
Standard error	95	142	116	111	158	161	175	368	171	224	263	281
Mean income deficit	4,851	4,432	5,206	4,566	4,345	4,858	5,447	4,670	5,663	5,242	4,875	5,685
Standard error	67	118	80	79	124	103	128	407	128	160	249	212
Deficit per family member	1,395	1,161	1,592	1,361	1,185	1,576	1,503	1,123	1,619	1,284	1,065	1,548

Source: "Size of Income Deficit for Families Below Poverty Level in 1988, by Type of Family, Race, and Hispanic Origin of Householder," *Money Income and Poverty Status in the United States: 1988*, 1989, p. 78. Primary source: U.S. Bureau of the Census, Current Population Reports, Series P-60, No. 166. *Notes:* Includes unrelated subfamilies, classified by sex of subfamily reference person. 1. Persons of Hispanic origin may be of any race.

★ 581 ★
Income Deficit of Individuals in Poverty

Numbers in thousands. Unrelated individuals as of March 1989.

Size of income deficit	Total			White			Black			Hispanic origin[1]		
	Total	Male	Female	Total	Male	Female	Total	Male	Female	Total	Male	Female
Total	7,071	2,846	4,225	5,316	2,050	3,266	1,509	681	828	597	326	271
Less than $250	582	195	387	460	151	309	92	36	57	17	8	9
$250 to $499	379	121	258	313	87	227	59	30	29	18	7	11
$500 to $999	893	250	643	688	174	513	178	68	110	69	23	46
$1,000 to $1,499	1,057	374	386	775	271	504	263	90	173	81	40	41
$1,500 to $1,999	731	260	471	522	196	326	194	59	135	57	38	18
$2,000 to $2,999	867	353	514	673	275	399	170	61	109	77	51	27

Continued.

Income Deficit of Individuals in Poverty
[Continued]

Size of income deficit	Total			White			Black			Hispanic origin[1]		
	Total	Male	Female	Total	Male	Female	Total	Male	Female	Total	Male	Female
$3,000 to $3,999	706	315	392	522	220	301	149	82	67	59	32	27
$4,000 to $4,999	541	289	252	397	207	190	110	57	53	48	34	13
$5,000 and over	1,316	690	626	965	469	496	293	197	96	171	92	78
In dollars												
Median income deficit	1,927	2,634	1,650	1,904	2,531	1,623	1,917	2,930	1,668	2,733	2,919	2,376
Standard error	45	118	54	55	129	69	78	300	84	248	335	471
Mean income deficit	2,616	3,064	2,314	2,593	3,034	2,316	2,634	3,128	2,229	3,171	3,308	3,006
Standard error	40	68	48	48	83	56	79	128	94	136	177	209

Source: "Size of Income Deficit for Unrelated Individuals Below Poverty Level in 1988, by Sex and Race and Hispanic Origin," *Money Income and Poverty Status in the United States: 1988*, 1989, p. 78. Primary source: U.S. Bureau of the Census, Current Population Reports, Series P-60, No. 166. *Note:* 1. Persons of Hispanic origin may be of any race.

★ 582 ★
Income Distribution

As of March of following year. For 1970 and 1975, persons 14 years old and over; thereafter, 15 years old and over. Based on Current Population Survey. See *Historical Statistics, Colonial Times to 1970*, series G 257- 268, for percent distribution by income level, and median income.

Sex, Year, Age, Race, Hispanic Origin, and Region	All persons (mil.)	Persons with Income									Median income (dol.)	Mean income (dol.)
		Total (mil.)	Percent distribution by income (in dollars) level--									
			1 to 1,999 or less[1]	2,000 -3,999	4,000 -5,999	6,000 -9,999	10,000 -14,999	15,000 -24,999	25,000 -34,999	35,000 and over		
White	83.5	76.7	16.8	11.1	11.1	16.9	15.1	17.9	6.9	4.2	8,279	11,621
Black	11.6	10.1	13.0	15.7	17.0	16.4	13.6	16.5	5.7	2.0	6,791	9,919
Hispanic[1]	6.8	5.3	18.6	13.9	13.2	20.0	13.4	14.3	4.4	2.2	6,611	9,303

Source: "Money Income of Persons — Percent Distribution by Income Level, Median, and Mean Income, by Sex, 1970 to 1987, and by Age, Race, Hispanic Origin, and Region, 1987," *Statistical Abstract*, 1989, p. 449. Primary source: U.S. Bureau of the Census, *Current Population Reports*, series P-60, No. 161, and unpublished data. *Note:* 1. Hispanic persons may be of any race.

★ 583 ★
Income Level

In dollars.

Year	Current Dollars				Constant (1987) Dollars			
	All races	White	Black	Hispanic[1]	All races	White	Black	Hispanic[1]
1970	3,177	3,354	1,869	[2]	9,299	9,817	5,470	[2]
1971	3,417	3,596	2,062	[2]	9,589	10,091	5,787	[2]
1972	3,769	3,968	2,300	[2]	10,239	10,780	6,248	[2]
1973	4,141	4,361	2,521	2,454	10,591	11,153	6,447	6,276
1974	4,445	4,677	2,718	2,735	10,244	10,779	6,264	6,303
1975	4,818	5,072	2,972	2,847	10,174	10,710	6,276	6,012
1976	5,271	5,556	3,286	3,179	10,523	11,092	6,560	6,347
1977	5,785	6,100	3,574	3,538	10,850	11,440	6,703	6,635
1978	6,455	6,797	4,034	3,961	11,245	11,841	7,028	6,900
1979	7,168	7,574	4,444	4,432	11,223	11,859	6,958	6,940
1980	7,787	8,233	4,804	4,865	10,740	11,355	6,626	6,710
1981	8,476	8,979	5,129	5,349	10,592	11,220	6,409	6,684

Continued.

Income Level
[Continued]

Year	Current Dollars				Constant (1987) Dollars			
	All races	White	Black	Hispanic[1]	All races	White	Black	Hispanic[1]
1982	8,980	9,527	5,360	5,448	10,573	11,218	6,311	6,415
1983	9,548	10,125	5,755	5,852	10,892	11,550	6,565	6,676
1984	10,328	10,939	6,277	6,401	11,301	11,969	6,868	7,004
1985	11,013	11,671	6,840	6,613	11,635	12,330	7,226	6,987
1986	11,670	12,352	7,207	7,000	12,096	12,803	7,470	7,256
1987	12,287	13,031	7,499	7,611	12,287	13,031	7,499	7,611

Source: Per Capita Money Income in Current and Constant (1987) Dollars, by Race and Hispanic Origin: 1970 to 1987," *Statistical Abstract,* 1989, p. 450. Primary source: U.S. Bureau of the Census, *Current Population Reports,* series P-60, No. 161. *Notes:* 1. Hispanic persons may be of any race. 2. Not available.

★ 584 ★
Income of Males

Age group and race	1940	1950	1960	1970	1980
25-34					
Black	6.7	6.4	16.2	12.7	16.8
White	23.0	21.2	21.7	20.3	21.3
35-44					
Black	10.7	8.2	12.6	14.5	15.9
White	32.9	26.5	28.3	24.9	19.4
45-54					
Black	15.0	16.2	13.3	21.4	20.6
White	40.7	31.3	32.1	31.2	22.2
55-64					
Black	16.8	11.5	13.8	20.5	19.3
White	42.3	30.0	30.3	29.5	22.0

Source: "Public Use Sample," *The Economic Progress of Black Men in America,* p. 85. Primary source: Census of Population, 1940-1980. *Notes:* Data for 1940 based on an estimate of hourly earnings. Annual earnings are divided by "full-time equivalent" weeks times 40 hours, assumed to be a full-time week.

★ 585 ★
Income Source and Income Characteristics
In dollars.

Characteristic	Black Per Capita	White Per Capita	Per Capita B/W	Aggre-gate Gap	Percent of Gap (bil.)	Gap
1987						
Wage & Salary	6,110.09	9,577.87	63.79	3,467.78	101.5	62.81
Nonfarm Self-Employed	121.11	777.59	15.58	656.48	19.2	11.88
Farm Self-Employed	4.07	71.64	5.68	71.64	2.0	1.24
Property	112.59	954.51	11.80	841.93	24.6	15.22

Continued.

Income Source and Income Characteristics
[Continued]

Characteristic	Black Per Capita	White Per Capita	Per Capita B/W	Aggre-gate Gap	Percent of Gap (bil.)	Gap
Transfer and Other Income[1]	1,172.61	1,660.79	70.61	488.18	14.3	8.85
Social Security and RR	491.80	792.87	62.03	301.07	8.8	5.45
Public Assistance	179.21	38.45	466.11	-140.76	-4.1	-2.54
Ret. & Annuities	198.47	527.04	37.69	328.41	9.6	5.94
Total	7,520.47	13,042.40	57.66	5,521.93	161.6	100%
1980						
Wage & Salary	5,388.25	8,703.55	61.92	3,314.30	87.7	68.56
Nonfarm Self-Employed	143.15	647.70	22.10	504.55	13.3	10.43
Farm Self-Employed[2]	2.36	83.63	2.82	81.27	2.1	1.68
Property	83.20	745.14	11.17	661.94	17.5	13.69
Transfer and Other Income[1]	1,190.70	1,462.72	81.41	271.98	7.2	5.63
Social Security and RR	539.11	706.65	76.29	167.54	4.4	3.47
Public Assistance	329.41	74.71	440.92	-254.70	-6.7	-5.27
Ret. & Annuities	146.98	388.91	37.79	241.93	6.4	5.00
Total	6,807.70	11,641.74	58.48	4,834.04	128.8	100%

Source: "Per Capita Income and Income Gaps by Source of Income (1987$)," *The State of Black America 1990*, January 1990, p. 39. Primary source: Calculated by author from data in U.S. Department of Commerce, Bureau of the Census, *Money Income of Households, Families, and Persons....* 1987, 1986, 1970. Extracted from: *The State of Black America*, January 1990. Published by permission. *Notes:* 1. Includes Social Security or Rail Ret. Income, Public Assistance or Welfare Payments, Supplemental Secondary Income, Ret./ Annuities, Veteran Payments, Unemployment and Workman's Comp., Alimony, etc. 2. Assumes that black income recipients receive the same mean income as white income recipients in this category.

★ 586 ★
Individual Income: Characteristics and Trends

Persons 15 years old and over as of March 1988. In 1987 dollars.

Type of income	1987 Black	1987 White	1987 Ratio: Black to White	1982 Black	1982 White	1982 Ratio: Black to White	1979 Black	1979 White	1979 Ratio: Black to White
United States									
Median Income									
Persons	8,419	12,509	0.67	7,875	11,252	0.70	8,561	11,783	0.73
Standard error	140	67	[1]	127	68	[1]	171	63	[1]
Median Earnings of Persons									
Both sexes	11,501	15,092	0.76	10,557	13,286	0.79	11,531	14,723	0.78
Standard error	163	75	[1]	238	62	[1]	164	94	[1]
Male	12,910	20,624	0.63	12,368	18,772	0.66	14,223	21,344	0.67
Standard error									
Female	10,402	10,605	0.98	9,182		1.02	9,331	9,364	1.00

Continued.

Individual Income: Characteristics and Trends
[Continued]

	1987			1982			1979		
Type of income	Black	White	Ratio: Black to White	Black	White	Ratio: Black to White	Black	White	Ratio: Black to White
Standard error	219	76	[1]	189	72	[1]	250	86	[1]
Ratio: Female to male median earnings	0.81	0.51	[1]	0.74	0.48	[1]	0.66	0.44	[1]
Median Earnings of Year-Round, Full-Time Workers									
Both sexes	17,066	22,231	0.77	15,980	20,951	0.76	17,627	22,576	0.78
Standard error	176	94	[1]	255	111	[1]	213	110	[1]
Male	19,014	26,677	0.71	18,247	25,426	0.72	19,937	27,276	0.73
Standard error	455	131	[1]	308	117	[1]	424	111	[1]
Female	16,002	17,034	0.94	14,279	15,489	0.92	14,831	16,033	0.93
Standard error	213	86	[1]	178	111	[1]	282	86	[1]
Ratio: Female to male median earnings	0.84	0.64	[1]	0.78	0.61	[1]	0.74	0.59	[1]
South									
Persons	7,902	12,109	0.65	7,242	11,150	0.65	7,557	11,397	0.66
Standard error	158	93	[1]	159	117	[1]	208	111	[1]
North and West									
Persons	9,391	12,785	0.73	8,679	11,300	0.77	9,812	11,969	0.82
Standard error	264	89	[1]	198	81	[1]	290	80	[1]

Source: "Selected Income Characteristics of Persons, by Region, Sex, and Race: 1987, 1982, and 1979," *The Black Population in the United States: March 1988*, p. 14.
Primary source: Current Population Reports Series P-20, No. 442, *The Black Population in the United States: March 1988. Note:* 1. Not applicable.

★ 587 ★
Individuals in Poverty: Characteristics

Numbers in thousands. Unrelated individuals as of March 1989.

	Total			White			Black			Hispanic origin[1]		
		Below poverty level			Below poverty level			Below poverty level			Below poverty level	
Characteristic	Total	No.	% of total	Total	No.	% of total	Total	No.	% of total	Total	No.	% of total
Educational Attainment												
Total, 25 years or older	29,655	5,570	18.8	25,275	4,107	16.3	3,638	1,293	35.5	1,548	455	29.4
No years of school completed	288	140	48.8	210	93	44.2	58	34	[3]	86	49	56.6
Elementary:												
Less than 8 years	2,219	1,078	48.6	1,571	690	43.9	589	366	62.2	375	175	46.7
8 years	1,906	649	34.1	1,642	516	31.5	220	114	51.7	101	34	33.8
High school:												
1 to 3 years	3,646	1,163	31.9	2,970	829	27.9	619	307	49.7	214	85	39.4
4 years	9,542	1,542	16.2	8,241	1,169	14.2	1,140	340	29.8	364	65	17.9
College: 1 year or more	12,054	998	8.3	10,642	811	7.6	1,012	132	13.1	408	48	11.7
Percent a high school graduate	72.8	45.6	[2]	74.7	48.2	[2]	59.2	36.5	[2]	49.9	24.8	[2]

Continued.

Individuals in Poverty: Characteristics
[Continued]

Characteristic	Total	Below poverty level		White	Below poverty level		Black	Below poverty level		Hispanic origin[1]	Below poverty level	
	Total	No.	% of total	Total	No.	% of total	Total	No.	% of total	Total	No.	% of total
Employment Status												
Employed	20,750	2,183	10.5	17,815	1,720	9.7	2,322	368	15.8	1,247	237	19.0
Unemployed	1,126	455	40.4	869	302	34.7	223	140	63.1	116	49	41.7
Not in labor force	12,434	4,430	35.6	10,601	3,291	31.0	1,550	1,001	64.4	495	311	62.8
In Armed Forces	30	3	3	30	3	3	4	4	3	5	1	3
Type of Residence												
Nonfarm	34,045	7,023	20.6	29,023	5,268	18.2	4,093	1,509	36.9	1,842	593	32.2
Farm	295	48	16.3	291	47	16.2	3	4	3	21	4	3
Inside metropolitan												
areas	27,865	5,283	19.0	23,554	3,884	16.5	3,510	1,206	34.4	1,712	538	31.4
Inside central cities	13,825	3,070	22.2	10,777	2,030	18.8	2,545	901	35.4	1,059	379	35.8
In poverty areas	3,628	1,347	37.1	2,017	631	31.3	1,446	657	45.4	475	223	46.9
Outside central cities	14,040	2,213	15.8	12,777	1,854	14.5	964	305	31.7	653	159	24.3
In poverty areas	740	270	36.4	546	173	31.6	182	92	50.6	98	38	38.2
Outside metropolitan												
areas	6,475	1,788	27.6	5,761	1,432	24.9	586	303	51.7	152	59	39.1
In poverty areas	1,475	591	40.0	1,057	358	33.9	355	202	57.0	51	24	3

Source: "Selected Characteristics of Unrelated Individuals, by Race and Hispanic Origin and Poverty Status in 1988," *Money Income and Poverty Status in the United States: 1988,* 1989, pp. 76-77. Primary source: U.S. Bureau of the Census, Current Population Reports, Series P-60, No. 166. *Notes:* 1. Persons of Hispanic origin may be of any race. 2. Not applicable. 3. Base less than 75,000. 4. Represents zero or rounds to zero.

★ 588 ★
Individuals in Poverty: Characteristics and Trends

Numbers in thousands. Persons as of March of the following year.

Year and characteristic	Under 18 years						18 to 64 years			65 years and over		
	All persons			Related children in families								
	Total	Below poverty No.	%	Total	Below poverty No.	%	Total	Below poverty No.	%	Total	Below poverty No.	%
All Races												
1988	63,743	12,584	19.7	62,892	12,058	19.2	150,761	15,812	10.5	29,022	3,482	12.0
1987	63,290	12,963	20.5	62,411	12,391	19.9	149,201	15,814	10.6	28,487	3,564	12.5
1986	62,948	12,876	20.5	62,009	12,257	19.8	147,631	16,017	10.8	27,975	3,477	12.4
1985	62,876	13,010	20.7	62,019	12,483	20.1	146,396	16,598	11.3	27,322	3,456	12.6
White												
1988	51,202	7,483	14.6	50,582	7,140	14.1	128,030	10,687	8.3	26,001	2,595	10.0
1987	51,009	7,842	15.4	50,351	7,448	14.8	126,992	10,703	8.4	25,602	2,704	10.6
1986	51,111	8,209	16.1	50,356	7,714	15.3	125,998	11,285	9.0	25,173	2,689	10.7
1985	51,031	8,253	16.2	50,358	7,838	15.6	125,258	11,909	9.5	24,629	2,698	11.0
Black												
1988	9,864	4,364	44.2	9,677	4,213	43.5	17,548	4,278	24.4	2,436	785	32.2
1987	9,729	4,441	45.6	9,541	4,287	44.9	17,244	4,362	25.3	2,387	774	32.4
1986	9,629	4,148	43.1	9,467	4,037	42.7	16,911	4,113	24.3	2,331	722	31.0
1985	9,545	4,157	43.6	9,405	4,057	43.1	16,667	4,052	24.3	2,273	717	31.5
Hispanic Origin[2]												
1988	7,003	2,653	37.9	6,907	2,598	37.6	12,056	2,501	20.7	1,005	225	22.4
1987	6,792	2,690	39.6	6,691	2,626	39.2	11,718	2,509	21.4	885	243	27.5

Continued.

Individuals in Poverty: Characteristics and Trends
[Continued]

Year and characteristic	Under 18 years						18 to 64 years			65 years and over		
	All persons			Related children in families				Below poverty			Below poverty	
		Below poverty			Below poverty							
	Total	No.	%	Total	No.	%	Total	No.	%	Total	No.	%
1986	6,646	2,507	37.7	6,511	2,413	37.1	11,206	2,406	21.5	906	204	22.5
1985	6,475	2,606	40.3	6,346	2,512	39.6	10,685	2,411	22.6	915	219	23.9

Source: "Poverty Status of Persons, by Age, Race, and Hispanic Origin: 1959 to 1988," *Money Income and Poverty Status in the United States: 1988,* 1989, pp. 60-61. Primary source: U.S. Bureau of the Census, Current Population Reports, Series P-60, No. 166. *Notes:* 1. Not available 2. Persons of Hispanic origin may be of any race.

★ 589 ★
Median Income in Selected States: Trends

State	1950	1960	1970	1980
Median Income White Males				
Alabama	1,809	3,367	5,688	11,610
Arkansas	1,423	2,486	4,510	9,742
Florida	2,239	3,743	5,878	11,356
Georgia	1,870	3,374	6,003	11,886
Louisiana	2,228	4,001	6,327	13,724
Mississippi	1,462	2,757	5,060	10,806
N. Carolina	1,872	3,035	5,295	10,681
S. Carolina	2,043	3,195	5,625	11,483
Tennessee	1,685	2,932	5,184	10,708
Texas	2,272	3,728	6,031	13,149
Virginia	2,255	3,734	6,339	12,786
Median Income Black Males				
Alabama	956	1,417	2,793	6,118
Arkansas	759	993	2,184	5,545
Florida	1,185	2,073	3,440	6,995
Georgia	919	1,489	3,116	6,771
Louisiana	997	1,565	2,866	6,815
Mississippi	605	890	2,034	5,251
N. Carolina	999	1,286	2,968	6,550
S. Carolina	801	1,135	3,013	6,549
Tennessee	1,142	1,598	3,173	6,670
Texas	1,203	1,917	3,597	8,118
Virginia	1,221	1,906	3,626	7,608
Median Income White Females				
Alabama	843	1,168	2,147	4,851
Arkansas	506	898	1,850	4,426
Florida	959	1,308	2,240	5,323
Georgia	986	1,438	2,612	5,633
Louisiana	920	1,245	2,071	5,099
Mississippi	775	1,120	2,124	4,829
N. Carolina	1,052	1,445	2,652	5,547
S. Carolina	1,172	1,523	2,764	5,578
Tennessee	859	1,182	2,229	4,968
Texas	860	1,170	2,112	5,464
Virginia	1,171	1,499	2,674	5,872

Continued.

Median Income in Selected States: Trends
[Continued]

State	1950	1960	1970	1980
Median Income Black Females				
Alabama	380	592	1,257	3,212
Arkansas	342	456	1,189	2,936
Florida	522	844	1,637	4,097
Georgia	389	660	1,465	3,903
Louisiana	512	744	1,352	3,302
Mississippi	330	412	932	3,126
N. Carolina	421	517	1,455	3,997
S. Carolina	363	462	1,256	3,731
Tennessee	470	674	1,593	3,749
Texas	460	750	1,618	4,440
Virginia	530	737	1,703	4,404

Source: Untitled Table, Unpublished Manuscript of the Southern Regional Council, (undated and unpaged). Primary source: Unpublished manuscript of the Southern Regional Council. Published by permission. Published by permission.

★ 590 ★
Men Without Earnings: Trends

Age	1939		1949		1959		1969		1979		1984	
	Black	White	Black	White	Black	White	Black	White	Black	White	Black	White
20-24	32	27	20	16	14	8	16	8	23	7	28	9
25-54	28	25	11	7	8	5	8	4	16	5	16	5
55-64	46	43	19	16	20	14	22	1	35	22	42	26
65+	72	74	55	9	63	61	68	65	78	71	81	78

Source: "Men With No Earnings (in percent), by Age and Race, 1939-1984," A Common Destiny: Blacks and American Society, 1989, p. 311. Primary source: Data from decennial censuses and Curent Population Surveys. Published by permission.

★ 591 ★
Parents of College Students: Income

Estimated parental income	All Institutions	Predominantly Black Colleges	Predominantly Black Colleges	
			Public	Private
Less than $6,000	3.0	8.8	9.1	8.2
$6,000-$9,999	2.8	7.5	7.7	7.0
$10,000-$14,999	4.8	8.8	8.7	9.0
$15,000-$19,999	5.3	8.5	8.6	8.7
$20,000-$24,999	7.0	10.5	11.2	9.4
$25,000-$29,999	7.0	8.7	8.7	8.7
$30,000-$34,999	9.3	8.4	8.1	8.8
$35,000-$39,999	9.0	7.5	7.7	7.2
$40,000-$49,999	12.8	9.4	9.6	9.0
$50,000-$59,999	11.8	7.7	7.2	8.3
$60,000-$74,999	10.8	7.6	7.1	8.4

Continued.

Parents of College Students: Income
[Continued]

Estimated parental income	All Institutions	Predominantly Black Colleges	Predominantly Black Colleges Public	Predominantly Black Colleges Private
$75,000-$99,999	7.2	3.9	3.7	4.2
$100,000-$149,999	4.8	1.6	1.4	1.9
$150,000 or more	4.5	1.1	0.9	1.5

Source: "Estimated Parental Income," *The American Freshman: National Norms for Fall 1989*, p. 44. Primary source: Cooperative Institutional Research Program, American Council on Education, University of California, Los Angeles, 1989. Figures for predominantly Black colleges includes all ethnic groups. Published by permission.

★ 592 ★
Poverty and the Elderly

Numbers in percent.

Group	Poverty Rate
Minorities:	
Blacks	31.5
Hispanics	23.9
Sex:	
Women	15.6
Black Women	34.8
Black Women living alone	54.5

Source: "Exceptionally High Poverty Rates among Elderly Groups in 1985," *On the Other Side of Easy Street*, 1987, p. 16. Primary source: The Villers Foundation, *On the Other Side of Easy Street: Myths and Facts about the Economics of Old Age*. Washington, DC, 1987. Name changed to Families USA Foundation. Published by permission.

★ 593 ★
Poverty and Workers' Years of School Completed

Numbers in thousands.

Years of school completed and race	Total	Men	Women	Below poverty level Total	Below poverty level Men	Below poverty level Women	At or above the poverty level Total	At or above the poverty level Men	At or above the poverty level Women
Total, 16 years and over	113,489	63,368	50,121	6,400	3,346	3,054	107,089	60,022	47,067
Less than 4 years of high school	18,516	11,616	6,900	2,466	1,453	1,013	16,051	10,163	5,888
8 years or less of high school	6,245	4,232	2,013	1,027	673	355	5,218	3,559	1,658
1 to 3 years of high school	12,271	7,384	4,888	1,438	780	658	10,833	6,604	4,229
4 years of high school only	45,979	24,226	21,750	2,620	1,196	1,424	43,355	23,030	20,325
1 to 3 years of college	23,083	11,954	11,128	867	413	454	22,215	11,541	10,674
4 years of college only	15,265	8,806	6,459	292	162	130	14,973	8,644	6,329
5 years of college or more	10,650	6,766	3,884	155	122	33	10,495	6,644	3,851
Median years of school completed	12.8	12.8	12.8	12.3	12.2	12.4	12.9	12.9	12.9
White 16 years and over	98,296	55,561	42,734	4,647	2,608	2,039	93,649	52,953	40,696
Less than 4 years of high school	15,276	9,791	5,485	1,787	1,141	646	13,489	8,649	4,480
8 years or less of high school	5,137	3,576	1,561	800	556	244	4,337	3,020	1,317
1 to 3 years of high school	10,139	6,214	3,924	987	585	402	9,152	5,629	3,522

Continued.

Poverty and Workers' Years of School Completed
[Continued]

Years of school completed and race	Total	Men	Women	Below poverty level			At or above the poverty level		
				Total	Men	Women	Total	Men	Women
4 years of high school only	39,297	21,213	18,714	1,872	927	945	38,055	20,286	17,769
1 to 3 years of college	20,039	10,489	9,551	642	316	326	19,397	10,173	9,224
4 years of college only	13,496	7,933	5,564	228	129	99	13,268	7,803	5,465
5 years of college or more	9,557	6,136	3,421	118	95	22	9,439	6,041	3,398
Median years of school completed	12.8	12.8	12.8	12.3	12.2	12.4	12.9	12.9	12.9
Black, 16 years and over	11,836	5,917	5,918	1,567	622	945	10,269	5,295	4,973
Less than 4 years of high school	2,789	1,578	1,211	622	274	348	2,167	1,304	863
8 years or less of high school	898	546	352	203	98	105	694	447	247
1 to 3 years of high school	1,891	1,033	859	418	176	243	1,473	857	616
4 years of high school only	5,128	2,520	2,608	706	242	464	4,422	2,278	2,144
1 to 3 years of college	2,323	1,095	1,228	186	81	105	2,138	1,014	1,124
4 years of college only	1,024	441	583	42	17	25	982	424	558
5 years of college or more	571	283	288	11	8	3	560	275	285
Median years of school completed	12.6	12.5	12.7	12.2	12.2	12.3	12.7	12.6	12.8

Source: "Poverty Status of Persons in the Labor Force 27 Weeks or More by Years of School Completed, Race, and Sex, 1987," *A Profile of the Working Poor,* December 1989, p. 20. Primary source: U.S. Department of Labor, Bureau of Labor Statistics.

★ 594 ★
Poverty in Relation to Educational Attainment

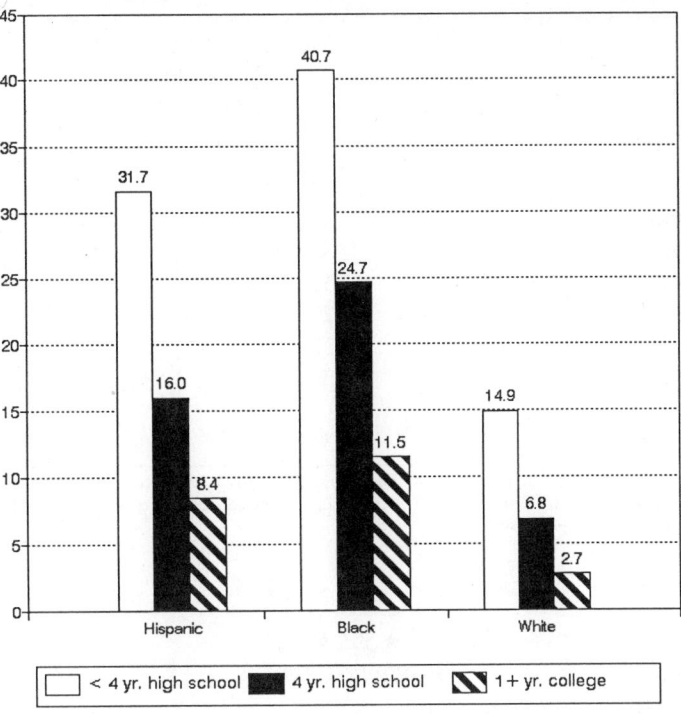

Race	Less than 4 years high school	Four years high school	1 or more years college
Hispanic	31.7	16.0	8.4
Black	40.7	24.7	11.5
White	14.9	6.8	2.7

Source: "Household Poverty Rate by Educational Attainment of Householder, 1988," *Black Issues in Higher Education*, January 18, 1990, p. 13. Primary source: The Decade of the Hispanic: A Sobering Economic Retrospective.

★ 595 ★
Poverty in the Big Cities

Metropolitan Area	Average Percentage of Population Poor in Census Tract of Typical Poor Person	
	Black	White
New York	36	20
Chicago	35	12
Los Angeles	29	16
Detroit	31	11
Philadelphia	37	12
Washington, D.C.	23	8
Baltimore	34	11
Houston	29	10

Continued.

Poverty in the Big Cities
[Continued]

Metropolitan Area	Average Percentage of Population Poor in Census Tract of Typical Poor Person	
	Black	White
Atlanta	32	10
Dallas	33	11
Newark	35	13
San Francisco	29	12
St. Louis	32	10
New Orleans	38	11
Average	32	12

Source: "Concentration of Poverty in Major Metropolitan Areas by Race, 1980," *A Common Destiny: Blacks And American Society,* 1989, p. 287. Primary source: Data from 1980 decennial census. Published by permission.

★ 596 ★
Poverty Level

Persons as of March 1988. Based on Current Population Survey.

Age and Region	Number Below Poverty Level (1,000)				Percent Below Poverty Level			
	All races[1]	White	Black	Hispanic[2]	All races[1]	White	Black	Hispanic[2]
Total	32,546	21,409	9,683	5,470	13.5	10.5	33.1	28.2
Under 16 years old	11,859	7,289	4,007	2,493	21.2	16.2	46.7	40.6
16-21 years old	3,455	2,148	1,144	565	15.9	12.1	36.0	27.5
22-44 years old	9,596	6,470	2,647	1,628	10.7	8.5	25.1	21.2
45-64 years old	4,145	2,905	1,077	536	9.1	7.4	23.5	20.4
65 years old and over	3,491	2,597	808	247	12.2	10.1	33.9	27.4
Northeast	5,476	3,860	1,391	1,232	11.0	8.9	28.8	36.6
Midwest	7,499	5,185	2,041	366	12.7	9.9	36.6	27.5
South	13,287	7,426	5,648	1,910	16.1	11.5	34.5	31.0
West	6,285	4,939	603	1,962	12.6	11.5	24.3	23.0

Source: "Persons Below Poverty, by Race, Hispanic Origin, Age, and Region: 1987," *Statistical Abstract,* 1989, p. 454. Primary source: U.S. Bureau of the Census, *Current Population Reports,* series P-60, No. 161. *Notes:* 1. Includes other races not shown separately. 2. Hispanic persons may be of any race.

★ 597 ★
Poverty Level

Persons as of March 1988.

| Characteristic | Number (1,000) | | | | | Percent Below Poverty Level | | | | |
| | | Market value | | Recipient value | | | Market Value | | Recipient value | |
	Current poverty definition	Valuing food and housing	Valuing food, housing, and medical benefits excluding institutional expenditures	Valuing food and housing	Valuing food housing, and medical benefits excluding institutional expenditures	Current poverty definition	Valuing food and housing	Valuing food, housing, and medical benefits excluding institutional expenditures	Valuing food and housing	Valuing food housing and medical benefits, excluding institutional expenditures
All persons	32,546	29,004	20,440	29,821	26,575	13.5	12.0	8.5	12.4	11.0
White	21,409	19,336	14,086	19,757	17,664	10.5	9.5	6.9	9.7	8.7
Black	9,683	8,349	5,475	8,713	7,768	33.1	28.5	18.7	29.8	26.5
Hispanic[1]	5,470	4,904	3,565	4,974	4,620	28.2	25.3	18.4	25.6	23.8

Source: "Persons Below Poverty Level and Poverty Rate, by Selected Characteristics, Using Alternative Methods of Valuing Noncash Benefits: 1987," *Statistical Abstract*, 1989, p. 457. Primary source: U.S. Bureau of the Census, *Estimates of Poverty Including the Value of Noncash Benefits: 1987*, Technical Paper 58. *Note:* 1. Hispanic persons may be of any race.

★ 598 ★
Poverty Rates

All persons	13.1
Race and Hispanic origin:	
White	10.1
Black	31.6
Other races	20.0
Hispanic origin[1]	26.8

Source: "Poverty Rates for Persons with Selected Characteristics: 1988," *Money Income and Poverty Status in the United States: 1988*, 1989, p. 6. Primary source: U.S. Bureau of the Census, Current Population Reports, Series P-60, No. 166. *Note:* 1. Persons of Hispanic origin may be of any race.

★ 599 ★
Poverty Rates: Trends

Year	Black	White	B/W
All Persons			
1988	31.6	10.1	3.13
1987	33.1	10.5	3.15
1986	31.1	11.0	2.83
1982	35.6	12.0	2.97
1980	32.5	11.4	2.85
1978	30.6	8.7	3.52
1970	33.5	9.9	3.38
Related Children under 18			
1988	44.1	14.1	3.06
1987	45.1	15.0	3.01

Continued.

Poverty Rates: Trends
[Continued]

Year	Black	White	B/W
1986	42.7	15.3	2.79
1982	47.3	16.5	2.87
1978	41.2	11.0	3.75
1970	41.5	10.5	3.95
Female-Headed Families			
1988	49.0	26.5	1.85
1987	53.8	26.4	2.04
1986	52.9	27.9	1.90
1982	57.4	28.7	2.00
1970	58.8	31.4	1.87

Source: "Poverty Rates for Selected Years (Percent of Population), The State of Black America 1990, January 1990, p. 34. Primary source: U.S. Department of Commerce, Bureau of the Census, *Money Income and Poverty Status in 1987*, Table 17.

★ 600 ★
Poverty Status: Trends

	Number below the poverty level, in thousands						Percent below the poverty level					
		In all families			In families with female householder, no husband present			In all families			In families with female householder, no husband present	
Year and race/ ethnicity	All persons	Total	House- holder	Related children under 18	Total	Related children under 18	All persons	Total	House- holder	Related children under 18	Total	Related children under 18
All races												
1959	39,490	34,562	8,320	17,208	7,014	4,145	22.4	20.8	18.5	26.9	49.4	72.2
1960	39,851	34,925	8,243	17,288	7,247	4,095	22.2	20.7	18.1	26.5	48.9	68.4
1965	33,185	28,358	6,721	14,388	7,524	4,562	17.3	15.8	13.9	20.7	46.0	64.2
1966	28,510	23,809	5,784	12,146	6,861	4,262	14.7	13.1	11.8	17.4	39.8	58.2
1970	25,420	20,330	5,260	10,235	7,503	4,689	12.6	10.9	10.1	14.9	38.1	53.0
1971	25,559	20,405	5,303	10,344	7,797	4,850	12.5	10.8	10.0	15.1	38.7	53.1
1972	24,460	19,577	5,075	10,082	8,114	5,094	11.9	10.3	9.3	14.9	38.2	53.1
1973	22,973	18,299	4,828	9,453	8,178	5,171	11.1	9.7	8.8	14.2	37.5	52.1
1974	23,370	18,817	4,922	9,967	8,462	5,361	11.2	9.9	8.8	15.1	36.5	51.5
1975	25,877	20,789	5,450	10,882	8,846	5,597	12.3	10.9	9.7	16.8	37.5	52.7
1976	24,975	19,632	5,311	10,081	9,029	5,583	11.8	10.3	9.4	15.8	37.3	52.0
1977	24,720	19,505	5,311	10,028	9,205	5,658	11.6	10.2	9.3	16.0	36.2	50.3
1978	24,497	19,062	5,280	9,722	9,269	5,687	11.4	10.0	9.1	15.7	35.6	50.6
1979	26,072	19,964	5,461	9,993	9,400	5,635	11.7	10.2	9.2	16.0	34.9	48.6
1980	29,272	22,601	6,217	11,114	10,120	5,866	13.0	11.5	10.3	17.9	36.7	50.8
1981	31,822	24,850	6,851	12,068	11,051	6,305	14.1	12.5	11.2	19.5	38.7	52.3
1982	34,398	27,349	7,512	13,139	11,701	6,696	15.0	13.6	12.2	21.3	40.6	56.0
1983	35,303	27,933	7,647	13,427	12,072	6,747	15.2	13.9	12.3	21.8	40.2	55.4
1984	33,700	26,458	7,277	12,929	11,831	6,772	14.4	13.1	11.6	21.0	38.4	54.0
1985	33,064	25,729	7,223	12,483	11,600	6,716	14.0	12.6	11.4	20.1	37.6	53.6
1986	32,370	24,754	7,023	12,257	11,944	6,943	13.6	12.0	10.9	19.8	34.2	54.4
1987	32,546	24,979	7,059	12,435	12,076	7,074	13.5	12.1	10.8	20.0	33.6	54.7
White[1]												
1960	28,309	24,262	6,115	11,229	4,296	2,357	17.8	16.2	14.9	20.0	39.0	59.9
1965	22,496	18,508	4,824	8,595	4,092	2,321	13.3	11.7	11.1	14.4	35.4	52.9
1970	17,484	13,323	3,708	6,138	3,761	2,247	9.9	8.1	8.0	10.5	28.4	43.1
1975	17,770	13,799	3,838	6,748	4,577	2,813	9.7	8.3	7.7	12.5	29.4	44.2
1980	19,699	14,587	4,195	6,817	4,940	2,813	10.2	8.6	8.0	13.4	28.0	41.6
1981	21,553	16,127	4,670	7,429	5,600	3,120	11.1	9.5	8.8	14.7	29.8	42.8

Continued.

Poverty Status: Trends
[Continued]

Year and race/ ethnicity	Number below the poverty level, in thousands						Percent below the poverty level					
		In all families			In families with female householder, no husband present			In all families			In families with female householder, no husband present	
	All persons	Total	House-holder	Related children under 18	Total	Related children under 18	All persons	Total	House-holder	Related children under 18	Total	Related children under 18
1982	23,517	18,015	5,118	8,282	5,686	3,249	12.0	10.6	9.6	16.5	30.9	46.5
1983	23,984	18,377	5,220	8,534	6,017	3,388	12.1	10.7	9.7	17.0	31.2	47.1
1984	22,955	17,299	4,925	8,086	5,866	3,377	11.5	10.1	9.1	16.1	29.7	45.9
1985	22,860	17,125	4,983	7,838	5,990	3,372	11.4	9.9	9.1	15.6	69.8	45.2
1986	22,183	16,393	4,811	7,714	6,171	3,522	11.0	9.4	8.6	15.3	30.6	46.3
1987	21,409	15,804	4,592	7,550	5,918	3,474	10.5	9.1	8.2	15.0	29.5	45.8
Black[1]												
1959	9,927	9,112	1,860	5,022	2,416	1,475	55.1	54.9	48.1	65.5	70.6	81.6
1966	8,867	8,090	1,620	4,774	3,160	2,107	41.8	40.9	35.5	50.6	65.3	76.6
1970	7,548	6,683	1,481	3,922	3,656	2,383	33.5	32.2	29.5	41.5	58.7	67.7
1975	7,545	6,533	1,513	3,884	4,168	2,724	31.3	30.1	27.1	41.4	54.3	66.0
1980	8,579	7,190	1,826	3,906	4,984	2,944	32.5	31.1	28.9	42.1	53.4	64.8
1981	9,173	7,780	1,972	4,170	5,222	3,051	34.2	33.2	30.8	44.9	56.7	67.7
1982	9,697	8,355	2,158	4,388	5,698	3,269	35.6	34.9	33.0	47.3	58.8	70.7
1983	9,882	8,376	2,161	4,273	5,736	3,187	35.7	34.7	32.3	46.2	57.0	68.3
1984	9,490	8,104	2,094	4,320	5,666	3,234	33.8	33.2	30.9	46.2	54.6	66.2
1985	8,926	7,504	1,983	4,057	5,342	3,181	31.3	30.5	28.7	43.1	53.2	66.9
1986	8,983	7,401	1,987	4,039	5,473	3,251	31.1	29.7	28.0	42.7	53.8	67.1
1987	9,683	7,952	2,149	4,297	5,797	3,394	33.1	31.8	29.9	45.1	54.8	68.3
Hispanic origin[2]												
1975	2,991	2,755	627	1,619	1,053	694	26.9	26.3	25.1	33.1	57.2	68.4
1980	3,491	3,143	751	1,718	1,319	809	25.7	25.1	23.2	33.0	54.5	65.0
1981	3,713	3,349	792	1,874	1,465	909	26.5	25.9	24.0	35.4	55.9	67.3
1982	4,301	3,865	916	2,117	1,601	990	29.9	29.2	27.2	38.9	60.1	71.8
1983	4,633	4,113	981	2,251	1,670	1,018	28.0	27.3	25.9	37.7	55.1	70.6
1984	4,806	4,192	991	2,317	1,764	1,093	28.4	27.4	25.2	38.7	56.2	71.0
1985	5,236	4,605	1,074	2,512	1,983	1,247	29.0	28.3	25.5	39.6	55.7	72.4
1986	5,117	4,469	1,085	2,413	1,921	1,194	27.3	26.5	24.7	37.1	52.9	66.7
1987	5,470	4,793	1,183	2,631	1,987	1,241	28.2	27.7	25.8	39.3	55.0	70.1

Source: "Poverty Status of Persons, Families, and Children Under 18 by Race/Ethnicity: 1959 to 1987," *Digest of Educational Statistics*, 1989, p. 25. Primary source: U.S. Department of Commerce, Bureau of the Census, *Current Population Reports*, Series P-60, No. 161. (This table was prepared October 1988.) *Notes:* 1. Includes persons of Hispanic origin. 2. Persons of Hispanic origin may be of any race.

★ 601 ★
Regional Household & Family Income: Trends

Households and families as of March 1988. In 1987 dollars.

Type of Income	1987			1982			1979		
	Black	White	Ratio: Black to White	Black	White	Ratio: Black to White	Black	White	Ratio: Black to White
United States									
Median Income by Type of Family									
Married-couple families	27,182	35,295	0.77 [1]	24,230	31,123	0.78 [1]	26,296	34,048	0.77 [1]
Standard error	701	163		421	140		504	146	
Female householder, no husband present	9,710	17,018	0.57 [1]	8,778	15,885	0.55 [1]	10,745	17,983	0.60 [1]
Standard error	300	300		266	291		291	268	
Male householder, no wife									

Continued.

Regional Household & Family Income: Trends
[Continued]

Type of Income	1987			1982			1979		
	Black	White	Ratio: Black to White	Black	White	Ratio: Black to White	Black	White	Ratio: Black to White
present	17,455	26,230	0.67	17,256	25,207	0.68	19,431	27,642	0.70
Standard error	1,242	562	1	1,153	706	1	1,460	884	1
South									
Median Income by Type of Family									
Married-couple families	25,293	33,390	0.76	22,870	29,303	0.78	23,579	31,442	0.75
Standard error	755	370	1	704	260	1	679	260	1
Female householder, no husband									
present	9,431	16,395	0.58	8,739	15,255	0.57	10,037	17,450	0.58
Standard error	414	576	1	339	431	1	449	454	1
Male householder, no wife									
present	15,002	23,058	0.65	15,882	24,755	0.64	18,691	23,784	0.79
Standard error	1,609	1,518	1	1,843	1,141	1	2,244	1,622	1
North and West									
Median Income by Type of Family									
Married-couple families	30,138	36,086	0.84	25,670	31,946	0.80	30,193	35,293	0.86
Standard error	836	193	1	587	164	1	941	193	1
Female householder, no husband									
present	10,001	17,282	0.58	8,816	16,253	0.54	11,333	18,098	0.63
Standard error	462	353	1	395	377	1	380	329	1
Male householder, no wife									
present	19,129	26,887	0.71	19,769	25,426	0.78	20,327	29,358	0.69
Standard error	1,212	549	1	3,018	869	1	2,215	1,072	1

Source: "Selected Income Characteristics of Households and Families, by Region, Sex, and Race: 1987, 1982, and 1979," *The Black Population in the United States: March 1988*, p. 12. Primary source: Current Population Reports, Series P-20, No. 442, *The Black Population in the United States: March 1988. Note:* 1. Not applicable.

★ 602 ★
Regional Money Income at Age 15 and Over

Numbers in thousands. Persons as of March 1988.

Total money income and region	All persons						Year-round, full-time workers					
	Black			White			Black			White		
	Both sexes	Male	Female	Both sexes	Male	Female	Both sexes	Male	Female	Both sexes	Male	Female
United States												
Total	21,221	9,603	11,618	161,341	77,823	83,518	7,641	3,972	3,668	67,085	41,809	25,276
Total with income	18,415	8,341	10,074	151,350	74,688	76,662	7,641	3,972	3,668	67,023	41,788	25,235
Median income (dollars)	8,419	11,101	6,796	12,509	18,854	8,279	17,300	19,385	16,211	23,040	27,468	17,775
Standard error (dollars)	140	219	142	67	129	57	178	459	219	103	142	126
Mean income (dollars)	11,945	14,391	9,919	17,553	23,643	11,621	19,844	21,951	17,563	27,655	32,148	20,216
Standard error (dollars)	134	233	143	72	123	65	226	365	242	125	178	123
South												
Total	11,723	5,253	6,469	51,758	24,968	26,790	4,313	2,259	2,055	21,616	13,192	8,424
Total with income	10,180	4,608	5,572	47,920	23,783	24,137	4,313	2,259	2,055	21,600	13,189	8,411
Median income (dollars)	7,902	10,486	6,056	12,109	17,564	8,300	15,987	17,162	14,925	21,658	26,284	6,741
Standard error (dollars)	158	253	208	93	217	104	226	350	333	162	241	168
Mean income (dollars)	11,064	13,304	9,212	17,013	22,766	11,345	18,296	19,971	16,456	26,388	31,048	19,080
Standard error (dollars)	151	254	172	126	215	110	251	386	302	214	311	204
North and West												
Total	9,498	4,349	5,149	109,583	52,855	56,728	3,327	1,714	1,614	45,468	28,617	16,851

Continued.

Regional Money Income at Age 15 and Over
[Continued]

Total money income and region	All persons						Year-round, full-time workers					
	Black			White			Black			White		
	Both sexes	Male	Female	Both sexes	Male	Female	Both sexes	Male	Female	Both sexes	Male	Female
Total with income	8,236	3,733	4,502	103,430	50,906	52,524	3,327	1,714	1,614	45,423	28,599	16,824
Median income (dollars)	9,391	12,028	7,499	12,785	19,429	8,269	19,402	22,171	17,585	23,753	28,019	18,421
Standard error (dollars)	264	324	217	89	147	65	310	511	295	127	168	149
Mean income (dollars)	13,033	15,733	10,794	17,803	24,052	11,747	21,850	24,561	18,972	28,258	32,655	20,785
Standard error (dollars)	194	348	195	85	143	77	332	559	314	147	208	147

Source: "Total Money Income in 1987 of Persons 15 Years Old and Over, by Sex, Region, and Race: March 1988," *The Black Population in the United States: March 1988*, pp. 28-29. Primary source: Current Population Reports, Series P-20, No. 442, *The Black Population in the United States: March 1988*. Represents zero or rounds to zero.

★ 603 ★
Regional Poverty Rates: Trends

Region and year	Northeast			Midwest			South			West		
	Black	White	Blk/ Wht	Black	White	Blk/ Wht	Black	White	Blk/ Wht	Black	White	Blk/ Wht
1988	22.9	8.4	2.7	34.8	8.7	4.0	34.3	11.6	3.0	23.6	11.3	2.1
1987	28.8	8.9	3.2	36.6	9.9	3.7	34.5	11.5	3.0	24.3	11.5	2.1
1986	24.0	8.9	2.7	34.5	10.6	3.3	33.6	11.8	2.8	21.7	12.3	1.8
1984	32.2	10.7	3.0	37.9	11.5	3.3	33.6	12.0	2.8	26.6	11.8	2.3
1980	30.7	8.9	3.4	33.3	8.9	3.7	35.1	12.2	2.9	19.0	10.4	1.8
1978	29.1	8.2	3.5	24.8	7.4	3.4	34.1	10.2	3.3	26.1	8.9	2.9
1970	20.0	7.7	2.6	25.7	8.9	2.9	42.6	12.4	3.4	20.4	10.6	1.9

Source: "Poverty Rates for Regions: Selected Years," The State of Black America 1990, January 1990, p. 36. Primary source: U.S. Department of Commerce, Bureau of the Census, *Money Income and Poverty Status...: 1987, 1988*, and Bureau of the Census, Current Population Reports Series P-60, *Characteristics of the Population Below Poverty Level*, 1984, 1978, 1970. Extracted from: *The State of Black America*, January 1990. Published by permission.

★ 604 ★
Residence and Poverty

For Blacks, poverty population = 8,953,000; for Whites, poverty population = 22,183,000. Numbers in percent.

Characteristics	Blacks	Whites
Central-City Poverty Area	42.8[1]	14.7[1]
Other Central-City Area	14.4	19.3
Suburban Poverty Area	7.7	4.7
Other Suburban Area	10.1	29.2
Nonmetropolitan Area	25.0	32.1

Source: "Poverty Distribution, by Race and Place of Residence, 1986," *A Common Destiny: Blacks And American Society*, 1989, p. 286. Primary source: Data from Current Population Surveys. *Note:* 1. Census tracts in which the poverty rate is 20 percent or higher. Published by permission.

★ 605 ★
Sources of Family Wealth

Instrument	Percentage	Mean Value of Assets (Dol.)
Automobiles	91	4,275
Savings Account	70	1,143
Home Ownership	59	32,146
Real Estate	11	2,288
IRA & Keogh	11	2,288
Stocks & Mutual Funds	9	3,157
Business Ownership	4	6,578
Money Market Funds/Bonds	3	953

Source: "Sources of Wealth among African-American Families," *Black Issues in Higher Education,* February 1, 1990, p. 27. Primary source: U.S. Bureau of the Census. .

★ 606 ★
The Economically Vulnerable Elderly

Characteristic	All Aged Blacks	Unrelated Aged Blacks Living Alone or With Nonrelatives	
		Males	Females
Poor	31.5	40.6	55.4
Economically Vulnerable	39.5	41.8	32.5
Poor and Economically Vulnerable	71.0	82.4	87.9

Source: "Poverty & Economic Vulnerability among Elderly Blacks," *On the Other Side of Easy Street,* 1987, p. 25. Primary source: The Villers Foundation, *On the Other Side of Easy Street: Myths and Facts about the Economics of Old Age.* Washington, DC, 1987. Name changed to Families USA Foundation. Published by permission.

★ 607 ★
The Poor: With Whom Do They Live?

For Blacks, poverty population = 7,680,000; for Whites, poverty population = 8,926,000. Numbers in percent.

	Blacks	Whites
Under 18		
Husband-wife family	8.1	10.0
Female-headed family	9.6	34.6
Other living arrangements	1.0	2.3
18 to 64		
Husband-wife family	29.9	11.1
Female-headed family	22.3	25.8
Other living arrangements	11.9	8.8

Continued.

The Poor: With Whom Do They Live?
[Continued]

	Blacks	Whites
65 and over	17.2	7.4

Source: "Poverty Distribution, by Race, Age, and Living Arrangements, 1970 and 1985," *A Common Destiny: Blacks And American Society*, 1989, p. 284. Primary source: Data from decennial census and 1985 Current Population Survey. Published by permission.

★ 608 ★
Trends in Individuals' Poverty Status

Numbers in thousands. Persons as of March of the following year.

	All persons			Persons in families						Unrelated individuals		
				All families			Families with female householder, no husband present					
		Below poverty level			Below poverty level			Below poverty level			Below poverty level	
Year and characteristic	Total	No.	%	Total	No.	%	Total	No.	%	Total	No.	%
All Races												
1988	243,526	31,878	13.1	208,042	24,173	11.6	32,372	12,103	37.4	34,340	7,071	20.6
1987	240,978	32,341	13.4	206,866	24,840	12.0	32,098	12,278	38.3	32,992	6,857	20.8
1986	238,554	32,370	13.6	205,459	24,754	12.0	31,152	11,944	38.3	31,679	6,846	21.6
1985	236,594	33,064	14.0	203,963	25,729	12.6	30,878	11,600	37.6	31,351	6,725	21.5
White												
1988	205,233	20,765	10.1	175,103	15,045	8.6	20,494	6,005	29.3	29,315	5,316	18.1
1987	203,603	21,249	10.4	174,479	15,643	8.9	20,344	6,041	29.7	28,290	5,174	18.3
1986	202,282	22,183	11.0	174,024	16,393	9.4	20,163	6,171	30.6	27,143	5,198	19.2
1985	200,918	22,860	11.4	172,863	17,125	9.9	20,105	5,990	29.8	27,067	5,299	19.6
Black												
1988	29,847	9,426	31.6	25,479	7,718	30.3	10,893	5,672	52.1	4,095	1,509	36.8
1987	29,360	9,577	32.6	25,123	7,901	31.4	10,797	5,862	54.3	3,977	1,471	37.0
1986	28,871	8,983	31.1	24,910	7,410	29.7	10,175	5,473	53.8	3,714	1,431	38.5
1985	28,485	8,926	31.3	24,620	7,504	30.5	10,041	5,342	53.2	3,641	1,264	34.7
Hispanic Origin[2]												
1988	20,064	5,379	26.8	18,101	4,721	26.1	3,762	2,074	55.1	1,864	597	32.0
1987	19,395	5,442	28.1	17,341	4,781	27.6	3,698	2,060	55.7	1,933	598	31.0
1986	18,758	5,117	27.3	16,880	4,469	26.5	3,631	1,921	52.9	1,685	553	32.8
1985	18,075	5,236	29.0	16,276	4,605	28.3	3,561	1,983	55.7	1,602	532	33.2

Source: "Poverty Status of Persons, by Family Relationship, Race, and Hispanic Origin: 1959 to 1988," *Money Income and Poverty Status in the United States: 1988*, 1989, p. 58-59. Primary source: U.S. Bureau of the Census, Current Population Reports, Series P-60, No. 166. *Notes:* Prior to 1979 persons in unrelated subfamilies were included in persons in families. Beginning in 1979 persons in unrelated subfamilies are included in all persons but are excluded from persons in families. 1. Not available 2. Persons of Hispanic origin may be of any race.

★ 609 ★
Type of Income and Percent of Recipients: Trends

| | 1987 | | | 1980 | | | 1970 | | |
Characteristic	Blk	Wht	Blk/ Wht	Blk	Wht	Blk/ Wht	Blk	Wht	Blk/ Wht
Wage or Salary	61.0	64.5	.74	59.2	63.3	.73	62.0	59.8	.75
Nonfarm Self-employment	2.0	6.5	.55	1.9	5.8	.74	2.3	5.5	.62
Farm Self-employment	.1	1.1	[1]	.2	1.2	.19	.7	2.3	.30
Property Income - All	24.1	61.6	.33	22.3	61.1	.33	5.3	24.3	.48
Interest Income	22.9	59.9	.33	[1]	[1]	[1]	[1]	[1]	[1]
Transfer and All Other	37.5	34.0	.70	39.1	34.0	.77	[1]	[1]	[1]

Continued.

Type of Income and Percent of Recipients: Trends
[Continued]

Characteristic	1987			1980			1970		
	Blk	Wht	Blk/Wht	Blk	Wht	Blk/Wht	Blk	Wht	Blk/Wht
Social Security or RR Retirement	15.8	18.9	.82	16.0	18.3	.81	10.9	13.6	.91
Public Asst & Supplemental	13.2	3.0	1.00	14.3	3.3	1.12	[1]	[1]	[1]
Public Asst & Welfare	8.5	1.6	.97	[1]	[1]	[1]	11.2	2.4	1.23
Supplemental	5.2	1.5	1.02	[1]	[1]	[1]	[1]	[1]	[1]
Retirement & Annuities	4.5	8.7	.80	3.3	6.8	.87	[1]	[1]	[1]

Source: "Percent with Income, Specified Type, and Ratio of Black/White Means," *The State of Black America 1990*, January 1990, p. 38. Primary source: U.S. Department of Commerce, Bureau of the Census, *Money Income of Households, Families, and Persons in the United States: 1987, Consumer Income*, Series P-60, No. 162. *Note:* 1. Not available.

★ 610 ★
Wage/Salary Workers' Median Weekly Earnings: Trends

Figures in dollars; ratios in percent.

Year	Black	White	Black/White
Total			
1988	314	394	0.797
1987	301	383	0.786
1986	302	383	0.789
1985	292	374	0.781
1984	290	371	0.782
1983	291	363	0.802
1981	291	361	0.806
1980	282	361	0.784
1979	311	385	0.808
Males			
1988	347	465	0.746
1987	326	450	0.724
1986	329	449	0.733
1985	322	441	0.730
1984	333	441	0.755
1983	338	448	0.754
1982	325	435	0.747
1981	326	435	0.749
1980	335	436	0.768
1979	351	467	0.752
Females			
1988	288	318	0.906
1987	275	307	0.896
1986	272	305	0.892
1985	267	298	0.896
1984	265	289	0.917
1983	261	287	0.909

Continued.

Wage/Salary Workers' Median Weekly Earnings: Trends
[Continued]

Year	Black	White	Black/White
1982	249	283	0.880
1981	252	271	0.930
1980	250	277	0.903
1979	258	281	0.918

Source: "Median Weekly Earnings of Full-Time Wage and Salary Workers by Race and Sex, 1979-1988," *The State of Black America 1990,* January 1990, p. 50. Primary source: Bureau of Labor Statistics, *Handbook of Labor Statistics,* June 1985, p. 94; *Employment and Earnings,* January 1986-89.

★ 611 ★
Wealth Distribution in 1984

Numbers in percent.

Characteristic	Blacks	Whites
Interest-bearing and checking accounts	8	21
Stocks and mutual funds	1	7
Business or professional firm or proprietorship	6	10
Motor vehicle	10	6
Real estate	75	53
Other	---	3

Source: "Wealth Distribution, by Race and Asset Type," *A Common Destiny: Blacks And American Society,* 1989, p. 293. Primary source: Data from 1984 Survey of Income and Program Participation. Published by permission.

★ 612 ★
Wealth: Amount and Type in 1987 Dollars

Figures in dollars.

Characteristic	Mean		Percent			Aggregate		
	Blk	Wht	Blk	Wht	B/W	Blk	Wht	Gap
Net Worth	22,141	99,435.65	100	100	23.45	210,538.20	7,115,165	637,450.40
Interest Earning at Financial Institutions	3429	18448.05	43.80	75.40	10.80	14,282.71	1,048,008.00	117,985.90
Regular Checking	655	1,035.90	3200	56.90	35.56	1,993.71	44,408.83	3,611.04
Stock & Mutual Funds	3,077	30,293.53	5.40	22.00	2.49	1,580.02	502,129.20	61,793.44
Equity in Business	37,188	70,548.90	4.0	14.00	15.06	14,144.89	744,151.10	79,774.02
Equity in Motor Vehicle	3,769	6,242.70	65.00	88.50	44.34	23,298.48	416,253.80	29.236.69
Equity in Home	32,722	56,814.32	43.80	67.30	37.47	136,284.90	2,880,818.00	227,301.50
Equity in Rental Property	41,722	80,761.23	6.69	10.10	33.75	26,184.63	614,564.10	51,379.19
Other Real Estate	15,777	38,386.89	3.30	10.90	12.43	4,950.72	315,330.10	34,846.92

Continued.

Wealth: Amount and Type in 1987 Dollars
[Continued]

Characteristic	Mean		Percent			Aggregate		
	Blk	Wht	Blk	Wht	B/W	Blk	Wht	Gap
U.S. Savings Bonds	602	2,870.31	7.40	16.10	9.63	423.34	34,817.44	3,970.95
IRA or Keogh	3,764	9,896.21	5.10	21.40	9.06	1,825.38	159,560.50	18,312.67

Source: "Wealth Ownership 1984 ($ 1987)," The State of Black America 1990, January 1990, p. 41. Primary source: U.S. Department of Commerce, Bureau of the Census, *Household Wealth and Asset Ownership: 1985*, Tables 1 and 3.

★ 613 ★
Work Experience and Ratio of Income/Poverty Threshold

Numbers in thousands. Persons as of March 1989.

Characteristic	Total			White			Black			Hispanic origin[1]		
		Below poverty level			Below poverty level			Below poverty level			Below poverty level	
	Total	No.	% of total	Total	No.	% of total	Total	No.	% of total	Total	No.	% of total
Work Experience in 1988												
Total 15 years and over	189,927	20,857	11.0	162,160	14,136	8.7	21,580	5,644	26.2	14,050	3,007	21.4
Worked	131,244	8,415	6.4	113,432	6,058	5.3	13,642	1,976	14.5	9,432	1,283	13.6
50 to 52 weeks	91,135	2,832	3.1	79,321	2,145	2.7	8,975	566	6.3	6,204	459	7.4
Full time	79,637	1,929	2.4	69,021	1,455	2.1	8,102	398	4.9	5,580	346	6.2
49 weeks or less[3]	40,109	5,583	13.9	34,112	3,912	11.5	4,667	1,410	30.2	3,228	823	25.5
Duration of unemployment:												
1 to 4 weeks	3,255	440	13.5	2,756	310	11.3	343	90	26.3	258	64	24.8
5 to 14 weeks	5,315	671	12.6	4,449	486	10.96	694	160	24.0	547	110	20.1
15 to 26 weeks	3,492	676	19.3	2,846	474	16.7	532	184	34.5	464	133	28.6
27 weeks or more	2,405	830	34.5	1,718	504	29.3	605	303	50.1	273	139	50.8
Did not work	57,779	12,404	21.5	48,007	8,047	16.8	7,781	3,663	47.1	4,545	1,718	37.8
Main reason did not work:												
Ill or disabled	8,034	2,631	32.8	6,127	1,662	27.1	1,705	884	51.9	605	267	44.2
Keeping house	18,127	4,111	22.7	15,654	2,821	18.0	1,825	1,064	58.3	2,037	842	41.3
Going to school	8,573	1,979	23.1	6,203	1,060	17.1	1,774	696	39.2	1,023	332	32.4
Unable to find work	1,573	911	57.9	877	458	52.2	624	401	64.3	161	117	72.9
Retired	20,482	2,362	11.5	18,450	1,809	9.8	1,623	480	29.6	614	104	17.0
All other reasons	990	410	41.4	694	237	34.1	229	138	60.0	105	55	52.0
In Armed Forces	904	38	4.2	721	32	4.4	158	6	3.6	73	7	[2]
Ratio of Income to Poverty Threshold[3]												
Under .50	243,526	12,773	5.2	205,233	7,610	3.7	29,847	4,528	15.2	20,064	2,151	10.7
Under .75	243,526	21,521	8.8	205,233	13,439	6.5	29,847	7,025	23.5	20,064	3,843	19.2
Under 1.25	243,526	42,649	17.5	205,233	29,185	14.2	29,847	11,362	38.1	20,064	6,789	33.8
Under 1.50	243,526	54,053	22.2	205,233	38,189	18.6	29,847	13,391	44.9	20,064	8,375	41.7
Under 1.75	243,526	65,265	26.8	205,233	47,394	23.1	29,847	15,021	50.3	20,064	9,689	48.3
Under 2.00	243,526	77,197	31.7	205,233	57,470	28.0	29,847	16,470	55.2	20,064	10,964	54.6
Under 3.00	243,526	122,632	50.4	205,233	96,378	47.0	29,847	21,663	72.6	20,064	14,772	73.6
Under 4.00	243,526	160,778	66.0	205,233	129,856	63.3	29,847	25,064	84.0	20,064	17,109	85.3

Source: "Age, Type of Residence, Region, Work Experience, and Ratio of Income to Poverty Threshold of Persons, by Race and Hispanic Origin and Poverty Status in 1988," *Money Income and Poverty Status in the United States: 1988*, 1989, pp. 66-67. Primary source: U.S. Bureau of the Census, Current Population Reports, Series P-60, No. 166. *Notes:* 1. Persons of Hispanic origin may be of any race. 2. Base less than 75,000. 3. For this data block, the figures in the column headed "below poverty level" represent the number below the specified multiple of the poverty level shown.

LABOR AND EMPLOYMENT

★ 614 ★
★ 614 ★
Age Distribution of the Employed

Data based on household interviews of the civilian noninstitutionalized population.

Race and occupation of longest employment	Estimated ever-worked population (thou.)	Length of longest job				
		All lengths	5 years or less	6-19 years	20 years or more	Un-known
White						
All persons	135,100	100.0	42.7	33.8	14.5	9.0
White-collar workers	66,815	100.0	43.4	37.0	13.8	5.8
Professional, technical, and kindred workers	19,383	100.0	38.6	39.9	15.8	5.6
Managers and administrators, except farm	12,900	100.0	28.0	42.8	21.5	7.7
Sales workers	8,603	100.0	49.8	31.9	11.6	6.7
Clerical and kindred workers	25,929	100.0	52.4	33.6	9.2	4.7
Blue-collar workers	41,604	100.0	39.3	36.1	16.4	8.2
Craftsmen and kindred workers	15,822	100.0	30.3	39.8	21.0	9.0
Operatives, except transport	17,091	100.0	44.1	35.2	14.2	6.4
Transport equipment operatives	3,722	100.0	32.7	40.7	15.5	11.1
Laborers, except farm	4,969	100.0	56.6	23.9	10.1	9.4
Farm workers	3,592	100.0	23.1	21.2	43.7	12.0
Farmers and farm managers	2,088	100.0	9.0	19.2	63.1	8.8
Farm laborers and farm foremen	1,504	100.0	42.6	24.1	16.8	16.6
Service workers	16,523	100.0	60.7	26.4	6.9	6.0
Service workers, except private household	15,474	100.0	60.9	26.4	6.6	6.1
Private household workers	1,049	100.0	57.7	26.0	11.1	5.2
Ever worked, occupation unknown	6,566	100.0	22.2	11.5	13.4	52.8
Black						
All persons	15,885	100.0	42.5	33.2	11.5	12.8
White-collar workers	4,702	100.0	50.8	34.2	6.2	8.7
Professional, technical, and kindred workers	1,334	100.0	41.1	40.9	8.7	9.4
Managers and administrators, except farm	533	100.0	43.9	35.5	9.8	10.9

Continued.

Age Distribution of the Employed
[Continued]

Race and occupation of longest employment	Estimated ever-worked population (thou.)	Length of longest job				
		All lengths	5 years or less	6-19 years	20 years or more	Un-known
Sales workers	381	100.0	56.4	29.1	2.6	11.8
Clerical and kindred workers	2,454	100.0	56.8	31.1	4.7	7.5
Blue-collar workers	5,608	100.0	38.2	36.7	13.7	11.3
Craftsmen and kindred workers	1,312	100.0	28.7	39.8	15.7	15.7
Operatives, except transport	2,498	100.0	44.3	37.8	10.1	7.8
Transport equipment operatives	654	100.0	29.4	39.4	18.5	12.7
Laborers, except farm	1,145	100.0	41.0	29.2	16.8	13.2
Farm workers	472	100.0	24.6	30.5	33.7	11.0
Farmers and farm managers	98	100.0	---	32.7	48.0	19.4
Farm laborers and farm foremen	373	100.0	31.1	30.0	29.8	9.1
Service workers	4,159	100.0	41.6	33.3	13.1	7.4
Service workers, except private household	3,190	100.0	52.6	31.3	8.4	7.6
Private household workers	970	100.0	24.7	39.9	28.6	6.8
Ever worked, occupation unknown	944	100.0	19.5	7.4	6.6	66.5

Source: "Number and Percent Distribution of Persons 17 Years of Age and Over Who Ever Worked by Length of Longest Employment: United States, 1980," Health Characteristics by Occupation and Industry of Longest Employment, June 1989, p. 20. Primary source: *Vital and Health Statistics*, Series 10, Data from the National Health Survey, No. 168. *Notes:* Relative standard errors of estimates from this table are found in appendix I, figures III and V. For official population estimates for more general use, see U.S. Bureau of the Census reports on the civilian population of the United States, in *Current Population Reports*, Series P-20, P-25, and P-60.

★ 615 ★
Blacks in Selected Occupations

Occupation	Total Americans Employed In Field	Percentage Black
Accountants and Auditors	1,416	7.5
Actors and Directors	96	7.2
Architects	157	2.1
Athletes	74	8.7
Bus Drivers	440	22.6
Cashiers	2,473	13.0
Cleaners and Servants	464	36.5
Computer Scientists	853	5.7
Construction Trades	5,142	7.2
Dentists	170	4.3
Editors and Reporters	253	5.6
Engineers	1,823	3.6

Continued.

Blacks in Selected Occupations
[Continued]

Occupation	Total Americans Employed In Field	Percen-tage Black
Executive and Managerial	14,848	5.7
Farmers	1,118	1.3
Food Counter Occupations	354	10.5
Garbage	50	38.1
Lawyers	741	3.0
Domestic Servants	646	26.7
Meat Butchers	266	19.0
Mechanics	4,550	7.7
Physicians	548	4.3
Pilots, Navigators	109	.2
Police and Detectives	803	15.1
Public Relations	159	5.5
Real Estate Sales	772	3.5
Secretaries, Typists	4,788	8.5
Service Occupations	15,556	17.6
Social Workers	527	17.6
Teachers, College	709	4.3
Teachers, Non-College	3,936	9.2

Source: "Where Blacks Are in Selected Occupations," *Black Enterprise* 20 (June 1990), p. 91. Primary source: Department of the Census. Reprinted in *Black Enterprise.*.

★ 616 ★
Changes in Employment Rates

	Total Workers 1983:1988 (in thousands)	Total Percent Change	Percent Change in Black Workers[1]	Percent Change in Hispanic Workers[1]
Total employed persons: 16 years and over	100,832: 114,968	+14	+24 10.1[1]	+56 7.2[1]
Occupation Sub-Category: Mathematical & Computer Scientist	463:732	+11	+116 7.3[1]	+83 3.0[1]
Health Diagnosing (physicians, dentists, etc.)	735:818	+11	-20 1.9[1]	+38 4.0[1]
Teachers, Colleges & Universities	606:700	+16	-44 2.1[1]	+127 3.5[1]
Teachers, Except College & University	3,365:3,773	+12	+9 8.7[1]	+63 3.7[1]
Social Scientists & Urban Planners	261:343	+31	+33	+116

Continued.

417

Changes in Employment Rates
[Continued]

	Total Workers 1983:1988 (in thousands)	Total Percent Change	Percent Change in Black Workers[1]	Percent Change in Hispanic Workers[1]
			6.9[1]	3.7[1]
Social, Recreation & Religious Workers	831:1,052	+27	+46	+61
			13.8[1]	4.7[1]
Lawyers & Judges	651:757	+16	-6	+133
			2.2[1]	1.8[1]

Source: "Decline/Rise in Employment Rates in Managerial Occupations by Race/Ethnicity in Selected Occupation Sub-Categories, 1983 and 1988," *Black Issues in Higher Education*," March 1, 1990, p. 29. Primary source: Extrapolated from: U.S. Department of Labor, Bureau of Labor Statistics, unpublished tabulations from the current population survey, 1983 and 1988. *Note:* 1. Percent of total workers in 1988.

★ 617 ★
Changes in Employment Rates

Selected Occupations	Total Workers (thou.) 1983	Total Workers (thou.) 1988	Total % Change	% Change in Black Workers (% of total workers in 1988)	% Change in Hispanic Workers (% of total workers in 1988)
Managerial & Professional Specialty Occupations	23,592	29,190	+24	+35 (6.1)	+74 (3.7)
Sales Occupations	11,818	13,747	+16	+50 (6.1)	+67 (5.3)
Administrative Support including Clerical	16,395	12,479	+11	+31 (11.3)	+45 (6.5)
Service Occupations Except Private Households & Protective Service	11,205	12,479	+11	+20 (17.4)	+65 (10.3)

Source: "Decline/Rise in Employment Rates in Selected Occupations by Race/Ethnicity, 1983 and 1988," *Black Issues in Higher Education*," March 1, 1990, p. 29. Primary source: U.S. Department of Labor, Bureau of Labor Statistics, unpublished tabulations from the current population survey, 1983 and 1988.

★ 618 ★
Characteristics of Employed College Students

For school year ending in year shown and summer of the previous year. Covers students enrolled full-time in undergraduate four year colleges. Based on sample and subject to sampling error; for details, see source. For definition of median, see Guide to Tabular Presentation.

Characteristic	Total (1,000)		Percent Employed--							
			Full-time[1]				Part-time[2]			
			School year		Summer		School year		Summer	
	1983	1985	1983	1985	1983	1985	1983	1985	1983	1985
Race:										
White	3,833.7	3,863.1	9.1	12.4	56.2	64.0	48.0	45.7	33.9	26.3
Black	377.4	381.9	12.6	16.1	47.8	51.5	36.7	41.2	26.5	31.2

Source: "Employed College Students, by Selected Characteristics: 1983 and 1985," *Statistical Abstract*, 1989, p. 151. Primary source: Simmons Market Research Bureau, Inc., New York, NY, *National College Study*, 1983 and 1985 (Copyright). *Notes:* 1. Thirty or more hours per week. 2. Less than 30 hours per week.

★ 619 ★
Characteristics of Occupation

Occupation	1940		1950		1960		1970		1980	
	Number	Percent	Number	Percent	Number	Percent	Number	Percent	Number	Percent
Managerial	62,220	33.2	112,020	37.5	121,762	25.7	170,035	21.8	487,432	31.1
Self-employed	49,760	26.5	73,560	24.6	63,357	13.4	34,893	4.5	21,781	1.4
Private salary	10,940	5.8	32,580	10.9	44,318	9.3	87,765	11.2	282,488	18.1
Government	1,240	0.7	5,250	1.8	12,282	2.6	46,388	5.9	181,847	11.6
Professional and technical[1]	125,300	66.8	186,930	62.5	352,298	74.3	611,334	78.2	1,077,482	68.9
Clergy	17,920	9.6	19,110	6.4	14,530	3.1	12,850	1.6	16,195	1.0
Engineers	300	0.2	2,730	0.9	12,049	2.5	13,679	1.8	36,019	2.3
Lawyers and judges	1,000	0.5	1,530	0.5	2,970	0.6	3,728	0.5	15,277	1.0
Physicians	4,160	2.2	4,500	1.5	9,983	2.1	6,106	0.8	13,509	0.9
Social workers	2,720	1.5	6,750	2.3	15,345	3.2	40,791	5.2	88,512	5.6
Teachers	67,660	36.0	90,180	30.2	150,743	31.8	240,073	30.7	424,755	27.1
Total	187,520	100.0	298,950	100.0	474,060	100.0	781,369	100.0	1,564,914	100.0

Source: "Selected White-Color Occupations Filled by Blacks, 1940-1980," *A Common Destiny: Blacks and American Society*, 1989, p. 170. Primary source: Data from decennial censuses. Published by permission. *Note:* 1. Includes other professions not listed below.

★ 620 ★
Characteristics of the Labor Force

Characteristics	All persons[1]	Ever worked				Never worked
		Total	Agriculture, forestry, and fisheries	Non-office based	Office based	
			Number in thousands			
Total[2]	160,149	154,002	5,139	54,048	87,319	6,146
Age						
17-44 years	92,722	89,575	2,286	29,293	53,518	3,147
45-64 years	43,536	42,416	1,434	16,717	22,240	1,120

Continued.

Characteristics of the Labor Force
[Continued]

Characteristics	All persons[1]	Ever worked				Never worked
		Total	Agriculture, forestry, and fisheries	Non-office based	Office based	
65 years and over	23,891	22,011	1,420	8,0374	11,561	1,880
Sex						
Male	74,665	74,757	3,908	34,235	32,316	908
Female	84,484	79,245	1,232	19,812	55,002	5,238
Race						
White	140,022	135,100	4,454	48,189	76,083	4,921
Black	16,842	15,885	518	5,004	9,487	957
Family income						
Less than $10,000	39,091	36,454	2,007	12,274	20,653	2,637
$10,000-$24,999	61,415	59,622	1,633	22,292	33,284	1,793
$25,000 or more	45,491	44,538	979	15,263	26,642	953
Percent distribution						
Total[2]	100.0	100.0	100.0	100.0	100.0	100.0
Age						
17-44 years	57.9	58.2	44.5	54.2	61.3	51.2
45-64 years	27.2	27.5	27.9	30.9	25.5	18.2
65 years and over	14.9	14.3	27.6	14.9	13.2	30.6
Sex						
Male	47.2	48.5	76.0	63.3	37.0	14.8
Female	52.8	51.4	24.0	36.6	63.0	85.2
Race						
White	87.4	87.7	86.7	89.2	87.1	80.1
Black	10.5	10.3	10.1	9.2	10.9	15.6
Family income						
Less than $10,000	24.4	23.7	39.0	22.7	23.6	42.9
$10,000-$24,999	38.3	38.7	31.8	41.2	38.1	29.2
$25,000 or more	28.4	28.9	19.0	28.2	30.5	15.5

Source: "Number and Percent Distribution of Persons 17 Years of Age and Over by Selected Characteristics, According to Work Status and Industrial Group of Longest Employment: United States, 1980," *Health Characteristics by Occupation and Industry of Longest Employment*, June 1980, p. 6. Primary source: *Vital and Health Statistics*, Series 10, Data from the National Health Survey, No. 168. *Notes:* 1. Includes persons of unknown industry. 2. Includes all other races not shown as separate categories and unknown family income.

★ 621 ★
Characteristics of the Labor Force

| Characteristics | All persons[1] | Ever worked | | | | | Never worked |
		Total	White-collar workers	Blue-collar workers	Farm workers	Service workers	
			Number in thousands				
Total[2]	160,149	154,002	72,895	48,058	4,177	21,120	6,146
Age							
17-44 years	92,722	89,575	43,018	27,193	1,678	12,985	3,147
45-64 years	43,536	42,416	20,602	13,640	1,194	4,921	1,120
65 years and over	23,891	22,011	9,274	7,225	1,305	3,214	1,880
Sex							
Male	75,665	74,757	27,276	33,827	3,256	5,899	908
Female	84,484	79,245	45,619	14,231	922	15,221	5,238
Race							
White	140,022	135,100	66,815	41,604	3,592	16,523	4,921
Black	16,842	15,885	4,702	5,608	472	4,159	957
Family income							
Less than $10,000	39,091	36,454	11,665	13,494	1,721	8,000	2,637
$10,000-$24,999	61,415	59,622	27,655	20,639	1,276	7,504	1,793
$25,000 or more	45,491	44,538	28,390	9,987	714	3,746	953
			Percent distribution				
Total[2]	100.0	100.0	100.0	100.0	100.0	100.0	100.0
Age							
17-44 years	57.9	58.2	59.0	56.6	40.2	61.5	51.2
45-64 years	27.2	27.5	28.3	28.4	28.6	23.3	18.2
65 years and over	14.9	14.3	12.7	15.0	31.2	15.2	30.6
Sex							
Male	47.2	48.5	37.4	70.4	78.0	27.9	14.8
Female	52.8	51.4	62.6	29.6	22.1	72.1	85.2
Race							
White	87.4	87.7	91.6	86.6	86.0	78.2	80.1
Black	10.5	10.3	6.4	11.7	11.3	19.7	15.6
Family income							
Less than $10,000	24.4	23.7	16.0	28.1	41.2	37.9	42.9
$10,000-$24,999	38.3	38.7	37.9	42.9	30.5	35.5	29.2
$25,000 or more	28.4	28.9	38.9	20.8	17.1	17.7	15.5

Source: "Number and Percent Distribution of Persons 17 Years of Age and Over by Selected Characteristics, According to Work Status and Occupational Group of Longest Employment: United States 1980," Health Characteristics by Occupation and Industry of Longest Employment, June 1989, p. 5. Primary source: Vital and Health Statistics, Series 10, Data from the National Health Survey, No. 168. *Notes:* 1. Includes persons of unknown industry. 2. Includes all other races not shown as separate categories and unknown family income.

★ 622 ★
Characteristics of the Labor Force

Sex and Occupation or Industry	1939	1949	1959	1969	1979	1984
Employed in major industry groupings						
Black men						
Agriculture, forestry, fisheries	42.5	24.9	12.7	5.3	2.8	3.4
Construction, manufacturing, mining	21.8	32.9	35.0	41.3	37.7	33.6
Transportation, communication, public utilities	6.5	9.0	8.2	9.9	12.6	12.6
Wholesale and retail trades	10.1	12.1	13.8	15.1	15.1	16.7
Service, including finance, insurance, real estate	15.8	15.6	17.4	21.1	24.7	27.5
Public Administration	1.6	3.9	5.6	7.3	7.0	6.2
Black women						
Agriculture, forestry, fisheries	16.1	9.4	3.6	1.4	0.6	0.4
Construction, manufacturing, mining	3.7	9.4	9.3	16.1	18.1	16.5
Transportation, communication, public utilities	0.2	0.9	1.0	3.0	5.2	5.4
Wholesale and retail trades	4.2	10.3	10.1	12.2	12.6	14.3
Service, including finance, insurance, real estate	73.9	65.9	65.0	61.4	55.4	56.5
Public Administration	0.6	2.2	3.8	5.9	8.0	6.9
Employed in major occupations						
Black men						
Professional	1.8	2.2	3.8	7.8	10.7	8.0
Proprietors, managers, officials	1.3	2.0	3.0	4.7	6.7	6.3
Clerical and sales	2.1	4.2	7.0	9.2	11.1	13.1
Craftsmen	4.4	7.8	9.5	13.8	17.1	15.8
Operatives	12.6	21.4	24.3	28.3	23.4	22.6
Domestic service	2.9	1.0	0.4	0.3	0.2	0.1
Other service	12.4	13.5	14.9	12.8	15.8	18.3
Farmers and farm workers	41.1	23.9	14.3	5.6	3.0	4.9
Nonfarm laborers	21.4	24.0	22.8	17.5	12.0	11.0
Black women						
Professional	4.3	5.7	6.0	10.8	14.8	13.9
Proprietors, managers, officials	0.7	1.4	1.8	1.9	3.7	5.2
Clerical and sales	1.4	5.4	10.8	23.4	32.4	33.1
Craftsmen	0.1	0.7	0.5	0.8	1.4	2.6
Operatives	6.2	14.9	14.1	17.6	14.9	12.0
Domestic service	60.0	42.0	35.2	17.5	6.5	5.9
Other service	10.5	19.1	21.4	25.7	24.3	24.8
Farmers and farm workers	16.0	9.3	9.6	1.6	0.6	0.5
Nonfarm laborers	0.8	1.5	0.6	0.7	1.4	1.8

Source: "Occupation and Industry of Employment for Black Men and Women (in percent), 1939-1984," *A Common Destiny: Blacks and American Society*, 1989, p. 273. Primary source: Bureau of Labor Statistics, decennial censuses. Published by permission.

★ 623 ★
Characteristics of the Unemployed

Numbers in percent.

	All Races	African American	White American
NUL Hidden Unemployment Rates			
Total Population	10.8	22.4	9.2
Male	8.7	19.0	7.5
Female	13.2	25.5	11.3
Teenagers	26.8	50.3	22.9
Male	26.0	48.1	22.5
Female	27.6	52.4	23.4
DOL Unemployment Rates			
Total Population	5.2	11.3	4.4
Male	4.7	10.7	4.0
Female	5.7	11.9	4.8
Teenagers	13.9	30.8	11.5
Male	13.4	27.8	11.3
Female	14.4	33.9	11.6

Source: "Unemployment by Age, Race and Sex, 3rd Quarter, 1989." National Urban League. *Quarterly Economic Report on The African American Worker*, Third Quarter, 1989, December, 1989, p. 3. Primary source: Prepared by the National Urban League Research Department from unpublished U.S. Bureau of Labor Statistics data. Extracted from *The Quarterly Economic Report of the African American Worker*. Published by permission.

★ 624 ★
Characteristics of Workforce

As of May. Multiple jobholders are employed persons who, either 1) had jobs as wage or salary workers with two employers or more; 2) were self employed and also held a wage and salary job; or 3) were unpaid family workers on their primary jobs but also held wage and salary job. Based on the Current Population Survey.

Characteristic	Employed (1,000)			Multiple Jobholders						
				Number (1,000)			Average weekly hours		Median weekly earnings[1]	
	Total	Male	Female	Total	Male	Female	All jobs	Secondary job	All jobs	Secondary job
Total	106,878	60,015	46,864	5,730	3,537	2,192	51.3	14.2	$343	$70
Race and Hispanic origin:										
White	93,555	53,222	40,333	5,286	3,291	1,995	51.1	14.0	344	69
Black	10,416	5,240	51,176	338	187	151	53.8	16.8	305	81
Hispanic origin[2]	6,489	3,984	2,505	194	125	69	51.1	15.1	355	66

Source: "Multiple Jobholders — Selected Characteristics: 1985," *Statistical Abstract*, 1989. p. 383. U.S. Bureau of Labor Statistics, *Monthly Labor Review*, November 1986, and unpublished data. *Notes:* 1. Data on wage and salary earnings only were collected for the primary job. Data on earnings from all sources were collected for the secondary job. 2. Hispanic persons may be of any race.

★ 625 ★
Civilian Employment

In thousands, except as indicated. Annual averages of monthly figures. Based on Current Population Survey, see text, section 1, and Appendix III for methodology. See also *Historical Statistics, Colonial Times to 1970*, Series D 11-19 and D 85-86.

Year and Race	Civilian noninsti-tutional population	Civilian Labor Force				Unemployed		Not in Labor Force	
		Total	Percent of population	Employed	Employment/population ratio[1]	Number	Percent of labor force	Number	Percent of Population
White:									
1955	98,880	58,085	58.7	55,833	56.5	2,252	3.9	40,798	41.3
1960	105,282	61,915	58.8	58,850	55.9	3,065	5.0	43,367	41.1
1965	113,284	66,137	58.4	63,445	56.0	2,691	4.1	47,147	41.6
1970	122,174	73,556	60.2	70,217	57.5	3,339	4.5	48,618	39.8
1975	134,790	82,831	61.5	76,411	56.7	6,421	7.8	51,959	38.5
1980	146,122	93,600	64.1	87,715	60.0	5,884	6.3	52,522	35.9
1981	147,908	95,052	64.3	88,709	60.0	6,343	6.7	52,856	35.7
1982	149,441	96,143	64.3	87,903	58.8	8,241	8.6	53,298	35.7
1983	150,805	97,021	64.3	88,893	58.9	8,128	8.4	53,784	35.7
1984	152,347	98,492	64.6	92,120	60.5	6,372	6.5	53,855	35.4
1985	153,679	99,926	65.0	93,736	61.0	6,191	6.2	53,753	35.0
1986	155,432	101,801	65.5	95,660	61.5	6,140	6.0	53,631	34.5
1987	156,958	103,290	65.8	97,789	62.3	5,501	5.3	53,669	34.2
Black:									
1973	14,917	8,976	60.2	8,128	54.5	846	9.4	5,941	39.8
1975	15,751	9,263	58.8	7,894	50.1	1,369	14.8	6,488	41.2
1980	17,824	10,865	61.0	9,313	52.2	1,553	14.3	6,959	39.0
1981	18,219	11,086	60.8	9,355	51.3	1,731	15.6	7,133	39.2
1982	18,584	11,331	61.0	9,189	49.2	2,142	18.9	7,254	39.0
1983	18,925	11,647	61.5	9,375	49.5	2,272	19.5	7,278	38.5
1984	19,348	12,033	62.2	10,119	52.3	1,914	15.9	7,315	37.8
1985	19,664	12,364	62.9	10,501	53.4	1,864	15.1	7,299	37.1
1986	19,989	12,654	63.3	10,814	54.1	1,840	14.5	7,335	36.7
1987	20,352	12,993	63.8	11,309	55.6	1,684	13.0	7,359	36.2

Source: "Employment Status of the Civilian Noninstitutional Population 16 Years Old and Over by Race: 1955 to 1987," *Statistical Abstract*, 1989, p. 377. Primary source: U.S. Bureau of the Census, *Employment and Earnings*, monthly. *Notes:* 1. Civilians employed as a percent of the civilian noninstitutional population.

★ 626 ★
Comparisons of Unemployment by Race

Weeks Unemployed	African-American			White		
	Total	Male	Female	Total	Male	Female
Less than 5	42.4	38.4	46.5	47.2	42.2	53.6
5-14	30.8	31.8	29.9	29.7	30.4	28.8
15-26	12.1	13.1	11.1	11.9	13.3	10.1
27 or more	14.7	16.7	12.5	11.2	14.1	7.6
Average wks	15.4	16.9	14.0	12.9	15.2	10.0

Source: "Percentage Comparison of African American and White Unemployment by Duration, 1988." *The State of Black America 1990*, January 1990, p. 214. Primary source: Bureau of Labor Statistics, *Employment and Earnings*, January 1989, Table 15, p. 176.

★ 627 ★
Distribution of Employed Workers - 1983

| | 1983 | | | | | |
| | Male | | | Female | | |
Occupation	Blk	Wht	B/W	Blk	Wht	B/W
Exec., Admin., & Managerial	5.8	13.5	0.43	4.9	8.3	0.59
Professional	6.4	12.1	0.53	11.2	14.3	0.78
Technicians & Related Support	2.0	2.8	0.71	3.4	3.3	1.03
Sales Occupations	4.7	11.5	0.41	7.3	13.5	0.54
Administrative Support	8.2	5.6	1.46	25.6	30.5	0.84
Private Households	.2	.1	2.0	5.7	1.7	3.35
Protective Service	4.1	2.4	1.67	.7	.5	1.40
Other Service	14.3	6.3	2.27	24.2	15.3	1.58
Precision Pro., Craft & Repair	15.7	20.5	.77	2.1	2.2	.95
Mach. Operators, Assem., & Insp.	11.6	7.6	1.53	11.5	9.0	1.28
Trans. and Material Movers	10.7	6.5	1.65	.9	.7	1.29
Handlers, Cleaners, Helpers, Labor	11.3	5.6	2.02	1.9	1.5	1.27
Farming, Forestry, & Fishing	5.2	5.5	.96	.6	1.4	.43

Source: "Occupational Distribution of Employed Workers 1988 and 1983." *The State of Black America*, January 1990, p. 48. Primary source: U.S. Department of Labor, Bureau of Labor Statistics, *Employment and Earnings*, January 1989 and January 1984.

★ 628 ★
Distribution of Employed Workers - 1988

| | 1988 | | | | | |
| | Male | | | Female | | |
Occupation	Blk	Wht	B/W	Blk	Wht	B/W
Exec., Admin., & Managerial	6.6	14.4	0.46	7.0	11.4	0.61
Professional	6.8	12.2	0.56	10.5	14.9	0.70
Technicians & Related Support	2.3	2.9	0.79	3.4	3.2	1.60
Sales Occupations	5.3	11.7	0.45	9.1	13.5	0.67
Administrative Support	9.3	5.3	1.75	26.2	28.7	0.91
Private Households	0.1	0.05	2.00	3.4	1.5	2.27
Protective Service	4.4	2.5	1.76	1.12	0.5	0.20
Other Service	13.6	6.0	2.27	23.6	14.6	1.62
Precision Pro., Craft & Repair	15.5	20.3	0.76	3.2	2.3	0.96
Mach. Operators, Assem., & Insp.	11.2	6.6	1.70	1.2	0.8	1.50
Trans. and Material Movers	10.7	7.3	1.47	9.9	5.9	1.68
Handlers, Cleaners, Helpers, Labor	10.9	6.0	1.82	2.1	1.6	1.31
Farming, Forestry, & Fishing	3.5	4.7	0.74	0.4	1.2	0.33

Source: "Occupational Distribution of Employed Workers 1988 and 1983." *The State of Black America*, January 1990, p. 48. Primary source: U.S. Department of Labor, Bureau of Labor Statistics, *Employment and Earnings*, January 1989 and January 1984.

★ 629 ★
Distribution of Labor Force

Occupation	Black Men 1972	Black Men 1980	White Men 1972	White Men 1980	Black Women 1972	Black Women 1980	White Women 1972	White Women 1980
Total Employed	4,347	4,704	45,769	5,033	3,406	4,394	27,305	36,043
Percent	100.0	100.0	100.0	100.0	100.0	100.0	100.0	100.0
Professional and technical	6.4	8.2	14.3	16.1	10.6	13.8	14.9	17.0
Managers and administrators	4.0	5.6	14.0	15.3	2.1	3.4	4.8	7.4
Sales	1.7	2.5	6.6	6.4	2.5	2.8	7.8	7.3
Clerical	7.6	8.4	6.8	6.2	22.7	29.3	36.2	36.0
Craft and kindred workers	14.8	17.6	21.2	21.5	.9	1.4	1.3	1.9
Operatives, except transport	17.4	15.5	12.1	10.7	14.8	13.8	12.5	9.4
Transport equipment operatives	10.3	9.9	5.7	5.4	.4	.7	.4	.7
Nonfarm laborers	17.4	13.0	6.8	6.5	.9	1.4	.9	1.2
Farm and farm managers	1.0	.4	3.4	2.6	-	-	.4	.4
Farm laborers and foremen	3.5	2.4	1.7	1.5	1.1	.5	1.5	1.3
Private household workers	.3	.1	-	-	16.4	7.4	3.0	1.9
Other service workers	15.8	16.4	7.3	7.9	27.6	25.4	16.2	16.0

Source: "Percent Distribution of Employed Persons by Occupation, Race, and Sex, 1972 and 1980," *Marital Status and Living Arrangements: March 1988*, p. 9. Primary source: Diane Nilsen Westcott, "Blacks in the 1970s: Did They Scale the Job Ladder?," *Monthly Labor Review*, June 1982, p. 30.

★ 630 ★
Earnings of Families

	Number Of Families (1,000)					Median Weekly Earnings (dollars)				
	1980	1984	1985	1986	1987	1980	1984	1985	1986	1987
White										
Total families with earners[1]	35,786	35,331	35,848	36,072	36,555	411	514	543	566	592
Married-couple families	30,316	29,585	29,899	29,865	30,095	438	557	589	615	547
One earner[2]	13,437	12,218	12,097	11,698	11,385	311	381	395	405	416
Husband	11,152	9,703	9,496	9,077	8,784	343	426	452	472	485
Wife	1,740	1,879	1,925	1,996	1,946	160	207	218	225	231
Two or more earners	16,878	17,368	17,802	18,167	18,710	542	689	723	755	785
Husband and wife only	11,448	12,017	12,394	12,656	13,232	511	656	691	720	748
Families maintained by women	4,140	4,510	4,616	4,786	4,959	233	299	311	320	329
Families maintained by men	1,331	1,236	1,333	1,420	1,501	374	442	475	476	492
Black										
Total families with earners[1]	4,503	4,579	4,668	4,810	4,942	299	366	378	391	412
Married-couple families	2,802	2,648	2,671	2,734	2,768	366	463	487	503	529
One earner[2]	1,103	967	902	978	924	210	260	257	267	289
Husband	769	634	580	615	581	244	309	292	307	335
Wife	279	281	257	289	264	151	188	206	209	215
Two or more earners	1,700	1,681	1,769	1,755	1,843	472	600	622	645	675
Husband and wife only	1,238	1,216	1,258	1,269	1,318	461	582	603	628	646
Families maintained by women	1,438	1,640	1,703	1,756	1,822	192	240	259	267	284
Families maintained by men	263	292	294	320	352	307	365	360	348	383
Hispanic origin[3]										
Total families with earners[1]	[4]	[4]	[4]	3,017	3,219	[4]	[4]	[4]	412	425

Continued.

Earnings of Families
[Continued]

	Number Of Families (1,000)					Median Weekly Earnings (dollars)				
	1980	1984	1985	1986	1987	1980	1984	1985	1986	1987
Married-couple families	4	4	4	2,272	2,411	4	4	4	459	473
One earner[2]	4	4	4	1,006	1,032	4	4	4	289	292
Husband	4	4	4	828	838	4	4	4	308	314
Wife	4	4	4	127	122	4	4	4	202	209
Two or more earners	4	4	4	1,266	1,379	4	4	4	603	615
Husband and wife only	4	4	4	809	884	4	4	4	582	592
Families maintained by women	4	4	4	538	575	4	4	4	273	285
Families maintained by men	4	4	4	207	234	4	4	4	380	418

Source: "Median Weekly Earnings of Families by Type of Family, Number of Earners, Race, and Hispanic Origin: 1980 to 1987," *Statistical Abstract*, 1989, p. 407. Primary source: U.S. Bureau of Labor Statistics, Bulletin 2307, and *Employment and Earnings*, January issues. *Notes:* 1. Excludes families in which there is no wage or salary earner or in which the husband, wife, or other person maintaining the family is either self-employed or in the Armed Forces. 2. Includes other earners, not shown separately. 3. Persons of Hispanic origin may be of any race. 4. Not available.

★ 631 ★
Employment in Health Occupations

Occupation	Black Percentage of Total
Physicians	2.7
Dentists	3.2
Registered nurses	6.7
Physician's assistants	7.7
Licensed practical nurses	17.7
Health technologies and technicians	12.7
Nursing aides, orderlies, and attendants	27.3
Therapists	7.6

Source: "Black Employment (as percentage of total employment) in Selected Health Occupations, 1983," *A Common Destiny: Blacks in American Society*, 1989, p. 437. Primary source: Fred McKinney. "Employment Implications of a Changing Health-Care System. In: Margaret C. Simms and Julianne M. Malveaux, eds. *Slipping Through the Cracks: The Status of Black Women*. New Brunswick, N.J.: Transaction Books, 1986, p. 437. Published in: *A Common Destiny: Blacks and American Society*, 1989, p. 437.

★ 632 ★
Employment in Industries

Company	Total Employees	Black Employees	Percent Black	Percent Black Managers	No. Blacks on Bd. of Directors
AT & T	302,895	43,469	14.4	7.7	2
Amtrak	22,031	5,481	24.9	13.4	2
Anheuser Busch	41,000	8,393	20.5[1]	30.0[1]	2
Atlantic Richfield	20,184	1,711	8.5	3.5	2
Avon Products	8,062	1,002	12.0	8.0	1

Continued.

Employment in Industries
[Continued]

Company	Total Employees	Black Employees	Percent Black	Percent Black Managers	No. Blacks on Bd. of Directors
Chase Manhattan	25,000	5,995	23.0	8.0	1
Chrysler	90,000	[2]	26.0[1]	11.4[1]	1
Coca-Cola	9,337	1,899	20.0	8.0	[2]
Eastman Kodak	75,324	5,574	7.4	2.6	1
Equitable	17,987	1,975	11.0	5.5	[2]
Exxon	41,410	5,844	14.1	5.4	[2]
Federal Express	56,098	13,650	24.0	8.0	[2]
Ford	180,500	29,421	16.3	7.5	1
Gannett	38,123	4,832	12.7	5.4	2
General Mills	71,773	10,534	14.8	5.6	1
General Motors	114,563	12,239	9.4	10.1	1
Hallmark	13,656	1,204	9.0	4.0	[2]
IBM	226,850	20,450	9.0	12.3	[2]
Johnson and Johnson	29,500	3,374	11.4	6.3	1
Kellogg	6,987	936	13.0	8.0	[2]
Kraft	37,453	4,567	12.2	4.9	1
McDonald's	118,159	30,659	25.9	16.8	1
Merck & Co.	15,000	1,456	9.7	4.0	1
N.C. Mutual	840	[2]	99.0	92.0	[2]
J. C. Penney	177,954	15,835	8.9	5.8	1
Pepsi-Cola	16,761	1,573	9.4	6.0	1
Philip Morris	68,500	[2]	27.1[1]	15.4[1]	1
Port Authority, NY/NJ	8,721	1,851	21.0	13.7	2
Proctor & Gamble	42,831	5,224	12.0	7.0	1
Ryder	32,473	4,655	14.3	6.5	[2]
J. E. Seagram & Sons	3,949	644	16.3	11.2	[2]
U.S. Armed Forces	2.1m	[2]	19.8	6.6	[2]
Xerox	53,162	[2]	13.8	11.4	[2]

Source: "Minority Representation in Selected Industries, February 1989, Group I", *Black Enterprise* 19 (February 1989), pp. 76-86. Primary source: *Black Enterprise* 19 (February 1989), pp. 76-86. Table compiled by the editors from data published in *Black Enterprise* 19 (February 1989), pp. 76-86. *Notes:* Group I includes industries with long-term commitment to affirmative action. 1. Minorities 2. No data given.

★ 633 ★

Employment in Industries

Company	Total Employees	Black Employees	Percent Black	Percent Black Managers	No. Blacks on Bd. of Directors
Aetna Life	41,023	5,033	12.3	2.7	1
Am Airlines	65,154	5,595	8.6	2.5	1
Apple Computers	6,979	205	3.0	1.8	[4]
Bristol Myers	34,100	[4]	18.6[2]	10.0[2]	[4]
Chevron	40,000	3,420	8.5	3.3	[4]
Digital	140,000	[4]	16.6[2]	10.0[2]	1
Gen Electric	198,550	21,760[2]	11.0[2]	4.7[2]	1

Continued.

Employment in Industries
[Continued]

Company	Total Employees	Black Employees	Percent Black	Percent Black Managers	No. Blacks on Bd. of Directors
Hewlett Packard	57,328	[4]	4.0[2]	10.6[3]	[4]
Inner City Broadcasting	175	89	5.0	[4]	100
Mobile	33,259	3,501	10.5	4.3	2
Russell, H.J.	490	236	48.0	58.0	[4]
Sears	95,000	64,770	18.8	7.5	1
Stroh Brewery	4,800	[4]	20.0[2]	10.0[2]	[4]
Time	22,800	4,020	17.0	7.0	1
US West	68,497	[4]	4.4	3.7	[4]

Source: "Minority Representation in Selected Industries, February 1989, Group II|1|." *Black Enterprise* 19 (February 1989), pp. 86-91. Primary source: *Black Enterprise* 19 (February 1989), pp. 86-91. Table compiled by the editors from data published in *Black Enterprise* 19 (February 1989), pp. 86-91. *Notes:* 1. Group II includes industries with a developing commitment to affirmative action. 2. Minorities. 3. Managers and supervisors. 4. No data supplied.

★ 634 ★

Employment of Civilians

Year	Total Population		Black/White
	Black	White	
1989[1]	56.9	63.8	0.892
1988	56.3	63.1	0.892
1987	55.6	62.3	0.892
1985	53.4	61.0	0.875
1982	49.4	58.8	0.840
1980	52.3	60.0	0.872
1970	53.7	57.4	0.936
Men (20 and Over)			
1989[1]	67.1	75.5	0.889
1988	67.0	75.1	0.892
1987	66.4	74.1	0.889
1985	64.6	74.3	0.870
1982	61.4	73.0	0.841
1980	65.8	75.6	0.870
1978	69.1	77.2	0.895
1972	73.0	79.0	0.924
Women (20 and Over)			
1989[1]	54.8	54.9	0.998
1988	53.9	54.0	0.998
1987	53.0	53.1	0.998
1985	51.0	51.0	1.000
1982	47.5	48.4	0.981
1980	49.1	47.8	1.027
1978	49.3	46.1	1.069
1972	46.5	40.6	1.145

Continued.

Employment of Civilians
[Continued]

| Year | Total Population | | Black/White |
	Black	White	
	Both Sexes (16 to 19)		
1989[1]	28.3	51.4	0.551
1988	27.5	51.0	0.539
1987	27.1	49.4	0.549
1985	24.6	48.5	0.507
1982	19.0	45.8	0.415
1980	23.9	50.7	0.471
1978	25.2	52.4	0.481
1972	25.2	46.4	0.543

Source: "Civilian Employment — Population Ratio by Race, Sex, and Age: Selected Years." *The State of Black America*, January 1990, p. 45. Primary source: Bureau of Labor Statistics. *Handbook of Labor Statistics*, June 1985, pp. 46,47; Employment and Earnings, January 1989 and October 1989. *Note:* 1. Average of first three quarters of 1989.

★ 635 ★
Employment Ratios

Numbers in percent.

Characteristics	All Races	African American	White American
Total	63.6	57.8	64.3
Male	73.7	64.4	74.8
Female	54.4	52.4	54.6
Teenagers	54.0	34.1	58.2
Male	56.5	37.0	60.8
Female	51.3	31.4	55.6

Source: "Employment-to-Population Ratio, 3rd Quarter, 1989." National Urban League. *Quarterly Economic Report on The African American Worker*, Third Quarter, 1989, December, 1989, p. 3. Primary source: Prepared by the National Urban League Research Department from unpublished U.S. Bureau of Labor Statistics data. Extracted from *The Quarterly Economic Report of the African American Worker*. Published by permission.

★ 636 ★
Employment Status of High School Graduates

| Race/ethnicity and level of education | Percent with specified level of education | Employment Status | | | | Average hourly wages of those employed (dol) | |
		Continuous full-time	Intermittent full-time	Part-time	Not in labor force	Continuous full-time	Intermittent full-time
Total, all persons	100	39	34	6	20	[2]	[2]
High school diploma	32	33	30	8	29	7.01	6.60
Some postsecondary education	30	42	33	6	19	7.17	7.18
1- or 2-year degree	12	40	37	9	14	7.59	7.65
Bachelor's degree	19	44	35	6	15	8.71	8.91

Continued.

Employment Status of High School Graduates
[Continued]

Race/ethnicity and level of education	Percent with specified level of education	Employment Status				Average hourly wages of those employed (dol)	
		Continuous full-time	Intermittent full-time	Part-time	Not in labor force	Continuous full-time	Intermittent full-time
Advanced degree	7	40	46	5	9	10.80	10.70
Race/ethnicity							
White							
Total	100	40	34	7	19	[2]	[2]
High school diploma	32	34	31	8	28	7.11	6.76
Some postsecondary education	29	42	33	7	18	7.32	7.36
1- or 2-year degree	12	41	37	9	13	7.70	7.84
Bachelor's degree	20	45	35	6	14	8.76	9.03
Advanced degree	8	41	47	5	8	10.86	10.55
Black							
Total	100	38	35	7	20	[2]	[2]
High school diploma	31	36	35	10	18	5.89	5.38
Some postsecondary education	38	43	32	5	20	5.85	6.29
1- or 2-year degree	12	32	44	10	14	6.58	6.33
Bachelor's degree	16	36	34	4	26	7.97	7.30
Advanced degree	4	37	32	7	24	10.66	[1]
Hispanic							
Total	100	41	27	5	26	[2]	[2]
High school diploma	42	30	23	6	41	7.26	5.90
Some postsecondary education	35	52	28	4	15	7.28	6.24
1- or 2-year degree	12	46	34	4	16	6.87	7.93
Bachelor's degree	8	54	27	8	11	8.94	[1]
Advanced degree	4	27	47	9	17	[1]	[1]

Source: "Employment Status and Hourly Wages of 1972 High School Graduates in Spring 1986, by Race/Ethnicity and Socioeconomic Status." *Digest of Education Statistics,* 1989, p. 364. Primary source: *Digest of Education Statistics,* 1989. U.S. Department of Education, National Center for Education Statistics, "National Longitudinal Study, 1972," unpublished tabulations. This table was prepared January 1989. *Notes:* 1. Too few respondents to produce reliable estimates. 2. Data not available.

★ 637 ★
Females in the Labor Force

Year	18-19 Years		20-24 Years		25-34 Years		35-44 Years		45-54 Years		55-64 Years	
	Black	White	Black	White	Black	White	Black	White	Black	White	Black	White
1955	43.2	52.0	46.7	45.8	51.3	32.8	56.0	39.9	54.8	42.7	40.7	31.8
1965	40.0	50.6	55.2	49.2	54.0	36.3	55.9	44.3	60.2	49.9	48.9	40.3
1975	45.1	60.4	56.2	65.4	61.4	53.5	61.7	54.9	56.8	54.3	43.8	40.7
1983	41.4	61.5	57.6	72.8	72.4	69.9	73.9	69.1	61.8	63.4	45.5	41.7

Source: "Labor Force Participation Rates of Females from 1955-1983 by Age and Race," *Equality and Excellence: The Educational Status of Black Americans,* 1985, p. 8. Primary source: *Employment and Training Report of the President,* 1982; *Employment and Earnings,* Bureau of Labor Statistics, November 1983.

★ 638 ★
High School Graduates Employed

In thousands, except percent. As of October. For civilian noninstitutional population 16 to 24 years old. High school graduates: Persons not enrolled in college who have completed 4 years of high school only. Dropouts: Persons not in regular school and who have not completed the 12th grade nor received a general equivalency degree. Based on Current Population Survey.

Employment, Status, Sex and Race	Graduates					Dropouts				
	1975[1]	1980	1985	1986	1987	1975[1]	1980	1985	1986	1987
Civilian population	10,518	11,622	10,381	9,993	9,339	4,906	5,252	4,323	4,143	4,252
White	6,591	7,638	6,732	6,533	6,153	1,875	2,310	1,887	1,844	1,929
Black	662	817	865	892	866	341	305	224	220	243
Unemployed [2]	1,158	1,228	1,118	976	813	765	894	757	679	574
Percent of labor force	13.6	12.5	12.7	11.5	10.2	25.3	25.2	25.9	24.3	20.5
White	917	924	729	640	549	547	638	584	480	416
Black	229	289	360	319	305	212	239	158	187	138

Source: "Employment Status of High School Graduates Not Enrolled in College and School Dropouts, by Sex and Race: 1975 to 1987," Statistical Abstract, 1989, p. 146. U.S. Bureau of Labor Statistics, Bulletin 2307, and unpublished data. Notes: 1. Population controls based on 1980 census. 2. Includes other races not shown separately.

★ 639 ★
Industry and Employees

In thousands, except percent. For civilian noninstitutional population 16 years and over. Annual averages of monthly figures. Based on Curent Population Survey; see text, section 1 and Appendix III. Data from 1985 forward not strictly comparable with earlier years due to changes in industrial classification.

Industry	1987		
		Percent	
	Total	Black	Hispanic[1]
Total employed	112,440	10.1	6.9
Agriculture	3,208	5.1	12.4
Mining	818	3.8	6.7
Construction	7,456	7.2	7.2
Manufacturing	20,935	10.3	8.2
Transportation, communication, and other public utilities	7,880	13.3	6.0
Wholesale and retail trade	23,392	8.0	7.1
Wholesale trade	4,580	5.8	7.0
Retail trade	18,812	8.5	7.2
Finance, insurance, real estate	7,763	7.9	5.7
Banking and other finances	3,421	8.1	6.0
Insurance and real estate	4,342	7.7	5.5
Services[2]	35,743	11.6	6.2
Business services[2]	4,706	11.4	6.6
Advertising	293	5.3	4.6
Service to dwellings and buildings	675	18.7	13.7
Personnel supply services	640	20.9	6.3
Business management/consulting	460	5.1	2.8
Computer and data processing	663	6.6	2.2
Detective/protectvie services	371	23.0	8.2
Automobile services	1,271	8.3	9.7
Personal services[2]	4,598	14.4	9.6
Private households	1,216	21.9	11.8

Continued.

Industry and Employees
[Continued]

Industry	1987		
	Total	Percent	
		Black	Hispanic[1]
Hotels and lodging places	1,597	13.1	10.6
Entertainment and recreation	1,353	8.0	7.1
Professional and related services[2]	22,963	11.7	5.1
Hospitals	4,444	16.4	5.5
Health services, except hospitals	4,034	11.1	5.3
Elementary, secondary schools	5,550	12.0	5.2
Colleges and universities	2,378	9.3	12.0
Social services	1,946	17.2	7.0
Legal services	1,138	5.0	3.8
Public administration[3]	5,246	14.6	5.7

Source: "Employment by Industry and by Selected Characteristics, 1987," Statistical Abstract, 1989, p. 391. Primary source: U.S. Bureau of Labor Statistics, Employment and Earnings, January issue. Notes: 1. Hispanic persons may be of any race. 2. Includes industries not shown separately. 3. Includes workers involved in uniquely governmental activities, e.g., judicial and legislative.

★ 640 ★
Labor Force

	1940	1950	1960	1970	1980
Agriculture					
25-34	32.5	16.6	8.2	4.0	1.9
35-44	29.3	17.3	9.0	4.4	2.3
45-54	36.0	19.7	12.2	5.9	3.3
55-64	48.2	27.2	15.7	9.8	4.7
Total	37.6	21.0	12.0	5.8	2.8
Private nonagriculture					
24-34	61.8	73.0	78.0	78.9	76.5
35-44	63.7	73.8	76.4	75.9	75.9
45-54	57.1	71.9	75.9	74.0	71.3
55-64	45.4	66.1	74.3	73.9	69.8
Total	56.5	70.9	76.1	75.8	74.7
Government					
25-34	5.7	10.4	13.8	17.1	21.6
35-44	7.0	8.9	14.6	19.7	21.8
45-54	6.9	8.4	11.9	20.1	25.3
55-64	6.5	6.7	10.0	16.4	25.5
Total	5.9	8.1	11.9	18.4	22.5

Source: "Distribution of Black Male Labor Force by Sector and Age," The Economic Progress of Black Men in America, p. 84. Primary Source: Census of Population, 1940-1980; Public Use Sample.

★ 641 ★
Labor Force

As of March. For civilian noninstitutional population, 16 years old and over. Based on Current Population Survey; see text, section 1 and Appendix III.

Presence and Age of Child	Total				White				Black			
	1975	1980	1985	1988	1975	1980	1985	1988	1975	1980	1985	1988
Wives, total	44.5	50.2	54.3	56.7	43.7	49.3	53.4	55.8	54.3	59.3	64.2	66.1
No children under 18	44.0	46.0	48.2	49.1	43.5	45.5	47.5	48.5	47.7	51.2	56.1	54.4
With children under 18	44.9	54.3	61.0	65.2	43.9	53.2	60.0	64.3	58.8	65.6	71.5	75.8
Under 6, total	36.8	45.3	53.7	57.4	35.0	43.5	52.3	56.3	56.4	63.4	69.3	71.7
Under 3	32.6	41.5	50.7	54.8	30.9	40.0	49.8	53.3	52.2	57.7	65.7	73.0
1 year or under	30.8	39.0	49.4	51.9	29.2	37.7	48.6	50.5	50.0	52.9	63.7	71.5
2 years	31.7	48.1	54.0	61.7	35.1	46.1	52.7	60.2	56.4	71.0	69.9	76.2
3 to 5 years	42.2	51.7	58.6	61.4	40.3	49.4	56.6	60.9	61.7	72.3	73.8	69.8
3 years	41.2	51.5	55.1	59.3	39.0	48.4	52.7	58.1	62.7	73.4	72.3	76.1
4 years	41.2	51.4	59.7	61.4	38.7	49.8	58.4	61.6	4.9	66.4	70.6	70.3
5 years	44.4	52.4	62.1	63.6	43.8	50.4	59.9	64.0	56.3	77.8	79.1	62.5
6 to 13 years	51.8	62.6	68.1	72.3	50.8	61.4	67.7	71.5	64.9	71.8	73.5	81.4
14 to 17 years	53.8	60.5	67.0	72.9	53.6	60.6	66.3	72.5	51.0	58.4	74.1	74.6

Source: "Labor Force Participation Rates for Wives, Husband Present, by Age of Own Youngest Child: 1975 to 1988," *Statistical Abstract*, 1989, p. 386. Primary source: U.S. Bureau of Labor Statistics, *Monthly Labor Review*, February 1986, and unpublished data.

★ 642 ★
Labor Force

As of March. For civilian noninstitutional population 25-64 years of age. Based on Current Population Survey; see text, section 1 and Appendix III.

Employment Status, Sex, and Race	Population, 25-64 years old (1,000)	Percent Distribution by School Years Completed							
		Elementary School			High School		College		
		0-4 years	5-7 years	8 years	1-3 years	4 years	1-3 years	4 years	5 years or more
White, total	104,889	1.5	2.7	3.0	10.0	40.7	18.7	13.5	9.8
Civilian labor force	81,887	1.0	2.0	2.3	8.5	40.1	19.7	15.0	11.4
Employed	78,599	1.0	1.9	2.2	8.1	39.8	19.9	15.3	11.7
Unemployed	3,287	2.2	4.6	4.2	17.7	45.6	15.9	7.5	2.3
Not in labor force	23,000	3.3	5.3	5.9	15.3	42.9	15.2	7.8	4.2
Black, total	13,439	2.2	4.9	3.9	18.9	41.0	16.7	7.7	4.7
Civilian labor force	9,984	1.1	3.2	2.8	15.5	43.0	19.2	9.5	5.7
Employed	8,984	1.2	3.0	2.8	14.5	42.4	19.8	10.2	6.1
Unemployed	1,001	.6	5.5	2.6	24.1	48.1	14.2	2.9	2.1
Not in labor force	3,455	5.2	9.7	7.3	28.8	35.3	9.2	2.7	1.9

Source: "Civilian Labor Force — Years of School Completed, by Sex and Race: 1988," *Statistical Abstract*, 1989, p. 384. Primary source: U.S. Bureau of Labor Statistics, unpublished data.

★ 643 ★
Labor Force

For civilian noninstitutional population 16 years old and over. Annual averages of monthly figures. Based on Current Population Survey; see text, section 1 and Appendix III.

Age and Race	Civilian Labor Force			Male (1,000)			Female (1,000)			Percent of Labor Force			
	Total (1,000)	Percent by age		Total	Employed	Unem-ployed	Total	Employed	Unem-ployed	Employed		Unemployed	
		Male	Female							Male	Female	Male	Female
White	103,290	100.0	100.0	57,799	54,647	3,132	45,510	43,142	2,369	94.6	94.8	5.4	5.2
16-19 years	6,893	6.1	7.4	3,547	2,999	548	3,347	2,900	447	84.6	86.6	15.4	13.4
20-24 years	12,764	11.6	13.3	6,717	6,150	568	6,047	5,598	449	91.5	92.6	8.5	7.4
25-34 years	29,956	29.4	28.5	16,963	16,084	879	12,993	12,345	648	94.8	95.0	5.2	5.0
35-44 years	24,581	23.7	24.0	13,674	13,138	536	10,907	10,459	448	96.1	95.9	3.9	4.1
45-54 years	15,792	15.5	15.0	8,945	8,596	350	6,847	6,620	227	96.1	96.7	3.9	3.3
55-64 years	10,497	10.7	9.4	6,200	5,991	209	4,297	4,172	124	96.6	97.1	3.4	2.9
65 years and over	2,806	3.0	2.4	1,733	1,690	43	1,073	1,047	25	97.5	97.6	2.5	2.3
Black	12,993	100.0	100.0	6,486	5,661	826	6,507	5,648	858	87.3	86.8	12.7	13.2
16-19 years	899	7.1	6.7	463	304	160	435	283	152	65.5	65.1	34.5	34.9
20-24 years	1,818	14.1	13.9	914	728	186	904	693	211	79.7	76.7	20.3	23.3
25-34 years	4,147	32.0	31.9	2,074	1,821	253	2,073	1,793	280	87.8	86.5	12.2	13.5
35-44 years	2,942	21.7	23.6	1,406	1,283	122	1,537	1,412	125	91.3	91.9	8.7	8.1
45-54 years	1,838	14.1	14.2	915	853	61	924	860	63	93.3	93.2	6.7	6.8
55-64 years	1,098	9.0	7.9	586	547	39	512	489	23	93.3	95.5	6.7	4.5
65 years and over	251	2.0	1.9	130 ·	124	.6	121	117	4	95.4	96.7	4.6	3.3

Source: "Civilian Labor Force — Employment Status by Sex, Race, and Age: 1987," *Statistical Abstract*, 1989, p. 379. Primary Source: U.S. Bureau of Labor Statistics, *Employment and Earnings*, monthly.

★ 644 ★
Labor Force

Characteristic	1940 -1960	1960 -1980
Ages 25-34		
Black		
0-11 yrs.	-2.8	-11.9
12-15 yrs.	-1.8	-4.2
16+ yrs.	-1.2	-2.8
Total	-2.6	-5.6
White		
0-11 yrs.	-1.2	-6.1
12-15 yrs.	-0.2	-1.6
16+ yrs.	+1.0	-0.9
Total	-0.5	-1.7
Ages 45-54		
Black		
0-11 yrs.	-2.6	-11.9
12-15 yrs.	-1.8	-5.4
16+ yrs.	+1.8	-3.0
Total	-2.2	-7.8
White		
0-11 yrs.	+0.3	-8.0
12-15 yrs.	+1.5	-3.7
16+ yrs.	+1.9	-1.0

Continued.

Labor Force
[Continued]

Characteristic	1940 -1960	1960 -1980
Total	+1.1	-4.3

Source: "Changes in Male Labor Force Participation Rates by Years of School, Race, and Age," *The Economic Progress of Black Men in America*, p. 31. Primary source: *The Economic Progress of Black Men in America* Tables 2.1, 2.2, and 2.3.

★ 645 ★
Labor Force

Age and years of school	1940	1950	1960	1970	1980
25-34					
0-11 yrs.	95.9	92.1	93.1	89.0	81.2
12-15	95.6	86.0	93.8	94.0	89.6
16+	96.7	89.6[1]	95.5	91.3	92.7
35-44					
0-11 yrs.	95.3	94.6	92.5	89.4	82.3
12-15	95.6	93.4	95.7	93.6	90.7
16+	96.9	95.6[1]	98.0	97.4	94.4
45-54					
0-11 yrs.	92.2	91.9	89.6	84.3	77.7
12-15	94.4	91.1	92.6	92.2	87.2
16+	94.8	95.1	96.6	95.7	93.6
55-64					
0-11 yrs.	87.5	82.6	76.6	72.2	59.1
12-15	95.3	80.7[1]	87.1	81.0	71.8
16+	89.1	92.9[1]	88.1	92.0	81.8
Total					
0-11 yrs.	93.8	91.4	88.8	83.6	74.2
12-15	95.7	88.5	93.7	92.6	88.0
16+	95.8	93.2	95.8	94.2	92.3

Source: "Black Male Civilian Labor Force Participation Rates by Age and Education," *The Economic Progress of Black Men in America*, p. 29. Primary source: Census of Population, 1940-1980, Public Use Sample. *Note:* 1. Less than 100 observations per call.

★ 646 ★
Labor Force

Race and age	1940	1950	1960	1970	1980
Blacks:					
25-34	96.0	91.0	93.4	91.4	87.8
35-44	95.3	94.5	93.3	91.2	87.9
45-54	92.3	91.9	90.1	86.4	82.3
55-59	90.8	83.5	82.9	79.5	70.1
60-64	83.8	74.2	70.0	66.6	54.9
Total	93.9	91.2	89.9	86.7	82.5

Continued.

Labor Force
[Continued]

Race and age	1940	1950	1960	1970	1980
Whites:					
25-34	97.2	94.6	96.7	95.8	95.0
35-44	96.8	97.0	97.2	96.5	95.8
45-54	94.0	94.2	95.1	94.2	91.7
55-59	89.6	87.7	89.7	88.5	82.2
60-64	80.9	80.0	80.0	74.9	61.1
Total	94.4	93.6	94.3	92.8	90.0
Difference in					
participation (white minus black):					
25-34	1.2	3.6	3.3	4.4	7.2
35-44	1.5	2.5	3.9	5.3	7.9
45-54	1.7	2.3	5.0	7.8	9.4
55-59	-1.2	4.2	6.8	9.0	12.1
60-64	-2.9	5.8	10.0	8.3	6.2
Total	0.5	2.4	4.4	6.1	7.5

Source: "Male Civilian Labor Force Participation Rates by Race and Age," *The Economic Progress of Black Men in America*, p. 28. Primary source: Census of Population, 1940-1980; Public Use Sample.

★ 647 ★
Labor Force

As of March. For civilian noninstitutional population 25-64 years of age. Based on Current Population Survey.

Sex, Race, and Years of School Completed	Total employed	Managerial/ professional	Tech./ sales/ administrative	Service[1]	Precision production[2]	Operators/ fabrica- tor[3]	Farming, forestry, fishing
			Number (1,000)				
Male, total:							
Less than 4 years of high school	7,807	460	617	908	2,257	2,967	596
4 years of high school only	18,402	2,212	3,287	1,776	5,418	4,936	774
1 to 3 years of college	9,342	2,427	2,694	812	1,885	1,296	227
4 years of college or more	14,367	9,588	3,140	410	591	479	159
White:							
Less than 4 years of high school	6,586	419	526	672	2,013	2,432	523
4 years of high school only	16,258	2,075	2,961	1,345	4,995	4,144	739
1 to 3 years of college	8,220	2,229	2,368	631	1,706	1,068	216
4 years of college or more	12,972	8,770	2,829	232	524	360	157
Black:							
Less than 4 years of high school	1,053	30	81	194	202	482	64
4 years of high school only	1,788	96	241	350	367	707	27
1 to 3 years of college	840	141	226	140	122	208	4
4 years of college or more	659	385	130	47	29	65	2
Female, total							
Less than 4 years of high school	4,812	287	1,048	1,830	227	1,330	88
4 years of high school only	17,437	2,273	9,225	3,275	513	1,982	171
1 to 3 years of college	8,640	2,508	4,663	997	155	269	48
4 years of college or more	9,586	6,502	2,537	533	69	103	41
White:							
Less than 4 years of high school	3,781	234	947	1,255	187	1,075	83
4 years of high school only	15,052	2,054	8,251	2,613	433	1,539	163
1 to 3 years of college	7,420	2,222	3,993	820	131	205	48
4 years of college or more	8,310	5,724	2,163	257	58	68	41
Black:							
Less than 4 years of high school	874	33	91	518	26	205	2
4 years of high school only	2,024	187	822	585	54	369	6

Continued.

Labor Force
[Continued]

Sex, Race, and Years of School Completed	Total employed	Managerial/ professional	Tech./ sales/ administrative	Service[1]	Precision production[2]	Operators/ fabrica- tor[3]	Farming, forestry, fishing
1 to 3 years of college	940	217	509	146	17	49	4
4 years of college or more	805	515	221	50	10	10	4

Source: "Occupation of Employed Civilians by Sex, Race, and Educational Attainment: 1988," *Statistical Abstract*, 1989, p. 390. Primary source: U.S. Bureau of Labor Statistics, unpublished data. *Notes:* 1. Includes private household workers. 2. Includes craft and repair. 3. Includes laborers. 4. Represents zero.

★ 648 ★
Labor Force

In thousands except percent. As of October. Civilian noninstitutional population. Based on Current Population Survey.

	Population		Civilian Labor Force			Employed		Unemployed		
			1980,	1987				1980,	1987	
Characteristic	1980	1987	total	Total	Percent[1]	1980	1987	total	Total	Rate[2]
Enrolled in school[3]	15,713	15,656	7,454	7,720	49.3	6,438	6,785	1,021	936	12.1
White	13,242	12,843	6,690	6,656	51.8	5,892	5,973	798	683	10.3
Below college	6,566	6,168	3,096	2,856	46.3	2,579	2,399	517	458	16.0
College level	6,678	6,675	3,592	3,800	56.9	3,310	3,575	282	225	5.9
Black	2,028	2,111	595	775	36.7	406	567	189	207	26.8
Below college	1,282	1,256	294	358	28.5	174	223	120	135	37.8
College level	747	855	300	417	48.7	230	345	70	72	17.3
Not enrolled[3]	21,390	17,796	17,464	14,671	82.4	15,021	13,062	2,443	1,608	11.0
White	18,103	14,747	15,121	12,406	84.1	13,318	11,288	1,803	1,117	9.0
Black	2,864	2,622	2,055	1,914	73.0	1,451	1,472	604	443	23.1

Source: "School Enrollment and Labor Force Status of Civilians 16 to 24 Years Old, by Selected Characteristics: 1980 and 1987," *Statistical Abstract*, 1989, p. 384. Primary source: U.S. Bureau of Labor Statistics, Bulletin 2192 and unpublished data. *Notes:* 1. Percent of civilian noninstitutional population. 2. Percent of civilian labor force in each category. 3. Includes other races not shown separately.

★ 649 ★
Labor Force

Characteristic	1950	1960	1970	1980
	Mean weeks per year[1]			
Black				
25-34	40.3	44.5	47.4	44.1
35-44	44.2	45.0	47.7	46.7
45-54	44.1	44.4	47.4	46.8
55-64	42.6	43.0	46.4	46.2
Total	43.6	44.4	47.3	45.9
White				
25-34	45.9	47.6	48.7	47.3
35-44	47.1	48.4	49.5	48.8
45-54	46.2	47.6	49.1	48.9
55-64	45.0	46.1	47.5	47.0
Total	46.2	47.6	48.8	47.9

Continued.

Labor Force
[Continued]

Characteristic	1950	1960	1970	1980

Mean hours worked per week[2]

Black				
25-34	41.8	40.6	40.2	40.0
35-44	43.2	41.0	40.8	41.1
45-54	43.4	40.6	40.4	40.7
55-64	43.3	39.8	39.4	39.8
Total	42.8	40.6	40.3	40.4
White				
25-34	44.6	44.0	43.3	43.5
35-44	46.0	45.3	44.8	45.2
45-54	45.7	44.8	44.1	44.5
55-64	44.6	43.2	42.6	42.7
Total	45.3	44.5	43.0	44.0

Source: "Weeks and Hours Worked for Men by Race and Age," *The Economic Progress of Black Men in America*, p. 47. Primary source: Census of Population, 1940-1980; Public Use Sample. *Notes:* 1. Weeks worked refer to male workers who worked during the preceding calendar year. 2. Hours worked refer to hours worked by male workers at work during the week of the census survey.

★ 650 ★
Labor Force

	Change in share of population out of the labor force, 1960-1980 (percentage point change)	Change in share of population receiving social security, 1960-1980 (percentage point change)	Change in social security recipients as percent of change in men out of the labor force, 1960-1980
Race and age			
Black men[1]			
25-34	5.6	1.6	28.5
35-44	5.4	2.9	53.7
45-54	7.8	5.5	70.5
55-59	12.8	9.5	74.2
60-64	15.1	31.1	206.0
White men			
25-34	1.7	0.8	47.1
35-44	1.4	1.7	121.4
45-54	3.4	3.4	100.0

Continued.

Labor Force
[Continued]

	Change in share of population out of the labor force, 1960-1980 (percentage point change)	Change in share of population receiving social security, 1960-1980 (percentage point change)	Change in social security recipients as percent of change in men out of the labor force, 1960-1980
55-59	7.5	6.1	81.3
60-64	18.9	30.5	161.4

Source: "Trends in Nonparticipation in the Labor Force and Social Security Recipient by Race," *The Economic Progress of Black Men in America,* p. 37. Primary source: Table was prepared from tables 2.1 and 2.6 in *The Economic Progress of Black Men in America. Notes:* Social Security Beneficiaries are essentially recipients of disability pensions up to age 62; recipients age 62-64 include recipients of old age pensions choosing the early retirement option. 1. Social Security data refer to nonwhite men.

★ 651 ★
Labor Force

Annual Averages.

Characteristics	1988		1987		1983		1982		1980	
	Black	White	Black	White	Black	White	Black	White	Black	White
Persons, 16 and Over										
Civilian Labor Force Participation Rate										
Both sexes	63.8	66.2	63.8	65.8	61.5	64.3	61.0	64.3	61.0	64.1
Male	71.0	76.9	71.1	76.8	70.6	77.1	70.1	77.4	70.3	78.2
Female	58.0	56.4	58.0	55.7	54.2	52.7	53.7	52.4	53.1	51.2
Unemployment Rate										
Both Sexes	11.7	4.7	13.0	5.3	19.5	8.4	18.9	8.6	14.3	6.3
Male	11.7	4.7	12.7	5.4	20.3	8.8	20.1	8.8	14.5	6.1
Female	11.7	4.7	13.2	5.2	18.6	7.9	17.6	8.3	14.0	6.5
Persons, 16 to 19 Years Old										
Civilian Labor Force Participation Rate										
Both Sexes	40.8	58.6	41.6	57.7	36.4	56.9	36.6	57.5	38.9	60.0
Male	43.8	60.0	43.6	59.0	39.9	59.4	39.8	60.0	43.2	63.7
Female	37.9	57.2	39.6	56.5	33.0	54.5	33.5	55.0	34.9	56.2
Unemployment Rate										
Both Sexes	32.4	13.1	34.7	14.4	48.5	19.3	48.0	20.4	38.5	15.5
Male	32.7	13.9	34.4	15.5	48.8	20.2	48.9	21.7	37.5	16.2
Female	32.0	12.3	34.9	13.4	48.2	18.3	47.1	19.0	39.8	14.8

Source: "Civilian Labor Force Participation and Unemployment Rates, by Sex and Race: 1988, 1987, 1983, 1982, and 1980," *The Black Population in the United States,* March 1988, p. 9. Primary source: *The Black Population in the United States:* March 1988.

★ 652 ★
Labor Force

In current dollars of usual weekly earnings. Data represent annual averages of quarterly data. Data revised since previously published. Based on Current Population Survey.

Characteristic	Number of Workers (1,000)				Median Weekly Earnings			
	1983	1985	1986	1987	1983	1985	1986	1987
All workers[1]	70,976	77,002	78,727	80,836	313	343	358	373
White	61,739	66,481	67,779	69,358	319	355	370	383
Male	37,378	40,030	40,471	41,150	387	417	433	450
Female	24,361	26,452	27,308	28,208	254	281	294	307
Black	7,373	8,393	8,654	9,050	261	277	291	301
Male	3,883	4,367	4,464	4,679	293	304	318	326
Female	3,490	4,026	4,190	4,371	231	252	263	275
Hispanic origin[2]	[3]	[3]	5,630	6,093	[3]	[3]	277	284
Male	[3]	[3]	3,622	3,874	[3]	[3]	299	306
Female	[3]	[3]	2,008	2,219	[3]	[3]	241	251

Source: "Full-Time Wage and Salary Workers — Numbers and median Weekly Earnings, by Selected Characteristics: 1983 to 1987," *Statistical Abstract*, 1989, p. 406. Primary source: U.S. Bureau of Labor Statistics, Bulletin 2307, and *Employment and Earnings*, January issues. *Notes:* 1. Includes other races, not shown separately. 2. Persons of Hispanic origin may be of any race. 3. Not available.

★ 653 ★
Labor Force

Age, sex, and race/ethnicity	Labor force participation rate[1]						Employment/population ratio[2]					
	Total	8 years or less[3]	High School		College		Total	8 years or less[3]	High School		College	
			1 to 3 years	4 years or more	1 to 3 years	4 years or more			1 to 3 years	4 years or more	1 to 3 years	4 years or more
Total, 16 years old and over	65.0	32.7	50.1	68.3	73.7	82.2	61.1	29.4	43.5	64.0	70.7	80.6
White[4]	65.4	33.5	51.1	67.8	73.2	82.1	62.1	30.3	45.2	64.2	70.6	80.7
Black[4]	62.2	29.1	46.3	73.2	79.6	85.9	53.9	24.9	35.7	62.8	72.8	82.8
Hispanic[5]	65.8	52.5	55.3	74.9	79.7	87.6	60.2	46.6	47.0	69.5	76.0	85.5
25 to 34 years old	82.9	60.3	73.3	82.2	85.4	89.6	78.0	53.5	62.4	76.5	81.8	87.7
White[4]	83.8	63.9	75.9	82.5	85.6	90.7	79.7	57.8	66.9	77.8	82.4	88.9
Black[4]	79.5	45.2	64.6	80.9	87.6	89.2	69.1	33.7	46.6	70.1	80.4	85.4
Hispanic[5]	77.5	68.5	71.5	78.6	84.3	89.8	72.1	61.8	61.8	73.8	81.0	87.7

Source: "Labor Force Participation of Persons 16 Years Old and Over, by Years of School Completed and Age, Sex, and Race/Ethnicity, March 1988," *Digest of Education Statistics*, 1989, p. 361. Primary source: U.S. Department of Labor, Bureau of Labor Statistics, Office of Employment and Unemployment Statistics, "Educational Attainment of Workers, March 1988." (This table was prepared December 1988). *Notes:* 1. Percent of the civilian population who are employed or seeking employment. 2. Number of persons employed as a percent of civilian population. 3. Includes persons reporting no school years completed. 4. Includes persons of Hispanic origin. 5. Persons of Hispanic origin may be of any race.

★ 654 ★
Labor Force

Race/ethnicity	1986	2000
White	79.5	73.9
Black	10.8	11.8
Hispanic	6.9	10.2
Asian	2.8	4.1

Source: "Racial and Ethnic Composition of Labor Force," *Detroit Free Press*, May 7, 1989, B-7. Primary source: Congressional Office of Technology Assessment, Rand Corporation.

★ 655 ★
Labor Force

In percent. As of March. Civilian noninstitutional population 25 to 64 years of age. Based on Current Population Survey.

Item	1970	1975	1977	1978	1979	1980
White: Total[1]	3.1	6.5	5.3	4.0	3.9	4.4
High school:						
1-3 years	4.5	10.1	8.4	6.7	6.5	7.8
4 years	2.7	6.5	5.2	4.0	3.9	4.6
College:						
1-3 years	2.8	5.1	4.6	2.9	3.1	3.9
4 years or more	1.3	2.4	2.8	2.0	2.0	1.8
Black: Total[1,2]	4.7	10.9	10.1	8.9	8.8	9.6
High school:						
1-3 years	5.2	13.5	11.7	10.7	10.6	11.7
4 years	5.2	10.7	10.1	9.3	9.3	9.5
College:						
1-3 years	3.5	9.8	10.5	6.7	6.7	9.0
4 years or more	.9	3.9	2.8	4.2	3.9	4.0

Source: "Unemployment Rates by Educational Attainment, Sex, and Race: 1970 to 1988," *Statistical Abstract*, 1989, p. 394. Primary source: U.S. Bureau of Labor Statistics, *Labor Force Statistics Derived from the Current Population Survey, 1948-87*, and unpublished data. *Notes:* 1. Includes persons reporting no school years completed. 2. For 1970 and 1975, data refer to Black and other workers.

★ 656 ★
Labor Force

In thousands, except as indicated. For civilian noninstitutional population 16 years old and over. Annual averages of monthly figures. See also *Historical Statistics, Colonial Times to 1970*, series D 87-101.

Unemployed workers, characteristics of Item and characteristic	1972	1975	1980	1982	1983	1984	1985	1986	1987
Unemployed									
Total[1]	4,882	7,929	7,637	10,678	10,717	8,539	8,312	8,237	7,429
Labor force time lost (percent)[2]	5.9	9.1	7.9	11.0	10.9	8.6	8.1	7.9	7.1
White	3,906	6,421	5,884	8,241	8,128	6,372	6,191	6,140	5,501
16-19 years old	1,021	1,413	1,291	1,534	1,387	1,116	1,074	1,070	995
20-24 years old	887	1,474	1,364	1,770	1,678	1,282	1,235	1,149	1,017
Black	906	1,369	1,553	2,124	2,272	1,914	1,864	1,840	1,684
16-19 years old	279	330	343	396	392	353	357	347	312

Continued.

Labor Force
[Continued]

Unemployed workers, characteristics of Item and characteristic	1972	1975	1980	1982	1983	1984	1985	1986	1987
20-24 years old	226	362	426	565	591	504	455	453	397
Hispanic[3]	5	508	620	929	961	800	811	857	751
Full time workers	3,806	6,523	6,269	9,006	9,075	7,057	6,793	6,708	5,979
Part time workers	1,077	1,408	1,369	1,672	1,642	1,418	1,519	1,529	1,446
Unemployment Rate (percent)[4]									
White	5.1	7.8	6.3	8.6	8.4	6.5	6.2	6.0	5.3
16-19 years old	14.2	17.9	15.5	20.4	19.3	16.0	15.7	15.6	14.4
20-24 years old	8.4	12.3	9.9	12.8	12.1	9.3	9.2	8.7	8.0
Black	10.4	14.8	14.3	18.9	19.5	15.9	15.1	14.5	13.0
16-19 years old	35.4	39.5	38.5	48.0	48.5	42.7	40.2	39.3	34.7
20-24 years old	16.3	24.5	23.6	30.5	31.4	26.1	24.5	24.1	21.8
Hispanic[3]	5	12.2	10.1	13.8	13.7	10.7	10.5	10.6	8.8
Experienced workers[4]	5.3	8.2	6.9	9.3	9.2	7.1	6.8	6.6	5.8
Women maintaining families[1]	7.2	10.0	9.2	11.7	12.3	10.4	10.5	9.9	9.3
White	5.8	8.5	7.3	9.4	9.2	7.8	8.1	7.8	6.8
Black	5	5	14.0	18.0	20.2	16.7	16.4	15.4	15.4
Married men, wife present[1]	2.8	5.1	4.2	6.5	6.5	4.6	4.3	4.4	3.9
White	2.6	4.8	3.9	6.0	6.0	4.3	4.0	4.0	3.6
Black	4.5	8.7	7.4	11.5	11.3	8.1	8.0	8.0	6.5

Source: "Unemployed Workers — Summary: 1972-1987," *Statistical Abstract*, 1989, p. 393. Primary source: U.S. Bureau of Labor Statistics, *Employment and Earnings*, monthly, and unpublished data. *Notes:* 1. Includes other races, not shown separately. 2. Aggregate hours lost by the unemployed and persons on part-time for economic reasons as a percent of potentially available labor force hours. 3. Hispanic persons may be of any race. 4. Wage and salary workers. 5. Not available.

★ 657 ★
Labor Force

Numbers in percent.

Characteristics	Total	African American	White American
3rd Quarter, 1989			
Total	67.1	65.1	67.3
Male	77.3	72.1	78.0
Female	57.7	59.4	57.4
Teenagers	62.7	49.3	65.7
Male	65.3	51.2	68.6
Female	60.0	47.5	62.8
2nd Quarter, 1989			
Total	66.5	63.9	66.8
Male	76.6	71.1	77.4
Female	57.3	58.1	57.1
Teenagers	56.9	43.1	60.2

Continued.

Labor Force
[Continued]

Characteristics	Total	African American	White American
Male	59.0	45.4	62.4
Female	54.7	40.7	58.0

Source: "Labor Force Participation Rates, 3rd Quarter, 1989, and 2nd Quarter, 1989." *Quarterly Economic Report on The African American Worker*, Third Quarter, 1989, December, 1989, p. 2. Primary source: Prepared by the National Urban League Research Department from unpublished U.S. Bureau of Labor Statistics data. Extracted from *The Quarterly Economic Report of the African American Worker*. Published by permission.

★ 658 ★
Labor Force

Because of rounding, sums of individual items may not equal totals.

Labor Force Status and Years of School Completed	Men			Women		
	White	Black	Hispanic	White	Black	Hispanic
Population, total	46,452	5,076	2,815	49,027	6,353	3,243
Elementary: 8 years or less	4,728	960	1,038	4,339	999	1,238
High School:						
1 to 3 years	5,222	996	371	5,891	1,460	484
4 years only	16,974	1,791	758	22,632	2,383	970
College						
1 to 3 years	7,921	818	374	8,183	934	333
4 years or more	11,607	512	277	7,983	597	217
Labor force, total	41,810	4,196	2,564	29,822	4,122	1,708
Elementary: 8 years or less	3,538	543	895	1,581	413	462
High School:						
1 to 3 years	4,394	797	328	2,850	783	234
4 years only	15,492	1,538	727	13,941	1,643	516
College:						
1 to 3 years	7,294	733	359	5,474	753	233
4 years or more	11,092	483	255	5,975	533	162
Labor force participation rate	90.0	82.7	91.1	60.8	64.9	52.7
Elementary: 8 years or less	74.8	67.0	86.4	36.4	41.3	37.3
High School:						
1 to 3 years	84.1	80.0	88.4	48.4	53.6	43.3
4 years only	91.3	85.9	95.9	61.6	69.5	63.5
College:						
1 to 3 years	92.1	89.6	96.0	66.9	80.6	70.0
4 years or more	95.6	94.3	92.1	75.8	89.3	74.7
Unemployment rate	7.2	15.0	10.5	6.4	12.8	11.1
Elementary: 8 years or less	12.0	17.3	13.4	14.5	11.4	18.0
High School:						
1 to 3 years	12.6	12.9	14.3	10.4	15.1	18.4
4 years only	8.3	17.3	8.8	6.8	15.6	7.0
College:						

Continued.

Labor Force
[Continued]

Labor Force Status and	Men			Women		
Years of School Completed	White	Black	Hispanic	White	Black	Hispanic
1 to 3 years	6.0	14.6	7.8	4.6	10.6	5.6
4 years or more	2.6	8.9	4.7	3.1	5.4	4.9

Source: "Labor Force Status of Persons 25 to 64 Years Old by Race, Hispanic Origin, and Years of School Completed, March 1982," *Marital Status and Living Arrangements: March 1988*, p. 9. Primary source: Ann McDougall Young, "Recent Trends in Higher Education and Labor Force Activity," *Monthly Labor Review*, February 1983, p. 40.

★ 659 ★
Labor Force

Characteristics	Black	White	B/W Ratio
1966			
Officials and Managers	0.9	9.0	.10
Professionals	1.1	7.1	.17
Technicians	2.2	4.7	.87
Sales Workers	2.1	7.9	.26
Clerical Workers	7.2	17.7	.41
Craftsmen	6.2	14.9	.42
Operatives	33.4	24.3	1.37
Laborers	25.0	7.7	3.25
Service Workers	21.8	6.5	3.25
Totals	100.0	100.0	---
1975			
Officials and Managers	3.0	12.0	.25
Professionals	2.5	9.0	.28
Technicians	3.4	5.1	.67
Sales Workers	4.7	9.5	.49
Clerical Workers	14.3	16.6	.86
Craftsmen	8.8	14.2	.62
Operatives	31.1	20.2	1.54
Laborers	15.4	6.8	2.26
Service Workers	16.8	6.6	2.50
Totals	100.0	100.0	---
1985			
Officials and Managers	4.5	13.7	.33
Professionals	4.6	13.5	.34
Technicians	4.6	6.3	.73
Sales Workers	7.0	9.7	.72
Clerical Workers	17.4	16.3	1.07
Craftsmen	8.0	11.4	.70
Operatives	24.6	16.0	1.54
Laborers	10.9	5.6	1.95
Service Workers	18.4	7.5	2.45

Continued.

Labor Force
[Continued]

Characteristics	Black	White	B/W Ratio
Totals	100.0	100.0	---

Source: "Occupational Distribution of Black and White Workers, 1966, 1975, 1985," *Black Employment in the Private Sector*, 1988, pp. 29-31. Primary source: Extracted from Billy J. Tidwell, *Black Employment in the Private Sector*. Washington, D.C.: National Urban League, July 1988. Published by permission. Employment Opportunity Report No. 1, *Job Patterns for Minorities and Women in Private Industry - 1966*, Table 2. EEO Report, *Job Patterns for Minorities and Women in Private Industry - 1975*, Table 1. EEO Report, *Job Patterns for Minorities and Women in Private Industry - 1985*, Table 1.

★ 660 ★
Labor Force

Characteristics	Blacks		Whites	
	Number	Percent	Number	Percent
1966				
Officials and Managers	0.9	-7.3	98	9.4
Professionals	1.3	-6.9	96.5	7.9
Technicians	4.1	-4.1	93.5	4.9
Sales Workers	2.3	-5.9	95.8	7.2
Clerical Workers	3.5	-4.7	94.1	5.5
Craftsmen	3.6	-4.6	93.8	5.2
Operatives	10.8	2.6	85.5	-3.1
Laborers	21.2	13.0	71.5	-17.0
Service Workers	22.4	14.2	72.7	-15.9
% of Total Employed		8.2		88.6
1975				
Officials and Managers	3.0	-7.2	94.6	10.8
Professionals	3.2	-7.5	92.5	8.7
Technicians	7.5	-3.2	87.9	4.1
Sales Workers	5.7	-5.0	90.6	6.8
Clerical Workers	9.4	-1.3	85.6	1.8
Craftsmen	7.0	-3.7	88.3	4.5
Operatives	15.4	4.7	78.1	-5.7
Laborers	20.0	9.3	69.1	-14.7
Service Workers	22.7	12	69.2	-14.6
% of Total Employed		10.7		83.8
1985				
Officials and Managers	4.6	-7.5	91.3	11.6
Professionals	4.6	-7.5	88.9	9.2
Technicians	9.1	-3.0	83.6	3.9
Sales Workers	9.3	-2.8	84.4	4.7
Clerical Workers	12.9	0.8	79.5	-0.2
Craftsmen	8.9	-3.2	83.9	4.2
Operatives	17.0	4.9	73.2	-6.5
Laborers	19.3	7.2	66.2	-13.6

Continued.

Labor Force
[Continued]

Characteristics	Blacks		Whites	
	Number	Percent	Number	Percent
Service Workers	23.7	11.6	64.0	-15.7
% of Total Employed		12.1		79.7

Source: "Black and White Participation Rates by Occupation, 1966, 1975, 1985," *Black Employment in the Private Sector*, 1988, pp. 32 - 34. Primary source: Extracted from Billy J. Tidwell, *Black Employment in the Private Sector.* Washington, D.C.: National Urban League, July 1988. Published by permission. EEO Report *Job Patterns for Minorities and Women in Private Industry - 1966*, Table 2. EEO Report, *Job Patterns for Minorities and Women in Private Industry - 1975*, Table 1. EEO Report, *Job Patterns for Minorities and Women in Private Industry - 1985*, Table 1.

★ 661 ★
Labor Force

Numbers in thousands. Persons 15 years old and over as of March, 1989.

Total money earnings	Total workers	Worked at full-time jobs				Worked at part-time jobs			
		Total	50 weeks or more	27 to 49 weeks	26 weeks or less	Total	50 weeks or more	27 to 49 weeks	26 weeks or less
Male									
White									
Number with earnings	61,550	53,120	42,716	6,330	4,074	8,430	3,123	1,944	3,364
Median earnings (dol.)	21,348	24,453	27,228	14,959	4,155	3,308	6,106	4,519	1,636
Standard error (dol.)	121	180	123	295	131	109	174	158	44
Mean earning (dol.)	25,419	28,398	31,804	19,303	6,814	6,647	10,068	8,822	2,213
Standard error (dol.)	158	169	190	394	261	281	491	866	114
Gini ratio	.438	.384	.337	.410	.551	.618	.544	.618	.473
Standard error	.0049	.0053	.0059	.0168	.0230	.0211	.0294	.0561	.1596
Black									
Number with earnings	6,687	5,561	4,108	797	656	1,126	317	207	601
Median earnings (dol.)	14,344	16,717	20,371	10,807	3,172	2,288	6,061	6,171	1,454
Standard error (dol.)	417	282	341	539	319	114	562	1,289	100
Mean earning (dol.)	17,134	19,700	23,374	13,338	4,428	4,458	7,495	7,706	1,738
Standard error (dol.)	346	385	466	549	296	343	629	734	406
Gini ratio	.445	.389	.325	.358	.485	.542	.410	.427	.427
Standard error	.0151	.0167	.0195	.0432	.0544	.0795	.0766	.0857	.1961
Hispanic[1]									
Number with earnings	5,564	4,924	3,608	796	521	640	250	129	261
Median earnings (dol.)	13,599	15,143	17,851	10,278	3,589	3,278	5,834	3,514	1,725
Standard error (dol.)	384	321	459	400	290	368	633	598	179
Mean earning (dol.)	16,903	18,389	21,697	12,257	4,485	5,549	8,673	4,808	2,701
Standard error (dol.)	381	413	513	554	421	482	971	675	478
Gini ratio	.428	.395	.340	.352	.485	.545	.464	.484	.524
Standard error	.0173	.0184	.0215	.0477	.0722	.0637	.0914	.1219	.1423
Female									
White									
Number with earnings	51,760	34,820	26,606	4,656	3,958	16,941	7,095	4,022	5,823
Median earnings (dol.)	11,105	15,633	17,819	10,713	3,146	3,725	6,579	4,336	1,570
Standard error (dol.)	87	97	139	192	118	75	94	98	32
Mean earning (dol.)	13,452	17,386	20,091	13,176	4,428	5,365	8,175	5,762	1,665
Standard error (dol.)	90	114	132	246	128	84	149	177	52

Continued.

Labor Force
[Continued]

Total money earnings	Total workers	Worked at full-time jobs				Worked at part-time jobs			
		Total	50 weeks or more	27 to 49 weeks	26 weeks or less	Total	50 weeks or more	27 to 49 weeks	26 weeks or less
Gini ratio	.453	.360	.297	.367	.489	.504	.409	.462	.352
Standard error	.0049	.0060	.0069	.0181	.0234	.0141	.0154	.0224	.0303
Black									
Number with earnings	6,691	5,337	3,985	711	640	1,625	556	309	760
Median earnings (dol.)	10,984	13,828	16,538	9,611	2,692	2,497	5,736	3,915	1,486
Standard error (dol.)	198	391	259	521	279	175	269	341	90
Mean earning (dol.)	12,628	15,202	17,811	10,765	3,894	4,174	6,514	5,024	2,118
Standard error (dol.)	218	240	169	478	275	297	370	498	507
Gini ratio	.425	.343	.274	.327	.477	.518	.364	.447	.521
Standard error	.0145	.0171	.0188	.0491	.0567	.0381	.0577	.0871	.0973
Hispanic[1]									
Number with earnings	3,865	2,866	1,966	428	473	998	374	196	429
Median earnings (dol.)	9,188	11,664	14,845	8,996	2,629	3,077	6,249	4,157	1,529
Standard error (dol.)	296	275	447	512	287	321	322	344	124
Mean earning (dol.)	11,286	13,790	16,860	11,080	3,479	4,096	6,854	4,581	1,467
Standard error (dol.)	302	367	453	704	312	238	456	444	133
Gini ratio	.450	.384	.300	.357	.452	.457	.354	.347	.292
Standard error	.0217	.0233	.0274	.0661	.0772	.0477	.0688	.1019	.0936

Source: "Work Experience in 1988 — Civilian Workers, by Total Earnings in 1988, Race, Hispanic Origin, and Sex," *Money Income and Poverty Status in the United States: 1988, 1989,* p. 52. Primary source: *Money Income and Poverty Status in the United States: 1988, 1989.* Note: 1. Persons of Hispanic origin may be of any race.

★ 662 ★
Labor Force

Numbers in thousands.

Characteristic	All races	Black	White
Labor Force Status in 1988[1]			
Both sexes, 16 years and over	184,613	20,692	158,194
In civilian labor force	121,669	13,205	104,756
Percent in civilian labor force	65.9	63.8	66.2
Employed	114,968	11,658	99,812
Unemployed	6,701	1,547	4,944
Percent unemployed	5.5	11.7	4.7
Not in labor force	62,944	7,487	53,439
Males, 16 years and over	87,857	9,289	75,855
In civilian labor force	66,927	6,596	58,317
Percent in civilian labor force	76.2	71.0	76.9
Employed	63,273	5,824	55,550
Unemployed	3,655	771	2,766
Percent unemployed	5.5	11.7	4.7
Not in labor force	20,930	2,694	17,538
Females, 16 years and over	96,756	11,402	82,340
In civilian labor force	54,742	6,609	46,439
Percent in civilian labor force	56.6	58.0	56.4
Employed	51,696	5,834	44,262

Continued.

Labor Force
[Continued]

Characteristic	All races	Black	White
Unemployed	3,046	776	2,177
Percent unemployed	5.6	11.7	4.7
Not in labor force	42,014	4,793	35,901
Occupations in 1988[1]			
Employed males, 16 years and over	63,273	5,824	55,550
Percent	100.0	100.0	100.0
Managerial and professional specialty	25.5	13.3	26.6
Technical, sales and administrative support	19.7	16.9	19.9
Service occupations	9.6	18.1	8.6
Farming, forestry, and fishing	4.5	3.5	4.7
Precision production, craft and repair	19.7	15.5	20.3
Operators, fabricators, and laborers	20.9	32.7	19.8
Employed females, 16 years and over	51,696	5,834	44,262
Percent	100.0	100.0	100.0
Managerial and professional specialty	25.2	17.5	26.3
Technical, sales, and administrative support	44.6	38.6	45.4
Service occupations	17.9	28.2	16.6
Farming, forestry, and fishing	1.1	0.4	1.2
Precision production, craft, and repair	2.3	2.2	2.3
Operators, fabricators, and laborers	8.9	13.1	8.2

Source: "Selected Economic Characteristics of Persons and Families, Sex and Race: 1988," *The Black Population in the United States,* March 1988, p. 20. Primary source: *The Black Population in the United States:* March 1988. *Note:* 1. Data on labor force and occupation are annual average.

★ 663 ★
Labor Force by Occupation

For civilian noninstitutional population 16 years old and over. Annual average of monthly figures. Based on Current Population Survey. Persons of Hispanic origin may be of any race.

Occupation	Total Employed (1,000)	Percent of Total		
		Female	Black	Hispanic
Managerial and professional specialty	27,742	44.3	6.2	3.7
Technical, sales, and administrative support	35,082	64.7	8.8	5.6
Service occupations	15,054	60.6	17.4	9.1
Precision production, craft, and repair	13,568	8.5	7.3	8.0
Operators, fabricators, and laborers	17,486	25.8	15.2	10.8
Farming, forestry, and fishing	3,507	15.8	6.5	13.2

Source: "Employed Civilians, by Occupation, Sex, and Race: 1987," *Statistical Abstract,* 1989, pp. 388-389. U.S. Bureau of Labor Statistics, *Employment and Earnings,* January 1988.

★ 664 ★
Labor Force in Southern Cities

Occupation	White Males	Black Males	Other Males	White Females	Black Females	Other Females
Officials/Administrators	89	3	1	6	1	
Professionals	82	4	1	11	2	
Technicians	84	6	1	7	1	1
Protective Service	86	9	5	2	1	
Paraprofessionals	26	14	3	36	20	2
Office/Clericals	15	2	1	68	11	4
Skilled Crafts	79	21				
Service Maintenance	32	53	12	1	2	
Total employed	59	22	5	11	3	1
Average central city labor force	44	11	3	28	11	1

Source: "Occupational Participation: Percent Within Eight Job Types, by Race, Sex, and Ethnic Group; Percent Within System Size and Average Labor Force, by Race, Sex, and Ethnic Group, for 16 Cities Combined, 1975," Southern Regional Council, "Background/Facts/Analysis," 1975, p. 1. Primary source: Southern Regional Council, "Background/Facts/Analysis," 1975. Published by permission.

★ 665 ★
Labor Force, Employment and Earnings - Part I

For civilian noninstitutional population 16 years old and over. Annual averages of monthly figures. Rates are based on annual average civilian noninstitutional population of each specified group and represent proportion of each specified group in the civilian labor force. Based on Current Population Survey; see text, section 1 and Appendix III. See also *Historical Statistics, Colonial Times to 1970*, series D 42-48.

| Race and Sex | Civilian Labor Force (millions) | | | | | | |
	1970	1975	1980	1985	1987	1995	2000
Total[1]	82.8	93.8	106.9	115.5	119.9	131.6	138.8
White	73.6	82.8	93.6	99.9	103.3	111.7	116.7
Male	46.0	50.3	54.5	56.5	57.8	60.5	62.3
Female	27.5	32.5	39.1	43.5	45.5	51.2	54.4
Black[2]	9.2	9.3	10.9	12.4	13.0	15.1	16.3
Male	5.2	5.0	5.6	6.2	6.5	7.4	7.9
Female	4.0	4.2	5.3	6.1	6.5	7.7	8.4
Hispanic[3]	[4]	[4]	6.1	7.7	8.5	11.8	14.1
Male	[4]	[4]	3.8	4.7	5.2	7.0	8.3
Female	[4]	[4]	2.3	3.0	3.4	4.7	5.8

Source: "Civilian Labor Force and Participation Rates by Race, Hispanic Origin, Sex and Age, 1970 to 1987, and Projections, 1995 and 2000," *Statistical Abstract*, 1989, p. 376. Primary source: U.S. Bureau of Labor Statistics, *Employment and Earnings*, monthly; *Monthly Labor Review*, September 1987, and unpublished data. *Notes:* 1. Beginning 1975, includes other races not shown separately. 2. For 1970, Black and other. 3. Hispanic persons may be of any race. 4. Not available.

★ 666 ★
Labor Force, Employment and Earnings - Part II

For civilian noninstitutional population 16 years old and over. Annual averages of monthly figures. Rates are based on annual average civilian noninstitutional population of each specified group and represent proportion of each specified group in the civilian labor force. Based on Current Population Survey. See also *Historical Statistics, Colonial Times to 1970*, series D 42-48.

Race and Sex	Participation Rate (percent)						
	1970	1985	1980	1985	1987	1995	2000
Total[1]	60.4	61.2	63.8	64.8	65.6	67.2	67.8
White	60.2	61.5	64.1	65.0	65.8	67.5	68.2
Male	80.0	78.7	78.2	77.0	76.8	75.9	75.3
Female	42.6	45.9	51.2	54.1	55.7	59.7	61.5
Black[2]	61.8	58.8	61.0	62.9	63.8	65.6	66.0
Male	76.5	71.0	70.6	70.8	71.1	71.4	70.7
Female	49.5	48.9	53.2	56.5	58.0	60.9	62.1
Hispanic[3]	[4]	[4]	64.0	64.6	66.4	69.7	68.7
Male	[4]	[4]	81.4	80.3	81.0	80.9	80.4
Female	[4]	[4]	47.4	49.3	52.0	54.7	56.9

Source: "Civilian Labor Force and Participation Rates by Race, Hispanic Origin, Sex and Age, 1970 to 1987, and Projections, 1995 and 2000," *Statistical Abstract*, 1989, p. 376. Primary source: U.S. Bureau of Labor Statistics, *Employment and Earnings*, monthly; *Monthly Labor Review*, September 1987,. and unpublished data. *Notes:* 1. Beginning 1975, includes other races not shown separately. 2. For 1970, Black and other. 3. Hispanic persons may be of any race. 4. Not available.

★ 667 ★
Labor Union Members - Part I

Annual averages of monthly data. Covers employed wage and salary workers 16 years old and over. Excludes self-employed workers whose businesses are incorporated although they technically qualify as wage and salary workers. Based on Current Population Survey.

Characteristic	Employed Wage and Salary Worker									
	Total (1,000)		Union members[1] (1,000)		Repre- sented by unions[2] (1,000)		Percent union members		Percent represented by union	
	1983	1987	1983	1987	1983	1987	1983	1987	1983	1987
White	77,046	85,525	14,844	13,972	17,182	15,712	19.3	16.3	22.3	18.4
Men	42,168	46,079	10,134	9,407	11,364	10,288	24.0	20.4	26.9	22.3
Women	34,877	39,446	4,710	4,565	5,818	5,424	13.5	11.6	16.7	13.8
Black	8,979	10,838	2,440	2,445	2,850	2,769	27.2	22.6	31.7	25.5
Men	4,477	5,329	1,420	1,381	1,615	1,531	31.7	25.9	36.1	28.7
Women	4,502	5,509	1,020	1,065	1,235	1,238	22.7	19.3	27.4	22.5
Hispanic[4]	[5]	7,215	[5]	1,234	[5]	1,371	[5]	17.1	[5]	19.0
Men	[5]	4,315	[5]	859	[5]	938	[5]	19.9	[5]	21.7
Women	[5]	2,900	[5]	374	[5]	434	[5]	12.9	[5]	15.0

Source: "Union Members, by Selected Characteristics: 1983 and 1987," *Statistical Abstract*, 1989, p. 416. Primary source: U.S. Bureau of Labor Statistics, *Employment and Earnings*, January issues. *Notes:* 1. Members of a labor union or an employee association similar to a labor union. 2. Members of a labor union or an employee association similar to a union as well as workers who report no union affiliation but whose jobs are covered by a union or an employee association contract. 3. For full-time employed wage and salary workers; 1983 revised since originally published. 4. Hispanic persons may be of any race. 5. Not available.

★ 668 ★
Labor Union Members - Part II

Annual averages of monthly data. Covers employed wage and salary workers 16 years old and over. Excludes self-employed workers whose businesses are incorporated although they technically qualify as wage and salary workers. Based on Current Population Survey.

	Median Usual Weekly Earnings (dol.)[3]							
	Total		Union members[1]		Repre-sented by union[2]		Not represented by unions	
	1983	1987	1983	1987	1983	1987	1983	1987
White	318	383	396	477	391	474	295	355
Men	387	450	423	501	421	500	362	419
Women	254	307	314	394	313	392	240	293
Black	261	301	31	399	324	395	222	268
Men	293	326	366	423	360	420	244	288
Women	231	275	292	357	287	355	209	251
Hispanic[4]	5	284	5	395	5	392	5	261
Men	5	306	5	418	5	417	5	276
Women	5	251	5	311	5	311	5	239

Source: "Union Members, by Selected Characteristics: 1983 and 1987," *Statistical Abstract*, 1989, p. 416. Primary source: U.S. Bureau of Labor Statistics, *Employment and Earnings*, January issues. *Notes:* 1. Members of a labor union or an employee association similar to a labor union. 2. Members of a labor union or an employee association similar to a union as well as workers who report no union affiliation but whose jobs are covered by a union or an employee association contract. 3. For full-time employed wage and salary workers; 1983 revised since originally published. 4. Hispanic persons may be of any race.

★ 669 ★
Level of Education

Characteristic	1940	1950	1960	1970	1980
Total U.S.					
White	9.03	9.85	10.65	11.65	12.83
Black	5.78	6.58	7.80	9.35	11.37
Difference[1]	3.25	3.27	2.85	2.31	1.46
South					
White	8.71	9.37	10.13	11.22	12.48
Black	5.13	5.88	6.91	8.53	10.89
Difference[1]	3.58	3.49	3.22	2.69	1.59
Non-South					
White	9.15	10.6	10.83	11.80	12.92
Black	7.31	7.98	8.94	10.20	11.91
Difference[1]	1.84	2.08	1.89	1.60	1.01

Source: "Mean Years of School of Male Wage Earners Ages 25-64 by Region and Race," *The Economic Progress of Black Men in America*, p. 55. Primary source: Census of Population, 1940-1980; Public Use Sample. *Note:* 1. White mean schooling minus black mean schooling.

★ 670 ★
Males in the Labor Force

Year	18-19 Years		20-24 Years		25-34 Years		35-44 Years		45-54 Years		55-64 Years	
	Black	White	Black	White	Black	White	Black	White	Black	White	Black	White
1955	75.7	71.7	89.7	86.4	95.8	97.5	96.2	98.2	93.2	96.8	83.1	89.2
1965	66.7	65.8	89.8	85.3	95.7	97.4	94.2	97.7	92.0	95.9	78.8	85.2
1975	57.5	72.8	78.4	85.5	89.4	95.8	90.0	96.4	84.6	92.9	68.7	76.5
1983	50.2	69.3	77.1	85.0	87.1	95.4	90.7	96.0	83.9	92.0	63.5	69.9

Source: "Labor Force Participation Rates of Males from 1955-1983 by Age and Race," *Equality and Excellence: The Educational Status of Black Americans,* 1985, p. 8. Primary source: *Employment and Training Report of the President, 1982; Employment and Earnings,* Bureau of Labor Statistics, November 1983.

★ 671 ★
Occupations in Selected Industries

Characteristic	Totals	Officials & Managers	Professionals	Technicians	Sales Workers	Clerical Workers	Craft Workers	Operatives	Laborers	Service Workers
Services										
Blacks	100.0	3.5	8.8	9.2	1.2	17.3	2.6	6.0	4.8	46.6
Whites	100.0	11.0	28.8	11.2	2.2	18.5	3.8	3.8	2.1	18.3
Retail Trade										
Blacks	100.0	5.1	0.6	0.7	35.3	9.6	2.1	6.0	8.9	31.7
Whites	100.0	12.4	1.7	1.0	43.2	9.9	3.0	4.3	5.3	19.3
Finance, Insurance, and Real Estate										
Blacks	100.0	7.6	8.0	6.2	2.4	66.4	1.0	1.8	1.1	5.5
Whites	100.0	20.3	13.9	6.0	5.2	50.0	1.0	1.0	0.5	2.1
Transportation and Public Utilities										
Blacks	100.0	7.3	3.9	3.5	5.2	33.4	13.3	18.6	10.8	4.0
Whites	100.0	15.7	9.8	5.5	5.1	21.2	21.0	14.7	4.7	2.3
Manufacturing										
Blacks	100.0	3.6	3.1	3.1	1.8	7.4	13.1	48.6	15.8	3.5
Whites	100.0	13.1	11.6	5.9	4.2	10.3	16.4	28.6	8.2	1.7

Source: "Black and White Occupational Distribution for Selected Industries, 1985." Billy J. Tidwell, *Black Employment in the Private Sector: A Twenty-Year Assessment.* National Urban League, Research Department, July 1988. Primary source: *Job Patterns for Minorities and Women in Private Industry,* EEO Report, 1985, Table 2.

★ 672 ★
Projected High-Growth Occupations: Participation

Occupation	Total Employed (1,000)			Black Percent of Total		
	1983	1984	1985	1983	1984	1985
Accountants and Auditors	1,105	1,234	1,265	5.5	5.5	5.9
Electrical and Electronic Engineers	(1,572)[1]	(1,627)[1]	544	(5.8)[1]	(2.6)[1]	3.4
Mechanical Engineers			272			2.2
Computer Systems Analysts	276	310	359	6.2	5.3	5.5
Physicians	519	520	492	3.2	5.0	3.7
Registered Nurses	1,372	1,402	1,447	6.7	7.6	6.8
Lawyers and Judges	651	678	671	2.7	2.6	3.3
Computer Programmers	443	507	534	4.4	5.3	6.4
Elementary School Teachers	1,350	1,322	1,360	11.1	9.9	11.1

Source: "Percent of Black Population in Projected High Growth Occupations 1983- 1985," *NAFEO INROADS*, April/May, 1988, p. 4. Primary source: *Statistical Abstract of the United States*, 1986, U.S. Department of Labor, Bureau of Labor Statistics. *Note:* 1. All engineers (data not provided by areas).

★ 673 ★
Ratios of Weekly Earnings

Characteristics	All years of school	0-7 years	8-11 years	High school	College
Ages 25-34[1]					
Non-South					
1940-1960	+7.1	+4.9	+10.7	+5.0	+0.5
1960-1980	+10.9	+13.4	+6.5	+9.9	+18.1
1940-1980	+18.0	+18.3	+17.2	+14.9	+18.6
South					
1940-1960	+10.2	+4.4	+4.6	+10.1	+12.7
1960-1980	+19.5	+19.2	+16.0	+16.3	+15.1
1940-1980	+29.7	+23.6	+20.6	+26.4	+27.8
All regions					
1940-1960	+14.8	+10.5	+9.3	+7.8	+8.7
1960-1980	+15.7	+22.0	+10.0	+10.7	+17.1
1940-1980	+30.5	+32.5	+19.3	+18.5	+25.8
Ages 45-54[2]					
Non-South					
1940-1960	+16.2	+19.0	+14.6	+18.1	+22.5
1960-1980	+7.0	+7.3	+10.6	+14.8	+23.5
1940-1980	+23.2	+26.3	+25.2	+32.9	+46.0
South					
1940-1960	+13.7	+12.8	+13.0	+22.9	+30.1
1960-1980	+13.2	+18.0	+11.3	+17.0	+8.2
1940-1980	+26.9	+30.8	+24.3	+39.9	+38.3
All regions					
1940-1960	+15.9	+16.7	+12.7	+21.3	+26.4

Continued.

Ratios of Weekly Earnings
[Continued]

Characteristics	All years of school	0-7 years	8-11 years	High school	College
1960-1980	+ 12.0	+ 15.3	+ 10.0	+ 14.8	+ 17.3
1940-1980	+ 27.9	+ 32.0	+ 22.7	+ 36.1	+ 43.7

Source: "Change in Black-White Weekly Earnings Ratios Between Cohorts by Education, Age, and Region," *The Economic Progress of Black Men in America*, p. 111 Primary source: *The Economic Progress of Black Men in America*. Washington, D.C.: U.S. Commission on Civil Rights, 1986. Clearing House Publication 91. *Notes:* 1. Percentage point change in black-white ratios for persons ages 25-34 in year t and persons 25-34 in year t+20, where t = 1940, 1960. 2. Percentage point change in black-white ratios for persons ages 45-54 in year t and persons 45-54 in year t+20, where t = 1940, 1960.

★ 674 ★
Unemployed

Race/ethnicity and years of school completed	Percent unemployed[1]								
	Total, 16 years and over	16 and 17 years	18 and 19 years	20 and 24 years	25 to 34 years	35 to 44 years	45 to 54 years	55 to 64 years	65 years and over
White[2]									
All education levels	5.0	17.3	12.7	7.8	4.9	3.9	3.0	3.3	2.0
8 years or less	9.4	32.3	32.4	14.5	9.5	10.2	7.6	6.5	2.5
1 to 3 years of high school	11.5	16.5	17.5	16.7	11.9	8.5	5.2	5.5	3.6
4 years of high school	5.3	15.0	10.4	8.6	5.7	4.9	3.1	2.8	1.5
1 to 3 years of college	3.5	4	6.0	4.7	3.7	3.4	2.3	2.4	1.7
4 of more years of college	1.7	4	4	4.2	2.0	1.3	0.9	1.4	2.0
Black[2]									
All education levels	13.3	34.5	40.6	22.4	13.1	9.0	7.4	5.3	6.5
8 years or less	14.5	57.6	36.8	25.5	15.7	9.8	8.0	4.1	
1 to 3 years of high school	23.0	32.5	57.4	38.3	27.9	15.3	4.6	4.1	17.0
4 years of high school	14.2	25.5	32.6	24.0	13.4	10.3	9.5	5.0	4
1 to 3 years of college	8.6	4	23.3	12.3	8.2	6.5	8.2	3.6	4
4 of more years of college	3.7	4	4	9.4	4.3	2.5	2.3	3.7	4
Hispanic origin[3]									
All education levels	8.5	27.0	20.1	10.6	7.0	7.2	5.7	6.9	3.8
8 years or less	11.2	34.5	29.9	12.5	9.7	11.5	8.3	10.2	7.9
1 to 3 years of high school	14.9	25.6	29.3	14.1	13.6	9.7	6.5	6.9	4
4 years of high school	7.2	12.9	9.8	10.6	6.1	6.8	4.9	4.0	4
1 to 3 years of college	4.6	4	11.4	7.6	4.0	3.7	2.0	1.6	4
4 of more years of college	2.3	4	-	3.4	2.4	1.1	2.5	5.3	4

Source: "Unemployment Rate of Persons 16 Years Old and Over, by Age, Sex, Race/Ethnicity, and Years of School Completed: March 1988," *Digest of Education Statistics,* 1989, p. 363. Primary Source: U.S. Department of Labor, Bureau of Labor Statistics, Office of Employment and Unemployment Statistics, "Educational Attainment of Workers, March 1988." *Notes:* 1. The unemployment rate is the percentage of individuals in the labor force who are not working and who made specific efforts to find employment sometime during the prior 4 weeks. The labor force includes employed and unemployed persons. 2. Includes persons of Hispanic origin. 3. Persons of Hispanic origin may be of any race. 4. Data not available.

★ 675 ★
Unemployed High School Graduates and Dropouts

Characteristic	1983	1984	1985	1986	1987	1988
All aged 20-24						
Graduates	17.6	12.9	12.6	13.1	10.7	10.7
Dropouts	31.5	26.6	25.1	23.7	22.7	20.5
White						
Graduates	15.0	10.7	10.4	10.7	9.0	8.6
Dropouts	27.6	22.5	22.4	19.7	17.0	16.7
Black						
Graduates	33.6	27.7	26.4	28.2	21.8	24.0
Dropouts	48.4	50.8	42.7	43.7	49.5	38.3
Hispanic						
Graduates	18.9	11.4	12.0	11.5	11.3	10.6
Dropouts	30.5	25.7	18.0	16.3	15.8	14.1
Male						
Graduates	19.3	13.6	13.0	13.6	11.0	10.4
Dropouts	32.1	26.3	25.1	23.8	22.7	18.8
Female						
Graduates	15.6	12.1	12.1	12.4	10.4	11.1
Dropouts	30.1	27.1	25.1	23.6	22.8	23.8

Source: "Unemployment Rates of High School Graduates and Dropouts, Aged 20-24, by Race and Ethnicity and Gender: March 1983- March 1988," *1989 Education Indicators*, n.d., p. 166. Primary source: U.S. Department of Labor, Bureau of Labor Statistics, "Educational Attainment of Workers, March (various years)." *Notes:* Dropouts are those who are identified as completing 1-3 years of high school.

★ 676 ★
Unemployment

	1940	1950	1960	1970	1980
Black					
25-34	10.0	7.3	7.9	4.6	11.3
35-44	9.7	6.4	7.9	4.2	8.1
45-54	9.0	4.9	7.0	4.0	7.5
55-64	9.2	6.5	8.3	3.9	6.1
Total	9.6	6.4	7.8	4.2	9.0
White					
25-34	7.7	3.5	3.7	2.8	5.6
35-44	6.5	3.0	3.2	2.3	3.7
45-54	7.4	3.3	3.8	2.4	3.5
55-64	9.6	4.2	4.7	2.9	3.8
Total	7.6	3.4	3.7	2.6	4.4
Black relative to white unemployment rate					
Ratio	1.3	1.9	2.1	1.6	2.0

Continued.

Unemployment
[Continued]

	1940	1950	1960	1970	1980
Difference	2.0	3.0	4.1	1.6	4.6

Source: "Male Unemployment Rates by Race and Age," *The Economic Progress of Black Men in America,* p. 41. Primary source: Census of Population, 1940-1980, Public Use Sample. *Note:* Unemployment as a percentage of the civilian labor force.

★ 677 ★
Unemployment

Charactersitic	1940	1950	1960	1970	1980
Black					
Less than 12 years					
Non-South	17.0	10.3	10.7	5.7	14.9
South	7.1	4.6	6.8	3.9	8.6
12 years or more					
Non-South	12.6	5.6	5.9	3.8	9.4
South	5.0	3.3	3.9	2.4	5.6
Total	9.6	6.4	7.8	4.2	9.0
White					
Less than 12 years					
Non-South	9.5	4.7	5.5	4.2	8.4
South	5.9	3.0	4.9	2.8	5.6
12 years or more					
Non-South	5.2	2.3	2.1	2.0	4.0
South	3.3	1.6	1.6	1.3	2.3
Total	7.6	3.4	3.7	2.6	4.4
Difference (black minus white)					
Less than 12 years					
Non-South	7.5	5.6	5.2	1.5	6.5
South	1.2	1.6	1.9	1.1	3.0
12 years or more					
Non-South	7.4	3.3	3.8	1.8	5.4
South	1.7	1.7	2.3	1.1	3.3
Total	2.0	3.0	4.1	1.6	4.6
Ratio (black divided by white)					
Less than 12 years					
Non-South	1.8	2.2	1.9	1.4	1.8
South	1.2	1.5	1.4	1.4	1.5
12 years or more					
Non-South	2.4	2.4	2.8	1.9	2.3
South	1.5	2.1	2.4	1.8	2.4
Total	1.3	1.8	2.1	1.6	2.0

Source: "Male Unemployment by Race, Education, and Region," *The Economic Progress of Black Men in America,* p. 44. Primary source: Census of Population, 1940-1980; Public Use Sample. *Note:* Ages 25-64.

★ 678 ★
Unemployment Insurance Coverage

| Characteristics | Tot | 1 mth | Length of Spell African American | | | 5+ |
			2 mths	3 mths	4 mths	
Some coverage	9.2	---	7.8	16.0	10.1	18.3
All mths	6.2	---	7.8	12.5	8.0	8.6
White						
Some coverage	18.2	---	17.7	27.4	21.4	40.9
All mths	13.0	---	17.7	22.6	15.1	22.8

Source: "Percentage Comparisons of African Americans and Whites with Unemployment Insurance Coverage by Duration of Unemployment." *The State of Black America 1990*, January 1990, p. 220. Primary source: U.S. Bureau of the Census, *Current Population Reports*, "Spells of Job Search and Layoff... and Their Outcomes," July 1989, Table H, p. 9. *Note:* 1. Spells beginning and ending between 1984 and 1986.

★ 679 ★
Unemployment Outcomes

| | African American | | White | |
	Found Job	Withdrew	Found Job	Withdrew
Both Sexes	52.7	47.3	71.0	29.0
Male	64.7	35.3	80.1	19.8
16-19	44.9	55.1	70.2	29.8
20-24	58.2	41.8	86.7	13.3
25-54	84.2	15.8	85.0	15.0
Female	44.6	55.4	62.8	37.2
16-19	40.8	59.2	62.9	37.1
20-24	42.7	57.3	66.2	33.8
25-54	46.9	53.1	62.1	37.9

Source: "Comparisons of Unemployment Outcomes Among African American and White Workers." *The State of Black America 1990*, January 1990, p. 222. Primary source: U.S. Bureau of the Census, *Current Population Reports*, "Spells of Job Search and Layoff... and Their Outcomes," July 1989, Table I, p. 10. *Note:* Spells beginning and ending between 1984 and 1986.

★ 680 ★
Unemployment Rates

Total Population	3rd Q. 1988	2nd Q. 1989	3rd Q. 1989
African American[1]			
NUL Unemployment	3,061	3,232	3,396
DOL Unemployment	1,543	1,547	1,544
Discouraged Workers	1,150	1,302	1,472
Part-time Unemployed	377	383	380
NUL CLF	14,603	14,717	15,186
DOL CLF	13,453	13,415	13,714

Continued.

Unemployment Rates
[Continued]

Total Population	3rd Q. 1988	2nd Q. 1989	3rd Q. 1989
Discouraged Workers	1,150	1,302	1,472
NUL Hidden Unemployment Rates	21.0	22.0	22.4
DOL Unemployment Rates	11.4	11.5	11.3
White American			
NUL Unemployment	10,483	10,529	10,227
DOL Unemployment	4,888	4,660	4,712
Discouraged Workers	3,542	4,047	3,658
Part-time Unemployed	2,053	1,822	1,857
NUL CLF	109,371	110,448	110,956
DOL CLF	105,829	106,401	107,298
Discouraged Workers	3,542	4,047	3,658
NUL Hidden Unemployment Rates	9.6	9.5	9.2
DOL Unemployment Rates	4.6	4.4	4.4

Source: "Department of Labor and National Urban League Unemployment Rates and Totals", National Urban League. *Quarterly Economic Report on The African American Worker,* Third Quarter, 1989, December, 1989, p. 2. Primary source: Prepared by the National Urban League Research Department from unpublished U.S. Bureau of Labor Statistics data. From *The Quarterly Economic Report of the African American Worker.* Published by permission. *Note:* 1. African Americans represents "Blacks only" data.

★ 681 ★
Unemployment Rates for Female Workers - Part I

	18-19 Years			20-24 Years			25-34 Years			35-44 Years		
Year	Black	White	B/W Ratios	Black	White	B/W Ratios	Black	White	B/W Ratios	Black	White	B/W Ratios
1955	21.4	7.7	2.8	13.0	5.1	2.5	10.2	4.3	2.4	5.5	3.8	1.4
1965	27.8	13.4	2.1	13.7	6.3	2.1	8.2	4.8	1.8	7.6	4.1	1.9
1975	38.3	16.1	2.4	22.5	11.2	2.0	12.9	8.5	1.5	8.6	6.6	1.3
1982	39.8	15.7	2.5	25.2	11.1	2.3	16.0	8.3	2.0	12.1	7.5	1.6
1983	56.1	14.9	3.8	32.5	9.6	3.4	18.6	7.1	2.6	10.1	5.2	2.0

Source: "Unemployment Rates and Unemployment Ratios for Female Workers by Race," *Equality and Excellence: The Educational Status of Black Americans,* 1985, p. 7. Primary source: *Employment and Training Report of the President, 1982; Employment and Earning,* Bureau of Labor Statistics, November 1983.

★ 682 ★
Unemployment Rates for Female Workers - Part II

Year	45-54 Years			55-64 Years		
	Black	White	B/W Ratios	Black	White	B/W Ratios
1955	5.2	3.4	1.4	5.5	2.2	2.5
1965	4.4	3.0	1.5	3.9	2.7	1.4
1975	6.7	5.8	1.2	5.3	5.1	1.0
1982	9.0	5.9	1.5	6.6	5.5	1.1
1983	9.7	5.0	2.0	7.8	4.0	2.0

Source: "Unemployment Rates and Unemployment Ratios for Female Workers by Race," *Equality and Excellence: The Educational Status of Black Americans*, 1985, p. 7. Primary source: *Employment and Training Report of the President, 1982; Employment and Earning*, Bureau of Labor Statistics, November 1983.

★ 683 ★
Unemployment Rates for Male Workers - Part I

Year	18-19 Years			20-24 Years			25-34 Years			35-44 Years		
	Black	White	B/W Ratios	Black	White	B/W Ratios	Black	White	B/W Ratios	Black	White	B/W Ratios
1955	12.9	10.4	1.2	12.4	7.0	1.8	8.6	2.7	3.2	8.2	2.7	3.2
1965	20.2	11.4	1.5	9.3	5.9	1.3	6.2	2.6	2.2	6.2	2.6	2.0
1975	32.9	17.2	1.9	22.9	13.2	1.7	11.9	6.3	1.9	11.9	6.3	1.9
1982	47.4	21.1	2.2	32.0	15.3	2.1	19.6	10.4	1.9	19.6	10.4	1.9
1983	42.7	18.3	2.3	30.4	11.4	2.7	14.8	7.2	2.1	14.8	7.2	2.1

Source: "Unemployment Rates and Unemployment Ratios 1955-1983 for Male Workers by Race," *Equality and Excellence: The Educational Status of Black Americans*, 1985, p. 7. Primary source: *Employment and Training Report of the President, 1982; Employment and Earning*, Bureau of Labor Statistics, November 1983.

★ 684 ★
Unemployment Rates for Male Workers - Part II

Year	45-54 Years			55-64 Years		
	Black	White	B/W Ratios	Black	White	B/W Ratios
1955	6.4	2.9	2.2	9.0	3.9	2.3
1965	5.1	2.3	2.2	5.4	3.1	1.7
1975	9.0	4.4	2.2	6.1	4.1	1.5
1982	10.0	6.3	1.6	11.9	5.8	2.2
1983	12.1	4.6	2.6	7.3	4.7	1.5

Source: "Unemployment Rates and Unemployment Ratios 1955-1983 for Male Workers by Race," *Equality and Excellence: The Educational Status of Black Americans*, 1985, p. 7. Primary source: *Employment and Training Report of the President, 1982; Employment and Earning*, Bureau of Labor Statistics, November 1983.

★ 685 ★
Unemployment Trends in Industries

Industry	3rd Q. 1988		2nd Q. 1989		3rd Q. 1989	
	African American	White American	African American	White American	African American	White American
Goods-Producing Industries	10.7	5.0	10.8	4.8	9.5	4.6
Construction	15.8	5.6	17.1	6.8	13.5	6.0
Manufacturing	9.1	4.6	8.8	4.2	10.0	4.2
Durable Goods	9.5	4.5	8.1	3.9	10.7	4.0
Primary Meals	11.5	3.9	12.1	1.6	13.8	2.6
Automobiles	11.3	5.5	8.0	4.8	9.7	6.7
Non-Durable Goods	8.7	4.9	9.6	4.6	9.3	4.6
Food	11.5	6.0	11.8	6.4	10.5	6.3
Textiles	5.5	4.3	4.7	4.2	6.9	4.6
Apparel	10.8	9.4	12.9	8.1	10.6	7.9
Service-Producing Industries	9.1	3.8	9.3	3.5	9.0	3.6
Transportation	5.6	2.8	7.6	3.0	7.5	3.1
Trade	14.2	5.0	14.0	4.7	14.0	4.7
Wholesale	9.6	3.7	9.2	3.1	9.9	3.3
Retail	14.9	5.3	14.7	5.0	14.6	5.0
Finance	7.2	2.5	6.7	2.8	8.2	3.4
Private Household Service	9.3	5.5	9.9	7.2	9.9	5.7
Misc. Service	8.7	3.6	8.3	3.1	8.5	3.5
Business, Repair	13.0	14.7	13.3	4.6	13.5	4.8
Personal Service	11.8	4.5	14.0	4.4	12.4	5.0
Professional Service	6.6	2.7	5.9	2.1	6.0	2.7
Public Administration	5.1	3.0	5.9	2.6	4.9	2.1
Federal	4.4	2.8	3.9	2.5	2.5	1.3
State	2.5	2.5	6.2	2.5	2.7	2.4
Local	3.9	2.4	6.5	1.6	8.1	2.5

Source: "Industrial Unemployment by Race (Percent Unemployed)." National Urban League. *Quarterly Economic Report on The African American Worker,* Third Quarter, 1989, December, 1989, p. 3. Primary source: Prepared by the National Urban League Research Department from unpublished U.S. Bureau of Labor Statistics data. Extracted from *The Quarterly Economic Report of the African American Worker.* Published by permission.

★ 686 ★
Where Do Male High School Graduates Go?

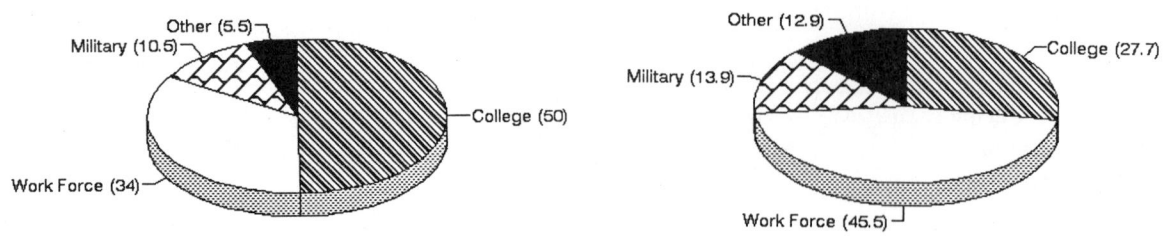

	College	Work Force	Military	Other
All males				
October 1979	46.0	41.7	8.6	3.7
October 1986	50.0	34.0	10.5	5.5
Black males				
October 1979	33.0	40.0[1]	21.0	6.0
October 1986	27.7	45.5[1]	13.9	12.9

Source: "Destinations of Recent Male and Black Male High School Graduates," *NAFEO INROADS*, October/November 1988, p. 11. Primary source: American Council on Education, Division of Policy Analysis and Research. *Notes:* The charts, above, show data for 'All Males' for October 1986 on the left and data for 'Black Males' for October 1986 on the right. 1. It should be noted that the percent of High School Graduates in the Work Force includes unemployed persons registered with the Labor Department as actively seeking employment.

★ 687 ★
Work Status of High School Dropouts: Trends

Numbers in thousands.

	Civilian noninstitutional population		Civilian labor force[1]				
				Labor force participation		Unemployed	
Year and race	Number	Percent	Number	rate	Employed	Number	Unemployment rate
1979-80 high school dropouts[2]							
in October 1980	739	100.0	471	63.7	322	149	31.6
White[3]	580	78.5	392	67.6	286	106	27.0
Black[3]	146	19.8	73	50.0	33	40	[4]
Hispanic origin[5]	91	12.3	60	65.9	43	17	[4]
1983-84 high school dropouts[6]							
in October 1984	601	100.0	387	64.4	258	129	33.3
White[3]	483	80.4	321	66.5	229	92	28.7
Black[3]	109	18.1	61	56.0	25	36	[4]
Hispanic origin[5]	91	15.1	47	51.6	32	15	[4]
1984-85 high school dropouts[7]							
in October 1985	612	100.0	413	67.5	266	147	35.6

Continued.

Work Status of High School Dropouts: Trends
[Continued]

Year and race	Civilian noninstitutional population		Civilian labor force[1]				
				Labor force participation rate		Unemployed	
	Number	Percent	Number		Employed	Number	Unemployment rate
White[3]	458	74.8	330	72.1	214	116	35.2
Black[3]	132	21.6	69	52.3	39	30	[4]
Hispanic origin[5]	106	17.3	73	68.9	40	33	[4]
1985-86 high school dropouts[8] in October 1986	562	100.0	359	63.9	259	100	27.9
White[3]	449	79.9	289	64.4	213	76	26.3
Black[3]	90	16.0	50	55.6	29	21	[4]
Hispanic origin[5]	127	22.6	77	60.6	58	19	24.7
1986-87 high school dropouts[9] in October 1987	502	100.0	333	66.4	207	126	37.8
White[3]	373	74.3	257	68.9	172	85	33.0
Black[3]	115	22.9	69	60.1	30	39	[4]
Hispanic origin[5]	57	11.4	37	[4]	22	15	[4]

Source: "Labor Force Status of 1979-80 to 1986-87 High School Dropouts 16 to 24 Years Old, by Sex and Race/Ethnicity: October 1980 to October 1987," *Digest of Education Statistics,* 1989, p. 326. Primary source: U.S. Department of Labor, Bureau of Labor Statistics, *Students, Graduates, and Dropouts, October 1980-82;* and *Employment of School-Age Youth, Graduates, and Dropouts,* various years, and "Nearly Half of College Freshmen Also Hold a Job or Are Looking for One," June 1987. (This table was prepared December 1988.) *Notes:* Data are based upon sample surveys of the civilian noninstitutional population. Percents are only shown when the base is 75,000 or greater. Even though the standard errors are large, smaller estimates are shown to permit users to combine categories in various ways. Because of rounding, details may not add to totals. 1. The labor force includes all employed persons plus those seeking employment. The labor force participation rate is the percentage of persons either employed or seeking employment. 2. Includes persons who dropped out of school between October 1979 and October 1980. 3. Includes persons of Hispanic origin. 4. Data not shown where base is less than 75,000. 5. Persons of Hispanic origin may be of any race. 6. Includes persons who dropped out of school between October 1983 and October 1984. 7. Includes persons who dropped out of school between October 1984 and October 1985. 8. Includes persons who dropped out of school between October 1985 and October 1986. 9. Includes persons who dropped out of school between October 1986 and October 1987.

★ 688 ★
Workplace Conditions

State	% Black Jobs	Rank
Massachusetts	35.3	1
	Adjusted	2
Alaska	33.7	3
California	33.4	4
	Adjusted	5
W. Virginia	32.7	6
Maryland	32	7
	Adjusted	8
Kansas	31.5	9
District of Columbia	31.4	10
	Adjusted	10
Rhode Island	31.4	10
Connecticut	29.2	13
	Adjusted	14

Continued.

Workplace Conditions
[Continued]

State	% Black Jobs	Rank
Illinois	28.6	15
Ohio	28.2	16
	Adjusted	17
Lousiana	27.8	18
New York	27.4	19
	Adjusted	20
Tennessee	27.3	21
Colorado	27.1	21
	Adjusted	23
Texas	26.7	24
New Jersey	26.2	25
	Adjusted	26
Pennsylvania	26	27
Virginia	25.7	28
	Adjusted	29
Florida	24.7	30
Georgia	24.4	31
	Adjusted	31
Mississippi	24.4	31
Kentucky	24.3	34
	Adjusted	35
Missouri	23.6	36
Delaware	23.4	37
	Adjusted	38
Oklahoma	23.3	39
Wisconsin	22.7	40
	Adjusted	41
Indiana	22.6	42
Alabama	22.5	43
	Adjusted	44
Michigan	22.2	45
Arkansas	21.7	46
	Adjusted	47
North Carolina	21	48
Nevada	18.7	49
	Adjusted	50
South Carolina	17.6	51
U.S.	31.9	

Source: "Blacks in Traditional White Male Jobs," *The Climate for Workers in the United States,* 1988, p. 43. Primary source: Southern Regional Council. *The Climate for Workers in the United States,* 1988. Published by permission.

MILITARY AFFAIRS

★ 689 ★
Armed Forces Officers from HBCUs

Year	Number
Military Science Graduates	
1987	629
1988	596
1989	543
1990 (proj.)	622

Source: "HBCU Production of Officers," *Black Issues in Higher Education*, April 12, 1990, p. 17. Primary source: CDT Data Base and BN Input Operations Dir (LLA) - 13 February, 1990 HBCU - Historically Black Colleges and Universities.

★ 690 ★
Armed Forces Qualifying Test Scores

Racial/Ethnic Group & Sex	Educational Level		
	Non-High School Graduate	GED Recipient	High School Diploma Graduate
White	438	512	543
Male	438	511	547
Female	437	513	539
Black	337	412	431
Male	341	407	430
Female	333	417	432
Hispanic	359	442	481
Male	358	451	495
Female	355	433	468
All Groups	419	494	524
Male	420	493	528
Female	418	495	520

Source: "Mean AFQT Standard Scores of American Youths (18-23 Years of Age by Sex, Racial/Ethnic Group, and Educational Level)," *Black Issues in Higher Education*, April 12, 1990, p. 26. Primary source: *Manpower for Military Occupations*, Office of the Assistant Secretary of Defense (Force Management and Personnel) *Notes:* Scores were standardized to a metric with a mean of 500 and a standard deviation of 100. American youth population includes all persons born between January 1, 1957 and December 31, 1962. White category includes all racial/ethnic groups other than Black or Hispanic. Black category does not include persons of Hispanic origin.

★ 691 ★
Black Army Personnel: Trends

Rank	1962	1972	1980	1986
Officers				
General	---	0.7	5.4	7.0
Colonel	0.1	1.6	4.5	5.0
Lt. Colonel	0.9	5.1	4.9	4.4
Major	2.5	5.1	4.4	6.8
Captain	5.2	3.7	7.5	12.7
1st Lieutenant	4.3	2.9	10.2	14.4
2nd Lieutenant	2.3	2.5	10.4	11.4
Total	3.2	3.9	7.2	10.4
Enlisted				
Sergeant Major	2.9	7.0	20.5	30.9
Master Sergeant	5.5	14.0	25.3	24.4
Sergeant 1st Class	7.8	19.6	24.7	25.5
Staff Sergeant	12.7	23.9	23.9	35.7
Sergeant	15.7	16.6	31.2	36.0
Specialist 4	13.0	13.5	37.2	29.9
Private 1st Class	10.8	15.9	39.0	23.6
Private	13.3	17.9	37.0	22.2
Recruit	11.4	18.3	27.0	22.8
Total	12.3	17.0	32.5	29.6

Source: "Black Participation in the U.S. Army (as a percentage of officers and enlisted personnel)," A Common Destiny: Blacks and American Society, 1989, p. 73. Primary source: Moskos, C.S., and John S. Butler. 1987. "Blacks in the Army: An American Success Story." *Atlantic Monthly*, October. Published by permission.

★ 692 ★
Coast Guard Personnel: Who Are They?

Average age: Enlisted: 28.03 yrs; Officer: 34.5 yrs; Warrant Officer: 40.26 yrs.

Characteristic	Number	Percent
Enlisted		
American Indian	339	1.13
Asian	497	1.66
Hispanic	11,286	4.29
Black	2,324	7.75
Other	25,555	85.18
Officer		
American Indian	10	.2
Asian	78	1.53
Hispanic	77	1.51
Black	79	1.55
Other	4,859	95.22
Warrant Officer		
American Indian	5	.36
Asian	55	3.93
Hispanic	14	1
Black	26	1.86

Continued.

Coast Guard Personnel: Who Are They?
[Continued]

Characteristic	Number	Percent
Other	1,300	92.86

Source: "A Look at Coast Guard Personnel," *Black Issues in Higher Education*, April 12, 1990, p. 24. Primary source: Coast Guaard Office of Personnel and Training.

★ 693 ★
Enlisted Military Personnel: Occupations

Occupational Group	White			Black			Hispanic		
	Male	Female	Both Sexes	Male	Female	Both Sexes	Male	Female	Both Sexes
Mgrs. & Prof.	6.94	11.25	7.33	7.45	7.58	7.47	6.75	9.46	6.99
Exec., Admin.	4.18	4.75	4.23	5.89	4.92	5.73	4.80	5.40	4.86
Prof. Spec.	2.76	6.51	3.10	1.56	2.66	1.74	1.95	4.07	2.14
T/S/A Supp.	18.95	49.06	21.66	33.83	64.61	39.00	26.09	54.07	28.58
Technical	7.87	14.95	8.51	9.83	13.27	10.41	8.27	13.00	18.69
Sales Occ.	0.21	0.23	0.21	0.47	0.26	0.43	0.31	0.39	0.32
Admin. Supp.	10.87	33.88	12.94	23.54	51.07	28.16	17.51	40.69	19.57
Service Occ.	8.90	12.48	9.23	10.16	10.75	10.28	8.10	10.67	8.33
Prot. Service	5.84	4.28	5.69	4.18	1.95	3.81	3.92	2.30	3.78
Svc. Ex. P.S.	3.07	8.21	3.53	6.00	8.80	4.67	4.18	8.38	4.55
Prec. Prod.	38.11	18.21	36.31	9.24	9.36	9.26	29.17	14.09	27.83
Mech. & Rep.	33.18	16.11	31.64	22.31	8.47	19.99	25.08	12.09	23.92
Const. Trades	1.91	0.51	1.79	1.66	0.23	1.42	2.42	0.47	1.57
Prec. Prod.	3.01	1.59	2.88	1.73	0.66	1.55	1.68	1.52	2.34
Oper., Fab.	14.06	8.63	13.57	24.43	7.52	21.59	14.98	11.53	14.67
Mach. Oper.	5.69	2.71	5.42	5.86	1.59	5.14	6.11	2.16	5.76
Fabricators	0.64	0.52	0.63	0.36	0.12	0.32	0.52	0.26	0.50
Prod. Inspect.	0.33	0.10	0.31	0.20	0.05	0.17	0.19	0.02	0.17
Trans. & Mat.	6.55	5.26	6.43	8.03	5.63	7.63	7.45	9.04	7.59
Handlers	0.85	0.05	0.77	0.98	0.13	0.84	0.70	0.05	0.65
Military[1]	13.04	0.37	11.90	14.88	0.18	12.40	14.91	0.18	13.60
Total	100.00	100.00	100.00	100.00	100.00	100.00	100.00	100.00	100.00

Source: "Occupational Distribution of Enlisted Personnel by Race-Ethnicity and Sex, 1988," *Black Issues in Higher Education*, April 12, 1990, pp. 16-17. Primary source: Defense Manpower Data Center (DMDC). *Notes:* 1. Military Specific Occupations with which there are no comparable civilian occupations.

★ 694 ★
Expectations of Qualification for Armed Forces

Characteristic	Rank
White male graduates	1
White female graduates	2
White male GEDs	3
White female GEDs	4
Hispanic male graduates	5

Continued.

Expectations of Qualification for Armed Forces
[Continued]

Characteristic	Rank
Hispanic female graduates	6
Hispanic male GEDs	7
White male nongraduates	8
White female nongraduates	9
Hispanic female GEDs	10
Black female graduates	11
Black male graduates	12
Black female GEDs	13
Black male GEDs	14
Hispanic male nongraduates	15
Hispanic female nongraduates	16
Black male nongraduates	17
Black female nongraduates	18

Source: "Population Subgroup (High School Graduates) Arranged in Order (from Highest to Lowest) by Expected Average Ability to Qualify for Enlistment," *Black Issues in Higher Education*, April 12, 1990, p. 26. Primary source: *Manpower for Military Occupations*, Office of the Assistant Secretary of Defense (Force Management and Personnel). *Notes:* Author Mark Eithelberg used mean AFQT standard scores of American youths (18-23 years of age) to infer the probable effect the military's education and aptitude standards would have on persons with different backgrounds. Data on eligibility of persons who actually apply to the military would be drawn from a narrower, more eligible population, due to factors such as self-selection and pre-screening by recruiters.

★ 695 ★
Military Population by Region: Assumptions and Projections

Rounded to thousands.

Region and division	Total	White	Black
United States	1,682,000	1,291,000	307,000
Northeast	116,000	95,000	15,000
New England	48,000	42,000	2,000
Middle Atlantic	68,000	53,000	13,000
Midwest	141,000	111,000	24,000
East North Central	67,000	54,000	11,000
West North Central	74,000	57,000	13,000
South	865,000	648,000	187,000
South Atlantic	562,000	424,000	119,000
East South Central	96,000	71,000	21,000
West South Central	207,000	153,000	47,000
West	560,000	437,000	81,000
Mountain	114,000	95,00	15,000
Pacific	446,000	342,000	66,000

Source: "Assumed Military Population in Each State, by Race:1989 to 2010," *Projections of the Population of States by Age, Sex, and Race: 1989-2010*, January 1990, p. 30. Primary source: These data are developed from July 1, 1988 estimates of the military population in each State.

★ 696 ★
Soldiers' Physical Fitness: 2-Mile Run Scores

Minutes:seconds.

Category	Male				Female			
	n	Mean	SD	Range	n	Mean	SD	Range
Total	1,006	14:55	2:05	10:06-24:00	254	17:45	2:21	12:30-27:24
Black	236	14:27	2:06	10:12-23:00	90	17:38	1:58	13:00-23:12
Hispanic	116	14:25	1:52	10:06-20:00	18	16:45	1:54	12:30-21:06
White	618	15:09	2:04	10:12-24:00	139	17:58	2:33	13:00-27:24

Source: "Army Physical Fitness Test 2- Mile Run Scores for Soldiers Assigned to a Variety of Units at an Army Post," *Assessing Physical Fitness and Physical Activity in Population-Based Surveys*, September 1989, p. 381. Primary source: Fitzgerald, P.I. Unpublished data from the U.S. Army Research Institute of Environmental Medicine, 1985.

★ 697 ★
Soldiers' Physical Fitness: Aerobic Fitness

Ml times kilogram to the power of -1 body weight times min to the power of -1.

Category	Male			Female		
	n	Mean	SD	n	Mean	SD
Combined	956	48.0	6.3	240	39.7	4.6
Black	213	48.5	6.3	84	38.4	4.1
Hispanic	103	48.0	6.8	17	41.3	4.2
White	603	47.9	6.2	131	40.3	4.7

Source: "VO 2 max of Soldiers Assigned to a Variety of Units and Occupations at one Army Post," *Assessing Physical Fitness and Physical Activity in Population-Based Surveys*, September 1989, p. 387. Primary source: Fitzgerald, P.I. Unpublished data from the U.S. Army Research Institute of Environmental Medicine, 1985.

★ 698 ★
Soldiers' Physical Fitness: Pushup Scores

Category	Male				Female			
	n	Mean	SD	Range	n	Mean	SD	Range
Total	1,014	50	15	13-99	255	32	12	10-78
Black	238	53	14	13-99	89	32	11	12-69
Hispanic	120	55	13	20-85	18	35	8	20-46
White	620	48	16	15-99	141	32	12	10-78

Source: "Army Physical Fitness Test Pushup Scores for Soldiers Assigned to a Variety of Units at a Large Army Post," *Assessing Physical Fitness and Physical Activity in Populaton-Based Surveys*, September 1989, p. 380. Primary source: Fitzgerald, P.I. Unpublished data from the U.S. Army Research Institute of Environmental Medicine, 1985.

★ 699 ★
Soldiers' Physical Fitness: Situp Scores

Category	Male				Female			
	n	Mean	SD	Range	n	Mean	SD	Range
Total	1,014	51	14	12-99	255	51	13	16-86
Black	239	57	12	25-99	89	51	12	26-75
Hispanic	116	55	12	33-84	18	55	10	40-71
White	621	50	15	12-99	141	50	13	16-86

Source: "Army Physical Fitness Test Situp Scores for Soldiers Assigned to a Variety of Units at an Army Post," *Assessing Physical Fitness and Physical Activity in Population-Based Surveys,* September 1989, p. 381. Primary source: Fitzgerald, P.I. Unpublished data from the U.S. Army Research Institute of Environmental Medicine, 1985.

★ 700 ★
Statistical Characteristics of U.S. Service Academies

Characteristic	Number
United States Naval Academy	
Number of applicants, Naval Academy Class of 1993	15,000
Number of entrants, Class of 1993	1,403
Current number, Black midshipmen, Class of 1993	83
Number of Hispanic midshipmen	82
Number of Native American midshipmen	13
Number of women	117
FY88 cost, four years at the Academy, per graduate (dol.)	150,195
Total graduation rate, 1981-1989 (%)	77.1
Graduation rate, Black midshipmen 1981-89 (%)	58.6
Graduation rate, Hispanic midshipmen 1981-87 (%)	72
Mean SAT scores, Class of 1993	
Verbal	576
Math	665
United States Military Academy	
Number of applicants, Class of 1993	12,859
Number of entrants, Class of 1993	1,356
Current number, Black cadets, Class of 1993	74
Number of Hispanic cadets	40
Number of Native American cadets	4
Number of women	124
Number of Asian Americans	67
FY88 cost, four years at the Academy, per graduate (dol.)	225,000
Total graduation rate, 1981-1989 (%)	72
Graduation rate, Black cadets 1981-89 (%)	68

Continued.

Statistical Characteristics of U.S. Service Academies
[Continued]

Characteristic	Number
Graduation rate, Hispanic cadets 1981-89 (%)	65
Mean SAT scores, Class of 1993	
Verbal	568
Math	645
United States Air Force Academy	
Number of applicants, Air Force Academy Class of 1993	14,819
Number of entrants, Class of 1993	1,381
Current number, Black cadets, Class of 1993	94
Number of Hispanic cadets	83
Number of Native American cadets	14
Number of women	130
FY88 cost, four years at the Academy, per graduate (dol.)	225,000
Total graduation rate, 1981-1989 (%)	62.9
Graduation rate, Black cadets 1981-89 (%)	60
Graduation rate, Hispanic cadets 1981-87 (%)	60
Mean SAT scores, Class of 1993	
Verbal	582
Math	668

Source: "U.S. Service Academies Statistical Portrait," *Black Issues in Higher Education,* April 26, 1990, p. 20. Primary source: *Black Issues in Higher Education.* .

★ 701 ★
U.S. Armed Services: Officers

Rank	Army	Navy	Marine Corps	Air Force	All Services
Commissioned officers	8.6	2.8	3.8	5.0	5.6
General	0.0	0.0	0.0	0.0	0.0
Lt. General	4.5	0.0	0.0	0.0	1.7
Maj. General	5.3	1.2	0.0	1.6	2.8
Brig. General	7.8	1.6	2.9	4.7	5.0
Colonel	4.6	0.8	0.3	1.9	2.4
Lt. Colonel	4.8	0.7	0.7	2.4	2.7
Major	4.8	1.8	1.9	2.3	2.9
Captain	9.3	3.7	5.0	5.5	6.4
1st Lieutenant	15.0	3.7	5.1	8.3	9.0
2nd Lieutenant	9.7	3.6	4.4	7.2	6.7

Continued.

U.S. Armed Services: Officers
[Continued]

Rank	Army	Navy	Marine Corps	Air Force	All Services
Warrant officers	6.1	5.1	7.3	---	6.0
All officers	8.2	2.9	4.1	5.0	5.6

Source: "Black Oficers in U.S. Armed Services, by Rank (as percentage of officers), June 1982," A Common Destiny: Blacks and American Society, 1989, p. 72. Primary source: Moskos, C.S., and John S. Butler. 1987. "Blacks in the Army: An American Success Story." *Atlantic Monthly*, October. Published by permission.

★ 702 ★
U.S. Service Academy New Officers: Trends

Service and Racial/Ethnic Group	1975	1978	1981	1984	1987	Total 1975-87
Army						
White	73.9	76.4	82.1	78.5	82.1	75.3
Black	4.7	8.3	5.9	21.0	12.8	8.8
Hispanic	1.6	2.5	0.6	0.4	2.0	1.2
Other/Unknown	19.8	12.9	11.4	9.2	3.1	14.1
All Groups	100.0	100.0	100.0	100.0	100.0	100.0
Navy						
White	93.1	93.0	92.6	89.2	89.6	91.5
Black	2.5	4.5	3.4	4.6	4.2	3.3
Hispanic	1.1	1.0	1.3	3.1	2.9	1.9
Other/Unknown	3.3	1.5	2.7	3.2	3.3	2.8
All Groups	100.0	100.0	100.0	100.0	100.0	100.0
Marine Corps						
White	90.6	92.9	94.9	89.5	88.2	91.3
Black	6.6	3.7	4.1	5.9	5.8	5.1
Hispanic	2.2	3.0	0.3	2.5	2.5	2.2
Other/Unknown	0.7	0.4	0.8	2.1	3.5	1.3
All Groups	100.0	100.0	100.0	100.0	100.0	100.0
Air Force						
White	91.9	87.8	88.8	89.1	89.6	89.5
Black	5.3	8.5	6.2	6.3	5.3	6.9
Hispanic	1.8	1.7	2.2	1.9	1.8	2.0
Other/Unknown	1.0	2.1	2.7	2.8	3.4	2.7
All Groups	100.0	100.0	100.0	100.0	100.0	100.0
All Services						
White	86.3	85.3	88.0	85.5	87.1	85.2
Black	4.6	7.0	5.2	7.8	7.4	6.6
Hispanic	1.6	1.9	1.3	1.7	2.2	1.7
Other/Unknown	7.6	5.8	5.5	5.0	3.3	6.6
All Groups	100.0	100.0	100.0	100.0	100.0	100.0

Source: "Percentage Distribution of New Officers, by Service and Racial/Ethnic Group, Selected Years, Fiscal 1975-87," *Black Issues in Higher Education*, April 26, 1990, p. 15. Primary source: Defense Manpower Data Center, special tabulations. *Notes:* "New Officers" refers to newly-commissioned officers who entered active duty at the pay grade of 0-1. Excludes warrant officers and some persons who received direct commissions.

MISCELLANY

Black "Firsts"

	Year
Colonel B.O. Davis, Jr. becomes the first black to command an Army Air Corps base in the United States.	1945
Kenny Washington and Woody Strode of the Los Angeles Rams become the first blacks to play in the National Football League (NFL).	1945
Jackie Robinson breaks the racial barrier in modern major league baseball when he joins the Brooklyn Dodgers.	1947
Wesley Brown becomes the first black to graduate from the U.S. Naval Academy.	1949
U.S. Congressman William L. Dawson becomes chair of the House Committee on Government Operations.	1949
Althea Gibson becomes the first black to play in the National Tennis Tournament at Forest Hills, Long Island.	1950
Gwendolyn Brooks is awarded the Pulitzer Prize for poetry.	1950
Chuck Cooper becomes the first black drafted and signed to play in the National Basketball Association (NBA). However, because of a quirk in the schedule, Earl Lloyd becomes the first black to play in the NBA by 1 day.	1950
Ralph J. Bunche is the first black American to receive the Nobel Peace Prize.	1950
B.O. Davis, Jr. becomes the first black general in the Air Force.	1954
Althea Gibson becomes the first black golfer to play on the Woman's Professional Golf Association tour.	1959
Charlie Sifford becomes the first black golfer to play on the Men's Professional Golf Association tour.	1961
Arthur Ashe becomes the first black named to the	

Continued.

Black "Firsts"
[Continued]

	Year
American Davis Cup team.	1963
Sidney Poitier becomes the first black to win an Oscar for best actor in a leading role (for 1963).	1964
David H. Blackwell becomes the first black elected to the National Academy of Sciences.	1965
Edward W. Brooke (R.-Mass.) elected first black U.S. Senator in the twentieth century.	1966
Robert C. Weaver is appointed the first black member of a president's cabinet, as secretary of the U.S. Department of Housing and Urban development.	1966
Andrew F. Brimmer becomes the first black member of the Federal Reserve Board.	1966
Richard G. Hatcher, Gary, Indiana, and Carl B. Stokes, Cleveland, Ohio, become first elected black mayors of major U.S. cities.	1967
Thurgood Marshall is appointed the first black justice of the U.S. Supreme Court.	1967
Henry Lewis becomes first black to head a symphony orchestra in the United States (New Jersey Symphony).	1968
Clifton R. Wharton, Jr., becomes first black president of a major, predominantly white university (Michigan State University).	1969
John M. Burgess becomes a bishop and the first black to head an Episcopal diocese in the United States (Boston).	1970
Joseph L. Searles becomes first black member of the New York Stock Exchange.	1970
Dance Theatre of Harlem, the first all-black classical ballet company in the United States, makes its debut at the Guggenheim Museum of Art in New York City.	1971
Samuel L. Gravely, Jr., becomes the first black admiral in the U.S. Navy.	1971
Major General Frederick E. Davidson becomes the first black commander of an Army division.	1972
Benjamin Hooks is appointed the first black member of	

Continued.

Black "Firsts"
[Continued]

	Year
the Federal Communications Commission.	1972
Barbara Jordan (D.-Texas) and Andrew Young (D.-Georgia) are the first blacks elected to the House of Representatives from the South in the Twentieth century.	1972
Daniel James, Jr., becomes the first black four-star general in the Air Force.	1975
Clifford Alexander, Jr., becomes the first black secretary of the Army.	1977
Marcus Alexis becomes the first black chair of the Interstate Commerce Commission.	1979
Thomas Bradley becomes the first black nominated to run for governor of a state by a major party (Democratic party).	1982
Roscoe Robinson, Jr., becomes the first four-star general in the Army.	1982

Source: "Selected Black Firsts in American Society: 1945-1982," *A Common Destiny: Blacks and American Society*, 1989, pp. 68-69. Primary source: Committee on the Status of Black Americans, National Research Council.

POLITICS AND ELECTIONS

★ 704 ★
Black Mayors of Cities

Name/City	Term Expires	Population[2]	% Black
Eugene Sawyer/Chicago, IL[1]	4/89	3,009,000	40.0
Thomas Bradley/Los Angeles, CA	7/89	3,259,000	17.0
W. Wilson Goode/Philadelphia, PA	12/91	1,642,000	40.2
Coleman Young/Detroit, MI	12/89	1,086,000	63.1
Kurt Schmoke/Baltimore, MD	12/91	763,000	54.8
Marion Barry, Jr./Washington, DC	12/90	626,000	70.0
Sidney Barthelemy/New Orleans, LA	3/90	545,000	55.3
Andrew Young/Atlanta, GA	12/89	421,000	66.6
Lionel J. Wilson/Oakland, CA	6/89	356,000	46.9
Sharpe James/Newark, NJ	6/90	316,000	46.9
Richard Arrington/Birmingham, AL	12/91	277,000	55.6
Richard C. Dixon/Dayton, OH	12/89	181,000	37.0
Thomas Barnes/Gary,IN	12/91	136,000	70.8
Jessie M. Rattley/Newport News, VA	6/90	154,000	31.5
Carrie Perry/Hartford, CT	12/89	137,000	33.9
Noel Taylor/Roanoke, VA	6/92	100,000	22.0
Edward Vincent/Inglewood, CA	11/90	102,000	57.3
Melvin Primas/Camden, NJ	6/89	82,000	53.0
Walter Tucker/Compton, CA	7/89	93,000	74.8
John Hatcher, Jr./East Orange, NJ	12/89	77,000	83.6
Walter L. Moore/Pontiac, MI	12/89	70,000	34.2
George Livingston/Richmond, CA	11/89	77,000	47.9
Edna W. Summers/Evanston Township, IL	4/89	72,000	21.4
Ronald A. Blackwood/Mt. Vernon, NY	12/91	68,000	48.7
Carl E. Officer/East St. Louis, IL	4/89	51,000	95.6
E. Pat Larkins/Pompano Beach, FL	3/89	66,000	17.2

Source: "Black Mayors of Cities with Population over 50,000, 1989," *Black Elected Officials,* 1989, p. 22. Primary source: *Black Elected Officials,* Joint Center for Political Studies, 1989. Name changed to Joint Center for Political and Economic Studies. Published by permission. *Notes:* 1. Mayors are listed by the population size of their respective cities, in decreasing order. 2. U.S. Bureau of the Census, 1986 population estimates.

★ 705 ★
Black Political Participation

	Democratic Conventions			Republican Conventions		
	Black		Total	Black		Total
Year	Delegates	Percent	Delegates	Delegates	Percent	Delegates
1912	0	0.0	1,094	65	6.0	1,078
1916	0	0.0	1,092	35	3.5	985
1920	0	0.0	1,094	29	2.9	984
1924	1	0.1	1,098	39	3.5	1,109
1928	0	0.0	1,100	49	4.4	1,098
1932	0	0.0	1,154	26	2.2	1,154
1936	12	1.0	1,204	45	4.5	1,003
1940	7	0.6	1,094	32	3.2	1,000
1944	11	0.9	1,176	18	1.7	1,057
1948	17	1.3	1,234	41	3.7	1,094
1952	33	2.6	1,230	29	2.4	1,206
1956	24	1.7	1,372	36	2.7	1,323
1960	46	3.0	1,521	22	1.6	1,331
1964	65	2.8	2,316	14	1.0	1,308
1968	209	6.7	3,084	26	1.9	1,333
1972	452	14.6	3,103	56	4.2	1,348
1976	323	10.6	3,048	76	3.4	2.259
1980	481	14.4	3,331	55	2.7	1,993
1984	697	17.7	3,933	69	3.1	2,235

Source: "Black Delegates at National Political Convention, 1912-1984," *A Common Destiny: Blacks and American Society*, 1989, p. 217. Primary source: Bain and Judith H. Parris. *Convention Decisions and Voting Records.* 2d ed. Washington, D.C.: Brookings Institution, 1973; and Monroe H. Work. *Negro Yearbook: An Encyclopedia of the Negro, 1937-1938.* Tuskegee, AL: Negro Yearbook Pub. Co., 1937: 102; for Democratic conventions of 1932-1984 from the Joint Center for Political Studies. *Blacks and the 1984 Democratic National Convention: A Guide.* Washington, D.C.: JCPS, 1984a: Table 2; data for Republican conventions from the Joint Center for Political Studies. *Blacks and the 1984 Democratic National Convention: A Guide.* Washington, D.C.: JCPS, 1984b: Table 1. Published in: *A Common Destiny: Blacks and American Society*, 1989. p. 217.

★ 706 ★
Black Political Participation

Region	1970	1986
Northeast	66	157
North Central	72	169
South	38	306
West	23	106
Territories	0	5
Total	199	743

Source: "Black State and Municipal Judges, by Region, 1970 and 1986," *A Common Destiny: Blacks and American Society*, 1989, p. 243. Primary source: Data for 1970 from Edward B. Toles. "Report of Black Lawyers and Judges in the United States, 1960-1970." *Congressional Record* (2 September): 30786-30788; and Joint Center for Political Studies. *Elected and Appointed Black Judges in the United States.* Washington, D.C.: JCPS, 1986. Published in: *A Common Destiny Blacks and American Society*, 1989, p. 243.

★ 707 ★
Black Political Participation

Year	Federal	State and Municipal	Total
1941	1	9	10
1951	3	23	26
1961	4	54	58
1970	19	199	218
1980	94	505	599
1986	98	743	841

Source: "Black Judges in the United States, 1941-1986," *A Common Destiny: Blacks and American Society,* 1989, p. 243. Primary source: Published by permission. Compiled from Vera Chandler Foster and Robert D. Reid. *The Negro in Politics.* In Jessie Parkhurst Guzman, ed. *Negro Yearbook: A Review of Events Affecting Negro Life, 1941-1946.* Tuskegee, AL: Tuskegee Institute, 1947, pp. 258-91; Jessie Parkhurst Guzman, ed. *Negro Yearbook.* William H. Wise, 1952; Edward B. Toles. "Report of Black Lawyers and Judges in the United States, 1960-1970." *Congressional Record* (2 September): 30786-30788; and the Joint Center for Political Studies. Elected and Appointed Judges in the United States. Washington, D.C.: NCPS, 1986. Published in: *A Common Destiny: Blacks and American Society,* 1989, p. 243.

★ 708 ★
Black Political Participation

Population of Municipality	Percent Black Population					
	South			Non-South		
	50-64%	65-79%	80-99%	50-64%	65-79%	80-99%
Less than 2,500	11	37	75	17	67	88
(N)	176	78	84	6	6	16
2,500 or more	12	45	100	58	75	78
(N)	93	20	9	12	8	18
Total	12	39	77	44	71	82
(N)	269	98	93	18	14	34

Source: "Incorporated Municipalities with Black Mayors, by Population, Racial Composition, and Region, 1985," A Common Destiny: Blacks and American Society, 1989, p. 241. Primary source: William O'Hare. "Racial Composition of Jurisdictions and the Election of Black Candidates," *Population Today* 14 (June 1986): 6-8. In: *A Common Destiny: Blacks and American Society,* 1989, p. 241. Published by permission.

★ 709 ★
Black Political Participation

Region and Race	Presidential Election Years						
	1964	1968	1972	1976	1980	1984	1988
United States							
White	70.7	69.1	64.5	60.9	60.9	61.4	59.1
Black	58.5	57.6	52.1	48.7	50.5	55.8	51.5
Difference	12.2	11.5	12.4	12.2	10.4	5.6	7.6
North and West							
White	74.7	71.8	67.5	62.6	62.4	63.0	60.4
Black	72.0	64.8	56.7	52.2	52.8	58.9	55.6
Difference	2.7	7.0	10.8	10.4	9.6	4.1	4.8

Continued.

Black Political Participation
[Continued]

Region and Race	Presidential Election Years						
	1964	1968	1972	1976	1980	1984	1988
South							
White	59.6	61.9	57.0	57.1	57.4	58.1	56.4
Black	44.0	51.6	47.8	45.7	48.2	53.2	48.0
Difference	15.6	10.3	9.2	11.4	9.2	4.9	8.4

Mid-Term Election Years

Region and Race	1966	1970	1974	1978	1982	1986	
United States							
White	57.0	56.0	46.3	47.3	49.9	47.0	
Black	41.7	43.5	33.8	37.2	43.0	43.2	
Difference	15.3	12.5	12.5	10.1	6.9	3.8	
North and West							
White	61.7	59.8	50.0	50.0	53.1	48.7	
Black	52.1	51.4	37.9	41.3	48.5	44.2	
Difference	9.6	8.4	12.0	8.7	4.6	4.5	
South							
White	45.1	46.4	37.4	41.1	42.9	43.5	
Black	32.9	36.8	38.0	33.5	38.3	42.5	
Difference	12.2	9.6	7.4	7.6	4.6	1.0	

Source: "Voter Participation (as a percentage of voting-age population), by Region and Race, 1964-1988," A Common Destiny: Blacks and American Society, 1989, p. 235. Primary source: U.S. Bureau of the Census. Published by permission.

★ 710 ★
Black Political Participation

Year	Blacks Regis-tered	Black Voting-Age Popu-lation	Regis-tration Rate (%)
1940	151,000	4,843,000	3.1
1946	595,000	4,869,000	12.2
1952	1,006,000	5,019,000	20.0
1956	1,238,000	4,955,000	25.0
1958	1,304,000	4,994,000	26.1
1960	1,463,000	5,090,000	28.7
1962	1,481,000	5,148,000	28.8
1964	2,165,000	5,173,000	41.9
1966	2,689,000	5,208,000	51.6
1968	3,112,000	5,299,000	58.7
1970	3,506,000	5,243,000	66.9
1972	3,448,000	6,178,000	55.8
1974	3,842,000	6,562,000	58.6
1976	4,149,000	6,931,000	59.9
1978	---	7,305,000	---
1980	4,254,000	7,718,000	55.1
1982	4,302,000	8,077,000	53.3

Continued.

Black Political Participation
[Continued]

Year	Blacks Regis-tered	Black Voting-Age Popu-lation	Regis-tration Rate (%)
1984	5,596,000	8,368,000	66.6
1986	5,796,000	8,957,000	64.7
1988	5,842,000	9,171,000	63.7

Source: "Black Registration in Southern States, 1940-1984," A Common Destiny: Blacks and American Society, 1989, p. 233. Primary source: Data for number of blacks registered from Voter Education Project; black voting-age population estimated by the committee. Published by permission.

★ 711 ★
Black State Legislators

	Total number of state legisla-tors	Total number of black legisla-tors	% black legisla-tors
Alabama	140	23	16.4
Alaska	60	1	1.7
Arizona	90	3	3.3
Arkansas	135	6	4.4
California	120	7	5.8
Colorado	100	4	4.0
Connecticut	187	8	4.3
Delaware	62	3	4.8
Florida	160	11	6.9
Georgia	236	30	12.
Hawaii	76	0	---
Idaho	126	0	---
Illinois	177	21	11.
Indiana	150	8	5.39
Iowa	150	1	0.7
Kansas	165	4	2.4
Kentucky	138	2	1.4
Louisiana	144	20	13.
Maine	186	0	---
Maryland	188	27	14.
Massachusetts	200	6	3.04
Michigan	148	16	10.
Minnesota	201	1	0.58
Mississippi	174	22	12.
Missouri	197	16	8.16
Montana	150	0	---
Nebraska	49	1	2.0
Nevada	63	3	4.8
New Hampshire	424	3	0.7

Continued.

Black State Legislators
[Continued]

	Total number of state legislators	Total number of black legislators	% black legislators
New Jersey	120	8	6.7
New Mexico	112	0	---
New York	210	21	10.0
North Carolina	170	15	8.8
North Dakota	150	0	---
Ohio	132	13	9.8
Oklahoma	149	5	3.4
Oregon	190	3	3.3
Pennsylvania	253	18	7.1
Rhode Island	150	6	4.0
South Carolina	170	21	12.4
South Dakota	105	0	---
Tennessee	132	13	9.8
Texas	181	15	8.3
Utah	104	0	---
Vermont	180	2	1.1
Virgin Islands	15	9	60.0
Virginia	140	10	7.1
Washington	147	3	2.0
West Virginia	134	1	0.7
Wisconsin	132	5	3.8
Wyoming	94	1	1.1
Total	7,466	416	5.6

Source: "Blacks in State Legislatures, January 1989," *Black Elected Officials*, 1989, p. 21. Primary source: *Black Elected Officials*, Joint Center for Political Studies, 1989. Name changed to Joint Center for Political and Economic Studies. Published by permission.

★ 712 ★
Distribution of Black Elected Officials - Education

	Education			
	Members, State Education Agencies	Members, University And College Boards	Members, Local School Boards	Other Education Officials
Alabama	2		86	2
Alaska			1	
Arizona		1	4	
Arkansas		1	84	
California		16	89	
Colorado			3	
Connecticut			15	
Delaware			5	
District of Columbia			8	

Continued.

Distribution of Black Elected Officials - Education
[Continued]

	Education			
	Members, State Education Agencies	Members, University And College Boards	Members, Local School Boards	Other Education Officials
Florida			15	2
Georgia			81	2
Hawaii			1	
Idaho				
Illinois		2	119	
Indiana			9	
Iowa			3	
Kansas			9	
Kentucky			9	
Louisiana	1		127	
Maine			1	
Maryland			4	
Massachusetts			11	
Michigan	1	14	84	
Minnesota			2	
Mississippi			107	8
Missouri		2	17	
Montana				
Nebraska			2	
Nevada		1	1	
New Hampshire				
New Jersey			79	
New Mexico			1	
New York			127	
North Carolina			82	
North Dakota				
Ohio	1		49	
Oklahoma			25	
Oregon				
Pennsylvania			20	
Rhode Island			1	
South Carolina		1	128	
South Dakota				
Tennessee			25	
Texas	2	6	93	
Utah				
Vermont				
Virginia				
Virgin Islands	10			
Washington			5	
West Virginia				
Wisconsin			4	
Wyoming			1	
Total	17	44	1,537	14

Source: "Black Elected Officials in the United States, January 1989," *Black Elected Officials*, 1989, pp. 14-15. Primary source: *Black Elected Officials*, 1989.

★713★
Distribution of Black Elected Officials - Municipal

	Municipal					Judicial and Law Enforcement					
	Mayors	Members, Municipal Governing Bodies	Members, Municipal Boards	Members, Neighbor-hood Advisory Commissions	Other Municipal Officials	Judges, State Courts of Last Resort	Judges, Other Courts	Magistrates, Justices of the Peace, Constables	Other Judicial Officials	Police Chiefs, Sheriffs, and Marshals	Other Law Enforcement Officials
Alabama	30	398				1	13	41	6	6	
Alaska		2									
Arizona		4									
Arkansas	24	147			17		2	37			
California	10	44	5		4	1	79		1	1	
Colorado		3					3		1		
Connecticut	2	31	2		2			2			
Delaware	3	11							1		
District of Columbia	1	10		222							
Florida	15	96	2		2	1	20			1	
Georgia	15	225	2		3		18	2	1	1	
Hawaii											
Idaho											
Illinois	18	152	45		18		23		1		
Indiana	1	28		4	2		3				
Iowa		3							1		
Kansas	1	4	1				2				
Kentucky	2	47					2	2	1	1	1
Louisiana	19	169			2		8	42	1	15	
Maine	1	1									
Maryland	8	56		1		1	11		3		
Massachusetts		13	6					1			
Michigan	10	80			17	1	52	4			
Minnesota	1	3					4			1	
Mississippi	25	282			3	1	1	56	10	6	
Missouri	16	87			6		10		2	2	
Montana											
Nebraska		1									
Nevada		2					2				
New Hampshire											
New Jersey	10	92							1		
New Mexico		1									
New York	2	30	5				48	1	1		
North Carolina	17	262				1	20		3	4	
North Dakota											
Ohio	9	101	3		9		28				
Oklahoma	13	47			21		1			1	
Oregon		2	1				2				
Pennsylvania	5	42			3	2	34	13	1		
Rhode Island		3									
South Carolina	17	131	1				1			5	
South Dakota	2	1									
Tennessee	2	41					9	6		1	
Texas	13	126	1				15	23		1	
Utah							1				
Vermont											
Virginia	6	73			3		1		8	3	
Virgin Islands											

Continued.

Distribution of Black Elected Officials - Municipal

[Continued]

	Municipal					Judicial and Law Enforcement					
	Mayors	Members, Municipal Governing Bodies	Members, Municipal Boards	Members, Neighbor-hood Advisory Commissions	Other Municipal Officials	Judges, State Courts of Last Resort	Judges, Other Courts	Magistrates, Justices of the Peace, Constables	Other Judicial Officials	Police Chiefs, Sheriffs, and Marshals	Other Law Enforcement Officials
Washington	1	5					5				
West Virginia		18			1		2	1	1		
Wisconsin		8					3			1	
Wyoming											
Total	299	2,882	74	227	113	9	425	231	44	50	1

Source: "Black Elected Officials in the United States, January 1989," *Black Elected Officials*, 1989, pp. 14-15. Primary source: *Black Elected Officials*, 1989.

★714★
Distribution of Black Elected Officials - National/State

State	Total[1]	Net Change since January 31, 1988	Federal		State			
			Sena-tors	Repre-sentatives	Gover-nors	Admin-istrators	Sena-tors	Repre-sentatives
Alabama	694	252					5	18
Alaska	4	0						1
Arizona	12	-1					1	2
Arkansas	318	-8					1	5
California	276	-10		4			2	5
Colorado	14	-1					1	3
Connecticut	63	0				1	3	5
Delaware	23	1					1	2
District of Columbia	242	-2		1				
Florida	179	3					2	9
Georgia	483	25		1			7	23
Hawaii	1	0						
Idaho	0	0						
Illinois	444	1		3		1	7	14
Indiana	68	1					2	6
Iowa	9	0					1	
Kansas	23	-5					1	3
Kentucky	68	-2					1	1
Louisiana	521	-3					5	15
Maine	3	0						
Maryland	118	-2		1			5	22
Massachusetts	38	3					1	5
Michigan	306	-10		2		1	2	14
Minnesota	12	0						1
Mississippi	646	68		1		1	2	20
Missouri	163	-2		2			3	13
Montana	0	0						
Nebraska	4	0					1	
Nevada	10	0					1	2
New Hampshire	3	2						3

Continued.

Distribution of Black Elected Officials - National/State
[Continued]

State	Total[1]	Net Change since January 31, 1988	Federal		State			
			Sena-tors	Repre-sentatives	Gover-nors	Admin-istrators	Sena-tors	Repre-sentatives
New Jersey	199	4		1			2	6
New Mexico	6	0				1		
New York	252	2		4			5	16
North Carolina	449	21					3	12
North Dakota	0	0						
Ohio	216	0		1			2	11
Oklahoma	115	3					2	3
Oregon	9	-1					2	1
Pennsylvania	139	2		1			3	15
Rhode Island	10	0					1	5
South Carolina	373	21					5	16
South Dakota	3	1						
Tennessee	146	1		1			3	10
Texas	312	12		1			2	13
Utah	1	0						
Vermont	2	1						2
Virginia	144	18				1	3	7
Virgin Islands	35	-1			1	1	9	
Washington	20	2					2	1
West Virginia	24	1						1
Wisconsin	24	1					1	4
Wyoming	2	-1					1	
Total	7,226	397	0	24	1	7	101	315

Source: "Black Elected Officials in the United States, January 1989," *Black Elected Officials,* 1989, pp. 14-15. Primary source: *Black Elected Officials,* Joint Center for Political Studies, 1989. Name changed to Joint Center for Political and Economic Studies. Published by permission. *Note:* 1. All kinds. See following tables.

★ 715 ★
Distribution of Black Elected Officials - Substate/County

State	Substate Regional		County		
	Members Regional Bodies	Other Regional Officials	Members, County Governing Bodies	Members, Other County Bodies	Other County Officials
Alabama			71		15
Alaska					
Arizona					
Arkansas					
California	4		8	1	2
Colorado					
Connecticut					
Delaware					
District of Columbia					
Florida			12	2	

Continued.

Distribution of Black Elected Officials - Substate/County
[Continued]

State	Substate Regional		County		
	Members Regional Bodies	Other Regional Officials	Members, County Governing Bodies	Members, Other County Bodies	Other County Officials
Georgia			98		4
Hawaii					
Idaho					
Illinois			38	2	1
Indiana			13		
Iowa			1		
Kansas			2		
Kentucky			1		
Louisiana			116	1	
Maine					
Maryland			6		
Massachusetts			1		
Michigan			24		
Minnesota					
Mississippi			67	52	4
Missouri			3		
Montana					
Nebraska					
Nevada			1		
New Hampshire					
New Jersey			7		1
New Mexico			1		
New York			13		
North Carolina			42	2	1
North Dakota					
Ohio			1	1	
Oklahoma			2		
Oregon			1		
Pennsylvania					
Rhode Island					
South Carolina			64	2	2
South Dakota					
Tennessee			47		1
Texas			16		
Utah					
Vermont					
Virginia			36		3
Virgin Islands		14			
Washington			1		
West Virginia					
Wisconsin			3		
Wyoming					
Total	4	14	696	63	34

Source: "Black Elected Officials in the United States, January 1989," *Black Elected Officials*, 1989, pp. 14-15.
Primary source: *Black Elected Officials*, 1989.

★ 716 ★
Distribution of Black Elected Officials

Region/division	Total		Federal		State		Substate regional		County		Mayors	
	N	%[1]	N	%[1]	N	%[1]	N	%[1]	N	%[1]	N	%[1]
Northeast	709	9.9	6	25.0	73	17.7	0	0.0	22	2.7	20	6.7
New England	119	1.7	0	0.0	26	6.3	0	0.0	1	0.1	3	1.0
Middle Atlantic	590	8.2	6	25.0	47	11.4	0	0.0	21	2.6	17	5.7
Midwest	1,272	17.7	8	33.3	88	21.3	0	0.0	89	11.2	58	19.4
East North Central	1,058	14.7	6	25.0	65	15.7	0	0.0	83	10.4	38	12.7
West North Central	214	3.0	2	8.3	23	5.6	0	0.0	6	0.8	20	6.7
South	4,855	67.5	6	25.0	226	54.7	0	0.0	667	84.1	210	70.2
South Atlantic	2,035	28.3	3	12.5	119	28.8	0	0.0	274	34.6	82	27.4
East South Central	1,554	21.6	2	8.3	61	14.8	0	0.0	258	32.5	59	19.7
West South Central	1,266	17.6	1	4.2	46	11.1	0	0.0	135	17.0	69	23.1
West	355	4.9	4	16.7	26	6.3	4	100.0	15	1.9	11	3.7
Mountain	45	0.6	0	0.0	12	2.9	0	0.0	2	0.3	0	0.0
Pacific	310	4.3	4	16.7	14	3.4	4	100.0	13	1.6	11	3.7
Total	7,191	100.0	24	100.0	413	100.0	4	100.0	793	100.0	299	100.0

Source: "Distribution of Black Elected Officials by Census Region/Division and Category of Office, January 1989," *Black Elected Officials,* 1989. Primary source: *Black Elected Officials,* Joint Center for Political Studies, 1989. Name changed to Joint Center for Political and Economic Studies. Published by permission. *Notes:* The 35 BEOs in the Virgin Islands are not included in this table because that territory is not included in the census divisions. 1. Percentage of all BEOs in category. Numbers have been force-rounded in some cases, to equal 100 percent.

★ 717 ★
Distribution of Black Elected Officials

Region/division	Other Municipal		Judicial/ Law enforcement		Education		% of U.S. blacks in region/div.
	N	%[1]	N	%[1]	N	%[1]	
Northeast	230	7.0	104	13.7	254	15.9	15.2
New England	58	1.8	3	0.4	28	1.8	1.5
Middle Atlantic	172	5.2	101	13.3	226	14.1	13.7
Midwest	573	17.4	138	18.2	318	19.9	16.5
East North Central	467	14.2	116	15.3	283	17.7	14.0
West North Central	106	3.2	22	2.9	35	2.2	2.5
South	2,420	73.4	420	55.2	906	56.5	60.2
South Atlantic	1,119	34.0	110	14.4	328	20.4	40.2
East South Central	771	23.4	164	21.6	239	14.9	8.2
West South Central	530	16.0	146	19.2	339	21.2	11.8
West	73	2.2	98	12.9	124	7.7	8.1
Mountain	10	0.3	9	1.2	12	0.7	1.0
Pacific	63	1.9	89	11.7	112	7.0	7.1
Total	3,296	100.0	760	100.0	1,602	100.0	100.0

Source: "Distribution of Black Elected Officials by Census Region/Division and Category of Office, January 1989," *Black Elected Officials,* 1989. Primary source: *Black Elected Officials,* 1989 *Notes:* The 35 BEOs in the Virgin Islands are not included in this table, because the territory is not included in the census divisions. 1. Percentage of all BEOs in category. Numbers have been force-rounded in some cases, to equal 100 percent.

★ 718 ★
Distribution of Elected Officials

Member of Congress/Principal City	District	% Black in District	% White in District	% Hispanic in District
Dellums (D-CA)/Oakland	8	27	60	7
Dixon (D-CA)/Los Angeles	28	39	38	28
Dymally (D-CA)/Compton	31	34	42	25
Hawkins (D-CA)/Los Angeles	29	50	32	37
Fauntroy (D-DC)/Washington, DC	At large	70	31	3
Lewis (D-GA)/Atlanta	5	65	34	1
Collins (D-IL)/Chicago	7	67	29	4
Savage (D-IL)/Chicago	2	70	25	7
Hayes (D-IL)/Chicago	1	92	6	1
Mfume (D-MD)/Baltimore	7	73	25	1
Conyers (DMI)/Detroit	1	71	27	2
Crockett (D-MI)/Detroit	13	71	26	3
Espy (D-MS)/Greenville	2	58	41	1
Clay (D-MO)/St. Louis	1	52	48	1
Wheat (D-MO)/Kansas City	5	23	75	3
Payne (D-NJ)/Newark	10	58	34	14
Flake (D-NY)/Jamaica	6	50	44	9
Towns (D-NY)/New York	11	47	29	38
Owens (D-NY)/Brooklyn	12	80	13	10
Rangel (D-NY)/New York	16	49	25	38
Stokes (D-OH)/Cleveland	21	62	36	1
Gray (D-PA)/Philadelphia	2	80	18	1
Ford (D-TN)/Memphis	9	57	42	1
Leland (D-TX)/Houston[1]	18	39	41	27

Source: "Congressional Districts Represented by Blacks, 1989," *Black Elected Officials*, 1989, p. 20. Primary source: *Black Elected Officials*, Joint Center for Political Studies, 1989. Name changed to Joint Center for Political and Economic Studies. Published by permission. *Notes:* Numbers may not add to 100% since Asian Americans are not included and according to the Bureau of the Census, persons of Spanish origin may be of any race. 1. Rep. Mickey Leland died in August 1989 while serving in the 101st Congress.

★ 719 ★
Distribution of Elected Officials by Sex

Office	Male	Female	Total
Federal	23	1	24
State	325	99	424
Substate	7	11	18
County	683	110	793
Municipal	2,658	937	3,595
Judicial/Law Enforcement	636	124	760
Education	1,080	532	1,612

Continued.

Distribution of Elected Officials by Sex
[Continued]

Office	Male	Female	Total
Total	5,412	1,814	7,226

Source: "Distribution of Male and Female Black Elected Officials," *Black Elected Officials*, 1989, p. 20. Primary source: *Black Elected Officials*, Joint Center for Political Studies, 1989. Name changed to Joint Center for Political and Economic Studies. Published by permission.

★ 720 ★
Elected Officials

	U.S. Offices		State Offices			City Offices			
Year	Senate	Represen-tative	Adminis-trator	Senate	Represen-tative	Mayor	Council	School Board	Total[1]
1941	0	1	0	3	23	0	4	2	33
1947	0	2	0	5	33	0	18	8	66
1951	0	2	0	1	39	0	25	15	82
1965	0	4	1	18	84	3	74	68	280
1970	1	9	1	31	137	48	552	362	1,469
1975	1	17	5	53	223	135	1,237	894	3,503
1980	0	17	6	70	247	182	1,809	1,149	4,890
1985	0	20	4	90	302	286	2,189	1,363	6,016

Source: "Black Elected Officials, by Selected Office Categories, 1941-1985," *A Common Destiny: Blacks and American Society*, 1989, p. 240. Primary source: Data for 1941-1947 from Jessie Parkhurst Guzman, ed. *Negro Yearbook.* Tuskegee, AL: Tuskegee Institute, 1947; Florence Murray, ed. *Negro Handbook, 1946-1947.* New York: Current Books, 1947; for 1965 from *Ebony* 20 (April, 1965): 191-97; Ebony. *The Negro Handbook.* Chicago: Johnson Pub. Co., 1966; U.S. Commission on Civil Rights, 1968; and Robert C. Weaver, "Federal Aid, Local Control, and Negro Participation." *Journal of Negro Education* 11 (January 1942): 47-59; and for 1970-1985 from the Joint Center for Political Studies, *Black Elected Officials: A National Roster.* Washington, D.C.: JCPS, 1985. Published in: A Common Destiny: Blacks and American Society, 1989, p. 240. Published by permission. *Notes:* 1. For 1965-1985 total includes all black elected officials, not just those in selected categories.

★ 721 ★
Elected Officials

Year	North-east	North Central	South	West	Total
1941	10	20	2	1	33
1947	21	35	6	4	66
1951	29	31	16	6	82
1965	63	104	87	26	280
1970	238	396	703	132	1,469
1975	503	869	1,913	218	3,503

Continued.

Elected Officials
[Continued]

Year	North-east	North Central	South	West	Total
1980	570	1,041	2,981	298	4,890
1985	694	1,150	3,801	371	6,016

Source: "Black Elected Officials, by Region, 1941-1985," A Common Destiny: Blacks and American Society, 1989, p. 238. Primary source: Data for 1941-1947 from Jessie Parkhurst Guzman, ed. *Negro Yearbook.* Tuskegee, AL: Tuskegee Institute, 1947; Florence Murray, ed. *Negro Handbook, 1946-1947.* New York: Current Books, 1947; for 1965 from *Ebony* 20 (April, 1965): 191-97; Ebony. *The Negro Handbook.* Chicago: Johnson Pub. Co., 1966; U.S. Commission on Civil Rights, 1968; and Robert C. Weaver, "Federal Aid, Local Control, and Negro Participation." *Journal of Negro Education* 11 (January 1942): 47-59; and for 1970-1985 from the Joint Center for Political Studies, *Black Elected Officials: A National Roster.* Washington, D.C.: JCPS, 1985. Published in: A Common Destiny: Blacks and American Society, 1989, p. 238. Published by permission. *Note:* Regions are those of the Bureau of the Census.

★ 722 ★
Female Black Elected Officials - Education

	Education			
	Members, State Education Agencies	Members, University And College Boards	Members, Local School Boards	Other Education Officials
Alabama	1		25	1
Alaska			1	
Arizona			1	
Arkansas			16	
California		6	42	
Colorado				
Connecticut			12	
Delaware			3	
District of Columbia			1	
Florida			1	
Georgia			26	
Hawaii				
Idaho				
Illinois		1	39	
Indiana			3	
Iowa			1	
Kansas			4	
Kentucky			2	
Louisiana			30	
Maine				
Maryland			3	
Massachusetts			5	
Michigan	1	8	27	
Minnesota				
Mississippi			22	
Missouri		1	6	
Montana				
Nebraska			2	

Continued.

Female Black Elected Officials - Education
[Continued]

	Education			
	Members, State Education Agencies	Members, University And College Boards	Members, Local School Boards	Other Education Officials
Nevada		1	1	
New Hampshire				
New Jersey			39	
New Mexico				
New York			65	
North Carolina			24	
North Dakota				
Ohio			18	
Oklahoma			8	
Oregon				
Pennsylvania			7	
Rhode Island				
South Carolina			41	
South Dakota				
Tennessee			7	
Texas		2	20	
Utah				
Vermont				
Virginia				
Virgin Islands	4			
Washington			1	
West Virginia				
Wisconsin			2	
Wyoming				
Total	7	19	505	1

Source: "Female Black Elected Officials in the United States, January 1989," *Black Elected Officials*, 1989, pp. 17-18. Primary source: *Black Elected Officials*, 1989.

★ 723 ★
Female Black Elected Officials - Municipal/Judicial

	Municipal					Judicial and Law Enforcement					
	Mayors	Members, Municipal Governing Bodies	Members, Municipal Boards	Members, Neighborhood Advisory Commissions	Other Municipal Officials	Judges, State Courts of Last Resort	Judges, Other Courts	Magistrates, Justices of the Peace, Constables	Other Judicial Officials	Chiefs, Sheriffs, and Marshals	Police Other Law Enforcement Officials
Alabama	9	117					2	7	2		
Alaska		1									
Arizona											
Arkansas	7	28			14			4			
California	2	9	3		2		18				
Colorado											
Connecticut	2	16	1		1			2			
Delaware										1	
District of Columbia		5		124							
Florida	4	24			2		1				
Georgia	2	44			2		6				
Hawaii											

Continued.

Female Black Elected Officials - Municipal/Judicial
[Continued]

	Municipal					Judicial and Law Enforcement					
	Mayors	Members, Municipal Governing Bodies	Members, Municipal Boards	Members, Neighbor-hood Advisory Commissions	Other Municipal Officials	Judges, State Courts of Last Resort	Judges, Other Courts	Magistrates, Justices of the Peace, Constables	Other Judicial Officials	Chiefs, Sheriffs, and Marshals	Police Other Law Enforcement Officials
Idaho											
Illinois	2	34	15		8		4		1		
Indiana		2		2	1		1				
Iowa		2							1		
Kansas											
Kentucky	1	11									
Louisiana	2	26					4	2			
Maine											
Maryland	2	16					2		2		
Massachusetts		5									
Michigan	4	18			13		15				
Minnesota		1					1				
Mississippi	5	60			3			4	3		
Missouri	4	24			1		1				
Montana											
Nebraska											
Nevada											
New Hampshire											
New Jersey		23									
New Mexico							1				
New York		5	3				6				
North Carolina	3	46					4				
North Dakota											
Ohio	3	29	3		5		10				
Oklahoma	3	18			16						
Oregon		1					1				
Pennsylvania	2	10				1	7				
Rhode Island											
South Carolina	5	26									
South Dakota											
Tennessee		7									
Texas	1	17					3	2			
Utah											
Vermont											
Virginia	2	18			1				2		
Virgin Islands											
Washington		1					1				
West Virginia		4			1			1	1		
Wisconsin		3									
Wyoming											
Total	65	651	25	126	70	1	88	22	13	0	0

Source: "Female Black Elected Officials in the United States, January 1989," *Black Elected Officials,* 1989, pp. 17-18. Primary source: *Black Elected Officials,* 1989.

★ 724 ★
Female Black Elected Officials - National/State

			Federal		State			
State	Total[1]	Net Change since January 31, 1988	Sena-tors	Repre-sentatives	Gover-nors	Admin-istrators	Sena-tors	Repre-sentatives
Alabama	171	83						4
Alaska	2	0						
Arizona	3	0					1	1
Arkansas	70	2						1
California	92	-2					1	3

Continued.

492

Female Black Elected Officials - National/State
[Continued]

State	Total[1]	Net Change since January 31, 1988	Federal		State			
			Senators	Representatives	Governors	Administrators	Senators	Representatives
Colorado	2	0						2
Connecticut	35	1					1	
Delaware	4	0						
District of Columbia	130	25						
Florida	37	3					1	1
Georgia	96	12						7
Hawaii	0	0						
Idaho	0	0						
Illinois	123	1		1			3	6
Indiana	14	1					2	1
Iowa	4	0						
Kansas	4	0						
Kentucky	14	-1						
Louisiana	74	1						3
Maine	0	0						
Maryland	34	1						8
Massachusetts	12	-1						2
Michigan	99	6						5
Minnesota	2	0						
Mississippi	123	20						1
Missouri	42	-4						3
Montana	0	0						
Nebraska	2	1						
Nevada	2	0						
New Hampshire	2	1						2
New Jersey	68	7					1	1
New Mexico	1	0						
New York	88	0					2	7
North Carolina	87	11						1
North Dakota	0	0						
Ohio	72	1						3
Oklahoma	49	1					2	1
Oregon	4	0						1
Pennsylvania	30	1					1	2
Rhode Island	0	0						
South Carolina	87	7						3
South Dakota	0	0						
Tennessee	19	3						2
Texas	50	1					1	3
Utah	0	0						
Vermont	1	1						1
Virginia	31	4					1	2
Virgin Islands	13	-1					1	
Washington	3	1						
West Virginia	7	1						
Wisconsin	10	1						3

Continued.

Female Black Elected Officials - National/State
[Continued]

State	Total[1]	Net Change since January 31, 1988	Federal		State			
			Senators	Representatives	Governors	Administrators	Senators	Representatives
Wyoming	1	0					1	
Total	1,814	189	0	1	0	0	19	80

Source: "Female Black Elected Officials in the United States, January 1989," *Black Elected Officials*, 1989, pp. 17-18. Primary source: *Black Elected Officials*, Joint Center for Political Studies, 1989. Name changed to Joint Center for Political and Economic Studies. Published by permission. *Notes:* 1. All kinds. See also tables for Substate/County, Municipal/Judicial, and Education following this table.

★ 725 ★
Female Black Elected Officials - Part I

Region/division	Total		Federal		State		Substate regional		County		Mayors	
	N	%[1]	N	%[1]	N	%[1]	N	%[1]	N	%[1]	N	%[1]
Northeast	236	13.1	0	0.0	20	20.4	0	0.0	4	3.6	4	6.2
New England	50	2.8	0	0.0	6	6.1	0	0.0	0	0.0	2	3.1
Middle Atlantic	186	10.3	0	0.0	14	14.3	0	0.0	4	3.6	2	3.1
Midwest	372	20.7	1	100.0	26	26.5	0	0.0	23	20.9	13	20.0
East North Central	318	17.7	1	100.0	23	23.4	0	0.0	21	19.1	9	13.8
West North Central	54	3.0	0	0.0	3	3.1	0	0.0	2	1.8	4	6.2
South	1,083	60.1	0	0.0	42	42.9	0	0.0	79	71.9	46	70.7
South Atlantic	513	28.4	0	0.0	24	24.6	0	0.0	39	35.5	18	27.7
East South Central	327	18.2	0	0.0	7	7.1	0	0.0	31	28.2	15	23.0
West South Central	243	13.5	0	0.0	11	11.2	0	0.0	9	8.2	13	20.0
West	110	6.1	0	0.0	10	10.2	3	100.0	4	3.6	2	3.1
Mountain	9	0.5	0	0.0	5	5.1	0	0.0	0	0.0	0	0.0
Pacific	101	5.6	0	0.0	5	5.1	3	100.0	4	3.6	2	3.1
Total	1,801	100.0	1	100.0	98	100.0	3	100.0	110	100.0	65	100.0

Source: "Distribution of Female Black Elected Officials by Census Region/Division and Category of Office, January 1989," *Black Elected Officials*, 1989, p. 16. Primary source: *Black Elected Officials*, Joint Center for Political Studies, 1989. Name changed to Joint Center for Political and Economic Studies. Published by permission. *Notes:* The 13 female BEO in the Virgin Islands are not included in this table, because the territory is not included in the census divisions. 1. Percentage of all BEOs in category. Numbers have been force-rounded in some cases, to equal 100 percent.

★ 726 ★
Female Black Elected Officials - Part II

Region/division	Other Municipal		Judicial/Law Law enforcement		Education		% of U.S. blacks in region/div.
	N	%[1]	N	%[1]	N	%[1]	
Northest	64	7.3	16	12.9	128	24.2	15.2
New England	23	2.6	2	1.6	17	3.2	1.5
Middle Atlantic	41	4.7	14	11.3	111	21.0	13.7
Midwest	161	18.5	34	27.4	114	21.6	16.5
East North Central	133	15.3	31	25.0	100	18.9	14.0

Continued.

Female Black Elected Officials - Part II
[Continued]

Region/division	Other Municipal		Judicial/Law Law enforcement		Education		% of U.S. blacks in region/div.
	N	%[1]	N	%[1]	N	%[1]	
West North Central	28	3.2	3	2.4	14	2.7	2.5
South	630	72.2	53	42.7	233	44.2	60.2
South Atlantic	313	35.9	20	16.1	99	18.8	40.2
East South Central	198	22.7	18	14.5	58	11.0	8.2
West South Central	119	13.6	15	12.1	76	14.4	11.8
West	17	2.0	21	17.0	53	10.0	8.1
Mountain	0	0.0	1	0.9	3	0.5	1.0
Pacific	17	2.0	20	16.1	50	9.5	7.1
Total	872	100.0	124	100.0	528	100.0	100.0

Source: "Distribution of Female Black Elected Officials by Census Region/Division and Category of Office, January 1989," *Black Elected Officials*, 1989, p. 16. Primary source: *Black Elected Officials*, 1989 *Notes:* The 13 female BEO in the Virgin Islands are not included in this table, because the territory is not included in the census divisions. 1. Percentage of all BEOs in category. Numbers have been force-rounded in some cases, to equal 100 percent.

★ 727 ★
Female Black Elected Officials - Substate/County

State	Substate Regional		County		
	Members Regional Bodies	Other Regional Officials	Members, County Governing Bodies	Members, Other County Bodies	Other County Officials
Alabama			1		2
Alaska					
Arizona					
Arkansas					
California	3		3		
Colorado					
Connecticut					
Delaware					
District of Columbia					
Florida			2	1	
Georgia			8		1
Hawaii					
Idaho					
Illinois			8		1
Indiana			2		
Iowa					
Kansas					
Kentucky					
Louisiana			7		
Maine					
Maryland			1		
Massachusetts					
Michigan			8		
Minnesota					

Continued.

Female Black Elected Officials - Substate/County
[Continued]

| State | Substate Regional | | County | | |
	Members Regional Bodies	Other Regional Officials	Members, County Governing Bodies	Members, Other County Bodies	Other County Officials
Mississippi			1	24	
Missouri			2		
Montana					
Nebraska					
Nevada					
New Hampshire					
New Jersey			3		1
New Mexico					
New York					
North Carolina			7	2	
North Dakota					
Ohio					
Oklahoma			1		
Oregon			1		
Pennsylvania					
Rhode Island					
South Carolina			11	1	
South Dakota					
Tennessee			3		
Texas			1		
Utah					
Vermont					
Virginia			3		2
Virgin Islands		8			
Washington					
West Virginia					
Wisconsin			2		2
Wyoming					
Total	3	8	75	28	7

Source: "Female Black Elected Officials in the United States, January 1989," *Black Elected Officials,* 1989, pp. 17-18. Primary source: *Black Elected Officials,* 1989.

★ 728 ★
Growth in Black Elected Officials by Sex

Year	Male BEOs	Female BEOs	Male BEO/ Female BEO Ratio
1975	2,973	530	5.71
1976	3,295	684	4.81
1977	3,529	782	4.51
1978	3,660	843	4.34
1979	3,725	882	4.22

Continued.

Growth in Black Elected Officials by Sex
[Continued]

Year	Male BEOs	Female BEOs	Male BEO/ Female BEO Ratio
1980	3,936	976	4.03
1981	4,017	1,021	3.93
1982	4,079	1,081	3.77
1983	4,383	1,223	3.58
1984[1]	4,441	1,259	3.52
1985	4,697	1,359	3.45
1986	4,942	1,482	3.33
1987	5,117	1,564	3.27
1988	5,204	1,625	3.20
1989	5,412	1,814	2.98

Source: "Total Numbers of Male and Female Black Elected Officials Since 1975," *Black Elected Officials,* 1989, p. 19. Primary source: *Black Elected Officials,* Joint Center for Political Studies, 1989. Name changed to Joint Center for Political and Economic Studies. Published by permission. *Notes:* 1. The 1984 figures reflect the number of blacks who took office during the seven-month period between July 1, 1983, and January 30, 1984.

★ 729 ★
Growth in Female Black Elected Officials

Year	Number	Percent Female BEO Growth	Percent Overall BEO Growth
1975	530	---	---
1976	684	29.1	13.6
1977	782	14.3	8.3
1978	843	7.8	4.5
1979	882	4.6	2.3
1980	976	10.6	6.6
1981	1,021	4.6	2.6
1982	1,081	9.7	2.4
1983	1,223	13.1	8.6
1984[1]	1,259	2.9	1.7
1985	1,359	10.8	6.2
1986	1,482	9.1	6.1
1987	1,564	5.5	4.0
1988	1,625	3.9	2.2
1989	1,814	11.6	5.8

Source: "Growth in the Number of Female Black Elected Officials, 1975-1989," *Black Elected Officials,* 1989, p. 19. Primary source: *Black Elected Officials,* Joint Center for Political Studies, 1989. Name changed to Joint Center for Political and Economic Studies. Published by permission. *Notes:* 1. The 1984 figures reflect the number of blacks who took office during the seven month period between July 1, 1983, and January 30, 1984.

★ 730 ★
Judges in U.S. Courts of Appeal

By Presidential administration, 1963-88. Numbers in percent.

	President Johnson's appointees 1963-68 (N=40)	President Nixon's appointees 1969-74 (N=45)	President Ford's appointees 1974-76 (N=12)	President Carter's appointees 1977-80 (N=56)	President Reagan's first term appointees 1981-84 (N=31)	President Reagan's second term appointees 1985-88 (N=47)
Sex						
Male	97.5	100.0	100.0	80.4	96.8	93.6
Female	2.5	0.0	0.0	19.6	3.2	6.4
Ethnicity						
White	95.0	97.8	100.0	78.6	93.5	100.0
Black	5.0	0.0	0.0	16.1	3.2	0.0
Hispanic	0.0	0.0	0.0	3.6	3.2	0.0
Asian	0.0	2.2	0.0	1.8	0.0	0.0
Education, undergraduate						
Public-supported	32.5	40.0	50.0	30.4	29.0	21.3
Private (not Ivy League)	40.0	35.6	41.7	50.0	45.2	55.3
Ivy League	17.5	20.0	8.3	19.6	25.8	23.4
None indicated	10.0	4.4	0.0	0.0	0.0	0.0
Occupation at nomination or appointment						
Politics or government	10.0	4.4	8.3	5.4	3.2	8.5
Judiciary	57.5	53.3	75.0	46.4	61.3	51.1
Law firm, large	5.0	4.4	8.3	10.8	9.6	14.9
Law firm, moderate	17.5	22.2	8.3	16.1	9.6	10.6
Law firm, small	7.5	6.7	0.0	5.4	0.0	2.1
Professor of law	2.5	2.2	0.0	14.3	16.1	10.6
Other	0.0	6.7	0.0	1.8	0.0	2.1
Occupational experience						
Judicial	65.0	57.8	75.0	53.6	70.9	53.2
Prosecutorial	47.5	46.7	25.0	32.1	19.3	34.0
Other	20.0	17.8	25.0	37.5	25.8	40.4
Religion						
Protestant	60.0	75.6	58.3	60.7	67.7	46.8
Catholic	25.0	15.6	33.3	23.2	22.6	36.2
Jewish	15.0	8.9	8.3	16.1	9.7	17.0
Political Party						
Democrat	95.0	6.7	8.3	89.3	0.0	0.0
Republican	5.0	93.3	91.7	5.4	100.0	95.7
Independent	0.0	0.0	0.0	5.4	0.0	2.1
Other	0.0	0.0	0.0	0.0	0.0	2.1
American Bar Association ratings						
Exceptionally well qualified	27.5	15.6	16.7	16.1	22.6	12.8
Well qualified	47.5	57.8	41.7	58.9	41.9	42.6
Qualified	20.0	26.7	33.3	25.0	35.5	44.7

Continued.

Judges in U.S. Courts of Appeal
[Continued]

	President Johnson's appointees 1963-68 (N=40)	President Nixon's appointees 1969-74 (N=45)	President Ford's appointees 1974-76 (N=12)	President Carter's appointees 1977-80 (N=56)	President Reagan's first term appointees 1981-84 (N=31)	President Reagan's second term appointees 1985-88 (N=47)
Not qualified	2.5	0.0	8.3	0.0	0.0	0.0
No report requested	2.5	0.0	0.0	0.0	0.0	0.0

Source: "Characteristics of Presidential Appointees to U.S. Courts of Appeals," *Sourcebook of Criminal Justice Statistics*, 1988, 1989, p. 98. Primary source: Sheldon Goldman "Reagan's Judicial Legacy: Completing the Puzzle and Summing up," *Judicature* 72 (April-May 1989), pp. 323-325. Table adapted by SOURCEBOOK staff. Reprinted by permission. *Notes:* These data were compiled from a variety of sources. Primarily used were questionnaires completed by judicial nominees for the Senate Judiciary Committee, transcripts of the confirmation hearings conducted by the Committee, and personal interviews. In addition, an investigation was made of various biographical directories including *The American Bench* (Sacramento: R.B. Forster), *Who's Who in American Politics* (New York: Bowker), *Martindale-Hubbell Law Directory* (Summit, NJ: Martindale-Hubbell Inc.), various regional editions of *Who's Who*, State legislative handouts, and relevant newspaper articles from the home State of nominees or appointees. Law firms are categorized according to the number of partners/associates: 25 or more associates for a large firm; 5 to 24 associates for a moderate firm; and 4 or less for a small firm. Percent subtotals for occupational experience sum to more than 100 because some appointees have had both judicial and prosecutorial experience. The American Bar Association's (ABA) ratings are assigned to candidates after investigation and evaluation by the ABA's Standing Committee on Federal Judiciary, which considers prospective Federal judiciary nominees only upon referral by the U.S. Attorney General or at the request of the United States Senate. The ABA's Committee evaluation is directed primarily to professional qualifications — competence, integrity, and judicial temperament. Factors including intellectual capacity, judgment, writing and analytical ability, industry, knowledge of the law, and professional experience are assessed. To be rated "exceptionally well qualified," the prospective nominee has to stand at the top of the legal profession in the community involved and have outstanding legal ability, wide experience, and the highest reputation for integrity and temperament. Similar high standing in the community is also required. To be rated "well qualified," the nominee has to have the Committee's strong affirmative endorsement and be regarded one of the best available for the vacancy from the standpoint of competence, integrity, and temperament. The evaluation of "qualified" indicates that it appears the prospective nominee would be able to perform satisfactorily as a Federal judge with respect to competence integrity, and temperament. When a nominee is found "not qualified," it means that the Committee's investigation indicates that the prospective nominee is not adequate from a standpoint of competence, integrity, or temperament (American Bar Association, *Standing Committee on Federal Judiciary* (Chicago: American Bar Association, 1980), pp. 3-5). Published by permission.

★ 731 ★
Percent Change in Black Elected Officials - Part I

	Total		Federal		State		Substate regional		County	
	BEOs N	% Change	N	% Change	N	% Change	N	% Change	N	% Change
1970	1,469	---	10	---	169	---	---	---	92	---
1971	1,860	26.6	14	40.0	202	19.5	---	---	120	30.4
1972	2,264	21.7	14	0.0	210	4.0	---	---	176	46.7
1973	2,621	15.8	16	14.3	240	14.3	---	---	211	19.9
1974	2,991	14.1	17	6.3	239	-0.4	---	---	242	14.7
1975	3,503	17.1	18	5.9	281	17.6	---	---	305	26.0
1976	3,979	13.6	18	0.0	281	0.0	30	---	355	16.4
1977	4,311	8.3	17	-5.6	299	6.4	33	10.0	381	7.3
1978	4,503	4.5	17	0.0	299	0.0	26	-21.2	410	7.6
1979	4,607	2.3	17	0.0	313	4.7	25	-3.8	398	-2.9
1980	4,912	6.6	17	0.0	323	3.2	25	0.0	451	13.3
1981	5,038	2.6	18	5.9	341	5.6	30	20.0	449	-0.4
1982	5,160	2.4	18	0.0	336	-1.5	35	16.7	465	3.6
1983	5,606	8.6	21	16.7	379	12.8	29	-17.1	496	6.7
1984[1]	5,700	1.7	21	0.0	389	2.6	30	3.4	518	4.4
1985	6,056	6.2	20	-4.8	396	1.8	32	6.7	611	18.0
1986	6,424	6.1	20	0.0	400	1.0	31	-3.2	681	11.4
1987	6,681	4.0	23	15.0	417	4.3	23	-25.8	724	6.3

Continued.

Percent Change in Black Elected Officials - Part I
[Continued]

	Total		Federal		State		Substate regional		County	
	BEOs N	% Change	N	% Change	N	% Change	N	% Change	N	% Change
1988	6,829	2.2	23	0.0	413	-1.0	22	-4.3	742	2.5
1989	7,226	5.8	24	4.2	424	2.7	18	-18.2	793	6.9

Source: "Change in Number of Black Elected Officials by Category of Office, 1970-1989," *Black Elected Officials*, 1989, p. 10. Primary source: *Black Elected Officials*, Joint Center for Political Studies, 1989. Name changed to Joint Center for Political and Economic Studies. Published by permission. *Notes:* 1. The 1984 figures reflect blacks who took office during the seven-month period between July 1, 1983 and January 30, 1984.

★ 732 ★
Percent Change in Black Elected Officials - Part II

	Municipal		Judicial/Law enforcement		Education	
	N	% Change	N	% Change	N	% Change
1970	623	---	213	---	362	---
1971	785	26.0	274	28.6	465	28.5
1972	932	18.7	263	-4.0	669	43.9
1973	1,053	13.0	334	27.0	767	14.6
1974	1,360	29.2	340	1.8	793	3.4
1975	1,573	15.7	387	13.8	939	18.4
1976	1,889	20.1	412	6.5	994	5.9
1977	2,083	10.3	447	8.5	1,051	5.7
1978	2,159	3.6	454	1.6	1,138	8.3
1979	2,224	3.0	486	7.0	1,144	0.5
1980	2,356	5.9	526	8.2	1,214	6.1
1981	2,384	1.2	549	4.4	1,267	4.4
1982	2,477	3.9	563	2.6	1,266	-0.1
1983	2,697	10.0	607	7.8	1,377	8.8
1984[1]	2,735	1.4	636	4.8	1,371	-0.4
1985	2,898	6.0	661	4.0	1,438	4.9
1986	3,112	7.4	676	2.3	1,504	4.6
1987	3,219	3.4	728	7.7	1,547	2.9
1988	3,341	3.8	738	1.4	1,550	0.2
1989	3,595	7.6	760	2.9	1,612	4.0

Source: "Change in Number of Black Elected Officials by Category of Office, 1970-1989," *Black Elected Officials*, 1989, p. 10. Primary source: *Black Elected Officials*, 1989. *Notes:* 1. The 1984 figures reflect blacks who took office during the seven-month period between July 1, 1983 and January 30, 1984.

★ 733 ★
Percentage of Black Elected Officials

State	Blacks as a percent of voting-age population	Elected Officials		
		Total	Black	%Black
Alabama	22.0	4,315	694	16.1
Alaska	3.8	1,865	4	[1]
Arizona	2.4	3,191	12	[1]
Arkansas	12.0	8,331	318	3.8
California	6.0	19,279	275	1.4
Colorado	4.0	8,035	14	[1]
Connecticut	4.0	9,929	63	0.6
Delaware	13.8	1,227	23	1.9
District of Columbia	65.9	325	242	74.5
Florida	13.0	5,368	179	3.3
Georgia	31.0	6,556	483	7.4
Hawaii	2.2	160	1	0.6
Idaho	101	4,678	0	[1]
Illinois	16.0	38,936	444	1.1
Indiana	9.0	11,355	68	0.6
Iowa	1.2	17,043	9	[1]
Kansas	5.0	16,410	23	[1]
Kentucky	5.0	7,481	68	0.9
Louisiana	27.0	4,985	521	10.5
Maine	[1]	7,147	3	[1]
Maryland	24.0	2,032	118	5.8
Massachusetts	4.0	13,888	38	[1]
Michigan	13.0	19,292	306	1.6
Minnesota	1.2	19,013	12	[1]
Mississippi	33.0	4,950	646	13.1
Missouri	10.0	17,115	163	1.0
Montana	[1]	5,646	0	[1]
Nebraska	2.7	15,064	4	[1]
Nevada	4.8	1,174	10	0.9
New Hampshire	[1]	6,883	3	[1]
New Jersey	12.0	9,345	199	2.1
New Mexico	1.6	2,096	6	[1]
New York	13.0	26,343	252	1.0
North Carolina	21.0	5,554	449	8.1
North Dakota	[1]	15,141	0	[1]
Ohio	9.0	19,750	216	1.1
Oklahoma	6.0	9,290	115	1.2
Oregon	1.2	8,366	9	[1]
Pennsylvania	8.0	33,242	139	[1]
Rhode Island	2.5	1,120	10	0.9
South Carolina	26.0	3,692	373	10.1
South Dakota	[1]	9,249	3	[1]
Tennessee	15.0	6,841	146	2.1
Texas	11.0	26,987	312	1.2
Utah	[1]	2,588	1	[1]
Vermont	[1]	8,021	2	[1]

Continued.

Percentage of Black Elected Officials
[Continued]

State	Blacks as a percent of voting-age population	Elected Officials		
		Total	Black	%Black
Virginia	18.0	3,118	144	4.6
Washington	2.4	8,032	20	[1]
West Virginia	3.1	2,838	24	0.8
Wisconsin	5.0	18,238	24	[1]
Wyoming	[1]	2,338	2	[1]
Total	11.1	503,862	7,191	1.4

Source: "Black Elected Officials as a Percentage of All Elected Officials, by State, January 1989."
Black Elected Officials, 1989, pp. 11-12. Primary source: *Black Elected Officials*, Joint Center for Political Studies, 1989. Name changed to Joint Center for Political and Economic Studies. Published by permission. *Notes:* The 35 BEOs in the Virgin Islands are not included in this table, because the Virgin Islands are not included in the 1987 Census of Government. 1. Less than 0.5 percent.

★ 734 ★
Presidential Appointees to Judgeships

By Presidential administration, 1963-88.

	President Johnson's appointees 1963-68 (N=122)	President Nixon's appointees 1969-74 (N=179)	President Ford's appointees 1974-76 (N=52)	President Carter's appointees 1977-80 (N=202)	President Reagan's first term appointees 1981-84 (N=129)	President Reagan's second term appointees 1985-88[1] (N=161)
Ethnicity						
White	93.4	95.5	88.5	78.7	93.0	91.9
Black	4.1	3.4	5.8	13.9	0.8	3.1
Hispanic	2.5	1.1	1.9	6.9	5.4	4.3
Asian	0.0	0.0	3.9	0.5	0.8	0.6

Source: "Characteristics of Presidential Appointees to U.S. District Court," *Sourcebook of Criminal Justice Statistics*, 1988, 1989, p. 98. Primary source: Sheldon Goldman, "Reagan's Judicial Legacy: Completing the Puzzle and Summing Up," *Judicature* 72 (April-May 1989), pp. 320-322. Table adapted by SOURCEBOOK staff. Reprinted by permission. *Notes:* Percent subtotals for occupational experience sum to more than 100 because some appointees have both judicial and prosecutorial experience. 1. One appointee classified as non-denominational. Published by permission.

★ 735 ★
Registered Voters for Specific Election

Numbers in thousands.

Age, sex, race, and Hispanic origin	All persons	Total registered	Registered specifically for 1988			Previously registered	Not reported whether previously registered
			Total[1]	First time	Not first time		
Number							
United States							
White	152,848	103,830	10,356	3,295	5,801	93,145	330
Black	19,692	12,700	966	407	458	11,684	50
Hispanic origin[2]	12,893	4,573	597	303	221	3,943	34
Northeast							
White	33,549	22,471	2,274	755	1,229	22,043	77
Black	3,410	1,879	131	61	66	1,740	7
Hispanic origin[2]	2,262	793	123	55	55	667	3
Midwest							
White	38,691	28,207	2,792	816	1,624	25,342	72
Black	3,960	2,965	296	119	154	2,650	19
Hispanic origin[2]	897	380	44	29	11	336	---
South							
White	49,163	32,756	2,683	918	1,467	29,954	120
Black	10,631	6,734	389	170	153	6,326	18
Hispanic origin[2]	4,134	1,732	172	89	57	1,541	19
West							
White	31,446	20,396	2,607	806	1,481	17,717	72
Black	1,690	1,123	150	57	86	967	5
Hispanic origin[2]	5,600	1,667	258	130	98	1,398	12
Percent distribution							
United States							
White	152,848	100.0	10.0	3.2	5.6	89.7	0.3
Black	19,692	100.0	7.6	3.2	3.6	92.0	0.4
Hispanic origin[2]	12,893	100.0	13.1	6.6	4.8	86.2	0.7
Northeast							
White	33,549	100.0	10.1	3.4	5.5	89.6	0.3
Black	3,410	100.0	7.0	3.2	3.5	92.6	0.4
Hispanic origin[2]	2,262	100.0	15.5	6.9	6.9	84.1	0.4
Midwest							
White	38,691	100.0	9.9	2.9	5.8	89.8	0.3
Black	3,960	100.0	10.0	4.0	5.2	89.4	0.6
Hispanic origin[2]	897	100.0	11.6	7.6	2.9	88.4	---
South							
White	49,163	100.0	8.2	2.8	4.5	91.4	0.4
Black	10,631	100.0	5.8	2.5	2.3	93.9	0.3
Hispanic origin[2]	4,134	100.0	9.9	5.1	3.3	89.0	1.1
West							
White	31,446	100.0	12.8	4.0	7.3	86.9	0.4

Continued.

Registered Voters for Specific Election
[Continued]

Age, sex, race, and Hispanic origin	All persons	Total registered	Registered specifically for 1988			Previously registered	Not reported whether previously registered
			Total[1]	First time	Not first time		
Black	1,690	100.0	13.4	5.1	7.7	86.1	0.4
Hispanic origin[2]	5,600	100.0	15.5	7.8	5.9	83.9	0.7

Source: "Persons Registered Specifically for the 1988 Election, by Age, Sex, Race, and Hispanic Origin, for the United States and Regions: November 1988." Voting and Registration in the Election of November 1988, 1989, pp. 66-67. Primary source: U.S. Bureau of the Census, Current Population Reports, Series P-20, No. 440, Voting and Registration in the Election of November 1988. *Notes:* 1. Includes 1,406,000 persons who said they had registered specifically for the 1988 election, but who did not report whether they were first time registrants in 1988. 2. Persons of Hispanic origin may be of any race.

★ 736 ★
Registered Voters for Specific Elections

Numbers in thousands. Civilian noninstitutional population.

Age, sex, race, and Hispanic origin	Total registered specifically for this election	First-time registrants			Not first-time registrants			Not reported whether first-time registrants
		Total[1]	Voted	Did not vote	Total[1]	Voted	Did not vote	
				Number				
United States								
White	10,356	3,295	2,808	420	5,801	5,345	432	1,260
Black	966	407	292	92	458	390	64	101
Hispanic origin[2]	597	303	237	61	221	192	28	72
Northeast								
White	2,274	755	661	81	1,229	1,219	71	297
Black	131	61	43	18	66	60	6	4
Hispanic origin[2]	123	55	45	7	55	54	1	13
Midwest								
White	2,792	816	672	118	1,624	1,541	78	352
Black	296	119	112	4	154	131	22	23
Hispanic origin[2]	44	29	24	3	11	9	---	4
South								
White	2,683	918	804	97	1,467	1,311	150	298
Black	389	170	99	51	153	124	25	66
Hispanic origin[2]	172	89	72	17	57	53	4	26
West								
White	2,607	806	672	125	1,481	1,339	139	320
Black	150	57	38	19	86	75	11	8
Hispanic origin[2]	258	130	97	34	98	75	22	30

Continued.

Registered Voters for Specific Elections
[Continued]

Age, sex, race, and Hispanic origin	Total registered specifically for this election	First-time registrants			Not first-time registrants			Not reported whether first-time registrants
		Total[1]	Voted	Did not vote	Total[1]	Voted	Did not vote	
				Percent distribution				
United States								
White	100.0	31.8	27.1	4.1	56.0	51.6	4.2	12.2
Black	100.0	42.1	30.2	9.5	47.4	40.4	6.6	10.5
Hispanic origin[2]	100.0	50.8	39.7	10.2	37.0	32.2	4.7	12.1
Northeast								
White	100.0	33.2	29.1	3.6	54.0	50.8	2.9	12.8
Black	100.0	46.6	32.8	13.7	50.4	45.8	4.6	3.1
Hispanic origin[2]	100.0	44.7	36.6	5.7	44.7	43.9	0.8	10.6
Midwest								
White	100.0	29.2	24.1	4.2	58.2	55.2	2.8	12.6
Black	100.0	40.2	37.8	1.4	52.0	44.3	7.4	7.8
Hispanic origin[2]	---	---	---	---	---	---	---	---
South								
White	100.0	34.2	30.0	3.6	54.7	48.9	5.6	11.1
Black	100.0	43.7	25.4	13.1	39.3	31.9	6.4	17.0
Hispanic origin[2]	100.0	51.7	41.9	9.9	33.1	30.8	2.3	15.1
West								
White	100.0	30.9	25.8	4.8	56.8	51.4	5.3	12.3
Black	100.0	38.0	25.3	12.7	57.3	50.0	7.3	5.3
Hispanic origin[2]	100.0	50.4	37.6	13.2	38.0	29.1	8.5	11.6

Source: "Persons Who Registered Specifically for the 1988 Election, by Whether First Time Registrants and Whether Voted, by Age, Sex, Race, and Hispanic Origin, for the United States and Regions: November 1988." Voting and Registration in the Election of November 1988, 1989, pp. 68-69. Primary source: U.S. Bureau of the Census, Current Population Reports, Series P-20, No. 440, Voting and Registration in the Election of November 1988. *Notes:* 1. Includes persons who did not report whether they had voted. 2. Persons of Hispanic origin may be of any race.

★ 737 ★
Trends in Voter Registration

Numbers in thousands.

Region, race, Hispanic origin, sex, and age	Presidential elections						Congressional elections			
	1988	1984	1980	1976	1972	1968	1986	1982	1978	1974
United States										
Total, voting age	178,098	169,963	157,085	146,548	136,203	116,535	173,890	165,483	151,646	141,299
Percent registered	66.6	68.3	66.9	66.7	72.3	74.3	64.3	64.1	62.6	62.2
White	67.9	69.6	68.4	68.3	73.4	75.4	65.3	65.6	63.8	63.5
Black	64.5	66.3	60.0	58.5	65.5	66.2	64.0	59.1	57.1	54.9
Hispanic origin[1]	35.5	40.1	36.3	37.8	44.4	[4]	35.9	35.3	32.9	34.9
Male	65.2	67.3	66.6	67.1	73.1	76.0	63.4	63.7	62.6	62.8
Female	67.8	69.3	67.1	66.4	71.6	72.8	65.0	64.4	62.5	61.7

Continued.

Trends in Voter Registration
[Continued]

Region, race, Hispanic origin, sex, and age	Presidential elections						Congressional elections			
	1988	1984	1980	1976	1972	1968	1986	1982	1978	1974
18 to 24 years	48.2	51.3	49.2	51.3	58.9	56.0[2]	42.0	42.4	40.5	41.3
25 to 44 years	63.0	66.6	65.6	65.5	71.3	72.4	61.1	61.5	60.2	59.9
45 to 64 years	75.5	76.6	75.8	75.5	79.7	81.1	74.8	75.6	74.3	73.6
65 years and over	78.4	76.9	74.6	71.4	75.6	75.6	76.9	75.2	72.8	70.2
North and West										
Total, voting age	117,373	112,376	106,524	99,403	93,653	81,594	114,689	110,126	102,894	96,505
Percent registered	67.1	69.0	67.9	67.7	73.9	76.5	64.9	65.2	63.8	63.3
White	68.5	70.5	69.3	69.0	74.9	77.2	66.2	66.7	64.9	64.6
Black	65.9	67.2	60.6	60.9	67.0	71.8	63.1	61.7	58.0	54.2
South										
Total, voting age	60,725	57,587	50,561	47,145	42,550	34,941	59,201	55,357	48,752	44,794
Percent registered	65.6	66.9	64.8	64.6	68.7	69.2	63.0	61.7	60.1	59.8
White	66.6	67.8	66.2	66.7	69.8	70.8	63.2	63.2	61.2	61.0
Black	63.3	65.6	59.3	56.4	60.0	61.6	64.6	56.9	56.2	55.5

Source: "Reported Registration, by Region, Race, Hispanic Origin, Sex, and Age: November 1968 to 1988." Voting and Registration in the Election of November 1988, 1989, p. 3. Primary source: U.S. Bureau of the Census, Current Population Reports, Series P-20, No. 440, Voting and Registration in the Election of November 1988. *Notes:* 1. Persons of Hispanic origin may be of any race. 2. Prior to 1972, includes persons 18 to 20 years old in Georgia and Kentucky, 19 and 20 in Alaska, and 20 years old in Hawaii. 4. Not available.

★ 738 ★
Voters and Voting - Part I

Numbers in thousands.

Race, Hispanic origin, sex, and type of respondent	All persons	Reported registered	Reported voted	Reported not voting					Do not know (voting)				
				Total	Registered				Total[1]	Registered			
					Yes	No	Do not know	Not reported		Yes	No	Do not know	Not reported
White													
All respondents[2]													
Both sexes	152,848	103,830	90,357	49,129	12,366	34,858	1,845	60	2,516	796	60	1,654	7
Male	73,119	48,836	42,662	23,576	5,539	16,983	1,024	31	1,584	505	46	1,031	2
Female	79,730	54,994	47,695	25,553	6,827	17,875	821	30	932	291	14	623	4
Reported by self													
Both sexes	80,781	57,945	50,658	26,310	7,103	18,652	535	19	102	17	---	84	---
Male	28,634	20,047	17,649	9,296	2,345	6,759	183	8	54	6	---	48	---
Female	52,147	37,898	33,008	17,014	4,758	11,893	352	11	47	11	---	36	---
Reported by other													
Both sexes	67,812	45,259	39,181	22,508	5,169	16,006	1,304	29	2,391	770	55	1,562	4
Male	42,519	28,531	24,792	14,155	3,163	10,135	839	18	1,516	496	40	979	---
Female	25,292	16,728	14,389	8,353	2,006	5,871	465	11	875	274	14	583	4
Black													
All respondents[2]													
Both sexes	19,692	12,700	10,144	7,405	2,260	4,727	411	7	866	271	6	586	3
Male	8,777	5,344	4,233	3,402	951	2,210	239	1	509	157	3	347	3
Female	10,915	7,356	5,911	4,003	1,309	2,517	172	6	357	114	3	240	---
Reported by self													
Both sexes	10,737	7,569	6,106	4,164	1,444	2,626	89	5	32	6	---	26	---
Male	3,634	2,458	1,979	1,422	475	920	26	1	16	1	---	14	---
Female	7,103	5,111	4,127	2,742	969	1,706	63	4	16	5	---	12	---
Reported by other													
Both sexes	8,436	5,089	4,007	3,219	809	2,085	322	2	831	262	6	560	3
Male	4,903	2,872	2,245	1,974	476	1,284	213	---	490	152	3	332	---
Female	3,534	2,216	1,762	1,245	334	801	109	2	341	110	3	228	---

Continued.

Voters and Voting - Part I
[Continued]

Race, Hispanic origin, sex, and type of respondent	All persons	Reported registered	Reported voted	Reported not voting					Do not know (voting)				
					Registered					Registered			
				Total	Yes	No	Do not know	Not reported	Total[1]	Yes	No	Do not know	Not reported
Hispanic Origin[3]													
All respondents[2]													
Both sexes	12,893	4,573	3,710	3,784	789	2,831	160	5	253	60	14	178	---
Male	6,398	2,143	1,753	1,795	362	1,329	103	1	163	26	13	125	---
Female	6,495	2,431	1,958	1,989	426	1,501	57	4	90	34	2	54	---
Reported by self													
Both sexes	6,270	2,387	1,968	1,989	410	1,549	26	4	7	---	---	7	---
Male	2,620	889	731	737	157	567	13	---	7	---	---	7	---
Female	3,651	1,498	1,237	1,252	253	982	13	4	---	---	---	---	---
Reported by other													
Both sexes	6,236	2,143	1,708	1,776	370	1,272	134	---	246	60	14	171	---
Male	3,597	1,228	1,003	1,050	200	761	90	---	156	26	13	118	---
Female	2,639	915	705	726	170	512	44	---	90	34	2	54	---

Source: "Reported Voting and Registration, by Race, Hispanic Origin, Sex, and Type of Respondent: November 1988." Voting and Registration in the Election of November 1988, 1989, p. 70. Primary source: U.S. Bureau of the Census, Current Population Reports, Series P-20, No. 440, Voting and Registration in the Election of November 1988. *Notes:* 1. Includes persons who reported on registration. 2. Includes not reported on type of respondent, not shown separately. 3. Persons of Hispanic origin may be of any race.

★ 739 ★
Voters and Voting - Part II

Numbers in thousands.

Race, Hispanic origin, sex, and type of respondent	Not reported (voting)		Not a U.S. citizen
	Total[1]	Not reported on registration	
White			
All respondents[2]			
Both sexes	3,999	3,668	6,849
Male	1,870	1,728	3,427
Female	2,129	1,940	3,422
Reported by self			
Both sexes	358	185	3,354
Male	126	77	1,509
Female	232	108	1,845
Reported by other			
Both sexes	275	126	3,457
Male	158	69	1,899
Female	116	57	1,559
Black			
All respondents[2]			
Both sexes	547	514	730
Male	238	230	396
Female	309	284	335
Reported by self			
Both sexes	59	41	376
Male	15	8	203
Female	44	32	173

Continued.

Voters and Voting - Part II
[Continued]

Race, Hispanic origin, sex, and type of respondent	Not reported (voting)		Not a U.S. citizen
	Total[1]	Not reported on registration	
Reported by other			
Both sexes	30	18	349
Male	5	4	189
Female	25	13	160
Hispanic Origin[3]			
All respondents[2]			
Both sexes	332	316	4,815
Male	140	138	2,547
Female	192	178	2,268
Reported by self			
Both sexes	17	9	2,290
Male	1	---	1,144
Female	16	9	1,146
Reported by other			
Both sexes	10	5	2,496
Male	5	5	1,384
Female	5	---	1,113

Source: "Reported Voting and Registration, by Race, Hispanic Origin, Sex, and Type of Respondent: November 1988." Voting and Registration in the Election of November 1988, 1989, p. 70. Primary source: U.S. Bureau of the Census, Current Population Reports, Series P-20, No. 440, Voting and Registration in the Election of November 1988. *Notes:* 1. Includes persons who reported on registration. 2. Includes not reported on type of respondent, not shown separately. 3. Persons of Hispanic origin may be of any race.

★ 740 ★
Voters and Voting

In thousands, except percent. Covers population 18 years old and over.

Year and Race	Total	AL	AR	FL	GA	LA	MS	NC	SC	TN	TX	VA
1980:												
White	24,981	1,700	1,056	4,331	1,800	1,550	1,152	2,314	916	2,200	6,020	1,942
Black	4,254	350	130	489	450	465	330	440	320	300	620	360
Percent of--												
White voting age pop.	71.9	81.4	76.9	67.7	63.0	74.8	98.9	70.1	58.5	78.5	75.1	62.2
Black voting age pop.	55.8	55.8	57.2	58.3	48.6	60.7	62.3	51.3	53.7	64.0	56.0	53.2
1982:												
White[1]	22,868	1,657	964	4,200	1,907	1,491	1,055	2,161	862	1,998	4,753	1,820
Black	4,302	437	145	500	467	468	340	436	321	310	548	330
1984:												
White[1]	27,999	1,828[2]	1,097[2]	4,983	2,102	1,701	1,211[2]	2,622	1,005	2,217[2]	7,030[2]	2,203[2]
Black	5,597	516[2]	171[2]	591	594	561	459[2]	619	389	362[2]	870[2]	464[2]
1986:												
White[3]	27,028[2]	1,807[2]	1,030[2]	4,677	1,990	1,580	1,193[2]	2,468	932	2,186[2]	7,068[2]	2,097[2]
Black	5,450[2]	509[2]	157[2]	576	576	551	450[2]	585	371	358[2]	875[2]	442[2]

Continued.

Voters and Voting
[Continued]

Year and Race	Total	AL	AR	FL	GA	LA	MS	NC	SC	TN	TX	VA
Percent of---												
White voting age pop.	69.9	77.5	67.2	66.9	62.3	67.8	91.6	67.4	53.4	70.0	79.0	60.3
Black voting age pop.	60.8	68.9	57.9	58.2	52.8	60.6	70.8	58.4	52.5	65.3	68.0	56.2

Source: "Voter Registration in 11 Southern States, by Race: 1980 to 1986," *Statistical Abstract*, 1989, p. 261. Primary source: Voter Education Project, Inc., Atlanta, GA, *Voter Registration in the South*, semiannual. *Notes:* 1. As of October, except Arkansas as of November. 2. Estimated. 3. As of August.

★ 741 ★
Voting and Registration

November 1988. Numbers in thousands. For meaning of symbols, see text.

Race, Hispanic origin, and residence	All persons	Reported registered		Reported voted		Reported that they did not vote[1]				
								Not registered		
		Number	Percent	Number	Percent	Total	Registered	Total[2]	Not a U.S. citizen	Do not know and not reported on registration[3]
White										
Total	123,648	85,181	68.9	74,846	60.5	48,802	10,334	38,468	5,708	5,427
Under $5,000	3,726	1,604	43.0	1,170	31.4	2,556	434	2,122	426	240
$5,000 to $9,999	8,177	4,170	51.0	3,300	40.4	4,878	871	4,007	776	345
$10,000 to $14,999	12,990	7,539	58.0	6,330	48.7	6,660	1,209	5,451	1,062	467
$15,000 to $19,999	21,184	13,642	64.4	11,672	55.1	9,512	1,970	7,542	1,097	863
$20,000 to $24,999	10,839	7,389	68.2	6,384	58.9	4,455	1,006	3,449	479	396
$25,000 to $34,999	20,634	15,031	72.8	13,440	65.1	7,194	1,592	5,602	644	730
$35,000 to $49,999	22,293	17,558	78.8	15,877	71.2	6,417	1,682	4,735	502	734
$50,000 and over	15,555	12,973	83.4	12,011	77.2	3,544	962	2,582	329	558
Income not reported	8,250	5,273	63.9	4,664	56.5	3,586	610	2,976	392	1,095
Black										
Total	15,614	10,130	64.9	8,157	52.2	7,457	1,973	5,484	558	1,206
Under $5,000	1,978	1,177	59.5	867	43.8	1,111	310	801	32	137
$5,000 to $9,999	2,409	1,506	62.5	1,146	47.6	1,263	360	903	67	143
$10,000 to $14,999	2,196	1,326	60.4	1,038	47.3	1,158	288	870	123	179
$15,000 to $19,999	3,021	1,910	63.2	1,512	50.0	1,510	399	1,111	165	208
$20,000 to $24,999	1,111	744	67.0	590	53.1	521	154	367	43	104
$25,000 to $34,999	1,696	1,249	73.7	1,036	61.1	660	213	447	24	89
$35,000 to $49,999	1,395	1,091	78.2	982	70.4	413	109	304	29	69
$50,000 and over	727	581	79.9	521	71.7	206	60	146	17	49
Income not reported	1,081	546	50.5	465	43.0	616	81	535		
Hispanic[4]										
Total	11,087	3,974	35.8	3,236	29.2	7,852	738	7,114	4,064	541
Under $5,000	950	246	25.9	179	18.8	771	67	704	353	65
$5,000 to $9,999	1,493	405	27.1	339	22.7	1,154	66	1,088	662	76
$10,000 to $14,999	1,984	506	25.5	386	19.5	1,598	119	1,478	946	82
$15,000 to $19,999	2,237	734	32.8	556	24.9	1,681	177	1,504	896	123
$20,000 to $24,999	886	310	35.0	229	25.9	657	81	576	319	34
$25,000 to $34,999	1,363	633	46.4	540	39.6	823	93	730	366	34
$35,000 to $49,999	1,019	580	56.9	508	49.8	512	72	439	189	34
$50,000 and over	526	368	70.0	336	63.9	190	32	158	80	15
Income not reported	630	192	30.5	162	25.7	467	30	437	253	78

Source: "Reported Voting and Registration of Family Members, by Race, Hispanic Origin, and Family Income." Voting and Registration in the Election of November 1988, 1989, p. 65. Primary source: U.S. Bureau of the Census, Current Population Reports, Series P-20, No. 440, Voting and Registration in the Election of November 1988. *Notes:* 1. Includes persons reported as "did not vote," "do not know," and "not reported" on voting. 2. In addition to those reported as "not registered," total includes those "not a U.S. citizen," and "do not know" and "not reported" on registration. 3. Includes "do not know" and "not reported" on citizenship. 4. Persons of Hispanic origin may be of any race.

★ 742 ★
Voting and Registration

November 1988. Numbers in thousands.

Race, sex, Hispanic origin, employment status, and class of worker	All persons	Reported registered		Reported voted		Reported that they did not vote[1]				
									Not registered	
		Number	Percent	Number	Percent	Total	Registered	Total[2]	Not a U.S. citizen	Do not know and not reported on registration[3]
White										
Both sexes										
Total	152,848	103,830	67.9	90,357	59.1	62,492	13,474	49,018	6,849	7,234
In civilian labor force	102,873	69,242	67.3	60,549	58.9	42,324	8,693	33,631	4,781	4,596
Employed	98,570	67,132	68.1	58,900	59.8	39,671	8,232	31,438	4,449	4,327
Agricultural industries	2,790	1,809	64.8	1,513	54.2	1,277	296	981	277	118
Self-employed workers[4]	1,453	1,139	78.4	979	67.4	474	160	314	54	42
Wage and salary workers	1,337	670	50.1	534	39.9	803	136	667	223	76
Nonagricultural industries	95,781	65,323	68.2	57,387	59.9	38,394	7,936	30,457	4,172	4,209
Private wage and salary workers	73,214	47,355	64.7	40,971	56.0	32,243	6,384	25,859	3,671	3,352
Government workers	14,282	12,029	84.2	11,086	77.6	3,196	943	2,253	186	443
Self-employed workers[4]	8,284	5,939	71.7	5,330	64.3	2,955	609	2,345	315	414
Unemployed	4,302	2,109	49.0	1,649	38.3	2,653	460	2,193	332	269
Not in labor force	49,976	34,589	69.2	29,808	59.6	20,168	4,781	15,387	2,068	2,638
Black										
Both sexes										
Total	19,692	12,700	64.5	10,144	51.5	9,548	2,557	6,991	730	1,522
In civilian labor force	13,066	8,553	65.5	6,905	52.8	6,162	1,649	4,513	577	996
Employed	11,751	7,797	66.3	6,359	54.1	5,392	1,437	3,955	526	916
Agricultural industries	156	77	49.2	50	32.3	105	26	79	7	14
Self-employed workers[4]	26	13	---	9	---	17	3	13	---	1
Wage and salary workers	130	64	49.4	41	31.7	89	23	66	7	13
Nonagricultural industries	11,595	7,720	66.6	6,309	54.4	5,286	1,411	3,876	519	902
Private wage and salary workers	8,413	5,335	63.4	4,221	50.2	4,192	1,113	3,078	429	706
Government workers	2,757	2,124	77.0	1,851	67.1	906	273	633	51	160
Self-employed workers[4]	425	261	61.5	237	55.8	188	24	164	39	35
Unemployed	1,315	757	57.5	545	41.5	770	211	558	52	80
Not in labor force	6,625	4,147	62.6	3,239	48.9	3,386	908	2,478	153	525

Source: "Reported Voting and Registration, by Race, Hispanic Origin, Sex, Employment Status, and Class of Worker." Voting and Registration in the Election of November 1988, 1989, p. 65. Primary source: U.S. Bureau of the Census, Current Population Reports, Series P-20, No. 440, Voting and Registration in the Election of November 1988. *Notes:* 1. Includes persons reported as "did not vote," "do not know," and "not reported" on voting. 2. In addition to those reported as "not registered," total includes those "not a U.S. citizen," and "do not know" and "not reported" on registration. 3. Includes "do not know" and "not reported" on citizenship. 4. Persons of Hispanic origin may be of any race.

★ 743 ★
Voting and Registration

November 1988. Numbers in thousands.

Region, race, Hispanic origin, sex, and age	All persons	Reported registered		Reported voted		Reported that they did not vote[1]				
									Not registered	
		Number	Percent	Number	Percent	Total	Registered	Total	Not a U.S. citizen	Do not know and not reported on registration
White										
Both Sexes										
Total, 18 years and over	152,848	103,830	67.9	90,357	59.1	62,492	13,474	49,018	6,849	7,234
18 to 20 years	8,824	4,047	45.9	3,045	34.5	5,778	1,002	4,777	440	775
21 to 24 years	12,268	6,231	50.8	4,750	38.7	7,518	1,481	6,037	832	833
25 to 34 years	35,914	21,238	59.1	17,963	50.0	17,950	3,275	14,676	2,313	1,712
35 to 44 years	30,139	21,296	70.7	18.964	62.9	11,175	2,332	8,843	1,395	1,150

Continued.

Voting and Registration
[Continued]

| Region, race, Hispanic origin, sex, and age | All persons | Reported registered | | Reported voted | | Reported that they did not vote[1] | | | | |
| | | | | | | | | Not registered | | |
		Number	Percent	Number	Percent	Total	Regis- tered	Total	Not a U.S. citizen	Do not know and not reported on regis- tration
45 to 54 years	20,903	15,689	75.1	14,206	68.0	6,697	1,483	5,214	890	829
55 to 64 years	18,892	14,816	78.4	13,346	70.6	5,547	1,470	4,077	560	739
65 to 74 years	15,771	12,876	81.6	11,638	73.8	4,133	1,238	2,895	234	626
75 years and over	10,137	7,637	75.3	6,444	63.6	3,693	1,193	2,500	184	570
Black										
Total, 18 years and over	19,692	12,700	64.5	10,144	51.5	9,548	2,557	6,991	730	1,522
18 to 20 years	1,543	662	42.9	429	27.8	1,114	232	882	74	165
21 to 24 years	2,024	1,114	55.1	820	40.5	1,204	294	910	80	201
25 to 34 years	5,262	3,045	57.9	2,200	41.8	3,062	845	2,217	258	442
35 to 44 years	3,778	2,566	67.9	2,135	56.5	1,643	432	1,211	175	248
45 to 54 years	2,548	1,902	74.6	1,639	64.3	909	263	646	63	160
55 to 64 years	2,114	1,574	74.5	1,382	65.4	731	192	540	51	151
65 to 74 years	1,526	1,205	78.9	1,060	69.5	466	144	322	29	100
75 years and over	896	632	70.5	478	53.3	418	154	264	---	55
Hispanic[1]										
Total, 18 years and over	12,893	4,573	35.5	3,710	28.8	9,183	863	8,320	4,815	660
18 to 20 years	1,104	270	24.5	171	15.5	933	99	834	362	81
21 to 24 years	1,557	404	25.9	276	17.7	1,281	128	1,154	667	72
25 to 34 years	3,959	1,182	29.9	940	23.7	3,020	243	2,777	1,693	213
35 to 44 years	2,626	1,005	38.3	841	32.0	1,785	164	1,621	976	123
45 to 54 years	1,569	629	40.1	538	34.3	1,031	91	940	583	81
55 to 64 years	1,218	643	52.8	553	45.4	665	91	574	340	42
65 to 74 years	537	301	56.1	269	50.1	268	32	235	90	31
75 years and over	325	139	42.8	124	38.1	201	15	186	105	17

Source: "Reported Voting and Registration, by Race, Hispanic Origin, Sex, and Age, for the United States and Regions." Voting and Registration in the Election of November 1988, 1989, pp. 16-17. U.S. Bureau of the Census, Current Population Reports, Series P-20, No. 440, Voting and Registration in the Election of November 1988. *Note:* 1. Hispanic persons may be of any race.

★ 744 ★
Voting Patterns

November 1988. Numbers in thousands.

| Race, Hispanic origin, and residence | All persons | Reported registered | | Reported voted | | Reported that they did not vote[1] | | | | |
| | | | | | | | | Not registered | | |
		Number	Percent	Number	Percent	Total	Registered	Total[2]	Not a U.S. citizen	Do not know and not reported on registra- tion[3]
United States										
All races										
Total	178,098	118,589	66.6	102,224	57.4	75,875	16,365	59,510	9,603	9,021
Metropolitan	139,134	91,345	65.7	79,505	57.1	59,630	11,841	47,789	9,098	7,525
In central cities	55,342	35,003	63.2	30,127	54.4	25,215	4,876	20,338	5,118	3,137
Outside central cities	83,792	56,342	67.2	49,378	58.9	34,415	6,964	27,450	3,980	4,338
Nonmetropolitan	38,964	27,243	69.9	22,719	58.3	16,245	4,524	11,721	506	1,496
White										
Total	152,848	103,830	67.9	90,357	59.1	62,492	13,474	49,018	6,849	7,234
Metropolitan	117,944	79,129	67.1	69,516	58.9	48,427	9,613	38,815	6,444	5,953
In central cities	41,777	26,911	64.4	8,511	56.2	18,313	3,446	14,867	3,556	2,103
Outside central cities	76,166	52,218	68.6	46,052	60.5	30,114	6,166	23,948	2,888	3,850
Nonmetropolitan	34,905	24,701	70.8	20,840	59.7	14,065	3,861	10,203	405	1,281

Continued.

Voting Patterns
[Continued]

Race, Hispanic origin, and residence	All persons	Reported registered		Reported voted		Reported that they did not vote[1]				
								Not registered		
		Number	Percent	Number	Percent	Total	Registered	Total[2]	Not a U.S. citizen	Do not know and not reported on registra-tion[3]
Black										
Total	19,692	12,700	64.5	10,144	51.5	9,548	2,557	6,991	730	1,522
Metropolitan	16,292	10,487	64.4	8,511	52.2	7,781	1,976	5,805	712	1,347
In central cities	11,107	7,251	65.3	5,957	53.6	5,150	1,294	3,857	506	924
Outside central cities	5,185	3,236	62.4	2,554	49.3	2,631	682	1,948	206	423
Nonmetropolitan	3,400	2,213	65.1	1,633	48.0	1,767	581	1,186	19	174
Hispanic[4]										
Total	12,893	4,573	35.5	3,710	28.8	9,183	863	8,320	4,815	660
Metropolitan	11,975	4,126	34.4	3,358	28.0	8,618	768	7,850	4,622	606
In central cities	6,792	2,202	32.4	1,805	26.6	4,987	398	4,590	2,778	379
Outside central cities	5,184	1,923	37.1	1,553	30.0	3,630	370	3,260	1,844	227
Nonmetropolitan	918	448	48.8	352	38.4	565	95	470	192	54

Source: "Reported Voting and Registration, by Race, Hispanic Origin, and Metropolitan-Nonmetropolitan Residence." Voting and Registration in the Election of November 1988, 1989, p. 41. Primary source: U.S. Bureau of the Census, Current Population Reports, Series P-20, No. 440, Voting and Registration in the Election of November 1988. *Notes:* 1. Includes persons reported as "did not vote," "do not know," and "not reported" on voting. 2. In addition to those reported as "not registered," total includes those "not a U.S. citizen," and "do not know" and "not reported" on registration. 3. Includes "do not know" and "not reported" on citizenship. 4. Persons of Hispanic origin may be of any race.

★ 745 ★
Voting Trends - November 1964

Numbers in thousands. Civilian noninstitutional population.

Characteristic	Voting-age population	Voted	
		Number	Percent
Race			
White	99,353	70,204	70.7
Black	10,340	6,048	58.5

Source: "Voting and Registration: November 1964." *Voting and Registration in the Election of November 1988,* 1989, p. 76. Primary source: U.S. Bureau of the Census, Current Population Reports, Series P-20, No. 440, *Voting and Registration in the Election of November 1988.*

★ 746 ★
Voting Trends - November 1968

Numbers in thousands. Civilian noninstitutional population.

Characteristic	Voting-age population	Registered		Voted	
		Number	Percent	Number	Percent
Race					
White	104,521	78,835	7534	72,213	69.1
Black	10,935	7,238	66.2	6,300	57.6

Source: "Voting and Registration: November 1968." *Voting and Registration in the Election of November 1988*, 1989, p. 75. Primary source: U.S. Bureau of the Census, Current Population Reports, Series P-20, No. 440, *Voting and Registration in the Election of November 1988.*

★ 747 ★
Voting Trends - November 1972

Numbers in thousands. Civilian noninstitutional population.

Characteristic	Voting-age population	Registered		Voted	
		Number	Percent	Number	Percent
Race and Hispanic Origin					
White	121,243	88,987	73.4	78,166	64.5
Black	13,493	8.837	65.5	7,032	52.1
Hispanic[1]	5,616	2,495	44.4	2,103	37.5

Source: "Voting and Registration: November 1972." *Voting and Registration in the Election of November 1988*, 1989, p. 74. Primary source: U.S. Bureau of the Census, Current Population Reports, Series P-20, No. 440, *Voting and Registration in the Election of November 1988. Note:* 1. Persons of Hispanic origin may be of any race.

★ 748 ★
Voting Trends - November 1976

Numbers in thousands. Civilian noninstitutional population.

Characteristic	Voting-age population	Registered		Voted	
		Number	Percent	Number	Percent
Race and Hispanic Origin					
White	129,316	88,329	68.3	78,808	60.9
Black	14,927	8,725	58.5	7,273	48.7
Hispanic[1]	6,594	2,494	37.8	2,098	31.8

Source: "Voting and Registration: November 1976." *Voting and Registration in the Election of November 1988*, 1989, p. 73. Primary source: U.S. Bureau of the Census, Current Population Reports, Series P-20, No. 440, *Voting and Registration in the Election of November 1988. Note:* 1. Persons of Hispanic origin may be of any race.

★ 749 ★
Voting Trends - November 1984

Numbers in thousands. Civilian noninstitutional population.

Characteristic	Voting-age population	Registered		Voted	
		Number	Percent	Number	Percent
Race and Hispanic Origin					
White	146,761	102,211	69.6	90,152	61.4
Black	18,432	12,223	66.3	10,293	55.8
Hispanic[1]	9,471	3,794	40.1	3,092	32.6

Source: "Voting and Registration: November 1984." *Voting and Registration in the Election of November 1988,* 1989, p. 71. Primary source: U.S. Bureau of the Census, Current Population Reports, Series P-20, No. 440, *Voting and Registration in the Election of November 1988. Note:* 1. Persons of Hispanic origin may be of any race.

★ 750 ★
Voting Trends

Numbers in thousands. Civilian noninstitutional population.

Charateristic	Voting-age population	Registered		Voted	
		Number	Percent	Number	Percent
Race and Hispanic Origin					
White	137,676	94,112	68.4	83,855	60.9
Black	16,423	9,849	60.0	8,287	50.5
Hispanic[1]	8,210	2,984	36.3	2,453	29.9

Source: "Voting and Registration: November 1980." Voting and Registration in the Election of November 1988, 1989, p. 72. Primary source: U.S. Bureau of the Census, Current Population Reports, Series P-20, No. 440, Voting and Registration in the Election of November 1988. *Note:* 1. Persons of Hispanic origin may be of any race.

POPULATION

★ 751 ★
1960-1987 Population

Year	Total	Black Number	Black Percent	Percent Change	White Number	White Percent	Percent Change
1960	180,671	19,006	10.5		160,023	88.6	
1961	183,691	19,437	10.6	2.3	162,533	88.5	1.6
1962	186,538	19,582	10.5	0.7	164,885	88.4	1.4
1963	189,277	20,255	10.7	3.4	167,104	88.3	1.3
1964	191,889	20,672	10.8	2.1	169,257	88.2	1.3
1965	194,303	21,064	10.8	1.9	171,205	88.1	1.2
1966	196,561	21,434	10.9	1.8	172,998	88.0	1.1
1967	198,712	21,780	11.0	1.6	174,695	87.9	1.0
1968	200,706	22,117	11.0	1.5	176,246	87.8	0.9
1969	202,677	22,431	11.1	1.4	177,782	87.7	0.9
1970	205,052	22,801	11.1	1.6	179,644	87.6	1.0
1971	207,661	23,240	11.2	1.9	181,663	87.5	1.1
1972	209,896	23,646	11.3	1.7	183,326	87.3	0.9
1973	211,909	24,029	11.3	1.6	184,782	87.2	0.8
1974	213,854	24,402	11.4	1.5	186,170	87.1	0.8
1975	215,973	24,778	11.5	1.5	187,629	86.9	0.8
1976	218,035	25,157	11.5	1.5	189,074	86.7	0.8
1977	220,329	25,559	11.6	1.6	190,649	86.6	0.8
1978	222,585	25,984	11.7	1.7	192,335	86.4	0.9
1979	225,055	26,417	11.7	1.7	194,094	86.2	0.9
1980	227,757	26,903	11.8	1.8	195,571	85.9	0.8
1981	230,138	27,328	11.9	1.6	197,132	85.7	0.8
1982	232,520	27,759	11.9	1.6	198,696	85.5	0.8
1983	234,799	28,178	12.5	1.5	200,216	85.3	0.8
1984	237,001	28,580	12.1	1.4	201,664	85.1	0.7
1985	239,283	29,002	12.1	1.5	203,156	84.9	0.7
1986	241,671	29,427	12.2	1.5	204,671	84.7	0.7
1987	243,827	29,857	12.2	1.5	206,190	84.6	0.7

Source: "Distribution of Blacks and Whites in Total U.S. Population by Number and Percent, 1967-1987 (Number in Thousands)," *NAFEO INROADS*, February/March-April/May, 1989, p. 11. U.S. Department of Commerce, Bureau of the Census, *Current Population Reports, Population Estimates and Projections*, Series P-25, Nos. 310, 519, 917, 990, and 1000. *Note:* Includes armed forces overseas.

515

★ 752 ★
Age Structure

Age Range	1985		1990		2000	
	Number	Percent	Number	Percent	Number	Percent
All ages	29.1	100	31.4	100	35.8	100
Male	13.8		14.9		17.0	
Female	15.3		16.5		18.7	
Infants/Toddlers						
Under 5	3.1	11	3.2	10	3.1	9
Male	1.5		1.6		1.6	
Female	1.5		1.6		1.5	
Childhood						
5-9 years	2.5	8	3.1	10	3.2	9
Male	1.3		1.6		1.6	
Female	1.2		1.5		1.6	
Early Adolescence						
10-14 years	2.5	8	2.5	8	3.2	9
Male	1.3		1.3		1.6	
Female	1.2		1.2		1.6	
Late Adolescence						
15-19 years	2.7	9	2.5	8	3.1	9
Male	1.4		1.3		1.6	
Female	1.3		1.3		1.5	
Young Adulthood						
20-24 years	3.0	10	2.7	9	2.6	7
Male	1.5		1.4		1.3	
Female	1.5		1.4		1.3	
Adulthood						
25-39 years	7.1	24	8.2	26	8.3	23
Male	3.4		3.9		4.1	
Female	3.8		4.3	4.2		
Middle Years						
40-64 years	5.8	20	6.5	21	9.2	26
Male	2.7		2.8		4.2	
Female	3.1		3.7	5.0		
Seniors						
65-84 years	2.2	8	2.2	7	2.2	7
Male	1.0		.8		.9	
Female	1.3		1.4		1.7	
Elders						
85-over	189[1]	1	257[1]	1	412[1]	1
Male	60[1]		77[1]		110[1]	
Female	129[1]		180[1]		302[1]	
Median	26.2		27.7		30.2	

Source: "African-American Age Structure Through the Life Span 1985 to 2000 (in millions)." *The State of Black America*, January 1990, p. 107. Primary source: U.S. Bureau of the Census, Current Population Reports, Series P-25, No. 952, *Projections of Population of the U.S. by Sex, 1983-2080. Note:* 1. Thousands.

★ 753 ★
Black Elderly in the Population

Characteristic	1985	2000	2020
Total 65+	8.1	8.5	9.9
65-74	8.4	9.0	10.4
75-84	8.1	7.9	9.4
85+	7.0	8.4	9.1

Source: "Black Proportion of Elderly Population," *Personnel for Health Needs of the Elderly Through Year 2020,* September 1987. Primary source: *Personnel for Health Needs of the Elderly Through Year 2020.* National Institute on Aging Administrative Document. September 1987 Report to Congress. National Institute on Aging, National Institutes of Health, Public Health Service, Department of Health and Human Services.

★ 754 ★
Black Family Types

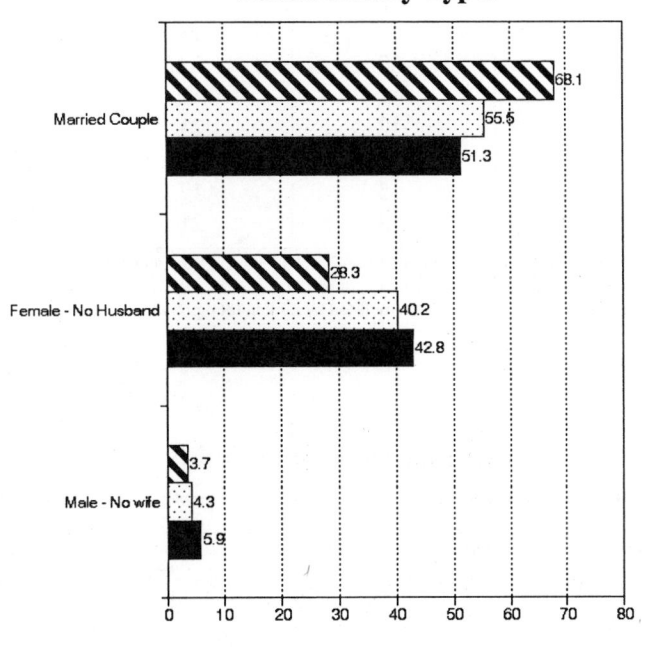

1988 ▨ 1980 ▧ 1970

In percent.

Characteristic	1970	1980	1988
Married-couple families	68.1	55.5	51.3
Female householder, no husband present	28.3	40.2	42.8
Male householder, no wife present	3.7	4.3	5.9

Source: "Black Families, by Type: 1970 to 1988," *Population Profile of the United States, 1989,* p. 36. Primary source: *Population Profile of the United States, 1989,* Special Studies, Bureau of the Census.

★ 755 ★
Black Population in Cities

City	1940	1960	1980
New York[1]	6	14	25
Chicago	8	23	40
Philadelphia	13	26	38
Detroit	9	29	63
Los Angeles	4	14	17
Cleveland	10	29	44
Baltimore	19	35	55
St. Louis	13	29	45
Boston	3	9	22
Pittsburgh	9	17	24
Washington, D.C.	28	54	70
San Francisco	<1	10	13
Milwaukee	2	9	23
Buffalo	3	13	27
New Orleans	30	37	55
Minneapolis	1	2	8
Cincinnati	12	21	34
Newark	21	34	58
Kansas City	5	17	27
Indianapolis	3	21	22

Source: "Black Percentage of Population of the 20 Largest U.S. Cities, 1940- 1980," *A Common Destiny: Blacks and American Society*, 1989, p. 62. Primary source: *A Common Destiny: Blacks and American Society*. Published by permission. *Note:* 1. Cities are listed by rank in total population in 1940.

★ 756 ★
Characteristics of Households

As of March, except as noted. Based on Current Population Survey, except as noted; see headnote, table 58. See also *Historical Statistics, Colonial Times to 1970*, series A 292-295 and A 320-334.

Characteristic	Number (1,000)					Percent Distribution				
	1970	1975	1980	1985	1987	1970	1975	1980	1985	1987
White										
Total	56,602	62,945	70,766	75,328	77,284	100.0	100.0	100.0	100.0	100.0
Family households	46,166	49,334	52,243	54,400	55,676	81.6	78.4	73.8	72.2	72.0
Married couple	41,029	42,951	44,751	45,643	46,410	72.5	68.2	63.2	60.6	60.1
Male householder[1]	1,038	1,257	1,441	1,816	2,038	1.8	2.0	2.0	2.4	2.6
Female householder[1]	4,099	5,126	6,052	6,941	7,227	7.2	8.1	8.6	9.2	9.4
Nonfamily households	10,436	13,612	18,522	20,928	21,608	18.4	21.6	26.2	27.8	28.0
Male householder	3,406	5,038	7,499	8,608	9,034	6.0	8.0	10.6	11.4	11.7
Female householder	7,030	8,574	11,023	12,320	12,574	12.4	13.6	15.6	16.4	16.3
Black										
Total	6,223	7,262	8,586	9,480	9,922	100.0	100.0	100.0	100.0	100.0
Family households	4,856	5,468	6,184	6,778	7,096	78.0	75.3	72.0	71.5	71.5
Married couple	3,317	3,343	3,433	3,469	3,742	53.3	46.0	40.0	36.6	37.7
Male householder[1]	181	211	256	344	386	2.9	2.9	3.0	3.6	3.9
Female householder[1]	1,358	1,915	2,495	2,964	2,967	21.8	26.4	29.1	31.3	29.9

Continued.

Characteristics of Households
[Continued]

Characteristic	Number (1,000)					Percent Distribution				
	1970	1975	1980	1985	1987	1970	1975	1980	1985	1987
Nonfamily households	1,367	1,793	2,402	2,703	2,826	22.0	24.7	28.0	28.5	28.5
Male householder	564	791	1,146	1,244	1,313	9.1	10.9	13.3	13.1	13.2
Female householder	803	1,002	1,256	1,459	1,513	12.9	13.8	14.6	15.4	15.2

Source: "White and Black Households, by Type: 1970 to 1987," *Statistical Abstract*, 1989, p. 46. Primary source: U.S. Bureau of the Census, *Census of Population: 1970, Persons of Spanish Origin*, PC(2)-1C; *Current Population Reports*, series P-20, No. 424 and earlier reports. *Note:* 1. No spouse present.

★ 757 ★
Characteristics of Population

In thousands, except as indicated. 1970 and 1980 data based on enumerated population as of April 1; other years based on estimated population as of July 1. Excludes Armed Forces overseas. See *Historical Statistics, Colonial Times to 1970*, Series A119-134.

Year, Sex, and Race	Total, all	Under 5	5- 9	10- 14	15- 19	20- 24	25- 29	30- 34	35- 39	40- 44	45- 49
1970, total[1,2]	203,235	17,163	19,969	20,804	19,084	16,383	13,486	11,437	11,113	11,988	12,124
Male	98,926	8,750	10,175	10,598	9,641	7,925	6,626	5,599	5,416	5,823	5,855
Female	104,309	8,413	9,794	10,206	9,443	8,458	6,859	5,838	5,697	6,166	6,269
White	178,098	14,464	16,941	17,724	16,412	14,327	11,850	10,000	9,749	10,633	10,868
Black	22,581	2,434	2,749	2,812	2,425	1,816	1,429	1,254	1,196	1,199	1,124
1980, total[1]	226,546	16,348	16,700	18,242	21,168	21,319	19,521	17,561	13,965	11,669	11,090
Male	110,053	8,362	8,539	9,316	10,755	10,663	9,705	8,677	6,862	5,708	5,388
Female	116,493	7,986	8,161	8,926	10,413	10,655	9,816	8,884	7,104	5,961	5,702
White[3]	194,713	13,414	13,717	15,095	17,681	18,072	16,658	15,157	12,122	10,110	9,693
Male[3]	94,924	6,882	7,034	7,730	9,008	9,102	8,363	7,565	6,014	4,991	4,755
Female[3]	99,788	6,532	6,683	7,365	8,673	8,970	8,295	7,592	6,108	5,119	4,938
Black[3]	26,683	2,459	2,509	2,691	3,007	2,749	2,342	1,904	1,469	1,260	1,150
Male[3]	12,612	1,240	1,265	1,353	1,500	1,313	1,095	879	667	571	519
Female[3]	14,071	1,220	1,245	1,338	1,506	1,436	1,247	1,025	801	689	632
1987, total[1]	243,400	18,252	17,661	16,485	18,459	19,790	21,980	21,335	18,738	15,567	12,350
Male	118,531	9,341	9,037	8,450	9,412	9,915	11,009	10,661	9,.273	7,639	6,025
Female	124,869	8,910	8,625	8,035	9,047	9,878	10,971	10,674	9,465	7,928	6,326
White	205,820	14,754	14,240	13,246	15,014	16,367	18,435	17,975	15,968	13,505	10,631
Male	100,589	7,567	7,305	6,803	7,664	8,238	9,313	9,071	7,994	6,696	5,239
Female	105,231	7,187	6,935	6,442	7,350	8,129	9,121	8,903	7,974	6,809	5,392
Black	29,736	2,745	2,728	2,589	2,790	2,762	2,811	2,593	2,108	1,546	1,323
Male	14,103	1,393	1,383	1,314	1,406	1,334	1,334	1,215	964	699	594
Female	15,633	1,352	1,345	1,275	1,384	1,428	1,477	1,378	1,144	846	729

Source: "Resident Population, by Age, Sex, and Race: 1970 to 1987," *Statistical Abstract*, 1989, p. 17. Primary source: U.S. Bureau of the Census, *Current Population Reports*, Series P-25, Nos. 870 and 1022. *Notes:* 1. Includes other races, not shown separately. 2. Official count. The revised 1970 resident population count is 203,302,031; the difference of 66,733 is due to errors found after release of the official series. 3. The race data shown for April 1, 1980 have been modified. See text, section 1 for explanation. 4. Not applicable.

★ 758 ★
Characteristics of Population

In thousands, except as indicated. 1970 and 1980 data based on enumerated population as of April 1; other years based on estimated population as of July 1. Excludes Armed Forces overseas. See *Historical Statistics, Colonial Times to 1970*, Series A119-134.

Year, Sex, and Race	50- 54	55- 59	60- 64	65- 74	75 and over	5- 13	14- 17	18- 24	16 and over	65 and over	Median age (yr.)
1970, total[1,2]	11,111	9,979	8,623	12,443	7,530	36,675	15,851	23,714	141,268	19,972	28.0
Male	5,351	4,769	4,030	5,440	2,927	18,687	8,069	11,583	67,347	8,367	26.8
Female	5,759	5,210	4,593	7,002	4,603	17,987	7,782	12,131	73,920	11,605	29.3
White	10,019	9,021	7,818	11,300	6,972	31,171	13,579	20,655	125,520	18,272	28.9
Black	990	874	734	1,043	501	5,009	2,073	2,721	14,053	1,544	22.4
1980, total[1]	11,710	11,615	10,088	15,581	9,969	31,159	16,247	30,022	171,196	25,549	30.0
Male	5,621	5,482	4,670	6,757	3,548	15,923	8,298	15,054	81,766	10,305	28.8
Female	6,089	6,133	5,418	8,824	6,420	15,237	7,950	14,969	89,429	15,245	31.3
White[3]	10,360	10,394	9,078	14,045	9,117	25,691	13,492	25,381	149,121	23,162	30.9
Male[3]	5,016	4,928	4,221	6,095	3,221	13,165	6,906	12,803	71,559	9,316	29.6
Female[3]	5,344	5,466	4,858	7,950	5,896	12,526	6,586	12,579	77,562	13,846	32.2
Black[3]	1,135	1,041	874	1,344	748	4,629	2,380	3,948	18,425	2,092	24.9
Male[3]	507	469	386	567	281	2,330	1,198	1,903	8,454	849	23.6
Female[3]	628	573	488	777	467	2,298	1,181	2,045	9,971	1,243	26.2
1987, total[1]	10,926	11,121	10,898	17,667	12,168	30,823	14,467	27,107	187,463	29,835	32.1
Male	5,285	5,298	5,068	7,824	4,295	15,784	7,414	13,615	89,892	12,119	31.0
Female	5,641	5,823	5,831	9,844	7,873	15,039	7,053	13,492	97,572	17,716	33.3
White	9,437	9,735	9,647	15,817	11,048	24,828	11,700	22,339	160,733	26,865	33.0
Male	4,412	4,673	4,507	7,028	3,877	12,744	6,003	11,264	77,454	10,905	31.9
Female	4,825	5,063	5,139	8,789	7,171	12,084	5,697	11,075	83,279	15,960	34.2
Black	1,169	1,112	1,012	1,518	930	4,786	2,235	3,848	21,116	2,448	27.2
Male	523	506	455	647	337	2,428	1,135	1,874	9,729	984	25.8
Female	646	607	557	871	594	2,358	1,100	1,974	11,386	1,465	28.5

Source: "Resident Population, by Age, Sex, and Race: 1970 to 1987," *Statistical Abstract*, 1989, p. 17. Primary source: U.S. Bureau of the Census, *Current Population Reports*, Series P-25, Nos. 870 and 1022. *Notes:* 1. Includes other races, not shown separately. 2. Official count. The revised 1970 resident population count is 203,302,031; the difference of 66,733 is due to errors found after release of the official series. 3. The race data shown for April 1, 1980 have been modified. See text, section 1 for explanation. 4. Not applicable.

★ 759 ★
Characteristics of Population

In thousands, except as indicated. Excludes Armed Forces abroad. For definition of median, see Guide to Tabular Presentation. See also *Historical Statistics, Colonial Times to 1970*, series A 73-81 and A 143-149.

Date	Race				Median Age (years)		
	White	Black Number	Black Percent	Other	All races	White	Black
Conterminous U.S.[1]							
1790 (Aug. 2)	3,172	757	19.3	[5]	[5]	[5]	[5]
1800 (Aug. 4)	4,306	1,002	18.9	[5]	[5]	16.0	[5]
1850 (June 1)	19,553	3,639	15.7	[5]	18.9	19.2	17.3
1860 (June 1)	26,923	4,442	14.1	79	19.4	19.7	17.7
1870 (June 1)	33,589	4,880	12.7	89	20.2	20.4	18.5
1880 (June 1)	43,403	6,581	13.1	172	20.9	21.4	18.0
1890 (June 1)	55,101	7,489	11.9	358	22.0	22.5	17.8
1900 (June 1)	66,809	8,834	11.6	351	22.9	23.4	19.4
1910 (Apr. 15)	81,732	9,828	10.7	413	24.1	24.5	20.8

Continued.

Characteristics of Population
[Continued]

Date	White	Black Number	Black Percent	Other	Median Age (years) All races	Median Age (years) White	Median Age (years) Black
1920 (Jan. 1)	94,821	10,463	9.9	427	25.3	25.6	22.3
1930 (Apr. 1)	110,287	11,891	9.7	597	26.4	26.9	23.5
1940 (Apr. 1)	118,215	12,866	9.8	589	29.0	29.5	25.3
1950 (Apr. 1)	134,942	15,042	10.0	713	30.2	30.8	26.2
United States							
1950 (Apr. 1)	135,150	15,045	9.9	1,131	30.2	30.7	26.2
1960 (Apr. 1)	158,832	18,872	10.5	1,620	29.5	30.3	23.5
1970 (Apr. 1)[2]	178,098	22,581	11.1	2,557	28.0	28.9	22.4
1980 (Apr. 1)[3]	194,713	26,683	11.8	5,150	30.0	30.9	24.9
1983 (July 1)[4]	199,849	28,055	12.0	6,379	30.9	31.8	26.0
1984 (July 1)[4]	201,290	28,457	12.0	6,730	31.2	32.1	26.3
1985 (July 1)[4]	202,769	28,870	12.1	7,097	31.5	32.4	26.6
1986 (July 1)[4]	204,312	29,306	12.2	7,478	31.8	32.7	26.9
1987 (July 1)[4]	205,820	29,736	12.2	7,845	32.1	33.0	27.2

Source: "Resident Population, by Race and Median Age: 1790 to 1987," *Statistical Abstract*, 1989, p. 16. *Notes:* 1. Excludes Alaska and Hawaii. 2. The revised 1970 resident population count is 203,302,031; which incorporates changes due to errors found after tabulations were completed. The race and sex data shown here reflect the official 1970 census count while the residence data comes from the tabulated count; see text, section 1. 3. The race data shown for April 1, 1980 have been modified; see text, section 1 for explanation. 4. Estimated. 5. Not available.

★ 760 ★
Characteristics of Population

In thousands, except percent. As of March, except as noted. Black population: Persons 18 years old and over. Except as noted, based on Current Population Survey.

Mairtal Status	Total 1970	Total 1980	Total 1985	Total 1987	Male 1970	Male 1980	Male 1985	Male 1987	Female 1970	Female 1980	Female 1985	Female 1987
Black												
Total	12,972	16,638	18,607	19,242	5,898	7,416	8,325	8,627	7,074	9,222	10,281	10,615
Single	2,668	5,070	6,439	6,583	1,435	2,540	3,149	3,220	1,233	2,530	3,290	3,363
Married	8,310	8,545	8,611	9,172	3,944	4,051	4,217	4,392	4,366	4,494	4,394	4,781
Widowed	1,427	1,627	1,791	1,594	307	308	324	309	1,120	1,319	1,468	1,286
Divorced	567	1,396	1,764	1,892	212	517	636	706	355	878	1,128	1,186
Percent of total:												
Total	100.0	100.0	100.0	100.0	100.0	100.0	100.0	100.0	100.0	100.0	100.0	100.0
Single	20.6	30.5	34.6	34.2	24.3	34.3	37.8	37.3	17.4	27.4	32.0	31.7
Married	64.1	51.4	46.3	47.7	66.9	54.6	50.7	50.9	61.7	48.7	42.7	45.0
Widowed	11.0	9.8	9.6	8.3	5.2	4.2	3.9	3.6	15.8	14.3	14.3	12.1
Divorced	4.4	8.4	9.5	9.8	3.6	7.0	7.6	8.2	5.0	9.5	11..0	11.2

Source: "Marital Status of the Black Population: 1970 to 1987," *Statistical Abstract*, 1989, p. 43. Primary source: U.S. Bureau of the Census, *Census of Population: 1970.*

★ 761 ★
Characteristics of Population

In thousands, except percent. As of March, except as noted. Black population: Persons 18 years old and over. Hispanic population: 1970, persons 14 years and over; thereafter, 18 years old and over. Except as noted, based on Current Population Survey.

Marital Status	Total				Male				Female			
	1970	1980	1985	1987	1970	1980	1985	1987	1970	1980	1985	1987
Black												
Total	12,972	16,638	18,607	19,242	5,898	7,416	8,325	8,627	7,074	9,222	10,281	10,615
Single	2,668	5,070	6,439	6,583	1,435	2,250	3,149	3,220	1,233	2,530	3,290	3,363
Married	8,310	8,545	8,611	9,172	3,944	4,051	4,217	4,392	4,366	4,494	4,394	4,781
Widowed	1,427	1,627	1,791	1,594	307	308	324	309	1,120	1,319	1,468	1,286
Divorced	567	1,396	1,764	1,892	212	517	636	706	355	878	1,128	1,186
Percent of total:												
Total	100.0	100.0	100.0	100.0	100.0	100.0	100.0	100.0	100.0	100.0	100.0	100.0
Single	20.6	30.5	34.6	34.2	24.3	34.3	37.8	37.3	17.4	27.4	32.0	31.7
Married	64.1	51.4	46.3	47.7	66.9	54.6	50.7	50.9	61.7	48.7	42.7	45.0
Widowed	11.0	9.8	9.6	8.3	5.2	4.2	3.9	3.6	15.8	14.3	14.3	12.1
Divorced	4.4	8.4	9.5	9.8	3.6	7.0	7.6	8.2	5.0	9.5	11.0	11.2
Hispanic[1]												
Total	5,872	7,888	10,848	12,111	2,838	3,787	5,322	6,014	3,033	4,101	5,526	6,098
Single	1,718	1,901	2,769	3,160	914	1,035	1,640	1,874	804	865	1,128	1,285
Married	3,666	5,176	6,799	7,507	1,801	2,541	3,272	3,652	1,864	2,635	3,525	3,855
Widowed	287	350	553	515	56	60	124	106	231	291	430	408
Divorced	201	460	727	929	67	151	285	380	134	310	442	549

Source: "Marital Status of the Black and Hispanic Populations: 1970 to 1987," *Statistical Abstract*, 1989, p. 43. Primary source: U.S. Bureau of the Census, *Current Population Reports. Note:* 1. Hispanic persons may be of any race. 1970 data as of April.

★ 762 ★
Characteristics of Population

As of March, except labor force status, annual average. Excludes members of Armed Forces except those living off post or with their families on post. Based on Current Population Survey.

Characteristic	Number (1,000)				Percent Distribution			
	White	Black	Mexican	Puerto Rican	Total population[1]	White	Black	Total[2]
Total persons	202,453	28,930	11,762	2,284	100.0	100.0	100.0	100.0
Under 5 years old	14,798	2,728	1,341	268	7.6	7.3	9.4	10.6
5-14 years old	27,441	5,283	2,553	482	14.2	13.6	18.3	19.6
15-44 years old	95,892	14,087	6,006	1,175	47.7	47.4	48.7	51.6
45-64 years old	39,149	4,501	1,373	280	18.8	19.3	15.6	13.3
65 years old and over	27,173	2,331	491	81	11.7	12.4	8.1	4.8
Years of School Completed								
Persons 25 years old and over	129,170	15,580	5,489	1,106	100.0	100.0	100.0	100.0
Elementary: 0-8 years	15,478	2,863	2,226	319	12.7	12.0	18.4	35.2
High school: 1-3 years	14,233	2,835	805	193	11.7	11.0	18.2	13.9
4 years	50,690	5,773	1,496	347	38.7	39.2	37.1	29.0
College: 1-3 years	22,265	2,442	642	160	17.1	17.2	15.7	13.3
4 years or more	26,505	1,667	320	88	19.9	20.5	10.7	8.6

Continued.

Characteristics of Population
[Continued]

Characteristic	Number (1,000)				Percent Distribution			
	White	Black	Mexican	Puerto Rican	Total population[1]	White	Black	Total[2]
Labor Force Status								
Civilians 16 years old and over	156,958	20,352	7,651	1,540	100.0	100.0	100.0	100.0
Civilian labor force	103,290	12,993	5,203	827	65.6	65.8	63.8	66.4
Employed	97,789	11,309	4,690	744	61.5	62.3	55.6	60.5
Unemployed	5,501	1,684	514	83	4.1	3.5	8.3	5.8
Unemployment rate[3]	5.3	13.0	9.9	10.1	5	5	5	5
Not in labor force	53,669	7,359	2,448	713	34.4	34.2	36.2	33.6
Family Type								
Total families	55,676	7,096	2,611	593	100.0	100.0	100.0	100.0
With own children[4]	26,717	4,184	1,769	432	49.5	48.0	59.0	64.9
Married couple	46,410	3,742	1,952	314	79.9	83.4	52.7	70.8
With own children[4]	21,787	2,023	1,359	214	38.2	39.1	28.5	46.2
Female householder, no spouse present	7,227	2,967	502	257	16.2	13.0	41.8	23.4
With own children[4]	4,141	2,025	347	209	9.8	7.4	28.5	16.6
Male householder, no spouse present	2,038	386	157	22	3.9	3.7	5.4	5.7
With own children[4]	789	136	63	9	1.5	1.4	1.9	2.2
Family Income, 1986								
Total families	55,676	7,096	2,611	593	100.0	100.0	100.0	100.0
Less than $5,000	1,947	994	208	105	4.7	3.5	14.0	8.7
$5,000-$9,999	3,747	1,146	365	116	7.8	6.7	16.1	14.6
$10,000-$14,999	5,047	977	441	81	9.7	9.1	13.8	15.2
$15,000-$24,999	10,875	1,435	629	110	19.6	19.5	20.2	22.4
$25,000-$34,999	10,332	1,043	432	80	18.1	18.6	14.7	16.5
$35,000-$49,999	11,461	878	323	56	19.6	20.6	12.4	12.5
$50,000 or more	12,267	624	212	44	20.7	22.0	8.8	10.2
Median income (dol.)	30,809	17,604	19,326	14,584	5	5	5	5
Persons below poverty level	22,183	8,983	3,333	898	13.6	11.0	31.1	27.3
Housing Tenure								
Total occupied units	77,284	9,992	2	2	100.0	100.0	100.0	100.0
Owner-occupied	51,657	4,505	2	2	64.0	66.8	45.4	40.6
Renter-occupied	24,289	5,245	2	2	34.3	31.4	52.9	57.2
No cash rent	1,338	172	2	2	1.7	1.7	1.7	2.3

Source: "Social and Economic Characteristics of the White, Black, and Hispanic Populations: 1987," *Statistical Abstract*, 1989, p. 38. Primary source: U.S. Bureau of the Census, *Current Population Reports*, P-60, No. 159 and P-20, No. 416. Labor force data are published by U.S. Bureau of Labor Statistics, *Employment and Earnings*, Januray 1988. *Notes:* 1. Hispanic persons may be of any race. 2. Not available. 3. Total unemployment as percent of civilian labor force. 4. Children under 18 years old. 5. Not applicable.

★ 763 ★
Characteristics of Population

As of March. Persons 18 years old and over. Excludes members of Armed Forces except those living off post or with their families on post. Based on Current Population Survey; see text, section 1 and Appendix III.

Sex and Race	1970	1975	1978	1979	1980	1981	1982	1983	1984	1985	1986	1987
Percent married:												
Male[1]	75.3	72.8	70.1	69.2	68.4	67.8	67.2	66.6	65.8	65.7	65.5	65.5
White	76.1	73.9	71.7	70.7	70.0	69.6	69.0	68.3	67.7	67.6	67.2	67.4
Black	66.9	62.7	57.6	55.7	54.6	53.5	53.1	52.2	50.6	50.7	51.7	50.9
Female[1]	68.5	66.7	64.2	63.5	63.0	62.4	61.9	61.4	60.8	60.4	60.5	60.5
White	69.3	68.0	65.9	65.2	64.7	64.1	63.7	63.3	62.8	62.7	62.4	62.5
Black	61.7	55.5	50.3	49.0	48.7	48.1	47.3	45.7	44.5	42.7	44.5	45.0
Percent divorced:												
Male[1]	2.5	3.7	4.7	4.8	5.2	5.7	5.9	5.8	6.1	6.5	6.6	6.7
White	2.4	3.6	4.5	4.5	5.0	5.5	5.7	5.7	6.0	6.4	6.6	6.6
Black	3.6	5.1	6.9	7.2	7.0	8.1	8.1	7.4	7.0	7.6	7.4	8.2
Female[1]	3.9	5.3	6.6	6.6	7.1	7.6	8.0	7.9	8.3	8.7	8.9	8.7
White	3.8	5.0	6.3	6.4	6.8	7.2	7.8	7.6	8.0	8.5	8.6	8.5
Black	5.0	7.5	9.3	8.9	9.5	10.3	9.6	10.5	11.0	11.0	11.6	11.2

Source: "Percent Married and Divorced of the Population, by Sex and Race: 1970 to 1987." Primary source: U.S. Bureau of the Census, *Current Population Reports*, series P-20, No. 423 and earlier reports. *Note:* 1. Includes other races, not shown separately.

★ 764 ★
Characteristics of Population

As of March, 1970 and 1975, persons 14 years old and over; beginning 1980, 15 years old and over.

Sex and Year	Race	
	White	Black
Male: 1970	32	62
1980	74	149
1985	98	179
1987	102	184
Female: 1970	56	104
1980	110	258
1985	142	326
1987	142	317

Source: "Divorced Persons per 1,000 Married Persons with Spouse Present, by Race, 1970 to 1987," *Statistical Abstract*, 1989, p. 43. Primary source: U.S. Bureau of the Census, *Current Population Reports*, series P-20, No. 423 and earlier reports.

★ 765 ★
Characteristics of Population

Characteristic	Male					Female				
	1960	1970	1980	1985	1987	1960	1970	1980	1985	1987
Total (million)[1,2]	7.5	8.3	9.9	11.0	12.1	9.0	11.5	14.2	15.8	17.7
Percent of total population	8.6	8.5	9.2	9.7	10.2	9.9	11.1	12.4	13.1	14.2
White (million)[1]	6.9	7.6	9.0	9.9	10.9	8.4	10.6	12.9	14.3	16.0
Black (million)[1]	.5	.7	.8	.9	1.0	.6	.9	1.2	1.3	1.5

Source: "Persons 65 Years Old and Over — Characteristics, by Sex: 1960 to 1987," *Statistical Abstract*, 1989, p. 36. Except as noted, U.S. Bureau of the Census, *Current Population Reports*, series P-20, No. 423 and earlier reports; series P-23, Nos. 57 and 59; series P-25, No. 1022; and series P-60, No. 160 and earlier reports; and unpublished data. *Notes:* 1. Civilian population as of March. Beginning 1980, excludes institutional population. 2. Includes other races, not shown separately.

★ 766 ★
Characteristics of the Population - Part I

Numbers in thousands.

Race, region, and marital status	Total, 15 years and over		15 to 24 years		25 to 34 years		35 to 44 years		45 to 54 years	
	Male	Female	Male	Female	Male	Female	Male	Female	Male	Female
Black										
United States										
Total	9,603	11,618	2,536	2,755	2,418	2,853	1,665	2,035	1,108	1,393
Percent	100.0	100.0	100.0	100.0	100.0	100.0	100.0	100.0	100.0	100.0
Never married	42.5	36.9	93.4	86.2	48.7	43.4	18.4	18.3	11.5	11.1
Married, spouse present	39.2	31.6	5.4	9.6	39.5	36.6	57.1	44.4	57.5	44.6
Married, spouse absent	6.3	9.5	0.4	3.0	5.2	10.7	10.0	15.1	10.4	15.0
Widowed	3.6	12.2	0.2	0.1	0.1	0.8	0.7	3.8	3.6	12.0
Divorced	8.5	9.8	0.6	1.1	6.5	8.5	13.8	18.4	17.1	17.3
South										
Total	5,253	6,469	1,397	1,590	1,336	1,580	915	1,117	589	736
Percent	100.0	100.0	100.0	100.0	100.0	100.0	100.0	100.0	100.0	100.0
Never married	41.1	36.0	92.8	83.8	44.5	41.9	16.5	16.4	12.6	11.3
Married, spouse present	40.8	32.9	5.9	11.0	44.0	39.6	59.2	47.6	58.4	44.6
Married, spouse absent	6.1	8.7	---	3.6	5.2	9.4	9.9	14.4	8.7	13.2
Widowed	3.8	13.2	0.2	0.1	0.1	1.0	1.1	3.9	4.9	13.5
Divorced	8.2	9.2	0.9	1.4	6.2	8.1	13.2	17.6	15.4	17.3
North and West										
Total	4,349	5,149	1,139	1,165	1,083	1,274	750	917	520	657
Percent	100.0	100.0	100.0	100.0	100.0	100.0	100.0	100.0	100.0	100.0
Never married	44.1	38.1	94.0	89.5	53.7	45.3	20.8	20.7	10.2	10.8
Married, spouse present	37.3	29.9	4.7	7.7	34.1	32.9	54.5	40.3	56.3	44.6
Married, spouse absent	6.5	10.6	0.9	2.1	5.2	12.2	10.0	16.0	12.3	16.9
Widowed	3.4	10.9	0.3	0.2	0.1	0.6	0.3	3.6	2.1	10.4
Divorced	8.8	10.6	0.2	0.5	6.7	9.0	14.4	19.3	19.0	17.4

Source: "Marital Status of Persons 15 Years Old and Over, by Age, Sex, Region, and Race: March 1988," *The Black Population in the United States*, March 1988, p. 23. Primary source: *The Black Population in the United States*: March 1988.

★ 767 ★
Characteristics of the Population - Part II

Numbers in thousands.

Race, region, and marital status	55 to 64 years		65 years and over	
	Male	Female	Male	Female
Black				
United States				
Total	916	1,158	960	1,424
Percent	100.0	100.0	100.0	100.0
Never married	7.6	5.1	2.9	6.2
Married, spouse present	53.1	38.8	62.5	27.1
Married, spouse absent	12.0	11.8	7.9	4.9
Widowed	10.2	30.5	19.7	55.3
Divorced	17.0	13.9	7.0	6.5
South				
Total	472	611	545	836
Percent	100.0	100.0	100.0	100.0
Never married	5.7	3.4	2.6	5.5
Married, spouse present	53.8	43.0	61.5	24.6
Married, spouse absent	13.3	8.8	8.8	5.3
Widowed	7.8	32.9	21.3	59.0
Divorced	19.5	11.9	5.9	5.7
North and West				
Total	443	547	414	588
Percent	100.0	100.0	100.0	100.0
Never married	9.7	6.9	3.4	7.1
Married, spouse present	52.1	34.0	64.0	30.8
Married, spouse absent	10.8	15.2	6.8	4.4
Widowed	12.9	28.0	17.4	50.2
Divorced	14.4	16.1	8.5	7.7

Source: "Marital Status of Persons 15 Years Old and Over, by Age, Sex, Region, and Race: March 1988," *The Black Population in the United States,* March 1988, p. 23. Primary source: *The Black Population in the United States:* March 1988.

★ 768 ★
Characteristics of the Population

Characteristic	Black	White
Total	29,333,000	203,869,000
Under 5 years	9.4	7.3
5 to 14 years	18.2	13.6
15 to 24 years	18.0	14.8
25 to 34 years	18.0	17.7
35 to 44 years	12.6	14.6
45 to 54 years	8.5	10.0
55 to 64 years	7.1	9.4
65 years and over	8.1	12.6

Source: "U.S. Population, by Age and Race: 1988," *The Black Population of the United States,* March 1988, p. 4. Primary source: *The Black Population of the United States:* March 1988.

★ 769 ★
Characteristics of the Population

Numbers in thousands.

Age and sex	1988 Black	1988 White	1985 Black	1985 White	1980 Black	1980 White
United States						
Age						
Total persons	29,333	203,869	28,151	199,117	26,033	191,905
Percent	100.0	100.0	100.0	100.0	100.0	100.0
Under 5 years	9.4	7.3	9.6	7.3	9.4	6.9
Under 18 years	33.4	25.1	33.9	25.6	36.1	27.3
18 years and over	66.6	74.9	66.1	74.4	63.9	72.7
18 to 24 years	12.3	10.6	13.4	11.7	14.3	12.9
65 years and over	8.1	12.6	7.9	12.2	7.8	11.4
Median age	27.3	33.1	26.4	32.2	24.8	30.8
Males per 100 females	87.8	95.7	87.6	95.1	87.3	95.0
South						
Age						
Total persons	16,403	64,813	14,937	63,148	13,599	59,597
Percent	100.0	100.0	100.0	100.0	100.0	100.0
Under 5 years	9.4	6.8	10.0	7.1	9.8	6.7
Under 18 years	34.2	24.7	34.3	24.9	36.7	27.3
18 years and over	65.8	75.3	65.7	75.1	63.3	72.7
18 to 24 years	12.6	10.4	13.3	11.5	14.4	12.3
65 years and over	8.4	12.8	8.8	12.6	8.9	11.7
Median age	26.8	33.6	26.3	32.7	24.5	31.3
Males per 100 females	85.7	95.8	87.4	95.0	86.8	96.5
North and West						
Age						
Total persons	12,931	139,056	13,214	135,969	12,435	132,307
Percent	100.0	100.0	100.0	100.0	100.0	100.0
Under 5 years	9.4	7.5	9.2	7.4	9.0	7.0
Under 18 years	32.3	25.3	33.4	25.9	35.4	27.3
18 years and over	67.7	74.7	66.6	74.1	64.6	72.7
18 to 24 years	12.0	10.6	13.7	11.7	14.1	13.2
65 years and over	7.8	12.5	7.0	12.0	6.7	11.3
Median age	28.0	32.8	26.6	32.0	25.2	30.6
Males per 100 females	90.6	95.6	87.8	95.1	87.8	94.3

Source: "Age and Sex of Persons, by Region and Race: March 1988, 1985, and 1980," *The Black Population in the United States*, March 1988, p. 5. Primary source: *The Black Population in the United States*: March 1988.

★ 770 ★
Children Living in Institutions

Type of Institution or Quarters	1960 Rate	1970 Rate	1980 Number	1980 Rate
All Races/Ethnic Groups	670	572	260,425	408
Institutions	370	342	167,306	262
Mental Hospital	---	27	16,494	26
Nursing Home	---	3	5,614	9
Correctional Institution	---	[1]	10,803	17
Other Institutions	---	312	134,395	211
Group Quarters	300	231	93,119	146
Rooming or Boarding House[2]	147	73	11,887	19
Military Quarters[3]	66	36	21,979	34
College Dormitory	27	27	24,541	38
Other Group Quarters	60	94	34,712	54
Whites	599	497	173,866	345
Institutions	351	304	113,795	226
Mental Hospital	---	25	12,584	25
Correctional Institution	---	[1]	5,505	11
Other Institutions	---	276	91,696	182
Group Quarters	248	192	60,071	119
Rooming or Boarding House[2]	88	55	7,311	15
Military Quarters[3]	72	38	17,202	34
College Dormitory	28	29	17,451	35
Other Group Quarters	59	71	18,107	36
Blacks[4]	1,122	1,004	57,120	607
Institutions	490	560	40,252	428
Mental Hospital	---	41	3,133	33
Nursing Home	---	3	1,170	12
Correctional Institution	---	[1]	4,371	46
Other Institutions	---	516	31,578	336
Group Quarters	632	444	16,868	179
Rooming or Boarding House[2]	517	174	1,681	18
Military Quarters[3]	26	25	2,844	30
College Dormitory	23	20	3,579	38
Other Group Quarters	67	226	8,764	93
Hispanics	[5]	508	26,856	476
Institutions		270	13,531	240
Mental Hospital		16	935	17
Nursing Home		4	340	6
Correctional Institution		[1]	923	16
Other Institutions		250	11,333	201
Group Quarters		239	13,325	236
Rooming or Boarding House[2]		80	2,223	39
Military Quarters[3]		31	1,662	29

Continued.

Children Living in Institutions
[Continued]

Type of Institution or Quarters	1960 Rate	1970 Rate	1980 Number	1980 Rate
College Dormitory		18	2,148	38
Other Group Quarters		110	7,292	129

Source: "Number and Rate (per 100,000) of Children (under Age 18) Living in Institutions or Group Quarters, 1960-1980," *U.S. Children and Their Families,* 1989, pp. 27-28. Primary source: Calculated from the following tables: 1960 U.S. Census of Population; Volume 1, Characteristics of the Population; Part 1, U.S. Summary; Table 182; 1970 U.S. Census of Population; Volume 1, Characteristics of the Population; Part 1, U.S. Summary; Section 2, Chapter D, Detailed Characteristics; Table 205; 1980 U.S. Census of Population; PC80-1- D1- A, U.S. Summary, Detailed Population Characteristics; Table 266. *Notes:* 1. In 1970, "Other institutions" include those in correctional facilities. 2. In 1960 and 1970, "Rooming or boarding house" included, among other categories, persons living in housing units in which 6 or more unrelated persons were living together. In 1980, this definition was changed from "6 or more" or "10 or more." Had the same definition been applied in 1980, a larger proportion of children would have been classified as living in rooming or boarding houses. 3. In 1960 and 1970, "military quarters" comprises only males living in military quarters. The figures for 1980 includes females as well. This adds about 7 percent to the number of persons in military quarters in 1980. In 1970 and 1980 persons stationed on ships are included in "military quarters." In 1960 these are included in "other group quarters." 4. The figures for 1960 are for non-whites, rather than for blacks. The great majority of non-whites in the U.S. are black. 5. Not available.

★ 771 ★
Children Under 18 Years Old

Number in millions.

Characteristic	1940	1950	1960	1970	1980	1985	Projected 1990	2000	2010
Race/Hispanic Origin									
White	35.5	41.3	55.5	59.1	52.5	51.1	51.9	53.5	50.5
Non-White	4.9	6.0	8.7	10.6	11.2	11.9	12.4	13.9	14.3
Black	1	1	1	9.5	9.5	9.6	10.3	11.4	11.5
Hispanic	1	1	1	1	5.3	6.3	7.1	8.7	9.7
Children as a percentage of total U.S. population	31	31	36	34	28	26	26	25	23

Source: "Number of Children Under 18 by Age and Race/Hispanic Origin, 1940- 2010," *U.S. Children and Their Families,* 1989, p. 3. Primary source: U.S. Bureau of the Census, 1970 Census Volume, *Characteristics of the Population, U.S. Summary,* Table 52, 1980 Census Volume, *General Population Characteristics, U.S. Summary,* Table 41, Current Population Reports, Series P-25, No. 311. *Estimates of the Population of the United States by Single Years of Age, Color, and Sex, 1900 to 1959,* pages 22-23, 42-43, Series P-25, No. 917, *Preliminary Estimates of the Population of the United States by Age, Sex, and Race: 1970 to 1981,* Table 2, Series P-25, No. 985, *Estimates of the Population of the United States by Age, Sex, and Race: 1980 to 1985,* Table 2, Series P-25, No. 985, *Projections of the Hispanic Population: 1983 to 2080,* Table 2, Series P-25, No. 952, *Projections of the Population of the United States by Age, Sex, and Race: 1983 to 2080,* Table 6. *Notes:* "Non-white" refers to all races other than white, and includes blacks, Indians, Japanese, Chinese, and any other race except white. Blacks comprise the great majority of non-whites. People of Hispanic origin can be of any race. 1. Not available.

★ 772 ★
Elderly Population

Race and age	1950	1960	1970	1980	1990	2000	2010	2020
White								
65+	8.4	9.6	10.2	11.9	13.6	14.0	14.9	18.6
70+	5.0	6.0	6.7	7.9	9.3	10.4	10.5	12.7
75+	2.7	3.3	3.9	4.7	5.9	7.0	7.3	7.9
80+	1.2	1.5	1.9	2.5	3.2	4.1	4.7	4.7
85+	0.4	0.5	0.7	1.1	1.5	2.7	3.4	3.5
Black								
65+	5.7	6.3	6.8	7.8	8.2	8.4	8.9	11.6
70+	3.0	3.7	4.1	4.9	5.6	6.0	6.1	7.4
75+	1.6	1.9	2.2	2.8	3.5	3.9	4.1	4.5
80+	0.8	0.9	1.1	1.4	1.8	2.3	2.6	2.7
85+	0.3	0.4	0.5	0.6	0.9	1.2	1.4	1.5

Source: "Elderly Population by Race (percentage of total population), 1950- 2020," A Common Destiny: Blacks and American Society, 1989, p. 426. Primary source: Data from decennial censuses and Census Bureau projections. Published by permission.

★ 773 ★
Families and Children

Numbers in millions.

Characteristic	1960	1970	1975	1980	1985	1987	1988
All families with related children	27.0	29.8	31.3	32.4	32.9	33.8	34.0
Type of Family							
Married-couple	24.1	26.1	25.9	25.6	25.0	25.6	25.5
Single parent:							
Female-headed	2.5	3.4	4.9	6.0	6.8	7.1	7.2
Male-headed	.3	.4	.5	.7	1.1	1.1	1.3
Percent Distribution							
Married-couple	89.3	87.5	82.6	79.1	76.0	75.6	75.2
Single parent:							
Female-headed	9.4	11.3	15.7	18.6	20.7	21.0	21.1
Male-headed	1.3	1.2	1.7	2.3	3.3	3.4	3.7
White families with related children	24.1	26.3	26.9	27.3	27.4	27.9	27.9
Percent Distribution							
Married-couple	1	1	1	83.7	81.0	80.4	80.3
Single parent:							
Female-headed	1	1	1	14.2	15.8	16.3	16.1
Male-headed	1	1	1	2.1	3.2	3.3	3.6
Black families with related children	1	3.4	3.9	4.3	4.5	4.8	4.9
Percent Distribution							
Married-couple	1	1	55.9	48.8	44.3	46.5	45.4
Single parent:							
Female-headed	1	1	41.4	48.0	51.8	49.6	50.1
Male-headed	1	1	2.7	3.2	3.9	3.9	4.5
Hispanic families with related children	1	1	2.5	3.0	3.9	4.4	4.6
Percent Distribution							
Married-couple	1	1	77.8	75.3	71.7	70.8	69.8

Continued.

Families and Children
[Continued]

Characteristic	1960	1970	1975	1980	1985	1987	1988
Single parent:							
Female-headed	[1]	[1]	18.7	20.1	23.0	23.4	23.4
Male-headed	3.5	4.6	5.3	5.8	6.8		

Source: "Number of Families with Related Children Under 18 and Percent Distribution by Family Type, 1960-1988," *U.S. Children and Their Families*, 1989, p. 21. Primary source: U.S. Bureau of the Census, Current Population Reports, Series P-60, No. 163, *Poverty in the United States: 1987*, February 1989, Table 3. *Notes:* The Census Bureau defines a "family" as a group of two or more persons related by birth, marriage, or adoption who reside together; all such persons are considered as members of one family. Every family must include a householder. Boarders with children who are unrelated to the householder are not included in the count of families. "Related children" in a family include the householder's own children under 18 and all other children in the household who are related to the householder by blood, marriage, or adoption. 1. Not available.

★ 774 ★
Geographic Distribution of Population

As of July 1.

Region, Division, and State	White						Black					
	Number (1,000)				Percent of total		Number (1,000)				Percent of total	
	1988	1989	1990	2000	1990	2000	1988	1989	1990	2000	1990	2000
U.S.	207,326	208,808	210,247	221,144	84.1	82.6	30,165	30,597	31,026	35,006	12.4	13.1
Region:												
New England	12,131	12,197	12,263	12,769	93.8	92.7	584	594	605	702	4.6	5.1
Middle Atlantic	31,504	31,475	31,451	31,110	83.9	81.8	4,982	5,040	5,100	5,661	13.6	14.9
East North Central	36,272	36,267	36,247	35,281	86.2	84.5	4,997	5,056	5,113	5,584	12.2	13.4
West North Central	16,424	16,442	16,457	16,405	92.9	91.9	865	874	882	958	5.0	5.4
South Atlantic	32,814	33,332	33,842	38,277	77.4	76.6	8,850	9,007	9,164	10,673	21.0	21.3
East South Central	12,235	12,301	12,364	12,782	79.3	78.5	3,070	3,096	3,122	3,354	20.0	20.6
West South Central	22,713	22,924	23,137	25,192	82.8	82.2	4,006	4,049	4,093	4,520	14.6	14.8
Mountain	12,462	12,672	12,876	14,572	92.0	90.9	340	348	356	432	2.5	2.7
Pacific	30,772	31,199	31,609	34,754	82.6	80.1	2,473	2,532	2,591	3,123	6.8	7.2

Source: "White and Black Population Projections, by State: 1988 to 2000," *Statistical Abstract*, 1989, p. 26. Primary source: U.S. Bureau of the Census, *Current Population Reports*, Series P-25, No. 1017.

★ 775 ★
Households with Children

Type of household	All Ethnic Groups	White	Black	Hispanic
All households	89.5	77.3	9.9	5.4
Households with members under 18[1]	34.3	28.4	4.9	3.1
Households with no members under 18	55.2	48.9	5.0	2.3
Average number of members under 18 per household with persons under 18	1.84	1.81	1.98	2.14
Households with children who are related to householder	33.8	27.9	4.8	3.1
Households with own children of householder				
under 18 years of age	31.9	26.7	4.2	2.9
6-17 years of age	23.6	19.5	3.3	2.1

Continued.

Households with Children
[Continued]

Type of household	All Ethnic Groups	White	Black	Hispanic
under 6 years of age	14.7	12.4	1.8	1.6
under 3 years of age	8.7	7.5	1.0	.9
	Percent Distribution			
All households	100.0	100.0	100.0	100.0
Households with members under 18[1]	38.4	36.7	49.3	57.9
Households with no members under 18	61.6	63.3	50.7	42.1
Households with children who are related to householder	37.8	36.1	48.4	56.8
Households with own children of householder				
under 18 years of age	35.6	34.6	42.2	25.8
6-17 years of age	26.4	25.2	33.7	38.3
under 6 years of age	16.4	16.1	18.4	29.1
under 3 years of age	9.8	9.7	10.0	16.3

Source: "Number and Proportion of U.S. Households with Children by Race and Hispanic Origin, March 1987," *U.S. Children and Their Families*, 1989, p. 19. Primary source: U.S. Bureau of the Census, Current Population Reports, Series P-20, No. 424, *Household and Family Characteristics: March 1987*, 1988, Tables 1, 21, and 22. *Notes:* 1. Includes households where the householder or spouse was under 18, as well as households with own or related children.

★ 776 ★
Households, Characteristics of

As of March, except as noted. Based on Current Population Survey, except as noted; see headnote, table 58. See also *Historical Statistics, Colonial Times to 1970*, series A 292-295 and A 320-334.

Characteristic	Number (1,000)					Percent Distribution				
	1970	1975	1980	1985	1987	1970	1975	1980	1985	1987
White										
Total	56,602	62,945	70,766	75,328	77,284	100.0	100.0	100.0	100.0	100.0
Family households	46,166	49,334	52,243	54,400	55,676	81.6	78.4	73.8	72.2	72.0
Married couple	41,029	42,951	44,751	45,643	46,410	72.5	68.2	63.2	60.6	60.1
Male householder[1]	1,038	1,257	1,441	1,816	2,038	1.8	2.0	2.0	2.4	2.6
Female householder[1]	4,099	5,126	6,052	6,941	7,227	7.2	8.1	8.6	9.2	9.4
Nonfamily households	10,436	13,612	18,522	20,928	21,608	18.4	21.6	26.2	27.8	28.0
Male householder	3,406	5,038	7,499	8,608	9,034	6.0	8.0	10.6	11.4	11.7
Female householder	7,030	8,574	11,023	12,320	12,574	12.4	13.6	15.6	16.4	16.3
Black										
Total	6,223	7,262	8,586	9,480	9,922	100.0	100.0	100.0	100.0	100.0
Family households	4,856	5,468	6,184	6,778	7,096	78.0	75.3	72.0	71.5	71.5
Married couple	3,317	3,343	3,433	3,469	3,742	53.3	46.0	40.0	36.6	37.7
Male householder[1]	181	211	256	344	386	2.9	2.9	3.0	3.6	3.9
Female householder[1]	1,358	1,915	2,495	2,964	2,967	21.8	26.4	29.1	31.3	29.9
Nonfamily households	1,367	1,793	2,402	2,703	2,826	22.0	24.7	28.0	28.5	28.5

Continued.

Households, Characteristics of
[Continued]

Characteristic	Number (1,000)					Percent Distribution				
	1970	1975	1980	1985	1987	1970	1975	1980	1985	1987
Male householder	564	791	1,146	1,244	1,313	9.1	10.9	13.3	13.1	13.2
Female householder	803	1,002	1,256	1,459	1,513	12.9	13.8	14.6	15.4	15.2

Source: "White and Black Households, by Type: 1970-1987," *Statistical Abstract*, 1989, p. 46. Primary source: U.S. Bureau of the Census, *Census of Population: 1970, Persons of Spanish Origin*, PC(2)-1C; *Current Population Reports*, series P-20, No. 424 and earlier reports. *Note:* 1. No spouse present.

★ 777 ★
Households, characteristics of

As of March. Based on Current Population Survey. See also *Historical Statistics, Colonial Times to 1970*, series A 335-349.

Characteristics of Householder and Size of Household	Number (mil.)							Percent Distribution				
	1970	1975	1980	1984	1985	1986	1987	1970	1975	1980	1985	1987
Total[1]	63.4	71.1	80.8	85.4	86.8	88.5	89.5	100.0	100.0	100.0	100.1	100.0
White	56.6	62.9	70.8	74.4	75.3	76.6	77.3	89.5	88.5	87.6	86.5	86.4
Black	6.2	7.3	8.6	9.2	9.5	9.8	9.9	9.8	10.2	10.6	10.9	11.1
Hispanic[2]	[3]	[3]	3.7	4.3	4.9	5.2	5.4	[3]	[3]	4.6	5.6	6.1

Source: "Households by Characteristic of Householder and Size of Household: 1970-1987," *Statistical Abstract*, 1989, p. 46. U.S. Bureau of the Census, *Current Population Reportss*, series P-20, No. 424 and earlier reports; and unpublished data. *Notes:* 1. Includes other races, not shown separately. 2. Hispanic persons may be of any race. 3. Not available.

★ 778 ★
Households, Characteristics of

As of March. Based on Current Population Survey.

Characteristic	Number of Households (1,000)			Percent Distribution			Persons per Household		
	Total	Black	Hispanic[1]	Total	Black	Hispanic[1]	Total	Black	Hispanic[1]
Total	89,479	9,922	5,418	100.0	100.0	100.0	2.66	2.91	3.42
Age of householder:									
15-24 years old	5,197	671	524	5.8	6.8	9.7	2.31	2.62	3.00
25-29 years old	9,652	1,159	845	10.8	11.7	15.6	2.65	2.92	3.31
30-34 years old	10,850	1,382	805	12.1	13.9	14.9	3.08	3.20	3.77
35-44 years old	18,704	2,109	1,300	20.9	21.3	24.0	3.37	3.44	3.97
45-54 years old	13,211	1,604	807	14.6	16.2	14.9	3.07	3.15	3.70
55-64 years old	12,868	1,301	589	14.4	13.1	10.9	2.37	2.56	2.98
65-74 years old	11,250	1,038	354	12.6	10.5	6.5	1.88	2.34	2.39
75 years old and over	7,748	658	192	8.7	6.6	3.5	1.57	1.90	2.09
Size of household:									
One person	21,128	2,499	810	23.6	25.2	15.0	1.00	1.00	1.00
Two persons	28,602	2,440	1,170	32.0	24.6	21.6	2.00	2.00	2.00
Three persons	16,159	1,951	1,048	18.1	19.7	19.3	3.00	3.00	3.00
Four persons	13,984	1,500	1,132	15.6	15.1	20.9	4.00	4.00	4.00
Five persons	6,162	797	695	6.9	8.0	12.8	5.00	5.00	5.00
Six persons	2,176	374	307	2.4	3.8	5.7	6.00	6.00	6.00

Continued.

Households, Characteristics of
[Continued]

Characteristic	Number of Households (1,000)			Percent Distribution			Persons per Household		
	Total	Black	Hispanic[1]	Total	Black	Hispanic[1]	Total	Black	Hispanic[1]
Seven persons or more	1,268	361	257	1.4	3.6	4.7	7.89	8.19	8.08

Source: "Household Characteristics, by Race, Hispanic Origin and Type: 1987," *Statistical Abstract*, 1989, p. 47. Primary source: U.S. Bureau of the Census, *Current Population Reports*, Series P-20, No. 24 an Series P-60, No. 159. *Note:* 1. Hispanic persons may be of any race.

★ 779 ★
Living Arrangements, Characteristics of - Part I

As of March. Based on current Population Survey which includes members of Armed Forces living off post or with families on post, but excludes other Armed Forces; see text, section 1 and Appendix III.

Age and Sex	All Races[1]				
	Total (1,000)	Percent living--			
		Alone	With spouse	With other relatives	With non-relatives
Male	89,368	9.2	58.5	25.3	7.0
15-19 years old	9,193	.4	1.2	95.6	2.8
20-24 years old	9,499	6.6	18.9	60.1	14.3
25-44 years old	37,671	10.3	64.7	15.5	9.5
45-64 years old	21,428	8.9	80.9	6.9	3.4
65 years old and over	11,578	15.6	74.9	6.9	2.6
65-74 years old	7,608	12.3	79.7	5.6	2.5
75 years old and over	3,970	21.8	65.9	9.6	2.7
Female	97,320	13.2	53.7	28.6	4.4
15-19 years old	8,994	.5	4.5	91.3	3.6
20-24 years old	9,859	5.5	32.8	49.6	12.0
25-44 years old	38,597	6.8	66.9	21.2	5.0
45-64 years old	23,472	12.6	69.8	15.6	2.0
65 years old and over	16,397	40.9	39.2	17.6	2.3
65-74 years old	9,624	33.5	51.0	13.9	1.6
75 years old and over	6,773	51.5	22.4	22.8	3.3

Source: "Living Arrangements of Persons 15 Years Old and Over, by Selected Characteristics: 1987," *Statistical Abstract*, 1989, p. 49. Primary source: U.S. Bureau of the Census, *Current Population Reports*, series P-20, No. 423. *Note:* 1. Includes other races not shown separately.

★ 780 ★
Living Arrangements, Characteristics of - Part II

As of March. Based on current Population Survey which includes members of Armed Forces living off post or with families on post, but excludes other Armed Forces; see text, section 1 and Appendix III.

Age and Sex	White Persons Percent Living--			Black Persons Percent Living--		
	Alone	With spouse	With other relatives	Alone	With spouse	With other relatives
Male	9.0	60.9	23.4	11.6	40.4	39.3
15-19 years old	.4	1.3	95.3	.4	.4	97.4
20-24 years old	6.9	20.8	57.8	4.6	9.3	75.1
25-44 years old	10.1	67.0	13.8	12.1	47.4	28.3
45-64 years old	8.1	82.9	6.1	17.1	61.2	14.3
65 years old and over	14.9	76.0	6.5	22.8	63.9	10.1
65-74 years old	11.7	81.1	5.0	20.0	65.9	9.9
75 years old and over	21.3	66.4	9.5	28.0	60.1	10.6
Female	13.6	56.6	25.3	12.2	32.7	51.6
15-19 years old	.6	5.1	90.5	.4	1.3	95.6
20-24 years old	5.7	36.2	45.3	4.5	15.7	72.5
25-44 years old	6.8	70.5	17.6	7.0	42.4	47.1
45-64 years old	12.2	73.0	12.8	17.6	44.0	35.9
65 years old and over	41.4	40.2	16.1	39.8	26.7	31.1
65-74 years old	33.6	52.6	12.2	35.4	34.0	28.6
75 years old and over	52.1	23.1	21.5	46.7	15.3	34.9

Source: "Living Arrangements of Persons 15 Years Old and Over, by Selected Characteristics: 1987," *Statistical Abstract*, 1989, p. 49. Primary source: U.S. Bureau of the Census, *Current Population Reports*, series P-20, No. 423. *Note:* 1. Includes other races not shown separately.

★ 781 ★
Married Couples

In thousands, 1970 data as of April; 1980 and 1987 data as of March. 1970, persons 14 years old and over; 1980 and 1987 persons 15 years old and over. 1980 and 1987 based on Current Population Survey.

Item	1970	1980	1987
Total married couples	44,597	49,714	52,286
Interracial married couples	310	651	799
All Black-White married couples	65	167	177
Husband Black, wife White	41	122	121
Wife Black, husband White	24	45	56
Other interracial married couples	245	484	622
Husband Black	8	20	33
Wife Black	4	14	8
Husband White	139	287	358
Wife White	94	163	223

Source: "Interracial Married Couples: 1970 to 1987," *Statistical Abstract*, 1989, p. 44. Primary source: U.S. Bureau of the Census, *Census of Population: 1970* Marital Status, PC(2)-4C; *Current Population Reports*, series P-20, No. 424 and earlier reports.

★ 782 ★
Men Married

Age group and race	1940	1950	1960	1970	1980
25-34					
Black	.740	.724	.740	.737	.563
White	.717	.803	.828	.822	.692
35-44					
Black	.819	.794	.789	.764	.704
White	.844	.870	.895	.887	.837
45-54					
Black	.799	.767	.789	.767	.719
White	.843	.852	.886	.892	.864
55-64					
Black	.765	.721	.757	.756	.742
White	.803	.809	.856	.874	.881

Source: "Proportion of Men Married with Wife Present by Age and Race," *The Economic Progress of Black Men in America*, p. 86. Primary source: Census of Population, 1940-1980; Public Use Sample.

★ 783 ★
Migration of Males from the South

Numbers in percent.

Year	Black	White
1940-50	26.3	1.8
1950-60	24.5	8.4
1960-70	19.3	3.3
1970-80	2.1	-1.3

Source: "Rates of Net Migration from the South for Men Ages 20-24," *The Economic Progress of Black Men in America*, p. 79. Primary source: *The Economic Progress of Black Men in America*. Washington, DC: U.S. Commission on Civil Rights, 1986. Clearing House Publication 91. *Notes:* These rates were calculated by comparing the share of males 20-24 years old living in the South in year *t* to the share of males 30-34 years old living in the South in year *t+10*.

★ 784 ★
Older Population

Range represents a 90- percent confidence interval.

Characteristic	85 years and over		100 years and over		100-104 years		105 years and over	
	Number	Range	Number	Range	Number	Range	Number	Range
Race, Sex								
White	2,044,961	2,043,104-2,046,818	11,167	10,609-11,725	10,368	9,763-10,973	799	484-1,114
Male	614,407	611,249-617,345	2,629	2,098-3,160	2,464	1,946-2,982	165	18-312
Female	1,430,554	1,427,390-1,433,718	8,538	7,869-9,207	7,904	7,225-8,583	634	351-917
Black	158,920	157,229-160,611	2,450	1,933-2,967	2,001	1,525-2,477	449	210-688

Continued.

★ 786 ★
Population Characteristics by Sex

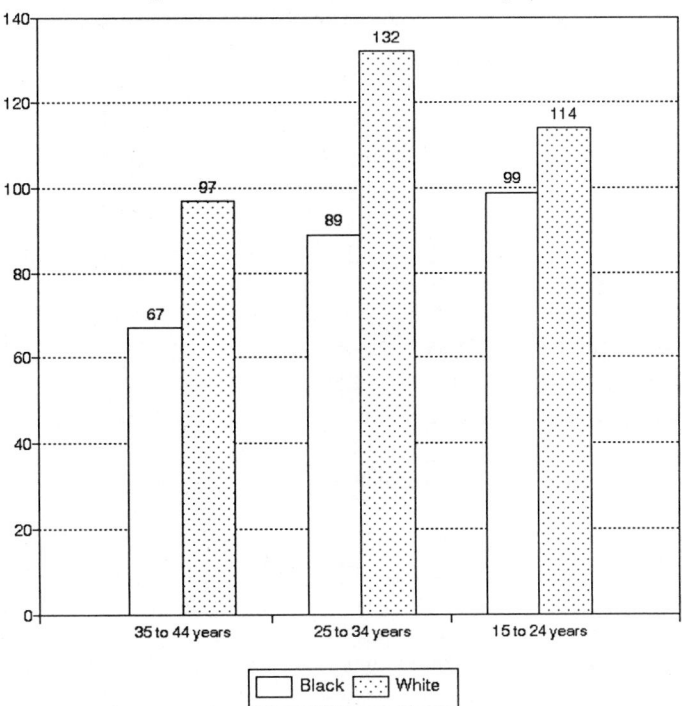

Males per 100 females.

Race	15 to 24 years	25 to 34 years	35 to 44 years
White	114	132	97
Black	99	89	67

Source: "Ration of Unmarried Men to Unmarried Women, by Selected Ages: 1988," *The Black Population in the United States*, March 1988, p. 6. Primary source: *The Black Population in the United States*: March 1988. *Note:* Unmarried includes never married, widowed, and divorced.

★ 787 ★
Population Growth

Numbers in thousands.

Race	March 1988 CPS[1,2]	1980 census[3]		Percent change, 1980-88[1]
		Civilian non-institutional population	Resident population	
Total population	241,155	222,461	226,546	8.4
Black	29,333	25,819	26,495	13.6
White	203,869	185,052	188,372	10.2

Source: "Population, by Race: March 1988 and April 1980," *The Black Population in the United States*, March 1988, p. 2. Primary source: *The Black Population in the United States*: March 1988. *Notes:* 1. Civilian noninstitutional population. 2. Estimates from the March 1988 CPS reflect the civilian noninstitutional population of the United States plus members of the Armed Forces in the United States living off post or with their families on post, but excludes all other members of the Armed Forces. 3. Data from the 1980 census are based on 100- percent tabulations of the population of the United States on April 1, 1980.

★ 788 ★
Population Projections - Part I

As of July 1. Includes Armed Forces overseas. Data are for middle series. Minus sign (-) indicates decrease.

Age, Sex, and Race	Population (1,000)					
	1988	1989	1990	1995	2000	2010
White, total	207,696	209,178	210,616	216,820	221,514	228,978
Under 5 years old	14,787	14,899	14,893	14,251	13,324	13,084
5-17 years old	36,469	36,317	36,537	38,493	38,569	35,258
18-24 years old	22,105	21,775	21,330	19,452	19,998	21,298
25-34 years old	36,749	36,798	36,620	33,680	29,988	29,585
35-44 years old	30,251	31,223	32,306	35,635	36,574	29,997
45-54 years old	20,838	21,450	21,950	26,879	31,618	35,860
55-64 years old	19,138	18,852	18,637	18,327	20,667	29,913
65-74 years old	15,983	16,188	16,380	16,681	15,811	17,875
75 years old and over	11,375	11,675	11,965	13,421	14,965	16,108
16 years old and over	162,390	163,468	164,465	169,665	175,579	186,417
Male	101,689	102,448	103,184	106,365	108,774	112,610
Female	106,007	106,730	107,432	110,455	112,739	116,368
Black, total	30,287	30,719	31,148	33,199	35,129	38,833
Under 5 years old	2,679	2,806	2,814	2,790	2,748	2,820
5-17 years old	7,082	7,095	7,170	7,697	7,895	7,809
18-24 years old	3,853	3,845	3,813	3,703	3,924	4,314
25-34 years old	5,562	5,639	5,685	5,534	5,264	5,590
35-44 years old	3,826	4,010	4,210	5,041	5,481	5,076
45-54 years old	2,558	2,620	2,686	3,261	4,106	5,369
55-64 years old	2,135	2,145	2,156	2,288	2,578	3,995
65-74 years old	1,545	1,576	1,608	1,762	1,848	2,277
75 years old and over	956	981	1,005	1,122	1,283	1,584
16 years old and over	21,592	21,920	22,226	23,860	25,708	29,467
Male	14,414	14,625	14,835	15,840	16,787	18,602
Female	15,874	16,094	16,313	17,359	18,342	20,231

Source: "Projections of the Total Population by Age, Sex, and Race: 1988 to 2010," *Statistical Abstract* 1989, p. 15. Primary source: U.S. Bureau of the Census, *Current Population Reports*, Series P-25, No. 1018.

★ 789 ★
Population Projections - Part II

As of July 1. Includes Armed Forces overseas. Data are for middle series. Minus sign (-) indicates decrease.

Age, Sex, and Race	Percent Distribution			Percent Change		
	1980-1990	1990-2000	2000-2010	1990	2000	2010
White, total	100.0	100.0	100.0	7.7	5.2	3.4
Under 5 years old	7.1	6.0	5.7	10.4	-10.5	-1.8
5-17 years old	17.3	17.4	15.4	-6.3	5.6	-8.6
18-24 years old	10.1	9.0	9.3	-16.7	-6.2	6.5
25-34 years old	17.4	13.5	12.9	13.6	-18.1	-1.3
35-44 years old	15.3	16.5	13.1	44.1	13.2	-18.0
45-54 years old	10.4	14.3	15.7	9.8	44.0	13.4

Continued.

Population Projections - Part II
[Continued]

Age, Sex, and Race	Percent Distribution			Percent Change		
	1980-1990	1990-2000	2000-2010	1990	2000	2010
55-64 years old	8.8	9.3	13.1	-4.5	10.9	44.7
65-74 years old	7.8	7.0	7.8	16.1	-3.5	13.1
75 years old and over	5.7	6.8	7.0	30.2	25.1	7.6
16 years old and over	78.1	79.3	81.4	9.6	6.8	6.2
Male	49.0	49.1	49.2	8.0	5.4	3.5
Female	51.0	51.9	50.8	7.4	4.9	3.2
Black, total	100.0	100.0	100.0	15.8	12.8	10.6
Under 5 years old	9.0	7.8	7.3	13.7	-2.3	2.6
5-17 years old	23.0	22.5	20.1	2.5	10.1	-1.1
18-24 years old	12.2	11.2	11.1	-5.4	2.9	9.9
25-34 years old	18.3	15.0	14.4	31.2	-7.4	6.2
35-44 years old	13.5	15.6	13.1	52.9	30.2	-7.4
45-54 years old	8.6	11.7	13.8	17.4	52.9	30.8
55-64 years old	6.9	7.3	10.3	12.1	19.6	55.0
65-74 years old	5.2	5.3	5.9	19.0	14.9	23.2
75 years old and over	3.2	3.7	4.1	33.1	27.7	23.5
16 years old and over	71.4	73.2	75.9	19.2	15.7	14.6
Male	47.6	47.8	47.9	16.2	13.2	10.8
Female	52.4	52.2	52.1	15.4	12.4	10.3

Source: "Projections of the Total Population by Age, Sex, and Race: 1988 to 2010," *Statistical Abstract* 1989, p. 15. Primary source: U.S. Bureau of the Census, *Current Population Reports*, Series P-25, No. 1018.

★ 790 ★
Population Projections

Includes Armed Forces overseas.

Year and Race	Total (Jan. 1-Dec. 31)						Rate per 1,000 Midyear Population				
	Population at start of period (1,000)	Net increase[1]		Natural increase		Net civilian immigration (1,000)	Net growth rate[1]	Natural increase		Death rate	Net civilian immigration rate
		Total (1,000)	Percent[2]	Births (1,000)	Deaths (1,000)			Total	Birth rate		
All Races[3]											
1988	244,938	2,212	.90	3,758	2,141	595	9.0	6.6	15.3	8.7	2.4
1989	247,150	2,180	.88	3,756	2,161	585	8.8	6.4	15.1	8.7	2.4
1990	249,330	2,125	.85	3,731	2,180	575	8.5	6.2	14.8	8.7	2.3
1995	259,238	1,767	.68	3,517	2,275	525	6.8	4.8	13.5	8.7	2.0
2000	267,498	1,522	.57	3,389	2,368	500	5.7	3.8	12.6	8.8	1.9
2010	281,894	1,351	.48	3,485	2,665	500	4.8	3.1	12.3	9.3	1.8
White											
1988	206,943	1,494	.72	2,990	1,854	358	7.2	5.5	14.4	8.9	1.7
1989	208,437	1,460	.70	2,982	1,872	350	7.0	5.3	14.3	8.9	1.7
1990	209,897	1,408	.67	2,955	1,888	340	6.7	5.1	14.0	9.0	1.6
1995	216,267	1,074	.50	2,744	1,966	296	5.0	3.6	12.7	9.1	1.4
2000	221,088	838	.38	2,602	2,038	273	3.8	2.5	11.7	9.2	1.2

Continued.

Population Projections
[Continued]

Year and Race	Total (Jan. 1-Dec. 31)							Rate per 1,000 Midyear Population				
	Population at start of period (1,000)	Net increase[1]		Natural increase		Net civilian immigra- tion (1,000)	Net growth rate[1]	Natural increase		Death rate	Net civilian immigra- tion rate
		Total (1,000)	Percent[2]	Births (1,000)	Deaths (1,000)			Total	Birth rate		
2010	228,637	674	.29	2,639	2,238	273	2.9	1.8	11.5	9.8	1.2
Black											
1988	30,072	432	1.43	621	250	60	11.2	12.2	20.5	8.3	2.0
1989	30,503	430	1.41	622	252	60	11.2	12.2	20.5	8.3	2.0
1990	30,934	426	1.38	620	254	60	13.7	11.8	19.9	8.1	1.9
1995	33,000	396	1.20	602	262	56	11.9	10.2	18.1	7.9	1.7
2000	34,939	379	1.08	597	272	54	10.8	9.3	17.0	7.7	1.5
2010	38,653	358	.93	616	312	54	9.3	7.8	15.8	8.1	1.4

Source: "Projected Components of Population Change: 1988-2010," *Statistical Abstract*, 1989, p. 14. Primary source: U.S. Bureau of the Census, *Current Population Reports*, series P-25, No. 1018. *Notes:* 1. Includes overseas admissions into, less discharges from, Armed Forces, not shown separately. 2. Percent of population at beginning of period. 3. Includes other races not shown separately.

★ 791 ★
Population Projections

Region, Division and State	Number (1,000)					Percent		
	Total, 18 years old and over	Race				Black	Other races[1]	Hispanic[2]
		White	Black	Other[1]	Hispanic[2]			
U.S.	182,628	156,578	20,441	5,609	13,021	11.2	3.1	7.1
Regions:								
New England	9,920	9,384	398	138	238	4.0	1.4	2.4
Middle Atlantic	28,482	24,351	3,494	637	1,935	12.3	2.2	6.8
East North Central	30,914	27,114	3,353	447	852	10.8	1.4	2.8
West North Central	13,037	12,232	579	226	153	4.4	1.7	1.2
South Atlantic	32,137	25,623	6,036	478	1,154	18.8	1.5	3.6
East South Central	11,284	9,199	2,010	74	46	17.8	.7	.4
West South Central	19,610	16,532	2,628	450	2,717	13.4	2.3	13.9
Mountain	9,691	9,009	231	450	1,193	2.4	4.6	12.3
Pacific	27,552	23,133	1,711	2,708	4,732	6.2	9.8	17.2

Source: "Projections of the Population 18 Years Old and Over, by Race and Hispanic Origin - States: 1988," *Statistical Abstract*, 1989, p. 23. Primary source: U.S. Bureau of the Census, *Current Population Reports*, Series P-25, No. 1019. *Notes:* 1. Virtually all persons of other races are Asian and Pacific Islanders, American Indians, Eskimos, and Aleuts. 2. Persons of Hispanic origin may be of any race.

★ 792 ★
Population Trends 1950-1986

Data based on decennial census updated by data from multiple sources.

Sex, race, and year	Total resident population	Under 1 year	1-4 years	5-14 years	15-24 years	25-34 years	35-44 years	45-54 years	55-64 years	65-74 years	75-84 years	85 years and over
					Numbers in thousands							
All races												
1950	150,697	3,147	13,017	24,319	22,098	23,759	21,450	17,343	13,370	8,340	3,278	577
1960	179,323	4,122	16,209	35,465	24,020	22,818	24,081	20,485	15,572	10,997	4,633	929
1970	203,212	3,485	13,669	40,746	35,441	24,907	23,088	23,220	18,590	12,435	6,119	1,511
1980	226,546	3,534	12,815	34,942	42,487	37,082	25,635	22,800	21,703	15,581	7,729	2,240
1986	241,096	3,768	14,384	33,860	39,021	42,779	33,070	22,815	22,232	17,332	9,060	2,776
White male												
1950	67,129	1,400	5,845	10,860	9,689	10,430	9,529	7,836	6,180	3,736	1,406	218
1960	78,367	1,784	7,065	15,659	10,483	9,940	10,564	9,114	6,850	4,702	1,875	331
1970	86,721	1,501	5,873	17,667	15,232	10,775	9,979	10,090	7,958	4,916	2,243	487
1980	94,976	1,487	5,402	14,773	18,123	15,940	11,010	9,774	9,151	6,096	2,600	621
1986	99,810	1,565	5,973	14,020	16,289	18,193	14,172	9,663	9,290	6,876	3,062	706
Black male												
1950	7,300	944[1]		1,442	1,162	1,105	1,003	772	460	299	113[2]	
1960	9,114	281	1,082	2,185	1,305	1,120	1,086	891	617	382	137	29
1970	10,748	245	975	2,784	2,041	1,226	1,084	979	739	461	169	46
1980	12,585	269	967	2,614	2,807	1,967	1,235	1,024	854	567	228	53
1986	13,892	289	1,091	2,667	2,759	2,488	1,593	1,092	951	633	262	67
White female												
1950	67,813	1,341	5,599	10,431	9,821	10,851	9,719	7,868	6,168	4,031	1,669	314
1960	80,465	1,714	6,795	15,068	10,596	10,204	11,000	9,364	7,327	5,428	2,441	527
1970	91,028	1,434	5,615	16,912	15,420	11,004	10,349	10,756	8,853	6,366	3,429	890
1980	99,835	1,412	5,127	14,057	17,653	15,896	11,232	10,285	10,325	7,951	4,457	1,440
1986	104,501	1,486	5,674	13,295	15,861	17,852	14,297	10,039	10,351	8,657	5,166	1,825
Black female												
1950	7,745	941[1]		1,446	1,300	1,260	1,112	796	443	322	125[2]	
1960	9,758	283	1,085	2,191	1,404	1,300	1,229	974	663	430	160	38
1970	11,832	243	970	2,773	2,196	1,456	1,309	1,134	868	582	230	71
1980	14,046	266	951	2,578	2,937	2,267	1,488	1,258	1,059	776	360	106
1986	15,413	283	1,058	2,596	2,837	2,797	1,906	1,347	1,155	858	430	145

Source: "Resident Population, according to Age, Sex, and Race: United States, Selected Years 1950-1986," *Health United States - 1988*, March 1989, p. 41. Primary source: U.S. Bureau of the Census: *1950 Nonwhite Population by Race*, Special Report P-E, No. 3B. Washington. U.S. Government Printing Office, 1951; Population estimates and projections. *Current Population Reports*, Series P-25, Nos. 499 and 1022. Washington. U.S. Government Printing Office, May 1973 and Mar. 1988; U.S. Bureau of the Census, *U.S. Census and Population: 1960, Number of Inhabitants*, PC(1)- A1, United States Summary, 1964. U.S. Bureau of the Census, *U.S. Census of Population: 1970, Number of Inhabitants*, Final Report PC(1)- A1, United States Summary, 1971; Unpublished data from the U.S. Bureau of the Census. *Notes:* Population figures are census counts as of April 1 for 1950, 1960, 1970, and 1980 and estimates as of July 1 for 1986. 1. Represents figure for "Under 1 year" and "1 to 4 years." 2. Represents figure for "75 to 85 years" and "85 years and over".

★ 793 ★
Poverty Level, Characteristics of

Numbers in thousands. Families as of March 1988.

Characteristic	1987 Black	1987 White	1982 Black	1982 White	1979 Black	1979 White
United States						
All persons	9,683	21,409	9,697	23,517	7,838	16,823
Percent below poverty level	33.1	10.5	35.6	12.0	30.9	8.9
Persons 65 years and over	808	2,597	811	2,870	716	2,840
Percent below poverty level	33.9	10.1	38.2	12.4	35.5	13.2
All related children under 18 years in families	4,297	7,550	4,388	8,282	3,695	5,759
Percent below poverty level	45.1	15.0	47.3	16.5	40.7	11.4
Families with a female householder, no husband present	3,394	3,474	3,269	3,249	2,851	2,560
Percent below poverty level	68.3	45.8	70.7	46.5	63.0	38.6
All other families	903	4,076	1,120	5,032	844	3,199
Percent below poverty level	19.8	9.5	24.1	11.6	18.5	7.3
South						
All persons	5,648	7,426	5,487	8,297	4,419	6,078
Percent below poverty level	34.5	11.5	37.6	13.4	33.9	10.6
Persons 65 years and over	560	1,064	587	1,352	490	1,208
Percent below poverty level	40.5	12.9	46.2	17.9	41.4	18.2
All related children under 18 years in families	2,511	2,465	2,435	2,781	2,112	1,997
Percent below poverty level	45.9	15.7	49.2	17.7	44.2	13.0
Families with a female householder, no husband present	1,865	1,028	1,698	947	1,548	654
Percent below poverty level	68.4	44.0	72.1	46.0	68.1	34.3
All other families	646	1,437	737	1,834	564	1,343
Percent below poverty level	23.6	10.7	28.4	13.4	22.5	10.0
North and West						
All persons	4,035	13,983	4,210	15,220	3,418	10,745
Percent below poverty level	31.3	10.1	33.3	11.3	27.7	8.2
Persons 65 years and over	249	1,532	224	1,517	227	1,631
Percent below poverty level	24.8	8.8	26.2	9.7	27.2	11.0
All related children under 18 years in families	1,785	5,085	1,953	5,500	1,584	3,762
Percent below poverty level	44.1	14.7	45.2	15.9	36.8	10.7
Families with a female householder, no husband present	1,529	2,446	1,570	2,302	1,303	1,907
Percent below poverty level	68.1	46.7	69.3	46.6	57.3	40.4
All other families	256	2,639	383	3,199	280	1,855
Percent below poverty level	14.2	9.0	18.6	10.8	13.6	6.1

Source: "Selected Characteristics of Persons Below the Poverty Level: 1987, 1982, and 1979," *The Black Population in the United States,* March 1988, p. 17. Primary source: *The Black Population in the United States*: March 1988.

★ 794 ★
Poverty Rates

Numbers in thousands. Families as of March 1988.

Characteristic	1987 Black	1987 White	1982 Black	1982 White	1979 Black	1979 White
United States						
Type of family						
All families	2,149	4,592	2,158	5,118	1,666	3,515
Percent below poverty level	29.9	8.2	33.0	9.6	27.6	6.8
Married-couple	454	2,440	543	3,104	437	2,058
Percent below poverty level	12.3	5.2	15.6	6.9	13.0	4.7
Female householder, no husband present	1,593	1,930	1,535	1,813	1,195	1,328
Percent below poverty level	51.8	26.7	56.2	27.9	49.2	22.3
All other families	102	223	79	201	34	130
Percent below poverty level	24.3	10.3	25.6	12.2	13.3	9.1
Householder 65 years and over	215	511	239	632	205	587
Percent below poverty level	23.7	5.4	29.4	7.3	25.9	7.2
South						
Type of family						
All families	1,237	1,636	1,177	1,850	922	1,297
Percent below poverty level	31.1	8.8	34.2	10.6	30.0	8.0
Female householder, no husband present	864	601	778	557	616	338
Percent below poverty level	52.6	26.1	56.4	28.0	52.8	20.2
All other families	373	1,034	399	1,294	306	960
Percent below poverty level	16.0	6.4	19.3	8.4	16.1	6.6
Householder 65 years and over	151	235	177	337	151	290
Percent below poverty level	27.9	7.4	36.3	11.4	31.4	11.2
North and West						
Type of family						
All families	913	2,957	981	3,268	745	2,218
Percent below poverty level	28.5	7.9	31.8	9.1	25.1	6.3
Female householder, no husband present	729	1,328	757	1,256	580	990
Percent below poverty level	50.9	26.9	56.0	27.8	46.0	23.1
All other families	183	1,628	224	2,012	166	1,228
Percent below poverty level	10.4	5.0	12.9	6.4	9.7	4.0
Householder 65 years and over	64	276	62	296	54	298
Percent below poverty level	17.6	4.4	19.1	5.2	17.5	5.6

Source: "Poverty Rates of Persons, by Race: 1979 to 1987," *The Black Population in the United States,* March 1988, p. 16.
Primary source: *The Black Population in the United States*: March 1988.

★ 795 ★
Racial Groups in Regions

Year	Black NE	Black NC	Black South	Black West	White NE	White NC	White South	White West
1980	3.6	5.7	90.3	0.4	31.1	39.8	23.9	5.2
1900	4.4	5.6	89.7	0.3	30.9	38.6	24.7	5.8
1910	4.9	5.5	89.0	0.5	31.0	35.8	25.1	8.0
1920	6.5	7.6	85.2	0.8	30.5	35.0	25.5	9.0
1930	9.7	10.6	78.7	1.0	30.1	33.7	25.1	9.8
1940	10.7	11.0	77.0	1.3	29.2	32.7	26.8	11.3

Continued.

Racial Groups in Regions
[Continued]

Year	Black				White			
	NE	NC	South	West	NE	NC	South	West
1950	13.4	14.8	68.0	3.8	27.7	31.2	27.3	13.8
1960[1]	16.1	18.8	59.9	5.8	26.1	30.2	27.4	16.3
1970	19.2	20.3	52.0	7.5	24.9	29.1	28.4	17.6
1980	18.3	20.1	53.0	8.5	22.3	27.1	31.3	19.3

Source: "Regional Distribution of Racial Groups," *The Economic Progress of Black Men in America*, p. 79. Primary source: *The Economic Progress of Black Men in America*. Washington D.C.: U.S. Commission on Civil Rights, 1986. Clearing House Publication 91. U.S. Bureau of the Census: *Historical Statistics of the U.S. Colonial Times to 1970*, Series A 172-194, p. 22; *Statistical Abstract 1982-83. Note:* 1. First year to include Alaska and Hawaii.

★ 796 ★
Region and Residence of the Population

Location	Total	Metropolitan residence		Non-Metropolitan residence
		Inside central cities	Outside central cities	
United States	82	57	25	18
South	70	43	27	30
North and West	98	75	23	2

Source: "Black Population, by Region and Metropolitan/Non-Metropolitan Residence: 1988," *The Black Population of the United States*, March 1988, p. 4. Primary source: *The Black Population in the United States*: March 1988.

★ 797 ★
Regional Distribution of the Black Population

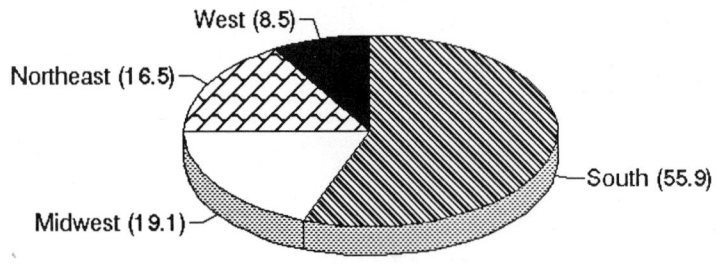

West (8.5)
Northeast (16.5)
Midwest (19.1)
South (55.9)

Region	Percent
South	55.9
Midwest	19.1
Northeast	16.5
West	8.5

Source: "Black Population, by Region: 1988," *The Black Population of the United States*, March 1988, p. 3. Primary source: *The Black Population of the United States*: March 1988.

★ 798 ★
Regional Distribution of the Population

Numbers in thousands.

Year and region	Number			Percent distribution			Black as a percent of total
	All races	Black	White	All races	Black	White	
1988							
Total	241,155	29,333	203,869	100.0	100.0	100.0	12.2
South	82,529	16,403	64,813	34.2	55.9	31.8	19.9
North and West	158,626	12,931	139,056	65.8	44.1	68.2	8.2
Male	117,260	13,717	99,671	100.0	100.0	100.0	11.7
South	39,920	7,571	31,712	34.0	55.2	31.8	19.0
North and West	77,339	6,147	67,959	66.0	44.8	68.2	7.9
Female	123,895	15,616	104,198	100.0	100.0	100.0	12.6
South	42,609	8,832	33,102	34.4	56.6	31.8	20.7
North and West	81,286	6,784	71,097	65.6	43.4	68.2	8.3
1980							
Total	223,160	26,033	191,905	100.0	100.0	100.0	11.7
South	74,046	13,599	59,597	33.2	52.2	31.1	18.4
North and West	149,114	12,435	132,307	66.8	47.8	68.9	8.3
Male	108,157	12,133	93,468	100.0	100.0	100.0	11.2
South	36,013	6,319	29,271	33.3	52.1	31.3	17.5
North and West	72,145	5,815	64,197	66.7	47.9	68.7	8.1
Female	115,002	13,900	98,437	100.0	100.0	100.0	12.1
South	38,033	7,280	30,326	33.1	52.4	30.8	19.1
North and West	76,969	6,620	68,111	66.9	47.6	69.2	8.6

Source: "Distribution of the Population, by Region, Sex, and Race: March 1988 and 1980," *The Black Population in the United States*, March 1988, p. 3. Primary source: *The Black Population in the United States*: March 1988.

★ 799 ★
Residence of the Population

Numbers in thousands.

Residence and region	All races	Black	White	Black as a percent of total
United States				
Total	241,155	29,333	203,869	12.2
Percent	100.0	100.0	100.0	[1]
All metropolitan areas	77.6	82.3	76.6	12.96
Inside central cities	31.0	57.2	26.7	22.4
Outside central cities	46.6	25.2	49.8	6.6
Nonmetropolitan areas	22.4	17.7	23.4	9.6
Nonfarm	20.9	17.4	21.7	10.1
Farm	1.5	0.3	1.7	2.6
Metropolitan areas of 1 million or more	103,404	15,796	82,865	15.3
Percent	100.0	100.0	100.0	[1]
Inside central cities	40.3	71.0	33.8	26.9
Outside central cities	59.7	29.0	66.2	7.4

Continued.

Residence of the Population
[Continued]

Residence and region	All races	Black	White	Black as a percent of total
Metropolitan areas under 1 million	83,775	8,348	73,280	10.0
Percent	100.0	100.0	100.0	[1]
Inside central cities	39.6	66.4	36.2	16.7
Outside central cities	60.4	33.6	63.8	5.5
South				
Total	82,529	16,403	64,813	19.9
Percent	100.0	100.0	100.0	[1]
All metropolitan areas	71.6	69.8	71.8	19.4
Inside central cities	28.8	43.2	25.1	29.8
Outside central cities	42.8	26.6	46.8	12.4
Nonmetropolitan areas	28.4	30.2	28.2	21.1
Nonfarm	27.0	29.6	26.5	21.8
Farm	1.4	0.6	1.7	8.1
Metropolitan areas of 1 million or more	26,561	5,902	20,006	22.2
Percent	100.0	100.0	100.0	[1]
Inside central cities	37.5	59.9	30.8	35.5
Outside central cities	62.5	40.1	69.2	14.3
Metropolitan areas under 1 million	32,529	5,551	26,560	17.1
Percent	100.0	100.0	100.0	[1]
Inside central cities	42.5	64.0	38.0	25.7
Outside central cities	57.5	36.0	62.0	10.7
North and West				
Total	158,626	12,931	139,056	8.2
Percent	100.0	100.0	100.0	[1]
All metropolitan areas	80.8	98.1	78.8	9.9
Inside central cities	32.2	74.9	27.5	19.0
Outside central cities	48.6	23.3	51.3	3.9
Nonmetropolitan areas	19.2	1.9	21.2	0.8
Nonfarm	17.7	1.9	19.4	0.9
Farm	1.6	---	1.8	---
Metropolitan areas of 1 million or more	76,844	9,894	62,859	12.9
Percent	100.0	100.0	100.0	[1]
Inside central cities	41.3	77.7	34.8	24.2
Outside central cities	58.7	22.3	65.2	4.9
Metropolitan areas under 1 million	51,247	2,796	46,719	5.5
Percent	100.0	100.0	100.0	[1]
Inside central cities	37.7	71.2	35.2	10.3
Outside central cities	62.3	28.8	64.8	2.5

Source: "Metropolitan-Nonmetropolitan Residence of the Population, by Region and Race: March 1988," *The Black Population in the United States*, March 1988, p. 22. Primary source: *The Black Population in the United States*: March 1988. *Note:* 1. Not applicable.

★ 800 ★
School Age Residents

In thousands.

Year	Total[1]	White[2]			Black[2]			Other races[2]		
		Total	Male	Female	Total	Male	Female	Total	Male	Female
1960	44,176	38,366	19,532	18,832	5,366	2,677	2,690	446	228	217
1961	45,263	39,220	19,975	19,246	5,575	2,782	2,792	469	238	232
1962	46,648	40,352	20,560	19,791	5,802	2,897	2,906	496	251	244
1963	48,070	41,524	21,164	20,361	6,025	3,009	3,016	520	264	257
1964	49,509	42,692	21,765	20,929	6,272	3,135	3,137	545	275	270
1965	49,900	42,891	21,872	21,019	6,440	3,220	3,221	567	285	281
1966	50,681	43,469	22,176	21,293	6,619	3,308	3,311	594	300	295
1967	51,357	43,969	22,438	21,529	6,768	3,383	3,384	622	314	310
1968	51,974	44,422	22,677	21,744	6,903	3,453	3,450	649	325	323
1969	52,386	44,697	22,826	21,871	7,016	3,511	3,505	673	338	336
1970	52,593	44,783	22,877	21,906	7,108	3,561	3,547	703	355	349
1971	52,562	44,644	22,809	21,834	7,182	3,600	3,583	737	371	365
1972	52,316	44,336	22,655	21,681	7,211	3,615	3,596	768	388	380
1973	51,910	43,898	22,434	21,464	7,213	3,617	3,596	799	405	394
1974	51,498	43,454	22,210	21,244	7,213	3,618	3,596	830	420	409
1975	51,044	42,950	21,956	20,994	7,199	3,611	3,588	895	456	440
1976	50,633	42,477	21,721	20,75	7,208	3,617	3,591	948	483	465
1977	49,897	41,737	21,350	20,386	7,167	3,600	6,568	994	506	487
1978	49,038	40,883	20,919	19,964	7,116	3,576	3,540	1,039	530	509
1979	48,041	39,910	20,427	19,484	7,037	3,538	3,498	1,094	560	536
1980	47,236	39,003	19,982	19,020	6,997	3,523	3,472	1,237	634	605
1981	46,353	38,118	19,532	18,586	6,924	3,491	3,433	1,310	672	639
1982	45,654	37,399	19,167	18,231	6,879	3,472	3,408	1,375	706	668
1983	45,129	36,859	18,899	17,960	6,842	3,457	3,384	1,428	733	698
1984	44,943	36,596	18,770	17,826	6,847	3,464	3,384	1,499	767	731
1985	44,975	36,502	18,727	17,775	6,897	3,493	3,406	1,575	805	768
1986	45,148	36,532	18,745	17,786	6,957	3,527	3,431	1,661	848	811
1987	45,290	36,528	18,747	17,780	7,021	3,563	3,458	1,741	888	853

Source: "Estimates of School Age Population, by Race and Sex, July 1, 1960 to July 1, 1987," *Digest of Educational Statistics,* 1989, p. 21. Primary source: U.S. Department of Commerce, Bureau of the Census, *Current Population Reports,* Series P-25, No. 519, No. 917, No. 1000, and No. 1022. (This table was prepared September 1988.) Published by permission. *Notes:* Some data have been revised from previously published figures. Because of rounding, details may not add to totals. 1. Includes persons 5 to 17 years old. 2. Includes persons of Hispanic origin.

★ 801 ★
Sex, Age and Race of Population

Represents number of males per 100 females. Total resident population.

Age	1987 (July 1)		
	Total[1]	White	Black
All ages	94.9	95.6	90.2
Under 14 years	104.9	105.4	103.1
14-24 years	102.4	102.9	97.9
25-44 years	98.8	100.8	86.9
45-64 years	91.8	93.2	81.8
65 years and over	68.4	68.3	67.1

Source: "Ratio of Males to Females, by Age Group, 1920 to 1987, and by Race, 1987," *Statistical Abstract*, 1989, p. 16. Primary source: U.S. Bureau of the Census, *U.S. Census of Population: 1930*, vol. II; *1940*, vol. II, part 1, and vol. IV, part 1; *1950*, vol. II, part 1; *1960*, vol. I, part 1; *1970*, vol. I, part B; and *Current Population Reports*, series P-25, No. 1022. *Note:* 1. Includes other races, not shown separately.

★ 802 ★
Young Adult Population Projections

	1985	1990	2000
Blacks	4.138	3.798	3.773
Whites	23.817	21.17	19.805

Source: "Projections of the Black and White Population for 18 to 24 Year Olds," *NAFEO INROADS*, February/March-April/May, 1989, p. 12. *Note:* Figures in millions.

THE PROFESSIONS

Academic Rank of Men Scientists/Engineers

Field and racial/ ethnic group	Academic rank			
	Total, four-year colleges & univer-sities[1]	Full professors	Associate Professor	Assistant Professor
Total, all fields[2]	174,500	79,600	41,700	26,400
White	156,700	72,900	37,300	23,000
Black	2,600	800	900	400
Asian	13,700	5,300	3,000	2,700
Native American	300	100	100	[4]
Hispanic[3]	2,800	900	700	600
Scientists, totals	151,400	68,300	37,000	22,900
White	137,500	62,900	33,600	20,500
Black	2,400	800	800	300
Asian	10,200	4,100	2,100	1,900
Native American	200	100	100	[4]
Hispanic	2,400	800	500	600
Engineers, total	23,100	11,300	4,700	3,500
White	19,200	10,000	3,700	2,500
Black	200	[4]	100	100
Asian	3,500	1,200	900	900
Native American	[4]	[4]	[4]	[4]
Hispanic	400	100	200	[4]

Source: "Doctoral Men Scientists and Engineers in Four-Year Colleges and Universities, by Field, Racial/Ethnic Group, and Academic Rank: 1987," Women and Minorities in Science and Engineering General:, January 1990, pp. 109-110. Primary source: National Science Foundation, SRS. *Notes:* 1. Includes instructor, other, and no report. 2. Detail will not add to total employed because a) racial and ethnic categories are not mutually exclusive and b) total employed includes other and no report. 3. Includes members of all racial groups. 4. Too few cases to estimate.

★ 804 ★
Academic Rank of Scientists/Engineers

Field and racial/ ethnic group	Academic rank			
	Total, four-year colleges & universities[1]	Full professors	Associate Professor	Assistant Professor
Total, all fields[2]	209,400	85,800	50,500	36,500
White	187,900	78,600	45,200	32,100
Black	3,700	1,000	1,200	800
Asian	16,000	5,700	3,500	3,300
Native American	300	100	100	[4]
Hispanic[3]	3,500	1,000	800	800
Scientists, total	185,700	74,500	45,600	32,700
White	168,300	68,500	41,400	29,400
Black	3,400	900	1,100	700
Asian	12,400	4,400	2,600	2,400
Native American	300	100	100	[4]
Hispanic	3,000	800	700	800
Engineers, total	23,600	11,400	4,900	3,700
White	19,600	10,000	3,800	2,700
Black	300	[4]	100	100
Asian	3,600	1,200	900	900
Native American	[4]	[4]	[4]	[4]
Hispanic	400	100	200	[4]

Source: "Doctoral Scientists and Engineers in Four-Year Colleges and Universities, by Field, Racial/Ethnic Group, and Academic Rank: 1987," Women and Minorities in Science and Engineering General:, January 1990, pp. 107-108 Primary source: National Science Foundation, SRS. *Notes:* 1. Includes instructor, other, and no report. 2. Detail will not add to total employed because a) racial and ethnic categories are not mutually exclusive and b) total employed includes other and no report. 3. Includes members of all racial groups. 4. Too few cases to estimate.

★ 805 ★
Academic Rank of Women Scientists/Engineers

Field and racial/ ethnic group	Academic rank			
	Total, four-year colleges & universities[1]	Full professors	Associate Professor	Assistant Professor
Total, all fields[2]	34,900	6,200	8,800	10,100
White	31,200	5,600	8,000	9,100
Black	1,100	100	300	400
Asian	2,300	400	400	500
Native American	100	[4]	[4]	[4]
Hispanic[3]	700	100	100	200
Scientists, totals	34,300	6,100	8,600	9,900
White	30,800	5,600	7,800	8,900
Black	1,100	100	300	400

Continued.

Academic Rank of Women Scientists/Engineers
[Continued]

Field and racial/ ethnic group	Academic rank			
	Total, four-year colleges & universities[1]	Full professors	Associate Professor	Assistant Professor
Asian	2,200	400	400	500
Native American	100	4	4	4
Hispanic	700	100	100	200
Engineers, total	600	100	100	200
White	500	100	100	200
Black	4	4	4	4
Asian	100	4	4	4
Native American	4	4	4	4
Hispanic	4	4	4	4

Source: "Doctoral Women Scientists and Engineers in Four-Year Colleges and Universities, by Field, Racial/Ethnic Group, and Academic Rank: 1987," Women and Minorities in Science and Engineering General:, January 1990, pp. 111-112. Primary source: National Science Foundation, SRS. *Notes:* 1. Includes instructor, other, and no report. 2. Detail will not add to total employed because a) racial and ethnic categories are not mutually exclusive and b) total employed includes other and no report. 3. Includes members of all racial groups. 4. Too few cases to estimate.

★ 806 ★
Applicants to Medical School

Howard University[1]	54
Morehouse College[1]	32
Harvard University	26
Xavier University (La.)[1]	26
UCLA	20
Johns Hopkins	17
Spelman College[1]	17
New York University	16
Stanford University	15
SUNY-Brooklyn College	15
University of Michigan	15

Source: "1988 Top Suppliers of Black Applicants to Medical School," *NAFEO INROADS*, December-January 1990, p. 13. *Note:* 1. Historically Black College. Published by permission.

★ 807 ★
Applications to Law School

Ethnic Group	American Indian	Black	Mexican American	Hispanic	Puerto Rican	Asian American
Year						
1988/89	300	4,510	740	1,730	880	2,460
1989/90	320	5,180	810	1,910	990	2,770
Percent change	+3.9	+15.0	+10.3	+10.7	+45.9	+12.7
National change - +7.2						

Source: "Law School Applications by Ethnic Group," *Black Issues in Higher Education*, June 7, 1990, p. 17. Primary source: Newsletter of the Law School Admission Council.

★ 808 ★
Characteristics of Medical School Faculty

	MD		PHD/OHD		MD-PHD/MD-OHD		Other	
	No	%	No	%	No	%	No	%
Female Ethnicity								
Native American	2	0.0	4	0.1	1	0.3	3	0.2
Asian	732	12.1	254	7.1	58	19.8	38	2.2
Black	238	3.9	52	1.5	3	1.0	80	4.6
Mexican American	14	0.2	8	0.2	-	-	3	0.2
Puerto Rican	85	1.4	10	0.3	-	-	15	0.9
Other Hispanic	110	1.8	39	1.1	2	0.7	22	1.3
White	4,465	74.0	2,998	83.5	213	72.7	1,436	82.0
Refused	234	3.9	148	4.1	9	3.1	51	2.9
Missing	157	2.6	78	2.2	7	2.4	104	5.9
Total	6,037	100.0	3,591	100.0	293	100.0	1,752	100.0
Male Ethnicity								
Native American	29	0.1	6	0.1	3	0.1	1	0.1
Asian	1,839	6.0	1,113	8.5	352	11.7	51	3.3
Black	527	1.7	120	0.9	32	1.1	51	3.3
Mexican American	92	0.3	27	0.2	4	0.1	4	0.3
Puerto Rican	246	0.8	27	0.2	5	0.2	8	0.5
Other Hispanic	561	1.8	113	0.9	47	1.6	20	1.3
White	25,794	83.3	10,962	83.3	2,444	80.9	1,129	72.1
Refused	1,017	3.3	537	4.1	94	3.1	46	2.9
Missing	680	2.2	259	2.0	40	1.3	255	16.3
Total	30,785	100.0	13,164	100.0	3,021	100.0	1,565	100.0

Source: "Distribution of U.S. Medical School Faculty by Sex, Ethnicity and Degree, 1988," *Black Issues in Higher Education*, November 9, 1989, p. 12. Primary source: Faculty Roster System, Number Book, AAMC, 1988. *Note:* 1. Other Health Doctorate.

★ 809 ★
Citizenship of Science/Engineering and Other Doctorate Recipients - Part I

	1975	1976	1977	1978	1979	1980
Total U.S. citizens						
S/E Ph.D.s	14,015	13,773	13,407	13,086	13,257	13,179
Non-S/E Ph.D.s	13,066	13,496	12,712	12,205	12,207	12,042
White U.S. citizens						
S/E Ph.D.s	12,837	12,586	12,100	11,484	11,601	11,647
Non-S/E Ph.D.s	11,515	11,787	10,965	10,327	10,319	10,346
Black U.S. citizens						
S/E Ph.D.s	240	246	265	278	288	261
Non-S/E Ph.D.s	759	849	851	755	768	771
Hispanic U.S. citizens						
S/E Ph.D.s	128	116	159	160	173	166
Non-S/E Ph.D.s	175	224	264	313	289	246
Asian U.S. citizens						
S/E Ph.D.s	192	240	246	275	301	323
Non-S/E Ph.D.s	94	94	93	115	127	135

Source: "Ph.D.s by Citizenship, Selected Racial/Ethnic Group, and Gender: 1975- 88, *Science and Engineering Indicators - 1989*, 1989, p. 227. Primary source: NSF, Division of Science Resources Studies.

★ 810 ★
Citizenship of Science/Engineering and Other Doctorate Recipients - Part II

	1981	1982	1983	1984	1985	1986	1987	1988
Total U.S. citizens								
S/E Ph.D.s	13,298	13,022	13,103	12,977	12,676	12,615	12,563	12,847
Non-S/E Ph.D.s	11,763	11,366	11,255	11,049	10,687	10,466	10,428	10,325
White U.S. citizens								
S/E Ph.D.s	11,873	11,804	11,866	11,684	11,424	11,406	11,260	11,559
Non-S/E Ph.D.s	10,107	9,872	9,833	9,665	9,333	9,220	9,210	9,126
Black U.S. citizens								
S/E Ph.D.s	273	270	269	282	260	238	222	231
Non-S/E Ph.D.s	740	777	653	671	652	585	545	574
Hispanic U.S. citizens								
S/E Ph.D.s	191	219	221	250	237	264	293	319
Non-S/E Ph.D.s	273	316	318	286	324	308	326	275
Asian U.S. citizens								
S/E Ph.D.s	327	318	341	380	371	394	440	441
Non-S/E Ph.D.s	138	134	151	132	145	137	102	171

Source: "Ph.D.s by Citizenship, Selected Racial/Ethnic Group, and Gender: 1975- 88, *Science and Engineering Indicators - 1989*, 1989, p. 227. Primary source: NSF, Division of Science Resources Studies.

★ 811 ★
Classification of Enrolled Dental Students

	Black	Hispanic	American Indian	Asian	Total
4th Year	258	245	17	469	989
3rd Year	215	295	15	488	1,013
2nd Year	241	303	8	506	1,058
1st Year	280	358	20	636	1,294
Total	994	1,201	60	2,099	4,354

Source: "Total Predoctoral Minority Enrollment in Dental Schools in the United States 1987-88," Black Issues in Higher Education, December 8, 1988, p. 18. Primary source: Council on Dental Education Annual Report, 1987-88, American Dental Association.

★ 812 ★
Dental School Enrollments: Trends

	Number	Percent
1976-77	955	4.5
1977-78	968	4.5
1978-79	977	4.5
1979-80	1,009	4.4
1980-81	1,022	4.5
1981-82	999	4.5
1982-83	1,001	4.6
1983-84	1,000	4.7
1984-85	1,037	5.0
1985-86	1,019	5.2
1986-87	1,032	5.5
1987-88	994	5.5
1988-89	984	5.7

Source: "Black Students Enrolled in Dental Schools 1976-1989," Black Issues in Higher Education, October 26, 1989, p. 6. Primary source: American Dental Association Supplement 3, Annual Report, 1976-77 - 1988-89.

★ 813 ★
Dental Schools with Minority Enrollment

	Black		Hispanic		Am. Indian		Asian		Total		
	M	F	M	F	M	F	M	F	M	F	T
Alabama	2	2	2	1	0	0	7	5	11	8	19
Baylor	5	7	18	8	0	0	24	23	47	38	85
Boston	6	4	29	27	0	0	25	20	60	51	111
Buffalo	3	2	2	3	0	0	2	4	7	9	16
Calif. LA	1	2	16	6	1	0	78	58	96	66	162
Calif. SF	8	8	22	11	1	1	64	67	95	87	182
Case Western	9	4	5	5	0	0	22	15	36	24	60
Colorado	1	1	12	7	0	2	5	2	18	12	30

Continued.

Dental Schools with Minority Enrollment
[Continued]

	Black		Hispanic		Am. Indian		Asian		Total		
	M	F	M	F	M	F	M	F	M	F	T
Columbia	7	4	2	10	0	0	40	28	49	42	91
Connecticut	2	0	2	4	0	0	6	4	10	8	18
Creighton	3	1	16	5	2	0	45	15	66	21	87
Detroit	6	4	3	1	0	1	6	5	15	11	26
Emory	0	0	0	0	0	0	0	0	0	0	0
F. Dickinson	20	15	14	10	0	0	13	6	47	31	78
Florida	8	9	32	22	0	0	8	7	48	38	86
Georgetown	5	11	22	19	0	0	21	22	48	52	100
Georgia	12	9	4	0	0	0	7	2	23	11	34
Harvard	1	1	3	1	0	0	17	17	21	19	40
Howard[1]	122	94	7	3	0	1	18	6	147	104	251
Illinois	3	5	13	5	0	0	34	27	50	37	87
Indiana	2	7	5	5	1	0	16	8	24	20	44
Iowa	2	4	5	3	0	0	18	6	25	13	38
Kentucky	4	3	1	0	0	0	1	0	6	3	9
Loma Linda	5	0	10	3	2	1	73	42	90	46	136
Louisiana	5	3	2	2	1	0	5	2	13	7	20
Louisville	1	4	4	3	0	1	2	4	7	12	19
Loyola	8	7	18	4	1	0	26	8	53	19	72
Marquette	8	19	77	24	3	0	39	28	127	71	198
Maryland	18	21	10	6	1	0	22	19	51	46	97
Meharry[1]	82	76	1	1	0	0	1	0	84	77	161
Michigan	16	23	3	4	1	0	19	10	39	37	76
Minnesota	0	2	1	0	1	0	8	9	10	11	21
Mississippi	0	9	1	0	0	0	1	0	2	9	11
Missouri K.C.	3	3	17	3	2	0	39	18	61	24	85
N. Carolina	12	10	0	1	3	1	3	3	18	15	33
Nebraska	0	1	4	1	2	1	2	4	8	7	15
New Jersey	7	5	15	4	0	0	6	10	28	19	47
New York	16	11	51	34	0	0	41	21	108	66	174
Northwestern	3	3	11	12	0	1	64	30	78	46	124
Ohio	11	6	14	2	0	1	23	6	48	15	63
Oklahoma	4	2	1	1	6	3	9	9	20	15	35
Oregon	0	1	2	1	2	0	14	6	18	8	26
Pacific	3	0	15	8	0	1	101	53	119	62	181
Pennsylvania	5	2	4	7	0	0	37	18	46	27	73
Pittsburgh	4	0	2	0	0	0	8	6	14	6	20
Puerto Rico	0	0	116	122	0	0	0	0	116	122	238
S. Calif.	3	2	12	10	1	0	135	74	151	86	237
S. Carolina	4	1	2	4	2	1	2	2	10	8	18
So. Illinois	4	1	0	2	0	0	8	6	12	9	21
Stony Brook	0	3	2	2	0	0	1	4	3	9	12
Temple	12	15	24	10	0	1	27	20	63	46	109
Tennessee	8	7	3	2	0	0	10	5	21	14	35
Texas, Houston	10	16	35	26	2	2	30	36	77	80	157
Texas, S.A.	6	1	46	20	0	0	14	6	66	27	93
Tufts	2	8	17	11	5	0	71	31	95	50	145
Virginia	5	5	5	4	0	0	23	22	33	31	64
W. Virginia	3	0	1	0	0	0	8	5	12	5	17

Continued.

Dental Schools with Minority Enrollment
[Continued]

	Black		Hispanic		Am. Indian		Asian		Total		
	M	F	M	F	M	F	M	F	M	F	T
Wash. Seattle	3	2	5	1	2	0	29	13	39	16	55
Washington S.L.	13	2	12	7	1	1	45	26	71	36	107
Total	516	468	778	498	43	20	1423	903	2760	1889	4649
Total for Each Minority	984		1276		63		2326				
% of Total D.S. Enrollment	5.76		7.46		0.37		13.61				27.20

Source: "Total Dental Schools with Minority Enrollment," Black Issues in Higher Education, October 26, 1989, p. 7. Primary source: American Dental Association. *Note:* 1. Historically Black Colleges.

★ 814 ★
Doctoral Male Scientists/Engineers at 4-Year Institutions

Field and racial/ ethnic group	Total, four-year colleges & univer- sities[1]	Tenure Track: Tenured	Tenure Track: Not tenured	Non-tenure track
Total, all fields[2]	174,500	104,400	24,500	12,500
White	156,700	96,000	21,300	10,700
Black	2,600	1,300	500	200
Asian	13,700	6,200	2,500	1,500
Native American	300	200	[4]	[4]
Hispanic[3]	2,800	1,400	500	300
Scientists, totals	151,400	91,000	20,700	11,300
White	137,500	84,300	18,500	9,800
Black	2,400	1,200	300	200
Asian	10,200	4,600	1,600	1,200
Native American	200	200	[4]	[4]
Hispanic	2,400	1,100	500	300
Engineers, total	23,100	13,300	3,800	1,200
White	19,200	11,600	2,700	900
Black	200	100	200	[4]
Asian	3,500	1,600	900	300
Native American	[4]	[4]	[4]	[4]
Hispanic	400	300	[4]	[4]

Source: "Doctoral Men Scientists and Engineers in Four-Year Colleges and Universities, by Field, Racial/Ethnic Group, and Tenure Status: 1987," Women and Minorities in Science and Engineering General:, January 1990, pp. 103-104. Primary source: National Science Foundation, SRS. *Notes:* 1. Includes tenure status unknown and no report. 2. Detail will not add to total employed because a) racial and ethnic categories are not mutually exclusive and b) total employed includes other and no report. 3. Includes members of all racial groups. 4. Too few cases to estimate.

★ 815 ★
Doctoral Scientists/Engineers at 4-Year Institutions

Field and racial/ ethnic group	Total, four-year colleges & univer-sities[1]	Tenure Track: Tenured	Tenure Track: Not tenured	Non-tenure track
Total, all fields[2]	209,400	116,900	32,200	18,600
White	187,900	107,500	28,200	16,200
Black	3,700	1,600	900	300
Asian	16,000	6,800	2,800	2,000
Native American	300	200	[4]	[4]
Hispanic[3]	3,500	1,600	700	400
Scientists, totals	185,700	103,500	28,100	17,300
White	168,300	95,700	25,300	15,300
Black	3,400	1,600	700	300
Asian	12,400	5,300	1,900	1,700
Native American	300	200	[4]	[4]
Hispanic	3,000	1,300	600	400
Engineers, total	23,600	13,400	4,100	1,300
White	19,600	11,700	2,900	900
Black	300	100	200	[4]
Asian	3,600	1,600	900	300
Native American	[4]	[4]	[4]	[4]
Hispanic	400	300	[4]	[4]

Source: "Doctoral Scientists and Engineers in Four-Year Colleges and Universities, by Field, Racial/Ethnic Group, and Tenure Status: 1987," Women and Minorities in Science and Engineering General:, January 1990, pp. 101-102. Primary source: National Science Foundation, SRS. *Notes:* 1. Includes tenure status unknown and no report. 2. Detail will not add to total employed because a) racial and ethnic categories are not mutually exclusive and b) total employed includes other and no report. 3. Includes members of all racial groups. 4. Too few cases to estimate.

★ 816 ★
Doctorate Degrees in Science and Engineering: Trends

Field, gender, and racial/ethnic group	1978	1979	1980	1981	1982	1983	1984	1985	1986	1987	1988
	Total, all degree recipients[1]										
Total, all fields	17,048	17,245	17,199	17,633	17,630	17,976	18,107	18,323	18,859	19,312	20,257
White	12,772	12,733	12,832	13,132	13,093	13,325	13,053	12,875	12,920	12,831	13,244
Black	437	470	483	519	507	505	556	538	477	454	487
Asian	1,901	2,051	2,046	2,099	2,222	2,367	2,628	2,884	2,957	3,333	3,740
Native American	22	29	26	26	37	28	31	40	50	50	43
Hispanic	420	488	465	545	483	516	532	563	611	627	673
Sciences, total	14,625	14,755	14,720	15,105	14,984	15,195	15,194	15,157	15,483	15,600	16,067
White	11,285	11,303	11,405	11,735	11,665	11,822	11,549	11,326	11,218	10,998	11,181
Black	404	416	426	461	454	438	490	466	428	398	420
Asian	1,271	1,337	1,320	1,321	1,411	1,492	1,629	1,752	1,857	2,048	2,283
Native American	20	25	23	22	34	27	28	39	44	42	39
Hispanic	343	403	389	453	395	416	452	477	516	531	549
Engineering, total	2,423	2,490	2,479	2,528	2,646	2,781	2,913	3,166	3,376	3,712	4,190

Continued.

Doctorate Degrees in Science and Engineering: Trends
[Continued]

Field, gender, and racial/ethnic group	1978	1979	1980	1981	1982	1983	1984	1985	1986	1987	1988
White	1,487	1,430	1.427	1,397	1,428	1,503	1,504	1,549	1,702	1,833	2,063
Black	33	54	57	58	53	67	66	72	49	56	67
Asian	630	714	726	778	811	875	999	1,132	1,100	1,285	1,457
Native American	2	4	3	4	3	1	3	1	6	8	4
Hispanic	77	85	76	92	88	100	80	86	95	96	124
U.S. citizens											
Total, all fields	13,086	13,257	13,179	13,298	13,022	13,103	12,977	12,676	12,615	12,563	12,847
White	11,484	11,601	11,647	11,873	11,805	11,866	11,684	11,424	11,406	11,260	11,559
Black	278	288	261	273	270	269	282	260	238	222	231
Asian	275	301	323	327	318	341	380	371	394	440	441
Native American	21	28	26	26	37	27	31	40	49	49	43
Hispanic	160	173	166	191	219	221	250	237	264	293	319
Sciences, total	11,825	11,964	11,924	12,128	11,853	11,940	11,738	11,397	11,232	11,005	11,069
White	10,410	10,516	10,579	10,864	10,790	10,850	10,622	10,327	10,177	9,929	10,032
Black	269	271	250	257	261	250	270	241	224	210	212
Asian	212	232	250	250	246	275	285	281	314	305	300
Native American	19	25	23	22	34	27	28	39	43	42	39
Hispanic	141	158	148	179	196	203	228	221	239	269	276
Engineering, total	1,261	1,293	1,255	1,170	1,169	1,163	1,239	1,279	1,383	1,558	1,778
White	1,074	1,085	1,068	1,009	1,015	1,016	1,062	1,097	1,229	1,331	1,527
Black	9	17	11	16	9	19	12	19	14	12	19
Asian	63	69	73	77	72	66	95	90	80	135	141
Native American	2	3	3	4	3	0	3	1	6	7	4
Hispanic	19	15	18	12	23	18	22	16	25	24	43

Source: "Science and Engineering Doctorate Recipients, by Field, Citizenship, Gender, and Racial/Ethnic Group: 1978-88," *Women and Minorities in Science and Engineering,* January 1990, pp. 149-156. Primary source: National Science Foundation, SRS. *Notes:* 1. Totals for racial/ethnic groups do not include individuals whose citizenship status is unknown.

★817★
Doctorates in Engineering: Trends

Item	1977-78	1978-79	1979-80	1980-81	1981-82	1982-83	1983-84	1984-85	1985-86	1986-87
Number of doctorates	2,423	2,494	2,479	2,528	2,644	2,780	2,915	3,165	3,376	3,716
Racial/ethnic group (percent) [1]										
American Indian	0.5	0.2	0.1	0.2	0.1	[2]	0.1	[2]	0.1	0.2
Asian	26.3	29.0	29.9	31.8	31.5	32.4	35.2	36.4	32.1	34.6
Black	1.4	2.1	2.3	2.3	2.0	2.4	2.3	2.3	1.5	1.5
Mexican-American	[3]	[3]	0.4	0.7	0.3	0.4	0.3	0.3	0.2	0.4
Puerto Rican	[3]	[3]	0.1	0.2	0.4	0.2	0.2	0.2	0.3	0.1
Other Hispanic	[3]	[3]	2.6	2.8	2.7	2.9	2.2	2.2	2.3	2.2
White	60.9	57.6	57.4	55.3	54.3	53.9	51.7	48.9	50.4	49.2
Other and unknown	7.4	7.8	7.1	6.6	8.6	7.3	7.8	9.7	12.5	11.9

Source: "Statistical Profile of Persons Receiving Doctor's Degrees in Engineering: 1977-78 to 1986-87," *Digest of Education Statistics,* 1989, p. 271. Primary source: National Academy of Sciences, National Research Council, Office of Scientific and Engineering Personnel, Doctorate Records File. (This table was prepared March 1989). *Notes:* The National Research Council's classification of degrees by field differs somewhat from that in most publications of the National Center for Education Statistics (NCES). The number of degrees also differs slightly from that reported in the NCES "Degrees and Other Formal Awards Conferred" survey. Because of rounding, percents may not add to 100.0. 1. Longitudinal comparisons by race/ethnicity should be done with extreme care, due to periodic changes in the survey. 2. Less than 0.05 percent. 3. Hispanic subcategories were not collected until 1980. Published by permission.

★ 818 ★
Engineering Fields at HBCUs

Fields	Number of Graduates 1985-86
Electrical	300
Mechanical	175
Civil	136
Architectural	44
Chemical	43
Industrial/Management	34
Computer	2

Source: "HBCUs Offer Engineering Degrees in a Variety of Fields," *NAFEO INROADS,* February-March/April-May, 1989, p. 6. Primary source: Neblett. R.F. "Minorities in Engineering: The Role of the HBCUs in Meeting a National Challenge," *NAFEO INROADS,* February-March/April-May, 1989, pp. 5-6. *Notes:* 1. Tuskegee, Howard, Southern, North Carolina A&T, Tennessee State and Prairie View A&M Universities. Published by permission.

★ 819 ★
Females in Engineering at HBCUs

University	1985-86 Graduates		
	Total	Female Number	Female % Total
Tuskegee	89	21	24
Howard	135	43	32
Southern University	174	13	7
North Carolina A&T	133	26	20
Tennessee State	88	11	13
Prairie View	115	34	30
Total	734	148	20
Total U.S.	78,178	11,264	14

Source: "Female Participation in Engineering at the HBCUs Exceeds the National Rate," *NAFEO INROADS,* February-March/April-May, 1989, p. 6. Primary source: Neblett, R.F. "Minorities in Engineering: The Role of the HBCUs in Meeting a National Challenge," *NAFEO INROADS,* February-March/April-May, 1989, pp. 5-6. HBCUs - Historically Black Colleges and Universities. Published by permission.

★ 820 ★
Fields of Women Scientists/Engineers

Field	Percent				
	Total	White	Black	Asian	Native Amer.
Total	100	100	100	100	100
Scientists, total	86	86	87	80	89
Physical	6	5	5	12	[1]
Mathematical	5	5	7	2	4
Computer specialists	23	24	21	24	15
Environmental	2	2	[1]	1	4
Life	15	15	10	15	37

Continued.

Fields of Women Scientists/Engineers
[Continued]

Field	Percent				
	Total	White	Black	Asian	Native Amer.
Psychologists	16	17	17	12	19
Social	19	19	27	14	15
Engineers, total	14	14	13	20	11

Source: "Field Distribution of Women Scientists and Engineers, by Racial Group: 1986," *Women and Minorities in Science and Engineering,* January 1990, p. 11. *Notes:* Detail may not add to total because of rounding. 1. Too few cases to estimate.

★ 821 ★
First-Professional Degrees Conferred

Major field of study and sex of student	Total	White non-Hispanic	Black non-Hispanic	Hispanic	Asian or Pacific Islander	American Indian/ Alaskan Native	Non-resident alien
All fields, total[1]	71,617	62,688	3,420	2,051	2,270	304	884
Men	46,522	41,149	1,835	1,303	1,420	183	632
Women	25,095	21,539	1,585	748	850	121	252
Dentistry (D.D.S. or D.M.S.), total	4,739	3,856	262	169	319	13	120
Men	3,602	3,006	169	120	218	11	78
Women	1,137	850	93	49	101	2	42
Medicine (M.D.), total	15,429	13,137	786	484	805	66	151
Men	10,431	9,003	437	319	534	36	102
Women	4,998	4,134	349	165	271	30	49
Optometry (O.D.), total	1,082	943	18	29	74	4	14
Men	697	625	8	20	33	3	8
Women	385	318	10	9	41	1	6
Osteopathic medicine (D.O.), total	1,618	1,498	26	25	45	13	11
Men	1,206	1,132	7	17	31	10	9
Women	412	366	19	8	14	3	2
Pharmacy (D.Pharm.), total	861	531	112	42	110	6	60
Men	351	236	37	16	27	6	29
Women	510	295	75	26	83	0	31
Podiatry (Pod.D. or D.P.) or podiatric medicine (D.P.M.), total	591	521	33	11	12	2	12
Men	468	423	18	8	8	2	9
Women	123	98	15	3	4	0	3
Veterinary medicine (D.V.M.), total	2,230	2,052	29	90	24	31	4
Men	1,150	1,035	12	73	11	16	3
Women	1,080	1,017	17	17	13	15	1
Chiropractic medicine (D.C. or D.C.M.), total	2,493	2,298	26	39	30	4	96
Men	1,864	1,723	16	28	25	3	69

Continued.

First-Professional Degrees Conferred
[Continued]

Major field of study and sex of student	Total	White non-Hispanic	Black non-Hispanic	Hispanic	Asian or Pacific Islander	American Indian/ Alaskan Native	Non-resident alien
Women	629	575	10	11	5	1	27
Law, general (LL.B or J.D.), total	36,056	32,242	1,735	1,054	694	152	179
Men	21,561	19,528	822	610	393	84	124
Women	14,495	12,714	913	444	301	68	55
Theological professions, general (B.D., M.Div., Rabbi), total	6,518	5,610	393	108	157	13	237
Men	5,192	4,438	309	92	140	12	201
Women	1,326	1,172	84	16	17	1	36

Source: "First-Professional Degrees Conferred by Institutions of Higher Education, by Racial/Ethnic Group, Major Field of Study, and Sex of Student: 1986-87," *Digest of Educational Statistics,* 1989, p. 251. Primary source: U.S. Department of Education, National Center for Educational Statistics, Integrated Postsecondary Education Data System (IPEDS), "Completions" survey. (This table was prepared June 1989.) *Notes:* 1. This tabulation excludes 938 men and 195 women whose racial/ethnic group could not be imputed. Because of imputation methods, field of study totals by race/ethnicity may differ slightly from field of study by sex. Data are preliminary.

★ 822 ★
From Applicants to Practitioners in Medicine

Factor	Year		
	1975	1980	1985
Applicants	5.4	7.2	7.4
Acceptees	6.2	6.2	5.8
First Year	6.0	6.0	6.1
Enrollment	6.2	5.7	5.8
Graduates	5.4	4.9	5.1
Practitioners	-	2.5	3.0

Source: "Medicine: Blacks as a Percent of Total (Impacting Factors)," *NAFEO INROADS,* October/ November, 1987, p. 3. Published by permission.

★ 823 ★
From Law School Applicant to Attorney: Trends

Factor	1975	Year 1980	1985
Applicants	-	-	7.4
Acceptees	-	-	-
First Year Entrants	5.2	5.1	5.4
Enrollment Medical School	4.4	4.4	4.9
Graduates	-	4.2	4.2[1]
Practitioners	-	4.2	2.6[1]

Source: "Parity Levels, Law: Blacks as a Percent of Total (Impacting Factors), *NAFEO INROADS*, October/November 1987, p. 4. NAFEO: National Association for Equal Opportunity in Education. *Note:* 1. 1984 data were used. Published by permission.

★ 824 ★
Parity in Law

Factor	Standards Population	High School Completions	College Enrollment
Applicants			
1975	-	-	-
1980	5.2	3.7	3.1
1985	4.7	3.3	3.4[1]
First Year Entrants			
1975	6.3	4.3	3.1
1980	6.7	5.2	4.5
1985	6.7	5.3	5.0
Enrollment Professional School			
1975	7.1	5.1	3.8
1980	7.4	5.9	5.3
1985	7.3	5.8	5.5
Graduates			
1975	-	-	-
1980	7.6	6.1	5.5
1985	7.9	6.5	6.2
Practitioners			
1975	-	-	-
1980	7.6	6.1	5.5
1985	9.5	8.1	7.8

Source: "Parity Levels, Law Profession (Blacks as a Percent of Total)," *NAFEO INROADS*, October/November 1987, p. 4. *Note:* 1. 1984 data were used. Published by permission.

★ 825 ★
Graduate Enrollment in Science/Engineering

Field, citizenship, and racial/ethnic background	1980[1]	1981[1]	1982	1983	1984	1985	1986	1987	1988
Total science and engineering	297,264	302,390	309,547	317,865	320,506	328,256	338,349	343,228	347,533
Total U.S. citizens	[2]	[2]	248,448	251,283	251,975	255,329	258,413	258,491	258,396
Black, non-Hispanic	8,033	7,832	8,997	9,241	8,883	8,769	8,870	8,765	9,395
Asian/Pacific Islander	6,555	6,219	7,168	7,927	8,746	10,526	11,355	12,867	14,020
Hispanic	5,662	5,776	7,211	7,931	7,897	7,928	8,250	8,446	8,438
White, non-Hispanic	178,508	170,576	198,190	207,211	205,612	206,818	211,184	211,589	212,028
Other or unknown	647	540	26,882	18,973	20,837	21,288	18,854	16,824	14,515
Foreign	[2]	[2]	61,099	66,582	68,531	72,927	79,936	84,737	89,137
Total science	227,121	228,017	231,369	232,541	233,391	238,017	242,555	246,226	250,555
Total U.S. citizens	[2]	[2]	194,320	192,362	191,614	192,790	193,427	193,754	195,075
Black, non-Hispanic	7,199	7,051	8,013	8,038	7,588	7,539	7,561	7,486	8,065
Asian/Pacific Islander	4,054	4,207	4,759	5,094	5,468	6,246	6,708	7,685	8,356
Hispanic	4,672	4,907	6,217	6,622	6,521	6,588	6,712	6,850	6,850
White, non-Hispanic	143,144	135,272	158,150	161,928	159,546	159,080	161,523	161,313	163,116
Other or unknown	572	432	17,181	10,680	12,491	12,619	11,023	10,420	8,688
Foreign	[2]	[2]	37,049	40,179	41,777	45,227	49,128	52,472	55,480
Engineering	70,143	74,373	78,178	85,324	87,115	90,239	95,794	97,002	96,978
Total U.S. citizens	[2]	[2]	54,128	58,921	60,361	62,539	64,986	64,737	63,321
Black, non-Hispanic	834	781	984	1,203	1,295	1,230	1,309	1,279	1,330
Asian/Pacific Islander	2,501	2,012	2,409	2,833	3,278	4,280	4,647	5,182	5,664
Hispanic	990	869	994	1,309	1,376	1,340	1,538	1,596	1,588
White, non-Hispanic	35,364	35,304	40,040	45,283	46,066	47,010	49,661	50,276	48,912
Other or unknown	75	108	9,701	8,293	8,346	8,679	7,831	6,404	5,827
Foreign	[2]	[2]	24,050	26,403	26,754	27,700	30,808	32,265	33,657

Source: "Science/Engineering Graduate Enrollment in Doctorate-Granting Institutions, by Field, Citizenship, and Racial/Ethnic Background: 1980-1988," *Science and Engineering Indicators - 1989*, 1989, pp. 216-217. Primary source: NSF, Division of Science Resources Studies. *Notes:* 1. For part-time students, distribution by citizenship was not requested prior to 1982. 2. Not available.

★ 826 ★
Graduate Support of Science/Engineering Doctorate Recipients

Field	Total known support	Family support	University					Federal support	Student loan	Other
			Total	Teaching assistant-ship	Research assistant-ship	Fellow-ship	Other			
Total										
Total, all fields	16,846	4,008	8,181	3,090	4,027	802	262	2,792	603	1,262
Sciences, total	13,389	3,490	6,286	2,651	2,757	660	218	2,230	574	809
Engineering, total	3,457	518	1,895	439	1,270	142	44	562	29	453
Men										
Total, all fields	12,302	2,602	6,244	2,308	3,224	559	153	2,083	318	1,055
Sciences, total	9,087	2,104	4,486	1,9063	2,036	430	114	1,574	292	631
Engineering, total	3,215	498	1,758	402	1,188	129	39	509	26	424

Continued.

Graduate Support of Science/Engineering Doctorate Recipients
[Continued]

| Field | Total known support | Family support | University | | | | | Federal support | Student loan | Other |
			Total	Teaching assistant- ship	Research assistant- ship	Fellow- ship	Other			
					Women					
Total, all fields	4,544	1,406	1,937	782	803	243	109	709	285	207
Sciences, total	4,302	1,386	1,800	745	721	230	104	656	282	178
Engineering, total	242	20	137	37	82	13	5	53	3	29
					White					
Total, all fields	12,067	3,288	5,463	2,091	2,586	575	211	2,104	532	680
Sciences, total	10,182	2,960	4,539	1,907	1,972	482	178	1,751	510	422
Engineering, total	1,885	328	924	184	614	93	33	353	22	258
					Black					
Total, all fields	435	120	177	62	75	31	9	55	18	65
Sciences, total	374	108	148	51	63	26	8	50	18	50
engineering, total	61	12	29	11	12	5	1	5	0	15
					Asian					
Total, all fields	3,213	386	2,054	754	1,134	139	27	461	11	301
Sciences, total	1,942	245	1,225	547	551	106	21	292	6	174
Engineering, total	1,271	141	829	207	583	33	6	169	5	127
					Native American					
Total, all fields	36	16	8	3	5	0	0	6	3	3
Sciences, total	32	15	7	2	5	0	0	5	3	2
Engineering, total	4	1	1	1	0	0	0	1	0	1
					Hispanic					
Total, all fields	605	117	230	80	111	31	8	97	28	133
Sciences, total	498	102	187	67	87	27	6	79	27	103
Engineering, total	107	15	43	13	24	4	2	18	1	30

Source: "Primary Source of Graduate Support Reported by 1988 Science and Engineering Doctorate Recipients, by Source, Field, Gender, and Racial/ Ethnic Group," *Women and Minorities in Science and Engineering*, January 1990, pp. 157-159. National Science Foundation, SRS. *Note:* Data are for all degree recipients regardless of citizenship.

★ 827 ★
HBCU Engineering Graduates: Trends

Year	Number of Minority Engineering Graduates, 6 HBCUs[1]		
	Total U.S.	Number	Percent Total U.S.
1974-75	1,435	183	12.8
1979-80	2,383	340	14.2
1985-86	4,107	466	11.3
1986-87	4,171	468	11.2

Source: "HBCUs Make a Significant Contribution to the Supply of Minority Engineers," *NAFEO INROADS*, February-March/April-May, 1989, p. 6. Primary source: Neblett, R.F. "Minorities in Engineering: The Role of the HBCUs in Meeting a National Challenge," *NAFEO INROADS*, February-March/April-May, 1989, pp. 5-6. HBCUs - Historically Black Colleges and Universities. *Notes:* 1. Tuskegee, Howard, Southern, North Carolina A&T, Tennessee State and Prairie View A&M Universities. Published by permission.

★ 828 ★
HBCU Female Science/Engineering Graduate Students: Trends

Field	Number							Average annual percent change		
	1980	1981	1982	1983	1984	1985	1986	1980-85	1985-86	1980-86
Total, all fields	1,335	1,377	1,452	1,554	1,613	1,502	1,467	2.4	-2.3	1.6
Engineering	19	16	25	37	41	36	59	13.6	63.9	20.8
Aerospace	0	0	0	0	0	0	0	0	0	0
Agricultural	0	0	0	0	0	0	0	0	0	0
Biomedical	0	0	0	0	0	0	0	0	0	0
Chemical	0	0	0	0	0	0	0	0	0	0
Civil	10	7	12	14	11	9	20	-2.1	122.2	12.2
Electrical	1	4	3	7	10	11	11	61.5	.0	49.1
Engineering Science	0	0	0	0	0	0	0	0	0	0
Industrial	3	1	0	5	5	7	0	18.5	-100.0	-100.0
Mechanical	1	0	1	2	7	7	3	47.6	-57.1	20.1
Metallurgical/Materials	0	0	0	0	0	0	0	0	0	0
Mining	0	0	0	0	0	0	0	0	0	0
Nuclear	0	0	0	0	0	0	0	0	0	0
Petroleum	0	0	0	0	0	0	0	0	0	0
Engineering, N.E.C.	4	4	9	9	8	2	25	-12.9	1150.0	35.7
Sciences, total	1,316	1,361	1,427	1,517	1,572	1,466	1,408	2.2	-4.0	1.1
Physical Sciences	73	85	104	122	112	113	85	9.1	-24.8	2.6
Astronomy	0	0	0	0	0	0	0	0	0	0
Chemistry	67	76	91	105	98	93	60	6.8	-35.5	-1.8
Physics	6	9	12	10	7	8	13	5.9	62.5	13.8
Physical sciences, N.E.C.	0	0	3	7	7	12	12	...	.0	...
Environmental Sciences	12	5	12	16	19	7	9	-10.2	28.6	-4.7
Atmospheric Sciences	0	0	0	0	0	0	0	0	0	0

Continued.

HBCU Female Science/Engineering Graduate Students: Trends
[Continued]

Field	Number							Average annual percent change		
	1980	1981	1982	1983	1984	1985	1986	1980-85	1985-86	1980-86
Geosciences	3	1	6	10	14	5	9	10.8	80.0	20.1
Oceanography	0	0	0	0	0	0	0	0	0	0
Environmental Sciences, N.E.C.	9	4	6	6	5	2	0	-26.0	-100.0	-100.0
Mathemical Sciences	86	81	95	96	104	100	105	3.1	5.0	3.4
Computer Sciences	38	54	82	86	99	84	83	17.2	-1.2	13.9
Life Sciences	374	386	436	431	417	417	360	2.2	-13.7	-.6
Agricultural Sciences	22	13	13	14	7	15	9	-7.4	-40.0	-13.8
Bioilogical Sciences	257	270	289	272	262	257	222	.0	-13.6	-2.4
Anatomy	3	3	5	3	2	7	6	18.5	-14.3	12.2
Biochemistry	3	9	11	7	7	5	5	10.8	.0	8.9
Biology	144	141	157	150	150	153	137	1.2	-10.5	-.8
Biometry/Epidemiology	0	0	0	0	0	0	0	0	0	0
Biophysics	0	0	0	0	0	0	0	0	0	0
Botany	15	20	35	35	6	9	11	-9.7	22.2	-5.0
Cell Biology	0	0	0	0	0	0	0	0	0	0
Ecology	0	0	0	0	0	0	0	0	0	0
Entomology/Parasitology	0	0	0	0	0	0	0	0	0	0
Genetics	9	10	19	15	18	17	18	13.6	5.9	12.2
Microbiology	12	17	13	18	16	12	8	.0	-33.3	-6.5
Nutrition	16	9	11	4	7	9	9	-10.9	.0	-9.1
Pathology	0	0	0	0	0	0	0	0	0	0
Pharmacology	14	13	14	15	12	11	9	-4.7	-18.2	-7.1
Physiology	9	9	4	5	9	11	5	4.1	-54.5	-9.3
Zoology	22	28	10	10	15	11	6	-12.9	-45.5	-19.5
Biosciences, N.E.C.	10	11	10	10	20	12	8	3.7	-33.3	-3.7
Health Sciences	95	103	134	145	148	145	129	8.8	-11.0	5.2
Dentistry	0	0	0	0	0	0	0	0	0	0
Neurology	0	0	0	0	0	0	0	0	0	0
Nursing	45	45	63	67	58	46	39	.4	-19.6	-3.2
Pharmaceutical Sciences	5	0	4	4	4	5	5	.0	.0	.0
Preventive Medicine/ Community Health	9	5	5	4	0	0	0	-100.0	...	-100.0
Speech Pathology/Audiology	36	45	53	56	78	82	81	17.9	-1.2	14.5
Veterinary Sciences	0	8	9	14	6	5	3	...	-40.0	...
Clinical Medicine, N.E.C.	0	0	0	0	2	0	0	...	...	...
Health Related, N.E.C.	0	0	0	0	0	7	3	...	-57.1	...
Psychology	149	158	130	207	242	227	252	8.8	11.0	9.2
Social Sciences	584	592	566	559	579	518	514	-2.4	-.8	-2.1
Agricultural Economics	5	5	6	9	9	8	8	9.9	.0	8.1
Anthropology	0	0	0	0	0	0	0	0	0	0
Economics (except Agricultural)	36	35	89	30	34	30	33	-3.6	10.0	-1.4

Continued.

HBCU Female Science/Engineering Graduate Students: Trends
[Continued]

Field	Number							Average annual percent change		
	1980	1981	1982	1983	1984	1985	1986	1980-85	1985-86	1980-86
Geography	0	0	0	0	0	0	0	0	0	0
History and Philosophy of Science	0	0	0	0	0	0	0	0	0	0
Linguistics	79	71	21	33	87	86	86	1.7	.0	1.4
Political Science	171	154	122	135	140	118	139	-7.2	17.8	-3.4
Sociology	66	130	110	109	110	109	102	10.6	-6.4	7.5
Sociology/Anthropology	46	52	64	72	60	37	33	-4.3	-10.8	-5.4
Social Sciences, N.E.C.	181	145	154	171	139	130	113	-6.4	-13.1	-7.6

Source: "Female Science/Engineering Graduates in Historically Black Colleges and Universities (HBCUs) by Field: 1980-86," *Selected Data on Historically Black Colleges and Universities, Academic Year 1986,* December 1987. Primary source: National Science Foundation. Figures include all area/ethnic groups enrolled.

★ 829 ★
HBCU Full-Time Science/Engineering Graduate Students: Trends

Type and Source of Major Support	Number							Average annual percent change		
	1980	1981	1982	1983	1984	1985	1986	1980-85	1985-86	1980-86
Total, all types:										
Total, all sources	2,322	2,504	2,326	2,322	2,411	2,389	2,198	.6	-8.0	-.9
Federal, total	622	597	591	553	611	718	575	2.9	-19.9	-1.3
Dept. of Defense	18	22	20	33	50	38	54	16.1	42.1	20.1
Dept. of HHS, total	318	218	231	220	225	215	210	-7.5	-2.3	-6.7
NIH	227	175	190	187	181	165	154	-6.2	-6.7	-6.3
Other HHS	91	43	41	33	44	50	56	-11.3	12.0	-7.8
NSF	85	103	70	50	39	25	33	-21.7	32.0	-14.6
All other federal	201	254	270	250	297	440	278	17.0	-36.8	5.6
Institutional support	674	625	643	673	609	428	481	-8.7	12.4	-5.5
Other outside support, total	113	93	141	176	114	105	173	-1.5	64.8	7.4
All other U.S.	70	67	105	136	94	80	150	2.7	87.5	13.5
Foreign	43	26	36	40	20	25	23	-10.3	-8.0	-9.9
Self-support	913	1,190	951	920	1,077	1,138	969	4.5	-14.9	1.0
Fellowships:										
Total, all sources	191	242	276	272	252	264	164	6.7	-37.9	-2.5
Federal, total	83	95	99	69	99	145	92	11.8	-36.6	1.7
Dept. of Defense	2	1	0	0	3	0	0	-100.0	...	-100.0
Dept. of HHS, total	34	23	17	15	18	30	16	-2.5	-46.7	-11.8
NIH	10	21	12	5	13	21	7	16.0	-66.7	-5.8
Other HHS	24	2	5	10	5	9	9	-17.8	.0	-15.1
NSF	14	26	12	10	7	10	5	-6.5	-50.0	-15.85
All other federal	33	45	70	44	71	105	71	26.0	-32.4	13.6
Institutional support	80	114	108	108	100	70	53	-2.6	-24.3	-6.6
Other outside support, total	28	33	69	95	53	49	19	11.8	-61.2	-6.3
All other U.S.	17	19	58	73	39	31	10	12.8	-67.7	-8.5
Foreign	11	14	11	22	14	18	9	10.4	-50.0	-3.3
Self-support	0	0	0	0	0	0	0	0	0	0

Continued.

HBCU Full-Time Science/Engineering Graduate Students: Trends
[Continued]

Type and Source of Major Support	Number							Average annual percent change		
	1980	1981	1982	1983	1984	1985	1986	1980-85	1985-86	1980-86
Traineeships:										
Total, all sources	239	226	216	220	208	174	178	-6.2	2.3	-4.8
Federal, total	194	211	189	185	185	155	130	-4.4	-16.1	-6.5
Dept. of Defense	0	0	1	5	1	0	0	...	...	...
Dept. of HHS, total	145	117	118	110	127	113	115	-4.9	1.8	-3.8
NIH	103	88	96	93	90	72	73	-6.9	1.4	-5.6
Other HHS	42	29	22	17	37	41	42	-.5	2.4	.0
NSF	38	43	37	19	8	1	2	-51.7	100.0	-38.8
All other federal	11	51	33	51	49	41	13	30.1	-68.3	2.8
Institutional support	41	11	20	25	18	18	38	-15.2	111.1	-1.3
Other outside support, total	4	4	7	10	5	1	10	-24.2	900.0	16.5
All other U.S.	4	4	3	0	1	1	3	-24.2	200.0	-4.7
Foreign	0	0	4	10	4	0	7	...	...	...
Self-support	0	0	0	0	0	0	0	0	0	0
Research Assistantships:										
Total, all sources	340	353	324	362	423	329	351	-.7	6.7	.5
Federal, total	258	214	229	243	274	274	260	1.2	-5.1	.1
Dept. of Defense	11	16	14	27	45	38	40	28.1	5.3	24.0
Dept. of HHS, total	100	74	85	85	76	65	70	-8.3	7.7	-5.8
NIH	99	66	77	80	76	65	65	-8.1	.0	-6.8
Other HHS	1	8	8	5	0	0	5	-100.0	...	30.8
NSF	27	28	18	18	18	14	23	-12.3	64.3	-2.6
All other federal	120	96	112	113	135	157	127	5.5	-19.1	.9
Institutional support	58	113	79	103	118	38	70	-8.1	84.2	3.2
Other outside support, total	24	26	16	16	31	17	21	-6.7	23.5	-2.2
All other U.S.	16	19	14	15	30	11	15	-7.2	36.4	-1.1
Foreign	8	7	2	1	1	6	6	-5.6	.0	-4.7
Self-support	0	0	0	0	0	0	0	0	0	0
Teaching Assistantships:										
Total, all sources	379	303	385	357	323	307	308	-4.1	.3	-3.4
Federal, total	24	6	16	3	7	52	35	16.7	-32.7	6.5
Dept. of Defense	0	0	0	0	0	0	0	0	0	0
Dept. of HHS, total	6	0	8	3	2	2	2	-19.7	.0	-16.7
NIH	1	0	2	3	0	2	2	14.9	.0	12.2
Other HHS	5	0	6	0	2	0	0	-100.0	...	-100.0
NSF	6	0	0	0	4	0	3	-100.0	...	-10.9
All other federal	12	6	8	0	1	50	30	33.0	-40.0	16.5
Institutional support	352	291	357	350	296	236	252	-7.7	6.8	-5.4
Other outside support, total	3	6	12	4	20	19	21	44.7	10.5	38.3
All other U.S.	3	6	12	4	20	19	21	44.7	10.5	38.3
Foreign	0	0	0	0	0	0	0	0	0	0
Self-support	0	0	0	0	0	0	0	0	0	0
Other Types of Support:										
Total, all sources	1,173	1,381	1,125	1,111	1,205	1,315	1,197	2.3	-9.0	.3
Federal, total	63	71	58	53	46	92	58	7.9	-37.0	-1.4
Dept. of Defense	5	5	5	1	1	0	14	-100.0	...	18.7

Continued.

HBCU Full-Time Science/Engineering Graduate Students: Trends
[Continued]

Type and Source of Major Support	Number							Average annual percent change		
	1980	1981	1982	1983	1984	1985	1986	1980-85	1985-86	1980-86
Dept. of HHS, total	33	4	3	7	2	5	7	-31.4	40.0	-22.8
NIH	14	0	3	6	2	5	7	-18.6	40.0	-10.9
Other HHS	19	4	0	1	0	0	0	-100.0	...	-100.0
NSF	0	6	3	3	2	0	0	...	...	...
All other federal	25	56	47	42	41	87	37	28.3	-57.5	6.8
Institutional support	143	96	79	87	77	66	68	-14.3	3.0	-11.7
Other outside support, total	54	24	37	51	5	19	102	-18.9	436.8	11.2
All other U.S.	30	19	18	44	4	18	101	-9.7	461.1	22.4
Foreign	24	5	19	7	1	1	1	-47.0	.0	-41.1
Self-support	913	1,190	951	920	1,077	1,138	969	4.5	-14.9	1.0

Source: "Full-Time Science/Engineering Graduates in Historically Black Colleges and Universities (HBCUs) by Field: 1980-86," *Selected Data on Historically Black Colleges and Universities, Academic Year 1986,* December 1987. Primary source: National Science Foundation. Figures include all area/ethnic groups enrolled.

★ 830 ★
HBCU Male Science/Engineering Graduate Students: Trends

Field	Number							Average annual percent change		
	1980	1981	1982	1983	1984	1985	1986	1980-85	1985-86	1980-86
Total, all fields	1,983	2,119	1,928	2,002	2,324	2,147	2,048	1.6	-4.6	.5
Engineering	245	226	242	274	364	306	315	4.5	2.9	4.3
Aerospace	0	0	0	0	0	0	0	0	0	0
Agricultural	0	0	0	0	0	0	0	0	0	0
Biomedical	0	0	0	0	0	0	0	0	0	0
Chemical	0	0	0	0	0	0	0	0	0	0
Civil	75	46	32	33	54	37	27	-13.2	-27.0	-15.7
Electrical	45	62	61	87	121	110	50	19.6	-54.5	1.8
Engineering Science	0	0	0	0	0	0	0	[1]	[1]	[1]
Industrial	23	6	8	18	32	13	0	-10.8	-100.0	-100.0
Mechanical	21	30	29	45	86	74	60	28.6	-18.9	19.1
Metallurgical/Materials	0	0	0	0	0	0	0	0	0	0
Mining	0	0	0	0	0	0	0	00	0	0
Nuclear	0	0	0	0	0	0	0	[1]	[1]	[1]
Petroleum	0	0	0	0	0	0	0	0	0	0
Engineering, N.E.C.	81	82	112	91	71	72	178	-2.3	147.2	14.0
Sciences, total	1,738	1,893	1,686	1,728	1,960	1,841	1,733	1.2	-5.9	[1]
Physical Sciences	175	199	182	197	235	207	214	3.4	3.4	3.4
Astronomy	0	0	0	0	0	0	0	0	0	0
Chemistry	128	141	135	145	171	135	136	1.1	.7	1.0
Physics	47	58	46	47	58	64	71	6.4	10.9	7.1
Physical sciences, N.E.C.	0	0	1	5	6	8	7	[1]	-12.5	[1]
Environmental Sciences	18	18	19	16	20	27	10	8.4	-63.0	-9.3
Atmospheric Sciences	0	0	0	0	0	0	0	0	0	0
Geosciences	6	1	7	6	9	12	10	14.9	-16.7	8.9
Oceanography	0	0	0	0	0	0	0	0	0	0
Environmental Sciences, N.E.C.	12	17	12	10	11	15	0	4.6	-100.0	-100.0
Mathemical Sciences	68	87	111	139	162	140	160	15.5	14.3	15.3
Computer Sciences	101	96	150	185	221	220	196	16.8	-10.9	11.7

Continued.

HBCU Male Science/Engineering Graduate Students: Trends
[Continued]

Field	Number							Average annual percent change		
	1980	1981	1982	1983	1984	1985	1986	1980-85	1985-86	1980-86
Life Sciences	467	449	422	421	410	311	306	-7.8	-1.6	-6.8
Agricultural Sciences	50	70	74	68	102	51	46	.4	-9.8	-1.4
Biological Sciences	383	340	316	321	274	222	225	-10.3	1.4	-8.5
Anatomy	4	5	5	5	4	4	3	.0	-25.0	-4.7
Biochemistry	18	12	11	11	12	6	9	-19.7	50.0	-10.9
Biology	218	182	177	173	151	114	92	-12.2	-19.3	-13.4
Biometry/Epidemiology	0	0	0	0	0	0	0	0	0	0
Biophysics	0	0	0	0	0	0	0	0	0	0
Botany	24	30	10	9	11	7	26	-21.8	271.4	1.3
Cell Biology	0	0	0	0	0	0	0	0	0	0
Ecology	0	0	0	0	0	0	0	0	0	0
Entomology/Parasitology	0	0	0	0	0	0	0	0	0	0
Genetics	4	6	6	12	11	13	14	26.6	7.7	23.2
Microbiology	9	10	11	8	8	9	6	.0	-33.3	-6.5
Nutrition	23	30	25	16	29	25	25	1.7	.0	1.4
Pathology	0	0	0	0	0	0	0	0	0	0
Pharmacology	28	21	21	21	13	4	8	-32.2	100.0	-18.8
Physiology	5	8	10	14	13	16	15	26.2	-6.3	20.1
Zoology	44	27	31	30	14	14	16	-20.5	14.3	-15.5
Biosciences, N.E.C.	6	9	9	22	8	10	11	10.8	10.0	10.6
Health Sciences	34	39	32	32	34	38	35	2.2	-7.9	.5
Dentistry	0	0	0	0	0	0	0	0	0	0
Neurology	0	0	0	0	0	0	0	0	0	0
Nursing	1	0	0	1	1	0	1	-100.0	[1]	10.0
Pharmaceutical Sciences	10	15	8	9	9	11	10	1.9	-9.1	.0
Preventive Medicine/Community Health	5	6	3	7	0	0	0	-100.0	[1]	-100.0
Speech Pathology/Audiology	3	3	5	3	3	2	2	-7.8	.0	-6.5
Veterinary Sciences	15	15	16	12	20	22	20	8.0	-9.1	4.9
Clinical Medicine, N.E.C.	0	0	0	0	1	0	0	[1]	[1]	[1]
Health Related, N.E.C.	0	0	0	0	0	3	2	[1]	-33.3	[1]
Psychology	142	110	97	177	194	177	167	4.5	-5.6	2.7
Social Sciences	767	934	705	543	718	759	680	-.2	-10.4	-2.0
Agricultural Economics	30	17	33	44	53	55	49	12.9	-10.9	8.5
Anthropology	0	0	0	0	0	0	0	0	0	0
Economics (except Agricultural)	139	215	195	76	101	131	114	-1.2	-13.0	-3.3
Geography	0	0	0	0	0	0	0	0	0	0
History and Philosophy of Science	0	0	0	0	0	0	0	0	0	0
Linguistics	45	33	3	10	50	43	43	-.9	.0	-.8
Political Science	279	298	164	162	252	227	250	-4.0	10.1	-1.8
Sociology	58	153	107	105	63	117	77	15.1	-34.2	4.8
Sociology/Anthropology	56	43	41	41	53	43	27	-5.1	-37.2	-11.4
Social Sciences, N.E.C.	160	175	162	155	146	143	120	-2.2	-16.1	-4.7

Source: "Male Science/Engineering Graduates in Historically Black Colleges and Universities (HBCUs) by Field: 1980-86," *Selected Data on Historically Black Colleges and Universities, Academic Year 1986,* December 1987. Primary source: National Science Foundation. Figures include all race/ethnic groups enrolled. *Note:* 1. Less than 0.05- percent change.

★ 831 ★
HBCU Part-Time Science/Engineering Graduate Students: Trends

Field	Number							Average annual percent change		
	1980	1981	1982	1983	1984	1985	1986	1980-85	1985-86	1980-86
Total, all fields	996	991	1,054	1,234	1,526	1,260	1,317	4.8	4.5	4.8
Engineering	73	72	75	116	147	69	177	-1.1	156.5	15.9
Aerospace	0	0	0	0	0	0	0	0	0	0
Agricultural	0	0	0	0	0	0	0	0	0	0
Biomedical	0	0	0	0	0	0	0	0	0	0
Chemical	0	0	0	0	0	0	0	0	0	0
Civil	17	10	13	13	27	4	15	-25.1	275.0	-2.1
Electrical	9	7	7	10	29	10	16	2.1	60.0	10.1
Engineering Science	0	0	0	0	0	0	0	...	...	...
Industrial	10	0	0	13	15	2	0	-27.5	-100.0	-100.0
Mechanical	5	5	4	13	30	10	3	14.9	-70.0	-8.2
Metallurgical/Materials	0	0	0	0	0	0	0	0	0	0
Mining	0	0	0	0	0	0	0	0	0	0
Nuclear	0	0	0	0	0	0	0	...	...	...
Petroleum	0	0	0	0	0	0	0	0	0	0
Engineering, N.E.C.	32	50	51	67	46	43	143	6.1	232.6	28.3
Sciences, total	923	919	979	1,118	1,379	1,191	1,140	5.2	-4.3	3.6
Physical Sciences	36	29	32	48	89	58	60	10.0	3.4	8.9
Astronomy	0	0	0	0	0	0	0	0	0	0
Chemistry	30	24	21	28	64	34	27	2.5	-20.6	-1.7
Physics	6	5	8	8	13	7	20	3.1	185.7	22.2
Physical sciences, N.E.C.	0	0	3	12	12	17	13	...	-23.5	...
Environmental Sciences	10	5	2	5	14	9	12	-2.1	33.3	3.1
Atmospheric Sciences	0	0	0	0	0	0	0	0	0	0
Geosciences	8	2	2	5	14	9	12	2.4	33.3	7.0
Oceanography	0	0	0	0	0	0	0	0	0	0
Environmental Sciences, N.E.C.	2	3	0	0	0	0	0	-100.0	...	-100.0
Mathemical Sciences	53	48	95	98	127	99	122	13.3	23.2	14.9
Computer Sciences	43	63	79	86	118	92	73	16.4	-20.7	9.2
Life Sciences	228	219	216	178	209	197	170	-2.9	-13.7	-4.8
Agricurtural Sciences	31	41	41	43	30	39	29	4.7	-25.6	-1.1
Bioilogical Sciences	149	131	118	82	114	110	99	-5.9	-10.0	-6.6
Anatomy	0	0	0	0	0	0	0	...	...	...
Biochemistry	0	0	0	0	0	0	0	0	0	0
Biology	115	103	92	63	83	95	80	-3.7	-15.8	-5.9
Biometry/Epidemiology	0	0	0	0	0	0	0	0	0	0
Biophysics	0	0	0	0	0	0	0	0	0	0
Botany	16	13	12	12	12	5	6	-20.8	20.0	-15.1
Cell Biology	0	0	0	0	0	0	0	0	0	0

Continued.

HBCU Part-Time Science/Engineering Graduate Students: Trends
[Continued]

Field	Number							Average annual percent change		
	1980	1981	1982	1983	1984	1985	1986	1980-85	1985-86	1980-86
Ecology	0	0	0	0	0	0	0	0	0	0
Entomology/Parasitology	0	0	0	0	0	0	0	0	0	0
Genetics	0	0	0	2	2	3	3	...	.0	...
Microbiology	0	0	0	0	0	1	0	...	-100.0	...
Nutrition	5	2	8	0	0	0	2	-100.0	...	-14.2
Pathology	0	0	0	0	0	0	0	0	0	0
Pharmacology	4	2	3	2	1	0	1	-100.0	...	-20.6
Physiology	0	0	0	0	0	1	1	...	.0	...
Zoology	5	10	2	2	11	2	5	-16.7	150.0	.0
Biosciences, N.E.C.	4	1	1	1	5	3	1	-5.6	-66.7	-20.6
Health Sciences	48	47	57	53	65	48	42	.0	-12.5	-2.2
Dentistry	0	0	0	0	0	0	0	0	0	0
Neurology	0	0	0	0	0	0	0	0	0	0
Nursing	27	22	23	21	30	12	10	-15.0	-16.7	-15.3
Pharmaceutical Sciences	0	0	0	0	0	0	0	0	0	0
Preventive Medicine/										
Community Health	0	5	2	1	0	0	0	...	...	...
Speech Pathology/Audiology	18	19	29	31	32	33	29	12.9	-12.1	8.3
Veterinary Sciences	3	1	3	0	3	3	3	.0	.0	.0
Clinical Medicine, N.E.C.	0	0	0	0	0	0	0	...	...	...
Health Related, N.E.C.	0	0	0	0	0	0	0	0	0	0
Psychology	113	115	107	252	263	245	236	16.7	-3.7	13.1
Social Sciences	440	440	448	451	559	491	467	2.2	-4.9	1.0
Agricultural Economics	4	2	20	3	13	22	19	40.6	-13.6	29.7
Anthropology	0	0	0	0	0	0	0	0	0	0
Economics (except Agricultural)	42	40	50	46	76	58	56	6.7	-3.4	4.9
Geography	0	0	0	0	0	0	0	0	0	0
History and Philosophy of Science	0	0	0	0	0	0	0	0	0	0
Linguistics	41	20	5	5	76	57	57	6.8	.0	5.6
Political Science	138	120	124	154	147	129	140	-1.3	8.5	.2
Sociology	56	89	89	78	76	85	88	8.7	3.5	7.8
Sociology/Anthropology	59	48	31	32	52	31	33	-12.1	6.5	-9.2
Social Sciences, N.E.C.	100	121	129	133	119	109	74	1.7	-32.1	-4.9

Source: "Part-Time Science/Engineering Graduates in Historically Black Colleges and Universities (HBCUs) by Field: 1980-86," *Selected Data on Historically Black Colleges and Universities, Academic Year 1986,* December 1987. Primary source: National Science Foundation. Figures include all area/ethnic groups enrolled.

★ 832 ★
HBCU Science/Engineering Graduate Students

Field	Total	U.S. Citizens						Foreign
		Black non-Hispanic	American Indian/Alaskan Native	Asian/Pacific Islander	Hispanic	White non-Hispanic	Other or unknown	
Total, all fields	3,515	1,779	2	76	19	344	93	1,202
Engineering	374	88	0	8	1	29	39	209
Aerospace	0	0	0	0	0	0	0	0
Agricultural	0	0	0	0	0	0	0	0
Biomedical	0	0	0	0	0	0	0	0
Chemical	0	0	0	0	0	0	0	0
Civil	47	3	0	1	1	9	0	33
Electrical	61	17	0	3	0	0	0	41
Engineering Science	0	0	0	0	0	0	0	0
Industrial	0	0	0	0	0	0	0	0
Mechanical	63	11	0	0	0	2	1	49
Metallurgical/Materials	0	0	0	0	0	0	0	0
Mining	0	0	0	0	0	0	0	0
Nuclear	0	0	0	0	0	0	0	0
Petroleum	0	0	0	0	0	0	0	0
Engineering, N.E.C.	203	57	0	4	0	18	38	86
Sciences, total	3,141	1,691	2	68	18	315	54	993
Physical Sciences	299	159	1	4	1	7	10	117
Astronomy	0	0	0	0	0	0	0	0
Chemistry	196	103	1	4	1	4	9	74
Physics	84	37	0	0	0	3	1	43
Physical sciences, N.E.C.	19	19	0	0	0	0	0	0
Environmental Sciences	19	3	0	0	0	7	0	9
Atmospheric Sciences	0	0	0	0	0	0	0	0
Geosciences	19	3	0	0	0	7	0	9
Oceanography	0	0	0	0	0	0	0	0
Environmental Sciences, N.E.C.	0	0	0	0	0	0	0	0
Mathemical Sciences	265	134	0	10	0	12	5	104
Computer Sciences	279	82	0	32	0	34	3	128
Life Sciences	666	390	1	13	15	61	6	180
Agricultural Sciences	55	22	0	1	0	6	0	26
Biological Sciences	447	272	1	9	5	14	5	141
Anatomy	9	7	0	0	0	1	0	1
Biochemistry	14	6	0	0	1	0	0	7
Biology	229	174	0	4	2	9	2	38
Biometry/Epidemiology	0	0	0	0	0	0	0	0
Biophysics	0	0	0	0	0	0	0	0
Botany	37	8	0	0	0	2	0	27
Cell Biology	0	0	0	0	0	0	0	0
Ecology	0	0	0	0	0	0	0	0
Entomology/Parasitology	0	0	0	0	0	0	0	0
Genetics	32	17	0	1	1	0	0	13
Microbiology	14	9	0	0	0	0	0	5
Nutrition	34	9	0	3	0	0	3	19
Pathology	0	0	0	0	0	0	0	0
Pharmacology	17	9	0	1	0	0	0	7
Physiology	20	10	0	0	0	0	0	10
Zoology	22	11	0	0	0	1	0	10
Biosciences, N.E.C.	19	12	1	0	1	1	0	4

Continued.

HBCU Science/Engineering Graduate Students
[Continued]

Field	Total	U.S. Citizens						Foreign
		Black non-Hispanic	American Indian/Alaskan Native	Asian/Pacific Islander	Hispanic	White non-Hispanic	Other or unknown	
Health Sciences	164	96	0	3	10	41	1	13
Dentistry	0	0	0	0	0	0	0	0
Neurology	0	0	0	0	0	0	0	0
Nursing	38	22	0	0	0	15	1	0
Pharmaceutical Sciences	15	0	0	0	0	7	0	8
Preventive Medicine/								
Community Health	0	0	0	0	0	0	0	0
Speech Pathology/Audiology	83	57	0	0	9	17	0	0
Veterinary Sciences	23	15	0	3	1	1	0	3
Clinical Medicine, N.E.C.	0	0	0	0	0	0	0	0
Health Related, N.E.C.	5	2	0	0	0	1	0	2
Psychology	419	232	0	1	1	169	5	11
Social Sciences	1,194	691	0	8	1	25	25	444
Agricultural Economics	57	10	0	0	0	2	0	45
Anthropology	0	0	0	0	0	0	0	0
Economics (except Agricutural)	147	45	0	0	0	0	7	95
Geography	0	0	0	0	0	0	0	0
History and Philosophy of Science	0	0	0	0	0	0	0	0
Linguistics	129	85	0	2	1	2	0	39
Political Science	389	232	0	1	0	1	18	137
Sociology	179	116	0	4	0	4	0	55
Sociology/Anthropology	60	48	0	0	0	0	0	12
Social Sciences, N.E.C.	233	155	0	1	0	16	0	61

Source: "Science/Engineering Graduates in Historically Black Colleges and Universities (HBCUs) by Field, Citizenship, and Racial/Ethnic Background: 1986," *Selected Data on Historically Black Colleges and Universities, Academic Year 1986,* December 1987. Primary source: National Science Foundation. Figures include all area/ethnic groups enrolled.

★ 833 ★
HBCU Science/Engineering Graduate Students: Trends

Field	Number							Average annual percent change		
	1980	1981	1982	1983	1984	1985	1986	1980-85	1985-86	1980-86
Total, all fields	3,318	3,496	3,380	3,556	3,937	3,649	3,515	1.9	-3.7	1.0
Engineering	264	242	267	311	405	342	374	5.3	9.4	6.0
Aerospace	0	0	0	0	0	0	0	0	0	0
Agricultural	0	0	0	0	0	0	0	0	0	0
Biomedical	0	0	0	0	0	0	0	0	0	0
Chemical	0	0	0	0	0	0	0	0	0	0
Civil	85	53	44	47	65	46	47	-11.6	2.2	-9.4
Electrical	46	66	64	94	131	121	61	21.3	-49.6	4.8
Engineering Science	0	0	0	0	0	0	0	...	...	...
Industrial	26	7	8	23	37	20	0	-5.1	-100.0	-100.0
Mechanical	22	30	30	47	93	81	63	29.8	-22.2	19.2
Metallurgical/Materials	0	0	0	0	0	0	0	0	0	0
Mining	0	0	0	0	0	0	0	0	0	0
Nuclear	0	0	0	0	0	0	0	...	...	...
Petroleum	0	0	0	0	0	0	0	0	0	0
Engineering, N.E.C.	85	86	121	100	79	74	203	-2.7	174.3	15.6
Sciences, total	3,054	3,254	3,113	3,245	3,532	3,307	3,141	1.6	-5.0	.5

Continued.

HBCU Science/Engineering Graduate Students: Trends
[Continued]

Field	Number							Average annual percent change		
	1980	1981	1982	1983	1984	1985	1986	1980-85	1985-86	1980-86
Physical Sciences	248	284	288	319	347	320	399	5.2	-6.6	3.2
Astronomy	0	0	0	0	0	0	0	0	0	0
Chemistry	195	217	226	250	269	228	196	3.2	-14.0	.1
Physics	53	67	58	57	65	72	84	6.3	16.7	8.0
Physical sciences, N.E.C.	0	0	4	12	13	20	19	...	-5.0	...
Environmental Sciences	30	23	31	32	39	34	19	2.5	-44.1	-7.3
Atmospheric Sciences	0	0	0	0	0	0	0	0	0	0
Geosciences	9	2	13	16	23	17	19	13.6	11.8	13.3
Oceanography	0	0	0	0	0	0	0	0	0	0
Environmental Sciences, N.E.C.	21	21	18	16	16	17	0	-4.1	-100.0	-100.0
Mathemical Sciences	154	168	206	235	266	240	265	9.3	10.4	9.5
Computer Sciences	139	150	232	271	3.0	304	279	16.9	-8.2	12.3
Life Sciences	841	835	858	852	827	728	666	-2.8	-8.5	-3.8
Agricultural Sciences	72	83	87	82	109	66	55	-1.7	-16.7	-4.4
Biological Sciences	640	610	605	593	536	479	447	-5.6	-6.7	-5.8
Anatomy	7	8	10	8	6	11	9	9.5	-18.2	4.3
Biochemistry	21	21	22	18	19	11	14	-12.1	27.3	-6.5
Biology	362	323	334	323	301	267	229	-5.9	-14.2	-7.3
Biometry/Epidemiology	0	0	0	0	0	0	0	0	0	0
Biophysics	0	0	0	0	0	0	0	0	0	0
Botany	39	50	45	44	17	16	37	-16.3	131.3	-.9
Cell Biology	0	0	0	0	0	0	0	0	0	0
Ecology	0	0	0	0	0	0	0	0	0	0
Entomology/Parasitology	0	0	0	0	0	0	0	0	0	0
Genetics	13	16	25	27	29	30	32	18.2	6.7	16.2
Microbiology	21	27	24	26	24	21	14	.0	-33.3	-6.5
Nutrition	39	39	36	20	36	34	34	-2.7	.0	-2.3
Pathology	0	0	0	0	0	0	0	0	0	0
Pharmacology	42	34	35	36	25	15	17	-18.6	13.3	-14.0
Physiology	14	17	14	19	22	27	20	14.0	-25.9	6.1
Zoology	66	55	41	40	29	25	22	-17.0	-12.0	-16.7
Biosciences, N.E.C.	16	20	19	32	28	22	19	6.6	-13.6	2.9
Health Sciences	129	142	166	177	182	183	164	7.2	-10.4	4.1
Dentistry	0	0	0	0	0	0	0	0	0	0
Neurology	0	0	0	0	0	0	0	0	0	0
Nursing	46	45	63	68	59	46	38	.0	-17.4	-3.1
Pharmaceutical Sciences	15	15	12	13	13	16	15	1.3	-6.3	.0
Preventive Medicine/Community Health	14	11	8	11	0	0	0	-100.0	...	-100.0
Speech Pathology/Audiology	39	48	58	59	81	84	83	16.6	-1.2	13.4
Veterinary Sciences	15	23	25	26	26	27	23	12.5	-14.3	7.4
Clinical Medicine, N.E.C.	0	0	0	0	3	0	0	...	...	...
Health Related, N.E.C.	0	0	0	0	0	10	5	...	-50.0	...
Psychology	291	268	227	384	436	404	419	6.8	3.7	6.3
Social Sciences	1,351	1,526	1,271	1,152	1,297	1,277	1,194	-1.1	-6.5	-2.0
Agricultural Economics	35	22	39	53	62	63	57	12.5	-9.5	8.5
Anthropology	0	0	0	0	0	0	0	0	0	0
Economics (except Agricultural)	175	250	284	106	135	161	147	-1.7	-8.7	-2.9
Geography	0	0	0	0	0	0	0	0	0	0
History and Philosophy of Science	0	0	0	0	0	0	0	0	0	0
Linguistics	124	104	24	43	137	129	129	.8	.0	.7
Political Science	450	452	286	297	392	345	389	-5.2	12.8	-2.4
Sociology	124	283	217	214	173	226	179	12.8	-20.8	6.3
Sociology/Anthropology	102	95	105	113	113	80	60	-4.7	-25.0	-8.5

Continued.

HBCU Science/Engineering Graduate Students: Trends
[Continued]

Field	Number							Average annual percent change		
	1980	1981	1982	1983	1984	1985	1986	1980-85	1985-86	1980-86
Social Sciences, N.E.C.	341	320	316	326	285	273	233	-4.4	-14.7	-6.2

Source: "Science/Engineering Graduates in Historically Black Colleges and Universities (HBCUs) by Field: 1980-86," *Selected Data on Historically Black Colleges and Universities, Academic Year 1986*, December 1987. Primary source: National Science Foundation. Figures include all area/ethnic groups enrolled.

★ 834 ★
Institutions with Top Minority Medical School Enrollment

University	Number of Hispanic Students[1]
Illinois, University of	92
San Antonio	86
TX, University of Dallas, Southwestern	77
Galveston	75
Los Angeles (UCLA & Drew Program)	64
San Francisco (& Berkeley Program)	57
Houston	53
San Diego	51
New Mexico	49
California, University of Irvine	45
California, University of Davis	39
Stanford	35
Caribe	34
Harvard	33
Puerto Rico	33
Arizona	30
Boston	30
New Jersey, UMDNJ-New Jersey Medical	28
Baylor	27
Iowa	26
Michigan, University of	26
SUNY Buffalo	24
Albert Einstein	23
Cornell	23
Michigan State	22
Washington, University of	22
Total, All U.S. Medical Schools	1,611

Source: "Top U.S. Medical Schools Enrolling Hispanics and Blacks (As of October, 1987, All Classes)," *Black Issues in Higher Education*, December 8, 1988, p. 18. Primary source: American Association of Medical Colleges 1987-88 Fall Enrollment Questionnaire. *Note:* 1. Mexican Americans and Mainland Puerto Ricans.

★ 835 ★
Institutions with Top Minority Medical School Enrollment

University	Number of Black Students
Howard[1]	276
Meharry[1]	232
Illinois, University of	154
Morehouse[1]	105
Wayne State	94
Temple	87
New Jersy, UMDNJ-New Jersey Medical	84
SUNY Brooklyn	83
North Carolina	80
Michigan, University of	71
Los Angeles (UCLA & Drew Program)	69
Hahnemann	66
Michigan State	58
Harvard	57
Georgetown	56
San Francisco (& Berkeley Program)	56
SUNY Buffalo	56
New York Medical	55
Pittsburgh	55
Maryland	50
Albert Einstein	49
Georgia, Medical College of	47
Louisiana State, New Orleans	46
Ohio State	46
Arkansas	45
SUNY Syracuse	45
Total, All U.S. Medical Schools	3,968

Source: "Top U.S. Medical Schools Enrolling Hispanics and Blacks (As of October, 1987, All Classes)," *Black Issues in Higher Education*, December 8, 1988, p. 18. Primary source: American Association of Medical Colleges 1987-88 Fall Enrollment Questionnaire. *Note:* 1. Historically Black College.

★ 836 ★
Law School Enrollment: Trends

Minority Classification	No. of Schools Reporting	Academic Year	Total
Black American	172/175	1985-86	6,051
	171/174	1984-85	5,955
	170/173	1983-84	5,967
	169/172	1982-83	5,852
Mexican American	172/175	1985-86	1,635
	171/174	1984-85	1,661

Continued.

Law School Enrollment: Trends
[Continued]

Minority Classification	No. of Schools Reporting	Academic Year	Total
	170/173	1983-84	1,744
	169/172	1982-83	1,739
Puerto Rican[1]	172/175	1985-86	412
	171/174	1984-85	407
	170/173	1983-84	450
	169/172	1982-83	418
Other Hispanic American	172/175	1985-86	1,632
	171/174	1984-85	1,439
	170/173	1983-84	1,302
	169/172	1982-83	1,249
American Indian or Alaskan Native	172/175	1985-86	462.5
	171/174	1984-85	429
	170/173	1983-84	441
	169/172	1982-83	406
Asian or Pacific Islander	172/175	1985-86	2,153
	171/174	1984-85	2,026
	170/173	1983-84	1,962
	169/172	1982-83	1,947

Source: "Minority Students Enrolled in J.D. Programs in Approved Law Schools," Black Issues in Higher Education, March 30, 1989, p. 21. Primary source: *A Review of Legal Education in the United States, Fall 1986,* American Bar Association. *Notes:* In March, 1983, the Office of the Consultant issued revised J.D. statistics based on a review of every law school questionnaire received between 1974 and 1982. Discrepancies were the result of inconsistent reporting of Hispanic students by some law schools. Appropriate adjustments were made, and some minor errors in transcription corrected. 1. 3 Puerto Rican schools not included; enrollment for ABA-approved law schools in Puerto Rico totaled 1,572 students; no data available from Oral Roberts University.

★ 837 ★
Law School Graduates: 1980-1984

Year	Black American Graduates	Total Law Graduates	Percent of Total
1980	1,461	35,059	4.2
1981	2,451	35,598	4.1
1982	1,563	34,846	4.5
1983	1,584	36,389	4.4
1984	1,548	36,687	4.2

Source: "Percentage of Black Americans Graduating from Law School in the Years 1980-1984," *NAFEO INROADS,* April/May, 1988, p. 4. Primary source: American Bar Association, 1985.

Medical School Applicants: Trends

The first part of the table shows the total number of applicants and the number of minority applicants for various entering years. The second part shows underrepresented minority applicants as a percentage of total applicants.

	1977	1978	1979	1980	1981	1982	1983	1984	1985	1986	1987

Number of applicants, for entering classes, 1977-1987

	1977	1978	1979	1980	1981	1982	1983	1984	1985	1986	1987
Black American	2,487	2,564	2,599	2,594	2,644	2,600	2,558	2,620	2,428	2,388	2,203
American Indian	122	133	151	147	160	137	161	150	125	121	123
Mexican American	487	433	457	449	515	504	507	555	518	507	466
Mainland Puerto Rican	203	1961	173	191	222	212	214	253	250	187	196
All underrepresented	3,299	3,321	3,380	3,381	3,541	3,453	3,440	3,578	3,321	3,203	2,988
All applicants	40,557	36,636	36,141	36,100	36,727	35,730	35,200	35,944	32,893	31,323	28,123

Minorities as a percentage of total applicants, for entering classes 1977-1987[1]

	1977	1978	1979	1980	1981	1982	1983	1984	1985	1986	1987
Black American	6.1	6.9	7.2	7.2	7.2	7.2	7.3	7.3	7.4	7.6	7.8
American Indian	0.3	0.4	0.4	0.4	0.4	0.4	0.5	0.4	0.4	0.4	0.4
Mexican American	1.2	1.2	1.3	1.2	1.4	1.4	1.4	1.5	1.6	1.6	1.7
Mainland Puerto Rican	0.5	0.5	0.5	0.5	0.6	0.6	0.6	0.7	0.8	0.6	0.7
All underrepresented	8.1	9.1	9.3	9.4	9.6	9.7	9.8	9.9	10.1	10.2	10.6
All applicants											

Source: "Medical School Appliacnts 1978 to 1987," *Black Issues in Higher Education,* December 8, 1988, p. 14. Primary source: *Minority Students in Medical Education: Facts and Figures IV,* Association of American Medical Colleges, March 1988. *Note:* 1. Percentages are rounded.

Medical School Enrollment: Trends

Total enrollment	77-78	78-79	79-80	80-81	81-82	82-83	83-84	84-85	85-86	86-87	87-88
Black American	3,587	3,537	3,627	3,708	3,884	3,869	3,892	3,944	3,849	3,892	3,968
American Indian	201	202	212	221	229	235	258	257	235	242	233
Mexican American	831	882	964	951	1,040	1,071	1,082	1,126	1,143	1,153	1,144
Mainland Puerto Rican	261	277	283	329	350	369	368	380	428	435	467
All underrepresented	4,880	4,898	5,086	5,209	5,503	5,544	5,600	5,707	5,655	5,722	5,812
All students	60,039	62,213	63,800	65,189	66,298	66,748	67,327	67,016	66,585	66,125	65,735

Source: "Medical School Enrollment," Black Issues in Higher Education, December 8, 1988, p. 13. Primary source: *Minority Students in Medical Education: Facts and Figures IV,* Association of American Medical Colleges, March, 1988.

Medical School Graduates: Trends

		1978	1979	1980	1981	1982	1983	1984	1985	1986	1987	1988
Black American	%	5.5	5.1	5.1	4.9	4.8	5.6	5.0	5.1	5.1	5.2	5.3
	n	791	760	768	766	763	883	818	828	824	820	850
American Indian	%	0.3	0.3	0.2	0.3	0.3	0.3	0.4	0.4	0.3	0.4	0.4
	n	46	49	33	43	45	45	59	65	49	63	58
Mexican American	%	1.1	1.3	1.3	1.3	1.4	1.4	1.4	1.5	1.4	1.4	1.5
	n	166	191	192	201	225	228	220	242	233	226	241
Mainland Puerto Rican	%	0.4	0.4	0.5	0.5	0.5	0.5	0.6	0.6	0.6	0.5	0.7
	n	62	62	73	76	74	75	94	89	89	81	112

Continued.

Medical School Graduates: Trends
[Continued]

		1978	1979	1980	1981	1982	1983	1984	1985	1986	1987	1988
All Underrepresented	%	7.4	7.1	7.0	6.9	7.0	7.8	7.3	7.5	7.4	7.5	7.9
	n	1,065	1,062	1,066	1,086	1,107	1,231	1,191	1,224	1,195	1,190	1,261
All Graduates	%	14,391	14,966	15,135	15,673	15,985	15,802	16,343	16,318	16,117	15,830	15,919

Source: "Medical School Graduates," Black Issues in Higher Education, October 26, 1989, p. 12. Primary source: *Minority Students in Medical Education: Facts and Figures III.* Association of American Medical Colleges, Office of Minority Affairs. *Notes:* Figures for 1978-1982 are taken from the LCME questionnaire. Figures from 1983-1988 are taken from the AAMC Section for Student Service, Reported Graduates Report. Reporting period differs slightly.

★ 841 ★
Medical School Graduates: Trends

Self-described ethnicity.

Characteristics	1983	1984	1985	1986	1987	1988	1989	% Change 1983-1989
Men								
White	10,060	10,226	9,769	9,401	9,029	8,898	8,577	-14.7
Underrepresented Minorities								
Black	495	440	456	474	458	441	396	-20.0
Amer. Indian/Alaskan Native	35	39	47	34	33	38	32	-8.6
Mexican Amer./Chicano	175	161	165	161	147	174	162	-7.4
Puerto Rican (Mainland)	50	62	51	52	53	69	78	56.0
Subtotal	755	702	719	721	691	722	668	-11.5
Other Men								
Subtotal	755	783	926	1,038	1,003	10,804	1,164	54.2
Total Men	11,570	11,711	11,414	11,160	10,723	10,704	10,409	-10.0
Women								
White	3,444	3,778	4,019	4,012	4,115	4,104	4,029	17.0
Underrepresented Minorities								
Black	388	378	372	350	362	409	425	9.5
Amer. Indian/Alaskan Native	12	20	18	15	30	20	25	108.3
Mexican Amer./Chicano	53	59	77	72	79	67	83	56.6
Puerto Rican (Mainland)	25	32	38	37	28	43	46	84.0
Subtotal	478	489	505	474	499	539	579	12.8
Other Women								
Subtotal	310	365	380	471	493	572	613	97.7
Total Women	4,232	4,632	4,904	4,957	5,107	5,215	5,221	23.4
Total Graduates								
White	13,504	14,004	13,788	13,413	13,144	31,002	12,606	-6.6
Underrepresented Minorities								
Black	883	818	828	824	820	850	821	-7.0
Amer. Indian/Alaskan Native	47	59	65	49	63	58	57	21.3
Mexican Amer./Chicano	228	220	242	233	226	241	245	7.5
Puerto Rican (Mainland)	75	94	89	89	81	112	124	65.3
Subtotal	1,233	1,191	1,224	1,195	1,190	1,261	1,247	1.1
Other Graduates								
Subtotal	1,065	1,148	1,306	1,509	1,496	1,656	1,777	66.9
Total Graduates	15,802	16,343	16,318	16,117	15,830	15,919	15,630	-1.1

Source: "U.S. Medical School Graduates by Race, Gender and Ethnicity," *Black Issues in Higher Education*, June 7, 1990, p. 11. Primary source: Association of American Medical Colleges.

★ 842 ★
Medicine

Year	Black American Graduates	Total Graduates	Percent of Total
1975	743	13,634	5.4
1976	752	13,614	5.5
1977	791	14,391	5.5
1978	760	14,966	5.1
1979	768	15,135	5.1
1980	766	15,673	4.9
1981	763	15,985	4.8
1982	883	15,802	5.6
1983	818	16,343	5.0
1984	828	16,318	5.1

Source: "Percentage of Black Americans Among the Medical School Graduates in the Years 1975 to 1984," *NAFEO INROADS*, April/May, 1988. p. 4. Primary source: Association of American Medical Colleges, 1986.

★ 843 ★
Minority Engineering Graduates and Freshman Enrollees: Trends

Characteristic	1984-85	1985-86	1986-87
B.S. Degrees	3,883	4,107	4,171
Percent of total			
B.S. degrees	5.0	5.3	5.5
B.S. Degrees of Blacks	2,043	2,114	2,182
Percent of total	2.6	2.7	2.9
Minority Freshmen			
in Engineering		10,588	9,585
Percent of total		10.4	9.7
Black Freshmen		6,374	5,873
Percent of total		6.0	5.9

Source: "Status of Minority Engineering Effort," *NAFEO INROADS*, February-March/April-May, 1989, p. 6. Primary source: Neblett, R.F. "Minorities in Engineering: The Role of the HBCUs in Meeting a National Challenge," *NAFEO INROADS*, February-March/April-May, 1989, pp. 5-6. HBCUs - Historically Black Colleges and Universities. Published by permission.

★ 844 ★
Minority Professional Workers, Scientists, and Engineers

Technical work force	Percent of total			
	1976		1986	
	Black	Asian	Black	Asian
Professional workers	1	1	7	1
Total scientists and engineers	2	5	2	5
Scientists	2	5	3	3
Engineers	1	4	2	5

Source: "Women and Racial Minorities as a Proportion of All Employed Scientists, Engineers, and Professional Workers," *Science and Technology Data Book*, 1989, p. 27. Primary source: National Science Foundation, SRS, and Department of Labor. Additional data may be obtained from Michael F. Crowley, SRS. Tel: (202) 634-4664. *Note:* 1. Not available.

★ 845 ★
New Scientists/Engineers: Employment Characteristics

Exclusive of full-time Graduate Students.

Field and rate	Total[1]	White	Black	Asian	Native American	Hispanic[2]
	Bachelor's Recipients[3]					
Total, all fields						
Labor Force Participation Rate	97.7	97.5	98.3	97.8	91.4	97.0
Unemployment Rate	2.4	2.3	3.4	3.5	7.8	4.4
Sciences, total						
Labor Force Participation Rate	97.2	96.9	98.5	98.1	90.0	95.9
Unemployment Rate	2.6	2.7	1.6	2.5	10.3	5.4
Engineering, total						
Labor Force Participation Rate	99.1	99.1	97.8	97.3	96.1	100.0
Unemployment Rate	2.0	1.3	8.5	5.0	.0	2.0
	Master's Recipients[3]					
Total, all fields						
Labor Force Participation Rate	97.3	97.4	97.4	93.1	99.3	99.6
Unemployment Rate	1.7	1.5	3.7	3.9	.0	.0
Sciences, total						
Labor Force Participation Rate	96.8	96.8	96.8	91.7	100.0	100.0
Unemployment Rate	1.8	1.7	2.2	3.4	.0	.0
Engineering, total						
Labor Force Participation Rate	98.6	99.0	99.8	95.1	98.8	98.6
Unemployment Rate	1.7	1.0	9.3	4.6	.0	.0

Source: "Selected Characteristics of Recent Science and Engineering Graduates, by Degree Level, Field, Gender, and Racial/Ethnic Group: 1988," Women and Minorities in Science and Engineering General:, January 1990, pp. 117-118. Primary source: National Science Foundation. *Notes:* 1. Detail will not average to total employed because a) racial and ethnic categories are not mutually exclusive and b) total employed includes other and no report. 2. Includes members of all racial groups. 3. Graduates who received their degrees in either academic year 1986 or 1987.

★ 846 ★
Parity in Medicine

| Factor | Standards | | |
	Population	High School Completions	College Enrollment
Applicants			
1975	6.1	4.1	2.8
1980	4.6	3.1	2.5
1985	4.7	3.3	3.1[1]
Acceptees			
1975	5.3	3.3	2.0
1980	5.6	4.1	3.5
1985	6.3	4.9	4.6
First Year Entrants			
1975	5.5	3.5	2.2
1980	5.8	4.3	3.7
1985	6.0	4.6	4.4
Enrollment Professional School			
1975	5.3	3.3	2.0
1980	6.1	1.6	4.0
1985	6.3	4.9	4.6
Graduates			
1975	6.1	4.1	2.8
1980	6.9	5.4	4.8
1985	7.0	6.9	5.3
Practitioners			
1975	-	-	-
1980	9.3	7.8	7.2
1985	9.1	7.7	7.4

Source: "Parity Levels, Medical Profession (Blacks as a Percent of Total)," *NAFEO INROADS,* October/November 1987, p. 3. *Note:* 1. 1984 data were used. Published by permission.

★ 847 ★
Participation in Arts and Leisure Activities

Represents percent of population 18 years old and over who participated at least once in the 12 months prior to the survey. Based on a survey conducted by the Bureau of the Census for the National Endowment for the Arts.

| Characteristic | Attended At Least Once | | | | | | Visited at least once - art museum or gallery | Read - novel, short stories, poetry, or plays |
	Jazz per- formance	Classical music per- formace	Opera per- formance	Musical plays	Plays	Ballet per- formance		
Average	10	13	3	17	12	4	22	56
White	9	14	3	18	12	5	23	58
Black	13	6	1	9	6	2	11	44
Other races	8	15	4	13	8	5	24	50

Source: "Participation Rates for Various Arts Performances and Leisure Activities by Selected Characteristics: 1985," *Statistical Abstract,* 1989, p. 231. Primary source: U.S. National Endowment for the Arts, *1985 Survey of Public Participation in the Arts.*

★ 848 ★
Professional Experience of Employed Scientists/Engineers

Field and racial/ ethnic group	Total Employed[1]	Professional Experience								
		1 or less	2-4	5-9	10-14	15-19	20-24	25-29	30-34	35 and over
Total, all fields[1]	4,626,500	104,200	584,200	726,700	680,900	625,800	526,500	459,600	359,200	417,400
White	4,190,400	91,600	522,800	646,500	607,200	564,900	469,300	419,700	38,100	402,100
Black	114,900	2,600	18,800	21,700	23,400	14,100	12,600	7,600	5,600	3,100
Asian	226,800	7,500	25,800	38,200	38,400	35,000	32,300	24,500	12,500	7,300
Native American	23,600	300	1,600	2,700	2,400	2,500	5,600	2,900	1,500	3,300
Hispanic[2]	93,400	3,000	18,900	19,500	13,900	13,200	7,800	6,400	3,900	3,800
Scientists, total	2,186,300	73,600	367,700	412,600	354,300	307,400	227,600	155,900	117,200	111,400
White	1,973,100	65,600	328,300	366,400	317,600	280,900	205,500	139,700	109,300	107,100
Black	73,700	1,800	14,400	14,900	15,100	8,800	7,000	4,800	3,200	800
Asian	94,000	4,500	15,100	19,800	15,900	12,400	9,800	9,000	3,800	2,100
Native American	10,300	[3]	1,200	1,600	600	400	3,200	1,200	700	1,200
Hispanic	46,100	2,000	13,100	10,000	6,400	7,300	2,900	1,500	1,500	600
Engineers, total	2,440,100	30,600	216,500	314,100	326,600	318,400	298,800	303,700	242,000	306,000
White	2,217,300	26,000	194,400	280,100	289,600	284,000	263,800	280,000	228,800	295,000
Black	41,300	800	4,500	6,800	8,300	5,300	5,700	2,800	2,400	2,300
Asian	132,800	3,000	10,700	18,400	22,500	22,600	22,500	15,600	8,700	5,200
Native American	13,300	200	400	1,100	1,800	2,100	2,500	1,700	800	2,100
Hispanic[2]	47,200	1,100	5,800	9,500	7,500	5,900	4,900	4,900	2,400	3,200

Source: "Employed Scientists and Engineers, by Field, Racial/Ethnic Group, and Years of Professional Experience: 1986," *Women and Minorities in Science and Engineering General:*, January 1990, pp. 77-78. Primary source: National Science Foundation, SRS. *Notes:* 1. Detail will not add to total employed because a) racial and ethnic categories are not mutually exclusive and b) total employed includes other and no report. 2. Includes members of all racial groups. 3. Too few cases to estimate.

★ 849 ★
Recent Dental School Enrollment and Graduates - Part I

Characteristics	Black				Hispanic				Native Amer.			
	Enroll		Grads		Enroll		Grads		Enroll		Grads	
	M	F	M	F	M	F	M	F	M	F	M	F
Total	499	484	101	92	772	506	184	112	39	18	9	5
Total each minority	983		193		1278		296		57	1	4	
Percent of total U.S. enrollment & grads	5.99[1]		4.48[1]		7.79[1]		6.88[1]		0.35[1]	0	.32[1]	

Source: "Dental School Minority Enrollment and Graduates by Ethnicity and Sex, 1989," *Black Issues in Higher Education,* June 7, 1990, p. 12. Primary source: American Dental Association *Note:* 1. Both sexes.

★ 850 ★
Recent Dental School Enrollment and Graduates - Part II

| Characteristics | Asian | | | | Total | | | | | |
| | Enroll | | Grads | | Enrollment | | | Grads | | |
	M	F	M	F	M	F	T	M	F	T
Total	1419	974	341	180	2729	1982	4711	635	389	1024
Total each minority	2329		521							
Percent of total U.S. enrollment & grads	14.58[1]		12.08[1]				28.70			23.75

Source: "Dental School Minority Enrollment and Graduates by Ethnicity and Sex, 1989," *Black Issues in Higher Education*, June 7, 1990, p. 12. Primary source: American Dental Association *Note:* 1. Both sexes.

★ 851 ★
Recent Science/Engineering Graduates: Employment

Exclusive or Full-time Graduate Students.

Field of degree	Total[1]	White	Black	Asian	Native Amer.	Hispanic[2]
Bachelor's Recipients[3]						
Total, all fields	484,800	407,400	19,700	18,400	2,500	15,800
Sciences, total	346,200	291,900	14,800	11,400	1,900	11,200
Engineering, total	138,600	115,400	4,900	7,100	700	4,600
Master's Recipients						
Total, all fields	86,500	67,600	2,600	7,700	300	2,600
Sciences, total	59,100	46,900	2,000	4,400	100	1,900
Engineering, total	27,300	20,700	500	3,300	200	700

Source: "Employed Recent Science and Engineering Graduates, by Degree Level, Field, Gender, and Racial/Ethnic Group: 1988," *Women and Minorities in Science and Engineering*, January 1990, pp. 73-74 National Science Foundation, SRS. *Notes:* Detail may not add to total because of rounding. 1. Detail will not add to total employed because a) racial and ethnic categories are not mutually exclusive and b) total employed includes other and no report. 2. Includes members of all racial groups. 3. Graduates who received their degrees in either academic year 1986 or 1987.

★ 852 ★
Recipients of Science/Engineering Bachelor's Degrees: Trends

Field	1977	1979	1981	1985	1987
Total, U.S. citizens and permanent residents[3]					
Total, all fields	383,618	384,318	386,280	392,883	389,290
Sciences, total	337,525	326,315	317,894	305,839	304,156
Engineering, total[2]	46,093	58,003	68,386	87,044	85,134
White, non-Hispanic[3]					
Total, all fields	341,726	340,603	338,715	342,814	332,524
Sciences, total	299,654	287,952	277,859	266,509	260,658
Engineering, total[2]	42,072	52,651	60,856	76,305	71,866

Continued.

Recipients of Science/Engineering Bachelor's Degrees: Trends
[Continued]

Field	1977	1979	1981	1985	1987
Black, non-Hispanic[3]					
Total, all fields	22,591	22,123	22,431	21,157	21,345
Sciences, total	21,206	20,348	19,982	18,015	17,925
Engineering, total[2]	1,385	1,775	2,449	3,142	3,420
Asian[3]					
Total, all fields	7,116	8,167	10,339	14,816	18,875
Sciences, total	5,905	6,309	7,273	9,809	12,497
Engineering, total[2]	1,211	1,858	3,066	5,007	6,378
Native Americans[3]					
Total, all fields	1,309	1,393	1,411	1,691	1,568
Sciences, total	1,174	1,229	1,216	1,382	1,285
Engineering, total[2]	135	164	195	309	283
Hispanic[3]					
Total, all fields	10,876	12,032	13,384	12,405	14,978
Sciences, total	9,586	10,477	11,564	10,124	11,791
Engineering, total[2]	1,290	1,555	1,820	2,281	3,187

Source: "Science and Engineering Bachelor's Degree Recipients, by Field and Racial/Ethnic Group: 1977, 1979, 1981, 1985, and 1987," *Women and Minorities in Science and Engineering,* January 1990, pp. 136-137. Primary source: National Science Foundation, SRS, and National Center for Education Statistics, Department of Education. *Notes:* Data by racial/ethnic group are collected on a biennial schedule. Imputations were done for racial/ethnic group nonresponse by field for 1977 through 1985 but not for 1987. Nonresponse for race/ethnicity was 11,075 in 1987. 1. Data on racial/ethnic group are collected by broad fields of study only; therefore, these data cannot be adjusted to the exact field taxonomies used by NSF. 2. Includes engineering technology. Racial/ethnic data for engineering and engineering technology can only be separated for 1985 and 1987. 3. Racial/ethnic categories are designated on the survey form. Data are provided by institutions. These categories include U.S. citizens and foreign citizens on permanent visas; data are not available by racial/ethnic groups for foreign citizens on temporary visas.

★ 853 ★
Salaries of Recent Science/Engineering Graduates

Exclusive of full-time Graduate Students.

Field of degree	Total[1]	White	Black	Asian	Native American	Hispanic[2]
Bachelor's Recipients[3]						
Total, all fields	25,100	25,100	23,000	27,500	18,000	25,000
Sciences, total	22,900	23,000	24,000	[4]	22,300	21,600
Engineering, total	30,000	30,000	29,100	30,000	[1]	29,200
Master's Recipients[3]						
Total, all fields	34,900	34,900	33,600	35,800	[4]	34,000

Continued.

Salaries of Recent Science/Engineering Graduates
[Continued]

Field of degree	Total[1]	White	Black	Asian	Native American	Hispanic[2]
Sciences, total	32,100	32,000	30,000	35,900	[4]	34,000
Engineering, total	37,900	38,000	35,300	[1]	32,100	33,300

Source: "Average Annual Salaries of Recent Science and Engineering Graduates, by Degree Level, Field, Gender, and Racial/Ethnic Group: 1988," *Women and Minorities in Science and Engineering,* January 1990, p. 121. Primary source: National Science Foundation. *Notes:* Salaries computed for full-time employed civilians. 1. Detail will not add to total employed because a) racial and ethnic categories are not mutually exclusive and b) total employed includes other and no report. 2. Includes members of all racial groups. 3. Graduates who received their degrees in either academic year 1986 or 1987. 4. Too few cases to estimate.

★ 854 ★
Science/Engineering Graduate Enrollment

U.S. Citizens only.

Field	Total[1] 1982	Total[1] 1988	White, non-Hispanic 1982	White, non-Hispanic 1988	Black non-Hispanic 1982	Black non-Hispanic 1988	Asian 1982	Asian 1988	Native American 1982	Native American 1988	Hispanic 1982	Hispanic 1988
Total, all fields	289,342	299,683	226,704	242,573	11,657	12,341	8,379	16,169	1,006	1,024	8,405	9,967
Sciences, total	229,957	230,707	183,328	189,682	10,513	10,791	5,632	9,771	835	879	7,304	8,232
Physical sciences	21,254	21,973	17,689	18,313	553	569	697	1,249	50	52	496	626
Mathematical sciences	12,668	12,670	10,158	10,139	357	432	492	751	42	32	290	333
Computer sciences	15,439	23,883	11,574	17,771	528	830	890	2,711	31	40	249	520
Environmental sciences	13,290	11,724	11,393	10,643	103	108	208	220	22	29	191	224
Life sciences	50,406	46,683	43,347	40,350	1,273	1,303	1,269	2,106	117	151	1,020	1,415
Psychology	38,704	42,941	30,321	36,129	1,643	1,956	441	755	139	178	1,471	1,751
Social sciences	18,196	70,833	58,846	56,337	6,056	5,593	1,635	1,979	434	397	3,587	3,363
Engineering, total	59,385	68,976	43,376	52,891	1,144	1,550	2,747	6,398	171	145	1,101	1,735
Chemical	4,659	4,103	3,850	3,382	85	84	312	334	14	24	101	135
Civil	9,638	9,174	7,103	7,462	139	198	410	649	22	22	221	288
Electrical	15,715	22,051	10,597	15,381	303	514	794	2,816	59	38	317	526
Industrial	7,905	9,267	5,948	7,632	250	300	288	476	19	15	175	278
Mechanical	7,407	10,326	5,333	7,863	100	200	336	912	14	12	113	217
Other engineering	14,061	14,055	10,545	11,171	267	254	607	1,211	43	34	174	291

Source: "Graduate Enrollment in Science and Engineering, by Field and Racial/Ethnic Group: 1982 and 1988," *Women and Minorities in Science and Engineering,* January 1990, p. 139. Primary source: National Science Foundation, SRS. *Notes:* Data are not collected on the racial/ethnic backgrounds of foreign citizens. 1. Total includes "other" and "unknown" racial/ethnic background.

★ 855 ★
Science/Engineering Graduate Students: Trends

Field, racial/ethnic group, and citizenship	1980[1]	1981[1]	1982	1983	1984	1985	1986	1987	1988
					Full-time				
Total science and engineering	208,232	212,083	216,012	223,135	224,701	227,486	236,748	240,966	245,463
Total U.S. citizens	161,547	161,566	162,868	165,673	165,736	163,977	166,651	167,312	167,741
White	124,732	118,478	132,383	139,962	139,116	135,971	139,563	138,582	139,345
Black	4,884	4,798	5,329	5,379	5,227	5,181	5,196	5,224	5,638
Hispanic	3,965	3,793	4,514	4,942	4,996	5,836	5,400	5,499	5,538
Asian	4,536	4,135	4,654	5,308	6,051	6,930	7,623	8,710	9,663
Other U.S. citizens	23,430	30,362	15,988	10,082	10,346	10,059	8,869	9,297	7,557
Foreign	46,691	50,517	53,144	57,462	58,965	63,509	70,097	73,654	77,722
Total sciences	166,293	167,266	167,325	170,445	170,727	172,669	177,717	180,614	183,807
Total U.S. citizens	137,111	135,950	134,993	135,222	134,369	132,658	134,028	134,351	134,516
White	106,391	100,439	111,231	116,040	114,419	111,774	113,859	113,080	113,664

Continued.

589

Science/Engineering Graduate Students: Trends
[Continued]

Field, racial/ethnic group, and citizenship	1980[1]	1981[1]	1982	1983	1984	1985	1986	1987	1988
Black	4,448	4,404	4,856	4,772	4,585	4,536	4,484	4,560	4,903
Hispanic	3,403	3,314	3,944	4,209	4,289	5,118	4,567	4,678	4,618
Asian	3,052	3,067	3,332	3,706	4,024	4,466	4,918	5,656	6,157
Other U.S. citizens	19,817	24,726	11,630	6,495	7,052	6,764	6,200	6,377	5,174
Foreign	29,188	31,316	32,332	35,223	36,358	40,011	43,689	46,263	49,291
Total engineering	41,939	44,817	48,687	52,690	53,974	54,817	59,031	60,352	61,656
Total U.S. citizens	24,436	25,616	27,875	30,451	31,367	31,319	32,623	32,961	33,225
White	18,341	18,039	21,152	23,922	24,697	24,197	25,704	25,502	25,681
Black	436	394	473	607	642	645	712	664	735
Hispanic	562	479	570	733	707	718	833	821	920
Asian	1,484	1,068	1,322	1,602	2,027	2,464	2,705	3,054	3,506
Other U.S. citizens	3,613	5,635	4,358	3,587	3,294	3,295	2,669	2,920	2,383
Foreign	17,503	19,201	20,812	22,239	22,607	23,498	26,408	27,391	28,431
Part-time									
Total science and engineering	89,032	90,307	93,535	94,730	95,805	100,770	101,601	102,262	102,070
Total U.S. citizens	[2]	[2]	85,580	85,610	86,239	91,352	91,762	91,179	90,655
White	53,776	52,098	65,807	67,249	66,496	70,847	71,621	73,007	72,683
Black	3,149	3,034	3,668	3,862	3,656	3,588	3,574	3,541	3,757
Hispanic	1,697	1,983	2,697	2,989	2,901	2,818	2,850	2,937	2,900
Asian	2,019	2,084	2,514	2,619	2,695	3,596	3,732	4,157	4,357
Other U.S. citizens	[2]	[2]	10,894	8,891	10,491	10,503	9,985	7,537	6,958
Foreign	[2]	[2]	7,955	9,120	9,566	9,418	9,839	11,083	11,415
Total sciences	60,828	60,751	64,044	62,096	62,664	65,348	64,838	65,612	66,748
Total U.S. citizens	[2]	[2]	59,327	57,140	57,245	60,132	59,399	59,403	60,559
White	36,753	34,833	46,919	45,888	45,127	48,034	47,664	48,233	49,452
Black	2,751	2,647	3,157	3,266	3,003	3,003	2,977	2,926	3,162
Hispanic	1,269	1,593	2,273	2,413	2,232	2,196	2,145	2,162	2,232
Asian	1,002	1,140	1,427	1,388	1,444	1,780	1,790	2,029	2,199
Other U.S. citizens	[2]	[2]	5,551	4,185	5,439	5,119	4,823	4,053	3,514
Foreign	[2]	[2]	4,717	4,956	5,419	5,216	5,439	6,209	6,189
Total engineering	28,204	29,556	29,491	32,634	33,141	35,422	36,763	36,650	35,322
Total U.S. citizens	[2]	[2]	26,253	28,470	28,994	31,220	32,363	31,776	30,096
White	17,023	17,265	18,888	21,361	21,369	22,813	23,957	24,774	23,231
Black	398	387	511	596	653	585	597	615	595
Hispanic	428	390	424	576	669	622	705	775	668
Asian	1,017	944	1,087	1,231	1,251	1,816	1,942	2,128	2,158
Other U.S. citizens	[2]	[2]	5,343	4,706	5,052	5,384	5,162	3,484	3,444
Foreign	[2]	[2]	3,238	4,164	4,147	4,202	4,400	4,874	5,226

Source: "Science/Engineering Graduate Enrollment in Doctorate-Granting Institutions, by Field, Racial/Ethnic Group, Citizenship, and Enrollment Status: 1980-88," *Science and Engineering Indicators - 1989*, 1989, p. 218-221. NSF, Division of Science Resources Studies. *Notes:* 1. For part-time students, distribution by citizenship was not requested prior to 1982. 2. Not available.

★ 856 ★
Science/Engineering Master's Degree Recipients: Trends

Field	1977	1979	1981	1985	1987
Total, U.S. citizens and permanent residents[3]					
Total, all fields[1]	67,633	65,204	64,698	64,604	64,718
Sciences, total	54,938	53,787	52,896	49,704	48,771
Engineering, total[2]	12,695	11,417	11,802	14,900	15,947
White, non-Hispanic[3]					
Total, all fields	60,890	58,616	57,610	56,479	56,166
Sciences, total	49,446	48,534	47,463	43,900	42,927

Continued.

Science/Engineering Master's Degree Recipients: Trends
[Continued]

Field	1977	1979	1981	1985	1987
Engineering, total[2]	11,444	10,082	10,147	12,579	13,239

Black, non-Hispanic[3]

Total, all fields	2,923	2,789	2,676	2,408	2,446
Sciences, total	2,683	2,543	2,416	2,049	2,013
Engineering, total[2]	240	246	260	359	433

Asian[3]

Total, all fields	2,042	2,268	2,580	3,703	3,891
Sciences, total	1,305	1,418	1,501	2,130	2,199
Engineering, total[2]	737	850	1,079	1,573	1,692

Native Americans[3]

Total, all fields	193	222	213	277	222
Sciences, total	170	198	182	228	159
Engineering, total[2]	23	24	31	49	63

Hispanic[3]

Total, all fields	1,585	1,309	1,619	1,737	1,993
Sciences, total	1,334	1,094	1,334	1,397	1,473
Engineering, total[2]	251	215	285	340	520

Source: "Science and Engineering Master's Degree Recipients, by Field and Racial/Ethnic Group: 1977, 1979, 1981, 1985, and 1987," *Women and Minorities in Science and Engineering*, January 1990, pp. 144-145. Primary source: National Science Foundation, SRS, and National Center for Education Statistics, Department of Education. *Notes:* Data by racial/ethnic group are collected on a biennial schedule. Imputations were done for racial/ethnic group nonresponse by field for 1977 through 1985 but not for 1987. Nonresponse for race/ethnicity was 4,070 in 1987. 1. Data on racial/ethnic group are collected by broad fields of study only; therefore, these data cannot be adjusted to the exact field taxonomies used by NSF. 2. Includes engineering technology. Racial/ethnic data for engineering and engineering technology can only be separated for 1985 and 1987. 3. Racial/ethnic categories are designated on the survey form. Data are provided by institutions. These categories include U.S. citizens and foreign citizens on permanent visas; data are not available by racial/ethnic groups for foreign citizens on temporary visas.

★ 857 ★
Science/Engineering Postdoctorates: Trends

Field	Total	White	Black	Asian	Native American	Hispanic
1977						
Total, all fields	9,755	8,172	104	1,354	6	136
Scientists, total	9,353	7,931	99	1,211	6	135
Engineers, total	402	241	5	143	0	1
1983						
Total, all fields	10,945	9,443	215	1,175	11	270
Scientist, total	10,620	9,318	215	975	11	212
Engineers, total	35	125	0	200	0	58

Continued.

Science/Engineering Postdoctorates: Trends
[Continued]

Field	Total	White	Black	Asian	Native American	Hispanic
				1985		
Total, all fields	11,796	9,830	213	1,629	51	249
Scientists, total	11,398	9,691	213	1,370	51	247
Engineers, total	398	139	0	259	0	2
				1987		
Total, all fields	12,296	10,068	233	1,853	24	275
Scientists, total	11,677	9,725	220	1,598	24	260
Engineers, total	619	343	13	255	0	15

Source: "Postdoctorates in Science and Engineering, by Field, Gender, and Racial/Ethnic Group: 1977, 1983, 1985, and 1987," *Women and Minorities in Science and Engineering*, January 1990, p. 166. Primary source: National Science Foundation, SRS.

★ 858 ★
Scientists and Engineers: Employment and Income

Characteristic	White	Black	Asian	Native American	Hispanic[1]
Unemployment rate	1.5	3.8	1.8	1.2	2.1
S/E underemployment rate	2.5	5.5	2.2	2.4	4.8
Average annual salary (in dol.)	38,700	31,500	39,100	41,000	34,600

Source: "Selecetd Characteristics of Scientists and Engineers: 1986," *Women and Minorities in Science and Engineering*, January 1990, p. 28. *Notes:* Primary source: National Science Foundation, SRS. 1. Includes members of all racial groups.

★ 859 ★
Scientists/Engineers: Employment Characteristics

Field and racial/ ethnic group	Labor force participation rate			Unemployment rate			S/E underemployment rate		
	Total	Men	Women	Total	Men	Women	Total	Men	Women
Total, all fields[1]	94.5	94.6	93.9	1.5	1.3	2.7	2.6	1.9	6.3
White	94.3	94.4	93.8	1.5	1.3	2.6	2.5	1.9	6.1
Black	97.2	97.6	96.4	3.8	2.8	6.0	5.5	3.7	9.7
Asian	96.3	97.0	93.9	1.8	1.9	1.6	2.2	1.8	4.1
Native American	96.0	95.9	96.8	1.2	1.3	[3]	2.4	1.1	13.1
Hispanic[2]	95.2	96.1	92.2	2.1	2.2	1.7	4.8	2.5	13.4
Scientists, total	95.3	95.9	94.0	1.9	1.6	2.7	4.3	3.3	7.0
White	95.2	95.8	93.8	1.8	1.5	2.6	4.2	3.3	6.7
Black	97.0	97.2	96.7	3.7	1.6	6.5	7.5	5.2	10.8
Asian	96.1	97.5	93.2	2.2	2.8	1.1	3.5	3.0	4.6
Native American	96.6	96.7	96.4	2.1	2.7	[3]	5.0	2.1	14.7
Hispanic	94.9	96.5	91.9	3.0	3.8	1.4	8.2	4.0	15.9
Engineers, total	93.8	93.8	93.6	1.2	1.2	2.5	1.0	1.0	2.3
White	95.3	95.3	95.3	1.2	1.1	2.5	1.0	.9	2.4

Continued.

Scientists/Engineers: Employment Characteristics
[Continued]

Field and racial/ ethnic group	Labor force participation rate			Unemployment rate			S/E underemployment rate		
	Total	Men	Women	Total	Men	Women	Total	Men	Women
Black	97.7	98.0	94.8	4.0	4.2	2.0	2.0	1.9	2.3
Asian	96.5	96.7	93.0	1.5	1.4	3.7	1.2	1.1	1.9
Native American	95.6	95.5	100.0	.4	.4	[3]	.4	.5	[3]
Hispanic	95.6	95.8	93.4	1.2	1.0	3.2	1.4	1.5	.8

Source: "Selected Employment Characteristics of Scientists and Engineers, by Field, Gender, and Racial/Ethnic Group: 1986," Women and Minorities in Science and Engineering General:, January 1990, pp. 113-114. Primary source: National Science Foundation, SRS. *Notes:* 1. Detail will not average to the total because a) racial and ethnic categories are not mutually exclusive and b) total employed includes other and no report. 2. Includes members of all racial groups. 3. Too few cases to estimate.

★ 860 ★
Senior Dental Student Enrollment: Trends

	1982 %	1983 %	1984 %	1985 %	1986 %	1987 %
American Indian	0.4	0.5	0.5	0.8	0.7	0.8
Asian	4.1	4.1	5.5	5.9	7.3	7.4
Black	3.8	2.7	2.6	2.8	3.1	3.2
Hispanic	2.4	3.0	3.4	4.3	4.4	5.4
White	85.0	86.5	85.5	83.6	82.4	80.5
No Response	4.3	3.3	2.5	2.6	2.3	2.7

Source: "Ethnicity of Senior Dental Students," Black Issues in Higher Education, March 30, 1989, p. 21. Primary source: *Survey of Dental Seniors, 1987*, American Association of Dental Schools.

★ 861 ★
Sex and Field of Employed Scientists/Engineers

Field and gender	Total Employed[1]	White	Black	Asian	Native American	Hispanic[2]
Total, all fields	4,626,500	4,190,400	114,900	226,800	23,600	93,500
Men	3,927,800	3,581,500	80,500	190,500	21,000	73,800
Women	698,600	608,900	34,500	36,300	2,700	19,600
Scientists, total	2,186,300	1,973,100	73,700	94,100	10,300	46,100
Men	1,586,700	1,448,300	43,600	65,000	7,900	29,800
Women	599,600	524,800	30,100	29,000	2,400	16,400
Physical scientists	288,400	261,800	6,200	15,400	1,000	4,800
Men	250,100	230,100	4,500	11,200	1,000	3,900
Women	38,300	31,700	1,700	4,200	[3]	900
Mathematical scientists	131,000	115,500	6,800	5,900	200	3,100
Men	97,100	85,200	4,500	5,100	100	1,900
Women	33,900	30,300	2,300	800	100	1,200
Computer specialists	562,600	497,100	18,900	36,100	2,200	9,300
Men	400,000	354,000	11,700	27,300	1,800	6,400
Women	162,500	143,000	7,200	8,800	400	2,900
Environmental scientists	111,300	105,800	1,000	2,100	400	1,800
Men	98,400	93,400	900	2,000	400	1,700

Continued.

Sex and Field of Employed Scientists/Engineers
[Continued]

Field and gender	Total Employed[1]	White	Black	Asian	Native American	Hispanic[2]
Women	12,900	12,400	100	200	100	200
Life scientists	411,800	377,900	8,800	15,000	2,800	9,900
Men	309,000	288,900	5,500	9,400	1,800	5,900
Women	102,800	89,100	3,300	5,600	1,000	4,100
Psychologists	253,500	234,100	9,100	5,200	1,900	5,900
Men	38,400	131,700	3,100	800	1,400	2,700
Women	115,200	102,500	6,000	4,400	500	3,100
Social scientists	427,800	380,800	22,900	14,200	1,700	11,400
Men	293,800	265,000	13,500	9,200	1,300	7,400
Women	134,000	115,800	9,400	5,000	400	4,000
Engineers, total	2,440,100	2,217,300	41,300	132,800	13,300	47,200
Men	2,341,100	2,133,200	36,900	125,500	13,100	44,000
Women	99,000	84,100	4,400	7,300	300	3,200

Source: "Employed Men and Women Scientists and Engineers, by Field, and Racial/Ethnic Group: 1986," *Women and Minorities in Science and Engineering,* January 1990, p. 69. Primary source: National Science Foundation, SRS. *Notes:* 1. Detail will not add to total employed because a) racial and ethnic categories are not mutually exclusive and b) total employed includes other and no report. 2. Includes members of all racial groups. 3. Too few cases to estimate.

★ 862 ★
Teachers, Characteristics of

In percent, except median. As of spring. Based on sample of all public school teachers and subject to sampling variability.

Characteristic	1976		1981			1986				
	Elementary	Secondary	Elementary	Junior high[1]	Senior high	Elementary	Junior high[1]	Senior high	Male	Female
Race										
White	89.7	91.8	90.8	89.4	94.0	89.3	86.7	92.0	90..6	89.2
Black	9.6	6.6	8.4	10.3	5.3	6.2	10.2	5.6	6.3	7.2
Other	.7[1]	1.5[1]	.8	.3	.7	4.5	3.1	2.4	3.0	3.7

Source: "Public Elementary and Secondary School Teachers — Selected Characteristics: 1976 to 1986," *Statistical Abstract,* 1989, p. 136. Primary source: National Education Association, Washington, DC, *Status of the American Public School Teacher, 1975-76, 1980-81, and 1985-86.* Note: 1. Does not include minorities of Spanish descent.

★ 863 ★
Top B.A. Producers of Engineering Degrees - Part I

Blacks	
Howard University[1]	113
North Carolina A&T Univ[1]	90
Prairie View A&M University[1]	78
Southern University[1]	73
CCNY (City College CUNY)	64
Georgia Inst. of Tech.	64
Tuskegee University[1]	64

Continued.

Top B.A. Producers of Engineering Degrees - Part I
[Continued]

North Carolina State U Raleigh	59
Northwestern University	41
Purdue University W. Lafayette	40
Polytechnic University	39
Pratt Institute	32
University of Maryland	30
University of Alabama	30
Tennessee State University[1]	27
NJ Inst. of Tech.	27
Univ. of Michigan Ann Arbor	27
Calif. State Univ. Long Beach	26
Stanford University	25
Univ. of DC	24
Mass. Institute of Technology	24
Univ. of Tenn. Knoxville	24
Cornell University	23
VAPolytechnic Inst. & State Univ.	23
GMI Engrg. & Mgmt. Inst	22
Mississippi State Univ.[1]	22
Clemson University	20
Calif. State Univ. Northridge	20
Illinois Institute of Tech.	20
Morgan State Univ.[1]	18
Univ. of Missouri Rolla	18
Rensselaer Polytechnic	18
Michigan State Univ.	16
US Naval Academy	16
Drexel University	15
U. Calif. Berkeley	15
Syracuse University	15
Ohio State University	15
Univ. of Virginia	15
Lawrence Tech. Univ.	15
All states and schools	2,122

Source: "Top Producers of Bachelor's Degrees in Engineering 1987-88," *Black Issues in Higher Education,* December 21, 1989, p. 25. Primary source: Engineering Manpower Commission of the American Association of Engineering Societies, Fall 1989 Report. *Note:* 1. Historically Black Colleges & Universities.

★ 864 ★
Top B.A. Producers of Engineering Degrees - Part II

Hispanics	
Univ. of Puerto Rico	533
Univ. of Florida	71
Texas A&M Univ.	66
Florida Intl. Univ.	66
Univ. of Miami	64
Univ. of Texas El Paso	58
Calif. State U. Long Beach	57
New Mexico State Univ.	56
Texas A&I Univ.	50
Univ. of Texas Austin	50
Calif. Poly. Pomona	45
Univ. of New Mexico	45
Univ. of Arizona	40
Univ. of Cal. Los Angeles	40
CCNY (City College CUNY)	40
Mass. Inst. of Technology	36
Cal. State Univ. Northridge	35
New Jersey Inst. of Tech.	34
San Diego State Univ.	26
Stanford University	26
Georgia Inst. of Tech.	26
Univ. of Cal. Berkeley	23
Univ. of Illinois Chicago	23
Stevens Inst. of Tech.	22
Illinois Inst. of Tech.	22
Univ. of Colorado Boulder	21
Florida Atlantic Univ.	21
Florida Inst. of Tech.	21
Calif. State Univ. Fresno	19
Cornell Univ.	19
Cal. Poly San Luis Obispo	18
Polytechnic Univ.	18
Univ. of Illinois Champaign	17
Arizona State Univ.	16
Univ. of Cal. Davis	16
Univ. of Southern California	16
Colorado School of Mines	16
Univ. of Central Florida	16
Manhattan College	16
Rensselaer Polytechnic	16
All States and Schools	1,996

Source: "Top Producers of Bachelor's Degrees in Engineering 1987-88," *Black Issues in Higher Education,* December 21, 1989, p. 25. Primary source: Engineering Manpower Commission of the American Association of Engineering Societies, Fall 1989 Report. *Note:* 1. Historically Black Colleges & Universities.

★ 865 ★
Top B.A. Producers of Engineering Degrees - Part III

Total Engineering Degrees	
Univ. of Illinois Champaign	1353
Purdue Univ. W. Lafayette	1155
Texas A&M	1122
Penn State Univ.	1089
Georgia Inst. of Technology	1031
NC State Univ. Raleigh	985
Ohio State Univ.	869
VA Polytechnic Inst. & State Univ.	860
Calif. State Univ. Long Beach	850
Univ. of Mich. Ann Arbor	809
Iowa State Univ.	791
Mass Inst. of Tech.	740
Univ. of Missouri Rolla	737
Univ. of Minnesota	735
Michigan Tech. Univ.	735
Univ. of Wisc. Madison	692
Auburn Univ.	691
Univ. of Florida	684
Univ. of Calif. Berkeley	681
Univ. of Maryland	660
Univ. of Texas Austin	647
Univ. of Washington	644
Northeastern Univ.	619
Rensselear Polytech	618
Cornell Univ.	583
Univ. of Arizona	578
Drexel Univ.	548
Clarkson Univ.	540
Univ. of Puerto Rico	533
Michigan State Univ.	527
Univ. of Southern Calif.	525
SUNY Buffalo	524
GMI Engrg & Mgmt. Inst.	505
Univ. of Missouri Columbia	503
Clemson University	462
Worcester Poly Institute	452
Rutgers Univ.	448
Univ. of Tenn. Knoxville	447
Arizona State Univ.	445
Cal. Poly Pomona	438
Lawrence Technical Inst.	438
All states and schools	68,824

Source: "Top Producers of Bachelor's Degrees in Engineering 1987-88," *Black Issues in Higher Education*, December 21, 1989, p. 25. Primary source: Engineering Manpower Commission of the American Association of Engineering Societies, Fall 1989 Report. *Note:* 1. Historically Black Colleges & Universities.

★ 866 ★
Total and Women's Enrollment in Medical School: Trends

Enrollment and race/ethnicity	Both sexes - Number			Women - Percent		
	1971-72	1977-78	1986-87	1971-72	1977-78	1986-87
Total enrollment						
All races	43,650	60,039	66,125	10.9	23.7	33.4
White	---	51,974	53,136	---	22.4	32.1
Minority	3,072	6,728	12,538	19.0	33.0	39.2
Black	2,055	3,587	3,892	20.4	38.2	49.2
Mexican American	252	831	1,153	9.5	22.7	34.2
Mainland Puerto Rican	76	261	435	17.1	34.1	37.2
Other Hispanic	---	426	1,933	---	23.2	34.0
American Indian	42	201	242	23.8	27.4	41.7
Asian	647	1,422	4,883	17.9	29.3	34.6
First-year enrollment						
All races	12,361	16,136	16,819	13.7	25.6	35.0
White	---	13,732	12,987	---	24.1	33.3
Minority	1,280	2,002	3,703	20.8	35.2	41.0
Black	882	1,085	1,174	22.7	40.8	51.1
Mexican American	118	246	331	8.5	26.8	36.6
Mainland Puerto Rican	40	68	111	15.0	33.8	40.5
Other Hispanic	---	157	512	---	27.4	37.9
American Indian	23	51	61	34.8	29.4	41.0
Asian	217	395	1,514	19.4	29.1	35.3

Source: "Total and First-Year Enrollment and Percent of Women in Schools of Medicine, according to Race and Ethnicity: United States, Academic Years 1971-72, 1977-78, and 1986-87," *Health United States - 1988,* March 1989, p. 138. Primary source: *Minorities and Women in the Health Fields, 1984,* Association of American Medical Colleges in Bureau of Health Professions, U.S. Government Printing Office, Washington, DC. .

★ 867 ★
Total Dental Predoctoral Enrollment: Schools & Trends

Dental School	1979	1980	1981	1982	1983	1984	1985	1986	1987	1988
U of Alabama	26	33	27	24	24	19	19	20	13	19
U of the Pacific	67	76	79	105	115	146	142	140	159	181
U of CA, SF	171	194	216	222	160	207	192	183	179	182
U of CA, LA	185	181	187	184	117	151	143	142	146	162
U of S. CA	189	160	171	173	190	208	212	215	214	237
Loma Linda U.	65	72	66	67	75	77	83	91	112	136
U of Colorado	15	12	15	15	9	13	15	18	26	30
U of Conn.	3	6	8	9	6	17	13	10	14	18
Georgetown U.[1]	38	38	57	43	53	91	93	114	120	100
Howard U.[2]	310	310	330	333	314	315	315	307	259	251
U of Florida	31	30	42	56	62	72	75	85	85	86
Emory U.[1]	20	26	31	27	32	44	19	15	8	[1]
Med.Col. of GA	28	30	30	27	21	21	23	31	31	34
Loyola U.	29	29	38	41	47	58	66	63	72	72
Northwestern U.	31	41	51	74	60	83	107	108	120	124
So. Illinois U.	3	5	15	21	24	26	23	26	28	21

Continued.

Total Dental Predoctoral Enrollment: Schools & Trends
[Continued]

Dental School	1979	1980	1981	1982	1983	1984	1985	1986	1987	1988
U of Illinois	52	64	72	67	76	71	74	76	88	87
Indiana U.	25	29	30	29	41	47	51	45	47	44
U of Iowa	22	26	25	23	19	18	18	23	30	38
U of Kentucky	15	12	10	9	7	9	7	11	11	9
U of Louisville	7	12	12	14	11	14	13	15	17	19
Louisiana St.U.	[1]	10	17	17	19	20	17	20	20	20
U of Maryland	65	63	67	86	88	103	112	97	102	97
Harvard U.	20	26	22	23	21	24	27	35	37	40
Boston U.	10	0	17	30	30	37	48	52	77	111
Tufts U.	41	47	49	51	59	61	83	109	144	145
U. of Detroit	9	9	10	11	13	11	15	16	24	26
U. of Michigan	57	52	49	50	51	59	60	71	84	76
U. of Minnesota	17	19	21	18	20	13	14	13	24	21
U. of Mississippi	18	13	9	9	15	11	11	9	11	11
U. of Missouri	43	43	46	56	52	59	61	73	83	85
Washington U., SL	38	49	58	54	64	58	75	81	100	107
Creighton U.	14	24	33	47	49	44	51	58	73	87
U. of Nebraska	4	6	10	6	6	12	9	12	12	15
F. Dickinson U.	18	22	37	51	65	56	65	65	69	78
NJ Dental Sch	49	73	70	74	68	65	57	42	41	47
Columbia U.	11	11	14	19	22	37	50	67	86	91
New York U.	34	35	31	37	54	67	76	107	136	174
SUNY, Stony Brook	4	4	6	7	7	9	9	14	9	12
SUNY, Buffalo	23	15	16	13	14	7	2	10	23	16
U. of NC	28	23	22	26	29	32	26	32	26	33
Ohio St. U.	24	27	30	38	40	43	45	44	63	63
Case Western U.	27	27	29	24	26	30	31	39	43	60
U. of Oklahoma	22	16	16	19	20	27	29	35	34	35
Oral Roberts U.[1]	4	5	10	9	11	6	[1]	[1]	[1]	[1]
Oregon Hlth Sci U.	14	22	26	26	27	31	26	25	28	26
Temple U.	19	24	20	22	22	31	43	59	82	109
U. of Pennsylvania	38	38	38	42	46	35	37	42	54	73
U. of Pittsburgh	25	24	20	24	22	17	20	16	17	20
Med U. of SC	5	8	8	7	9	11	11	11	14	18
Meharry Med Coll.[2]	186	210	189	165	168	177	177	165	168	161
U. of Tennessee	10	14	21	26	24	24	23	23	33	35
Baylor Coll.	16	16	21	30	38	46	47	61	67	85
U. of Texas, Houston	62	73	83	95	100	117	125	135	155	157
U. of Texas, SA	68	72	75	96	95	89	77	79	76	93
VA Comm. U.	33	32	40	44	58	49	87	47	47	64
U. of WA, Seattle	42	56	60	54	51	56	48	47	51	55
W. Virginia U.	2	1	0	3	6	9	13	12	14	17
Marquette U.	13	22	37	49	66	95	132	155	195	198
U. of Puerto Rico	257	261	264	261	259	261	266	270	253	238
Total	2,710	2,878	3,103	3,282	3,283	3,644	3,768	3,987	4,354	4,649

Source: "Total Predoctoral Enrollment of Minority Students, 1979-1988," *Black Issues in Higher Education*, October 26, 1989, p. 13. Primary source: American Dental Association *Notes:* 1. The predominantly dental education program has been discontinued. 2. Historically Black College.

★ 868 ★
Veterinary Medicine Schools: Teaching Faculty

College/University	Black		Hispanic		American Indian		Asian		Total Minority Faculty[1]	Total Faculty[1]
	M	F	M	F	M	F	M	F		
North Carolina State U.	1	0	1	0	1	0	0	0	3	119
U. of Tennessee	1	1	1	0	0	0	0	0	3	71
Colorado State U.	0	0	0	0	3	2	0	0	5	157
U. of Georgia	2	0	2	0	4	0	0	0	8	116
Iowa State U.	1	0	2	1	5	0	0	0	9	118
Michigan State U.	4	2	0	0	4	0	0	0	10	116
Oregon State U.	0	0	0	0	1	0	0	0	1	30
U. of Missouri-Columbia	1	0	1	1	3	0	0	0	6	81
Texas A&M U.	0	0	1	1	2	0	1	0	5	149
VA-MD Col. of Veterinary Medicine-VA Tech	0	0	2	0	5	0	0	0	7	84
U. of Wisconsin	1	0	0	0	1	0	0	0	2	80
Auburn U.	0	0	0	0	1	0	0	0	1	86
Oklahoma Statue U.	0	0	0	0	2	0	0	0	2	71
NY State Col. of Veterinary Medicine-Cornell	1	0	4	0	6	1	0	0	12	163
Mississippi State U.	0	0	0	0	1	1	0	0	2	58
U. of Minnesota	0	0	2	1	7	0	0	0	10	105
U. of California-Davis	2	0	1	1	11	1	0	1	17	157
U. of Pennsylvania	0	1	2	0	5	0	0	0	8	106
Washington State U.	1	0	1	0	6	0	0	0	8	83
U. of Illinois	1	0	1	0	0	3	0	0	5	106
Ohio State U.	2	0	3	0	3	2	0	0	10	102
Louisiana State U.	2	0	2	0	1	0	0	0	5	91
Kansas State U.	0	0	0	0	2	0	1	0	3	85
Tuskegee U.[2]	33	6	1	0	7	0	0	0	47	54
U. of Florida	2	1	1	1	2	0	0	0	7	103
Tufts U.	0	0	0	0	0	0	0	0	0	67
Purdue U.	5	0	0	0	1	0	0	0	6	84
U. of Montreal-St. Hyacinthe	0	0	0	0	0	0	0	0	0	63
Western Col. of Veterinary Medicine-Saskatchewan	0	0	0	0	0	0	0	0	0	91
U. of Guelph-Ontario	0	0	0	0	0	0	0	0	0	92
Atlantic Veterinary College-Price Edward Island	0	0	0	0	0	0	0	0	0	64
U. of Idaho-Dept. of Veterinary Science	0	0	0	0	0	0	0	0	0	15
Montana Statue U.-Veterinary Research Dept.	0	0	0	0	0	0	0	0	0	9
Pennsylvania State U.-Dept. of Veterinary Science	0	0	0	0	2	1	0	0	3	23
South Dakota State U.-Dept. of Veterinary Science	0	0	0	0	0	0	0	0	0	15
U. of Nebraska-Dept. of										

Continued.

Veterinary Medicine Schools: Teaching Faculty
[Continued]

College/University	Black		Hispanic		American Indian		Asian		Total Minority Faculty[1]	Total Faculty[1]
	M	F	M	F	M	F	M	F		
Veterinary Science	0	0	3	0	1	0	0	0	4	25
Total	60	11	31	6	87	11	2	1	209	3,039

Source: "Minority Teaching Faculty in Veterinary Schools," *Black Issues in Higher Education*, March 15, 1990, p. 28. Primary source: Complied from the Association of American Veterinary Medical Colleges, 1989-90 Comparative Data Report. *Notes:* 1. Excludes lecturers. 2. Historically Black College/University.

★ 869 ★
Veterinary Medicine Students

College/University	Black		Hispanic		Asian		American Indians		Alaska Native		Total Minority Students[1]	Total Student Enrollment
	M	F	M	F	M	F	M	F	M	F		
North Carolina State U.	2	2	0	4	0	0	1	1	0	0	10	270
U. of Tennessee	1	3	1	1	0	0	0	0	0	0	6	170
Colorado State U.	1	0	7	0	3	0	2	0	1	0	14	500
U. of Georgia	0	1	4	3	0	0	0	0	0	0	8	300
Iowa State U.	0	1	5	4	6	4	0	1	0	0	21	343
Michigan State U.	1	3	3	5	2	3	1	1	0	0	1	140
Oregon State U.	0	0	0	0	0	0	1	0	0	0	6	257
U. of Missouri-Columbia	1	1	0	3	1	0	0	0	0	0	39	478
Texas A&M U.	2	2	10	17	2	6	0	0	0	0	39	478
VA-MD Col. of Veterinary Medicine-VA Tech	1	2	1	1	2	2	0	1	0	0	10	312
U. of Wisconsin	0	1	0	1	0	2	2	1	0	0	7	303
Auburn U.	1	0	3	0	0	0	0	0	0	0	4	351
Oklahoma State U.	0	4	0	0	0	2	1	4	0	0	11	259
NY State Col. of Veterinary Medicine-Cornell	2	10	5	12	0	4	2	4	0	0	39	318
Mississippi State U.	0	0	0	0	0	0	0	0	0	0	0	170
U. of Minnesota	0	1	1	3	0	4	0	1	0	0	10	259
U. of California-Davis	1	5	6	20	4	18	0	2	0	0	56	474
U. of Pennsylvania	0	4	2	1	3	3	0	0	0	0	13	419
Washington State U.	1	1	2	6	3	10	1	1	0	0	25	308
U. of Illinois	0	0	1	0	1	1	0	0	0	0	3	323
Ohio State U.	1	3	2	8	4	8	0	1	0	0	27	506
Louisiana State U.	7	2	6	3	0	0	1	0	0	0	19	264
Kansas State U.	0	0	6	4	0	1	1	2	0	0	14	378
Tuskegee U.[2]	58	85	9	9	4	0	0	0	0	0	165	210
U. of Florida	2	6	12	8	1	1	1	1	0	0	32	317
Tufts U.	0	0	1	0	1	7	0	0	0	0	9	268
Purdue U.	0	0	3	3	0	2	1	0	0	0	9	245
U. of Montreal-St. Hyacinthe	0	0	0	0	0	0	0	0	0	0	0	290
Western Col. of Veterinary Medicine-Saskatchewan	0	0	0	0	0	0	0	0	0	0	0	283
U. of Guelph-Ontario	0	0	0	0	0	0	0	0	0	0	0	400
Atlantic Veterinary College-Prince Edward Island	0	0	0	0	0	0	0	0	0	0	0	185
Total	82	137	90	116	37	78	15	21	1	0	577	9,681

Source: "Minority Professional Degree Students," *Black Issues in Higher Education*, March 15, 1990, p. 27. Primary source: Association of American Veterinary Medical Colleges, 1989-90 Comparative Data Report. *Notes:* 1. Excludes Pacific Islanders. 2. Historically Black College/University.

★ 870 ★
Women Doctoral Scientists/Engineers at 4-Year Institutions

Field and racial/ ethnic group	Total, four-year colleges & univer- sities[1]	Tenure Track: Tenured	Tenure Track: Not tenured	Non-tenure track
Total, all fields[2]	34,900	12,600	7,700	6,100
White	31,200	11,500	6,900	5,500
Black	1,100	300	300	100
Asian	2,300	600	400	500
Native American	100	[4]	[4]	[4]
Hispanic[3]	700	200	200	100
Scientists, totals	34,300	12,400	7,500	6,000
White	30,800	11,400	6,700	5,400
Black	1,100	300	300	100
Asian	2,200	600	300	500
Native American	100	[4]	[4]	[4]
Hispanic	700	200	200	100
Engineers, total	600	100	200	100
White	500	100	200	100
Black	[4]	[4]	[4]	[4]
Asian	100	[4]	[4]	[4]
Native American	[4]	[4]	[4]	[4]
Hispanic	[4]	[4]	[4]	[4]

Source: "Doctoral Women Scientists and Engineers in Four-Year Colleges and Universities, by Field, Racial/ Ethnic Group, and Tenure Status: 1987," Women and Minorities in Science and Engineering General:, January 1990, pp. 105-106. Primary source: National Science Foundation, SRS. Notes: 1. Includes tenure status unknown and no report. 2. Detail will not add to total employed because a) racial and ethnic categories are not mutually exclusive and b) total employed includes other and no report. 3. Includes members of all racial groups. 4. Too few cases to estimate.

★ 871 ★
Working Female Scientists/Engineers: Primary Work Activity

Field and racial/ ethnic group	Total Employed[1]	Research	Development	Management of R&D	General management	Teaching	Production/ inspection	Reporting, statistical work, and computing
Total, all fields[2]	698,600	79,000	73,200	31,400	102,500	81,500	53,600	131,700
White	608,900	69,900	63,000	27,500	86,600	73,600	45,000	114,400
Black	43,500	2,600	2,000	2,000	6,400	2,800	3,400	7,100
Asian	36,300	4,800	5,200	1,70	6,300	2,600	3,700	8,200
Native American	2,700	200	100	[4]	900	200	100	300
Hispanic[3]	19,600	2,200	2,100	20	2,900	3,500	1,500	2,400
Scientists, total	599,600	70,200	41,000	27,000	93,600	77,500	34,600	122,400
White	524,800	61,800	35,200	24,100	79,100	70,400	28,700	107,300
Black	30,100	2,600	1,100	1,900	5,800	2,800	2,300	5,800
Asian	29,000	4,200	3,000	1,00	5,800	2,100	2,600	7,500
Native American	2,400	200	[4]	[4]	900	200	100	100
Hispanic	16,400	2,000	1,100	100	2,600	3,400	800	2,200
Engineers, total	99,000	8,900	32,200	4,300	8,900	3,900	19,000	9,400
White	84,100	8,100	27,900	3.400	7,500	3,200	16,300	7,100
Black	4,400	[4]	800	100	500	[4]	1,100	1,300
Asian	7,300	500	2,300	700	600	500	1,100	700

Continued.

Working Female Scientists/Engineers: Primary Work Activity
[Continued]

Field and racial/ ethnic group	Total Employed[1]	Research	Development	Management of R&D	General management	Teaching	Production/ inspection	Reporting, statistical work, and computing
Native American	300	[4]	100	[4]	[4]	[4]	[4]	100
Hispanic	3,200	200	1,100	[4]	400	100	800	200

Source: "Employed Women Scientists and Engineers, by Field, Racial/Ethnic Group, and Selected Primary Work Activity: 1986," Women and Minorities in Science and Engineering General:, January 1990, pp. 97-100. Primary source: National Science Foundation, SRS. *Notes:* 1. Includes consulting, other, and no report. 2. Detail will not add to total employed because a) racial and ethnic categories are not mutually exclusive and b) total employed includes other and no report. 3. Includes members of all racial groups. 4. Too few cases to estimate.

★ 872 ★
Working Female Scientists/Engineers: Professional Experience

Field and racial/ ethnic group	Total Employed[1]	Professional Experience								
		1 or less	2-4	5-9	10-14	15-19	20-24	25-29	30-34	35 and over
Total, all fields[1]	698,600	32,200	188,000	185,000	119,600	67,900	35,400	18,000	12,900	13,600
White	608,900	28,400	164,500	159,300	104,500	60,600	31,400	15,000	11,700	12,200
Black	34,500	1,200	7,900	8,700	7,900	2,100	2,100	700	1,000	200
Asian	36,300	1,800	8,200	11,300	5,700	3,500	1,700	1,700	200	1,200
Native American	2,700	100	700	1,000	100	200	[3]	500	[3]	[3]
Hispanic[2]	19,600	700	8,200	5,600	2,300	1,400	600	100	[3]	100
Scientists, total	599,600	29,000	155,600	153,700	107,500	62,600	32,500	15,900	10,100	11,500
White	524,800	25,700	136,300	132,400	94,400	56,000	29,00	13,600	9,200	10,100
Black	30,100	1,000	6,900	7,400	7,500	1,800	2,100	700	800	200
Asian	29,000	1,400	6,400	9,400	4,300	3,100	1,300	1,000	100	1,200
Native American	2,400	[3]	600	900	100	200	[3]	500	[3]	[3]
Hispanic	16,400	600	7,100	4,400	1,900	1,300	500	100	[3]	100
Engineers, total	99,000	3,300	32,500	31,300	12,100	5,300	2,900	2,100	2,800	2,200
White	84,100	2,700	28,200	26,900	10,100	4,600	2,400	1,400	2,500	2,200
Black	4,400	100	1,000	1,300	300	300	[3]	[3]	100	[3]
Asian	7,300	300	1,900	1,900	1,400	400	400	700	[3]	[3]
Native American	300	[3]	100	100	100	[3]	[3]	[3]	[3]	[3]
Hispanic[2]	3,200	100	1,100	1,200	400	100	100	[3]	[3]	[3]

Source: "Employed Women Scientists and Engineers, by Field, Racial/Ethnic Group, and Years of Professional Experience: 1986," Women and Minorities in Science and Engineering General:, January 1990, pp. 81-82. Primary source: National Science Foundation, SRS. *Notes:* 1. Detail will not add to total employed because a) racial and ethnic categories are not mutually exclusive and b) total employed includes other and no report. 2. Includes members of all racial groups. 3. Too few cases to estimate.

★ 873 ★
Working Male Scientists/Engineers: Primary Work Activity

Field and racial/ ethnic group	Total Employed[1]	Research	Development	Management of R&D	General management	Teaching	Production/ inspection	Reporting, statistical work, and computing
Total, all fields[2]	3,927,800	314,400	802,300	367,200	781,100	276,300	529,000	341,100
White	3,581,500	285,200	717,80	339,300	724,000	251,500	480,900	308,500
Black	80,500	4,200	13,500	5,300	19,300	8,000	11,600	8,100
Asian	190,500	18,600	55,600	15,800	25,800	14,300	24,000	17,200
Native American	21,000	1,000	3,600	2,500	3,700	500	3,900	1,600
Hispanic[3]	73,800	5,800	13,200	6,100	14,800	3,900	12,200	7,900
Scientists, total	1,586,700	221,300	141,300	135,500	289,400	223,300	124,400	237,200
White	1,448,300	202,200	126,200	124,000	266,200	203,900	111,500	214,800
Black	43,600	3,100	2,600	1,900	12,700	7,400	3,000	6,300
Asian	65,000	11,600	10,400	5,200	7,100	10,200	5,600	11,500
Native American	7,900	800	100	1,700	1,000	400	1,400	1,100
Hispanic	29,800	3,700	2,200	3,000	6,200	2,800	2,500	5,200
Engineers, total	2,341,100	93,100	661,000	231,700	491,700	53,000	404,600	103,900
White	2,133,200	83,000	591,500	215,30	457,800	47,600	369,400	93,700
Black	36,900	1,000	10,800	3,400	6,600	600	8,600	1,800
Asian	125,500	6,900	45,200	10,600	18,700	4,100	18,400	5,700
Native American	13,100	200	3,500	800	2,700	[4]	2,500	400
Hispanic	44,000	2,100	11,000	3,200	8,600	1,100	9,700	2,700

Source: "Employed Men Scientists and Engineers, by Field, Racial/Ethnic Group, and Selected Primary Work Activity: 1986," Women and Minorities in Science and Engineering General:, January 1990, pp. 93-96. Primary source: National Science Foundation, SRS. *Notes:* 1. Includes consulting, other, and no report. 2. Detail will not add to total employed because a) racial and ethnic categories are not mutually exclusive and b) total employed includes other and no report. 3. Includes members of all racial groups. 4. Too few cases to estimate.

★ 874 ★
Working Male Scientists/Engineers: Professional Experience

Field and racial/ ethnic group	Total Employed[1]	Professional Experience								
		1 or less	2-4	5-9	10-14	15-19	20-24	25-29	30-34	35 and over
Total, all fields[1]	3,927,800	72,000	396,200	541,700	561,300	557,900	491,100	441,600	346,300	403,800
White	3,581,500	63,200	358,300	487,200	502,700	504,300	437,900	404,600	326,400	389,800
Black	80,500	1,400	10,900	12,900	15,600	12,000	10,600	6,900	4,600	2,900
Asian	190,500	5,800	17,600	26,900	32,700	31,500	30,700	22,800	12,300	6,100
Native American	21,000	200	900	1,700	2,300	2,300	5,600	2,300	1,400	3,300
Hispanic[2]	73,800	2,300	10,700	14,000	11,600	11,800	7,200	6,200	3,900	3,800
Scientists, total	1,586,700	44,600	212,100	258,900	246,800	244,800	195,100	139,900	107,100	99,900
White	1,448,300	39,900	192,000	234,000	223,200	224,800	176,500	126,100	100,100	97,000
Black	43,600	800	7,400	7,400	7,500	7,000	4,900	4,100	2,400	600
Asian	65,000	3,100	8,700	10,400	11,600	9,200	8,600	7,900	3,600	900
Native American	7,900	[3]	600	700	600	200	3,200	700	700	1,200
Hispanic	29,800	1,300	6,000	5,700	4,500	6,000	2,400	1,400	1,500	500
Engineers, total	2,341,100	27,300	184,100	282,700	314,500	313,100	296,000	301,600	239,300	303,800
White	2,133,200	23,300	166,300	253,200	279,500	279,500	261,400	278,500	226,300	292,800
Black	36,900	600	3,500	5,500	8,000	5,000	5,700	2,800	2,200	2,300
Asian	125,500	2,700	8,900	16,500	21,100	22,200	22,100	14,900	8,600	5,200

Continued.

Working Male Scientists/Engineers: Professional Experience
[Continued]

Field and racial/ ethnic group	Professional Experience									
	Total Employed[1]	1 or less	2-4	5-9	10-14	15-19	20-24	25-29	30-34	35 and over
Native American	13,100	200	300	1,000	1,700	2,100	2,500	1,700	800	2,100
Hispanic[2]	44,000	1,000	4,700	8,300	7,000	5,800	4,800	4,900	2,400	3,200

Source: "Employed Men Scientists and Engineers, by Field, Racial/Ethnic Group, and Years of Professional Experience: 1986," *Women and Minorities in Science and Engineering General:*, January 1990, pp. 79-80. Primary source: National Science Foundation, SRS. *Notes:* 1. Detail will not add to total employed because a) racial and ethnic categories are not mutually exclusive and b) total employed includes other and no report. 2. Includes members of all racial groups. 3. Too few cases to estimate.

★ 875 ★
Working Scientists/Engineers: Primary Work Activity

Field and racial/ ethnic group	Total Employed[1]	Research	Development	Management of R&D	General management	Teaching	Production/ inspection	Reporting, statistical work, and computing
Total, all fields[2]	4,626,500	393,500	875,500	398,600	875,500	357,800	582,600	472,800
White	4,190,400	355,000	780,800	366,800	810,600	325,100	526,000	422,900
Black	114,900	6,800	15,400	7,300	25,700	10,800	15,000	15,200
Asian	226,800	23,300	60,800	17,500	32,100	16,900	27,700	25,400
Native American	23,600	1,200	3,700	2,500	4,600	700	3,900	1,800
Hispanic[3]	93,400	8,100	15,300	6,300	17,700	7,400	13,700	10,300
Scientists, total	2,186,300	291,500	182,200	162,600	383,000	300,800	159,000	359,600
White	1,973,100	263,900	161,400	148,200	345,300	274,300	140,200	322,000
Black	73,700	5,700	3,800	3,800	18,600	10,200	5,300	12,100
Asian	94,000	15,900	13,400	6,200	12,800	12,300	8,200	19,000
Native American	10,300	900	200	1,700	1,800	700	1,500	1,200
Hispanic	46,100	5,700	3,300	3,100	8,800	6,200	3,300	7,400
Engineers, total	2,440,100	102,000	693,200	236,000	500,600	56,900	423,600	113,200
White	2,217,300	91,100	619,400	218,700	465,400	50,800	385,700	100,800
Black	41,300	1,100	11,700	3,500	7,100	600	9,700	3,200
Asian	132,800	7,500	47,400	11,400	19,300	4,600	19,500	6,400
Native American	13,300	200	3,500	800	2,800	[4]	2,500	600
Hispanic	47,200	2,400	12,000	3,200	9,000	1,100	10,400	2,900

Source: "Employed Scientists and Engineers, by Field, Racial/Ethnic Group, and Selected Primary Work Activity: 1986," Primary source: National Science Foundation, SRS. *Notes:* 1. Includes consulting, other, and no report. 2. Detail will not add to total employed because a) racial and ethnic categories are not mutually exclusive and b) total employed includes other and no report. 3. Includes members of all racial groups. 4. Too few cases to estimate.

RELIGION

★ 876 ★
Attendance at Church

Year	Whites		Blacks	
	Percent	Number	Percent	Number
1978	34.0	1,107	36.7	147
1980	41.0	1,103	50.0	128
1983	35.2	1,186	39.5	147
1984	42.9	1,053	57.3	157

Source: "People Saying They Attend Church with People of the Other Race," A Common Destiny: Blacks and American Society, 1989, p. 94. Primary source: Compiled from Milton J. Yinger, *Black Americans and Predominantly White Churches*. Paper prepared for the Committee on the Status of Black Americans, National Research Council, Washington, D.C., and C. Kirk Hadaway, David G. Hackett and James F. Miller. *Review of Religious Research* 25 (March): 204-219. Published in: A Common Destiny: Blacks and American Society, p. 94.

★ 877 ★
Religious Bodies

Name of religious body	Date of Statistics	No. of Churches	Inclusive Membership
African Methodist Episcopal Church	1981	6,200	2,210,000
African Methodist Episcopal Zion Church	1987	6,060	1,220,000
Apostolic Faith Mission Church of God	1989	18	6,200
Apostolic Overcoming Holy Church of God	1988	177	12,479
The Bible Church of Christ	1988	6	6,405
Bible Way Church of Our Lord Jesus Christ, World Wide	1970	350	30,000
Christian Methodist Episcopal Church	1983	2,340	718,922
Church of God in Christ	1982	9,982	3,709,661
Church of God in Christ, International	1982	300	200,000
Church of God (Which He Purchased With His Own Blood)	1986	7	800
Church of the Living God (C.W.F.F.)	1985	170	42,000
Church of Our Lord Jesus Christ of the Apostolic Faith	1954	155	45,000
The Coptic Orthodox Church	1989	40	160,000

Continued.

Religious Bodies
[Continued]

Name of religious body	Date of Statistics	No. of Churches	Inclusive Membership
Free Christian Zion Church of Christ	1956	742	22,260
House of God, Which is the Church of the Living God, the Pillar and Ground of the Truth	1956	107	2,350
Kodesh Church of Immanuel	1980	5	326
National Baptist Convention of America	1956	11,398	2,668,799
National Baptist Convention, U.S.A., Inc.	1958	26,000	5,500,000
National Primitive Baptist Convention	1975	606	250,000
Pentecostal Assemblies of the World	1960	550	4,500
Progressive National Baptist Convention	1967	655	521,692
Reformed Methodist Union Episcopal Church	1983	18	3,800
Reformed Zion Union Apostolic Church	1965	50	16,000
Second Cumberland Presbyterian Church in U.S.	1959	121	30,000
Triumph the Church and Kingdom of God in Christ	1972	475	54,307
United Holy Church of America	1960	470	28,890
Total 26 Denominations		67,002	17,464,651

Source: "Black Denominations in the United States," [A Selected List], *Yearbook of American and Canadian Churches,* 1989. Primary source: *Yearbook of American and Canadian Churches, 1989.* Nashville: Abingdon Press, 1989. Published by permission. *Notes:* The 26 denominations have been identified as composed predominantly of Black members as determined by reference to various sources of information available to the *Yearbook of American and Canadian Churches.* Organized religion is one of the most segregated institutions in the United States with an estimated 90 percent of Blacks in Black churches. The greatest number of Black Christians are found in various Baptist churches, followed by the Methodist denominations and the Pentecostal bodies. The twenty-six denominations account for the overwhelming Black membership in the United States. Some small, predominantly Black, religious bodies may be omitted from the tabulation and the editor of the *Yearbook* would be glad to receive details concerning them.

★ 878 ★
Religious Denominations

Denomination (Year of Founding)	Membership	
	Early 1940s	Early 1980s
National Baptist Convention, U.S.A., Inc. (1895)	4,022,000	6,300,000
Church of God in Christ (1895)	300,000	3,710,000
National Baptist Convention of America (1917)	2,352,000	2,500,000
African Methodist Episcopal Church (1816)	869,000	2,210,000
African Methodist Episcopal Zion Church (1822)	489,000	1,202,000
Christian Methodist Episcopal Church (1870)	382,000	719,000
National Primitive Baptist Convention	44,000	250,000

Continued.

Religious Denominations
[Continued]

Denomination (Year of Founding)	Membership	
	Early 1940s	Early 1980s
Progressive National Baptist Convention (1961)	---	200,000

Source: "Membership in Major Black Religious Denominations," A Common Destiny: Blacks and American Society, 1989, p. 174. Primary source: Compiled from Florence Murray, ed. *Negro Handbook, 1946-47.* New York: Current Books, 1947: 153-55; *Yearbook of American and Canadian Churches, 1987.* Nashville: Abingdon Press, 1987: 1- A; and C. Eric Lincoln. *Race, Religion, and the Continuing American Dilemma.* New York: Hill and Wang, 1984: 88. In: A Common Destiny: Blacks and American Society, 1989, p. 174. Published in: A Common Destiny: Blacks and American Society, 1989, p. 217. Published by permission.

★ 879 ★
Religious Preferences of College Students

Characteristic	Predominantly Black Colleges	Predominantly Black Private Colleges
Baptist	58.8	51.9
Buddhist	0.2	0.2
Congregational	0.6	0.7
Eastern Orthodox	0.0	0.0
Episcopal	1.6	1.7
Islamic	1.2	1.0
Jewish	0.0	0.0
LDS (Mormon)	0.0	0.0
Lutheran	0.7	1.0
Methodist	10.4	12.0
Presbyterian	1.7	1.9
Quaker	0.1	0.2
Roman Catholic	9.3	13.6
Seventh Day Adventist	0.7	0.6
Other Protestant	1.6	1.5
Other religion	7.3	7.1
None	5.5	6.4
Born-Again Christian		
Yes	50.5	51.3
No	49.5	48.7

Source: "Students' Religious Preferences," *The American Freshmen: National Norms for Fall 1989,* p. 45. Primary source: *The American Freshmen: National Norms for Fall 1989.* Published by permission.

SOCIAL SERVICES

★ 880 ★
Homeless Adults in Cities

Percentages are weighted. Numbers in percent.

Race	Home- less with Children	Home- less Alone
Black	54	39
White	22	49
Hispanic	20	9
Other	4	3

Source: "Selected Characteristics of Service-Using Homeless Adults With and Without Children in Cities Over 100,000, 1987," *U.S. Children and Their Families*, 1989, p. 33. Primary source: Burt, Martha and Barbara Cohen, "Feeding the Homeless: Does the Prepared Meals Provision Help?" Report to Congress on the Prepared Meals Provision, Volume II, Urban Institute, October 1988. Tables 2, 7, 21, and 25.

★ 881 ★
Medicaid Recipients

In thousands, except percent. Represents number of persons as of March of following year who were enrolled at any time in year shown. Person did not have to receive medical care paid for by Medicaid in order to be counted.

Poverty Status	1986			
	Total[1]	White	Black	Hispanic[2]
Persons covered, total	19,739	12,689	6,200	2,833
Below poverty level	12,805	7,635	4,643	2,029
Above poverty level	6,934	5,054	1,557	804
Percent of total population	8.3	6.3	21.5	16.5
Below poverty level	41.0	35.9	53.0	42.8
Above poverty level	3.3	2.8	7.8	6.5

Source: "Medicaid — Selected Characteristics of Persons Covered: 1986," *Statistical Abstract*, 1989, p. 363. Primary source: U.S. Bureau of the Census, *Current Population Reports*, series P-60, No. 155, and earlier and forthcoming reports. *Notes:* 1. Includes other races not shown separately. 2. Hispanic persons may be of any race.

★ 882 ★
Social Insurance and Human Service

In thousands, except percent. As of March. Covers civilian noninstitutional population and members of Armed Forces living off post or with their families on post. Persons are classified as having a work disability if they (1) have a health problem or disability which prevents them from working or which limits the kind of amount of work they can do: (2) have a service connected disability or ever retired or left a job for health reasons; (3) did not work in survey reference week or previous year because of long-term illness or disability; or (4) are under age 65, and are covered by Medicare or received Supplemental Security Income. Based on Current Population Survey; see text, section 1 and Appendix III.

Age and Participation Status in Assistance Program	White	Black	Hispanic[1]
Persons with work disability	10,544	2,512	1,011
16-24 years old	963	291	125
25-34 years old	1,874	464	189
35-44 years old	1,957	433	217
45-54 years old	1,852	502	190
55-64 years old	3,898	822	290
Percent work disabled of total population	7.9	13.7	8.2
16-24 years old	3.5	6.1	3.7
25-34 years old	5.2	8.8	5.0
35-44 years old	6.6	11.7	8.3
45-54 years old	9.1	20.1	12.8
55-64 years old	20.4	39.6	25.4
Percent of work disabled-			
Receiving Social Security income	29.7	30.0	23.4
Receiving food stamps	14.4	37.0	31.5
Covered by Medicaid	17.8	37.0	32.8
Residing in public housing	2.5	12.7	7.3
Residing in subsidized housing	2.5	4.5	3.9

Source: "Persons with Work Disability, by Selected Characteristics: 1988," *Statistical Abstract*, 1989, p. 360. Primary source: U.S. Bureau of the Census, unpublished data. *Note:* 1. Hispanic persons may be of any race.

★ 883 ★
Social Insurance and Human Service

Covers civilian workers as of March of following year who had earnings in year shown. Based on Current Population Survey.

Race and Hispanic Origin	Number with Coverage (1,000)					Percent of Total Civilian Workers				
	Total[1]	$5,000 - $14,999	$15,000 - $24,999	$25,000 - $34,999	$35,000 and over	Total[1]	$5,000 - $14,999	$15,000 - $24,999	$25,000 - $34,999	$35,000 and over
Total[2]	49,578	10,333	15,983	11,365	10,395	42.6	29.3	60.9	73.4	76.0
White	43,090	8,495	13,636	10,093	9,626	42.9	28.9	59.9	73.1	75.8
Black	5,152	1,594	1,941	929	467	41.2	33.2	70.3	78.1	80.7
Hispanic[3]	2,444	708	878	472	283	30.1	21.0	52.0	65.9	74.7

Source: "Pension Plan Coverage of Civilian Workers by Wage or Salary Income: 1986," *Statistical Abstract*, 1989, p. 356. U.S. Bureau of the Census, *Current Population Reports*, series P-60, forthcoming report. *Notes:* 1. Includes workers with income under $5,000, not shown separately. 2. Includes other races, not shown separately. 3. Hispanic persons may be of any race.

★ 884 ★
Social Insurance and Human Services

Women as of spring 1986. Covers civilian noninstitutional population. Child support data are for women with own children under 21 years of age present from absent fathers. Alimony data are for ever-divorced and currently separated women. Based on Current Population Survey; see text, section 1 and Appendix III. For definition of mean, see Guide to Tabular Presentation.

Recipiency Status of Women	Unit	Total[1]	Race White	Black	Hispanic[2]
Child Support					
All women, total	1,000	8,808	6,341	2,310	813
Payments awarded[3]	1,000	5,396	4,476	839	342
Percent of total	Percent	61.3	70.6	36.3	42.1
Due child support payment in 1985	1,000	4,381	3,651	657	282
Received payment	1,000	3,243	2,722	473	192
Percent of due	Percent	74.0	74.6	72.0	68.1
Did not receive payment	1,000	1,138	929	184	90
Payments not awarded	1,000	3,411	1,865	1,471	471
Mean money income:					
Women received payments	Dollars	14,776	15,052	13,297	11,505
Mean child support	Dollars	2,215	2,294	1,754	2,011
Women did not receive payments	Dollars	10,837	10,854	10,477	9,430
Women not awarded payments	Dollars	7,998	8,746	6,969	6,308
Women with incomes below the poverty level in 1985, total	1,000	2,797	1,569	1,190	414
Payments awarded[3]	1,000	1,130	787	322	100
Received payments in 1985	1,000	595	411	174	43
Mean income from child support	Dollars	1,383	1,463	1,085	(B)
Did not receive payment	1,000	310	221	83	31
Payments not awarded	1,000	1,668	782	868	314
Alimony					
All women, total	1,000	19,156	16,039	2,766	1,196
Payments awarded[3]	1,000	2,803	2,539	220	132
Received payments in 1985	1,000	616	559	44	29
Mean income from alimony	Dollars	3,733	3,858	(B)	(B)
Did not receive payment	1,000	225	193	25	13
Payments not awarded	1,000	16,354	13,500	2,546	1,064
Women with incomes below the poverty level in 1985, total	1,000	3,716	2,670	973	410
Payments awarded	1,000	434	378	49	35
Percent of total	Percent	11.7	14.2	5.0	8.5

Source: "Child Support and Alimony — Selected Characteristics of Women: 1985," Statistical Abstract, 1989, p. 368. Primary source: U.S. Bureau of the Census, Current Population Reports, series P-23, No. 152. Notes: 1. Includes other items not shown separately. 2. Hispanic women may be of any race. 3. Includes women who were not supposed to receive payments in 1985, not shown separately.

SPORTS AND LEISURE

★ 885 ★
Additions to Division I College Basketball, 1979-1988

Year	# Teams Added	# From Predomin- antly Black Institutions
1979-80	3	1
1980-81	7	3
1981-82	11	1
1982-83	3	1
1983-84	2	0
1984-85	7	1
1985-86	1	1
1986-87	8	0
1987-88	3	0
1988-89	3	0
Totals:		
N	48	8
%	100.0	16.7

Source: "Welcome to Division I," *The Sporting News 1989-90 College Basketball Yearbook,* October 1989, p. 138. Primary source: Compiled by the editors from data in *The Sporting News,* TSN series # 5, *1989-90 College Basketball Yearbook.* . Published by permission.

★ 886 ★
College Basketball Coaches: 1989-90

Region & Conference	Number Teams	Number Black American Coaches
South		
Atlantic Coast	8	0
Southeastern	10	1
Metro	8	0
American South	6	0
Colonial Athletic Association	8	0
Ohio Valley	7	1[1]

Continued.

College Basketball Coaches: 1989-90
[Continued]

Region & Conference	Number Teams	Number Black American Coaches
Sun Belt	8	0
Big South	7	0
Mid-Eastern Athletic Conference	9	6[1]
Southern	8	0
East		
Big East	9	1
Atlantic 10	10	1
Ivy League	8	0
Metro Atlantic Athletic	12	0
East Coast	8	0
North Atlantic	7	1
Northeast	9	0
Midwest		
Big Ten	10	2
Mid-Continent	8	0
Mid-American	9	0
Near West		
Big Eight	8	0
Southwest	9	1
Missouri Valley	8	0
Far West		
Pacific-10	10	1
Western Athletic	9	0
Big West	10	0
Big Sky	9	0
West Coast	8	0
Major Independents	3	0
Other Independents	12	0
Totals:		
N	255	15
%	100.0	5.9

Source: "Conference Data," The Sporting News 1989-90 College Basketball Yearbook, October 1989, pp. 69, 72, 73, 77, 79, 81, 83, 85, 87, 91, 94, 95, 97, 99, 101, 104, 105, 107, 109, 113, 117, 119, 124, 125, 127, 130, 131, 133, 135, 136, and 139. Primary source: Compiled by the editors from data in *The Sporting News, TSN Series #5, 1989-90 College Basketball Yearbook. Note:* 1. Historically or Predominantly Black Institutions. Published by permission.

★ 887 ★
College Football Award Winners

Award/Trophy	Years	Number of awards	Number awarded to Black Athlete	Year of first award to Black Athlete
Heisman Trophy[1]	1935-1988	54	17	1961
Outland Trophy[2]	1946-1988	43	10	1955
Lombardi Award[3]	1970-1988	19	9	1972

Source: "Award Winners: Heisman Trophy, Outland Trophy, Lombardi Award," *The Sporting News 1989 College Football Yearbook*, July 1989, p. 187. Primary source: Compiled by the editors from The Sporting News, TSN Series #3, *The Sporting News 1989 College Football Yearbook. Notes:* 1. Honoring the outstanding college football player in the United States, presented by the Downtown Athletic Club of New York. 2. Honoring the outstanding interior lineman, selected by the Football Writers Association of America. 3. Honoring the outstanding college lineman of the year, sponsored by the Rotary Club of Houston. Published by permission.

★ 888 ★
Final Four Basketball: All-Stars and MVPs

Year(s)	All-Tournament Players		Black American MVP
	Total No.	# Black Amer.	
1989	5	4	Yes
1988	5	3	Yes
1987	5	4	Yes
1986	5	4	Yes
1985	5	4	Yes
1984	5	4	Yes
1983	5	3	No
1982	5	5	Yes
1981	5	2	Yes
1980	3[1]	3	Yes (No.)
1970-1979	[2]	[2]	5
1960-1969	[2]	[2]	4
1950-1959	[2]	[2]	3
1940-1949	[2]	[2]	0

Source: "Tournament MVPs" and "80s All-Tournament," *The Tennessean*, April 2, 1990, p. 4- D Primary source: Compiled by the editors from information in "Tournament MVPs" and "80s All-Tournament," *The Tennessean*, (Nashville, TN) April 2, 1990, p. 4- D. *Notes:* 1. Two spots vacated. 2. Data not supplied.

★ 889 ★
Fishermen and Hunters: Trends

Covers persons 16 years old and over. Sportsmen are anyone who fished or hunted. Based on the National Surveys of Fishing, Hunting, and Wildlife-Associated Recreation conducted by the Bureau of the Census.

Characteristic	Number (1,000)		Percent of Population who participated	
	1980	1985	1980	1985
Total persons	46,713	50,288	27	28
White	43,161	46,582	29	13
Black	2,709	2,521	15	14
Other races	843	1,185	18	18

Source: "Sportsmen — Selected Characteristics: 1980 and 1985," *Statistical Abstract*, 1989, p. 230. Primary source: 1980, U.S. Fish and Wildlife Service and U.S. Bureau of the Census, *1980 National Survey of Fishing, Hunting, and Wildlife-Associated Recreation*; and 1985, U.S. Fish and Wildlife Service, 1985 *National Survey of Fishing, Hunting, and Wildlife-Associated Recreation.*.

★ 890 ★
Professional Baseball: Black American Team Leaders, 1989

Category	National League		American League		Total
	East	West	East	West	
Batting Average	1	4	4	2	11
At-bats	1	1	2	3	7
Runs	3	3	4	3	13
Hits	0	3	2	1	6
Total Bases	0	4	3	3	10
Doubles	0	1	3	1	5
Triples	2	2	3	3	10
Home Runs	0	4	3	2	9
Runs Batted In	0	2	2	4	8
Stolen Bases	4	2	5	5	16
Slugging Percentage	0	4	3	3	10
On-Base Percentage	1	3	3	1	8
Wins	0	0	0	1	1
Earned-Run Average	1	0	0	0	1
Complete Games	0	0	0	0	0
Shutouts	0	0	0	0	0
Saves	0	0	1	0	1
Innings Pitched	1	0	0	1	2
Strikeouts	1	0	0	0	1
# Teams	6	6	7	7	26

Source: "1989 Leaders," *The Sporting News 1990 Baseball Yearbook*, March 1990, pp. 73, 77, 79, 83, 85, 89, 91, 95, 97, 101, 103, 107, 111, 115, 117, 121, 123, 127, 129, 133, 135, 139, 141, 145, 147, and 151. Primary source: Compiled by the editors from *The Sporting News 1990 Baseball Yearbook*. Published by permission.

★ 891 ★
Professional Baseball: League Batting Leaders, 1989

| Category | Leaders | | | | | |
| | National League | | American League | | Total | |
	Total	Black American	Total	Black American	Total	Black American
Batting Average	10	4^1	10	2^1	20	6^2
Runs	10	3	9	3^1	19	6
Hits	8	1^1	10	2^1	18	3^2
Doubles	10	3	10	1	20	4
Triples	8	4	9	3	17	7
Home Runs	9	3^1	10	4^1	19	7^2
Runs Batted In	9	3^1	9	3	18	6
Total Bases	10	4^1	10	3	20	7
Walks	10	4	9	6^1	19	10
On-Base Percentage	10	4^1	10	4	20	8
Slugging Percentage	10	4^1	10	5	20	9
Extra-Base Hits	10	4	10	3	20	7
Multi-Hit Games	7	1^1	9	3^1	16	4^2
Stolen Bases	10	1^1	10	5^1	20	6^2
Grand Slams	5	2	3	1	8	3
Hitting Streaks	5	2^1	5	0	10	2

Source: "1989 N.L. and A.L. Batting Leaders," *The Sporting News 1990 Baseball Yearbook*, March 1990, pp. 153-154. Primary source: Compiled by the editors from *The Sporting News 1990 Baseball Yearbook. Notes:* 1. Includes #1 in League. 2. Includes #1 in both Leagues. Published by permission.

★ 892 ★
Professional Baseball: League Pitching Leaders, 1989

| Category | Leaders | | | | | |
| | National League | | American Leaders | | Total | |
	Total	Black American	Total	Black American	Total	Black American
Wins	9	0	5	1	14	1
Earned-Run Average	10	0	10	0	20	0
Complete Games	7	0	8	1	15	1
Winning Percentage	10	0	10	2	20	2
Strikeouts	10	0	10	1	20	1
Games	9	0	8	1	17	1
Saves	10	0	8	0	18	0
Shutouts	10	0	6	0	16	0
Winning Streaks	3	0	5	0	8	0
Innings Pitched	9	0	10	0	19	0

Source: "1989 N.L. and A.L. Pitching Leaders," *The Sporting News 1990 Baseball Yearbook*, March 1990, pp. 153-154. Primary source: Compiled by the editors from *The Sporting News 1990 Baseball Yearbook.* Published by permission.

★ 893 ★
Professional Basketball: Draft, Rosters, and Coaches

Division/ Team	1989 NBA Draft		1989-90 Roster		Black Head Coach	Assistant Coaches	
	Number Choices	Number Black American	Number Players	Number Black American		Number	Number Black American
Atlantic							
Boston Celtics	2	1	12	7		2	0
Miami Heat	3	2	12	8		2	0
New Jersey Nets	2	2	13	8		2	1
New York Knicks	1	1	13	11	X	3	0
Philadelphia 76ers	3	3	17	13		1	1
Washington Bullets	3	2	13	10	X	2	0
Central							
Atlanta Hawks	2	2	13	11		2	1
Chicago Bulls	3	3	12	9		3	1
Cleveland Cavaliers	2	2	15	12	X	2	0
Detroit Pistons	1	1	14	11		2	0
Indianapolis Pacers	2	2	13	8		2	0
Milwaukee Bucks	1	0	13	6		3	1
Orlando Magic	2	2	14	9		2	0
Midwest							
Charlotte Hornets	1	1	13	7		2	1
Dallas Mavericks	3	2	13	10		2	0
Denver Nuggets	3	2	13	9		2	1
Houston Rockets	0	-	16	11	X	3	1
Minneapolis Timberwolves	3	2	14	9		1	0
San Antonio Spurs	1	1	11	9		4	2
Utah Jazz	2	2	11	5		4	0
Pacific							
Golden State Warriors	1	1	12	7		2	0
Los Angeles Clippers	3	3	11	8		2	0
Los Angeles Lakers	1	0	11	8		2	0
Phoenix Suns	4	4	17	11		3	2
Portland Trailblazers	2	2	15	11		2	0
Sacramento Kings	1	1	11	8		1	0
Seattle Supersonics	2	2	11	10	X	2	1
Number	54	46	353	246	5	60	13
Percent	100.0	85.2	100.0	69.7	1	100.0	21.7

Source: "1989 NBA Draft: Team by Team," and "(Team) Data," *The Sporting News 1989-90 Pro Basketball Yearbook,* September 1989, pp. 137, 70, 72, 75, 77, 79, 81, 83, 85, 87, 89, 91, 93, 95, 99, 101, 103, 105, 107, 109, 111, 113, 115, 117, 119, 121, 123, and 125. Primary source: Compiled by the editors from *The Sporting News 1989-90 Pro Basketball Yearbook. Note:* 1. Base too small for percentage to be reliable. Published by permission.

★ 894 ★
Professional Basketball: NBA Leaders, 1988-89

	Leaders	
Category	Total	Black American
Points	12	10
Field Goals	9	8
Free Throws	10	4
Assists	10	7
Steals	10	8
Rebounds	10	6
Blocked Shots	10	6
3-pt. Field Goals	9	6

Source: "1988-89 Individual Leaders," *The Sporting News 1989-90 Pro Basketball Yearbook,* September 1989, p. 144. Primary source: Compiled by the editors from *The Sporting News 1989-90 Pro Basketball Yearbook.* Published by permission.

★ 895 ★
Professional Football: 1991 First- and Second-Round Draft Picks

Conference/ Division	First Round		Second Round		First 2 Rounds	
	# Picks	# Black Americans	# Picks	# Blacks Americans	# Picks	# Blacks Americans
National Football Conference[1]						
East[2]	3	3	5	4	8	7
Central[3]	5	5	5	4	10	9
West[4]	4	2	5	5	9	7
American Football Conference[1]						
East[5]	6	5	4	4	10	9
Central[6]	3	3	4	3	7	6
West[7]	4	3	5	4	9	7
Total	25	21	28	24	53	45

Source: "NFL Draft Through 5 Rounds," *The Tennessean,* April 23, 1990, p. D-6. Primary source: New York Associated Press. Compiled by the editors from data in *The Tennessean. Notes:* 1. Some conference teams had no first-or second-round draft pick. 2. Dallas Cowboys, New York Giants, Philadelphia Eagles, Phoenix Cardinals, Washington Redskins. 3. Chicago Bears, Detroit Lions, Green Bay Packers, Tampa Bay Buccaneers. 4. Atlanta Falcons, Los Angeles Rams, New Orleans Saints, San Francisco 49ers. 5. Buffalo Bills, Indianapolis Colts, Miami Dolphins, New England Patriots, New York Jets. 6. Cleveland Browns, Cincinnati Bengals, Houston Oilers, Pittsburgh Steelers. 7. Denver Broncos, Kansas City Chiefs, Los Angeles Raiders, San Diego Chargers.

★ 896 ★
Socioeconomic Differences in NCAA Athletes

	Black	Non-Black
Student-Athletes in Football, Basketball and Other Sports at Division I Institutions:		
Football/Basketball	39.0	61.0
Other Sports	8.0	92.0
Socioeconomic Status of Football and Basketball Players:		

Continued.

618

Socioeconomic Differences in NCAA Athletes
[Continued]

	Black	Non-Black
Low (0-42.64)	49.0	13.0
Middle (42.65-56.39)	42.0	58.0
High (56.5-67.93)	8.0	29.0
Football and Basketball Players Reporting Amounts of Money They or Their Parents Have Had to Borrow for College:		
Low ($0)	70.0	67.0
Middle ($1-1,999)	7.0	6.0
High ($2,000-37,000)	24.0	28.0
Amount of Money Football and Basketball Players Report Having After Expenses Each Month:		
Low ($0-25)	61.0	40.0
Middle ($26-124)	18.0	28.0
High ($125-800)	21.0	32.0

Source: "NCAA Athletic Statistics Portray Socioeconomic Disparity," *Black Issues in Higher Education*, September 14, 1989, p. 19. *The Experiences of Black Intercollegiate Athletes at NCAA Division I Institutions, 1989*; American Institutes for Research, Palo Alto, CA.

★ 897 ★
Student Athlete Drug Use

	Alcohol	Cocaine	Marijuana	Smokeless Tobacco	Anabolic Steroids	Major Pain Medication
Caucasian	91	5	28	31	5	36
Black	78	4	23	11	3	34
Other[1]	83	1	26	30	1	29

Source: "Drug Use Among Black and White Athletes," *Black Issues in Higher Education*, November 9, 1989, p. 4. Primary source: Michigan State University. Survey, 1989. *Note:* 1. Includes Asian-Americans and Native Americans.

★ 898 ★
Winning College/University Basketball Coaches - Part I

Minimum five years as Division I head coach; includes record at four-year colleges only.

Rank, Coach, School	Yrs.	By Percentages		
		Won	Lost	Pct.
1. Jerry Tarkanian, Nevada-Las Vegas	21	536	117	.821
2. John Chaney, Temple[1]	17	397	109	.785
3. Dean Smith, North Carolina	28	667	190	.778
4. Jim Boeheim, Syracuse	13	317	101	.758
5. John Thompson, Georgetown[1]	17	399	135	.747
6. Denny Crum, Louisville	18	436	148	.747
7. Bruce Stewart, Middle Tennessee State	7	172	60	.741
8. Bob Knight, Indiana	24	512	189	.730
9. Lou Carnesecca, St. John's	21	460	170	.730

Continued.

Winning College/University Basketball Coaches - Part I
[Continued]

Rank, Coach, School	By Percentages			
	Yrs.	Won	Lost	Pct.
10. Boyd Grant, Colorado State	11	239	97	.711
11. Charlie Spoonhour, SW Missouri State	6	130	54	.707
12. Kevin Mackey, Cleveland State	6	129	54	.705
13. Gale Catlett, West Virginia	17	359	151	.704
14. Nolan Richardson, Arkansas[1]	9	196	83	.703
15. Joey Meyer, DePaul	5	108	46	.701
16. Digger Phelps, Notre Dame	19	391	167	.701
17. Don Haskins, Texas-El Paso	28	542	232	.700
18. Bob Huggins, Cincinnati	8	168	72	.700
19. Don Corbett, North Carolina A&T	18	352	155	.694
20. Billy Tubbs, Oklahoma	15	336	148	.694

Source: "Winningest Active Coaches," *The Sporting News 1989-90 College Basketball Yearbook*, October 1989, p. 162. Primary source: *The Sporting News*, TSN Series #5, *1989-90 College Basketball Yearbook*. American coach and Predominantly or Historically Black Institution. *Notes:* The following coaches' records are different when games forfeited in accordance with NCAA Council actions are taken into account: Jerry Tarkanian (530-114,.823 winning percentage), Lou Henson (535-249,.682), Gene Bartow (514-270,.656), Bob Knight (514-187,.733), Eldon Miller 446- 2283,.612), Hugh Durham (428-234,.647) and Lute Olson (328-148,.689). 1. Black American coach.

★ 899 ★
Winning College/University Basketball Coaches - Part II

Minimum five years as Division I head coach; includes record at four-year colleges only.

Rank, Coach, School	By Victories Wins
1. Dean Smith, North Carolina	667
2. Norman Sloan, Florida	627
3. Don Haskins, Texas-El Paso	542
4. Lefty Driesell, James Madison	540
5. Jerry Tarkanian, Nevada-Las Vegas	536
6. Lou Henson, Illinois	533
7. Norm Stewart, Missouri	528
8. Gene Bartow, Alabama-Birmingham	513
9. Bob Knight, Indiana	512
10. Glenn Wilkes, Stetson	497
11. Tom Young, Old Dominion	496
12. Lou Carnesecca, St. John's	460
13. Eldon Miller, Northern Iowa	444
14. Denny Crum, Louisville	436
14. Bill Foster, Northwestern	436
16. Shelby Metcalf, Texas A&M	429
16. Hugh Durham, Georgia	429
18. Bill Foster, Miami (Fla.)	418
19. Butch Van Breda Kolff, Hofstra	417
20. John Thompson, Georgetown[1]	399
21. John Chaney, Temple[1]	397
22. Digger Phelps, Norte Dame	391
23. Johnny Orr, Iowa State	389
24. Pete Carril, Princeton	388

Continued.

Winning College/University Basketball Coaches - Part II
[Continued]

Rank, Coach, School	By Victories Wins
25. Bob Hallberg, Illinois-Chicago	372
26. Cy McClairen, Bethune-Cookman[2]	361
27. Gale Catlett, West Virginia	359
28. Don Corbett, N.C. A&T[2]	352
28. Murray Arnold, Western Ky	352
30. Tom Davis, Iowa	351
31. Gerald Myers, Texas Tech	344
32. Rollie Massimino, Villanova	340
33. Billy Tubbs, Oklahoma	336
34. Jim Valvano, N.C. State	327
35. Lute Olson, Arizona	326
36. George Blaney, Holy Cross	324
37. Dale Brown, Louisiana State	317
37. Jim Boeheim, Syracuse	317
39. Paul Evans, Pittsburgh	311
40. Lou Campanelli, California	306
41. Carroll Williams, Santa Clara	302
42. Gordon Stauffer, Nicholls State	298
43. Jim Calhoun, Connecticut	295
43. Tom Penders, Texas	295
45. Jud Heathcote, Michigan State	291
45. Frank Kerns, Georgia Southern	291
47. Mike Krzyewski, Duke	275
48. Bob Dye, Boise State	272
49. Neil McCarthy, New Mexico State	270
50. James Oliver, Alabama State[2]	269

Source: "Winningest Active Coaches," *The Sporting News 1989-90 College Basketball Yearbook,* October 1989, p. 162. Primary source: *The Sporting News,* TSN Series #5, *1989-90 College Basketball Yearbook.* American coach and Predominantly or Historically Black Institution. *Notes:* The following coaches' records are different when games forfeited in accordance with NCAA Council actions are taken into account: Jerry Tarkanian (530-114,.823 winning percentage), Lou Henson (535-249,.682), Gene Bartow (514-270,.656), Bob Knight (514-187,.733), Eldon Miller 446- 2283,.612), Hugh Durham (428-234,.647) and Lute Olson (328-148,.689). 1. Black American coach 2. Black.

★ 900 ★
Young Adults and Voluntary "Joining"

Young adult characteristics	Percent participating in voluntary organizations[1]											
	Sports teams or clubs	Church activities	Social or hobby clubs	Union trade farm, or other professional associates	Literary, art discussion or study	Community groups[2]	Youth organi-zations	PTA or other academic group	Political clubs	Organized volunteer work[3]	Service organi-zations[4]	Other voluntary group
Total	36.0	32.2	21.8	17.7	10.8	9.4	9.2	7.0	6.2	5.8	4.0	9.6
Race/Ethnicity												
White, non-Hispanic	36.5	30.6	22.3	18.2	10.2	8.5	8.7	6.4	5.9	5.5	3.9	9.7
Black, non-Hispanic	31.9	44.2	21.5	14.9	13.1	16.2	12.0	12.0	8.2	6.8	4.0	10.3
Hispanic	34.6	32.4	17.1	15.8	11.6	8.5	9.5	5.6	6.9	4.3	4.7	7.1

Continued.

Young Adults and Voluntary "Joining"
[Continued]

Young adult characteristics	Percent participating in voluntary organizations[1]											
	Sports teams or clubs	Church activities	Social or hobby clubs	Union trade farm, or other professional associates	Literary, art discussion or study	Community groups[2]	Youth organi-zations	PTA or other academic group	Political clubs	Organized volunteer work[3]	Service organi-zations[4]	Other voluntary group
Asian	41.4	31.0	28.7	27.3	23.2	10.5	10.8	9.1	5.9	14.1	5.9	10.3
American Indian	41.1	30.0	27.9	19.7	8.9	13.0	11.6	6.5	9.6	4.2	7.2	7.8

Source: "Participation of Young Adults in Voluntary Organizations by Selected Characteristics: 1984 to 1986, "*Digest of Education Statistics*, 1989, p. 376. Primary source: U.S. Department of Education, National Center for Education Statistics, High School and Beyond. (This table was prepared October 1987). *Notes:* Some adults participated in more than one organization. 1. Sample survey in 1986 based on people who were high school seniors in spring 1980. Respondents to the survey were asked about their voluntary participation in selected organizations over the previous 24- month period. 2. Includes participation in community centers, neighborhood improvement, or social action associations or groups. 3. E.g., hospital volunteer. 4. Includes participation in organizations such as Rotary, Junior Chamber of Commerce, Veterans, etc.

VITAL STATISTICS

★ 901 ★
Age-Adjusted Causes of Death: Trends

Data are based on the National Vital Statistics System.

Sex, race, and cause of death	1950[1]	1960[1]	1970	1980	1983	1984	1985	1986
	Deaths per 100,00 resident population							
All races								
All causes	841.5	760.9	714.3	585.8	550.5	549.9	546.1	541.7
Diseases of heart	307.6	286.2	253.6	202.0	188.8	183.6	180.5	175.0
Cerebrovascular diseases	88.8	79.7	66.3	40.8	34.4	33.4	32.3	31.0
Malignant neoplasms	125.4	125.8	129.9	132.8	132.6	133.5	133.6	133.2
Respiratory system	12.8	19.2	28.4	36.4	37.9	38.4	38.8	39.0
Colorectal	19.0	17.7	16.8	15.5	14.9	15.0	14.8	14.4
Prostate[2]	13.4	13.1	13.3	14.4	14.6	14.5	14.6	15.0
Breast[3]	22.2	22.3	23.1	22.7	22.7	23.2	23.2	23.1
Chronic obstructive pulmonary diseases	4.4	8.2	13.2	15.9	17.4	17.7	18.7	18.8
Pneumonia and influenza	26.2	28.0	22.1	12.9	11.8	22.2	13.4	13.5
Chronic liver disease and cirrhosis	8.5	10.5	14.7	12.2	10.2	10.0	9.6	9.2
Diabetes mellitus	14.3	13.6	14.1	10.1	9.9	9.5	9.6	9.6
Accidents and adverse effects	57.5	49.9	53.7	42.3	35.3	35.0	34.7	35.2
Motor vehicle accidents	23.3	22.5	27.4	22.9	18.5	19.1	18.8	19.4
Suicide	11.0	10.6	11.8	11.4	11.4	11.6	11.5	11.9
Homicide and legal intervention	5.4	5.2	9.1	10.8	8.6	8.4	8.3	9.0
White Male								
All causes	963.1	917.7	893.4	754.3	698.4	689.9	688.7	679.8
Diseases of heart	381.1	375.4	347.6	277.5	257.8	249.5	244.5	234.8
Cerebrovascular diseases	87.0	80.3	68.8	41.9	35.2	33.9	32.8	31.1
Malignant neoplasms	130.9	141.6	154.3	160.5	158.9	159.0	159.2	158.8
Respiratory system	21.6	34.6	49.9	58.0	58.0	58.4	58.2	58.0
Colorectal	19.8	18.9	18.9	18.3	17.8	17.8	17.6	17.2
Prostate	13.1	12.4	12.3	13.2	13.4	13.3	13.3	13.8
Chronic obstructive pulmonary diseases	6.0	13.8	24.0	26.7	27.6	27.6	28.5	28.1
Pneumonia and influenza	27.1	31.0	26.0	16.2	15.3	15.8	17.4	17.5
Chronic liver disease and cirrhosis	11.6	14.4	18.8	15.7	13.4	13.2	12.6	12.2
Diabetes mellitus	11.3	11.6	12.7	9.5	9.2	9.0	9.2	9.1
Accidents and adverse effects	80.9	70.5	76.2	62.3	51.8	51.3	50.4	51.1
Motor vehicle accidents	35.9	34.0	40.1	34.8	27.8	28.4	27.6	28.7
Suicide	18.1	17.5	18.2	18.9	19.3	19.7	19.9	20.5
Homicide and legal intervention	3.9	3.9	7.3	10.9	8.4	8.2	8.1	8.4
Black Male								
All causes	1,373.1	1,246.1	1,1318.6	1,112.8	1,019.6	1,011.7	1,024.0	1,026.9
Diseases of heart	415.5	381.2	375.9	327.3	308.2	300.1	301.0	294.3
Cerebrovascular diseases	146.2	141.2	124.2	77.5	64.2	62.8	60.8	58.9

Continued.

Age-Adjusted Causes of Death: Trends
[Continued]

Sex, race, and cause of death	1950[1]	1960[1]	1970	1980	1983	1984	1985	1986
Malignant neoplasms	126.1	158.5	198.0	229.9	232.2	234.9	231.6	229.0
Respiratory system	16.9	36.6	60.8	82.0	83.3	85.9	84.4	83.9
Colorectal	13.8	156.0	17.3	19.2	19.0	19.9	19.5	19.3
Prostate	16.9	22.2	25.4	29.1	29.9	29.7	30.3	30.3
Chronic obstructive pulmonary diseases	-	-	-	20.9	22.2	22.8	23.9	24.6
Pneumonia and influenza	63.8	70.2	53.8	28.0	24.3	25.2	26.8	27.2
Chronic liver disease and cirrhosis	8.8	14.8	33.1	30.6	22.8	22.5	23.4	20.8
Diabetes mellitus	11.5	16.2	21.2	17.7	17.7	17.6	17.7	17.9
Accidents and adverse effects	105.7	100.0	119.5	82.0	66.2	64.7	66.7	66.9
Motor vehicle accidents	39.8	38.2	50.1	32.9	26.4	27.2	27.7	29.2
Suicide	7.0	7.8	9.9	11.1	10.5	11.2	11.3	11.5
Homicide and legal intervention	51.1	44.9	82.1	71.9	53.8	50.8	49.9	55.9
White Female								
All causes	645.0	555.0	501.7	411.1	392.7	391.3	390.6	387.7
Diseases of heart	223.6	197.1	167.8	134.6	126.7	124.0	121.7	119.0
Cerebrovascular diseases	79.7	68.7	56.2	35.2	29.6	28.9	27.9	27.1
Malignant neoplasms	119.4	109.5	107.6	107.7	108.5	109.9	110.3	110.1
Respiratory system	4.6	5.1	10.1	18.2	21.0	21.6	22.6	23.1
Colorectal	19.0	17.0	15.3	13.3	12.5	12.8	12.3	12.0
Breast	22.5	22.4	23.4	22.8	22.7	23.1	23.3	23.0
Chronic obstructive pulmonary diseases	2.8	3.3	5.3	9.2	11.3	11.8	12.9	13.3
Pneumonia and influenza	18.9	19.0	15.0	9.4	8.6	8.8	9.8	9.9
Chronic liver disease and cirrhosis	5.8	6.6	8.7	7.0	6.0	5.9	5.6	5.4
Diabetes mellitus	16.4	13.7	12.8	8.7	8.6	8.0	8.1	8.1
Accidents and adverse effects	30.6	25.5	27.2	21.4	18.3	18.5	18.4	18.4
Motor vehicle accidents	10.6	11.1	14.4	12.3	10.3	10.9	10.8	11.0
Suicide	5.3	5.3	7.2	5.7	5.6	5.6	5.3	5.4
Homicide and legal intervention	1.4	1.5	2.2	3.2	2.8	2.9	2.9	2.9
Black female								
All causes	1,106.7	916.9	814.4	631.1	590.4	585.3	589.1	588.2
Diseases of heart	349.5	292.6	251.7	201.1	191.5	186.6	186.8	185.1
Cerebrovascular diseases	155.6	139.5	107.9	61.7	53.8	51.8	50.3	47.6
Malignant neoplasms	131.9	127.8	123.5	129.7	129.8	131.0	130.4	132.1
Respiratory system	4.1	5.5	10.9	19.5	22.0	21.4	22.5	23.3
Colorectal	15.0	15.4	16.1	15.3	15.1	15.3	16.1	15.2
Breast	19.3	21.3	21.5	23.3	24.4	26.1	25.3	25.8
Chronic obstructive pulmonary diseases	-	-	-	6.3	7.6	8.1	8.7	8.9
Pneumonia and influenza	50.4	43.9	29.2	12.7	10.2	11.3	12.4	13.1
Chronic liver disease and cirrhosis	5.7	8.9	17.8	14.4	10.8	10.3	10.1	93.3
Diabetes mellitus	22.7	27.3	30.9	22.1	21.1	20.5	21.1	21.4
Accidents and adverse effects	38.5	35.9	35.3	25.1	21.9	20.1	20.7	21.0
Motor vehicle accidents	10.3	10.0	13.8	8.4	7.5	7.6	8.2	8.5
Suicide	1.7	1.9	2.9	2.4	2.1	2.3	2.1	2.4
Homicide and legal intervention	11.7	11.8	15.0	13.7	11.2	11.0	10.8	11.8

Source: "Age-Adjusted Death Rates for Selected Causes of Death, according to Sex and Race: United States, Selected Years 1950-86, *Health United States - 1988,* March 1989, pp. 62-63. National Center for Health Statistics: *Vital Statistics Rates in the United States, 1940-1960,* by R. D. Grove and A.M. Hetzel, DHEW Pub. No. (PHS) 1677. Public Health Service, Washington. U.S. Government Printing Office, 1968; Unpublished data from the Division of Vital Statistics; *Vital Statistics of the United States,* Vol. II, Mortality, Part A, 1950-89, Public Health Service, Washington. U.S. Government Printing Office; Data computed by the Division of Analysis from data compiled by the Division of Vital Statistics. *Notes:* For data years shown, the code numbers for cause of death are based on the then current *International Classification of Diseases,* which are described in Appendix II, tables IV and V of original source. 1. Includes deaths of nonresidents of the United States. 2. Male only. 3. Female only.

★ 902 ★
AIDS Deaths at 13 and Older

Data are based on reporting by State health departments.

Race/ethnicity and transmission category	Number, by year of death								Percent distribution			
	All[1,2]	1982	1983	1984	1985	1986	1987	1988[2]	All[1,2]	1984	1986	1988[2]
Total[3]	43,093	420	1,373	3,077	5,914	9,874	12,613	9,521	100.0	100.0	100.0	100.0
Male homosexual/bisexual	27,053	244	816	1,915	3,821	6,409	7,774	5,917	62.8	62.2	64.9	62.2
Intravenous drug use	7,947	82	275	588	1,067	1,684	2,419	1,759	18.4	19.1	17.1	18.5
Male homosexual/bisexual and intravenous drug use	3,254	38	129	294	444	744	921	660	7.6	9.6	7.5	6.9
Hemophilia/coagulation disorder	452	6	6	24	70	96	140	109	1.1	0.8	1.0	1.1
Born in Caribbean/African countries	676	29	72	74	99	123	160	98	1.6	2.4	1.3	1.0
Heterosexual[4]	1,061	3	15	42	104	221	353	319	2.5	1.4	2.2	3.4
Sexual contact with intravenous drug user	728	3	9	35	71	151	243	214	1.7	1.1	1.5	2.3
Transfusion	1,349	3	19	64	169	320	446	324	3.1	2.1	3.2	3.4
Undetermined[5]	1,301	15	41	76	140	277	400	335	3.0	2.5	2.8	3.5
Race/ethnicity												
White, not Hispanic	25,480	206	739	1,804	3,586	5,995	7,387	5,617	100.0	100.0	100.0	100.0
Male homosexual/bisexual	19,676	159	573	1,409	2,840	4,709	5,594	4,288	77.2	78.1	78.6	76.3
Intravenous drug use	1,587	14	63	101	206	306	513	365	6.2	5.6	5.1	6.5
Male homosexual/bisexual and intravenous drug use	1,986	14	73	184	278	480	569	376	7.8	10.2	8.0	6.7
Hemophilia/coagulation disorder	392	6	5	21	57	85	120	97	1.5	1.2	1.4	1.7
Born in Caribbean/African countries	1	-	-	1	-	-	-	-	0.0	0.1	-	-
Heterosexual[4]	312	1	2	5	27	70	98	109	1.2	0.3	1.2	1.9
Sexual contact with intravenous drug user	152	1	-	4	9	34	52	52	0.6	0.2	0.6	0.9
Transfusion	1,035	3	15	51	126	250	338	249	4.1	2.8	4.2	4.4
Undetermined[5]	491	9	8	32	52	95	155	133	1.9	1.8	1.6	2.4
Black, not Hispanic	11,889	141	422	820	1,525	2,531	3,544	2,790	100.0	100.0	100.0	100.0
Male homosexual/bisexual	4,551	54	148	287	585	1,013	1,352	1,074	38.3	35.0	40.0	38.5
Intravenous drug use	4,459	41	133	321	584	950	1,338	1,052	37.5	39.2	37.5	37.7
Male homosexual/bisexual and intravenous drug use	889	11	38	72	115	182	252	211	7.5	8.8	7.2	7.6
Hemophilia/coagulation disorder	29	-	-	1	6	3	12	7	0.2	0.1	0.1	0.3
Born in Caribbean/African countries	671	29	72	73	98	122	158	98	5.6	8.9	4.8	3.5
Heterosexual[4]	558	1	8	24	53	97	206	165	4.7	2.9	3.8	5.9
Sexual contact with intravenous drug user	419	1	5	19	42	72	153	125	3.5	2.3	2.8	4.5
Transfusion	195	-	1	10	27	39	70	48	1.6	1.2	1.5	1.7
Undetermined[5]	537	5	22	32	57	125	156	135	4.5	3.9	4.9	4.8
Hispanic	5,366	71	202	424	762	1,274	1,575	1,023	100.0	100.0	100.0	100.0
Male homosexual/bisexual	2,580	30	89	198	372	641	752	485	48.1	46.7	50.3	47.4
Intravenous drug use	1,875	26	77	163	272	422	563	338	34.9	38.4	33.1	33.0
Male homosexual/bisexual and intravenous drug use	361	13	17	37	49	77	95	69	6.7	8.7	6.0	6.7
Hemophilia/coagulation disorder	27	-	1	2	5	8	6	5	0.5	0.5	0.6	0.5
Born in Caribbean/African countries	4	-	-	-	1	1	2	-	0.1	-	0.1	-
Heterosexual[4]	186	1	5	13	24	52	48	43	3.5	3.1	4.1	4.2
Sexual contact with intravenous drug user	156	1	4	12	20	45	38	36	2.9	2.8	3.5	3.5
Transfusion	85	-	2	2	10	23	25	23	1.6	0.5	1.8	2.3
Undetermined[5]	248	1	11	9	29	50	84	60	4.6	2.1	3.9	5.9

Source: "Acquired Immunodeficiency Syndrome (AIDS) Deaths, according to Race/Ethnicity and Transmission Category, for Persons 13 Years of Age and Over: United States, 1982-88," *Health United States - 1988*, March 1989, p. 86-87. Primary source: Centers for Disease Control, Center for Infectious Diseases, AIDS Program. *Notes:* The AIDS case definition was changed in September 1987 to allow for the presumptive diagnosis of AIDS-associated diseases and conditions and to expand the spectrum of human immunodeficiency virus-associated diseases reportable as AIDS. Excludes residents of U.S. territories. 1. Includes deaths prior to 1982. 2. Data are as of November 30, 1988, and reflect reporting delays. 3. Includes all other races not shown separately. 4. Includes persons who have had heterosexual contact with a person with human immunodeficiency virus (HIV) infection or at risk of HIV infection. 5. Includes persons for whom risk information is incomplete (because of death, refusal to be interviewed, or loss to followup), persons still under investigation, men reported only to have had heterosexual contact with prostitutes, and interviewed persons for whom no specific risk is identified.

★ 903 ★
Birth Control

Refers to women 15-44 years old at time of abortion.

	White				Black and Other			
	Women 15-44 years old (1,000)	Abortions			Women 15-44 years old (1,000)	Abortions		
		Number (1,000)	Rate per 1,000 women	Ratio per 1,000 live births		Number (1,000)	Rate per 1,000 women	Ratio per 1,000 live births
1972	38,532	455.3	11.8	175	6,056	131.5	21.7	223
1975	40,857	701.2	17.2	276	6,749	333.0	49.3	565
1976	41,721	784.9	18.8	296	7,000	394.4	56.3	638
1977	42,567	888.8	20.9	333	7,247	427.9	59.0	679
1978	43,427	969.4	22.3	356	7,493	440.2	58.7	665
1979	44,266	1,062.4	24.0	373	7,750	435.3	56.2	625
1980	44,942	1,093.6	24.3	376	8,106	460.3	56.5	642
1981	45,494	1,107.8	24.3	377	8,407	469.6	55.9	645
1982	46,049	1,095.2	23.8	373	8,630	478.7	55.5	646
1983	46,506	1,084.4	23.3	376	8,834	490.6	55.5	670
1984	47,023	(NA)	(NA)	(NA)	9,038	(NA)	(NA)	(NA)
1985	47,512	(NA)	(NA)	(NA)	9,242	(NA)	(NA)	(NA)

Source: "Legal Abortions — Estimated Number, Rate, and Ratio, by Race: 1972 to 1985," *Statistical Abstract*, 1989, p. 70. Primary source: 1972, U.S. Centers for Disease Control, Atlanta, GA, *Abortion Surveillance, Annual Summary, 1972*, 1974 and the Alan Guttmacher Institute; 1975-1981, S.K. Henshaw and E. Blaine eds., *Abortion Services in the United States, Each State and Metropolitan Area 1981- 1982*, The Alan Guttmacher Institute,, New York, NY, 1985 (copyright); 1982 and 1983, S.K. Henshaw, "Characteristics of U.S. Women Having Abortions, 1982-1983," *Family Planning Perspectives*, vol. 19, No. 1, Jan./ Feb. 1987, The Alan Guttmacher Institute, New York, NY; 1984 and 1985, S.K. Henshaw, J.D. Forrest and J. Von Vort, "Abortion Services in the United States, 1984 and 1985," *Family Planning Perspectives*, vol. 19, No. 2, March/April 1987, The Alan Guttmacher Institute, New York, NY.

★ 904 ★
Birth Control

Number of abortions from surveys conducted by source; characteristics from the U.S. Centers for Disease Control's (CDC) annual abortion surveillance summaries, with adjustments for changes in States reporting data to the CDC each year.

Characteristic	Number (1,000)							Percent Distribution			Abortion Ratio[1]		
	1973	1975	1979	1980	1981	1982	1983	1973	1980	1983	1973	1980	1983
Total legal abortions	745	1,034	1,498	1,554	1,577	1,574	1,575	100.0	100.0	100.0	193	300	304
Race of woman													
White	549	701	1,062	1,094	1,108	1,095	1,084	73.7	70.4	68.8	178	274	274
Black and other	196	333	435	460	470	479	491	26.3	29.6	31.2	252	392	401

Source: "Legal Abortions, by Selected Characteristics: 1973 to 1983," *Statistical Abstract*, 1989, p. 70. Primary Source: 1973-1981, S.K. Henshaw and E. Blaine, eds., *Abortion Services in the United States, Each State and Metropolitan Area 1981-1982*, The Alan Guttmacher Institute, New York, NY, 1985 (copyright); 1982 and 1983. S.K. Henshaw, "Characteristics of U.S. Women Having Abortions. 1982-1983." *Family Planning Perspectives*, vol. 19, No. 1. Jan/Feb. 1987, The Alan Guttmacher Institute, New York, NY. *Notes:* 1. Number of abortions per 1,000 abortions and live births. Live births are those which occurred from July 1 of year shown through June 30 of the following year (to match time of conception with abortions).

★ 905 ★
Birth Control by Contraceptives

Based on the 1982 National Survey of Family Growth.

Contraceptive Status and Method	All Women[1]	Race White	Race Black
All women (1,000)	54,099	45,367	6,985
Percent Distribution			
Sterile	27.2	27.7	23.7
Surgically sterile	25.7	26.1	22.2
Contraceptively sterile[2]	17.8	18.3	14.9
Noncontraceptively sterile	7.8	7.8	7.3
Nonsurgically sterile[3]	1.5	1.6	1.5
Pregnant,postpartum	5.0	4.8	5.6
Seeking pregnancy	4.2	4.0	5.4
Other nonusers	26.9	26.2	29.6
Not sexually active[4]	19.5	19.9	16.1
Sexually active[4]	7.4	6.4	13.5
Nonsurgical contraceptors	36.7	37.2	35.7
Pill	15.6	15.1	19.8
IUD	4.0	3.9	4.7
Diaphragm	4.5	5.0	1.8
Condom	6.7	7.2	3.2
Foam	1.3	1.4	1.4
Rhythm[5]	2.2	2.2	1.6
Other methods[6]	2.5	2.4	3.1

Source: "Contraceptive Use by Women, 15-44 Years Old, by Race and Method of Contraception: 1982," *Statistical Abstract*, 1989, p. 69. Primary source: U.S. National Center for Health Statistics, *Advance Data from Vital and Health Statistics*, No. 102 and unpublished data. *Notes:* 1. Includes other races, not shown separately. 2. Includes sterility of the husband or a current partner. Persons who had sterilizing operation and who gave as one reason that they had already had all the children they wanted. 3. Persons sterile from illness, accident, or congenital conditions. 4. Those having intercourse in the last 3 months before the survey. 5. Periodic abstinence and natural family planning. 6. Withdrawal, douche, suppository and less frequently used methods.

★ 906 ★
Birth Projections

As of June.

Year	Lifetime Births to White Wives Aged--			Lifetime Births to Black Wives Aged--		
	18-24	25-29	30-34	18-24	25-29	30-34
1971	2,353	2,577	2,936	2,623	3,112	3,714
1975	2,147	2,233	2,564	2,489	2,587	3,212
1980	2,130	2,146	2,223	2,155	2,426	2,522
1985	2,177	2,227	2,139	2,242	2,259	2,521
1987	2,192	2,228	2,180	2,199	2,333	2,281

Source: "Lifetime Births Expected per 1,000 Wives: 1971 to 1987," *Statistical Abstract*, 1989, p. 69. Primary source: U.S. Bureau of the Census, *Current Population Reports*, series P-20, No. 427, and earlier reports.

★ 907 ★
Birth Rates

Total fertility rates per 1,000.

Race/ethnicity	1940	1950	1960	1965	1970	1975	1980	1985	1986
Total	2.30	3.09	3.65	2.91	2.48	1.77	1.84	1.84	1.84
White	2.23	2.98	3.53	2.78	2.39	1.69	1.75	1.75	1.74
Non-White	2.87	3.93	4.52	3.81	3.07	2.28	2.32	2.26	2.28
Black	[3]	[3]	4.54	3.83	3.10	2.24	2.27	2.20	2.23
Total Hispanic[1]							2.53		
Mexican							2.90		
Puerto Rican							2.05		
Cuban							1.30		
Other Hispanic[2]							2.06		
Non-Hispanic							1.81		
White							1.69		
Black							2.35		

Source: "Average Number of Children Born per Woman, 1940-1986," *U.S. Children and Their Families*, 1989, p. 7. Primary source: National Center for Health Statistics, 1988, *Vital Statistics of the United States, 1986*, Vol. I, Natality, Table 1-6 and NCHS, S.J. Ventura, "Births of Hispanic Parentage, 1980," *Monthly Vital Statistics Report*, Vol. 32, No. 6, Supplement, Table 5. *Notes:* Total fertility rates show the number of children that *would* be born to 1,000 women if they were subject at each year to the observed age specific fertility rates in a given year. Dividing by 1,000 gives the average number of children that a typical woman would bear under the same assumptions. Because the total fertility rate is unaffected by differences in the age composition of women 15-49, it is a useful statistic for comparing fertility across different populations. 1. Data on Hispanic origin were obtained from 22 reporting states, accounting for about 90 percent of all Hispanic origin births in the United States, but for only about 57% of all births in the nation. To calculate total fertility rates, it is necessary to know the number of women in each age and ethnicity category. For the states reporting Hispanic origin information on their birth certificates, such data are currently only available during census years. 2. Includes Central and South American and other and unknown Hispanics. 3. Not available.

★ 908 ★
Birth Rates

Race	Percent of All Births Occurring Outside Marriage, by Race/Hispanic Origin						
	1950	1960	1970	1975	1980	1985	1986
White	1.8	2.3	5.7	7.3	11.0	14.5	15.7
Non-white	18.0	21.6	34.9	44.2	48.5	51.4	52.4
Black	[2]	[2]	37.6	48.8	55.3	60.1	61.2
Hispanic	[2]	[2]	[2]	[2]	23.6	29.5	31.6
Non-Hispanic	[2]	[2]	[2]	[2]	18.5	21.6	22.8

Non-Marital Birth Rate[1]

	1950	1960	1970	1975	1980	1985	1986
White	6.1	9.2	13.9	12.4	17.6	21.8	23.2
Non-white	71.2	98.3	89.9	79.0	77.2	73.2	74.8
Black	[2]	[2]	95.5	84.2	82.9	78.8	80.9

Continued.

Birth Rates
[Continued]

Race	Percent of All Births Occurring Outside Marriage, by Race/Hispanic Origin						
	1950	1960	1970	1975	1980	1985	1986
Hispanic	2	2	2	2	52.0	2	2
Non-Hispanic	2	2	2	2	27.7	2	2

Source: "Births to Unmarried Women, 1950-1986," *U.S. Children and Their Families*, 1989, p. 15. Primary source: National Center for Health Statistics, *Vital Statistics of the United States*, Annual Natality Volumes for 1950, 1960, 1970, 1975, 1980, 1985, and 1986; *Monthly Vital Statistics Report*, "Advance Report of Final Natality Statistics, 1986," Vol. 37, No. 3, Supplement, Table 27; *Monthly Vital Statistics Report*, "Births of Hispanic Parentage, 1985," Vol. 36, No. 11, Supplement, Table 6; *Monthly Vital Statistics Report*, "Births of Hispanic Parentage, 1980, "Vol. 32, No. 6, Supplement, Tables 1 and 11. *Notes:* Data on Hispanic origin are based on information from 22 reporting states in 1980 and from 23 reporting states and the District of Columbia in 1985 and 1986. 1. Births per 1,000 unmarried women aged 15-44. 2. Not available.

★ 909 ★
Birth Rates and Educational Level

Characteristic	Current Age of Woman						Total Number of of Children (mil.)
	18-24 Years		25-34 Years		35-44 Years		
	Children Born per 1,000 Women	Percent Childless	Children Born Per 1,000 Women	Percent Childless	Children Born Per 1,000 Women	Percent Childless	
Total	429	71.7	1,369	31.6	2,089	15.6	71.3
All Races							
Less than H.S.	885	49.0	2,162	12.0	2,919	8.8	15.7
High School	478	66.9	1,529	22.9	2,138	12.2	32.2
Some college	158	87.7	1,241	33.7	1,938	15.1	13.5
College/more	79	93.6	728	57.4	1,611	26.6	10.0
White							
Less than H.S.	837	50.9	2,061	13.1	2,760	9.0	11.3
High School	427	69.6	1,487	24.2	2,114	12.1	26.6
Some college	140	89.2	1,204	35.1	1,913	15.5	11.1
College/more	60	94.8	720	58.3	1,577	28.2	8.6
Black							
Less than H.S.	1,078	39.8	2,553	8.3	3,557	8.0	3.7
High School	756	51.7	1,777	15.0	2,375	11.9	4.8
Some college	286	76.6	1,411	25.7	2,124	11.1	1.9
College/more	290	81.0	878	43.7	1,848	16.2	.8
Hispanic[1]							
Less than H.S.	1,085	43.4	2,381	11.9	3,185	6.6	4.1
High School	505	65.2	1,732	18.6	2,582	9.4	2.4
Some college	235	81.9	1,373	26.6	2,166	9.2	.8
College/more	2	2	621	63.0	1,544	28.5	2

Source: "Children Ever Born Per 1,000 Women and Percent Childless, by Education and Race/Hispanic Origin, June 1987," *U.S. Children and Their Families*, 1989, p. 12. Primary source: U.S. Bureau of the Census, Current Population Reports, *Fertility of American Women: June 1987*, Series P-20, No. 427, Table 2. *Notes:* 1. Persons of Hispanic Origin may be of any race. 2. Population base too small to provide reliable estimates.

★ 910 ★
Birth Rates at ages 15-44: Trends

Race of child and year	Total	Live-birth order				
		1	2	3	4	5 or higher
		Live births per 1,000 women 15-44 years of age				
All races						
1950	106.2	33.3	32.1	18.4	9.2	13.2
1955	118.3	32.8	31.8	23.1	13.3	17.3
1960	118.0	31.1	29.2	22.8	14.6	20.3
1965	96.6	29.8	23.4	16.6	10.7	16.1
1970	87.9	34.2	24.2	13.6	7.2	8.7
1975	66.0	28.1	20.9	9.4	3.9	3.7
1980	68.4	29.5	21.8	10.3	3.9	2.9
1981	67.4	29.0	21.6	10.2	3.8	2.8
1982	67.3	28.6	22.0	10.2	3.8	2.6
1983	65.8	27.8	21.5	10.1	3.7	2.6
1984	65.4	27.4	21.7	10.1	3.7	2.6
1985	66.2	27.6	22.0	10.4	3.8	2.5
1986	65.4	27.2	21.6	10.3	3.8	2.5
White						
1950	102.3	33.3	32.3	17.9	8.4	10.4
1955	113.7	32.6	32.0	22.9	12.6	13.6
1960	113.2	30.8	29.2	22.7	14.1	16.4
1965	91.4	28.9	23.0	16.2	10.2	13.1
1970	84.1	32.9	23.7	13.3	6.8	7.4
1975	62.5	26.7	20.3	8.8	3.5	3.1
1980	64.7	28.4	21.0	9.5	3.4	2.4
1981	63.9	28.1	20.9	9.4	3.3	2.3
1982	63.9	27.7	21.3	9.5	3.3	2.2
1983	62.4	26.8	20.9	9.4	3.3	2.1
1984	62.2	26.4	21.1	9.4	3.2	2.0
1985	63.0	26.5	21.4	9.7	3.3	2.0
1986	61.9	26.0	20.9	9.6	3.3	1.9
Black						
1960	153.5	33.6	29.3	24.0	18.6	48.0
1965	133.9	35.7	26.2	19.4	14.6	38.0
1970	115.4	43.3	27.1	16.1	10.0	18.9
1975	87.9	36.9	24.2	12.6	6.3	8.0
1980	88.1	35.2	25.7	14.5	6.7	6.0
1981	85.4	33.8	25.2	14.3	6.6	5.7
1982	84.1	33.0	24.9	14.2	6.5	5.4
1983	81.7	32.3	24.1	13.7	6.3	5.2
1984	81.4	32.2	24.1	13.9	6.3	5.1
1985	82.2	32.4	24.5	13.9	6.3	5.1
1986	82.4	32.5	24.5	14.1	6.3	4.9

Source: "Birth Rates for Women 15-44 Years of Age, according to Live Birth Order and Race of Child: United States, Selected Years 1950-86," *Health United States - 1988,* p. 43. Primary source: National Center for Health Statistics: *Vital Statistics of the United States,* 1986, Vol. 1, Natality. Public Health Service, DHHS, Hyattsville, Md. To be published. *Notes:* Data are based on births adjusted for underregistration for 1950 and 1955 and on registered births for all other years. Beginning in 1970, births to nonresidents of the United States are excluded. Figures for live-birth order not stated are distributed.

★ 911 ★
Births

Births in thousands, except as indicated. Beginning 1970, excludes births to nonresidents of U.S. Minus sign (-) indicates decrease. See also *Historical Statistics, Colonial Times to 1970*, series B 1, B 5-10, and B 12-20.

Item		1960	1965	1970	1975	1979	1980	1981	1982	1983	1984	1985	1986
	Live births[1]	4,258	3,760	3,731	3,144	3,494	3,612	3,629	3,681	3,639	3,669	3,761	3,757
	Average annual percent change[2]	.8	-2.5	-.2	-3.4	2.7	3.4	.5	1.4	-1.1	.8	2.5	-.1
White		3,601	3,124	3,091	2,552	2,808	2,899	2,909	2,942	2,904	2,924	2,991	2,970
Black		602	581	572	512	576	590	588	593	586	593	608	621
	Birth rate per 1,000 population	23.7	19.4	18.4	14.6	15.6	15.9	15.8	15.9	15.5	15.5	15.8	15.6
White		22.7	18.3	17.4	13.6	14.5	14.9	14.8	14.9	14.6	14.5	14.8	14.5
Black		31.9	27.7	25.3	20.7	22.0	22.1	21.6	21.4	20.9	20.8	21.1	21.2
	Plural birth ratio[3]	20.4	20.1	18.1[4]	19.2	19.5	19.3	19.7	19.9	20.3	20.3	21.0	21.6
White		19.3	19.0	17.3[4]	18.5	18.6	18.5	18.8	18.8	19.2	19.6	19.8	20.4	21.2
Black		6		6	22.8[4]	23.1	24.2	24.1	24.7	24.1	24.5	24.2	25.3	24.9
	Birth rate per 1,000 women[5]	118.0	96.6	87.9	66.0	67.2	68.4	67.4	67.3	65.8	65.4	66.2	65.4
White[5]		113.2	91.4	84.1	62.5	63.4	64.7	63.9	63.9	62.4	62.2	63.0	61.9
Black[5]		153.5	133.2	115.4	87.9	88.3	88.1	85.4	84.1	81.7	81.4	82.2	82.4
	Birth rate per 1,000 men	94.8	77.4	71.5	53.8	55.8	57.0	56.3	56.4	55.3	55.0	55.7	54.9
White		89.8	72.3	67.1	49.8	51.6	52.9	52.3	52.5	51.5	51.2	51.9	50.9
Black		6		6	107.4	82.1	83.7	83.8	81.2	79.8	78.0	77.6	78.2	78.3

Source: "Births and Birth Rates: 1960 to 1986," *Statistical Abstract*, 1989, p. 62. Primary Source: U.S. National Center for Health Statistics, *Vital Statistics of the United States*, annual; and unpublished data. *Notes:* 1. Includes other races not shown separately. 2. For explanation, see Guide to Tabular Presentation for 1960, change from 1055. 3. Per 1,000 live births. 4. 1971. 5. Per 1,000 women, 15-44 years old in specified group. 6. Not available.

★ 912 ★
Births

As of June. Covers civilian noninstitutional population. Since the number of women who had a birth during the 12- month period was tabulated and not the actual numbers of births some small underestimation of fertility for this period may exist due to the omission of: (1) Multiple births (2) Two or more live births spaced within the 12- month period (the woman is counted only once), (3) Women who had births in the period and who did not survive to the survey date, (4) Women who were in institutions and therefore not in the survey universe. These losses may be somewhat offset by the inclusion in the CPS of births to immigrants who did not have their children born in the United States and births to nonresident women. These births would not have been recorded in the vital registration system. Based on Current Population Survey (CPS).

	Total 18 to 44 years old			18 to 29 years old			30 to 44 years old		
		Women who have had a child in the last year			Women who have had a child in the last year			Women who have had a child in the last year	
Characteristic	Number of women (1,000)	Total births per 1,000 women	First births per 1,000 women	Number of women (1,000)	Total births per 1,000 women	First births per 1,000 women	Number of women (1,000)	Total Births per 1,000 women	First births per 1,000 women
Total[1]	52,139	71.0	27.4	24,265	103.9	48.0	27,874	42.3	9.4
White	43,634	68.5	27.5	20,091	100.3	48.4	23,543	41.3	9.6
Black	6,734	83.2	24.8	3,402	123.0	44.6	3,331	42.5	4.6
Hispanic	4,296	95.8	24.4	2,239	126.7	40.2	2,057	62.1	7.3

Source: "Social and Economic Characteristiics of Women, 18-44 Years Old, Who Have Had A Child In The Last Year: 1987," *Statistical Abstract*, 1989, p. 67. U.S. Bureau of the Census, *Current Population Reports*, series P-20, No. 427. *Notes:* 1. Includes women of other races and women with family income not reported, not shown separately. 2. Hispanic persons may be of any race.

★ 913 ★
Births to Young Unmarried Women

Age	All races	White	Black	His-panic
Total under 20 years	58.7	45.1	90.0	51.9
Under 15 years	91.8	82.4	98.7	79.0
15-17 years	70.9	57.8	95.4	60.6
18-19 years	50.7	38.0	85.5	53.8

Source: "Percentage of Births to Unmarried Women Younger Than 20, by Age and Race, 1985." *The Urban League Review* 12 (Summer 1988/ Winter 1988-89), p. 12. Primary source: Pittman, K., and Adams, G. *Teenage Pregnancy: An Advocate's Guide to the Numbers.* A Publication of the Adolescent Pregnancy Prevention Clearinghouse. Washington, D.C.: Children's Defense Fund, 1988, p. 19.

★ 914 ★
Characteristics of Births - Part I

Births per 1,000 women 15-44 years old in specified racial group. Live-birth order refers to number of children born alive. Figures for births of order not stated are distributed. See also *Historical Statistics, Colonial Times to 1970*, series B 20-27.

Live-birth order	All Races[1]					White				
	1960	1970	1980	1985	1986	1960	1970	1980	1985	1986
Total	118.0	87.9	68.4	66.2	65.4	113.2	84.1	64.7	63.0	61.9
First birth	31.1	34.2	29.5	27.6	27.2	30.8	32.9	28.4	26.5	26.0
Second birth	29.2	24.2	21.8	22.0	21.6	29.2	23.7	21.0	21.4	20.9
Third birth	22.8	13.6	10.3	10.4	10.3	22.7	13.3	9.5	9.7	9.6
Fourth birth	14.6	7.2	3.9	3.8	3.8	14.1	6.8	3.4	3.3	3.3
Fifth birth	8.3	3.8	1.5	1.4	1.4	7.5	3.4	1.3	1.1	1.1
Sixth and seventh	7.6	3.2	1.0	.8	.8	6.1	2.7	.8	.7	.6
Eighth and over	4.3	1.8	.4	.3	.3	2.8	1.2	.3	.2	.2

Source: "Birth Rates, by Live-Birth Order and Race: 1960 to 1986," *Statistical Abstract*, 1989, p. 64. Primary source: U.S. National Center for Health Statistics. *Vital Statistics of the United States*, annual and unpublished data. *Note:* 1. Includes other races, not shown separately.

★ 915 ★
Characteristics of Divorced Persons

Year and sex	Total	Race		Hispanic[1]
		White	Black	
Both sexes:				
1988	133	124	263	137
1980	100	92	203	98
1970	47	44	83	61
1960	35	33	62	[2]
Male:				
1988	110	102	216	106
1980	79	74	149	64
1970	35	32	62	40
1960	28	27	45	[2]

Continued.

Characteristics of Divorced Persons
[Continued]

Year and sex	Total	Race		Hispanic[1]
		White	Black	
Female:				
1988	156	146	311	167
1980	120	110	258	132
1970	60	56	104	81
1960	42	38	78	[2]

Source: "Divorced Persons per 1,000 Married Persons with Spouse Present, by Age, Sex, Race, and Hispanic Origin: 1988, 1980, 1970 and 1960," *Marital Status and Living Arrangements: March 1988*, p. 60. Primary source: U.S. Bureau of the Census, Current Population Reports, Series P-20, No. 444. *Marital Status and Living Arrangements: March 1988*. Source of 1970 Hispanic data: 1970 Census of Population, Vol.11, 1C, *Persons of Spanish Origin*. Source of 1960 Black data: *1960 Census of Population*, Vol. 11, 1C, Nonwhite Population by Race. *Notes:* 1. Persons of Hispanic origin may be of any race. 2. Not Available.

★ 916 ★
Characteristics of Live Births: Trends

Data are based on the National Vital Statistics System.

Race of child and characteristic	1970	1975	1980	1981	1982	1983	1984	1985	1986
	Percent of live births								
Birth weight:[1]									
Less than 2,500 grams	7.94	7.39	6.84	6.81	6.75	6.82	6.72	6.75	6.81
Less than 1,500 grams	1.17	1.16	1.15	1.16	1.18	1.19	1.19	1.21	1.21
Age of mother:									
Less than 18 years	6.3	7.6	5.8	5.4	5.2	5.0	4.8	4.7	4.8
18-19 years	11.3	11.3	9.8	9.4	9.0	8.7	8.3	8.0	7.8
Unmarried mothers	10.7	14.3	18.4	18.9	19.4	20.3	21.0	22.0	23.4
Education of mother:									
Less than 12 years	30.8	28.6	23.7	22.9	22.3	21.7	20.9	20.6	20.4
16 years or more	8.6	11.4	14.0	14.8	15.3	15.9	16.4	16.7	17.1
Prenatal care began:									
1st trimester	68.0	72.4	76.3	76.3	76.1	76.2	76.5	76.2	75.9
3rd trimester or no prenatal care	7.9	6.0	5.1	5.2	5.5	5.6	5.6	5.7	6.0
White									
Birth weight:[1]									
Less than 2,500 grams	6.84	6.26	5.70	5.67	5.63	5.67	5.59	5.64	5.64
Less than 1,500 grams	0.95	0.92	0.90	0.90	0.92	0.93	0.92	0.94	0.93
Age of mother:									
Less than 18 years	4.8	6.0	4.5	4.3	4.1	3.9	3.7	3.7	3.7
18-19 years	10.4	10.3	9.0	8.6	8.2	7.9	7.4	7.1	6.9
Unmarried mothers	5.7	7.3	11.0	11.6	12.1	12.8	13.4	14.5	15.7
Education of mother:									
Less than 12 years	27.0	25.0	20.7	19.9	19.3	18.7	18.0	17.8	17.6
16 years or more	9.5	12.7	15.6	16.4	17.0	17.7	18.4	18.7	19.2
Prenatal care began:									
1st trimester	72.4	75.9	79.3	79.4	79.3	79.4	79.6	79.4	79.2
3rd trimester or no prenatal care	6.2	5.0	4.3	4.3	4.5	4.6	4.7	4.7	5.0

Continued.

Characteristics of Live Births: Trends
[Continued]

Race of child and characteristic	1970	1975	1980	1981	1982	1983	1984	1985	1986
Black									
Birth weight:[1]									
Less than 2,500 grams	13.86	13.09	12.49	12.53	12.40	12.59	12.36	12.42	12.53
Less than 1,500 grams	2.40	2.37	2.44	2.47	2.51	2.55	2.56	2.65	2.66
Age of mother:									
Less than 18 years	14.7	16.1	12.2	11.4	11.1	10.9	10.6	10.3	10.4
18-19 years	16.6	16.8	14.3	13.9	13.5	13.4	13.1	12.7	12.4
Unmarried mothers	37.4	49.0	55.2	56.0	56.7	58.2	59.2	60.1	61.2
Education of mother:									
Less than 12 years	51.0	45.1	36.2	35.4	34.8	34.2	33.1	32.3	31.7
16 years or more	2.8	4.4	6.3	6.6	6.8	6.8	7.0	7.1	7.3
Prenatal care began:									
1st trimester	44.4	55.8	62.7	62.4	61.5	61.5	62.2	61.8	61.6
3rd trimester or no prenatal care	16.6	10.5	8.8	9.1	9.6	9.7	9.6	10.0	10.6
Asian and Pacific Islander[2]									
Birth weight:[1]									
Less than 2,500 grams	8.43	7.04	6.55	6.61	6.63	6.51	6.53	6.11	6.38
Less than 1,500 grams	1.12	0.80	0.91	0.91	0.87	0.87	0.91	0.84	0.87
Age of mother:									
Less than 18 years	3.3	2.7	1.7	1.8	1.8	1.7	1.8	1.8	1.9
18-19 years	7.1	5.8	4.3	4.4	4.4	3.9	3.8	3.7	3.7
Unmarried mothers	7.8	8.5	7.8	7.5	8.4	9.0	9.6	10.1	10.6
Education of mother:									
Less than 12 years	21.7	18.5	20.0	21.9	22.2	20.7	19.3	18.5	17.3
16 years or more	20.0	27.5	30.2	29.0	28.9	29.7	30.2	30.1	31.1
Prenatal care began:									
1st trimester	67.8	73.9	74.7	74.4	74.4	74.9	75.6	75.0	75.6
3rd trimester or no prenatal care	6.8	4.5	6.1	6.2	6.2	6.1	6.0	6.1	5.9
American Indian[3]									
Birth weight:[1]									
Less than 2,500 grams	7.99	6.61	6.47	6.27	6.17	6.43	6.16	5.88	6.16
Less than 1,500 grams	0.98	1.04	0.96	0.90	1.04	1.06	1.03	0.98	1.01
Age of mother:									
Less than 18 years	7.5	11.0	8.8	8.5	8.0	7.9	7.4	7.1	7.4
18-19 years	13.3	15.8	14.3	14.0	13.5	12.9	12.6	12.0	11.8
Unmarried mothers	19.8	27.9	33.5	35.2	36.3	38.7	39.8	40.7	42.3
Education of mother:									
Less than 12 years	57.6	50.6	41.8	40.7	39.5	38.8	38.0	36.9	36.8
16 years or more	3.0	2.8	4.2	4.4	4.5	4.3	4.5	4.6	4.6
Prenatal care began:									
1st trimester	41.7	49.3	58.7	59.3	60.5	59.7	60.0	60.3	60.7
3rd trimester or no prenatal care	25.6	19.5	13.3	12.9	12.4	12.7	12.4	11.5	11.6

Source: "Live Births, according to Race of Child and Selected Characteristics: United States, Selected Years 1970-86," *Health United States - 1988*, March 1989, p. 47. Primary source: *Vital Statistics of the United States*. U.S. Government Printing Office, Washington, DC. *Notes:* Data on education of mother are not available from California, Texas, and Washington. Other States do not have data on marital status, education, and/or month prenatal care began for certain years before 1980. 1. Before 1979, data are for infants weighing 2,500 grams or less at birth. 2. Includes Chinese, Japanese, Filipino, Hawaiian (Includes part Hawaiian), Guamian (1970 and 1975), and other Pacific Islander (starting in 1980). 3. Includes Aleut and Eskimo.

★ 917 ★
Death by Suicide: Trends

Data are based on the National Vital Statistics System.

Sex, race, and age	1950[1]	1960[1]	1970	1980	1983	1984	1985	1986
	Deaths per 100,000 resident population							
All races								
All ages, age adjusted	11.0	10.6	11.8	11.4	11.4	11.6	11.5	11.9
All ages, crude	11.4	10.6	11.6	11.9	12.1	12.4	12.3	12.8
Under 1 year	-	...	...	...	...	...	...	...
1-4 years	-	...	...	...	...	...	...	...
5-14 years	0.2	0.3	0.3	0.4	0.6	0.7	0.8	0.8
15-24 years	4.5	5.2	8.8	12.3	11.9	12.5	12.9	13.1
25-34 years	9.1	10.0	14.1	16.0	15.8	15.5	15.2	15.7
35-44 years	14.3	14.2	16.9	15.4	14.6	15.1	14.6	15.2
45-54 years	20.9	20.7	20.0	15.9	16.2	16.2	15.6	16.4
55-64 years	27.0	23.7	21.4	15.9	16.5	17.3	16.7	17.0
65-74 years	29.3	23.0	20.8	16.9	17.7	18.8	18.5	19.7
75-84 years	31.1	27.9	21.2	19.1	22.3	22.0	24.1	25.2
85 years and over	28.8	26.0	20.4	19.2	19.0	18.4	19.1	20.8
White male								
All ages, age adjusted	18.1	17.5	18.2	18.9	19.3	19.7	19.9	20.5
All ages, crude	19.0	17.6	18.0	19.9	20.6	21.3	21.5	22.3
Under 1 year	-	...	...	...	...	...	...	...
1-4 years	-	...	...	...	...	...	...	...
5-14 years	0.3	0.5	0.5	0.7	0.9	1.1	1.3	1.2
15-24 years	6.6	8.6	13.9	21.4	20.6	22.0	22.7	23.6
25-34 years	13.8	14.9	19.9	25.6	26.2	25.8	25.4	26.4
35-44 years	22.4	21.9	23.3	23.5	23.2	23.7	23.5	23.9
45-54 years	34.1	33.7	29.5	24.2	25.5	25.3	25.1	26.3
55-64 years	45.9	40.2	35.0	25.8	27.4	28.8	28.6	28.7
65-74 years	53.2	42.0	38.7	32.5	33.2	35.6	35.3	37.6
75-84 years	61.9	55.7	45.5	45.5	52.5	52.0	57.1	58.9
85 years and over	61.9	61.3	50.3	52.8	56.8	55.8	60.3	66.3
Black male								
All ages, age adjusted	7.0	7.8	9.9	11.1	10.5	11.2	11.3	11.5
All ages, crude	6.3	6.4	8.0	10.3	9.9	10.6	10.8	11.1
Under 1 year {	-	...	...	...	...	...	...	...
1-4 years {		...	...	...	...	...	...	...
5-14 years	-	0.1	0.1	0.3	0.5	0.5	0.6	0.8
15-24 years	4.9	4.1	10.5	12.3	11.5	11.2	13.3	11.5
25-34 years	9.3	12.4	19.2	21.8	19.1	20.7	19.6	21.3
35-44 years	10.4	12.8	12.6	15.6	14.0	16.5	14.9	17.5
45-54 years	10.4	10.8	13.8	12.0	12.1	11.6	13.5	12.8
55-64 years	16.5	16.2	10.6	11.7	11.6	13.4	11.5	9.9
65-74 years	10.0	11.3	8.7	11.1	13.6	13.8	15.8	16.1
75-84 years {	6.2	6.6	8.9	10.5	15.8	15.1	15.6	16.0
85 years and over {		6.9	10.3	18.9	12.7	11.1	7.7	17.9
White female								
All ages, age adjusted	5.3	5.3	7.2	5.7	5.6	5.6	5.3	5.4
All ages, crude	5.5	5.3	7.1	5.9	5.9	5.9	5.6	5.9

Continued.

Death by Suicide: Trends
[Continued]

Sex, race, and age		1950[1]	1960[1]	1970	1980	1983	1984	1985	1986
Under 1 year		-	...	...	...	...	...	...	...
1-4 years		-	...	...	...	...	...	...	...
5-14 years		0.1	0.1	0.1	0.2	0.3	0.3	0.5	0.5
15-24 years		2.7	2.3	4.2	4.6	4.6	4.7	4.7	4.7
25-34 years		5.2	5.8	9.0	7.5	7.2	6.6	6.4	6.2
35-44 years		8.2	8.1	13.0	9.1	8.2	8.4	7.7	8.3
45-54 years		10.5	10.9	13.5	10.2	9.9	10.0	9.0	9.6
55-64 years		10.7	10.9	12.3	9.1	9.1	9.1	8.4	9.0
65-74 years		10.6	8.8	9.6	7.0	7.9	7.8	7.3	7.7
75-84 years		8.4	9.2	7.2	5.7	6.6	6.8	7.0	8.0
85 years and over		8.9	6.1	6.1	5.8	5.3	5.1	4.7	5.0
Black female									
All ages, age adjusted		1.7	1.9	2.9	2.4	2.1	2.3	2.1	2.4
All ages, crude		1.5	1.6	2.6	2.2	2.0	2.2	2.1	2.3
Under 1 year	{	-	...	...	...	...	...	...	...
1-4 years	{		...	...	...	...	...	...	...
5-14 years		-	0.0	0.2	0.1	0.6	0.2	0.2	0.2
15-24 years		1.8	1.3	3.8	2.3	2.7	2.4	2.0	2.3
25-34 years		2.6	3.0	5.7	4.1	2.9	3.5	3.0	3.8
35-44 years		2.0	3.0	3.7	4.6	3.5	3.2	3.6	2.8
45-54 years		3.5	3.1	3.7	2.8	3.0	3.5	3.2	3.2
55-64 years		1.1	3.0	2.0	2.3	1.7	3.1	2.2	4.2
65-74 years		1.9	2.3	2.9	1.7	1.3	2.5	2.0	2.8
75-84 years	{	2.4	1.3	1.7	1.4	1.3	0.5	4.5	2.6
85 years and over	{		-	3.2	-	2.3	0.8	1.4	-

Source: "Death Rates for Suicide, according to Sex, Race, and Age: United States, Selected Years 1950-86," *Health United States - 1988,* March 1989, p. 74. Primary source: *Vital Statistics of the United States.* National Center for Health Statistics, U.S. Government Printing Office, Washington, DC. *Notes:* For data years shown, the code numbers for cause of death are based on the then current *International Classification of Diseases,* which are described in Appendix II, tables IV and V. 1. Includes deaths of nonresidents of the United States.

★ 918 ★
Death Rates

Deaths per 100,000 population in specified group. Beginning in 1970, excludes deaths of nonresidents of U.S.

Year and characteristic	Total[1]	Diseases of the heart	Malignant neoplasms	Accidents and adverse effects	Cerebro-vascular diseases	Chronic obstructive pulmonary diseases[2]	Pneumonia, flu	Suicide	Diabetes mellitus	Chronic liver disease, cirrhosis
White										
Male: 1960, age-adjusted	917.7	375.4	141.6	70.6	80.3	[3]	31.0	17.5	11.6	14.4
1970, age-adjusted	893.4	347.6	154.3	76.2	68.3	[3]	26.0	18.2	12.7	18.8
1980, age-adjusted	745.3	277.5	160.5	62.3	41.9	26.7	16.2	18.9	9.5	15.7
1985, age-adjusted	688.7	244.5	159.2	50.4	32.8	28.5	17.4	19.9	9.2	12.6
1986, age-adjusted	679.8	234.8	158.8	51.1	31.1	28.1	17.5	20.5	9.1	12.2
Female:1960, age-adjusted	555.0	197.1	109.5	25.4	68.7	[3]	19.0	5.3	13.7	6.6
1970, age-adjusted	501.7	167.8	107.6	27.2	56.2	[3]	15.0	7.2	12.8	8.7
1980, age-adjusted	411.1	134.6	107.7	21.4	35.2	9.2	9.4	5.7	8.7	7.0
1985, age-adjusted	390.6	121.7	110.3	18.4	27.9	12.9	9.8	5.3	8.1	5.6
1986, age-adjusted	387.7	119.0	110.1	18.4	27.1	13.3	9.9	5.4	8.1	5.4
Black										
Male: 1960, age-adjusted	1,246.1	381.2	158.5	100.0	141.2	[3]	70.2	7.8	16.2	14.8

Continued.

Death Rates
[Continued]

Year and characteristic	Total[1]	Dis-eases of the heart	Malig-nant neo-plasms	Accidents and adverse effects	Cerebro-vascular diseases	Chronic obstruc-tive pul-monary diseases[2]	Pneu-monia, flu	Suicide	Diabetes mellitus	Chronic liver disease, cirrhosis
1970, age-adjusted	1,318.6	375.9	198.0	119.5	122.5	[3]	53.8	9.9	21.2	33.1
1980, age-adjusted	1,112.8	327.3	229.9	82.0	77.5	20.9	28.0	11.1	17.7	30.6
1985, age-adjusted	1,024.0	301.0	231.6	66.7	60.8	23.9	26.8	11.3	17.7	23.4
1986, age-adjusted	1,026.9	294.3	229.0	66.9	58.9	24.6	27.2	11.5	17.9	20.8
Female: 1960, age-adjusted	916.9	292.6	127.8	35.9	139.5	[3]	43.9	1.9	27.3	8.9
1970, age-adjusted	814.4	251.7	123.5	35.3	107.9	[3]	29.2	2.9	30.9	17.8
1980, age-adjusted	631.1	201.1	129.7	25.1	61.7	6.3	12.7	2.4	22.1	14.4
1985, age-adjusted	589.1	186.8	130.4	20.7	50.3	8.7	12.4	2.1	21.1	10.1
1986, age-adjusted	588.2	185.1	132.1	21.0	47.6	8.9	13.1	2.4	21.4	9.3

Source: "Death Rates by Selected Causes and Selected Characteristics: 1960 to 1986," *Statistical Abstract*, 1989, p. 80. Primary source: U.S. National Center for Health Statistics, *Vital Statistics of the United States,* annual. *Notes:* 1. Includes other causes, not shown separately. 2. Includes allied conditions. 3. Data not available on a comparable basis with later years.

★ 919 ★
Death Rates

Rates are per 1000,000 population. Excludes deaths of nonresidents of the U.S. Beginning 1979, deaths classified according to the ninth revision of the *International Classification of Diseases.*

Cause of Death and Age	White						Black					
	Male			Female			Male			Female		
	1970	1980	1986	1970	1980	1986	1970	1980	1986	1970	1980	1986
Total[1]	101.9	97.1	85.8	42.4	36.3	33.2	183.2	154.0	131.1	51.7	42.6	37.4
Motor vehicle accidents	39.1	35.9	29.2	14.8	12.8	11.5	44.3	31.1	28.6	13.4	8.3	8.5
All other accidents	38.2	30.4	25.7	18.3	14.4	12.8	63.3	46.0	36.4	22.5	18.6	14.5
Suicide	18.0	19.9	22.3	7.1	5.9	5.9	8.0	10.3	11.1	2.6	2.2	2.3
Homicide	6.8	10.9	8.6	2.1	3.2	3.0	67.6	66.6	55.0	13.3	13.5	12.1
15-24 years old	130.7	138.6	118.8	64.9	37.3	34.3	234.3	162.0	147.6	45.5	35.0	31.8
25-34 years old	96.6	118.4	102.5	23.8	29.0	25.9	384.4	256.9	207.6	76.0	49.4	44.8
35-44 years old	85.7	94.1	80.6	25.8	29.2	25.2	345.2	218.1	179.9	77.2	43.2	35.7
45-54 years old	87.5	90.8	78.6	30.4	31.8	26.9	303.3	207.3	148.9	65.5	40.2	30.9
55-64 years old	101.5	92.3	82.1	36.3	33.8	29.9	242.4	188.5	133.8	56.0	47.3	41.4
65 years old and over	216.9	163.9	155.4	122.4	87.2	81.7	220.0	215.8	187.1	107.9	102.9	81.2
65-74 years old	128.0	116.7	105.7	57.7	46.4	44.4	217.4	182.2	146.1	81.5	68.7	54.8
75-84 years old	229.3	209.2	204.3	149.0	101.5	94.4	236.0	261.4	240.9	140.1	137.5	95.9
85 years old and over	466.7	438.5	428.8	391.4	268.1	222.9	271.8	379.2	364.2	214.3	235.7	193.8

Source: "Death Rates from Accidents and Violence: 1970 to 1986," *Statistical Abstract*, 1989, p. 83. Primary source: U.S. National Center for Health Statistics, *Vital Statistics of the United States,* annual. *Note:* 1. Includes persons under 15 years old, not shown separately.

★ 920 ★
Deaths - Part I

Age	Total[1]			Male					
				White			Black		
	1970	1980	1986	1970	1980	1986	1970	1980	1986
All ages[1,2]	11.6	11.9	12.8	18.0	19.9	22.3	8.0	10.3	11.1
10-14 years old	.6	.8	1.5	1.1	1.4	2.4	.3	.5	1.5
15-19 years old	5.9	8.5	10.2	9.4	15.0	18.2	4.7	5.6	7.1
20-24 years old	12.2	16.1	15.8	19.3	27.8	28.4	18.7	20.0	16.0
25-34 years old	14.1	16.0	15.7	19.9	25.6	26.4	19.2	21.8	21.3
35-44 years old	16.9	15.4	15.2	23.3	23.5	23.9	12.6	15.6	17.5
45-54 years old	20.0	15.9	16.4	29.5	24.2	26.3	13.8	12.0	12.8
55-64 years old	21.4	15.9	17.0	35.0	25.8	28.7	10.6	11.7	9.9
65 years and over	20.8	17.8	21.5	41.1	37.5	45.6	8.7	11.4	16.2
65-74 years old	20.8	16.9	19.7	38.7	32.5	37.6	8.7	11.1	16.1
75-84 years old	21.2	19.1	25.2	45.5	45.5	58.9	8.9	10.5	16.0
85 years and over	19.0	19.2	20.8	45.8	52.8	66.3	8.7	18.9	17.9

Source: "Suicide Rates, by Sex, Race, and Age Group: 1970 to 1986," *Statistical Abstract*, 1989, p. 84. Primary source: U.S. National Center for Health Statistics, *Vital Statistics of the United States*, annual. *Notes:* 1. Includes other races not shown separately. 2. Includes other age groups not shown separately.

★ 921 ★
Deaths - Part II

Age	Female					
	White			Black		
	1970	1980	1986	1970	1980	1986
All ages[1,2]	7.1	5.9	5.9	2.6	2.2	2.3
10-14 years old	.3	.3	.7	.4	.1	.4
15-19 years old	2.9	3.3	4.1	2.9	1.6	2.1
20-24 years old	5.7	5.9	5.3	4.9	3.1	2.4
25-34 years old	9.0	7.5	6.2	5.7	4.1	3.8
35-44 years old	13.0	9.1	8.3	3.7	4.6	2.8
45-54 years old	13.5	10.2	9.6	3.7	2.8	3.2
55-64 years old	12.3	9.1	9.0	2.0	2.3	4.2
65 years and over	8.5	6.5	7.5	2.6	1.4	2.4
65-74 years old	9.6	7.0	7.7	2.9	1.7	2.8
75-84 years old	7.2	5.7	8.0	1.7	1.4	2.6
85 years and over	5.8	5.8	5.0	2.8	---	---

Source: "Suicide Rates, by Sex, Race, and Age Group: 1970 to 1986," *Statistical Abstract*, 1989, p. 84. Primary source: U.S. National Center for Health Statistics, *Vital Statistics of the United States*, annual. *Notes:* 1. Includes other races not shown separately. 2. Includes other age groups not shown separately.

★ 922 ★
Deaths

Rates are per 1,000 population for specified groups. Except as noted, excludes deaths of nonresidents of the U.S. Excludes fetal deaths. For explanation of age-adjustment, see text, section 2. The standard population for this table is the total population of the United States enumerated in 1940. See also *Historical Statistics, Colonial Times to 1970*, series B 167-173 and B 181-192.

Sex and Race	1960[1]	1970	1975	1979	1980	1981	1982	1983	1984	1985	1986	1987 prel.[1,2]
Deaths (1,000)[3]	1,712	1,921	1,893	1,914	1,990	1,978	1,975	2,019	2,039	2,086	2,105	2,127
White (1,000)	1,505	1,682	1,660	1,676	1,739	1,731	1,729	1,766	1,782	1,819	1,831	1,853
Male (1,000)	861	942	918	910	934	925	919	932	935	950	953	957
Female (1,000)	644	740	743	766	805	806	810	834	847	869	879	896
Black (1,000)	196	226	218	221	233	229	227	233	236	244	250	251
Male (1,000)	108	128	124	124	130	127	126	128	129	134	137	137
Female (1,000)	88	98	94	96	103	101	101	105	107	111	113	114
Death rates[3]	9.5	9.5	8.8	8.5	8.8	8.6	8.5	8.6	8.6	8.7	8.7	8.7
White	9.5	9.5	8.9	8.7	8.9	8.8	8.7	8.8	8.9	9.0	9.0	9.0
Male	11.0	10.9	10.0	9.6	9.8	9.7	9.5	9.6	9.5	9.6	9.5	9.5
Female	8.0	8.1	7.8	7.7	8.1	8.0	8.0	8.2	8.2	8.4	8.4	8.5
Black	10.4	10.0	8.8	8.4	8.8	8.4	8.2	8.3	8.3	8.5	8.5	8.4
Male	11.8	11.9	10.6	10.0	10.3	9.9	9.6	9.6	9.6	9.8	9.9	9.7
Female	9.1	8.3	7.3	7.0	7.3	7.1	6.9	7.1	7.1	7.3	7.3	7.3
Age-adjusted death rates[3]	7.6	7.1	6.2	5.8	5.9	5.7	5.5	5.5	5.5	5.5	5.4	5.4
White	7.3	6.8	6.0	5.5	5.6	5.4	5.3	5.3	5.2	5.2	5.2	5.1
Male	9.2	8.9	8.0	7.4	7.5	7.2	7.1	7.0	6.9	6.9	6.8	6.7
Female	5.6	5.0	4.4	4.0	4.1	4.0	3.9	3.9	3.9	3.9	3.9	3.9
Black	10.7	10.4	8.9	8.1	8.4	8.0	7.8	7.8	7.7	7.8	7.8	7.7
Male	12.5	13.2	11.6	10.7	11.1	10.7	10.4	10.2	10.1	10.2	10.3	10.1
Female	9.2	8.1	6.7	6.1	6.3	6.0	5.8	5.9	5.9	5.9	5.9	5.8

Source: "Deaths and Death Rates, by Sex and Race: 1960 to 1987," *Statistical Abstract*, 1989, P. 74. Primary source: U.S. National Center for Health Statistics, *Vital Statistics of the United States*, annual; and unpublished data. *Notes:* 1. Includes deaths of nonresidents of the U.S. 2. Based on a 10 percent sample of deaths. 3. Includes other races, not shown separately.

★ 923 ★
Deaths

Number of deaths per 100,000 population in specified group.

Sex, Year, and Race	All ages[1]	Under 1 yr. old	1-4 yr. old	5-14 yr. old	15-24 yr. old	25-34 yr. old	35-44 yr. old	45-54 yr. old	55-64 yr. old	65-74 yr. old	75-84 yr. old	85 yrs. old and over
Male[2]												
White: 1970	1,087	2,113	84	48	171	177	344	883	2,203	4,810	10,099	18,552
1980	983	1,230	66	35	167	171	257	699	1,729	4,036	8,830	19,097
1985	960	1,039	52	30	136	157	241	609	1,614	3,717	8,500	18,789
1987, prel.[3,4]	952	939	54	30	145	167	251	578	1,555	3,586	8,200	18,456
Black: 1970	1,187	4,299	151	67	321	560	957	1,778	3,257	5,803	9,455	12,222
1980	1,034	2,587	111	47	209	407	690	1,480	2,873	5,131	9,232	16,099
1985	977	2,135	89	41	174	347	642	1,283	2,623	4,889	9,298	15,046
1987, prel.[3,4]	973	2,218	85	46	195	370	674	1,244	2,474	4,592	9,239	14,957
Female[2]												
White: 1970	813	1,615	66	30	62	84	193	463	1,015	2,471	6,699	15,980
1980	806	963	49	23	56	65	138	373	876	2,067	5,402	14,980
1985	837	787	40	19	48	59	121	340	864	2,028	5,171	14,579

Continued.

Deaths
[Continued]

Sex, Year, and Race	All ages[1]	Under 1 yr. old	1-4 yr. old	5-14 yr. old	15-24 yr. old	25-34 yr. old	35-44 yr. old	45-54 yr. old	55-64 yr. old	65-74 yr. old	75-84 yr. old	85 yrs. old and over
1987, prel.[3,4]	851	730	44	18	50	64	116	335	858	2,012	5,076	14,642
Black: 1970	829	3,369	129	44	112	231	533	1,044	1,986	3,861	6,692	10,707
1980	733	2,124	84	31	71	150	324	768	1,561	3,057	6,212	12,367
1985	728	1,757	71	28	60	136	278	654	1,502	2,962	6,252	12,155
1987, prel.[3,4]	727	1,781	51	26	64	140	295	644	1,466	2,879	5,980	11,921

Source: "Death Rates, by Age, Sex, and Race: 1960 to 1987," *Statistical Abstract*, 1989, p. 74. Primary source: U.S. National Center for Health Statistics, *Vital Statistics of the United States*, annual; and unpublished data. *Notes:* 1. Includes unknown age. 2. Includes other races not shown separately. 3. Includes deaths of nonresidents. 4. Based on a 10- percent sample of deaths.

★ 924 ★
Deaths

In thousands. Excludes deaths of nonresidents of the U.S. Deaths classified according to ninth revision of *International Classification of Diseases*.

Age, Sex, and Race	Total[1]	Diseases of heart	Malignant neoplasms	Accidents and adverse effects	Cerebro-vascular diseases	Chronic obstructive pulmonary diseases[2]	Pneumonia flu	Suicide	Chronic liver diseases cirrhosis	Diabetes mellitus
White										
Both sexes, total[3]	1,831.1	681.4	412.2	80.3	130.0	71.1	62.3	28.4	21.9	30.3
Under 15 years old	38.7	1.2	1.5	6.0	.1	.1	.7	.2	4	4
15-24 years old	31.8	.7	1.8	17.5	.2	.1	.2	4.6	4	.1
25-34 years old	41.5	2.5	4.6	13.9	.6	.2	.5	5.9	.7	.5
35-44 years old	52.5	9.3	12.1	8.3	1.5	.4	.7	4.6	2.2	.9
45-54 years old	90.4	26.2	30.9	5.7	3.2	1.8	1.1	3.5	3.6	1.5
55-64 years old	234.5	79.6	85.1	6.4	8.9	9.4	3.3	3.6	6.2	4.3
65-74 years old	425.8	159.1	7.4	23.6	23.6	24.1	8.8	3.2	5.9	8.3
75-84 years old	519.3	216.9	105.4	8.6	46.3	25.4	20.1	2.2	2.7	9.4
85 years old and over	395.8	185.6	40.8	6.4	45.5	9.6	26.9	.6	.6	5.2
Black										
Both sexes, total[3]	250.3	77.7	52.0	12.6	18.0	4.9	6.7	1.9	3.7	6.3
Under 15 years old	14.8	.5	.3	1.8	.1	.1	.3	4	4	4
15-24 years old	7.1	.3	.3	1.9	.1	.1	.1	.4	4	4
25-34 years old	13.7	1.2	.9	2.5	.3	.1	.3	.6	.4	.1
35-44 years old	16.3	2.9	2.5	1.7	.8	.1	.5	.3	.9	.3
45-54 years old	22.6	6.3	6.2	1.1	1.4	.4	.5	.2	.9	.6
55-64 years old	41.2	13.8	12.6	11.2	2.6	1.0	.8	.1	.9	1.3
65-74 years old	55.1	20.1	15.4	1.0	4.4	1.6	1.2	.1	.5	1.8
75-84 years old	50.8	20.2	10.3	.9	5.2	1.1	1.7	.1	.2	1.5
85 years old and over	28.5	12.5	3.6	.5	3.1	.4	1.4	4	4	.7

Source: "Deaths, by Selected Cause and Selected Characteristics: 1966," *Statistical Abstracts*, 1989, p. 79. Primary source: U.S. National Center for Health Statistics, *Vital Statistics of the United States*, annual. *Notes:* 1. Includes other causes, not shown separately. 2. Includes allied conditions. 3. Includes those deaths with age not stated. 4. Fewer than 50.

★ 925 ★
Deaths due to Cerebrovascular Diseases: Trends

Data are based on the National Vital Statistics System.

Sex, race, and age	1950[1]	1960[1]	1970	1980	1983	1984	1985	1986
			Deaths per 100,000 resident population					
All races								
All ages, age adjusted	88.8	79.7	66.3	40.8	34.4	33.4	32.3	31.0
All ages, crude	104.0	108.0	101.9	75.1	66.5	65.3	64.1	62.1
Under 1 year	5.1	4.1	5.0	4.4	3.9	3.0	3.6	2.9
1-4 years	0.9	0.8	1.0	0.5	0.4	0.4	0.3	0.3
5-14 years	0.5	0.7	0.7	0.3	0.3	0.3	0.2	0.2
15-24 years	1.6	1.8	1.6	1.0	0.8	0.8	0.8	0.7
25-34 years	4.2	4.7	4.5	2.6	2.2	2.2	2.1	2.2
35-44 years	18.7	14.7	15.6	8.5	7.3	7.5	7.2	7.1
45-54 years	70.4	49.2	41.6	25.2	22.8	22.6	21.1	20.4
55-64 years	195.3	147.3	115.8	65.2	57.6	55.8	54.3	53.0
65-74 years	549.7	469.2	384.1	219.5	182.2	177.0	171.3	164.1
75-84 years	1,499.6	1,491.3	1,254.2	788.6	652.7	626.2	605.8	573.8
85 years and over	2,990.1	3,680.5	3,234.6	2,288.9	1,912.5	1,883.8	1,837.5	1,762.6
White male								
All ages, age adjusted	87.0	80.3	68.8	41.9	35.2	33.9	32.8	31.1
All ages, crude	100.5	102.7	93.5	63.3	55.5	53.8	52.5	50.5
Under 1 year	5.9	4.3	4.5	3.8	4.0	2.6	3.7	2.5
1-4 years	1.1	0.8	1.2	0.4	0.5	0.3	0.3	0.2
5-14 years	0.5	0.7	0.8	0.2	0.2	0.2	0.2	0.2
15-24 years	1.6	1.7	1.6	1.0	0.8	0.8	0.7	0.7
25-34 years	3.4	3.5	3.2	2.0	1.9	1.8	1.8	1.8
35-44 years	13.1	11.3	11.8	6.5	5.5	5.9	5.4	5.7
45-54 years	53.7	40.9	35.6	21.7	19.1	19.3	18.0	16.5
55-64 years	182.2	139.0	119.9	64.2	56.5	54.3	54.2	51.4
65-74 years	569.7	501.0	420.0	240.4	197.1	190.4	183.7	171.4
75-84 years	1,556.3	1,564.8	1,361.6	854.8	714.8	671.1	651.1	617.3
85 years and over	3,127.1	3,734.8	3,317.6	2,236.9	1,862.9	1,846.4	1,747.8	1,697.0
Black male								
All ages, age adjusted	146.2	141.2	124.2	77.5	64.2	62.8	60.8	58.9
All ages, crude	122.0	122.9	108.7	73.1	61.3	60.0	58.5	57.1
Under 1 year {	2.5	8.5	12.2	11.2	7.5	8.2	9.8	8.0
1-4 years {		1.9	1.4	0.6	0.2	0.8	0.8	0.5
5-14 years	0.7	0.9	0.8	0.5	0.4	0.6	0.1	0.2
15-24 years	3.3	3.7	3.0	2.1	1.4	1.2	1.3	1.1
25-34 years	12.0	12.8	14.6	7.7	5.9	5.7	5.7	6.1
35-44 years	59.3	47.4	52.7	29.2	24.3	26.0	25.9	27.2
45-54 years	211.9	166.1	136.2	182.1	74.1	72.9	70.6	68.2
55-64 years	522.8	439.9	343.4	189.8	163.8	159.0	151.6	144.3
65-74 years	783.6	899.2	780.0	472.8	388.0	379.8	358.9	337.8
75-84 years {	1,504.9	1,475.2	1,442.6	1,067.6	844.1	819.5	817.6	809.9
85 years and over {		2,700.0	2,315.4	1,873.2	1,479.4	1,395.2	1,363.1	1,350.7
White female								
All ages, age adjusted	79.7	68.7	56.2	35.2	29.6	28.9	27.9	27.1
All ages, crude	103.3	110.1	109.8	88.8	79.8	79.2	78.1	76.2
Under 1 year	2.9	2.6	3.2	3.3	2.5	2.6	2.2	1.8
1-4 years	0.6	0.5	0.6	0.4	0.2	0.3	0.3	0.2

Continued.

Deaths due to Cerebrovascular Diseases: Trends
[Continued]

Sex, race, and age		1950[1]	1960[1]	1970	1980	1983	1984	1985	1986
5-14 years		0.4	0.6	0.6	0.3	0.3	0.3	0.3	0.2
15-24 years		1.2	1.4	1.1	0.7	0.7	0.6	0.7	0.6
25-34 years		2.9	3.4	3.4	2.0	1.6	1.6	1.6	1.6
35-44 years		13.6	10.1	11.5	6.7	5.6	5.6	5.3	5.0
45-54 years		55.0	33.8	30.5	18.7	16.9	17.0	15.4	15.5
55-64 years		156.9	103.0	78.1	48.7	42.6	42.0	39.7	40.1
65-74 years		498.1	383.3	303.2	172.8	144.6	140.9	138.0	136.3
75-84 years		1,471.3	1,444.7	1,176.8	730.3	602.0	580.9	559.4	530.7
85 years and over		3,017.9	3,795.7	3,316.1	2,367.8	1,986.5	1,962.5	1,923.0	1,837.3
Black female									
All ages, age adjusted		155.6	139.5	107.9	61.7	53.8	51.8	50.3	47.6
All ages, crude		128.3	127.7	112.1	77.9	70.5	68.5	68.0	65.0
Under 1 year	{	2.8	6.7	9.1	6.4	7.3	3.3	5.3	5.3
1-4 years	{		1.3	1.4	0.5	0.5	0.5	0.5	0.4
5-14 years		0.6	1.0	0.8	0.3	0.4	0.4	0.3	0.3
15-24 years		4.2	3.4	3.0	1.7	1.6	1.7	1.5	1.0
25-34 years		15.9	17.4	14.3	7.0	5.1	6.1	5.6	6.0
35-44 years		75.0	57.4	49.1	21.6	20.1	19.2	19.3	18.5
45-54 years		248.9	166.2	119.4	61.9	55.7	50.3	49.8	46.4
55-64 years		567.7	452.0	272.5	138.7	126.0	112.6	111.3	109.4
65-74 years		754.4	830.5	673.4	362.2	308.4	304.6	281.5	268.5
75-84 years	{	1,496.7	1,413.1	1,337.8	918.6	786.7	803.4	775.4	710.7
85 years and over	{		2,578.9	2,504.8	1,896.3	1,603.1	1,470.7	1,585.6	1,504.1

Source: "Death Rates for Cerebrovascular Diseases, according to Sex, Race, and Age: United States, Selected Years 1950-86," *Health United States - 1988*, March 1989, p. 67. Primary source: *Vital Statistics of the United States*. National Center for Health Statistics, U.S. Government Printing Office, Washington, DC. *Notes:* For data years shown, the code numbers for cause of death are based on the then current *International Classification of Diseases*, which are described in Appendix II, tables IV and V. 1. Includes deaths of nonresidents of the United States.

★ 926 ★
Deaths due to Heart Disease: Trends

Data are based on the National Vital Statistics System.

Sex, race, and age	1950[1]	1960[1]	1970	1980	1983	1984	1985	1986
				Deaths per 100,000 resident population				
All races								
All ages, age adjusted	307.6	286.2	253.6	202.0	188.8	183.6	180.5	175.0
All ages, crude	355.5	369.0	362.0	336.0	329.2	323.5	323.0	317.5
Under 1 year	3.5	6.6	13.1	22.8	26.0	26.1	24.5	26.1
1-4 years	1.3	1.3	1.7	2.6	2.5	2.4	2.1	2.5
5-14 years	2.1	1.3	0.8	0.9	0.9	1.0	0.9	0.9
15-24 years	6.8	4.0	3.0	2.9	2.6	2.7	2.8	2.8
25-34 years	19.4	15.6	11.4	8.3	8.3	8.0	8.2	8.6
35-44 years	86.4	74.6	66.7	44.6	39.3	38.7	38.0	37.5
45-54 years	308.6	271.8	238.4	180.2	164.7	156.7	152.9	144.6
55-64 years	808.1	737.9	652.3	494.1	463.0	450.3	439.1	424.2
65-74 years	1,839.8	1,740.5	1,558.2	1,218.6	1,139.2	1,102.7	1,080.6	1,043.0

Continued.

Deaths due to Heart Disease: Trends
[Continued]

Sex, race, and age	1950[1]	1960[1]	1970	1980	1983	1984	1985	1986
75-84 years	4,310.1	4,089.4	3,683.8	2,993.1	2,816.3	2,748.6	2,712.6	2,637.5
85 years and over	9,150.6	9,317.8	8,468.0	7,777.1	7,335.5	7,251.0	7,275.0	7,178.7
White male								
All ages, age adjusted	381.1	375.4	347.6	277.5	257.8	249.5	244.5	234.8
All ages, crude	433.0	454.6	438.3	384.0	370.9	361.8	358.9	348.6
Under 1 year	4.1	6.9	12.0	22.5	24.1	24.6	23.8	26.0
1-4 years	1.1	1.0	1.5	2.1	2.2	2.2	1.7	2.1
5-14 years	1.7	1.1	0.8	0.9	0.9	0.9	0.8	0.9
15-24 years	5.8	3.6	3.0	2.9	2.7	2.8	3.0	3.0
25-34 years	20.1	17.6	12.3	9.1	9.6	9.2	9.2	9.5
35-44 years	110.6	107.5	94.6	61.8	55.3	54.0	52.4	51.7
45-54 years	423.6	413.2	365.7	269.8	243.0	231.2	224.4	208.8
55-64 years	1,081.7	1,056.0	979.3	730.6	674.1	655.5	635.6	610.3
65-74 years	2,308.3	2,297.9	2,177.2	1,729.7	1,603.6	1,533.0	1,501.0	1,440.9
75-84 years	4,907.3	4,839.9	4,617.6	3,883.2	3,664.3	3,579.3	3,532.9	3,405.2
85 years and over	9,950.5	10,135.8	9,693.0	8,958.0	8,503.4	8,416.4	8,396.3	8,138.4
Black male								
All ages, age adjusted	415.5	381.2	375.9	327.3	308.2	300.1	301.0	294.3
All ages, crude	348.4	330.6	330.3	301.0	288.5	282.2	285.0	281.3
Under 1 year	4.8	13.9	33.5	42.8	54.5	48.4	46.7	49.8
1-4 years		3.8	3.9	6.3	5.1	4.4	4.4	5.3
5-14 years	6.4	3.0	1.4	1.3	1.5	1.5	1.5	1.4
15-24 years	18.0	8.7	8.3	8.3	6.6	6.7	7.2	6.7
25-34 years	51.9	43.1	41.6	30.3	27.5	27.5	29.1	29.3
35-44 years	198.1	168.1	189.2	136.6	115.9	121.1	122.0	123.6
45-54 years	624.1	514.0	512.8	433.4	398.2	384.6	382.4	365.1
55-64 years	1,434.0	1,236.8	1,135.4	987.2	928.0	895.9	882.6	864.9
65-74 years	2,140.1	2,281.4	2,237.8	1,847.2	1,804.5	1,734.7	1,738.4	1,673.1
75-84 years	4,107.9	3,533.6	3,783.4	3,578.8	3,457.5	3,375.7	3,450.0	3,407.3
85 years and over		6,037.9	6,330.8	6,819.5	5,907.9	6,015.9	6,098.5	6,268.7
White female								
All ages, age adjusted	223.6	197.1	167.8	134.6	126.7	124.0	121.7	119.0
All ages, crude	289.4	306.5	313.8	319.2	321.5	319.3	320.7	319.0
Under 1 year	2.7	4.3	7.0	15.7	19.3	20.3	18.3	19.1
1-4 years	1.1	0.9	1.2	2.1	2.1	2.0	1.6	2.1
5-14 years	1.9	0.9	0.7	0.8	0.8	0.9	0.9	0.7
15-24 years	5.3	2.8	1.7	1.7	1.6	1.8	1.7	1.6
25-34 years	12.2	8.2	5.5	3.9	3.8	3.7	3.8	4.1
35-44 years	40.5	28.6	23.9	16.4	14.5	14.1	14.3	13.8
45-54 years	141.9	103.4	91.4	71.2	67.4	63.1	62.1	59.8
55-64 years	460.2	383.0	317.7	248.1	237.5	236.1	225.8	221.4
65-74 years	1,400.9	1,229.8	1,044.0	796.7	745.6	735.3	713.7	693.9
75-84 years	3,925.2	3,629.7	3,143.5	2,493.6	2,332.4	2,273.1	2,233.3	2,180.2
85 years and over	9,084.7	9,280.8	8,207.5	7,501.6	7,133.7	7,044.7	7,089.3	7,021.3
Black female								
All ages, age adjusted	349.5	292.6	251.7	201.1	191.5	186.6	186.8	185.1

Continued.

Deaths due to Heart Disease: Trends
[Continued]

Sex, race, and age		1950[1]	1960[1]	1970	1980	1983	1984	1985	1986
All ages, crude		289.9	268.5	261.0	249.7	248.1	244.6	248.1	250.8
Under 1 year	{	3.9	12.0	31.3	43.6	45.6	45.1	39.5	42.8
1-4 years	{		2.8	4.2	4.4	3.6	4.3	5.2	4.8
5-14 years		8.8	3.0	1.8	1.7	1.1	1.4	1.7	1.5
15-24 years		19.8	10.0	6.0	4.6	4.4	4.3	4.6	4.6
25-34 years		52.0	35.9	24.7	15.7	13.6	12.5	13.1	15.3
35-44 years		185.0	125.3	99.8	61.7	53.0	52.8	50.4	50.1
45-54 years		526.8	360.7	290.9	202.4	182.8	174.1	172.6	172.5
55-64 years		1,210.7	952.3	710.5	530.1	517.7	499.6	500.4	479.0
65-74 years		1,659.4	1,680.5	1,553.2	1,210.3	1,159.8	1,127.1	1,133.6	1,108.3
75-84 years	{	3,499.3	2,926.9	2,964.1	2,707.2	2,660.1	2,618.9	2,606.0	2,623.5
85 years and over	{		5,650.0	5,669.8	5,796.5	5,298.4	5,315.0	5,441.0	5,698.6

Source: "Death Rates for Diseases of Heart, according to Sex, Race, and Age: United States, Selected Years 1950-86," *Health United States - 1988*, March 1989, p. 66. Primary source: *Vital Statistics of the United States*. National Center for Health Statistics, U.S. Government Printing Office, Washington, DC. *Notes:* For data years shown, the code numbers for cause of death are based on the then current *International Classification of Diseases*, which are described in Appendix II, tables IV and V. 1. Includes deaths of nonresidents of the United States.

★ 927 ★
Deaths due to Malignant Neoplasms: Trends

Data are based on the National Vital Statistics System.

Sex, race, and age	1950[1]	1960[1]	1970	1980	1983	1984	1985	1986
			Deaths per 100,000 resident population					
All races								
All ages, age adjusted	125.4	125.8	129.9	132.8	132.6	133.5	133.6	133.2
All ages, crude	139.8	149.2	162.8	183.9	189.3	191.8	193.3	194.7
Under 1 year	8.7	7.2	4.7	3.2	3.6	3.1	3.0	2.6
1-4 years	11.7	10.9	7.5	4.5	4.7	4.0	3.8	4.0
5-14 years	6.7	6.8	6.0	4.3	3.9	3.6	3.5	3.4
15-24 years	8.6	8.3	8.3	6.3	5.6	5.5	5.4	5.4
25-34 years	20.0	19.5	16.5	13.7	12.8	13.0	13.1	13.1
35-44 years	62.7	59.7	59.5	48.6	45.6	46.6	45.7	45.3
45-54 years	175.1	177.0	182.5	180.0	172.2	170.5	169.1	165.7
55-64 years	39.9	396.8	423.0	436.1	443.0	448.4	450.5	444.4
65-74 years	692.5	713.9	754.2	817.9	829.3	835.1	838.3	847.0
75-84 years	1,153.3	1,127.4	1,168.0	1,232.3	1,254.7	1,272.3	1,281.0	1,287.3
85 years and over	1,451.0	1,450.0	1,417.3	1,594.6	1,583.4	1,604.0	1,591.5	1,612.0
White male								
All ages, age adjusted	130.9	141.6	154.3	160.5	158.9	159.0	159.2	158.8
All ages, crude	147.2	166.1	185.1	208.7	213.8	512.1	217.2	218.8
Under 1 year	9.6	7.9	4.3	3.5	3.5	2.7	3.1	3.0
1-4 years	13.1	13.1	8.5	5.4	5.3	4.4	4.4	4.7
5-14 years	7.6	8.0	7.0	5.2	4.4	4.1	4.0	3.9
15-24 years	9.9	10.3	10.6	7.8	6.7	6.8	6.5	6.8
25-34 years	17.7	18.8	16.2	13.6	12.6	12.5	13.0	13.5
35-44 years	44.5	46.3	50.1	41.1	38.3	38.5	39.5	37.7
45-54 years	150.8	164.1	172.0	175.4	166.7	164.0	161.2	158.5

Continued.

644

Deaths due to Malignant Neoplasms: Trends

[Continued]

Sex, race, and age	1950[1]	1960[1]	1970	1980	1983	1984	1985	1986
55-64 years	409.4	450.9	498.1	497.4	499.5	504.5	508.4	504.3
65-74 years	798.7	887.3	997.0	1,070.7	1,063.7	1,064.1	1,061.2	1,063.3
75-84 years	1,367.6	1,413.7	1,512.7	1,779.7	1,805.3	1,806.9	1,820.1	1,827.0
85 years and over	1,732.7	1,791.4	1,948.1	2,375.6	2,416.3	2,438.6	2,424.5	2,462.3
Black male								
All ages, age adjusted	126.1	158.5	198.0	229.9	232.2	234.9	231.6	229.0
All ages, crude	106.6	136.7	171.6	205.5	210.5	214.0	212.2	211.4
Under 1 year {	8.2	6.8	5.3	4.5	3.9	3.2	2.4	1.7
1-4 years {		7.9	7.6	5.1	4.7	3.5	3.3	3.1
5-14 years	5.8	4.4	4.8	3.7	4.1	3.6	3.6	3.8
15-24 years	7.9	9.7	9.4	8.1	5.6	6.4	6.4	6.3
25-34 years	18.0	18.4	18.8	14.1	14.7	15.8	14.7	14.2
35-44 years	55.7	72.9	81.3	73.8	70.7	74.4	71.2	71.4
45-54 years	211.7	244.7	311.2	333.0	315.5	314.1	313.6	303.6
55-64 years	490.8	579.7	689.2	812.5	821.6	841.7	803.3	776.0
65-74 years	636.4	938.5	1,168.9	1,417.2	1,457.4	1,44.9	1,448.7	1,455.1
75-84 years {	853.5	1,053.3	1,624.8	2,029.6	2,196.8	2,226.3	2,238.3	2,249.2
85 years and over {		1,155.2	1,635.9	2,393.9	2,219.0	2,471.4	2,507.7	2,620.9
White female								
All ages, age adjusted	119.4	109.5	107.6	107.7	108.5	109.9	110.3	110.1
All ages, crude	139.9	139.8	149.4	170.3	177.9	181.7	183.7	185.6
Under 1 year	7.8	6.8	5.4	2.7	3.5	2.9	3.0	2.4
1-4 years	11.3	9.7	6.9	3.6	4.4	3.8	3.5	3.4
5-14 years	6.3	6.2	5.4	3.7	3.4	3.3	3.1	3.1
15-24 years	7.5	6.5	6.2	4.7	4.6	4.3	4.3	4.2
25-34 years	20.9	18.8	16.3	13.5	12.3	12.8	12.6	12.1
35-44 years	74.5	66.6	62.4	50.9	48.0	49.0	47.0	47.4
45-54 years	185.8	175.7	177.3	166.4	160.0	160.0	160.6	155.6
55-64 years	362.5	329.0	338.6	355.5	366.8	370.0	374.1	369.4
65-74 years	616.5	562.1	554.7	605.2	627.4	638.6	645.3	658.7
75-84 years	1,026.6	939.3	903.5	905.4	919.5	944.2	949.2	956.4
85 years and over	1,348.3	1,304.9	1,179.4	1,266.8	1,265.7	1,284.3	1,270.9	1,283.6
Black female								
All ages, age adjusted	131.9	127.8	123.5	129.7	129.8	131.0	130.4	132.1
All ages, crude	111.8	113.8	117.3	136.5	140.7	142.9	143.9	146.7
Under 1 year {	7.0	6.7	3.3	3.0	3.3	2.5	4.3	2.8
1-4 years {		6.9	5.7	3.9	3.1	3.1	2.5	4.3
5-14 years	3.9	4.8	4.0	3.4	3.6	3.3	3.0	2.9
15-24 years	8.8	6.9	6.4	5.7	5.0	4.3	4.3	4.7
25-34 years	34.3	31.0	20.9	18.3	17.3	16.5	17.0	17.8
35-44 years	119.8	102.4	94.6	73.5	68.9	74.3	69.5	72.2
45-54 years	277.0	254.8	228.6	230.2	217.8	215.1	208.1	215.3
55-64 years	484.6	442.7	404.8	450.4	452.9	462.2	465.4	451.6
65-74 years	477.3	541.6	615.8	662.4	694.2	685.8	694.2	717.5
75-84 years {	605.3	696.3	763.3	923.9	972.4	1,013.7	1,014.6	1,017.9
85 years and over {		728.9	896.8	1,159.9	1,132.6	1,154.9	1,228.8	1,254.5

Source: "Death Rates for Malignant Neoplasms, according to Sex, Race, and Age: United States, Selected Years 1950-86," *Health United States - 1988*, March 1989, p. 68. Primary source: *Vital Statistics of the United States*. National Center for Health Statistics, U.S. Government Printing Office, Washington, DC. *Notes:* For data years shown, the code numbers for cause of death are based on the then current *International Classification of Diseases*, which are described in Appendix II, tables IV and V. 1. Includes deaths of nonresidents of the United States.

Deaths due to Malignant Neoplasms: Trends
[Continued]

Sex, race, and age		1950[1]	1960[1]	1970	1980	1983	1984	1985	1986
75-84 years	{	605.3	696.3	763.3	923.9	972.4	1,013.7	1,014.6	1,017.9
85 years and over	{		728.9	896.8	1,159.9	1,132.6	1,154.9	1,228.8	1,254.5

Source: "Death Rates for Malignant Neoplasms, according to Sex, Race, and Age: United States, Selected Years 1950-86," *Health United States - 1988*, March 1989, p. 68. Primary source: *Vital Statistics of the United States*. National Center for Health Statistics, U.S. Government Printing Office, Washington, DC. *Notes:* For data years shown, the code numbers for cause of death are based on the then current *International Classification of Diseases*, which are described in Appendix II, tables IV and V. 1. Includes deaths of nonresidents of the United States.

★ 928 ★
Deaths due to Motor Vehicle Accidents: Trends

Data based on the National Vital Statistics System.

Sex and race	1950[1]	1960[1]	1970	1980	1983	1984	1985	1986
				Deaths per 100,000 resident population				
White male								
All ages, age adjusted	35.9	34.0	40.1	34.8	27.8	28.4	27.6	28.7
All ages, crude	35.1	31.5	39.1	35.9	28.5	29.1	28.2	29.2
Under 1 year	9.1	8.8	9.1	7.0	5.7	3.9	4.5	4.1
1-4 years	13.2	11.3	12.2	9.5	8.3	7.5	7.6	7.0
5-14 years	12.0	10.3	12.6	9.8	8.4	8.4	8.5	8.7
15-24 years	58.3	62.7	75.2	73.8	57.0	59.1	57.4	62.6
25-34 years	39.1	38.6	47.0	46.6	37.0	37.3	35.5	37.3
35-44 years	30.9	28.4	35.2	30.7	24.3	24.3	24.1	23.7
45-54 years	31.6	29.7	34.6	26.3	21.2	21.7	20.9	20.8
55-64 years	41.9	34.4	39.0	23.9	19.9	20.9	20.6	19.9
65-74 years	59.1	45.5	46.2	25.8	22.5	24.0	21.7	22.4
75-84 years	86.4	66.8	69.2	43.6	39.8	41.8	41.2	42.9
85 years and over	79.3	61.9	72.0	57.3	54.7	52.6	56.4	51.6
Black male								
All ages, age adjusted	39.8	38.2	50.1	32.9	26.4	27.2	27.7	29.2
All ages, crude	37.2	33.1	44.2	31.1	25.2	26.4	26.7	28.6
Under 1 year {	9.0	6.8	10.6	7.8	3.6	5.7	5.9	8.0
1-4 years {		12.7	16.9	13.7	10.9	9.8	10.7	10.7
5-14 years	9.7	10.4	16.1	10.5	8.5	8.7	8.9	9.6
15-24 years	41.6	46.4	58.1	34.9	28.3	31.9	32.1	35.3
25-34 years	57.4	51.0	70.4	44.9	35.9	36.8	37.2	41.7
35-44 years	45.9	43.6	59.5	41.2	33.6	33.8	35.4	35.1
45-54 years	49.9	48.1	61.4	39.1	32.4	28.5	29.9	31.4
55-64 years	58.8	47.3	62.1	40.3	31.2	31.5	34.3	31.9
65-74 years	48.5	46.1	54.9	41.8	29.6	35.5	30.0	27.2
75-84 years {	61.8	51.8	51.5	46.5	41.7	45.0	42.2	53.1
85 years and over {		58.6	53.8	34.0	28.6	57.1	36.9	62.7
White female								
All ages, age adjusted	10.6	11.1	14.4	12.3	10.3	10.9	10.8	11.0
All ages, crude	10.9	11.2	14.8	12.8	10.8	11.5	11.4	11.5

Continued.

Deaths due to Motor Vehicle Accidents: Trends
[Continued]

Sex and race		1950[1]	1960[1]	1970	1980	1983	1984	1985	1986
Under 1 year		7.8	7.5	10.2	7.1	4.8	4.4	3.9	4.6
1-4 years		10.1	8.3	9.6	7.7	6.0	5.4	5.7	6.0
5-14 years		5.6	5.3	6.9	5.7	4.7	5.1	5.2	4.9
15-24 years		12.6	15.6	22.7	23.0	18.8	20.1	20.1	21.5
25-34 years		9.0	9.0	12.7	12.2	10.7	11.0	10.0	10.8
35-44 years		8.1	8.9	12.3	10.6	8.8	9.4	9.4	8.4
45-54 years		10.8	11.4	14.3	10.2	8.5	8.9	8.9	8.5
55-64 years		15.0	15.3	16.1	10.5	9.3	10.3	9.9	9.6
65-74 years		20.9	19.3	22.1	13.4	12.6	13.0	14.3	14.4
75-84 years		25.4	23.8	28.1	19.0	17.9	20.6	19.9	20.5
85 years and over		22.3	22.2	18.9	15.3	14.0	13.8	15.1	14.7
Black female									
All ages, age adjusted		10.3	10.0	13.8	8.4	7.5	7.6	8.2	8.5
All ages, crude		10.2	9.7	13.4	8.3	7.6	7.8	8.3	8.5
Under 1 year	{	7.0	8.1	11.9	5.3	5.1	5.1	7.8	5.3
1-4 years	{		8.8	12.6	9.5	8.0	6.9	6.8	6.9
5-14 years		6.2	5.9	9.3	5.2	4.3	4.4	4.3	4.8
15-24 years		11.5	9.9	13.4	8.0	8.6	8.4	9.1	9.1
25-34 years		10.7	9.8	13.3	10.6	7.4	9.0	9.2	10.3
35-44 years		11.1	11.0	16.1	8.3	7.3	8.6	9.1	8.7
45-54 years		10.6	11.8	16.4	9.1	8.7	6.4	8.2	8.7
55-64 years		14.0	14.0	17.1	9.3	8.1	8.5	9.5	10.9
65-74 years		12.7	14.2	16.3	8.5	9.6	9.7	9.6	9.7
75-84 years	{	17.6	8.8	14.3	11.1	15.1	13.7	15.0	10.0
85 years and over	{		21.1	17.5	12.3	7.8	9.8	9.4	11.0

Source: "Death Rates for Motor Vehicle Accidents, according to Sex, Race, and Age: United States, Selected Years 1950-86," *Health United States - 1988*, March 1989, p. 72. Primary source: *Vital Statistics of the United States*, National Center for Health Statistics, U.S. Government Printing Office, Washington, DC. *Notes:* For data years shown, the code numbers for cause of death are based on the then current *International Classification of Diseases*, which are described in Appendix II, tables IV and V. 1. Includes nonresidents of the U.S.

★ 929 ★
Deaths from Breast Malignancies: Trends

Data are based on the National Vital Statistics System.

Race and age	1950[1]	1960[1]	1970	1980	1983	1984	1985	1986
	Deaths per 100,000 resident population							
All races								
All ages, age adjusted	22.2	22.3	23.1	22.7	22.7	23.2	23.2	23.1
All ages, crude	24.7	26.1	28.4	30.6	31.6	32.5	32.7	32.8
Under 25 years	0.1	0.1	0.0	0.0	0.1	0.0	0.0	0.0
25-34 years	3.8	3.8	3.9	3.3	3.2	3.3	3.0	3.1
35-44 years	20.8	20.2	20.4	17.9	16.6	18.5	17.5	18.3
45-54 years	46.9	51.4	52.6	48.1	45.9	45.8	46.1	45.4
55-64 years	70.4	70.8	77.6	80.5	81.9	82.0	83.6	80.9
65-74 years	94.0	90.0	93.8	101.1	104.9	108.0	107.7	109.9
75-84 years	139.8	129.9	127.4	126.4	130.9	136.2	137.7	136.2

Continued.

Deaths from Breast Malignancies: Trends
[Continued]

Race and age		1950[1]	1960[1]	1970	1980	1983	1984	1985	1986
85 years and over		195.5	191.9	157.9	169.3	175.1	180.0	175.9	180.0
White									
All ages, age adjusted		22.5	22.4	23.4	22.8	22.7	23.1	23.3	23.0
All ages, crude		25.7	27.2	29.9	32.3	33.3	34.2	34.6	34.6
Under 25 years		0.1	0.0	0.0	0.0	0.1	0.0	0.0	0.0
25-34 years		3.7	3.6	3.7	3.0	3.0	3.1	2.8	2.7
35-44 years		20.8	19.7	20.2	17.3	16.0	17.4	16.7	17.3
45-54 years		47.1	51.2	53.0	48.1	45.3	45.3	46.5	44.4
55-64 years		70.9	71.8	79.3	81.3	82.8	82.2	84.2	81.8
65-74 years		96.3	91.6	95.9	103.7	106.9	110.1	110.0	112.4
75-84 years		143.6	132.8	129.6	128.4	133.1	138.3	140.4	139.7
85 years and over		204.2	199.7	161.9	171.7	178.6	183.7	178.9	182.7
Black									
All ages, age adjusted		19.3	21.3	21.5	23.3	24.4	26.1	25.3	25.8
All ages, crude		16.4	18.7	19.7	22.9	84.4	26.3	25.6	26.2
Under 25 years		0.1	0.2	0.1	0.0	0.1	0.0	0.1	0.1
25-34 years		4.9	6.1	5.9	5.3	4.6	5.0	4.4	5.6
35-44 years		21.0	24.8	24.4	24.1	23.8	28.9	26.3	28.3
45-54 years		46.5	54.4	52.0	52.7	55.3	55.5	54.4	59.1
55-64 years		64.3	63.2	64.7	79.9	82.9	90.5	88.5	83.6
65-74 years		67.0	72.3	77.3	84.3	95.0	100.1	99.3	100.5
75-84 years	{	81.0	87.5	101.8	114.1	120.6	128.2	121.0	112.1
85 years and over	{		92.1	112.1	149.9	143.4	149.6	152.5	162.1

Source: "Death Rates for Malignant Neoplasm of Breast for Females, according to Race and Age: United States, Selected Years 1950-86," *Health United States - 1988*, March 1989, p. 70. Primary source: *Vital Statistics of the United States*. National Center for Health Statistics, U.S. Government Printing Office, Washington, DC. *Notes:* For data years shown, the code numbers for cause of death are based on the then current *International Classification of Diseases*, which are described in Appendix II, tables IV and V. 1. Includes deaths of nonresidents of the United States.

★ 930 ★
Deaths of Infants

Deaths per 1,000 live births, by place of residence. Represents deaths of infants under 1 year old, exclusive of fetal deaths. Excludes deaths of nonresidents of the United States. See *Historical Statistics, Colonial Times to 1970*, Series B143-147, for U.S. total by race.

Division and State	Total[1]		White		Black	
	1980	1986	1980	1986	1980	1986
U.S.	12.6	10.4	11.0	8.9	21.4	18.0
New England	10.5	8.8	10.1	8.2	17.7	18.2
Middle Atlantic	12.8	10.4	11.1	8.7	21.1	17.8
East North Central	13.0	11.1	10.9	9.3	24.4	20.9
West North Central	11.3	9.7	10.5	8.9	21.3	17.5
South Atlantic	14.5	11.7	11.6	9.2	21.6	18.3
East South Central	14.5	11.6	11.8	9.3	21.8	17.8
West South Central	12.7	10.1	11.1	8.8	19.8	16.3

Continued.

Deaths of Infants
[Continued]

Division and State	Total[1]		White		Black	
	1980	1986	1980	1986	1980	1986
Mountain	11.0	9.3	10.7	9.0	19.5	15.7
Pacific	11.2	9.1	10.9	8.8	17.8	16.0

Source: "Infant Mortality Rates, by Race - States: 1980 and 1986," *Statistical Abstract*, 1989, p. 77. Primary source: U.S. National Center for Health Statistics, *Vital Statistics of the United States*, annual; and unpublished data. *Note:* 1. Includes other races, not shown separately.

★ 931 ★
Fertility Rate

Excludes Alaska prior to 1959 and Hawaii prior to 1960. Prior to 1960, based on births adjusted for underregistration; thereafter, registered births only. Beginning 1970, excludes births to nonresidents of United States. The total fertility rate is the number of births that 1,000 women would have in their lifetime if, at each year of age, they experienced the birth rates occurring in the specified year. A total fertility rate of 2,110 represents "replacement level" fertility for the total population under current mortality conditions (assuming no net immigration). The intrinsic rate of natural increase is the rate that would eventually prevail if a population were to experience at each year of age, the birth rates and death rates occurring in the specified year and if those rates remained unchanged over a long period of time. Minus sign (-) indicates decrease.

Annual Average and Year	Total Fertility Rate		Intrinsic Rate of Natural Increase	
	White	Black and other	White	Black and other
1940-1944	2,460	3,010	3.9	9.8
1945-1949	2,916	3,485	10.9	17.2
1950-1954	3,221	4,185	15.4	25.7
1955-1959	3,549	4,716	19.5	30.7
1960-1964	3,326	4,326	17.1	27.7
1965-1969	2,512	3,362	6.4	18.6
1970-1974	1,997	2,680	-2.5	9.1
1975-1979	1,685	2,270	-8.5	3.0
1980-1984	1,731	2,262	-7.3	3.0
1985-1986	1,748	2,272	-6.7	3.2
1965	2,783	3,808	10.3	23.1
1966	2,603	3,532	7.9	20.4
1967	2,447	3,299	5.6	18.2
1968	2,366	3,108	4.2	16.0
1969	2,360	3,061	4.1	15.4
1970	2,385	3,067	4.5	14.4
1971	2,161	2,920	.8	12.6
1972	1,907	2,628	-3.9	8.6
1973	1,783	2,444	-6.5	5.7
1974	1,749	2,339	-7.2	4.0
1975	1,686	2,276	-8.6	3.0
1976	1,652	2,223	-9.3	2.1
1977	1,703	2,278	-8.1	3.2
1978	1,668	2,264	-8.8	2.9
1979	1,715	2,310	-7.7	3.8
1980	1,749	2,323	-7.0	4.0
1981	1,726	2,275	-7.4	3.3
1982	1,742	2,264	-7.0	3.0

Continued.

Fertility Rate
[Continued]

| Annual Average and Year | Total Fertility Rate | | Intrinsic Rate of Natural Increase | |
	White	Black and other	White	Black and other
1983	1,718	2,225	-7.5	2.5
1984	1,719	2,224	-7.4	2.4
1985	1,754	2,263	-6.6	3.1
1986	1,741	2,281	-6.8	3.3

Source: "Total Fertility Rate and Intrinsic Rate of Natural Increase: 1940 to 1986," *Statistical Abstract*, 1989, p. 64.

★ 932 ★
Fetal Death Rates: Trends

Data are based on the National Vital Statistics System.

| Geographic Division and State | Fetal deaths per 1,000 live births plus fetal deaths[1] | | | | | | | | |
| | All races | | | White | | | Black | | |
	1974-76	1979-81	1984-86	1974-76	1979-81	1984-86	1974-76	1979-81	1984-86
United States	10.8	9.1	7.9	9.6	8.1	7.0	16.8	14.3	12.6
New England	8.9	7.2	6.7	8.7	7.0	6.4	12.9	10.1	11.3
Maine	6.4	7.1	6.4	6.5	7.1	6.4	[2]	[2]	[2]
New Hampshire	7.8	6.3	5.7	7.7	6.3	5.8	[2]	[2]	[2]
Vermont	8.0	6.6	6.8	8.0	6.5	6.8	[2]	[2]	[2]
Massachusetts	9.1	6.5	6.7	9.0	6.3	6.3	11.9	9.1	12.0
Rhode Island	12.0	10.7	7.6	11.9	10.6	7.5	16.8[2]	13.5[2]	10.7[2]
Connecticut	9.1	8.0	6.9	8.7	7.7	6.3	13.3	10.7	11.1
Middle Atlantic	11.4	10.6	9.1	10.5	9.6	8.2	15.9	15.2	13.4
New York	11.5	11.5	9.6	10.6	10.6	8.6	15.2	15.4	13.6
New Jersey	10.2	8.5	8.0	9.4	7.3	6.9	14.1	13.1	12.6
Pennsylvania	12.0	10.4	9.0	11.0	9.5	8.3	19.3	17.0	13.9
East North Central	10.1	8.4	7.1	9.1	7.5	6.3	15.8	13.0	11.0
Ohio	9.9	8.5	7.4	9.1	7.9	6.7	14.8	12.7	11.2
Indiana	10.4	8.6	7.4	9.5	8.0	6.9	18.0	13.7	11.6
Illinois	11.0	9.3	7.9	9.4	7.9	6.7	16.9	14.3	12.2
Michigan	9.8	7.4	5.8	8.9	6.7	5.3	14.3	11.1	8.1
Wisconsin	8.4	7.2	6.5	8.0	7.0	5.9	14.2	11.1	13.5
West North Central	9.6	8.0	6.7	9.2	7.5	6.3	15.9	13.3	10.6
Minnesota	8.7	6.8	6.5	8.6	6.7	6.4	13.9[2]	11.2[2]	9.6
Iowa	9.1	7.3	6.6	9.0	7.3	6.5	14.4[2]	9.4[2]	9.6[2]
Missouri	10.4	9.0	6.7	9.5	8.1	6.1	15.9	14.3	10.5
North Dakota	9.9	8.5	6.3	9.6	8.4	6.1	[2]	[2]	[2]

Continued.

Fetal Death Rates: Trends
[Continued]

Geographic Division and State	Fetal deaths per 1,000 live births plus fetal deaths[1]								
	All races			White			Black		
	1974-76	1979-81	1984-86	1974-76	1979-81	1984-86	1974-76	1979-81	1984-86
South Dakota	9.8	8.0	6.8	9.4	7.0	6.4	[2]	[2]	[2]
Nebraska	9.1	8.4	7.2	8.8	8.2	6.9	15.1[2]	12.4[2]	12.0[2]
Kansas	10.4	8.1	6.7	9.9	7.6	6.3	18.3	12.5	11.4
South Atlantic	12.7	11.3	9.6	10.6	9.4	7.9	18.2	16.0	14.2
Delaware	10.6	8.9	7.6	9.5	7.5	6.6	14.4	13.6	10.9
Maryland	10.1	8.9	8.4	8.7	7.3	6.8	14.2	13.0	12.5
District of Columbia	15.7	14.1	13.1	10.6[2]	10.8[2]	7.6	16.5	14.9	14.7
Virginia	14.2	13.0	10.5	11.9	11.3	8.9	22.3	18.5	16.3
West Virginia	11.2	9.5	8.1	10.9	9.3	8.1	20.1[2]	14.3[2]	10.2[2]
North Carolina	12.8	10.4	8.6	10.4	8.4	7.3	18.3	15.0	12.0
South Carolina	14.2	12.4	10.9	10.6	9.1	8.1	19.9	17.2	15.3
Georgia	14.4	14.5	11.5	12.0	11.9	9.4	18.9	18.9	15.5
Florida	11.4	9.8	8.8	9.7	8.4	7.1	16.5	13.9	13.9
East South Central	13.4	10.7	9.2	10.8	8.7	7.5	20.4	16.0	13.9
Kentucky	10.9	9.5	8.1	10.3	9.0	7.5	18.2	14.4	13.6
Tennessee	12.1	9.4	7.3	10.7	8.2	6.6	17.4	13.5	9.7
Alabama	13.7	11.2	10.6	10.5	8.8	8.2	19.8	15.5	15.0
Mississippi	17.9	13.7	11.8	12.7	9.1	7.9	23.5	18.5	16.1
West South Central	10.8	8.6	7.7	9.7	7.7	7.0	15.4	12.7	11.3
Arkansas	11.7	9.6	7.8	9.7	7.8	6.7	17.7	15.2	11.1
Louisiana	11.3	10.0	8.8	8.6	7.6	6.7	15.6	14.0	12.4
Oklahoma	9.8	9.1	7.9	9.1	8.4	7.6	15.1	14.9	10.9
Texas	10.7	8.0	7.4	10.0	7.6	6.9	14.7	10.7	10.7
Mountain	9.5	8.0	7.0	9.2	7.9	6.9	15.8	12.4	10.5
Montana	9.5	7.1	7.4	9.2	6.9	7.1	[2]	[2]	[2]
Idaho	8.6	7.4	7.2	8.2	7.4	7.0	[2]	[2]	[2]
Wyoming	10.8	7.8	6.9	10.7	8.0	6.9	[2]	[2]	[2]
Colorado	11.5	9.7	8.6	11.4	9.5	8.4	16.9	14.5	12.1
New Mexico	9.1	7.5	5.7	8.7	7.3	5.8	16.4[2]	12.0[2]	5.4[2]
Arizona	8.9	7.6	6.4	8.3	7.3	6.2	14.3[2]	11.8	8.8
Utah	8.4	7.5	6.6	8.2	7.4	6.6	[2]	[2]	[2]
Nevada	8.5	8.1	7.0	7.9	7.6	6.5	13.4[2]	11.8[2]	13.2[2]
Pacific	9.3	7.9	6.7	8.7	7.5	6.4	14.4	12.2	10.7
Washington	8.6	7.4	6.2	8.4	7.2	6.0	15.1	12.6	8.5
Oregon	8.7	7.1	6.5	8.5	7.0	6.5	14.8[2]	10.9[2]	8.0[2]
California	9.2	7.9	6.7	8.7	7.5	6.4	14.3	12.2	10.9

Continued.

Fetal Death Rates: Trends
[Continued]

Geographic Division and State	Fetal deaths per 1,000 live births plus fetal deaths[1]								
	All races			White			Black		
	1974-76	1979-81	1984-86	1974-76	1979-81	1984-86	1974-76	1979-81	1984-86
Alaska	9.2	7.8	6.7	9.7	7.3	6.3	[2]	11.9[2]	8.6[2]
Hawaii	13.8	11.1	8.8	15.8	14.2	8.1	20.6[2]	12.9[2]	11.8[2]

Source: "Fetal Death Rates, according to Race, Geographic Division, and State: United States, Average Annual 1974-76, 1979-81, and 1984-86," *Health United States - 1988*, March 1989, p. 58. Primary source: *Division of Vital Statistics.* National Cenetr for Health Statistics, U.S. Government Printing Office, Washington, DC. *Notes:* 1. Deaths of fetuses of 20 weeks or more gestation 2. Data for States with fewer than 5,000 live births for the 3- year period are considered unreliable. Data for States with fewer than 1,000 births are considered highly unreliable and are not shown.

★ 933 ★
Homicides & Related Deaths: Trends

Data are based on the National Vital Statistics System.

Sex, race, and age	1950[1]	1960[1]	1970	1980	1983	1984	1985	1986

Deaths per 100,000 resident population

All races

All ages, age adjusted	5.4	5.2	9.1	10.8	8.6	8.4	8.3	9.0
All ages, crude	5.3	4.7	8.3	10.7	8.6	8.4	8.3	9.0
Under 1 year	4.4	4.8	4.3	5.9	5.3	6.5	5.3	7.4
1-4 years	0.6	0.7	1.9	2.5	2.3	2.4	2.4	2.7
5-14 years	0.5	0.5	0.9	1.2	1.0	1.3	1.2	1.1
15-24 years	6.3	5.9	11.7	15.6	12.4	12.0	12.1	14.2
25-34 years	9.9	9.7	16.6	19.6	15.4	14.7	14.7	16.1
35-44 years	8.8	8.1	13.7	15.1	11.8	11.3	11.3	11.4
45-54 years	6.1	6.2	10.1	11.1	8.7	8.5	8.1	8.3
55-64 years	4.0	4.2	7.1	7.0	6.1	5.8	5.7	5.4
85-74 years	3.2	2.8	5.0	5.7	4.3	4.2	4.3	4.4
75-84 years	2.6	2.4	4.0	5.2	4.9	4.4	4.3	4.6
85 years and older	2.3	2.4	4.5	5.3	5.0	4.3	4.1	4.7

White male

All ages, age adjusted	3.9	3.9	7.3	10.9	8.4	8.2	8.1	8.4
All ages, crude	3.9	3.6	6.8	10.9	8.6	8.3	8.2	8.6
Under 1 year	4.3	3.8	2.9	4.3	3.3	4.9	3.7	5.4
1-4 years	0.4	0.6	1.4	2.0	1.7	1.9	1.9	1.9
5-14 years	0.4	0.4	0.5	0.9	0.9	0.9	1.1	0.9
15-24 years	3.7	4.4	7.9	15.5	11.5	11.1	11.2	12.5
25-34 years	5.4	6.2	13.0	18.9	14.9	14.1	13.9	14.6
35-44 years	6.4	5.5	11.0	15.5	12.4	11.8	11.5	11.6
45-54 years	5.5	5.0	9.0	11.9	9.1	9.4	8.6	8.6
55-64 years	4.4	4.3	7.7	7.8	6.4	6.3	6.3	6.0
65-74 years	4.1	3.4	5.6	6.9	4.6	4.2	4.5	4.3
75-84 years	3.5	2.7	5.1	6.3	4.6	4.2	4.5	4.6
85 years and older	1.8	2.7	7.0	6.4	5.6	5.3	3.9	4.4

Black male

All ages, age adjusted	51.1	44.9	82.1	71.9	53.8	50.8	49.9	55.9

Continued.

Homicides & Related Deaths: Trends
[Continued]

Sex, race, and age		1950[1]	1960[1]	1970	1980	1983	1984	1985	1986
All ages, crude		47.3	36.6	67.5	66.6	51.4	48.7	48.4	55.0
Under 1 year	{	1.8	10.3	14.3	18.6	14.0	20.1	16.0	22.5
1-4 years	{		1.7	5.1	7.2	7.2	5.0	6.5	9.3
5-14 years		1.8	1.4	4.2	2.9	3.1	3.2	3.2	3.2
15-24 years		58.9	46.4	102.5	84.3	66.8	61.5	66.1	79.2
25-34 years		110.5	92.0	158.5	145.1	102.0	96.2	94.3	108.0
35-44 years		83.7	77.5	126.2	110.3	82.0	78.1	76.3	79.4
45-54 years		54.6	54.8	100.6	83.8	57.8	57.1	51.1	56.3
55-64 years		35.7	31.8	59.8	55.6	46.7	40.6	37.8	35.4
65-74 years		18.7	19.1	40.6	33.9	28.1	30.3	27.6	30.0
75-84 years	{	11.5	16.1	18.9	27.6	32.4	28.3	21.5	27.9
85 years and older	{		10.3	23.1	17.0	27.0	28.6	16.9	25.4
White female									
All ages, age adjusted		1.4	1.5	2.2	3.2	2.8	2.9	2.9	2.9
All ages, crude		1.4	1.4	2.1	3.2	2.8	2.9	2.9	3.0
Under 1 year		3.9	3.5	2.9	4.3	3.7	4.0	4.3	5.1
1-4 years		0.6	0.5	1.2	1.5	1.2	1.7	1.6	1.4
5-14 years		0.4	0.3	0.5	1.0	0.7	0.9	0.8	0.8
15-24 years		1.3	1.5	2.7	4.7	3.7	4.3	3.6	4.3
25-34 years		1.9	2.0	3.4	4.3	4.1	3.9	4.4	4.4
35-44 years		2.2	2.2	3.2	4.1	3.5	3.4	3.6	3.5
45-54 years		1.6	1.9	2.2	3.0	2.9	2.7	2.9	2.8
55-64 years		1.3	1.5	2.0	2.1	2.2	2.2	2.3	1.9
65-74 years		1.1	1.1	1.7	2.5	2.0	1.9	2.2	2.2
75-84 years		1.2	1.2	2.5	3.3	3.1	2.9	3.1	3.1
85 years and older		1.9	1.5	2.0	4.0	3.8	2.6	3.2	3.3
Black female									
All ages, age adjusted		11.7	11.8	15.0	13.7	11.2	11.0	10.8	11.8
All ages, crude		11.5	10.4	13.2	13.5	11.3	11.2	11.0	12.1
Under 1 year	{	2.6	13.8	10.7	12.8	15.3	16.4	10.3	17.0
1-4 years	{		1.7	6.3	6.4	6.3	6.7	6.3	6.8
5-14 years		1.2	1.0	2.0	2.2	1.4	3.1	2.0	2.3
15-24 years		16.5	11.9	17.7	18.4	15.7	14.8	14.2	16.2
25-34 years		26.6	24.9	25.6	25.8	19.9	19.3	19.8	21.9
35-44 years		17.8	20.5	25.1	17.7	14.8	14.4	14.8	14.8
45-54 years		8.5	12.7	17.5	12.5	9.5	7.5	9.0	8.5
55-64 years		3.6	6.8	8.1	8.9	6.3	6.7	6.4	6.8
65-74 years		3.4	3.3	7.7	8.6	7.0	6.8	7.2	8.7
75-84 years	{	4.0	2.5	5.7	6.7	11.3	9.8	7.6	8.6
85 years and older	{		2.6	11.1	8.5	8.5	7.5	11.5	13.1

Source: "Death Rates for Homicide and Legal Intervention, according to Sex, Race, and Age: United States, Selected Years 1950-86," *Health United States - 1988*, March 1989, p. 73. Primary source: National Center for Health Statistics, *Vital Statistics of the United States*: Vol. II, Mortality, Part A, 1950-86, U.S. Government Printing Office, Washington, DC. *Notes:* For data years shown, the code numbers for cause of death are based on the then current *International Classification of Diseases*, which are described in Appendix II, tables IV and V. 1. Includes deaths of nonresidents of the United States.

★ 934 ★
Infant and Maternal Deaths

Deaths per 1,000 live births, except as noted. Beginning 1970, excludes deaths of nonresidents of U.S. See also *Historical Statistics, Colonial Times to 1970*, Series B 136-147.

Item	1960	1970	1975	1977	1978	1979	1980	1981	1982	1983	1984	1985	1986
Infants deaths[1]	26.0	20.0	16.1	14.1	13.8	13.1	12.6	11.9	11.5	11.2	10.8	10.6	10.4
White	22.9	17.8	14.2	12.3	12.0	11.4	11.0	10.5	10.1	9.7	9.4	9.3	8.9
Black	44.3	32.6	26.2	23.6	23.9	21.8	21.4	20.0	19.6	19.2	18.4	18.2	18.0
Maternal deaths[2]	37.1	21.5	12.8	11.2	9.6	9.6	9.2	8.5	7.9	8.0	7.8	7.8	7.2
White	26.0	14.4	9.1	7.7	6.4	6.4	6.7	6.3	5.8	5.9	5.4	5.2	4.9
Black	103.6	59.8	31.3	29.2	25.0	25.1	21.5	20.4	18.2	18.3	19.7	20.4	18.8
Neonatal deaths[3]	18.7	15.1	11.6	9.9	9.5	8.9	8.5	8.0	7.7	7.3	7.0	7.0	6.7
White	17.2	13.8	10.4	8.7	8.4	7.9	7.5	7.1	6.8	6.4	6.2	6.1	5.8
Black	27.8	22.8	18.3	16.1	15.5	14.3	14.1	13.4	13.1	12.4	11.8	12.1	11.7

Source: "Infant, Maternal, and Neonatal Mortality Rates, and Fetal Mortality Ratios, by Race: 1960 to 1986," *Statistical Abstract*, 1989, p. 76. Primary source: U.S. National Center for Health Statistics, *Vital Statistics of the United States*, annual; and unpublished data. *Notes:* 1. Represents deaths of infants under 1 year old, exclusive of fetal deaths. 2. Per 100,000 live births from deliveries and complications of pregnancy, childbirth, and the puerperium. Beginning 1979 deaths are classified according to the ninth revision of the *International Classification of Diseases*; for the earlier years classified according to the revision in use at the time; see text, section 2. 3. Represents deaths of infants under 28 days old, exclusive of fetal deaths.

★ 935 ★
Infant Deaths in Southern States

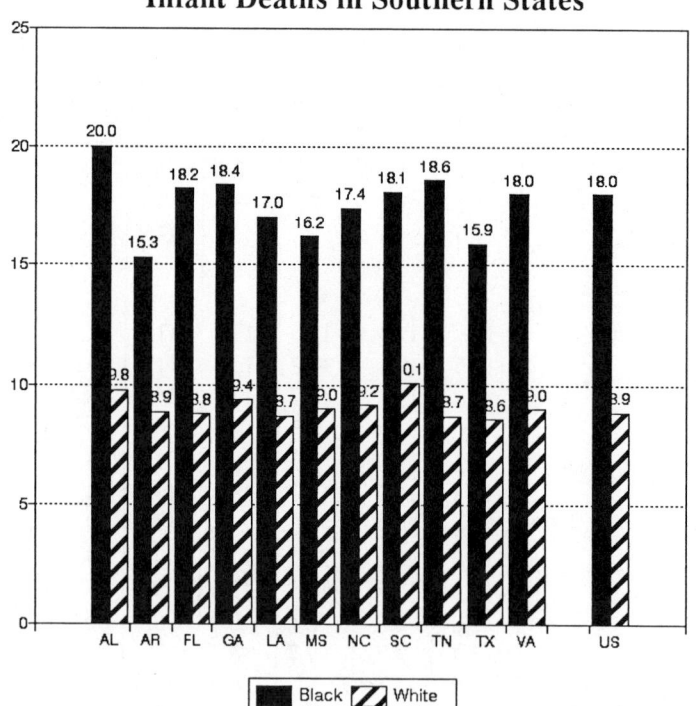

Southern States by Race: 1985.

	Black	White
Alabama	20.0	9.8
Arkansas	15.3	8.9
Florida	18.2	8.8
Georgia	18.4	9.4
Lousiana	17.0	8.7

Continued.

Infant Deaths in Southern States
[Continued]

	Black	White
Mississippi	16.2	9.0
North Carolina	17.4	9.2
South Carolina	18.1	10.1
Tennessee	18.6	8.7
Texas	15.9	8.6
Virginia	18.0	9.0
Total U.S.	18.0	8.9

Source: "Infant Death Rate per 1,000 Live Births," "Legislative Bulletin," 1989, p. 2. Primary source: "Legislative Bulletin," Spring, 1989. Published by permission of the Southern Regional Council.

★ 936 ★
Infant Feeding

Data for 1970-1975 based on 1976 National Survey of Family Growth (NSFG) and for 1976-1981 on 1982 NSFG. Based on a sample and subject to sampling variability.

Characteristic of Mother	Percent Breast-fed at all						Percent Breast-fed 3 months or more					
	1970-1971	1972-1973	1974-1975	1976-1977	1978-1979	1980-1981	1970-1971	1972-1973	1974-1975	1976-1977	1978-1979	1980-1981
Total babies	24.3	23.6	32.4	42.2	44.3	52.5	10.6	10.8	15.0	25.7	28.5	32.6
White	25.8	25.6	35.5	46.2	48.1	57.2	11.2	11.4	16.6	29.0	31.2	35.8
Black	12.8	12.9	16.4	19.5	24.4	24.5	6.2	6.9	6.4	11.5	14.2	12.1

Source: "Breast-Feeding by Characteristic of Mother and Birth Year of Baby: 1970 to 1981," *Statistical Abstract*, 1989, p. 65. Primary source: Pratt, William F. et al., "Understanding U.S. Fertility: Findings from the National Survey of Family Growth, Cycle III," *Population Bulletin*. vol. 39, No. 5 (Population Reference Bureau, Inc., Washington, DC, 1984).

★ 937 ★
Infant Mortality and Fetal Death Rates

Data based on the National Vital Statistics System.

Race and year	Infant mortality rate[1] Deaths per 1,000 live births				Fetal death rate[2]	Late fetal death rate[3]	Peri-natal mortality rate[4]
	Total	Neonatal Under 28 days	Neonatal Under 7 days	Post neo-natal			
All Races							
1950[5]	29.9	20.5	17.8	8.7	18.4	14.9	32.5
1960[5]	26.0	18.7	16.7	7.3	15.8	12.1	28.6
1970	20.0	15.1	13.6	4.9	14.0	9.5	23.0
1975	16.1	11.6	10.0	4.5	10.6	7.8	17.7
1980	12.6	8.5	7.1	4.1	9.1	6.2	13.2
1981	11.9	8.0	6.7	3.9	8.9	5.9	12.6
1982	11.5	7.7	6.4	3.8	8.8	5.9	12.3
1983	11.2	7.3	6.1	3.9	8.4	5.4	11.5
1984	10.8	7.0	5.9	3.8	8.1	5.2	11.0
1985	10.6	7.0	5.8	3.7	7.8	4.9	10.7
1986	10.4	6.7	5.6	3.6	7.7	4.7	10.3

Continued.

Infant Mortality and Fetal Death Rates
[Continued]

Race and year	Infant mortality rate[1] Deaths per 1,000 live births				Fetal death rate[2]	Late fetal death rate[3]	Peri-natal mortality rate[4]
	Total	Neonatal		Post neo-natal			
		Under 28 days	Under 7 days				
Provisional data:							
1985[5]	10.6	6.9	---	3.6	---	---	---
1986[5]	10.4	6.7	---	3.7	---	---	---
1987[5]	10.0	6.5	---	3.4	---	---	---
White							
1950[5]	26.8	19.4	17.1	7.7	16.6	13.3	30.1
1960[5]	22.9	17.2	15.6	5.7	13.9	10.8	26.2
1970	17.8	13.8	12.5	4.0	12.3	8.6	21.1
1975	14.2	10.4	9.0	3.8	9.4	7.1	16.0
1980	11.0	7.5	6.2	3.5	8.1	5.7	11.9
1981	10.5	7.1	5.9	3.4	8.0	5.5	11.3
1982	10.1	6.8	5.6	3.3	7.9	5.4	11.0
1983	9.7	6.4	5.4	3.3	7.4	5.0	10.3
1984	9.4	6.2	5.1	3.3	7.3	4.8	9.9
1985	9.3	6.1	5.0	3.2	7.0	4.5	9.6
1986	8.9	5.8	4.8	3.1	6.7	4.3	9.1
Black							
1950[5]	43.9	27.8	23.0	16.1	32.1	---	---
1960[5]	44.3	27.8	23.7	16.5	---	---	---
1970	32.6	22.8	20.3	9.9	23.2	---	---
1975	26.2	18.3	15.7	7.9	16.8	11.4	26.9
1980	21.4	14.1	11.9	7.3	14.4	8.9	20.7
1981	20.0	13.4	11.4	6.6	13.8	8.2	19.4
1982	19.6	13.1	11.1	6.6	13.8	8.1	19.1
1983	19.2	12.4	10.6	6.8	13.5	7.7	18.2
1984	18.4	11.8	10.2	6.5	12.7	7.3	17.4
1985	18.2	12.1	10.3	6.1	12.6	7.1	17.4
1986	18.0	11.6	10.1	6.3	12.5	7.0	17.0

Source: "Infant Mortality Rates, Fetal Death Rates, and Perinatal Mortality Rates, According to Race: United States, Selected Years 1950-1987," *Health United States - 1988*, March 1989, p. 54. Primary source: National Center for Health Statistics: *Vital Statistics of the United States*, Vol. II, Mortality, Part A, 1950-83. Public Health Service. Washington. U.S. Government Printing Office. 1984-86, to be published; Annual summary of births, marriages, divorces, and deaths, United States, 1985. *Monthly Vital Statistics Report*. Vol. 34, No. 13. DHHS Pub. No. (PHS) 86-1120. Sept. 19, 1986; Annual summary of births, marriages, divorces, and deaths, United States, 1987. *Monthly Vital Statistics Report*. Vol. 36, No. 13. DHHS Pub. No. (PHS) 87-1120. July 29, 1988. Public Health Service. Hyattsville, MD; Data computed by the Division of Analysis from data compiled by the Division of Vital Statistics. *Notes:* 1. Infant mortality is number of deaths of infants under 1 year per 1,000 live births. Neonatal deaths occur within 28 days of birth; postneonatal deaths occur 28-365 days after birth. Deaths within 7 days are early neonatal deaths. 2. Number of deaths of fetuses of 20 weeks or more gestation per 1,000 live births plus fetal deaths. 3. Number of fetal deaths of 28 weeks or more gestation per 1,000 live births plus late fetal deaths. 4. Number of late fetal deaths plus infant deaths within 7 days of birth per 1,000 live births plus late fetal deaths. 5. Includes births and deaths of nonresidents of the United States.

★ 938 ★
Infant Mortality in Southern States

State		1980	1985	1986
Alabama		15.1	12.6	13.3
	White	11.6	10.4	9.8
	Black	21.6	17.0	20.0
Arkansas		12.7	11.6	10.3
	White	10.3	10.9	8.9
	Black	20.0	14.2	15.3
Florida		14.6	11.3	11.0
	White	11.8	9.2	8.8
	Black	22.8	17.8	18.2
Georgia		14.5	12.7	12.5
	White	10.8	9.5	9.4
	Black	21.0	19.0	18.4
Louisiana		14.3	11.9	11.9
	White	10.5	8.6	8.7
	Black	20.6	17.2	17.0
Mississippi		17.0	13.7	12.4
	White	11.1	9.3	9.0
	Black	23.7	18.9	16.2
North Carolina		14.5	11.8	11.5
	White	12.1	9.4	9.2
	Black	20.0	17.8	17.4
South Carolina		15.6	14.2	13.2
	White	10.8	9.6	10.1
	Black	22.9	21.8	18.1
Tennessee		13.5	11.4	11.0
	White	11.9	8.9	8.7
	Black	19.3	20.2	18.6
Texas		12.2	9.8	9.5
	White	11.2	9.0	8.6
	Black	19.3	20.2	18.6
Virginia		13.6	11.5	11.1
	White	11.9	9.3	9.0
	Black	19.8	19.4	18.0

Source: "Change in Infant Mortality by Race, 1980-1986," "Legislative Bulletin," 1989, p. 2. Primary source: Computed by the Southern Regional Council from USNCHS: Vital Statistics of the U.S., 1980, 1985, and 1986, U.S. Department of HEW: Vital Statistics of the U.S. Published by permission of the Southern Regional Council.

★ 939 ★
Infant Mortality in the South and Non-South

Location	1960	1970	1980	1985
South	31.2	22.6	13.9	11.4
Non-South	24.3	19.1	12.1	10.3

Source: "Changes in Infant Mortality, 1960-1985," "Legislative Bulletin," 1980, p. 1 Published by permission of the Southern Regional Council.

★ 940 ★
Infant Mortality Rates

	1950	1960	1970	1975	1980	1985	1986	1987	1988
All Races	29.2	26.0	20.0	16.1	12.6	10.6	10.4	10.0[1]	9.9[1]
Whites	26.8	22.9	17.8	14.2	11.0	9.3	8.9	[2]	[2]
Blacks	43.9	44.3	32.6	26.2	21.4	18.2	18.0	[2]	[2]
Hispanics							8.0		
Mexican							7.7		
Puerto Rican							8.6		
Cuban							5.5		
Other Hispanic							9.1		

Source: "Infant Deaths Per 1,000 Live Births, 1950-1988," *U.S. Children and Their Families*, 1989, p. 171. Primary source: Hispanic rates are based on data from 18 reporting states and the District of Columbia. National Center for Health Statistics, "Advance Report of Final Mortality Statistics, 1986," *Monthly Vital Statistics Reports*, Vol. 37, No. 6, Supplement, Table 13 and 20; "Annual Summary, 1987," *Monthly Vital Statistics Report*, Vol. 36, No. 13, Table 11; "Births, Marriages, Divorces, and Deaths for 1988," *Monthly Vital Statistics Report*, Vol. 37, No. 12. *Notes:* The infant mortality rate is the number of deaths of children under age 1 per *1,000* live births. It is not a percentage. 1. Provisional data. 2. Not available.

★ 941 ★
Infant Mortality Rates: Trends

Data are based on the National Vital Statistics System.

Geographic Division and State	All races			White			Black		
	1974-76	1979-81	1984-86	1974-76	1979-81	1984-86	1974-76	1979-81	1984-86
Postneonatal deaths per 1,000 live births									
United States	4.4	4.1	3.7	3.7	3.5	3.2	7.9	7.1	6.3
New England	3.3	2.9	2.7	3.1	2.8	2.5	6.0	4.8	5.1
Maine	3.8	3.8	3.0	3.8	3.8	3.1	[1]	[1]	[1]
New Hampshire	3.1	2.9	3.1	3.1	2.9	3.1	[1]	[1]	[1]
Vermont	3.1	3.5	2.9	3.1	3.5	2.9	[1]	[1]	[1]
Massachusetts	3.2	2.8	2.7	3.0	2.7	2.4	6.3	4.7	5.7
Rhode Island	3.7	3.0	2.7	3.6	2.6	2.6	[1]	9.4[1]	4.0[1]
Connecticut	3.1	2.8	2.4	2.8	2.6	2.2	5.7	4.3	4.6
Middle Atlantic	4.0	3.7	3.4	3.3	3.0	2.7	7.3	6.8	6.3
New York	4.2	3.8	3.4	3.5	3.2	2.8	6.9	6.4	5.9
New Jersey	3.9	3.7	3.3	3.0	2.7	2.5	7.9	7.6	7.0
Pennsylvania	3.7	3.5	3.3	3.2	3.0	2.8	7.6	7.7	6.6
East North Central	4.4	4.1	3.7	3.7	3.4	3.1	8.5	8.0	6.9
Ohio	4.1	3.9	3.7	3.7	3.4	3.2	7.2	7.2	6.3
Indiana	4.2	3.8	3.7	3.9	3.3	3.4	7.1	7.9	6.4
Illinois	4.9	4.6	3.9	3.6	3.3	2.9	9.9	9.2	7.8
Michigan	4.6	4.1	3.6	3.8	3.5	3.0	8.4	7.1	6.4
Wisconsin	3.7	3.6	3.6	3.4	3.3	3.3	7.3	7.5	6.1

Continued.

Infant Mortality Rates: Trends
[Continued]

Geographic Division and State	All races			White			Black		
	1974-76	1979-81	1984-86	1974-76	1979-81	1984-86	1974-76	1979-81	1984-86
West North Central	3.9	3.8	3.6	3.5	3.5	3.3	7.8	7.1	6.4
Minnesota	3.8	3.7	3.5	3.5	3.5	3.4	8.3[1]	7.9[1]	5.9[1]
Iowa	3.2	3.6	3.1	3.1	3.5	3.1	5.9[1]	8.6[1]	4.7[1]
Missouri	4.3	4.1	3.9	3.7	3.6	3.4	8.0	7.1	6.9
North Dakota	3.5	3.8	3.7	3.1	3.5	3.5	[1]	[1]	[1]
South Dakota	5.6	4.9	5.1	4.1	3.7	3.8	[1]	[1]	[1]
Nebraska	3.9	3.8	3.5	3.6	3.6	3.2	11.1[1]	7.3[1]	6.4[1]
Kansas	3.7	3.4	3.6	3.5	3.1	3.4	6.0[1]	6.2	5.9
South Atlantic	4.9	4.5	3.9	3.7	3.5	3.0	7.9	7.1	6.1
Delaware	3.7	3.6	3.4	3.1	3.0	2.5	6.1[1]	5.5[1]	6.3[1]
Maryland	4.0	3.8	3.6	3.4	3.1	3.0	5.7	5.7	5.1
District of Columbia	5.5	5.7	4.9	2.4[1]	2.0[1]	2.7[1]	6.1	6.5	5.6
Virginia	4.3	3.7	3.5	3.6	3.3	2.9	6.8	5.3	5.7
West Virginia	4.6	4.2	3.6	4.5	4.1	3.5	5.7[1]	7.4[1]	6.0[1]
North Carolina	5.2	4.5	4.0	3.7	3.5	3.2	8.5	7.0	6.2
South Carolina	6.0	5.3	4.5	4.0	3.7	3.2	9.3	7.6	6.7
Georgia	5.4	5.0	4.1	3.8	3.5	3.1	8.3	7.7	6.0
Florida	4.8	4.7	3.8	3.5	3.6	3.0	8.6	8.1	6.7
East South Central	5.3	4.7	4.2	3.9	3.7	3.3	8.9	7.4	6.6
Kentucky	4.4	4.2	3.8	4.2	4.0	3.6	7.0	6.7	5.7
Tennessee	4.4	4.2	3.9	3.8	3.6	3.3	6.9	6.3	6.0
Alabama	5.7	5.0	4.2	3.9	3.6	3.0	9.2	7.4	6.6
Mississippi	6.9	5.8	5.1	3.9	3.5	3.2	10.3	8.2	7.2
West South Central	4.7	4.3	3.8	4.0	3.7	3.4	7.6	7.0	6.2
Arkansas	5.0	5.1	4.4	3.7	3.9	3.8	8.6	8.8	6.6
Louisiana	4.7	4.7	4.1	3.4	3.4	2.8	6.8	6.8	6.2
Oklahoma	5.0	4.6	4.1	4.6	4.2	4.0	8.5	7.9	6.4
Texas	4.7	4.1	3.7	4.1	3.7	3.3	7.9	6.6	6.0
Mountain	4.7	4.1	4.0	4.2	3.8	3.8	6.6	6.9	6.1
Montana	4.5	4.2	4.6	4.1	3.7	4.3	[1]	[1]	[1]
Idaho	4.3	3.9	4.5	4.2	4.0	4.5	[1]	[1]	[1]
Wyoming	5.0	3.6	4.9	4.8	3.4	4.9	[1]	[1]	[1]
Colorado	4.4	3.7	3.9	4.3	3.7	3.8	6.3[1]	5.1[1]	6.7[1]
New Mexico	6.0	4.4	4.0	5.1	3.8	3.7	[1]	7.3[1]	6.9[1]
Arizona	5.0	4.3	3.9	4.0	3.6	3.5	5.1[1]	6.9[1]	5.6[1]
Utah	3.6	3.9	3.8	3.3	3.9	3.8	[1]	[1]	[1]
Nevada	5.3	4.9	4.1	4.9	4.5	4.1	9.4[1]	9.1[1]	6.3[1]
Pacific	4.3	3.9	3.7	4.1	3.8	3.6	6.9	6.1	6.2

Continued.

Infant Mortality Rates: Trends
[Continued]

Geographic Division and State	All races			White			Black		
	1974-76	1979-81	1984-86	1974-76	1979-81	1984-86	1974-76	1979-81	1984-86
Washington	4.9	4.4	4.6	4.7	4.2	4.6	6.7[1]	6.9[1]	6.0[1]
Oregon	4.9	4.4	4.8	4.8	4.4	4.8	8.7[1]	4.8[1]	7.0[1]
California	4.1	3.8	3.4	3.9	3.7	3.3	6.9	6.1	6.1
Alaska	6.1	5.5	5.3	4.8	4.3	4.4	[1]	[1]	[1]
Hawaii	3.4	3.0	3.1	3.9	2.5	2.5	[1]	[1]	7.3[1]

Source: "Postneonatal Mortality Rates, according to Race, Geographic Division, and State: United States, Average Annual 1974-76, 1979-81, and 1984-86," *Health United States - 1988*, March 1989, p. 57. Primary source: *Division of Vital Statistics.* National Center for Health Statistics, U.S. Government Printing Office, Washington, DC. *Notes:* 1. Data for States with fewer than 10,000 live births for the 3- year period are considered unreliable. Data for States with fewer than 2,000 births are considered highly unreliable and are not shown.

★ 942 ★
Inmate Suicides in Local Jails

By selected characteristics, United States, 1979 and 1986.

Selected characteristics	1979	1986
Race		
White	67.3	71.6
Black	21.6	15.7
Other[1]	11.1	12.7

Source: "Estimated Percent Distribution of Inmate Suicides in Local Jails," *Sourcebook of Criminal Justice Statistics, 1988,* 1989, p. 608. Primary source: Lindsay M. Hayes and Joseph R. Rowan, *National Study of Jail Suicides: Seven Years Later* (Alexandria, VA: National Center on Institutions and Alternatives, 1988), pp. 21-36, Appendix A. Table adapted by SOURCEBOOK staff. Reprinted by permission. *Notes:* A second survey was mailed to all jails in both 1979 and 1986 that experienced at least one suicide, in order to gather descriptive information on the suicide victim and incident. This second survey yielded data on 344 of the 419 suicides occurring in 1979, for a response rate of 82 percent. In the 1986 survey, information was gathered for 339 out of 401 suicides for an 85 percent response rate. 1. For 1979, "other" includes Spanish/Mexican, American Indian, and unspecified. For 1986, "other" includes Spanish heritage, Chicano, Mexican American, and American Indian.

★ 943 ★
Leading Causes of Death

Rank	<1	1-14	15-24	25-34	35-44	45-54	55-64	65+	Total[1]
1	Perinatal Conditions 6,051	Accidents 1,498	Homicide 2,296	Homicide 2,761	Heart Diseases 2,509	Heart Diseases 6,530	Heart Diseases 14,252	Heart Diseases 49,960	Heart Diseases 74,976
2	Congenital Anomalies 1,443	Malignant Neoplasms 282	Accidents 1,792	Accidents 2,117	Malignant Neoplasms 2,145	Malignant Neoplasms 6,111	Malignant Neoplasms 12,557	Malignant Neoplasms 26,532	Malignant Neoplasms 48,728
3	Pneumonia and Influenza 279	Homicide 256	Suicide 399	Heart 974	Accidents 1,398	Cerebrovascular Disease 1,494	Cerebrovascular Disease 2,903	Cerebrovascular Disease 13,062	Cerebrovascular Disease 18,554
4	Heart Diseases 277	Congenital Anomalies 251	Heart Diseases 314	Malignant Neoplasms 780	Homicide 1,275	Accidents 1,177	Diabetes 1,325	Diabetes 3,505	Accidents 11,862
5	Accidents	Heart Disease	Malignant Neoplasm	Suicide	Liver Diseases & Cirrhosis	Liver Diseases & Cirrhosis	Accidents	Pneumonia and Influenza	Homicide

Continued.

Leading Causes of Death
[Continued]

Rank	<1	1-14	15-24	25-34	35-44	45-54	55-64	65+	Total[1]
	267	160	301	505	835	992	1,225	3,204	6,376
6	Meningitis	Pneumonia & Influenza	Congenital Anomalies	Liver Disease & Cirrhosis	Cerebrovascular Diseases	Homicide	Liver Disease & Cirrhosis	Bronchitis Asthma Emphysema	Perinatal Conditions
	106	88	88	412	677	720	974	2,443	6,097
7	Septicemia	Anemias	Cerebrovascular Diseases	Cerebrovascular Diseases	Pneumonia & Influenza	Diabetes	Bronchitis Asthma Emphysema	Accidents	Diabetes
	96	80	85	266	274	550	921	2,388	5,788
8	Homicide	Bronchitis Asthma Emphysema	Anemias	Pneumonia & Influenza	Suicide	Pneumonia & Influenza	Pneumonia & Influenza	Nephritis & Nephrosis	Pneumonia & Influenza
	81	64	84	218	253	413	700	2,301	5,227
9	Nephritis Asthma 71	Meningitis & Nephrosis 48	Bronchitis Emphysema 65	Diabetes Asthma 125	Diabetes 240	Bronchitis Emphysema 320	Nephritis Asthma 581	Septicemia & Nephrosis 1,610	Bronchitis Emphysema 4,066
10	Cerebrovascular Diseases 41	Perinatal Conditions 40	Pneumonia & Influenza 52	Anemias 99	Bronchitis Asthma Emphysema 144	Nephritis & Nephrosis 225	Homicide 491	Arterosclerosis 1,596	Liver Disease & Cirrhosis 3,822
Residual[2]	2,530	809	1,054	2,677	2,982	3,796	5,878	17,095	45,412
Total	11,242	3,578	6,529	10,954	12,832	22,328	41,811	123,694	232,968

Source: "Ten Leading Causes of Death for Blacks by Age Group," *Black Issues in Higher Education*, December 7, 1989, p. 12. Primary source: "High Risk Racial and Ethnic Groups - Blacks, Hispanics, 1970-1983," Centers for Disease Control, 1986. *Notes:* 1. Excludes persons of unknown age 2. Deaths from all other causes.

★ 944 ★
Life and Death Projections

Age in 1986 (years)	Expectation of Life in Years					Expected Deaths per 1,000 Alive at Specified Age[1]				
	Total	White		Black		Total	White		Black	
		Male	Female	Male	Female		Male	Female	Male	Female
At birth	74.8	72.0	78.8	65.2	73.5	10.36	10.02	7.80	20.04	16.09
1	74.6	71.7	78.4	65.5	73.7	.72	.76	.57	1.16	.96
5	70.7	67.8	74.6	61.7	69.9	.29	.30	.22	.51	.43
10	65.8	62.9	69.6	56.8	65.0	17	.18	.13	.30	.20
15	60.9	58.0	64.7	52.0	60.1	.63	.88	.39	.88	.36
20	56.2	53.4	59.9	47.3	55.3	1.09	1.58	.52	2.07	.66
25	51.5	48.8	55.0	42.8	50.5	1.18	1.60	.52	2.98	1.00
30	46.8	44.2	50.1	38.5	45.2	1.33	1.69	.60	3.98	1.55
35	42.1	39.5	45.3	34.3	41.1	1.61	1.95	.79	5.27	2.07
40	37.4	34.9	40.5	30.3	36.6	2.20	2.54	1.27	7.11	3.09
45	32.9	30.4	35.8	26.4	32.2	3.22	3.72	2.03	9.10	4.42
50	28.5	26.1	31.2	22.7	28.0	5.17	6.00	3.39	13.03	6.78
55	24.3	21.9	26.8	19.3	24.0	8.10	9.94	5.35	17.96	9.70
60	20.4	18.2	22.6	16.1	20.3	12.87	16.14	8.70	26.24	15.39
65	16.8	14.8	18.7	13.4	17.0	19.10	24.28	13.41	35.69	21.15

Source: "Expectation of Life and Expected Deaths, by Race, Sex, and Age: 1986," *Statistical Abstract*, 1989, p. 73. Primary source: U.S. National Center for Health Statistics, *Vital Statistics of the United States*, annual. *Notes:* 1. Based on the proportion of the cohort who are alive at the beginning of an indicated age interval who will die before reaching the end of that interval. For example, out of every 1,000 people alive and exactly 50 years old at the beginning of the period, between 5 and 6 (5.17) will die before reaching their 51st birthdays.

★ 945 ★
Life Expectancy

Prior to 1960, excludes Alaska and Hawaii. Beginning 1970, excludes deaths of nonresidents of the United States. See also *Historical Statistics, Colonial Times to 1970*, series B 116-125.

Age and Sex	White					Black		
	1959-1961	1969-1971	1979-1981	1985	1986	1979-1981	1985	1986
Average Expectation of Life in Years								
At birth:								
Male	67.6	67.9	70.8	71.9	72.0	64.1	65.3	65.2
Female	74.2	75.5	78.2	78.7	78.8	72.9	73.5	73.5
Age 20:								
Male	50.3	50.2	52.5	53.3	53.4	46.5	47.4	47.3
Female	56.3	57.2	59.4	59.8	59.9	54.9	55.3	55.3
Age 40:								
Male	31.7	31.9	34.0	34.7	34.9	29.5	30.2	30.3
Female	37.1	38.1	40.2	40.4	40.5	36.3	36.6	36.6
Age 50:								
Male	23.2	23.3	25.3	25.8	26.1	22.0	22.5	22.7
Female	28.1	29.1	31.0	31.1	31.2	27.8	27.9	28.0
Age 65:								
Male	13.0	13.0	14.3	14.6	14.8	13.3	13.3	13.4
Female	15.9	16.9	18.6	18.7	18.7	17.1	17.0	17.0
Annual Deaths Expected per 1,000								
Alive at Specified Age								
At birth:								
Male	25.9	20.1	12.3	10.6	10.0	23.0	19.9	20.0
Female	19.6	15.3	9.7	8.0	7.8	19.3	16.5	16.1
Age 20:								
Male	1.6	1.9	1.8	1.5	1.6	2.2	1.9	2.1
Female	.6	.6	.6	.5	.5	.7	.6	.7
Age 40:								
Male	3.3	3.4	2.6	2.5	2.5	6.9	6.7	7.1
Female	1.9	1.9	1.4	1.3	1.3	3.2	2.9	3.1
Age 50:								
Male	9.6	8.9	7.1	6.2	6.0	14.9	13.1	13.0
Female	4.7	4.7	3.8	3.5	3.4	7.7	6.7	6.8
Age 65:								
Male	33.9	33.9	27.4	24.9	24.3	38.5	36.1	35.7
Female	17.4	15.6	13.6	13.5	13.4	21.6	20.9	21.2
Number Surviving to Specified Age								
per 1,000 Born Live								
Age 20:								
Male	959	965	975	979	979	961	967	966
Female	971	976	984	986	986	972	976	976
Age 40:								
Male	924	926	940	946	944	885	898	891
Female	953	958	969	973	973	941	948	946

Continued.

Life Expectancy
[Continued]

Age and Sex	White					Black		
	1959-1961	1969-1971	1979-1981	1985	1986	1979-1981	1985	1986
Age 50:								
Male	874	877	901	912	910	801	819	812
Female	925	929	947	953	954	896	908	905
Age 65:								
Male	658	663	724	745	748	551	581	581
Female	807	816	848	856	857	733	749	749

Source: "Selected Life Table Values: 1959 to 1986," *Statistical Abstract*, 1989, p. 72. Primary source: U.S. National Center for Health Statistics, *U.S. Life Tables and Actuarial Tables, 1959-61, 1969-71, and 1979-81*; and *Vital Statistics of the United States*, annual; and unpublished data.

★ 946 ★
Life Expectancy

In years. Prior to 1960, excludes Alaska and Hawaii. Beginning 1970, excludes deaths of nonresidents of the United States. See also *Historical Statistics, Colonial Times to 1970*, series B 107-115.

Year	White			Black and Other			Black		
	Total	Male	Female	Total	Male	Female	Total	Male	Female
1950	69.1	66.5	72.2	60.8	59.1	62.9	1	1	1
1955	70.5	67.4	73.7	63.7	61.4	66.1	1	1	1
1960	70.6	67.4	74.1	63.6	61.1	66.3	1	1	1
1965	71.0	67.6	74.7	64.1	61.1	67.4	1	1	1
1970	1.7	68.0	75.6	65.3	61.3	69.4	64.1	60.0	68.3
1971	72.0	68.3	75.8	65.6	61.6	69.8	64.6	60.5	68.9
1972	72.0	68.3	75.9	65.7	61.5	70.1	64.7	60.4	69.1
1973	72.2	68.5	76.1	66.1	62.0	70.3	65.0	60.9	69.3
1974	72.8	69.0	76.7	67.1	62.9	71.3	66.0	61.7	70.3
1975	73.4	69.5	77.3	68.0	63.7	72.4	66.8	62.4	71.3
1976	73.6	69.9	77.5	68.4	64.2	72.7	67.2	62.9	71.6
1977	74.0	70.2	77.9	68.9	64.7	73.2	67.7	63.4	72.0
1978	74.1	70.4	78.0	69.3	65.0	73.5	68.1	63.7	72.4
1979	74.6	70.8	78.4	69.8	65.4	74.1	68.5	64.0	72.9
1980	74.4	70.7	78.1	69.5	65.3	73.6	68.1	63.8	72.5
1981	74.8	71.1	78.4	70.3	66.1	74.4	68.9	64.5	73.2
1982	75.1	71.5	78.7	71.0	66.8	75.0	69.4	65.1	73.7
1983	75.2	71.7	78.7	71.1	67.2	74.9	69.6	65.4	73.6
1984	75.3	71.8	78.7	71.3	67.4	75.0	69.7	65.6	73.7
1985	75.3	71.9	78.7	71.2	67.2	75.0	69.5	65.3	73.5
1986	75.4	72.0	78.8	71.2	67.2	75.1	69.4	65.2	73.5
1987, prel.	75.5	72.1	78.8	71.6	67.6	75.4	69.7	65.4	73.8

Source: "Expectation of Life at Birth: 1950 to 1987," *Statistical Abstract*, 1989, p. 71. Primary source: U.S. National Center for Health Statistics, *Vital Statistics of the United States*, annual; and unpublished data. *Note:* 1. Not available.

★947★
Life Expectancy at Birth & 65: Trends

Data are based on the National Vital Statistics System.

Specified age and year	All races			White			Black		
	Both sexes	Male	Female	Both sexes	Male	Female	Both sexes	Male	Female
				Remaining life expectancy in years					
1900[1,2]	47.3	46.3	48.3	47.6	46.6	48.7	33.0[3]	32.5[3]	33.5[3]
1950[2]	68.2	65.6	71.1	69.1	66.5	72.2	60.7	58.9	62.7
1960[2]	69.7	66.6	73.1	70.6	67.4	74.1	63.2	60.7	65.9
1970	70.9	67.1	74.8	71.7	68.0	75.6	64.1	60.0	68.3
1975	72.6	68.8	76.6	73.4	69.5	77.3	66.8	62.4	71.3
1980	73.7	70.0	77.4	74.4	70.7	78.1	68.1	63.8	72.5
1981	74.2	70.4	77.8	74.8	71.1	78.4	68.9	64.5	73.2
1982	74.5	70.9	78.1	75.1	71.5	78.7	69.4	65.1	73.7
1983	74.6	71.0	78.1	75.2	71.7	78.7	69.6	65.4	73.6
1984	74.7	71.2	78.2	75.3	71.8	78.7	69.7	65.6	73.7
1985	74.7	71.2	78.2	75.3	71.9	78.7	69.5	65.3	73.5
1986	74.8	71.3	78.3	75.4	72.0	78.8	69.4	65.2	73.5
Provisional data:									
1985[2]	64.7	71.2	78.2	75.3	71.8	78.7	69.5	75.3	73.7
1986[2]	74.9	71.3	78.3	75.4	72.0	78.9	69.6	65.5	73.6
1987[2]	74.9	71.5	78.3	75.5	72.1	78.8	69.7	65.4	73.8
At 65 years									
1900-1902[1,2]	11.9	11.5	12.2	---	11.5	12.2	---	10.4	11.4
1950[2]	13.9	12.8	15.0	---	12.8	15.1	13.9	12.9	14.9
1960[2]	14.3	12.8	15.8	14.4	12.9	15.9	13.9	12.7	15.1
1970	15.2	13.1	17.0	15.2	13.1	17.1	14.2	12.5	15.7
1975	16.1	13.8	18.1	16.1	13.8	18.2	15.0	13.1	16.7
1980	16.4	14.1	18.3	16.5	14.2	18.4	15.1	13.0	16.8
1981	16.7	14.3	18.6	16.7	14.4	18.7	15.5	13.4	17.3
1982	16.8	14.5	18.7	16.9	14.5	18.8	15.7	13.5	17.5
1983	16.7	14.5	18.6	16.8	14.5	18.7	15.5	13.4	17.3
1984	16.8	14.6	18.6	16.9	14.6	18.7	15.5	13.5	17.2
1985	16.7	14.6	18.6	16.8	14.6	18.7	15.3	13.3	17.0
1986	16.8	14.7	18.6	16.9	14.8	18.7	15.4	13.4	17.0
Provisional data:									
1985[2]	16.8	14.6	18.6	16.8	14.6	18.7	15.5	13.3	17.2
1986[2]	16.9	14.8	18.6	17.0	14.8	18.8	15.5	13.6	16.9
1987[2]	16.9	14.8	18.6	17.0	14.9	18.7	15.6	13.6	17.2

Source: "Life Expectancy at Birth and at 65 Years of Age, according to Race and Sex: United States, Selected Years 1900-1987," *Health United States - 1988,* March 1989, p. 53. Primary source: *Vital Statistics Rates in the United States, 1940-1960; Vital Statistics of the United States, 1970; Monthly Vital Statistics Report, 1987-1988.* National Center for Health Statistics, U.S. Government Printing Office, Washington, DC. *Notes:* 1. Death registration area only. The death registration area increased from 10 States and the District of Columbia in 1900 to the coterminous United States in 1933. 2. Includes deaths of nonresidents of the United States. 3. Figure is given for the all other population.

★ 948 ★
Life Expectancy Rates

Numbers in years.

Characteristics	1970	1975	1980	1985	1986	1987[1]
At birth						
Total	70.8	72.6	73.7	74.7	74.8	74.9
Black Males	60.0	62.4	63.8	65.3	65.2	65.4
White males	68.0	69.5	70.7	71.9	72.0	72.1
Black females	68.3	71.3	72.5	73.5	73.5	73.8
White females	75.6	77.3	78.1	78.7	78.8	78.8
At age 1						
Total	72.3	73.7	74.7	75.5	[2]	75.7
Black Males	63.5	65.4	65.2	66.7	[2]	[2]
White males	69.4	70.6	71.6	72.6	[2]	[2]
Black females	71.4	74.0	73.7	74.8	[2]	[2]
White females	76.8	78.1	78.9	79.4	[2]	[2]
At age 18						
Total	73.0	74.3	75.2	76.0	[2]	[2]
Black Males	64.5	66.1	65.9	67.1	[2]	[2]
White males	70.1	74.6	72.2	73.1	[2]	[2]
Black females	64.5	66.1	74.2	75.2	[2]	[2]
White females	77.3	78.6	79.3	79.7	[2]	[2]

Source: "Average Age to Which People May Expect to Live, for Persons at Birth, Age 1, and Age 18, by Sex and Race, 1970-1987," *U.S. Children and Their Families,* 1989, p. 161. Primary source: U.S. Department of Health and Human Services, *Vital Statistics of the United States, Volume II. Mortality. Part A,* for the years indicated, Tables 5 or 6. *Notes:* Prior to 1980, data reported for blacks are for non-whites. Most non-whites are black. If the data were available for blacks alone, they would show slightly lower life expectancies. 1. Provisional data. 2. Not available.

★ 949 ★
Live Birth Characteristics

Represents registered births. Excludes births to nonresidents of the U.S. Data are available on race of mother from all States, but data on Hispanic origin of mother are available from only 23 States and the District of Columbia. However, approximately 90 percent of all births to Hispanic mothers occur to residents of these 23 States.

Race and Hispanic Origin	Number of birth (1000)		Birth to Teenage Mothers, Percent of total		Birth to Unmarried Mothers, Percent of of total		Percent of Mothers Beginning Prenatal Care During				Percent of Birth with Low birth weight[1]	
							First trimester		Third trimester or no care			
	1985	1986	1985	1986	1985	1986	1985	1986	1985	1986	1985	1986
Total	3,761	3,757	12.7	12.6	22.0	23.4	76.2	75.9	5.7	6.0	6.8	6.8
White	2,991	2,970	10.8	10.6	14.5	15.7	79.4	79.2	4.7	5.0	5.6	5.6
Black	608	621	23.0	22.8	60.1	61.2	61.8	61.6	10.0	10.6	12.4	12.5
American Indian	43	43	19.1	19.2	40.7	[4]	60.3	[4]	11.5	[4]	5.9	6.2
Asian and Pacific Islander[2]	116	119	5.5	5.6	10.1	[4]	75.0	[4]	6.1	[4]	6.1	6.4
Filipino	21	22	5.8	5.9	12.1	[4]	77.2	[4]	4.6	[4]	6.9	7.3
Chinese	18	18	1.1	1.1	3.7	[4]	82.4	[4]	4.2	[4]	5.0	4.9
Japanese	10	10	2.9	3.0	7.9	[4]	85.8	[4]	2.6	[4]	5.9	5.6
Hispanic origin[3]	373	389	16.5	16.4	29.5	31.6	61.2	60.3	12.5	13.0	6.2	6.1
Mexican	243	246	17.5	17.4	25.7	27.9	59.9	58.9	12.9	13.4	5.8	5.6
Puerto Rican	35	37	20.9	20.9	51.1	52.6	58.3	57.2	15.5	17.4	8.7	9.2
Cuban	10	10	7.1	6.8	16.1	15.8	72.5	81.8	3.7	4.2	6.0	5.5

Source: "Live Births, by Race and Type of Hispanic Origin — Selected Characteristics: 1985 and 1986," *Statistical Abstract,* 1989, p. 64. Primary source: U.S. National Center for Health Statistics, *Vital Statistics of the United States,* annual; and unpublished. *Notes:* 1. Births less than 2,500 grams (5 lb.-8 oz.). 2. Includes races not shown separately. 3. Hispanic persons may be of any race. Includes other types, not shown separately. 4. Not available.

★ 950 ★
Live Births & Birth Rates: Trends

Data are based on the National Vital Statistics System.

Race of child and year	Live birth	Crude birth rate[1]	Live birth per 1,000 women by age of woman								
			10-14 years	15-17 years	18-19 years	20-24 years	25-29 years	30-34 years	35-39 years	40-44 years	45-49 years
All races											
1950	3,632,000	24.1	1.0	40.7	132.7	196.6	166.1	103.7	52.9	15.1	1.2
1955	4,097,000	25.0	0.9	44.5	157.9	241.6	190.2	116.0	58.6	16.1	1.0
1960	4,257,850	23.7	0.8	43.9	166.7	258.1	197.4	112.7	56.2	15.5	0.9
1965	3,760,358	19.4	0.8	36.6	124.5	195.3	161.6	94.4	46.2	12.8	0.8
1970	3,731,386	18.4	1.2	38.8	114.7	167.8	145.1	73.3	31.7	8.1	0.5
1975	3,144,198	14.6	1.3	36.1	85.0	113.0	108.2	52.3	19.5	4.6	0.3
1980	3,612,258	15.9	1.1	32.5	82.1	115.1	112.9	61.9	19.8	3.9	0.2
1981	3,629,238	15.8	1.1	32.1	81.7	111.8	112.0	61.4	20.0	3.8	0.2
1982	3,680,537	15.9	1.1	32.4	80.7	111.3	111.0	64.2	21.1	3.9	0.2
1983	3,638,933	15.5	1.1	32.0	78.1	108.3	108.7	64.6	22.1	3.8	0.2
1984	3,669,141	15.5	1.2	31.1	78.3	107.3	108.3	66.5	22.8	3.9	0.2
1985	3,760,561	15.8	1.2	31.1	80.8	108.9	110.5	68.5	23.9	4.0	0.2
1986	3,756,547	15.6	1.3	30.6	81.0	108.2	109.2	69.3	24.3	4.1	0.2
White											
1950	3,108,000	23.0	0.4	31.3	120.5	190.4	165.1	102.6	51.4	14.5	1.0
1955	3,485,000	23.8	0.3	35.4	145.7	235.8	186.6	114.0	56.7	15.4	0.9
1960	3,600,744	22.7	0.4	35.5	154.6	252.8	194.9	109.6	54.0	14.7	0.8
1965	3,123,860	18.3	0.3	27.8	111.9	189.0	158.4	91.6	44.0	12.0	0.7
1970	3,091,264	17.4	0.5	29.2	101.5	163.4	145.9	71.9	30.0	7.5	0.4
1975	2,551,996	13.6	0.6	28.0	74.0	108.2	108.1	51.3	18.2	4.2	0.2
1980	2,898,732	14.9	0.6	25.2	72.1	109.5	112.4	60.4	18.5	3.4	0.2
1981	2,908,669	14.8	0.5	25.1	71.9	106.3	111.3	60.2	18.7	3.4	0.2
1982	2,942,054	14.9	0.6	25.2	70.8	105.9	110.3	63.3	20.0	3.5	0.2
1983	2,904,250	14.6	0.6	24.8	68.3	102.6	108.0	64.0	21.0	3.5	0.2
1984	2,923,502	14.5	0.6	23.9	68.1	101.4	107.7	66.1	21.7	3.5	0.2
1985	2,991,373	14.8	0.6	24.0	70.1	102.8	110.0	68.1	22.7	3.6	0.2
1986	2,970,439	14.5	0.6	23.4	69.8	101.5	108.3	68.9	23.3	3.7	0.2
Black											
1960	602,264	31.9	4.3	---	---	295.4	218.6	137.1	73.9	21.9	1.1
1965	581,126	27.7	4.3	99.3	227.6	243.1	180.4	111.3	61.9	18.7	1.4
1970	572,362	25.3	5.2	101.4	204.9	202.7	136.3	79.6	41.9	12.5	1.0
1975	511,581	20.7	5.1	85.6	152.4	142.8	102.2	53.1	25.6	7.5	0.5
1980	589,616	22.1	4.3	73.6	138.8	146.3	109.1	62.9	24.5	5.8	0.3
1981	587,797	21.6	4.1	70.6	135.9	141.2	108.3	60.4	24.2	5.6	0.3
1982	592,641	21.4	4.1	71.2	133.3	139.1	106.9	60.4	24.4	5.4	0.4
1983	586,027	20.9	4.1	70.1	130.4	137.7	103.4	59.2	24.7	5.2	0.3
1984	592,745	20.8	4.3	69.7	132.0	137.9	103.2	59.5	24.8	5.1	0.2
1985	608,193	21.1	4.5	69.8	137.1	140.8	105.1	60.7	25.5	4.9	0.3
1986	621,221	21.2	4.6	70.0	141.0	143.7	105.9	62.2	25.5	5.1	0.3

Source: "Live Births, Crude Birth Rates, and Birth Rates by Age of Mother, according to Race of Child: United States, Selected Years 1950-86," *Health United States - 1988*, p. 42. Primary source: *Vital Statistics of the United States, 1986*. National Center for Health Statistics. *Notes:* Data are based on births adjusted for underregistration for 1950 and on registered births for all other years. Beginning in 1970, births to nonresidents of the United States are excluded. 1. Live births per 1,000 population.

★ 951 ★
Live Births of Low Birth Weight

Numbers in percent.

Characteristic	1960	1970	1975	1980	1985	1986	1987
Low birth weight							
Less than 2,500 grams							
All races and origins	7.7	7.9	7.4	6.8	6.8	6.8	6.9
White	6.8	6.8	6.3	5.7	5.6	5.6	5.7
Black[1]	12.8	13.9	13.1	12.5	12.4	12.5	12.7
Hispanic origin	[2]	[2]	[2]	6.1	6.2	6.9	6.2
Cuban				5.6	6.0	5.5	5.9
Mexican				.6	5.8	5.6	5.7
Puerto Rican				8.9	8.7	9.2	9.3
Non-Hispanic origin				7.0	6.9	7.0	7.1
Less than 1,500 grams							
All races	1.2	1.2	1.1	1.2	1.2	1.2	1.2
White	1.0	1.0	.9	.9	.9	.9	.9
Black[1]	2.1	2.4	2.3	2.4	2.7	2.7	2.7

Source: "Percentage of Live Births of Low Birth Weight (Less Than 2500 and Less Than 1500 Grams), 1960-1987," *U.S. Children and Their Families,* 1989 p. 167. Primary source: National Center for Health Statistics, *Health, United States, 1982,* Table 24; *Monthly Vital Statistics Report,* Vol. 31, No. 8. Supplement, November, 1982, Tables 13, 20, Vol. 35, No. 4, Supplement, July 1986, Table 25; Vol. 38, No. 3, Supplement, June 1989, Tables 27 and 29. Birth figures for Hispanic infants in 1985-87 are based on data for 23 States and the District of Columbia which report Hispanic origin of the mother on the birth certificate. These states accounted for 90 percent of the Hispanic population in 1980. *Notes:* Prior to 1979, low birth weight and extremely low birth weight were defined as weighing 2,500 grams or less, and weighing 1,500 grams or less, respectively. In 1979, the definition was changed so that low birth weight was defined as weighing less than 2,500 grams and extremely low birth weight as weighing less than 1,500 grams. The pounds and ounces equivalents of these figures are as follows: 2,500 grams or less = 5 lbs. 9 oz. or less; 1,500 grams or less = 3 lbs. 5 oz. or less; less than 2,500 grams = 5 lbs. 8 oz. or less; less than 1,500 grams = 3 lbs. 4 oz. or less. Non-Hispanic infants are white, black, and other infants not of Hispanic origin in the same 23 states that report data on origin. 1. In 1960, data are for all non-whites. 2. Not available.

★ 952 ★
Live Births: Trends

Represents registered births. Beginning 1970, excludes births to nonresidents of the U.S.

Year	Births Attended (1,000)			Median Birth Weight (lbs.-oz.)			Percent of Birth with Low Birth Weight[4]			Percent of Births By Period In Which Prenatal Care Began	
	In hospital[1]	Not in hospital		Total[3]	White	Black	Total[3]	White	Black	1st trimester	3d trimester or no prenatal care
		Physician	Midwife and other[2]								
1960	4,114	49	94	7 lb.-5 oz.	7 lb.-6 oz.	6 lb.-15 oz.	7.7	6.8	12.8	NA	NA
1965	3,661	33	66	7 lb.-4 oz.	7 lb.-5 oz.	6 lb.-14 oz.	8.3	7.2	13.8	NA	NA
1970	3,708	5	18	7 lb.-4 oz.	7 lb.-5 oz.	6 lb.-14 oz.	7.9	6.8	13.9	68.0	7.9
1975	3,105	11	28	7 lb.-5 oz.	7 lb.-7 oz.	6 lb.-15 oz.	7.4	6.3	13.1	72.4	6.0
1977	3,278	13	36	7 lb.-6 oz.	7 lb.-8 oz.	6 lb.-15 oz.	7.1	5.9	12.8	74.1	5.6
1978	3,301	12	21	7 lb.-6 oz.	7 lb.-8 oz.	6 lb.-15 oz.	7.1	5.9	12.9	74.9	5.4
1979	3,460	12	22	7 lb.-7 oz.	7 lb.-8 oz.	6 lb.-15 oz.	6.9	5.8	12.6	75.9	5.1
1980	3,576	12	24	7 lb.-7 oz.	7 lb.-8 oz.	7 lb.-0 oz.	6.8	5.7	12.5	76.3	5.1
1981	3,592	11	27	7 lb.-7 oz.	7 lb.-8 oz.	7 lb.-0 oz.	6.8	5.7	12.5	76.3	5.2
1982	3,642	10	28	7 lb.-7 oz.	7 lb.-8 oz.	7 lb.-0 oz.	6.8	5.6	12.4	76.1	5.5
1983	3,600	10	29	7 lb.-7 oz.	7 lb.-8 oz.	7 lb.-0 oz.	6.8	5.7	12.6	76.2	5.6
1984	3,631	10	28	7 lb.-7 oz.	7 lb.-9 oz.	7 lb.-0 oz.	6.7	5.6	12.4	76.5	5.6

Continued.

Live Births: Trends
[Continued]

Year	Births Attended (1,000)			Median Birth Weight (lbs.-oz.)			Percent of Birth with Low Birth Weight[4]			Percent of Births By Period In Which Prenatal Care Began	
	In hospital[1]	Not in hospital		Total[3]	White	Black	Total[3]	White	Black	1st trimester	3d trimester or no prenatal care
		Physician	Midwife and other[2]								
1985	3,722	10	29	7 lb.-7 oz.	7 lb.-9 oz.	7 lb.-0 oz.	6.8	5.6	12.4	76.2	5.7
1986	3,720	9	27	7 lb.-7 oz.	7 lb.-9 oz.	7 lb.-0 oz.	6.8	5.6	12.5	75.9	6.0

Source: "Live Births, by Place of Delivery; Median and Low-Birth Weight, and Prenatal Care: 1960 to 1986," *Statistical Abstract*, 1989, p. 65 Primary source: U.S. National Center for Health Statistics, *Vital Statistics of the United States*, annual; and unpublished data. *Notes:* 1. Includes all births in hospitals or institutions and in clinics. 2. Includes births with attendant not specified. 3. Includes other races not shown separately. 4. Through 1978, births of 2,500 grams (5 lb.-8 oz.) or less at birth; thereafter, less than 2,500 grams. and other races.

★ 953 ★
Married Women's Childbirth Expectations: Trends

Data based on reporting of birth expectations by currently married of the civilian noninstitutionalized population.

Race and year	All ages 18-34 years	18-19 years	20-21 years	22-24 years	25-29 years	30-34 years
Expected births per currently married woman						
All races						
1967	3.1	2.7	2.9	2.9	3.0	3.3
1971	2.6	2.3	2.4	2.4	2.6	3.0
1975	2.3	2.2	2.2	2.2	2.3	2.6
1980	2.2	2.1	2.2	2.1	2.2	2.2
1985	2.2	2.1	2.2	2.2	2.2	2.2
1986	2.3	2.2	2.2	2.3	2.3	2.2
1987	2.2	2.1	2.2	2.2	2.2	2.2
White						
1967	3.0	2.7	3.0	2.8	3.0	3.2
1971	2.6	2.3	2.4	2.4	2.6	2.9
1975	2.3	2.2	2.1	2.1	2.2	2.6
1980	2.2	2.1	2.2	2.1	2.1	2.2
1985	2.2	2.0	2.2	2.2	2.2	2.1
1986	2.2	2.1	2.2	2.3	2.2	2.2
1987	2.2	2.0	2.2	2.2	2.2	2.2
Black						
1967	3.5	...	2.5	3.0	3.4	4.3
1971	3.1	...	2.4	2.8	3.1	3.7
1975	2.8	...	2.6	2.5	2.6	3.2
1980	2.4	...	2.2	2.1	2.4	2.5
1985	2.4	...	...	2.3	2.3	2.5
1986	2.4	...	...	2.4	2.3	2.6
1987	2.3	...	...	2.2	2.3	2.3
Percent of expected births already born						
1967	70.2	26.9	33.2	47.8	76.1	92.7
1971	69.4	25.3	32.5	46.7	74.4	93.7

Continued.

Married Women's Childbirth Expectations: Trends
[Continued]

Race and year	All ages 18-34 years	18-19 years	20-21 years	22-24 years	25-29 years	30-34 years
1975	68.8	27.5	30.7	43.9	70.9	93.0
1980	67.0	29.5	32.9	44.9	67.4	89.7
1985	64.2	27.9	30.9	41.8	60.2	84.4
1986	64.7	20.0	30.4	41.8	59.5	84.8
1987	66.5	27.8	36.4	43.8	62.0	83.8
White						
1967	68.9	24.2	30.1	46.2	75.1	92.9
1971	68.9	23.7	31.4	45.3	74.1	93.8
1975	68.2	24.9	29.4	42.3	70.5	93.2
1980	66.3	28.6	31.8	43.5	64.0	90.0
1985	63.3	25.7	30.6	40.4	59.4	84.1
1986	63.8	28.6	28.7	40.5	58.6	84.8
1987	65.6	27.0	36.0	42.0	60.9	83.6
Black						
1967	82.8	...	65.7	67.9	87.9	92.3
1971	74.8	...	43.0	57.5	81.0	93.4
1975	76.4	...	43.3	61.0	78.4	91.8
1980	74.7	...	46.1	58.9	73.8	90.0
1985	77.1	...	...	62.3	72.8	91.4
1986	75.7	...	...	59.7	70.2	90.0
1987	77.8	...	...	55.4	76.6	89.7

Source: "Lifetime Births Expected by Currently Married Women and Percent of Expected Births Already Born, according to Age and Race: United States, Selected Years 1967-87," *Health United States - 1988*, March 1989, p. 45. Primary source: *Current Population Reports*, U.S. Government Printing Office, Washington, DC. .

★ 954 ★
Maternal Mortality Rates: Trends

Data are based on the National Vital Statistics System.

Race and age	1950[1]	1960[1]	1970	1980	1983	1984	1985	1986
	Deaths per 100,000 live births							
All races								
All ages, age adjusted	73.8	32.2	21.5	9.6	8.0	7.4	7.9	7.0
All ages, crude	83.3	37.1	21.5	9.2	8.0	7.8	7.8	7.2
Under 20 years	70.7	22.7	18.9	7.6	5.4	6.3	6.9	5.9
20-24 years	47.6	20.7	13.0	5.8	7.5	4.3	5.4	5.7
25-29 years	63.5	29.8	17.0	7.7	6.6	6.9	6.4	5.8
30-34 years	107.7	50.3	31.6	13.6	9.1	11.5	8.9	7.8
35 years and over[2]	222.0	104.3	81.9	36.3	20.7	21.9	25.0	21.4
White								
All ages, age adjusted	53.2	22.4	14.5	7.0	5.9	5.0	5.1	4.7
All ages, crude	61.1	26.0	14.4	6.7	5.9	5.4	5.2	4.9
Under 20 years	44.9	14.8	13.9	5.9	4.4[3]	4.3[3]	4.3[3]	4.1[3]
20-24 years	35.7	15.3	8.4	4.3	4.9	2.0[3]	3.4	3.7

Continued.

Maternal Mortality Rates: Trends
[Continued]

Race and age	1950[1]	1960[1]	1970	1980	1983	1984	1985	1986
25-29 years	45.0	20.3	11.2	5.5	5.2	5.7	4.7	3.6
30-34 years	75.9	34.3	18.8	9.4	6.0	7.8	5.2	5.2
35 years and over[2]	174.1	73.9	59.6	25.8	17.3	16.0	17.8	16.1
Black								
All ages, age adjusted	---	92.1	64.2	24.0	19.3	20.9	22.2	19.3
All ages, crude	---	103.6	59.8	21.5	18.3	19.7	20.4	18.8
Under 20 years	---	54.8	31.8	12.8	7.0[3]	11.4[3]	12.1[3]	10.6[3]
20-24 years	---	56.9	41.0	13.4	20.2	15.2	14.0	13.9
25-29 years	---	92.8	63.8	21.4	16.0	15.6	18.4	19.3
30-34 years	---	150.6	115.6	41.9	31.1	37.9	35.8	29.0
35 years and over[2]	---	299.5	204.7	96.5	41.4[3]	67.6[3]	72.6	58.6[3]

Source: "Maternal Mortality Rates for Complications of Pregnancy, Childbirth, and the Puerperium, according to Race and Age: United States, Selected Years 1950-86," *Health United States - 1988*, March 1989, p. 71. Primary source: *Vital Statistics of the United States*; *Current Population Reports*. National Center for Health Statistics, U.S. Government Printing Office, Washington, DC. *Notes:* For data years shown, the code numbers for cause of death are based on the then current *International Classification of Diseases*, which are dscribed in Appendix II, tables IV and V. 1. Includes deaths of nonresidents of the United States. 2. Rates computed by relating deaths of women 35 years and over to live births to women 35-49 years. 3. Based on fewer than 20 deaths.

★ 955 ★
Mortality by Cardiovascular Disease

	Percent decrease	
Race and sex	Observed mortality[1]	Expected mortality[2]
White males	14	7
White females	15	8
Black males	13	13
Black females	20	16

Source: "Percent Decrease in Age-Adjusted Rates for Observed and Expected Coronary Heart Disease Mortality," *Nutrition Monitoring in the United States*, September 1989. Primary source: Rowland, M.L. and R. Fulwood. "Coronary Heart Disease Risk Factor Trends in Blacks Between the First and Second National Health and Nutrition Surveys, United States, 1971-80." *American Heart Journal* 108: 771-79. *Notes:* Age adjusted by direct method to the total U.S. population as estimated at the midpoint of the 1976-80 NHANES II. 1. From the Division of Vital Statistics. 2. Predicted from NHANES I and NHANES II survey data based on Framingham risk model.

★ 956 ★
Mortality Rates

Children	1-4	5-14
Male		
White	52.4	29.9
Black	89.0	41.3
Female		
White	39.7	19.4
Black	70.3	28.1

Source: "Mortality Rates for Children Aged 1-14, by Race, 1985," *A Common Destiny: Blacks and American Society,* 1989, p. 405. Primary source: National Center for Health Statistics. Published by permission. *Note:* Mortality rate is deaths per 100,000 children aged 1-14.

★ 957 ★
Motor Vehicle Deaths

Per 100,000 persons in age group.

Population Groups	1979	1980	1982	1984	1985	1986
All teenagers						
Ages 12-14	9.4	9.3	8.2	7.9	8.6	9.1
Ages 15-19	44.6	43.0	35.0	34.6	33.9	37.6
White males						
Ages 12-14	12.7	12.7	11.5	10.6	11.6	12.4
Ages 15-19	72.1	69.1	56.5	54.4	51.9	58.4
White females						
Ages 12-14	7.4	6.8	6.0	6.4	6.7	6.9
Ages 15-19	25.7	25.6	20.7	22.1	22.8	24.8
Black males						
Ages 12-14	7.7	8.9	7.3	6.8	9.6	9.0
Ages 15-19	24.5	24.4	20.9	21.2	21.9	25.6
Black females						
Ages 12-14	2.9	3.0	3.7	1.7	2.6	3.1
Ages 15-19	8.7	6.7	7.7	7.0	7.5	8.0

Source: "Number of Motor Vehicle Deaths, 1979-1986," *U.S. Children and Their Families,* 1989, p. 183. Primary source: National Center for Health Statistics, unpublished work tables prepared by the Mortality Statistics Branch, Division of Vital Statistics, 1989.

★ 958 ★
Neonatal Mortality Rates

Data are based on the National Vital Statistics System.

Geographic Division and State	All races			White			Black		
	1974-76	1979-81	1984-86	1974-76	1979-81	1984-86	1974-76	1979-81	1984-86
Neonatal deaths per 1,000 live births[1]									
United States	11.6	8.5	6.9	10.4	7.5	6.0	18.3	13.9	11.9
New England	10.5	7.8	6.4	10.1	7.4	6.0	18.6	13.9	13.2
Maine	9.7	6.1	5.7	9.7	6.2	5.8	[1]	[1]	[1]

Continued.

Neonatal Mortality Rates
[Continued]

Geographic Division and State	All races			White			Black		
	1974-76	1979-81	1984-86	1974-76	1979-81	1984-86	1974-76	1979-81	1984-86
New Hampshire	9.9	7.2	6.4	9.9	7.2	6.4	[1]	[1]	[1]
Vermont	10.2	5.5	6.1	10.3	5.5	6.1	[1]	[1]	[1]
Massachusetts	10.0	7.6	6.2	9.8	7.3	5.7	14.2	11.7	12.2
Rhode Island	11.1	9.3	6.5	10.6	9.1	6.2	22.2[1]	13.7[1]	10.5[1]
Connecticut	12.0	9.0	7.3	10.6	7.9	6.3	22.9	16.7	14.9
Middle Atlantic	12.0	9.0	7.3	10.6	8.0	6.4	19.0	14.0	11.4
New York	11.9	9.0	7.4	10.3	7.9	6.7	18.8	13.7	10.5
New Jersey	11.4	8.4	7.1	10.0	7.2	6.2	17.6	13.3	11.5
Pennsylvania	12.6	9.3	7.2	11.4	8.5	6.2	21.0	15.2	13.8
East North Central	11.8	8.9	7.4	10.5	7.7	6.2	19.4	15.7	13.8
Ohio	11.5	8.7	6.8	10.5	7.8	6.1	18.4	14.7	11.1
Indiana	11.0	8.4	7.4	10.3	7.8	6.7	18.0	13.9	13.7
Illinois	13.3	10.1	8.1	11.2	8.3	6.5	21.3	16.7	14.1
Michigan	11.7	9.0	7.9	10.3	7.5	6.2	18.9	16.8	16.5
Wisconsin	9.6	6.9	5.9	9.5	6.7	5.4	13.8	10.8	11.7
West North Central	11.1	7.6	6.0	10.5	7.1	5.6	19.0	14.0	10.5
Minnesota	10.2	6.7	5.5	10.2	6.5	5.5	15.3[1]	15.3[1]	9.0
Iowa	10.8	7.2	5.8	10.6	7.1	5.7	24.4[1]	14.2[1]	9.1[1]
Missouri	11.8	8.8	6.6	10.6	8.0	5.7	19.2	13.8	11.1
North Dakota	11.7	8.0	4.7	11.7	7.7	4.7	[1]	[1]	[1]
South Dakota	12.0	6.4	6.0	11.5	5.9	5.5	[1]	[1]	[1]
Nebraska	10.6	7.2	6.3	10.2	6.8	6.0	20.3[1]	15.2[1]	11.4[1]
Kansas	10.9	7.6	5.9	10.5	7.1	5.6	17.9	14.1	10.1
South Atlantic	12.8	9.9	8.1	10.8	8.0	6.4	18.1	14.6	12.7
Delaware	11.0	11.2	9.0	9.8	7.9	7.4	15.4	21.9	14.5
Maryland	12.6	9.9	8.2	10.9	8.1	6.4	18.1	14.4	12.7
District of Columbia	21.5	18.4	16.0	14.8[1]	11.6[1]	7.7	22.8	19.8	18.4
Virginia	12.6	9.8	8.1	10.6	8.4	6.5	19.6	14.7	13.2
West Virginia	13.5	8.7	7.0	13.2	8.4	6.7	20.9[1]	15.7[1]	14.9[1]
North Carolina	13.4	9.7	7.8	11.6	7.8	6.4	17.8	14.1	11.8
South Carolina	14.0	11.0	9.5	11.4	8.2	7.1	18.2	15.3	13.5
Georgia	12.1	9.4	8.6	10.0	7.4	6.5	16.1	13.0	12.6
Florida	11.9	9.5	7.2	9.9	7.9	5.9	18.1	14.3	11.5
East South Central	13.1	9.2	7.9	11.0	7.5	6.4	18.8	13.6	12.0
Kentucky	11.3	8.0	7.1	11.0	7.5	6.7	15.0	13.0	11.4
Tennessee	12.1	9.0	7.5	10.5	7.6	5.8	18.1	14.2	13.2
Alabama	14.2	9.2	8.7	11.6	7.5	6.9	19.2	12.5	12.2
Mississippi	15.4	10.9	8.4	11.3	7.6	6.2	19.9	14.4	11.0

Continued.

Neonatal Mortality Rates
[Continued]

Geographic Division and State	All races			White			Black		
	1974-76	1979-81	1984-86	1974-76	1979-81	1984-86	1974-76	1979-81	1984-86
West South Central	12.3	8.3	6.6	11.1	7.4	5.9	18.0	12.8	10.1
Arkansas	12.0	7.5	6.5	10.9	6.6	5.9	15.5	10.5	8.9
Louisiana	13.6	9.8	7.8	10.7	7.5	5.9	18.3	13.7	11.0
Oklahoma	11.7	7.8	6.7	11.5	7.6	6.7	18.5	11.7	10.5
Texas	12.1	8.1	6.2	11.1	7.4	5.8	18.4	12.6	9.7
Mountain	10.1	7.0	5.6	10.0	6.9	5.6	16.0	12.2	8.8
Montana	11.6	7.0	5.0	12.0	7.1	4.9	[1]	[1]	[1]
Idaho	9.6	6.1	6.0	9.6	6.1	6.0	[1]	[1]	[1]
Wyoming	11.6	7.6	6.4	11.9	7.7	6.5	[1]	[1]	[1]
Colorado	9.9	6.5	5.5	9.8	6.4	5.3	14.3	10.3	10.0
New Mexico	10.9	7.3	5.9	11.2	7.5	6.0	20.4[1]	11.2[1]	6.4[1]
Arizona	10.0	8.2	5.7	9.7	8.1	5.6	16.1[1]	14.3	9.1
Utah	8.7	6.4	5.4	8.7	6.4	5.4	[1]	[1]	[1]
Nevada	11.9	6.6	5.2	11.2	6.1	5.2	18.4[1]	13.2[1]	8.0[1]
Pacific	9.3	7.0	5.8	9.0	6.8	5.6	14.2	10.8	9.9
Washington	10.3	6.8	5.7	10.2	6.9	5.6	14.8	8.0	9.7
Oregon	9.3	6.9	4.9	9.3	6.8	4.9	13.2[1]	11.0[1]	9.1[1]
California	9.1	7.0	5.9	8.7	6.8	5.7	14.1	11.0	9.9
Alaska	10.1	8.0	5.7	8.1	7.0	5.2	[1]	15.0[1]	7.5[1]
Hawaii	9.6	7.1	6.2	9.7	7.9	5.4	8.0[1]	6.8[1]	9.3[1]

Source: "Neonatal Mortality Rates, according to Race, Geographic Division, and State: United States, Average Annual 1974-76, 1979-81, and 1984-86," *Health United States - 1988*, March 1989, p. 56. Primary source: Division of Vital Statistics, National Center for Health Statistics, U.S. Government Printing Office, Washington, DC. *Notes:* 1. Data for States with fewer than 5,000 live births for the 3- year period are considered unreliable. Data for States with fewer than 1,000 births are considered highly unreliable and are not shown.

★ 959 ★
Percent of Low Birth Weight

Mother's Age and Race	1960	1970	1975	1980	1985	1986	1987
All Races							
All Ages	7.7	7.9	7.4	6.8	6.8	6.8	6.9
<15	16.0	16.6	14.1	14.6	12.9	13.8	13.7
15-17	9.9	10.5	11.1	10.5	10.2	10.3	10.2
18-19			9.3	8.8	8.7	8.7	8.8
20-24	7.4	7.4	7.1	6.9	6.9	7.0	7.1
25-29	6.9	6.9	6.1	5.8	5.9	6.0	6.1
30-34	7.5	7.5	6.8	5.9	6.0	6.1	6.2
35-39	7.9	8.7	8.2	7.0	6.9	6.9	6.9
40+	8.4	9.2	9.5	8.3	8.4	8.3	7.9
Whites							
All Ages	6.8	6.8	6.3	5.7	5.6	5.6	5.7
<15	11.5	12.5	11.3	11.2	10.5	11.1	10.4

Continued.

Percent of Low Birth Weight
[Continued]

Mother's Age and Race	1960	1970	1975	1980	1985	1986	1987
15-17	8.3	8.6	8.1	8.6	8.4	8.5	8.4
18-19				7.2	7.3	7.2	7.3
20-24	6.5	6.4	6.0	5.7	5.7	5.7	5.8
25-29	6.2	6.2	5.4	5.0	5.0	5.1	5.1
30-34	6.7	6.7	6.1	5.1	5.2	5.2	5.2
35-39	7.3	7.8	7.3	6.2	6.0	6.0	6.0
40+	7.9	8.4	8.7	7.4	7.4	7.1	7.1
Blacks[1]							
All Ages	12.8	13.9	13.1	12.5	12.4	12.5	12.7
<15	18.8	19.1	16.2	17.2	14.8	15.8	16.2
15-17	15.9	15.7	14.8	14.2	13.9	13.6	13.4
18-19				13.7	13.0	12.8	12.8
20-24	12.6	13.4	12.8	12.6	12.0	12.2	12.3
25-29	11.5	12.2	11.2	11.2	12.0	12.2	12.5
30-34	11.9	12.3	11.8	11.1	12.4	12.5	13.0
35-39	11.8	13.4	13.2	11.7	12.7	12.9	13.4
40+	11.1	12.9	13.0	12.3	13.7	14.7	12.9

Source: "Percent of Live Births That Were of Low Birth Weight by Mother's Age and Race, 1960-1987," *U.S. Children and Their Families*, 1989, p. 169. Primary source: National Center for Health Statistics, *Monthly Vital Statistics Report*, "Advance Report of Final Natality Statistics," Vol. 35, No. 4, Supplement, Table 15; Vol. 31, No. 8, Supplement, Table 13; "Trends in Births to Older Mothers," by Stephanie Ventura, Vol. 31, No. 2, Supplement (2), Table 8; "Advance Report of Final Natality Statistics," Vol. 36, No. 4, Supplement, Table 15; Vol. 37, No. 3, Supplement, Table 15; and Vol. 38, No. 3, Supplement, June 1989, Table 15. *Notes:* Since 1979, low birth weight has been defined as less than 2500 grams or 5 pounds 8 ounces or less. 1. 1960 data are for all nonwhites.

★ 960 ★
Premature Infant Birth Rates: Trends

Data based on the National Vital Statistics System.

Geographic division and State	All races			White			Black		
	1974-1976[1]	1979-1981	1984-1986	1974-1976[1]	1979-1981	1984-1986	1974-1976[1]	1979-1981	1984-1986
Infants weighing less than 2,500 grams at birth per 100 total live births									
United States	7.4	6.9	6.8	6.2	5.7	5.6	13.1	12.5	12.4
New England	6.7	6.2	5.9	6.3	5.8	5.5	12.1	11.8	11.7
Maine	6.1	5.7	5.2	6.1	5.7	5.2	[2]	[2]	[2]
New Hampshire	6.5	5.4	5.1	6.5	5.4	5.0	[2]	[2]	[2]
Vermont	6.4	6.1	5.7	6.4	6.1	5.7	[2]	[2]	[2]
Massachusetts	6.6	6.0	5.8	6.3	5.6	5.4	10.9	11.0	10.7
Rhode Island	6.7	6.3	6.3	6.4	5.8	5.8	12.2[2]	11.4[2]	11.4[2]
Connecticut	7.1	6.9	6.6	6.3	6.0	5.6	13.4	13.1	13.1
Middle Atlantic	7.8	7.1	6.9	6.5	5.9	5.6	13.7	12.8	12.5
New York	8.0	7.5	7.1	6.7	6.1	5.7	13.4	12.5	12.1
New Jersey	7.8	7.2	6.9	6.4	5.7	5.5	13.8	13.1	12.4
Pennsylvania	7.3	6.6	6.7	6.3	5.6	5.6	14.2	13.4	13.7

Continued.

Premature Infant Birth Rates: Trends
[Continued]

Geographic division and State	All races			White			Black		
	1974-1976[1]	1979-1981	1984-1986	1974-1976[1]	1979-1981	1984-1986	1974-1976[1]	1979-1981	1984-1986
East North Central	7.2	6.8	6.7	6.0	5.5	5.4	13.5	13.3	13.2
Ohio	7.2	6.7	6.6	6.3	5.7	5.6	13.3	13.0	12.1
Indiana	6.5	6.4	6.4	5.9	5.6	5.7	11.8	12.2	11.8
Illinois	7.7	7.4	7.2	6.0	5.5	5.4	13.9	13.9	31.8
Michigan	7.4	6.9	6.9	6.2	5.7	5.4	13.6	13.2	13.9
Wisconsin	5.9	5.4	5.3	5.5	4.8	4.6	12.4	12.7	21.3
West North Central	6.3	5.7	5.7	5.7	5.2	5.1	13.3	12.4	12.2
Minnesota	5.5	5.2	4.9	5.4	4.9	4.7	12.8[2]	11.5[2]	11.2
Iowa	5.7	5.0	5.1	5.6	4.8	4.9	12.0[2]	11.1[2]	11.0[1]
Missouri	7.3	6.7	6.7	6.1	5.6	5.6	13.7	12.7	12.7
North Dakota	5.3	4.8	4.9	5.1	4.7	4.7	[2]	[2]	[2]
South Dakota	6.0	5.2	5.3	5.7	4.9	5.0	[2]	[2]	[2]
Nebraska	6.0	5.5	5.4	5.7	5.2	5.0	12.1[2]	12.6[2]	11.6[2]
Kansas	6.4	6.1	6.1	5.9	5.6	5.5	13.0	12.1	12.1
South Atlantic	8.3	8.0	7.8	6.4	6.1	5.9	13.0	12.5	12.4
Delaware	7.8	7.7	7.4	6.2	5.6	5.9	13.4	14.5	12.2
Maryland	8.0	7.9	7.6	6.2	5.9	5.4	13.1	12.4	12.4
District of Columbia	12.7	12.9	12.7	6.8[2]	6.0[2]	5.1	13.8	14.3	14.6
Virginia	7.6	7.4	7.1	6.2	5.9	5.6	12.5	12.0	11.6
West Virginia	7.3	6.8	6.9	7.2	6.6	6.7	11.4[2]	12.4[2]	12.3[2]
North Carolina	8.5	8.0	7.9	6.6	6.1	6.1	13.1	12.3	12.4
South Carolina	9.0	8.8	8.6	6.4	6.1	6.1	13.1	12.7	12.7
Georgia	8.9	8.6	8.1	6.6	6.2	6.0	13.1	12.6	12.2
Florida	8.0	7.6	7.5	6.3	6.0	6.0	12.8	12.1	12.3
East South Central	8.1	7.8	7.9	6.5	6.2	6.3	12.4	12.2	12.2
Kentucky	7.2	6.9	7.4	6.7	6.4	6.5	21.2	11.9	12.3
Tennessee	7.9	8.0	7.9	6.5	6.4	6.4	13.1	13.3	12.9
Alabama	8.4	7.9	8.0	6.4	5.7	5.9	12.2	11.9	12.0
Mississippi	9.1	8.7	8.7	6.3	5.7	6.0	12.3	11.9	11.9
West South Central	7.9	7.3	7.1	6.6	6.0	5.9	13.3	12.5	12.5
Arkansas	8.1	7.4	7.7	6.6	5.8	6.3	12.7	12.1	12.3
Louisiana	9.1	8.6	8.6	6.5	6.0	5.8	13.0	12.7	13.1
Oklahoma	7.6	6.6	6.4	7.0	6.1	5.9	14.1	11.8	11.6
Texas	7.6	7.0	6.8	6.6	6.0	5.9	31.5	12.6	12.2
Mountain	7.2	6.6	6.6	7.0	6.4	6.4	13.3	12.2	12.2
Montana	6.9	5.6	5.8	6.7	5.5	5.7	[2]	[2]	[2]
Idaho	5.8	5.2	5.3	5.8	5.2	5.2	[2]	[2]	[2]
Wyoming	8.9	7.1	7.0	8.7	7.0	7.0	[2]	[2]	[2]
Colorado	8.9	8.1	7.7	8.7	7.8	7.3	14.7	13.6	13.6
New Mexico	8.5	7.7	7.2	8.5	7.7	7.4	12.5[2]	11.8[2]	9.7[2]
Arizona	6.5	6.1	6.2	6.3	5.9	6.0	11.6[2]	11.3	11.8
Utah	5.4	5.3	5.6	5.4	5.3	5.5	[2]	[2]	[2]

Continued.

Premature Infant Birth Rates: Trends
[Continued]

Geographic division and State	All races			White			Black		
	1974-1976[1]	1979-1981	1984-1986	1974-1976[1]	1979-1981	1984-1986	1974-1976[1]	1979-1981	1984-1986
Nevada	7.7	6.9	7.0	7.0	6.3	6.2	14.0[2]	12.1[2]	12.2[2]
Pacific	6.2	5.8	5.8	5.5	5.1	5.1	11.5	11.1	11.6
Washington	5.8	5.2	5.2	5.5	4.9	4.8	10.3	10.0	10.5
Oregon	5.6	5.0	5.1	5.4	4.8	5.0	12.1[2]	10.5[2]	10.8[2]
California	6.2	5.9	6.0	5.6	5.2	5.2	11.6	11.2	11.7
Alaska	5.3	5.3	4.8	4.9	4.9	4.2	[2]	6.9[2]	8.6[2]
Hawaii	7.7	7.0	6.9	5.9	5.8	5.6	[2]	9.4[2]	8.8[2]

Source: "Infants Weighing Less Than 2,500 Grams at Birth, according to Race of Child, Geographic Division, and State: United States, Average Annual 1979-81, and 1984-86," *Health United States - 1988*, March 1989, p. 48. *Notes:* 1. Before 1979, data are for infants weighing 2,500 grams or less at birth. 2. Data for States with fewer than 5,000 live births for the 3- year period are considered unreliable. Data for States with fewer than 1,000 births are considered highly unreliable and are not shown.

★ 961 ★
Projections in Lifetime Births

As of June. Covers currently married women in the civilian noninstitutional population. Data limited to wives reporting on birth expectations. Based on Current Population Survey.

Year and Number of Births Expected	Total[1]	Race		Hispanic[2]
		White	Black	
1975:				
None	4.8	4.9	3.0	3.2
One	10.9	10.8	10.7	10.6
Two	49.0	49.8	40.0	40.4
Three	23.2	23.3	22.4	25.2
Four or more	12.1	11.1	24.0	20.5
1980:				
None	5.9	6.0	4.0	2.8
One	13.3	13.2	14.4	9.4
Two	51.1	51.5	45.3	44.3
Three	20.5	20.4	22.2	24.2
Four or more	9.3	8.8	14.2	19.4
1987:				
None	4.8	5.0	3.5	1.9
One	12.7	12.6	15.5	10.4
Two	50.7	51.0	47.3	43.5
Three	23.3	23.4	21.3	29.5
Four or more	8.5	7.9	12.3	14.6

Source: "Lifetime Births Expected by Wives, 18-34 Years Old — Percent Distribution: 1975 to 1987," *Statistical Abstract*, 1989, p. 69. Primary source: U.S. Bureau of the Census, *Current Population Reports*, series P-20, No. 427, and earlier reports. *Notes:* 1. Includes other races, not shown separately. 2. Hispanic persons may be of any race.

★ 962 ★
Region of Residence and Infant Mortality

Data based on the National Vital Statistics System.

Geographic Division and State	All races			White			Black		
	1974-76	1979-81	1984-86	1974-76	1979-81	1984-86	1974-76	1979-81	1984-86

Infant deaths per 1,000 live births

Geographic Division and State	All races			White			Black		
United States	16.0	12.5	10.6	14.1	11.0	9.2	26.2	21.0	18.2
New England	13.8	10.7	9.2	13.2	10.2	8.5	24.6	18.7	18.3
Maine	13.4	9.9	8.8	13.5	10.1	8.9	[1]	[1]	[1]
New Hampshire	12.9	10.0	9.5	13.0	10.1	9.5	[1]	[1]	[1]
Vermont	13.4	9.0	9.1	13.4	9.0	9.0	[1]	[1]	[1]
Massachusetts	13.2	10.4	8.8	12.8	10.0	8.2	20.5	16.4	17.9
Rhode Island	14.9	12.3	9.1	14.2	11.6	8.8	29.0[1]	23.1[1]	14.5[1]
Connecticut	15.1	11.8	9.8	13.4	10.5	8.5	28.7	21.0	19.5
Middle Atlantic	16.0	12.7	10.7	13.9	11.0	9.1	26.3	20.8	17.7
New York	16.1	12.8	10.8	13.8	11.1	9.4	25.7	20.2	16.3
New Jersey	15.3	12.1	10.4	13.0	9.9	8.6	25.5	20.9	18.6
Pennsylvania	6.3	12.8	10.5	14.6	11.5	9.0	28.5	22.2	20.4
East North Central	16.2	13.0	11.1	14.2	11.1	9.3	28.0	23.8	20.7
Ohio	15.6	12.6	10.5	14.2	11.2	9.3	25.6	21.9	17.4
Indiana	15.3	12.2	11.1	14.2	11.1	10.1	25.1	21.8	20.0
Illinois	18.2	14.6	12.0	14.8	11..7	9.4	31.2	25.9	21.9
Michigan	16.3	13.1	11.5	14.1	11.0	9.2	27.3	24.0	22.9
Wisconsin	13.3	10.5	9.4	12.9	10.0	8.7	21.1	18.3	17.8
West North Central	15.0	11.4	9.6	14.0	10.6	9.0	26.8	21.1	16.9
Minnesota	14.0	10.3	9.0	13.7	10.0	8.9	23.5[1]	23.1[1]	14.9
Iowa	14.0	10.8	8.9	13.7	10.5	8.8	30.3[1]	22.8[1]	13.7[1]
Missouri	16.2	12.9	10.4	14.3	11.6	9.1	27.2	20.9	17.9
North Dakota	15.2	11.7	8.4	14.7	11.2	8.1	[1]	[1]	[1]
South Dakota	17.6	11.2	11.0	15.6	9.6	9.4	[1]	[1]	[1]
Nebraska	14.5	11.0	9.8	13.8	10.4	9.2	31.4[1]	22.5[1]	17.8[1]
Kansas	14.6	11.0	9.4	14.0	10.2	8.9	24.0	20.3	15.9
South Atlantic	17.7	14.4	12.0	14.5	11.5	9.4	26.0	21.6	18.8
Delaware	14.8	14.8	12.4	12.9	10.9	9.9	21.5	27.4	20.8
Maryland	16.6	13.7	11.2	14.2	11.2	11.5	23.7	20.0	17.7
District of Columbia	27.0	24.1	21.0	17.2[1]	13.7[1]	10.4	28.8	26.3	24.0
Virginia	16.9	13.5	11.6	14.2	11.7	9.6	26.4	20.0	18.9
West Virginia	18.0	12.9	10.7	17.7	12.5	10.3	26.5[1]	23.2[1]	20.9[1]
North Carolina	18.5	14.3	11.9	15.4	11.3	9.5	26.4	21.1	18.0
South Carolina	20.0	16.3	14.0	15.4	11.9	10.3	27.6	22.9	20.2
Georgia	17.4	14.4	12.7	13.8	10.9	9.6	24.4	20.8	18.6
Florida	16.7	14.2	11.0	13.4	11.5	8.8	26.8	22.4	18.1

Continued.

Region of Residence and Infant Mortality
[Continued]

Geographic Division and State	All races			White			Black		
	1974-76	1979-81	1984-86	1974-76	1979-81	1984-86	1974-76	1979-81	1984-86
East South Central	18.4	13.9	12.1	15.0	11.3	9.7	27.7	21.0	18.6
Kentucky	15.7	12.2	10.9	15.1	11.5	10.3	22.0	19.7	17.2
Tennessee	16.5	13.2	11.4	14.3	11.2	9.1	25.0	20.4	19.2
Alabama	20.0	14.2	12.9	15.3	11.1	9.9	28.4	19.9	18.8
Mississippi	22.3	16.7	13.5	15.2	11.1	9.4	30.2	22.7	18.2
West South Central	17.1	12.7	10.4	15.1	11.1	9.3	25.6	19.8	16.3
Arkansas	16.9	12.7	11.0	14.6	10.5	9.7	24.1	19.3	15.5
Louisiana	18.3	14.5	11.9	14.1	10.9	8.7	25.0	20.6	17.2
Oklahoma	16.8	12.3	10.7	16.1	11.8	10.7	27.0	19.6	16.9
Texas	16.8	12.2	9.9	15.2	11.1	9.1	26.3	19.3	15.7
Mountain	14.7	11.1	9.6	14.2	10.7	9.4	22.7	19.0	14.9
Montana	16.1	11.3	9.6	16.1	10.8	9.1	[1]	[1]	[1]
Idaho	13.8	10.0	10.5	13.8	10.0	10.5	[1]	[1]	[1]
Wyoming	16.6	11.1	11.4	16.7	11.1	11.4	[1]	[1]	[1]
Colorado	14.3	10.2	9.4	14.1	10.1	9.1	20.6	15.4	16.7
New Mexico	16.9	11.7	9.9	16.3	11.3	9.7	29.1[1]	18.5[1]	13.3[1]
Arizona	15.0	12.6	9.5	13.7	11.7	9.1	21.3[1]	21.3	14.7
Utah	12.3	10.3	9.1	12.0	10.3	9.1	[1]	[1]	[1]
Nevada	17.2	11.5	9.4	16.2	10.5	9.3	27.8[1]	22.3[1]	14.2[1]
Pacific	13.5	10.9	9.5	13.1	10.6	9.2	21.1	16.9	16.0
Washington	15.1	11.2	10.2	14.9	11.1	10.2	21.4	14.9	15.7
Oregon	14.2	11.3	9.7	14.1	11.3	9.7	21.9[1]	15.8[1]	16.2[1]
California	13.2	10.8	9.3	12.6	10.4	8.9	21.1	17.1	16.1
Alaska	16.2	13.6	10.9	12.8	11.2	9.7	[1]	20.3[1]	15.6[1]
Hawaii	13.0	10.0	9.4	13.5	10.4	8.0	13.0[1]	11.4[1]	16.6[1]

Source: "Infant Mortality Rates, According to Race, Geographic Division, and State: United States, Average Annual 1974-76, 1979-81, and 1984-86," *Health United States - 1988*, March 1989, p. 55. Primary source: Division of Vital Statistics, National Center for Health Statistics. *Notes:* 1. Data for states with fewer than 5,000 live births for the 3- year period are considered unreliable. Data for states with fewer than 1,000 births are considered highly unreliable and are not shown.

★ 963 ★
Teen Suicide Deaths

Population Groups	1960	1970	1975	1980	1985	1986
All teenagers						
Ages 12-14	[1]	[1]	[1]	1.2	2.4	2.3
Ages 15-19	3.6	5.9	7.5	8.5	10.0	10.2
White males						
Ages 12-14	[1]	[1]	[1]	2.1	3.8	3.5

Continued.

Teen Suicide Deaths
[Continued]

Population Groups	1960	1970	1975	1980	1985	1986
Ages 15-19	5.9	9.4	12.9	15.0	17.3	18.2
White females						
Ages 12-14	[1]	[1]	[1]	.5	1.4	1.1
Ages 15-19	1.6	2.9	3.1	3.3	4.1	4.1
Black males						
Ages 12-14	[1]	[1]	[1]	.9	1.9	2.3
Ages 15-19	2.9	4.7	6.1	5.6	8.2	7.1
Black females						
Ages 12-14	[1]	[1]	[1]	.2	.6	.6
Ages 15-19	1.1	2.9	1.5	1.6	1.5	2.1

Source: "Number of Teen Suicide Deaths, 1960-1986," *U.S. Children and Their Families*, 1989, p. 189. Primary source: National Center for Health Statistics, unpublished work tables prepared by the Mortality Statistics Branch, Division of Vital Statistics, 1989. *Note:* 1. Not available.

★ 964 ★
Unmarried Mothers

Excludes births to nonresidents of U.S. Data for 1970 and 1975 include estimates for States in which marital status data were not reported. Beginning in 1980, marital status is inferred from a comparison of the child's and parents' surnames on the birth certificate for those States that do not report on marital status. No estimates included for misstatements on birth records or failures to register births. See also *Historical Statistics, Colonial Times to 1970*, series B 28-35.

Race of Child and Age of Mother	1970	1975	1980	1985	1986
Number (1,000)					
Total live births[1]	398.7	447.9	665.7	828.2	878.5
White	175.1	186.4	320.1	433.0	466.8
Black	215.1	249.6	325.7	365.5	380.3
Percent Distribution					
Total[1]	100.0	100.0	100.0	100.0	100.0
White	43.9	41.6	48.1	52.3	53.1
Black	54.0	55.7	48.9	44.1	43.3
All Births in Racial Groups					
Total[1]	10.7	14.2	18.4	22.0	23.4
White	5.7	7.3	11.0	14.5	15.7
Black	37.6	48.8	55.2	60.1	61.2
Birth Rate[2]					
Total[1,3]	26.4	24.5	29.4	32.8	34.3
White[3]	13.8	12.4	17.6	21.8	23.2
Black[3]	95.5	84.2	81.4	78.8	80.9

Source: "Births to Unmarried Women, by Race of Child and Age of Mother: 1970 to 1986", *Statistical Abstract*, 1989, p. 66. Primary Source: U.S. National Center for Health Statistics, *Vital Statistics of the United States*, annual and unpublished data. *Notes:* 1. Includes other races not shown separately. 2. Rate per 1,000 unmarried women (never-married, widowed, and divorced) estimated as of July 1. 3. Covers women aged 15-44 years.

★ 965 ★
Unmarried Mothers

As of June. Covers civilian noninstitutional population. Refers to women never-married at time of survey. Based on Current Population Survey.

Item	White Single Women			Black Single Women		
	Total 18-44 years	18-29 years	30-44 years	Total 18-44 years	18-29 years	30-44 years
1980						
Single women (1,000)	9,862[1]	8,557	1,305[2]	2,327[1]	1,888	439[2]
Percent by number of children born:						
None	93.5	93.9	90.5	52.2	56.7	32.6
One	4.9	4.7	5.9	24.5	26.0	18.5
Two or more	1.6	1.3	3.6	23.3	17.3	49.0
Children ever born (1,000)	898[1]	666	232[2]	2,199[1]	1,325	874[2]
Rate per 1,000 women	91	78	178	945	702	1,991
1987						
Single women (1,000)	11,679	9,511	2,168	3,124	2,347	778
Percent by number of children born:						
None	88.3	89.6	82.4	46.6	53.6	25.4
One	7.1	6.9	8.3	26.9	25.1	32.0
Two or more	4.6	3.5	9.3	26.6	21.2	42.5
Children ever born (1,000)	2,220	1,502	718	3,187	1,929	1,257
Rate per 1,000 women	190	158	331	1,020	822	1,616

Source: "Children Ever Born to Single Women, by Age and Race of Woman: 1980 and 1987", *Statistical Abstract*, 1989, p. 68. Primary source: U.S. Bureau of the Census, *Current Population Reports*, series P-20, Nos. 375 and 427. *Notes:* 1. Covers single women, 18-49 years old. 2. Covers single women, 30-39 years old.

★ 966 ★
Who Dies from AIDS ?

Data are based on reporting from State health departments.

Age, sex, and race/ethnicity	Number, by year of death								Percent Distribution
	All years[1,2]	1982	1983	1984	1985	1986	1987	1988[2]	All years[1,2]
Total[3]	43,790	431	1,402	3,122	6,010	10,010	12,843	9,657	...
Male									
All males, 13 years and over[3]	39,551	384	1,271	2,849	5,510	9,107	11,514	8,651	100.0
White, not Hispanic	24,408	197	716	1,751	3,456	5,765	7,031	5,354	61.7
Black, not Hispanic	9,957	121	368	691	1,331	2,123	2,936	2,294	25.2
Hispanic	4,861	65	177	380	686	1,154	1,448	920	12.3
Female									
All females, 13 years and over[3]	3,542	36	102	228	404	767	1,099	870	100.0
White, not Hispanic	1,072	9	23	53	130	230	356	263	30.3
Black, not Hispanic	1,932	20	54	129	194	408	608	496	54.5
Hispanic	504	6	25	44	76	120	127	103	14.3

Continued.

Who Dies from AIDS ?

[Continued]

Age, sex, and race/ethnicity	Number, by year of death								Percent Distri-bution
	All years[1,2]	1982	1983	1984	1985	1986	1987	1988[2]	All years[1,2]
Children									
All children, under 13 years[3]	697	11	29	45	96	136	230	136	100.0
White, not Hispanic	183	4	6	8	26	30	63	42	26.3
Black, not Hispanic	368	6	19	26	56	73	111	71	52.8
Hispanic	137	1	4	11	13	31	52	21	19.7

Source: "Acquired Immunodeficiency Syndrome (AIDS) Deaths, according to Age, Sex, and Race/Ethnicity: United States, Selected Years 1982-88," *Health United States - 1988*, March 1989, p. 83. Primary source: Centers for Disease Control, Center for Infectious Diseases, AIDS Program, *Health United States - 1988*, March 1989, p. 83. *Notes:* The AIDS case definition was changed in September 1987 to allow for the presumptive diagnosis of AIDS-associated diseases and conditions and to expand the spectrum of human immunodeficiency virus-associated diseases reportable as AIDS. Excludes residents of U.S. territories. 1. Includes deaths prior to 1982. 2. Data are as of November 30, 1988, and reflect reporting delays. 3. Includes all other races not shown separately.

★ 967 ★
Women and Children

As of June. Based on Current Population Survey, See *Historical Statistics, Colonial Times to 1970*, series B 49-66.

Age	Percent Childless Among Women Ever Married 1987				Children Ever Born per 1,000 Women Ever Married 1987			
	Total[1]	White	Black	Hispanic[2]	Total[1]	White	Black	Hispanic[2]
Total	18.6	19.5	11.3	12.1	1,785	1,732	2,246	2,240
18-19 years old	49.8	51.0	[3]	[3]	635	606	[3]	[3]
20-24 years old	39.8	41.0	24.9	19.9	940	903	1,332	1,369
25-29 years old	25.9	27.1	14.4	17.6	1,385	1,339	1,782	1,746
30-34 years old	15.6	16.1	9.5	8.1	1,788	1,752	2,098	2,335
35-39 years old	11.5	12.1	7.8	5.6	2,113	2,047	2,689	2,749
40-44 years old	10.2	10.3	8.7	7.8	2,329	2,279	2,777	3,047

Source: "Childless Women and Children Ever Born, by Age of Woman, 1987," *Statistical Abstracts*, 1989, p. 68 Primary source: U.S. Bureau of the Census, *Current Population Reports*, series P-20, No. 427 and earlier reports. *Notes:* 1. Includes other races not shown separately. 2. Hispanic persons may be of any race. 3. Base figure too small to meet standards for reliability of derived figure.

reports.

Burt, Martha and Barbara Cohen. "Feeding the Homeless: Does the Prepared Meals Provision Help?" Report to Congress on the Prepared Meals Provision. Volume 2. Urban Institute, October 1988. Tables 2, 7, 21, and 25.

Cancer among Blacks and Other Minorities: Statistical Profiles. U.S. Department of Health and Human Services, Public Health Service, National Institutes of Health, National Cancer Institute, n.d.

The Chronicle of Higher Education. weekly, except August and December. Available from *The Chronicle*, 1255 23rd Street, N.W., Washington, DC 20037. Concentrates on subjects of interest to higher education and often includes tables.

The Climate for Workers in the United States. The Second Biennial Report from the Southern Labor Institute; a special project of the Southern Regional Council. Atlanta: Southern Regional Council, 1988.

The College Board Review. quarterly. The College Board, 45 Columbus Avenue, New York, NY 10023-6992.

Conciatore, J. "Business School Accreditation System That Excludes Black Colleges Due for Change." *Black Issues in Higher Education* 7, No. 2 (March 29, 1990): 5-6.

————. "Military Testing and Standards Barriers for Some Minorities." *Black Issues in Higher Education* 7, No. 3 (April 12, 1990): 1, 26-28.

Cooper, S., P. Buffler, and C. Cooper. *Health Characteristics by Occupation and Industry of Longest Employment*. National Center for Health Statistics. *Vital and Health Statistics* 10: 168, 1989. DHS Publication No. (PHS) 89-1596.

Criminal Victimization in the United States, 1987. A National Crime Survey Report. U.S. Department of Justice, Office of Justice Programs, Bureau of Justice Statistics. Washington, D.C.: NCJ-115-524, June 1989.

Curran, J. W., H. W. Jaffe, A. M. Hardy, W. M. Morgan, R. M. Selik, and T. J. Dondero. "Epidemiology of HIV Infection and AIDS in the United States. *Science* 239 (4840): 610-616. In *A Common Destiny: Blacks and American Society*, 1989. Table, 8-5, p. 420.

Davis, James A., and Tom W. Smith. "General Social Surveys, 1972-1987." *Public Opinion Quarterly* 43 (Winter 1987): 463-76. In *A Common Destiny: Blacks and American Society*, 1989. Table 3-2, pp. 128-29.

Demographics, Standards, and Equity: Challenges in College Admissions, Report of a Survey of Undergraduate Admissions Policies, Practices, and Procedures. Sponsored by American Association of Collegiate Registrars and Admissions Officers, The American College Testing Program, The College Board, Educational Testing Service, National Association of College Admission Counselors. November 1986.

Detroit Free Fress. daily. Available from the press at 321 West Lafayette Boulevard, Detroit, MI 48231.

Digest of Education Statistics, 1989. 25th ed. U.S. Department of Education, Office of Educational Research and Improvement. National Center for Education Statistics, Washington, D.C. NCES 89-643.

Equality and Excellence: The Educational Status of Black Americans. A Special Report of The College Entrance Examination Board, New York, 1985. College Board Publications, Box 886, New York, NY 10101.

Gender and Campus Race Differences in Black Student Academic Performance, Racial Attitudes and College Statistics. Southern Education Foundation, Atlanta, GA 30303, March 1986. A part of the Higher Education Program Research Series, with data taken from the National Study of Black College Students, University of Michigan.

Goldman, Sheldon. "Reagan's Judicial Legacy: Completing the Puzzle and Summing Up." *Judicature* 72 (April-May 1989): 320-22, 323-25. In *Sourcebook of Criminal Justice Statistics — 1988*, p. 98. Table adapted by *Sourcebook* staff.

Hawkins, Darnell F. "Paper Prepared for the Committee on The Status of Black Americans, National Research Council, Washington, D.C." In *A Common Destiny: Blacks and American Society*, 1989. Table 9-1, p. 461.

Health of Black and White Americans, 1985-87. National Center for Health Statistics, U.S. Department of Health and Human Services, Public Health Service, Centers for Disease Control. Hyattsville, Md., January 1990. (PHS) 90-1599.

Health United States, 1988. U.S. Department of Health and Human Services, Public Health Service, Centers for Disease Control, National Center for Health Statistics, Hyattsville, Md., March 1989. DHHS Pub. No. (PHS)89-1232. The 13th annual report on the nation's health status.

Henderson, L. J. "Budget and Tax Strategy: Implications for Blacks." In *The State of Black America 1990*, January 1990, pp. 53-71.

Jamieson, Katherine M., and Timothy J. Flanagan, eds. *Sourcebook of Criminal Justice Statis-*

tics—1988. Eds. Katherine U.S. Department of Justice, Bureau of Justice Statistics. Washington, D.C.: U.S. Government Printing Office, 1989. U.S. Department of Justice, Bureau of Justice Statistics. Washington, D.C. U.S. Government Printing Office, 1989. A project supported by a grant to The Hinderlang Criminal Justice Research Center, Albany, N.Y. Available from Superintendent of Documents, U.S. Government Printing Office, Washington, DC 20402.

Jaynes, Gerald D., and Robin M. Williams, Jr., eds. *A Common Destiny: Blacks and American Society*. Committee on the Status of Black Americans, Commission on Behavioral and Social Sciences and Education, National Research Council. Washington, D.C.: National Academy Press, 1989. Presents information on black life in relation to American society and includes both statistical and evaluative data.

Joint Center for Political Studies. [Now Joint Center for Political and Economic Studies.] *Black Elected Officials: A National Roster*. 18th ed. Washington, D.C.: Joint Center for Political Studies Press, 1989. Documents the election of blacks to public office. Available from University Press of America, 4720 Boston Way, Lanham, MD 20706.

Kirsch, Irvin S., and Ann Jungeblut. "Literacy's Profiles of America's Young Adults." Princeton, N.J.: Educational Testing Service. In *A Common Destiny: Blacks and American Society*, 1989. Table 7-4, p. 353.

Kleppner, Paul. "Who Voted? The Dynamics of Electoral Turnout, 1870-1980. New York: Praeger, 1982. Data from Current Population Surveys. In *A Common Destiny: Blacks and American Society*, 1989. Table 5-9, p. 236.

Lefall, L. D. "Health Status of Black Americans." In *The State of Black America 1990*, January 1990, pp. 121-142.

Legislative Bulletin. quarterly. Southern Legislative Research Council, a project of the Southern Regional Council. Atlanta: Southern Regional Council, 60 Walton Street, N.W., Atlanta, GA 30303-2199. Provides data to legislators who represent poor and minority constituencies on Southern states.

LeVee, William N., ed. *New Perspectives on HIV-Related Illnesses: Progress in Health Services Research*. Conference Proceedings, Miami, Fla., May 17-19, 1989. National Center for Health Services Research and Health Care Technology Assessment. Public Health Service, U.S. Department of Health and Human Services. September 1989. National Center for Health Services Research Publications and Information Branch, Room 18-12, 5600 Fishers Lane, Rockville, MD 20857.

Life Sciences Research Office, Federation of American Societies for Experimental Biology. *Nutrition Monitoring in the United States: An Update Report on Nutrition Monitoring*. Prepared for the U.S. Department of Agriculture and the U.S. Department of Health and Human Services, DHHS Publication No. (PHS) 89-1255. Public Health Service. Washington, D.C.: U.S. Government Printing Office, September 1989. Superintendent of Documents, U.S. Government Printing Office, Washington, D.C. 20402.

McGhee, James D. *Running the Gauntlet: Black Men in America*. Washington, D.C.: National Urban League, 1984.

McKinney, Fred. "Employment Implications of a Changing Health-Care System." In: *Slipping Through the Cracks: The Status of Black Women*, edited by Margaret C. Simms and Julianne M. Malveaux, p. 437. New Brunswick, N.J.: Transaction Books, 1986. Reprinted in *A Common Destiny: Blacks and American Society*, 1989. Table 8-12, p. 437.

Moskos, C. S., and John S. Butler. "Blacks in the Army: An American Success Story." *The Atlantic Monthly* (October 1987). In *A Common Destiny: Blacks and American Society*, 1989. Table 2-3, p. 72; Table 2-4, p. 73.

Moyer, M. Eugene. "A Revised Look at the Number of Uninsured Americans." *Health Affairs*, Summer 1989.

Myers, Samuel L., Jr., and William J. Sabol. "Crime and the Black Community: Issues in the Understanding of Race and Crime in America." Paper prepared for the Committee on the Status of Black Americans, National Research Council, Washington, D.C. In *A Common Destiny: Blacks and American Society*, 1989. Table 9-4, p. 471.

NAACP Legal Defense and Educational Fund, Inc. Periodic news releases present data on variables of interest to the source. Included in this volume are the releases "Execution Update" and "Death Row, U.S.A." National Office: Suite 1600, 99 Hudson Street, New York, NY 10013. Regional offices in Washington, D.C. and Los Angeles, Calif.

NAFEO Inroads. A bimonthly newsletter. Individual issues contain various reports on the status of black higher education and related factors, with emphasis on Historical Black Colleges and Universities (HBCUs) and Equal Opportunity Enrollment Institutions (EOEIs) that are members of NAFEO (National Association for Equality of Opportunity in Higher Education), and other Predominantly Black Institutions (PBIs). NAFEO, Black Higher Education Center, Lovejoy Building, 400 12th Street, N.E., Washington, DC 10002.

National Center for Health Statistics. *Assessing Physical Fitness and Physical Activity in Population-Based Surveys*. Thomas F. Drury, ed. DHHS Pub. No. (PHS) 89-1253. Public Health Service. Washington, D.C.: U.S. Government Printing Office, 1989. Superintendent of Documents, U.S. Government Printing Office, Washington, DC 20402.

National Center for Health Statistics. *Health, United States, 1989*; and *Prevention Profile* (in

Health United States, 1989). Hyattsville, Md.: Public Health Service, 1990. DHHS Pub. No. (PHS) 90-1232. This edition of the annual publication adds to the report on health status and conditions data relating the 1990 objective for various health states to the current status. Available from the Superintendent of Documents, U.S. Government Printing Office, Washington, DC 20402.

National Churches of Christ in the United States of America, New York. *Yearbook of American and Canadian Churches, 1989*. Nashville, Tenn.: Abingdon Press, 1989.

National Institute on Aging. Administrative Document: *Personnel for Health Needs of the Elderly through Year 2020*. September 1987 Report to Congress. U.S. Department of Health and Human Services. National Institute on Aging, National Institutes of Health, Bethesda, MD. 20892.

National Institute on Justice: Research in Action. U.S. Department of Justice, Office of Justice Program, National Institute of Justice. Washington, D.C., December 1989, NCJ 120742. Newsletter issued through a program of the National Institute of Justice.

National Science Board. *Science and Engineering Indicators — 1989*. Washington, D.C.: U.S. Government Printing Office, 1989. (NSB 89-1). Superintendent of Documents, U.S. Government Printing Office, Washington, DC 20402.

The New York Times. daily. Available from 229 West 43rd Street, New York, NY 10036.

NIMH. *Mental Health United States, 1987*, edited by R. W. Manderscheid and S. A. Barrett. DHHS Publication No. (ADM) 87-1518. Washington, D.C.: U.S. Government Printing Office, 1987.

1989 Education Indicators. U.S. Department of Education, Office of Educational Research and Improvement, National Center for Education Statistics, Information Services. NCES 89-653. Superintendent of Documents, U.S. Government Printing Office, Washington, DC 20402.

O'Hare, William. "Incorporated Municipalities with Black Mayors, by Population, Racial Composition, and Region, 1985. *Population Today* 14 (June) 6-8. In *A Common Destiny: Blacks and American Society*, 1989. Table 5-12, p. 241.

Personnel for Health Needs of the Elderly through Year 2020. National Institute on Aging Administrative Document. September 1987 Report to Congress. U.S. Department of Health and Human Services. National Institute on Aging, National Institutes of Health, Public Health Service, Department of Health and Human Services.

Pittman, K. J. "Reading and Writing as Risk-Reduction: The School's Role in Preventing

Teenage Pregnancies." *The Urban League Review* 12, Nos. 1 & 2 (Summer 1988/Winter 1988-89): 55-69.

A Profile of the Working Poor. U.S. Department of Labor, Bureau of Labor Statistics, December 1989, Bulletin 2345. Superintendent of Documents, U.S. Government Printing Office, Washington, DC 20402.

The Quarterly Economic Report on the African American Worker. Research Department, National Urban League, December 1989.

Research Perspectives on Depression and Suicide in Minorities. U.S. Department of Health and Human Services, Public Health Service, Alcohol, Drug Abuse and Mental Health Administration, Washington, D.C. Proceedings of a workshop sponsored by the National Institite of Mental Health, December 7-8, 1989.

Science and Technology Data Book. (NSF 88-332). Washington, D.C., 1989.

Sekcenski, E. S. *Discharges from Nursing Homes: 1985 National Nursing Survey.* Vital Health Statistics 13 (103), 1990. This issue of *Vital and Health Statistics* presents detailed information on the characteristics of individuals discharged from nursing homes, including discharge status, stay duration, dependencies, pre- and post-discharge living arrangements, and primary sources of payment. DHHS Publication No. (PHS) 90-1764.

Selected Data on Historical Black Colleges, Academic Year 1986. Washington, D.C.: National Science Foundaion, December 1987. Tables derived from (a) surveys of institutions that grant a graduate science or engineering degree and/or meet a specific criterion of amount budgeted for research and development, (b) surveys of 15 agencies with Federal obligations to universities and colleges for science and engineering funding, and (c) the Survey of Graduate Science and Engineering Students and Postdoctorates.

The State of Black America 1990. New York: National Urban League, 1990. Annual. National Urban League, Inc., 500 East 62nd Street, New York, NY 10021.

The Supporting News. TSN Series Nos. 1-5. Yearbooks providing statistical and other information on, respectively, professional and college baseball, professional football, college football, professional basketball, and college basketball. Sporting News Publishing Co., 121 N. Lindbergh Boulevard, St. Louis, MO. 63132.

Swinton, D. H. "Economic Status of Black Americans During the 1980s: A Decade of Limited Progress." In *The State of Black America, 1990.* January 1990, pp. 25-52.

The Tennessean. daily. Available from 1100 Broadway, Nashville, TN 37203.

Tidwell, Billy J. *Black Employment in the Private Sector: A Twenty-Year Assessment*. National Urban League, July 1988.

———. "Racial Composition of Jurisdictions and the Election of Black Candidates." *Population Today* 14 (June 1986): 6-8. In *A Common Destiny: Blacks and American Society*, 1989. Table 5-12, p. 241.

———. "The Unemployment Experience of African Americans: Some Important Correlates and Consequences." *The State of Black America 1990*. January 1990, pp. 213-23.

UNCF 1989 Statistical Report. United Negro College Fund, Inc. New York: n.d.

The Urban League Review: A Policy Research Journal of the National Urban League. Published semiannually by the Research Department, National Urban League. *The Urban League Review*, 1111 14th Street, N.W., 6th Floor, Washington, DC 20005.

U.S. Bureau of the Census. Current Population Reports, Population Characteristics Series P-20, No. 422. *The Black Population in the United States: March 1990*. Washington, D.C.: U.S. Government Printing Office, 1989. Superintendent of Documents, U.S. Government Printing Office, Washington, DC 20402.

———. Series P-20, No. 444. *Marital Status and Living Arrangements: March 1988*. Washington, D.C.: U.S. Government Printing Office, 1989.

———. Series P-20, No. 440. *Voting and Registration in the Election of November 1988*. Washington, D.C.: U.S. Government Printing Office, 1989.

———. Series P-60, No. 166. *Money Income and Poverty Status in the United States: 1988 (Advance Data from the March 1989 Current Population Survey)*. Washington, D.C.: U.S. Government Printing Office, 1989.

U.S. Bureau of the Census. Department of Commerce. *Population Profile of the United States, 1989*. Current Population Reports, Special Studies, Series P-23, No. 159. Washington, D.C., April 1989.

U.S. Bureau of the Census. *Statistical Abstract of the United States: 1989*. 109th ed. Washington, D.C., 1989. Provides a standard summary of statistics on the social, political, and economic organization of the United States and serves as a guide to other statistical publications and sources. Available from Superintendent of Documents, U.S. Government Printing Office, Washington, DC 20402.

U.S. Congress. House. *U.S. Children and Their Families: Current Conditions and Recent Trends, 1989*. A Report together with Additional Views of the Select Committee on Children,

Youth, and Families. 101st Cong., 1st Sess. Washington, D.C. U.S. Government Printing Office, 1989.

The Villers Foundation. [Now Families USA Foundation.] "On the Other Side of Easy Street: Myths and Facts About the Economics of Old Age." Washington, D.C., January 1987. [1334 G Street, N.W., Washington, DC 20005.]

Vital and Health Statistics, Series 10. Data from the National Health Survey, No. 168.

Wescott, Diane Nilsen, "Blacks in the 1970s: Did They Scale the Job Ladder?" *Monthly Labor Review* (June 1982): 32.

Wiley, E., III. "Coast Guard Trying to Prove It's Serious about Minority Progress." *Black Issues in Higher Education* 7, No. 3 (April 12, 1990): 12-24.

————. "HBCUs Main Source of Black Officers, but Some Question Preparation." *Black Issues in Higher Education* 7, No. 3 (April 12, 1990): 17-18.

Women and Minorities in Science and Engineering. National Science Foundation, Washington, DC 20550. NSF 99-301.

Yinger, J. Milton. "Black Americans and Predominantly White Churches." Paper prepared for the Committee on the Status of Black Americans, National Research Council, Washington, D.C. In *A Common Destiny: Blacks and American Society*, 1989. Table 2-6, p. 94.

Young, Ann McDougall. "Recent Trends in Higher Education and Labor Force Activity." *Monthly Labor Review* (February 1983): 40.

INDEX

Page numbers immediately follow the index terms. Values in brackets are table numbers.

Abortions, p. 626, [904]

Abortions, legal, p. 626, [903, 904]

Abortion, attitudes toward, p. 21, 25, [43, 54]

Achievement/aptitude, p. 105, 108, 134, 473, [174, 180, 219, 220, 703]

Achievement/aptitude, college students, p. 115, [192]

Achievement/aptitude, computers, p. 120, [196]

Achievement/aptitude, eighth graders, p. 104, [173]

Achievement/aptitude, GRE scores, p. 107, 213, 252, [178, 325, 377]

Achievement/aptitude, high school courses taken, p. 176, [276]

Achievement/aptitude, high school grade-point averages, p. 113, [188]

Achievement/aptitude, history, p. 182, [284]

Achievement/aptitude, literacy, p. 203, [309]

Achievement/aptitude, literature, p. 182, [284]

Achievement/aptitude, mathematics, p. 103, 119, 134, 206, 227, 228, 258, [171, 194, 219, 220, 314, 342, 344, 382]

Achievement/aptitude, reading, p. 214, 216, 229, [326, 329, 345]

Achievement/aptitude, reading scores, p. 203, [309]

Achievement/aptitude, SAT scores, p. 107, 133, 226, 227, [177, 218, 340, 341, 342]

Achievement/aptitude, science, p. 103, 134, 233, [172, 219, 220, 351]

Achievement/aptitude, teacher candidates, p. 238, [358]

Achievement/aptitude, teachers, p. 240, [361]

Achievement/aptitude, writing, p. 256, [381]

Adoptions, p. 290, [434]

Adults, educational attainment, p. 259, [384]

Adults, elderly, p. 361, 401, 410, [530, 592, 606]

Adults, homeless, p. 609, [880]

Adults, hypertension in, p. 340, 364, [500, 535]

Adults, overweight, p. 318, 350, [469, 513]

Adults, with diabetes, p. 299, [443]

AIDS, p. 324, 340, 362, [476, 501, 534]

AIDS, characteristics of victims, p. 680, [966]

AIDS, death rates, p. 625, [902]

AIDS, in children, p. 302, 340, [447, 499]

AIDS, in young adults, p. 302, [447]

AIDS, incidence, p. 315, 339, [466, 498]

AIDS, risk, p. 315, [466]

AIDS, source of, p. 340, [499]

AIDS, testing for, p. 24, [51]

AIDS, transmitted by, p. 625, [902]

Alcohol, drinking age, p. 22, [45]

Alcohol, use by teenagers, p. 362, [533]

Allied health fields, p. 562, [821]

American College Testing scores, p. 242, [363]

Amniocentesis, among older expectant mothers, p. 302, [448]

Aptitude and achievement, Armed Forces Qualifying Test scores, p. 465, [690]

Armed Forces, officers, p. 465, 471, [689, 701]

Army, personnel, p. 466, [691]

Army, physical fitness scores, p. 469, 470, [696, 697, 698, 699]

Arrests of persons, p. 46, [80]

Arrests, after previous imprisonment, p. 82, [135]

Arrests, and type of crime, p. 91, [151]

Arrests, for federal offenses, p. 68, [110]

Art museums and galleries, attendance, p. 585, [847]

Arts performances, attendance, p. 585, [847]

Aspirations, college students, p. 141, 207, [230, 316]

Attitudes, p. 100, 141, 156, 207, 357, [167, 230, 251, 316, 524]

Attitudes, college faculty, p. 3, 4, [5, 6, 7]

Attitudes, college students, p. 8, 17, [16, 35]

Attitudes, crime-related, p. 9, 10, [19, 20, 21]

Attitudes, eighth graders' expected occupations, p. 2, [2]

Attitudes, ethical/moral standards, p. 22, [46, 47]

Attitudes, of 8th graders toward school, p. 15, [31]

Attitudes, of college freshmen, p. 24, [52]

Attitudes, of eighth graders, p. 1, [1]

Attitudes, of public school parents/teachers, p. 18, [39]

Attitudes, of teenagers, p. 20, [41]

Attitudes, racial, p. 6, 156, [12, 251]

Attitudes, toward abortion, p. 21, 25, [43, 54]

Attitudes, toward alcohol, p. 22, [45]

Attitudes, toward busing, p. 4, [8]

Attitudes, toward community problems, p. 15, [32]

Attitudes, toward crime, p. 6, 13, [13, 27]

Attitudes, toward death penalty, p. 17, 18, 25, [36, 38, 53]

Attitudes, toward drug abuse, p. 7, 18, [14, 37]

Attitudes, toward drug dealers, p. 20, [42]

Attitudes, toward drug-related crime, p. 8, [17]

Attitudes, toward firearms, p. 2, 10, [3, 21]

Attitudes, toward gun regulation, p. 3, 21, [4, 44]

Attitudes, toward interracial dating, p. 5, [9]

Attitudes, toward justice system, p. 11, 13, [24, 28]

Attitudes, toward law enforcement, p. 7, [15]

Attitudes, toward lawyers, p. 22, [46]

Attitudes, toward legal justice, p. 7, [15]

Attitudes, toward national problems, p. 16, 17, [33, 34]

Attitudes, toward police, p. 12, 14, 22, [25, 29, 47]

Attitudes, toward public school education, p. 18, [39]

Attitudes, toward registration of firearms, p. 10, [22]

Attitudes, toward same race, p. 5, [11]

Attitudes, toward sex education & related topics, p. 5, [10]

Attitudes, toward Supreme Court, p. 8, 12, 14, 23, [18, 26, 30, 50]

Attitudes, toward the death penalty, p. 19, 26, [40, 55]

Attorneys, number, p. 564, [824]

Automobile dealers, p. 36, [70]

Automobile dealerships, p. 28, 43, [57, 77]

Bachelor's degrees, field, p. 111, [184]

Bachelor's degrees, in education, p. 113, [187]

Banks, p. 28, 32, 41, [58, 62, 75]

Banks, assets, p. 28, [58]

Banks, characteristics of, p. 32, [62]

Banks, deposits, p. 28, [58]

Banks, leading, p. 41, [75]

Banks, loans, p. 28, [58]

Banks, selected, p. 41, [75]

Banks, size of staff, p. 28, [58]

Baseball, professional league leaders, p. 615, 616, [890, 891, 892]

Basic skills, of young mothers, p. 288, [430]

Basic skills, of young parents, p. 260, [385]

Basketball, coaches, p. 612, 619, 620, [886, 898, 899]

Basketball, college, p. 612, 614, [885, 888]

Basketball, professional, p. 617, [893]

Basketball, professional league leaders, p. 618, [894]

Behavior, high school seniors' extracurricular activities, p. 10, [23]

Birth control, p. 627, [905]

Birth expectations, p. 627, [906]

Birth order, p. 630, [910]

Birth rates, p. 628, 629, 630, 631, 632, [907, 908, 909, 910, 911, 914]

Birth rates, crude, p. 666, [950]

Birth rates, premature infants, p. 674, [960]

Birth weight, p. 667, 673, [951, 959]

Births, p. 627, 665, 676, 679, 680, [906, 949, 961, 964, 965]

Births expected, p. 676, [961]

Births out-of-wedlock, p. 632, [913]

Births, age of mother, p. 666, [950]

Births, as related to prenatal care, p. 352, [518]

Births, characteristics of, p. 633, 665, [916, 949]

Births, live, p. 633, 666, 667, 673, [916, 950, 951, 959]

Births, low birth weight, p. 361, [531]

Births, married women's expectations, p. 668, [953]

Births, single women, p. 680, [965]

Black elderly, p. 517, [753]

Black mayors, p. 476, [704]

Black mayors in municipalities, p. 478, [708]

Black mayors, distribution of, p. 476, [704]

Black men, educational level, p. 199, 452, [304, 669]

Black men, employed, p. 435, 436, 438, 452, [644, 645, 646, 649, 669]

Black men, employment rates, p. 436, [645]

Black men, unemployed, p. 456, 457, [676, 677]

Black population, characteristics of, p. 522, [762]

Black religious denominations, p. 607, [878]

Blacks in cities, p. 518, [755]

Blacks in the economy, p. 422, [622]

Black-White residential segregation, p. 376, [552]

Books and reading, p. 585, [847]

Breast feeding, p. 655, [936]

Business and economics, p. 427, 428, [632, 633]

Business income, p. 34, [66]

Businesses, p. 28, 29, 30, 33, 34, 36, 38, 39, 41, 42, 43, [58, 59, 60, 65, 66, 67, 69, 70, 72, 74, 75, 76, 77]

Businesses, growth leaders, p. 31, [61]

Businesses, income, p. 34, [67]

Businesses, leading, p. 31, [61]

Businesses, location of, p. 32, [64]

Businesses, minority-owned, p. 35, [68]

Business, enrollment in schools of, p. 110, [182]

Busing, attitudes toward, p. 4, [8]

Cancer, age-adjusted rates, p. 301, [445, 446]

Cancer, geographic distribution of cases, p. 330, [484]

Cancer, histologic type, p. 307, [456]

Cancer, incidence, p. 301, 305, [446, 452]

Cancer, mortality, p. 301, [445]

Cancer, mortality rates, p. 305, [452]

Cancer, site, p. 301, 304, 305, 306, [445, 446, 450, 452, 454]

Cancer, survival rates, p. 304, 305, 306, [450, 453, 454, 455]

Capital punishment, p. 84, 85, [140, 141, 142]

Centenarians, p. 536, [784]

Centenarians, living arrangements, p. 538, [785]

Child abuse, p. 47, [82]

Child neglect, characteristics of, p. 47, [82]

Childless women, p. 681, [967]

Children, p. 286, [427]

Children in families, p. 262, 269, 271, 272, [390, 399,

401, 402]

Children in group quarters, p. 528, [770]

Children in households, p. 531, [775]

Children in institutions, p. 528, [770]

Children in poverty, p. 286, [427]

Children in the U.S., p. 529, [771]

Children, abuse of, p. 262, [388]

Children, activity limitations, p. 309, [460]

Children, adopted, p. 290, [434]

Children, after-school conditions, p. 263, [391]

Children, child support of, p. 262, [389]

Children, computer competence, p. 120, [196]

Children, distribution in families, p. 530, [773]

Children, family income of, p. 270, [400]

Children, father-absent, p. 282, [421]

Children, health insurance coverage, p. 308, [457]

Children, health ratings, p. 308, [458]

Children, in extended families, p. 266, [395]

Children, in father-absent homes, p. 279, [416]

Children, in poverty, p. 267, [397]

Children, iron deficiency, p. 342, [503]

Children, living arrangements of, p. 373, [547, 548]

Children, living conditions, p. 528, [770]

Children, not living with parents, p. 264, [392]

Children, physician visits, p. 309, [459]

Children, pre-primary school enrollment, p. 232, [349]

Children, residence area, p. 289, [433]

Children, with AIDS, p. 302, 340, [447, 499]

Children, with parents in household, p. 279, [417]

Children, with working mothers, p. 261, 282, [387, 422]

Cholesterol, incidence of high-risk, p. 341, [502]

Cholesterol, mean intake, p. 327, [481]

Church attendance, p. 606, [876]

Churches, p. 606, [877]

Cities, segregation in, p. 376, [551]

Civilian employment ratio, p. 429, [634]

Coast Guard, personnel, p. 466, [692]

College and university enrollment, p. 571, [830]

College faculty, UNCF institutions, p. 130, [212]

College faculty, veterinary medicine, p. 600, [868]

College faculty, with doctorates, p. 251, [376]

College freshmen, attitudes toward college, p. 24, [52]

College freshmen, degree aspirations, p. 242, [364]

College freshmen, financial assistance, p. 243, [365]

College freshmen, majors/career choices, p. 243, [366]

College freshmen, parental income, p. 400, [591]

College students, achievement/aptitude, p. 115, [192]

College students, aspirations, p. 141, 207, [230, 316]

College students, attitudes, p. 5, 6, 8, 17, 156, [9, 11, 12, 16, 35, 251]

College students, computer use, p. 133, [216]

College students, employed, p. 419, [618]

College students, enrollment, p. 151, [245]

College students, faculty-student relationships, p. 156, [251]

College students, financial aid, p. 133, 163, 164, [217, 258, 259]

College students, first/second generation, p. 205, [313]

College students, full-time, p. 169, [266]

College students, graduation rates, p. 133, [217]

College students, high school grade-point averages, p. 113, [188]

College students, majors/career choices, p. 107, 131, 205, 227, 252, [177, 213, 313, 342, 377]

College students, occupational striving, p. 23, [48]

College students, outcomes, p. 135, [221]

College students, part-time, p. 169, [266]

College students, self-concept, p. 23, [49]

College students, withdrawal rates, p. 133, [217]

College, completion rates, p. 122, [199]

Colleges & universities, p. 128, 608, [210, 879]

Colleges & universities, academic competition, p. 100, [167]

Colleges & universities, acceptance rates, p. 101, 109, 121, 168, [169, 181, 198, 264]

Colleges & universities, acceptances, p. 102, [170]

Colleges & universities, accreditation, p. 172, [270]

Colleges & universities, accreditation, specialized, p. 173, [271]

Colleges & universities, admissions, p. 101, 165, 168, [169, 260, 264]

Colleges & universities, applicants to medical school, p. 553, 581, [806, 838]

Colleges & universities, applications, p. 101, 107, 168, [169, 179, 264]

Colleges & universities, athletics, p. 619, 620, [898, 899]

Colleges & universities, basketball, p. 612, 614, [885, 886, 888]

Colleges & universities, college participation by age, p. 131, [214]

Colleges & universities, control, p. 155, 186, 188, [249, 290, 292]

Colleges & universities, date established, p. 155, 188, [249, 292]

Colleges & universities, degrees awarded, p. 113, 137, [186, 225]

Colleges & universities, degrees conferred, p. 99, 111, 113, 140, 158, 162, 171, 190, 204, 208, [165, 184, 187, 228, 229, 254, 257, 268, 269, 297, 312, 317, 318]

Colleges & universities, degrees conferred, p. 215, 232, 235, 236, 237, 238, 251, 580, 583, 594, 596, 597, [327, 350, 354, 355, 356, 357, 375, 837, 842, 863, 864, 865]

Colleges & universities, dental school enrollment, p. 556, 598, [813, 867]

Colleges & universities, endowment, p. 123, [201]

Colleges & universities, enrollment, p. 114, 115, 123,

124, 125, 126, 139, 148, 151, 153, 165,
167, 176, 184, 186, 201, 202, 220, 247, 254, 258, 462,
567, 569, 573, 575, 576,
[189, 190, 193, 202, 203, 204, 205, 206, 226, 242, 246,
247, 261,
263, 275, 287, 289, 306, 307, 333, 334, 369, 379, 383,
686, 828, 829, 831, 832, 833]
Colleges & universities, expenditures, p. 190, [296]
Colleges & universities, faculty, p. 3, 115, 129, 130, 132,
136, 155, 170, 234, 249, 250, 551, 552, [6, 191, 211, 212,
215, 223, 250, 267, 353, 372, 373, 803, 804]
Colleges & universities, faculty, p. 552, 558, 559, 602,
[805, 814, 815, 870]
Colleges & universities, faculty fields of study, p. 139,
[227]
Colleges & universities, faculty ranks, p. 127, 128, [207,
208]
Colleges & universities, faculty salaries, p. 128, 225,
250, [209, 339, 374]
Colleges & universities, faculty source of bachelor's
degree, p. 112, [185]
Colleges & universities, faculty teaching fields, p. 241,
[362]
Colleges & universities, financial aid, p. 163, [258]
Colleges & universities, financial support, p. 188, [293]
Colleges & universities, freshmen, p. 165, 166, 167, 246,
[261, 262, 263, 367]
Colleges & universities, graduate enrollment, p. 565,
[825]
Colleges & universities, HBCUs, p. 202, [308]
Colleges & universities, level, p. 155, 186, 188, [249,
290, 292]
Colleges & universities, loan default rates, p. 122, 240,
[200, 360]
Colleges & universities, majors/career choices, p. 243,
309, [366, 461]
Colleges & universities, majors/career fields, p. 110,
[182]
Colleges & universities, majors/careers, p. 166, [262]
Colleges & universities, medical school enrollment, p.
578, 579, [834, 835]
Colleges & universities, newer PBIs, p. 207, [315]
Colleges & universities, number, p. 186, [290]
Colleges & universities, research & development
support, p. 156, 157, [252, 253]
Colleges & universities, selectivity, p. 121, [198]
Colleges & universities, sports, p. 612, [886]
Colleges & universities, student athletes, p. 618, 619,
[896, 897]
Colleges & universities, Traditionally Black
Institutions, p. 248, [371]
Colleges & universities, transfer students, p. 174, 175,
189, 248, [272, 273, 274, 294, 370]

Colleges & universities, type of institution, p. 148, [242]
Community problems, attitudes, p. 15, [32]
Computer science, high school credits, p. 177, [277]
Computers, achievement/aptitude, p. 120, [196]
Computers, college students, p. 133, [216]
Computers, exposure to, p. 239, [359]
Computer, elementary/secondary students, p. 145,
[235]
Contraceptives, p. 627, [905]
Crime, p. 2, 3, 6, 7, 8, 9, 10, 11, 12, 13, 14, 17, 18, 19, 20,
21, 22, 23, 25, 26, [3, 4, 13, 15, 17, 18, 19, 20, 21, 24, 25,
26, 27, 29, 30, 36, 38, 40, 42, 44, 47, 50, 53, 55]
Crime victims, p. 48, 53, 69, 71, [84, 91, 112, 115]
Crime, against law enforcement officers, p. 74, [119,
120]
Crime, and age of victims, p. 45, [78, 79]
Crime, and neighborhood type, p. 48, [83]
Crime, arrestees, p. 60, [97]
Crime, arrests, p. 91, [151]
Crime, attitudes toward, p. 6, 13, [13, 27]
Crime, burglary, p. 64, [104]
Crime, characteristics of victims, p. 48, 51, 52, 57, 63,
64, 65, 66, 67, 69, 70, 78, 88, 92, 94, 96, [83, 87,
88, 89, 90, 96, 102, 103, 104, 105, 106, 107, 108,
111, 114, 126, 146, 153, 156, 161]
Crime, committed by multiple-offenders, p. 76, [123]
Crime, committed by single-offenders, p. 89, [149]
Crime, committed by strangers, p. 51, 54, 94, [87, 92,
156]
Crime, defendant detention rate, p. 68, [109]
Crime, economic loss, p. 57, 88, 92, [96, 146, 153]
Crime, educational level of victims, p. 49, 50, [85, 86]
Crime, federal, p. 68, [109]
Crime, federal offenses, p. 68, [110]
Crime, homicide, p. 74, 78, 93, [119, 120, 128, 155]
Crime, hospitalization caused by, p. 69, [111]
Crime, households victimized, p. 72, [116]
Crime, injury caused by, p. 78, 89, [126, 149]
Crime, juvenile, p. 95, [158]
Crime, larceny, p. 66, [107]
Crime, manslaughter, p. 78, 93, [128, 155]
Crime, motor vehicle theft, p. 88, 93, [146, 154]
Crime, motor vehicle thefts, p. 87, [144]
Crime, multiple-offenders, p. 94, [157]
Crime, of violence, p. 76, 89, [123, 149]
Crime, offender-victim, p. 93, [155]
Crime, offender-victim race, p. 76, 89, [123, 149]
Crime, offender/victim race, p. 94, [157]
Crime, rate, p. 91, [152]
Crime, reports to police, p. 51, [87]
Crime, residence-area of victims, p. 52, 75, [89, 121,
122]
Crime, robbery and assault, p. 78, [126]

Crime, robbery/theft, p. 88, 92, [146, 153]

Crime, theft, p. 67, [108]

Crime, types, p. 49, 50, 51, 52, 54, 57, 63, 64, 65, 66, 70, 75, 75, 81, 82, 91, 96, [85, 86, 87, 88, 89, 90, 92, 96, 102, 103, 105, 106, 113, 114, 121, 122, 133, 134, 151, 152, 161]

Crime, unreported to police, p. 63, 64, [102, 103]

Crime, victim self-protective measures, p. 52, [88]

Crime, victims, p. 95, [158, 159]

Crime, victims' household tenure, p. 70, [114]

Crime, violent, p. 95, [158, 159]

Crime, work-time lost due to, p. 96, [161]

Death expectancy, p. 661, [944]

Death penalty, attitudes toward, p. 17, 18, 19, 25, 26, [36, 38, 40, 53, 55]

Death penalty, executions, p. 62, [100]

Death penalty, women executed, p. 61, [99]

Death rates, p. 625, 636, 637, 639, [902, 918, 919, 922, 923]

Death rates, age-adjusted, p. 623, [901]

Death rates, AIDS, p. 680, [966]

Death rates, fetal, p. 650, [932]

Death rates, from breast malignancies, p. 647, [929]

Death rates, from cerebrovascular diseases, p. 641, [925]

Death rates, from heart disease, p. 642, [926]

Death rates, from malignant neoplasms, p. 644, [927]

Death rates, homicide, p. 652, [933]

Death rates, infant, p. 655, 677, [937, 962]

Death rates, legal intervention, p. 652, [933]

Death rates, maternal, p. 669, [954]

Death rates, motor vehicle accidents, p. 646, [928]

Death rates, neonatal, p. 671, [958]

Death rates, postneonatal mortality, p. 658, [941]

Death rates, suicide, p. 635, [917]

Deaths, p. 636, 637, 639, 640, [918, 919, 922, 923, 924]

Deaths by accident, p. 637, [919]

Deaths by suicide, p. 638, [920, 921]

Deaths by violence, p. 637, [919]

Deaths of infants, p. 648, [930]

Deaths, causes of, p. 623, [901]

Deaths, characteristics of, p. 636, 640, [918, 924]

Deaths, infant, p. 654, 657, [934, 935, 938]

Deaths, maternal, p. 654, [934]

Deaths, neonatal, p. 654, [934]

Deaths, suicide, p. 678, [963]

Death, accidental, p. 671, [957]

Death, infant, p. 657, [939]

Death, leading causes, p. 660, [943]

Death, motor vehicle, p. 671, [957]

Degrees awarded, bachelor's, p. 113, 159, 587, [186, 255, 852]

Degrees awarded, business/management, p. 113, [186]

Degrees awarded, doctorates, p. 555, 559, [809, 810, 816]

Degrees awarded, education, p. 113, [186]

Degrees awarded, engineering, p. 559, 587, 590, [816, 852, 856]

Degrees awarded, fields, p. 159, 222, 223, [255, 336, 337]

Degrees awarded, higher education, p. 200, [305]

Degrees awarded, level, p. 200, [305]

Degrees awarded, master's, p. 590, [856]

Degrees awarded, science, p. 559, 587, 590, [816, 852, 856]

Degrees awarded, UNCF institutions, p. 137, [225]

Degrees conferred, associate, p. 158, [254]

Degrees conferred, bachelor's, p. 111, 215, 235, [184, 327, 354]

Degrees conferred, Doctor of Philosophy, p. 208, [317]

Degrees conferred, doctoral, p. 161, [256]

Degrees conferred, doctorates, p. 99, 100, 119, 140, 162, 190, 208, 216, 232, 237, [165, 166, 195, 228, 257, 297, 318, 328, 350, 356]

Degrees conferred, doctorates in education, p. 140, [229]

Degrees conferred, education, p. 171, 238, [269, 357]

Degrees conferred, engineering, p. 560, 594, 596, 597, [817, 863, 864, 865]

Degrees conferred, fields, p. 161, [256]

Degrees conferred, fields of study, p. 158, [254]

Degrees conferred, first-professional, p. 562, [821]

Degrees conferred, HBCUs, p. 171, [268]

Degrees conferred, higher education, p. 251, [375]

Degrees conferred, in education, p. 113, [187]

Degrees conferred, law, p. 580, [837]

Degrees conferred, master's, p. 204, 236, [312, 355]

Degrees conferred, medicine, p. 583, [842]

Degrees conferred, percent change, p. 221, [335]

Degrees conferred, physical science doctorates, p. 208, [318]

Degrees conferred, postsecondary, p. 209, [319]

Degrees conferred, social science doctorates, p. 237, [356]

Degrees, doctoral, p. 100, 136, 222, 246, [166, 224, 336, 368]

Degrees, fields of study, p. 209, [319]

Degrees, highest earned, p. 187, [291]

Degrees, master's, p. 223, [337]

Degrees, of medical school faculty, p. 554, [808]

Degrees, science and engineering, p. 136, [224]

Delegates to conventions, p. 477, [705]

Democratic conventions, p. 477, [705]

Dentistry, p. 562, [821]

Dentistry, enrollment, p. 586, 587, 593, [849, 850, 860]

Dentistry, professional care, p. 329, [483]

Diabetes, p. 333, [492]
Diabetes, in adults, p. 299, [443]
Disabled workers, p. 610, [882]
Diseases, p. 324, [476]
Diseases, cerebrovascular, p. 641, [925]
Diseases, heart, p. 642, [926]
Divorced persons, p. 632, [915]
Divorced persons, comparative data, p. 632, [915]
Doctorate recipients, characteristics, p. 119, [195]
Doctorates, baccalaureate origins of recipients, p. 110, [183]
Doctorates, citizenship of recipients, p. 555, [809, 810]
Doctorates, college faculty, p. 251, [376]
Doctorates, degrees awarded, p. 555, [809, 810]
Doctorates, degrees conferred, p. 99, 100, 140, 216, [165, 166, 228, 328]
Doctorates, engineering, p. 560, [817]
Doctorates, fields of recipients, p. 162, [257]
Doctorates, fields of study, p. 99, [165]
Doctorates, in education, p. 140, [229]
Doctorates, institutions awarding degrees, p. 249, [372]
Doctorates, science, p. 232, [350]
Doctorates, science and engineering, p. 555, [809, 810]
Doctorates, time to degree, p. 246, [368]
Drugs, abuse, p. 7, 18, [14, 37]
Drugs, and crime, p. 8, [17]
Drugs, and teenagers, p. 18, [37]
Drugs, arrests for, p. 68, [110]
Drugs, attitudes toward dealers, p. 20, [42]
Drugs, heroin, p. 367, [540]
Drugs, use by prisoners, p. 56, [95]
Earnings, black/white ratios, p. 454, [673]
Earnings, of families, p. 426, [630]
Earnings, weekly, p. 454, [673]
Education, p. 1, 2, 3, 4, 5, 6, 8, 10, 15, 17, 18, 23, 24, 267, 272, 288, 309, 382, 391, 392, 397, 400, 403, 442, 462, 465, 470, 549, 551, 552, 554, 556, 558, 559, 561, 562, 563, 564, 565, 567, 569, 571, 573, 575, 576, 579, 580, 581, 581, 582, 583, 584, 585, 586, 587, 589, 590, 592, 593, 594, 596, 597, 598, 600, 601, 602, 618, 619, 620, 629, [1, 2, 5, 6, 7, 10, 12, 16, 23, 31, 35, 39, 48, 49, 52, 396, 403, 430, 461, 559, 575, 577, 587, 591, 594, 655, 686, 687, 689, 700, 800, 803, 804, 805, 808, 811, 812, 813, 814, 815, 816, 820, 821, 822, 823, 826, 828, 829, 830, 831, 832, 833, 836, 837, 838, 839, 840, 841, 842, 843, 845, 846, 849, 850, 852, 854, 856, 859, 861, 863, 864, 865, 866, 867, 868, 869, 870, 896, 897, 898, 899, 909]
Educational attainment, p. 564, [824]
Educational attainment, and age, p. 106, [176]
Educational attainment, and income, p. 382, 391, [559, 575]
Educational attainment, and individual characteristics, p. 219, [331]
Educational attainment, and poverty, p. 384, 401, [561, 593]
Educational attainment, and poverty rate, p. 403, [594]
Educational attainment, and poverty status, p. 106, 267, [176, 396]
Educational attainment, and type of family, p. 267, [396]
Educational attainment, arrestees, p. 60, [97]
Educational attainment, at age 18 and over, p. 142, [232]
Educational attainment, by region, p. 218, 219, [330, 331]
Educational attainment, college completion rates, p. 122, [199]
Educational attainment, crime victims, p. 49, 50, [85, 86]
Educational attainment, dental school graduates, p. 586, 587, [849, 850]
Educational attainment, Doctor of Philosophy, p. 208, [317]
Educational attainment, doctorates, p. 119, 216, [195, 328]
Educational attainment, high school and beyond, p. 169, [265]
Educational attainment, high school graduates, p. 141, 143, 462, [231, 233, 686]
Educational attainment, high school graduates, change in percent, p. 144, [234]
Educational attainment, highest degree earned, p. 187, [291]
Educational attainment, highest educational level, p. 187, [291]
Educational attainment, householders, p. 272, [403]
Educational attainment, individual, p. 397, [587]
Educational attainment, law school graduates, p. 564, [823]
Educational attainment, medical school graduates, p. 581, 582, [840, 841]
Educational attainment, of medical school faculty, p. 554, [808]
Educational attainment, postsecondary, p. 98, [164]
Educational attainment, postsecondary degrees, p. 209, [319]
Educational attainment, prisoners, p. 84, [139]
Educational attainment, young adults, p. 259, [384]
Education, achievement/aptitude, p. 104, 107, 113, 115, 119, 120, 133, 134, 182, 206, 213, 214, 216, 226, 227, 228, 229, 233, 252, 256, [173, 177, 178, 188, 192, 194, 196, 218, 219, 220, 284, 314, 325, 326, 329, 340, 341, 342, 344, 345, 351, 377, 381]
Education, adult, p. 106, [175]
Education, advanced placement tests, p. 256, [380]

Education, attitudes toward, p. 18, [39]
Education, basic skills, p. 260, 288, [385, 430]
Education, characteristics of participants, p. 106, [175]
Education, children after-school, p. 263, [391]
Education, college freshmen, p. 24, 242, 243, 246, [52, 364, 365, 366, 367]
Education, college resources, p. 202, [308]
Education, computer exposure, p. 239, [359]
Education, continuing, p. 101, [168]
Education, degrees awarded, p. 159, 200, 559, 590, [255, 305, 816, 856]
Education, degrees conferred, p. 100, 161, 221, [166, 256, 335]
Education, doctoral degrees, p. 246, [368]
Education, doctorates, p. 100, 222, [166, 336]
Education, eighth grade school attendance patterns, p. 228, [343]
Education, enrollment, p. 589, [854]
Education, financial aid to college students, p. 164, [259]
Education, high school, p. 219, [332]
Education, high school courses taken, p. 176, [276]
Education, high school curricula, p. 254, [378]
Education, high school dropouts, p. 177, 178, [278, 279]
Education, high school graduates, p. 98, 125, 179, 180, 181, 210, [163, 204, 280, 281, 282, 283, 320]
Education, high school students, p. 135, [222]
Education, level of, p. 191, 193, 194, 196, 198, 199, 259, [298, 299, 300, 301, 302, 303, 384]
Education, literacy, p. 203, [310]
Education, majors/career choices, p. 107, [178]
Education, master's degrees, p. 223, [337]
Education, of eighth graders, p. 1, [1]
Education, postdoctorates, p. 591, [857]
Education, secondary school principals, p. 234, [352]
Education, student, p. 565, [826]
Education, teacher competency, p. 240, [361]
Education, vocational, p. 101, [168]
Elderly, p. 530, [772]
Elderly population, p. 517, [753]
Elected officials, p. 481, 483, 484, 485, 488, 496, 499, 500, 501, [712, 713, 714, 715, 718, 719, 728, 731, 732, 733]
Elected officials by office, p. 487, [716, 717]
Elected officials by region, p. 487, [716, 717]
Elected officials, changes in, p. 499, 500, [731, 732]
Elected officials, characteristics of, p. 481, 483, 484, 485, 488, 489, [712, 713, 714, 715, 718, 720]
Elected officials, distribution of, p. 481, 483, 484, 485, 487, 488, [712, 713, 714, 715, 716, 717, 718, 719]
Elected officials, female, p. 488, 490, 491, 492, 494, 495, 496, [719, 722, 723, 724, 725, 726, 727, 728]
Elected officials, geographical distribution, p. 489, [721]

Elected officials, growth of, p. 496, [728]
Elected officials, male, p. 488, 496, [719, 728]
Elected officials, male and female, p. 488, 496, [719, 728]
Elected officials, percentage of, p. 501, [733]
Elementary/secondary students, computer use, p. 145, [235]
Employed females, p. 431, [637]
Employed males, p. 453, [670]
Employed workers, p. 425, [627, 628]
Employed workers, distribution of, p. 425, [627, 628]
Employees, characteristics of, p. 292, [435]
Employees, federal, p. 293, [436]
Employees, law enforcement, p. 78, 79, 89, 90, [127, 129, 148, 150]
Employees, length of service, p. 415, [614]
Employees, state and local government, p. 292, [435]
Employment, p. 416, 423, 424, 425, 429, 432, 437, 449, 450, 451, [615, 624, 625, 627, 628, 634, 639, 647, 663, 665, 666]
Employment benefits, p. 610, [883]
Employment rates, characteristics of, p. 417, 418, [616, 617]
Employment rates, trends in, p. 417, 418, [616, 617]
Employment ratios, p. 430, [635]
Employment status, p. 435, [643]
Employment, college & university faculty, p. 132, [215]
Employment, colleges & universities, p. 115, [191]
Employment, distribution, p. 415, [614]
Employment, engineers, p. 584, 587, 592, 593, [845, 851, 859, 861]
Employment, family, p. 274, 278, [405, 414]
Employment, high school dropouts, p. 462, [687]
Employment, high school graduates, p. 254, [379]
Employment, householders, p. 272, [403]
Employment, individual, p. 397, [587]
Employment, industry and acute conditions, p. 325, [479]
Employment, industry and chronic health conditions, p. 335, [495]
Employment, industry and disability days, p. 319, [471]
Employment, leaders in, p. 32, [63]
Employment, maternal, p. 261, 282, [387, 422]
Employment, of participants in education, p. 101, [168]
Employment, private industries, p. 446, [660]
Employment, rates of, p. 434, [641]
Employment, scientists, p. 584, 587, 592, 593, [845, 851, 859, 861]
Employment, scientists/engineers, p. 592, [858]
Employment, work-loss days, p. 368, [541]
Employment, years of, p. 415, [614]
Energy, mean intake, p. 327, [481]
Engineering, p. 560, [817]

Engineering, degrees, p. 561, [818]

Engineering, degrees awarded, p. 559, 587, 590, [816, 852, 856]

Engineering, females in, p. 561, [819]

Engineering, fields, p. 561, [818]

Engineering, foreign national enrollment, p. 145, [236]

Engineering, freshmen, p. 583, [843]

Engineering, graduate enrollment, p. 589, [854]

Engineering, graduate students, p. 567, 569, 571, 575, 576, [828, 829, 830, 832, 833]

Engineering, graduates, p. 567, 583, [827, 843]

Engineering, HBCUs, p. 561, [819]

Engineering, minority enrollment, p. 145, [236]

Engineering, postdoctorates, p. 591, [857]

Engineering, support for graduate students, p. 565, [826]

Engineering, women enrollment, p. 145, [236]

Engineering, workers, p. 584, [844]

Engineers, college faculty, p. 551, 552, 558, 559, 602, [803, 804, 805, 814, 815, 870]

Engineers, employment, p. 584, 587, 592, 593, [845, 851, 859, 861]

Engineers, experience, p. 586, 603, 604, [848, 872, 874]

Engineers, fields, p. 561, 593, [820, 861]

Engineers, salaries, p. 588, [853]

Engineers, women, p. 561, [820]

Engineers, work activity, p. 602, 604, 605, [871, 873, 875]

Enrollment, p. 147, 148, 154, 231, [240, 241, 248, 348]

Enrollment, 4-year colleges, p. 98, [163]

Enrollment, by state of higher education institution, p. 184, [287]

Enrollment, by student disability status, p. 139, [226]

Enrollment, by type of institution, p. 153, [247]

Enrollment, characteristics of, p. 146, 231, [237, 238, 348]

Enrollment, college, p. 114, 123, 124, 125, 126, 176, 254, [189, 190, 202, 203, 205, 206, 275, 379]

Enrollment, college students, p. 151, 169, [245, 266]

Enrollment, colleges, p. 146, 148, [237, 238, 241]

Enrollment, colleges & universities, p. 115, 125, 165, 167, 186, 201, 220, 247, 258, 462, [193, 204, 261, 263, 289, 306, 333, 334, 369, 383, 686]

Enrollment, dental school, p. 556, 598, [811, 812, 813, 867]

Enrollment, dental students, p. 593, [860]

Enrollment, elementary school, p. 144, 150, [234, 244]

Enrollment, engineering, p. 589, [854]

Enrollment, for ages 3-34, p. 230, [347]

Enrollment, graduate, p. 565, 589, [825, 854, 855]

Enrollment, high school, p. 148, [241]

Enrollment, higher education, p. 139, 148, 153, 182, 183, 184, 185, 202, [226, 242, 247, 285, 286, 287, 288, 307]

Enrollment, in health occupation programs, p. 309, [461]

Enrollment, in independent colleges, p. 151, [245]

Enrollment, in schools of business, p. 110, [182]

Enrollment, K-12, p. 189, [295]

Enrollment, law school, p. 564, 579, [823, 824, 836]

Enrollment, males, p. 154, [248]

Enrollment, medical school, p. 563, 578, 579, 581, 585, 598, [822, 834, 835, 839, 846, 866]

Enrollment, postsecondary, p. 210, [320]

Enrollment, preprimary, p. 147, 232, [239, 240, 349]

Enrollment, programs for gifted/talented students, p. 149, [243]

Enrollment, public school, p. 212, [324]

Enrollment, science, p. 589, [854]

Enrollment, science/engineering, p. 565, 589, [825, 855]

Enrollment, science/engineering, graduate students, p. 573, 576, [831, 833]

Enrollment, secondary school, p. 144, 150, [234, 244]

EOEIs, p. 115, 155, 176, 186, [191, 249, 275, 290]

Faculty tenure status, p. 128, [210]

Families, p. 373, 448, 530, 544, 545, 609, [547, 662, 773, 773, 793, 794, 880]

Families in poverty, p. 283, 287, [423, 428]

Families with children, p. 271, 530, [401, 773]

Families, adopted children, p. 290, [434]

Families, by region, p. 288, [431]

Families, characteristics, p. 273, 288, 517, [404, 431, 754]

Families, child abuse, p. 262, [388]

Families, economic characteristics of, p. 522, [762]

Families, employment, p. 274, 278, [405, 414]

Families, extended, p. 266, [395]

Families, father-absence, p. 262, 279, 282, [389, 416, 421]

Families, in poverty, p. 267, [397]

Families, income, p. 261, 268, 270, 275, 276, 278, 289, 380, 381, 384, 390, 391, [386, 398, 400, 407, 408, 409, 413, 432, 556, 557, 562, 574, 576]

Families, income, p. 392, 393, 411, [577, 580, 608]

Families, mothers who work, p. 261, 282, [387, 422]

Families, parents in household, p. 279, [417]

Families, parents not in household, p. 264, [392]

Families, poverty, p. 287, 411, [429, 608]

Families, residence area, p. 289, [433]

Families, size of, p. 269, [399]

Families, social class, p. 277, [410, 411]

Families, sources of wealth, p. 410, [605]

Families, structure, p. 277, [411, 412]

Families, type, p. 273, 278, 279, 288, [404, 414, 415, 431]

Families, unemployment, p. 274, 276, 278, [405, 408, 414]

Families, with computers, p. 239, [359]

Families, with young mothers, p. 288, [430]

Families, with young parents, p. 260, [385]

Family, p. 232, 308, 309, 379, 380, 381, 384, 390, 391, 392, 393, 405, [349, 457, 459, 460, 554, 556, 557, 562, 574, 576, 577, 580, 599]

Family, p. 406, 410, 411, 426, [600, 605, 607, 608, 630]

Family earnings, p. 426, [630]

Family earnings, median weekly, p. 426, [630]

Family groups, p. 272, [402]

Family income, p. 264, 265, 275, 281, [393, 394, 406, 419, 420]

Family, characteristics, p. 272, [403]

Family, poverty status, p. 406, [600]

Fats, mean intake, p. 327, [481]

Female officials, distribution of, p. 490, 491, 492, 494, 495, [722, 723, 724, 725, 726, 727]

Female officials, growth in, p. 497, [729]

Females, employed, p. 431, [637]

Females, unemployed, p. 459, 460, [681, 682]

Fertility rates, p. 628, 629, 649, [907, 909, 931]

Finances, colleges & universities, p. 188, [293]

Financial institutions, p. 32, 34, [62, 66]

Firearms, attitudes toward, p. 10, [22]

Football, award winners, p. 614, [887]

Football, NFL draft, p. 618, [895]

Government, federal, p. 156, 157, [252, 253]

Grades K-12, percent change in enrollment, p. 150, [244]

HBCUs, p. 114, 115, 120, 166, 171, 172, 173, 174, 175, 176, 186, 188, 189, 190, 202, 238, 248, 465, 553, 556, 561, 567, 569, 573, 575, 576, 578, 579, 598, 600, 601, [190, 191, 197, 262, 268, 269, 270, 271, 272, 273, 274, 275, 290, 292, 294, 297, 308, 357, 370, 689, 806, 813, 818, 827, 828, 829, 831, 832, 833, 834, 835, 867, 868, 869]

HBCUs-Historically Black Colleges & Universities, p. 561, [818]

Health, p. 24, 56, 619, [51, 95, 897]

Health and medical care, p. 469, 470, 670, [696, 697, 698, 699, 955]

Health conditions, activity limitations, p. 309, 359, [460, 527]

Health conditions, activity limitations due to, p. 311, 335, 336, [462, 495, 496]

Health conditions, acute, p. 295, 296, 297, 298, 325, 348, [438, 439, 440, 441, 479, 511]

Health conditions, AIDS, p. 24, 302, 315, 339, 340, 362, [51, 447, 466, 498, 499, 501, 534]

Health conditions, blood pressure, p. 304, 324, [451, 478]

Health conditions, cancer, p. 301, 304, 305, 306, 307, 330, [445, 446, 450, 452, 453, 454, 455, 456, 484]

Health conditions, cholesterol, p. 341, [502]

Health conditions, chronic, p. 311, 312, 335, 336, 346, [462, 463, 495, 496, 509]

Health conditions, diabetes, p. 299, [443]

Health conditions, disability due to, p. 320, [472]

Health conditions, disability due to work, p. 319, [471]

Health conditions, drug use/abuse, p. 619, [897]

Health conditions, heart disease, p. 299, [442]

Health conditions, hypertension, p. 340, 364, [500, 535]

Health conditions, overweight, p. 318, 328, 350, [469, 482, 513]

Health conditions, self-assessment, p. 298, [441]

Health conditions, smoking, p. 312, 314, 315, 361, [464, 465, 467, 531]

Health examinations, amniocentesis, p. 302, [448]

Health examinations, characteristics, p. 330, [485]

Health insurance, p. 331, [486]

Health insurance, of unemployed workers, p. 332, [490]

Health occupations, p. 427, [631]

Health occupations, choice of, p. 309, [461]

Health occupations, employment in, p. 427, [631]

Health practices, characteristics of, p. 333, [491]

Health, activity limitations due to, p. 312, 324, [463, 477]

Health, bed days, p. 294, [437]

Health, characteristics of hospitalized persons, p. 303, 317, 338, 344, [449, 468, 497, 506]

Health, children's health ratings, p. 308, [458]

Health, children's physician visits, p. 309, [459]

Health, cholesterol intake, p. 327, [481]

Health, dental care, p. 329, [483]

Health, disability due to, p. 321, [473]

Health, energy, p. 327, [481]

Health, fat intake, p. 327, [481]

Health, hospital discharges, p. 323, 338, 344, 358, [475, 497, 506, 525]

Health, hospitalization, p. 303, 317, 326, 338, 344, 349, [449, 468, 480, 497, 506, 512]

Health, insurance, p. 332, [489]

Health, insurance coverage, p. 308, 331, 332, 366, [457, 487, 488, 538]

Health, medical care, p. 345, [507]

Health, nutritional deficiencies, p. 342, 345, [503, 504, 508]

Health, of the elderly, p. 361, [530]

Health, physical fitness, p. 469, 470, [696, 697, 698, 699]

Health, prenatal care, p. 352, 353, [518, 519]

Health, professional care, p. 326, 349, 357, 365, 366, [480, 512, 524, 537, 539]

Health, self-assessment, p. 317, 323, 334, 335, 358, 360, 366, [468, 475, 493, 494, 525, 528, 539]

Health, work-loss due to, p. 368, [541]

Heart disease, risk factors, p. 299, [442]

Heroin, use, p. 367, [540]

High school dropouts, employment status, p. 462, [687]
High school dropouts, labor force status, p. 177, [278]
High school dropouts, percent, p. 178, [279]
High school dropouts, unemployed, p. 456, [675]
High school graduates, college enrollment, p. 98, [163]
High school graduates, credits, p. 179, 180, 181, [280, 281, 282, 283]
High school graduates, educational attainment, p. 98, 141, 143, [164, 231, 233]
High school graduates, employment, p. 254, [379]
High school graduates, employment of, p. 430, [636]
High school graduates, postsecondary enrollment, p. 210, [320]
High school graduates, socioeconomic status, p. 141, [231]
High school graduates, unemployed, p. 456, [675]
High school seniors, attitudes, p. 11, 12, 13, 14, [24, 25, 26, 27, 28, 29, 30]
High school students, courses, p. 135, [222]
High school, advanced courses, p. 225, [338]
High school, curricula, p. 254, [378]
High school, graduation rates, p. 219, [332]
High school, remedial courses, p. 225, [338]
High school, science/mathematics credits, p. 177, [277]
Higher education, degrees awarded, p. 200, [305]
Higher education, degrees conferred, p. 251, [375]
Higher education, enrollment, p. 182, 183, 185, [285, 286, 288]
Hispanic population, characteristics of, p. 522, [762]
Historically Black Colleges & Universities, p. 115, 156, 157, 594, 596, 597, [193, 252, 253, 863, 864, 865]
History, achievement/aptitude, p. 104, [173]
Homeless, p. 609, [880]
Homeless in cities, p. 609, [880]
Homicide, p. 88, 652, [147, 933]
Homicides, race of victims, p. 61, [98]
Homicide, of law enforcement officers, p. 74, [119, 120]
Hospitalization, and employment industry, p. 326, [480]
Hospitalization, and occupational category, p. 349, [512]
Hospitalization, characteristics, p. 361, [529]
Hospitalization, payment of bills, p. 362, [532]
Households, Black, p. 533, [777, 778]
Households, characteristics of, p. 262, 372, 531, 532, [390, 546, 775, 776]
Households, Hispanic, p. 533, [777, 778]
Households, income, p. 380, 381, 390, 392, [556, 557, 574, 577]
Households, race of, p. 518, [756]
Households, victimized by crime, p. 72, [116]
Household, value of, p. 389, 390, [572, 573]
Housing, p. 372, 528, [546, 770]
Housing units, characteristics of, p. 370, 371, [543, 544, 545]
Housing units, occupied, p. 374, [549]
Housing units, trends in occupancy, p. 374, [549]
Housing, characteristics of, p. 375, [550]
Housing, occupied, p. 375, 377, [550, 553]
Housing, of children, p. 373, [547, 548]
Housing, owner-occupied, p. 369, 370, [542, 544]
Housing, segregated, p. 376, [551, 552]
Housing, value and rent, p. 377, [553]
Hypertension, in adults, p. 340, 364, [500, 535]
Illiteracy, male, p. 204, [311]
Income, p. 64, 65, 66, 67, 106, 128, 225, 250, 267, 268, 270, 272, 278, 294, 297, 303, 311, 334, 338, 344, 357, 359, 360, 368, 592, [104, 105, 106, 107, 108, 176, 209, 339, 374, 396, 397, 398, 400, 403, 413, 437, 440, 449, 462, 493, 497, 506, 524, 527, 528, 541, 858]
Income and wealth, p. 265, 275, 281, [394, 406, 419, 420]
Income comparisons, p. 395, [584]
Income, absence of earnings, p. 400, [590]
Income, aggregate, p. 392, [579]
Income, and educational attainment, p. 382, [559]
Income, and health, p. 294, 295, 297, 303, 311, 344, 357, 359, 360, [437, 438, 440, 449, 462, 506, 524, 527, 528]
Income, and health self-assessment, p. 334, [493]
Income, and work-days lost, p. 368, [541]
Income, black:white ratio, p. 396, 407, [586, 601]
Income, by educational attainment, p. 391, [575]
Income, by family type, p. 391, [576]
Income, by region, p. 268, 278, 396, 407, 408, [398, 413, 586, 601, 602]
Income, characteristics of, p. 381, 383, 386, 387, 388, 389, 394, [558, 560, 565, 566, 567, 568, 569, 570, 571, 583]
Income, comparisons, p. 411, [609]
Income, deficit, p. 393, [580, 581]
Income, distribution characteristics, p. 392, [578]
Income, distribution of, p. 264, 265, 394, [393, 394, 582]
Income, economic vulnerability, p. 410, [606]
Income, engineers, p. 588, [853]
Income, families, p. 267, 268, 270, 275, 276, 379, 390, 407, [396, 398, 400, 407, 409, 554, 574, 601]
Income, family, p. 272, 278, 380, 381, 384, 392, 393, 411, [403, 413, 556, 557, 562, 577, 580, 608]
Income, full-time workers, p. 385, [563]
Income, gaps, p. 392, 395, [579, 585]
Income, household, p. 380, 381, 407, [556, 557, 601]
Income, in selected southern states, p. 399, [589]
Income, individual, p. 380, 381, 393, 397, 398, 411, 414, [556, 557, 581, 587, 588, 608, 613]
Income, married-couples, p. 261, [386]
Income, median, p. 289, [432]
Income, of burglary victims, p. 64, [104]

Income, of crime victims, p. 65, 66, 94, [105, 106, 156]
Income, of families, p. 289, [432]
Income, of full-time workers, p. 385, [564]
Income, of larceny victims, p. 66, [107]
Income, of theft victims, p. 67, [108]
Income, of wage/salary workers, p. 412, [610]
Income, of year-round workers, p. 385, [564]
Income, parents, p. 400, [591]
Income, per capita, p. 379, 392, 395, [554, 579, 585]
Income, poverty, p. 106, 267, 272, 384, 393, 397, 398, 403, 405, 411, 414, [176, 396, 403, 562, 580, 581, 587, 588, 594, 599, 608, 613]
Income, poverty rates, p. 401, 403, 405, 409, 410, [592, 595, 598, 603, 604, 606, 607]
Income, poverty status, p. 380, 384, 401, [555, 561, 593]
Income, regional, p. 289, 409, [432, 603]
Income, scientists, p. 588, [853]
Income, scientists/engineers, p. 592, [858]
Income, source, p. 395, [585]
Income, spending, and wealth, p. 376, [551]
Income, total money, p. 278, 390, 408, [413, 574, 602]
Income, type, p. 411, [609]
Income, wealth, p. 413, [611, 612]
Income, weekly, p. 395, 412, [584, 610]
Income, year-round workers, p. 385, [563]
Industrial companies, p. 39, [74]
Industrial service companies, p. 36, [70]
Industries, characteristics of employees, p. 427, 428, [632, 633]
Industries, employment in, p. 427, 428, [632, 633]
Industries, occupations in, p. 453, [671]
Industries, types of, p. 36, [69]
Industry, p. 432, [639]
Infant feeding, p. 655, [936]
Infant mortality, p. 658, [940]
Infant mortality rates, p. 648, [930]
Infants, death rates, p. 655, 677, [937, 962]
Infants, premature, p. 674, [960]
Inmates, criminal history, p. 81, [132]
Insurance companies, p. 29, 33, [59, 65]
Insurance companies, leading, p. 38, [72]
Insurance companies, ranked, p. 38, [72]
Insurance, health, p. 331, 332, 366, [486, 489, 490, 538]
Insurance, type of health coverage, p. 331, 332, [487, 488]
Interracial dating, attitudes toward, p. 5, [9]
Intervention, legal, p. 652, [933]
Jail inmates, p. 81, [131]
Judges, p. 478, [707]
Judges, characteristics of, p. 498, [730]
Judges, federal, p. 498, 502, [730, 734]
Judges, federal appointees, p. 498, 502, [730, 734]
Judges, municipal, p. 477, [706]

Judges, regional distribution of, p. 477, [706]
Judges, state, p. 477, [706]
Justice system, attitudes toward, p. 11, 13, [24, 28]
Juveniles, confinement facilities, p. 63, [101]
Labor, p. 79, 90, 101, 170, 177, 234, 249, 254, 261, 272, 282, 368, 380, 384, 397, 401, 414, 467, 563, 584, 585, 592, 593, [129, 150, 168, 267, 278, 353, 372, 379, 387, 403, 422, 541, 555, 561, 587, 593, 613, 693, 822, 844, 845, 846, 858, 859, 861]
Labor and employment, p. 32, 34, 96, 115, 132, 293, 319, 320, 325, 335, 336, 348, 349, 419, 422, 427, 428, 431, 432, 439, 440, 443, 447, 450, 453, 459, 460, 463, 522, 581, [63, 66, 161, 191, 215, 436, 471, 472, 479, 495, 496, 511, 512, 618, 622, 632, 633, 637, 638, 650, 651, 657, 661, 664, 670, 681, 682, 683, 684, 688, 762, 840]
Labor force and unions, p. 451, 452, [667, 668]
Labor force, Black male, p. 433, [640]
Labor force, characteristics of, p. 415, 419, 421, 422, 426, 434, 437, 441, 444, 447, 448, [614, 620, 621, 622, 629, 641, 642, 647, 653, 658, 661, 662]
Labor force, civilian, p. 424, 435, 449, 450, 451, [625, 643, 663, 665, 666]
Labor force, composition of, p. 442, [654]
Labor force, distribution, p. 445, 446, [659, 660]
Labor force, earnings, p. 441, [652]
Labor force, educational level, p. 434, [642]
Labor force, employment, p. 441, [652]
Labor force, ethnic composition, p. 442, [654]
Labor force, full-time, p. 447, [661]
Labor force, high school graduates, p. 462, [686]
Labor force, participation rates, p. 441, [653]
Labor force, part-time, p. 447, [661]
Labor force, projections in, p. 442, [654]
Labor force, racial composition, p. 442, [654]
Labor force, status of high school dropouts, p. 177, [278]
Labor union members, p. 451, 452, [667, 668]
Law, p. 562, [821]
Law enforcement, attitudes toward, p. 7, [15]
Law enforcement, cases litigated, p. 46, [81]
Law enforcement, employees, p. 78, 79, 89, 90, [127, 129, 148, 150]
Law enforcement, executions, p. 61, [98]
Law enforcement, officers slain, p. 74, [120]
Law enforcement, prisoners, p. 81, [133]
Law enforcement, probationers, p. 81, [133]
Law school applicants, p. 554, [807]
Lawyers, attitudes toward, p. 22, [46]
Legal justice, attitudes toward, p. 7, [15]
Legal justice, prison terms, p. 82, [134]
Legislators, p. 480, [711]
Legislators, distribution of, p. 480, [711]
Leisure activities, p. 585, [847]

Life expectancy, p. 661, 663, 664, 665, [944, 946, 947, 948]

Life table values, characteristics of, p. 662, [945]

Literacy, in young adults, p. 203, [310]

Live births, p. 632, 667, [914, 952]

Live births and prenatal care, p. 667, [952]

Live births, weights, p. 667, [952]

Living arrangements, p. 534, 535, [779, 780]

Males, p. 454, 536, [673, 783]

Males, employed, p. 453, [670]

Males, unemployed, p. 460, [683, 684]

Marriages, interracial, p. 535, [781]

Married persons, p. 521, [760]

Married women, childbirth expectations, p. 668, [953]

Mathematics, p. 134, [219, 220]

Mathematics, achievement/aptitude, p. 103, 104, 119, 227, 228, [171, 173, 194, 342, 344]

Mathematics, courses taken, p. 135, [222]

Mathematics, high school credits, p. 177, [277]

Mathematics, proficiency, p. 206, [314]

Mayors, p. 476, 478, [704, 708]

Medicaid recipients and payments, p. 609, [881]

Medical care, not received, p. 345, [507]

Medicine, p. 562, [821]

Medicine, applicants to medical school, p. 553, 563, 585, [806, 822, 846]

Medicine, characteristics of medical school faculty, p. 554, [808]

Men married, characteristics, p. 536, [782]

Mental health, age of inpatients, p. 300, [444]

Mental health, diagnoses, p. 343, 354, [505, 520]

Mental health, duration of hospital stay, p. 343, [505]

Mental health, facility types, p. 300, 343, 354, 355, 356, [444, 505, 520, 521, 523]

Mental health, inpatient services, p. 300, 343, 354, 355, 356, [444, 505, 520, 521, 522, 523]

Mental health, Vietnam veterans, p. 364, [536]

Migration of males, p. 536, [783]

Migration rates, p. 536, [783]

Military, p. 364, 462, [536, 686]

Military, Army personnel, p. 466, [691]

Military, assumed regional population, p. 468, [695]

Military, Coast Guard personnel, p. 466, [692]

Military, enlisted personnel, p. 467, [693]

Military, enlistees, p. 462, [686]

Military, new service academy officers, p. 472, [702]

Military, officers, p. 465, 471, [689, 701]

Military, qualification for, p. 465, 467, [690, 694]

Military, selected characteristics of service academies, p. 470, [700]

Military, Vietnam veterans, p. 364, [536]

Minority employment, p. 427, 428, [632, 633]

Morbidity, indicators, p. 361, [530]

Mortality, p. 670, [955]

Mortality of children, p. 671, [956]

Mortality rates, p. 671, [956]

Mortality rates, infant, p. 655, 677, [937, 962]

Mortality rates, maternal, p. 669, [954]

Mortality rates, neonatal, p. 671, [958]

Mortality rates, postneonatal, p. 658, [941]

Mortality, decrease in, p. 670, [955]

Mortality, infant, p. 654, 657, [935, 938, 939]

Mothers, household heads, p. 282, [421]

Motor vehicle accidents, death rates, p. 646, [928]

NAACP, cases litigated, p. 46, [81]

National political conventions, p. 477, [705]

National problems, attitudes, p. 16, 17, [33, 34]

Neoplasms, malignant, p. 644, [927]

Neoplasms, malignant breast, p. 647, [929]

Non-marital birth rates, p. 628, [908]

Nursing home discharges, p. 347, [510]

Nursing homes, characteristics, p. 347, [510]

Nursing homes, discharges, p. 318, 322, 350, 351, [470, 474, 514, 515]

Nutrition, deficiencies, p. 342, 345, [503, 504, 508]

Occupational distribution of Blacks, p. 416, [615]

Occupations, p. 416, 419, 437, 445, 446, 450, [615, 619, 647, 659, 660, 664]

Occupations in industries, p. 453, [671]

Occupations, and acute conditions, p. 348, [511]

Occupations, and chronic health conditions, p. 336, [496]

Occupations, and disability days, p. 320, [472]

Occupations, college faculty, p. 127, 128, 155, 234, 249, [207, 208, 250, 353, 372]

Occupations, distribution of, p. 453, [671]

Occupations, eighth graders' expectations, p. 2, [2]

Occupations, enlisted military personnel, p. 467, [693]

Occupations, managerial, p. 419, [619]

Occupations, professional and technical, p. 419, [619]

Occupations, projected high growth, participation in, p. 454, [672]

Occupations, secondary school principals, p. 234, [352]

Occupations, teachers, p. 18, 210, [39, 321]

Officials, elected, p. 497, [729]

Older Americans, p. 530, [772]

Older population, living arrangements, p. 538, [785]

Organizations, joined voluntarily, p. 621, [900]

Parents, father-absence, p. 262, 279, [389, 416]

Parents, income, p. 400, [591]

Parents, not in household, p. 264, [392]

Parents, present in household, p. 279, [417]

PBIs, p. 120, [197]

PBIs, newer ones, p. 207, [315]

Pension plan, p. 610, [883]

Physical fitness, of Army personnel, p. 469, 470, [696,

697, 698, 699]

Physician contacts, patient characteristics, p. 352, [517]

Physicians, number, p. 563, 585, [822, 846]

Police, attitudes toward, p. 12, 14, 22, [25, 29, 47]

Police, knowledge of crimes, p. 78, 93, [128, 155]

Political participation, p. 478, [707]

Political participation, young adults, p. 26, [56]

Politics, p. 26, [56]

Population, p. 123, 124, 131, 230, 376, 468, 628, [202, 203, 214, 347, 552, 695, 907]

Population trends, p. 516, [752]

Population, age groups, p. 550, [801]

Population, age of, p. 519, 520, 526, 540, [757, 758, 768, 788, 789]

Population, age trends, p. 543, [792]

Population, annual change, p. 515, [751]

Population, assumed military, p. 468, [695]

Population, changes in, p. 541, [790]

Population, characteristics of, p. 522, 525, 526, 527, 536, 539, [762, 766, 767, 768, 769, 784, 786, 787]

Population, distribution of, p. 546, 547, [797, 798]

Population, divorced, p. 522, 524, [761, 763, 764]

Population, enrolled in school, p. 230, [347]

Population, growth of, p. 539, [787]

Population, location of, p. 546, [796]

Population, married, p. 522, 524, [761, 763]

Population, married persons, p. 524, [764]

Population, median age, p. 520, [759]

Population, metropolitan residents, p. 547, [799]

Population, nonmetropolitan residents, p. 547, [799]

Population, older persons, p. 525, [765]

Population, projections of, p. 531, 541, 542, 550, [774, 790, 791, 802]

Population, race of, p. 519, 520, 540, 550, [757, 758, 759, 788, 789, 801]

Population, regional concentration, p. 546, 547, [797, 798]

Population, residence of, p. 546, 547, [796, 799]

Population, resident, p. 519, 520, [757, 758, 759]

Population, school age, p. 549, [800]

Population, sex of, p. 519, 520, 540, 550, [757, 758, 759, 788, 789, 801]

Population, sex trends, p. 543, [792]

Population, single, p. 522, [761]

Population, trends in, p. 516, [752]

Population, unmarried, p. 539, [786]

Population, widowed, p. 522, [761]

Population, young adults, p. 550, [802]

Poverty, p. 404, 405, 545, [596, 597, 794]

Poverty level, characteristics of, p. 544, [793]

Poverty level, persons below, p. 544, [793]

Poverty, and area of residence, p. 409, [604]

Poverty, and educational attainment, p. 106, 267, 384,

401, 403, [176, 396, 561, 593, 594]

Poverty, and living arrangements, p. 410, [607]

Poverty, and the elderly, p. 401, 410, [592, 606]

Poverty, and type of family, p. 106, 267, [176, 396]

Poverty, children, p. 406, [600]

Poverty, children residing in area, p. 289, [433]

Poverty, families in, p. 267, 285, [397, 426]

Poverty, family, p. 406, 287, [600, 429]

Poverty, individual, p. 398, 411, [588, 608]

Poverty, individuals, p. 406, [600]

Poverty, of workers, p. 380, [555]

Poverty, older persons, p. 284, [424]

Poverty, persons in, p. 285, [425, 426]

Poverty, rates, p. 403, 405, 409, [595, 598, 599, 603, 604]

Poverty, rates of, p. 545, [794]

Poverty, status, p. 272, 410, 414, [403, 607, 613]

Poverty, threshold, p. 414, [613]

Predominantly Black Institutions, dates of establishment, p. 151, [246]

Predominantly Black Institutions, newer ones, p. 151, [246]

Prenatal care, first trimester, p. 353, [519]

Prison inmates, p. 80, [130]

Prisoners, p. 77, 81, [125, 131, 132]

Prisoners, arrests after release, p. 82, [135]

Prisoners, criminal history, p. 84, [138]

Prisoners, current offense, p. 54, [93]

Prisoners, drug use, p. 56, [95]

Prisoners, educational attainment, p. 84, [139]

Prisoners, executed, p. 61, 62, [99, 100]

Prisoners, facilities, p. 63, [101]

Prisoners, in California, p. 81, [133]

Prisoners, in state institutions, p. 96, [160]

Prisoners, jurisdiction, p. 73, [118]

Prisoners, juveniles, p. 63, [101]

Prisoners, parole outcomes, p. 77, [124]

Prisoners, recidivism rates, p. 83, 87, [136, 145]

Prisoners, sentence length, p. 86, [143]

Prisoners, state, p. 80, [130]

Prisoners, testing for AIDS, p. 24, [51]

Prisoners, time served, p. 86, [143]

Prisoners, under death sentence, p. 73, 83, [118, 137]

Prisoners, young adults, p. 87, [145]

Prisoners, youth, p. 54, 97, [93, 162]

Prisons, Death Row inmates, p. 56, [94]

Prisons, racial characteristics, p. 77, [125]

Prisons, racial composition, p. 72, [117]

Professional care, characteristics of hospital stay, p. 361, [529]

Professional care, dental, p. 326, 329, 349, [480, 483, 512]

Professional care, dentists, p. 365, [537]

Professional care, hospital discharges, p. 323, 338, 344,

358, [475, 497, 506, 525]

Professional care, hospitalization, p. 303, 317, 326, 338, 344, 349, [449, 468, 480, 497, 506, 512]

Professional care, medical, p. 325, 326, 348, 349, 352, 359, [479, 480, 511, 512, 517, 526]

Professional care, nursing homes, p. 318, 322, 350, 351, [470, 474, 514, 515, 516]

Professional care, personal home care, p. 351, [516]

Professional care, physician contacts, p. 352, 357, 359, 366, [517, 524, 526, 539]

Professional care, physician visits, p. 309, [459]

Professional care, physicians, p. 365, [537]

Professional care, short-stay hospitals, p. 361, [529]

Professions, p. 22, 202, 427, [46, 307, 631]

Professions, degrees conferred, p. 562, [821]

Professions, dentistry, p. 556, 586, 587, 593, 598, [811, 812, 813, 849, 850, 860, 867]

Professions, engineering, p. 551, 552, 558, 559, 560, 561, 565, 567, 569, 571, 573, 575, 576, 583, 584, 586, 587, 588, 589, 590, 591, 592, 593, 594, 596, 597, 602, 603, 604, 605, [803, 804, 805, 814, 815, 816, 817, 818, 819, 820, 826, 827, 828, 829, 830, 831, 832, 833, 843, 844, 845, 848, 851, 852, 853, 854, 856, 857, 858, 859, 861, 863, 864, 865, 870, 871, 872, 873, 874, 875]

Professions, enrollment toward degree, p. 202, [307]

Professions, law, p. 554, 564, 579, 580, [807, 823, 824, 836, 837]

Professions, medicine, p. 553, 554, 563, 578, 579, 581, 582, 583, 585, 598, [806, 808, 822, 834, 835, 838, 839, 840, 841, 842, 846, 866]

Professions, scientists, p. 584, [844]

Professions, veterinary medicine, p. 600, 601, [868, 869]

Professions, workers, p. 584, [844]

Psychiatric inpatients, age, p. 300, [444]

Race, p. 93, [155]

Racial groups, geographic distribution, p. 545, [795]

Racial groups, regional distribution, p. 545, [795]

Reading, achievement/aptitude, p. 104, 216, 229, [173, 329, 345]

Reading, illiteracy, p. 204, [311]

Reading, proficiency, p. 214, [326]

Receiverships, p. 39, [73]

Religion, p. 210, 606, 608, [321, 877, 879]

Religions, p. 607, [878]

Religions, student preferences, p. 608, [879]

Religious denominations, p. 606, 607, [877, 878]

Republican conventions, p. 477, [705]

Salaries, college faculty, p. 128, 225, 250, [209, 339, 374]

Savings and loan companies, p. 30, 42, [60, 76]

School age population, p. 549, [800]

School dropouts, p. 432, [638]

School dropouts, characteristics of, p. 229, [346]

Schools, characteristics of, p. 211, [323]

Schools, private, p. 210, [321]

Schools, private secondary, p. 211, [322]

Schools, public, p. 211, 212, [323, 324]

Science, achievement/aptitude, p. 103, 104, 134, [172, 173, 219, 220]

Science, courses taken, p. 135, [222]

Science, degrees awarded, p. 559, 587, [816, 852]

Science, graduate enrollment, p. 589, [854]

Science, graduate students, p. 567, 569, 571, 575, 576, [828, 829, 830, 832, 833]

Science, high school credits, p. 177, [277]

Science, physical, p. 208, [318]

Science, postdoctorates, p. 591, [857]

Science, proficiency, p. 233, [351]

Science, social, p. 237, [356]

Science, support for graduate students, p. 565, [826]

Science/engineering, enrollment, p. 565, 589, [825, 855]

Scientists, college faculty, p. 551, 552, 558, 559, 602, [803, 804, 805, 814, 815, 870]

Scientists, employment, p. 584, 592, 593, [845, 859, 861]

Scientists, experience, p. 586, 603, 604, [848, 872, 874]

Scientists, fields, p. 593, 561, [861, 820]

Scientists, salaries, p. 588, [853]

Scientists, women, p. 561, [820]

Scientists, work activity, p. 602, 604, 605, [871, 873, 875]

Scientists/engineers, employment, p. 592, [858]

Scientists/engineers, income, p. 592, [858]

Secondary school teachers, p. 211, [322]

Self-concept, college students, p. 23, [49]

Service companies, p. 39, [74]

Sex education, attitudes toward, p. 5, [10]

Smoking, and low birth weights, p. 361, [531]

Smoking, rates, p. 312, 314, 315, [464, 465, 467]

Social class, of families, p. 277, [410, 411]

Social services, p. 308, 331, 332, 458, [457, 487, 488, 678]

Socioeconomic status, of high school graduates, p. 141, [231]

Socioeconomic status, of NCAA athletes, p. 618, [896]

Sports, athlete drug use, p. 619, [897]

Sports, basketball, p. 619, 620, [898, 899]

Sports, coaches, p. 612, 619, 620, [886, 898, 899]

Sports, college basketball, p. 612, 614, [885, 886, 888]

Sports, fishing, p. 615, [889]

Sports, football, p. 614, [887]

Sports, hunting, p. 615, [889]

Sports, professional baseball, p. 615, 616, [890, 891, 892]

Sports, professional basketball, p. 617, 618, [893, 894]

Sports, professional football, p. 618, [895]

Sports, student athletes, p. 619, [897]

SREB states, p. 189, [295]

State legislators, distribution of, p. 480, [711]

Students, employment of, p. 438, [648]

Suicides, p. 638, 660, [920, 921, 942]

Suicides, inmate, p. 660, [942]

Suicide, death rates, p. 635, [917]

Supreme Court, attitudes toward, p. 8, 12, 14, 23, [18, 26, 30, 50]

Survival rates, cancer, p. 306, [455]

TBIs, p. 112, [185]

Teachers K-12, p. 189, [295]

Teachers, applicant achievement/aptitude, p. 238, [358]

Teachers, competency, p. 240, [361]

Teachers, elementary, p. 594, [862]

Teachers, private school, p. 210, [321]

Teachers, secondary, p. 594, [862]

Teen suicides, p. 678, [963]

Teenage pregnancies, p. 632, [913]

Teenagers, alcohol use, p. 362, [533]

Teenagers, attitudes, p. 20, [41]

Teenagers, drug abuse, p. 18, [37]

Tests, for advanced placement, p. 256, [380]

Tests, for Armed Forces, p. 465, [690]

Tests, of teacher competency, p. 240, [361]

Theology, p. 562, [821]

Thrift companies, p. 39, [73]

Thrift companies, asset, p. 37, [71]

Thrifts, minority, p. 37, [71]

Traditionally Black Institutions, p. 248, [371]

UNCF institutions, p. 123, 130, 137, 163, 165, 190, 220, 247, 251, [201, 212, 225, 258, 260, 296, 333, 369, 376]

Unemployed, p. 439, [650]

Unemployed females, p. 459, 460, [681, 682]

Unemployed males, p. 460, [683, 684]

Unemployed workers, p. 424, 442, [626, 655, 656]

Unemployed workers, educational level, p. 442, [655]

Unemployed, characteristics of, p. 423, 424, [623, 626]

Unemployment, p. 442, 456, 461, [655, 656, 675, 685]

Unemployment in industries, p. 461, [685]

Unemployment insurance coverage, p. 458, [678]

Unemployment outcomes, p. 458, [679]

Unemployment rate, p. 455, [674]

Unemployment, and income, p. 276, [408]

Unemployment, and poverty, p. 287, [429]

Unemployment, families, p. 276, [408]

Unemployment, rate of, p. 440, 458, [651, 680]

Unemployment, trends in, p. 458, [680]

Unmarried women, births, p. 679, [964]

Unmarried women, pregnancies, p. 632, [913]

Veterinary medicine, faculty, p. 600, [868]

Veterinary medicine, students, p. 601, [869]

Vietnam veterans, mental health, p. 364, [536]

Vital statistics, p. 45, 178, 230, 290, 301, 303, 304, 305, 306, 317, 323, 338, 344, 352, 358, [78, 79, 279, 347, 434, 445, 446, 449, 450, 452, 453, 454, 455, 468, 475, 497, 506, 518, 525]

Vital statistics, high school dropouts, p. 178, [279]

Vital statistics, percent of population enrolled in school, p. 230, [347]

Voter participation, p. 478, [709]

Voter participation in regions, p. 478, [709]

Voter registration, p. 505, 508, [737, 740]

Voters, p. 505, [737]

Voters and voting, p. 503, 504, 506, 507, [735, 736, 738, 739]

Voters and voting, characteristics of, p. 510, [743]

Voters, characteristics of, p. 510, [742]

Voters, registered, p. 479, [710]

Voting, p. 478, 511, [709, 744]

Voting age population, p. 479, [710]

Voting and registration, p. 509, [741]

Voting practices, p. 511, [744]

Voting trends, p. 512, 513, 514, [745, 746, 747, 748, 749, 750]

Voting, historical patterns, p. 512, 513, 514, [745, 746, 747, 748, 749, 750]

Wealth, amount, p. 413, [612]

Wealth, family sources of, p. 410, [605]

Wealth, type, p. 413, [611, 612]

Weight, birth weight related to smoking, p. 361, [531]

Weight, excess, p. 318, 328, 350, [469, 482, 513]

Women, p. 494, [725, 726]

Women and alimony, p. 611, [884]

Women and births, p. 631, [912]

Women and child support, p. 611, [884]

Women giving birth, p. 681, [967]

Women householders, p. 280, [418]

Women, executed, p. 61, [99]

Work force, multiple jobholders, p. 423, [624]

Workers, full-time, p. 382, [559]

Workplace, conditions of, p. 463, [688]

Work, disability days, p. 319, 320, [471, 472]

Work, experience, p. 414, [613]

Writing, proficiency, p. 256, [381]

Young adults, college enrollment, p. 258, [383]

Young adults, college participation rates, p. 131, [214]

Young adults, literacy, p. 203, [310]

Young adults, political participation, p. 26, [56]

Young adults, voluntary organizations, p. 621, [900]

Young adults, with AIDS, p. 302, [447]

Youth, incarcerated, p. 54, [93]

Youth, prisoners, p. 97, [162]